Adolescence

Adolescence

Laurence Steinberg
Temple University

Sixth Edition

McGraw
Hill

Boston   Burr Ridge, IL   Dubuque, IA   Madison, WI   New York   San Francisco   St. Louis
Bangkok   Bogotá   Caracas   Kuala Lumpur   Lisbon   London   Madrid   Mexico City
Milan   Montreal   New Delhi   Santiago   Seoul   Singapore   Sydney   Taipei   Toronto

McGraw-Hill Higher Education

*A Division of The **McGraw-Hill** Companies*

ADOLESCENCE, SIXTH EDITION

Published by McGraw-Hill, a business unit of The McGraw-Hill Companies, Inc., 1221
Avenue of the Americas, New York, NY 10020. Copyright © 2002, 1999, 1996, 1993
by The McGraw-Hill Companies, Inc. All rights reserved. Previous editions © 1989, 1985
by Alfred A. Knopf, Inc. All rights reserved. No part of this publication may be reproduced
or distributed in any form or by any means, or stored in a database or retrieval system, without
the prior written consent of The McGraw-Hill Companies, Inc., including, but not limited to,
in any network or other electronic storage or transmission, or broadcast for distance learning.

Some ancillaries, including electronic and print components, may not be available to customers
outside the United States.

This book is printed on acid-free paper.

International   2 3 4 5 6 7 8 9 0 QWV/QWV 0 9 8 7 6 5 4 3 2 1
Domestic   3 4 5 6 7 8 9 0 QWV/QWV 0 9 8 7 6 5 4 3 2

ISBN 0–07–241456–1
ISBN 0–07–112488–8 (ISE)

Vice president and editor-in-chief: *Thalia Dorwick*
Editorial director: *Jane E. Karpacz*
Senior sponsoring editor: *Rebecca H. Hope*
Developmental editor: *Rita Lombard*
Senior marketing manager: *Chris Hall*
Project manager: *Jane E. Matthews*
Senior production supervisor: *Sandy Ludovissy*
Designer: *K. Wayne Harms*
Cover/interior designer: *Kay Fulton*
Cover image: *Laurence Monnenet/Stone*
Photo research coordinator: *John C. Leland*
Photo research: *Connie Gardner Picture Research*
Supplement producer: *Tammy Juran*
Media technology lead producer: *David Edwards*
Compositor: *GTS Graphics, Inc.*
Typeface: *10/12 Minion*
Printer: *Quebecor World*

The credits section for this book begins on page 516 and is considered an extension
of the copyright page.

Library of Congress Cataloging-in-Publication Data

Steinberg, Laurence D., 1952–
  Adolescence / Laurence D. Steinberg. —6th ed.
    p.   cm.
  Includes bibliographical references and indexes.
  ISBN 0–07–241456–1
  1. Adolescent psychology.   I. Title.

BF724 .S75   2002
305.235—dc21   2001030697
                                                     CIP

INTERNATIONAL EDITION ISBN 0–07–112488–8
Copyright © 2002. Exclusive rights by The McGraw-Hill Companies, Inc., for manufacture
and export. This book cannot be re-exported from the country to which it is sold by McGraw-Hill.
The International Edition is not available in North America.

www.mhhe.com

For Wendy and Ben

About the Author

Laurence Steinberg, Ph.D., is the Distinguished University Professor and Laura H. Carnell Professor of Psychology at Temple University. He graduated from Vassar College in 1974 and from Cornell University in 1977, where he recieved his Ph.D. in human development and family studies. He is a Fellow of the American Psychological Association and former president of the Society for Research on Adolescence.

Dr. Steinberg's own research has focused on a range of topics in the study of contemporary adolescence, including parent-adolescent relationships, adolescent employment, high school reform, and juvenile crime and justice. He has been the recipient of numerous honors, including the John P. Hill Award for Outstanding Contributions to the Study of Adolescence, given by the Society for Research on Adolescence, and the Society for Adolescent Medicine's Gallagher Lectureship. Dr. Steinberg also has been recognized for excellence in research and teaching by the University of California, the University of Wisconsin, and Temple University, where he was honored in 1994 as one of that university's Great Teachers.

In addition to *Adolescence,* Dr. Steinberg is the author or co-author of more than 150 scholarly articles on growth and development during the teenage years, as well as the books *You and Your Adolescent: A Parent's Guide for Ages 10 to 20* (with Ann Levine); *When Teenagers Work: The Psychological and Social Costs of Adolescent Employment* (with Ellen Greenberger); *Crossing Paths: How Your Child's Adolescence Triggers Your Own Crisis* (with Wendy Steinberg); *Studying Minority Adolescents: Conceptual, Methodological, and Theoretical Issues* (with Vonnie McLoyd); and *Beyond the Classroom: Why School Reform Has Failed and What Parents Need to Do* (with Bradford Brown and Sanford Dornbusch). •

Brief Contents

Contents

Part I
The Fundamental Changes
of Adolescence   19

Chapter 2
Cognitive Transitions   58

Chapter 3
Social Transitions   92

Part II
The Contexts of Adolescence   123

Chapter 4
Families   124

Part III
Psychosocial Development During Adolescence   253

Chapter **8**
Identity   254

Chapter **9**
Autonomy   286

Preface

In 1976, the first time I was asked to teach a semester-long course in adolescent development, my graduate advisor, John Hill—who at that time had been teaching adolescent development for 10 years—took me aside. "Getting them to learn the stuff is easy," John said, smiling. "Unfortunately, you'll only have about 3 weeks to do it. It'll take you 10 weeks just to get them to unlearn all the junk they're sure is true."

He was right. I would present study after study documenting that turmoil isn't the norm for most adolescents, that most teenagers have relatively good relationships with their parents, that adolescence isn't an inherently stressful period, and so on, and my students would nod diligently. But five minutes later someone would tell the class about his or her cousin Billy, who had either run away from home, attempted to set his parents' bedroom on fire, or refused to say a word to either his mother or his father for eight years.

As most instructors discover, teaching adolescent development is both exhilarating and exasperating. Every student comes into class an expert; for many of them, adolescence wasn't very long ago. No good instructor wants to squelch the interest and curiosity most students bring with them when they first come into a class. But no conscientious teacher wants to see students leave with little more than the preconceptions they came in with and an even firmer conviction that social scientists who study human development are out of touch with the "real" world.

One of my other mentors, Urie Bronfenbrenner, once wrote that the science of child development had found itself caught between "a rock and a soft place"—between rigor and relevance. Teachers of adolescent development find themselves in the same boat. How do you present scientific research on adolescent development in ways students find interesting, believable, relevant, and worth remembering when the term is over? I hope this book will help.

ABOUT THE SIXTH EDITION

About the time of the publication of the first edition of *Adolescence* in 1985, the study of development during the second decade of the life cycle suddenly became a hot topic. New journals devoted exclusively to the study of adolescence began publication; established journals in the field of child development became deluged with submissions on adolescence; more and more well-trained scholars specializing in the study of adolescent development appeared on the scene. During the 14 years between the publication of the first and fifth editions of this text, our understanding of adolescent development expanded dramatically, and this expansion has continued at a rapid pace since the previous edition was published in 1999.

The sixth edition of this textbook reflects this new and more substantial knowledge base. Although the book's original organization has been retained, the material in each chapter has been significantly updated and revised. Nearly *700* new studies have been cited since the fifth edition alone.

Our knowledge about adolescent development has grown dramatically in the past three years. Readers will find expanded sections in this edition about behavior genetics and adolescent development, brain growth and development, adolescent decision making and risk taking, neighborhood and community effects on development, sibling relationships, juvenile crime and justice, the impact of parental remarriage and postdivorce custodial arrangements, romance and dating, adolescents' use of the mass media and the Internet, school violence and aggression, and depression. These additions, corrections, and expansions are natural responses to the development of new knowledge in a dynamic growing scientific field.

Perhaps the greatest expansion of knowledge during the past decade about development during the second decade of life has been about adolescents growing up in poverty, about adolescents from ethnic minority groups, and about adolescents from parts of the world other than North America. This has permitted increased coverage of the ways in which the course of development during adolescence is affected by economics, ethnicity, and culture. Instead of presenting this material in boxed inserts or in a separate chapter, however, I have incorporated this information into the text in order to show when and how patterns of adolescent development vary across class, ethnicity, and region.

This edition of *Adolescence* retains a feature that ran throughout the past several editions. A box entitled "The Sexes" in each chapter considers in detail whether a particular pattern of adolescent development is different for boys and for girls. I emphasize the word *whether* here, for in many instances the scientific evidence suggests that the similarities between the sexes are far more striking than the differences. Some of the topics I examine are whether or why there are sex differences in the impact of early pubertal maturation, in cognitive abilities, in rates of depression, in relations with mothers and fathers, in intimacy, in math and science achievement, and in the nature of the transition into adulthood.

A second set of boxed inserts is continued here in response to the positive feedback I've received from readers. Although most instructors (and virtually all students) who have used this text have enjoyed its "dejargonized" writing style, some felt that including more information about research design and methods would be useful. Each chapter in this edition contains a boxed feature entitled "The Scientific Study of Adolescence," which examines in detail one particular study discussed in that chapter and teaches students about an important aspect of research methods, design, or statistics. Among the topics covered in this series are, for example, the difference between an independent and a dependent variable, the meaning of a statistical interaction, how researchers use electronic beepers to study adolescents' moods, why correlation is not causation, statistical power, the Q-Sort procedure, and the use of meta-analysis in examining a research literature.

ADOLESCENT DEVELOPMENT IN CONTEXT

If there is a guiding theme to *Adolescence*, it is this: Adolescent development cannot be understood apart from the context in which young people grow up. Identity crises, generation gaps, and peer pressure may be features of adolescent life in contemporary society, but

their prevalence has more to do with the nature of our society than with the nature of adolescence as a period in the life cycle. In order to understand how adolescents develop in contemporary society, students need first to understand the world in which adolescents live and how that world affects their behavior and social relationships. I have therefore devoted a good deal of attention in this book to the contexts in which adolescents live—families, peer groups, schools, neighborhoods, and work and leisure settings—to how these contexts are changing, and to how these changes are changing the nature of adolescence.

ORGANIZATION

The overall organization of this book has not changed since the last edition. Specifically, the chapters about psychosocial development during adolescence are separate from those about the contexts of adolescence. In this way, the psychosocial concerns of adolescence—identity, autonomy, intimacy, sexuality, and achievement—are presented as central developmental concerns that surface across, and are affected by, different settings.

This book contains an introduction and 13 chapters, which are grouped into three parts: the fundamental biological, cognitive, and social changes of the period (Part I); the contexts of adolescence (Part II); and psychosocial development during the adolescent years (Part III). The Introduction presents a model for studying adolescence that was developed by the late John Hill and that serves as the organizational framework for the text. I have found the framework to be extremely helpful in teaching adolescent development, and I highly recommend using it. However, if the model does not fit with your course outline or your own perspective on adolescence, it is possible to use the text without using the framework. Each chapter is self-contained, so it is not necessary to assign chapters in the sequence in which they are ordered in the text. However, if you choose to use the model presented in the Introduction, it may be helpful to follow the text organization.

THEORY AND METHODS

One of the things you will notice about *Adolescence* when you thumb through the contents is that the ubiquitous chapters about "theories of adolescence" and "research methods" are missing. The chapter titles are indeed missing, but the material isn't. After teaching adolescence for many years, I am convinced that students seldom remember a word of the chapters about theory and methods because the information in them is presented out of context. Therefore, although there is plenty of theory in this text, it is presented when it is most relevant, in a way that shows students how research and theory are related. At the beginning of the chapter on intimacy, for example, Sullivan's perspective on intimacy (and on psychosocial development in general) is presented, and then the relevant research is examined. Similarly, the research methods and tools used in the study of adolescence are discussed in the context of specific studies that illustrate the powers—or pitfalls—of certain strategies. Many of these research issues are spotlighted in the boxed material on "The Scientific Study of Adolescence," which appears in each chapter. Overall, my approach has been to blend theory, research, and practical applications in a way that shows students how the three depend on each other. For students unfamiliar with theories in developmental psychology, I have included a brief overview of this material in the Introduction.

LEARNING AIDS

I have included three types of learning aids in this edition of *Adolescence* that are designed to help students get the most out of their reading.

- **Recaps** follow coverage of key concepts within each chapter. These summaries highlight the important information that students have just read.
- **Food for Thought** questions, which appear within each chapter, are designed to help students both retain what they've read and think critically about the nature of adolescence while they are reading.
- A **Web Researcher** question concludes each chapter by challenging students, in a step-by-step process, to use the Internet in order to bring together and apply concepts they've just read about.

SUPPLEMENTARY MATERIALS

Please consult your local McGraw-Hill representative to learn about the availability of supplements that accompany *Adolescence*, 6th edition.

For the Instructor

- **Instructor's Resource Manual with Test Questions by Dale Grubb, Baldwin Wallace College** This comprehensive manual continues to be a valuable resource for both new and seasoned instructors. New features include a Total Teaching Package Outline, which combines a traditional chapter outline with instructions on exactly how and where to use all of the supplementary materials McGraw-Hill offers. The accompanying test questions have been extensively revised and updated to correlate to the new edition. Each item is linked to learning objectives that are used consistently across the supplements.

- **Computerized Test Bank on CD-ROM by Dale Grubb, Baldwin Wallace College** This CD-ROM is a Macintosh/Windows hybrid that works on either platform, offering the complete set of test items included in the printed Test Bank. This affords an instructor maximum flexibility in editing and selecting test questions.

- **Instructor's Resource CD-ROM** This teaching tool offers you the opportunity to customize McGraw-Hill materials to create your lecture presentations. Resources included on the CD-ROM are the Instructor's Resource Manual, Computerized Test Bank, PowerPoint presentation slides, and images from the Image Database with a fully functioning editing feature. You can add your own lecture notes to the CD-ROM and can organize the images to correspond to your particular classroom needs.

- **Online Learning Center** This extensive website, designed to accompany *Adolescence*, offers an array of resources for both instructor and student. PowerPoint presentations, author-selected images from the database with a fully functioning editing feature, Web links, recommended readings, and the innovative, chapter-concluding **Web Researcher** feature, can all be found by logging on to the text site at www.mhhe.com/steinberg6.

- **McGraw-Hill's Developmental Supersite** This comprehensive site serves as a portal through which instructors and students can access each text-specific online learning center as well as many universally useful teaching and study tools. Visit us at www.mhhe.com/developmental.

● **Annual Editions—Adolescent Psychology** Published by Dushkin/McGraw-Hill, this is a collection of articles on topics related to the latest research and thinking in adolescent development. These editions are updated annually and contain helpful features, including a topic guide, an annotated table of contents, unit overviews, and a topical index. An Instructor's Guide containing testing materials to accompany the Annual Edition is also available.

● **PageOut—Build Your Own Course Web Site in Less Than an Hour**. You don't have to be a computer whiz to create a website. Especially with an exclusive McGraw-Hill product called PageOut.™ It requires no prior knowledge of HTML, no long hours of coding, and no design skills on your part. Visit us at www.pageout.net.

● **PowerPoint™ Lectures** Available on the Internet and as part of the Instructor's Resource CD-ROM, these presentations are designed to enhance both large- and small-section lectures by including visual representations of key chapter material in the text. You have the option of modifying these presentations or using them as they are. Visit us at www.mhhe.com/steinberg6.

For the Student

● **Study Guide by Nancy Dodge Reyome, State University of New York at Potsdam, and Chris Bjornsen, Longwood College** The revised Study Guide includes learning objectives, a chapter outline and brief overview, and a wide variety of quizzing tools, such as multiple-choice, fill-in-the blank, and true-or-false questions complete with answer keys. Students can further prepare themselves for exams with the inclusion of comprehensive practice tests, as well as critical thinking questions, which can be useful as a study group tool. Recommendations for further readings are also included, as well as critical thinking exercises, which can be used as useful study group tools.

● **PowerWeb** This dynamic website, accessible by using a password card shrink-wrapped for free with each new copy of *Adolescence*, 6th edition, offers a suite of original web-based materials for the adolescent development course. PowerWeb is the first Internet tool to help students learn how to research on-line. The site offers daily and weekly course updates, access to key articles on important course topics, and self-assessment built into the site.

● **Online Learning Center** The official website for the text contains chapter outlines, practice quizzes that can be e-mailed to the professor, links to relevant websites, recommended readings, interactive crosswords and flashcards, and the text's new, chapter-concluding **Web Researcher** feature. Log on to www.mhhe.com/steinberg6.

● **McGraw-Hill's Developmental Supersite** This comprehensive website serves as a portal through which instructors and students can access each text-specific on-line learning center, as well as many universally useful teaching and study tools. Visit us at www.mhhe.com/developmental.

● **Student and Instructor Supplement Users—We Want to Hear from You!** If you are currently using a McGraw-Hill supplement, we'd like to hear from you. In an effort to improve the quality of future supplements, we invite you to visit our text website and complete an evaluation form. This completed form will be e-mailed directly to the editors and will be considered as we develop future supplements for adolescence. This form can be found at www.mhhe.com/socscience/devel/index.mhtml.

ACKNOWLEDGMENTS

Revising a textbook at a time when so much new information is available is a challenge that requires much assistance. Over the years, my students have suggested many ways in which the text might be improved, and I have learned a great deal from listening to them. I am especially grateful to Amanda Sheffield Morris, who ably tracked down and organized much of the new research published in the three years between editions; and to several colleagues, including: Mary Louise Arnold, University of Toronto; Melissa M. Brown, State University of New York–Brockport; Nancy Darling, Penn State University; Gypsy M. Denzine, Northern Arizona University; Andrew J. Fuligni, New York University; Arthur Gonchar, University of La Verne, California; Karen G. Howe, The College of New Jersey; Patricia A. Jarvis, Illinois State University; Belinda Blevins Knabe, University of Arkansas at Little Rock; Radhi Al-Mabuk, University of Northern Iowa; Beth

Manke, University of Houston; and Dorothy J. Shedlock, State University of New York–Oswego, who provided critiques of the previous edition and made suggestions that improved this one.

I also wish to thank my colleagues at McGraw-Hill, including Jane Matthews, project manager; Wayne Harms, designer; John Leland, photo researcher; Tammy Juran, supplement producer; and, especially, Rita Lombard, developmental editor; Rebecca Hope, senior sponsoring editor; Sharon Geary, director of development; and Jane Karpacz, editorial director, who helped develop this edition of the book.

Finally, my thanks to the many colleagues and students across the country who took the time to write during the past dozen years with comments and suggestions based on their firsthand experiences using *Adolescence* in the classroom. They have improved the text with each edition.

Laurence Steinberg

Visual Preview

NEW!
Web Researcher

This web-based critical thinking question appears before the summary in each chapter and challenges students to apply concepts learned, and do on-line research via recommended hot links on the text's on-line learning center at www.mhhe.com/steinberg6. Additional multiple-choice questions further test student understanding and offer comprehensive feedback on all chosen answers, so that students fully grasp the reasoning behind correct or incorrect answers.

Recaps

Periodic summaries are placed at key points throughout each chapter and provide a good review tool for students.

NEW!
Food for Thought

This critical thinking feature appears periodically throughout each chapter and tests students' grasp and understanding of key concepts.

Chapter 6 Schools 223

observers have noted that most schools are not structured to promote psychosocial development, with their excessive focus on conformity and obedience and their lack of encouragement for creativity, independence, and self-reliance (Friedenberg, 1967). This certainly comes through loud and clear when adolescents are asked about their classroom experiences. But there are very many good schools, in which students not only learn the academic material taught in classes but also learn about themselves, their relationships with others, and their society. Schools differ from each other, and it is difficult to generalize about the impact of schools on adolescent development without knowing more about the particular school in question.

It is also important to recognize that, despite adults' intentions and objectives, students do not view school solely in terms of its academic agenda. In one study, the researchers asked a sample of seventh- through twelfth-graders to list the best and worst things about school. The best things? "Being with my friends" and "meeting new people." The worst? Homework, tests, and the school's restrictive atmosphere (Brown et al., 1992). Adults may evaluate schools in terms of their contribution to adolescents' cognitive and career development, but for the typical adolescent, school is the main setting for socializing. When we ask about the consequences of leaving school early, we must take into account the impact this has on the individual's social, as well as cognitive, development.

Studies also show that students' experiences within a school can vary widely according to the track they are in, the peer group they belong to, and the extracurricular activities in which they participate. It seems safe to say that academically talented and economically advantaged students have a more positive experience in school than do their less capable or less affluent counterparts—positive not only with respect to what they learn in class but also with respect to the impact of school on their feelings about themselves as individuals. Their teachers pay more attention to them, they are more likely to hold positions of leadership in extracurricular organizations, and they are more likely to experience classes that are engaging and challenging. In other words, the structure of a school—its size, its tracking policy, and its curricula—provides different intellectual and psychosocial opportunities for students who occupy dif-

ferent places within that structure. Not surprisingly, a study of Swedish adolescents found a great deal of variability in students' feeling about school: About 25 percent enjoyed school a great deal, about 25 percent detested school (and felt that their friends in school were their only salvation), and the remainder felt ambivalent (Andersson, 1994). The best answer to the question "How do schools affect adolescent development?" then, is another question: "Which schools, which adolescents, and in what respects?"

Web Researcher What is the average class size in elementary schools, high schools, liberal arts colleges, and large universities? How many students do teachers in each of these institutions see in a week? How much time do they spend with each student? How might these differences relate to the goals and means of instruction, the types of assignments teachers give, and students' experience in the classroom? Go to www.mhhe.com/steinberg6 for further information.

KEY TERMS

charter schools
comprehensive high school
education vouchers
Forgotten Half
gifted students
higher-order thinking
junior high school
learning disability
mainstreaming
middle school
school climate
secondary education
self-fulfilling prophecy
social capital
student engagement
tracking

Chapter 6 Schools 215

RECAP
In an effort to understand better how various types of school environments influence adolescent achievement, researchers have compared students in segregated versus desegregated schools and in private versus public ones. In general, the effects of desegregation on student achievement are very modest, and there appear to be advantages for students who attend Catholic, but not necessarily all types of private, schools.

Food for Thought
How do you feel about vouchers? about charter schools?

THE IMPORTANCE OF SCHOOL CLIMATE

Thus far, we have seen that certain elements of the school's social organization—size, age grouping, tracking, and so forth—can affect students' behavior and achievement. But these factors are important mainly because they influence what takes place in classrooms and in other school settings. Indeed, most social scientists and educators now agree that the school-related factors which are most important in influencing learning and psychosocial development during adolescence concern the more immediate environment of the school and classroom. The good schools, the classroom environments encourage dialogue between teachers and students and among students, and learning is emphasized over memorization (Newmann et al., 1996). Various aspects of the **school climate** have important effects on youngsters' learning and achievement (Rutter, 1983). Specifically, the way teachers interact with students, the way classroom time is used, and the sorts of standards and expectations that teachers hold for their students are all more important than the size of the school, the way that age groups are combined, and the racial composition of the school. One reason that tracking makes a difference, for example, is that classes in different tracks have very different climates.

What sort of climate brings out the best in students? Considered together, the results of several studies indicate that the same factors which influence positive adolescent adjustment at home appear to be important at school. Specifically, students achieve and

are engaged more in school more when they attend schools that are *responsive* and *demanding*. Moreover, academic functioning and psychological adjustment affect each other, so that a positive school climate—where relationships between students and teachers are positive, teachers are supportive, and teachers are demanding—enhances adolescents' psychological well-being, as well as their achievement (Blum & Rinehart, 2000; Phillips, 1997; Roeser & Eccles, 1998; Roeser, Eccles, & Sameroff, 1999; Rowan, Chiang, & Miller, 1997).

Generally speaking, both students and teachers are more satisfied in classes that combine a moderate degree of structure with high student involvement and high teacher support. In these classes, teachers encourage their students' participation but do not let the class get out of control. Classes that are too task-oriented—particularly when they also emphasize teacher control—tend to make students feel anxious, uninterested, and unhappy (Moos, 1978). The pattern of classroom variables that is associated with positive student behavior and attitudes, then, is reminiscent of the *authoritative* family environment (see chapter 4). Similarly, an overemphasis on control in the classroom in the absence of support is reminiscent of the *authoritarian* family, whereas a lack of clarity and organization is reminiscent of both the *indulgent* family and the *indifferent family*—and these styles may affect adolescents detrimentally. Students do best when their teachers spend a high proportion of time on lessons (rather than on setting up equipment or dealing with discipline problems) and when teachers begin and end lessons on time, provide clear feedback to students about what is expected of them and about their performance, and give ample praise to students when they perform well (Rutter, 1983). A good high school teacher, in other words, bears a striking resemblance to a good parent (Wentzel, 1994).

Students in schools in which teachers are supportive but firm and maintain high, well-defined standards for behavior and academic work have stronger bonds to their school and more positive achievement motives; these beliefs and emotions, in turn, lead to fewer problems, better attendance, lower rates of delinquency, and higher scores on tests of achievement (see figure 6.3) (Roeser et al., 1996). This pattern is remarkably similar to that uncovered in studies comparing public and private high schools (Coleman et al., 1982). In these studies, too, the students' achievement was higher in schools that were somewhat more structured and demanding—no matter whether the school was public or private.

The Sexes

Retained for several editions, "The Sexes" appears in each chapter and considers in detail whether a particular pattern of adolescent development is different for boys and for girls. It focuses on such topics as whether or why there are sex differences in the impact of early pubertal maturation, in cognitive abilities, in rates of depression, in relations with mothers and fathers, in intimacy, in math and science achievement, and in the nature of the transition into adulthood.

The Scientific Study of Adolescence

Each chapter contains this boxed feature, which examines in detail one particular study discussed in that chapter and teaches students about an important aspect of research methods, design, or statistics. Among the topics covered in this series are the difference between an independent and dependent variable, the meaning of a statistical interaction, how researchers use electronic beepers to study adolescents' moods, and why correlation is not causation.

Chapter Outline

At the beginning of each chapter, an outline previews the major topics included in the chapter.

Chapter 2

Cognitive Transitions

End of Chapter Key Terms

These are defined in the glossary and bolded in the text body of each chapter.

Morgan, & Colbert, 1996; Leadbeater & Bishop, 1994; Roye & Balk, 1996). Studies suggest that a lack of support is an especially dire problem among poor Hispanic adolescent mothers (Wasserman et al., 1990). Together, these and other studies suggest that the best arrangement for a teenage mother may be to live independently from her own parents but to be able to rely on them for emotional support and child care (Coley & Chase-Lansdale, 1998).

Because it is so important for young mothers to have an adequate income and the chance for adequate employment, many policymakers have called for changes in the ways that schools and other social institutions treat pregnant students and for changes in the provision of day care (Sandfort & Hill, 1996; Seitz & Apfel, 1993, 1994). Among the most important are adaptations in school schedules and the development of school-based child-care centers, so that pregnant students can remain in school after the birth of their child; the expansion of subsidized child care for young mothers who are out of school, so that the economic benefits of having a job are not outweighed by the costs of suitable child care during the workday; and the expansion of family planning services for adolescent mothers, so that they can prevent yet another pregnancy. Unfortunately, evaluations of programs aimed at enhancing teen mothers' employability, decreasing their reliance on welfare, or preventing their subsequent pregnancies have been largely disappointing (Coley & Chase-Lansdale, 1998), although there have been occasional successes reported in the literature (e.g., Solomon & Liefeld, 1998).

 Food for Thought
Describe trends in teenage childbearing over the past 50 years. Does the public's concern over teenage childbearing match the data? Why or why not?

Web Researcher Check out one or more websites aimed at gay, lesbian, or bisexual teenagers. What seem to be the dominant issues and concerns? Go to www.mhhe.com/steinberg6 for further information.

KEY TERMS

AIDS (acquired immune deficiency syndrome)
androgens
autoerotic behavior
chlamydia
gender identity
gonorrhea
herpes
HIV (human immunodeficiency virus)
human ecology
human papilloma virus
permissive societies
restrictive societies
risk factor
semirestrictive societies
serial monogamy
sex-role behavior
sexual orientation
sexual socialization
sexually transmitted infections (STIs)
sociosexual behaviors
testosterone

RECAP
Preventing teenage pregnancy has been extremely difficult, and most sex education programs developed during the past two decades have failed in this respect. There are approximately 1 million teenage pregnancies each year in the United States, about half of which are carried full-term. Research indicates that teenagers are not harmed psychologically by aborting their pregnancy or by placing their infant up for adoption, but studies of the consequences of teenage childbearing indicates that the short- and long-term problems for the teenage mother may be considerable. Although there are occasional success stories, teenage parents are more likely than their peers to experience disruptions in their educational and occupational development. Studies clearly show that adolescent mothers who have social support from family or friends and who are able to complete high school fare far better than those who do not.

Introduction

Adolescent Development in Context

A few years ago, I was asked to provide expert testimony in three different legal cases involving teenagers. In one, a 14-year-old boy had created an Internet site about a math teacher whom he felt had humiliated him in class. The site contained a mixture of profanity, violent imagery, and juvenile humor, of the sort one might find in *Mad* magazine or on the television show *South Park*. The boy had circulated the site to his friends, as a way of getting back at the teacher. Now, he was being sued by his teacher, who claimed that his website had so ruined her reputation that she could no longer teach. I was asked to comment on whether what the student had done was "normal" for a teenager his age.

The second case involved a challenge to a new Colorado law concerning adolescents and abortion. The law required that all parents of minors (individuals not yet 18 years old) seeking an abortion be notified before a physician could perform the operation. Although many other states have similar laws, they usually allow exceptions, if, for example, the adolescent is afraid of how her parents might react. Under these circumstances, the teenager can meet with a judge, who can hear the adolescent's story and authorize the procedure without having to notify the young person's parents. The new Colorado law was much more restrictive. It permitted such exceptions only when the adolescent could prove that her parents had abused her. I was asked whether I thought it was ever appropriate for a pregnant adolescent to seek an abortion without telling her parents.

The third case was one you may have heard about. It involved the fatal school shootings in Jonesboro, Arkansas, committed by two students who were 11 and 13 years old at the time. In response to this tragic incident, the state legislature was considering lowering the age at which juvenile offenders could be treated as adults. Under this proposal, juveniles would have their cases heard in adult court, rather than in juvenile court, and, if convicted, they would receive punishments identical to those given to adults who had committed similar crimes—serving time in adult prison, for example, rather than being sent to a training school designed specifically for delinquents. Some lawmakers wanted the age at which juveniles could be transferred to the adult criminal justice system lowered to 10. I was asked to discuss what is known about child and adolescent development and how this information might be relevant to the proposed change in the law.

Take a moment to think about each of these issues. Discuss them with your friends and family members. Should a 14-year-old student be held liable for his criticism of a teacher? If an adult were to circulate a similar website about someone he or she worked for, a lawsuit might very well be filed. But what about a teenager? Should an adolescent be held to the same standards as an adult?

Should a pregnant adolescent be able to obtain an abortion without notifying her parents? Should she be able to obtain contraception without her parents' knowing? see a psychologist? have cosmetic surgery? At what age do you think individuals are mature enough to make these sorts of decisions on their own?

And how should we respond to young offenders? "Do the adult crime, do the adult time" may sound fair from the perspective of crime victims, but does it make sense in light of what we know about adolescent development? Can a 12-year-old fully appreciate the consequences of his actions? Does someone this age have a sufficient understanding of court procedures to be competent to stand trial? Can we accurately assess how dangerous an adolescent might be in the future? That is, is it possible to predict whether a young adolescent will commit more crimes in the future by looking at his past history and current behavior?

These are all difficult and complicated questions without easy answers. And, although what you will learn in this book will not provide clear-cut answers to these questions—in fact, there are no clear-cut answers to them—you will certainly think about them in a more sophisticated, knowledgeable way after you've finished this course. In fact, you might want to write down you answers to these questions now and revisit them after you've finished the book. You may be surprised at how your views have changed. •

A MULTIDISCIPLINARY APPROACH TO ADOLESCENCE

What is the nature of adolescents' identity development in a changing world? How should society deal with problems of youth unemployment, adolescent AIDS, teenage pregnancy, alcohol abuse, and juvenile crime? What is the best way to prepare young people for the roles of adulthood? Should adolescents be required to obtain their parents' consent in order to receive medical or mental health services? How should the criminal justice system treat youthful offenders, such as those involved in the Jonesboro shootings?

Answering these questions requires a thorough understanding of adolescents' psychological development, and in this book we will examine how—and why—people's hopes and plans, their fears and anxieties, and their questions and concerns change as they grow into adulthood. But answering these difficult questions also requires knowledge of how individuals develop physically, how their relationships with parents and friends change, how young people as a group are viewed and treated by society, how adolescence in our society differs from adolescence in other cultures, and how the nature of adolescence itself has changed over the years. In other words, a complete understanding of adolescence in contemporary society depends on being familiar with biological, social, sociological, cultural, and historical perspectives on adolescence.

In this book, we look at adolescence from a *multidisciplinary* perspective—a perspective that draws on a variety of disciplines. Each discipline provides a view of adolescence that helps, in its own way, to further our understanding of this period of the life cycle. We will look at contributions to the study of adolescence made by biologists, psychologists, educators, sociologists, historians, and anthropologists. The challenge ahead of us in this book is not to try to determine which perspective on adolescence is best but to find ways in which to integrate contributions from different disciplines into a coherent and comprehensive viewpoint on the nature of adolescent development in contemporary society.

THE BOUNDARIES OF ADOLESCENCE

Let's begin with a fairly basic question. When does adolescence begin and end? Perhaps we can gain some insight into this question by examining the word itself.

The word *adolescence* is Latin in origin, derived from the verb *adolescere*, which means "to grow into adulthood." In all societies, adolescence is a time of growing up, of moving from the immaturity of childhood into the maturity of adulthood, of preparation for the future (Larson, in press). **Adolescence** is a period of transitions: biological, psychological, social, and economic. It is an exciting time of life. Individuals become interested in sex and become biologically capable of having children. They become wiser, more sophisticated, and better able to make their own decisions. Adolescents are permitted to work, to get married, and to vote. And, eventually, adolescents are expected to be able to support themselves financially.

For the purposes of this book, *adolescence* is defined, roughly speaking, as the second decade of the life span. Although at one time *adolescence* may have been synonymous with the teenage years (from 13 to 19), the adolescent period has been lengthened considerably in the past century, both because young people mature earlier physically (we will discuss this in chapter 1) and because so many individuals remain economically dependent on their parents well after they turn 20. Because of these changes, it makes more sense to think of adolescence as beginning around age 10 and ending in the early twenties.

As you can see in the accompanying box, there are a variety of boundaries that one might draw between childhood and adolescence, as well as between adolescence and adulthood. Although it may seem frustrating, determining the beginning and ending of adolescence is more a matter of opinion than absolute fact. Whereas a biologist would place a great deal of emphasis on the attainment and completion of puberty, an attorney would look instead at important age breaks designated by law, whereas an educator might draw attention to differences between students enrolled in different grades in school. Is a biologically mature fifth-grader an adolescent or a child? Is a 20-year-old college student who lives at home an adolescent or an adult? It all depends on the boundaries one uses to define the period.

Rather than argue about which boundaries are the correct ones, it probably makes more sense to think of development during adolescence as involving a *series* of transitions from immaturity into maturity (Arnett & Taber, 1994; Graber & Brooks-Gunn, 1996; Hoffman, 1996). Some of these passages are long and some are short; some are smooth and others are rough. And not all of them occur at the same time. Consequently, it is quite possible—and perhaps even likely—that an individual will mature in some respects before he or she matures in others. The various aspects of adolescence have different beginnings and different endings for every individual. Every young person is a child in some ways, an adolescent in other ways, and an adult in still others.

RECAP

A thorough understanding of adolescent development in contemporary society depends on being familiar with numerous perspectives on adolescence. Among the most important are those drawn from psychology, biology, history, sociology, education, and anthropology. Within all of these perspectives, adolescence is viewed as a transitional period whose chief purpose is the preparation of children for adult roles. Rather than viewing adolescence as having a specific beginning and a specific ending, it makes more sense to think of the period as being composed of a series of passages—biological, psychological, social, and economic—from immaturity into maturity.

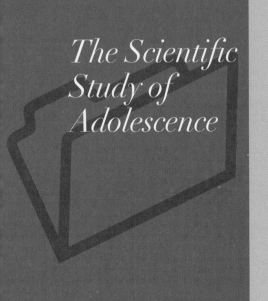

The Scientific Study of Adolescence

The Boundaries of Adolescence

One problem that students of adolescence encounter early is a fundamental one: deciding when adolescence begins and ends, what the boundaries of the period are. Different theorists have proposed various markers, but there is little agreement on this issue.

The following are some examples of the ways in which adolescence has been distinguished from childhood and adulthood, which we will examine in this book. Which boundaries make the most sense to you?

Perspective	When Adolescence Begins	When Adolescence Ends
Biological	Onset of puberty	Development of capacity for sexual reproduction
Emotional	Beginning of detachment from parents	Attainment of separate sense of identity
Cognitive	Emergence of more advanced reasoning abilities	Consolidation of advanced reasoning abilities
Interpersonal	Beginning of a shift in interest from parental to peer relations	Development of capacity for intimacy with peers
Social	Beginning of training for adult work, family, and citizen roles	Full attainment of adult status and privileges
Educational	Entrance into junior high school	Completion of formal schooling
Legal	Attainment of juvenile status	Attainment of majority status
Chronological	Attainment of designated age of adolescence (e.g., 10 years)	Attainment of designated age of adulthood (e.g., 22 years)
Cultural	Entrance into period of training for a ceremonial rite of passage	Completion of ceremonial rite of passage

Food for Thought

Of all the different ways in which we draw boundaries around the adolescent period, which ones make the most sense to you? Which ones are least useful?

Early, Middle, and Late Adolescence

Although adolescence may span a 10-year period, most social scientists and practitioners recognize that so much psychological and social growth takes place during this decade that it makes more sense to view the adolescent years as composed of a series of phases than as one homogeneous stage. A 13-year-old whose interests center around rap music and soccer, for example, has little in common with an 18-year-old who is contemplating marriage, worried about pressures at work, and beginning a college career.

Social scientists who study adolescence usually differentiate among **early adolescence,** which covers the period from about age 10 through age 13; **middle adolescence,** from about age 14 through age 18; and **late adolescence** (or *youth,* as it is sometimes known), from about age 19 through age 22 (Arnett, 2000; Kagan & Coles, 1972; Keniston, 1970; Lipsitz, 1977). These divisions, as you

▲ *One significant aspect of the transition from childhood into adolescence is the young person's entry into the labor force.* (Thomas Craig/Picture Cube)

may have guessed, correspond to the way in which many societies group young people in educational institutions; they are the approximate ages that customarily mark attendance at middle or junior high school, high school, and college. In discussing development during adolescence, we will need to be sensitive not only to differences between adolescence and childhood, or between adolescence and adulthood, but to differences among the various phases of adolescence itself.

A FRAMEWORK FOR STUDYING ADOLESCENT DEVELOPMENT

In order to organize information from a variety of perspectives, this book uses a framework that is based largely on a model suggested by late psychologist John Hill (1983). The framework is organized around three basic components: the *fundamental changes* of adolescence, the *contexts* of adolescence, and the *psychosocial developments* of adolescence.

The Fundamental Changes of Adolescence

What, if anything, is distinctive about adolescence as a period in the life cycle? According to Hill, there are three features of adolescent development that give the period its special flavor and significance: (1) the onset of puberty, (2) the emergence of more advanced thinking abilities, and (3) the transition into new roles in society. We refer to these three sets of changes—biological, cognitive, and social—as the *fundamental changes of adolescence.* They are changes that occur universally; virtually without exception, all adolescents in every society go through them.

● **Biological Transitions**   The chief elements of the biological changes of adolescence—which together are referred to as **puberty**—involve changes in the young person's physical appearance (including breast development in girls, the growth of facial hair in boys, and a dramatic increase in height for both sexes) and the attainment of reproductive capability—the ability to conceive children (Graber, Petersen, & Brooks-Gunn, 1996).

Chapter 1 describes not only the biological changes that occur in early adolescence but also the impact of puberty on the adolescent's psychological development and social relations. Puberty requires adaptation on the part of young people and those around them. The adolescent's self-image, for example, may be temporarily threatened by marked changes in physical appearance. The body changes, the face changes, and, not surprisingly, the way the adolescent feels about himself or herself changes. Relationships inside the family are transformed by the adolescent's greater need for privacy and by his or her interest in forming intimate relationships with peers. Girls may suddenly feel uncomfortable about being physically

▲ *Social scientists who study adolescence usually differentiate among three periods: early adolescence (approximately 11 through 14 years of age), middle adolescence (15 through 18 years), and late adolescence (18 through 21 years).* (David S. Strickler/Picture Cube; Rick Smolan/Stock, Boston)

affectionate with their fathers, and boys with their mothers. And, of course, adolescents' friendships are altered by newly emerging sexual impulses and concerns.

• **Cognitive Transitions**   The word *cognitive* is used to refer to the processes that underlie how people think about things. Memory and problem solving are both examples of cognitive processes. Changes in thinking abilities, which are dealt with in chapter 2, constitute the second of the three fundamental changes of the adolescent period. The emergence of more sophisticated thinking abilities is one of the most striking changes to take place during adolescence. Compared with children, for example, adolescents are much better able to think about hypothetical situations (that is, things that have not yet happened but will or things that may not happen but could) and are much better able to think about abstract concepts, such as friendship, democracy, and morality (Moshman, 1998).

The implications of these cognitive changes are also far-reaching. The ability to think more capably in hypothetical and abstract terms affects the way adolescents think about themselves, their relationships, and the world around them. We will see, for example, that teenagers' abilities to plan ahead, to argue with their parents, to solve chemistry problems, and to resolve moral dilemmas are all linked to changes in the way they think. Even the way that day-to-day decisions are made is affected. For the first time, individuals become able to think in logical ways about what their lives will be like in the future, about their relationships with friends and family, and about politics, religion, and philosophy.

• **Social Transitions**   All societies distinguish between individuals who are thought of as children and those who are seen as ready to become adults. Our society, for example, distinguishes between people who are "underage," or minors, and people who have reached the age of majority. It is not until adolescence that individuals are permitted to drive, marry, and vote. Such changes in rights, privileges, and responsibilities—which are examined chapter 3—constitute the third set of fundamental changes that occur at adolescence: social changes. In some cultures, the social changes of adolescence are marked by a formal ceremony—a **rite of passage.** In others, the transition is less clearly demarcated. Still, a change in social status is a universal feature of adolescence (Ford & Beach, 1951).

Society's redefinition of the individual provokes reconsideration of the young person's capabilities and competencies. As the young person's treatment by society changes, so do relationships around the home, at school, and in the peer group. Changes in social status also permit young people to enter new roles and engage in new activities, such as marriage and work, which dramatically alter their self-image and relationships with others. The adolescent, on the verge of becoming an adult, has choices to consider that previously did not exist for him or her.

> **RECAP**
>
> *Three features of adolescence give the period its special flavor and distinctiveness: the biological changes of puberty, the emergence of more advanced thinking abilities, and the transition of the individual into new roles in society. These three sets of universal changes are referred to as the fundamental changes of adolescence.*

Food for Thought

Of the three sets of fundamental changes that define adolescence, which seems to you to be the most important?

The Three Fundamental Changes of Adolescence

- Biological transitions
- Cognitive transitions
- Social transitions

The Contexts of Adolescence

Although all adolescents experience the biological, cognitive, and social transitions of the period, the *effects* of these changes are not uniform for all young people. Puberty makes some adolescents feel attractive and self-assured, but it makes others feel ugly and self-conscious. Being able to think in hypothetical terms makes some youngsters thankful that they grew up with the parents they have, but it prompts others to run away in search of a better life. Reaching 18 years of age prompts some teenagers to enlist unhesitatingly in the military or apply for a marriage license; for others, however, becoming an adult is frightening and unsettling.

If the fundamental changes of adolescence are universal, why are their effects so varied? Why aren't all individuals affected in the same ways by puberty, by changes in thinking, and by changes in social and legal status? The answer lies in the fact that the psychological impact of the biological, cognitive, and social changes of adolescence is shaped by the environment in which the changes take place. In other words, psychological

▲ *The implications of the cognitive changes of adolescence are far-reaching.* (Michelle Bridwell/PhotoEdit)

development during adolescence is a product of the interplay between a set of three very basic and universal changes and the context in which these changes are experienced. According to the **ecological perspective on human development,** whose main proponent has been Urie Bronfenbrenner (1979), we cannot understand development without examining the settings, or context, in which it occurs.

Consider, for example, two 14-year-old girls growing up in neighboring communities. When Alice went through puberty, around age 13, her parents responded by restricting her social life because they were afraid that Alice would become too involved with boys and neglect her schoolwork. Alice felt that her parents were being unfair and foolish. She rarely had a chance to meet any boys she wanted to date, anyway. All the older boys went to the high school across town. Even though she was in the eighth grade, she was still going to school with fifth-graders. And she couldn't meet anyone through work, either. Her school would not issue work permits to any student under the age of 16.

Maria's adolescence was very different. For one thing, when she had her first period, her parents took her aside and discussed sex and pregnancy with her. They explained how various contraceptives work and made an appointment for Maria to see a gynecologist in town, in case she ever needed to discuss something with a doctor. Although she was still only 14 years old, Maria knew that she would begin dating soon, because in her community the junior and senior high schools had been combined into one large school, and the older boys frequently asked the younger girls out. In addition, since there was no prohibition at her school against young teenagers working, Maria decided to get a job; she knew she would need money to buy clothes if she were going to start dating.

Two teenage girls: Each goes through puberty, each grows intellectually, and each moves closer in age to becoming an adult, yet they grow up under very different circumstances—in different families, in different schools, with different groups of peers, and under different work conditions. Both are adolescents, but their adolescent experiences are markedly different. And, as a result, each girl's psychological development will follow a unique course.

Alice's and Maria's worlds may seem quite different from one another, yet the two girls share many things, at least in comparison with two girls growing up in different parts of the world or in different historical eras. Imagine how different your adolescence would have been if you had grown up without going to high school and had had to work full-time from the age of 12. Imagine how different it would have been to grow up 100 years ago—or how different it will be to grow up 100 years from today. And imagine how different adolescence is for a youngster whose family is very poor and for one whose family is very rich. Even siblings growing up within the same family have different growing-up experiences, depending on their birth order within the family and various other factors (Hetherington, Reiss, & Plomin, 1994). You can see that it is impossible to generalize about the nature of adolescence without taking into account the surroundings and circumstances in which young people grow up.

For this reason, the second component of our framework is the *context of adolescence*. In modern societies, four main contexts affect the development and behavior of young people: families, peer groups, schools, and work and leisure settings. But it is not enough to consider these settings in isolation, because they themselves are located within a community, which influences how they are structured and what takes place in them. It would be naïve, for example, to discuss the impact that "school" has on adolescent development without recognizing that a school in an affluent suburban community is likely very different from one in the inner city or in a remote rural area. Moreover, the community in which these settings are located is itself embedded in a broader context defined by culture, geography, and historical time (Bronfenbrenner, 1979). The nature and structure of these contexts—both proximal and distant—dramatically affect the way in which the fundamental changes of adolescence are experienced. To the extent that one adolescent's world differs from another's, the two young people will have very different experiences during the adolescent years.

Although young people growing up in modern America share some experiences with young people all over the world, their development is distinctively different from that of young people in other societies, especially those in less affluent and less industrialized nations, because their families, peer groups, schools, work settings, and social institutions are different (Larson, in press). In other words, the contexts of adolescence are themselves shaped and defined by the larger society in which young people live. In this book, we will be especially interested in how the contexts of adolescence have changed in contemporary industrialized society and in the implications of these changes for adolescent development.

As in discussions of young people's psychological development, it is important when discussing families, peer groups, schools, and work and leisure settings to differentiate among the phases of adolescence. Take adolescent peer groups, for example. During early adolescence, peer groups are usually composed of teenagers of the same sex. During middle adolescence, peer groups become a context in which males and females interact. And, during late adolescence, the large peer groups of earlier phases begin to disintegrate.

Let us now briefly survey how the contexts of adolescence have changed as society has changed.

● **Families** Frequent moves, high rates of divorce, increasing numbers of single-parent households, and more and more working mothers have become characteristic of family life in contemporary America (Hernandez, 1997). In chapter 4, we will look at these changes and try to assess how they are affecting young people's psychological development. We will also examine how the entire family system adapts to the transition from childhood into adolescence (Grotevant, 1997).

▲ *As family life has changed, so has the context in which adolescents develop.* (B. Daemmrich/Image Works)

● **Peer Groups**   Over the past 100 years, age-segregated peer groups—groups of people of the same age who spend most of their time together—have come to play an increasingly important role in the socialization and development of teenagers (Brown, Theobald, & Klute, in press). But has the rise of peer groups been a positive or negative influence on young people's development? In chapter 5, we will discuss how peer groups have changed adolescence in contemporary America.

● **Schools**   Chapter 6 examines schools as a context for adolescent development. Since the 1930s, Americans have turned more and more to schools as a setting to occupy, socialize, and educate adolescents (Hechinger, 1993). But how good a job are schools doing? What should schools do to help prepare adolescents for adulthood? And how should schools for adolescents be structured? These are three of the many difficult questions we will be examining.

● **Work and Leisure**   If you've been to a large shopping mall or fast-food restaurant lately, you know that many of today's teenagers are working. But did you know that more adolescents have jobs now than at any other time in the past 40 years (Steinberg & Cauffman, 1995)? In chapter 7, we will look at the world of adolescent work and at how part-time jobs are affecting young people's psychological development and well-being. We will also take a look at adolescents' leisure activities—their involvement in extracurriculars, their use of the mass media, and so forth (e.g., Brown & Witherspoon, in press).

> **RECAP**
>
> *Although the fundamental biological, cognitive, and social transitions of adolescence are universal, they occur in a given social context that varies from individual to individual and across space and time. The most important elements of the context of adolescent development are the family, the peer group, schools, and work and leisure settings.*

> *Food for Thought*
>
> *Think about the context in which you went through adolescence and compare it with the context in which your parents went through the same period of development. How are these contexts different from each other? How might these differences have resulted in different adolescent experiences for you and your parents?*

The Four Contexts of Adolescence

• Families
• Peer groups
• Schools
• Work and leisure

The Psychosocial Developments of Adolescence

Five sets of developmental issues are paramount during adolescence: **identity, autonomy, intimacy, sexuality,** and **achievement.** These five sets of *psychosocial issues,* as well as certain psychosocial problems that may arise at adolescence, constitute the third, and final, component of our framework. Theorists use the word **psychosocial** to describe aspects of development that are both psychological and social. Sexuality, for instance, is a psychosocial issue because it involves psychological change (that is, changes in the individual's emotions, motivations, and behavior) as well as changes in the individual's social relations with others.

Of course, identity, autonomy, intimacy, sexuality, and achievement are not concerns that arise for the first time during the adolescent years and psychological or social problems can and do occur during all periods of the life cycle. Nor do psychosocial concerns disappear when an adolescent becomes an adult. These five sets of issues are present throughout the entire life span, from infancy through late adulthood. They represent basic developmental challenges that all people face as they grow and change: discovering and understanding who they are as individuals (identity); establishing a healthy sense of independence (autonomy); forming close and caring relationships with other people (intimacy); expressing sexual feelings and enjoying physical contact with others (sexuality); and being successful and competent members of society (achievement).

Although these are not new concerns to the adolescent, development in each of these areas takes a special turn during the adolescent years. Understanding how and why such psychosocial developments take place during adolescence is a special concern of social scientists interested in this age period. We know that individuals form close relationships before adolescence, for example, but why is it during adolescence that intimate relationships with opposite-sex agemates first develop? We know that infants struggle with learning how to be independent, but why during adolescence do individuals need to be more on their own and make some decisions apart from their parents? We know that children fantasize about what they will be when they grow up, but why is it not until adolescence that these fantasies are transformed into serious concerns? Part 3 of this book (chapters 8–13) discusses changes in each of the five psychosocial areas and examines several common psychosocial problems.

● **Identity**   Chapter 8 deals with changes in identity, self-esteem, and self-conceptions. At adolescence, a variety of important changes occur in the realm of identity (Harter, 1997). The adolescent may wonder who he or she really is and where he or she is headed (Erikson, 1968). Coming to terms with these questions may involve a period of experimentation—a time of trying on different personalities in an attempt to discover one's true self. As you will read, the adolescent's quest for

identity is a quest not only for a personal sense of self, but for recognition from others and from society that he or she is a unique individual.

● **Autonomy**   Adolescents' struggle to establish themselves as independent, self-governing individuals—in their own eyes and in the eyes of others—is a long and occasionally difficult process, not only for young people but for those around them, too. Chapter 9 focuses on three sorts of concerns that are of special importance to developing adolescents: becoming less emotionally dependent on parents, becoming able to make independent decisions, and establishing a personal code of value and morals (Douvan & Adelson, 1966; Steinberg, 1990).

● **Intimacy**   During adolescence, important changes take place in the individual's capacity to be intimate with others, especially with peers. As we will see in chapter 10, friendships emerge for the first time during adolescence that involve openness, honesty, loyalty, and the exchange of confidences, rather than simply shared activities and interests (Berndt, 1996). Dating takes on increased importance; as a consequence, so does the capacity to form a relationship that is trusting and loving (Furman, Brown, & Feiring, 1999).

● **Sexuality**   Sexual activity generally begins during the adolescent years. Becoming sexual is an important aspect of development during adolescence—not only because it transforms the nature of relationships between adolescents and their peers but also because it raises for the young person a range of trying and difficult questions. Chapter 11 discusses these concerns, including efforts to incorporate sexuality into a still developing sense of self, to resolve questions about sexual values and morals, and to come to terms with the sorts of relationships into which one is prepared—or not prepared—to enter (Rodgers, 1996). We will also look at sex education, contraceptive use, the dangers of sexually transmitted infections, and adolescent childbearing.

● **Achievement**   In chapter 12, we will examine changes in individuals' educational and vocational behavior and plans. Important decisions—many with long-term consequences—about schooling and careers are made during adolescence. Many of these decisions depend on adolescents' achievement in school, on their evaluations of their own competencies and capabilities, on their aspirations and expectations for the future, and on the direction and advice they receive from parents, teachers, and friends (Eccles, Wigfield, & Schiefele, 1997).

● **Psychosocial Problems**   In chapter 13, we will look at three sets of problems typically associated with adolescence: drug and alcohol use and abuse, delinquency and other "externalizing problems," and depression and other "internalizing" problems. In each case, we will examine the prevalence of the problem, the factors believed to contribute to its development, and approaches to prevention and intervention.

RECAP

Five sets of psychosocial concerns are paramount during adolescence. These issues involve developing self-understanding (identity), establishing a healthy sense of independence (autonomy), forming close and caring relationships with others (intimacy), expressing sexual feelings and enjoying physical contact with others (sexuality), and being successful and competent members of society (achievement). Although these are not new concerns in adolescence, development in each of these areas takes a special turn during the adolescent years. A number of specific psychosocial problems are associated with adolescence, although they affect only a minority of young people. Among the most important are drug and alcohol use, delinquency and other externalizing problems, and depression and other internalizing problems.

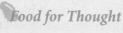

Food for Thought

Identity, autonomy, intimacy, sexuality, and achievement are life-long issues that have special significance during adolescence. Think back to your adolescence. Which of these issues posed the most difficult challenges for you? Why?

The Psychosocial Issues and Problems of Adolescence

- Identity
- Autonomy
- Intimacy
- Sexuality
- Achievement
- Psychosocial problems

A Framework for Studying Adolescent Development

- Fundamental changes
- Contexts
- Psychosocial issues and problems

THEORETICAL PERSPECTIVES ON ADOLESCENCE

It is useful to organize theoretical perspectives on adolescence around an issue that has long dominated discussions about the nature of this period of the life span: To what extent is adolescence shaped by the fundamental biological changes of the period, and to what extent is it defined by the environment in which the individual develops? Whereas some theories construe adolescence as a biologically defined period, others view it as contextually determined. Still others fall somewhere between the two extremes of this continuum. The purpose of this brief overview is not to argue for one approach over another but, rather, to demonstrate how each of these views has helped us gain a better understanding of the nature of adolescence.

Biological Theories

The fact that biological change during adolescence is noteworthy is not a matter of dispute. How important this biological change is in defining the psychosocial issues of the period is, however, in dispute. Theorists who have taken a biological—or, more accurately, a biosocial—view of adolescence stress the hormonal and physical changes of puberty as driving forces. The most important biosocial theorist was G. Stanley Hall (1904), considered the "father" of the scientific study of adolescence.

Hall, who was very much influenced by the work of Charles Darwin, the author of the theory of evolution, believed that the development of the individual parallels the development of the human species, a notion referred to as his theory of recapitulation. Infancy, in his view, is equivalent to the time during our evolution when we were primitive, like animals. Adolescence, in contrast, was seen as a time that parallels the evolution of our species into civilization. For Hall, the development of the individual through these stages is determined primarily by instinct—by biological and genetic forces within the person—and hardly influenced by the environment.

The most important legacy of Hall's view of adolescence is the notion that adolescence is inevitably a period of storm and stress. He believed that the hormonal changes of puberty cause upheaval, both for the individual and for those around the young person. Because this turbulence is biologically determined, it is unavoidable. The best that society can do is to find ways of managing the young person, whose "raging hormones" invariably lead to difficulties.

Although scientists no longer believe that adolescence is an inherently stressful period, much contemporary work continues to emphasize the role that biological factors play in shaping the adolescent experience. Indeed, the study of the impact of puberty on adolescent psychosocial development has been, and continues to be, a central question for the field. In addition, current work from the biosocial tradition explores the genetic bases of individual differences in adolescence, as well as the socio-biological bases of adolescent behavior.

Organismic Theories

Our next stop on the continuum is in the domain of organismic theorists. Like biosocial theorists, organismic theorists also stress the importance of the biological changes of adolescence. However, unlike their biosocial counterparts, organismic theories also take into account the ways in which contextual forces interact with and modify the impact of these biological imperatives.

If you have had previous coursework in developmental psychology, you have encountered the major organismic theorists, since they have long dominated the study of development. Three of these theorists, in particular, have had a great influence over the study of adolescence: Sigmund Freud (1938), Erik Erikson (1968), and Jean Piaget (Inhelder & Piaget, 1958). Although each of these theorists is classified as organismic, the theories they developed emphasized different aspects of individual growth and development.

For Freud, development was best understood in terms of the psychosexual conflicts that arise at different points in development. In psychoanalytic theory, adolescence is also seen as a time of upheaval—as was the case in Hall's view. According to Freud, the hormonal changes of puberty upset the psychic balance that had been achieved during the prior psychosexual stage, called latency. Because the hormonal changes of puberty are responsible for marked increases in sexual drive, the adolescent is temporarily thrown into a period of intrapsychic crisis, and old psychosexual conflicts, long buried in the unconscious, are revived. Freud and his followers believed that the main challenge of adolescence is to restore a psychic balance and resolve these conflicts. Although the process is driven by the hormonal changes of puberty, the specific conflicts faced by the young person were seen as dependent on his or her early experiences in the family.

Freud himself actually had very little to say specifically about adolescence. But his daughter, Anna Freud (1958), extended much of her father's thinking to the study of development during the second decade of life. Today, this work is carried on by neo-Freudians, such as Peter Blos (1979), whose theories of adolescent development we will explore in detail in chapter 9.

In Erikson's theory, the emphasis was on the psychosocial crises characteristic of each period of growth. Like Freud, Erikson also believed that internal, biological developments move the individual from one developmental stage to the next. But, unlike Freud, Erikson stressed the psychosocial, rather than the psychosexual, conflicts faced by the individual at each point in time. Whereas Freud emphasized the development of the id—that part of the psyche believed to be dominated by instinctual urges—Erikson emphasized the development of the ego—that part of the psyche believed to regulate thought, emotion, and behavior.

Erikson proposed eight stages in psychosocial development, each characterized by a specific "crisis," that arises at that point in development because of the interplay between the internal forces of biology and the unique demands of society. In Erikson's theory, which we will look at in detail in chapter 8, adolescence is seen as a period that revolves around the crisis of identity versus identity diffusion, a crisis that is shaped both by the changes of puberty and by the specific demands that society places on young people. According to Erikson, the challenge of adolescence is to resolve the identity crisis successfully and to emerge from the period with a coherent sense of who one is and where one is headed.

Freud and Erikson both emphasized emotional and social development. For Piaget, development can best be understood by examining changes in the nature of thinking, or cognition. Piaget believed that, as children mature, they pass through stages of cognitive development; in each stage, from birth to adolescence, their ways of thinking are qualitatively distinct. According to his view, understanding the distinctive features of thought and reasoning at each stage can give us insight into the overall development of the individual at that point in time.

In Piaget's theory, which is discussed in detail in chapter 2, adolescence marks the transition from concrete to abstract thought. According to this model, adolescence is the period in which individuals become capable of thinking in hypothetical terms, a development that permits a wide expansion of logical abilities. As you will see, many of the familiar changes in behavior that we associate with adolescence have been attributed to these changes in cognitive abilities. Piaget's views have been applied to the study of moral development, social development, and education.

As is the case with the other organismic theories, Piaget's theory of cognitive development emphasizes the interplay between biological and contextual forces. The development of higher-order thinking in adolescence, for example, is influenced both by the internal biological changes of the developmental period and by changes in the intellectual environment encountered by the individual.

Learning Theories

As we move across the theoretical continuum from extreme biological views to extreme environmental ones, we encounter a group of theories that shift the emphasis from biological forces to contextual ones. Whereas organismic theorists tend to emphasize the interaction between biological change and environmental demand, learning theorists stress the context in which behavior takes place. The capacity of the individual to learn from experience is assumed to be a biological given. What is of interest to learning theorists is the content of what is learned.

Learning theorists are not especially developmental in their approach and, as a consequence, have little to say specifically about adolescence as a developmental period. Indeed, for learning theorists, the basic processes of human behavior are the same during adolescence as they are during other periods of the life span. But learning theorists have been extremely influential in the study of adolescent development because they have helped us understand how the specific environment in which an adolescent lives can shape the individual's behavior.

There are two general categories of learning theorists. One group, called behaviorists, emphasizes the processes of reinforcement and punishment as the main influences on adolescent behavior. The main proponent of this view was B. F. Skinner (1953), whose theory of operant conditioning has had a tremendous impact on the entire field of psychology. Within an operant conditioning framework, reinforcement is defined as the process through which a behavior is made more likely to occur again, whereas punishment is defined as the process through which a behavior is made less likely to occur again. From this vantage point, adolescent behavior can be seen as nothing more or less than the product of the various reinforcements and punishments to which the individual has been exposed.

An adolescent who strives to do well in school, for example, does so because he or she has been reinforced for this behavior, or has been punished for not behaving this way, in the past.

A related approach is taken by social learning theorists, such as Albert Bandura (Bandura & Walters, 1959), who also emphasize the ways in which adolescents learn how to behave. However, in contrast to behaviorists, social learning theorists place more weight on the processes of modeling and observational learning. That is, adolescents learn how to behave not simply by being reinforced and punished by forces in the environment but also by watching and imitating those around them. As is clear throughout this text, social learning approaches to adolescence have been very influential in explaining how adolescents are affected by the child-rearing methods their parents use and by the influence, or pressure, of their peers.

Sociological Theories

The emphasis within the biosocial, organismic, and learning theories is mainly on forces within the individual or within the individual's specific environment in shaping his or her development and behavior. In contrast, sociological theories of adolescence attempt to understand how adolescents, as a group, come of age in society. Instead of emphasizing differences among individuals in their biological makeup or their experiences in the world, sociological theorists emphasize the factors that all adolescents or groups of adolescents—by virtue of their sharing age, ethnicity, gender, or another demographic feature—have in common.

Sociological theories of adolescence have often focused on relations between the generations and have tended to emphasize the difficulties young people have in making the transition from adolescence into adulthood, especially in industrialized society. Two themes have dominated these discussions. One theme, concerning the marginality of young people, emphasizes the difference in power that exists between the adult and the adolescent generations. Two important thinkers in this vein are Kurt Lewin (1951) and Edgar Friedenberg (1959). Although the view that adolescents are second-class citizens was more influential 40 years ago than today, contemporary applications of this viewpoint stress the fact that many adolescents are prohibited from occupying meaningful roles in society and therefore experience frustration and restlessness. Some theorists have argued that adults have forced

▲ *Your experiences as a teenager were the product of a unique set of cultural and historical forces at work in the context in which you came of age. These young women will forever remember their adolescent experiences as refugees during the war in Bosnia.* (Wesley Boexe/Photo Researchers)

adolescents into occupying one and only one role—that of student—which is an inherently powerless and "infantilizing" position for young people. This was one explanation given for the student movements of the 1960s (e.g., Braungart, 1980).

A modification of this view focuses on differences within the adolescent population. According to this viewpoint, the adolescent's social class, or socioeconomic status, as it is formally known, structures his or her experience of growing up. Theorists such as August Hollingshead (1949/1975) and Robert Havighurst (1952) have emphasized the fact that the experience of adolescence differs markedly as a function of the young person's family background. They argue that it is impossible to generalize about the nature of adolescence because it varies so much depending on the resources of the adolescent's family.

The other theme in sociological theories of adolescence concerns intergenerational conflict or, as it is more commonly known, the generation gap. Theorists such as Karl Mannheim (1952) and James Coleman (1961) stressed the fact that adolescents and adults grow up under different social circumstances and therefore develop different sets of attitudes, values, and beliefs. As a consequence, there is inevitable tension between the adolescent and the adult generations. Some writers, such as Coleman, have gone so far as to argue that adolescents develop a different cultural viewpoint—a counterculture—which may be hostile to the values or beliefs of adult society.

Although sociological theories of adolescence clearly place the emphasis on the broader context in which adolescents come of age, there is still a theme of inevitability that runs through their approach. Mannheim, for example, believed that, because modern society changes so rapidly, there will always be problems between generations because each cohort comes into adulthood with different experiences and beliefs. Similarly, Lewin believed that marginality is an inherent feature of adolescence because adults always control more resources and have more power than young people.

Historical and Anthropological Approaches

Our final stop on the continuum takes us to the extreme environmental position. Historians and anthropologists who study adolescence share with sociologists an interest in the broader context in which young people come of age, but they take a much more relativistic stance. Historical perspectives, such as those offered by Glen Elder (1998), Joseph Kett (1977), and Thomas Hine (1999), stress the fact that adolescence as a developmental period has varied considerably from one historical era to another. As a consequence, it is impossible to generalize about such issues as the degree to which adolescence is stressful, the developmental tasks of the period, and the nature of intergenerational relations. Historians would say that these issues all depend on the social, political, and economic forces present at a given time. Even something as basic to our view of adolescence as the identity crisis, they say, is a social invention that arose because of industrialization and the prolongation of schooling. Before the industrial revolution, when most adolescents followed in their parents' occupation, crises over identity did not exist.

One group of theorists has taken this viewpoint to its logical extreme. These theorists, called *inventionists,* argue that adolescence is entirely a social invention (Bakan, 1972). Inventionists believe that the way in which we divide the life cycle into stages—drawing a boundary between childhood and adolescence, for example—is nothing more than a reflection of the political, economic, and social circumstances in which we live. They point out that, although puberty has been a feature of development for as long as humans have lived, it was not until the rise of compulsory education that we began treating adolescents as a distinct group. This suggests that social conditions, not biological givens, define the nature of adolescent development.

A similar theme is echoed by anthropologists who study adolescence, the most important of whom were Ruth Benedict (1934) and Margaret Mead (1928). Benedict and Mead, whose work is examined in chapter 3, pointed out that societies vary considerably in the ways in which they view and structure adolescence. As a consequence, these thinkers viewed adolescence as a culturally defined experience—stressful and difficult in societies that saw it this way but calm and peaceful in societies that had an alternative vision. Benedict, in particular, drew a distinction between continuous and discontinuous societies. In continuous societies (typically, nonindustrialized societies with little social change), the transition from adolescence to adulthood is gradual and peaceful. In discontinuous societies (typically, industrialized societies characterized by rapid social change), the transition into adulthood is abrupt and difficult.

RECAP

Major theories about adolescence can be organized along a continuum, with biological theories at one end, and historical and anthropological theories at the other. In the middle of the continuum are organismic, learning, and sociological theories. These perspectives vary in the degree to which they view adolescence as a biologically determined period of development versus a socially constructed one.

Food for Thought

Theorists who emphasize the biological nature of adolescence would have a difficult time accepting the view of those who argue that adolescence is merely an invention, that exists at some times and not others or in some, but not all, cultures. Is there a way to reconcile these two points of view?

STEREOTYPES VERSUS SCIENTIFIC STUDY

One of the oldest debates in the study of adolescence is whether adolescence is an inherently stressful time for individuals. G. Stanley Hall likened adolescence to the turbulent, transitional period in the evolution of the human species from savagery into civilization. "Adolescence is a new birth," Hall wrote. "Development is less gradual, suggestive of some ancient period of storm and stress" (1904, p. 6). Long before Hall, in the eighteenth century, French philosopher Jean-Jacques Rousseau had described adolescence by drawing an analogy to a violent storm: "As the roaring of the waves precedes the tempest, so the murmur of rising passions announces the tumultuous change. . . . Keep your hand upon the helm," he warned parents, "or all is lost" (Rousseau, 1762/1911, pp. 172–173).

Although neither Hall nor Rousseau had any scientific evidence that adolescence is any more stormy than childhood or adulthood, their portrayal of teenagers as passionate, fickle, and unpredictable persists today. For example, people still tend to think of adolescence as a difficult and stressful time. A 12-year-old girl once told me that her mother had been telling her that she was going to go through a difficult time when she turned 14—as if a magical, internal alarm clock was set to trigger "storm and stress" on schedule.

The girl's mother wasn't alone in her view of adolescence, of course. Sometime this week, turn on the television and note how teenagers are depicted. If they are not portrayed as juvenile delinquents—the usual role in which they are cast—adolescents are depicted as sex-crazed idiots (if they are male); giggling schoolgirls (if

they are female); or tormented lost souls, searching for their place in a strange, cruel world (if they aren't delinquent, sex-crazed, or giggling). One study of local television news in California, for example, found that over half the stories on youth were about violence (Dorfman Woodruff, Chavez, & Wallack,1997).

Adolescents are one of the most stereotyped groups in contemporary society; as a consequence, they are one of the most misunderstood (Adelson, 1979; Arnett, 1999; Males, 1996, 1998). Indeed, one study of college students demonstrated that most of the undergraduates enrolled in an adolescent development course believed that

Table I.1   How stereotyped are your views of adolescence?
One group of researchers has developed a questionnaire designed to measure people's beliefs about adolescence. Make a copy of this questionnaire and fill it out today, before you read any further in the text. Then do the same thing at the end of the course and compare your answers.

Instructions: For each characteristic or behavior, please mark the probability that a typical adolescent possesses that characteristic or displays that behavior. (Another way to think about this is to mark the proportion of adolescents that you believe possess the characteristic or display the behavior.) Move quickly through the list; don't think too long about each item.

	0% definitely no										100% definitely yes
Active	0	10	20	30	40	50	60	70	80	90	100
Adventurous	0	10	20	30	40	50	60	70	80	90	100
Ambitious	0	10	20	30	40	50	60	70	80	90	100
Anxious	0	10	20	30	40	50	60	70	80	90	100
Awkward	0	10	20	30	40	50	60	70	80	90	100
Caring	0	10	20	30	40	50	60	70	80	90	100
Conforming to peers	0	10	20	30	40	50	60	70	80	90	100
Confused	0	10	20	30	40	50	60	70	80	90	100
Considerate	0	10	20	30	40	50	60	70	80	90	100
Dates	0	10	20	30	40	50	60	70	80	90	100
Depressed	0	10	20	30	40	50	60	70	80	90	100
Distractible	0	10	20	30	40	50	60	70	80	90	100
Easily influenced by friends	0	10	20	30	40	50	60	70	80	90	100
Emotional	0	10	20	30	40	50	60	70	80	90	100
Energetic	0	10	20	30	40	50	60	70	80	90	100
Faddish	0	10	20	30	40	50	60	70	80	90	100
Friendly	0	10	20	30	40	50	60	70	80	90	100
Fun-loving	0	10	20	30	40	50	60	70	80	90	100
Generous	0	10	20	30	40	50	60	70	80	90	100
Hardworking	0	10	20	30	40	50	60	70	80	90	100
Helpful	0	10	20	30	40	50	60	70	80	90	100
Honest	0	10	20	30	40	50	60	70	80	90	100
Impulsive	0	10	20	30	40	50	60	70	80	90	100

adolescence is an inherently stressful period (Holmbeck & Hill, 1988). After completing the course, however—which, incidentally, used an earlier edition of this textbook—the students were less likely to endorse this view.

The tremendous growth of the scientific literature on adolescence over the past two decades has, fortunately, led to more accurate views of normal adolescence among practitioners who work with young people (Stoller, Offer, Howard, & Koenig, 1996), although a trip to the "Parenting" section of your local bookstore will quickly reveal that the storm and stress stereotype is still alive and well (Steinberg, 2001b). Today, most experts do not dismiss the storm and stress viewpoint as entirely incorrect but see the difficulties that some adolescents have as due largely to the cultural context within which young people grow up. Adolescents are more stressed in contemporary industrialized societies, for example, than they are in nonindustrialized, traditional ones, al-

though this may change as globalization brings some of the more stressful aspects of adolescence to less industrialized parts of the world (Arnett, 1999).

You have no doubt come into this course with many convictions about adolescence. These beliefs are based in part on your own experiences as a teenager (Buchanan & Holmbeck, 1998) and in part on the images of adolescents to which you have been exposed over the years—in books, on film, and on television. As several writers have pointed out, even scientists' portrayal of teenagers is influenced by the broader social and historical context in which they work. To the extent that we *want* to see adolescents as different from adults, we exaggerate the differences between teenagers and their elders and portray young people as "out of control due to hormonal storms" (Lesko, 1996, p. 157). During periods of economic downturns, for instance, when jobs are scarce, scholars depict adolescents as immature, unstable, and in

	0% definitely no									100% definitely yes
Inquisitive	0	10	20	30	40	50	60	70	80	90	100
Insecure	0	10	20	30	40	50	60	70	80	90	100
Intelligent	0	10	20	30	40	50	60	70	80	90	100
Interested in school	0	10	20	30	40	50	60	70	80	90	100
Into clothes	0	10	20	30	40	50	60	70	80	90	100
Listens to music	0	10	20	30	40	50	60	70	80	90	100
Materialistic	0	10	20	30	40	50	60	70	80	90	100
Rebellious	0	10	20	30	40	50	60	70	80	90	100
Reckless	0	10	20	30	40	50	60	70	80	90	100
Restless	0	10	20	30	40	50	60	70	80	90	100
Rude	0	10	20	30	40	50	60	70	80	90	100
Sad	0	10	20	30	40	50	60	70	80	90	100
Selfish	0	10	20	30	40	50	60	70	80	90	100
Sexually active	0	10	20	30	40	50	60	70	80	90	100
Smokes	0	10	20	30	40	50	60	70	80	90	100
Social	0	10	20	30	40	50	60	70	80	90	100
Spends time with friends	0	10	20	30	40	50	60	70	80	90	100
Stubborn	0	10	20	30	40	50	60	70	80	90	100
Takes risks	0	10	20	30	40	50	60	70	80	90	100
Tests limits	0	10	20	30	40	50	60	70	80	90	100
Uses drugs	0	10	20	30	40	50	60	70	80	90	100
Uses alcohol	0	10	20	30	40	50	60	70	80	90	100

Source: Buchanan, Holmbeck, Allison, & Hughes, 1996.

need of more schooling, whereas during periods of war, the same age group is portrayed as mature, responsible, and competent (Enright, Levy, Harris, & Lapsley, 1987). Presumably, these characterizations serve a broader, if hidden, agenda—during depressions, there are fewer jobs to go around, and adults may need to see adolescents as incapable of working, whereas the reverse is true during wartime, when even youngsters are needed to help in factories and on farms. In all likelihood, today's calls for treating youthful offenders as adults have more to do with politicians' desires to take advantage of public concerns about crime than with any real changes that have taken place in young people themselves (Bernard, 1991). Nevertheless, recent public opinion polls indicate that contemporary adults view adolescents very negatively, describing them as rude, irresponsible, wild, and disrespectful (Public Agenda, 1999).

One of the goals of this book is to provide a more realistic understanding of adolescent development in contemporary society—an understanding that reflects the best scientific knowledge available. Some of the results of this scientific research will not mesh with your own experiences and beliefs; others will.

As you read the material, you should think about your personal experiences as an adolescent, but you should also try to look beyond them and be willing to question the "truths" about teenagers that you have grown accustomed to believing over the years. This does not mean that your experiences were not valid ones or your recollections inaccurate. Rather, your experiences as a teenager were the product of a unique set of forces that have made you the individual you are today. The person who sits next to you in class—or the person who right now, in a distant region of the world, is thinking back to his or her adolescence—was probably exposed to different forces than you and probably had a different set of adolescent experiences as a consequence.

RECAP

Although it is commonly believed that adolescence is an inherently difficult time, there is little scientific support for this idea. Adolescence is a period of change, but the degree to which it is stressful is dependent on the broader context within which people come of age. One important goal of the study of adolescence is to understand the factors that make the period difficult for some individuals but not for others.

Food for Thought

If adolescence is not inevitably a period of storm and stress, why is it so often portrayed in this way?

KEY TERMS

achievement

adolescence

autonomy

early adolescence

ecological perspective on human development

identity

intimacy

late adolescence

middle adolescence

psychosocial

puberty

rite of passage

sexuality

I

The Fundamental Changes of Adolescence

Chapter 1

Biological Transitions

According to an old joke, there are only two things in life that one can be sure of—death and taxes. To this brief list one might add puberty—the physical changes of adolescence—for, of all the developments that take place during the second decade of life, the only truly inevitable one is physical maturation. Not all adolescents experience identity crises, rebel against their parents, or fall head over heels in love, but virtually all undergo the biological transitions associated with maturation into adult reproductive capability.

Puberty, however, is considerably affected by the context in which it occurs. Physical development is influenced by a host of environmental factors, and the timing and rate of pubertal growth vary across regions of the world, socioeconomic classes, ethnic groups, and historical eras. In contemporary America, the average girl reaches **menarche**—the time of first menstruation—between her twelfth and thirteenth birthdays. However, among the Lumi people of New Guinea, the typical girl does not reach menarche until after 18 years of age (Eveleth & Tanner, 1990). Imagine how great a difference those five years make in transforming the nature of adolescence. Picture how different American high schools would be if sexual maturation did not occur until after graduation.

Physical and sexual maturation profoundly affect the way in which adolescents view themselves and the way in which they are viewed and treated by others. Yet the social environment exerts a tremendous impact on the meaning of puberty and on its psychological and social consequences; indeed, as you will read in this chapter, the social environment even affects the *timing* of puberty (i.e., whether a person matures early or late). In some societies, pubertal maturation brings with it a series of complex initiation rites that mark the passage of the young person into adulthood socially as well as physically. In other societies, recognition of the physical transformation from child into adult takes more subtle forms. Parents may merely remark, "Our little boy has become a man," when they discover that he needs to shave. Early or late maturation may be cause for celebration or cause for concern, depending on what is admired or derogated in a given peer group at a given point in time. In the fifth grade, developing breasts may be a source of embarrassment; but in the ninth grade, it may be just as embarrassing *not* to have developed breasts.

In sum, even the most universal aspect of adolescence—puberty—is hardly universal in its impact on the young person. In this chapter, we will examine just how and why the environment in which adolescents develop exerts its influence even on something as fundamental as puberty. ●

PUBERTY: AN OVERVIEW

Puberty derives from the Latin word *pubertas,* which means "adult." Technically, the term refers to the period during which an individual becomes capable of sexual reproduction; that is, it denotes the series of biological changes leading up to reproductive capability. More broadly speaking, however, puberty encompasses all the physical changes that occur in the growing girl or boy as the individual passes from childhood into adulthood.

The following are the five chief physical manifestations of puberty (Marshall, 1978):

1. A *rapid acceleration in growth,* resulting in dramatic increases in both height and weight

2. The *development of primary sex characteristics,* including the further development of the gonads, or sex glands, which are the testes in males and the ovaries in females

▲ *Although puberty is a universal feature of adolescence, individuals develop physically at different ages and at different rates.* (David Young Wolff/PhotoEdit)

3. The *development of secondary sex characteristics,* which involves changes in the genitals and breasts; the growth of pubic, facial, and body hair; and the further development of the sex organs

4. *Changes in body composition*—specifically, in the quantity and distribution of fat and muscle

5. *Changes in the circulatory and respiratory systems,* which lead to increased strength and tolerance for exercise

Each of these sets of changes is the result of developments in the endocrine and central nervous systems, many of which begin years before the external signs of puberty are evident—some occur even before birth.

RECAP

The term puberty *refers to the physical changes that occur in the growing girl or boy as the individual passes from childhood into adulthood. The chief physical manifestations are the growth spurt, the further development of the gonads, the development of secondary sex characteristics, changes in body composition, and changes in circulation and respiration.*

The Endocrine System

The **endocrine system** produces, circulates, and regulates levels of hormones in the body. **Hormones** are highly specialized substances secreted by one or more endocrine glands. **Glands** are organs that stimulate particular parts of the body to respond in specific ways. Just as specialized hormones carry messages to particular cells in the body, so are the body's cells designed to receive hormonal messages selectively. For example, one of the many effects of the hormone adrenaline, secreted by the adrenal gland, is to stimulate the heart to increase its activity. The heart responds to adrenaline but not to all other hormones.

Puberty may appear to be rather sudden, judging from its external signs, but, in fact, it is part of a gradual process that begins at conception (Petersen & Taylor, 1980). You may be surprised to learn that no new hormones are produced and no new bodily systems develop at puberty. Rather, some hormones that have been present since before birth increase, and others decrease.

The endocrine system receives its instructions to increase or decrease circulating levels of particular hormones from the central nervous system—chiefly, the brain. The system works somewhat like a thermostat.

Hormonal levels are set at a certain point, just as you might set a thermostat at a certain temperature. By setting your room's thermostat at 60°F, you are instructing your heating system to go into action when the temperature falls below this level. Similarly, when a particular hormonal level in your body dips below the endocrine system's **set point** for that hormone, secretion of the hormone increases; when the level reaches the set point, secretion temporarily stops. And, as is the case with a thermostat, the setting level, or set point, for a particular hormone can be adjusted up or down, depending on environmental or internal bodily conditions.

Such a **feedback loop** becomes increasingly important at the onset of puberty. Long before early adolescence—in fact, during infancy—a feedback loop develops involving the **pituitary gland** (which controls hormone levels in general), the **hypothalamus** (the part of the brain that controls the pituitary gland), and the **gonads** (in males, the testes; in females, the ovaries), a feedback loop known as the **HPG axis** (for *h*ypothalamus, *p*ituitary, *g*onads). The gonads release the sex hormones—**androgens** and **estrogens** (see figure 1.1). Although one typically thinks of androgens as "male" hormones and estrogens as "female" hormones, both types of hormones are produced by each sex, and both are present in males and females at birth. During adolescence, however, the average male produces more androgens than estrogens, and the average female produces more estrogens than androgens (Petersen & Taylor, 1980).

The hypothalamus responds to the levels of sex hormones circulating in the body. Your HPG axis is set to maintain certain levels of androgens and estrogens. When these levels fall below the set points, the hypothalamus no longer inhibits the pituitary, thus permitting it to stimulate the release of sex hormones by the gonads and other, puberty-related hormones by the adrenal gland. When sex-hormone levels reach the set point, the hypothalamus responds by inhibiting its stimulation of the pituitary gland.

Hormones play two very different roles in adolescent development; they perform both an **organizational role** and an **activational role** (Coe, Hayashi, & Levine, 1988; Collaer & Hines, 1995). Long before adolescence—in fact, prenatally—hormones shape, or *organize,* the brain in ways that may not be manifested in behavior until childhood or even adolescence. Generally speaking, until about eight weeks after conception, the human brain is "feminine" unless and until it is exposed to certain "masculinizing" hormones, such as testosterone. Because levels of testosterone are higher among males than females while the brain is developing, males, in general, end up with a more "masculinized" brain than females. This sex difference in brain organization predetermines certain patterns of behavior, many of which may not actually appear until much later (Collaer & Hines, 1995). Studies of sex differences in aggression, for example, show that, even though some of these differences may not appear until adolescence, they likely result from the impact of prenatal hormones, rather than from hormonal changes at puberty.

In other words, the presence or absence of certain hormones early in life may program the brain and nervous system to develop in certain ways later on. Because we may not see the resulting changes in behavior until adolescence, it is easy to conclude mistakenly that the behaviors result from hormonal changes specific to puberty. In reality, however, exposure to certain hormones before birth may set a sort of alarm clock, which does not go off until adolescence. Just because the alarm clock rings at the same time that puberty begins does not mean that puberty caused the alarm to go off.

Other changes in behavior at adolescence occur, however, because of changes in hormone levels at puberty; these hormonal changes are said to *activate* the changes in behavior. For instance, the increase in certain hormones at puberty is thought to stimulate the development of secondary sex characteristics, such as the growth of pubic hair. Other hormonal changes at adolescence, controlled by the adrenal gland, may stimulate an increase in individuals' sex drive (McClintock & Herdt, 1996).

Still other changes during puberty are likely to be results of an *interaction* between the organizational and activational effects of hormones (Collaer & Hines, 1995). Hormones that are present during the development of the fetus may organize a certain set of behaviors (for example, the brain may be set up to have us later engage in sexual behavior), but certain changes in those hormones at puberty may be needed to activate the pattern; that is, individuals may not become motivated to engage in sex until puberty.

What Triggers Puberty?

Although the HPG axis is active long before adolescence—before birth, in fact—it is relatively quiet during much of childhood. Something happens during middle childhood, though, that reawakens the HPG axis and signals it that the body is ready for puberty.

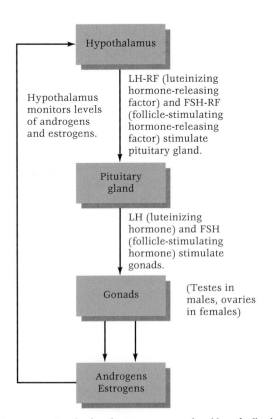

Hypothalamus

Hypothalamus monitors levels of androgens and estrogens.

LH-RF (luteinizing hormone-releasing factor) and FSH-RF (follicle-stimulating hormone-releasing factor) stimulate pituitary gland.

Pituitary gland

LH (luteinizing hormone) and FSH (follicle-stimulating hormone) stimulate gonads.

Gonads

(Testes in males, ovaries in females)

Androgens Estrogens

Figure 1.1   Levels of sex hormones are regulated by a feedback system composed of the hypothalamus, pituitary gland, and gonads. (Grumbach, Roth, Kaplan, & Kelch, 1974)

▲ *The timing of puberty is affected by experience as well as heredity. Exercise can affect the onset of puberty. (Li-Hua Lan/ The Image Works)*

Although scientists are not entirely certain, there is increasing evidence that rising levels of a protein produced by fat cells, **leptin,** may be the most important signal (Spear, 2000). This idea is consistent with observations that individuals may not go through puberty until they have accumulated a certain amount of body fat and is consistent with research showing that stress, illness, nutritional deficiencies, excessive exercise, and excessive thinness can all delay the onset of puberty (Frisch, 1983; McClintock, 1980). The signal carried by rising levels of leptin instructs the hypothalamus both to stop doing things that have been inhibiting puberty and to start doing things that set it in motion (Spear, 2000). As a result of both of these processes, the hypothalamus initiates a cascade of hormonal events that ultimately result in the sexual maturation of the individual.

During and just before puberty, the pituitary also secretes hormones that act on the thyroid and on the adrenal cortex, as well as hormones that stimulate overall bodily growth. The release of these substances is also under the control of the hypothalamus. The thyroid and adrenal cortex, in turn, secrete hormones that cause various physical (somatic) changes to take place at puberty. Research also indicates that early feelings of sexual attraction to others—most individuals report that their first sexual attraction took place around age 10, before they went through puberty—may be stimulated by maturation of the adrenal glands, called **adrenarche** (McClintock & Herdt, 1996). Changes at puberty in the brain system that regulates the adrenal gland are also important because this is the brain system that controls how we respond to stress (Spear, 2000).

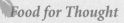

Food for Thought

In a study of monkeys that was done some years ago, it was found that male monkeys who had been castrated (i.e., had their testes removed) shortly after birth still showed the onset of many of the changes in sexual behavior at adolescence normally observed among males of this species (Coe et al., 1988). How does the distinction between the organizational and activational effects of hormones help account for this?

SOMATIC DEVELOPMENT

The effects of the endrocrinological changes of puberty on the adolescent's body are remarkable. Consider the dramatic changes in physical appearance that occur during the short span of early adolescence. One enters puberty looking like a child but within four years or so has the physical appearance of a young adult. During this relatively brief period of time, the average individual grows nearly 12 inches taller, matures sexually, and develops an adult-proportioned body.

Changes in Stature and the Dimensions of the Body

The simultaneous release of growth hormone, thyroid hormones, and androgens stimulates rapid acceleration in height and weight. This dramatic increase in stature is referred to as the **adolescent growth spurt.** What is most incredible about the adolescent growth spurt is not so much the absolute gain of height and weight that typically occurs but the speed with which the increases take place. Think for a moment of how quickly very young children grow. At the time of **peak height velocity**—the time at which the adolescent is growing most rapidly—he or she is growing at the same rate as a toddler. For boys, peak height velocity averages about 4.1 inches (10.5 centimeters) per year; for girls, it averages about 3.5 inches (9.0 centimeters) (J. Tanner, 1972).

Figure 1.2 shows just how remarkable the growth spurt is in terms of height. The graph on the left presents information on absolute height and indicates that, as you would expect, the average individual increases in height throughout infancy, childhood, and adolescence. As you can see, there is little gain in

RECAP

The onset of puberty is regulated by a feedback loop in the endocrine system, called the HPG axis, involving the hypothalamus, the pituitary, and the gonads—ovaries in females, testes in males. Increases in some hormones and decreases in others, as a result of activity along the HPG axis, result in the internal and external changes associated with puberty. Sex hormones play two roles in adolescent development: organizational and activational. Long before puberty, they organize the brain in ways that are not manifested until adolescence. And at puberty, they activate new patterns of behavior. There is increasing evidence that rising levels of a protein produced by fat cells, leptin, may signal the hypothalamus to set the hormonal changes of puberty in motion.

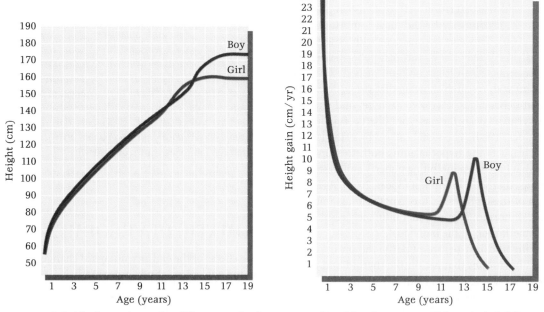

Figure 1.2   Left: *height (in centimeters) at different ages for the average male and female youngster.* Right: *gain in height per year (in centimeters) for the average male and female youngster. Note the adolescent growth spurt.* (Adapted from Marshall, 1978)

height after the age of 18. But look at the right-hand graph, which shows the *average increase in height per year* (i.e., the *rate* of change) over the same age span. Here you can see the acceleration in height at the time of peak height velocity.

Figure 1.2 also indicates quite clearly that the growth spurt occurs, on the average, about two years earlier among girls than among boys. In general, as you can see by comparing the two graphs, boys tend to be somewhat taller than girls before age 11; then girls tend to be taller than boys between ages 11 and 13; finally, boys tend to be taller than girls from about age 14 on. You may remember what this was like during fifth and sixth grades. Sex differences in height can be a concern for many young adolescents when they begin socializing with members of the opposite sex, especially if they are tall, early-maturing girls or short, late-maturing boys.

During puberty, the composition of the skeletal structure also changes; bones become harder, more dense, and more brittle. One marker of the conclusion of puberty is the closing of the ends of the long bones in the body, which terminates growth in height. Interestingly, there are ethnic differences in some of these skeletal changes, with bone density increasing significantly more during puberty among African American than among white youngsters. Some experts believe that this

ethnic difference in adolescence may account for the fact that, during adulthood, African American women are less likely than white women to develop osteoporosis, and they have fewer bone fractures (Gilsanz, Roe, Mora, Costin, & Goodman, 1991).

Much of the height gain during puberty results from an increase in torso length rather than in leg length. The sequence in which various parts of the body grow is fairly regular. Extremities—the head, hands, and feet—are the first to accelerate in growth. Then accelerated growth occurs in the arms and legs, followed by torso and shoulder growth. In concrete terms, "a boy stops growing out of his trousers (at least in length) a year before he stops growing out of his jackets" (J. Tanner, 1972, p. 5).

Young adolescents often appear to be out of proportion physically—as though their noses or legs were growing faster than the rest of them. It's not an optical illusion. The parts of the body do not all grow at the same rate or at the same time during puberty. This **asynchronicity in growth** can lead to an appearance of awkwardness or gawkiness in the young adolescent, who may be embarrassed by the unmatched accelerated growth of various parts of the body. It is probably little consolation for the young adolescent to be told that an aesthetic balance probably will be restored within a few years; nevertheless, this is what usually happens.

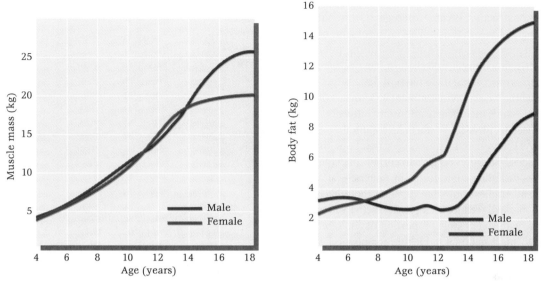

Figure 1.3   *During preadolescence, important sex differences emerge in body composition that continue through adolescence. These graphs reflect muscle and body fat for individuals of average height at each age. Note the changes in muscle mass* (left) *and body fat* (right). (Adapted from Gumbach et al., 1974)

The spurt in height during adolescence is accompanied by an increase in weight, which results from an increase in both muscle and fat. However, there are important sex differences along these latter two dimensions. In both sexes, muscular development is rapid and closely parallels skeletal growth, but muscle tissue grows faster in boys than in girls (see figure 1.3). Body fat increases for both sexes during puberty, but more so for females than for males and at a somewhat faster rate for girls, especially during the years just before puberty. For boys, there is actually a slight decline in body fat just before puberty. The result of these sex differences in growth is that boys finish adolescence with a muscle-to-fat ratio of about 3:1, but the comparable ratio for girls is approximately 5:4. This has important implications for understanding why sex differences in strength and athletic ability often appear for the first time during adolescence. According to one estimate, about half of the sex difference in physical performance during early adolescence results simply from the difference in body fat (Smoll & Schutz, 1990). Before puberty, there are relatively few sex differences in muscle development and only slight sex differences in body fat.

The rapid increase in body fat that occurs among females in early adolescence frequently prompts young girls to become overly concerned about their weight—even when their weight is within the normal range for their height and age (Smolak, Levine, & Gralen, 1993).

Although most girls diet unnecessarily during this time in response to the increase in body fat, the young women who are most susceptible to feelings of dissatisfaction with their bodies during this phase of development are those who mature early, begin dating early, and come from relatively more affluent families (Dornbusch et al., 1981; Smolak, Levine, & Gralen, 1993). African American females seem less vulnerable to these feelings of body dissatisfaction than other girls, and consequently they are less likely to diet, presumably because of ethnic differences in conceptions of the ideal body type. Even among African American youngsters, however, dieting is common in early adolescence (Halpern & Udry, 1994). Many studies point to adolescence as the period of greatest risk for the development of eating disorders, such as anorexia and bulimia.

Accompanying the gains in strength that occur during early adolescence are increases in the size and capacity of the heart and lungs and, consequently, in exercise tolerance. In all these areas, the rate and magnitude of the gains favor males over females. By the end of puberty, boys are stronger, have "larger hearts and lungs relative to their size, a higher systolic blood pressure, a lower resting heart rate, a greater capacity for carrying oxygen to the blood, . . . a greater power for neutralizing the chemical products of muscular exercise, such as lactic acid," higher blood hemoglobin, and more red blood cells (Petersen & Taylor, 1980, p. 129).

It is tempting to attribute these sex differences purely to hormonal factors, because androgens, which are present at higher levels in the prenatal environments of males versus females, and which increase during puberty in males at a much faster rate than in females, are closely linked to growth along these physical dimensions. In addition, with age, such environmental factors as diet and exercise become increasingly important influences on sex differences in physical performance (Smoll & Schutz, 1990). As Petersen and Taylor (1980) point out, there are strong social pressures on girls to curtail "masculine" activities—including some forms of exercise—at adolescence, and studies show that girls are more likely than boys to markedly reduce their physical activity in preadolescence, with a very large proportion of adolescent girls failing to meet national guidelines for physical activity (Goran et al., 1998; Savage & Scott, 1998). Moreover, adolescent girls' diets, especially those of African American girls, are generally less adequate nutritionally than the diets of boys, particularly in important minerals, such as iron (Johnson, Johnson, Wang, Smiciklas-Wright, & Guthrie, 1994). Both factors could result in sex differences in muscular development and exercise tolerance. Thus, sex differences in physical ability are influenced by a variety of factors, of which hormonal differences are but one part of an extremely complicated picture. Along with many other of the body's organs, the brain changes in size, structure, and function at puberty, a series of developments that we will discuss in chapter 2.

RECAP

The dramatic increase in stature that occurs during puberty is referred to as the adolescent growth spurt. On average, girls experience the growth spurt about two years earlier than boys. Important changes also take place in the relative proportions of body fat and muscle, and these changes leave boys relatively more muscular and with a lower proportion of body fat. Many girls react to the increase in body fat at puberty by dieting unnecessarily.

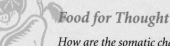

Food for Thought

How are the somatic changes of puberty different for males and females? Why might some of these changes make adolescents feel awkward about or unhappy with their body? Why might body dissatisfaction be greater among adolescent girls than boys? Is this biological, cultural, or a combination of the two?

Sexual Maturation

Puberty brings with it a series of developments associated with sexual maturation. In both boys and girls, the development of the **secondary sex characteristics** is typically divided into five stages, often called **Tanner**

Table 1.1   The sequence of physical changes at puberty

Boys		Girls	
Characteristic	Age of First Appearance (Years)	Characteristic	Age of First Appearance (Years)
1. Growth of testes, scrotal sac	$10-13\frac{1}{2}$	1. Growth of breasts	7–13
2. Growth of pubic hair	10–15	2. Growth of pubic hair	7–14
3. Body growth	$10\frac{1}{2}-16$	3. Body growth	$9\frac{1}{2}-14\frac{1}{2}$
4. Growth of penis	$11-14\frac{1}{2}$	4. Menarche	$10-16\frac{1}{2}$
5. Change in voice (growth of larynx)	About the same time as penis growth	5. Underarm hair	About two years after pubic hair
6. Facial and underarm hair	About two years after pubic hair appears	6. Oil- and sweat-producing glands (acne occurs when glands are clogged)	About the same time underarm hair
7. Oil- and sweat-producing glands, acne	About the same time as underarm hair		

Source: Goldstein, B. (1976). *Introduction to human sexuality.* Belmont, CA: Star.

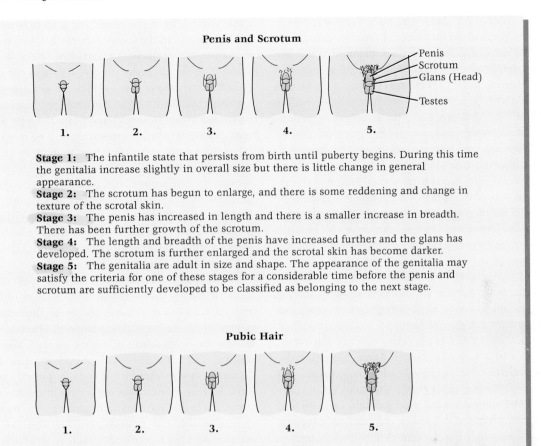

Penis and Scrotum

1.   2.   3.   4.   5.

Penis
Scrotum
Glans (Head)
Testes

Stage 1:   The infantile state that persists from birth until puberty begins. During this time the genitalia increase slightly in overall size but there is little change in general appearance.

Stage 2:   The scrotum has begun to enlarge, and there is some reddening and change in texture of the scrotal skin.

Stage 3:   The penis has increased in length and there is a smaller increase in breadth. There has been further growth of the scrotum.

Stage 4:   The length and breadth of the penis have increased further and the glans has developed. The scrotum is further enlarged and the scrotal skin has become darker.

Stage 5:   The genitalia are adult in size and shape. The appearance of the genitalia may satisfy the criteria for one of these stages for a considerable time before the penis and scrotum are sufficiently developed to be classified as belonging to the next stage.

Pubic Hair

1.   2.   3.   4.   5.

Stage 1:   There is no true pubic hair, although there may be a fine velus over the pubes similar to that over other parts of the abdomen.

Stage 2:   Sparse growth of lightly pigmented hair, which is usually straight or only slightly curled. This usually begins at either side of the base of the penis.

Stage 3:   The hair spreads over the pubic symphysis and is considerably darker and coarser and usually more curled.

Stage 4:   The hair is now adult in character but covers an area considerably smaller than in most adults. There is no spread to the medial surface of the thighs.

Stage 5:   The hair is distributed in an inverse triangle as in the female. It has spread to the medial surface of the thighs but not up the linea alba or elsewhere above the base of the triangle.

Figure 1.4   The five pubertal stages of penile and pubic hair growth. (Morris & Udry, 1980)

stages, after the British pediatrician who devised the categorization system.

● **Sexual Maturation in Boys**   The sequence of developments in secondary sex characteristics among boys is fairly orderly (see table 1.1). Generally, the first stages of puberty involve growth of the testes and scrotum, accompanied by the first appearance of pubic hair. Approximately one year later, the growth spurt in height begins, accompanied by growth of the penis and further development of pubic hair—now of a coarser texture and darker color. The five Tanner stages of penis and pubic hair growth in boys are shown in figure 1.4.

The emergence of facial hair—first at the corners of the upper lip, next across the upper lip, then at the upper parts of the cheeks and in the midline below the lower lip, and finally along the sides of the face and the lower border of the chin—and body hair are relatively late developments in the pubertal process. The same is true for the deepening of the voice, which is gradual and generally does not occur until very late adolescence. During puberty, there are changes in the skin as well; the skin becomes rougher, especially around the upper arms and thighs, and there is increased development of the sweat glands, which often gives rise to acne, skin eruptions, and increased oiliness of the skin.

During puberty, there are slight changes in the male breast—to the consternation and embarrassment of many boys. Breast development is largely influenced by the estrogen hormones. Both estrogens and androgens are present in both sexes and increase in both sexes at puberty, although in differing amounts. In the male adolescent, the areola (the area around the nipple) increases in size, and the nipple becomes more prominent. Some boys show a slight enlargement of the breast, although in most cases this development is temporary.

Other, internal changes occur that are important elements of sexual maturation. At the time that the penis develops, the seminal vesicles, the prostate, and the bilbo-urethral glands also enlarge and develop. The first ejaculation of seminal fluid generally occurs about one year after the beginning of accelerated penis growth, although this is often determined culturally, rather than biologically, since for many boys first ejaculation occurs as a result of masturbation (J. Tanner, 1972). One interesting observation about the timing and sequence of pubertal changes in boys is that boys are generally fertile (i.e., capable of fathering a child) before they have developed an adultlike appearance. The opposite is true for girls.

● **Sexual Maturation in Girls**   The sequence of development of secondary sex characteristics among girls (shown in table 1.1) is somewhat less regular than it is among boys. Generally, the first sign of sexual maturation is the elevation of the breast—the emergence of the so-called breast bud. In about one-third of all adolescent girls, however, the appearance of pubic hair precedes breast development. The development of pubic hair follows a sequence similar to that in males—generally from sparse, downy, light-colored hair to more dense, curled, coarse, darker hair. Breast development often occurs concurrently and generally proceeds through several stages. In the bud stage, the areola widens, and the breast and nipple are elevated as a small mound. In the middle stages, the areola and nipple be-

come distinct from the breast and project beyond the breast contour. In the final stages, the areola is recessed to the contour of the breast, and only the nipple is elevated. The female breast undergoes these changes at puberty regardless of changes in breast size. Changes in the shape and definition of the areola and nipple are far better indicators of sexual maturation among adolescent girls than is breast growth alone. The five Tanner stages of breast and pubic hair growth in girls are shown in figure 1.5.

As is the case among boys, puberty brings important internal changes for adolescent girl that are associated with the development of reproductive capacity. In girls, these changes involve the development and growth of the uterus, vagina, and other aspects of the reproductive system. In addition, the labia and clitoris enlarge.

As is apparent in table 1.1, the growth spurt is likely to occur during the early and middle stages of breast and pubic hair development. Menarche, the beginning of menstruation, is a relatively late development, which reflects the culmination of a long series of hormonal changes (Dorn et al., 1999). Hence, it is incorrect to use menarche as a marker for the onset of puberty among girls. A great deal of pubertal development has taken place long before the adolescent girl begins to menstruate. Generally, full reproductive function does not occur until several years after menarche, and regular ovulation follows menarche by about two years (Hafetz, 1976). Unlike boys, therefore, girls generally appear physically mature before they are capable of reproduction.

RECAP

One of the most important physical changes of puberty is the development of secondary sex characteristics—the changes in outward appearance that signal the onset of reproductive maturity. These changes include the growth of pubic hair, changes in the appearance of the sex organs, and breast development.

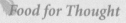 *Food for Thought*

Think about the changes in secondary sex characteristics that take place during puberty. Why might humans have evolved so that puberty occurs on the "outside" of the body as well as internally?

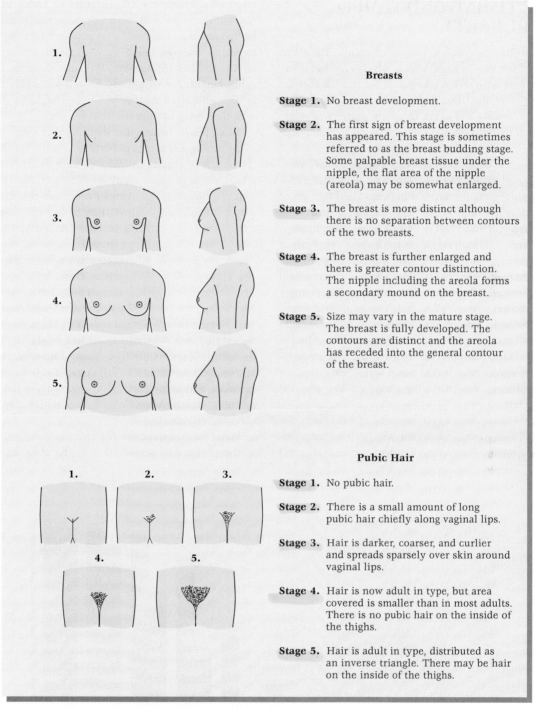

Breasts

Stage 1. No breast development.

Stage 2. The first sign of breast development has appeared. This stage is sometimes referred to as the breast budding stage. Some palpable breast tissue under the nipple, the flat area of the nipple (areola) may be somewhat enlarged.

Stage 3. The breast is more distinct although there is no separation between contours of the two breasts.

Stage 4. The breast is further enlarged and there is greater contour distinction. The nipple including the areola forms a secondary mound on the breast.

Stage 5. Size may vary in the mature stage. The breast is fully developed. The contours are distinct and the areola has receded into the general contour of the breast.

Pubic Hair

Stage 1. No pubic hair.

Stage 2. There is a small amount of long pubic hair chiefly along vaginal lips.

Stage 3. Hair is darker, coarser, and curlier and spreads sparsely over skin around vaginal lips.

Stage 4. Hair is now adult in type, but area covered is smaller than in most adults. There is no pubic hair on the inside of the thighs.

Stage 5. Hair is adult in type, distributed as an inverse triangle. There may be hair on the inside of the thighs.

Figure 1.5   The five pubertal stages for breast and pubic hair growth. (Marshall & Tanner, 1969. Reprinted by permission of BMJ publishing Group)

THE TIMING AND TEMPO OF PUBERTY

You may have noted that, thus far, no mention has been made about the "normal" ages at which various pubertal changes are likely to take place. The truth is that the variations in the timing of puberty (the age at which puberty begins) and in the tempo of puberty (the rate at which maturation occurs) are so great that it is misleading to talk even about average ages.

The onset of puberty can occur as early as age 7 years in girls and $9\frac{1}{2}$ in boys, or as late as 13 in girls and $13\frac{1}{2}$ in boys. In girls, the interval between the first sign of puberty and complete physical maturation can be as short as a year and a half or as long as six years. In boys, the comparable interval ranges from about two years to five years (J. Tanner, 1972). Within a totally normal population of young adolescents, some individuals will have completed the entire sequence of pubertal changes before others have even begun. In more concrete terms, it is possible for an early-maturing, fast-maturing youngster to complete pubertal maturation by the age of 10 or 11—two years before a late-maturing youngster has even begun puberty and seven years before a late-maturing, slow-maturing youngster has matured completely.

There is no relation between the age at which puberty begins and the rate at which pubertal development proceeds. The timing of puberty may have a small effect on the ultimate adult stature or bodily dimensions of the individual, with late maturers, on average, being taller than early maturers as adults, and early maturers, on average, being somewhat heavier—at least among females (St. George, Williams, & Silva, 1994). Adult height and weight are far more strongly correlated with height and weight before childhood than with the timing of puberty, however.

Many people believe that there are ethnic differences in the timing and rate of pubertal maturation, although the results of studies in this area have been inconclusive. One large-scale study of U.S. youngsters does indicate, however, that African American females may mature significantly earlier than their white counterparts (the study did not include enough youngsters from other ethnic groups to make statistical comparisons). For example, whereas the average age of menarche among white U.S. girls is closer to 13, among African American girls, it is closer to 12. And, as figure 1.6 shows, more than 27 percent of African American girls, but less than 7 percent of white girls, have entered puberty by age 7 (Herman-Giddens et al., 1997). Although the reasons for this ethnic difference are not known, one possibility is that African American girls are more frequently exposed to chemicals in the environment, such as synthetic hormones, which may stimulate earlier puberty.

What factors underlie the tremendous variations in the timing and tempo of puberty? Why do some

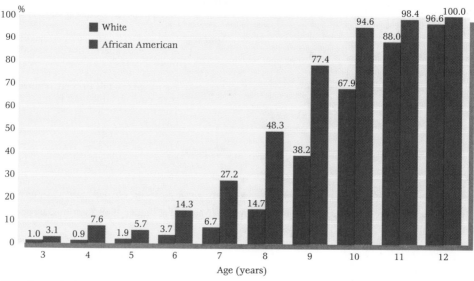

Figure 1.6   Prevalence of African American and white girls at different ages who show signs of either breast development or pubic hair. (Herman-Giddens et al., 1997)

individuals mature relatively early and others relatively late?

Researchers who study variability in the onset and timing of puberty approach the issue in two ways. One strategy involves the study of differences among individuals (that is, studying why one individual matures earlier or faster than another). The other involves the study of differences among groups of adolescents (that is, studying why puberty occurs earlier or more rapidly in certain populations than in others). Both sets of studies point to both genetic and environmental influences on the timing and tempo of puberty.

Individual Differences in Pubertal Maturation

Differences in the timing and rate of puberty among individuals growing up in the same general environment result chiefly, but not exclusively, from genetic factors. Comparisons between pairs individuals who are genetically identical (identical twins) and pairs who are not reveal patterns of similarity in pubertal maturation indicating that the timing and tempo of an individual's pubertal maturation are largely inherited (Marshall, 1978).

Despite this powerful influence of genetic factors, the environment plays an important role. In all likelihood, every individual inherits a predisposition to develop at a certain rate and to begin pubertal maturation at a certain time. But this predisposition is best thought of as upper and lower age limits, not a fixed absolute. Whether the genetic predisposition that each person has to mature around a given age is actually realized, and the time within the predisposed age boundaries at which he or she actually goes through puberty, are subject to the influence of the environment. In this respect, the timing and rate of pubertal maturation are the product of an interaction between nature and nurture, between one's genetic makeup and the environmental conditions under which one has developed.

By far the two most important environmental influences on pubertal maturation are nutrition and health. Puberty occurs earlier among individuals who are better nourished throughout their prenatal, infant, and childhood years. Not surprisingly, then, girls who are taller or heavier than their peers mature earlier (St. George et al., 1994). In contrast, delayed puberty is more likely to occur among individuals with a history of protein and/or caloric deficiency. Chronic illness during childhood and adolescence is also associated with delayed puberty, as is excessive exercise.

For example, girls in ballet companies or in other rigorous training programs often mature later than their peers (Frisch, 1983). Generally speaking, then, after genetic factors, an important determinant of the onset of puberty is the overall physical well-being of the individual from conception through preadolescence (Marshall, 1978).

Interestingly, a number of studies suggest that social as well as physical factors in the environment influence the onset of maturation, especially in girls. Several studies, for example, have found that puberty may occur somewhat earlier among girls who have grown up in less cohesive, or more conflict-ridden, family environments or in households in which a stepfather is present (e.g., Ellis & Garber, 2000; Ellis, McFadyen-Ketchum, Dodge, Pettit, & Bates, 1999; Graber, Brooks-Gunn, & Warren, 1995; Moffitt, Caspi, Belsky, & Silva, 1992; Steinberg, 1988; Surbey, 1990). One explanation for the finding that distant family relations may accelerate pubertal maturation is that distance in the family may induce a very small amount of stress, which, in turn, may affect hormonal secretions

▲ The age at which adolescents mature physically varies around the world. On average, teenagers in highly industrialized countries, such as Japan, mature earlier than their counterparts in developing nations, where health and nutritional problems slow physical growth. (R. M. Collins, III/Image Works)

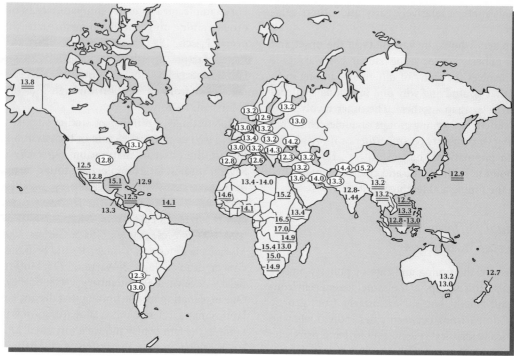

Figure 1.7 *The average menarcheal age of adolescent girls varies in different regions of the world.* (Adapted from Eveleth & Tanner, 1976)

in the adolescent (Graber et al., 1995). Puberty may be sped up by *small* amounts of stress; a great deal of stress, however, is likely to slow maturation (Ellis & Garber, 2000). In addition, the presence of a stepfather may expose the adolescent girl to **pheromones** (chemicals secreted by animals that stimulate certain behaviors in other members of the species) that stimulate pubertal maturation. In general, among humans and other mammals, living in proximity to one's close biological relatives appears to slow the process of pubertal maturation, whereas exposure to unrelated members of the opposite sex may accelerate it (Izard, 1990; Surbey, 1990).

Although it may seem surprising that something as biological as puberty can be influenced by factors in our social environment, scientists have long known that our social relationships can indeed affect our biological functioning. One of the best-known examples of this is that women who live together—such as dormitory roommates—find that their menstrual periods begin to synchronize over time (Graham, 1991; McClintock, 1980).

Group Differences in Pubertal Maturation

Researchers typically study group differences in puberty by comparing average ages of menarche in different regions. Most of these studies have indicated that genetic factors play an extremely small role in determining group differences in pubertal maturation (Eveleth & Tanner, 1990). Differences among countries in the average rate and timing of puberty are more likely to reflect differences in their environments than differences in their populations' gene pools (Morabia, Costanza, & World Health Organization, 1998).

The influence of the broader environment on the timing and tempo of puberty can be seen in more concrete terms by looking at three sorts of group comparisons: (1) comparisons of the average age of menarche across countries, (2) comparisons among socioeconomic groups within a country, and (3) comparisons within a population during different eras. (Although menarche does not signal the onset of puberty, researchers often use the average age of menarche when comparing the timing of puberty across different groups or regions.)

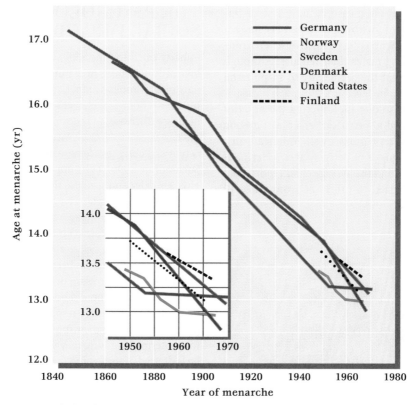

Figure 1.8 *The age at menarche has declined considerably over the past 150 years. This decline is known as the secular trend.*
(Adapted from Eveleth & Tanner, 1976)

First, consider variations in the age of menarche across different regions of the world. Figure 1.7 presents median menarcheal ages throughout the world, across regions that vary considerably in typical dietary intake and health conditions. As you can see, the average age at menarche generally is lower in those countries where individuals are less likely to be malnourished or to suffer from chronic disease. For example, in Western Europe and in the United States, the median menarcheal age ranges from about 12.5 years to 13.5 years. In Africa, however, the median menarcheal age ranges from about 14 years to about 17 years. The range is much wider across the African continent because of the much greater variation in environmental conditions there.

When we look *within* a specific region, we find that, almost without exception, girls from affluent homes reach menarche before economically disadvantaged girls. In comparisons of affluent and poor youngsters from the United States, Hong Kong, Tunis, Baghdad, and South Africa, for example, differences in the average menarcheal ages of economically advantaged and disadvantaged youngsters within each

of these regions range from about 6 months to about 18 months.

Finally, we can examine environmental influences on the timing of puberty by looking at changes in the average age of menarche over the past two centuries. Because nutritional conditions have improved during the past 150 years, we would expect to find a decline in the average age at menarche over time. This is indeed the case, as can be seen in figure 1.8. Generally, "children have been getting larger and growing to maturity more rapidly" (Eveleth & Tanner, 1990, p. 205). This pattern, referred to as the **secular trend,** is attributable not only to improved nutrition but also to better sanitation and better control of infectious diseases. In most European countries, maturation has become earlier by about three to four months per decade. For example, in Norway 150 years ago, the average age of menarche may have been about 17 years. Today, it is between 12 and 13 years. Similar declines have been observed over the same time period in other industrialized nations and, more recently, in developing countries. The secular trend is less well documented among boys, in part because there is no easily measured indicator of puberty, such as menarche, in boys and in part because reproductive development is less sensitive to environmental stimuli among males than females. Although some data suggest that the secular trend in pubertal maturation appears to be leveling off in most industrialized nations, other studies indicate that the onset of puberty has continued to occur earlier, at least among girls. Today, a significant minority of American girls show one or more signs of puberty by age 7 (Herman-Giddens et al., 1997), and the average child reports first feeling sexually attracted to others at around age 10 (McClintock & Herdt, 1996).

RECAP

There is considerable variation in the timing and tempo of puberty. As a result, a group of adolescents of the same chronological age will contain youngsters whose physical maturity varies considerably. The most important influence on the timing of maturation is genetic. But, in addition, adolescents who have been well nourished and healthy during childhood go through puberty earlier than their peers. Because of improvements in nutrition and health care, young people mature earlier today than they did centuries ago, a phenomenon known as the secular trend.

Food for Thought

Data seem to indicate that the trend toward earlier puberty has been much greater among females than males. Can you speculate on why this might be?

THE PSYCHOLOGICAL AND SOCIAL IMPACT OF PUBERTY

Puberty can affect the adolescent's behavior and psychological functioning in a number of ways as figure 1.9 illustrates (Brooks-Gunn, Graber, & Paikoff, 1994). First, puberty's biological changes can have a direct effect on behavior. Increases in testosterone at puberty are directly linked, for example, to an increase in sex drive and sexual activity among adolescent boys (Halpern, Udry, & Suchindran, 1996). (The impact of hormonal change on girls' sex drive and sexual activity is more complicated, as you will read in chapter 11.)

Second, the biological changes of puberty cause changes in the adolescent's self-image, which in turn may affect how he or she behaves. For example, a boy who has recently gone through puberty may seek more privacy at home when he is dressing or bathing. He closes his door more often and is more modest around his parents than he used to be. If they are responsive to his discomfort, his parents will change their routines around the house. Before entering his room, they will knock and wait to see if he is dressed—something they did not have to do before.

Finally, biological change at puberty transforms the adolescent's appearance, which in turn may elicit changes on how *others* react to the teenager. These changes in reactions may provoke changes in the adolescent's behavior. An adolescent girl who has recently matured physically may find herself suddenly receiving the attention of older boys, who had not previously paid her much heed. She may feel nervous about all the extra attention and may be confused about how she should respond to it. Moreover, she must now make decisions about how much time she wishes to devote to dating and how she should behave when out on a date.

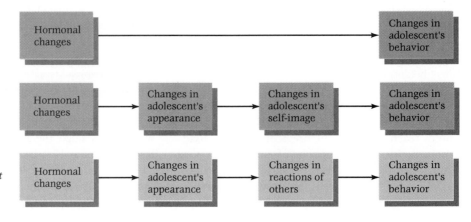

Figure 1.9   The biological changes of puberty can affect the adolescent's behavior in at least three ways.

▲ *One sign that attitudes toward menstruation have changed in the past 50 years is that advertisements for tampons and sanitary napkins have become far more explicit and far less mysterious. As a consequence, today's adolescent girls receive messages about the meaning of maturation that are very different from those of 40 or 50 years ago. Here are two excerpts from magazine advertments for sanitary napkins—one from the 1950s, the other from the 1990s. (KOTEX is a registered trademark of Kimberly-Clark Corporation. These advertisements reprinted by permission. All rights reserved.)(Right: David Young Wolff/PhotoEdit)*

Young people's reactions to the changes brought on by puberty, and others' reactions to them, are influenced by the broader social environment, where messages about physical attractiveness, sexuality, and sexual maturation change, often markedly, from era to era. Although it is difficult to imagine an era in which adolescents, especially girls, did not obsess about their shape, size, and sexual allure, adolescent females' preoccupation with their body is a relatively recent phenomenon, created largely by marketers of clothing, undergarments, cosmetics, weight-loss programs, and "feminine" products (Brumberg, 1997). Contemporary society's views of puberty and physical maturation are expressed through television commercials, newspaper and magazine advertisements, and depictions of young adolescents in films and other media. People cannot help but be influenced by these images, and the expectations they associate with puberty as well as the meaning they give it determine the reactions puberty brings out in them. Consider, for example, the treatment of menstruation in each of the advertisements shown above. What sorts of reactions might each of the ads foster?

Researchers have generally taken two approaches to studying the psychological and social consequences of puberty. One approach is to look at individuals who are at various stages of puberty, either in a **cross-sectional study** (in which groups of individuals are compared at different stages of puberty) or in a **longitudinal study** (in which the same individuals are tracked over time as they move through the stages of puberty). Studies of this sort examine the immediate impact of puberty on young people's psychological development and social relations. Researchers might ask, for example, whether youngsters' self-esteem is higher or lower during puberty than before or after.

A second approach compares the psychological development of early and late maturers. The focus of these studies is not so much on the absolute impact of puberty but on the effects of differential timing of the changes. Here, a typical question might be whether early maturers are more popular in the peer group than late maturers are.

The Immediate Impact of Puberty

Studies of the psychological and social impact of puberty indicate that physical maturation, regardless of whether it occurs early or late, affects the adolescent's self-image, mood, and relationships with parents. As you will read, however, the short-term consequences of puberty may be more taxing on the adolescent's family than on the adolescent.

● **Puberty and Self-Esteem**   Research suggests that puberty is a potential stressor with temporary adverse psychological consequences for girls (but not boys), but only when it is coupled with other changes that necessitate adjustment (Simmons & Blyth, 1987). Indeed, studies suggest that the impact of puberty on adolescents' psychological functioning is, to a great extent, shaped by the social context in which puberty takes place (Brooks-Gunn & Reiter, 1990; Susman, 1997). Accordingly, the impact of puberty on mental health varies by gender and across ethnic groups, with girls more adversely affected than boys and with white girls, in particular, at greatest risk for developing a poor body image (Rosenblum & Lewis, 1999; Siegel, Yancey, Aneshensel, & Schuler, 1999). Given the premium placed in contemporary society on thinness, the increase in body dissatisfaction among white girls that takes place at puberty is, not surprisingly, linked to specific concerns girls have about their hips, thighs, waist, and weight (Rosenblum & Lewis, 1999). Interestingly, the way adolescents feel about their physical appearance when they begin adolescence remains remarkably stable over time, regardless of whether their actual attractiveness changes (Rosenblum & Lewis, 1999).

● **Adolescent Moodiness**   Although an adolescent's self-image could be expected to be changed during a time of dramatic physical development, it could also be the case that self-esteem or self-image is a reasonably stable characteristic, with long and sturdy roots reaching back to childhood. For this reason, some researchers have turned their attention to the impact of puberty on more transient states, such as mood. One reason for this focus is that adolescents are thought to be moodier, on average, than either children or adults. One study, in which adolescents' moods were monitored repeatedly by electronic pagers, for example, showed that adolescents' moods fluctuate during the course of the day more than the moods of adults do (Csikszentmihalyi & Larson, 1984) (see figure 1.10).

Many adults assume that adolescent moodiness is directly related to the hormonal changes of puberty (Petersen, 1985). Is there any scientific evidence that the hormonal changes of puberty cause adolescents to be moody or, for that matter, that these hormonal changes affect the adolescent's psychological functioning or behavior at all?

According to several comprehensive reviews of research on hormones and adolescent mood and behavior, the direct connection between hormones and mood, although apparent, is not very strong (Buchanan, Eccles, & Becker, 1992; Flannery, Torquati, & Lindemeier, 1994). When studies do find a connection between hormonal changes at puberty and adolescent mood or behavior, the effects are strongest early in puberty, when the system is being "turned on" and when hormonal levels are highly variable. For example, studies indicate that *rapid* increases in many of the hormones associated with puberty—such as testosterone, estrogen, and various adrenal androgens—especially when the increases take place very early in adolescence, may be associated with increased irritability, impulsivity, aggression (in boys), and depression (in girls). One interpretation of these findings is that it is not so much the absolute increases in these hormones during puberty but their rapid fluctuation early in puberty that may affect adolescents' moods. Once the hormone levels stabilize at higher levels, later in puberty, their negative effects appear to wane (Buchanan et al., 1992). There is also evidence, which is discussed in chapter 2, that important changes take place in early adolescence in the regions of the brain that play major roles in the processing of emotion (Spear, 2000).

Even still, most researchers agree that the impact of hormonal change on mood and behavior in adolescence is greatly influenced by environmental factors (Susman, 1997). An excellent illustration of the way in which hormones and environment interact at puberty comes from the work of psychologist Jeanne Brooks-Gunn and her colleagues (Brooks-Gunn, 1987, 1989; Brooks-Gunn, Graber, & Paikoff, 1994; Brooks-Gunn & Warren, 1989), who have been studying the development of psychological problems, such as depression and aggression, in young girls around the time of puberty. Although rapid increases in hormones early in puberty are associated with depressed mood in girls, it turns out that stressful life events, such as problems in the family, in school, or with friends, play a far greater role in the development of depression than do hormonal changes. Moreover, as she and others point out, it is possible that changes in the environment—in levels of stress, for instance—

Table 1.2   *Five patterns of adolescent moodiness*

Pattern	Size of Mood Change	Rate of Mood Change	Typical Mood	Intensity of Mood
I	Very large	Very fast	Positive	Very high
II	Small	Average	Positive	Low
III	Small	Slow	Negative	Very low
IV	Very large	Average	Negative	High
V	Average	Slow	Very negative	High

Source: Bence, 1992.

affect hormonal activity, which in turn may affect adolescents' mood.

Interestingly, not only is there little evidence that adolescents' moodiness results from the storm and stress of raging hormones, but there is also research that questions the very idea that adolescents are inherently moodier than children. Psychologists Mihaly Csikszentmihalyi and Reed Larson (1984; Larson & Lampman-Petraitis, 1989) had teenagers carry electronic pagers similar to the ones physicians carry, and the researchers paged them periodically throughout the day. When the adolescents were paged, they filled out forms noting how they were feeling, what they were doing, where they were, and whom they were with. By looking at changes in mood across activities and settings, the researchers were able to determine the correlates of adolescent moodiness.

Their findings suggest that adolescent mood swings parallel their changes in activities. Over the course of a day, a teenager may shift from elation to boredom, back again to happiness, and then to anger. But this shifting appears to have more to do with shifts in activities—elated when seeing a girlfriend, bored in social studies class, happy when having lunch with friends, and angry when assigned extra work at the fast-food restaurant—than with internal, biological changes. More important, comparisons of youngsters between the ages of 9 and 15 did not show increases in moodiness during the transition into adolescence. Although adolescents may be moodier than adults, it is probably because they change activities and contexts more often than adults do.

How can we reconcile these scientific studies, which provide little support for the notion that adolescents are especially prone to mood swings, with the popular portrayals of teenagers as exceedingly moody? One suggestion is that there is a great deal of variability within the adolescent population in moodiness. In one study of adolescents, for example, five distinct patterns of mood change were identified (Bence, 1992) (see table 1.2). One group showed considerable fluctuation in mood over the course of a week, but members typically were in a positive mood (these youngsters bounced back up to positive moods quickly after being in a bad mood). A second group was, on average, equally positive as the first but showed much less mood fluctuation. The third group was similar to the second, in that members showed little fluctuation in mood; however, in contrast to the second group, the third group was generally in a slightly bad mood. The fourth group, like the first, showed considerable fluctuation in mood but was generally in a bad mood (that is, members dropped back down to negative moods quickly after being in a positive mood). Finally, the fifth group was composed of youngsters whose mood did not fluctuate greatly but who were in an extremely negative mood most of the time.

● **Changes in Sleep Patterns**   One fascinating finding on hormones and behavior in adolescence concerns adolescents' sleep preferences. Many parents complain that their teenage children go to bed too late in the evening and sleep too late in the morning. It now appears that the emergence of this pattern—called a **delayed phase preference**—is directly related to the biological changes of puberty (Carskadon, Acebo, Richardson, Tate, & Seifer, 1997). Thus, physically mature teenagers who are forced to maintain a sleep schedule similar to that of prepubertal individuals have biological reasons to feel energetic when it is time to go to bed and lethargic in the morning. When allowed to regulate their own sleep schedules (as on weekends), most teenagers will stay up until around 1 A.M. and sleep until about 10 A.M. It is therefore ironic that many school districts ask

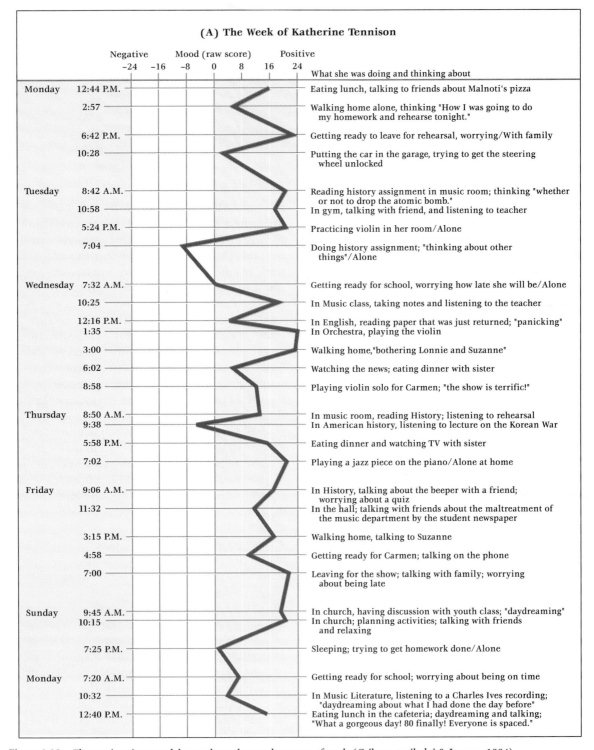

Figure 1.10   *Fluctuations in two adolescents' moods over the course of week.* (Csikszentmihalyi & Larson, 1984)

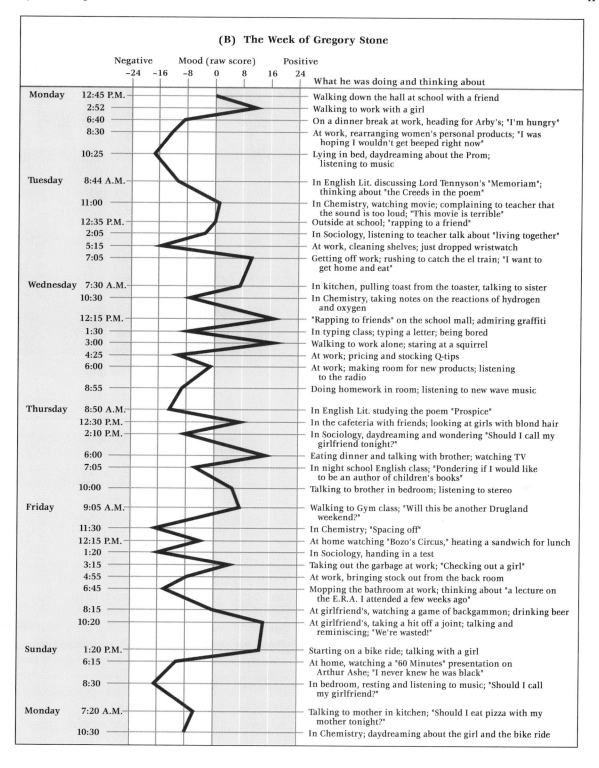

(B) The Week of Gregory Stone

		Negative		Mood (raw score)		Positive	What he was doing and thinking about
		−24 −16 −8 0 8 16 24					
Monday	12:45 P.M.						Walking down the hall at school with a friend
	2:52						Walking to work with a girl
	6:40						On a dinner break at work, heading for Arby's; "I'm hungry"
	8:30						At work, rearranging women's personal products; "I was hoping I wouldn't get beeped right now"
	10:25						Lying in bed, daydreaming about the Prom; listening to music
Tuesday	8:44 A.M.						In English Lit. discussing Lord Tennyson's "Memoriam"; thinking about "the Creeds in the poem"
	11:00						In Chemistry, watching movie; complaining to teacher that the sound is too loud; "This movie is terrible"
	12:35 P.M.						Outside at school; "rapping to a friend"
	2:05						In Sociology, listening to teacher talk about "living together"
	5:15						At work, cleaning shelves; just dropped wristwatch
	7:05						Getting off work; rushing to catch the el train; "I want to get home and eat"
Wednesday	7:30 A.M.						In kitchen, pulling toast from the toaster, talking to sister
	10:30						In Chemistry, taking notes on the reactions of hydrogen and oxygen
	12:15 P.M.						"Rapping to friends" on the school mall; admiring graffiti
	1:30						In typing class; typing a letter; being bored
	3:00						Walking to work alone; staring at a squirrel
	4:25						At work; pricing and stocking Q-tips
	6:00						At work; making room for new products; listening to the radio
	8:55						Doing homework in room; listening to new wave music
Thursday	8:50 A.M.						In English Lit. studying the poem "Prospice"
	12:30 P.M.						In the cafeteria with friends; looking at girls with blond hair
	2:10 P.M.						In Sociology, daydreaming and wondering "Should I call my girlfriend tonight?"
	6:00						Eating dinner and talking with brother; watching TV
	7:05						In night school English class; "Pondering if I would like to be an author of children's books"
	10:00						Talking to brother in bedroom; listening to stereo
Friday	9:05 A.M.						Walking to Gym class; "Will this be another Drugland weekend?"
	11:30						In Chemistry; "Spacing off"
	12:15 P.M.						At home watching "Bozo's Circus," heating a sandwich for lunch
	1:20						In Sociology, handing in a test
	3:15						Taking out the garbage at work; "Checking out a girl"
	4:55						At work, bringing stock out from the back room
	6:45						Mopping the bathroom at work; thinking about "a lecture on the E.R.A. I attended a few weeks ago"
	8:15						At girlfriend's, watching a game of backgammon; drinking beer
	10:20						At girlfriend's, taking a hit off a joint; talking and reminiscing; "We're wasted!"
Sunday	1:20 P.M.						Starting on a bike ride; talking with a girl
	6:15						At home, watching a "60 Minutes" presentation on Arthur Ashe; "I never knew he was black"
	8:30						In bedroom, resting and listening to music; "Should I call my girlfriend?"
Monday	7:20 A.M.						Talking to mother in kitchen; "Should I eat pizza with my mother tonight?"
	10:30						In Chemistry; daydreaming about the girl and the bike ride

▲ *Studies indicate that parent-adolescent conflict may increase during puberty.* (Stewart Cohen/Tony Stone Images)

adolescents to report to school even *earlier* than younger children, since this demand clearly conflicts with the natural sleep preferences of adolescents. Indeed, one study found that adolescents were least alert between the hours of 8 and 9 A.M. (when most schools start) and were most alert after 3 P.M., when the school day is over (Allen & Mirabell, 1990).

Although individuals' preferred bedtime gets later as they move from childhood into adolescence, the amount of sleep they need each night remains constant, at around nine hours. Yet in one study of more than 3,000 Rhode Island high school students, it was found that only one-fifth of the students got at least eight hours of sleep on an average school night and that nearly half got seven hours or less (Wolfson & Carskadon, 1998). There is now a clear consensus among scientists that most American teenagers are not getting enough sleep, and that inadequate sleep is associated in adolescence with poorer mental health (more depression and anxiety) and lowered school performance. In the Rhode Island study, for example, the students who were earning grades of *C* or lower were going to bed 40 minutes later and sleeping about 25 minutes less each night than their classmates whose grade-point averages were *B* or better. The students with poorer

grades also reported staying up considerably later on weekends than they did on school nights. Despite many adolescents' belief that catching up on their sleep on weekends makes up for sleep deprivation during the week, research indicates that having markedly different bedtimes on weekend versus weekday evenings contributes to further sleep-related problems (Wolfson & Carskadon, 1998).

● **Puberty and Family Relationships**   Research into the impact of puberty on family relationships has pointed to a fairly consistent pattern—namely, that puberty appears to increase conflict and distance between parents and children. The distancing effect of puberty on adolescent-parent relationships is not as strong in single-parent homes (Anderson, Hetherington, & Clingempeel, 1989) and not as consistently observed in ethnic minority families, however (Molina & Chassin, 1996; Sagrestano, McCormick, Paikoff, & Holmbeck, 1999). Among white families, though, several studies show that, as youngsters mature from childhood toward the middle of puberty, distance between them and their parents increases, and conflict intensifies, especially between the adolescent and his or her mother (Laursen, Coy, & Collins, 1998; Paikoff & Brooks-Gunn, 1991). The change that takes place is reflected in an increase in "negatives" (e.g., conflict, complaints, anger) and, to a lesser extent, a decrease in "positives" (e.g., support, smiles, laughter) (Flannery et al., 1994; Holmbeck & Hill, 1991). Although negative interchanges may diminish after the adolescent growth spurt, adolescents and their parents do not immediately become as close as they were before the adolescents entered puberty. Interestingly, puberty increases distance between children and their parents in most species of monkeys and apes, and some writers have suggested that the pattern seen in human adolescents has some evolutionary basis (Steinberg, 1987a).

Because this connection between pubertal maturation and parent-child distance is not affected by the age at which the adolescent goes through puberty—in other words, the pattern is seen among early as well as late maturers—it suggests that something about puberty in particular transforms the parent-child bond. To date, it is unknown whether this effect results from the hormonal changes of puberty, from changes in the adolescent's physical appearance, or from changes in adolescent psychological functioning, which in turn affect family relationships. Moreover, because few studies of family relationships at puberty have examined multiple aspects of adolescent development simultaneously, it is difficult to say whether the patterns of change in family relationships that many studies have found do, in fact, result from puberty and not from another change taking place at the same time in the adolescent or in the parent (Paikoff & Brooks-Gunn, 1991).

Whatever underlying mechanism that is involved, one interpretation of these studies is that developments occurring around the time of puberty can upset the interpersonal balances established during childhood, causing temporary periods of disruption in the family system. During a son's or daughter's childhood, families develop patterns of relationships that are comfortable and workable, but they may find that puberty disrupts the patterns to which they have grown accustomed. They have developed a certain way of discussing things and a certain way of including the children in discussions. However, as the children go through puberty, they may want to be treated more like adults and may want to have greater say in family decisions. Consequently, families may experience a temporary period of conflict or tension when

sons and daughters enter early adolescence. It may take some time for the individual and the family to achieve a new equilibrium that takes into account the changes brought on by puberty.

Puberty may have an effect on relationships in the peer group, too. One study of adolescents' social networks—the people they are most likely to see and spend time with—found that adolescents who were physically mature were less likely than their less developed peers to name adults as people who were important to them, and they were more likely to name other adolescents (Garbarino, Burston, Raber, Russell, & Crouter, 1978). This finding suggests that pubertal maturation may influence adolescents' interests and energies toward the peer group. Boys and girls who are physically mature are more likely than less mature age-mates to be involved in cross-sex activities, such as having a boyfriend or girlfriend and going out on dates (Crockett & Dorn, 1987), although this depends on the social norm of the adolescent's peer group and the prevailing expectations about the age at which teenagers should begin dating (Dornbush et al., 1981; Gargiulo, Attie, Brooks-Gunn, & Warren, 1987).

The Impact of Specific Pubertal Events

Several studies have focused specifically on adolescents' attitudes toward and reactions to particular events at puberty, such as girls' reactions to menarche or breast development, and boys' reactions to their first ejaculation. In general, most adolescents react positively to the biological changes associated with puberty, especially those associated with the development of secondary sex characteristics. One study of adolescent girls' attitudes towards breast development, for example, found that most of the girls greeted this change positively (Brooks-Gunn, Newman, Holderness, & Warren, 1994).

Girls' reactions to menarche are more varied, however, in part because the onset of menstruation is "not just one of a series of physiological events during puberty, but is also a sociocultural event . . . imbued with special meaning" (Brooks-Gunn & Ruble, 1979, p. 1). Cultural beliefs concerning menarche and the specific information that a young woman receives from parents, teachers, friends, and health practitioners all influence how she greets and experiences menarche (Brooks-Gunn & Ruble, 1982).

Adolescent girls' attitudes toward menarche are less negative today than they appear to have been in the past (Grief & Ulman, 1982; Ruble & Brooks-Gunn, 1982), a change that may be attributable to the more open presentation of information about menstruation in schools and in the media in recent years (Merskin, 1999). In general, among today's adolescent girls, menarche is typically accompanied by gains in social maturity, peer prestige, and self-esteem—as well as by heightened self-consciousness (Brooks-Gunn & Reiter, 1990). Nevertheless, many young women have developed a negative image of menstruation before reaching adolescence, and they enter puberty with ambivalent attitudes about menarche—a mixture of excitement and fear (Moore, 1995; Ruble & Brooks-Gunn, 1982).

Interestingly, one set of studies indicates that a strong negative bias toward menstruation before menarche may actually be associated with greater menstrual discomfort. Menstrual symptoms are reported to be more severe among women who expect menstruation to be uncomfortable, among girls whose mothers lead them to believe that menstruation will be an unpleasant or uncomfortable experience, and in cultures that label menstruation as an important event. In addition, girls who experience menarche early, relative to their peers, or who are otherwise unprepared for puberty report more negative reactions to the event (Koff & Rierdan, 1996; Rierdan, Kobb, & Stubbs, 1989).

Far less is known about boys' reactions to their first ejaculation, an experience that we might consider analogous to menarche in girls. Although most boys are not very well prepared for this event by their parents or other adults, first ejaculation does not appear to cause undue anxiety, embarrassment, or fear. It is interesting to note, however, that, in contrast to girls, who generally tell their mothers shortly after they have begun menstruating and tell their girlfriends soon thereafter, boys, at least in the United States, do not discuss their first ejaculation with either parents or friends (Gaddis & Brooks-Gunn, 1985; Stein & Reiser, 1994). In other cultures, the event may be experienced somewhat differently. For example, one study of first ejaculation among adolescent boys in Nigeria found not only that the boys were not upset by the event but also that they told their friends about the experience very soon after it occurred (Adegoke, 1993). Cultural differences in boys' responses to their first ejaculation are likely related to differences in how different cultures view masturbation. As is the case with girls and menarche, boys' reactions to their first ejaculation are more positive when they have been prepared for the event (Stein & Reiser, 1994).

RECAP

Although puberty may cause temporary disruption in the adolescent's social relationships and changes in sleep patterns, research has not shown that puberty is inherently stressful or associated with dramatic changes in mood or behavior. Puberty may be associated with increases in negative moods, but only during the very early stages of hormonal change, when hormone levels are fluctuating widely. More important than puberty itself is how puberty is viewed within the context in which the adolescent matures, as well as the extent to which the adolescent has been prepared psychologically for the biological changes of the era.

Food for Thought

Examine the two mood diagrams that were presented in figure 1.10. Can you draw any generalizations about the role of context in mood fluctuation?

The Impact of Early or Late Maturation

Adolescents who mature relatively early or relatively late stand apart from their peers physically and may, as a consequence, elicit different sorts of reactions and expectations from those around them. Moreover, individual adolescents may be all too aware of whether they are early or late relative to their agemates, and their feelings about themselves are likely to be influenced by their comparisons. Indeed, adolescents' *perceptions* of whether they are an early or a late maturer are more strongly related to their feelings about their physical maturation than whether they actually are early or late (Dubas, Graber, & Petersen, 1991), and adolescents' behavior is related to how old they feel, not simply to how physically mature they actually are (Galambos, Kolaric, Sears, & Maggs, 1999). Nevertheless, early and late maturers are often treated differently by others and view themselves differently; as a result, they may behave differently. As we will see, however, early and late maturation have different consequences in the immediate present and the long run; different consequences in different contexts; and, most important, different consequences for boys and girls.

● **Early Versus Late Maturation Among Boys**   The first studies to compare early- and late-maturing boys suggested that it is an advantage to mature earlier than one's peers. Drawing on data collected as part of the Oakland Growth Study (a longitudinal study begun early in the twentieth century), psychologist Mary Jones and her colleagues compared early- and late-maturing boys on a variety of psychological tests and measures of interpersonal relationships (Jones, 1957, 1965; Jones & Bayley, 1950; Mussen & Jones, 1957, 1958). They found that late maturers were seen by their peers as more childish and were less popular and less likely to have held leadership positions. On personality measures, late-maturing boys exhibited stronger feelings of inadequacy, more negative self-concepts, and less self-assurance.

More recent studies of early versus late maturation have confirmed many of the findings from these earlier studies. As was the case a half-century ago, late-maturing boys today have relatively lower self-esteem and stronger feelings of inadequacy, whereas early-maturing boys are more popular and have a more positive self-image (Graber, Lewinsohn, Seeley, & Brooks-Gunn, 1997). Consistent with this, a study of adolescents' daily moods indicates that boys who are more physically mature than their peers report more frequent feelings of positive affect, attention, strength, and being in love (Richards & Larson, 1993).

With regard to behavior, however, the data on early versus late maturers is quite consistent: In general, early maturers are more likely than their peers to get involved in antisocial or deviant activities, including truancy, minor delinquency, and problems at school (Duncan, Ritter, Dornbusch, Gross, & Carlsmith, 1985), and they are more likely to use drugs and alcohol and engage in other risky activity (Andersson & Magnusson, 1990; Silbereisen, Kracke, & Crockett, 1990; Williams & Dunlop, 1999). One reasonable explanation is that boys who are more physically mature develop friendships with older peers and that these friendships lead them into activities that are problematic for the younger boys. Once involved with these older peer groups, the early maturers' higher rate of delinquency and substance use increases over time through their social contacts (Silbereisen, Petersen, Albrecht, & Kracke, 1989). Thus, early puberty seems to play more of a direct role in the initiation than in the intensification of substance use.

It is clear that early-maturing boys enjoy some psychological advantages over late maturers during early adolescence, when some boys have matured physically but others have not. But what about later during adolescence, when the late maturers have caught up? At least one study points to some interesting advantages

▲ *These adolescents are all the same chronological age, despite their markedly different physical appearances. Among boys, early maturation is associated with greater popularity and higher self-esteem. Although early-maturing girls are also more popular with their peers, they report more emotional difficulties than young women who mature later.* (Alan Carey/Image Works)

for late-maturing boys, despite their initially lower popularity with peers. Although early and late maturers exhibit similar psychological profiles before they enter adolescence, during the time of pubertal onset, as well as one year later, late maturers show significantly higher ratings on measures of intellectual curiosity, exploratory behavior, and social initiative. Interestingly, early maturers experience more frequent and more intense temper tantrums during puberty (Livson & Peskin, 1980).

Why might this be? One explanation is that late maturers have the advantage of a longer preadolescent period, giving them more time to prepare psychologically for the onset of puberty (Peskin, 1967). This preparation may be important if rapid increases in hormones at puberty provoke changes in mood. Many theorists believe that the middle childhood and preadolescent years are extremely important periods for the development of coping skills—skills that prove valuable during adolescence and adulthood. Although puberty by no means marks the end of the growth of coping abilities, it does come as an abrupt interruption to the more re-laxed preadolescent era. A later puberty, and hence a longer preadolescence, might allow for coping skills to develop more fully before adolescence. This may ac-count in part for the apparently better coping skills demonstrated by late maturers—not only during pu-berty but as adults.

Do the psychological and interpersonal differences that are observed between early and late maturers during adolescence persist into adulthood? In order to answer such questions, a series of follow-up studies conducted 25 years later looked at the adult personalities of males who had been studied during adolescence (Livson & Peskin, 1980). At age 38, the early maturers were more responsi-ble, more cooperative, more self-controlled, and more so-ciable. At the same time, though, early maturers had also grown up to be more conforming, conventional, and hu-morless. Their peers who had been late maturers re-mained somewhat more impulsive and more assertive but turned out to be more insightful, more inventive, and more creatively playful. What had happened?

One interpretation is that, because of their more adultlike appearance, the early-maturing boys had been pushed into adult roles earlier than their peers. They were more likely to be asked to assume responsibility, to take on leadership positions, and to behave in a more grown-up manner. But this early press toward adult-hood may have come too soon and may have stifled a certain amount of creativity and risk taking.

Have you gone to any gatherings of former high school classmates? Did you discover that some of the people you had remembered as extremely mature and socially successful during high school have turned out to be not all that interesting a few years after gradua-tion? Perhaps too much leadership, responsibility, so-cial success, and maturity during the high school years interferes with the sort of psychological development that makes for interesting and creative adults. Many psychologists believe that adolescents may benefit in the long run from having an extended period of time during which they are *not* being pushed into adulthood.

In short, success and social status may come too eas-ily and too early for early-maturing boys, leaving them with less need to develop creative or flexible solutions to life's problems and less time to experiment with new roles and identities. In contrast, late-maturing young-sters, experiencing more difficulty in achieving social standing and recognition because of their immature physical appearance, may be forced to develop more in-ventive means of problem solving and greater cognitive and social flexibility. In other words, the greater diffi-culty that late maturers face as early adolescents may lead to their developing coping skills that prove useful when they reach adulthood. Unfortunately, however, at least one study of late-maturing boys indicates that heavy drinking may be one of the "coping" behaviors that persists into young adulthood (Andersson & Magnusson, 1990).

● **Early Versus Late Maturation in Girls**   Early re-search on this issue, again conducted by researchers working on the Oakland Growth Study, suggested that, in contrast to boys, early-maturing girls are at a disad-vantage—although the findings were far less consistent than they were in the studies of boys (Jones, 1949; Jones & Mussen, 1958). Early-maturing girls were found to be "less popular, less poised, less expressive, and more sub-missive, withdrawn, and unassured then [their] age-mates" (Livson & Peskin, 1980, p. 71). Like the late-maturing boy, the early-maturing girl is out of step with her peers. And, since girls mature about two years ear-lier than boys, the early-maturing girl is not only more physically advanced than her female peers but far more advanced than nearly all her male classmates as well. In these studies, the late-maturing girls were more likely to be seen as attractive, sociable, and expressive.

As is the case with research on early- and late-maturing boys, more recent research on girls has tended to corroborate the findings of the earlier studies, but we have learned a good deal more about the development of early-maturing girls, in particular, in the ensuing years. A number of studies find that early-maturing girls have more emotional difficulties than do girls who mature on time or late, including lowered self-image and higher rates of depression, anxiety, eat-ing disorders, and panic attacks (Aro & Taipale, 1987; Ge, Conger, & Elder, 1996; Graber et al., 1997; Hayward et al., 1997). These difficulties seem to have a great deal to do with girls' feelings about their weight, because early maturers are, almost by definition, heavier than their late-maturing peers (Petersen, 1988). In societies that define as physically attractive the thin, "leggy" woman, a late-maturing girl will look more like this image than an early-maturing girl will.

Whether earlier maturation has a negative effect on the young girl's feelings about herself appears to de-pend on the broader context in which maturation takes place, however. For example, studies of American girls generally find that early-maturing girls have lower self-esteem and a poorer self-image because of our cultural preference for thinness and our national ambivalence about adolescent sexuality (Brooks-Gunn & Reiter, 1990). In Germany, however, where sex education is more open and attitudes toward adolescent sexuality are less conflicted, early-maturing girls are found to have *higher* self-esteem (Silbereisen et al., 1989).

Interestingly, even *within* the United States, the impact of physical maturation appears to depend on the social context in which teenagers live (Dyer & Tiggemann, 1996). One study of suburban Chicago youngsters, for example, found that the girls' body image was significantly higher in one community than in another—despite comparable levels of physical maturation between the two groups. One factor that differentiated the two communities was "cliquishness": In the more cliquish high school, girls were less satisfied with the way they looked, perhaps because cliquish girls place more emphasis on physical appearance in determining popularity (Richards, Boxer, Petersen, & Albrecht, 1990).

Although some early-maturing girls may have self-image difficulties, their popularity with peers is not jeopardized. Indeed, some studies indicate that early maturers are more popular than other girls, especially, as you would expect, when the index of popularity includes popularity with boys (Simmons, Blyth, & McKinney, 1983). Ironically, it may be in part because the early maturer is more popular with boys that she reports more emotional upset: At a very early age, pressure to date and, perhaps, to be involved in a sexual relationship may take its toll on the adolescent girl's mental health. Consistent with this, research indicates that early-maturing girls are more vulnerable to emotional distress when they have relatively more opposite-sex friendships (Ge et al., 1996) and when they are in schools with older peers (for example, sixth-graders who are in a school that also has seventh- and eighth-graders) (Blyth, Simmons, & Zakin, 1985). Again, we see the importance of context.

Like their male counterparts, early-maturing girls are also more likely to become involved in deviant activities, including delinquency and drug and alcohol use; are more likely to have school problems; and are more likely to experience early sexual intercourse (Aro & Taipale, 1987; Caspi & Moffitt, 1991; Flannery, Rowe, & Gulley, 1993; Ge et al., 1996; Graber et al., 1997; Magnusson, Stattin, & Allen, 1986). This is true in Europe as well as in the United States (Silbereisen et al., 1989). These problems appear to arise because early-

maturing girls are more likely to spend time with older adolescents, especially older adolescent boys, who initiate them into activities that might otherwise be delayed (Magnusson et al., 1986). Girls with a history of problem behavior prior to puberty appear most susceptible to the adverse effects of early maturation (Caspi & Moffitt, 1991) (see "The Scientific Study of Adolescence: Early Maturation and Girls' Problem Behavior—Activation or Accentuation?").

Again, however, it is important to consider the role of context in interaction with pubertal change. Although it is generally true that early-maturing girls are more likely to engage in delinquent behavior than are their late-maturing peers, a study of New Zealand youngsters indicates that this may hold true only for girls who attend coeducational high schools (Caspi, Lynam, Moffitt, & Silva, 1993). Early-maturing girls in all-female schools are no more likely than late maturers to be involved in delinquent activities, presumably because there are far fewer opportunities for delinquency in same-sex schools. Thus, although early puberty may predispose girls toward more frequent and earlier deviance, this predisposition may be realized only in an environment that permits the behavior—such as a school that places early-maturing girls in close contact with older boys.

One study of the adult personalities of women who had been either early or late maturers suggests some interesting parallels between the personality development of early-maturing girls and late-maturing boys (Peskin, 1973). Both sets of youngsters may have self-esteem problems during adolescence, but both appear to be somewhat more psychologically advanced than their peers during adulthood. Like late-maturing boys, early-maturing girls may be forced to develop coping skills during adolescence that have some long-term positive effects.

At the same time, however, more recent research indicates that the earlier involvement of early-maturing girls in problem behavior may adversely affect their long-term educational achievement. In one study of Swedish girls, for example, the researchers found that the school problems of the early-maturing adolescent girls persisted over time, leading to the development of negative attitudes toward school and lower educational aspirations. In young adulthood, there were marked differences between the early- and late-maturing girls' levels of education; for example, the late-maturing girls were twice as likely as the early-maturing girls to continue beyond the compulsory minimum number of years of high school (Magnusson et al., 1986).

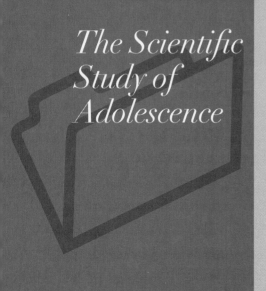

The Scientific Study of Adolescence

Early Maturation and Girls' Problem Behavior—Activation or Accentuation?

As you know, researchers have observed for some time now that early physical maturation in both boys and girls is associated with higher rates of problem behavior, including delinquency, drug and alcohol use, and precocious sexual activity. But does early maturation by itself actually cause problem behavior to emerge at adolescence? Or are the two variables associated in some other fashion?

In order to examine this question, psychologists Avshalom Caspi and Terrie Moffitt drew on data from an extensive study of 15-year-old New Zealand girls who had been studied since birth (Caspi & Moffitt, 1991). One of the interesting features of the data set used by the researchers was that measures of problem behavior had been gathered on the adolescents both during childhood, well before the onset of puberty (at age 9), and during adolescence, after puberty had begun (at ages 13 and 15). The researchers used age at menarche as their indicator of early

(menarche before age 13), on-time (menarche between 13 and 14), and late (menarche after age 14) maturation. They looked to see whether problem behavior increased between 13 and 15 to a greater degree among early maturers than among the other girls.

As hypothesized, and consistent with other studies, Caspi and Moffitt noted a larger increase in problem behavior between ages 13 and 15 among the early-maturing girls. However, when they further broke down the early-maturing sample into two smaller groups—girls who had shown high rates of problem behavior before puberty and those who had not—they saw an interesting pattern: Early maturation was associated with an increase in problem behavior only among those girls who had a history of difficulties. As you can see in the accompanying figure, the discrepancy in problem behavior between early maturers and other girls is far more evident in the group of girls who had been rated high

---

RECAP

Psychologists have long been interested in the consequences of early versus late physical maturation. In general, early maturation brings with it more social advantages for boys and girls, but very early maturation may be somewhat of a psychological liability for girls, at least in the United States. For both sexes, however, early physical maturation is associated with more problem behavior, including drug and alcohol use, delinquency, and precocious sexual activity. This may be because early maturers see themselves as being more adult and, consequently, as being more entitled to engage in these activities. It is important to keep in mind, however, that early maturation has different effects in different social contexts.

Food for Thought

What are the major advantages and disadvantages of early pubertal maturation? of late maturation? How are these advantages and disadvantages similar, and how are they different, between males and females? How might the advantages and disadvantages of being early, on time, or late vary across historical eras?

EATING DISORDERS

Although a variety of nutritional and behavioral factors can lead to weight gains during adolescence, gaining weight can sometimes result directly from the physical changes of puberty. Not only does the ratio of body fat to muscle increase markedly during puberty, but the body's basal metabolism rate also drops about 15 percent. The **basal metabolism rate** is the minimal amount of energy one uses when resting. A person's weight is partly dependent on this rate.

Because adolescence is a time of dramatic change in physical appearance, the young person's overall self-in problem behavior before adolescence. Indeed, within the group of girls who had been rated low in problem behavior at age 9, there were no differences at all between early and on-time maturers in terms of problem behavior.

Does early maturation cause problem behavior during adolescence? Not entirely; rather, early maturation appears to accentuate, or magnify, differences between individuals that existed prior to adolescence. Why should this be so?

According to Caspi and Moffitt, early puberty is stressful, and stress, they suggest, tends to bring out differences between individuals. Although we tend to think of stress as something that changes people in dramatic ways, Caspi and Moffitt say that just the opposite is true: During times of stress, not only do we not change markedly but we also become even *more* like we were before the stress occurred.

Interestingly, in another analysis, these and other researchers used the same data set to examine the possibility that problem behavior leads to early puberty, rather than the reverse (Moffitt, Caspi, Belsky, & Silva, 1992).

Although, like other researchers, they found that earlier maturation is associated with higher levels of family conflict in childhood, they found no evidence that early puberty follows higher levels of behavior problems.

Source: Caspi, A., & Moffitt, T. (1991). Individual differences and personal transitions: The sample case of girls at puberty. *Journal of Personality and Social Psychology, 61,* 157–168.

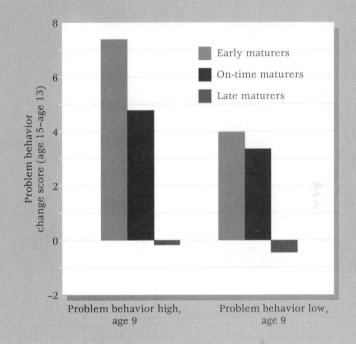

image is very much tied to his or her body image. Deviation from the ideal physique can lead to loss of self-esteem and other problems in the adolescent's self-image. In light of the tremendous emphasis that contemporary society places on being thin, particularly for females, it comes as no surprise to learn that the normal weight gain and change in body composition that accompanies puberty leads many adolescents, especially girls, to become extremely concerned about their weight.

Many adolescents, of course, have legitimate concerns about being overweight. According to national surveys, for example, nearly 20 percent of adolescents in the United States are overweight, and about 5 percent are obese—that is, they are more than 20 percent over the maximum recommended weight for their height— and an additional 15 percent are seriously overweight (Gans, 1990). Current research indicates that obesity is a result of an interplay of genetic and environmental factors (Friedman & Brownell, 1995).

Research on the *psychological* consequences of obesity has not led to consistent conclusions, with some

studies showing higher levels of psychological distress (e.g., depression, low self-esteem) among obese individuals, especially during adolescence, but many studies show no such effect (Friedman & Brownell, 1995). Nevertheless, because nearly 80 percent of obese adolescents will be obese adults, obesity during adolescence places the individual at much higher risk for other health problems, including hypertension (high blood pressure), high cholesterol levels, and diabetes (Must, Jacques, Dallal, Bajema, & Dietz, 1992). The high prevalence of obesity among African American females, in particular, poses a serious risk to the cardiovascular health of this group (Flynn & Fitzgibbon, 1996; Morrison, Payne, Barton, Khoury, & Crawford, 1994). Often, a program of intense physical exercise combined with proper nutrition can help youngsters lose weight (Kimm, 1995).

Health-care professionals have been concerned not only about adolescents who are obese but also about adolescents who have unhealthy attitudes toward eating and toward their body image (French, Story, Downes,

The Effects of Early Maturation

Researchers are still trying to make sense of the complicated pattern of findings that emerges from comparisons of early and late maturers, but one fact is clear: Early maturation brings many more disadvantages for girls than it does for boys. Psychologists have offered several explanations for this sex difference. The explanations all are compatible, but they derive from very different premises.

One explanation might be termed the "deviance" hypothesis (Simmons & Blyth, 1987). Simply put, youngsters who stand far apart from their peers—in physical appearance, for instance—may experience more psychological distress than adolescents who blend in more easily. Studies of adolescents who stand out physically in other ways—obese students and students who attend schools in which they are clearly in a racial minority—support the view that standing out too much can be an unfortunate disadvantage (Blyth et al., 1980; Simmons et al., 1983). Because girls mature earlier than boys, on average, early-maturing girls mature much earlier than their male and female agemates. This makes them stand out at a time when they would rather fit in and, as a result, may make them more vulnerable. This explanation would also account for the lower self-esteem of late-maturing boys, who are deviant toward the other extreme.

A second explanation focuses on "developmental readiness." Here the notion is that psychological distress results when youngsters have experiences before they are psychologically ready for them (Simmons & Blyth, 1987). If puberty is a challenge that

Resnick, & Blum, 1995). Egged on by advertisers, who promote the idea that thin is beautiful—middle-class white girls define bodily perfection as being five feet seven inches tall and 110 pounds—many adolescents respond to normal bodily changes at puberty by dieting, often unnecessarily (Brumberg, 1997). Studies, for example, indicate that more than half of all adolescent girls consider themselves overweight and have attempted to diet (Fisher et al., 1995). Psychologists use the term **disordered eating** to refer to patterns of behaviors and attitudes about eating that are unhealthy. Disordered eating can range from unnecessary preoccupation with weight and body image to full-blown clinical eating disorders, such as anorexia and bulimia. Studies show that disordered eating is associated with a range of psychological problems associated with stress, including poor body image, depression, alcohol and tobacco use, and poor interpersonal relationships (French et al., 1995; Graber, Brooks-Gunn, Paikoff, & Warren, 1994; Neumark-Sztainer, Story, Dixon, & Murray, 1998), although it is not clear whether these problems precede, or follow from, disordered eating (Leon, Fulkerson, Perry, Keel, & Klump, 1999).

In contemporary America, as the expression goes, one can never be too rich or too thin. Studies of magazines aimed particularly at women and adolescent girls reveal clear and consistent messages implying that women cannot be beautiful without being slim and suggesting a range of products designed to promote weight loss. Between 1970 and 1990, moreover, the images used in these magazines' advertisements changed, with the ideal body shape becoming slimmer and less curvaceous (Guillen & Barr, 1994). Ironically, research indicates that adolescents' attempts to control their weight through intensive dieting, the use of laxatives and appetite suppressants, and deliberate vomiting leads to weight *gain,* not loss (Stice, Cameron, Killen, Hayward, & Taylor, 1999). Girls whose mothers have their own body image problems are especially likely to engage in extreme weight-loss behaviors (Benedikt, Wertheim, & Love, 1998), as are those who report more negative relationships with their parents (Archibald, Graber, & Brooks-Gunn, 1999). Interestingly, among Hispanic American girls, those who are more acculturated (i.e., "Americanized") are signficantly more likely to develop disordered eating than are those who are less acculturated (Gowen, Hayward, Killen, Robinson, & Taylor, 1999).

Not everyone is genetically or metabolically meant to be as thin as fashion magazines tell people they

requires psychological adaptation by the adolescent, perhaps younger adolescents are less able than older ones to cope with the challenge. Because puberty occurs quite early among early-maturing girls (some may begin maturing at age 8 or 9 and may experience menarche at age 10), it may tax their psychological resources. Early maturation among boys, because it occurs at a much later age, would pose less of a problem. The developmental readiness hypothesis has been used to account for the finding that older youngsters (eighth-graders) fare better during the transition from elementary to secondary school than do younger students (sixth-graders). This perspective also helps account for the fact that, in puberty, late-maturing boys seem better able than early maturers to control their temper and their impulses (Peskin, 1967).

A final explanation concerns the cultural desirability of different body types (Petersen, 1988). Early maturation for girls means leaving behind the culturally admired state of thinness. Among girls, the ratio of fat to muscle increases dramatically at puberty, and many girls feel distressed when they mature because they gain weight. Early maturers experience this weight gain at a time when most of their peers are still girlishly thin. One interesting study showed that, in ballet companies—where thinness is even more important than in the culture at large—late maturers, who can retain the "ideal" shape much longer than earlier maturers, have fewer psychological problems than even on-time girls do (Brooks-Gunn & Warren, 1985). In contrast, at puberty boys move from a culturally undesirable state for males (being short and scrawny) to a culturally admired one (being tall and muscular). Early maturers enjoy the special advantage of being tall and muscular before their peers and therefore are more likely to react well to puberty. The fact that the effects of early maturation on girls' self-esteem vary across cultures suggests that contextual factors need to be taken into account in explaining this pattern of sex differences.

Whatever the explanation, the fact that early-maturing girls are at heightened risk for temporary psychological problems, at least in the United States, is an important fact for parents and school counselors to bear in mind. Unfortunately, as long as our culture overvalues thinness and encourages the view that females should be judged on the basis of their physical appearance rather than their abilities, values, or personality, the risks of early puberty will probably persist. Adults can help by being supportive, by helping the early-maturing girl to recognize her strengths and positive features—physical and nonphysical alike—and by preparing her for puberty before it takes place.

should be. Some young women become so concerned about gaining weight that they take drastic—and dangerous—measures to remain thin. Some go on eating binges and then force themselves to vomit to avoid gaining weight, a pattern associated with an eating disorder called **bulimia.** In the more severe cases, young women who suffer from an eating disorder called **anorexia nervosa** actually starve themselves in an effort to keep their weight down. Adolescents with these sorts of eating disorders have an extremely disturbed body image. They see themselves as overweight when they are actually underweight. Some anorexic youngsters may lose between 25 and 50 percent of their body weight. As you would expect, bulimia and anorexia, if untreated, lead to a variety of serious physical problems; in fact, nearly 20 percent of anorexic teenagers inadvertently starve themselves to death.

Anorexia and bulimia both began to receive a great deal of popular attention during the 1980s, because of their dramatic nature and their frequent association in the mass media with celebrities. Perhaps because of this attention, initial reports characterized these eating disorders as being of epidemic proportion. Although unhealthy eating and unnecessary dieting may be prevalent among teenagers, careful studies indicate that the incidence of genuine anorexia and genuine bulimia is rather small (Fisher et al., 1995). Fewer than one-half of 1 percent of adolescents are anorexic, and only about 3 percent are bulimic (American Psychiatric Association, 1994). Anorexia and bulimia are far more common among females than males, however, and are rarely seen before puberty.

Although the incidence of anorexia and bulimia is small, the proportion of adolescents who are unhappy with their body shape or weight is not. This is especially the case among female adolescents from relatively more affluent backgrounds, which no doubt accounts for the greater incidence of anorexia and bulimia in this population (Gardner, Friedman, & Jackson, 1999). In one study, for example, more than one-third of the girls whose weight was considered normal by medical and health standards believed that they were overweight—including 5 percent who actually were underweight by medical criteria. (Less than 7 percent of normal-weight boys, and no underweight boys, described themselves as being overweight.) In this study, more than 70 percent of the girls reported that they would like to be thinner than they are (as opposed to one-third of the boys), and more than 80 percent said that being thinner would make them happier, more successful, and more popular (Paxton et al., 1991).

▲ *Although it is far less glamorous and less well publicized than anorexia or bulimia, obesity is the most common eating disorder. According to national surveys, nearly 20 percent of adolescents in the United States are overweight, and about 5 percent of adolescents are obese.* (Bob Daemmrich/Stock Boston)

Not surprisingly, dissatisfaction with one's body is likely to lead to the development of eating problems (Attie & Brooks-Gunn, 1989). Some researchers caution, however, that a large number of adolescents who are "watching their weight" are engaging in behaviors that are perfectly normal, even healthy (Nichter, Ritenbaugh, Nichter, Vukovic, & Aickin, 1995).

Unfortunately, many girls gain weight during puberty, and, for early adolescent girls, being overweight is highly correlated with being rated as unattractive by others (Rosenblum & Lewis, 1999). Despite adults' wishes that girls would not place so much emphasis on being thin, research indicates that the widespread belief among adolescent girls that being slim will increase their popularity, especially with boys, is based in reality (see figure 1.11) (Halpern, Udry, Campbell, & Suchindran, 1999). This places many girls in a difficult situation, as one team of researchers noted:

> Most girls in our sample reported that having a boyfriend was either somewhat or very important to them, and virtually all girls saw physical attractiveness as important. As adolescent girls experience the weight and fat gains that accompany and follow puberty, they must reconcile these gains with their belief that slimness is an important factor in dating and popularity with boys. . . . For White girls and Black girls with college-educated mothers, more

body fat, even among non-obese girls, strongly lowered the probability of dating. . . . The 5 ft 3 in. girls who weighed 110 pounds was twice as likely to date as a girl of the same height and level of pubertal maturity who weighed 126 pounds. . . . Obviously, these adolescent girls had not carried out the sort of probability calculations that we have presented here, but adolescents, White adolescents in particular, believe that slimness is important to the likelihood of dating. Our data indicate that they are right. (Halpern et al., 1999, p. 732)

Initial reports on the prevalence of disordered eating among adolescent girls led to the conclusion that eating disorders are especially common among affluent, suburban, white and Asian American girls (e.g., Condit, 1990). More recent studies do not support this contention, however, suggesting either that the initial conclusions were incorrect or that there have been changes over time in the links among disordered eating, ethnicity, and socioeconomic status. Whatever the explanation, contemporary research indicates that disordered eating and body dissatisfaction have been reported among poor, as well as affluent, teenagers and among African American and Hispanic, as well as Asian American and white, youngsters (Davis & Gergen, 1994; Fisher et al., 1995; Pastore, Fisher, & Friedman, 1996a; Robinson et al., 1996; Schreiber et al., 1996). There is some evidence, however, that African Americans have more flexible conceptions of beauty that tolerate a wider range of body types, including body types that other ethnic groups view as overweight (Flynn & Fitzgibbon, 1996; Parker et al., 1995, Thompson, Sargent, & Kemper, 1996).

Several theories have been proposed to account for the onset of anorexia and bulimia during adolescence (see Condit, 1990). One perspective emphasizes the biological basis for anorexia, in particular, since there is strong evidence that anorexia is both genetically and hormonally influenced (Holland, Sicotte, & Treasure, 1988; Leibowitz, 1983). Unfortunately, it is difficult in hormonal studies to separate cause and effect: Changes in hormone levels can effect weight loss, but starvation and dieting also affect hormone levels.

A second view emphasizes psychological factors. Some theorists have proposed that anorexia is related to the adolescent's attempts to assert her autonomy within an overly controlling family system (Bruch, 1973; Killian, 1994; Minuchin, Rosman, & Baker, 1978). Others have suggested that anorexia is a sort of avoidance mechanism that reflects the young woman's fears of entering adulthood (Crisp, 1983). One of the consequences of starvation during early adolescence, for example, is that pubertal development is severely delayed (Surbey, 1987).

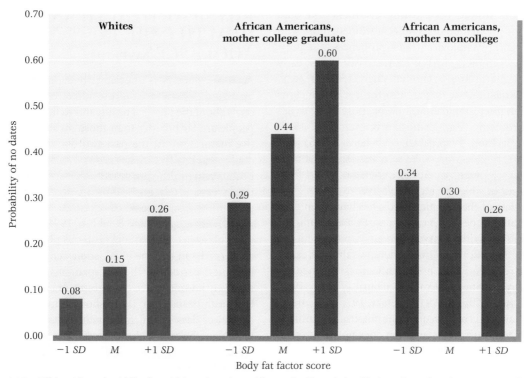

Figure 1.11   *White girls and middle-class African American girls are significantly less likely to date when they are not as slim as their peers. The same is not true for less affluent black girls, however.* (Halpern et al., 1999)

A third school of thought views eating disorders as part of a more general syndrome of psychological distress. Many studies have pointed to links between eating disorders and other serious mental health problems, such as depression, obsessive-compulsive disorder, and substance abuse; many anorexic and bulimic women display such psychological problems along with their eating disorder (Casper & Jabine, 1996; Leon, Fulkerson, Perry, & Dube, 1994; Munoz & Amado, 1986; Rastam, Gillberg, & Gillberg, 1996; Strober, Freeman, Bower, & Rigali, 1996). These studies suggest that anorexia and bulimia may be best understood not as independent or unique disorders but as particular manifestations of a more general underlying psychological problem—called *internalized distress*—which can be displayed in a variety of ways. (As you will read in chapter 13, many different psychological disorders in adolescence occur together, or "covary.") In support of this view, there is some evidence that the medications that are successful in treating depression and obsessive-compulsive disorder are useful in treating anorexia (Condit, 1990).

Finally, because anorexia and bulimia are 10 times more common in females than males, it is likely that broader social forces are a main factor in the development of these eating disorders (Brumberg, 1988). Research indicates, for example, that girls who are early maturers and early daters are likely to report greater dissatisfaction with their bodies and to be at greater risk for disordered eating (Cauffman & Steinberg, 1996; Smolak et al., 1993; Swarr & Richards, 1996) and that girls who turn to popular magazines, such as *Seventeen, Sassy,* and *Glamour,* for information about dieting and appearance are more likely to have a high drive for thinness and disturbed patterns of eating (Levine, Smolack, & Hayden, 1994). One interesting study showed, for example, how bulimia became socially "contagious" in a college sorority (Crandall, 1988). This researcher found that, over the course of the academic year, the women's eating behavior became more and more like that of their sorority friends—even in a sorority in which binge eating was the norm. Other research indicates that girls' attitudes toward eating and dieting are influenced by the attitudes of their parents and friends (Mukai, 1996).

Just because cultural conditions contribute to the development of anorexia nervosa doesn't mean that individual characteristics do not play a role as well. It may be that cultural conditions predispose females more than males toward these eating disorders and that, within the population of adolescent women, those who have certain psychological traits (proneness to depression, for example), physical characteristics (e.g., early pubertal maturation), familial characteristics (e.g., strained relations with parents), or social concerns (e.g., high interest in dating) may be more likely to develop problems (e.g., Cauffman & Steinberg, 1996; Frank & Jackson, 1996; Swarr & Richards, 1996). The onset of eating disorders, like so many aspects of adolescent development, cannot be understood apart from the context in which young people live.

A variety of therapeutic approaches have been used successfully in the treatment of anorexia and bulimia, including individual psychotherapy and cognitive-behavior modification, group therapy, family therapy, and, more recently, the use of antidepressant medication (Agras, Schneider, Arnow, Raeburn, & Telch, 1989; Condit, 1990; Killian, 1994; Vigersky, 1977). The treatment of anorexia often requires hospitalization initially in order to ensure that starvation does not progress to fatal or near-fatal levels (Mitchell, 1985).

RECAP

Many writers link the emergence of eating problems in adolescence to the biological changes of puberty, which typically include increases in weight and changes in body composition. Disordered eating can range from mild disturbances in attitudes and diet to serious and potentially life-threatening clinical disorders, such as anorexia. Although many adolescents, especially girls, are unhappy with their body and concerned about being overweight—even when their weight is perfectly normal—clinical eating disorders such as anorexia and bulimia are actually quite rare. Nevertheless, studies indicate that individuals with eating disorders are at risk for a wide range of other mental health problems, including depression, substance abuse, and other forms of internalized distress. Current thinking suggests that eating disorders are caused by a complex interplay of biological and environmental factors.

Food for Thought

Boys may not show the symptoms of anorexia or bulimia to the extent that girls do, but many boys are overly concerned about their body and weight nevertheless. What might be some signs in an adolescent male that could indicate problems in this area?

PHYSICAL HEALTH AND HEALTH CARE IN ADOLESCENCE

Although puberty is undoubtedly the most important biological development of the adolescent decade, concerns about the physical health and well-being of young people are far broader than those involving reproductive maturation. In the past two decades, the field of **adolescent health care** has grown rapidly, as health educators and health-care practitioners have come to better understand that the health-care needs of young people differ from those of children and adults in important respects (Slap & Jablow, 1994).

Adolescence is a paradox as far as physical health is concerned. On the one hand, adolescence is one of the healthiest periods in the life span, characterized by a relatively low incidence of disabling or chronic illnesses (e.g., asthma, cancer), fewer short-term hospital stays, and fewer days in which individuals stay home sick in bed. Nonetheless, in the United States, nearly 1 in 15 adolescents has at least one disabling or chronic illness, with the main causes of disability being mental disorders, such as depression; respiratory illnesses, such as asthma; and muscular and skeletal disorders, such as arthritis (Ozer, Macdonald, & Irwin, in press). Fortunately, in the past 50 years, the rates of death and disability resulting from illness and disease during adolescence have decreased substantially, and new medical technologies and better health-care delivery have improved the physical well-being of children, especially those with chronic illness and disabling medical conditions (Gans, 1990). Adolescents are far less likely than individuals of any other age to seek and receive medical care through traditional office visits to practitioners, however. Moreover, there are large socioeconomic and ethnic disparities in adolescents' access to care, with poor and ethnic minority youth far less likely to have adequate health insurance and health-care access than affluent or white youth (Ozer et al., in press).

The most virulent threat to adolescent health comes from unhealthy behaviors (such as drug use), violence (both self-inflicted and inflicted by others), and risky activity (such as unprotected sexual intercourse or drunk driving). In some senses, then, many of the improvements made in preventing and treating the traditional medical problems of the period—those having to do with chronic illnesses—have been offset by what some scientists call the "new morbidity and mortality" of adolescence (Hein, 1988b). Contributors to this new morbidity and mortality include accidents (especially automobile accidents), suicide, homicide, substance abuse (including tobacco and alcohol use), and sexually transmitted diseases (including AIDS).

The contrast between the old and new mortalities of adolescence is readily apparent. Fifty years ago, illness and disease accounted for more than twice as many deaths among teenagers as violence or injury, but the reverse is true today, although deaths due to accidents, mainly automobile accidents, have fallen dramatically in the past two decades (Ozer et al., in press). According to recent estimates, approximately 45 percent of all teenage deaths result from car accidents and other unintentional injuries, and another 30 percent are a result of homicide or suicide (Ozer et al., in press). Adolescents are involved in more driving accidents than are adults primarily because they are less experienced behind the wheel (at any age, new drivers are more likely to have accidents than seasoned drivers) but also because adolescents are more likely to take chances while driving—perhaps because they are likely to be driving with other teenagers who encourage risk-taking (Simpson, 1996). Adolescents are also more likely than other age groups to be injured as pedestrians and bicyclists in traffic accidents (Hingson & Howland, 1993). One piece of good news is that, although alcohol contributes greatly to automobile accidents among young drivers, the rate of alcohol-related traffic fatality among young people has dropped dramatically in recent years (Sells & Blum, 1996).

The consensus among health-care experts, then, is that the most significant threats to the health of today's youth arise from psychosocial rather than from natural causes (Ozer et al., in press). Unlike many other periods of the life span (such as infancy or old age), when we are more vulnerable to disease and illness, most of the health problems of teenagers are preventable. Moreover, patterns of diet, smoking, and exercise established during adolescence persist into adulthood (Kelder, Perry, Klepp, & Lytle, 1994). As a result of this recognition, the focus in the field of adolescent health has shifted away from traditional medical models (in which the emphasis is on the assessment, diagnosis, and treatment of disease) toward more community-oriented, educational approaches (in which the emphasis is on the prevention of illness and injury and the promotion of good health) (Millstein, Petersen, & Nightingale, 1993; Susman, Koch, Maney, & Finkelstein, 1993).

In other words, instead of asking how we can best treat sick adolescents, experts in adolescent health care are now asking how we can encourage adolescents to take the steps necessary to prevent illness and disability. How can we help adolescents reduce **health-compromising behav-**iors, such as violence, drug use, unsafe driving, and unprotected sexual intercourse, and increase **health-enhancing behaviors,** such as eating properly, exercising adequately, and wearing seat belts? Current efforts include providing teenagers education about alcohol and other drug use, accident prevention, safe sex, and proper nutrition, as well as encouraging health-care professionals to do more direct screening for risky health practices among their adolescent patients—as one group of experts put it, "Don't Ask, They Won't Tell" (Blum, Beuhring, Wunderlich, & Resnick, 1996, p. 1767).

Adolescent medicine expert Charles Irwin, Jr. (1993), has suggested that parents, practitioners, and educators who are interested in helping adolescents live healthier lives keep in mind the "five As" of successful health promotion:

Anticipatory guidance. Establish a trusting relationship with the young person prior to adolescence.

Ask. Query adolescents directly about their health-enhancing and health-compromising behaviors.

Advise. Give advice about health promotion, even if the young person doesn't ask for it.

Assist. Encourage the adolescent to participate in programs that promote health.

Arrange. Arrange follow-up visits or consultations to monitor the adolescent's progress.

A variety of new, wide-reaching strategies for promoting adolescent health have been attempted in recent decades. Among the most popular of the latest wave involve **school-based health centers.** These are located in or adjacent to schools, and they provide such services as physical examinations, the treatment of minor injuries, health education programs, dental care, and counseling related to substance abuse, sexuality, and mental health. They often are set up to serve poor youth, who generally are less likely to receive medical and dental care than are their more affluent counterparts.

School-based health centers became increasingly popular because they are positioned to address the most pressing problems in adolescent health care: the fact that most adolescent health problems are preventable, the fact that adolescents underutilize conventional medical services, and the fact that adolescents often want their health-care needs to remain confidential. Although the development of these centers has generated controversy in a number of communities because some school-based health centers distribute contraceptives (a practice that upsets many adults), studies show that the vast majority of visits to these centers are for injuries,

▲ *School-based health centers deliver important services to adolescents, including contraceptive information and counseling.* (J. Stettenheim/Saba)

acute illnesses (e.g., influenza, strep throat), and mental health services (e.g., counseling). Visits for family planning services account for only 10 percent of visits to school-based clinics (Scales, 1991).

How well are school-based health centers working? Recent evaluations of several school-based health programs—including those designed to improve adolescents' physical and mental health, those designed to reduce drug and alcohol use, and those designed to reduce teenage pregnancy—have been inconsistent. Although most programs have shown some success in increasing adolescents' understanding of health-related issues (e.g., how AIDS is spread) and knowledge about health risks (e.g., the dangers of cocaine use), few programs have been markedly successful in changing adolescents' *behavior,* particularly after the program was completed (Kisker & Brown, 1996; Millstein et al., 1993). Why is this so? As is the case in studies of adults, studies of adolescents indicate that it is far easier to alter what individuals know than it is to change how they behave.

As many experts point out, health behavior is influenced by a large number of factors, of which knowledge is only one component (e.g., Leventhal & Keeshan, 1993). Changes in the context in which adolescents live (e.g., the accessibility of handguns, the availability of illicit drugs, the role models to which young people are exposed) must accompany changes in adolescents' knowledge and un-

derstanding if lasting health promotion is to be accomplished. For example, investigations of the impact of changing one element of the broader context of adolescent health—the legal drinking age—have found that raising the age leads to a significant decline in accidental death rates among young automobile drivers and pedestrians, as well as in the rates of unintentional injuries not involving cars and homicides (Jones, Pieper, & Robertson, 1992).

Improving the health of young people is an especially important concern among those working with adolescents who are poor or from ethnic minority groups, because these youngsters are at greater risk for many of the old as well as the new morbidities and mortalities of adolescence (Ozer et al., in press; Singh & Yu, 1996a). Nonwhite youngsters, for example, are relatively more likely than white youngsters to suffer from a chronic illness (Ozer et al., in press); to be obese or to have high blood pressure or high cholesterol levels (National Heart, Lung, and Blood Institute Growth and Health Study Research Group, 1992); to be physically inactive (Wolf et al., 1993); to be victims of violent crimes (Earls, Cairns, & Mercy, 1993); to contract AIDS (Sells & Blum, 1996); to die from drowning (Warneke & Cooper, 1994); or to be murdered (Sorenson, Richardson, & Peterson, 1993). Homicide is the leading cause of death for African American adolescents, accounting for almost half of all deaths in this ethnic group, and homicide is largely responsible for higher mortality rates among Hispanic youth (Ozer et al., in press). American Indian/Alaska Native males have suicide rates four times higher than any other racial/ethnic group (Ozer et al., in press). Yet, despite their generally poorer health, minority youngsters less likely to have access to sources of medical care, less likely to visit the doctor when ill, and less likely to have health insurance (Lieu, Newacheck, & McManus, 1993).

The terrible combination of poor health and poor access to health care is even more concentrated among the sizable proportion of adolescents who live in poverty, a disproportionate number of whom are from ethnic minority backgrounds (Klerman, 1993). There is now convincing evidence that the links between health and socioeconomic status are strong and pervasive across various sorts of health problems, with physical and mental health problems increasing linearly as one moves down the socioeconomic ladder (Adler, 1994; Keating & Hertzman, 2000) Because increases in the size of the adolescent population over the next several decades worldwide will be concentrated among poor and minority youth (Fussell & Greene, in press), the most daunting challenge facing health-care providers and policymakers will be finding ways of minimizing or even eliminating the socioeconomic and ethnic disparities in health and health care that currently exist around the world (Ozer et al., in press).

RECAP

Today, in contrast to 50 years ago, the most important physical health problems in adolescence have psychosocial rather than natural causes. This new morbidity and mortality of adolescence is caused by such preventable phenomena as automobile accidents, violence, substance abuse, and unprotected sex. New approaches to adolescent health care, emphasizing prevention and health promotion instead of treatment, are being studied. Among the most important innovations are school-based health centers.

Food for Thought

What is meant by the distinction between the old and the new health problems of adolescence? Given this distinction, what do you think are the most important things society should do to minimize health problems during this period of development?

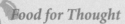

Web Researcher A Girl Scout troop asks you to run a session on feeling good about yourself during the transition to adolescence. You know that sleep and good nutrition are important parts of feeling good about yourself that often get neglected because of busy schedules and worries about their looks. What would you tell them, and how might you help them take what you have to say to heart? Go to **www.mhhe.com/steinberg6** for further information.

KEY TERMS

activational role of hormones
adolescent growth spurt
adolescent health care
adrenarche
androgens
anorexia nervosa
asynchronicity in growth
basal metabolism rate
bulimia
cross-sectional study
delayed phase preference
disordered eating
endocrine system
estrogens
feedback loop
glands
gonads
health-compromising behaviors
health-enhancing behaviors
hormones
HPG axis
hypothalamus
leptin
longitudinal study
menarche
organizational role of hormones
peak height velocity
pheromones
pituitary gland
school-based health centers
secondary sex characteristics
secular trend
set point
Tanner stages

Chapter 2

Cognitive Transitions

Changes in cognition, or thinking, represent the second in a set of three fundamental changes that occur during adolescence—the others being the biological changes of puberty and the transition of the adolescent into new social roles. Like developments in the other two domains, the cognitive transitions of adolescence have far-reaching implications for the young person's psychological development and social relations. Indeed, the expansion of thought during adolescence represents as significant an event and as important an influence on the adolescent's development and behavior as puberty. ●

CHANGES IN COGNITION

Most people would agree that adolescent are "smarter" than children. Not only do teenagers know more than children—after all, the longer we live, the more opportunities we have to acquire new information—but adolescents actually think in ways that are more advanced, more efficient, and generally more effective. This can be seen in five chief ways (Keating, 1990):

1.   During adolescence, individuals become better able than children to think about what is possible, instead of limiting their thought to what is real.

2.   Adolescents become better able to think about abstract things.

3.   During adolescence, individuals begin thinking more often about the process of thinking itself.

4.   Adolescents' thinking tends to become multidimensional, rather than being limited to a single issue.

5.   Adolescents are more likely than children to see things as relative, rather than as absolute.

Let's look at each of these advantages—and some of their implications—in greater detail.

Thinking About Possibilities

The adolescent's thinking is less bound to concrete events than is that of the child. Children's thinking is oriented to the here and now—that is, to things and events that they can observe directly. But adolescents are able to consider what they observe against a backdrop of what is possible. Put another way, for the child, what is possible is what is real; for the adolescent, what is real is but one subset of what is possible. Children, for example, do not wonder, the way adolescents often do, about the ways in which their personalities might change in the future or the ways in which their lives might be affected by different career choices. For the young child, you are who you are. But for the adolescent, who you are is just one possibility of who you could be.

This does not mean that the child is incapable of imagination or fantasy. Even young children have vivid and creative imaginations. Nor does it mean that children are unable to conceive of things being different from the way they observe them to be. Rather, the advantage that adolescents enjoy over children when it comes to thinking about possibilities is that adolescents are able to move easily between the specific and the abstract, to generate alternative possibilities and explanations systematically, and to compare what they actually observe with what they believe is possible.

We can illustrate this development by looking at the following problem. How would you approach it?

> Imagine four poker chips, one red, one blue, one yellow, and one green. Make as many different combinations of chips, of any number, as you can. Use the notations *R, B, Y,* and *G* to record your answers. (Adapted from Elkind, Barocas, & Rosenthal, 1968)

How did you tackle this problem? Did you need to use real poker chips to solve the problem? Probably not. In all likelihood, you used some sort of system, beginning perhaps with the case of zero chips (don't worry, a lot of people forget this one) and then proceeding on to one-chip combinations *(R, B, Y, G)*, two-chip combinations *(RB, RY, RG, BY, BG, YG)*, three-chip combinations *(RBY, RBG, RYG, BYG)*, and finally the single four-chip combination *(RBYG)*. More important, you probably did not approach the problem haphazardly. You probably used an abstract system for generating the possibilities that you had in mind before being faced with the poker-chip problem—a system that you can apply across a variety of similar tasks. Although preadolescent children might be able to solve the problem correctly—in the sense that they might, with luck, generate all the possible combinations—children are far less likely than teenagers to use a systematic approach (Neimark, 1975).

The adolescent's ability to reason systematically in terms of what is possible comes in handy in a variety of scientific and logical problem-solving situations. For instance, the study of mathematics in junior and senior high school (algebra, geometry, and trigonometry) often requires that you begin with an abstract or theoretical formulation—for example, "the square of a right triangle's hypotenuse is equal to the sum of the squares of the other two sides" (the Pythagorean theorem). This theorem, after all, is a proposition about the possible rather than the real. It is a statement about all *possible* right triangles, not just triangles that we might actually observe. In mathematics, we learn how to apply these theorems to concrete examples (that is, real triangles). Scientific experimentation—in biology, chemistry, and physics—also involves the ability to generate possibilities systematically. In a chemistry experiment in which you are trying to identify an unknown substance by performing various tests, you must first be able to imagine alternative possibilities for the substance's identity in order to know what tests to conduct.

The adolescent's use of this sort of thinking is not limited to scientific situations. It is seen in the types of arguments adolescents use, in which they are more able than younger children to envision and therefore anticipate the possible responses of an opponent and to have handy a counterargument or a series of counterarguments (Clark & Delia, 1976). Many parents believe that their children become more argumentative during adolescence. What probably happens is that their children become *better arguers.* An adolescent does not accept other people's points of view unquestioningly but, instead, evaluates them against other theoretically possible beliefs. As you will read in chapter 4, this improvement in the adolescent's intellectual ability may contribute to the bickering and squabbling that often occur between teenagers and their parents (Smetana, 1989).

Related to the adolescent's increased facility with thinking about possibilities is the development of **deductive reasoning.** Deductive reasoning is a type of logical reasoning in which you draw logically necessary conclusions from a general set of premises, or givens. For example, consider the following problem:

All hockey players wear mouth guards.

Kim is a hockey player.

Does Kim wear a mouth guard?

Individuals who are able to reason deductively are able to understand that the correct conclusion (that Kim wears a mouth guard) necessarily follows from the first two statements. No additional knowledge about hockey, or about Kim, is necessary to reach the correct answer. Contrast this problem with the following one:

Kim, John, Julie, Tom, Liz, and Kendra are hockey players.

Kim, John, Julie, Tom, Liz, and Kendra all wear a mouth guard.

Do all hockey players wear mouth guards?

This problem, in contrast to the first, cannot be solved using deductive reasoning, because no one answer to the question necessarily follows from the first two statements. Instead, this problem is likely to be solved using **inductive reasoning,** in which an inference is made based on the accumulated evidence that one has. For this problem, your answer to the question would likely vary, depending on how many people were listed in the first two statements, your knowledge of hockey, your own experience playing contact sports, and so on. And, rather than being certain of your answer, you would have different degrees of confidence in your conclusion, depending on the amount of information you had. In other words, whereas the conclusions derived from deductive inferences are guaranteed to be true by virtue of their inherent logic, conclusions derived from inductive inferences vary in their likelihood of being true (Galotti, Komatsu, & Voelz, 1997). Inductive reasoning is used by people of all ages, even very young children (Jacobs & Portenza, 1991). Indeed, we all use inductive reasoning often in everyday situations (e.g., you find out that many of your classmates have gotten poor grades on a test, so you start to worry that you will, too). Deductive reasoning is seldom seen before adolescence, however. Many researchers see the development of deductive reasoning as the major intellectual accomplishment of adolescence (Klaczynski & Narasimham, 1998).

Related to the development of deductive reasoning is the emergence of hypothetical thinking, or "if-then" thinking, as it is sometimes called. In order to think hypothetically, you need to see beyond what is directly observable and apply logical reasoning to anticipate what might be possible. The ability to think through hypotheses is an enormously powerful tool. Being able to plan ahead, being able to see the future consequences of an action, and being able to provide alternative explanations of events are all dependent on being able to hypothesize effectively.

Thinking in hypothetical terms also permits us to suspend our beliefs about something in order to argue in the abstract. Being capable of assuming a hypothetical stance is important when it comes to debating an issue, since doing so permits us to understand the logic behind the other person's argument, without necessarily agreeing with its conclusion. Playing devil's advocate, for example—as when you formulate a position contrary to what you really believe in order to challenge someone else's reasoning—requires the ability to think in hypothetical terms. Studies show that, prior to adolescence, individuals have difficulty in dealing with propositions that are contrary to fact, unless they are part of a larger fictional story (Markovits & Valchon, 1989). For example, a 7-year-old boy would have trouble answering the question "Where would flying cows build nests?" He might say, "Cows don't fly," unless he had heard about flying cows in a story that was clearly fantasy-based.

Of course, hypothetical thinking also has implications for the adolescent's social behavior. It helps the young person take the perspective of others by enabling him or her to think through what someone else might be thinking or feeling, given that person's point of view ("If I were in that person's shoes, I would feel pretty angry"). Hypothetical thinking helps in formulating and arguing one's viewpoint, because it allows adolescents to think a step ahead of the opposition—a cognitive tool that comes in quite handy when dealing with parents ("If they come back with 'You have to stay home and clean up the garage,' then I'll remind them about the time they let Susan go out when she had chores to do"). And hypothetical thinking plays an important role in decision-making abilities, because it permits the young person to plan ahead and to foresee the consequences of choosing one alternative over another ("If I choose to go out for the soccer team, then I am going to have to give up my part-time job").

Thinking About Abstract Concepts

The appearance of more systematic, abstract thinking is the second notable aspect of cognitive development during adolescence. Children's thinking is more concrete and more bound to observable events and objects than is that of adolescents. This difference is clearly evident when we consider the ability to deal with abstract concepts—things that cannot be experienced directly through the senses.

For example, adolescents find it easier than children to comprehend the sorts of higher-order abstract logic inherent in puns, proverbs, metaphors, and analogies. When presented with verbal analogies, children are more likely than adolescents to focus on concrete and familiar associations among the words than on the abstract, or conceptual, relations among them. Consider the following analogy, for example:

Sun : Moon : : Asleep : ?

a. Star
b. Bed
c. Awake
d. Night

Instead of answering *awake*—which is the best answer of the four given—children would be more likely to respond with *bed* or *night,* since both of these words have stronger associations with the word *asleep*. It is generally not until early adolescence that individuals are able to discern the abstract principles underlying analogies—in the example, the principle involves antonyms—and therefore solve them correctly (Sternberg & Nigro, 1980).

The adolescent's greater facility with abstract thinking also permits the application of advanced reasoning and logical processes to social and ideological matters. This is clearly seen in the adolescent's increased facility and interest in thinking about interpersonal relationships, politics, philosophy, religion, and morality—topics that involve such abstract concepts as friendship, faith, democracy, fairness, and honesty. As some writers have pointed out, the ability to think abstractly may prompt many adolescents to spend time thinking about the meaning of life itself (Hacker, 1994). The growth of social thinking—generally referred to as social cognition—during adolescence is directly related to the young person's improving ability to think abstractly. In this chapter, we will examine the ways in which social thinking improves in adolescence.

Thinking About Thinking

A third noteworthy gain in cognitive ability during adolescence involves thinking about thinking itself, a process sometimes referred to as **metacognition.** Metacognition often involves monitoring one's own cognitive activity during the process of thinking—when you consciously use a strategy for remembering something (such as *Every Good Boy Deserves Fun,* for the notes of the treble clef in music notation) or when you appraise your own comprehension of something you are reading before going on to the next paragraph. Studies show that using such strategies significantly aids adolescents in problem-solving situations (Chalmers & Lawrence, 1993).

Not only do adolescents manage their thinking more than children do, but they are also better able to explain to others the processes they are using. For instance, in the poker-chip problem mentioned earlier, an adolescent would be able to describe the strategy to you ("First I took the single-chip possibilities, then I took the different pairs . . ."), whereas a child would probably just say, "I thought of everything I could." When asked, adolescents can explain not only *what* they know but also *why* knowing what they know enables them to think differently and solve problems more effectively (Reich, Oser, & Valentin, 1994). Adolescence is an important time for changes in our understanding of knowledge and how it is acquired (Schommer, Calvert, Gariglietti, & Bajaj, 1997). In addition, adolescents are much better able than children to understand that people do not have complete control over their mental activity. One study found, for example, that adolescents and adults are much more likely than children to understand that it is impossible to go for a long period of time without thinking about anything, that we often have thoughts that we do not want to have, and that unwanted thoughts we try to get rid of often return (Flavell, Green, & Flavell, 1998).

Another interesting way in which thinking about thinking becomes more apparent during adolescence is in increased introspection, self-consciousness, and intellectualization. When we are introspective, after all, we are thinking about our own emotions. When we are self-conscious, we are thinking about how others think about us. And, when we intellectualize, we are thinking about our own thoughts. All three processes play an important role in the adolescent's psychological growth. As we will see in chapter 8, for example, these processes permit the sorts of self-examination and exploration that are important components of the young person's attempt to establish a coherent sense of identity.

These intellectual advances may occasionally result in problems for the young adolescent, particularly before he or she adjusts to having such powerful cognitive tools. Being able to introspect, for instance, may lead to periods of extreme self-absorption—a form of "adolescent egocentrism" (Elkind, 1967). Adolescent egocentrism results in two distinct problems in thinking, which help explain some of the seemingly odd beliefs and behaviors of teenagers (Goossens, Seiffge-Krenke, & Marcoen, 1992). The first, the **imaginary audience,** involves having such a heightened sense of self-consciousness that the teenager imagines that his or her behavior is the focus of everyone else's concern and attention. For example, a teenager who is going to a concert with 4,000 other people may worry about

dressing the right way because "everybody will notice." Given the cognitive limitations of adolescent egocentrism, it is difficult to persuade a young person that the "audience" is not all that concerned with his or her behavior or appearance.

A second related problem is called the **personal fable.** The personal fable revolves around the adolescent's egocentric (and erroneous) belief that his or her experiences are unique. For instance, a young man whose relationship with a girlfriend had just broken up might tell his sympathetic mother that she could not possibly understand what it feels like to break up with someone—even though breaking up is something that most people have experienced plenty of times during their adolescent and young adult years. In some respects, adherence to a personal fable of uniqueness provides some protective benefits, in that it enhances adolescents' self-esteem and feelings of self-importance. Sometimes holding on to a personal fable can actually be quite dangerous, however, as in the case of a sexually active adolescent who believes that pregnancy simply won't happen to her or a careless driver who believes that he will defy the laws of nature by taking hairpin turns on a road at breakneck speed. Much of the risk-taking behavior engaged in by adolescents can be explained partly in terms of the personal fable (Lapsley, Flannery, Gottschlich, & Raney, 1996).

Although the concept of adolescent egocentrism rings true, several researchers have found it difficult to confirm that the various manifestations of adolescent egocentrism actually peak in early adolescence, as predicted (Gray & Hudson, 1984; Riley, Adams, & Neilsen, 1984). Instead, certain aspects of adolescent egocentrism, such as the personal fable and the imaginary audience, may remain present throughout the adolescent and adult years (Goossens et al., 1992; Quadrel, Fischoff, & Davis, 1993). Ask any *adult* cigarette smoker if he or she is aware of the scientific evidence linking cigarette smoking with heart and lung disease, and you'll see that it is quite common for adults to hold personal fables.

One problem with many of these studies of adolescent egocentrism is that they rely on fairly simple questionnaires to assess rather complicated belief systems invoked in real-life situations (Elkind, 1985). For example, it is easy to imagine that the adolescent who worried about being seen by "everyone" at a rock concert might not appear so egocentric in his responses to a hypothetical dilemma posed in a questionnaire. This difference, of course, would raise doubts about whether

▲ *Adolescent egocentrism can contribute to a heightened sense of self-consciousness.* (Don Smetzer/Tony Stone)

adolescent egocentrism is an entirely cognitive phenomenon, since we would expect that cognitive deficiencies would show up in questionnaire assessments. It may be that Elkind is right about the increased prevalence of egocentrism during early adolescence but wrong about the processes that underlie it (Lapsley & Murphy, 1985). Indeed, one study found that adolescents' egocentrism was more closely tied to their interpersonal understanding than to their general cognitive ability (Jahnke & Blanchard-Fields, 1993). One guess is that adolescents are egocentric for emotional and social, not cognitive, reasons. Another is that adolescents are overly concerned about what others think of them not because they are cognitively compromised but because, in the highly social world in which adolescents live, other people's opinions have genuine and important consequences (Bell & Bromnick, 2000). It's like the old joke: "Just because you're paranoid doesn't mean that people aren't following you."

Thinking in Multiple Dimensions

A fourth way in which thinking changes during adolescence involves the ability to think about things in a multidimensional fashion. Whereas children tend to think about things one aspect at a time, adolescents can see things through more complicated lenses. For instance, in a baseball game, when a certain hitter comes up to the plate, a preadolescent who knows that the hitter has a good home-run record might exclaim that the batter will hit the ball out of the park. An adolescent, however, would consider the hitter's record in relation to the specific pitcher on the mound and would weigh both factors, or dimensions, before making a prediction (perhaps this player hits homers against left-handed pitchers but strikes out against righties).

The ability to think in multidimensional terms is evident in a variety of situations. Obviously, adolescents can give much more complicated answers than children to questions such as "Why did the Civil War begin?" or "How did Jane Austen's novels reflect the changing position of women in European society?" Thorough answers to these sorts of questions require thinking about several dimensions simultaneously.

The development of a more sophisticated understanding of probability is also made possible by improvements in being able to think in multidimensional terms. Suppose I give you a set of beads that contains both blue beads and yellow ones. Now I ask you to divide them into two containers, so that the containers have different numbers of beads overall but so that the probability of reaching into a container and picking a blue bead is the same for each. In order to do so, you need to vary the number of blue beads *and* the number of yellow beads between the two containers, since the probability of drawing a blue bead is a function of both the number of blue beads and the number of yellow beads. It is not until early adolescence that individuals can solve this sort of problem successfully (Falk & Wilkening, 1998).

However, as is the case with other gains in cognitive ability, the increasing capability of individuals to think in multiple dimensions has consequences for their behavior and thinking outside of academic settings, too. Adolescents describe themselves and others in more differentiated and complicated terms ("I'm both shy and extroverted") and find it easier to look at problems from multiple perspectives ("I know that's the way you see it, but try to look at it from her point of view"). Being able to understand that people's personalities are not one-sided and that social situations can have different interpretations, depending on one's point of view, permits the adolescent to have far more sophisticated—and far more complicated—relationships with people.

One interesting manifestation of adolescents' ability to look at things in multiple dimensions concerns the development of their understanding of sarcasm. As an adult, you understand that the meaning of a speaker's statement is communicated by a combination of what is said, how it is said, and the context in which it is said. If I turn to you during a boring lecture, roll my eyes, and say, in an exaggeratedly earnest tone, "This is the most interesting lecture I've ever heard," you would know that I actually mean just the opposite. But you know this only if you pay attention to my inflection and to the context, as well as the content, of my statement. Only by attending simultaneously to multiple dimensions of speech can we distinguish between the sincere and the sarcastic. Because our ability to think in multidimensional terms improves during adolescence, we would predict improvements as well in our ability to understand when someone is being sarcastic.

In one study designed to look at this question, children, adolescents, and adults were presented with different stories, in which an interaction between two people was followed by a remark that was sincere, deliberately deceptive, or sarcastic (Demorest, Meyer, Phelps, Gardner, & Winner, 1984). The participants in the study were then asked what the true meaning and intent of the remark were. Children under 9 years old had difficulty picking out sarcastic remarks. Individuals' understanding of sarcasm increased somewhat between 9 and 13, and it continued to increase during the adolescent years.

Why do young adolescents laugh hysterically when Beavis and Butthead say such things as "He said 'erector set' "? Adolescents' increased facility in thinking along multiple dimensions permits them to appreciate satire, metaphor, and the ways in which language can be used to convey multiple messages, as in *double-entendres*—expressions that have two meanings, one of them usually off-color. Teenagers' new-found ability to use and appreciate sarcasm and satire helps explain why *Mad* magazine, *The Simpsons*, and *South Park* have such strong appeal for this age group.

Adolescent Relativism

A final aspect of thinking during adolescence concerns the way in which adolescents look at things. Children tend to see things in absolute terms—in black and white. Adolescents, in contrast, tend to see things as relative. They are more likely to question others' assertions and less likely to accept "facts" as absolute truths.

This increase in relativism can be particularly exasperating to parents, who may feel as though their adolescent children question everything just for the sake of argument. Difficulties often arise, for example, when adolescents begin seeing parents' values that they had previously considered absolutely correct ("Moral people do not have sex before they are married") as completely relative ("Get a life, Dad").

Adolescents' belief that everything is relative can become so overwhelming that they may begin to become extremely skeptical about many things (Chandler, 1987). In fact, once adolescents begin doubting the certainty of their prior beliefs, they may come to feel as if everything is uncertain or that no knowledge is completely reliable. Some theorists have suggested that adolescents pass through such a period of extreme skepticism on the way toward reaching a more sophisticated understanding of the complexity of knowledge.

> ### RECAP
> *Changes in cognition, or thinking, are the second of three sets of fundamental changes that occur during adolescence. Adolescents show five main advantages in thinking over children: in thinking in terms of what is possible, not only what is real; in thinking about abstract things; in thinking about the process of thinking itself (referred to as metacognition); in thinking in multidimensional terms; and in seeing knowledge as relative, rather than as absolute.*

> ### Food for Thought
> *The main cognitive changes of adolescence are usually seen as intellectual improvements, but are they always advantageous? Can you think of any circumstances under which one or more of the five changes discussed in the "Changes in Cognition" section would be disadvantageous?*

THEORETICAL PERSPECTIVES ON ADOLESCENT THINKING

Although there is general agreement that adolescents' thinking is different from and more advanced than children's, there is far less consensus about the processes underlying the cognitive differences between children and adolescents. Part of the lack of agreement stems from the

Table 2.1   The four stages of cognitive development, according to Piaget

Stage	Approximate Ages	Chief Characteristics
Sensorimotor	Birth–2 years	Discovery of relationships between sensation and motor behavior
Preoperational	2–6 years	Use of symbols to represent objects internally, especially through language
Concrete operations	6–11 years	Mastery of logic and development of rational thinking
Formal operations	11+ years	Development of abstract and hypothetical reasoning

various points of view that theorists have taken toward the issue of cognitive development in general. Because researchers working from different theoretical perspectives have posed different research questions, used different tasks to measure cognitive growth, and emphasized some aspects of cognitive activity more than others, their studies provide different but theoretically compatible pictures of mental development during adolescence. The two theoretical viewpoints that have been especially important are the **Piagetian perspective** and the **information-processing perspective.** Although these two views of adolescent thinking begin from different assumptions about the nature of cognitive development in general, each provides valuable insight into why thinking changes during adolescence.

The Piagetian View of Adolescent Thinking

● **Piaget's Theory of Cognitive Development**   Generally, theorists who follow Piaget and take a **cognitive-developmental view** of intellectual development argue that cognitive development proceeds through a fixed sequence of qualitatively distinct stages; that adolescent thinking is fundamentally different from the type of thinking used by children; and that, during adolescence, individuals develop a special type of thinking that they use in a variety of situations.

According to Piaget, cognitive development proceeds through four stages: the **sensorimotor period** (from birth until about age 2), the **preoperational period** (from about age 2 until about age 5), the period of **concrete operations** (from about age 6 until early adolescence), and, finally, the period of **formal operations** (from adolescence through adulthood). These stages are presented in table 2.1. Each stage is characterized by a particular type of thinking, with earlier stages of thinking being incorporated into new, more advanced, and more adaptive forms of reasoning. According to Piaget, transitions into higher stages of reasoning are

most likely to occur at times when the child's biological readiness and the increasing complexity of environmental demands interact to bring about cognitive disequilibrium.

Given the emphasis that Piaget placed on the interaction between biological change and environmental stimulation in provoking intellectual growth, it comes as no surprise that early adolescence—a time of dramatic biological maturation and equally noteworthy changes in environmental demands—is viewed in Piagetian theory as an extremely important period in cognitive development.

Piaget believed that at the heart of formal-operational thinking is the use of an abstract system of **propositional logic**—a system based on theoretical, or formal, principles of logic (hence the term *formal operations*). Formal reasoning can be applied just as easily to hypothetical events as to real ones; it is just as effective in dealing with abstract concepts as with concrete things; and it is just as useful for thinking about alternatives to what really exists as it is for thinking about reality itself. Consider the significance of being able to understand the following example of propositional logic:

If *A* is true or *B* is true, then *C* is true.

This is a logical relationship that is encountered in all sorts of situations, ranging from scientific problem solving (for example, "if the solution turns blue or yellow, then it must contain the mineral copper") to understanding social relationships ("If Bob asks Susan out or if Judy calls me to do something this Friday night, then Bob and Judy must have broken up"). Once the form of the logic is understood—that either *A* or *B* is sufficient to demonstrate that *C* is true—it can be applied to all sorts of events (real as well as possible, concrete as well as abstract) merely by changing what *A*, *B*, and *C* stand for. Although concrete-operational thinkers are able to imagine alternative and hypothetical situations, they are unable to think about them in as systematic a way as formal-operational thinkers can.

Just because adolescents can use propositional logic, however, does not mean that they are always consciously aware of doing so. In the example, for instance, we would hardly expect that an adolescent who is trying to figure out whether two friends are still dating consciously runs through the *A*s, *B*s, and *C*s of propositional logic. But you do not have to be aware of using propositional logic to use it effectively.

● **The Growth of Formal-Operational Thinking**
Piagetian theorists believe that the use of propositional logic—the foundation of formal-operational thinking—is the chief feature of adolescent thinking that differentiates it from the type of thinking children use. Adolescents' thinking can be distinguished from the thinking of children in several respects—among them, in thinking about possibilities, in thinking multidimensionally, and in thinking about abstract concepts. The connection between these types of thinking and the development of formal operations is clear: In order to think about alternatives to what really exists, in order to think in multidimensional terms, and in order to think systematically about concepts that are not directly observable, you must have a system of reasoning that works just as well in abstract, imagined, and complicated situations as it does in concrete ones. The system of propositional logic provides the basis for precisely this sort of reasoning.

The development of formal thinking appears to take place in two steps. During the first step, characteristic of early adolescence, formal thinking is apparent, but it has a sort of "now you see it, now you don't" quality. Young adolescents may demonstrate formal thinking at some times but at others may be able to think only in concrete terms; they may use formal operations on some tasks but not on others; they may reason formally under some but not all testing situations (Markovits et al., 1996). Virtually all adolescents go through this period of "emergent formal operations" (Kuhn, Langer, Kohlberg, & Haan, 1977). It is not until middle or even late adolescence that formal-operational thinking becomes consolidated and integrated into the individual's general approach to reasoning (Markovits & Valchon, 1990).

Whereas virtually all adolescents have the potential to develop formal-operational thinking, and most can and do demonstrate it from time to time, not all adolescents (or, for that matter, all adults) develop formal-operational thinking or use it regularly and in a variety of situations. At least some research suggests that adolescents who, as children, had more secure relationships with their parents are more likely to display formal thinking than are their insecure peers (Jacobsen, Edelstein, & Hofmann, 1994), as are young people who have received explicit instruction in deductive reasoning (Morris & Sloutsky, 1998). Consistent with the notion that certain types of schooling may facilitate the development of formal reasoning, one analysis of French students' reasoning abilities found that adolescents in the 1990s performed significantly better on tests of reasoning than their counterparts who were tested 20 or 30 years earlier (Flieller, 1999).

More important, the extent to which formal-operational thinking is displayed consistently by an individual depends a great deal on the conditions under which his or her reasoning is assessed. It is important, therefore, to differentiate between *competence* (i.e., what the adolescent is capable of doing) and *performance* (i.e., what the adolescent actually does in the assessment situation [Overton, 1990]). Much research, on adults as well as adolescents, indicates that gaps between individuals' logical reasoning abilities and their actual use of logical reasoning in everyday situations are very large, with everyday decision making fraught with logical errors that cannot be explained by cognitive incompetence (Klaczynski, in press).

The **competence-performance distinction** is nicely illustrated in a series of studies by Willis Overton and his colleagues (O'Brien & Overton, 1982; Overton, Ward, Noveck, Black, & O'Brien, 1987; Ward & Overton, 1990). The researchers found that adolescents' performance on sophisticated logical reasoning tasks varies as a function of both their underlying cognitive competence and the features of the task itself. Older adolescents have an easier time on reasoning tasks when the questions are personally relevant (e.g., questions about things that happen in schools) than when they are irrelevant (i.e., questions about things that happen to people when they retire from work), but younger adolescents have difficulty regardless of the relevance of the questions (see box "The Scientific Study of Adolescence"). One interpretation of this is that having the underlying competence (as did the older, but not the younger, adolescents) is a necessary, but not sufficient, condition for performing well. Ultimate performance depends on contextual factors as well and may vary from one task to the next (Ward & Overton, 1990).

Separating Competence and Performance in Studies of Adolescent Reasoning

Experts agree that a complete understanding of the development of intellectual abilities in adolescence necessitates distinguishing between what adolescents can do and what they do do. This distinction, known as the competence-performance distinction, has been extensively investigated by Willis Overton and his colleagues in a series of studies of adolescent reasoning. In these studies, adolescents are asked to solve a series of logical problems modeled after the Wason selection task. In the Wason selection task, individuals are presented with cards, on which are printed logical problems similar to the following:

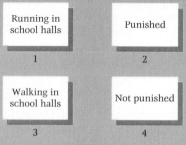

The students are then given the following instructions: Each of the cards has information about a student attending school. On one side of the card is a student's behavior in school. On the other side of the card is whether or not the student has been punished for that behavior. Here is a rule: *If a student is caught running in the school halls, then the student must be punished.* Select the card or cards that you would definitely need to turn over to decide whether or not the rule is being broken. Which card or cards would you need to turn over to decide if the rule is being broken? (The answer appears at the end of this box.)

Because some formal operational reasoning is needed to solve these problems, students' answers to a series of these problems can be scored for the presence and extent of formal reasoning. But how can the researchers disentangle students' formal reasoning competence from their formal reasoning performance? If a student does not solve the problem correctly, is that an indication of diminished competence or merely of diminished performance?

In one study designed to examine this (Ward & Overton, 1990), the

Although its influence has waned considerably in the past two decades (see Bjorklund, 1997), the Piagetian perspective on cognitive development during adolescence has stimulated a great deal of research on how young people think (Lourenço & Machado, 1996). Generally, the concept of formal operations as defined by Piaget and his followers describes many of the changes in thinking observed during the adolescent years. Specifically, the theory helps explain why adolescents are better able than children to think about possibilities, to think multidimensionally, and to think about thoughts.

Where the Piagetian perspective on adolescent cognitive development falls short is in its claim that cognitive development proceeds in a stagelike fashion and that the stage of formal operations is the stage of cognitive development characteristic of adolescence (Keating, 1990). Rather, research suggests that advanced reasoning capabilities (which may or may not be synonymous with what Piaget termed "formal operations") develop gradually and continuously from childhood through adolescence and beyond, probably in more of a quantitative fashion than was proposed by Piaget. Rather than talking about a stage of cognitive activity characteristic of adolescence, then, it is more accurate to depict these advanced reasoning capabilities as skills that are used by older children more often than younger ones, by some adolescents more often than by other adolescents, and by individuals when they are in certain situations (especially familiar situations) more often than when they are in other situations (Kuhn, Garcia-Mila, Zohar, & Andersen, 1995).

researchers presented adolescents with a mixture of problems, which varied in their relevance to adolescents' lives. The most relevant problem concerned students' misbehavior in school; the least relevant problem concerned the situation of older individuals who had retired from work. The researchers hypothesized that having relevant problems to solve would improve adolescents' performance, but only among those adolescents who had the underlying competence to reason formally. In order to test this hypothesis, the problems were given to sixth-, ninth-, and twelfth-grade students. Presumably, if the hypothesis were correct, the relevance of the task would only affect the performance of the older students.

This is precisely what the researchers found, as you can see in the accompanying figure. Among the sixth-graders, only about 20 percent of the problems were solved correctly, regardless of whether the task was relevant. Among the ninth- and twelfth-graders, however, students were more than twice as successful when given relevant problems than when given less relevant ones. The researchers concluded from this study that the competence to reason deductively does not become available until early adolescence and that the relevance of the content of tasks used to assess logical reasoning is an important influence on adolescents' performance, once they have achieved the necessary level of competence.

The fact that the relevance of the task had different effects at different grade levels is an example of what researchers call a **statistical interaction.** A statistical interaction is found when one factor (in this case, task relevance) affects an outcome variable (in this case, performance on the task) differently at different levels of another factor (in this case, grade level). If a researcher were to find that a certain teaching strategy affects boys' and girls' learning differently, that would be another example of a statistical interaction.

The correct solution to the problem presented at the beginning of this box is to turn over the first and fourth cards. Turning over both of these, but not the second and third ones, is necessary to determine whether the rule is being broken.

Source: Ward, S., & Overton, W. (1990). Semantic familiarity, relevance, and the development of deductive reasoning. *Developmental Psychology, 26,* 488–493.

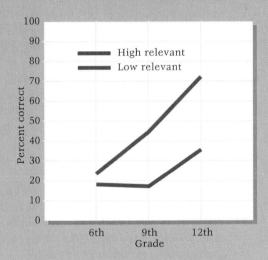

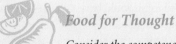

The Information-Processing View of Adolescent Thinking

During the past two decades, a different view of cognitive development during adolescence has emerged, partly in response to criticisms of the Piagetian perspective. Some scientists point out that the Piagetian approach has not been especially helpful in pinpointing exactly *what* it is that changes as individuals mature into and through adolescence. If we are left only with the conclusion that cognitive growth between childhood and adolescence reflects changes in "logical reasoning abilities," we have not moved a great deal closer to understanding which *specific* aspects of intellectual development during adolescence are the most important ones. Just what is it about the ways that adolescents think about things that makes them better problem solvers than children? This question has been the focus of researchers working from a second theoretical vantage point: the information-processing perspective.

Information-processing researchers apply the same techniques to understanding human reasoning that computer scientists use in writing programs. Suppose that you were asked to develop a computer program to solve the poker-chip problem presented in the section on "Thinking About Possibilities" in this chapter. A first step in the program might involve determining how many different-colored chips are contained in the set. But, as you know if you have ever written a computer program, this first step is actually quite complicated when broken down into discrete tasks. It involves (1) perceiving what color the first chip is, (2) storing this information in memory, (3) considering the second chip and deciding what color it is, (4) storing this information in memory, (5) retrieving the color of the first chip from memory, (6) retrieving the color of the second chip from memory, (7) comparing these two bits of information, (8) determining whether the colors are the same or different, and (9) storing the results of the comparison in memory. And these nine steps take us only as far as comparing the first two chips. Imagine how involved a program would have to be in order to perform more complicated tasks.

Information-processing theorists argue that it is possible to look at human intelligence in much the same way. When broken down into its component processes, human thinking involves such "subprograms" as paying attention to a stimulus, encoding information, retrieving information, comparing different pieces of information, and making decisions based on such comparisons. Obviously, deficiencies in any of these component functions will interfere with accurate problem solving. In the poker-chip problem, for example, perceiving the colors incorrectly will lead to mistakes in the solution. The ways in which component processes are combined also will affect the results. For example, if we try to compare the two chips' colors

before storing the color of the first chip in memory, we will not be able to solve the problem.

Some arrangements of component processes are not only more accurate than others but also more efficient. Suppose you have successfully determined that the first two poker chips are, indeed, different in color. What is your next step? Do you compare the third chip with both the first and the second chips before moving on to the fourth chip, or do you compare the third with the first and then compare the fourth with the first? If you work out this problem, you will find that one approach is more efficient than the other.

● **Changes in Information-Processing Abilities During Adolescence**   Studies of changes in specific components of information processing have focused on five areas in which improvement occurs during adolescence: attention, memory, processing speed, organization, and metacognition. Together, these gains help explain why adolescents are better than children at abstract, multidimensional, and hypothetical thinking.

First, there are advances in individuals' ability to pay *attention*. Improvements are seen both in **selective attention,** in which adolescents must focus on one stimulus (such as a reading assignment) and tune out another (such as the electronic beeping of a younger brother's video game), and in **divided attention,** in which adolescents must pay attention to two sets of stimuli at the same time (such as studying while listening to music) (Higgins & Turnure, 1984; Schiff & Knopf, 1985). Improvements in attention mean that adolescents are better able than children to concentrate and stay focused on complicated tasks, such as reading and comprehending difficult material (Casteel, 1993).

Second, during adolescence our *memory* abilities improve. This is reflected both in **working memory,** which involves our ability to remember something for a brief period of time, such as 30 seconds, and in **long-term memory** (being able to recall something from a long time ago) (Keating, 1990). When we think of the importance of memory in problem solving, we typically think of having to retrieve facts that we have memorized deliberately—one aspect of long-term memory. For example, can you recall the name of the stage of thinking that precedes the stage of formal operations in Piaget's theory? (If not, refer to page 66.)

However, working memory is extremely important in problem solving as well. For example, in order to solve multiple-choice questions successfully, you need to be able to remember each alternative answer long

▲ *Improvements in divided attention* (left) *and selective attention* (right) *abilities enable adolescents to tune out interference and focus on the task at hand.* (Patrick Waston/Waston Media Services; Mary Kate Denny/PhotoEdit)

enough to compare it with the other choices as you read them. Think for a moment of how frustrating it would be to solve a multiple-choice problem if, by the time you had read the final potential answer, you had forgotten the first one. Studies show that working memory skills for both verbal and visual information increase between childhood and adolescence and over the course of adolescence (Hale, Bronik, & Fry, 1997). This increase in our ability to hold information in temporary storage contributes to the development of reading skills during adolescence (Siegel, 1994).

One illustration of how improvements in working memory might account for adolescents' advantages over children in problem solving comes from studies of individuals' solutions to problems involving analogies (Sternberg, 1977; Sternberg & Nigro, 1980; Sternberg & Rifkin, 1979). Through a series of experiments in which different types of analogies were presented to third-graders, sixth-graders, ninth-graders, and college students, Sternberg and his colleagues examined age differences in the use and organization of cognitive processes. The major difference between younger and older subjects concerned the incomplete nature of the younger ones' information processing. Although older and younger subjects appeared to use similar processes, the older ones used them in a far more exhaustive fashion. For example, in determining the relation between pairs of terms, the third- and sixth-graders tended to curtail

their information processing prematurely, before all possible relations had been considered.

The researchers attribute this premature termination to information overload in working memory. Because adolescents are able to hold more information in immediate memory than children can, they are more successful in the sorts of tasks (such as analogies) that require repeated comparisons between newly encoded information and information that has been stored previously. Running out of storage space before all necessary information has been encoded results in information-processing errors.

A third component of information processing that may be closely related to the observed improvements in memory is an increase in the sheer *speed of information processing* (Hale, 1990; Kail, 1991a, 1991b; Kail & Hall, 1994). Regardless of the type of cognitive task used, researchers find that older adolescents process the information necessary to solve the problem faster than early adolescents, who, in turn, process information faster than preadolescents. This fact would certainly help explain age differences in performance on timed tests (such as standardized achievement tests). Generally, the size of the improvement in the speed of information processing that occurs with age becomes smaller over the course of adolescence, so that the difference in speed between a 9-year-old and a 12-year-old is greater than that between a 12-year-old and a 15-year-old, which, in turn, is greater than that between a 15-year-old and an 18-year-old (Kail, 1991b). In fact, speed of processing does not appear to change very much between middle adolescence and young adulthood (Hale, 1990).

A fourth type of information-processing gain seen in adolescence involves improvements in individuals' *organizational strategies* (Siegler, 1988). Adolescents are more "planful" than children—they are more likely to approach a problem with an appropriate information-processing strategy in mind and are more flexible in their ability to use different strategies in different situations (Plumert, 1994). Psychologist Ann Brown (1975), for example, has suggested that the use of mnemonic devices and other organizational strategies helps account for differences in the performance of older and younger children on tasks requiring memory and, moreover, that older children are better able to judge when the use of such strategies is likely to be helpful and when it is not. For instance, think for a moment about how you approach learning the information in a new textbook chapter. After years of studying, you are probably well aware of particular strategies that work well for you (underlining, highlighting, taking notes, writing in the margin of the textbook), and you begin a reading assignment with these strategies in mind. Because children are not as planful as adolescents, their learning is not as efficient. Developmental differences in planfulness during childhood and adolescence can be seen quite readily by comparing individuals' approaches to the guessing game "20 Questions." With age, individuals' strategies become increasingly more efficient (Drumm & Jackson, 1996).

Finally, individuals' *knowledge about their own thinking processes* improves during adolescence. One of the most important gains to occur in adolescence is in the realm of metacognition—thinking about thinking. Adolescents are more likely than children to think about their own thoughts—a tendency that helps explain their greater self-consciousness. However, from an information-processing perspective, adolescents' heightened self-consciousness results from advances in basic metacognitive abilities. Self-consciousness may be more a cognitive than an emotional phenomenon: For the first time, the adolescent is capable of thinking about thinking about thinking.

Of course, advances in metacognition are more a blessing than a curse. Because adolescents are better able to think about their own thoughts, they are much better at monitoring their own learning processes. For example, during the course of studying, adolescents are more able than children to step back from time to time and assess how well they are learning the material. Doing this enables them to pace their studying accordingly—to speed up and skim the material if they feel that they are learning it easily or to slow down and repeat a section if they feel that they are having a hard time (e.g., Baker & Brown, 1984).

New Directions for Theories About Adolescent Thinking

There is no doubt that many specific aspects of information processing improve during the adolescent years. What remains to be seen is whether and how understanding these specific cognitive gains can help account for the broader changes in thinking described at the beginning of this chapter—in abstraction, in hypothetical thinking, or in relativism, for example. To many theorists, the quantitative approach to thinking advocated by information-processing theorists leaves something out: the intuitive feeling that adolescents think in a way that is qualitatively different from children.

Several researchers have attempted to integrate findings on improvements in adolescents' information-processing abilities within a cognitive-developmental framework similar to Piaget's. One such theorist, neo-Piagetian theorist Robbie Case (1985), for example, argued, like Piaget, that cognitive development proceeds in discrete stages. Unlike Piaget, however, Case believed that the differences between stages can best be described not in terms of logical abilities but in terms of the cognitive components studied by information-processing theorists. For example, although Case, like information-processing theorists, believed that improvements in working memory or information-processing speed help explain gains in intellectual performance, he believed that these improvements occur in a stagelike fashion (Marini & Case, 1994). Moreover, Case theorized that transitions from one stage to another are closely linked to physical changes in the brain.

With regard to adolescence, Case argued that the gains in attention, memory, speed, organization, and metacognition that are enjoyed during the adolescent years permit the individual to think in a more automatic way. For instance, think about how automatically you drive a car now in contrast to when you were first learning how. This **automatization** of thinking frees up cognitive resources for the adolescent, which enables him or her to approach problems in a structurally more sophisticated way. In other words, as the basic elements of information processing become more automatic—second nature, we might say—the adolescent is better able to devote conscious cognitive processes to more complicated tasks.

To other theorists, such as Paul Klaczynski (in press), the most interesting question about cognitive development during adolescence is not why or how individuals develop logical reasoning abilities but why individuals' behavior is so often illogical despite the cognitive skills they have developed. This is a fascinating question that is not really addressed by either the Piagetian or the information-processing approach to adolescent cognition. Young children behave illogically because they have not yet developed certain cognitive tools, such as deductive reasoning. But why do adolescents (and adults) behave illogically, when they possess the skills necessary for sophisticated logical thought? Klaczynski suggests that there are two different cognitive systems at work—one that is analytic and that uses the sort of deductive reasoning presumed to develop during the formal operational period and another that is more intuitive, which uses short-cuts, or heuristics, that are based on past experience, gut feelings, and unconscious processes. Why, if given the choice, do most individuals prefer to participate in a lottery in which there are 10 winning tickets out of 100 versus one in which there is 1 winning ticket out of 10? Even though the odds of winning are identical, there is something about having 10 chances to win instead of 1 that many people find intuitively more appealing. Why do educational efforts to provide adolescents with logical evidence about the risks of unprotected sex, smoking, or driving without wearing a seatbelt have such a poor track record? Klaczynzki has argued that a full appreciation of the ways in which adolescents think in everyday situations necessitates taking into account both the development of logical reasoning and the development, or persistence, of thinking that is often at odds with logic.

> RECAP
>
> *Adolescent thinking has been described from the information-processing perspective. According to this view, advances in thinking during adolescence result from quantitative increases in such skills as attention, memory, processing speed, organization, and metacognition. Information-processing theorists attempt to break down problem solving into its specific components in order to understand exactly what it is that develops as individuals mature intellectually.*

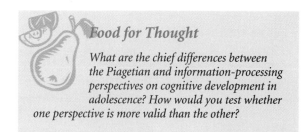

> *Food for Thought*
>
> *What are the chief differences between the Piagetian and information-processing perspectives on cognitive development in adolescence? How would you test whether one perspective is more valid than the other?*

THE ADOLESCENT BRAIN

Scientists have long wondered whether the sorts of changes in thinking and behavior that occur during adolescence can be linked to actual changes in the brain. After all, early adolescence is a time of tremendous improvement in abstract thinking, and there is considerable brain maturation during this time period. For many years, researchers searched for evidence that the sheer growth in the size of the brain that takes place around puberty is somehow related to the expansion of intellectual abilities. These attempts proved futile, however (Keating, 1990).

Recent improvements in the study of brain maturation—including studies of brain growth and development in other animals; studies of changes in brain chemistry in humans and other species; and, perhaps most important, studies of human brains using various imaging techniques, such as **functional magnetic resonance imaging (fMRI)** and **positron emission tomography (PET)** have shed new light on this issue. PET and fMRI studies allow researchers to take pictures of individuals' brains and compare their structure and functioning. Studies using fMRI have been especially important in research on brain development in adolescence, because the technique, unlike PET, is noninvasive and can be used with children as well as adults. Using fMRI, researchers have looked at activity in various regions of the brain while individuals are performing a variety of tasks (e.g., tests of memory, vision, problem solving). It is possible, therefore, to study whether adolescents and adults show different patterns of brain activity while performing the same task (e.g., Pine et al., 2000a).

Taken together, these strands of research point to several aspects of brain maturation in adolescence that may be linked to behavioral, emotional, and cognitive development during this period (Spear, 2000). First, there appears to be considerable remodeling of synapses (the connections between brain cells, or neurons), possibly associated with a decrease in overall

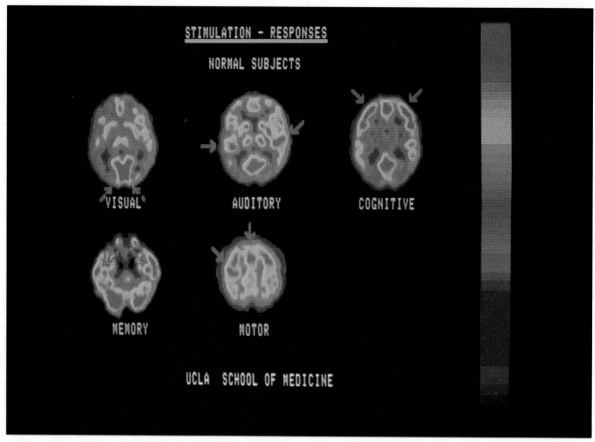

▲ *Examples of images of the brain captured by PET.* (PhotoEdit)

synapse number, on certain parts of the brain, especially the **cortex,** leading to much more efficient and more focused information processing. Although one might think that a loss of synapses would be associated with worse, rather than better, information processing, this is not always the case. Indeed, early in life many more synapses are produced in the brain than are necessary for competent information processing, and information processing is improved by the selective pruning of excessive and unnecessary neuronal connections. This pruning may help account for some of the cognitive advances that adolescents have over children.

Second, there are changes in levels of several neurotransmitters (the chemicals that permit the transfer of electrical charges between neurons), including the neurotransmitters dopamine and serotonin, in the parts of the brain that process emotional stimuli—most notably, areas of the **limbic system.** These changes may make individuals more emotional, more responsive to stress, and at the same time less responsive to rewards.

Some scientists believe that this diminished sensitivity to rewards may stimulate adolescents to seek higher levels of novelty, take more risks, and experiment with drugs in an effort to get the same levels of reward from the environment that they were able to get before adolescence. In other words, there may be a neurochemical basis for adolescents' frequent complaint of boredom. More seriously, though, a decline in reward sensitivity in adolescence is thought to increase individuals' vulnerability to depression, substance abuse, and other mental health problems (Spear, 2000).

Finally, full maturation of the **prefrontal cortex** is not complete until sometime between adolescence and early adulthood. The prefrontal cortex is the part of the brain that is active when we are engaged in complicated cognitive activities, such as planning, decision making, goal setting, and metacognition. During early adolescence a great deal of **synaptic pruning** appears to take place in this region of the brain. In addition, there is continued **myelination** of the prefrontal cortex

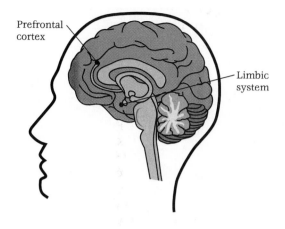

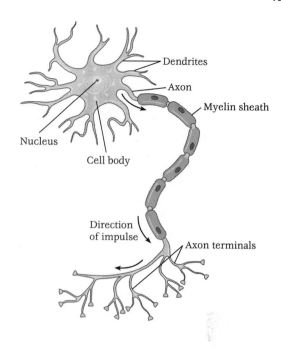

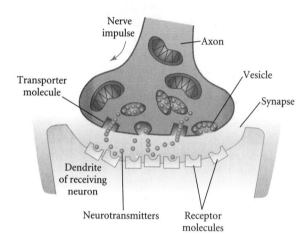

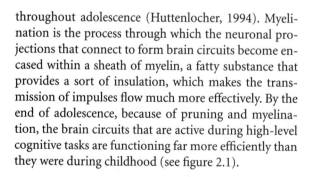

Figure 2.1   Among the most important brain changes to take place at adolescence are those in the prefrontal cortex and limbic system. In the prefrontal cortex, synaptic pruning and myelination improve the efficiency of information processing. In the limbic system, changes in levels of certain neuro-transmitters, such as dopamine, affect reward sensitivity.

throughout adolescence (Huttenlocher, 1994). Myelination is the process through which the neuronal projections that connect to form brain circuits become encased within a sheath of myelin, a fatty substance that provides a sort of insulation, which makes the transmission of impulses flow much more effectively. By the end of adolescence, because of pruning and myelination, the brain circuits that are active during high-level cognitive tasks are functioning far more efficiently than they were during childhood (see figure 2.1).

INDIVIDUAL DIFFERENCES IN INTELLIGENCE IN ADOLESCENCE

For the most part, theorists who have studied adolescent cognitive development from a Piagetian or information-processing framework have focused on the universals in adolescent intellectual growth. How does thinking change as individuals move into adolescence? What processes drive cognitive development as children become teenagers? What cognitive competencies do all adolescents share?

In contrast, other theorists have been more interested in studying individual differences in intellectual abilities. How can we account for different patterns of intellectual growth within the adolescent population? How large are individual differences in intelligence in adolescence? Are some adolescents brighter than others? If so, why, and in what ways?

The Measurement of IQ

In order to answer questions about the relative intelligence of individuals, psychologists have had to devise ways of assessing intelligence, which has been no easy feat, since there is considerable disagreement over what

▲ *Standardized intelligence tests, or IQ tests, are often used to study individual differences in cognitive abilities during adolescence. Critics of such tests argue that they measure just one type of intelligence—"school smarts"—and neglect other, equally important skills, such as social intelligence, creativity, and "street smarts."* (Arthur Grace/Stock, Boston)

"intelligence" really is. Today, the most widely used measures are intelligence tests, or IQ (for "intelligence quotient") tests. A variety of such tests exists, including the Stanford-Binet, the Wechsler Intelligence Scale for Children (WISC-R), and the Wechsler Adult Intelligence Scale (WAIS-III).

The IQ test is one of the most widely used—and most widely misused—psychological instruments ever developed. Initially developed by French psychologist Alfred Binet in 1905, the first intelligence test was devised in response to the French government's interest in better predicting which children would profit from formal schooling. Thus, although Binet's test—and the many others that would be developed over the years—was designed to yield a measure of intelligence, the test was devised with a very specific type of intelligence in mind: the type of intelligence it takes to succeed in formal educational institutions. Even the best IQ tests used today measure only a very specific type of intelligence.

An individual's performance on an IQ test is usually presented not as a raw score but as a relative score in comparison with the scores of other individuals of the same age and from approximately the same **cohort** (a group of people born during the same historical era). Comparison scores are collected every so often, so that the comparison group for individuals taking the test at any given time is valid, representative, and up-to-date. The score of 100 is used to designate the midway point: An IQ score below 100 indicates a poorer test performance than half of the comparison group; a score above 100 indicates a better performance than half the comparison group. In other words, the higher an individual's IQ, the smaller the number of agemates who perform equally or better on the same test.

Although an individual's score on an intelligence test is often reported in terms of his or her overall IQ, intelligence tests actually comprise a series of tests, and it is usually possible to look at performance in different areas independently. The WISC-R and the WAIS-III, for example, both contain two groups of tests: *verbal tests,* which include measures of vocabulary, general information, comprehension, and arithmetic abilities, and *performance tests,* which include block design, mazes, picture completion, and picture arrangement.

The IQ test represents only one of many ways of assessing intelligence in adolescence. Indeed, many theorists have argued that its exclusive focus on "school smarts"—the sorts of abilities that are related to scholastic success—yields a one-sided picture of what it means to be an intelligent person. Two of the more well-known attempts to expand on this narrow definition come from the work of Robert Sternberg (1988) and Howard Gardner (1983). Many of Sternberg and Gardner's ideas formed the basis for the best-selling book *Emotional Intelligence,* by journalist Daniel Goleman (1995).

● **Sternberg's "Triarchic" Theory** Sternberg proposed a triarchic, or three-part, theory of intelligence. He argued that a thorough assessment of an individual's intellectual capabilities requires that we look at three distinct but interrelated types of intelligence: *componential intelligence*, which involves our abilities to acquire, store, and process information; *experiential intelligence*, which involves our abilities to use insight and creativity; and *contextual intelligence,* which involves our ability to think practically. Componential intelligence is closest to the type of intelligence measured on traditional intelligence tests. Experiential intelligence is closest to what we call creativity. Contextual intelligence is closest to what we might call "street smarts." All individuals have all three types of intelligence, but some individuals are stronger in one respect than in others. You probably can think of individuals who are good test takers but who are not particularly creative or sensible. According to Sternberg's model, these individuals are high in componential intelligence but low in experiential and contextual intelligence.

More important, Sternberg's view forces us to look at individuals who are not good test takers, but who are creative or street smart, as being equally intelligent as individuals who score high on IQ tests—but intelligent in a different way. He argues that society needs individuals with all types of intelligence and that it is time we started assessing—and encouraging—experiential and contextual intelligence as much as we do componential intelligence (Matthews & Keating, 1995).

● **Gardner's Theory of Multiple Intelligences** Howard Gardner's theory of multiple intelligences also stresses that there is more to being smart than being "book smart." He has proposed that there are seven types of intelligence: verbal, mathematical, spatial, kinesthetic (movement), self-reflective, interpersonal, and musical. According to his view, for example, outstanding athletes, such as basketball star Michael Jordan, have a well-developed kinesthetic intelligence, which allows them to control their bodies and process the movements of others in extraordinarily capable ways. Although conventional tests of intelligence emphasize verbal and mathematical abilities, these are not the only types of intelligence that we possess—nor are they the only types that we should value.

Intelligence Test Performance in Adolescence

Although ideas about the existence of different forms of intelligence have become popular in the past decade, most research in the psychometric tradition has used traditional IQ tests to investigate the nature of intelligence during adolescence. Assessments based on IQ tests have been used to examine two seemingly similar but actually very different questions. First, how *stable* are IQ scores during adolescence? Second, do the sorts of mental abilities that are assessed via intelligence tests *improve* during adolescence?

It is easy to confuse these questions. At first glance, they seem to be asking the same thing. But consider this: Individuals' IQ scores remain remarkably stable during the adolescent years, yet during the same time period their mental abilities improve dramatically. Although this might seem contradictory, it is not. Studies of stability examine changes in individual's *relative* standing over time, whereas studies of change examine changes in individuals' *absolute* scores.

Consider height, for example. Children who are taller than their peers during middle childhood are likely to be taller than their peers during adulthood as well; children who are about average in height remain so throughout childhood and adulthood; and children who are shorter than their peers at one point in time are likely to be shorter than their peers later on. Height, therefore, is a very stable trait. But this does not mean that individuals don't grow between childhood and adolescence.

Like height, scores on intelligence tests are characterized by high stability and a good deal of change during childhood and adolescence. To the question "How stable are IQ scores during adolescence?" the answer, then, is very stable. As figure 2.2 indicates, intelligence test scores become increasingly stable during childhood (at around age 6 or 7) and are remarkably stable during

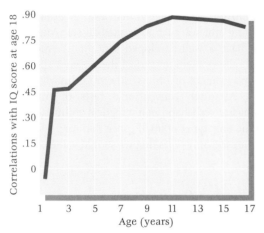

Figure 2.2   *Average correlations between individuals'*
intelligence test scores at various ages from 1 to 17 and their
scores at age 18. By age 11, the correlation is over .90.
(Adapted from Bayley, 1949)

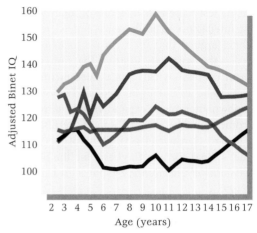

Figure 2.3   *For some individuals, IQ scores fluctuate very*
little during childhood and adolescence. However, for others,
variations of 20 or 30 points occur. Here are five common
patterns of change in IQ scores during childhood and
adolescence. Note how much the patterns differ in their relative
stability over time. (Adapted from McCall et al., 1973)

adolescence. To put it more concretely, youngsters who score higher than their peers on intelligence tests during early adolescence are likely to score higher throughout the adolescent years. In fact, research indicates that certain measures of intellectual performance taken during the first year of life—not IQ tests, but measures of speed of information processing—are significantly predictive of IQ test performance in early adolescence (Rose & Feldman, 1995). This does not mean, however, that individuals' intellectual performance remains fixed or is not susceptible to change.

A 10-year-old boy whose score is average for his age has an IQ of about 100. If his score were stable—that is, if he were to remain about average in comparison with his peers—his score would remain at about 100. Even if he were to become more intelligent over time, as any normal child would, his IQ score probably would not change very much, because the score would always reflect his performance relative to his peers. If his abilities were to increase at the same rate as his agemates', his relative standing would not change. In other words, when an individual's IQ scores are fairly stable, a graph of those scores over a period of time produces a relatively straight, horizontal line.

For most individuals, this is indeed what happens. But some studies suggest that not everyone follows this pattern of high stability (McCall, Applebaum, & Hogarty, 1973; Moffitt, Caspi, Harkness, & Silva, 1993). After graphing many individuals' IQ scores during childhood and adolescence, one group of researchers

was able to identify five patterns—some very stable but others very unstable (McCall et al., 1973). Their findings are shown in figure 2.3. As expected, most individuals fell into cluster number 1; that is, their scores were extremely stable over the 17-year period. But many youngsters' scores fluctuated considerably. In other words, although most adolescents' IQ scores remain stable throughout adolescence, not all do.

A study by Terrie Moffitt and her colleagues (Moffitt et al., 1993) indicates, however, that, although some individuals show fluctuation in IQ scores between childhood and adolescence, ultimately most individuals end up with IQ scores as adolescents that are not very different from their scores as children. In this study, for example, the average amount of change over a seven-year period (from age 7 to age 13) among the individuals whose scores fluctuated at all was only 5 IQ points, which is not a change of much practical significance.

In absolute terms, however, do mental abilities increase during adolescence? Figure 2.4 shows the growth of mental abilities as assessed by standardized tests. As you can see, abilities assessed by conventional IQ tests increase dramatically through childhood and adolescence, reaching a plateau sometime during early adulthood. Thus, despite the fact that IQ scores remain stable during adolescence, individuals do become smarter as they get older—a fact that argues strongly in favor of educational interventions designed to stimulate

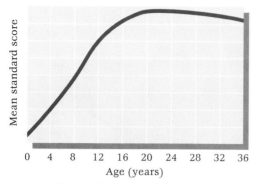

Figure 2.4 The growth of mental abilities from birth to age 36. (Adapted from Bayley, 1949)

intellectual development during adolescence. In fact, research shows that extended schooling enhances individuals' performance on standardized tests of intelligence (Ceci & Williams, 1999). Whereas individuals who had dropped out of school early showed unchanging—and relatively lower—scores on intelligence tests during adolescence, students who remained in school, especially those in the more advanced tracks, showed impressive gains in verbal ability over time.

Another widely used—and equally controversial—measure of aptitude in adolescence is the SAT. The SAT is intended not to measure an adolescent's present level of accomplishment (i.e., his or her academic achievement) but to predict his or her likelihood of success in college. Like the IQ test, therefore, the SAT is a measure of "school smarts," and scores on this test should be so viewed. The SAT does not measure such important characteristics as insight, creativity, and practical intelligence.

Given that the SAT was created in order to predict high school students' college success, it is only fair that it be evaluated in this light. How well does the SAT predict success in college courses? The answer is well, but not perfectly. Knowing an individual's SAT scores helps foretell how well he or she will do in college, but SAT scores are only one of many useful predictive factors. Because of this, most college admissions committees rely on many additional pieces of information about an applicant's academic record, including the difficulty of the student's high school curriculum and the student's class rank (Moll, 1986).

Interestingly, one study reported that scores on the mathematics section of the SAT may be a more valid predictor of college math grades for males than for females (Wainer & Steinberg, 1992). In this study, the researchers began with a sample of 47,000 college men and women, who were then matched on their performance in college math classes (and on the difficulty of the math classes they took). If the SAT is an equally valid predictor of achievement for males and females, the researchers reasoned, then males and females who earn comparable grades in math classes should have had comparable SAT scores as high school students. This was not the case, however. Among college students earning *As* in math classes, for example, the men had scored 36 points higher on the mathematics subsection of the SAT than had the women. Any college admissions committee that rejects a woman in favor of a man on the basis of their SAT mathematics scores is making an ill-informed decision.

Culture and Intelligence

Much of our current thinking about the nature of intelligence has been influenced by the work of Russian psychologist Lev Vygotsky (1930/1978), who emphasized the broader context in which intellectual development occurs (Rogoff, 1997). According to this view, it is essential that we understand the nature of the environment in which an adolescent develops in terms of its demands for intelligent behavior and its opportunities for learning. Individuals develop and use intellectual skills not simply as a function of their cognitive maturation but also in response to the everyday problems they are expected to solve. Young street merchants in Brazil, for example, who might not perform well on standardized tests of math knowledge, nevertheless use sophisticated mathematical skills during transactions with customers (Guberman, 1996). The very same children who perform poorly on school-based tests of knowledge may excel when faced with an equally challenging test of competence in the real world—such as figuring out the most efficient route between school and home through a dangerous neighborhood.

Vygotsky argued that children and adolescents learn best in everyday situations when they encounter tasks that are neither too simple nor too advanced, but just slightly more challenging than their abilities permit them to solve on their own. Within this so-called **zone of proximal development,** young people, through close collaboration with a more experienced instructor (whether an adult or another child), are stimulated to reach for the more advanced level of performance. The role of the instructor is to help structure the learning situation so that it is within the

Are There Differences in Mental Abilities at Adolescence (Anymore)?

For many years, social scientists had asserted that there are sex differences in mental abilities and that these differences emerge for the first time during adolescence (Maccoby & Jacklin, 1974). Although adolescent males and females did not show overall differences in IQ scores, studies showed that females enjoyed a small advantage in tests of verbal ability, whereas males had a small advantage in tests of spatial ability and, to a lesser extent, mathematics. What was especially interesting about the pattern, however, was that boys' and girls' scores on math and verbal tests were comparable before puberty. Experts offered a number of explanations for this pattern of sex differences and, in particular, for their emergence in early adolescence. One explanation concerned the hormonal changes of puberty. As noted in chapter 1, levels of androgens and estrogens change at puberty in different degrees for males and females. Because individuals with higher androgen levels score better on tests of spatial ability—this is true whether they are male or female—it has been argued that the male advantage in tests of spatial ability at adolescence may result from the higher level of androgens (Petersen & Taylor, 1980).

A second explanation focused on the fact that girls are more likely, on average, to mature earlier than boys. Researchers speculated that the development of certain brain functions is altered by the onset of puberty and, specifically, that the onset of puberty curtails some developments in the structure of the brain that are related to spatial ability. Since girls mature earlier than boys, it was rea-soned that their development of spatial abilities may be curtailed earlier (Waber, 1977). If this theory were true, however, one would expect that early maturers in general—whether male or female—would show worse spatial abilities than later maturers. But this is not the case, casting doubt on the idea that females' earlier maturation is the reason for their poorer performance on tests of spatial intelligence (Newcombe & Dubas, 1987).

A third account—that sex differences in mental abilities are social, not biological, in origin—has received the most support. The argument here is that boys and girls are rewarded for different interests and for showing different abilities. During elementary school, boys and girls take the same courses and are therefore expected to show similar intellectual strengths and weaknesses. However, once young people begin taking elective courses, males and females may be led down different educational paths by their guidance counselors, parents, and friends (Klebanov & Brooks-Gunn, 1992). Males, for example, are more likely to be encouraged to pursue advanced courses in math and science, whereas females are more likely to be steered away from these classes (Fennema & Sherman, 1977). Consistent with this explanation, studies have found that differences in individuals' mathematical and scientific abilities are more closely related to their attitudes toward math and science, the courses they take in school, and their prior knowledge of the content area (which reflects achievement, not ability) than to their gender

reach of the student—a structuring process called **scaffolding.** If you watch good parents, teachers, or coaches at work, you will probably observe a great deal of scaffolding.

Studying cognitive development in context clearly points out the problems in measuring intelligence through standardized testing (Neisser et al., 1996). Indeed, the problem of defining intelligence adequately is perhaps no more readily apparent than when issues of ethnic and racial differences in intelligence are raised. In general, studies find that, within the United States, African American and Hispanic American

(Byrnes & Takahira, 1993; Paulsen & Johnson, 1983). If, beginning in adolescence, girls are told, implicitly or explicitly, that math is not interesting, their performance in this area may decline. In some countries, where educational opportunities and expectations for boys and girls are comparable—as is the case in elementary school in Scotland and Hungary—gender differences in math and science are virtually nonexistent (Beller & Gafni, 1996).

Perhaps the clearest support for the idea that sex differences in mental abilities are socialized rather than biologically determined comes from several examinations of males' and females' test scores. According to Carol Jacklin, who in 1974 had coauthored the initial study documenting reliable sex differences in mental abilities, by the end of the 1980s many of the differences in males' and females' performance either had vanished or had diminished substantially (Jacklin, 1989). This is true with regard to both verbal and math abilities and to performance on many (but not all) tests of achievement and intelligence (Feingold, 1993; Hyde & Linn, 1988; Marsh, 1989; Stumpf & Stanley, 1996). The fact that more recent contrasts of males' and females' scores have shown much smaller sex differences than were found in earlier studies suggests to many experts that the changes in sex roles and educational opportunities that have taken place in recent decades are now beginning to be reflected on measures such as the SAT and various tests of achievement (Feingold, 1988). Between 1987 and 1994, for example, the gender gap in math SAT scores declined by 20 percent. Between 1984 and 1993, the gender gap on the Advanced Placement Test in Computer Science narrowed as well (Stumpf & Stanley, 1996).

▲ Recent studies of sex differences in mental abilities have shown that the old gender gap in math abilities, favoring boys, has disappeared. Male and female adolescents also score equally well in tests of verbal ability. (Tony Freeman/ PhotoEdit)

It appears now that the only reliable sex difference in mental abilities during adolescence is in the area of spatial ability, where males outperform females by a slight margin. You may recall taking standardized tests in which you were asked to imagine how an irregular, three-dimensional object would appear if it were rotated in certain ways; this is a test of spatial ability. The male advantage on many tests of spatial performance emerges before age 10 and is more or less constant during the adolescent years (Johnson & Meade, 1987; Voyer, Voyer, & Bryden, 1995). It is now known that any observed sex differences in math test scores are entirely due to sex differences in spatial ability (Casey, Nuttall, Pezaris, & Benbow, 1995).

The reasons for the sex difference in spatial skill involve a complicated mix of biological and social factors, as indicated by a series of studies examining the interactive effects of gender, genetics, family composition, and experience in activities that involve spatial ability (Casey, Nuttall, & Pezaris, 1999). As expected, the researchers found that the girls who grew up with brothers and who frequently participated in activities with them that could potentially facilitate the development of spatial abilities (e.g., doing carpentry, building model airplanes, playing with Legos) did, in fact, have better spatial skills as adolescents, but that this was true only among girls who were genetically predisposed toward better spatial ability. Like most aspects of adolescent development, then, sex differences in spatial ability are the product of an interactive set of biological and environmental influences.

youngsters typically score lower on standard IQ tests than do their white peers (Anastasi, 1988). But how are we to interpret this finding? Does this mean that minority youngsters are less "intelligent" than white youth? Or does it mean that the tests we use to assess intelligence are unfairly biased against minority children?

In recent years, experts have leaned toward the latter explanation. They point out that IQ tests, which were initially developed and standardized on populations of individuals of European descent, are loaded with questions that reflect the experiences and values of middle-class whites. These critics suggest that whites would do similarly poorly on intelligence tests designed by and for ethnic minority individuals (Miller-Jones, 1989). In addition, language differences between minority and nonminority youth (especially if English is not the minority youngster's first language) may lead to apparent differences in intelligence when the testing is performed in English.

These criticisms have lead to calls for **culture-fair tests**—intelligence tests that attempt to reduce sources of ethnic or cultural bias. Such tests tend to be based less on verbal skills (thus avoiding the language problems of many tests) and more on the sorts of items included on the performance scales of traditional IQ tests.

Even with the advent of culture-fair testing, the notion that there is such a thing as intelligence and that this thing is the same in all cultural and ethnic groups is difficult for many experts to accept. The skills that contribute to intelligent behavior in a nonindustrialized farming and hunting community, or on the streets of an inner-city community, are likely very different from those that contribute to intelligence in a high school science class, yet it is clear that the standard tests used in assessing intelligence place nearly exclusive emphasis on the intellectual skills that are chiefly helpful in educational settings. It is essential for practitioners to keep in mind that any assessment of a youngster's intelligence must take into account the nature and purpose of the test used, the circumstances of the assessment, the background of each child, and the context in which the child has developed (Keating, 1995).

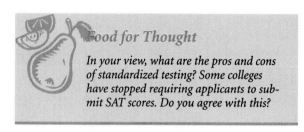

Food for Thought

In your view, what are the pros and cons of standardized testing? Some colleges have stopped requiring applicants to submit SAT scores. Do you agree with this?

ADOLESCENT THINKING IN CONTEXT

Just as it is important to ask how the broader context influences the cognitive development of the adolescent, it is also important to ask how the cognitive developments of adolescence influence the young person's interactions with his or her environment. After all, most of the thinking we do occurs in everyday situations, not just when we are taking tests designed to see how able we are.

As the understanding of adolescent thinking has expanded, researchers have begun to look beyond laboratory experiments and standardized tests in an effort to examine how the cognitive changes of adolescence actually affect teenagers' day-to-day thoughts and actions. Do advances in propositional logic and information-processing abilities make a difference in the real world? In order to look at this issue, psychologists and educators have studied the practical side of adolescent thinking in three domains: in social situations, in risk taking, and in the classroom.

Changes in Social Cognition

Many of the examples of adolescent thinking that we have looked at in this chapter have involved reasoning about scientific problems and physical objects. But the same sorts of gains in intellectual abilities that are observed in young people's thinking in these realms are apparent in their reasoning about social phenomena as well. **Social cognition** involves such cognitive activities as thinking about people, thinking about social relationships, and thinking about social institutions (Lapsley, 1989).

It is not difficult to imagine that adolescents' advanced abilities in thinking about possibilities, thinking in multiple dimensions, and thinking about abstract concepts make them more sophisticated than children when it comes to reasoning about social

RECAP

Some researchers have focused on the measurement and assessment of individual differences in mental abilities during adolescence—in particular, differences in intelligence. In recent years, several theorists, such as Sternberg and Gardner, have proposed alternatives to the view that intelligence can be captured adequately on standardized tests, arguing that true intelligence is defined by skills in addition to those assessed in tests of school smarts, such as the IQ test or the SAT. Accordingly, many critics have called for intelligence tests that are more culture-fair. Today, scientists who study intellectual development are especially interested in ways in which the broader context influences cognitive growth, through the everyday challenges and opportunities for learning that the context provides.

matters. Compared with those of children, adolescents' conceptions of interpersonal relationships are more mature, their understanding of human behavior is more advanced, their ideas about social institutions and organizations are more complex, and their ability to figure out what other people think is far more accurate. Gains in the area of social cognition help account for many of the psychosocial advances typically associated with adolescence—advances in the realms of identity, autonomy, intimacy, sexuality, and achievement. Individual differences in social cognitive abilities also help explain why some adolescents have more social problems than others do (Lenhart & Rabiner, 1995).

Studies of social cognition during adolescence typically fall into three categories: studies of *impression formation*, which examine how individuals form and organize judgments about other people; studies of *social perspective taking*, which examine how, and how accurately, individuals make assessments about the thoughts and feelings of others; and studies of *morality and social conventions*, which examine individuals' conceptions of justice, social norms, and guidelines for social interaction.

● **Impression Formation** During preadolescence and adolescence, individuals' impressions of other people develop mainly in five directions (Hill & Palmquist, 1978). First, impressions become progressively *more differentiated*. Adolescents are more likely than children to describe people—themselves as well as others—in more narrowly defined categories and with more differentiated attributes. Whereas children tend to use fairly global descriptors, such as gender and age, adolescents are more likely to describe other people in terms of such things as interests and personality characteristics, although the particular sets of attributes adolescents use to describe other people may vary across cultures (Crystal, Watanabe, Weinfurt, & Wu, 1998). A second trend in the development of impression formation is toward *less egocentric* impressions, meaning that adolescents are more likely to be aware that their impressions of others are personal viewpoints and are therefore subject to disagreement. Third, their impressions of other people become *more abstract;* that is, impressions become less rooted in such concrete attributes as physical characteristics or personal possessions and more tied to such abstract things as attitudes and motives. Fourth, adolescents come to make *greater use of inference* in their impressions of others. Compared with children, adolescents are more likely to interpret the feelings of others and to

infer the motives, beliefs, and feelings of others, even when specific information of this sort is not directly observable. Finally, adolescents' impressions of others are *more highly organized*. Adolescents are more likely than children, for example, to make judgments of others that link personality traits to the situations in which they are likely to be expressed ("She's impatient when she works with other people") and to reconcile apparently discrepant information about people into a more complex impression ("He's friendly toward girls but not at all friendly toward boys").

Together, these gains in impression formation mark the beginning of the development of an **implicit personality theory**—a theory of why people are the way they are (Barenboim, 1981). As we will see in chapter 10, the development of this implicit personality theory has important implications for the development of intimate relationships.

● **Social Perspective Taking** Related to the gains in impression-formation abilities are considerable improvements in the adolescent's **social perspective taking**—the ability to view events from the perspectives of others. According to Robert Selman (1980), who has studied this development extensively, children become better able as they grow older to step back from their own point of view and to see that others may view an event from a different, but equally valid, perspective. Not only are adolescents more capable of discerning another person's perspective on an issue or event, but they are also better able to understand that person's perspective on their own point of view.

According to Selman, the development of social perspective taking progresses through a series of stages. During the preadolescent stage in the development of perspective taking, youngsters can put themselves in others' shoes but do not yet see how the thoughts and feelings of one person may be related to the thoughts and feelings of another. During early adolescence, with the progression into what Selman calls **mutual role taking,** the young adolescent can be an objective third party and can see how the thoughts or actions of one person can influence those of another. In thinking about two friends, for instance, an adolescent at this level would be able to look at the friends' relationship and see how each person's behavior affects the other's.

Later in adolescence, perspective taking develops an in-depth, societal orientation. The adolescent at this level understands that the perspectives that people have on each other are complicated, are often unconscious, and are influenced by larger forces than individuals can

▲ *Advances in social cognition enhance adolescents' ability to reason with others.* (Billy Barnes/PhotoEdit)

control—including each person's position in society or within a social institution. For example, you are able to understand that your perspective on the instructor teaching your class is influenced not only by your own personality and by the instructor's but also by forces inherent in the way the relationship of professor and student is defined.

Ultimately, an adolescent's gains in social perspective-taking abilities lead to improvements in communication, as he or she becomes more capable of formulating arguments in terms that are more likely to be understood by someone whose opinion is different. One study (Clark & Delia, 1976), for example, looked at how well youngsters of different ages were able to persuade other people to do something for them—such as convincing their parents to buy them a new stereo. The researchers found that the adolescents were more likely to use reasoning that pointed out advantages to their parents ("If I have my own stereo in my room, you won't be bothered by my music") than to use reasoning that simply stated the case from their own point of view ("I really need to have my own stereo; all the other kids do"). A major shift in reasoning took place during early adolescence, coinciding with the transition into the stage of mutual role taking. Although one might think that parents find it more difficult to deal with a teenager who is more persuasive, studies suggest that, when adolescents are able to take their parents' perspective in an

argument, family communication becomes more effective and more satisfying (Silverberg, 1986).

● **Conceptions of Morality and Social Convention**
The realization that individuals' perspectives vary, and that their opinions may differ as a result, leads to changes in the ways that issues regarding morality and social convention are approached. Changes in moral reasoning during adolescence have been investigated extensively, and we will examine this body of research in detail in chapter 9. Briefly, during childhood, moral guidelines are seen as absolutes emanating from such authorities as parents and teachers; judgments of right and wrong are made according to concrete rules. During adolescence, however, such absolutes and rules come to be questioned, as the young person begins to see that moral standards are subjective and are based on points of view that are subject to disagreement. Later in adolescence comes the emergence of reasoning that is based on such moral principles as equality, justice, and fairness—abstract guidelines that transcend concrete situations and can be applied across a variety of moral dilemmas (Kohlberg, 1976).

The development of individuals' understanding of **social conventions**—the social norms that guide day-to-day behavior—follows a similar course (Smetana, 1994; Turiel, 1978). During middle childhood, social conventions—such as waiting in line to buy movie tickets—are seen as arbitrary and changeable, but adherence to them is not; compliance with such conventions is based on rules and on the dictates of authority. When you were 7 years old, you might not have seen why people had to wait in line to buy movie tickets; however, when your mother or father told you to wait in line, you waited. By early adolescence, however, conventions are seen as arbitrary and changeable in both their origins and their enforcement; conventions are merely social expectations. As an adolescent, you begin to realize that people wait in line because they are expected to, not because they are forced to. Indeed, young adolescents often see social conventions as *nothing but* social expectations and, consequently, as insufficient reasons for compliance. You can probably imagine youngsters in their midteens saying something like this: "Why wait in a ticket line simply because other people are lined up? There isn't a *law* that forces you to wait in line, is there?"

Gradually, however, adolescents begin to see social conventions as means used by society to regulate people's behavior. Conventions may be arbitrary, but we

Table 2.2   *Differences between preadolescent and adolescent thinking in four social cognitive domains*

Domain	Preadolescent Thought	Adolescent Thought
Impressions of others (*e.g., Barenboim*)	Impressions are global, egocentric, concrete, disorganized, and haphazard.	Impressions are differentiated, objective, abstract, and organized into a coherent whole.
Role taking (*e.g., Selman*)	Child is able to put self in other's shoes but has difficulty seeing how one person's perspective affects another's.	Adolescent is able to take third-party perspective and to see the bigger, societal picture.
Moral reasoning (*e.g., Kohlberg*)	Morals are based on concrete rules handed down by authorities.	Morals come out of agreements between people or out of abstract principles.
Social conventions (*e.g., Turiel*)	Conventions are based on the rules and dictates of authorities.	Conventions are based on expectations or grow out of social norms.

follow them because we all share an understanding of how people are expected to behave in various situations. In fact, high schoolers see conventions as so ingrained in the social system that individuals follow them partly out of habit. We wait in line for theater tickets not because we want to comply with any rule but because it is something we are accustomed to doing.

Ultimately, individuals come to see that social conventions serve a function in coordinating interactions among people. Social norms and expectations are derived from and maintained by individuals' having a common perspective and agreeing that, in given situations, certain behaviors are more desirable than others, because such behaviors help society and its institutions function more smoothly. Without the convention of waiting in line to buy movie tickets, the pushiest people would always get tickets first. The older adolescent can see that waiting in line not only benefits the theater but also preserves everyone's right to a fair chance to buy tickets. In other words, we wait in line patiently because we all agree that it is better if tickets are distributed fairly.

Table 2.2 summarizes some of the important differences in social cognitive abilities between preadolescents and adolescents. As you can see, across all four domains, thinking becomes more abstract, more hypothetical, and more relativistic between childhood and adolescence.

Together, these gains in social cognitive abilities help account for gains in individuals' social competence during adolescence. As you will read in chapter 10, adolescents who have more sophisticated social cognitive abilities (i.e., more advanced perspective-taking abilities and more sophisticated impression-formation

skills) actually behave in more socially competent ways (Ford, 1982; Lenhart & Rabiner, 1995). Although there is more to social competence than social cognition, being able to understand social relationships in a more advanced way is an important component of being able to behave in a more advanced way.

RECAP

The cognitive developments of adolescence are reflected in young people's behavior in real-world situations, as well as in laboratory experiments. One area of inquiry that has received a good deal of attention is the development of social cognition. Studies show that thinking about social relationships and social institutions—like thinking in general—becomes more abstract, more multidimensional, and more relativistic throughout the adolescent period.

 *Food for Thought*

In what ways does popular culture aimed at adolescents—television, movies, magazines, and music—take advantage of the relatively more sophisticated social-cognitive abilities that emerge at this time?

Adolescent Risk Taking

A second practical application of research into adolescent thinking involves the study of adolescent risk taking. In chapter 1, we noted that many of the health problems of the adolescent period are the result of

▲ *Research on cognitive development during adolescence has been aimed at understanding the thought processes behind adolescent risk taking.* (Dugald Bremner/Tony Stone)

behaviors that can be prevented—behaviors such as substance abuse, reckless driving, and unprotected sex. The Centers for Disease Control, a government agency that monitors the health of Americans, now surveys teenagers annually and asks whether they have engaged in various behaviors during the previous 30 days (Centers for Disease Control, 2000). The most recent survey revealed that about 16 percent of high school students rarely or never use a seat belt. Of the teenagers who ride motorcycles, 38 percent report rarely or never wearing a helmet. Studies of young adolescents have found that nearly 80 percent of boys and 60 percent of girls take unnecessary risks while skateboarding or riding bikes; that more than one-third of both sexes have been passengers in cars driven by intoxicated drivers; that two-thirds of sixth-graders have experimented with alcohol, and half have smoked cigarettes; and that one-fifth of seventh-graders are sexually active (with only half using contraception) (Ozer, Macdonald, & Irwin, in press). Nor is risk taking prevalent only among American youth: A study of Danish adolescents found that half of all 14- to 15-year-olds had driven a bicycle while intoxicated, that one-fifth were regular cigarette smokers, and that one-sixth had had sexual intercourse without using contraception (Arnett & Balle-Jensen, 1993). In

general, risk taking is much more common among males than females, although there is some evidence that this gender gap has been narrowing (Byrnes, Miller, & Schafer, 1999).

Some writers have suggested that we look at these behaviors as resulting from decisions that adolescents make—for instance, decisions to drink alcohol, to drive fast, or to have intercourse without using contraception—and that we need to understand better the cognitive processes behind such decision making. One line of research has attempted to examine whether adolescents make risky decisions because of deficiencies in their developing cognitive abilities (Furbey & Beyth-Marom, 1992).

A number of writers have looked at adolescent risk taking from a perspective called **behavioral decision theory** (Fischoff, 1988; Fischoff & Quadrel, 1995; Kahneman, Slovic, & Tversky, 1982). According to this theory, all behaviors can be analyzed as the outcome of a process that involves (1) identifying alternative choices, (2) identifying the consequences that follow each choice, (3) evaluating the desirability of each possible consequence, (4) assessing the likelihood of each possible consequence, and (5) combining all this information according to a decision rule (Beyth-Marom, Austin, Fischoff, Palmgren, & Jacobs-Quadrel, 1993). For example, an adolescent girl who is trying to decide whether to accept a ride home from a party with friends who had been drinking would (1) identify the choices (to accept the ride or not); (2) identify the consequences ("If I accept the ride, and we get into an accident, I could be seriously hurt"; "if I don't accept the ride, my friends will make fun of me for being a loser"); (3) evaluate the desirability of each consequence ("Appearing like a loser to my friends is bad, but being in an accident would be terrible"); (4) assess the likelihood of each consequence ("My friends probably won't really change their opinion of me just because I turn down the ride, and my friend who is driving is so drunk that he really might get into an accident"); and (5) combine all the information according to a decision rule ("All things considered, I

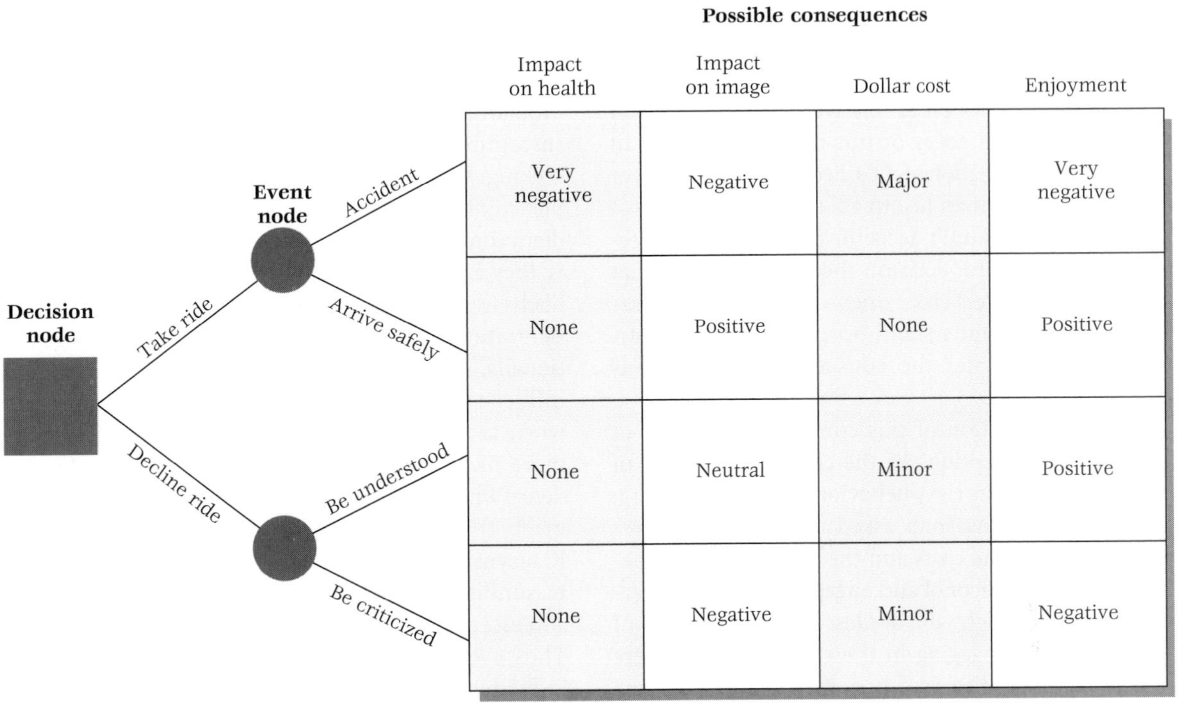

Possible consequences

	Impact on health	Impact on image	Dollar cost	Enjoyment
Accident	Very negative	Negative	Major	Very negative
Arrive safely	None	Positive	None	Positive
Be understood	None	Neutral	Minor	Positive
Be criticized	None	Negative	Minor	Negative

Decision node — Take ride — Event node — Accident / Arrive safely

Decline ride — Be understood / Be criticized

Figure 2.5   The process of deciding whether to accept a ride home from a friend who has been drinking, according to behavioral decision theory. (Fischoff et al., 1995)

think I won't take the ride"). Figure 2.5 shows what this decision-making process looks like.

From the perspective of behavioral decision theory, then, it is important to ask whether adolescents use different processes than adults do in identifying, estimating, and evaluating various behavioral options and consequences. If risky decisions are the result of faulty information processing—in attention, memory, metacognition, or organization, for example—perhaps it makes sense to train adolescents in these basic cognitive abilities as a means of lessening their risk taking.

According to most studies, however, adolescents make decisions using the same basic cognitive processes that adults use (Beyth-Marom et al., 1993; Furbey & Beyth-Marom, 1992). This is true even regarding issues as complicated as deciding whether to abort a pregnancy (Lewis, 1987). The major gains in information processing appear to occur between childhood and adolescence, rather than between adolescence and adulthood (Keating, 1990; Steinberg & Cauffman, 1996).

A second possibility that is often suggested is that adolescents are more likely to feel invulnerable—that

is, more likely to subscribe to the personal fable that they will not be harmed by potentially harmful experiences. However, there is no evidence for the widely held belief that adolescents are more likely to subscribe to personal fables than are adults (Quadrel et al., 1993). More important, studies indicate that adolescents are no more likely than adults to perceive themselves as invulnerable. *Both* age groups are equally likely to underestimate their likelihood of being harmed by potentially harmful experiences (Quadrel et al., 1993).

If adolescents use the same decision-making processes as adults, and if adolescents are no more likely than adults to think of themselves as invulnerable, why, then, do adolescents behave in ways that are excessively risky? One answer may involve the different ways in which adolescents and adults evaluate the desirability of various consequences (Moore & Gullone, 1996). For example, an individual's decision to try cocaine at a party may involve evaluating a number of consequences, including the legal and health risks, the pleasure the drug may induce, and the way in which one will be judged (both positively and negatively) by the other people present. Although an adult and an adolescent may both consider all these consequences, the adult may place relatively more weight on the health risks of trying the drug, whereas the adolescent may place relatively more weight on the social consequences of not trying. Although an adult may see an adolescent's decision to value peer acceptance more than health as irrational, an adolescent may see the adult's decision as equally incomprehensible. Behavioral decision theory reminds us that all decisions—even risky ones—can be seen as rational, once we understand how an individual estimates and evaluates the consequences of various courses of action.

A nice illustration of this comes from a study of adolescents' perceptions of the costs and benefits of engaging in various risky behaviors (Small, Silverberg, & Kerns, 1993). This study asked adolescents of different ages to rate the costs and the benefits of such behaviors as using alcohol and engaging in sexual intercourse. Interestingly, the adolescents' perceptions of the benefits of engaging in the risky behaviors were not nearly as predictive of how they behaved as were their perceptions of costs. The adolescents' perceptions of costs were highly predictive of their behavior, however, the more costly an adolescent thought engaging in a given behavior would be, the less likely he or she was to engage in that behavior. A similar case has made for understanding why adolescents risk exposing themselves to HIV infection by having unprotected sex: Many adolescents do not believe that the costs of unprotected sex are sufficiently great to avoid the risky behavior (Gardner & Herman, 1990).

In all likelihood, of course, neither adolescents' nor adults' decisions are always made in as straightforward or rational a way as suggested by behavioral decision theory. Nevertheless, this approach has opened up a new way of thinking about adolescent risk taking. Instead of looking at risky decisions as the result of irrational or faulty judgment, experts are now trying to understand where and how adolescents obtain the information they use in reaching their conclusions and how accurate the information is. If, for example, adolescents underestimate the likelihood of getting pregnant following unprotected sex, sex education efforts might focus on teaching teenagers the actual probability.

We should also keep in mind that emotional and contextual factors, as well as cognitive ones, contribute to adolescent risk taking. Several researchers have noted that adolescents may differ from adults in

important ways that are not captured by cognitive measures of decision making (Lightfoot, 1997; Maggs, Almeida, & Galambos, 1995; Scott, Reppucci, & Woolard, 1995; Steinberg & Cauffman, 1996), such as susceptibility to peer pressure, impulsivity, and fun seeking. With respect to emotional factors, for example, studies show that individuals who are overconfident, competitive, and high in **sensation seeking** (that is, they enjoy novel and intense experiences) are more likely to engage in various types of risky behaviors than are their peers (Miller & Byrnes, 1997). Additionally, adolescents' reasoning, like that of adults, is influenced by their desires, motives, and interests; when faced with a logical argument, adolescents are more likely to accept faulty reasoning or shaky evidence when they agree with the substance of the argument than when they do not (Klaczynski, 1997; Klaczynski & Gordon, 1996). Although this sort of reasoning bias declines between preadolescence and adolescence, even late adolescents are biased thinkers. Thus, even though adolescence is a time during which individuals acquire more sophisticated reasoning abilities, individuals use these competencies selectively, using advanced logic to question strong evidence that contradicts their opinion but setting aside these logical abilities when accepting flimsy evidence that supports their pre-existing belief (Klaczynzki & Narasimham, 1998).

Perhaps more important in explaining the rise in risk taking during adolescence than age differences in personality or reasoning are age differences in the nature of the contexts in which individuals spend time. A good deal of adolescents' risk taking takes place in contexts in which they are unsupervised by parents and other adults and where they are exposed to tremendous peer pressure to engage in risky behavior (Byrnes, 1997). Children who have personalities that have made them more prone to take risks may only be able to act on their impulses as adolescents, when their behavior is less closely controlled by adults. Adolescents living in large cities, for example, have more opportunities for risk taking because they are less closely monitored by parents and other adults. As well, risk taking may be less prevalent in settings that attempt to limit opportunities for risky behavior through legal or institutional means, such as having a higher legal drinking age or a higher legal driving age (Arnett & Balle-Jensen, 1993). More research is needed on how these various cognitive, emotional, and contextual factors interact in shaping risk-taking behavior.

RECAP

Researchers have examined adolescent risk taking from a cognitive point of view. Contrary to popular wisdom, which holds that adolescents are bad decision makers, studies suggest that adolescents make decisions in much the same way that adults do. Research also indicates that adolescents are no more likely than adults to suffer from feelings of invulnerability. The current consensus is that young people sometimes behave in risky ways not because of faulty decision making but because they evaluate the possible consequences of their actions differently than adults do and because a variety of emotional and social factors influence their judgment.

Food for Thought

Think back to some things that you did in adolescence that adults might have considered risky. Did they seem risky to you at the time? Do they seem risky when you think about them now?

Adolescent Thinking in the Classroom

Given the sorts of changes in thinking that occur during the adolescent years, one would hope that schools and teachers adapt their methods and curricula to mesh better with the developing cognitive abilities of their students. In theory, adolescents' ability to think in more advanced ways—whether in terms of abstraction, multidimensionality, relativism, or another dimension—should permit them to think more critically about a wide range of issues. However, the prevalence of **critical thinking** among American high school students—thinking that is in-depth, analytical, and discriminating—has been less than staggering. Most assessments of adolescent achievement in recent years indicate that American youth have difficulty thinking in the sophisticated ways that the theories and research suggest they should be capable of. Part of the reason, some critics contend, is that adolescents are rarely asked to think in this fashion (Linn & Songer, 1991; Ravitch, 1995).

To what can we attribute this gap between theory and practice? According to some writers, our educational system does not encourage or stimulate the type of thinking that adolescents have the potential for. Although research indicates that it is possible, for ex-

ample, to stimulate the development of formal-operational thinking (e.g., Danner & Day, 1977; Siegler, Liebert, & Liebert, 1973), few junior or senior high school classes are set up to do so. Rather than encouraging adolescents to think in abstract or relativistic ways, for instance, most secondary school classes reward the rote memorization of concrete facts and the parroting back of the teacher's correct answer. According to one expert, opportunities for real give-and-take in adolescents' schools account for less than 10 percent of the total time spent on instruction (Sternberg, 1994). At a time when adolescents are becoming capable of seeing that most issues are too complicated to have one right answer, an educational program that stifles this developing ability works against individuals' developmental inclinations. Although attempts have been made to make the instruction of adolescents more compatible with researchers' understanding of their cognitive development, these efforts have not been widespread. However, studies show that teaching that takes advantage of adolescents' developing reasoning abilities can result in their more sophisticated understanding of the subject matter, especially in science classes (Linn & Songer, 1991, 1993). Studies show that opportunities to engage in hands-on experiments contribute to adolescents' understanding of scientific principles (Penner & Klahr, 1996).

The gap between what adolescents can do (i.e., their *competence*) and their actual school achievement (i.e., their *performance*) may be especially large among youth who attend English-speaking schools but who speak another language or dialect when not in school, as one study of native Hawaiian youth indicates (Feldman, Stone, & Renderer, 1990). Although the students in this research attended schools in which the instruction was in Standard English, they spoke Hawaiian Creole-English at home and with their friends. The researchers found that, even though the students were functioning at a high cognitive level, they were uncomfortable speaking in class because of their language background, and this lack of verbal engagement interfered with their learning. One hypothesis is that speaking in class aids in the process of encoding the information, which facilitates learning. Presumably, all groups of youngsters whose in-school and out-of-school languages are very different are at risk for this disadvantage.

Criticisms also have been leveled against schools' lack of attempts to deliberately enhance adolescents' information-processing skills. As our society becomes more information-dependent—some social commentators have talked about information overload—it is important that adolescents learn how to better manage and use this wealth of data. A number of writers have argued that schools can and should teach adolescents ways of focusing attention, improving short- and longterm memory, organizing information, and monitoring thought processes (Baron & Sternberg, 1987; Gagne, 1985; Glazer & Bassok, 1989). In other words, these experts believe that information-processing skills can be taught and that educators should make a more conscious effort to do so. Moreover, they point to recent advances in research on adolescent information processing as providing the foundation for an overhaul of our secondary school curricula.

RECAP

Research on cognitive development in adolescence suggests a number of ways that schools might change in order to better match classroom instruction to the developing capabilities of adolescent students. Unfortunately, however, little has been done to change the way that adolescents are taught, and few high school programs are designed to stimulate the development of formal operations or more sophisticated information-processing skills.

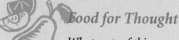

Food for Thought

What sorts of things could schools do to promote more critical thinking among adolescents? How much of this was done in the high school you attended?

Web Researcher Pick a risky behavior that teenagers are believed to engage in and find out whether they really do take more risks than adults. How might behavioral decision theory explain these differences? Do you think changes in their cognitive abilities make them more or less vunerable to risk? Go to www.mhhe.com/steinberg6 for further information.

KEY TERMS

automatization

behavioral decision theory

cognitive-developmental view

cohort

competence-performance distinction

concrete operations

cortex

critical thinking

culture-fair tests

deductive reasoning

divided attention

formal operations

functional magnetic resonance imaging (fMRI)

imaginary audience

implicit personality theory

inductive reasoning

information-processing perspective

limbic system

long-term memory

metacognition

mutual role taking

myelination

personal fable

Piagetian perspective

positron emission tomography (PET)

prefrontal cortex

preoperational period

propositional logic

scaffolding

selective attention

sensation seeking

sensorimotor period

social cognition

social conventions

social perspective taking

statistical interaction

synaptic pruning

working memory

zone of proximal development

Chapter 3

Social Transitions

When did you know that you had finally become an adolescent? When you finished elementary school? Went to your first boy-girl party? Were allowed to be out at night without an adult?

What defined your transition into adulthood? Getting your first job? Getting your driver's license? Going off to college? Getting married?

Transitions into and out of adolescence vary all over the world. For example, among the Thonga, an agrarian society in the southeastern region of Africa, an adolescent girl at the time of her first menstruation, goes to an older woman of her choosing and announces that she has come of age (Ford & Beach, 1951). At this point, a seclusion period of one month commences, and

> three or four girls, undergoing the initiation ceremony together, are shut up in a hut, and when they come out, must always wear over their face a veil consisting of a very dirty and greasy cloth. Every morning they are led to the pool, and their whole body is immersed in the water as far as the neck. Other initiated girls or women accompany them, singing obscene songs, and drive away with sticks any man who happens to be on the road, as no man is allowed to see a girl during this period. . . . When the cortege of women accompanying the initiated has returned home, the nubile girls are imprisoned in the hut. They are teased, pinched, scratched by the adoptive mothers or by other women; they must also listen to the licentious songs which are sung to them. . . . They are also instructed in sexual matters, and told that they must never reveal anything about the blood of the menses to a man. . . . At the end of the month the adoptive mother brings the girl home to her true mother. She also presents her with a pot of beer. A feast takes place on this occasion. (Junod, 1927, cited in Ford & Beach, 1951, p. 175)

Along with the biological changes of puberty and changes in thinking abilities, changes in social roles and status constitute yet another universal feature of development during adolescence. All societies differentiate among individuals on the basis of how old they are (although not all use chronological age as the defining criterion).

In all societies, adolescence is a period of social transition for the individual. Over the course of the adolescent years, the individual ceases to be viewed by society as a child and comes to be recognized as an adult. Although the specific elements of this social passage from childhood into adulthood vary across time and space, the presence during adolescence of some sort of recognition that the individual's status has changed—a **social redefinition** of the individual—is universal. Indeed, some theorists have argued that the nature of adolescence is influenced far more by the way in which society defines the economic and social roles of young people than by the biological or cognitive changes of the period.

To be sure, the process of social redefinition at adolescence is less vivid and less ceremonial in contemporary America than it is among the Thonga. We do not seclude young people from the rest of society at the onset of puberty, nor, with the exception of certain religious ceremonies, do we mark the passage into adulthood with elaborate rituals. However, just because the social transition of adolescence is less explicit in contemporary society than it is in many traditional cultures does not mean that the passage is any less significant.

The study of social transitions at adolescence provides an interesting vehicle through which we can compare adolescence across different cultures and historical epochs. Although certain features of the social passage from childhood into adulthood are universal, considerable differences exist between the processes of social redefinition in industrialized society and those in more traditional cultures, as well as between different cultural groups within contemporary society. In examining some of these differences, you will come to understand better how the way in which society structures the transition of adolescents into adult roles influences the nature of psychosocial development during the period.

Because young people go through puberty earlier today than individuals did 100 years ago, and because they stay in school longer, the adolescent period has been lengthened and the transition into adulthood prolonged. Today, young people are caught between the world of childhood and the world of adulthood for an extremely long time, with only a vague sense of when—and how—they become adults. Indeed, in the minds of many social scientists who study adolescence in modern society, the social passage of young people into adult roles is too long, too vague, and too rocky (Chisholm & Hurrelmann, 1995; Nightingale & Wolverton, 1993). And, as we will see, the passage from adolescence into adulthood is especially difficult among young people growing up in poverty. ●

RECAP

Changes in social definition make up the third set of fundamental transformations that define adolescence as a period of development. Although the specific elements of the social passage from childhood into adulthood vary from one society to another, all societies recognize that the social status of the individual changes during the adolescent period.

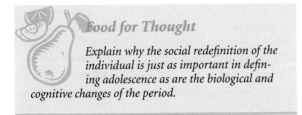

SOCIAL REDEFINITION AND PSYCHOSOCIAL DEVELOPMENT

Like the biological and cognitive transitions of adolescence, the social transitions have important consequences for the young person's psychosocial development. Indeed, from a sociological or an anthropological perspective, it is social redefinition at adolescence—rather than, for example, puberty—that has the most profound impact on the individual's development and behavior. In the realm of *identity,* for example, the attainment of adult status may transform a young woman's self-concept, causing her to feel more adultlike and to think more seriously about future work and family roles. Doing for the first time such things as reporting to work, going into a bar, and registering to vote all make us feel older and more mature. In turn, these new activities and opportunities may prompt self-evaluation and introspection.

Becoming an adult member of society, accompanied as it is by shifts in responsibility, independence, and freedom, also has an impact on the development of *autonomy.* In contrast to the child, the adolescent-turned-adult is permitted to make a wider range of decisions that may have serious long-term consequences (Scott, Reppucci, & Woolard, 1995). A young man who has reached the drinking age, for example, must decide how he should handle this new privilege. Should he go along with the crowd and drink every weekend night, or should he follow his parents' example and abstain from drinking? And, in return for the privileges that come with adult status, adolescents are expected to behave in a more responsible fashion. Receiving a driver's license carries with it the obligation of driving safely. Thus, the attainment of adult status provides chances for the young person to exercise autonomy, as well as chances to develop a greater sense of independence.

Changes in social definition often bring with them changes in the sorts of relationships and interpersonal behaviors that are permitted and expected. Social redef-

inition at adolescence is therefore likely to raise new questions and concerns for the young person about *intimacy*—including, in particular, such matters as dating and marriage. Many parents prohibit their children from dating until they have reached an "appropriate" age, and not until the **age of majority** (the legal age for adult status) are individuals allowed to marry without first gaining their parents' permission. In certain societies, young people may even be *required* to marry when they reach adulthood, entering into a marriage that was arranged while they were children.

Changes in status at adolescence may also affect development in the domain of *sexuality.* In contemporary society, for example, laws governing sexual behavior (such as the definition of statutory rape) typically differentiate between individuals who have and have not attained adult status. By becoming an adult in a legal sense, the young person may be confronted with the need for new and different decisions about sexual activity. One problem continuing to face contemporary society is whether sexually active individuals who have not yet attained adult legal status should be able to make independent decisions about such adult matters as abortion and contraception.

Finally, reaching adulthood often has important implications in the realm of *achievement.* For instance, in contemporary society, it is not until adult status is attained that one can enter the labor force as a full-time employee. Not until young people have reached a designated age are they permitted to leave school of their own volition. In less industrialized societies, becoming an adult typically entails entrance into the productive activities of the community. Together, these shifts are likely to prompt changes in the young person's skills, aspirations, and expectations.

ADOLESCENCE AS A SOCIAL INVENTION

Because so many of the psychological changes of adolescence are linked to the changes that accompany society's redefinition of the individual, many writers have argued that adolescence, as a period in the life cycle, is mainly a social invention (e.g., Fasick, 1994; Lapsley, Enright, & Serlin, 1985). These writers, often referred to as **inventionists,** point out that, although the biological and cognitive changes characteristic of the period are important in their own right, adolescence is defined primarily by the ways in which society recognizes (or does not recognize) the period as distinct from childhood or adulthood.

Many of our images of adolescence are influenced by the fact that society draws lines between adolescence and childhood (for instance, the boundary between elementary and secondary school) and between adolescence and adulthood (for instance, the age at which one can hold a job). Inventionists stress that it is because we *see* adolescence as distinct that it, in fact, exists as such. They point to cultures and historical periods in which adolescence either is not recognized at all or is viewed very differently. Many of these theorists view the behaviors and problems characteristic of adolescence in contemporary society as having to do with the particular way that adolescence is defined by society, rather than the result of the biological or cognitive givens of the period. This is an entirely different view than that espoused by writers such as G. Stanley Hall, for example, who saw the psychological changes of adolescence as driven by puberty and, as a result, by biological destiny.

RECAP

Some writers, called inventionists, have argued that adolescence is more a social invention than a biological or cognitive phenomenon. They suggest that our conception of adolescence—its nature and whether it exists as a separate period—is determined largely by forces in the broader social environment. Changes in the broader environment, therefore, can change the very nature of adolescence.

Food for Thought

Explain the inventionist perspective on adolescence. What evidence would you use to support this argument? What evidence would you use to argue against it?

Have there always been adolescents? Although this question seems like a simple one with an obvious answer, its answer is very complicated. Naturally, there have always been individuals between the ages of 10 and 20. However, according to the inventionist view, adolescence as we know it in contemporary society did not really exist until the industrial revolution of the middle of the nineteenth century (Fasick, 1994). Prior to that time, in the agricultural world of the sixteenth and seventeenth centuries, children were treated primarily as miniature adults, and people did not make precise distinctions

among children of various ages (the term *child* referred to anyone under the age of 18 or even 21). Children provided important labor to their families, and they learned early in their development the roles they were expected to fulfill later in life. The main distinction between children and adults was not based on their age or their abilities but on whether they owned property (Modell & Goodman, 1990). As a consequence, there was little reason to label some youngsters as "children" and others as "adolescents"—in fact, the term *adolescent* was not widely used before the nineteenth century.

With industrialization, however, came new patterns of work, schooling, and family life. Adolescents were among the most dramatically affected by these changes. First, because the economy was changing so rapidly, away from the simple and predictable life known in agrarian society, the connection between what individuals learned in childhood and what they would need to know in adulthood became increasingly uncertain. Although a man may have been a farmer, his son would not necessarily follow in his footsteps. One response to this uncertainty was that parents, especially in middle-class families, encouraged adolescents to spend time preparing for adulthood within societal institutions, such as schools. Instead of working side-by-side with their parents and other adults at home, as was the case before industrialization, nineteenth-century adolescents were increasingly more likely to spend their days with peers of the same age, preparing for the future.

Inventionists have been quick to point out that the redefinition of adolescence as a time of preparation, rather than participation, suited society's changing economic needs as well (Fasick, 1994). One initial outcome of industrialization was a shortage of job opportunities, because machines were used to replace workers. Although adolescents provided inexpensive labor, they were competing with adults for a limited supply of jobs. One way of protecting adults' jobs was to remove adolescents from the labor force, by turning them into full-time students. In order to accomplish this, society needed to begin discriminating between individuals who were "ready" for work and those who were not. And, although there was very little factual basis for the distinction, society began to view adolescents as less capable and as more in need of guidance and training—as a way of rationalizing what was little more than age discrimination. Individuals who, earlier in the century, would have been working side-by-side with adults were now seen as too immature or too unskilled to carry out similar tasks—even though the individuals themselves hadn't changed in any meaningful way. As noted in the Introduction, society's view of adolescents' capability and maturity has changed dramatically when their labor has been sorely needed, such as during wartime (Enright, Levy, Harris, & Lapsley, 1987).

A less cynical view of the events of the late nineteenth century emphasizes the genuine desire of some adults to protect adolescents from the dangers of the new workplace, rather than the selfish desire to protect adults' jobs from teenagers. Industrialization brought with it worrisome changes in community life, especially in the cities. Many factories were dangerous working environments, filled with new and unfamiliar machinery. The disruption of small farming communities and the growth of large urban areas because of the shift from agriculture to industry were accompanied by increases in crime and in "moral degeneracy." **Child protectionists** argued that young people needed to be kept away from the labor force for their own good. In addition to the rise of schools during this time, the early twentieth century saw the growth of many organizations aimed at protecting young people, such as the Boy Scouts and similar adult-supervised youth clubs (Modell & Goodman, 1990).

For whatever reason, it was not until the late nineteenth century—about 100 years ago—that adolescence came to be viewed as we view it today: a lengthy period of preparation for adulthood, in which young people, in need of guidance and supervision, remain economically dependent on their elders. This view started within the middle class—where parents had more to gain by keeping their children out of the labor force and educating them for a better adulthood—but it spread quickly throughout much of society. Because the workplace has continued to change in ways that make the future uncertain, the idea of adolescence as a distinctive period of preparation for adulthood has remained intact.

Two other modifications of the definition of adolescence also gave rise to new terminology and ideas. The first of these concerns the use of the term **teenager,** which was not employed until about 50 years ago. In contrast to the term *adolescent, teenager* suggests a more frivolous and lighthearted age, during which individuals concern themselves with such things as cars and cosmetics. An important social change that led to the invention of the teenager was the increased affluence and economic freedom enjoyed by American adolescents during the late 1940s and early 1950s (Fasick, 1994; Hine, 1999). Advertisers recognized that these young people represented an important consumer group

▲ Although adolescence was invented during the late nineteenth century, it was not until the middle of the twentieth century that our present-day image of the teenager was created. An important contributor to this image was the mass media— magazines such as Seventeen *cultivated the picture of the happy-go-lucky teenager as a way of targeting advertisements toward the lucrative adolescent market.* (Courtesy of *Seventeen* magazine. Photographed exclusively for *Seventeen* by Francesco Scavullo)

and—with the help of new publications, such as *Seventeen* magazine—began cultivating the image of the happy-go-lucky teenager as a means of targeting ad campaigns toward the lucrative adolescent market (Greenberger & Steinberg, 1986).

A second term whose acceptance grew as a result of social change is **youth,** which was used long before *adolescent.* However, prior to industrialization, *youth* had a very vague and imprecise meaning and could refer to someone as young as 12 or as old as 24 (Modell & Goodman, 1990). Gradually—and during the 1960s, in particular—the growth of the college population and the rise in student activism across the country focused attention on individuals who were somewhere between adolescence and young adulthood—those in the 18- to 22-year-old range. Many adults referred to the changes they saw in attitudes and values among college students as the "youth movement." One theorist went so far as to argue that youth is a separate stage in the life cycle, psychologically as well as chronologically distinct from adolescence and adulthood (Keniston, 1970). Indeed, many college students are unsure about whether they are adolescents or adults, since they may feel mature in some respects (e.g., keeping up an apartment, being involved in a serious dating relationship) but immature in others (e.g., having to depend on parents for economic support, having to have an advisor approve class schedules). Although it may strike you as odd to think of 22-year-olds as adolescents, the lengthening of formal schooling in contemporary society has altered the way we define adolescence, because most young people continue their education past high school and are forced to delay their transition into many adult work and family roles. By this definition, many 22-year-olds (and many individuals who are even older) are still not adults. Indeed, one writer has argued that the transition to adulthood has become so delayed in many industrialized societies that we think of the existence of a new stage in life—"emerging adulthood"—which may last for some individuals until their late twenties (Arnett, 2000).

It is important to note that, when it is said that adolescence (or the teenager or youth) is in part a social invention, that does not mean that its significance is in any way diminished or that it is somehow less real than if it were an entirely biological phenomenon. Democracy, after all, is a social invention, too, but its creation and development have had profound effects on the way we live. As with other social inventions, the notion that there should be a distinct period of adolescence has endured over time and has had important and very concrete repercussions. However, as with other social constructs, the nature of adolescence changes over time, and it will continue to change as we revise our notions of what it means to grow from childhood into adulthood.

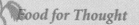

Food for Thought

Historians agree that social conditions during the second half of the nineteenth century led to the invention of adolescence as we know it today. What changes in the nature of adolescence have taken place since that time? What are your predictions for how adolescence will change in the twenty-first century?

CHANGES IN STATUS

"The most casual survey of the ways in which different societies have handled adolescence makes one fact inescapable," wrote anthropologist Ruth Benedict in her classic work, *Patterns of Culture*. "[E]ven in those cultures which have made the most of the trait, the age upon which they focus their attention varies over a great range of years. . . . The puberty they recognize is social, and the ceremonies are a recognition in some fashion or other of the child's new status of adulthood. . . . In order to understand [adolescence] . . . we need . . . to know what is identified in different cultures with the beginning of adulthood and their methods of admitting to the new status" (Benedict, 1934, p. 25).

Changes in social definition at adolescence typically involve a two-sided alteration in status. On the one hand, the adolescent is given certain privileges and rights that are typically reserved for the society's adult members. On the other hand, this increased power and freedom generally are accompanied by increased expectations for self-management, personal responsibility, and social participation.

We can find examples of this double shift in social status in all societies, across a variety of interpersonal, political, economic, and legal arenas.

Changes in Interpersonal Status

In many societies, individuals who have been recognized as adults are usually addressed with adult titles. They also are expected to maintain different sorts of social relationships with their parents, with the community's elders, and with young people whose status has not yet changed. On holidays such as Thanksgiving, some large families set two tables: a big table for the adults and a smaller, children's table. When a young person is permitted to sit at the big table, it is a sign that he or she has reached a new position in the family. These interpersonal changes are typically accompanied by new interpersonal obligations—for example, being expected to take care of and set a proper example for the younger members of the family.

Changes in Political Status

With the attainment of adult status, the young person is often permitted more extensive participation in the community's decision making. Among the Navaho, for example, it is only following a formal initiation ceremony that adolescents are considered members of the Navaho People and are permitted full participation in ceremonial life (Cohen, 1964). In contemporary America, attaining the age of majority brings the right to vote; however, in return for this increased power usually come new obligations. In most societies, young adults are expected to serve their communities in cases of emergency or need, and in many cultures training for warfare is often demanded of young people once they attain adult status (Benedict, 1934).

Changes in Economic Status

Attaining adult status also has important economic implications that again entail obligation as well as privilege. In some societies, only adults may own property and maintain control over their income (Miller, 1928). In many American states, for example, any income that a youngster earns before the age of 16 is technically the property of the young person's parents.

Entrance into certain work roles is also restricted to adults. In most industrialized societies, employment is regulated by child labor laws, and the attainment of a prescribed age is a prerequisite to employment in certain occupations. Among the Tikopia (Melanesia), one of the first privileges accorded boys when they reach adolescence is accompanying older males on fishing expeditions (Fried & Fried, 1980). In most communities, however, once young people have attained the economic status and rights of adults, they are expected to contribute to the economic well-being of their community. They are depended on to partici-

pate in the community's productive activities and to carry out the labor expected of adults. In contemporary society, the young adult's economic responsibilities to the broader community may entail having to pay taxes for the first time. In some families, adolescents who are permitted to work must contribute to their family's support.

Changes in Legal Status

In most societies, not until adult status is attained is the young person permitted to participate in a variety of activities that are typically reserved for adults. Gambling, purchasing alcoholic beverages, and driving are but three of the many privileges we reserve in America for individuals who have reached the legal age of adulthood. In many cultures, the eating of certain foods is restricted to individuals who have been admitted to adult society (Mead, 1928).

Once an adolescent is designated as an adult, however, he or she is also subject to a new set of laws and must expect to be treated differently by the legal institutions of the society, compared with how he or she was treated as a child. In the United States, for example, certain activities that are permissible among adults, such as not showing up for school (e.g., truancy) and leaving

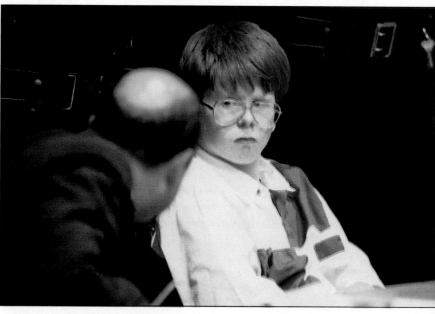

▲ *During the mid-1990s, many adults demanded that juveniles accused of violent crimes be tried as adults. This 14-year-old was tried as an adult and found guilty of murdering a preschooler.* (Karen Garver/Sipa Press)

one's home without informing others (e.g., running away), are considered offenses when they are committed by young people. (Indeed, the term **status offense** refers to a behavior that is viewed as a problem because of the young person's status as a juvenile.) Even certain crimes, when committed by a minor, are adjudicated in a separate **juvenile justice system,** which operates under different rules and principles from those used by the criminal justice system, where adults are tried.

Unfortunately, development during the adolescent years is so rapid and so variable that it is difficult to know at what chronological age a line should be drawn between legally viewing someone as an adult and viewing someone as a child (Steinberg & Cauffman, 1996). There is especially great disagreement about how we should view, and treat, young people who commit serious violent offenses (Fagan & Zimring, 2000; Grisso & Schwartz, 2000). If someone has committed a violent crime, should he or she be treated as a child (and processed as a delinquent) or as an adult (and processed as a criminal)? Should young teenagers and adults who are convicted of the same crime receive the same penalties? In one study, it was found that American jurors were significantly more likely to recommend the death penalty for an individual convicted of first-degree murder if he were 16 or older than if he were 15 or younger, suggesting that many people draw the line at 16. Interestingly, this is where the U.S. Supreme Court has drawn the line as well (Britner, Crosby, & Jodl, 1994).

Many other issues surrounding the legal status of adolescents remain vague and confusing. Two U.S. Supreme Court cases indicate just how inconsistent the views of adolescents' status are (Moshman, 1993). In one case, *Hazelwood v. Kuhlmeier,* the Court ruled that a public high school may censor articles written by students for their school newspaper, on the grounds that adolescents are "immature" enough to need the protection of "wiser" adults, yet the same Court also ruled, in

Board of Education v. Mergens, that students who want to form a Bible study group have the right to meet on campus because high school students are "mature" enough to understand that a school can permit the expression of ideas that it does not necessarily endorse.

There are many other examples of this sort of inconsistency. For example, courts have ruled that teenagers have the right to obtain contraceptives without their parents' approval. But they also have upheld laws forbidding adolescents access to cigarettes and to magazines that, although vulgar, are not considered so obscene that they are outlawed among adults (Zimring, 1982). Is there a pattern to this inconsistency? In general, legal decisions have tended to restrict the behavior of adolescents when the behavior in question is viewed as potentially damaging to the young person (buying cigarettes, for example) but have supported adolescent autonomy when the behavior is viewed as having potential benefit (using contraceptives).

RECAP

Changes in the individual's social definition at adolescence typically revolve around changes in status in four domains: interpersonal, political, economic, and legal (see table 3.1). In each of these domains, individuals are given greater privileges but are expected to take increased responsibility for self-management and social participation.

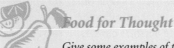 *Food for Thought*

Give some examples of the ways in which individuals' status changes in contemporary society as they move into and through adolescence.

Table 3.1   Some consequences of attaining adult status

	In Traditional Societies	In Contemporary Societies
Interpersonal	Addressed with adult title by other members of community	Permitted to sit with grown-ups for special occasions
Political	Permitted to participate in community decision making	Eligible to vote
Economic	Permitted to own property	Permitted to work
Legal	Permitted to consume certain foods	No longer dealt with in a separate juvenile justice system

THE PROCESS OF SOCIAL REDEFINITION

Social redefinition during adolescence is not a single event but a series of events that may occur over a relatively long time. In contemporary America, the process of redefinition typically begins at the age of 15 or 16, when the young person is first permitted to drive, to work, and to leave school. However, in most states, the social redefinition of the adolescent continues well into the young adult years. Some privileges, such as voting, are not conferred until the age of 18, and others, such as purchasing alcoholic beverages, are not conferred until the age of 21, five or six years after the redefinition process begins. Even in societies that mark the social redefinition of the young person with a dramatic and elaborate **initiation ceremony,** the social transformation of the individual from a child into an adult may span many years, and the initiation ceremony may represent just one element of the transition. In fact, the initiation ceremony usually marks the beginning of a long period of training and preparation for adulthood, rather than the adolescent's final passage into adult status (Cohen, 1964).

In many cultures, the social redefinition of young people occurs in groups. That is, the young people of a community are grouped with peers of approximately the same age—a *cohort*—and move through the series of status transitions together. One of the results of such age-grouped social transitions is that very strong bonds are formed among youngsters who have shared certain rituals. In many American high schools, for example, attempts are made to create class spirit or class unity by fostering bonds among students who will graduate together. In many Latino communities, adolescent girls together participate in an elaborate sort of coming-out celebration, called the **quinceañera.** On college campuses, fraternities and sororities may conduct group initiations that involve difficult or unpleasant tasks, and special ties may be forged between brothers or sisters who have pledged together.

The timetable for the process of social definition is highly variable within and across societies, and it is affected by economics, politics, and culture. For instance, research on rural youth growing up in America (e.g., Elder, Conger, Foster, & Ardelt, 1992; Schonert-Reichl & Elliott, 1994) points to the tremendous impact that the farm crisis of the 1980s had on youngsters' hopes and plans, which in turn affected their transition into adult roles. A poor economy compelled many rural youth to leave the communities in which they grew up, a decision that was often accompanied by feelings of depression and unhappiness (Elder, King, & Conger, 1996).

Social and political changes in Eastern Europe also have affected the nature of the adolescent transition, which, in turn, affects adolescents' well-being (Crockett & Silbereisen, 2000). One study of German adolescents after the unification of Germany, for example, found that youngsters who were recent immigrants from Eastern Europe had age expectations for various transitions (such as drinking alcohol without adults present and falling in love for the first time) that were, on average, about two years later than were the expectations of their West German–born counterparts or immigrants who had been living in unified Germany for a longer period of time (Schmitt-Rodermund & Silbereisen, 1993). Another study found that adolescents of European descent from the United States, Australia, and Hong Kong have faster timetables than do those of Asian descent (Feldman & Rosenthal, 1994).

Although the specific ceremonies, signs, and timetables of social redefinition during adolescence vary from one culture to another, several general themes characterize the process in all societies. First, social redefinition usually entails the *real or symbolic separation of the young person from his or her parents.* In traditional societies, this may take the form of **extrusion:** During late childhood, children are expected to begin sleeping in households other than their own. Youngsters may spend the day with their parents, but they spend the night with friends of the family, with relatives, or in a separate residence reserved for preadolescent youngsters (Cohen, 1964). In America, during earlier times, it was customary for adolescents to leave home temporarily and live with other families in the community, either to learn occupational skills (i.e., as apprentices) or to work as domestic servants (Kett, 1977). Interestingly, the placing out of adolescents from their parents' home often coincided with puberty (Katz, 1975). In contemporary societies, the separation of adolescents from their parents takes somewhat different forms. They are sent to summer camps, to boarding schools, or, as is more common, to college.

A second aspect of social redefinition during adolescence entails the *accentuation of physical and social differences between males and females* (Ford & Beach, 1951; Schlegel & Barry, 1991). This accentuation of differences occurs partly because of the physical changes of puberty and partly because adult work and family roles are generally highly sex-differentiated. Many societies separate

▲ *Formal rites of passage from childhood into adolescence or from adolescence into adulthood are rare in contemporary society. Certain religious ceremonies, such as the confirmation or the Bar Mitzvah (pictured here), are as close as we come to initiation rites in contemporary America.* (Peter Southwick/ Stock, Boston)

males and females during religious ceremonies, have individuals begin wearing sex-specific articles of clothing (rather than clothing permissible for either gender), and keep males and females apart during initiation ceremonies. Some traditional societies practice what is called **brother-sister avoidance:** After puberty, a brother and sister may not have any direct contact or interaction until one or both are married (Cohen, 1964).

The separation of males and females in adolescence is not limited to traditional societies. In earlier times in America (and to a certain extent in many other industrialized societies today), males and females were separated during adolescence in educational institutions, either by excluding adolescent girls from secondary and higher education, grouping males and females in different schools or different classrooms, or having males and females follow different curricula. In present-day America, many of these practices have been discontinued because of legal rulings prohibiting discrimination, but some elements of accentuated sex differentiation and sex segregation during adolescence still exist: in residential arrangements, in styles of dress, in athletic activities, and in household chores (Hill & Lynch, 1983; Medrich, Roizen, Rubin, & Buckley, 1982; White & Brinkerhoff, 1981). And many contemporary ceremonies designed to recognize the young person's passage into adulthood either are limited to one sex (e.g., debutante balls or the quinceañera, each of which is for young women) or differentiate between males and females (e.g., the **Bar Mitzvah** and the **Bas Mitzvah** ceremonies for Jewish males and females, respectively).

Third, social redefinition during adolescence typically entails the *passing on of cultural, historical, and practical information* from the adult generation to the newly inducted cohort of young people. This information may concern (1) matters thought to be important to adults but of limited utility to children (for example, information about the performance of certain adult work tasks); (2) matters thought to be necessary for adults but unfit for children (for example, information regarding sex); or (3) matters concerning the history or rituals of the family or community (for example, how to perform certain ceremonies). In traditional societies, initiates are often sent to some sort of "school," in which they are instructed in the productive activities of the community (hunting, fishing, farming). Following puberty, boys and girls receive instruction about sexual relations, moral behavior, and societal lore (Fried & Fried, 1980; Miller, 1928).

In contemporary society, too, adolescence is a time of instruction in preparation for adulthood. Elementary school students, for example, are generally not taught a great deal about sexuality, work, or financial matters; such coursework is typically reserved for high school students. We also restrict entrance into certain "adult" activities (such as attending sexually explicit movies) until the adolescent is believed to be old enough to be exposed to them.

Because formal initiation ceremonies are neither very common nor very meaningful in modern society, students sometimes overlook important similarities between the processes of social redefinition in traditional and contemporary societies. Practices such as extrusion, brother-sister avoidance, and **scarification** (the intentional creation of scars on a part or parts of the body, often done as part of an initiation ceremony) are alien and seem odd to us. However, if we look beneath the surface, at the meaning and significance of each culture's practices, we find many common threads. In contemporary society, for example, our own form of brother-sister avoidance begins at puberty: Once adolescents have reached puberty, brothers and sisters are more likely to seek privacy from each other when dressing or bathing. And, although we do not practice anything as "alien" as scarification, we do have our share of body rituals, which often are not seen until adolescence and which might seem equally alien to someone unfamiliar with our society: the punching of holes in earlobes and other parts of the body (ear or body piercing), the scraping of hair from faces and legs (shaving), the permanent decoration of skin (tattoos), and the application of brightly colored paints to lips, eyes, and cheeks (makeup).

RECAP

Certain themes are common to the process of social redefinition across many societies. These include the real or symbolic separation of young people from their parents; the accentuation of differences between males and females; and the passing on of cultural, historical, or practical information deemed important for adulthood.

Food for Thought

Social redefinition in contemporary society is often so familiar that we overlook it. Can you think of examples of social definition practices within your own community that parallel practices in more traditional cultures?

VARIATIONS IN SOCIAL TRANSITIONS

Different societies recognize and orchestrate the passage into adult status at different times and in different ways. In this respect, although the presence of social redefinition in a general sense is a universal feature of adolescent development, there is considerable diversity in the nature of the transition. Examining social redefinition from cross-cultural and historical perspectives provides a valuable means of contrasting the nature of adolescence in different social contexts. Two very important dimensions along which societies differ in the process of social redefinition are in the explicitness, or *clarity*, of the transition and in the smoothness, or *continuity*, of the passage.

Variations in Clarity

Initiation ceremonies are in many ways religious ceremonies. As such, they are most often used in societies in which a shared religious belief unites the community and structures individuals' daily experiences. Universal, formal initiation ceremonies, therefore, have never been prevalent in American society, largely because of the diversity of the population and the general separation of religious experience from everyday affairs.

There are, however, factors other than the presence of formal rites of passage that determine how clear the transition into adult status is to the young person and society. One such factor concerns the extent to which various aspects of the status change occur at about the same time for an individual and during the same general time period for adolescents growing up together (Elder, 1980). When transitions into adult work, family, and citizenship roles occur close in time, and when most members of a cohort experience these transitions at about the same age, the passage into adulthood takes on greater clarity. If all young people were to graduate from high school, enter the labor force, and marry at the age of 18, this age would be an implicit boundary between adolescence and adulthood, even without a formal ceremony. However, when different aspects of the passage occur at different times, and when adolescents growing up in a similar environment experience these transitions in a different order and along different schedules, the boundary between adolescence and adulthood is made more cloudy.

● **The Clarity of Social Redefinition in Contemporary American Society** When did you become an adolescent? When did you (or when will you) become an adult? If you are like most individuals in contemporary society, your answers to these questions are not clear-cut. We have no formal ceremonies marking the transition from childhood into adolescence, nor do we have any to mark the passage from adolescence into adulthood. Although in many religious, cultural, and social groups young adolescents undergo an initiation ceremony of sorts—the confirmation, the Bar Mitzvah, the quinceañera, and the coming-out parties of debutantes are some examples—rarely does such a rite have much significance outside the youngsters' family, circle of friends, or religious community. School graduation ceremonies perhaps come the closest to universal rites of passage in contemporary society, but school graduation does not bring with it many meaningful or universal changes in social status, responsibilities, or privileges. As a result, social redefinition in contemporary society does not give the adolescent any clear indication of when his or her responsibilities and privileges as an adult begin.

Attaining adult status is essentially an individual matter in contemporary society, and the absence of

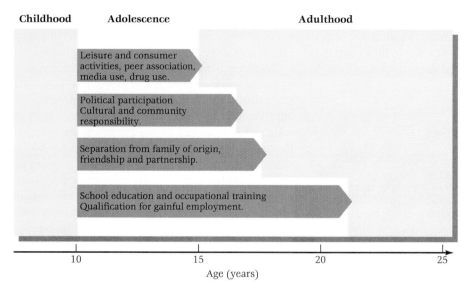

Childhood   Adolescence   Adulthood

Leisure and consumer activities, peer association, media use, drug use.

Political participation Cultural and community responsibility.

Separation from family of origin, friendship and partnership.

School education and occupational training Qualification for gainful employment.

10   15   20   25

Age (years)

Figure 3.1   In contemporary society, different aspects of the passage into adulthood occur at different ages. (Chisholm & Hurrelmann, 1995)

clear-cut and universal markers of the passage make the process confusing. It is often difficult for young people to tell when they have reached adulthood. As figure 3.1 illustrates, some aspects of the passage into adulthood are complete by age 15, whereas others may last well into the early twenties. Even laws governing what individuals can, and cannot, do, are inconsistent. In many states, for example, the age for starting employment is 15; for leaving high school, 16; for attending restricted (R-rated) movies without parents, 17; for voting, 18; and, for drinking, 21.

In short, we have few universal markers of adulthood—adolescents are treated as adults at different times by different people in different contexts (Alsaker, 1995; Arnett & Taber, 1994). A young person may be legally old enough to drive, but his parents may feel that 16 is too early and may refuse to let him use the family car. Another may be treated like an adult at work, where she works side-by-side with people three times her age, but she may be treated like a child at home. A third may be viewed as an adult by her mother but as a child by her father. It is little wonder, in light of the mixed and sometimes contradictory expectations facing young people, that for many adolescents the transition into adult roles is a difficult passage to navigate. In the middle of the twentieth century, social psychologist Kurt Lewin (1948) introduced the term **marginal man** to describe the adolescent's position in society—caught in a transitional space between childhood and adulthood. Many commentators believe that adolescents continue to be marginalized today.

Because contemporary society does not send clear or consistent messages to young people about when adolescence ends and adulthood begins, it is possible for young people living within the same society to have widely varying views of their own social status and beliefs about age-appropriate behavior (Arnett, 1994; Nurmi, 1993). For this reason, it is instructive to ask people what they *think* defines the transition to adulthood, as a way of gauging the way in which adult status is conceptualized by the broader society. Psychologist Jeffrey Arnett has examined conceptions of adulthood in contemporary North America and has contrasted this with the ways in which adult status has been viewed in other cultures and at other points in time (Arnett, 1998). His analysis points to three interesting trends.

First, in modern industrialized society, there is less of an emphasis than in traditional societies (i.e., those with limited industry) on the attainment of specific roles (e.g., worker, spouse, parent) as defining characteristics of adulthood and more emphasis on the development of various character traits indicative of self-reliance (e.g., responsible, independent, self-controlled). For example, among contemporary American youth, "accepting responsibility for one's self" was the most frequently mentioned criterion, whereas among Inuit adolescents in the Canadian Arctic, the most important was the establishment of a marriagelike relationship by moving into a separate household with a prospective mate. Of the role-related transitions viewed as important among contemporary youth, being able to support oneself financially was the most important defining criterion of adulthood. Perhaps for this reason, less than

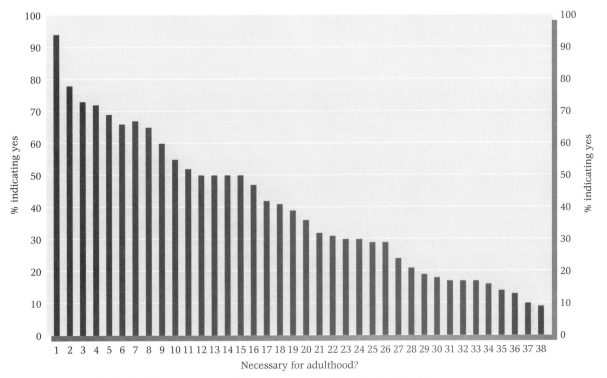

1. Accept responsibility for the consequences of your actions
2. Decide on personal beliefs and values independently of parents or other influences
3. Financially independent from parents
4. Capable of running a household (man)
5. Establish a relationship with parents as an equal adult
6. Avoid committing petty crimes like shoplifting and vandalism
7. Capable of running a household (woman)
8. Use contraception if sexually active and not trying to conceive a child
9. No longer living in parents' household
10. Avoid drunk driving
11. Capable of keeping family physically safe (man)
12. Learn always to have good control of your emotions
13. Capable of supporting a family financially (man)
14. Capable of caring for children (woman)
15. Capable of caring for children (man)
16. Capable of keeping family physically safe (woman)
17. Capable of supporting a family financially (woman)
18. Avoid using illegal drugs
19. Reached age 18
20. Make lifelong commitments to others
21. Drive an automobile safely and close to the speed limit
22. Reached age 21
23. Avoid becoming drunk
24. Capable of fathering children (man)
25. Capable of bearing children (woman)
26. Have no more than one sexual partner
27. Obtained driver's license
28. Settle into a long-term career
29. Not deeply tied to parents emotionally
30. Avoid using profanity/vulgar language
31. Married
32. Employed full-time
33. Purchased a house
34. Committed to a long-term love relationship
35. Have at least one child
36. Grow to full height
37. Finished with education
38. Have had sexual intercourse

Figure 3.2   *Contemporary young adults' notions of what defines adulthood emphasize personality traits more than role transitions.* (Arnett, 1998)

one-third of college undergraduates see themselves unambiguously as adults (Arnett, 1998).

Second, over time, there has been a striking decline in the importance of family roles—marriage and parenthood—as defining features of the transition from adolescence to adulthood. In early American society, for example, the role of head of household was an especially important indicator of adult status for males, and

entering the roles of wife and mother defined adulthood for females. In contrast, in Arnett's surveys of contemporary youth, in which he asked whether certain accomplishments were necessary for an individual to be considered an adult, only 17 percent of the respondents indicated that being married was necessary, and only 14 percent indicated that it was necessary to become a parent (Arnett, 1998). (See figure 3.2.)

Finally, the defining criteria of adulthood have become more or less the same for males and females in contemporary industrialized society, unlike the case in traditional societies or during previous eras. In nonindustrialized cultures, the requirements for male adulthood were to be able to "provide, protect, and procreate," whereas, for females, the requirements for adulthood were to care for children and run a household. Contemporary youth, in contrast, view the various indicators of adult status as equally important (or equally unimportant) for males and females (Arnett, 1998).

Given the absence of clear criteria that define adult status in contemporary North America, it is little surprise that, among people of the same age, some may feel older than their chronological agemates, whereas others might feel less mature. How old an adolescent feels affects his or her behavior; adolescents who feel older spend more time with opposite-sex peers, feel more autonomous, spend more time with antisocial peers, and engage in more problem behavior. Interestingly, in one study, the highest levels of problem behavior were reported by boys who felt markedly older than their actual age (Galambos, Kolaric, Sears, & Maggs, 1999).

● The Clarity of Social Redefinition in Traditional Cultures
Unlike the case in contemporary society, social redefinition during adolescence is clearly recognized in most traditional cultures. Typically, the passage from childhood into adolescence is marked by a formal initiation ceremony, which publicly proclaims the young person's entrance into a new position in the community (Ford & Beach, 1951). For boys, such ceremonies take place at the time of puberty, at the attainment of a designated chronological age, or at a time when the community decides that the individual is ready for the status change. For girls, initiation is more often linked to puberty and, in particular, to the onset of menstruation. In both cases, the initiation ceremony ritualizes the passing of the young person out of childhood and, if not directly into adulthood, into a period of training for it.

In many initiation ceremonies, the adolescent's physical appearance is changed, so that other members of the community can distinguish between initiated and uninitiated young people. For example, new types of clothing may be worn following initiation, or some sort of surgical operation or scarification may be performed to create a permanent means of marking the individual's adult status. In most traditional societies,

there is no mistaking which individuals are adults and which are still children.

● The Clarity of Social Redefinition in Previous Eras
The transition into adulthood may actually have been even more disorderly and cloudy during the early nineteenth century than it is today. According to historian Joseph Kett (1977), many young people at that time moved back and forth between school, where they were viewed as children, and work, where they were viewed as adults. Moreover, timetables for the assumption of adult roles varied considerably from one individual to the next, because those roles were highly dependent on family and household needs rather than on generally accepted age patterns of school, family, and work transitions. Adolescents might have been working and living away from home, but if the family needed them—because, let's say, someone became ill—they would leave the job and move back in with their parents. During the middle of the nineteenth century, in fact, many young people were neither enrolled in school nor working, occupying a halfway stage that was not quite childhood but not quite adulthood (Katz, 1975). Industrialization excluded many young people from the labor force, and only adolescents from affluent families were able to afford private school. Descriptions of adolescent idleness during that era are strikingly reminiscent of descriptions of unemployed, out-of-school youth today. Indeed, concern about juvenile misbehavior was one factor that encouraged the development of public high schools.

One study comparing adolescents' transitions today with those of their counterparts 100 years ago indicates that the passage into adulthood may have been more prolonged as well as less clearly defined during the nineteenth century than it is today. Using census data and historical documents, social historian John Modell and his colleagues compared the timing and patterning of adolescents' transitions in 1970 with those in 1880 (Modell, Furstenberg, & Hershberg, 1976). The researchers examined five transitions, all of which can be thought of as indicators of the passage into adulthood: exit from school, entry into the labor force, departure from home, first marriage, and establishment of an independent household. They were interested in the extent to which these transitions were negotiated along a common timetable and clustered around a narrow age period.

Compared with contemporary youth, adolescents living in the late nineteenth century underwent family-

Age (years) at time of transition

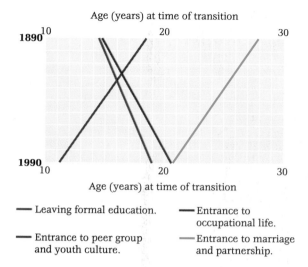

Figure 3.3   *A century ago, the passage into adulthood may have been even more prolonged and less clear than it is today.* (Chisholm & Hurrelmann, 1995)

— Leaving formal education.

— Entrance to peer group and youth culture.

— Entrance to occupational life.

— Entrance to marriage and partnership.

RECAP

The process of social definition varies from society to society in its clarity. In some societies, as well as within certain religious and cultural groups, adolescence is marked by a formal initiation ceremony and specific rites of passage, which clearly mark the redefinition of the individual. In others, however, the transition from childhood into adulthood is vague and poorly defined. This absence of clarity is especially the case in industrialized societies.

Food for Thought

Explain how societies vary in the clarity with which they recognize the transition from childhood to adulthood. Are there steps that could be taken in contemporary society to make the transition clearer than it presently is?

related transitions (leaving home, getting married, and setting up an independent household) somewhat later, and they made school- and work-related transitions (leaving school and entering the labor force) much earlier. As figure 3.3 indicates, the passages into the work and family roles of adulthood were much more spread out over time a century ago. Over the past 100 years, however, the timing of family-related and nonfamily-related transitions have converged, and the age range during which young people make these transitions is narrower and more universal now than it was 100 years ago (Chisholm & Hurrelmann, 1995; Modell & Goodman, 1990). Interestingly, though, there are some sex differences in the way in which different elements of the transition are ordered, as the box on pages 108-109 describes.

In this respect, it appears as though the transition into adult status today has greater uniformity, if not greater clarity, than it did during much of the nineteenth century. As Modell and his colleagues suggest, those "who see today's period of youth as extended, normless, [and] lacking bounds" would do well to compare the structure of the adolescent passage as it exists today with that of 100 years ago (Modell et al., 1976, p. 31). Although the notion of "emerging adulthood" (e.g., Arnett, 2000) may ring true today as a way of describing the prolonged transition into adult roles experienced by many young people, it is by no means a new phenomenon.

Variations in Continuity

Well-known anthropologist Ruth Benedict (1934), after surveying many societies, pointed out that a second way in which the process of social redefinition varies across cultural and historical contexts is along the dimension of *continuity*—the extent to which the adolescent's transition into adulthood is gradual or abrupt. Gradual transitions, in which the adolescent assumes the roles and status of adulthood bit by bit, are referred to as **continuous transitions.** Transitions that are not so smooth, and in which the young person's entrance into adulthood is more sudden, are referred to as **discontinuous transitions.** Children who grow up working on the family farm and continue this work as adults have a continuous transition into adult work roles. In contrast, children who do not have any work experience while they are growing up and who enter the labor force for the first time when they graduate from college have a discontinuous transition into adult work roles.

● **The Continuity of the Adolescent Passage in Contemporary Society**   In contemporary society, we tend to exclude young people from the world of adults; we give them little direct training for adult life and then thrust them rather abruptly into total adult independence. Transitions into adulthood in contemporary society are therefore more discontinuous than in other cultural or

The Sexes

Similarities and Differences in the Transition into Adulthood

The transition from adolescence to adulthood in America is marked by several related changes in social roles. Among the most important events in this transition are the completion of formal schooling, the entrance into the full-time labor force, marriage, and parenthood. One way to think about the transition into adulthood, therefore, is to think about the transition out of one role (student) and into three other roles (worker, spouse, and parent) (Marini, 1984).

Because these four transitions do not occur simultaneously, it is interesting to ask how they might be related to one another over time. Do most individuals finish school before taking on a full-time job, or does entry into the world of work precede leaving school? How do transitions into family roles, such as spouse and parent, link up with nonfamily transitions? For instance, do individuals become adults in nonfamily roles (that is, by leaving school and entering the workforce) before or after they become adults with respect to family roles? Is one sequence more common than another?

Sociologist Margaret Marini has examined these questions by looking at the way in which role transitions during young adulthood are ordered in contemporary America. Using data collected as a part of a longitudinal follow-up of individuals who had been high school students during the late 1950s, Marini was able to look at the relations among the role transitions out of school and into work, marriage, and parenthood. Although Marini found that about half of all males and females followed one particular sequence of role transitions, she also found several important differences between males' and females' patterns that have implications for understanding sex differences in educational and occupational attainment.

The most common sequence followed for both sexes was (1) exit from school, (2) entrance into work, (3) entrance into marriage, and (4) entrance into parenthood. But half of all the individuals did not follow this "normative" path toward adulthood. One-fifth of the women and nearly one-third of the men had taken a full-

historical contexts. Consider, for example, three of the most important roles of adulthood that individuals are expected to carry out successfully—worker, parent, and citizen. Adolescents in contemporary society receive little preparation for all three positions. For instance, young people are segregated from the workplace throughout most of their childhood and early adolescent years and receive little direct training in school relevant to the work roles they will likely find themselves in as adults. The transition into adult work roles, therefore, is fairly discontinuous—and often difficult—for most young people in industrialized society. And, according to former U.S. Secretary of Labor Ray Marshall, writing with his colleague, Robert Glover, "America has the worst approach to school-to-work transition of *any* industrialized nation" (Glover & Marshall, 1993, p. 588, italics added).

During the early 1990s, and with the enthusiastic backing of President Clinton, many American educa-

tors and policymakers began calling for changes in our educational system in order to improve the **school-to-work transition** (e.g., Kazis, 1993; Rosenbaum et al., 1992; Stern, Finkelstein, Stone, Latting, & Dornsife, 1994). These writers argued that many individuals have difficulty making this transition successfully because there really exists only one acceptable way of making this passage—through higher education—and not all individuals can, or want to, make the transition via this route. Moreover, this transition is inherently discontinuous, which makes it harder to negotiate.

However, is it possible to create a route from high school to adult work that doesn't involve college? Many critics of the American educational system say that it is. They point out that, in other industrialized countries, many different possibilities for high school students exist other than going to college—including, most important, the option of taking a formal

time job before finishing school; some worked while in school, and others left school for a time and returned later. One-fifth of the women and nearly one-quarter of the men married before finishing school, and about 1 in 10 men and women had married and become parents before their education was finished.

In general, the longer an individual stayed in school, the less likely he or she was to follow the expected sequence—primarily because longer schooling made it more likely that at least one of the transitions would occur before education was completed. At the turn of the century, for example, the average age by which most individuals had completed school was still a few years younger than the average age by which even the youngest members of the generation had married. By 1930, however, individuals were staying in school longer and marrying earlier, so that there were large numbers of individuals who were leaving school and marrying at about the same age. By 1960, these trends had continued to the point where substantial numbers of individuals were marrying before finishing their education. Although between 1960 and 1980 the tendency toward younger and younger marriages that had characterized the first half of the century began to reverse itself, the average age at which individuals completed their education continued to increase. As a result, the time frame within which individuals finished school and got married remained fairly narrow (Modell & Goodman, 1990).

A similar pattern is found in individuals' entrance into the labor force. Although individuals are staying in school longer than they did 100 years ago, they have barely delayed their entry into the labor force. These findings counter the widely held belief that entering into work or family commitments before finishing school necessarily impedes educational attainment. As Marini notes, more research is needed on the long-term occupational experiences of students who marry or work before completing school.

Why have men been somewhat more likely than women to combine their schooling with work or family commitments? Women who went on to higher levels of education were especially likely to delay taking on family roles. Marini suggests that women's traditional family roles—and, in particular, their greater involvement in domestic responsibilities—make it more difficult for them to move between student and nonstudent roles and make marriage and parenthood "less compatible with the continuation of education for women than for men" (Marini, 1984, p. 78). As she writes, "Although for men the continuation of education does not permit direct fulfillment of the traditional male role of provider, because of its future payoff for the well-being of the family, it is viewed as an investment in the family's future. Women's educational and occupational pursuits tend to be viewed as secondary to those of their husbands" (p. 78). Put simply, men find it easier than women to become both spouse and parent while still in school. Because becoming a spouse and parent interrupts the process of educational attainment more for women than for men, it may be more important for women to delay taking on family roles until after they have finished school, or they risk compromising their careers. Indeed, Marini has pointed out that the earlier transition into parenthood among women than men and its greater educational cost for women are main factors in the generally lower occupational attainment of women. Although it is possible for men and women to marry and become parents before they stop being students, the costs of deviating from the "normative" sequence are not equal for the two sexes.

youth apprenticeship; this provides structured, work-based learning, which likely leads to a high-quality job. Typically, a high school student combines time in an apprenticeship with time in school as he or she gradually makes the transition from school to work. Among the most successful models of youth apprenticeships are those developed in Germany, in which young people during their last few years of high school can spend one or two days per week in school and the remainder of the week at a job supervised by master workers. Unlike American high school students, who have difficulty finding good jobs after graduation, German graduates who complete a youth apprenticeship program usually enter a high-quality job within a few days of finishing school (Rosenbaum et al., 1992). Although some writers have questioned whether the German model can be copied directly in the United States, there is hope that a version of an apprenticeship system can be developed successfully in America. At the very least, some critics have argued that for many young people in the United States, high school as it now exists is far too long (Botstein, 1997).

Actually, the transition of young people into adult family roles is even more abrupt than is their transition into work roles. Before actually becoming a parent, most young people have little training in child rearing and other related matters. Families are relatively small today, and youngsters are likely to be close in age to their siblings; as a result, few opportunities exist for participating in child-care activities at home. Schools generally offer little, if any, instruction in family relationships and domestic activities. And, with childbirth generally taking place in hospitals rather than at home, few young people today have the opportunity of observing a younger sibling's birth.

Passage into adult citizenship and decision-making roles is also highly discontinuous in contemporary Western society. Adolescents are permitted few opportunities for independence and autonomy in school and are segregated from most of society's political institutions until they complete their formal education. Young people are permitted to vote once they turn 18 years old, but they have received little preparation for participation in government and community roles before this time.

Nearly 70 years ago, anthropologist Ruth Benedict (1934) pointed out that the degree of stress individuals experience at adolescence is related to the degree of continuity they experience in making the transition into adulthood; the more discontinuous the passage, the more stressful it is likely to be. Benedict's view suggests that adolescent turmoil, if it exists, is more likely a consequence of environmental than biological factors.

It is of little surprise, then, that some young people today have difficulty in assuming adult roles and responsibilities. Instead of being gradually socialized into work, family, and citizenship positions, adolescents in modern society typically are segregated from activities in these arenas during most of their childhood and youth, yet young people are supposed to be able to perform these roles capably on reaching the age of majority. With little preparation in meaningful work, adolescents are expected to find, get, and keep a job immediately after completing their schooling. With essentially no training for marriage or parenting, they are expected to form their own families, manage their own households, and raise their own children soon after they reach adulthood. And, without any previous involvement in community activities, they are expected on reaching the age of majority to vote, pay taxes, and behave as responsible citizens.

● **The Continuity of the Adolescent Passage in Traditional Cultures**   The high level of discontinuity found in contemporary America is not characteristic of adolescence in traditional societies. Consider the socialization of young people in Samoa, for example. From early childhood on, youngsters are involved in work tasks that have a meaningful connection to the work they will perform as adults. They are involved in the care of younger children, in the planting and harvesting of crops, and in the gathering and preparation of food. Their entrance into adult work roles is gradual and continuous, with work tasks being graded to children's skills and intelligence. Young people are charged with

the socialization of their infant brothers and sisters, particularly during middle childhood, when they are not yet strong enough to make a substantial contribution to the community's fishing and farming activities. Gradually, young people are taught the fundamentals of weaving, boating, fishing, building, and farming. By the time they have reached late adolescence, Samoan youngsters are well trained in the tasks they will need to perform as adults (Mead, 1928).

Such continuity is generally the case in societies in which hunting, fishing, and farming are the chief work activities. As Margaret Mead (1928) observed, the emphasis in these societies is on informal education in context, rather than on formal education in schools. Children are typically not isolated in separate educational institutions, and they accompany the adult members of their community in daily activities. Adolescents' preparation for adulthood, therefore, comes largely from observation and hands-on experience in the same tasks that they will continue to carry out as adults. Typically, boys learn the tasks performed by adult men, and girls learn those performed by adult women. When work activities take adults out of the community, it is not uncommon for children to travel with their parents on work expeditions (Miller, 1928).

● **The Continuity of the Adolescent Passage in Previous Eras**   During earlier periods in American history, the transition into adult roles and responsibilities began at an earlier age and proceeded along a more continuous path than generally is the case today. This is especially true with regard to work. During the eighteenth century, of course, and well into the early part of the nineteenth century, when many families were engaged in farming, a good number of adolescents were expected to work on the family farm and to learn the skills necessary to carry on the enterprise. Some youngsters, generally boys, accompanied their fathers on business trips, learning the trades of sales and commerce (Kett, 1977)—a pattern reminiscent of that found in many traditional societies.

Many other young people left home relatively early—some as early as age 12—to work for nonfamilial adults in the community or in nearby villages (Katz, 1975; Kett, 1977). Even as recently as the midnineteenth century, it was common for young adolescents to work as apprentices, learning skills and trades in preparation for the work roles of adulthood; others left home temporarily to work as servants or to learn domestic skills. The average nineteenth-century youngster in Europe

▲ *In societies in which hunting, farming, and fishing are the primary work activities, young people often are taught the skills they will need as adult workers by accompanying—and observing—their elders in daily activities rather than by attending school.* (Owen Franken/Stock, Boston)

and America left school well before the age of 15 (Chisholm & Hurrelmann, 1995; Modell, Furstenberg, & Hershberg, 1976).

However, census data and historical documents—such as letters, diaries, and community histories—indicate that, although adolescents of 100 years ago took on full-time employment earlier in life than they typically do today, they were likely to live under adult supervision for a longer period than is usual in contemporary society. That is, although the transition into work roles may have occurred earlier in the nineteenth century than in the twentieth century, this transition was made in the context of semi-independence, rather than complete emancipation (Katz, 1975; Kett, 1977; Modell & Goodman, 1990). This semi-independent period—which for many young people spanned the decade from about ages 12 to 22, and even beyond—may have increased the degree of continuity of the passage into adulthood by providing a time during which young people could assume certain adult responsibilities gradually (Katz, 1975). The semi-independence characteristic of adolescence in the nineteenth century had

largely disappeared by 1900, however (Modell & Goodman, 1990).

Socialization for family and citizenship roles may also have been more continuous in previous historical eras. Living at home during the late-adolescent and early-adult years, particularly in the larger families characteristic of households 100 years ago, contributed to the preparation of young people for future family life. It was common for the children in a family to span a wide age range, and remaining at home undoubtedly placed the older adolescent from time to time in child-rearing roles (President's Science Advisory Committee, 1974). As opposed to today's adolescents, who typically have little experience with infants, adolescents 100 years ago were more likely to have fed, dressed, and cared for their younger siblings. They were also expected to assist their parents in maintaining the household (Modell et al., 1976), and this experience probably made it easier for young people to manage when they eventually established a home separate from their parents. Leaving one's parents' home earlier and living independently before marriage encourages young women

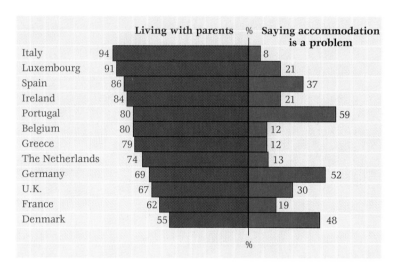

Figure 3.4 *In many industrialized countries, a significant percentage of youth live with their parents well into their midtwenties. Note the wide variation in the proportion of youth in various countries who consider this a problem.* (Chisholm & Hurrelmann, 1995)

to develop less traditional attitudes, values, and plans than their counterparts who live with their parents as young adults (Waite, Goldscheider, & Witsberger, 1986). Interestingly, individuals from single-parent homes, stepfamilies, adoptive families, and foster homes tend to leave home at an earlier age than do their peers whose biological parents remain married (Aquilino, 1991; Mitchell, Wister, & Burch, 1989).

Recent reports of changes in home-leaving are noteworthy, however, and suggest that this aspect of the transition into adulthood may be changing in many industrialized countries: On average, individuals are living with their parents longer today than was the case 40 years ago; more than half of all U.S. 18- to 24-year-olds (nearly 60 percent of males, and about 50 percent of females) either live with or are supported by their parents—up from 40 percent in 1960 (U.S. Bureau of the Census, 1999). Most experts attribute this trend to the increased cost of housing, which makes it difficult for individuals to move out of their parents' home (or give up their parents' financial support) and establish a separate residence. A similar trend has taken place in Western Europe, where there was a substantial increase during the 1980s in the proportion of youth who were living with their parents well into their midtwenties (Chisholm & Hurrelmann, 1995) (see figure 3.4). In several countries, as figure 3.4 indicates, this living arrangement is not something young people are very happy about.

The current impact of the economy on adolescents' home-leaving reaffirms the importance of looking at the broader context in defining what normal adolescence is. In 1960, because it was the exception to live at home past high school, individuals who did so were usually viewed as being less independent or less mature than their peers. However, now that living at home has become the norm, it is no longer viewed as an index of maturity. Above all, we need to keep in mind that, because adolescence is in part defined by society, its nature changes along with society.

Recent economic changes in many postindustrial societies have had a particularly strong effect on the expectations and plans of working-class adolescents (Bettis, 1996) and those living in rural areas (Crockett & Bingham, 2000). Many such teenagers are anxious and uncertain about their future, given the shrinking number of well-paying, blue-collar jobs and the limited economic opportunities for individuals without a college degree. One researcher, after interviewing working-class students in an urban high school, put it this way:

The old rules of the industrial order no longer apply, but the new rules of a postindustrial society, if there are any, are not yet in place. The majority of students know that there are no industrial jobs for them. They know that they cannot follow their parents to the factories of the North End, for these factories have downsized or relocated. Many have watched their parents and relatives lose their supposedly secure and lifelong industrial jobs. . . .

The students have also seen their older friends either unemployed or working in low-skill, low-paying jobs, including those in fast-food restaurants, valet parking, security, retail, and telemarketing. Many students do not want these types of jobs and the future with which they are associated. But what are their options? Many say that they must and will attend college; however, with their low grade-point-averages, their failure to

▲ *Major historical events, such as the Great Depression, may temporarily alter the transition to adulthood. During the Depression, many adolescent boys had to leave school and enter the workforce full-time at an unusually early age. Many adolescent girls also were forced to leave school early, in order to assume adult responsibilities at home.* (Bettmann Newsphotos)

pass the ninth grade–level state-mandated proficiency tests, and little knowledge of how to apply to colleges, their chances of entering and graduating from college are small.

One student put it this way:

Interviewer: Do you ever talk about your future career and educational plans with friends your own age?
Scott: Yeah.
Interviewer: What do they say?
Scott: Well, that is, they don't have any motivation.
Interviewer: No motivation?
Scott: No. They just say, well, go up to, get out of high school and then, they haven't got no plans. (Bettis, 1996, p. 111)

Indeed, some massive historical events, such as the 1991 war in the Persian Gulf and the economic reces-

sion of the early 1980s, may temporarily alter the nature of the adolescent passage and may produce exceptions to general historical trends. One such event was the Great Depression of the early 1930s. Sociologist Glen Elder, Jr., has examined the impact of growing up during this era on adolescents' behavior and development (Elder, 1974), and many of his findings are relevant to the issue of continuity in the adolescent passage. Elder looked at the data collected during the Depression as part of a longitudinal study of individuals living in Oakland, California. The group Elder focused on was born between 1920 and 1921 and thus were preadolescents during the worst years of the Depression.

Elder found that the youngsters whose families experienced economic hardship during these years were more likely to be involved in adultlike tasks at an earlier age than were their more privileged peers. The boys, for example, were more likely to work and to help support their

The Scientific Study of Adolescence

Does Leaving Home Too Early Cause Problems for Adolescents?

Scientists often have difficulty in determining whether two factors that are associated with each other, or correlated, have any causal connection to each other. For example, we might find that smart people eat a great deal of fish (i.e., that intelligence and eating fish are correlated), but it wouldn't necessarily be correct to conclude on the basis of this finding that eating fish causes people to become smarter. It might be the case, instead, that smart people are more aware of the nutritional benefits of eating seafood and choose to eat seafood more often—in which case, we might be correct in saying that being smart causes people to eat more fish. Or another factor—living near the ocean, for example—may be associated both with being smart and with eating fish, making it only appear that intelligence and fish eating are independently related. It is far more difficult to demonstrate that one thing causes another than to show that the two are merely correlated.

An example of the difference between correlation and causation is found in a study of early home-leaving and problem behavior (Stattin & Magnusson, 1994a). The researchers followed a sample of urban youth from Solna, a community near Stockholm, from birth onward. All the individuals had been born between 1955 and 1958. Data were collected each year during the children's first 18 years of life and again at the ages of 21, 25, and 36 years. The median age for leaving home in this sample was 18 for girls and 20 for boys (a **median** is a type of average, defined as the score above and below which there are equal numbers of people in a sample) (see accompanying figure). In the study of home-leaving, the researchers focused their attention on females.

When the researchers computed the correlation between age of leaving home and various indicators of the women's behavioral adjustment, they discovered that earlier home-leaving was associated, in young adulthood, with earlier marriage, more childbearing, and lower educational attainment, measured in terms of years of school completed. But did

families; the girls were more likely to play a major role with household chores. And both the boys and the girls were more likely to marry and enter into full-time employment relatively early. Thus, some aspects of the semi-independent stage of adolescence that had become uncommon by 1930 may have reappeared during the Great Depression. For many youngsters growing up during this time period, the adolescent passage may have resembled that of an earlier era.

Research on contemporary German and Polish youngsters by Rainer Silbereisen and his colleagues (Silbereisen, Schwarz, Nowak, Kracke, & von Eye, 1993) indicates that, still today, growing up under adversity is associated with an earlier transition into adult roles and behaviors. Whether "earlier" means "better" is a matter of some debate, however; as you will read in chapter 8, some writers believe that adolescents profit psychologically from having a relatively long period of time to develop without being burdened by adult responsibilities.

RECAP

In addition to the clarity of the adolescent passage, societies also vary in the extent to which the passage is continuous or discontinuous. In a continuous passage, the adolescent assumes the roles and status of adulthood bit by bit, with a good deal of preparation and training along the way. In a discontinuous passage, the adolescent is thrust into adulthood abruptly, with little prior preparation. Contemporary industrialized societies generally are characterized by a discontinuous passage into adulthood.

Food for Thought

Many commentators have remarked on the tremendous discontinuity characteristic of the adolescent transition in modern society. However, in light of the nature of adult roles in contemporary society, is it really possible to make the transition more continuous than it currently is?

114

leaving home early *cause* these outcomes? Before you conclude that it did, think about the difference between correlation and causation.

Because the researchers had collected data throughout the women's lives, they were able to examine the correlation between various indicators of adjustment during childhood and early adolescence and the age of leaving home later on. The results showed that the young women who chose to leave home earlier than their peers may have been different from their agemates long before leaving home. The women who left home relatively early had shown, throughout childhood and early adolescence, more strained family relations, poorer adjustment, more impulsivity, more aggression, higher rates of school problems, lower educational aspirations, more drug and alcohol use, earlier sexual activity, and more sexual partners. Instead of early home-leaving causing lower educational attainment, then, it appears as though having more modest educational plans precedes early home-leaving. In other words, girls who have lower educational aspirations by midadolescence may complete less school and may also choose to leave home early. By the same token, girls who are more sexually active than their peers may marry earlier and may also choose to leave home early.

As the old social science maxim goes, "correlation is not causation."

Source: Stattin, H., & Magnusson, C. (1996). Leaving home at an early age among female adolescents: Antecedents, adolescent adjustment, and future life implications. *New Directions for Child Development, 71*, 53–69.

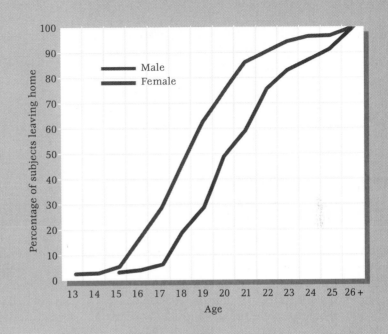

THE TRANSITION INTO ADULTHOOD IN CONTEMPORARY SOCIETY

It is not known for certain whether the discontinuity characteristic of the passage into adulthood today impedes the adolescent's psychosocial development and responsible assumption of adult roles. But many social scientists have speculated that these consequences may result. Identity development, as one example, is probably made more difficult by the higher levels of confusion and inconsistency that surround the social passage into adulthood in modern society. Erik Erikson (1968) and other theorists view identity development during adolescence as the result of the interplay between the young person's growing self-awareness and society's changing view of him or her. It is not difficult to see, then, how an "identity crisis" might be intensified by not knowing whether one is an adult or a child or when the change in social definition takes place.

In recent years, observers of adolescence in America have suggested that the discontinuity in the passage into adulthood has become so great that many youngsters, especially those not bound for college, are having tremendous problems negotiating the passage into adult roles (Hamburg, 1986; Kazis, 1993; National Research Council, 1993; William T. Grant Foundation, 1988). One national commission found that society had so neglected the needs of noncollege-bound adolescents that its report called them "the Forgotten Half" (William T. Grant Foundation, 1988). Another prestigious panel, in a disheartening volume, estimated that nearly 7 million young Americans—about one-quarter of adolescents 10 to 17 years old—are at risk of failing to achieve productive adult lives (National Research Council, 1993).

These observers point to problems many young people experience in developing a coherent sense of identity, establishing a healthy sense of autonomy, and making informed decisions about commitments to family and work. They note that the lack of clarity and

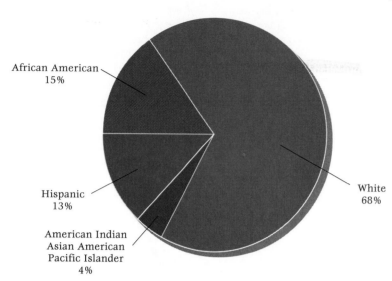

African American
15%

Hispanic
13%

American Indian
Asian American
Pacific Islander
4%

White
68%

Figure 3.5   *At the end of the twentieth century, youngsters from minority backgrounds accounted for about one-third of the U.S. adolescent population.* (Wetzel, 1987)

continuity in the transition into adulthood may contribute to some of the problems faced by adolescents in contemporary society and may contribute to some of the problems faced by contemporary society in dealing with young people. Many social scientists believe that our relatively high rates of divorce, family violence, youth unemployment, juvenile delinquency, and teenage alcoholism stem in part from the confusing and contradictory nature of the passage into adulthood in modern society (National Research Council, 1993).

The Transitional Problems of Poor and Minority Youth

No discussion of the transitional problems of young people in America today is complete without noting that youngsters from some minority groups—African American, Hispanic American, and American Indian youth, in particular—have more trouble negotiating the transition into adulthood than do their white and Asian American counterparts as a result of many factors, including poverty, discrimination, and segregation (Garcia Coll et al., 1996). Youngsters from minority backgrounds make up a substantial and growing portion of the adolescent population in America. By the end of the twentieth century, about 15 percent of the youth population was African American, and another 13 percent was Hispanic American. Approximately 4 percent of the youth population was composed of Asian American, Pacific Islander, and American Indian youth. In other words, about one-third of the youth population in the year 2000 was from minority groups

(Wetzel, 1987) (see figure 3.5). Moreover, approximately 20 percent of the school-age population at the end of the twentieth century was composed of children from immigrant families, primarily from Mexico, Central and South America, and Asia (National Research Council, 1995). By the year 2020, ethnic minority children will account for nearly half of all U.S. children (Pallas, Natriello, & McDill, 1989).

One curiosity within studies of ethnic minority youth and the transition to adulthood concerns the better than expected mental health and school performance of immigrant adolescents in the United States. For reasons not entirely understood, foreign-born adolescent immigrants have better mental health, exhibit less problem behavior, and perform better in school than adolescents from the same ethnic group who are native-born Americans (Harris, 1999; Kao, 1999; Rumbaut, 1997). Indeed, one of the most interesting findings to emerge from research on immigrant adolescents is that Americanization appears to be associated with worse, not better, outcomes.

● **The Effects of Poverty on the Transition into Adulthood**   Growing up in poverty may profoundly impair youngsters' ability to move easily between adolescence and adulthood. Poverty is associated with failure in school, unemployment, and out-of-wedlock pregnancy, all of which contribute to transitional difficulties (Edelman & Ladner, 1991; National Research Council, 1993). Because minority youngsters are more likely than other teenagers to grow up in poverty, they are more likely than other youth to encounter transitional problems during middle and late adolescence

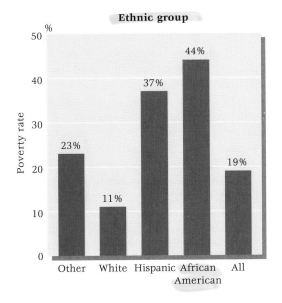

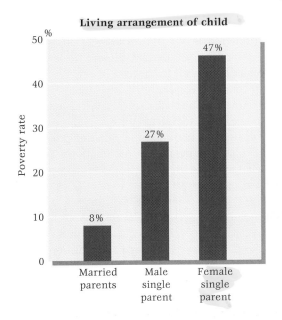

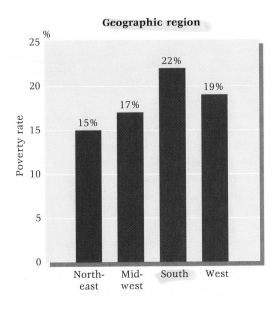

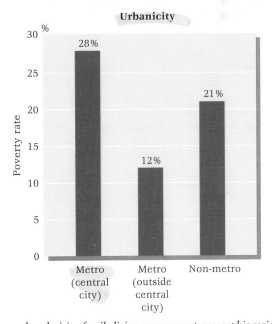

Figure 3.6   *Poverty rates among adolescents in the United States vary by ethnicity, family living arrangement, geographic region, and urbanicity.* (Sum & Fogg, 1991)

(see figure 3.6). Poverty is especially high among adolescents living in single-parent families, in the South, and in urban and rural (as opposed to suburban) communities (Sum & Fogg, 1991).

Whereas growing up amid poverty early in life has a strong adverse effect on individuals' cognitive ability, experiencing poverty during adolescence has an especially negative effect on young people's school achieve-

ment (Guo, 1998). School dropout rates are much higher among Hispanic American and American Indian teenagers than among other groups, and college enrollment is lower among African American, Hispanic American, and American Indian youth. Unemployment is much higher among African American, Hispanic American, and American Indian teenagers. African American and Hispanic American youth are more likely to be victimized by crime and exposed to violence (Bowen & Bowen, 1999; DuRant, Getts, Cadenhead, & Woods, 1995; Paschall, Ennett, & Flewelling, 1996; Singh & Yu, 1996a; Warner & Weist, 1996). And rates of out-of-wedlock births are higher among African American and Hispanic American teenagers than among white teenagers (Wetzel, 1987). All these factors disrupt the transition into adulthood by limiting individuals' economic and occupational success. Poverty impedes the transition to adulthood among all teenagers, regardless of race, of course; however, because minority youth are more likely to grow up poor, they are more likely to have transitional problems.

As William Julius Wilson documented in his widely cited book *The Truly Disadvantaged,* the situation is particularly grave for poor minority youngsters growing up in the inner city (Wilson, 1987). Many of these young people grow up without knowing a single adult "whose stable employment supports an even modest standard of family life" (Wilson, cited in Nightingale & Wolverton, 1993, p. 480). As two writers for the Carnegie Council on Adolescent Development noted with depressing clarity,

> Those who have succeeded in attaining a solid standard of living often have moved away from the city to the suburbs, further depriving young people of role models. Such young people have no experience working or living among people with . . . different kinds of jobs and their choices are limited to poorly paying and unrewarding jobs or quick money from drug running. Often the only role models available in areas of concentrated poverty are gang members or drug dealers, who appear to have what adolescents desperately want, respect and money.
>
> In these neighborhoods, often adult women were adolescent mothers themselves. Their daughters, in turn, may see a child of their own as the only hope for affection and respect, and perhaps even stability. However, the babies quickly become demanding toddlers. Usually the fathers of these children do not marry or provide family support. Too early child-bearing can have disastrous consequences for both mother and child, including dropping out of school and long-term unemployment for the mother, and low birth-weight and other health problems for the child. (Nightingale & Wolverton, 1993, p. 480)

● The Effects of Growing Up in a Poor Neighborhood

One factor contributing to the especially worrisome situation of poor youth is that poverty became much more concentrated during the 1970s and 1980s, with greater and greater clustering of poor families into economically and racially segregated communities. In response to this,

and taking the lead from Wilson's ideas about the devastating impact of concentrated poverty outlined in The Truly Disadvantaged, a number of researchers have turned their attention to the study of adolescents in poor neighborhoods (for a review, see Leventhal & Brooks-Gunn, 2000). Their aim is to see whether neighborhood poverty, in addition to family poverty, is predictive of adolescent problems (e.g., Brooks-Gunn, Duncan, Klebanov, & Sealand, 1993; Coulten & Pandey, 1992; Duncan, 1994; Ensminger, Lamkin, & Jacobson, 1996; Sampson, 1997). Generally, researchers hypothesize that living in a community that has a high proportion of poor families affects adolescents for the worse, regardless of their own family's situation. For instance, even if an adolescent lives in an economically stable, supportive household, he or she may be adversely affected by growing up in a community that has a high unemployment rate (because there are fewer employed role models with whom to identify), few resources (such as parks and libraries), and a high crime rate (as is often the case in poor neighborhoods) (National Research Council, 1993). Exposure to concentrated poverty is an especially prevalent problem among nonwhite adolescents. Close to 90 percent of all residents of the poorest neighborhoods in the United States are from ethnic minority groups (National Research Council, 1993).

There is growing evidence that coming of age amid concentrated poverty has negative effects on adolescent behavior and mental health, as well as on the transition to adulthood, and that these effects are above and beyond those attributable to growing up in a poor family. Adolescents growing up in impoverished communities are more likely than their peers from equally poor households, but better neighborhoods, to bear children as teenagers and to achieve less in, or even drop out, of high school—two factors that seriously interfere with the successful transition into adulthood (Leventhal & Brooks-Gunn, 2000). Interestingly, it seems to be the absence of affluent neighbors, rather than the presence of poor neighbors, that places adolescents in impoverished communities at greatest academic risk (Duncan, 1994; Ensminger et al., 1996). In addition, adolescents who grow up in poor neighborhoods are more likely to engage in a range of antisocial behaviors, including crime, delinquency, and violence (Leventhal & Brooks-Gunn, 2000).

How might concentrated neighborhood poverty adversely affect the behavior and development of adolescents? At least three mechanisms have been suggested. First, some writers (e.g., Crane, 1991; Simons, Johnson, Beaman, Conger, & Whitbeck, 1996) suggest that social

▲ *A variety of psychological and social problems are more common among adolescents who grow up in poverty.* (Peter Byron/PhotoEdit)

problems are contagious; they are spread from one adolescent to another in a pattern not unlike a medical epidemic. To the extent that poverty increases behavior problems, adolescents living in poor neighborhoods come into contact with deviant peers all the more often. Adolescents who associate with delinquent peers are more likely to be drawn into criminal and delinquent activity in the peer group (Simons et al., 1996). Not all poor neighborhoods have high rates of juvenile crime, however; indeed, at least one study indicates that inner-city adolescents growing up in moderately poor neighborhoods are more at risk for antisocial behavior than are those growing up in extremely poor ones (Seidman et al., 1998).

Second, poverty in neighborhoods breeds social isolation and social disorganization, undermining a neighborhood's sense of **collective efficacy**—the extent to which neighbors trust each other, share values, and can count on each other to monitor the activities of youth in the community (Sampson, Raudenbusch, & Earls, 1997). A lack of collective efficacy is associated with poor and ineffective parenting, family conflict, diminished social support among community members, and poor communitywide supervision of adolescents (Bowen & Chapman, 1996; Brooks-Gunn et al., 1993; Paschall & Hubbard, 1998; Sampson, 1997; Sampson & Lamb, 1994; Simons et al., 1996). When parents are not effective in supervising and monitoring their teenagers, for example, and when

teenagers have little social support from parents or other adults, the teenagers are more likely to get into trouble (Bowen & Chapman, 1996; McCabe, Barnett, & Robbins, 1996). Studies also indicate that poverty is associated with harsh, inconsistent, and punitive parenting, and these factors, in turn, are linked to adolescent misbehavior (Conger et al., 1992; Patterson, Reid, & Dishion, 1992; Simons et al., 1996).

Finally, adolescents who grow up in poor neighborhoods are far more likely than other youth to be exposed to chronic community violence, and repeated exposure to violence and other types of stress increases the risk of behavioral and emotional problems (Biafora, Warheit, Vega, & Gil, 1994; DuRant, Cadenhead, Pendergrast, Slavens, & Linder, 1994; Osofsky, 1997; Stevenson, 1998). A study of young adolescents in Philadelphia, for example, indicated that 96 percent of the students in an urban middle school knew someone who had been robbed, beaten, stabbed, shot, or murdered. Two-thirds of these students had been personally robbed, beaten up, stabbed, shot, or caught in gun cross fire. Nearly three-quarters of the youngsters reported hearing gunfire in their neighborhood (Cambell & Schwartz, 1996). In another study, of poor New York City teenagers, half of the students reported knowing someone who had been murdered, 61 percent had witnessed a robbery, 59 percent had witnessed a beating, 37 percent had witnessed a shooting, and 31 percent had witnessed a stabbing (Pastore, Fisher, & Friedman, 1996b). Adolescents who themselves have been exposed to violence are more likely to engage in violent behavior, to think about killing themselves, and to report symptoms of depression, post-traumatic stress disorder, and substance abuse (Cambell & Schwartz, 1996; DuRant, et al., 1994, 1995; Gorman-Smith & Tolan, 1998; Pastore et al., 1996b). It is important to note, though, that it is exposure to violence, rather than living in a poor neighborhood, that increases adolescents' risk for aggression (Paschall & Hubbard, 1998).

Growing up amid concentrated poverty is a risk factor for young people all over the world, of course (Staub, 1996). Approximately 100 million children and adolescents are growing up on the streets of large cities worldwide (Campos et al., 1994). One study of street youth in Brazil, for example, compared youngsters "on" the street (that is, youth who were working and contributing to the welfare of their families) with youngsters "of" the street (youth who were homeless and without stable adult supervision); as you might expect, the homeless youngsters were at great risk for involvement in crime, drug use, violent victimization, and dangerous sex (Campos et al., 1994).

What Can Be Done to Ease the Transition?

A variety of suggestions have been offered for making the transition into adulthood smoother for all young people, especially those who are not college-bound, including restructuring secondary education, expanding work and volunteer opportunities, and improving the quality of community life for adolescents and their parents. Some groups have called for expanded opportunities in the workplace as a way of making the high school years more of a bridge between adolescence and adulthood (Kazis, 1993). Other groups have suggested that adolescents be encouraged to spend time in voluntary, nonmilitary service activities—such as staffing day-care centers, working with the elderly, and cleaning up the environment—for a few years after high school graduation, so that they can learn responsibility and adult roles (Children's Defense Fund, 1989). Still others have pointed out that adolescents cannot come of age successfully without the help of adults and that programs are needed to strengthen families and communities and bring adolescents into contact with adult mentors (National Research Council, 1993). Overall, most experts agree that a comprehensive approach to the problem is needed and that such an approach must simultaneously address the educational, employment, interpersonal, and health needs of adolescents from all walks of life (Dryfoos, 1990).

In recent years, there has been growing interest in mentoring programs for at-risk adolescents, many of whom have few relationships with positive adult role models (DuBois, Holloway, Valentine, & Cooper, in press; Grossman, 1999). Among the best known mentoring programs is Big Brothers/Big Sisters, which has more than 500 branches across the United States. Mentoring programs seek to pair adults with young people through community- and school-based efforts designed to facilitate positive youth development, improve academic achievement, and deter antisocial behavior.

Evaluations of mentoring programs indicate that they have a small but significant positive effect on youth development. On average, adolescents who have been mentored are less likely to have problems in school, are less likely to use drugs and alcohol, and are less likely to get into trouble with the law. Not surprisingly, the impact of mentoring varies as a function of the characteristics of the mentor, the young person, and their relationship (DuBois et al., in press; Grossman, 1999). In general, mentoring tends to be more successful when the mentor maintains a steady presence in the young person's life over an extended period of time (at least two years), has frequent contact with the young person, and involves the adolescent in a wide range of recreational, social, and instrumental activities (Grossman, 1999; Roth, Brooks-Gunn, Murray, & Foster, 1998).

RECAP

Many social commentators have argued that the vague and discontinuous nature of the adolescent passage in contemporary society has contributed to numerous psychological and behavioral problems among today's youth. These difficulties are more severe among adolescents who are not bound for college, and especially so among poor, minority youth living in pockets of concentrated poverty within the inner city, where exposure to crime and violence is chronic. Most experts agree that a comprehensive approach to the problem is needed and that such an approach must simultaneously address the educational, employment, interpersonal, and health needs of adolescents from all walks of life.

Food for Thought

Inner-city neighborhoods typically come to mind when we think of adolescents growing up in poverty, but many poor adolescents live in rural, not urban, areas. In what ways is poverty different for urban versus rural youth? How does this affect the nature of adolescence in each type of community?

Web Researcher Photographs can sometimes startle us by violating our expectations about how people should behave. Find 10 or 20 photographs of adolescents from different historical periods. In what ways does it seem as if adolescents made a faster transition from childhood to adulthood than they do now? In what ways does it seem that their transition was slower? Can you draw any conclusions? Go to www.mhhe.com/steinberg6 for further information.

KEY TERMS

age of majority
Bar (Bas) Mitzvah
brother-sister avoidance
child protectionists

collective efficacy
continuous transitions
discontinuous transitions
extrusion
initiation ceremony
inventionists
juvenile justice system
marginal man
median
quinceañera
scarification
school-to-work transition
social redefinition
status offense
teenager
youth
youth apprenticeship

II

The Contexts of Adolescence

Chapter

Families

The next time you are in a bookstore, take a look at the books in the section on parent-adolescent relationships. Judging from the titles—such as *How to Survive Your Child's Adolescence*—you would think that stress and strain between teenagers and their parents is commonplace, even normal. In contrast to advice books on infancy, which emphasize normative development, books for parents of teenagers tend to focus on problems (Steinberg, 2001). And, like the popular writings on the subject, a great deal of the scientific writing about families during adolescence has focused on conflict between parents and teenagers. But is there a **generation gap** between adolescents and their parents? If so, how wide is it? The answer may surprise you.

Despite popular stereotypes of storm and stress in the adolescent's family, scientific studies indicate that there is very little emotional distance between young people and their parents. Although some adolescents and their parents have serious interpersonal problems, the overwhelming majority of adolescents feel close to their parents, respect their parents' judgment, feel that their parents love and care about them, and have a lot of respect for their parents as individuals (Public Agenda, 1999; Steinberg, 2001). In fact, one-fifth of American teenagers say that their top concern is that they don't have enough time with their parents; ironically, less than one-tenth of parents say that *their* top concern is that they don't have enough time with their kids (YMCA, 2000).

To be sure, there are times when adolescents and parents have their problems. But so are there times when younger children and their parents have problems, and when adults and *their* parents do. No systematic studies demonstrate that family problems are any more likely to occur during adolescence than at other times in the life span. Most research indicates that, among the 25 percent of teenagers and parents who report having problems, about 80 percent had problematic relations during childhood (Rutter, Graham, Chadwick, & Yule, 1976). The bottom line is that only about 5 percent of families who enjoy positive relations during childhood can expect to develop serious problems during adolescence.

When we look at intergenerational differences in values and attitudes, we also find little evidence in support of a generation gap—or, at least, of schism as large as many people have been led to believe exists. Adolescents and their parents have similar beliefs about the importance of hard work, about educational and occupational ambitions, and about the personal characteristics and attributes that they feel are important and desirable (Gecas & Seff, 1990). Indeed, when it comes to more basic values—

▲ *Many popular advice books for parents of teenagers, such as this one, incorrectly portray adolescence as an inherently difficult time.* (Michael Newman/PhotoEdit)

concerning religion, work, education, and the like—diversity *within* the adolescent population is much more striking than are differences *between* the generations. Socioeconomic background, for instance, has a much stronger influence on individuals' values and attitudes than does age, and adolescents are more likely to share their parents' values than those of other teenagers who have a different background. Wealthy adolescents growing up in affluent suburbs, for example, have educational and career plans that resemble their parents' plans for them, and their plans are very different from those of poor adolescents growing up in less prosperous areas.

However, in matters of personal taste there is often a gap between the generations, most clearly evident in styles of dress, preferences in music, and patterns of leisure activity. The explanation for this gap is not surprising: Adolescents are more likely to be influenced by their friends than by their parents in these matters, and, as a consequence, disagreements and differences in opinion between old and young often result. Indeed, it is over these matters that much of the bickering that occurs in families takes place (Montemayor, 1983). A mother and daughter may argue about such things as the daughter's curfew, how the daughter spends her spare time, whether the daughter keeps her room clean enough, or what sorts of clothes the daughter wears. Unlike values, which develop gradually over time and are shaped from an early age, preferences and tastes are far more transitory and subject to the immediate influences of the social environment. Because adolescents spend a great deal of time with their friends (and because a good deal of that time is spent in social activities in which taste in clothes, music, and so on is especially important), teenagers' tastes are shaped to a large measure by forces outside the family. Conflict between adolescents and parents is generally less frequent in ethnic minority than in nonminority families, although the topics of disagreement are similar across ethnic groups (Barber, 1994; Kupersmidt, Burchinal, Leff, & Patterson, 1992).

Why do parents and teenagers argue over mundane issues, such as household chores, clothing, and the adolescents' choice of friends? According to research by Judith Smetana (1988a, 1988b, 1989; Smetana & Asquith, 1994; Yau & Smetana, 1996), a major contributor to adolescent-parent bickering is the fact that teenagers and their parents define the issues of contention very differently. Smetana studies parent-adolescent relations by having parents and teenagers discuss various issues while they are being videotaped and then analyzing the conversations. Parents are likely to see these as issues of right and wrong—not in a moral sense, but as matters of custom or convention. For instance, a mother who disapproves of her daughter's outfit may say, "People just don't dress that way to go to school." Adolescents, in contrast, are likely to define the same issues as matters of personal choice. The daughter may respond by saying, "*You* wouldn't dress this way for school, but *I* do."

Smetana believes that teenagers and their parents often clash more over the *definition* of the issue (that is, as a matter of custom versus a matter of personal choice) than over the specific details. The struggle, then, is over who has the authority—and into whose jurisdiction the issue falls. Because early adolescence is a time during which adolescents' reasoning abilities are changing—recall the dramatic cognitive developments discussed in chapter 2—there are changes in the ways that individuals under-

▲ One source of conflict between teenagers and parents involves the different ways that they define the same issues. Making sure that the adolescent's bedroom is tidy often is seen by parents as an area over which they have jurisdiction. Teenagers, however, tend to see their rooms as their own private space and decisions about neatness as matters of personal choice. (Elizabeth Crews/The Image Works)

stand family rules and regulations. As a consequence of normal cognitive development, a child who is willing to accept his parents' views of right and wrong—who doesn't question his mother when she says, "We do not leave clothes on the floor"—grows into an adolescent who understands that some issues are matters of personal choice, rather than social convention ("It's *my* room, so why should it bother *you?*"). ●

RECAP

Although popular books for parents of teenagers present adolescence as a problematic time for the family, the notion that a wide gap exists between the generations is largely a myth. When parents and adolescents disagree, it tends to be over mundane, day-to-day issues, not over major values or priorities. Many disagreements between parents and teenagers stem from the different perspectives that they bring to the discussion: Parents typically see the issues as matters of right or wrong, whereas adolescents see them as matters of personal choice.

FAMILY RELATIONSHIPS AT ADOLESCENCE

Although it is incorrect to characterize adolescence as a time of conflict in most families, it is important to keep in mind that adolescence is a period of change and reorganization in family relationships and daily interactions, with adolescents spending increasingly less time in family activities, especially in activities with the family as a group (see figure 4.1) (Larson, Richards, Moneta, Holmbeck, & Duckett, 1996). It is to these processes of change and reorganization in the adolescent's family that we now turn.

Relationships in families change most dramatically during the times when individual family members are changing or when the family's circumstances are changing, since it is during these times that the family's previously established equilibrium is upset. Not surprisingly, one period in which family relationships usually change a great deal is adolescence.

The specific concerns and issues characteristic of families at adolescence arise not just because of the changing needs and concerns of the young person but also because of changes in the adolescent's parents and changes in the needs and functions of the family as a unit. You already have some understanding of the changes adolescents go through and how these affect the family system. However, to fully understand the changing nature of family relationships during the adolescent years, we must take into account not only the characteristics of the developing young person but also the characteristics of the adolescent's parents and of families at this stage.

The Adolescent's Parents at Midlife

Today, the typical parent is close to 40 years old when his or her first child enters early adolescence. Some research suggests that the period surrounding age 40 can be a potentially difficult time for many adults. Indeed, some theorists have gone so far as to describe it as a time of **midlife crisis** (Farrell & Rosenberg, 1981; Levinson, 1978).

If we look at the nature of these midlife crises in some detail, we find that the developmental concerns of parents and adolescents are complementary (Steinberg & Steinberg, 1994). First, consider the issue of biological change. At the same time that adolescents are entering into a period of rapid physical growth and sexual maturation and ultimately the period of the life span that society has labeled one of the most physically attractive, their parents are beginning to feel increased concern about their own bodies, their physical attractiveness, and their sexual appeal (Gould, 1972).

A second overlap of crises concerns perceptions of time and the future. While adolescents are beginning to develop the ability to think systematically about the future and do, in fact, begin to look ahead, their parents are beginning to feel that the possibilities for change are limited. While adolescents' about the future are becoming more expansive, their parents' ideas are probably becoming more limited. An important shift in time perspective takes place during midlife: Before this phase in the life cycle, we tend to measure time in terms of how long we have been alive; after midlife, we are more likely to see things in terms of how much longer we have to live (Neugarten & Datan, 1974). One reason for this shift may be that midlife adults are reminded of their mortality because they see their own parents aging.

Finally, consider the issues of power, status, and entrance into the roles of adulthood. Adolescence is the time when individuals are on the threshold of gaining a great deal of status. Their careers and marriages lie ahead of them, and choices seem limitless. For their parents, in contrast, many choices have already been made—some successfully, others perhaps less so. Most adults reach their occupational plateau—the point at which they can tell how successful they are likely to be—during midlife, and many must deal with whatever gap exists between their early aspirations and their actual achievements (Gould, 1972). In sum, for adolescents, this phase in the family life cycle is a time of boundless horizons; for their parents, it is a time of coming to terms with choices made when they were younger.

This overlap of crises is likely to have an impact on family relationships (Hamill, 1994; Steinberg & Steinberg, 1994). A father who is worried about his own physical health suddenly feels uncomfortable about playing tennis each weekend with his growing son, as

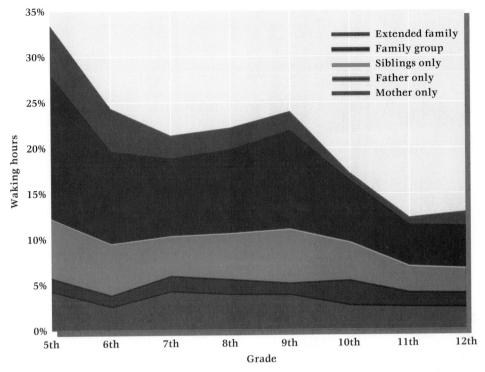

Figure 4.1 *Age differences in the amount of time adolescents spend with family members.* (Larson et al., 1996)

they did for years when the son was younger. They may have to find new activities that they can share together. An adolescent girl with big plans for the future finds it difficult to understand why her father seems so cautious and narrow-minded when she asks him for advice. She may react by turning to her friends more often. An adolescent boy finds his mother's constant attention annoying; he doesn't see that, to her, his interest in independence signifies the end of an important stage in her career as parent. The adolescent's desire for autonomy, in particular, may be especially stressful for parents (Small, Eastman, & Cornelius, 1988). Although none of these situations may cause family conflict, each requires a period of adjustment on the part of parents and their children.

This generalization about the collision of adolescence and midlife must be tempered by the fact that recent decades have seen important changes in both the age at which individuals marry and the age at which they have their first child. The average age at marriage has increased by several years since 1970, for both men (who now tend to marry in their late twenties) and women (who tend to marry in their midtwenties). Although it had been common in the past for couples to

begin having children soon after marriage, proportionately more couples today are delaying childbearing until they have become established in their careers. As a consequence of both of these changes, adults tend to be older today when their children reach adolescence than was the case three decades ago. Although psychologists have studied the impact of this change on parents' relationships with their infants (e.g., Parke, 1988), it is not known how being an older parent affects relationships during adolescence.

In families with middle-aged adults, however, adjusting to adolescence may take more of a toll on the mental health of parents than on the mental health of adolescents (Steinberg & Steinberg, 1994). One study found that nearly two-thirds of mothers and fathers describe adolescence as the most difficult stage of parenting (Pasley & Gecas, 1984), and several studies have found this period in the family life cycle to be a low point in parents' marital and life satisfaction (Gecas & Seff, 1990).

Parents may be especially adversely affected by the transition of their child into adolescence if the child is of the same sex as the parent. Mothers of daughters and fathers of sons, for example, show more psychological distress, report less satisfaction with their

▲ *For many adults, midlife is a time of heightened introspection and personal reevaluation. Because many parents are at this stage in the life cycle when their children are teenagers, the so-called midlife crisis of adulthood may coincide with the identity crisis of adolescence.* (Ellis Herwig/Stock, Boston)

marriage, and experience more intense midlife identity concerns as their children begin to mature physically, get involved in dating relationship, and distance themselves from their parents emotionally. Parents who are deeply involved in work outside the home or who have an especially happy marriage may be buffered against some of these negative consequences, however, whereas single mothers may be especially vulnerable to these effects (Kalil & Eccles, 1993; Mac-Dermid & Crouter, 1995; Silverberg, Marczak, & Gondoli, 1996; Silverberg & Steinberg, 1987, 1990; Steinberg & Silverberg, 1987; Steinberg & Steinberg, 1994). Studies also show that parents who have high self-esteem have better relationships with their adolescents than do parents who think more poorly of themselves (Small, 1988). These studies of the factors that influ-

ence parental mental health during the adolescent years are important, because research shows that parents who are emotionally distressed (e.g., depressed, anxious, self-doubting) feel and are less effective in the parental role (Gondoli & Silverberg, 1997).

Changes in Family Needs and Functions

It is not only individual family members who undergo change during the family's adolescent years. The family *as a unit* changes as well in its economic circumstances, its relationship to other social institutions, and its functions. One of the most important changes undergone by the family during adolescence is financial: Family finances are likely to be strained during adolescence. Children grow rapidly during puberty, and clothing for adolescents is expensive. Keeping up with the accoutrements of the peer culture—the CDs, the cosmetics, the clothes, and the high-priced video, computer, and stereo equipment—may push a family budget to the limit. Many families also begin saving money for anticipated large expenditures, such as the adolescent's college education. And, in some families, parents may find themselves having to help support their own parents at a time when their children are still economically dependent. The financial demands placed on parents in the "sandwich generation" (that is, sandwiched between their adolescent children and their aging parents) require considerable adjustment.

In addition to these financial pressures, the adolescent's family must cope with the increasing importance of two contexts in which the young person spends time and invests energy: the peer group and, later in adolescence, the workplace (Larson & Richards, 1994a). During the early stages of the life cycle, the child's social world is fairly narrow, and the family is the central setting. As the child grows, the school begins to take on increased significance, and relationships and concerns revolving around school must be balanced with those revolving around the family. During late childhood and early adolescence, however, the peer group becomes a setting in which close ties are formed. Families may have a tough time adjusting to the adolescent's increasing interest in forgoing family activities for peer activities. They may have arguments about the teenager's reluctance to give up time with his or her friends, or on the job, for family outings.

Finally, important changes in family functions also take place during adolescence. During infancy and childhood, the functions and responsibilities of the family are fairly clear: nurturance, protection, and socialization. Although all these roles are still important during adolescence, adolescents are more in need of support than nurturance, guidance more than protection, and direction more than socialization. Making the transition from the family functions of childhood to the family functions of adolescence is not necessarily easy, for the shift often upsets the equilibrium established during childhood. The transition is further complicated in contemporary society, in which preparation for adulthood—one of the chief tasks of adolescence that was once carried out primarily by the family—is increasingly done by other institutions, such as the school. Many families may feel at a loss to figure out just what their role is during adolescence.

Transformations in Family Relations

Together, the biological, cognitive, and social transitions of adolescence, the changes experienced by adults at midlife, and the changes undergone by the family during this stage in the family life cycle set in motion a series of transformations in family relationships. In most families, there is a movement during adolescence from asymmetrical and unequal patterns of influence and interaction to patterns in which parents and their adolescent children are on a more equal footing. And there is some evidence that early adolescence—when this shift toward more egalitarian relationships first begins—may be a time of temporary disruption in the family system.

Studies of family interaction suggest that early adolescence is a time during which young people begin to try to play a more forceful role in the family but parents may not yet acknowledge the adolescents' input. As a result, young adolescents may interrupt their parents more often but have little impact. By middle adolescence, however, teenagers act and are treated much more like adults. They have more influence over family decisions, but they do not need to assert their opinions through interruptions and similarly immature behavior (Grotevant, 1997).

Increases in the assertiveness and influence of adolescents as they get older are consistent with their changing needs and capabilities. In order to adapt successfully to the changes triggered by the child's entrance into adolescence, family members must have a shared sense of what they are experiencing and how they are changing, yet studies show that, in many families, parents and children live in separate realities, perceiving their day-to-day experiences in very different ways (Larson & Richards, 1994a). A mother and son, for example, may have a conversation about the boy's schoolwork, and, although she may experience the conversation as a serious discussion, he may perceive it as an argument. Families have more difficulties when individual members have more divergent perceptions of family life (Larson & Richards, 1994a; Paikoff, Carlton-Ford, & Brooks-Gunn, 1993).

The adolescent's biological and cognitive maturation likely play a role in unbalancing the family system during early adolescence. Several researchers have demonstrated that family relationships change during puberty, with conflict between adolescents and their parents increasing slightly and closeness between adolescents and their parents diminishing (Grotevant, 1997; Holmbeck,

1996; Larson et al., 1996; Steinberg, 1981, 1987b; Susman et al., 1987). Although puberty seems to distance adolescents from their parents, it is not associated with familial storm and stress, and rates of outright conflict between parents and children are not dramatically higher during adolescence than before or after (Laursen, Coy, & Collins, 1998). Rather, disagreements between parents and teenagers are more likely to take the form of bickering over day-to-day issues, such as household chores, than outright fighting. Similarly, the diminished closeness is more likely to be manifested in increased privacy on the part of the adolescent and diminished physical affection between teenagers and parents, rather than any serious loss of love or respect between parents and children (Montemayor, 1983, 1986). Research suggests that the distancing effect of puberty is temporary, though, and that relationships may become less conflicted and more intimate during late adolescence (Thornton, Orbuch, & Axinn, 1995). Nevertheless, studies indicate that the more frequent bickering characteristic of early adolescence may take a modest toll on parents' mental health (Steinberg, 2001).

In any event, it does appear that the beginning of adolescence is a somewhat more strained time for the family than earlier or later. Part of the problem may be that conflicts between teenagers and parents tend to be resolved not through compromise but through submission (i.e., giving in) or disengagement (e.g., walking away), neither of which enhances the quality of their relationship (Laursen & Collins, 1994). Interestingly, one study found that, in Asian American households, the increase in conflict did not occur until later in adolescence (Greenberger & Chen, 1996), consistent with the finding, discussed in chapter 3, that the timetable for the development of independence may be slower in Asian than in non-Asian households.

Several researchers have studied changes in adolescents' cognitive abilities and how these changes may reverberate throughout the family. Changes in the ways adolescents view family rules and regulations may contribute to increased conflict between them and their parents (Smetana, 1989). Research also indicates that early adolescence is a time of changes in youngsters' views of family relationships and in family members' expectations of each other. For example, one study asked adolescents of different ages to characterize their actual and ideal families in terms of how close and dominant different family members were (Feldman & Gehring, 1988). With age, the gap between the adolescents' actual and ideal portraits widened, indicating

that, as they became older, the adolescents became more aware of their families' shortcomings—at least in comparison with what they believed a perfect family is like. This realization does not necessarily lead adolescents to reject their parents, but it does lead to a more balanced, and probably more accurate, appraisal of them (Youniss & Smollar, 1985).

Psychologist W. Andrew Collins (1988, 1990) has examined changes in children's and parents' expectations for each other during adolescence and how "violations" of these expectations can cause family conflict. A child may enter adolescence expecting that it will be a time of great freedom, for example, whereas the parents may view the same period as one in which tighter reins are necessary. Alternatively, another child, perhaps influenced by television sitcoms portraying happy families, may imagine that adolescence will be a time of increased closeness and shared activities in the family, only to be disappointed to find that his or her parents have been looking forward to having time to themselves. It is easy to see how differences in expectations about what adolescence is going to be like can escalate into arguments and misunderstandings. For this reason, psychologists have been studying the sorts of beliefs that children and parents have about adolescence and where they turn for sources of information (Steinberg, 1990).

RECAP

Adolescence is a time of reorganization in family relationships, with adolescents gaining increasingly more power and becoming increasingly more assertive. These transformations in family relations are sparked by the biological, cognitive, and social maturation of the adolescent. Many of the changes in family relations that occur at adolescence affect the psychological well-being of the adolescent's middle-aged parents as well as the teenager; indeed, in some regards, adolescence may be a more difficult time for the parents than for the teenager. In general, parents who have some strong interests outside the family and who have a positive sense of self-esteem cope better with the changes of adolescence than do other parents.

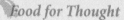

Food for Thought

Most research on changes in family relations at adolescence has been focused on firstborn children. Do you think the results would differ in studies of later-borns?

FAMILY RELATIONSHIPS AND ADOLESCENT DEVELOPMENT

Thus far, we have looked at the sorts of issues and concerns faced by most families during the adolescent years. In our focus on the experiences that all families share, however, we have not addressed the very important questions of how relationships differ from family to family and whether these differences have important consequences for the developing adolescent. Some parents are stricter than others. Some adolescents are given a great deal of affection, whereas others are treated more distantly. In some households, decisions are made through open discussion and verbal give-and-take; in other households, parents lay down the rules, and children are expected to follow them. To what extent are different patterns of family relationships associated with different patterns of adolescent development? Are some styles of parenting more likely than others to be associated with healthy development?

Before we try to answer these questions, several cautions are in order. Although our tendency is to see children's behavior as the result of their parents' behavior, socialization is actually a two-way, not a one-way, street (Collins, Maccoby, Steinberg, Hetherington, & Bornstein, 2000). It is known, for example, that parents who use physical punishment (e.g., spanking, hitting) are more likely to have aggressive adolescents (Bandura & Walters, 1959). But we cannot be sure whether (1) physical punishment leads to adolescent aggression; (2) adolescent aggression leads to parents' using physical punishment; (3) another factor is correlated with parents' using physical punishment and with adolescent aggression (e.g., a genetic predisposition to behave aggressively, which adolescents inherit from their parents); or (4) a combination of these causal and correlational factors is at work. Thus, when we look at the findings concerning parenting practices and adolescent development, we must remember that, just as parents affect their adolescents' behavior, so do adolescents affect their parents' behavior, thereby playing a role in shaping their own development (Ge et al., 1995; Ge, Conger, Cadoret, Neiderheiser, Yates, Throughton, & Stewart 1996; Lerner, Castellino, & Perkins, 1994).

It is also the case that various types of parenting affect different adolescents differently. The adolescent's **temperament** often changes the impact of the parent's behavior. For example, although it is well established that adolescents whose parents are hostile or aloof are more likely to exhibit antisocial behavior (e.g., Dobkin, Tremblay, & Sacchitelle, 1997), the link between negative parenting and adolescent problem behavior is far stronger among teenagers who are temperamentally more prone to anger (Stice & Gonzales, 1998) (see figure 4.2). Furthermore, adolescents who have a greater genetic risk for developing problems are more likely to evoke from their parents the sort of behavior that has been shown to lead to the development of behavior problems (O'Connor, Deater-Deckard, Fulker, Rutter, & Plomin, 1998). Researchers who study parent-adolescent relationships have become increasingly aware of the need to look not only

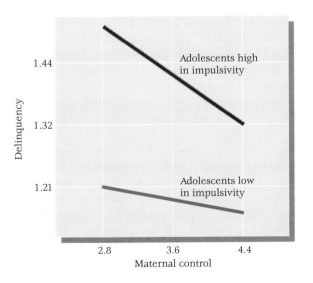

Figure 4.2 Adolescents who are temperamentally different are affected in different ways by the same parenting. Too little control by mothers predicts delinquency among adolescents who are impulsive, but not among their peers who have more self-control. (Adapted from Stice & Gonzales, 1998)

Are There Sex Differences in Adolescents' Family Relationships?

Do daughters and sons have different sorts of relationships with their mothers and fathers? Several studies have offered a tentative answer to this question, and it is a surprising one.

In general, differences between the family relations of sons and those of daughters are minimal (Russell & Saebel, 1997; Silverberg, Tennenbaum, & Jacob, 1992). Although there are occasional exceptions to the rule, sons and daughters report similar degrees of closeness to their parents, similar amounts of conflict, similar types of rules (and disagreements about those rules), and similar patterns of activity (Hill & Holmbeck, 1987; Montemayor & Brownlee, 1987; Youniss & Ketterlinus, 1987). Observational studies of interactions between parents and adolescents indicate that sons and daughters interact with their parents in remarkably similar ways (Cooper & Grotevant, 1987; Hauser et al., 1987).

Does this mean that sex differences in the family are absent? Not entirely. These studies also indicate that the sex of the adolescent's parent may be a more important influence on family relationships than the sex of the adolescent. Recent reviews of studies of adolescent-parent relations indicate that teenagers—males and females alike—relate very differently to their mothers than to fathers (Collins & Russell, 1991; Holmbeck, Paikoff, & Brooks-Gunn, 1995). Adolescents tend to be closer to their mothers, to spend more time alone with their mothers, and to feel more comfortable talking to their mothers about problems and other emotional matters. Fathers are more likely to be perceived as relatively distant authority figures, who may be consulted for "objective" information

Figure 4.3   A scheme for classifying parenting types. (Maccoby & Martin, 1983)

at the impact of parenting on the adolescent but also at how experiences in the family and in other contexts interact with genetic factors in influencing behavior and development (Collins et al., 2000; Rutter, 1997).

Parenting Styles and Their Effects

There are a variety of ways to characterize parents' behavior toward their children. One of the most useful approaches derives from the work of psychologist Diana Baumrind (1978). According to her work and that of oth-

ers in this vein, two aspects of the parent's behavior toward the adolescent are critical: parental responsiveness and parental demandingness (Maccoby & Martin, 1983). **Parental responsiveness** is the degree to which the parent responds to the child's needs in an accepting, supportive manner. **Parental demandingness** is the extent to which the parent expects and demands mature, responsible behavior from the child. Parents vary on each of these dimensions. Some are warm and accepting, whereas others are unresponsive and rejecting; some are demanding and expect a great deal of their child, whereas others are permissive and demand very little.

Because parental responsiveness and demandingness are more or less independent of each other—that is, it is possible for a parent to be very demanding without being responsive, and vice versa—it is possible to look at various combinations of these two dimensions (see figure 4.3). Many studies of parents and children indicate that the fourfold classification scheme presented in figure 4.3 is very important in understanding the impact of parents' behavior on the child, and psychologists have given labels to the four prototypes presented in the figure. A parent who is very responsive but not at all demanding is labeled

(such as help with homework) but who are rarely sought for support or guidance (such as help for problems with a boyfriend or girlfriend). Interestingly, adolescents also fight more often with their mothers than with their fathers, but this higer level of conflict does not appear to jeopardize the closeness of the mother-adolescent relationship. It seems safe to say that relationships between adolescents and their mothers are more emotionally intense in general and that this intensity has both positive and negative manifestations (Apter, 1990; Larson & Richards, 1994).

One of the most interesting findings to emerge from these studies concerns the father-daughter relationship, in particular. Most researchers have found that this relationship is especially distant (Larson & Richards, 1994), although the reasons are not certain. Some theorists have speculated that unconscious taboos against incest make it difficult for fathers and daughters to remain close after puberty, whereas others have suggested that the general emotional inexpressiveness of fathers put daughters off more than sons (Youniss & Ketterlinus, 1987). However, it seems clear that this relationship is the flattest, emotionally speaking, in the family. Whether and in what ways this affects the daughter's development is not known.

Why should mothers and fathers have such different sorts of relationships with their adolescent children? One explanation concerns differences in the socialization of men and women. For example, women in Western cultures are socialized to be more emotionally expressive than men, and this may give them talents and capabilities that permit them to form closer relationships with their children. Growing up in a household in which mothers are emotionally accessible and fathers are emotionally distant only furthers this tendency, for this provides role models for adolescents to imitate. A somewhat different explanation concerns differences in the maternal and paternal roles. The mother's role in this culture traditionally has included more of an expressive, or emotional, component, whereas the father's role may be more "instrumental" (Parsons, 1949). Moreover, until relatively recently, patterns of work and family life were so different for mothers and fathers that it may have been difficult for fathers—whatever their socialization—to form close relationships with their children. Mothers may be closer than fathers simply because they spend more time with their children as their children develop, and time together may foster and strengthen emotional bonds.

Whatever the explanation, however, the consistency with which studies of parents and adolescents uncover different patterns of relations for mothers and fathers is striking—especially in light of changes that have taken place in sex roles in contemporary society. Although researchers cannot be sure of the origins of these differences, they are fairly confident that the differences exist, even in today's families. In discussing the parent-adolescent relationship, clearly we need to pay attention to sex differences—not necessarily the differences between sons and daughters, however, but the differences between mothers and fathers.

---

indulgent, whereas one who is equally responsive but also very demanding is labeled *authoritative*. Parents who are very demanding but not responsive are *authoritarian*; parents who are neither demanding nor responsive are labeled *indifferent*.

Authoritative parents are warm but firm. They set standards for the child's conduct but form expectations that are consistent with the child's developing needs and capabilities. They place a high value on the development of autonomy and self-direction but assume the ultimate responsibility for their child's behavior. Authoritative parents deal with their child in a rational, issue-oriented manner, frequently engaging in discussion and explanation with their children over matters of discipline.

Authoritarian parents place a high value on obedience and conformity. They tend to favor more punitive, absolute, and forceful disciplinary measures. Verbal give-and-take is not common in authoritarian households, because the underlying belief of authoritarian parents is that the child should accept without question the rules and standards established by the parents. They tend not to encourage independent behavior and, instead, place a good deal of importance on restricting the child's autonomy.

Indulgent parents behave in an accepting, benign, and somewhat more passive way in matters of discipline. They place relatively few demands on the child's behavior, giving the child a high degree of freedom to act as he or she wishes. Indulgent parents are more likely to believe that control is an infringement on the child's freedom that may interfere with the child's healthy development. Instead of actively shaping their child's behavior, indulgent parents are more likely to view themselves as resources that the child may or may not use.

Indifferent parents try to do whatever is necessary to minimize the time and energy that they must devote to interacting with their child. In extreme cases, indifferent parents are neglectful. They know little about their child's activities and whereabouts, show little interest in their child's experiences at school or with friends, rarely converse with their child, and rarely consider their child's opinion when making decisions. Rather than raising their child according to a set of beliefs about what is good for the child's development (as

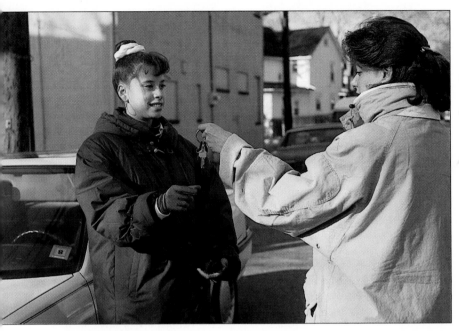

▲ *Authoritative parents are warm, firm, and fair in exercising their authority over the adolescent while granting an appropriate degree of independence.* (Rhoda Sidney/Stock, Boston)

ling, Mounts, & Dornbusch, 1994; Steinberg, 2001). Although exceptions to these general patterns have been noted, the evidence linking authoritative parenting and healthy adolescent development is remarkably strong, and it has been found in studies of a wide range of ethnicities, cultures, regions, social classes, and family structures (Carson, Chowdhury, Perry, & Pati, 1999; Dornbusch, Ritter, Liederman, Roberts, & Fraleigh, 1987; Forehand, Miller, Dutra, & Chance, 1997; Ge, Best, Conger, & Simons, 1996; Hetherington et al., 1999; Juang & Silbereisen, 1999; Pilgrim, Luo, Urberg, & Fang, 1999; Slicker, 1998; Steinberg, Mounts, Lamborn, & Dornbusch, 1991; Weiss & Schwartz, 1996). Indeed, the evidence in support of the advantages of authoritative parenting is so strong that some experts have suggested that the question "Which type of parenting benefits teenagers the most?"

do the other three parent types), indifferent parents are "parent-centered"—they structure their home life primarily around their own needs and interests.

This fourfold categorization provides a useful way of summarizing and examining some of the relations between parenting practices and adolescent psychosocial development. Generally speaking, young people who have been raised in authoritative households are more psychosocially competent than peers who have been raised in authoritarian, indulgent, or indifferent homes. Adolescents raised in authoritative homes are more responsible, more self-assured, more adaptive, more creative, more curious, more socially skilled, and more successful in school. Adolescents raised in authoritarian homes, in contrast, are more dependent, more passive, less socially adept, less self-assured, and less intellectually curious. Many adolescents raised in indulgent households are often less mature, more irresponsible, more conforming to their peers, and less able to assume positions of leadership. Many adolescents raised in indifferent homes are often impulsive and more likely to be involved in delinquent behavior and in precocious experiments with sex, drugs, and alcohol (Fuligni & Eccles, 1993; Kurdek & Fine, 1994; Lamborn, Mounts, Steinberg, & Dornbusch, 1991; Pulkkinen, 1982; Steinberg, Lamborn, Dar-

need not be studied anymore (Steinberg, 2001).

At the other extreme, parenting that is indifferent, neglectful, or abusive has been shown consistently to have harmful effects on the adolescent's mental health and development, leading to depression and a variety of behavior problems, including, in cases of physical abuse, aggression toward others (Crittenden, Claussen, & Sugarman, 1994; Sheeber, Hops, Alpert, Davis, & Andrews, 1997; Strauss & Yodanis, 1996). Severe psychological abuse (excessive criticism, rejection, or emotional harshness) appears to have the most deleterious effects (McGee, Wolfe, & Wilson, 1997; Rohner, Bourque, & Elordi, 1996; Simons, Johnson, & Conger, 1994).

Why is authoritative parenting associated with healthy adolescent development? First, authoritative parents provide an appropriate balance between restrictiveness and autonomy, giving the adolescent opportunities to develop self-reliance while providing the sorts of standards, limits, and guidelines that developing individuals need (Rueter & Conger, 1995a, 1995b, 1998). Authoritative parents, for instance, are more likely to give children more independence gradually as they get older, which helps children develop self-reliance and self-assurance. Because of this, authoritative parenting promotes the development of adolescents' competence (Glasgow, Dornbusch, Troyer, Steinberg, & Ritter, 1997; Steinberg, Elmen, & Mounts, 1989) and enhances their ability to withstand a variety of potentially negative influences, including life stress (Barrera, Li, & Chassin, 1995; Hagan, MacMillan, & Wheaton, 1996; McCabe, 1997; McIntyre & Dusek, 1995; Wagner, Cohen, & Brook, 1996) and exposure to antisocial peers (Curtner-Smith & MacKinnon-Lewis, 1994; Kim, Hetherington, & Reiss, 1999; Mason, Cauce, Gonzales, & Hiraga, 1994; Mounts & Steinberg, 1995).

Second, because authoritative parents are more likely to engage their children in verbal give-and-take, they are likely to promote the sort of intellectual development that provides an important foundation for the development of psychosocial competence (Rueter & Conger, 1998). Authoritative parents, for example, are less likely than other parents to assert their authority by turning adolescents' personal decisions (e.g., over what type of music they listen to) into "moral" issues (Smetana, 1995; Smetana & Asquith, 1994). Family discussions in which decisions, rules, and expectations are explained help the child understand social systems and social relationships. This understanding plays an important part in the development of reasoning abilities, role taking, moral judgment, and empathy (Baumrind, 1978; Krevans & Gibbs, 1996).

Third, because authoritative parenting is based on a warm parent-child relationship, adolescents are more likely to identify with, admire, and form strong attachments to their parents, which leaves them more open to their parents' influence (Bogenschneider, Small, & Tsay, 1997; Darling & Steinberg, 1993; Reimer, Overton, Steidl, Rosenstein, & Horowitz, 1996; Sim, 2000). Adolescents who have had warm, close relationships with their parents are more likely, for example, to have similar attitudes and values (Brody, Moore, & Glei, 1994). Adolescents who are raised by nonauthoritative parents, in contrast, often end up having friends their parents disapprove of, including those involved in antisocial activity (Kim et al., 1999).

Finally, the child's own behavior may play a role in shaping authoritative parenting practices (Lewis, 1981a; Stice & Barrera, 1995). Children who are responsible, self-directed, curious, and self-assured elicit from their parents warmth, flexible guidance, and verbal give-and-take. In contrast, children who are aggressive, dependent, or less psychosocially mature in other ways may provoke parents' behavior that is excessively harsh, passive, or distant (Rueter & Conger, 1998). Par-

ents may enjoy being around children who are responsible, independent, and willing to tell them about their activities and whereabouts, and they may treat them more warmly as a result; what often appears to be "effective parental monitoring" may actually be the end result of a parent-adolescent relationship in which the adolescent willingly discloses information to the parent (Kerr & Stattin, 2000; Kerr, Stattin, & Trost, 1999). In contrast, children who are continually acting up make their parents short-tempered, impatient, or distant. In other words, the relationship between adolescent competence and authoritative parenting may be the result of a reciprocal cycle in which the child's psychosocial maturity leads to authoritative parenting, which in turn leads to the further development of maturity (Lerner et al., 1994; Repetti, 1996; Steinberg et al., 1989).

Ethnic Differences in Parenting Practices

A number of researchers have asked whether parents from different ethnic groups vary in their child rearing and whether the relation between parenting and adolescent outcomes is the same across ethnic groups. These, of course, are two different questions: The first concerns average differences between groups in their approaches to parenting (e.g., whether ethnic minority parents are stricter than white parents), whereas the second concerns the correlation between parenting practices and adolescent adjustment in different groups (e.g., whether the effect of strictness is the same in ethnic minority families as it is in white families).

In general, researchers find that authoritative parenting is less prevalent among African American, Asian American, and Hispanic American families than among white families, no doubt reflecting the fact that parenting practices are linked to cultural values and beliefs (Dornbusch et al., 1987; Steinberg et al., 1991; Steinberg, Dornbusch, & Brown, 1992; Yau & Smetana, 1996). Nevertheless, even though authoritative parenting is less common in ethnic minority families, its *effects* on adolescent adjustment are beneficial in all ethnic groups (Knight, Virdin, & Roosa, 1994; Mason, Cauce, Gonzales, & Hiraga, 1996; Steinberg et al., 1992). In other words, ethnic minority youngsters, for the most part, benefit just as much from parenting that is responsive and demanding as do their nonminority peers (Steinberg, 2001).

Research has also indicated that authoritarian parenting (high in demandingness but low in responsiveness) is more prevalent among ethnic minority

▲ *Research indicates important ethnic differences in parenting practices during adolescence. In general, Asian American parents are stricter than their counterparts from other cultures.* (Michael Newman/PhotoEdit)

(Formoso, Ruiz, & Gonzales, 1997; Rohner & Pettengill, 1985; Smetana & Gaines, 2000; Yau & Smetana, 1996). If they focus too much on parents' strictness when observing family relationships, white researchers may mislabel other ethnic groups' approaches to child rearing (which appear very controlling but which are neither aloof nor hostile) as authoritarian (Gonzales et al., 1996). Similar arguments have been made about the misinterpretation of strictness among American parents who are very religious conservative Protestants, a group that now makes up between 20 and 25 percent of the U.S. population (Gunnoe, Hetherington, & Reiss, 1999; Wilcox, 1998).

Autonomy and Attachment in the Adolescent's Family

Several studies of conversations between adolescents and their parents have examined the factors in the nature of parent-adolescent communication that contribute to healthy adolescent development. In these studies, families are asked to discuss a problem together, and their interaction is taped and later analyzed. Generally speaking, families with psychologically competent teenagers interact in ways that permit family members to express their autonomy while remaining attached, or connected, to other family members (Grotevant, 1997; Rathunde, 1996; Silverberg et al., 1992). In these families, verbal give-and-take is the norm, and adolescents (as well as parents) are encouraged to express their own opinions, even if this sometimes leads to disagreement. At the same time, however, the importance of maintaining close relationships in the family is emphasized, and individuals are encouraged to consider how their actions may affect other family members (Rueter & Conger, 1995a, 1995b). Indeed, adolescents who are permitted to assert their own opinions within a family context that is secure and loving develop higher self-esteem and more mature coping abilities. Adolescents whose autonomy is squelched are at risk for developing feelings of depression, and those who do not feel connected are more likely than their peers to develop behavior problems (Allen, Hauser, Bell, & O'Conner,

than among white families, even after taking ethnic differences in socioeconomic status into account (Chao, 1994; Dornbusch et al., 1987; Steinberg, Lamborn, Dornbusch, & Darling, 1992). As opposed to research on authoritative parenting, however, which suggests comparable effects across ethnic groups, research on authoritarian parenting indicates that the adverse effects of this style of parenting may be greater among white youngsters than among their ethnic minority counterparts (Chao, 1994; Dornbusch et al., 1987; Lamborn, Dornbusch, & Steinberg, 1996; Steinberg et al., 1994). Several explanations have been offered for this finding.

First, some writers have suggested that, because ethnic minority families are more likely to live in dangerous communities, authoritarian parenting, with its emphasis on control, may not be as harmful and may even carry some benefits. Second, as several researchers (Chao, 1994; Gonzales, Cauce, & Mason, 1996) have pointed out, the distinction between authoritative and authoritarian parenting may not always make sense when applied to parents from other cultures. For example, nonwhite parents frequently combine a very high degree of strictness (like white authoritarian parents) with warmth (like white authoritative parents)

1994; Allen, Hauser, Eickholt, Bell, & O'Conner, 1994; Hauser, Powers, & Noam, 1991).

Rather than posing attachment and autonomy as opposites, studies of family interaction indicate that the path to healthy psychological development during adolescence is likely to combine the two. In other words, adolescents appear to do best when they grow up in a family atmosphere that permits the development of individuality against a backdrop of close family ties (Cooper, Grotevant, & Condon, 1983; Grotevant & Cooper, 1986). In these families, conflict between parents and adolescents can play a very important and positive role in the adolescent's social and cognitive development, because individuals are encouraged to express their opinions in an atmosphere that does not risk severing the emotional attachment (Cooper, 1988). In chapter 10, we will look more closely at the nature of attachment between parents and adolescents.

RECAP

Psychologists have identified four basic styles of parenting during adolescence: authoritative, authoritarian, indulgent, and indifferent. In general, adolescents from authoritative homes fare the best on measures of psychological adjustment, whereas adolescents from indifferent homes fare worst. Authoritative parenting, which has been shown to benefit adolescents from a variety of ethnic backgrounds, is composed of three main factors: warmth, structure, and autonomy support. Studies of parent-adolescent interaction show, as well, that the healthiest families are those that permit the adolescent to develop a sense of autonomy while staying emotionally attached to the family.

Food for Thought

Our discussion has focused mainly on the consequences of growing up with parents who use various styles of parenting. But what makes parents choose the sort of parenting style they use? Why are some parents authoritative but others not?

Adolescents' Relationships with Siblings

Far more is known about adolescents' relations with their parents than about their relations with brothers and sisters. During the past 10 years, however, research on ado-

lescence and the family moved beyond studies of parent-adolescent relationship to also include research on the family system (e.g., Rueter & Conger, 1994), the extended family (e.g., Clingempeel et al., 1992; Spieker & Bensley, 1994), and siblings. There has been a particular surge of interest in sibling relationships and the ways in which siblings influence adolescent development.

In general, sibling relationships have characteristics that set them apart from both other family relationships (such as those between adolescents and their parents) and other relationships with peers (such as those between adolescents and their close friends) (Furman & Buhrmester, 1985; Raffaelli & Larson, 1987). In one study, for example, young adolescents were asked to rate several types of relationships (for example, with parents, siblings, friends, grandparents) along similar dimensions. As you can see in figure 4.4, sibling relationships were rated like those with parents for companionship and importance, but they were rated more like friendships with respect to power, assistance, and satisfaction.

Over the course of adolescence, adolescents' relationships with siblings, and especially with younger siblings, become more egalitarian but more distant and less emotionally intense (Anderson & Starcher, 1992; Buhrmester & Furman, 1990). Despite these changes over time, there is considerable stability in the quality of sibling relationships between childhood and adolescence, and siblings who are relatively closer during middle childhood are relatively closer as young adolescents (Dunn, Slomkowski, & Beardsall, 1994).

The sibling relationship in adolescence is an emotionally charged one, marked by conflict and rivalry but also nurturance and social support (Lempers & Clark-Lempers, 1992). As children mature from childhood to early adolescence, sibling conflict increases (Brody et al., 1994), with adolescents reporting more negativity in their sibling relationships, compared with their relationships with peers (Buhrmester & Furman, 1990). Negative interactions between siblings are especially common in families under economic stress (Conger, Conger, & Elder, 1994). High levels of conflict in early adolescence gradually diminish as adolescents move into middle and late adolescence. As siblings mature, relations become more egalitarian and supportive, and, as with the parent-adolescent relationship, siblings become less influential as adolescents expand their relations outside the family (Hetherington et al., 1999).

Several researchers have uncovered important interconnections among parent-child, sibling, and peer relationships in adolescence. A considerable amount of

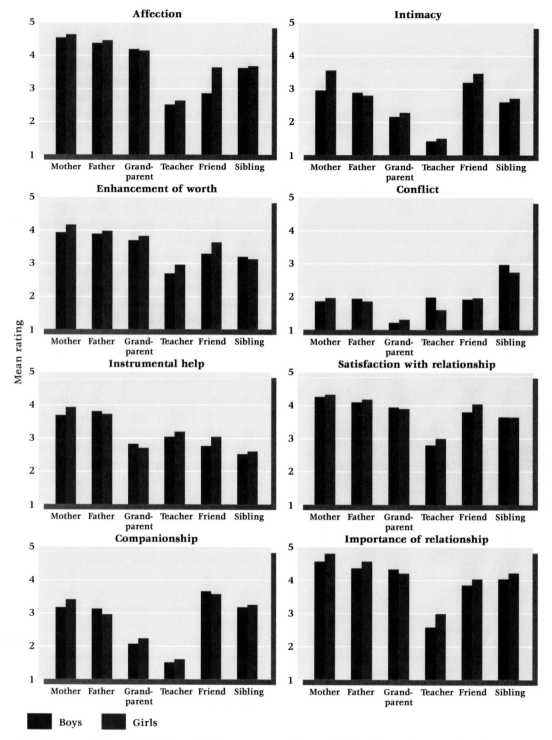

Figure 4.4   *These graphs show similarities and differences among adolescents' relationships with parents, friends, siblings, and significant others.* (Furman & Buhrmester, 1985)

research indicates that the quality of the parent-adolescent relationship influences the quality of relations among adolescent brothers and sisters, which in turn influences adolescents' relationships with peers (e.g., Brody et al., 1994; MacKinnon-Lewis, Starnes, Volling, & Johnson, 1997). Harmony and cohesiveness in the parent-adolescent relationship are associated with less sibling conflict and a more positive sibling relationship (e.g., Hetherington et al., 1999). In contrast, adolescents who experience maternal rejection and negativity are more likely to display aggression with siblings. By the same token, children and adolescents learn much about social relationships from sibling interactions, and they bring this knowledge and experience to friendships outside the family (Brody, Stoneman, & McCoy, 1994; McCoy, Brody, & Stoneman, 1994). In poorly functioning families, aggressive interchanges between unsupervised siblings may provide a training ground within which adolescents learn, practice, and perfect antisocial and aggressive behavior (Bank, Reid, & Greenley, 1994).

The quality of the sibling relationship affects not only adolescents' peer relations but also their adjustment in general (Seginer, 1998). Positive sibling relationships contribute to adolescent school competence, sociability, autonomy, and self-worth (e.g., Hetherington et al., 1999; Rowe et al., 1989). Having a close sibling relationship can partially ameliorate the negative effects of not having friends in school (East & Rook, 1992), and siblings can serve as sources of advice and guidance (Tucker, Barber, & Eccles, 1997). At the same time, siblings can influence the development of problem behavior (Conger et al., 1997). For example, younger sisters of childbearing adolescents are more likely to engage in early sexual activity and to become pregnant during adolescence (e.g., East 1996b). Siblings also influence each other's drug use and antisocial behavior (e.g., Rowe et al., 1989).

> **RECAP**
>
> *In general, adolescents' relations with siblings are different from those with parents or with friends. Over the course of adolescence, adolescents' relationships with siblings—and especially with younger siblings—become more equal but more distant and less emotionally intense. Studies show that the quality of the adolescent's sibling relationships is affected by the quality of the parent-child relationship and that the quality of adolescent-sibling relationships affects the nature of the adolescent's relationships with peers.*

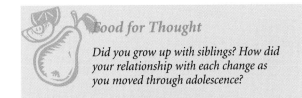

Food for Thought

Did you grow up with siblings? How did your relationship with each change as you moved through adolescence?

Behavioral Genetics and Adolescent Development

One topic of interest to researchers who study adolescents and their siblings concerns how closely siblings resemble each other in various characteristics, such as intelligence, personality, and interests. Recent advances in the study of **behavioral genetics** have provided new insights into this issue, as well as a host of others concerning the joint impact of genes and environment on development. Researchers examine these questions by studying adolescents who are twins, to see whether identical twins are more similar than fraternal twins (e.g., Elkins, McGue, & Iacono, 1997); by studying adolescents who have been adopted, to see whether adopted adolescents are more like their biological parents than like their adoptive parents (e.g., Deater-Deckard & Plomin, 1999); and by studying adolescents and their siblings in stepfamilies, to see whether similarity between siblings varies with their biological relatedness (e.g., Hetherington, Reiss, & Plomin, 1994). In addition to examining whether and how much given traits are genetically versus environmentally determined, researchers also ask how these two sets of factors interact (e.g., whether the same environment affects people with different genetic makeups in different ways, or whether people with different genetic makeups evoke different reactions from their environment) (Collins et al., 2000).

In studies of genetic and environmental influences on adolescent development, researchers distinguish between two types of environmental influences. **Shared environmental influences** are factors in the environment that individuals, such as siblings, have in common and that make them similar in personality and behavior. **Nonshared environmental influences** are factors in the environments of individuals that are not similar and that, as a consequence, make individuals different from one another (Plomin & Daniels, 1987). In studies of siblings, nonshared environmental influences can include factors within the family as well as outside it. For example, if two siblings are treated very differently by their parents, this is

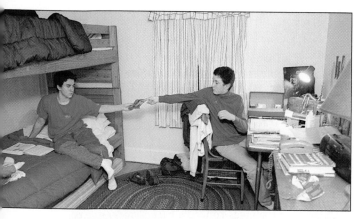

▲ *Because siblings live in close proximity to each other, they have added opportunities for both positive and negative interaction.* (Patrick Watson/Watson Media Services)

considered a nonshared environmental influence. Ineed, there is some evidence that this sort of nonshared environment—that is, the nonshared environment that results from people having different experiences within what would appear to be the same context—is the most important (Turkheimer & Waldron, 2000). Studies indicate that both genetic and nonshared environmental influences, such as parental differential treatment, peer relations, and school experiences, are particularly strong in adolescence. In contrast, shared environmental factors, such as parental personality, a family's socioeconomic status, and the neighborhood in which two siblings live, are less influential (e.g., McGue et al., 1996; Pike et al., 1996).

Genetic factors strongly influence aggression, antisocial behavior, and delinquency. Evidence suggests that aggressive behavior is more biologically driven than other behaviors, although shared and nonshared influences on adolescents' antisocial behavior, including aggression, also have been found (Deater-Deckard & Plomin 1999; Eley, Lichenstein, & Stevenson, 1999). Genetic factors also have been linked to emotional distress in adolescence, such as risk for suicide and depressed mood (Blumenthal & Kupfer, 1988; Jacobson & Rowe, 1999).

Research also has found strong genetic influences on adolescent competence, self-image, and intelligence. Adolescents' self-perceptions of their scholastic competence, athletic competence, physical appearance, social competence, and general self-worth are moderately heritable, with little evidence for shared environmental influences (McGuire et al., 1994; McGuire, Manke, Saudino, Reiss, Hetherington, & Plomin, 1999). Intelligence in adolescence (as indexed by IQ) is also under strong genetic control, with genetic influences compounding over time and ultimately becoming more in-

fluential than the family environment, although genetic influences on school performance, in contrast to intelligence, are more modest (Loehlin et al., 1989; Teachman, 1997). In general, genetic influences on intelligence are stronger in families with highly educated parents, consistent with the general notion that the influence of genes is typically higher in more favorable environments (Rowe et al., 1999).

When researchers study the impact of the family context on adolescent development, they assume that they are studying an environmental, rather than a genetic, influence. But one of the most interesting findings to emerge in recent years is that assessments of the adolescent's family may also reflect features of the adolescent's and parents' genetic makeup. Actual and reported levels of conflict, support, and involvement in the family, for example, are significantly influenced by adolescents' genetic makeup (Neiderhiser, Pike, Hetherington, & Reiss, 1998), in part because adolescents who display hostile and antisocial behaviors are more likely than adolescents not prone to these problems to elicit negative behaviors from their parents (Ge, et al., 1996), and in part because the same genetic factors that may make adolescents prone to fighting (e.g., irritability) may make them prone to be critical of their parents when questioned about their family (Neiderhiser et al., 1999). Because of this, it is important to be cautious when interpreting research on adolescent development in the family context. As it turns out, there is growing evidence that at least some of the impact of parenting on adolescent adjustment, depression, and antisocial behavior can be explained by the genetic transmission of these characteristics from parents to their children (Neiderhiser et al., 1999).

Although many traits are influenced by genetic factors, genes in no way determine cognitive, emotional, or social development (Collins et al., 2000). Given the fact that the environment plays an important role in shaping development, and in view of research suggesting that the family context is an important influence, how can we explain the fact that siblings who grow up in the same family often turn out to be very different from one another? One answer is that siblings may have very different family experiences, both because they are treated differently by their parents and because they often perceive similar experiences in different ways (Anderson, Hetherington, Reiss, & Howe, 1994; Hoffman, 1991; Mekos, Hetherington, & Reiss, 1996; O'Connor, Hetherington, Reiss, & Plomin, 1995; Plomin & Daniels, 1987). One brother may describe his family as very close-knit, whereas another may have experienced it as very distant. One girl describes her family life as plagued with argument and conflict; her sister describes it as peaceful and agreeable. In other words, even though we may assume that children growing up in the same family have shared the same environment, this may not really be the case.

As one might expect, unequal treatment from mothers or fathers often creates conflict among siblings (Brody et al., 1987) and is linked to problem behaviors, such as depression and antisocial behavior (Reiss et al., 1995). Studies show that differences in siblings' real and perceived family experiences are related to different patterns of development (Anderson et al., 1994; Conger & Conger, 1994; Mekos et al., 1996). In general, better-adjusted adolescents are more likely than their siblings to report that their relationship with their mother was close, that their relations with brothers or sisters were friendly, that they were involved in family decision making, and that they were given a high level of responsibility around the house (Daniels, Dunn, Furstenberg, & Plomin, 1985). Despite this evidence for differential treatment and its potentially adverse influence on adolescent development, adolescents report that 75 percent of parental treatment is not differential. Interestingly, studies show that youngsters generally appreciate the reasons for parents treating siblings differently and that sibling relationships are strained only when this differential treatment is perceived as unfair (Kowal & Kramer, 1997).

In addition to the fact that siblings have different experiences inside their family, siblings also may have very different experiences outside the family—at school, with friends, in the neighborhood. These contexts provide yet another source of nonshared environmental influence. Because factors other than the family environment shape adolescent development and behavior, siblings may turn out to be very different if they have divergent experiences outside the home.

● **Adolescents and Adoption** Studies of the psychological development of adolescents who have been adopted have yielded mixed and often contradictory results. Although several earlier studies reached the conclusion that adopted individuals have many more psychological problems than individuals raised by their biological parents, more recent research, on larger and more representative samples, has questioned this conclusion. Much appears to depend on the age at which the child was adopted, with a higher incidence of problems seen among adolescents who had been adopted relatively later in childhood, rather than in infancy. By and large, though, it appears that any differences observed between adopted and nonadopted adolescents

are quite small and vary a great deal depending on the specific measure of adjustment examined. In general, adopted individuals show slightly higher rates of delinquency and substance use and poorer school performance, but lower rates of withdrawal and interpersonal problems, and higher rates of prosocial behavior (Sharma, McGue, & Benson, 1998).

RECAP

Behavioral genetics researchers distinguish among three types of influences: genetic influences, shared environmental influences, and nonshared environmental influences. Research has demonstrated strong genetic contributions to a wide variety of traits, including intelligence, competence, depression, and antisocial inclinations. At the same time, however, studies of siblings find that many brothers and sisters, who share many genes, are very different. These differences are attributed to the influence of nonshared environmental factors.

Food for Thought

What factors might contribute to siblings having different experiences in the same family?

THE ADOLESCENT'S FAMILY IN A CHANGING SOCIETY

If there is one word that has best characterized the nature of family life in America as we have moved into the twenty-first century, that word is *diversity*. As you read in chapter 3, a large and growing proportion of American adolescents are from ethnic minority families, and a large number of these youngsters are foreign-born or recent immigrants. In addition to this ethnic diversity, today's adolescents grow up in a vast array of family forms, from the traditional two-parent, stay-at-home-mother structure that dominated the demographic landscape of the late 1950s, to blended, dual-career stepfamilies that gained prominence in the mid-1990s. Some adolescents have parents who are in their midforties (the most common age among parents of teenagers), but many have parents who are younger than 30, and a substantial number have parents who are in their fifties or sixties. About one-fifth of youngsters are only children, but one-sixth have three or more siblings. Nearly one-fifth of American adolescents today grow up in poverty, but almost one-

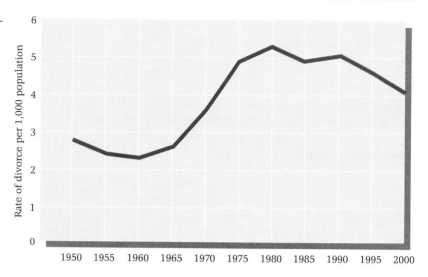

Figure 4.5   *The divorce rate rose dramatically between 1960 and 1980 but has more or less leveled off since then.*

third live in families whose circumstances can be described as relatively luxurious (Hernandez, 1997).

In America and in many comparably industrialized countries, the family has undergone a series of profound changes during the past 30 years that have diversified its form and, as a result, adolescents' daily experiences. Increased rates of divorce, childbearing outside of marriage, and maternal employment, as well as a changing international economy and accelerating geographic mobility, all have dramatically altered the world in which children and adolescents grow up. Although some of the most striking trends in family life slowed during the early 1990s, they did not reverse, by any means. The divorce rate, the proportion of single-parent families, and the rate of maternal employment, all of which skyrocketed during the 1970s and 1980s, stabilized at their historically high levels at the beginning of the 1990s and have changed very little since then (Hernandez, 1997; Kilborn, 1996).

Questions about whether these changes have weakened the family's influence over young people or have harmed young people continue to generate heated debate. According to some observers, the all-too-familiar problems of young people—low achievement test scores, high rates of alcohol and drug use, sexual precocity, violence in the schools—are due to changes in the family (e.g., Cornwell, Eggebeen, & Meschke, 1996; Uhlenberg & Eggebeen, 1986). Others, less pessimistic, have noted that, although the prototypical, *Leave It to Beaver* family style of the 1950s has become less common, the new types of families are commendable in their own right and strong in their own ways (Parke & Buriel, 1998; Weisner & Garnier, 1995). According to many, supporting and strengthening today's families—in all their diversity—is more

important than wringing our hands over the passing of family forms of the 1950s.

Just how dramatic have the changes in American family life been over the past half-century? Consider four of the most important shifts: increases in the rate of divorce, increases in the number of single parents, increases in the rate of mothers' employment, and increases in the proportion of families living in poverty. These shifts have transformed the nature of family life for many young people.

As you can see from figure 4.5, the rate of divorce has increased markedly since 1950, rising steadily, and at times rapidly, until 1980. (The divorce rate increased most dramatically after 1965 and peaked around 1980.) By 1979, the divorce rate in the United States had become the highest in the world (Hetherington, 1981). Between 1980 and 1999, the rate of divorce remained more or less constant, rising somewhat in some years but falling in others (National Center for Vital Statistics, 2000). **Demographers** (social scientists who study changes in the composition of the population) estimate that two-thirds of all first marriages are likely to disrupt through divorce or separation and that nearly half of all American children born during the 1990s—today's young teenagers—will experience their parents' divorce and will spend approximately five years in a single-parent household (Hernandez, 1997; Hetherington, Henderson, & Reiss, 1999). In addition, a sizable percentage of youngsters will spend time in a single-parent household from birth; nearly one-third of children living in single-parent homes live with a parent who has never been married (Weinraub & Gringlas, 1995). When youngsters live with only one of their natural

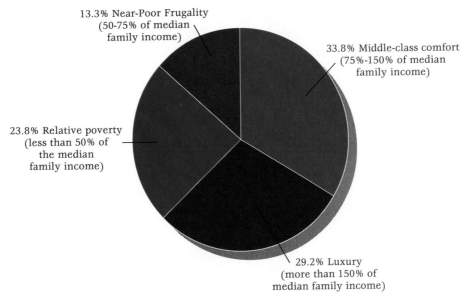

13.3% Near-Poor Frugality
(50-75% of median
family income)

33.8% Middle-class comfort
(75%-150% of median
family income)

23.8% Relative poverty
(less than 50% of
the median
family income)

29.2% Luxury
(more than 150% of
median family income)

Figure 4.6   The proportions of adolescents living at various income levels. (Hernandez, 1997)

parents, either in single-parent or in two-parent house-holds, it is nearly always with the mother; only about 20 percent of children whose parents have been divorced live with their father (Hetherington et al., 1999). It is also the case that a substantial number of adolescents who are classified as living in single-parent households actually live with more than one adult, often with the unmarried partner of the child's parent (Eggebeen, Snyder, & Manning, 1996; Manning & Lichter, 1996).

There are important racial and ethnic differences in these patterns of family life, however. African American youngsters are far more likely than other youngsters to experience parental divorce and to be born outside of marriage, and they are far less likely to experience their parents' remarriage (Hetherington, Bridges, & Insabella, 1998). As a consequence, African American adolescents spend longer periods of time in single-parent households than do other adolescents. Whereas about 75 percent of all white children and nearly two-thirds of all Hispanic children live with two parents, only about one-third of African American children do (U.S. Bureau of the Census, 1999b).

Because more than 75 percent of divorced men, and two-thirds of divorced women remarry, most youngsters whose parents separate also experience living in a stepfamily. And, because the rate of divorce is higher for second marriages than first marriages (60 percent versus 50 percent), most youth whose parents remarry will experience yet a second divorce. Moreover, because divorces generally occur faster in remarriages—one-fourth happen within five years—many children confront a second divorce before they have finished adapting to having a stepparent (Hetherington et al., 1999).

Another trend worth noting concerns maternal employment. Among women with school-aged children, full-time employment has increased steadily since 1950. Today, 75 percent of all married women with adolescent children are employed, and more than 45 percent of these mothers work full-time. Nearly 80 percent of single mothers with adolescent children are employed outside the home, and more than half of these mothers are employed full-time. Among elementary school children, nearly three-quarters have mothers in the labor force, nearly 40 percent in full-time jobs (Hernandez, 1997).

Finally, since the mid-1970s, after years of steady decline in the proportion of children living at or near the poverty line, there has been a substantial increase in the proportion of poor children in the United States. Today, nearly 25 percent of all adolescents grow up in poor families (i.e., families whose household income, adjusted for family size, is less than half the national average), and another 15 percent are classified as near-poor. Approximately one-third of adolescents live in middle-class comfort, and another 30 percent enjoy very high family incomes (50 percent higher than the average family income) (Hernandez, 1997) (see figure 4.6). As figure 4.7 indicates, the gap between the very poor and the very wealthy has widened in the past 30

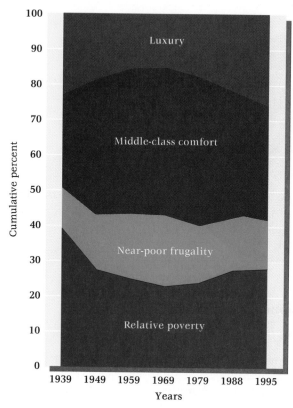

Figure 4.7   In the past 30 years, the proportion of children living in either poverty or luxury has increased, while the proportion of middle-class children has diminished. (Hernandez, 1997)

years, with relative increases in both poor and affluent children and a shrinkage of the population of children living in middle-class comfort. Poverty, as noted in chapter 3, is much more likely to touch the lives of non-white children; between 40 and 50 percent of African American and Hispanic American children grow up in poverty in the United States. Among the many contributors to the increase in poverty during recent decades has been the erosion of blue-collar jobs; a decline in government benefits for families, such as Aid for Families with Dependent Children (Huston Mcloyd, & Garcia Coll, 1994); and the rise in single-parent families (40 percent of white single-mother households and 60 percent of nonwhite single-mother households are poor). One reason for the large disparity in poverty rates between white and nonwhite children, in fact, is the racial disparity in rates of single parenthood: Because nonwhite children are more likely to be raised in single-parent homes, they are more likely to be poor (Hernandez, 1997).

In summary, few adolescents live in the idealized— perhaps even romanticized— family structure that was common before 1960: the two-parent family with the father as the only breadwinner. In fact, less than 15 percent of all adolescents live in this sort of arrangement today. Many adolescents live in single-parent households, almost always with their mothers, and most adolescents have mothers who work outside the home. Of the young people living in two-parent families, a substantial number—close to 15 percent—live with only one of their biological parents (Hernandez, 1997). And a shockingly high number of adolescents grow up under severe economic disadvantage.

RECAP

Four of the most important changes that have occurred among American families with adolescents are the increase in the rate of divorce, the increase in the prevalence of single-parent households, the increased participation of mothers in the labor force, and the increase in the proportion of families living in poverty. Half of all individuals born during the 1990s will experience their parents' divorce, and more than half of these youngsters will experience living in a stepfamily. As a consequence of this, as well as the large number of children born to nonmarried mothers, most children born in the 1990s will spend at least part of their childhood or adolescence in a single-parent household. About 80 percent of contemporary teenagers have mothers who are employed outside the home. And nearly one-quarter of all adolescents grow up in poverty; poverty is especially common among ethnic minority families.

Food for Thought

What demographic trends do you predict for the next several decades? Do you foresee changes in the rates of divorce, remarriage, maternal employment, or poverty?

ADOLESCENT DEVELOPMENT AND THE CHANGING FAMILY

To what extent has the changed nature of the American family changed the nature of adolescent development? How do divorce, absent fathers, working mothers, and economic stress affect adolescents' development?

Many individuals are certain that the answer to these questions is "For the worse." However, before we jump to this conclusion, it is important to raise two considerations. First, although increases in adolescents' problems between 1950 and 1980—as indexed by such indicators as drug use, suicide, and poor school achievement—occurred alongside many of these shifts in family life, it is difficult to say that the family changes caused the changes in adolescent behavior. Social scientists who have argued that the decline in family life has led to these problems (e.g., Uhlenberg & Eggebeen, 1986) have had a hard time explaining why adolescents' psychological and behavioral well-being took a turn for the *better* in the early 1980s, despite the continued "demise" of the family (see Furstenberg, 1990a). Moreover, the one group of young people whose psychological and behavioral profile improved most markedly in the past 10 years—poor, minority youngsters—experienced the most dramatic "decline" in family life during this time.

Second, because the conditions under which divorce, single parenthood, and maternal employment take place vary tremendously from family to family, it is hard to generalize about their effects on adolescents. (In contrast, it is relatively easy to generalize about the effects of poverty on adolescents, which are almost always negative.) To some young people, divorce brings a welcome end to family conflict and tension; to others, it may be extremely disruptive psychologically. Some young people living just with their mothers see their fathers more often than do their peers who live in homes where the father ostensibly is present. And, although for some adolescents having an employed mother means curtailed family time and less contact with her, for others a mother who is employed provides an important role model and added opportunities to take on responsibility around the household. In other words, the variations *within* various family structures are likely to be more important than the differences among them. This is readily apparent when we look at how adolescents are affected by parental divorce.

Adolescents, Divorce, and Single-Parent Families

Three decades ago, any discussion of adolescents and divorce would likely have started with the assumption that living one parent was not as good as living with two and, consequently, that children whose parents divorced would be at a distinct disadvantage, relative to those whose parents remained married. Over the past 25 years, however, researchers' ideas about divorce and its impact on the adolescent have changed dramatically, as new and better studies have challenged, clarified, and tempered the conclusions of past research. Although it is still the consensus of most social scientists that adolescents from divorced homes have more difficulties than those from nondivorced homes, the explanation for this difference is far more complicated than the conventional wisdom that "two parents are better than one" or that "all children need a mother *and* a father."

Three sets of findings have questioned these simple assertions. First, a growing body of research suggests that the number of parents in the adolescent's house matters far less than the quality of the relationships the young person has with the important adults in his or her life (Buchanan, Maccoby, & Dornbusch, 1996; Hardesty, Wenk, & Morgan, 1995; Hines, 1997; McKeown et al., 1997). Adolescents from stepfamilies, for example, have as many, if not more, problems than those from single-parent homes, even though adolescents in stepfamilies have the ostensible benefit of two parents in the home (Allison & Furstenberg, 1989; Hetherington et al., 1999; Jeynes, 1999). In addition, youngsters from single-parent families who have not experienced divorce (for example, youngsters who have lost a parent through death or youngsters with a single mother who has *never* been married) have fewer difficulties than their counterparts from divorced or remarried homes (Demo & Acock, 1996). Finally, adolescents in two-parent homes do not always have warm and close relationships with their parents; indeed, adolescents living in "father-absent" homes have higher self-esteem than adolescents who live in two-parent homes but who feel that their fathers have little interest in them (Clark & Barber, 1994). In fact, adolescents in divorced, single-parent families describe their parents as friendlier than do adolescents whose parents are married (Asmussen & Larson, 1991) and are in a relatively more positive mood when with their family than when with friends (Larson & Gillman, 1996). Adolescents and their parents argue less often in divorced households, perhaps because single parents tend to be more permissive in their child rearing, which may make for less parent-adolescent conflict (Smetana, Yau, Restrepo, & Braeges, 1991).

Second, several longitudinal studies have indicated that it is the *process* of going through a divorce, not the resulting family structure, that matters most for adolescents' mental health (Buchanan et al., 1996; Hetherington et al., 1998). In general, most studies show that the period of greatest difficulty for most adolescents is, as you would think, right around the time of the disruption itself. Although many young people show signs of difficulty —among them, problems in school, more behavior problems, and more anxiety —immediately after their parents divorce or remarry, by the time two years have passed most of these children have adjusted to the change and behave comparably to their peers whose biological parents have remained married (Hetherington et al., 1998). Although adolescents whose parents have divorced have, on average, more problems than those whose parents remain married, the vast majority of individuals with divorced parents do not have significant problems (Hetherington et al., 1998).

Third, research has linked the adverse consequences of divorce to a number of factors not specifically due to having a single parent or an absent father (see Hetherington et al., 1998, for a review). These include the *exposure of the children to marital conflict* (Amato & Keith, 1991a; Forehand et al., 1991; Vandewater & Lansford, 1998); *disorganized or disrupted parenting* (Fauber, Forehand, McCombs, & Wierson, 1990; Forehand, Thomas, Wierson, Brody, & Fauber, 1990; Hetherington et al., 1992; Shucksmith, Glendinning, & Hendry, 1997); or *marked increases in the degree of stress experienced by the household* (Hetherington et al., 1998; Thomson, Hanson, & McLanahan, 1994). Adolescents living in two-parent families in which no divorce has occurred are also harmed by marital conflict, disrupted parenting (especially parenting that is too lenient, too harsh, or inconsistent), and family stress, such as loss of income. In other words, the adverse temporary effects of divorce or remarriage on youngsters' well-being appear to reflect the heightened conflict, disorganization, and stress surrounding the event, not the divorce or remarriage per se. Experts now believe that the most important pathway through which divorce may adversely affect adolescent adjustment is through its direct and indirect impact on the quality of parenting to which the child is exposed (Hetherington et al., 1998).

Finally, although some of the apparent effects of parental divorce are the result of exposure to such stressors as marital conflict and disorganized parenting, at least some of the differences between adolescents whose parents have divorced and those whose parents have not are due to genetic differences between the teenagers. Adults who divorce are different from those who do not with respect to many traits that have strong genetic origins—such as aggression, antisociality, and predispositions to various sorts of emotional and behavioral problems, such as depression—and these traits are passed on from parents to children. At least part of the reason that adolescents from divorced homes may have more problems than their peers is that they have inherited from their divorced parents some of the same traits that influenced their parents' divorce (O'Connor, Caspi, DeFries, & Plomin, 2000).

There also are interesting differences among children in how vulnerable they are to the short-term effects of divorce. In general, immediate problems are relatively more common among boys, younger children, children with a difficult temperament, children who do not have supportive relationships with adults outside the immediate family, and youngsters whose parents divorce during childhood or preadolescence. Especially interesting, if somewhat disheartening, is the finding that contact after the divorce between the child and his or her noncustodial father does not invariably reduce the adverse effects of marital dissolution and sometimes may make things worse, especially in African American families (Thomas, Farrell, & Barnes, 1996). *Financial* support from fathers, however, is associated with less problem behavior (Furstenberg, Morgan & Allison, 1987).

▲ *Contact with members of one's extended family may play an especially important role in the socialization of African American youth.* (Bill Bachman/PhotoEdit)

Studies of African American youth indicate that social support from friends and relatives outside the family is an especially important resource for inner-city children growing up in single-parent homes (Mason, Cauce, Gonzales, Hiraga, & Grove, 1994; Salem, Zimmerman, & Notaro, 1998; Taylor, 1996; Taylor, Casten, & Flickinger, 1993; Taylor & Roberts, 1995). Support from kin, in particular, appears to increase single parents' effectiveness in child rearing, and this, in turn, tends to limit adolescents' misbehavior. This support can come from relatives living apart from, or within, the adolescent's household. For example, one study of African American youngsters found that children growing up in homes headed by their mothers and grandmothers fared significantly better than did those growing up in single-parent homes or in stepfamilies (Barbarin & Soler, 1993). These studies, as well as others, remind us that relatives other than parents may play an extremely important role in adolescents' lives, especially within ethnic groups that historically have placed a great deal of importance on maintaining close ties to extended family members. Single parenthood and extensive contact with the extended family have been salient features of African American family life for more than 100 years (Ruggles, 1994).

The Impact of Marital Conflict

Although divorce is generally associated with short-term difficulties for the adolescent, several studies show that at least some of the differences between adolescents from divorced versus nondivorced homes were present before the parents divorced (Cherlin et al., 1991), although not all researchers report this (e.g., Forehand, Armistead, & David, 1997). In one sample of British youngsters who were followed from birth into adulthood, 7-year-olds whose parents *eventually* divorced had more educational and behavior problems than did 7-year-olds whose parents did not divorce (Cherlin, Chase-Lansdale, & McRae, 1998; Elliott & Richards, 1991). One explanation for this is that the children in the households that later divorced were exposed to higher levels of marital unhappiness and conflict and strained parent-child relationships, both of which are known to increase children's difficulties (Amato & Booth, 1996; Forehand, Neighbors, Devine, & Armistead, 1994).

The recognition that exposure to marital conflict, apart from and in addition to divorce itself, has harmful effects on children's development has prompted many researchers to study why and how the quality of the adolescent's parents' marriage affects the teenager's mental health and behavior (Davies & Cummings, 1994; Erel & Burman, 1995; Feldman & Fisher, 1997; Fincham, 1994; Harold & Conger, 1997; Rogers & Holmbeck, 1997). Several conclusions have emerged from this research. First, children are more adversely affected by marital conflict when they are aware of it than when it is more covert (Feldman & Wentzel, 1995; Harold & Conger, 1997). For this reason, marital conflict is particularly harmful when it is especially hostile, physically violent, or frightening (Buehler et al., 1998; Gordis, Margolin, & St. John, 1997; Harold & Conger, 1997; Osofsky, 1995). Exposure to overt marital conflict and domestic violence has been linked to a wide range of adolescent problems, including aggression, delinquency, and other types of acting-out behavior (Harold & Conger, 1997; Krishnakumar & Buehler, 1996; Sim & Vuchinich, 1996).

Second, children are more negatively affected when the marital conflict leads to feelings of insecurity, self-blame, or threat. Adolescents who blame themselves for their parents' conflict, whose feelings of security are challenged, or who are drawn into their parents' arguments are more likely to feel anxious, depressed, and distressed (Buehler, Krishnakumar, Anthony, Tittsworth, & Stone, 1994; Davies & Cummings, 1994).

Finally, marital conflict more adversely affects the adolescent when the conflict disrupts the quality of the parent-child relationship. Adolescents are directly affected by exposure to their parents' conflict, to be sure, but several studies have found as well that tension between spouses spills over into the parent-child relationship, making mothers and fathers more hostile, more irritable, and less effective as parents (Almeida & Wethington, 1996; Davies & Cummings, 1994; Fine & Kurdek, 1995; Harold, Fincham, Osborne, & Conger, 1977). Adolescents who perceive their parents as hostile or uncaring are more likely than their peers to report a wide range of emotional and behavior problems.

The Longer-Term Effects of Divorce

Social scientists have also looked at the longer-term (more than two or three years) consequences of divorce. These studies, for example, look at elementary school children whose parents divorced when the children were in preschool or at adolescents whose parents split up during the youngsters' elementary school years. Presumably, if the adverse effects of divorce were

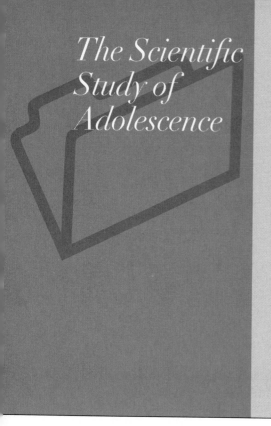

The Scientific Study of Adolescence

Parental Divorce and the Well-Being of Adolescents

Research into the impact of divorce on adolescent development burgeoned during the 1980s, with dozens of studies appearing in the scientific literature in a relatively short period of time. When so many studies on one topic appear so quickly, the overall pattern of results usually appears inconsistent and contradictory, with some studies showing significant effects and others not. This happened in the early years of research on the long-term impact of divorce; some scientists concluded that children from divorced homes are at a psychological disadvantage, whereas others argued that they are not.

Apparent inconsistency in research fidings is especially likely when the **effect size** under consideration is small—that is, when the absolute size of the difference between comparison groups (e.g., adolescents from divorced versus nondivorced homes) is not very large. In order for a small effect to be statisticaly significant, the study sample needs to be sufficiently large. for example, a correlation of .25 (which most social scientists would consider a small to moderate effect), would be statistically significant in a sample of 60 cases, but not in a sample of 50 cases. (A **correlation** is a measure of the strength of an association between two variables, which can range from −1.0 to 1.0, with a correlation of .00 indicative of no association whatsoever). Two researchers studying the same phenomenon could come to opposite conclusions (i.e., one saying a finding is significant and the other saying it is not) simply because they had different

attributable solely to the immediate problems of adjusting to a new household structure, or were due to exposure to intense marital conflict before and during the divorce, these effects would dissipate in a few years.

Research on the longer-term consequences of parental divorce has yielded very interesting findings, and in recent years psychologists have changed their tune a bit. Initially, studies of children whose parents divorced early in life suggested that most of the adverse effects disappear within three years. Research on elementary school children whose parents had divorced indicated that, after a few years, the children were functioning essentially as well as children whose parents had remained married (e.g., Hetherington, 1981).

More recent research, however, indicates that this conclusion may have been somewhat optimistic. Specifically, some studies show that many individuals whose parents divorce during preadolescence and adolescence demonstrate adjustment difficulties later, even after two or three years (e.g., Hetherington, 1993). The problems typically seen in greater frequency among individuals from divorced homes include higher rates of drug and alcohol use, more behavior problems, precocious sexual activity, and poorer school performance (Allison & Furstenberg, 1989; Astone & McLanahan, 1991; Hetherington & Stanley-Hagan, 1995; Sandefur,

McLanahan, & Wojtkiewicz, 1992; Zimiles & Lee, 1991); poorer interpersonal relationships with members of the opposite sex in late adolescence and young adulthood, including more negative attitudes toward marriage, and higher rates of divorce (McLanahan & Bumpass, 1988; Summers, Forehand, Armistead, & Tannenbaum, 1998; Tasker & Richards, 1994; Wallerstein & Blakeslee, 1989); and, with the exception of African American and Hispanic American males, lower levels of occupational attainment as adults (Amato & Keith, 1991b). Some research indicates that individuals whose parents divorced during childhood or adolescence continue to have adjustment problems well into their thirties (Cherlin et al., 1998) (see figure 4.8). These effects do not appear to be ameliorated by parental remarriage; adolescents from stepfamilies score similarly, or worse, on measures of longer-term adjustment, as do adolescents from single-parent, divorced homes (Allison & Furstenberg, 1989; Hetherington et al., 1998).

To what can we attribute these "sleeper" effects—effects of divorce that may not be apparent until much later in the child's development? Two possible explanations come to mind. The first is that the ways in which adjustment difficulties are expressed may not surface until adolescence. For example, social

sample sizes. The size of one's sample affects one's power to detect an effect.

How do social scientists make sense of a literature in which many studies with varying sample sizes have been reported? One useful way is to statistically combine the results of various studies through a procedure called **meta-analysis.** In a meta-analysis, the researchers track down all the scientifically acceptable research published on a topic and essentially calculate the average effect observed across the many studies. They then interpret this average effect size relative to the total number of adolescents who have been participants in the studies.

Sociologists Paul Amato and Bruce Keith did just that in a meta-analysis of studies of divorce and children's well-being (Amato & Keith, 1991a). They examined the results of 92 studies, which collectively involved more than 13,000 children. The studies compared youngsters from divorced versus nondivorced homes on a wide range of outcomes, including academic achievement, behavior problems, psychosocial adjustment, and family relations. Amato and Keith were able to break down the studies by various characteristics of the samples, so that they could examine separately the effects of divorce on girls versus boys, children versus adolescents, and so on.

The researchers concluded that, although divorce clearly diminishes youngsters' well-being, the average effect size is quite small. Thus, although there are significant differences between children from divorced versus nondivorced homes in school achievement, behavior problems, psychosocial adjustment, and family relations—all favoring individuals from nondivorced homes—the absolute difference in the groups' scores was seldom substantial. The largest effects were observed in studies of behavior problems and father-child relations, whereas the differences observed in studies of psychosocial adjustment were trivial. (Studies of other outcomes fell between these two extremes.)

In general, the reported effects tended to be stronger for school-age individuals than for preschoolers or college students; interestingly, the effects were comparable for boys and girls. One especially intriguing finding is that the effects of divorce seem to be smaller among youngsters from the United States than among those from other countries. The explanation is that divorce is more common in the United States than abroad, and, as a consequence, children from divorced homes in the United States are less likely to be stigmatized and more likely to have access to psychological services (such as counseling) that may attenuate the negative impact of family disruption.

Source: Amato, P., & Keith, B. (1991a). Parental divorce and the well-being of children: A meta-analysis. *Psychological Bulletin, 110,* 26–46.

---

scientists believe that increased drug use and higher rates of early pregnancy are consequences of the lower level of parental monitoring found in divorced homes (e.g., Dornbusch et al., 1985; McLanahan & Bumpass, 1988). However, because younger children—even poorly monitored ones—are unlikely to use drugs or be sexually active, no matter what their family background, the effect of the poor monitoring is not seen until adolescence, when individuals might begin using drugs and having sex.

A second explanation concerns the particular developmental challenges of adolescence (Sessa & Steinberg, 1991). Adolescence is a time when individuals first begin experimenting with intimate, sexual relationships. If having one's parents divorce or being exposed to marital conflict early in life affects one's conceptions of relationships or views of commitment (Belsky, Steinberg, & Draper, 1991; Franklin, Janoff-Bulman, & Roberts, 1990; Tasker & Richards, 1994), it makes sense that some of the effects of early parental divorce will not be manifested until the adolescent begins dating and getting seriously involved with others of the opposite sex. These initial forays into intimate relationships may recall old and difficult psychological conflicts that had remained latent for some time (Wallerstein & Blakeslee, 1989).

Custody, Contact, and Conflict Following Divorce

After a divorce, do adolescents fare better or worse in various kinds of living arrangements? Does contact with the nonresidential parent contribute to the adolescent's well-being?

Studies to date indicate that it is the nature of the relationship between the adolescent's divorced parents, not which one he or she lives with, that makes a difference (Buchanan et al., 1996; Downey, Ainsworth-Darnell, & Dufur, 1998; Hetherington et al., 1998). In the years immediately following a divorce, children may fare a bit better in the custody of the parent of the same sex, but these effects are not long-lasting; over time, it appears that both male and female adolescents fare equally well either in dual custody or in the sole custody of their mothers (Buchanan et al., 1996; Donnelly & Finkelhor, 1992; Downey, 1995). More important, especially for adolescents who have dual residences, are two factors: (1) whether the ex-spouses continue to fight and place the child between them and (2) whether the adolescent's discipline is consistent across the two households. Adolescents whose parents have a congenial, cooperative relationship and who receive consistent appropriate discipline from both homes report less

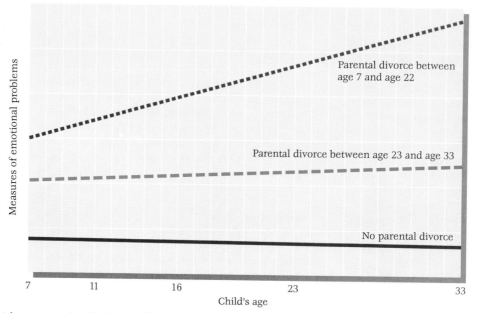

Figure 4.8   A long-term study of British individuals illustrates two interesting points about the effects of divorce on the development of emotional problems. First, at age 7, individuals whose parents eventually divorced already *had more emotional problems than other children. Second, the emotional problems associated with parental divorce during childhood or adolescence increased over time and persisted well into adulthood.* (Cherlin et al., 1998)

emotional difficulty and fewer behavior problems than those whose parents fight or are inconsistent with each other (Buchanan et al., 1996; Coiro & Emery, 1996; Donnelly & Finkelhor, 1992; Kitzmann & Emergy, 1994; Simons, Whitbeck, Beaman, & Conger, 1994).

Adolescents whose parents have divorced also differ in the extent to which they have contact with the parent they no longer live with—typically, their father. Generally speaking, contact between adolescents and their father following a divorce diminishes very quickly after the father moves out, and contact declines rapidly over time, especially among men who remarry or enter into a new romantic relationship (Stephens, 1996). Although conventional wisdom suggests that adolescents ought to benefit from maintaining a close relationship with their nonresidential parent, research on this has been inconsistent. Some studies find that adolescents benefit from regular postdivorce contact with their nonresident parent, but others find that such contact matters very little, and still others find that extensive postdivorce contact with the nonresidential parent can have harmful effects on children's well-being (see Amato & Rezac, 1994; Hetherington & Stanley-Hagan, 1995). The critical factor appears to be the level of conflict between

the divorced parents: Adolescents benefit from contact with their nonresidential parent when conflict between the divorced mother and father is minimal, but they suffer from such contact when the conflict is intense. In essence, "children adjust better to the loss of contact with the noncustodial parent than to continued exposure and involvement in parental conflict" (Hetherington & Stanley-Hagan, 1995, p. 241).

One recent study examined the sorts of disclosure that take place between recently divorced mothers and their daughters (Koerner, Jacobs, & Raymond, 2000). The researchers were especially interested in two topics of conversation: the mother's complaints and anger about her ex-husband and the mother's concerns about finances (both common concerns among recently divorced women). Not all mothers shared their feelings about these topics with their child. As one put it,

> I try really hard not to say anything negative about my ex-husband to my children. We agreed when we got divorced to always do what was best for our children. So far, so good. (Koerner et al., 2000, p. 305)

Among mothers who did disclose, however, an important motive for doing so turned out not to be the mothers' need for a confidante but, rather, their desire to shape daughters' impressions of them and the circumstances surrounding the divorce. Here's one example:

> I talk to her about anything. Complaints I have about her father. [Alison] thinks the divorce is all my fault. Her Dad has been absent for two years. He called on occasion and sent presents on Christmas and B-Days. While he was gone Alison turned him into some sort of God in her mind. Now that he has returned to the area he wants little or nothing to do with his kids. When Alison complains, I make statements like, "Alison, you're starting to see the side of your Dad that I was married to" or "He never gave me any time either." (Koerner et al., 2000, p. 305)

Consistent with other research indicating that adolescents fare worse when they are drawn into their divorced parents' conflict, in this study the daughters whose mothers complained to them about their ex-husband or discussed their financial concerns reported more psychological distress in the form of anxiety, depression, tension, and psychosomatic complaints.

RECAP

Research on divorce indicates that the period of greatest difficulty is the time immediately after the event and that such difficulty is largely attributable to the exposure of the child to marital conflict, disrupted parenting, and family stress. Although most youngsters ultimately adapt to parental divorce, new research indicates that certain adjustment or behavior problems may appear or reappear in adolescence. These include academic problems, increased drug and alcohol use, and difficulties in romantic relationships. It is important to remember, however, that differences between adolescents from divorced versus nondivorced homes tend to be small; moreover, there is considerable variability within the population of adolescents whose parents have divorced. In addition, at least some of the apparent effects of divorce are likely due to genetic differences between family members from divorced versus nondivorced households.

Food for Thought

What are the ways in which, and the processes through which, adolescents are affected by their parents' divorce? Based on the available research, what advice would you give to teenagers' parents who are considering divorce?

Remarriage

Many adolescents growing up in stepfamilies—especially if the remarriage occurred during early adolescence rather than childhood—have more problems than their peers (Hetherington et al., 1999). For example, youngsters growing up in single-parent homes are more likely than those in intact homes to be involved in delinquent activity, but adolescents in stepfamilies are even more at risk for this sort of problem behavior than are adolescents in single-parent families (Dornbusch et al., 1985; Steinberg, 1987c). In part, this is because they are exposed to a double dose of marital conflict—normal, everyday conflict between the parent and stepparent and additional conflict between ex-spouses (Hanson, McLanahan, & Thomson, 1996; MacDonald & DeMaris, 1995) and because they are exposed to a new set of potentially difficult issues that arise in the blending of children from two marriages (Hetherington et al., 1999).

Like the short-term effects of divorce, the short-term effects of remarriage vary among children, although not necessarily in the same ways. In general, girls show more difficulty in adjusting to remarriage than do boys, and older children have more difficulty than do younger children (Hetherington, 1993; Lee, Burkham, Zimiles, & Ladewski, 1994; Needle, Su, & Doherty, 1990; Vuchinich, Hetherington, Vuchinich, & Clingempeel, 1991; Zimiles & Lee, 1991). One explanation for this is that both boys and younger children have more to gain from their mother's remarriage than do girls or older children, who may have become accustomed to having a single mother (Hetherington, 1991). Over time, however, gender differences in adjustment to remarriage disappear, and, in remarriages that have lasted more than five years, the adjustment of males is similar to that of females (Hetherington et al., 1999).

Remarriage during the adolescent years may be extremely stressful when families are unable to accommodate the new stepparent relationship. Given what is known about family reorganization and change during adolescence, having to integrate a new type of relationship into a family system that is already undergoing a great deal of change may be more than some families can cope with (Kurdek & Fine, 1995). Many adolescents find it difficult to adjust to a new authority figure's moving into the household, especially if that person has different ideas about rules and discipline, and particularly if the new authority figure is not legally married to the child's biological parent (Buchanan et al., 1996;

Hetherington et al., 1999). This appears to be especially true when the adolescent in question is already somewhat vulnerable, either because of previous psychological problems or because of a very recent divorce or another stressful event.

By the same token, many stepparents find it difficult to join a family and not be accepted immediately by the children as the new parent. Stepparents may wonder why love is not forthcoming from their stepchildren, many of whom act critical, resistant, and sulky (Vuchinich et al., 1991). Although many stepfathers and their adolescent stepchildren do establish positive relations, the lack of a biological connection between stepparent and stepchild—coupled with the stresses associated with divorce and remarriage—may make this relationship especially vulnerable to problems (Hetherington et al., 1999). Adolescents in remarried households fare better when their stepparents can establish a consistent, supportive, authoritative style of discipline (Crosbie-Burnett & Giles-Sims, 1994; Henry & Lovelace, 1995; Hetherington et al., 1999).

The findings of this research underscore the need—particularly as remarriage becomes a more common part of American family life—to understand the special problems that may arise in the course of family reorganization. Several studies indicate that children's adjustment declines somewhat each time they must cope with a change in their family's organization (e.g., Capaldi & Patterson, 1991; Kurdek, Fine, & Sinclair, 1995), presumably because parenting may become less effective during each family transition (Forgatch, DeGarmo, & Knutson, 1994; Kurdek & Fine, 1993). As the field's understanding of stepfamily relationships grows, it should become easier to anticipate stepfamily problems before they occur, to prepare families in the process of reorganization for the transition they are about to make, as well as to provide special services for families who need help. Given the fact that the benefits of authoritative parenting are just as strong in divorced and remarried families as they are in other homes, experts believe that clinicians who work with families that have undergone marital transitions should help parents learn and adopt this sort of parenting style (Hetherington et al., 1999).

One factor that seems to make a very big difference in the adjustment of children in stepfamilies is the nature of the relationships they have with their *noncustodial* parents—that is, the biological parents with whom they do *not* live. Children in stepfamilies fare better when there is consistency in discipline between their custodial and noncustodial parents and when they have a good relationship with the noncustodial parents, especially in the years immediately following the remarriage (Anderson, 1992; Bray, Berger, Tiuch, & Boethel, 1993; Buchanan & Maccoby, 1993; Gunnoe, 1994). Having a close relationship with the noncustodial parent does not appear to undermine the relationship with the custodial parent (Buchanan & Maccoby, 1993).

RECAP

Because adolescents' mental health suffers somewhat each time their family situation changes, young people growing up in stepfamilies may be at even greater risk than their peers in single-parent, divorced homes. In general, girls show more difficulty in adjusting to remarriage than boys do in the short term, and older children have more difficulty than younger children. One factor that seems to make a difference in adolescents' adjustment to remarriage is the quality of the relationship they maintain with their noncustodial biological parent.

Food for Thought

Although many people believe that two parents are better than one, research on adolescent adjustment after remarriage doesn't support this. Why do you think this is true?

Parental Employment and Adolescent Adjustment

The increase in women's participation in the labor force has prompted a good deal of research on the effects of maternal employment on adolescent development. The label *maternal employment* is a misnomer, of course, because most children whose mothers work have fathers who are employed as well. It is important to remember that most studies of "maternal employment" are really studies of the impact of having both parents employed, not simply studies of the impact of having an employed mother. The impact of "paternal employment" by itself is unknown, because there are too few families with employed mothers and nonemployed fathers to make a comparison.

Adolescents whose mothers are employed differ from those whose mothers are not, in several respects. In general, maternal employment during adolescence has quite positive effects on daughters but more mixed or negligible effects on sons, especially in middle-class and professional families (Bronfenbrenner & Crouter, 1982). Not surprisingly, in these social classes, girls whose mothers work outside the home have higher career aspirations than do girls whose mothers do not work, but this is not necessarily the case for boys (Hoffman, 1974). Because daughters are more likely than sons to identify with their mother, girls' occupational plans are more influenced by having a mother work than are boys' plans.

One especially interesting finding concerns the impact of maternal employment on adolescents' academic achievement. A number of studies have found that, in middle-class and upper-middle-class homes, full-time maternal employment during the high school years is associated with lowered school performance among boys, but not among girls (Bogenschneider & Steinberg, 1994; Bronfenbrenner & Crouter, 1982; Wolfer & Moen, 1996). This effect is not found in homes where mothers work part-time, nor is it found in working-class and lower-class households. Presumably, the added income from mothers' work in poorer families makes up for any negative effects it has on boys' schooling.

Researchers have been puzzled by this sex difference. Why are boys, but not girls, adversely affected in school by full-time maternal employment? One explanation concerns the impact of maternal employment on parental monitoring, in general, and in relation to school, in particular (Bogenschneider & Steinberg, 1994; Crouter, MacDermid, McHale, & Perry-Jenkins, 1990; Muller, 1995). Boys are more adversely affected by less vigilant parental monitoring than girls are, because boys tend to be more active and more prone to getting into trouble. Also, children who are monitored more carefully by their parents tend to do better in school than their peers do (Steinberg et al., 1989). If one effect of having two parents work full-time is interference with parental monitoring, it may have a more negative effect on boys than on girls. Consistent with this, adolescents with employed parents who monitor them carefully do not seem to show special problems (Jacobson & Crockett, 2000).

A second explanation concerns the effect on adolescents' family relationships when two parents work. At least one study finds that adolescents whose mothers work have more arguments with their mothers and with their siblings than do those whose mothers are not employed (Montemayor, 1984). This is especially the

▲ *Maternal employment has quite positive effects on the development of adolescent females, who have higher career aspirations than girls whose mothers are not employed. The impact of maternal employment on sons is mixed, however, especially in middle-class or professional families.* (Patrick Watson/Watson Media Services)

case in families in which the working parents report high levels of work stress (Crouter, Bumpus, Maguire, & McHale, 1999). Part of the increase in conflict appears due to the increased demands for household work placed on the children of working mothers (Montemayor, 1984). It is possible that boys react more negatively than girls to having to help out around the house, and this may contribute to more frequent family arguments in households with sons. If conflict at home depresses school performance, this may help explain why boys, but not girls, whose mothers work full-time do less well in school.

Above all, however, studies indicate far more similarities than differences in the daily experiences of adolescents with employed versus nonemployed mothers (Duckett & Richards, 1995; Richards & Duckett, 1994). Experts believe that the most important factor may be the way in which the family perceives the mother's employment, rather than her employment per se. Children whose mothers are happily employed are much more likely to benefit from the experience than are children whose mothers would prefer not to work or who have jobs with which they are unhappy. When a mother is happy to be working, when her work is not so demanding as to be stressful, and when her spouse and family are appreciative of her employment, her youngster is more likely to develop self-reliance and independence and less likely to develop problems (Galambos, Sears, Almeida, & Kolaric, 1995; Hoffman, 1974). In contrast, adolescent girls who perceive their mothers to have been held back occupationally are more likely than their peers to report depression and psychosomatic distress (Silverstein, Perlick, Clauson, & McKoy, 1993).

RECAP

Research on maternal employment indicates that its effects depend on the sex of the adolescent and the attitude of the mother, as well as other family members, toward her work. Maternal employment has positive effects on daughters but mixed effects on sons, especially where school performance is concerned. Children whose mothers are happy with their employment are more likely to benefit than are children whose mothers don't wish to work or dislike their jobs. All in all, however, research suggests that the daily experiences of adolescents whose mothers are employed are not significantly different from those of adolescents whose mothers are not employed.

Food for Thought

Researchers have had difficulty studying the effects of paternal employment, because there are so few adolescents growing up in households in which fathers do not work, which would be needed for a comparison group. Can you speculate, however, about how such research might turn out if it were possible to do the appropriate studies?

Economic Stress and Poverty

Although many psychologists have focused their attention on the effects of maternal employment on adolescent development, in recent years there has been an upsurge in interest in the relation between parents' *unemployment* and adolescents' well-being and, in particular, in the ways in which adolescents' mental health is affected by changes in their family's financial situation. Much of this research was stimulated by the economic recession of the early 1980s, during which many adults became unemployed and many families lost substantial income.

To date, the studies of family income loss and adolescent adjustment suggest a number of parallels with the research on divorce and remarriage. Like divorce, income loss tends to be associated with disruptions in

parenting, which in turn lead to increases in adolescent difficulties, including a diminished sense of mastery, increased emotional distress, academic difficulties, and delinquency (Conger, Conger, Matthews, & Elder, 1999; Elder, Caspi, & van Nguyen, 1986; Elder, van Nguyen, & Caspi, 1985; Kloep, 1995; Lempers, Clark-Lempers, & Simmons, 1989). Although males and females alike are adversely affected by their family's economic problems, the pathways through which this occurs may differ between the sexes. For girls, financial difficulty is likely to lead to more demands for maturity and increased responsibility around the house (perhaps to take over some of the mother's duties while she works or looks for employment) (Elder, 1974; Flanagan, 1990). This may contribute to their developing more pessimistic expectations about their own occupational futures, since they may develop more traditional views and find it difficult to envision a satisfying career outside the home (Galambos & Silbereisen, 1987). For boys, in contrast, disruptions in family finances seem to lead to more frequent conflict, especially with fathers (Elder, van Nguyen, & Caspi, 1985; Flanagan, 1990). Boys whose fathers have been laid off may lose respect for them and challenge their authority. The resulting disruption in family functioning may lead to more involvement in problem behavior and more irresponsibility.

A series of studies of rural families during the American farm crisis of the 1980s by sociologists Rand Conger and Glen Elder sheds light on some of the processes through which economic strain on the family can adversely affect adolescents' psychological development (Conger, Ge, Elder, Lorenz, & Simons, 1994; Conger et al., 1992, 1993, 1999; Elder, Conger, Foster, & Ardelt, 1992; Ge & Conger, 1995) (see figure 4.9). Financial strain increases mothers' and fathers' feelings of depression, worsens parents' marriages, and causes conflicts between parents and adolescents over money. These consequences, in turn, make parents more irritable, which adversely affects the quality of their parenting. Studies show that parents under economic strain are less involved, less nurturing, harsher, and less consistent in their discipline (McLoyd, 1990).

The family climate created by economic strain puts adolescents at risk for a wide variety of problems. As you now know, adolescents who are exposed to harsh, uninvolved, and inconsistent parenting are at greater risk for a wide range of psychological and behavior problems. When adolescents are repeatedly exposed to marital conflict—especially when it is not resolved—

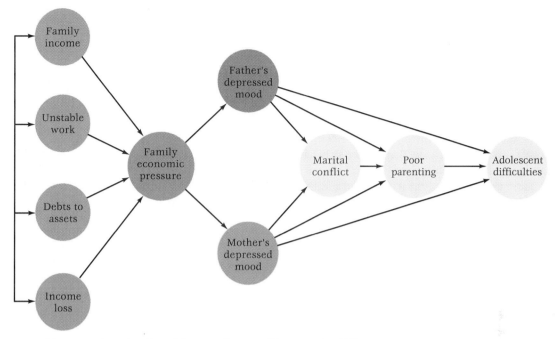

Figure 4.9   *How economic strain affects adolescent adjustment.* (Conger et al., 1993)

they are more likely to become aggressive and depressed (Cummings, Ballard, El-Sheikh, & Lake, 1991). And, when adolescents themselves are the recipients of aggressive parenting, they are likely to imitate this behavior in their relationships with siblings (Conger et al., 1994) and later, in their own marriage (Strauss & Yodanis, 1996) and with their children (Simons, Whitbeck, Conger, & Chyi-In, 1991).

Researchers have also studied the impact on adolescents of growing up amid chronic economic disadvantage (Brody, Stoneman et al., 1994; Felner et al., 1995; McLoyd, Jayartne, Ceballo, & Borquez, 1994; Sampson & Laub, 1994), a condition disproportionately likely to characterize the lives of African American and Hispanic American youth, especially those living in inner-city and rural communities. In general, persistent poverty, like temporary economic strain, undermines parental effectiveness, making mothers and fathers harsher, more depressed, less vigilant, and if married, more embroiled in marital conflict. These consequences all have negative effects on adolescent adjustment, which are manifested in increases in anxiety and depression, more frequent conduct problems, and diminished school performance (Conger, Patterson, & Ge, 1995; Taylor, Roberts, & Jacobson, 1997). Interestingly, there appear to be few differences in the behavior, values, or family relationships between adolescents in families who are on welfare and adolescents whose families are not, calling into question the notion that welfare undermines parental effectiveness, contributes to adolescents' development of undesirable beliefs and values about work, or encourages problem behavior among teenagers (Kalil & Eccles, 1998).

Growing up poor affects adolescents' mental health through other means as well. Poor children are more likely to be victims of violence, which is associated with higher rates of depression (Fitzpatrick, 1993; Whitbeck, Hoyt, & Ackley, 1996); to feel more alienated from school (Felner et al., 1995); and to be exposed to high levels of stress (Felner et al., 1995; Masten, Miliotis, Graham-Bermann, Ramirez, & Neemann, 1993). Although few scientific studies have been conducted on homeless adolescents, research suggests that these youngsters share many of the same problems with other youth who experience chronic poverty—problems that include higher rates of depression and suicidal thoughts, academic difficulties, and behavior problems (Masten et al., 1993; Unger, Kipke, Simon, Montgomery, & Johnson, 1997; Yoder, Hoyt, & Whitbeck, 1998; Zima, Wells, & Freeman, 1994). About 5 percent of American adolescents experience at least one night of homelessness each year (Ringwalt, Greene, Robertson, & McPheeters, 1998).

Studies of families living under poverty also tell us what parents living in poor neighborhoods can do to help protect their children from the adverse consequences of growing up in poor inner-city or rural neighborhoods (Brody, Stoneman, & Flor, 1996; Early & Eccles, 1994; Elder & Ardelt, 1992; Furstenberg, 1996; Jarrett, 1995). In general, families fare better when they have adequate sources of social support (Mason, Cauce, Gonzales, Hiraga, & Grove, 1994; Taylor, 1996; Taylor & Roberts, 1995) and when they have strong ties to religious institutions (Brody, Stoneman, Flor, & McCrary, 1994; Brody et al., 1996). In addition, two specific sets of family management strategies used by parents in poor neighborhoods seem to work: (1) *promotive strategies,* which attempt to strengthen the adolescent's competence through effective child rearing within the home environment or through involving the child in positive activities outside the home, and (2) *restrictive strategies,* which attempt to minimize the child's exposure to dangers in the neighborhood (Furstenberg, Cook, Eccles, Elder, & Sameroff, 1999; Jarrett, 1995). Studies indicate that a combination of promotive strategies as well as moderately (but not overly) restrictive strategies may be especially beneficial to adolescents living in impoverished communities. Although adolescents in poor neighborhoods benefit from consistent parental monitoring—perhaps even from monitoring that is more vigilant than that used by families from more advantaged communities—they do not thrive when their parents exercise control that is excessive (McCarthy, Lord, Eccles, Kalil, & Furstenberg, 1992).

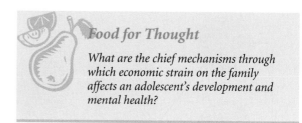

Food for Thought

What are the chief mechanisms through which economic strain on the family affects an adolescent's development and mental health?

THE IMPORTANCE OF THE FAMILY IN ADOLESCENT DEVELOPMENT

Amid all of the diversity that exists among families with adolescents—diversity in background, income, parenting style, and household composition—one finding stands out above all others: No other factor seems to influence adolescent adjustment more than the quality of his or her relationships at home. As one team of experts concluded on the basis of a comprehensive study of the lives, behavior, and health of 90,000 American teenagers:

> Across all of the health outcomes examined, the results point to the importance of family and the home environment for protecting adolescents from harm. What emerges most consistently as protective is the teenager's feeling of connectedness with parents and family. Feeling loved and cared for by parents matters in a big way. (Blum & Rinehart, 2000, p. 31)

Study after study finds that adolescents who feel that their parents or guardians are there for them—caring, involved, and accepting—are healthier, happier, and more competent than their peers, no matter how health, happiness, or competence is assessed. This conclusion holds true regardless of the adolescent's sex, ethnicity, social class, or age and across all types of families, whether married or divorced, single-parent or two-parent, rich or poor. Despite the tremendous growth and psychological development that take place as individuals leave childhood on the road toward adulthood, despite society's pressures on young people to grow up fast, despite all the technlogical and social innovation that has transformed family life—and contrary to claims that parents don't make a difference (e.g., Harris, 1998)—the fact of the matter remains that adolescents continue to need the love, support, and guidance of adults who genuinely care about their development and well-being.

RECAP

Adolescents whose families have suffered severe economic losses, or who live in chronic poverty, are at heightened risk for psychological difficulties and problem behavior. Research on economic strain and its impact on the adolescent indicates that the main effects of financial stress are transmitted to the adolescent through the negative impact they have on parents' mental health and marital relations. Parents under financial strain are harsher, more inconsistent, and less involved as parents, which, in turn, leads to problems for their children. Effective parents living in poor communities must actively manage their adolescent's activities and relationships to promote the development of competence while minimizing exposure to risk.

Web Researcher Enter a chat room for parents of
teenagers and monitor the conversation for a few days.
What topics seem most likely to generate interest?
How good is the advice given? Go to
www.mhhe.com/steinberg6 for further information.

KEY TERMS

authoritarian parents
authoritative parents
behavioral genetics
correlation
demographers
effect size
generation gap
indifferent parents
indulgent parents
meta-analysis
midlife crisis
nonshared environmental influences
parental demandingness
parental responsiveness
shared environmental influences
temperament

Chapter 5

Peer Groups

It is about 8:30 in the morning. A group of teenagers congregates in the hallway in front of its first-period classroom. The teens are discussing their plans for the weekend. As the first-period bell sounds, they enter the classroom and take their seats. For the next four hours (until there is a break in their schedule for lunch), they will attend class in groups of about 30—30 adolescents to 1 adult.

At lunch, the clique meets again to talk about the weekend. They have about 45 minutes until the first afternoon period begins. After lunch, they spend another two hours in class—again, in groups of about 30. The school day ends, and the clique reconvenes. They are going over to someone's house to hang out for the rest of the day. Everyone's parents are working. They are on their own. At about 6 in the evening, they disperse and head home for dinner. A few will talk on the phone that night. Some will get together to study. They will see one another first thing the next morning.

When you stop to think about it, adolescents in modern society spend a remarkable amount of time with their peers. In fact, American teenagers spend more time talking to their friends each day than in any other single activity (Csikszentmihalyi, Larson, & Prescott, 1977). High school students in the United States and Europe spend twice as much of their time each week with peers as with parents or other adults—even discounting time in class (Brown, Theobald, & Klute, in press; Larson & Verma, 1999). Virtually all adolescents spend most of each weekday with their peers while at school, and the vast majority also see or talk to their friends in the afternoon, in the evening, and over the weekend (Larson & Verma, 1999). Even when adolescents work in part-time jobs, they are more likely to work with people their own age than with adults (Greenberger & Steinberg, 1986). And studies show that adolescents' moods are most positive when the teens are with their friends, that time spent with friends becomes more rewarding over the course of adolescence, and, as figure 5.1 illustrates, that teenagers' moods become more positive over the course of the week, as the weekend approaches (Larson, 1983; Larson & Richards, 1991).

American society is very age segregated. From the time youngsters enter school at the age of 5 until they graduate at age 18 or so, they are grouped with children their own age. They have little contact with people who are older or younger, outside of relatives. Because schools play such an important role in determining children's friendships, age grouping carries over into after-school, weekend, and vacation activities. Little League, scouting, church groups—all are structured in a way that groups people by age.

In contemporary society, **peer groups** (groups of people who are roughly the same age) have become an increasingly important context in which adolescents spend time (Harris, 1995). Modernization has led to more and more age segregation—in schools, in the workplace, and in the community. Today's teenagers spend far more time in the exclusive company of their peers than their counterparts did in the past. Indeed, the rise of peer groups in modern society gives adolescence in contemporary America some of its most distinctive features. And the role of peers in shaping adolescent psychosocial development has become increasingly important.

For these reasons, understanding how adolescent peer groups form and what takes place within their boundaries is critical to understanding adolescent development in contemporary society. No discussion of adolescent identity development is complete without an examination of how and why teenagers derive part of their identity from the group they spend time with. No discussion of adolescent friendship is complete without an examination of teenagers' cliques and how they are formed. And no discussion of adolescent sexuality is complete without an examination of how, and when, peer groups change from same-sex groups to mixed-sex groups. •

THE ORIGINS OF ADOLESCENT PEER GROUPS IN CONTEMPORARY SOCIETY

Contact between adolescents and their peers is found in all cultures. But not all societies have peer groups that are as narrowly defined and age segregated as those in modern-day America. Although adolescent peer relationships are universal, age-segregated peer groups are not. In earlier times, for example, interactions among youngsters occurred largely in the context of mixed-age groups composed of infants, children, and adolescents (Hartup, 1977). And much interaction among children occurred in the presence of their parents, because adults and children were not isolated from one another during the day. Even today, in societies that are less industrialized, and in Asian countries, young people spend a good part of the day in contact with their parents. For example, in India, adolescents spend about 40 percent of their waking hours with

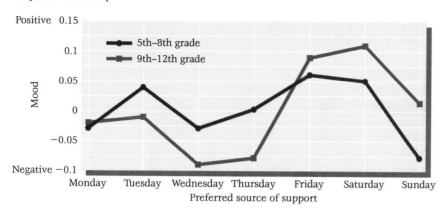

Figure 5.1 As the weekend approaches, and adolescents anticipate spending more time with their friends, their mood takes a marked turn for the better. (Larson & Richards, 1998)

family members; in the United States, by the time an adolescent is a senior in high school, less than 15 percent of his or her waking hours are spent with family (Larson & Verma, 1999).

In contemporary America and Europe, however, age segregation is the norm, a fact of life that is clearly reflected in the tremendous amount of time that teenagers spend with their peers (Larson & Verma, 1999). The causes of age segregation have to do with the ways in which our schools, our work, and our population are structured.

The Educational Origins of Adolescent Peer Groups

Educators first developed the idea of free public education, with students grouped by age (a practice called **age grading**), in the middle of the nineteenth century (President's Science Advisory Committee, 1974). In so doing, they established an arrangement that would eventually touch all American youngsters and encourage the development and maintenance of age-segregated peer groups.

It was not until the second quarter of the twentieth century that most adolescents were directly affected by educational age grouping, however. Attending elementary school may have been common, but, until 1930 or so, high school was a luxury available only to the very affluent. In other words, adolescent peer groups based on friendships formed in school were not prevalent until the 1930s.

What about adolescents growing up before 1930? Did they have peer groups similar to those that adolescents have today? No one knows for sure, but it is fairly certain that the forces encouraging adolescents to associate almost exclusively with people of the same age were not as

▲ *The physical separation of teenagers and adults has increased during the past four decades, due to changing patterns of housing and employment. In contemporary society, many adolescents spend a good deal of their free time without contact with adults.* (Billy Barnes/PhotoEdit)

strong at the beginning of the twentieth century as they are today. Youngsters who were not in school were generally working and living at home, where they were likely to have a good deal of contact with adults and children (Modell, Furstenberg, & Hershberg, 1976). Even the youngsters from families wealthy enough to send their children to high school typically attended academies where children of different ages were mixed together, and it was not uncommon during the nineteenth century for "peer" groups to be composed of individuals ranging in age from 14 to 20 (President's Science Advisory Committee, 1974). Today, in contrast, virtually all American adolescents spend the years between ages 10 and 16 in age-graded schools, and fewer than 25 percent leave school before graduating at the age of 17 or 18 (William T. Grant Foundation, 1988).

The impact of this educational age grading on adolescents' social life has been staggering. In one survey, in which seventh- through tenth-grade students were asked to list the people who were important to them, over two-thirds of the same-sex peers they mentioned were from the same grade in their school (Blyth, Hill, & Thiel, 1982). Participation in organized activities outside of school also contributes to age segregation. One study found that close to 80 percent of sixth-graders are involved in at least one nonschool club, extracurricular activity group, or youth organization in which they are likely to have contact only with peers of the same age (Medrich, Roizen, Rubin, & Buckley, 1982). When students are free to mix with people of different ages while at school, they are more likely to do so, especially during early adolescence (Gray & Feldman, 1997), perhaps because there is such wide variability in physical development at this point in development.

Work, Family Life, and Adolescent Peer Groups

A second set of factors related to the rise of adolescent peer groups concerns changes in the workplace, or, more precisely, changes in the relationship between work and other aspects of daily life. With industrialization came more stringent and more carefully monitored child labor laws, which restricted adolescents' participation in the world of work (Bakan, 1972; Modell & Goodman, 1990). Because the implementation of tougher child labor laws coincided with the rise of secondary education, adolescents and adults (who had once shared the same daily activity—work) went their separate ways. Adolescents spent the day in school, and adults were at work.

The segregation of adolescents from adults also has been fueled by the rise in maternal employment. The movement of mothers out of the home and into the workplace furthered the trend—already set in motion by suburbanization—toward the development of residential neighborhoods dominated by young people during weekday mornings and afternoons. Today, between 2 million and 6 million school-age youngsters come home from school to houses with no adults present, and an additional half-million care for themselves in the morning, before school begins (Berman, Winkleby, Chesterman, &

Boyce, 1992; Richardson, Radziszewska, Dent, & Flay, 1993). We will look at the implications of after-school activities for adolescent development in Chapter 7, when we take a look at how adolescents spend their free time.

Changes in the Population

Perhaps the most important factor in the rise of adolescent peer groups in recent years has been the rapid growth of the teenage population between 1955 and 1975, a trend that repeated itself during the 1990s. Following the end of World War II, many parents wanted to have children as soon as possible, creating the postwar **baby boom.** The products of this baby boom became adolescents during the 1960s and early 1970s,

▲ *Changes in patterns of work and family life have resulted in a large number of young people who are not supervised by their parents after school. Affluent, suburban, and white children are most likely to be home alone.* (Myrleen Ferguson Cate/ PhotoEdit)

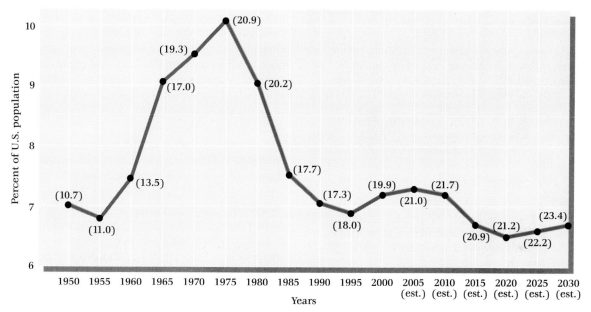

Figure 5.2   The percentage of the U.S. population comprising 15- to 19-year-olds reached its highest level in 1975. It began to increase again in 1990. Figures in parentheses indicate the number of 15- to 19-year-olds, in millions. (United Nations Population Division, 1976; U.S. Bureau of the Census, 1996)

creating an "adolescent boom" for about 15 years. As you can see from figure 5.2, the size of the population from ages 15 to 19 nearly doubled between 1955 and 1975 and, more important, rose from less than 7 percent of the total population to over 10 percent. During the mid-1970s, more than one out of every six Americans were teenagers. One reason for the growth of peer groups, therefore, was the sheer increase in the number of peers that young people had.

This trend, as you can see in figure 5.2, turned downward in 1975, and the relative size of the adolescent population decreased until 1990. However, during the last decade of the twentieth century—when the products of the baby boom began raising adolescents of their own—the size of the teenage population began increasing once again, although in relative terms it has remained, and will continue to remain, at around 7 percent of the U.S. population. In the year 2000, the population of 15- to 19-year-olds in the United States numbered about 20 million. An additional 20 million individuals were between 10 and 14 at that time, meaning that, as we entered the twenty-first century, approximately one in seven individuals in this country was an adolescent. The proportion of the population that is adolescent is estimated to remain at about this level through the next half-century (U.S. Bureau of the Census, 2000).

Social scientists are interested in tracking the size of the adolescent population for several reasons. First, changes in the size of the adolescent population may warrant changes in the allocation of funds for social services, educational programs, and health care, since adolescents' needs are not the same as those of children and adults.

Second, changes in the size of the adolescent population have implications for understanding the behavior of cohorts. A cohort is a group of individuals born during a given era, such as the baby boom generation (born in the late 1940s and early 1950s), Generation X (born in the early 1970s), and Generation Y (the adolescent children of the baby boomers, born in the 1980s). Baby boomers, many of whom were adolescents in the early and mid-1970s, for example, were members of a very crowded cohort, which meant that they encountered a relatively high degree of competition from each other for places in college, jobs, and so on. The size of this cohort also meant that it could attract a great deal of public attention, from politicians to advertisers. In contrast, members of Generation X, who were adolescents in the late 1980s and early 1990s, were members of a much smaller cohort, with less competition among individuals but with far less clout in the larger society. Generation Y, which will be larger than Generation X, will also likely be more influential.

Food for Thought

How has the significance of the peer group changed over the past century? What implications do you think this has for adolescent development?

THE ADOLESCENT PEER GROUP: A PROBLEM OR A NECESSITY?

Is the rise of peer groups in modern society a problem that needs to be remedied, or is it an inevitable—perhaps even necessary—part of life in contemporary America? This question has sparked some of the hottest arguments in the study of adolescence during the past 25 years (Brown, in press). On one side are those who say that age segregation has led to the development of a separate **youth culture,** in which young people maintain attitudes and values that are different from—even contrary to—those of adults. On the other side are those who argue that industrialization and modernization have made peer groups more important, that adults alone can no longer prepare young people for the future, and that peer groups play a vital and needed role in the socialization of adolescents for adulthood (Harris, 1995). Let's look at both sides of the debate.

Is There a Separate Youth Culture?

The belief that age segregation has fueled the development of a separate—and troublesome—youth culture was first expressed by sociologist James Coleman, whose book *The Adolescent Society* (1961) presented the findings of an extensive study of the social worlds of 10 American high schools. Even though this book was published more than 40 years ago, many of the concerns Coleman expressed have echoed repeatedly

over the past four decades. Indeed, when adults today complain about the questionable morals and poor character of today's young people, they are saying nothing different than Coleman and other commentators were saying in the middle of the twentieth century. Indeed, there probably has not been a generation of adults that hasn't complained about the character and behavior of the young.

Coleman worried about the relatively low value the adolescents in his study placed on academic success. Although the parents he surveyed felt that academic achievement should be a priority for their youngsters, the adolescents lived in a social world in which academic success was frowned on, in which doing well in school did not earn the admiration of peers. Whereas their parents may have been pleased by straight-*A* report cards, the high school students in the study said that being a good student carried little weight with their friends. Although Coleman's study is more than 40 years old, its findings still ring true. It probably is fair to say that academic achievement is not valued any more by American teenagers today than it was four decades ago (Bishop, 1999; Meyer, 1994; Steinberg, 1996).

What should we make of the fact that adolescents, relative to adults, do not place a great deal of emphasis on doing well in school? According to some observers, age segregation has so strengthened the power of the peer group that American adolescents have become alienated and unfamiliar with the values of adults. No longer are young people interested in the things their parents want for them, these commentators say. In fact, teenagers have become separated from adult society to such an extent that they have established their own society—a separate youth culture that undermines parents' efforts to encourage academic excellence and, instead, emphasizes sports, dating, and partying.

According to this view, problems such as youth unemployment, teenage suicide, juvenile crime and delinquency, drug and alcohol use, and premarital pregnancy can be attributed to the rise of peer groups and the isolation of adolescents from adults. Many observers of the adolescent scene have noted that all these problems increased dramatically after 1940, as peer groups became more prominent and age segregation became more prevalent (e.g., Bronfenbrenner, 1974). The argument, then, is that the rise in adolescents' problems can be linked directly to the rise in the power of adolescent peer groups. Although this view is widely held among adults, at least one study indicates that it may not be entirely true.

▲ *Studies show that, in most high schools, athletic and social success are more reliable routes to popularity with peers than is academic success.* (Polly Brown/Picture Cube)

In this study, the researcher contrasted the peer orientation of young people at three points in time. Identical questionnaires assessing how much adolescents looked to their parents and friends for advice on a range of issues were given to groups of teenagers from the same community in 1963, 1976, and 1982 (Sebald, 1986). As might have been predicted, between 1963 and 1976 the adolescents became more oriented toward their peers and less toward their parents. Between 1976 and 1982, however—a period of time during which rates of adolescent problems increased—this trend reversed itself somewhat, as the adolescents' orientation toward their peers diminished. During this later period, the boys' orientation toward their parents increased, but the girls' continued to decline, although at a less dramatic rate. The adolescents' values were more similar to those of their parents during the early 1980s than

they were during the late 1960s and early 1970s (Gecas & Seff, 1990).

As B. Bradford Brown (1990), an expert on adolescent peer groups, has noted, the nature and strength of adolescent peer influence vary a great deal from one historical period to the next. We must be cautious about generalizing images of adolescent peer pressure derived from one point in time to all generations of young people. The strength of peer influence also may vary from one context to another. One study of Canadian adolescents, for example, found that most of the students preferred to be remembered as outstanding students (rather than as great athletes or popular adolescents), and other studies have found that students' preferences for how they will be remembered vary a great deal by sex, age, and where they fit into the social structure of the school (Brown, 1990).

These cautions notwithstanding, it seems obvious to even the most casual observer that peers play a more important role in the lives of adolescents in modern society than they did in previous eras. But has the rise of adolescent peer groups in modern society really caused so many problems?

Unfortunately, this question is very difficult to answer. Although it is true that age segregation has increased over the past 50 years, society has changed in other ways during the same time—ways that may also have contributed to increases in such problems as crime and drug use. In many regards, the world is a far more stressful place to grow up in now than it was in the past. Families move every few years. Divorce is commonplace. Adolescents experience enormous pressures from parents, peers, and the mass media (Meyer, 1994). Is it any wonder that problems such as suicide and alcohol abuse are on the rise?

To be sure, contemporary adolescents spend more *time* in peer groups than adolescents did in past eras. But it is not known if today's young people are any more susceptible to the influence of their friends than their counterparts were previously, nor is it known if teenagers are any worse off because peer groups have come to play a more prominent role in modern society. In fact, studies of peer pressure indicate that most teenagers feel that their friends are likely to pressure them not to use drugs or to engage in sexual activity. Adolescents do, however, report a good deal of pressure to drink alcohol, and this pressure increases during the adolescent years (Brown, Clasen, & Eicher, 1986), and few adolescents report that their friends pressure them to do well in school (Steinberg, 1996). Thus, adolescents exert *both* positive and negative influences on each other, and it is incorrect to describe the peer group as a monolithic, negative influence. More to the point, some theorists have suggested that peer groups—regardless of how they influence adolescent behavior—are inevitable and *necessary* byproducts of modernization and essential to the transmission of cultural information (Harris, 1995). Let's now look at their point of view.

The Need for Peer Groups in Modern Society

In less industrialized societies, political, economic, and social institutions revolve around the family. Occupation, choice of spouse, place of residence, treatment under society's laws, and participation in governing the community are all tied to the identity of one's relatives.

Individuals' family ties determine with whom they can trade and how much they pay for various commodities. In short, the ways in which adults are expected to behave depends on which family they come from.

Because not all adults are expected to behave in the same way in these kinship-based societies, it is not possible to educate or socialize all young people in one large group, since they all have to learn somewhat different sets of norms. Norms for behavior that vary from person to person are called **particularistic norms.** Suppose, for example, that the rules for driving were particularistic—that the rules of the road were different for every person. Perhaps people from families who had lived in the community for a long time would be allowed to drive at 75 miles an hour, but people from families who were new to the area would have to drive at 55. Under a particularistic system such as this, having driver education courses for high school students wouldn't make much sense, because each student would have to learn a different set of rules.

In societies in which norms are particularistic, grouping adolescents by age and sending them off to school is not an effective strategy for socializing them for adulthood, since their family ties, not their age, determine what their rights and responsibilities are. The socialization of adolescents in kinship-based societies is best accomplished in family groups, where elders can pass on the family's particular values and norms to their younger relatives.

In contemporary societies, things are quite different. Modernization has eroded much of the family's importance as a political, social, and economic unit. Generally speaking, in modern society, all individuals are expected to learn the same set of norms, because the rules governing behavior apply equally to all members of the community. These norms are called **universalistic norms.** When you walk into a department store to buy something or when you go into a voting booth to vote, it generally makes no difference who your relatives are. Whom you may marry, what kind of work you do, where you live, and how you are treated under the law are not based on family lineage. The norms that apply to you apply to everyone. Under these circumstances, it is not wise to limit the socialization of adolescents to the family, because doing so does not ensure that all youngsters will learn the same set of norms (Harris, 1995). In societies that require individuals to learn universalistic norms, it is more efficient to group together by age all the individuals who are to be socialized (Eisenstadt, 1956). Teaching is better done in schools than left up to individual families. One of the

▲ *In postfigurative societies, cultural change is slow. As a result, the socialization and education of adolescents are performed almost exclusively by their elders. In cofigurative societies, such as ours, where cultural change takes place at a faster rate, much of the socialization and education of adolescents is performed by peers.* (Paul Conklin/PhotoEdit; Harry Wilkes/Stock, Boston)

reasons we have driver education classes, for example, is that our rules for driving are universalistic—the same for everyone—and we need to make sure that individuals learn a common set of regulations, not simply the ones their parents teach them.

As the family has become a less important political and economic institution, universalistic norms have come to replace particularistic ones. And this has required a change in the way in which adolescents are prepared for adulthood. Not only has modernization created age groups, but it has also made them absolutely necessary. Without systematic age grouping in schools, it would be impossible to prepare young people for adulthood. And, because age grouping in schools carries over into activities outside of school, the need for universal, school-based education has created age-segregated peer groups.

Some theorists do not see this as a bad thing. They feel that, as society has become more technologically advanced, adolescents have come to play a valuable role in preparing one another for adulthood. According to anthropologist Margaret Mead (1928/1978), the way in which young people are best socialized for adulthood depends on how fast their society is changing. In some cultures, cultural change is so slow that what a child

needs to know to function as an adult changes very little over time. Mead called these **postfigurative cultures;** they socialize children almost exclusively through contact with the culture's elders, because the way in which older generations have lived is almost identical to the way in which subsequent generations will live.

Imagine, for a moment, growing up in a world in which you had to know only what your grandparents knew in order to survive. In this age of laptop computers, CD-ROMs, satellites, cellular phones, and space shuttles, growing up in a world in which very little changes over 50 years seems almost impossible to imagine. Fifty years ago, television had barely been on the market. Strange as it may seem to us now, however, most societies until fairly recently have been postfigurative—and they still are in much of the developing world. In other words, until fairly recently, adolescents could learn exclusively from their elders what they needed to know to be successful adults.

During the past 100 years, contemporary societies have shifted away from being postfigurative cultures to become **cofigurative cultures,** in which the socialization of young people is accomplished not merely through contact between children and their elders but also through contact between people of the same age. In cofigurative cultures, society changes so quickly that much of what parents are able to teach their children may be outdated by the time their children become adults. Today, we live in a cofigurative society. For adolescents in contemporary America, peers have become role models as important as parents and grandparents. As a result of such rapid change, adolescents increasingly need to turn to members of their own generation for advice, guidance, and information.

If you were a teenager living in a postfigurative culture, you might ask your grandfather for advice about how to hunt or farm. But, if you were a teenager in today's cofigurative culture, to whom would you turn for advice about how to surf the Internet to research a term paper? Would you turn to your friends, who probably have grown up with computers in their homes and schools, or to your grandparents, who may never even have used a computer?

Mead believed that, as cofigurative cultures changed even more rapidly, they would be replaced by **prefigurative cultures,** in which young people would become adults' teachers. We already may be living in a prefigurative culture. Instead of parents asking, "Why can't Johnny read?" teenagers ask, "Why can't Mom and Dad figure out how to burn their own CDs?"

Do these analyses mean that the adolescents of the future will cease to profit from having close relationships with adults? Of course not. As we saw in chapter 4, young people will always need the support, affection, and advice of their elders. But understanding how peer groups have been made necessary by modernization casts the issue of age segregation in a new light. Despite whatever problems may have been caused by the rise of peer groups in contemporary society, there may be little we can—or should—do to make adolescent peer groups less important.

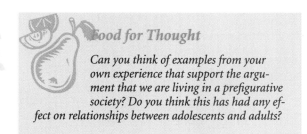

Food for Thought

Can you think of examples from your own experience that support the argument that we are living in a prefigurative society? Do you think this has had any effect on relationships between adolescents and adults?

THE NATURE OF ADOLESCENT PEER GROUPS

Changes in Peer Groups During Adolescence

Visit any elementary school playground and you will readily see that peer groups are an important feature of the social world of childhood. However, even though peer groups exist well before adolescence, during the teenage years they change in significance and structure. Four specific developments stand out (Brown, 1990; in press).

First, *there is a sharp increase during adolescence in the sheer amount of time individuals spend with their peers* and in the relative time they spend in the company of peers versus adults. If we count school as being a setting in which adolescents are mainly with agemates, well over half of the typical adolescent's waking hours are spent with peers, as opposed to only 15 percent with adults—including parents (a good deal of the remaining time is spent alone or with a combination of adults and agemates). Indeed, during the transition into adolescence, there is a dramatic drop in the amount of time adolescents spend with parents; for boys this is mainly replaced by time spent alone, whereas for girls, this is replaced by time alone and time with friends (see figure 5.3) (Larson & Richards, 1991). There are important ethnic and gender differences in patterns of time use, however: The decline in time spent with family members and the dramatic increase in time spent with peers in early adolescence are more striking among European American girls than among boys and African American youth (Larson, Richards, Sims, & Dworkin, in press).

When asked to list the people in their life who are most important to them—their **significant others**—nearly half the people adolescents mention are people of their own age. By sixth grade, adults other than parents account for less than 25 percent of the typical adolescent's social network—the people he or she interact with most regularly. And, among early-maturing teenagers, this figure is only about 10 percent (Brown, 1990).

RECAP

Social scientists have long debated whether the prominent role played by peer groups in the socialization of young people is cause for concern or celebration. On the one side are commentators who suggest that the rise of peer groups has contributed to the development of a separate youth culture that is hostile toward adult values. On the other side are those who point to the necessary and valuable educational role played by peer groups in quickly changing societies such as ours.

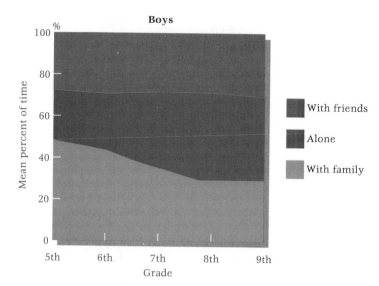

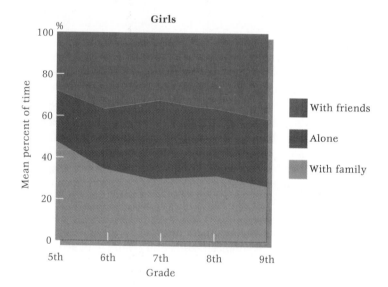

Figure 5.3   *Changes in how individuals spend leisure time during early adolescence.* (Larson & Richards, 1991)

Second, during adolescence, *peer groups function much more often without adult supervision* than they do during childhood (Brown, 1990). Groups of younger children typically play where adults are present or in activities that are organized or supervised by adults (e.g., Little League, Brownies), whereas adolescents are granted far more independence. A group of teenagers may go off to the mall or the movies on their own or deliberately congregate at the home of someone whose parents are out.

Third, during adolescence, *increasingly more contact with peers is with opposite-sex friends.* During childhood, peer groups are highly sex segregated, a phenomenon known as **sex cleavage.** This is especially true of children's peer activities in school and other settings organized by adults, although somewhat less so of their more informal activities, such as neighborhood play (Maccoby, 1990). During adolescence, however, an increasingly larger proportion of an individual's significant others are opposite-sex peers, even in public settings (Brown, 1990). This movement toward opposite-sex peers seems to stimulate changes in the structure of the peer group.

Finally, whereas children's peer relationships are limited mainly to pairs of friends and relatively small groups—three or four children at a time, for example—*adolescence marks the emergence of larger* collectives of peers, or crowds. (Adolescents still have close friendships, of course, which we will look at in chapter 10.) In junior high school cafeterias, for example, the popular crowd sits in one section of the room, the "brains" in another, and the "druggies" in yet a third (see Eder, 1985). These crowds typically develop their own minicultures, which include particular styles of dressing, talking, and behaving. Studies show that it is not until early adolescence that individuals can confidently list the various crowds that characterize their schools and reliably describe the stereotypes that distinguish the crowds from each other (Brown, Mory, & Kinney, 1994).

These changes in peer relations have their origins in the biological, cognitive, and social transitions of adolescence. Puberty stimulates adolescents' interest in opposite-sex relationships and distances adolescents from their parents, which helps explain why adolescents' social networks increasingly include more opposite-sex peers and fewer adults. The cognitive changes of adolescence permit a more sophisticated understanding of social relationships, an understanding that may allow the sort of abstract categorization that leads to grouping individuals into crowds. And changes in social definition may stimulate changes in peer relations as a sort of adaptive response: The larger, more anonymous social setting of the secondary school, for instance, may force adolescents to seek out individuals whom they perceive as having common interests and values, perhaps as a way of recreating the smaller, more intimate groups of childhood (Brown, in press). Instead of floundering in a large, impersonal high school cafeteria, the adolescent who belongs to the "cheerleader" crowd, or even the "nerds," may head directly for his or her place at a familiar table.

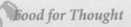

Food for Thought

In what ways do peer groups change during adolescence? How do the biological, cognitive, and social transitions of adolescence affect the ways in which peer groups are structured and function?

Cliques and Crowds

In order to better understand the significance of peer relations during adolescence, it is helpful to think of adolescents' peer groups as organized around two related, but different, structures (Brown, 1990). **Cliques** are small groups of between 2 and 12 individuals—the average is 5 or 6—generally of the same sex and, of course, the same age (Dunphy, 1969; Hollingshead, 1949/1975). Cliques can be defined by common activities (e.g., the "drama" group, a group of students who study together regularly, etc.) or simply by friendship (e.g., a group of girls who have lunch together every day or a group of boys who have known each other for a long time). The importance of the clique, whatever its basis, is that it provides the main social context in which adolescents *interact* with each other. The clique is the social setting in which adolescents hang out, talk to each other, and form close friendships. Some cliques are more open to outsiders than others (i.e., the members are less "cliquish"), but virtually all cliques are small enough so that the members feel that they know each other well and appreciate each other more than people outside the clique do (Brown, 1990).

One study examined the structure, prevalence, and stability of cliques among ninth-graders in five high schools within a large American school district (Ennett & Bauman, 1996). Based on interviews with students over a one-year period, the researchers categorized adolescents as *clique members* (individuals who have most of their interactions with the same small group of people), *liaisons* (individuals who interact with two or more adolescents who are members of cliques but who themselves are not part of a clique), and *isolates* (individuals who have few or no links to others in the network) (see figure 5.4). Three interesting patterns emerged. First, despite the popular image of adolescents as cliquish, fewer than half the adolescents in any school were members of cliques.

> **RECAP**
>
> *The structure of peer groups changes as individuals move into adolescence. First, there is an increase in the amount of time individuals spend in the exclusive company of their peers. Second, peer groups function outside adult supervision more during adolescence than before. Third, during adolescence, increasingly more time is spent with opposite-sex peers. Finally, during adolescence, larger collectives of peers, called crowds, begin to emerge. These transformations are linked to the biological, cognitive, and social transitions and definitional changes of adolescence.*

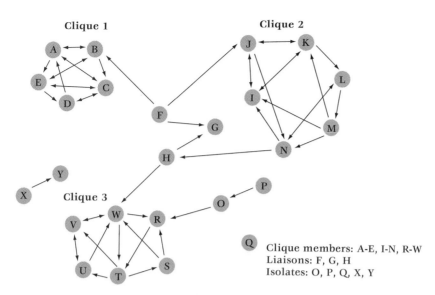

Clique members: A-E, I-N, R-W
Liaisons: F, G, H
Isolates: O, P, Q, X, Y

Second, the girls were more likely than the boys to be members of cliques, whereas the boys were more likely than the girls to be isolates (see also Urberg, Degirmencioglu, Tolson, & Halliday-Scher, 1995). Finally, the adolescents' positions in their school's social network was relatively stable over time. The adolescents who were members of cliques in the ninth grade were clique members in tenth grade; ninth-grade isolates remained, for the most part, isolates one year later.

Cliques are quite different from crowds in structure and purpose. **Crowds** are "large, reputation-based collectives of similarly stereotyped individuals who may or may not spend much time together" (Brown, 1990, p. 177). In contemporary American high schools, typical crowds are "jocks," "brains," "nerds," "populars," "druggies," and so on. The labels for these crowds vary from school to school ("jocks" versus "sportos," "populars" versus "trendies"), but their generic presence is commonplace, at least in the United States and Canada, and you can probably recognize these types of crowds from your own school experience. In contrast to cliques, crowds are not settings for adolescents' intimate interactions or friendships but, instead, serve three broad purposes: to locate adolescents (to themselves and to others) within the social structure of the school, to channel adolescents into associations with some peers and away from others, and to provide contexts that reward certain lifestyles and disparage others (Brown, 1996; Brown, Dolcini, & Leventhal, 1995; Brown et al., 1994). Al-

though most European schools have the crowds that Americans call "populars," "druggies," and "toughs," as well as crowds organized around certain types of music (e.g., "metalheads"), athletically oriented crowds ("jocks") and academically oriented crowds ("brains," "nerds") are rarely found (Arnett, in press). The absence of a "jock" crowd is attributable to the absence of school-sponsored teams in Europe (adolescents join sports clubs in the community, instead). The absence of "brains" and "nerds" is likely due to the different sorts of attitudes that European and American teenagers have toward achievement.

Membership in a crowd is based mainly on reputation and stereotype, rather than on actual friendship or social interaction. This is very different from membership in a clique, which, by definition, hinges on shared activity and friendship. In concrete terms—and perhaps ironically—an adolescent does not actually have to have "brains" as friends, or to hang around with "brainy" students, to be a member of the "brain" crowd. If he dresses as a "brain," acts as a "brain," and takes honors courses, then he is a "brain," as far as his crowd membership goes. The fact that crowd membership is based on reputation and stereotype can be very difficult for individual adolescents, who—if they do not change their reputations early on in high school—may find themselves stuck, at least in the eyes of their peers, in a crowd that they do not wish to belong to (or that they do not see themselves as a part of) (Brown, Freeman, Huang, & Mounts, 1992). This also means that some individuals can be members of more than one crowd simultaneously, if their reputation is such (Mory, 1994).

The images adolescents have of various crowds in their schools are often highly stereotyped and caricatured, and adolescents tend to inflate the positive qualities of their own crowd, while exaggerating the negative qualities of others (Mory, 1992). In one study (cited in Brown et al., 1994), in which teenagers were asked about the crowds in their school, responses such as the following were given:

Oh, yeah; they all wear these tight-fitting jeans and sit around the commons in between classes like they own the place!

You'd be crazy to walk down the B-wing by yourself because the headbangers, they, like, attack you.

They all wear glasses and "kiss up" to teachers, and after school they all tromp uptown to the library, or they go over to somebody's house and play some stupid computer game until 9:00 at night—and then they go right to bed, 'cause their mommies make 'em!

Whether every "popular" wears tight-fitting jeans, every "headbanger" stalks other adolescents, or every "nerd" goes to sleep at 9 P.M. doesn't really matter. What is more important, perhaps, is that their peers believe that they do.

Although an adolescent's closest friends are almost always members of the same clique, some of them may belong to a different crowd, especially when one crowd is close in lifestyle to the other (Urberg, Degitmencioglu, Tolson, & Halliday-Scher, 1995). Thus, for example, a "brain" will have some friends who are also "brains" and some who are "nerds" but few, if any, who are "druggies" (Brown et al., 1994).

More important, crowds are not simply clusters of cliques; the two different structures serve entirely different purposes. Because a clique is based on activity and friendship, it is the important setting in which the adolescent learns social skills—how to be a good friend to someone else, how to communicate with others effectively, how to be a leader, how to enjoy someone else's company, and even how to break off a friendship that is no longer satisfying. These and other social skills are important in adulthood as well as in adolescence. In contrast, because crowds are based on reputation and stereotype, not interaction, they probably contribute more to the adolescent's sense of identity and self-conceptions—for better and for worse—than to his or her actual social development.

RECAP

Social scientists distinguish between crowds and cliques. Crowds are larger and more vaguely defined groups that are based on reputation. Contrary to the stereotype of a homogeneous youth culture, research has indicated that the social world of adolescents is composed of many distinct subcultures. In order to understand how peers influence adolescent development, it is essential to know which peer group a youngster is part of.

Food for Thought

Think back to your own high school experience. What were the major crowds in your school? What common characteristics did you share with the people who were in your clique?

Changes in Clique and Crowd Structure over Time

Studies of the structure of adolescents' peer groups often make use of a research technique called **participant observation.** In this approach, the researcher establishes rapport with a group of individuals in order to infiltrate and eventually join the group. In *Inside High School* (Cusick, 1973), for example, the author pretended to be a newcomer to the community and attended high school for a year to learn more about the adolescents' social world. As an observer who is also a participant, the researcher can observe the group's behavior under condition that are more natural and more private than would otherwise be the case. Overhearing a 10-minute conversation in a high school locker room can be more informative than interviewing a student for three hours, if the student feels uncomfortable or uneasy.

Observational studies of young people indicate that there are important changes in the structure of cliques and crowds during the adolescent years (e.g., Dunphy, 1963). During early adolescence, adolescents' activities revolve around same-sex cliques. Adolescents at this stage are not yet involved in parties and typically spend their leisure time with a small group of friends, playing sports, talking, or simply hanging around.

Somewhat later, as boys and girls become more interested in one another—but before dating actually begins—boys' and girls' cliques come together. This is clearly a transitional stage. Boys and girls may go to parties together, but the time they spend there actually involves interaction with peers of the same sex. When youngsters are still uncomfortable about dealing with members of the opposite sex, this setting provides an opportunity in which adolescents can learn more about opposite-sex peers without having to be intimate and without having to risk losing face. It is not unusual, for example, at young adolescents' first mixed-sex parties for groups of boys and girls to position themselves on opposite sides of a room, watching each other but seldom interacting.

The peer group then enters a stage of structural transformation, generally led by the clique leaders. As youngsters become interested in dating, part of the group begins to divide off into mixed-sex cliques, while other individuals remain in the group but in same-sex cliques. The shift into dating is usually led by the clique leaders, with other clique members following along. For instance, a clique of boys whose main activity is playing basketball may discover that one of the guys they look up to has become more interested in going out with girls on Saturday nights than in hanging out at the schoolyard. Over time, they will begin to follow his lead, and their clique at the schoolyard will become smaller and smaller.

During middle adolescence, mixed-sex cliques become more prevalent. In time, the peer group becomes composed entirely of heterosexual cliques. One clique might consist of the drama students—male and female students who know each other from acting together in school plays. Another might be composed of four girls and four boys who like to drink on the weekends. The staff of the school yearbook might make up a third.

Finally, during late adolescence, the peer group begins to disintegrate. Pairs of dating adolescents begin to split off from the activities of the larger group. The larger peer group is replaced by loosely associated sets of couples. Couples may go out together from time to time, but the feeling of being in a crowd has disappeared. This pattern—in which the couple becomes the focus of social activity—persists into adulthood.

When viewed from a structural point of view, the peer group's role in the development of intimacy is quite clear. Over time, the structure of the peer group

▲ *By late adolescence, same-sex peer groups have mainly disintegrated. Adolescents are more likely to spend their leisure time as members of couples.* (Tom McCarthy/Unicorn Stock Photos)

changes to become more in keeping with adolescents' changing needs and interests. As we will see in chapter 10, the adolescent's capacity for close relationships develops first through friendships with peers of the same sex. Only later does intimacy enter into opposite-sex relationships. Thus, the structure of the peer group changes during adolescence in a way that parallels the adolescent's development of intimacy: As the adolescent develops increasing facility in close relationships, the peer group moves from the familiarity of same-sex activities to contact with opposite-sex peers but in the safety of the larger group. It is only after adolescent males and females have been slowly socialized into dating roles—primarily by modeling their higher-status peers—that the safety of numbers is no longer needed, and adolescents begin pairing off.

There also are changes in peer crowds during this time. Many of these changes reflect the growing cognitive sophistication of the adolescent, as described in chapter 2. For example, as adolescents mature intellectually, they come to define crowds more in terms of abstract and global characteristics (e.g., "preppies," "nerds," "jocks") than in terms of concrete, behavioral features (e.g., "the ballet crowd," "the Play Station crowd," "the kids who play basketball on 114th Street") (O'Brien & Bierman, 1988). As you know, this shift

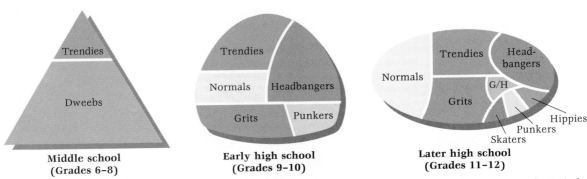

Figure 5.5   Developmental changes in crowd structure. Line widths indicate the degree of impermeability among crowds. Vertical location indicates each crowd's position in the school's peer-status hierarchy. Note: G/H = "grit-headbangers." (Brown, Mory, & Kinney, 1994)

from concrete to abstract is a general feature of cognitive development in adolescence. In addition, as adolescents become more cognitively capable, they become more consciously aware of the crowd structure of their school and their place in it (Brown et al., in press).

Over the course of adolescence, the crowd structure also becomes more differentiated, more permeable, and less hierarchical, which allows adolescents more freedom to change crowds and enhance their status (Kinney, 1993). For example, in a study of peer crowds in one small midwestern city, the researcher found that, over the course of adolescence, the crowd structure shifted in middle school, early high school, and late high school. During middle school, there was a clear, small in-group ("trendies") and a larger out-group ("dweebs"). During early high school, there was one high-status crowd ("trendies"), two other socially acceptable crowds ("headbangers" and "normals"), and two less desirable groups ("grits" and "punkers"). During late high school, the status differences among "trendies," "normals," and "headbangers" were negligible, and "hybrid" crowds (e.g., "grit-headbangers") were common (see figure 5.5). This change over time permitted some individuals who were low in status during middle-school to "recover" during high school.

As crowds become increasingly more salient influences on adolescents' view of their social world, they come to play an increasingly important role in structuring adolescent social behavior (O'Brien & Bierman, 1988). By ninth grade, there is nearly universal agreement among students in a school about their school's crowd structure, and students' assessment of the strength of peer group influence is very high. Between ninth and twelfth grades, however, the significance of the crowd

structure begins to decline, and the salience of peer pressure wanes. As we will see in chapter 9, this pattern of an increase and then a decline in the salience of peer crowds parallels developmental changes in adolescents' susceptibility to peer pressure. In other words, as crowds become more important in defining the teenager's social world—between early and middle adolescence—adolescents become more likely to accede to their influence. As crowds become less important, however—between middle adolescence and late adolescence—their influence over the adolescent's behavior weakens as well (Brown, 1990; Gavin & Furman, 1989).

Just as the changes in the structure of cliques play a role in the development of intimacy during adolescence, changes in the salience of crowds over the adolescent years play an important role in adolescent identity development. In chapter 8, we will see that adolescence is frequently a time for experimentation with roles and identities. During the early adolescent years, before adolescents have "found" themselves, the crowd provides an important basis for self-definition (Newmann & Newmann, 1976). By locating themselves within the crowd structure of their school—through style of dress, language, or choice of hangouts—adolescents wear badges that say, "This is who I am." At a time when adolescents may not actually know just who they are, associating with a crowd provides them with a rudimentary sense of identity.

As adolescents become more secure about their identity as individuals, however, the need for affiliation with a crowd diminishes. Indeed, by the time they have reached high school, older adolescents are likely to feel that remaining a part of a crowd *stifles* their sense of identity and self-expression (Larkin, 1979; Varenne,

1982). The breakup of the larger peer group in late adolescence may both foreshadow and reflect the emergence of each adolescent's unique and coherent sense of self (Brown et al., in press).

RECAP

Social scientists have charted changes in the structure of cliques and crowds over the course of adolescence. Cliques, which begin as same-sex groups of individuals, gradually merge to form larger, mixed-sex groups, as adolescents begin dating and socializing with peers of the opposite sex. In late adolescence, these groups begin to break down, as adolescents' social lives start to revolve more around couple-based activities. Crowds, which peak in importance during the midadolescence years, become more differentiated and more permeable during high school, and their influence becomes less salient.

Food for Thought

Why do crowds and cliques change over the course of adolescence? How do these changes affect—and how are they affected by—the development of the individual adolescent?

ADOLESCENTS AND THEIR CROWDS

The Social Map of Adolescence

The idea of a single youth culture has not held up very well in recent research. Most ethnographic studies of high schools indicate that the social world of adolescents is far more multifaceted than this (e.g., Cusick, 1973). One helpful scheme for mapping the social world of adolescent crowds was suggested by Rigsby and McDill (1975) and was later modified by Brown (1990).

According to this model, adolescents' crowds can be placed along two dimensions: (1) how involved they are in the institutions controlled by adults, such as school and extracurricular activities, and (2) how involved they are in the informal, peer culture (see figure 5.6). "Jocks" and "populars," for example, are quite involved in the peer culture, but they are also very involved in the institutions valued by adults (sports and school orga-

nizations, for example). "Brains" and "nerds," in contrast, are also involved in adult-controlled organizations (in their case, academics), but they tend to be less involved in the peer culture. "Partyers" are on the opposite side of the map from "nerds": These adolescents are very involved in the peer culture but are not involved in adult institutions. "Toughs" and adolescents who are members of delinquent gangs are not involved in either the peer culture or adult institutions. Other crowds, such as "normals" and "druggies," fall between these extremes. This conceptualization points to an important limitation of Coleman's view of a monolithic adolescent society: His description of adolescents as fun-loving and anti-intellectual accurately described one segment of the adolescent society—a segment known in some schools as "partyers"—but not all young people in general.

Crowds as Reference Groups

Knowing where an adolescent fits into the social system of the school can often tell a fair amount about the individual's behavior and values. This is because crowds contribute to the definition of norms and standards for such things as clothing, leisure, and tastes in music. Being a "jock" means more than simply being involved in athletics; it means wearing certain types of clothes, listening to certain types of music, spending Saturday nights in certain hangouts, and using a particular slang. These adolescents accept many of the values of the adults around them but also value many elements of the contemporary peer culture.

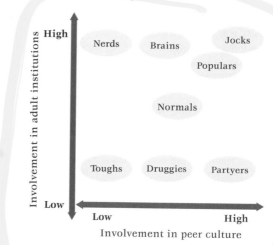

Figure 5.6   A model for mapping the social world of adolescent peer groups. (Brown, 1990)

The Scientific Study of Adolescence

How "Nerds" Become "Normals"

"Popular films and television shows about adolescents and schools," writes sociologist David Kinney, "usually include a certain type of teenager who is frequently ridiculed and rejected by his or her peers. These adolescents are often portrayed as awkward, intelligent, shy, unattractive social outcasts with unfashionable hair and dress styles. . . . They are called 'nerds,' 'dweebs,' 'dorks,' 'geeks,' 'brainiacs,' and 'computer jocks' " (Kinney, 1993, p. 21). What happens to "nerds" as they move through adolescence? One surprising finding from Kinney's research is that many individuals who are "nerds" early in adolescence become "normals" by the end of high school.

In order to study the day-to-day experiences of "nerds" and their interactions with other students, Kinney conducted an **ethnography** of the social interaction and peer culture in a high school in a small midwestern city. In contrast to survey or experimental research, which is typically quantitative (that is, the data collected can be quantified), ethnographic research is qualitative. The researcher spends a considerable amount of time observing interactions within the setting, inter-

viewing many adolescents, and writing field notes, much as an anthropologist would do to study a foreign culture. Ethnogrphic approaches can be extremely useful in studying social relationships, because they provide rich, descriptive data. Indeed, those who study adolescent peer culture have learned a great deal more from qualitative research than from quantitative studies.

How do ethnographers go about establishing themselves in the setting? As Kinney explains,

> I attempted to carve out a neutral identity for myself at the school by making and maintaining connections with students in a wide variety of peer groups and by being open to their different viewpoints. During my initial contacts with the students and before I conducted the interviews, I stressed that I would be the only one to listen to the audiotapes and that neither the school nor any individual students would be identified. . . . I also distanced myself from adult authority figures by dressing in jeans and casual shirts and by emphasizing my status as a college student writing a

Another way of putting this is that adolescents' crowds serve as **reference groups.** They provide their members with an identity in the eyes of other adolescents. Adolescents judge one another on the basis of the company they keep. Individuals become branded on the basis of whom they hang around with. Such labels as "jocks," "brains," "socies," "druggies," and "leathers" serve as shorthand notations—whether accurate or inaccurate—to describe what someone is like as a person and what he or she holds as important.

Crowd membership is important not only because crowds are used by adolescents when talking about one another but also because membership in a crowd is often the basis for an adolescent's own identity. A girl who runs with the "preppies" identifies herself as such by wearing their "uniform," shopping in their stores, and speaking their language. After a while, preppiness becomes part of her own self-concept; she wouldn't think

of dressing or talking in a different way. Or consider the boys whose clique is held together by a dislike of school. Since this attitude toward school is continuously reinforced by the clique, each boy's feelings about school become strengthened, and not liking school becomes part of each boy's identity. Even if something very positive happens at school, it becomes difficult for someone in the clique to admit that it makes him feel good about himself. Doing well on a test or receiving a compliment from a teacher is likely to be dismissed as unimportant.

Because the adolescent's peer group plays such an important role as a reference group and a source of identity, the nature of the crowd with which an adolescent affiliates is likely to have an important influence on his or her behavior, activities, and self-conceptions (Sussman et al., 1994). Brown and his colleagues have studied how peer group membership—that is, which

paper about teenagers' high school experiences. (1993, p. 25).

At the time, Kinney was a graduate student collecting data for his doctoral dissertation. Kinney asked students to recall their middle school experiences. Following is an excerpt of an interview he conducted with two students, "Ross" and "Ted," who had been "nerds":

Ross: And middle school—

Ted: We were just nerds. I mean—

Ross: Yeah—

Ted: people hated us.

Ross: Well, they didn't hate us, but we weren't—

Ted: popular. Which was either you were popular or you weren't.

Ross: In middle school it's very defined. There's popular people and unpopular people. It's just very— rigid. You were popular or unpopular. That's it.

Ted: And there wasn't people that were in between.

Ross: Oh no!

Ted: You just had one route [to becoming popular], and then there was the other. And we were the other, and—basically you were afraid of getting laughed at about

anything you did because if you did one thing that was out of the ordinary, and you weren't expected to do anything out of the ordinary, then you were laughed at and made fun of, and you wouldn't fit the group at all, and then, of course, you were excluded and then you didn't even exist.

Ross: You got "nuked," so to speak. (Kinney, 1993, p. 27)

Kinney discovered, however, that many individuals who had been "nuked" in middle school had managed to transform themselves from "nerds" into "normals" sometime during high school. For some, this transition was accomplished because the high school peer structure was more differentiated and more permeable. As opposed to middle school, where there were only two groups—the popular and the unpopular—in high school there were more socially acceptable groups with which to affiliate. For others, the transition to "normal" came about through gains in self-assurance that came with physical and social development. And, for others still, the transformation was facilitated by the development of a more congnitively sophisticated, confident view of the social hierarchy—one that permitted them to reject the prem-

ise that whatever the "trendies" valued was necessarily desirable. As one young woman put it,

If you have confidence, you can overlook people who put you down 'cause there are always people who are going to put you down. And [when you have confidence], you don't have to worry about what I think are the more trivial things in life, like appearance or being trendy. (Kinney, 1993, p. 33)

In essence, the transformation of "nerds" to "normals" was enabled by a combination of factors both within the context (e.g., the increasing differentiation and permeability of the peer crowd system) and within the adolescent (e.g., the physical, cognitive, and social maturation of the individual) (Brown, 1996). Kinney's study reminds us of the potential for growth and change during the adolescent years, even for individuals who begin the period at a social disadvantage.

Source: Kinney, D. (1993). From nerds to normals: The recovery of identity among adolescents from middle school to high school. *Sociology of Education, 66,* 21–40.

peer group the adolescent affiliates with—may affect the adolescent's development and behavior (Brown, 1996). Although most adolescents feel pressure from their friends to behave in ways that are consistent with their crowd's values and goals, the specific nature of the pressure varies from one crowd to another. Adolescents who are part of the "druggie" crowd report much more peer pressure to engage in misconduct, for example, than do adolescents in the "jock" crowd (Clasen & Brown, 1985).

Crowd membership can also affect the way adolescents feel about themselves. Adolescents' self-esteem is higher among students who are identified with peer groups that have relatively more status in their school. In the high schools that Brown studied, the "jocks" and "socies" were highest in status, and the "druggies" and "toughs" were lowest. Students who were identified with the higher-status groups had higher self-esteem

than did those who were identified with the lower-status groups (Brown & Lohr, 1987). As the authors wrote, "Crowds are not merely fertile grounds for bolstering self-esteem through identity testing or building supportive social relationships. Crowd labels also provide one feedback on one's comparative standing among peers, which in turn may enhance or depreciate self-esteem" (Brown & Lohr, 1987, p. 53).

Researchers do not know how the social structure of adolescent crowds differs for minority and nonminority adolescents, because most of the research to date has been conducted in predominantly white high schools. Some research indicates that at least some of the basic distinctions among crowds that were found in studies of predominantly white high schools (e.g., academically oriented crowds, partying crowds, deviant crowds, and trendy crowds) also exist among adolescents from ethnic minority groups (e.g., Brown & Mounts, 1989;

▲ *In multiethnic high schools, peer groups often divide along ethnic lines.* (Mary Kate Denny/PhotoEdit)

Fordham & Ogbu, 1986). There is some evidence, however, that, in multiethnic high schools, the adolescents divide first across ethnic lines and then into the more familiar adolescent crowds within ethnic groups. Thus, in a large urban high school, there may be separate groups of African American "jocks" and white "jocks," of Hispanic American "populars" and African American "populars," and so on (Steinberg et al., 1996). Interestingly, in multiethnic schools, adolescents from one ethnic group are less likely to see crowd distinctions within other ethnic groups than they are in their own group. Thus, to white students, all Asian American adolescents are part of the "Asian" crowd, whereas the Asian American students see themselves as divided into "brains," "populars," and so on (Brown & Mounts, 1989).

There is also reason to believe that the meaning associated with belonging to various crowds differs among ethnic groups. According to one team of researchers, for example, in predominantly African

American high schools, the adolescents who are in the "brain" crowd were ridiculed (Fordham & Ogbu, 1986). In the inner-city schools they studied, the students who were high achievers were labeled "brainiacs" and were ostracized for "acting white." Similarly, in some schools it may be admirable to be a "jock," whereas in others it may be frowned upon. Thus, the values we associate with being in one crowd as opposed to another may not be constant across all school contexts.

Of course, many adolescents develop passing acquaintances with peers who are neither close friends nor members of the same crowd. In one fascinating analysis of messages inscribed in high school yearbooks over nearly 70 years, sociologist Peggy Giordano (1995) found some commonalities among inscriptions written by classmates who weren't close friends. In general, three rules dictated the content of yearbook inscriptions, regardless of when or where they were written: (1) say something nice about the receiver; (2) talk about your relationship with the receiver; and (3) give the receiver some advice, words of wisdom, or good wishes. The following are some examples, from very different eras:

> Bill, It took me almost all of the 4th hour to get to sign your book so you know you are real hip and popular. Best of luck wherever you are. Marguerite (1955)

> You're a real sweet girl with an $A+$ personality. Best of luck always. Thanks for all the answers you gave me for English. Ellen (1961)

> Huntley, It's been fun knowing you in trig. this year. In the future, when you are asked a question try to give them a short answer. Johnny (1965)

> Janie, I hate to be like everybody else and just write a lot of things you know they never mean, so I'll just say what I feel. I think you're a really great person. Remember all the fun we had serving. Lots of luck, Lisa (1972)

> Karri, We've had fun together (I hope) at the basketball games. Don't worry about your best friend Ann cause you have a friend in me. Amber (1980)

> Katie, your a great friend with a great butt. Get a tighter pair of pants for bowling. Brian (1990)

Of course, these inscriptions are very different from those written by close friends:

> Missy,
> . . . know I'll leave out something, but most importantly of all: we did all those tons of things together. Again my mind drifts to Myrtle Beach—the ultimate. The greatest

moment and memory of our lives and of course we did it together. Well maybe we weren't connected at the elbow but adjoining rooms was close enough. . . . so many memories . . . you and me are the only ones who can understand them. You and me have shared a lot these past few years. I can't think of anyone else I have trusted or talked or cared about more than you. You have been my best friend and will be always. I'll miss you. Jennifer (1987)

RECAP

Although the specific crowd names may differ from school to school, and from one ethnic group to the next, most high schools have relatively similar crowd structures, with some version of "jocks," "populars," "brains," "nerds," and "toughs." Adolescents' crowds can be mapped on two distinct dimensions: how involved they are in adult institutions, such as school, and how involved they are in the peer culture. Because they often serve as reference groups, crowds play an important role in the adolescent's identity development.

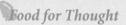

Food for Thought

What does it mean to say that crowds serve as reference groups for adolescents? How might membership in one crowd, as opposed to another, affect an adolescent's development? What happens to someone who wants to change crowds?

ADOLESCENTS AND THEIR CLIQUES

What draws adolescents into one clique and not another? Because cliques serve as a basis for adolescents' friendships and play an important role in their social development, many researchers have studied the determinants of clique compositions.

Similarity Among Clique Members

The most important influence on the composition of cliques is similarity. Adolescents' cliques typically are composed of people who are of the same age and the same race, from the same socioeconomic background, and—at least during early and middle adolescence—of the same sex (Ennett & Bauman, 1996).

● **Age Segregation**   Age grouping in junior and senior high schools makes it unlikely for an individual to have friends who are substantially older or younger. A tenth-grader who is enrolled in tenth-grade English, tenth-grade math, tenth-grade history, and tenth-grade science simply does not have many opportunities to meet adolescents who are in different grades. Age segregation in adolescents' cliques does, indeed, appear to result mostly from the structure of schools (Shrum, Cheek, & Hunter, 1988). When an adolescent's friends come from a different school, those friends are just as likely to be younger or older as they are to be the same age (Blyth et al., 1982).

● **Sex Segregation**   During the early and middle adolescent years, cliques also tend to be composed of adolescents of the same sex (Ennett & Bauman, 1996). This sex cleavage begins in childhood and continues through most of the adolescent years, although it is stronger among white students than among African American students (Filardo, 1996; Hallinan, 1981; Sagar, Schofield, & Snyder, 1983), and it weakens later in adolescence (Shrum et al., 1988). The causes of sex segregation in adolescents' cliques are more interesting than the causes of age segregation, because schools do not separate boys and girls into different classes. Why, then, do adolescent males and females separate themselves into different cliques? Psychologist Eleanor Maccoby, an expert on gender and development, has suggested several reasons (Maccoby, 1990).

First, cliques are formed largely on the basis of shared activities and interests. Generally speaking, preadolescent and early adolescent boys and girls are interested in different things. It is not until adolescents begin dating that boys' cliues and girls' cliques mix, presumably because dating provides a basis for common activity.

A second reason for the sex cleavage in adolescent peer groups concerns young adolescents' sensitivity about sex roles. Over the course of childhood, boys and girls become increasingly concerned about behaving in ways that are judged to be sex-appropriate. When boys show an interest in dolls, they are often told either explicitly (by parents, friends, and teachers) or implicitly (by television, books, and other mass media), "Little boys don't play with dolls. Those are for girls." And, when girls start wrestling or roughhousing, they are often reprimanded and told to "act like ladies."

As a consequence of these continual reminders that there are "boys' activities" and "girls' activities," early adolescents—who are trying to establish a sense of

Two findings from studies of adolescent peer groups emerge over and over again. First, a strong sex cleavage limits the interaction between adolescent boys and girls—at least until dating begins. Second, adolescents have very little contact with peers from other races, even when they attend desegregated schools that have been developed to increase cross-racial interaction.

One curiosity that has been uncovered, as noted in this chapter, is that, although the race cleavage seems to characterize boys' as well as girls' interaction, it is much stronger among adolescent girls than boys. Specifically, although boys and girls alike are likely to interact more often with adolescents of the same race, the likelihood of white boys interacting with African American boys is much greater than the likelihood of white girls interacting with African American girls. Indeed, several studies suggest that cliques of young adolescent African American girls are among the most socially isolated of all adolescent groups (Damico & Sparks, 1986). This isolation seems to work both ways: White students of both sexes are less likely to talk to African American girls than to any other group, and African American girls are less likely than any other group to initiate contact with whites.

No one is quite sure why African American females face this predicament, but at least three hypotheses are offered.

identity—are very concerned about acting in sex-appropriate ways. This makes it very difficult for an adolescent girl to be part of a boys' clique, in which activities are likely to be dominated by athletics and other physical pursuits, or for a boy to be a part of a girls' clique, in which activities are likely to revolve around clothing, grooming, and talk about boys (Schofield, 1981). Adolescents who go against prevailing sex-role norms by forming friendships with members of the opposite sex may be teased about being "fags" or may be ostracized by their peers because they are "perverts." Ironically, once dating becomes the norm, adolescents who *don't* have relationships with peers of the opposite sex become the objects of equally strong suspicion and social rejection.

● **Social-Class Segregation**   One of the most important studies ever undertaken of adolescents' peer groups is *Elmtown's Youth* (Hollingshead, 1949/1975). In this study of adolescents in the midwestern community of Elmtown, sociologist August Hollingshead examined the relation between the social position of adolescents' families and the composition of teenagers' cliques. He was interested in determining whether the adolescents' cliques were segregated along class lines.

Hollingshead used such indicators as income, residence, and reputation in the community to sort families into five groups defined by **social class.** In the highest class were families who were very affluent, lived in the best neighborhoods, and were known in the community as powerful and respected families. These "upper-class" families had lived in the community for a long time and belonged to all the exclusive clubs and organizations. In the "lower class" were families who were poor, lived on the "wrong" side of town, and were not highly regarded in the community. Between these extremes were three groups of families: the hard-working but not very well off "working-class" families; the comfortable but not especially affluent "middle-class" families; and the "upper-middle-class" families, who had money but did not quite have the reputation and prestige of the families in the highest class.

Hollingshead found that adolescents do, in fact, associate chiefly with peers from the same social class. More than 60 percent of each adolescent's close friendships in Elmtown High School were between teenagers from the same background. Of the remaining clique relationships, the vast majority were between adolescents of adjacent social classes (for example, between middle-class adolescents and upper-middle-class adolescents). Almost never did adolescents from one social class associate with students from a class that was two steps higher or lower.

Hollingshead found similar patterns when he looked at the adolescents' best friends and dating relationships: Rarely were social-class lines crossed, and, when they were, it was virtually always between adolescents of

One researcher has suggested that a special tension exists between white and African American girls that does not exist between white and African American boys (Schofield, 1981). She suggests that, as sex and romance become more important during early adolescence, students become increasingly competitive for the attention of opposite-sex students. Although both boys and girls seek this attention, it may be more important for girls, who may rely more on the prestige derived from dating popular boys as an index of their social status in school. Boys, in contrast, may look more to athletics for status and may be slightly less concerned about getting the attention of girls in their classes. The heightened concern for male attention introduces a greater level of competition into adolescent girls' social relations, and this competition may underlie white and African American girls' reluctance to interact.

An alternative explanation concerns the special role that white girls may play in the communication network of the school. One team of researchers has suggested that, from an early age, white girls try to develop personalized relationships with their teachers (Damico & Sparks, 1986). By junior high school, these girls have become an important source of "inside information" for students in the school about teachers and classes. Thus, white girls may find themselves more centrally located within the school's social network than are African American girls. African American girls may receive fewer social overtures from other students because they are perceived as less tied into the school's network.

Finally, sex differences in the degree to which peer interaction is racially segregated may be based on differences between the activity patterns of girls and boys in general. As you will read in chapter 10, adolescent boys are more likely than girls to spend time in large-group activities, such as sports, and girls are more likely to spend time talking in pairs or in small groups. The large-group activities of boys may simply provide greater opportunities for cross-racial interaction to take place—as when white and African American students are on the same team. In contrast, the focus of adolescent girls on more intimate peer relations may make them less likely to interact with individuals whom they perceive—correctly or not—to have different values and norms for behavior. In other words, sex differences in the structure of adolescent peer activities may make cross-racial contact easier for boys than for girls.

adjacent classes. Moreover, the adolescents became even more class conscious as they got older.

Several other studies conducted since the time of *Elmtown's Youth* have confirmed the enduring importance of social class in influencing an adolescent's position in the high school peer network. In one five-school study of cliques, for example, cliques were just as class-segregated as they had been found to be by Hollingshead many decades earlier. Within each clique, about 60 percent of the adolescents came from the same social class, even though each school was considerably more diverse in its social-class composition as a whole (Ennett & Bauman, 1996). Clique-based friendships between adolescents who were from very different social backgrounds were seldom observed.

● **Race Segregation** Race is not a strong determinant of clique composition during childhood, but, like social class, it becomes increasingly powerful as youngsters get older, at least within the United States (Shrum et al., 1988). By middle and late adolescence, adolescents' peer groups typically are racially segregated, with very few race-mixed cliques present in most high schools (Ennett & Bauman, 1996). This appears to be the case, although somewhat less so, even within schools that have been desegregated (Schofield, 1981).

There are several explanations for racial separation in adolescents' peer groups. First, because adolescents' cliques are often segregated along socioeconomic lines, peer groups that appear to be segregated because of race actually may be separated on the basis of social class, since disproportionately higher numbers of minority youngsters come from economically poorer families. This explanation helps account for the race cleavage in desegregated schools, which often bring together youngsters not only of different racial backgrounds but from varying economic backgrounds and neighborhoods as well. Even among adolescents who do have cross-racial friendships at school, few report seeing those friends outside of school (DuBois & Hirsch, 1990).

Another reason for the strong racial split in adolescents' cliques appears to be the differential levels of academic achievement of adolescents from different ethnic groups (Schofield, 1981). As you will read in chapter 12, on average, white and Asian adolescents earn significantly higher grades in school than do African American and Hispanic adolescents (Steinberg Dornbusch & Brown, 1992). Adolescents who are friends usually have similar attitudes toward school, similar educational aspirations, and similar school achievement levels (Savin-Williams & Berndt, 1990). Racial differences in school achievement may lead to racial separation in adolescent peer groups through tracking and other mechanisms (Hallinan & Williams, 1989).

A third reason for racially segregated peer groups—according to one study of adolescents in a desegregated school—is attitudinal. In this school, the white adolescents perceived their African American peers as aggressive, threatening, and hostile. The African American students felt that the white students were conceited, prejudiced, and unwilling to be friends with them. These perceptions, which fed on each other, made the formation of interracial peer groups unlikely. The more the white students felt that the African American students were hostile, the more the white students acted distant and kept to themselves. The more the white students acted this way, however, the more likely the African American students were to feel rejected, and the more hostile they became. In many schools, adolescents' lack of familiarity with youngsters from other racial groups results in misperceptions of the others' attitudes and motives, and this misunderstanding limits interracial interaction (Schofield, 1981). In general, white students are less apt to initiate contact with African American students than vice versa (Sagar et al., 1983).

One way out of this cycle of misunderstanding is to bring white and African American youngsters together from an early age, before they have had time to build up prejudices and stereotypes. Interracial school busing, for example, has been far more successful in communities that began such programs during elementary school than in districts that implemented them for the first time at the high school level. If white and African American children grow up together from an early age, they are less likely to misunderstand each other and less likely to go off into separate peer groups purely on the basis of race.

Indeed, one study of Canadian adolescents indicated that racial segregation in adolescent peer relationships is far less common in Canada than in the United States (Maharaj & Connolly, 1994). According to the researchers, one reason for this is that the broader cultural context in Canada is more tolerant of diversity than that in the United States and more aggressive in its approach to multicultural education and ethnic integration.

Of course, not all adolescents have especially strong preferences for friends from the same ethnic background. One comparison of two Chinese immigrant girls in a U.S. high school illustrates this point (Shih, 1998). One of the girls, Christine, had a strong preference for friends who were not only Chinese but were also Chinese immigrants. Although she initially was open-minded about having friends who were not Chinese, she came to feel psychologically distant from them—that she had little in common with them and that they made fun of her speech and behavior. Denise, in contrast, was eager to become Americanized, and

went out of her way to acquire the slang, customs, and attitudes of mainstream American adolescent culture. She saw having non-Chinese friends as a way of facilitating her Americanization, and she actively sought them for this reason.

Common Interests Among Friends

Thus far we have seen that adolescents' cliques are usually composed of adolescents who are the same age, in the same grade in school, from the same social class, and of the same race. But what about factors beyond these? Do adolescents who associate with one another also share certain interests and activities? Generally speaking, they do. Three factors appear to be especially important in determining adolescent clique membership and friendship patterns: orientation toward school, orientation toward the teen culture, and involvement in antisocial activity. In general, this is true for both white youth (e.g., Berndt, 1982) and nonwhite youth (e.g., Tolson, Halliday-Scher, & Mack, 1994).

● **Orientation Toward School**   Adolescents and their friends tend to be similar in their attitudes toward school, in their school achievement, and in their educational plans (Berndt, 1982; Epstein, 1983b; Wentzel & Caldwell, 1997). Adolescents who earn high grades, study a great deal, and plan to go on to college usually have friends who share these activities and aspirations. One reason for this is that how much time a student devotes to schoolwork affects his or her involvement in other activities. Someone who is always studying will not have many friends who are out late at night partying, because the two activities conflict. By the same token, someone who wants to spend afternoons and evenings out having fun will find it difficult to remain friends with someone who prefers to stay home and study. Students also may influence each other's academic performance. Given two students with similar records of past achievement, the student whose friends do well in school is likely to achieve more than the student whose friends do not do as well (Epstein, 1983a). Similarly, adolescents whose friends are disruptive in school tend to become more disruptive over time (Berndt & Keefe, 1995).

● **Orientation Toward the Teen Culture**   Adolescents and their friends generally listen to the same type of music, dress similarly, spend their leisure time in similar types of activities, and have similar patterns of drug use

(Berndt, 1982). It would be very unlikely, for example, for a "jock" and a "druggie" to be part of the same clique, because their interests and attitudes are so different. In most high schools, it is fairly easy to see the split between cliques—in how people dress, where they eat lunch, how much they participate in the school's activities, and how they spend their time outside of school.

● **Involvement in Antisocial Activity**   A number of studies, involving both boys and girls from various ethnic groups, indicate that antisocial, aggressive adolescents may gravitate toward each other, forming deviant peer groups (Bukowski, Peters, Sippola, & Newcomb, 1993; Cairns, Cairns, Neckerman, Gest, & Gariepy, 1988; Dishion, Patterson, Stoolmiller, & Skinner, 1991; Fergusson, Woodward, & Horwood, 1999; Laird, Pettit, Dodge, & Bates, 1999). That is, contrary to the popular belief that antisocial adolescents do not have friends, or that they are interpersonally inept, these studies show that such youngsters do have friends, but their friends tend also to be antisocial. Although one would not necessarily want to label all of these peer groups delinquent, since they are not always involved in criminal activity, understanding the processes through which antisocial peer groups form provides some insight into the development of delinquent peer groups, or gangs. **Gangs** are deviant peer groups that can be identified by name (often denoting a neighborhood or part of the city) and common symbols ("colors," tattoos, hand signs, jewelry, etc.) (Branch, 1995; Harris, 1994; Winfree, Bäckström, & Mays, 1994).

According to several studies (Dishion et al., 1991; Kim et al., 1999), the process of antisocial peer group formation begins in the home. Problematic parent-child relationships that are coercive and hostile lead to the development of an antisocial disposition in the child, and this disposition contributes, in elementary school, to school failure and rejection by classmates (Dishion et al., 1991). (Aggression in elementary and middle school often leads to peer rejection.) Rejected by the bulk of his classmates, an aggressive boy "shops" for friends and finds that he is accepted only by other aggressive boys. Once these friendships are formed, the boys, like any other adolescents, reward each other for participating in a shared activity—in their case, antisocial behavior.

Similar findings on the role of the family in friendship choice have been reported in studies of crowd selection and susceptibility to peer influence (Brown, Mounts, Lamborn, & Steinberg, 1993; Curtner-Smith & MacKinnon-Lewis, 1994; Mason et al., 1996; Melby, 1995). That

is, parents play a role in socializing certain traits in their children, and these orientations, whether toward aggression or academic achievement, predispose adolescents toward choosing certain friends or crowds with which to affiliate. Once in these cliques or crowds, adolescents are rewarded for the traits that led them there in the first place, and these traits are strengthened. Thus, a child who is raised to value academics will perform well in school and will likely select friends who share this orientation. Over time, these friends will reinforce the youngster's academic orientation and strengthen his or her school performance. By the same token, antisocial adolescents, who are drawn toward other antisocial peers, become more antisocial over time as a result (Vitaro, Tremblay, Kerr, Pagani, & Bukowski, 1997).

The finding that adolescents become more antisocial when they spend time with antisocial peers has prompted some experts to question the wisdom of group-based interventions for adolescents with conduct problems (Dishion, McCord, & Poulin, 1999). Several studies of programs designed to diminish adolescents' delinquency or aggression, for example, have found that, instead of having the desired effect, the programs actually *increased* participants' problem behavior—that is, the programs had what scientists call **iatrogenic effects.** (Iatrogenic effects are the undesirable consequences of well-intentioned treatments—for example, when the side effects of a medication are far worse than the problem it is intended to treat.) Evidently, when antisocial adolescents spend time with like-minded peers, even in therapeutic settings, they may teach each other how to be "more effective" delinquents and may reward each other for misbehavior. Knowing that group treatments for antisocial behavior have iatrogenic effects is obviously important for the design of programs for delinquent and aggressive youth.

Are adolescent gangs merely a peer group whose main focus revolves around antisocial activity, or do they have unique characteristics? Research indicates that gangs both resemble and differ from other sorts of peer groups. On the one hand, as a study of Mexican American female gang members, or *cholas*, points out, adolescent gangs look much like other types of adolescent cliques, in that they are groups of adolescents who are similar in background and orientation, who share common interests and activities, and who use the group to derive a sense of identity (Harris, 1994). On the other hand, however, the processes that lead adolescents to join gangs are not the same as those that lead to membership in other sorts of peer groups. More specifically, gang members tend to be more isolated from family, to have more emotional and behavior problems, and to have poorer self-conceptions than other adolescents, including other adolescents who are not gang members but who are involved in antisocial activity (Dukes, Martinez, & Stein, 1997; Esbensen, Deschenes, & Winfree, 1999; Harper & Robinson, 1999). But a study of Puerto Rican male adolescents from New York City suggests that the actual relationships that antisocial adolescents have with their clique-mates may be less satisfying than are those between other adolescents and their friends (Pabon, Rodriguez, & Gurin, 1992). This study found that, although antisocial peers spent a great deal of time together, they did not describe their relationships as emotionally close or intimate. Rather, most of the boys felt estranged from each other. As the researchers point out, this finding has implications for the design of interventions aimed at controlling delinquency by involving antisocial peer groups in positive activities; in the absence of their shared interest in antisocial activities, delinquent peers may have little reason to maintain their friendship.

Similarity Between Friends: Selection or Socialization?

Because antisocial activities seem to be such a strong determinant of clique composition, many adults have expressed concern over the influence of peers in the socialization of delinquent activity and drug and alcohol use. Parents often feel that, if their youngster runs with the wrong crowd, he or she will acquire undesirable interests and attitudes. They express concern, for instance, when their child starts spending time with peers who seem to be less interested in school or more involved with drugs. But which comes first, joining a clique or being interested in a clique's activities? Do adolescents develop interests and attitudes because their friends influence them in this direction, or is it more the case that people with similar interests and tastes are likely to become friends?

This question has been examined in several large-scale studies that have tracked adolescents and their friendships over time (e.g., Curran, Stice, & Chassin, 1997; Dobkin, Tremblay, Mâsse, & Vitaro, 1995; Ennett & Bauman, 1994; Farrell & Danish, 1993; Kandel, 1978; Mounts & Steinberg, 1995; Poulin, Dishion, & Haas, 1999; Stein, Newcomb, & Bentler, 1987). By examining patterns of attitudinal and behavioral change over time and comparing these shifts with patterns of friendship formation and change, the researchers can examine whether adolescents are attracted to one another because of their initial similarity (what social scientists refer to as *selection*), whether they become similar because friends influence each other (what is referred to as *socialization*), or a combination of both.

In general, studies indicate that both selection and socialization are at work, across a variety of attitudinal and behavioral domains, including school achievement, drug use, mental health, and delinquency (Hartup, 1996). Adolescents who use alcohol or tobacco, for example, are more likely to choose other alcohol or tobacco users as friends (an example of selection), but spending time with friends who use these substances increases adolescents' own use as well (an example of socialization) (Curran et al., 1997; Urberg, Degirmencioglu, & Pilgrim, 1997). Similarly, adolescents who report more depressive symptoms are likely to choose other depressed adolescents as friends, which, in turn, negatively affects their own mood and that of their friends (Baker, Milich, & Manolis, 1996; Hogue & Steinberg, 1995). Conversely, aggressive adolescents who have few friends—and few aggressive friends, in particular—are likely to become less aggressive over time (Botvin & Vitaro, 1995).

Parents, of course, are inclined to blame the peer group for any of their adolescent's misbehavior, but studies that look simultaneously at selection and socialization suggest that this may not be justified. When it comes to antisocial activities, such as delinquency or drug use, it appears as if birds of a feather flock together, at least to some extent. How much of adolescents' similarity to their friends is due to selection, and how much is due to socialization? The answer depends on what and who is being studied. It looks as if selection is a somewhat stronger factor, at least as far as delinquency is concerned (Dobkin et al., 1995), whereas selection and socialization are about equally forceful when it comes to drug use (Curran et al., 1997; Emmett & Bauman, 1994; Kandel, 1978). And peer influence on antisocial behavior is generally stronger among European American adolescents than in other cultural groups, a finding that has emerged in several studies conducted at different historical times and in different parts of the world (Chen, Greenberger, Lester, Dong, & Guo, 1998).

How stable are adolescents' friendships over time? In general, adolescents' cliques show only moderate stability over the course of the school year—with some members staying in the clique, others leaving, and new ones joining—although cliques become more stable during the later years of high school (Cairns, Leung, Buchanan, & Cairns, 1995; Degirmencioglu, Tolson, & Urberg, 1993). Although the actual composition of adolescents' cliques may shift over time, the defining characteristics of their cliques and their best friends do not (Hogue & Steinberg, 1995; Luo, Urberg, Rao, & Fang, 1995; Neckerman, Cairns, & Cairns, 1993). That is, even though some members of an adolescent's clique may leave and may be replaced by others, the new members are likely to have attitudes and values that are quite similar to the former members'. Even best friends are likely to change during the school year: One study found that only about one-third of junior and senior high school students who were surveyed in the fall of a school year renamed the same person as their best friend in the spring, although that person was usually listed as a friend (Degirmencioglu et al., 1993; Degirmencioglu, Urberg, Tolson, & Richard, 1998).

RECAP

Cliques are small groups of adolescents who are friends who see each other regularly. For this reason, cliques play an important role in the development of social skills and intimacy. Generally, adolescents form cliques with peers who are similar in background, in orientation toward school, in orientation toward the peer culture, and in their level of involvement in antisocial activities. Although clique members influence each other's behavior and values, research has also shown that adolescents select their friends to begin with on the basis of similarity.

Food for Thought

How could research distinguish between similarity among friends that is due to socialization and similarity that is due to selection?

POPULARITY AND REJECTION IN ADOLESCENT PEER GROUPS

Thus far our discussion has focused on how and why crowds and cliques serve as the basis for adolescents' social activities. But what about the *internal* structure of peer groups? Within a clique or a crowd, what determines which adolescents are popular and which ones are disliked?

The chief determinant of a youngster's popularity during adolescence is his or her social skill. Popular adolescents act appropriately in the eyes of their peers, are skilled at perceiving and meeting the needs of others, and are confident without being conceited. Additionally, popular adolescents are friendly, cheerful, good-natured, humorous, and—you may be surprised to learn—intelligent (Hartup, 1983; Hollingshead, 1949/1975). Popular adolescents and adolescents with satisfying friendships are more knowledgeable specifically about what it takes to make and keep friends than are adolescents who are less well accepted by their peers (Jarvinen & Nicholls, 1996; Wentzel & Erdley, 1993). Although many determinants of popularity are common across cultures, some differ: For example, shyness, which is clearly a social liability in American peer groups, may be an asset among children in China (Chen, Rubin, & Li, 1995).

Despite these broad generalizations about the determinants of popularity, it is important to note that there are many routes to popularity within adolescent peer groups. One recent study of preadolescent and young adolescent boys indicates that there are at least two distinct types of popular boys, at least at that age (Rodkin, Farmer, Pearl, & Van Acker, 2000). One group, whom the researchers described as "model" boys, had the characteristics typically identified in studies of popular youth: They were physically and academically competent, friendly, and neither shy nor aggressive. A second group of popular boys, however, whom the researchers described as "tough," were extremely aggressive, physically competent, and average or below average in friendliness, academic competence, and shyness. This, as well as several other studies, indicates that, contrary to the notion that aggressive children are invariably rejected by their classmates, there are some youngsters— both boys and girls—who are aggressive and popular at the same time (Bowker, Bukowski, Hymel, & Sippola, 2000). Other research suggests that it is the combination of aggression and poor emotion regulation that leads to problems with peers (Pope & Bierman, 1999).

Two ethnographic studies of early adolescent girls provide insight into the dynamics of popularity. Ethnographer Donna Eder (1985) spent two years in a middle school, observing interactions among early adolescent girls in various extracurricular and informal settings (in the cafeteria, in the hallway, at school dances). In this school, the cheerleaders were considered the elite crowd,

▲ *In general, popularity in the adolescent peer group is associated with social competence—popular teenagers are friendly, cheerful, and humorous. Status in the peer group, in contrast, has more to do with leadership and capability in highly valued activities.* (Richard Hutchings/Photo Researchers)

and girls who made the cheerleading squad were immediately accorded social status. Other girls then attempted to befriend the cheerleaders as a means of increasing their own status. This, in turn, increased the cheerleaders' popularity within school, since they became the most sought-after friends. The girls who were successful in cultivating friendships with the cheerleaders then became a part of this high-status group and became more popular themselves. This popularity had a price, however, as one eighth-grader explained to the researcher:

> A lot of times, people don't talk to the popular kids because they're kind of scared of them and they don't know their real personality. So that's kind of a bummer when you're considered to be popular because you don't usually meet a lot of other people because they just go, "Oh." (Eder, 1985, p. 162)

Paradoxically, popularity in many cases led to these girls' being disliked. As Eder explains,

> There are limits to the number of friendships that any one person can maintain. Because popular girls get a high number of affiliative offers, they have to reject more offers of friendship than other girls. Also, to maintain their

higher status, girls who form the elite group must avoid associations with lower-status girls. . . . These girls are likely to ignore the affiliative attempts of many girls, leading to the impression that they are stuck-up. . . . Shortly after these girls reach their peak of popularity, they become increasingly disliked. (Eder, 1985, p. 163)

In another study, the researcher spent time observing and interviewing a group described by teachers as the "dirty dozen" (Merten, 1997). This group of girls was "considered 'cool,' 'popular,' and 'mean.' They are a combination of cute, talented, affluent, conceited, and powerful" (p. 178). The researcher was interested in understanding "why a clique of girls that was popular and socially sophisticated was also renowned for its meanness" (p. 188). The answer, he discovered, was that meanness was one of the ways that the clique ensured that no one member became stuck-up as a result of her popularity in the eyes of her classmates. Thus, although it was important for the clique members to maintain their popular image, if any clique member appeared to become *too* popular, the other members would turn on her, undermining her standing with other girls by gossiping, starting rumors, and deliberately attempting to disrupt her friendships. The following quote, from a girl whose friends had turned on her, will sound all too familiar:

> Gretchen was starting to get really mad at me. I talked to her about it and I asked her what was wrong. She just said, "Oh, I heard something you said about me." But I didn't say anything about her. Sara was mad at me. I don't know why. She started being mad at me and then she started making things up that [she said] I said. Sara told Brenda and Gretchen so that they would get mad at me, too. So now I guess Gretchen has made up something and told Wellesley. They are all mad at me and laughing and everything. (Merten, 1997, p. 182)

Ironically, one of the potential costs of being popular in adolescence is that, if one's popularity becomes too great, one faces the possibility of being the object of other classmates' meanness.

Although popularity clearly has some costs, in general the advantages of being popular far outweigh the disadvantages. Being popular (accepted or well-liked by a large number of people) is not the same as having close and intimate friendships (Asher, Parker, & Walker, 1996), but the two often go hand in hand (Bukowski, Pizzamiglio, Newcomb, & Hoza, 1996; Franzoi et al., 1994). Compared with their less popular agemates, popular adolescents are more likely to have close and intimate friendships, participate in social activities with peers, participate in extracurricular activities, and receive more social recognition (such as being selected as the leader of a school organization) (Franzoi et al., 1994). Part of the overlap between social acceptance and friendship stems from the fact that many of the characteristics that make adolescents popular are the same as those that make them sought-after as friends—chief among them, having good social skills.

Social scientists have shown that it is important to distinguish among three types of unpopular, or disliked, adolescents (Bierman & Wargo, 1995; Coie, Terry, Lenox, Lochman, & Hyman, 1995; French, Conrad, & Turner, 1995; Hatzichristou & Hopf, 1996; Hymel, Bowker, & Woody, 1993; Olweus, 1993; Parkhurst & Asher, 1992). One set of unpopular adolescents is overly *aggressive;* they are likely to get into fights with other students, are more likely to be involved in antisocial activities, and often are involved in bullying. A second set of unpopular adolescents are *withdrawn;* these adolescents are exceedingly shy, timid, and inhibited and are themselves more likely to be the victims of bullying. A third group of unpopular youngsters are *aggressive-*

withdrawn. Like other aggressive youngsters, aggressive-withdrawn children have problems controlling their hostility; however, like other withdrawn children, they tend to be nervous about initiating friendships with other adolescents.

Most studies of the peer relations of aggressive children has focused on children who are overtly aggressive (either physically or verbally). This has led researchers to focus relatively more attention on the social relationships of rejected boys than girls, because boys exhibit more overt aggression than girls. A series of studies by psychologist Nikki Crick, however, indicates that girls also act aggressively toward peers but that their aggression is often social, not physical, in its expression (Crick, 1996; Crick, Bigbee, & Howes, 1996; Crick & Grotpeter, 1995). In particular, Crick has studied the use of **relational aggression**—aggression intended to harm other adolescents through deliberate manipulation of their social standing and social relationships. Individuals who use relational aggression try to hurt others by excluding them from social activities, damaging their reputations with others, or withdrawing attention and friendship. Although relational aggression was first noticed in observations of girls, recent research suggests that both genders use it but that girls are more distressed by it (Galen & Underwood, 1997; Paquette & Underwood, 1999). Although relational aggression is more covert than fighting or yelling, the use of relational aggression is nevertheless associated with rejection by peers (Crick, 1996; Rys & Bear, 1997). Interestingly, adolescents whose aggression is atypical for their gender (i.e., girls who are highly physically aggressive and boys who are highly relationally aggressive) show more maladjustment than do their peers whose aggression is more gender-typical (Crick, 1997).

Being unpopular has negative consequences for adolescents' mental health and psychological development—peer rejection is associated with subsequent depression, behavior problems, and academic difficulties (DeRosier, Kupersmidt, & Patterson, 1994; Kupersmidt, Burchinal, & Patterson, 1995; Kupersmidt & Coie, 1990; Morison & Masten, 1991; Olweus, 1993; Parker & Asher, 1987; Patterson & Stoolmiller, 1991). But studies show that the specific consequences of peer rejection may differ among rejected youth who are aggressive versus those who are withdrawn. Aggressive children who are rejected are often likely to end up in peer groups with other aggressive youngsters, and they are at risk for conduct problems and involvement in antisocial activity (Feldman, Rosenthal, Brown, & Canning, 1995; French et al.,

1995; Rubin, Chen, McDougall, Bowker, & McKinnon, 1995; Underwood, Kupersmidt, & Coie, 1996). In contrast, rejected, withdrawn children are likely to feel exceedingly lonely and are at risk for low self-esteem, depression, and diminished social competence (Hoza, Molina, Bukowski, & Sippola, 1995; Rubin et al., 1995). Adolescents who are both aggressive and withdrawn are at the greatest risk of all (Morison & Masten, 1991; Parkhurst & Asher, 1992; Rubin, LeMare, & Lollis, 1990).

Many psychologists believe that unpopular youngsters lack some of the social skills and social understanding necessary to be popular with peers. According to findings from an extensive program of research by Kenneth Dodge and his colleagues, unpopular aggressive children are more likely than their peers to think that other children's behavior is deliberately hostile, even when it is not (Crick & Dodge, 1994, 1996; Dodge, 1986; Dodge & Coie, 1987). Numerous studies have now confirmed that this so-called **hostile attributional bias** plays a central role in the aggressive behavior of rejected adolescents (Astor, 1994; Courtney & Cohen, 1996; Crick & Dodge, 1994; Waldman, 1996). When accidentally pushed while waiting in line, for instance, unpopular aggressive children are more likely than others to believe that the person who did the pushing did it on purpose and, consequently, to retaliate. A study of African American adolescents found that deficits in social information processing may characterize overly aggressive African American youngsters as well (Graham, 1993; Graham & Hudley, 1994).

Not surprisingly, the inferences that adolescents draw from the behavior of others vary in part as a function of the adolescents' ethnic and cultural background. In one fascinating study, the reactions of African American and Mexican American adolescents to videotapes of various social situations were compared (Rotheram-Borus & Phinney, 1990). In one situation, for example, a boy was rejected for a team. Whereas the African American adolescents who saw the videotape said that, in a similar situation, they would get angry or leave, the Mexican American youngsters said that they would feel hurt but would not leave. In another vignette, two teenagers were working at a table on which the necessary supplies were close to one adolescent but not to the other. In response to this video, the Mexican American adolescents were more likely to say simply that the adolescent who was closer to the supplies should hand them to the other teenager, wheras the African American adolescents were more likely to say that, if they were the adolescent farther from the supplies, they would be upset and would reach over and get what they needed.

These differences in social information processing likely reflect cultural differences in the emphases placed on group solidarity and cooperation—two things that tend to be highly valued in Mexican American families.

What about unpopular, withdrawn children? What are their social skills deficits? In general, research shows that unpopular, withdrawn children are excessively anxious and uncertain around other children, often hovering around the group without knowing how to break into a conversation or activity (Rubin et al., 1990). Their hesitancy, low self-esteem, and lack of confidence make other children feel uncomfortable, and their submissiveness makes them easy targets for bullying (Olweus, 1993; Salmivalli, 1998). Many of these youngsters are especially sensitive to being rejected, a trait that may have its origins in early experiences with parents (Downey, Lebolt, Rincón, & Freitas, 1998). Unfortunately, the more these children are teased, rejected, and victimized, the more hesitant they feel, and the more they blame themselves for their victimization, which only compounds their problem—creating a cycle of victimization (Graham & Juvonen, 1998; Hymel, Rubin, Rowden, & LeMare, 1990). For example, young adolescents who are victimized by their peers typically develop problems that lead to further peer rejection and victimization (Hodges, & Perry, 1999). However, children who are victimized but who have a best friend are less likely to be caught in the cycle (Hodges, Bouvin, Vitaro, & Bukowski, 1999).

Can unpopular adolescents be helped? Several teams of psychologists have experimented with various interventions designed to improve the social skills of unpopular adolescents. These social competence training programs have focused on three strategies. One type of program has been designed to teach social skills—self-expression, the questioning of others about themselves, and leadership (Kelley & de Armaa, 1989; Repinski & Leffert, 1994). These social skills intervention programs have been shown to improve adolescents' abilities to get along with peers. A second approach has been to have unpopular adolescents participate with popular ones in group activities under the supervision of psychologists. Programs such as this have been shown to improve adolescents' self-conceptions and their acceptance by others (Bierman & Furman, 1984). Finally, some social competence programs focus on a combination of behavioral and cognitive abilities, including social problem solving (e.g., Greenberg & Kusche, 1998; Weissberg, Caplan, & Harwood, 1991). Social problem-solving programs, such as PATHs (Providing Alternative THinking Solutions), are designed to improve individuals' abilities to judge social situations and figure out acceptable ways of behaving. Adolescents are taught to calm down and think before they react, to decide what the problem is, to figure out what their goal is, and to think of positive approaches toward reaching that goal. Instead of lashing out at a classmate who grabbed the last basketball from a gym closet, for example, a hot-tempered boy who had been through this sort of social skills program might calm himself down, tell himself that his goal is to play basketball rather than get into a fight, and approach another student to ask if he can get into a game. PATHs has been shown to effectively reduce behavior problems among elementary school children (Conduct Problems Prevention Research Group, 1999).

> ## RECAP
>
> *Popular adolescents tend to be socially skilled, intelligent, humorous, and friendly. Unpopular adolescents tend to fall into three categories: aggressive adolescents, withdrawn adolescents, and aggressive-withdrawn adolescents. In general, adolescents who are rejected by their peers are at risk for a wide variety of psychological and behavior problems, including academic failure, conduct problems, and depression. Numerous interventions have been designed to improve adolescents' social competence, including those that focus on improving unpopular adolescents' social skills and social understanding.*

> ### Food for Thought
>
> *Based on research on the determinants of popularity and rejection in adolescence, do you think it is possible to turn unpopular adolescents into popular ones? If so, what sorts of interventions would you design to help unpopular teenagers?*

THE PEER GROUP AND PSYCHOSOCIAL DEVELOPMENT

Regardless of the structure or norms of a particular peer group, peers play an extremely important role in the psychological development of adolescents. Problematic peer relationships are associated with a range of serious psychological and behavior problems during adolescence and adulthood. Individuals who are un-popular or who have poor peer relationships during adolescence are more likely than their socially accepted peers to be low achievers in school, to drop out of high school, to have a range of learning disabilities, to show higher rates of delinquent behavior, and to suffer from an array of emotional and mental health problems as adults (Savin-Williams & Berndt, 1990). Although it is likely that poorly adjusted individuals have difficulty making friends, there is now good evidence that psychological problems result from—as well as cause—problems with peers (Bagwell, Newcomb, & Bukowski, 1998; Brendgen, Vitaro, & Bukowski, 2000; Buhrmester & Yin, 1997; Coie et al., 1995; Hymel et al., 1990; Kupersmidt & Coie, 1990; McCoy, 1996; Parker & Asher, 1987; Parker & Seal, 1996; Windle, 1994; Woodward & Fergusson, 1999).

Peers also play a crucial role in promoting (or hindering) normal psychosocial development. In the realm of identity, peers provide the sorts of models and feedback that adolescents cannot get from adults. In the context of the peer group, young people can try on various roles and personalities and can experiment with different identities with greater ease than at home. And the peer group may serve as a way station in the development of identity as adolescents begin to develop a separate sense of self that is differentiated from the family (Brown et al., 1986). Experience in the peer group also can be an important influence on adolescents' self-image.

Experience in the peer group also is vital for the development and expression of autonomy. The process of developing more mature and more independent relationships with parents is accompanied by the establishment of more mature relationships with peers. In addition, the peer group provides a context for adolescents to test out decision-making skills in an arena where there are no adults present to monitor and control their choices (Hill & Holmbeck, 1986).

Intimacy and sexuality, of course, are much more common between peers than between adolescents and adults, for a variety of reasons. Perhaps most critical is that both intimacy and sexuality require interaction between two individuals who are relative equals. Moreover, sexual relationships and close intimacy within the family context would be likely to disrupt important functions of family relationships (Hartup, 1977). It is therefore the adolescent's peer group that generally plays the central role in socializing youngsters in appropriate sexual behavior and in the development of the capacity for intimate friendship (Sullivan, 1953b).

Finally, peers are an important influence on adolescent achievement. Although peers may play a less influential role than parents or teachers in influencing adolescents' long-term educational and occupational plans, peers are a significant influence on adolescents' day-to-day school behaviors and feelings, including how much they value school, how much effort they devote to their studies, and how well they perform in class (Epstein, 1983a; Steinberg, 1996). Peers seem to be an especially important influence on the achievement of ethnic minority youth (Steinberg, Dornbusch, & Brown, 1992).

Adolescents consider the time they spend with peers to be among the most enjoyable parts of the day (Csikszentmihalyi & Larson, 1984). One reason is that activities with friends are typically organized around having a good time, in contrast to activities with parents, which are more likely to be organized around household chores and the enforcement of parental rules (Larson, 1983; Montemayor, 1982). Rather than being competing institutions, the family and the peer group seem to provide contrasting opportunities for adolescent activites and behaviors. The family is organized around work and other tasks, and it may be important in the socialization of responsibility and achievement. The peer group provides more frequent opportunities for interaction and leisure, which contributes to the development of intimacy and enhances the adolescent's mood and psychological well-being.

Web Researcher Popular media—especially advertising—are designed to influence behavior. Look at websites aimed at teenagers. What methods do advertisers and web designers use to influence their audiences? Look for subtle techniques, such as product placements, as well as more blatant bids for attention. What parallels do you see between these techniques and the kinds of peer influences adolescents experience in real life? If you found differences between the behavior of adolescents who spent time on these different sites, would you conclude that they result from the sites' influence, or might other processes be operating as well? Go to www.mhhe.com/steinberg6 for further information.

KEY TERMS

age grading

baby boom

cliques

cofigurative cultures

crowds

ethnography

gangs

hostile attributional bias

iatrogenic effects

participant observation

particularistic norms

peer groups

postfigurative cultures

prefigurative cultures

reference groups

relational aggression

sex cleavage

significant others

social class

universalistic norms

youth culture

Chapter 6

Schools

Although we naturally think of schools as educational institutions, they are also potentially important tools of social intervention, because it is through schools that the greatest number of young people can most easily be reached. For this reason, the study of schools is extremely important to social scientists and policymakers who are interested in influencing adolescent development. In fact, one way to understand the ways in which adults want adolescents to change is to examine proposals for school reform. During the 1950s, for example, when politicians felt that the United States had lost its scientific edge to the former Soviet Union, schools were called upon to see to it that students took more courses in math and science (Conant, 1959). When social scientists felt that adolescents were growing up unfamiliar with the world of work—as they did in the 1970s—schools were asked to provide opportunities for work-study programs and classes in career education (President's Science Advisory Committee, 1974). In the 1990s, as society grappled with a broad array of social problems affecting and involving youth—problems such as violence, AIDS, and drug abuse—we once again looked to schools for assistance and asked that schools implement a wide array of preventive interventions (Dryfoos, 1993). Toward the end of the 1990s, amid growing concerns that our inner-city schools were not producing graduates who could compete for high-skills jobs, and in response to a public that was growing increasingly interested in alternatives to public education, schools were called upon to raise standards for all students (e.g., Ravitch, 2001). It is difficult to forecast what the next wave of school reform proposals will bring, but we can be sure that, as we move into the twenty-first century, schools will continue to play a central role in the development and implementation of a wide range of social policies concerning young people.

Because of the important and multifaceted role it has come to play in modern society, the secondary educational system—**secondary education** refers to middle schools, junior high schools, and high schools—has been the target of a remarkable amount of criticism, scrutiny, and social science research. Parents, teachers, educational administrators, and researchers debate what schools should teach, how schools should be organized, and how schools might best teach their students. They debate such issues as whether high schools should stick to instructing students in the basics—reading, writing, and arithmetic—or should offer a more diverse range of classes and services designed to prepare young people for adulthood socially and emotionally, as well as intellectually. They ask such questions as whether early adolescents should be schooled in separate middle or junior high schools, whether students should be grouped by ability ("tracked"), and whether certain classroom atmospheres are preferable to others.

These questions have proved difficult to answer. Nevertheless, they remain extremely important. Virtually all American adolescents under the age of 16 and the vast majority of 16-and 17-year-olds are enrolled in school. More than half of all youth now continue their education beyond high school graduation—in technical schools, colleges, and universities. During most of the year, the typical American student spends more than one-third of his or her waking hours each week in school or in school-related activities, although only a portion of this time is actually spent on schoolwork (Larson & Verma, 1999). Not only are schools the chief educational arena for adolescents in America, but they also play an extremely important role in defining the young person's social world and in shaping the adolescent's developing sense of identity and autonomy. It is therefore crucial that we understand how best to structure schools. •

SECONDARY EDUCATION IN AMERICA

Consider the data presented in figure 6.1. Today, virtually all young people from ages 14 to 17 are enrolled in school. But, in 1930, only about half of this age group were students, and at the turn of the twentieth century only 1 in 10 attended school (D. Tanner, 1972; William T. Grant Foundation, 1988).

Not only are there considerably more youngsters enrolled in school today than there were 50 years ago, but today's students also spend more days per year in school. In 1920, for example, the average school term was 162 days, and the average student attended only 121 days, or 75 percent of the term. By 1968, however, the school term had been lengthened to nearly 180 days, which is still the national average today, and the typical student attends 90 percent of the term (National Education Commission on Time and Learning, 1994; President's Science Advisory Committee, 1974). In many European countries, the school year is even longer. In England, for example, high school students

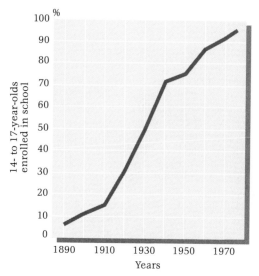

Figure 6.1   The proportion of the 14- to 17-year-old population enrolled in school increased dramatically between 1910 and 1940. Today, nearly 95 percent of individuals this age are in school. (D. Tanner, 1972; William T. Grant Foundation, 1988)

spend 220 days in school each year (Consortium on Productivity in the Schools, 1995).

Although some critics of American schools have called for lengthening our school year (National Commission on Excellence in Education, 1983), others have pointed out that simply expanding the school year, without changing what takes place in school, may be misguided (National Education Commission on Time and Learning, 1994). For example, although today the typical school offers a six-period day, with about 5.6 hours of classroom time, studies show that students spend only 40 percent of their time on such core academic subjects as math, English, history, and science, about half the time devoted to basic academic instruction in European schools (Consortium on Productivity in the Schools, 1995; National Education Commission on Time and Learning, 1994). Clearly, then, it would be possible to increase the amount of time students spend on academic matters considerably without lengthening the school day at all.

Adolescents also remain in school for more years now than they did in past eras. In 1924, fewer than one-third of all youngsters entering the fifth grade eventually graduated from high school; today, about 75 percent of all fifth-graders will eventually graduate on time, and a substantial number of those who do not graduate on schedule eventually get their diploma

through equivalency programs or continuation schools. Over the course of the twentieth century, then, schools became increasingly prominent settings in the life of the average American adolescent.

The Origins of Compulsory Education

The rise of secondary education in America was the result of several historical and social trends at the turn of the twentieth century. Most important were industrialization, urbanization, and immigration.

Following widespread industrialization during the late nineteenth century, the role of children and young adolescents in the workplace changed dramatically. With the economy expanding, many families who at one time had needed their children in the labor force for financial reasons were able to make ends meet without the labor of their young. Furthermore, as the nature of the workplace changed, employers recognized that they needed workers who were more skilled and more reliable than youngsters. The few unskilled jobs that remained required strength beyond the capacity of many youth (Church, 1976). Social reformers also expressed concerns about the dangers children faced working in factories, and organized labor—an increasingly powerful force during the early 1900s—sought to protect not only the welfare of children but also the security of their own employment. Child labor laws narrowed and limited the employment of minors (Bakan, 1972). Together, these changes in the workplace kept many youngsters out of the labor force.

During the same period, the nature of life in American cities was also changing markedly. Industrialization brought with it urbanization and, along with the rising rate of immigration during the early twentieth century, new problems for urban centers. The effects of a rapidly expanding economy were seen in the tenements and slums of America's cities: poor housing, overcrowded neighborhoods, and crime. Eager to improve living conditions for the urban masses, social reformers envisioned education as a means of improving the life circumstances of the poor and working classes. And, eager to ensure that the problems of cities did not get out of hand, many saw compulsory secondary education as a means of social control. High schools would take thousands of idle young people off the streets, it was argued, and keep them in a social institution in which they could be supervised and kept out of trouble. Eager, too, to see that foreign-born immigrants were well socialized into the American way of life, reformers presented universal secondary education as a necessary part of the process of Americanization: It was a way of homogenizing a population characterized by increasing—and, to many, increasingly uncomfortable—ethnic and cultural diversity (Church, 1976; D. Tanner, 1972). By 1915, the idea of universal compulsory education for adolescents had gained widespread acceptance.

The Rise of the Comprehensive High School

Prior to the early twentieth century, before secondary education became compulsory, high schools were designed for the elite. In curriculum, staff, and student composition, they were similar to the colleges of the day—the emphasis being, for the most part, on classical liberal arts instruction (Church, 1976; D. Tanner, 1972).

By 1920, however, educators had begun to see a need for curricular reform. Compulsory secondary education had changed the social composition of the schools; many educators argued for a corresponding diversification in the secondary school curriculum. Now that secondary education was aimed at the masses, schooling was seen not merely as a means of intellectual training but also as a way of preparing youth for life in modern society. It was argued that education, especially for the majority, should include preparation for work and citizenship roles.

The 1920s marked the birth of what came to be known as the **comprehensive high school,** an educational institution that promised to meet the needs of a diverse and growing population of young people. Classes in general education, college preparation, and vocational education were all housed under one roof. As you saw in figure 6.1, the proportion of high school–age individuals enrolled in school jumped dramatically in the years between World War I and World War II—from 32 percent in 1920 to over 73 percent in 1940. This was also a time of tremendous change in the high school curriculum. During these years, new courses were added in music, art, family life, health, physical education, and other subjects designed to prepare adolescents for family and leisure as well as work roles.

The high school had come a long way from its exclusive focus at the turn of the century on the intellectual development of the socioeconomic elite. By the 1950s, its concern had broadened to include the social and intellectual development of all young people. And, today, despite continuing questioning and criticism, the comprehensive high school remains the cornerstone of the American system of secondary education.

RECAP

Schools play an extremely important role in structuring the nature of adolescence in modern society. In the United States, virtually all individuals between 14 and 17 years old are enrolled in school. One hundred years ago, fewer than 10 percent of this age group were students. Now, the average American adolescent's school year consists of 180 six-hour days. A number of social forces combined to lead the development of compulsory education for adolescents in America. Among the most important were industrialization, immigration, and urbanization. During the 1920s, the high school as we know it today—the comprehensive high school—was born. By 1940, nearly three-fourths of high school–aged individuals were enrolled in school.

Food for Thought

The comprehensive high school was invented within a specific historical context. Does it make sense within today's society? If not, what alternative or alternatives would you suggest?

SCHOOL REFORM: PAST AND PRESENT

Suppose you were asked to make a list of the things you think young people need to know in order to function as competent, responsible, and satisfied adults. Which items on your list should be the responsibility of high schools? Should high school curricula be limited to the traditional academic subjects, or should schools play a broader role in preparing young people for adulthood by providing instruction more directly relevant to work, family, leisure, and citizenship? Should students receive instruction only in English, mathematics, science, and social studies, or should they take courses as well in "general education"—in subjects such as art, home economics, health, sex education, driver education, and personal finance? Which courses should be required, and which should be left as electives? If you were to discuss these questions with your classmates, you would probably find little agreement.

Over the past decade or so, politicians and parents have sounded the cry for schools to scale down their general education offerings and place greater emphasis on the traditional academic subjects: English, mathematics,

▲ *During the second quarter of the twentieth century, high schools began to play an increasingly important role in the lives of American adolescents.* (Culver)

science, social studies, and a new "basic"—computer science (Consortium on Productivity in the Schools, 1995; Consortium on Renewing Education, 1998; National Education Commission on Time and Learning, 1994; Ravitch, 1995). Several social commentators have argued that educators—in high schools and colleges alike—have lost sight of the common core of knowledge and values that serves as the intellectual foundation of our society (Bloom, 1987; Botstein, 1997; Hirsch, 1996).

To observers who are unfamiliar with the history of America's high schools, this plea for limiting the high school curriculum to the "essentials" sounds like a fresh and timely idea. Although returning to the basics may be seen as a welcome change, however, this is by no means the first time that education critics have called for a more rigorous and more focused curriculum. Similar calls were heard during the 1950s, in response to the perceived threat of the former Soviet Union's space program.

Actually, the current cry for more rigor in our schools is in part a reaction to curricular changes that took place 30 years ago. During the early 1970s, educa-

tion reformers claimed that schools were not preparing young people for the roles they would encounter as adults (Church, 1976). They felt that adolescents should spend less time in school and more time in community and work settings. Programs such as career education and experiential education were implemented in many school districts, so that young people could receive hands-on experience in the real world (President's Science Advisory Committee, 1974). During this time, students also became more vocal and demanded more courses in relevant and practical subject areas. Schools began to offer an increasingly wide range of electives for students to choose among.

The students of the 1970s clearly took advantage of these opportunities. In the late 1970s, over 40 percent of all high school students were taking a general— rather than a college preparatory or vocational— course of study, and 25 percent of their educational credits came from work experience outside of school, from remedial coursework, and from courses aimed at personal growth and development (National

Commission on Excellence in Education, 1983). Still today less than half of the school day is spent on core academic subjects, a carryover from the 1970s focus on relevance (Consortium on Productivity in the Schools, 1995; National Education Commission on Time and Learning, 1994).

During the 1980s, however, the pendulum swung back toward the basics. Why? The achievement test scores of American high school students had been falling steadily. Cross-cultural comparisons of student achievement consistently placed American youngsters at or near the bottom of the international list. As one team of investigators put it,

> A close examination of American children's academic achievement rapidly dispels any notion that we face a problem of limited scope. The problem is not restricted to a certain age level or to a particular academic subject. Whether we look at the average scores for schools or at the scores for individuals, we find evidence of serious and pervasive weakness. (Stevenson & Stigler, 1992, p. 50)

Partly in response to these worrisome findings, several proposals called for more demanding curricula (e.g., Finn, 1991). One set of writers bemoaned what they called the "shopping-mall high school," where students were given too much freedom in choosing courses, and schools were more concerned with keeping students happy than with seeing that genuine and important learning took place (Powell, Farrar, & Cohen, 1985). Noting that America was losing its competitive edge in the world market, education reformers called for more academic rigor in the schools as a means of preparing young people for the workplace of the future. One group, for example, called for schools to implement more demanding academic requirements, tougher standards for graduation, and longer school days (National Commission on Excellence in Education, 1983). Another recommended that schools spend at least 5.5 hours daily on instruction in core academic subjects (National Education Commission on Time and Learning, 1994). Whereas school reformers of the 1970s had demanded more relevant curricula, reformers of the 1980s demanded more rigorous ones.

During the late 1980s, yet another type of school reform received widespread attention. This time, however, the focus shifted from the content of the curriculum to the process of learning. Education reformers called for more emphasis in the classroom on higher-order thinking—whether in the teaching of basics or in the teaching of electives (Newmann, 1992; Newmann, Marks, & Gamoran, 1996). **Higher-order thinking** is stimulated when students are encouraged to interpret, analyze, and evaluate information, rather than simply memorizing or applying it in a routine way. In social studies, for example, asking students to discuss why political revolts occur may stimulate higher-order thinking, whereas asking them simply to memorize (and regurgitate) the dates of important political revolutions probably will not.

School reformers in the late 1990s continued to call for schools to place a greater emphasis on higher-order thinking but stressed that this focus needed to be accompanied by a return to rigorous and universal performance standards. Many commentators argued that schools had, by the late 1980s, become so focused on the process of learning that they had lost sight of the importance of having a strong and challenging curriculum (Hirsch, 1996; Ravitch, 1995). Once again, the pendulum swung back toward concerns about the content of the curriculum.

The stimulation of higher-order thinking and the implementation of rigorous and demanding curricula sound like admirable goals. However, as with all education reforms, the reasons behind these goal are embedded in a particular historical and economic context. Why, early in the 1990s, would education reformers suddenly become interested in restructuring the curriculum toward the promotion of higher-order thinking? Beginning in the late 1980s, it had become apparent that American adolescents were sorely deficient in skills requiring in-depth analysis, which did not bode well for our country's competitiveness in an international economy, that was increasingly centered on high-skilled jobs. As the president of the National Urban League put it in a 1997 speech,

> The Big Three [auto makers] expect to hire 173,000 new auto workers over the next seven years. These jobs will pay up to $70,000 with overtime. In other words, these are "good jobs." But to get one of these jobs as an auto worker, applicants must pass a reading test, math test, spatial relations test—and a drug test. . . . And that's merely the beginning of the selection process. Those who pass the initial battery of tests are then assigned to a team with several other survivors. The team is given a description of [a] portion of the assembly line in an auto factory, along with job descriptions of those on that section of the line. The team has several hours to come up with ways of improving the productivity of that segment of the manufacturing process. Those that come up with solid recommendations will be offered jobs. This is what one needs to know and be able to do just in order to land a job as an auto worker. We're not even talking about what's required to become an auto executive, auto dealer, auto salesperson, or auto parts supplier.

By the mid-1990s, it had become apparent that vast numbers of American students were graduating from high school deficient not only in higher-order abilities but also in basic academic skills and knowledge. According to the National Assessment of Educational Progress, in the mid-1990s, the percentage of students who scored at or above proficiency on reading and mathematics ranged from about 10 percent in Louisiana, California, and the District of Columbia to around 35 percent in North Dakota, Maine, and Minnesota (Education Trust, 1996). The need for remedial education—on college campuses and in the workplace—had risen substantially (Steinberg, 1998). And, according to carefully conducted international comparisons, after two decades of school reform, American students still ranked below the international average in math, and just barely above average in science (American Federation of Teachers, 1997). At the end of the twentieth century, many observers questioned whether the comprehensive public high school should—or could—

continue to play a central role in the education of adolescents. Increasing numbers of parents began looking at other options—among them, charter schools (public schools that are given more freedom to set their own curricula), vouchers to be used for private school tuition, and home schooling.

Education in the Inner Cities

Although concerns about the demise of American education raged during the late 1990s, some commentators argued that the sense of crisis had been overblown by politicians and mass media keen on stirring up public concern and discrediting public education. The problem of low student achievement, they argued, was not an across-the-board problem but was concentrated mainly among poor and minority youngsters living in inner cities and rural areas (Berliner & Biddle, 1995).

Although other critics (e.g., Stedman, 1998; Steinberg 1996) disagreed with this assessment, arguing

▲ *Higher-order thinking is stimulated when students are encouraged to interpret, analyze, and evaluate information, rather than simply memorize or apply it in a routine way.* (Bob Daemmrich/Stock Boston)

that poor achievement was a problem *everywhere,* virtually all social scientists concurred that the education crisis, and its implications for the future of the labor force, had become distressingly urgent within inner-city public schools. Indeed, the achievement gap between white and nonwhite youngsters, which had been closing for some time, grew *wider* during the 1990s, especially in large urban school districts. In the District of Columbia, for example, which serves a predominantly African American population, only 5 percent of all eighth-graders are judged proficient in math. In California, white students who are proficient in math outnumber Latino youngsters by a ratio of 5 to 1. In New York, proficient white students outnumber proficient African American students by a ratio of 8 to 1. As one set of writers pointed out, "One recent report on urban education concluded that because of the continued failure to educate city children, many people now dismiss urban schools 'as little more than human storehouses to keep young people off the streets'" (Kantor & Brenzel, 1992, pp. 278–279).

Why has school reform failed in so many urban schools? Experts point to several reasons. First, the increasing concentration of poverty into certain inner-city communities (see chapter 3) has produced a population of students with very grave academic and behavior problems—problems that few schools are equipped or able to address. Recent surveys of American high school students indicate that so many are afraid of being victimized that 15 percent of all boys and 8 percent of all girls across the country carry a gun to school, with even higher percentages in inner-city schools (Centers for Disease Control, 2000b). Second, many urban school districts are burdened by huge administrative bureaucracies that often impede reform and stand in the way of educational innovation. Finally, the erosion of job opportunities in inner-city communities has left many students with little incentive to remain in school or to devote a great deal of effort to academic pursuits (Kantor & Brenzel, 1992).

By the early 1990s, it had become evident to economists that merely training our students in basics was not going to help build a competitive workforce for the next century (Jackson & Hornbeck, 1989; National Center on Education and the Economy, 1990). According to one analysis, the world's workplace had become split into two markedly different sectors: One was composed of low-paying jobs that required little skill or training, whereas the other was composed of high-paying jobs that required advanced training and well-developed intellectual skills, including higher-order

thinking abilities. Most industrialized countries have made a concerted effort to expand the high-skill sector of their workplace, because these jobs are more lucrative for their economy as well as for their workers. However, in order to maintain this expansion, it is necessary to develop a steady pool of highly skilled workers. In the words of this analysis, America's choice was clear: "High skills or low wages" (National Center on Education and the Economy, 1990). This recognition has fueled much of the current debate over the past decade about how best to reform America's schools.

Characteristics of Good Schools

Actually, for all the debate about how schools ought to be reformed, there is a fair degree of consensus among experts about the characteristics of good schools for adolescents (Linney & Seidman, 1989). First and foremost, good schools emphasize intellectual activities (Ravitch, 1995). They create this atmosphere in various ways, depending on the nature and size of the student body, but in these good schools a common purpose—quality education—is valued and shared by students, teachers, administrators, and parents (Lee, Smith, & Croninger, 1997). Learning is more important to students than are school athletics and social activities, and seeing that students learn is more important to teachers and administrators than seeing that they graduate.

Second, good schools have teachers who are committed to their students and who are given a good deal of freedom and autonomy by the school administration in the way that this commitment is expressed in the classroom (Lee & Smith, 1996; Lee et al., 1997). In all schools, of course, teachers have curricular requirements that they must fulfill. However, in good schools, teachers are given relatively more authority to decide how their lessons are planned and how their classes are conducted. When teachers are given this sort of say in school governance, they may find it easier to make a commitment to the shared values of the institution.

Third, good schools constantly monitor themselves and their students in order to become even better. Rather than viewing questions and concerns about school policies and practices as threatening, principals and other administrators welcome opportunities for dialogue and discussion. When school personnel encourage flexibility, openness to change, and the exchange of ideas, they set a tone for the entire school that may even affect the classroom and may result in more stimulating student-teacher interaction (Goodlad, 1984).

Fourth, good schools are well integrated into the communities they serve (Coleman & Hoffer, 1987). Active attempts are made to involve parents in their youngsters' education. Links are forged between the high school and local colleges and universities, so that advanced students may take more challenging and more stimulating courses for high school credit. Bridges are built between the high school and local employers, so that students begin to see the relevance of their high school education to their occupational futures.

Finally, and perhaps obviously, good schools are composed of good classrooms. In good classrooms, students are active participants in the process of education, not passive recipients of lecture material. The atmosphere is orderly but not oppressive. Innovative projects replace rote memorization as a way of encouraging learning. Students are challenged to think critically and to debate important issues, rather than being asked simply to regurgitate yesterday's lessons (Newmann et al., 1996).

RECAP

Educators have long debated the nature of the high school curriculum. During the 1970s, educators clamored for relevance. During the 1980s, the pendulum swung back to basics. During the early 1990s, the fashion became higher-order thinking. In the late 1990s, calls for rigorous academic standards became familiar, as the public grew increasingly worried about the competitiveness of American students in an international economy, that increasingly is reliant on high technology and high-skilled jobs. Although experts disagree about how widespread America's achievement problem is, there is broad consensus that inner-city public schools are failing to prepare students for this new labor market. Educators agree that good schools (1) emphasize intellectual activities, (2) have committed teachers who are given autonomy, (3) monitor their own progress, (4) are well integrated into their community, and (5) have a high proportion of classrooms in which students are active participants in their education.

Food for Thought

Why do calls for school reform focus on such different issues at different points in time? What is the current focus? Does this make sense to you?

THE SOCIAL ORGANIZATION OF SCHOOLS

In addition to debating curricular issues, social scientists who have been interested in school reform have also discussed the ways in which secondary schools should be organized. Because the organization of a school affects students' day-to-day experiences, variations in school organization can have profound effects on adolescents' development and behavior. In this section, we will examine the research on five aspects of school organization: (1) school and classroom size; (2) various approaches to age grouping and, in particular, how young adolescents should be grouped; (3) tracking, or the grouping of students in classes according to their academic abilities; (4) school desegregation; and (5) public versus private schools.

School Size and Class Size

As the idea of the comprehensive high school gained widespread acceptance, educators attempted to deliver a wider range of courses and services under a single roof. As a consequence, schools became larger and larger over the course of the twentieth century. By the end of the 1990s, in many metropolitan areas, it had grown common for students to attend enormous schools, with enrollments of several thousand students.

When it comes to school size, however, is bigger necessarily better? Do students who attend larger schools reap any psychological advantages as a result? A fair amount of research conducted over the past 40 years says no. Indeed, one of the most consistent conclusions to emerge from recent evaluations of school reform efforts is that student performance and interest in school improve when schools are made less bureaucratic and more intimate. Numerous studies indicate that students achieve more and behave better when they attend smaller schools, which create a cohesive sense of community and encourage students to form strong bonds with the institution (Lee et al., 1997; Roeser, Midgley, & Urdan, 1996).

Although the move to reorganize large secondary schools into more personal institutions gained wider and wider acceptance during the 1990s, some of the most interesting data about the effects of school size on adolescents actually come from a series of studies conducted more than 35 years ago (Barker & Gump, 1964). These researchers were interested in how the size of a school influences the variety of classes and extracurricular activities available to students as well as the students' participation in them. The researchers found, as expected, that large schools offer more varied instruction than small schools. But they also discovered that the variety of courses offered in a school increases substantially only when the size of the school increases dramatically. Although a school with 2,000 students might offer 50 different classes, a school with 4,000 students might offer only 60. In order to realize the diversity in offerings that many advocates of the comprehensive high school had envisioned, schools would have to be very, very large.

Perhaps the most interesting findings of this early research on school size and its effects on students concern participation in nonacademic activities, however. One might expect that, in addition to providing a more varied curriculum, large schools would be able to offer a more diverse selection of extracurricular activities to their students, and indeed they do. Large schools can afford to have more athletic teams, after-school clubs, and student organizations. In fact, nearly four times as many nonacademic activities are available to students attending very large high schools as are available to students in small schools.

However, because large schools also contain so many more students, actual participation in various activities is only half as high in large schools as in smaller ones. As a result, in larger schools, students tend more often to be observers than participants in school activities. For instance, during the fall, a small school and a large school might each field teams in football, soccer, and cross-country running, together requiring a total of 100 students. An individual's chances of being 1 of those 100 students are greater in a school that has only 500 students than in a school with an enrollment of 4,000.

Because students in small schools are more likely than students in large schools to be active in a wider range of activities, they are more likely to report doing things that help them develop their skills and abilities, that allow them to work closely with others, and that make them feel needed and important. In a small school, chances are that, sooner or later, most students will find themselves on a team, in the student government, or in an extracurricular organization. Students in small schools also are more likely to be placed in positions of leadership and responsibility, and they more often report having done things that made them feel confident and diligent. School size especially affects the participation of students whose grades are not very good. In large schools, academically marginal students often feel like outsiders; they rarely get involved in school activities. In small schools, however, these students feel a sense of involvement and obligation equal to that of more academically successful students.

In short, although large schools may be able to offer more diverse curricula and provide greater material resources to their students, the toll that school size may take on student learning and engagement appears to exceed the benefits of size (Lee & Smith, 1995). Experts now agree that the ideal size of a school for adolescents is between 500 and 1,000 students (Entwisle, 1990).

Unfortunately, policymakers do not always implement social science findings in ways that accurately reflect the research evidence. Encouraged by the results of research on smaller *schools*, many politicians began calling for smaller *classes*. However, in contrast to studies of schools, studies of classrooms indicate that variations within the typical range of classroom sizes—from 20 to 40 students—do not generally affect students' scholastic achievement once they have reached adolescence; small classes may benefit very young children, who may need more individualized instruction (e.g., up until third grade), but adolescents in classes with 40 students learn just as much as students in classes with 20 students (Mosteller, Light, & Sachs, 1996; Rutter, 1983). More important, without changes in instruction, changes in class size alone are unlikely to have an effect on students (Bennett, 1987). One important exception to this conclusion involves situations that call for highly individualized instruction or tutoring, where smaller classes *do* appear to be more effective. For example, in remedial education classes, where teachers must give a great deal of attention to each student, small classes are valuable. One important implication of these findings is that it may be profitable for schools that maintain regular class sizes of 25 or 30 students to increase the size of these classes by a student or two in order to free instructors and to trim the size of classes for students who need specialized, small-group instruction (Rutter, 1983).

Age Grouping and School Transitions

A second issue that social scientists have examined in the study of school structure and organization concerns the way in which schools group students of different ages and the frequency with which students are expected to change schools. Early in the twentieth century, most school districts separated youngsters into an elementary school (which had either six or eight grades) and a secondary school (which had either four or six grades). Students changed schools once (either after sixth or eighth grade).

Many educators felt that the two-school system was

▲ *Generally speaking, research has shown that adolescents in large classes learn just as much as adolescents in small ones. An important exception, however, is remedial education. Here, adolescents benefit from smaller classes and one-on-one instruction.* (Meri Houtchens-Kitchens/Picture Cube)

unable to meet the special needs of young adolescents, however, whose intellectual and emotional maturity was greater than that expected in elementary school but not yet at the level necessary for high school. During the early years of compulsory secondary education, the establishment of separate schools for young adolescents began, and the **junior high school** was born (Hechinger, 1993). In more recent years, the **middle school**—a three- or four-year school housing the seventh and eighth grades, with one or more younger grades—has gained in popularity, replacing the junior high school in many districts. Proponents of middle schools point to the earlier maturation of young people today and the greater similarity of fifth- and sixth-graders to their older peers than to their younger ones.

What is known about the differential effects of these various arrangements? From the point of view of the developing adolescent, are some organizational schemes superior to others? The evidence favors middle schools over junior high schools (Entwisle, 1990). Middle schools are typically smaller and less departmentalized, which promotes students' sense of community; young adolescents, especially, are less likely to feel lost in smaller schools. In addition, teachers in middle schools are more likely to engage in team-teaching, to teach only one grade level, and to teach in their area of specialization. For these reasons,

middle schools are likely to be better environments both academically and socially than junior high schools.

Although most experts now agree that middle schools are preferable to junior high schools, there is still considerable room for improvement in existing middle schools. One well-publicized report on this subject was issued by the Carnegie Corporation's Council on Adolescent Development (1989). Among the most important recommendations made were to divide middle schools into units of between 200 and 500 students in order to reduce students' feelings of anonymity, to hire teachers who have special training in adolescent development, and to strengthen ties between schools and the communities in which they are located.

Researchers also have examined how changing schools affects student achievement and behavior. In many of these studies, researchers have compared school arrangements in which students remain in elementary school until eighth grade—that is, where they have one school change—with arrangements in which they move from elementary school into middle or junior high school and, later, into high school—where they change schools twice. In general, this research suggests that school transitions, whenever they occur, can disrupt the academic performance, behavior, and self-image of adolescents. This disruption is generally temporary, however; over time, most youngsters adapt successfully to changing schools, especially when other aspects of their life—family and peer relations, for example—remain stable and supportive and when the new school environment is well suited for adolescents (Anderman & Midgley, 1996; DuBois, Eitel, & Felner, 1994; Gillock & Reyes, 1996; Koizumi, 1995; Lord, Eccles, & McCarthy, 1994; Teachman, Paasch, & Carver, 1996; Wigfield & Eccles, 1994).

Jacquelynne Eccles and her colleagues have conducted the most comprehensive research to date on school transitions during the early adolescent years (Eccles, Lord, & Midgley, 1991; Eccles et al., 1993; Roeser, Eccles, & Freedman-Doan, 1999). Eccles has argued that the classroom environment in the typical junior high school is quite different from that in the typical elementary school. Not only are junior high schools larger and less personal, but also junior high school teachers hold different beliefs about students than do elementary school teachers— even when they teach students of the same chronological age (Midgley, Berman, & Hicks, 1995). For example, teachers in junior high schools are less likely to trust their students and more likely to emphasize control and discipline. They also tend to be more likely to believe that students' abilities are fixed and not easily modified through instruction. Eccles points out that it is little surprise that students experience a drop in self-esteem and in achievement motivation when they enter junior high school, given the change in environments they experience and given the mismatch between what adolescents need developmentally and what the typical junior high school context provides. The issue, according to her, is not that the adolescents must make a transition; it is the nature of the transition they must make. Indeed, although students' self-esteem drops during the transition into junior high school, it increases somewhat during the early junior high school years, suggesting that the initial decline reflects students' temporary difficulties in adapting to the new environment (Wigfield, Eccles, Mac Iver, Reuman, & Midgley, 1991). Consistent with this, junior high school students attending more personal, less departmentalized schools do better in school than their peers in more rigid and more anonymous schools (Lee & Smith, 1993). Not surprisingly, changing schools is easier on students who move into small, rather than large, institutions (Russell, Elder, & Conger, 1997).

Why do junior high school teachers differ from those who teach elementary school? At this point, the answer is not clear-cut. It does not seem that the individuals who choose to become junior high teachers differ all that much from those who choose to teach younger grades. Rather, Eccles has suggested that the organization and anonymity of junior high schools have a negative effect on the teachers who work in them, which in turn affects the way they interact with students. This is consistent with a large body of evidence that students are more engaged in school when their teachers themselves are more engaged in their work (Louis & Smith, 1992).

Eccles also points out that cultural stereotypes about adolescence may have a negative influence on junior high school teachers' beliefs. Many adults believe that adolescence is an inevitably difficult time—not only for teenagers themselves but also for those who work with them. To the extent that teachers come into the classroom with negative images of adolescence as a stage in the life cycle—that teenagers are inherently unruly, unteachable, or perplexing—their preconceptions may interfere with their work as educators (Midgley, Feldlaufer, & Eccles, 1988). One of the most important influences on the adolescent's experience in school is the climate of the classroom.

The fact that many teachers of young adolescents have negative, or even erroneous, perceptions of this stage in the life cycle is not at all surprising, given the lack of specialized training in early adolescence that most teachers of

middle grades have received. According to one report, only about one-third of middle school principals report that the teachers in their school had specialized college coursework that focused on middle-grades education and that only about one-third had done student teaching at this grade level. Even among teachers who had received specialized middle-grades training, half felt that their training was poor or inadequate (Scales & McEwin, 1994).

It is important to remember that, although some aspects of the transition into secondary school may be difficult for students to negotiate, not all students experience the same degree of stress during the transition. One recent study identified four distinct groups of students (Roeser et al., 1999) (see figure 6.2). About 30 percent of the children were highly motivated, well-adjusted, and high achieving while in elementary school, and they did not have difficulties making the transition into secondary school. A second group, about 10 percent of the sample, who had multiple academic and psychological problems before the transition, had particular difficulty with the transition from elementary to middle school, but no special problems with the transition into high school, presumably because they were already disengaged from academics entirely. Indeed, by the time these young adolescents were ready for high school, they had become so alienated from school and discouraged about their own ability that they viewed school as uninteresting and unimportant. A third group of students (another 30 percent) showed declines in their motivation and feelings of competence during the transition out of elementary school, as well as declines in their school performance and mental health during the transition into high school. Finally, a fourth group (another 30 percent) showed increases in psychological distress over the course of the transition, but no appreciable changes in academic motivation or performance. One possibility is that aspects of the transition unrelated to academics (e.g., changes in peer relations) distressed these adolescents.

Not surprisingly, students who have more academic and psychosocial problems before making a school transition cope less successfully with it (Anderman, 1996; Berndt & Mekos, 1995; Carlson et al., 1999; Roeser et al., 1999; Safer, 1986). Factors other than a student's prior record may also influence the nature of the adolescent's transition to middle or high school. Students who experience the transition earlier in adolescence have more difficulty with it than those who experience it later (Simmons & Blyth, 1987). And adolescents who have close friends before and during the transition adapt more successfully to the new school environment, although the benefits of

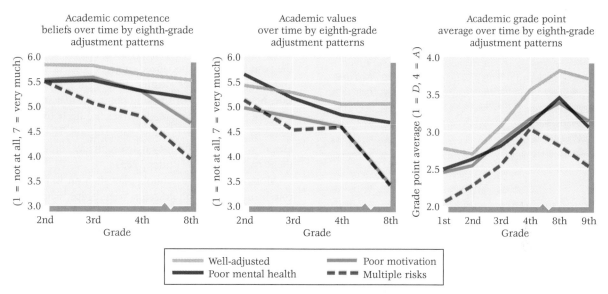

Figure 6.2 *Although many studies find a general drop in school performance and academic engagement during the transition into middle school, not all adolescents show this pattern.* (Roeser et al., 1999)

staying with one's friends may accrue only to students who had been doing well previously; students who had been doing poorly adjust better if they enroll in a different school from their friends (Schiller, 1999).

Evidently, then, the transition into secondary school is not the sort of stressor that has uniform effects on all students. More vulnerable adolescents, adolescents with fewer sources of social support, and adolescents moving into more impersonal schools may be more susceptible to the adverse consequences of this stressor than their peers are. Not surprisingly, one study of poor, inner-city youngsters found significant negative effects of the school transition on adolescents' self-esteem, achievement, classroom preparation, perceptions of the school environment, reports of social support, and participation in extracurricular activities (Seidman, Aber, Allen, & French, 1996; Seidman, Allen, Aber, Mitchell, & Feinman, 1994). Another study of Texas adolescents found that African American and, especially, Mexican American youngsters were more likely than their white peers to experience a variety of difficulties during the transition out of elementary school—including receiving poor grades, getting into trouble with teachers, and being hassled by other students (Munsch & Wampler, 1993).

One study by a team of investigators at the University of Vermont suggests that low-income students' adjustment to middle school may be enhanced as a result of an intervention targeted at their *parents* (Bronstein et al., 1998). The researchers had parents participate in an 11-week program designed to increase their understanding of adolescent development and their effectiveness as parents. The children whose parents had participated in the program were functioning better psychologically and behaviorally, both immediately after the program and one year later, than were their counterparts whose parents had not participated. Moreover, the children whose parents had participated did not show the decline in functioning that often is associated with the transition into middle school. In general, parental support is associated with better adolescent adjustment during school transitions (Isakson & Jarvis, 1999).

RECAP

Educators have long debated how best to structure schools for young adolescents. Generally speaking, smaller schools, although not necessarily smaller classes, are more effective. With respect to age grouping, middle schools seem slightly preferable to junior high schools, but research on the transition from elementary school into secondary school, or from one secondary school to another, indicates that changing schools can be difficult for some students, especially for those who have academic or behavior problems at the time of the transition. Researchers point to features of the secondary school environment that may be problematic and, more generally, to a mismatch between the school environment and the developmental needs of young adolescents.

Food for Thought

*What are the best organizational envi-
ronments of schools for adolescents? How
do the characteristics of these environments mesh well with the psychosocial
needs of individuals at this point in their development?*

Tracking

In some schools, students with different academic abilities and interests do not attend classes together. Some
classes are designated as more challenging and more rigorous and are reserved for students who are identified as
especially capable. Other classes in the same subject area
are designated as average classes and are taken by most
students. Still others are designated as remedial classes
and are reserved for students having academic difficulties.
The process of separating students into different levels of
classes within the same school is called ability-grouping,
or **tracking.** Not all high schools use tracking systems. In
some schools, students with different abilities take all
their classes together.

Even among schools that use tracking, there are important differences in the implementation of the tracking
system (Jones, Vanfossen, & Ensminger, 1995). Some
schools are more inclusive in their tracking, permitting a
relatively high proportion of students into the highest
track (even, perhaps, some students whose abilities do not
warrant such placement). Other schools are more exclusive, limiting the places in the highest track to a privileged
few (even if this means placing some high-ability students
in the lower tracks). And still other schools are "meritocratic," placing students in tracks that match their abilities. In general, inclusive tracking is found in schools
where principals have confidence in their students, where
teachers influence track placement, and where there is
open communication between students and teachers. Exclusive tracking is more likely to be found in smaller,
more affluent schools where principals lack confidence in
their students, where teachers have high professional
standards, and where there is little information flow between staff and students. Meritocratic tracking is found
more often in larger schools (Kilgore, 1991).

Educators have debated the pros and cons of tracking
for years. On the positive side, proponents of tracking
note that ability-grouping allows teachers to design class

lessons that are more finely tuned to students' abilities;
tracking may be especially useful at the high school level,
where students must master certain basic skills before
they can learn such specialized subjects as science, math,
and foreign languages (Rutter, 1983). On the negative
side, however, critics of tracking point out that students
who are placed in the remedial track are likely to be labeled by their peers as "slow" or "stupid." Their self-
esteem may suffer, and they may eventually come to see
themselves as failures (Rutter, 1983).

Moreover, because schools play such an important
role in influencing adolescents' friendships, when students are tracked, they tend to socialize only with peers
from the same academic group (Rosenbaum, 1976).
Tracking can thereby contribute to the polarization of the
student body into various subcultures that feel hostile toward each other. The students in the advanced track may
feel academically superior and may look down on other
students, and the students in the remedial track may feel
angry and resentful. Some critics of tracking also point
out that decisions about track placements often discrimi-
nate against poor and minority students and may hinder
rather than enhance their academic progress (Ayalon,
1994; Oakes, 1995; Rosenbaum, 1976; Wells & Serna,
1996). Some school counselors assume, for example, that
minority or poor youngsters are not capable of handling
the work in advanced classes and may assign them to average or remedial classes, where less material is covered
and the work is less challenging (Vanfossen, Jones, &
Spade, 1987). Other studies, however, indicate that a student's ability has a stronger influence than his or her
background on the youngster's initial track placement
(Alexander & Cook, 1982; Dauber, Alexander, & Entwisle,
1996) but that middle-class and white students who are
initially placed in lower tracks are more likely to move
into higher ones, in part because middle-class parents are
frequently successful in "lobbying" their child's school for
a changed track placement (Hallinan, 1996; Oakes, 1995;
Wells & Serna, 1996).

In many respects, then, early track placements set in
motion a sort of educational trajectory, that is often difficult to change, without the deliberate intervention of the
student's parents (Alexander & Cook, 1982; Dauber et al.,
1996; Dornbusch, 1994; Hallinan, 1992, 1996; Stevenson,
Schiller, & Schneider, 1994). Junior high track placements
in mathematics, for example, determine which sorts of
math courses a student is eligible to take in high school,
which in turn determine which colleges he or she may apply to. Moreover, because students are assigned to different tracks initially on the basis of test scores and other

indicators of aptitude, and because students in the lower tracks receive an inferior education, the net effect of tracking over time is to increase pre-existing differences among students. The students who need the most help are assigned to the tracks in which the quality of instruction is the poorest. In other words, in a school that uses tracking, the academically "rich get richer, and the poor get poorer." Although students in the lower tracks get the short end of the educational stick, there are some exceptions—for example, schools in which classes in the lower tracks are taught by strong teachers who insist on maintaining high standards (Gamoran, 1993; Hallinan, 1994).

Research on tracking in high schools indicates quite clearly that students in different tracks have markedly different opportunities to learn (Gamoran, 1987, 1996; Stevenson et al., 1994). Students in the more advanced tracks receive more challenging instruction and better teaching, and they are more likely to engage in classroom activities that emphasize higher-order thinking rather than rote memorization. Being placed in a more advanced track has a positive influence on school achievement (how much is actually learned over time), on subsequent course selection (the curriculum to which a student is exposed), and on ultimate educational attainment (how many years of schooling a student completes) (Gamoran & Mare, 1989; Lee & Bryk, 1989; Natriello, Pallas, & Alexander, 1989).

Literally hundreds of studies have been done on the impact of tracking on student achievement (Hallinan, 1996). Unfortunately, this research suggests both positive and negative effects and, more important, different effects among students in different tracks. More specifically, tracking has positive effects on the achievement of high-tracked students, negative effects on low-tracked students, and negligible effects on students in the middle or average track (Fuligni, Eccles, & Barber, 1995; Hallinan, 1996). Because of this, decisions about whether to implement tracking in nontracked schools, or whether to "detrack" schools that use ability-grouping, are typically quite controversial; not surprisingly, parents of students in the higher tracks favor the practice, whereas parents of students in the lower tracks oppose it (Wells & Serna, 1996).

Even in schools that do not have formal tracking, of course, teachers may group students within the same class into ability groups. In such an arrangement, students may have a wider range of peers with whom to compare themselves than they would in separate tracks, since their classes are much more diverse in composition. The impact of this comparison process on both students and teachers is quite interesting. For high-ability students,

within-classroom ability-grouping raises their expectations for achievement and raises their teachers' evaluations of them; for low-ability students, the opposite is true: The students have lowered expectations and get worse grades from their teachers (Reuman, 1989). Presumably, both adolescents and teachers make their evaluations based on unstated comparisons, and, in mixed classes with ability groups, the high-ability students look better, and the low-ability students look worse, than they would in a conventionally tracked school or in a school in which ability-grouping is not used (Marsh, Chessor, Craven, & Roche, 1995). As is the case with tracking, within-classroom ability-grouping also exposes students in different groups to different levels of educational quality, with students in the high-ability groups receiving more challenging instruction and more engaging learning experiences (Catsambis, 1992).

Related to the issue of tracking are questions concerning the placement of individuals who are considered **gifted students** and of those who have a **learning disability.** Adolescents who are gifted score 130 or higher on an intelligence test. Adolescents with a learning disability are those whose actual performance is significantly poorer than their expected performance (based on intelligence tests and the like) and whose difficulty with academic tasks cannot be traced to an emotional problem, such as coping with a parental divorce, or sensory dysfunction, such as a visual or hearing impairment. Most learning disabilities are presumed to be neurological in origin (Lovitt, 1989).

Educators have debated whether gifted students and those with learning disabilities are best served by instruction in separate classes (for example, in enriched classes for gifted students or in special education classes for students with a learning disability) or by **mainstreaming,** the integration of all students with special needs into regular classrooms. Pros and cons of each approach have been identified. On the one hand, separate special education programs can be tailored to meet the specific needs of students and can target educational and professional resources in a cost-effective way. On the other hand, however, segregating students on the basis of their academic ability may foster social isolation and stigmatization—either for being "stupid" or for being a "brainiac."

Generally speaking, educators have tended to favor mainstreaming over separate classrooms for adolescents with special needs. (Mainstreaming, whenever possible, is required by federal law in the case of adolescents with disabilities.) Their argument has been that the psychological costs of separating adolescents with special academic

Ability-Grouping, Coeducation, and Sex Differences in Mathematics Achievement

Although elementary school girls generally outscore boys on tests of math achievement, junior and senior high school boys are more likely to take advanced math classes, and, among higher-performing students, boys are more likely to outperform girls (Davenport et al., 1998; Hedges & Nowell, 1995; Oakes, 1990). Sex differences in course enrollment are important, because students emerging from high school with little preparation in mathematics are unlikely to be able to enter certain college programs (such as engineering) or to pursue certain occupations (such as scientist) that require training in math. Decisions that young women make early in their education, therefore, may have important long-term implications for their educational and occupational futures.

Many psychological explanations have been offered for the flip-flop in math achievement during early adolescence, including that (1) girls come to see math achievement as part of the masculine role and develop negative attitudes toward math, as a consequence; (2) girls have fewer role models of successful mathematicians or scientists and, consequently, are less likely to aspire to enter these fields; and (3) girls receive pressure from their male peers not to excel in math class (Hallinan & Sorensen, 1987). We examine some of these explanations in chapter 12 as part of our discussion of psychological aspects of adolescent achievement. As Hallinan and Sorensen point out, however, psychological explanations of sex differences in math achievement ignore the organizational aspects of schools that may have important effects. In particular, they suggest that tracking biases in the math curriculum operate against the assignment of girls to high-ability math classes.

These researchers examined mathematics ability-group assignments in a large sample of fourth-through seventh-graders. They were interested in whether assignment to the high-

needs from their peers outweigh the potential academic benefits. Studies of gifted youngsters have found, for example, that those who are integrated into regular classrooms have more positive academic self-conceptions than do those in special classes (Marsh et al., 1995; Schneider, Clegg, Byrne, Ledingham, & Crombie, 1989). Even with mainstreaming, adolescents who have learning disabilities may suffer psychological consequences related to their problems in school. Compared with average-achieving students, adolescents with learning disabilities report more social and behavior difficulties and, not surprisingly, more problems in coping with school. They are also more likely than other adolescents to have poor peer relations, are less likely to participate in school-based extracurricular activities, and are more likely to drop out of school (Lovitt, 1989). Given the tremendous importance society places on school success, it is not difficult to see why students who have difficulties learning suffer psychological, as well as scholastic, problems.

RECAP

In general, educational research on ability-grouping, or tracking, reveals that the rich get richer and the poor get poorer. Over time, students who are placed in the more advanced tracks achieve more than those in lower tracks, in part because the quality of instruction in the higher tracks is superior. In contrast, students placed in the lower tracks or in low-ability groups within classrooms receive a markedly inferior education than do those in the higher tracks or groups, and, once a student is placed in a lower track, it is very difficult for the student to move up. Tracking also may contribute to the polarization of the student body into various subcultures that feel hostile toward each other. Even in the case of gifted adolescents or adolescents with learning disabilities, educators generally recommend mixing students of different ability levels instead of separating them.

ability group was influenced by the student's math ability, by his or her gender, or by a combination of both. They found, not surprisingly, that a student's ability weighed heavily in the assignment process, with more able students being more likely to be assigned to the high-ability group. But they also found that high-ability girls were less likely to be assigned to the high-ability group than were boys of comparable talent (Hallinan & Sorensen, 1987). Studies also show that girls are less likely than boys to be moved from a lower math track into a higher one (Hallinan, 1996).

Even within math classes, teachers interact differently with males than with females. Teachers are more likely to communicate to girls who are having difficulty that their problem is related to a lack of ability, whereas they are more likely to communicate to boys who are having difficulty that their problem results from a lack of effort. As a consequence, girls may be more likely than boys to develop feelings of helplessness when it comes to learning math, and they may emerge with negative perceptions of their own abilities (Henderson & Dweck, 1990).

Moreover, the biased assortment of youngsters into math tracks has long-term implications for future course selection. An adolescent girl who is not assigned to a high-ability math class—despite her talent—may come to develop more negative attitudes toward math than she might have otherwise and may miss opportunities to pursue careers that require advanced mathematics training. Indeed, girls are less likely than boys to receive advice, encouragement, and counseling to take advanced courses in math or to prepare for careers that would require these courses (Lee, Marks, & Byrd, 1994).

Is this sort of sexism diminished in single-sex schools? One investigation involving 60 private schools—20 coeducational, 20 boys' schools, and 20 girls' schools—says not necessarily. The researchers observed classes in these schools and carefully noted both subtle and blatant forms of sexism, such as a teacher's ignoring a young woman's interest in science or providing female students with less challenging math instruction than was warranted. Somewhat surprisingly, these sorts of practices existed even in girls' schools, despite the hope that girls might encounter less sexist instruction in a single-sex environment. Although a number of academically demanding girls' schools were less sexist than the norm, there was considerable variation among the girls' schools studied. For example, the researchers observed the teachers in girls' schools "talking down to girls, making academic activities more palatable by 'wrapping calculus in a nontechnical package,' setting up expectations that students would have difficulty with assignments by offering help before it was required or requested, or promulgating an attitude that 'trying hard is as important as succeeding' with difficult undertakings" (Lee et al., 1994, p. 114). In contrast, the boys' schools were more likely to use an aggressive style of teaching that encouraged students to state their views assertively and to expect the intense scrutiny of their teachers and peers. Sexism was just as pronounced in the coeducational schools, however, especially in science classes. In one chemistry class that was observed, for example, the female teacher responded positively to boys who spoke out without raising their hands, yet she reprimanded girls for the same behavior. Another chemistry teacher at a different coeducational school told the researchers that he believed that "girls are not suited to 'do' science" (Lee at al., 1994, p. 108).

Food for Thought

Did you go to a high school in which tracking was used? If so, what were some of the unintended consequences of that policy? If not, how would your school have been different if tracking had been implemented?

School Desegregation

Since the landmark U.S. Supreme Court rulings in *Brown v. Board of Education of Topeka* (1954, 1955), many of the nation's school districts have enacted changes aimed at desegregating their schools. Underlying the Court's rulings was the belief that segregation in schools impedes the academic and economic progress of students from racial minorities and, in addition, fosters hostility and misunderstanding between individuals of different backgrounds. Even if racially segregated schools appear equivalent on various indices of quality (for example, the amount of money spent on educational materials and programs), segregated schools are "inherently unequal," the Court argued, because "to separate [African American youngsters] from others solely because of their race generates a feeling of inferiority as to their status in the community that may affect their hearts and minds in a way unlikely ever to be undone" (*Brown v. Board of Education of Topeka*, 1954). Since the Court's rulings, many school districts have adopted measures designed to create voluntary desegregation (for example, permitting families to choose among various schools within a large catchment area, rather than assigning students to specific schools on the basis of their residence). Others have enacted policies aimed at mandatory desegregation (assigning students of different racial backgrounds to specific schools in

▲ *Research on the presumed positive effects of school desegregation has not been encouraging. One reason is that many desegregated schools are integrated in theory but not in practice. In many so-called integrated schools, segregation continues through tracking and other structural arrangements.* (Peter Southwick/Stock, Boston)

order to create predetermined racial balances) (Bradley & Bradley, 1977). Nonetheless, many schools in the United States remain segregated because of strong and continuing residential segregation (Rivkin, 1994).

Despite the clear legal basis for desegregation, research into the short-term effects of desegregation programs on high school students has not been overwhelmingly encouraging. Several sets of studies point to this disappointing conclusion. First, research indicates that desegregation has surprisingly little impact on the achievement levels of either minority or white youngsters (Entwisle, 1990).

Second, there is some evidence that minority youngsters' self-esteem is higher when they attend schools in which they are in the majority—a phenomenon true not only for African American youth but for all youth; in general, students fare better psychologically when the cultural environment of their neighborhood is conso-

nant with the cultural environment of their school (Arunkumar & Midgley, 1996; Gray-Little & Carels, 1997; Hudley, 1995; Nieto et al., 1996; Phelan, Yu, & Davidson, 1994; Rosenberg, 1975). The difficulties associated with attending school where one is in a distinct minority were tellingly illustrated in a study by Patricia Phelan and colleagues (Phelan et al., 1994). Consider the following excerpts from the researchers' interviews with students:

Ivonne, Mexican American female: Well, I kind of feel uncomfortable. Not many Mexicans and Hispanics are in [my] classes. They [other students] probably think of me as weird, because they probably have this view that most Hispanics are dumb or something. They have that opinion, you know, [Hispanics] get bad grades. So, I don't know why I feel uncomfortable. I just . . . it means you're not really with any other . . . many people. Maybe by the end of the year they will realize that I belong. (Phelan et al., 1994, p. 425)

Trinh, Vietnamese American female: [Because I'm Vietnamese] I notice the little things more often than other people. Just like, I don't really get noticed by all the popular people. OK, everyone in the class, I know their names and everything. . . . Like being Vietnamese . . . like they have a lot of Americans in here. That there are more of them, and when you're alone, you're nervous over little things. (Phelan et al., 1994, p. 425)

Sonia, Mexican American female: Yeah, it's weird, 'cause most teachers, you know—white teachers—some of them are kind of prejudiced. . . . It's probably the way they look at you, the way they talk, you know when they're talking about something—about something like when they talk about the people who are going to drop out, and they . . . look around, look around [at you].

And then Mr. Kula, when he's talking about teenage pregnancy or something like that. He turns around and he looks at us. It's like—he tries to look around the whole room, so we won't notice but like he mostly like tries to tell us, tries to get it through our heads, you know. Sometimes I think he's prejudiced. And sometimes I think he's trying to help us. (Phelan et al., 1994, p. 431)

Third, as discussed in chapter 5, interracial contact, even in desegregated schools, is rare, largely because of the reluctance on the part of white students to form cross-racial friendships (Hallinan & Teixeira, 1987). Fourth, studies indicate that, immediately following the imposition of a desegregation program, white enrollment in a school declines as white families move or withdraw their children from the public school (although the high rate of "white flight" appears to be most pronounced during the first year of a desegregation program and slows shortly thereafter) (Wilson, 1985).

As several commentators have pointed out, however, focusing on the short-term impact of desegregation on achievement or self-esteem may provide only a very narrow means of assessing its costs and benefits (Braddock, 1985; Wells, 1995). For example, African Americans who attend desegregated high schools are more likely to graduate and to continue their education in desegregated institutions, and African American students who attended racially mixed high schools adjust more successfully to integrated colleges than do their peers who attended segregated high schools (Adan & Felner, 1995). Because African Americans graduating from predominantly white colleges earn more when they enter the labor force than do those who attend predominantly minority colleges, it seems that youngsters who attend desegregated high schools may reap advantages in the labor force later on, as young adults. Moreover, African American graduates of predominantly white

schools are more likely to work in integrated environments, have integrated networks of friends, and live in integrated neighborhoods during adulthood (Wells, 1995). Together, these studies suggest that desegregated high school programs do benefit minority youth but that the benefits may not be apparent until adulthood. Furthermore, these studies suggest that desegregation during high school helps break down racial barriers in society at large.

It also may not be advisable to make generalizations about the impact of school desegregation without looking further at the processes inside the school and how they are affected (or not affected) by its racial composition. De facto segregation may be maintained even in desegregated schools through tracking, seating assignment, ability-grouping within classrooms, and class scheduling (Entwisle, 1990). To assess the situation, one would need information about how the school's policies and procedures were changed and about how students, teachers, and administrators responded to the changes. Not all desegregated schools are the same (Campbell, 1977). Consider, for example, the differences between two desegregated schools. Each has achieved racial balance; however, in one school, minority and white students are taught in different classes but, in the other, the classes are all integrated. Obviously, it makes little sense to view these schools as having similar environments merely because they are both classified as desegregated.

Finally, not all children and families respond in the same way to changes in the racial composition of their school. Some parents and students are enthusiastic about such changes, whereas others are apprehensive. Thus, in any comprehensive study of the effects of school desegregation, it would be important to know how children of different ages are affected, how children from different racial and socioeconomic backgrounds are affected, how parents' attitudes toward desegregation affect the child's reaction, and so forth. These and other factors are likely to mediate the impact of desegregation on the adolescent (St. John, 1975).

Public Schools Versus Private Schools

Although the vast majority of students attending secondary school in America are enrolled in public schools, a substantial minority attend private schools, either parochial (i.e., with a religious affiliation) or independent. In the past, researchers cared little about studying differences between private and public

▲ *Although social scientists disagree over their interpretation, studies show that adolescents attending parochial schools generally achieve at a higher level than those attending public schools.* (Mimi Forsyth/Monkmeyer)

schools; however, during the late 1980s and early 1990s, many education policymakers suggested that one way to improve schools would be to give parents more of a choice in determining where their child was enrolled, in order to force schools to compete with each other for the best students. One concrete suggestion linked to such school choice programs was that states should provide parents with **education vouchers,** which could be used to purchase education at a school of their choosing—private or public. Another was that states should permit the development of **charter schools**—independent public schools that are freer to operate as they wish, outside of some of the constraints imposed by the state's education bureaucracy. In light of these suggestions, researchers became interested in studying whether some types of schools produce more high-achieving students than others do.

Initial investigations of this by sociologist James Coleman and his colleagues (e.g., Coleman & Hoffer, 1987; Coleman, Hoffer, & Kilgore, 1982) pointed to clear advantages for students attending private high schools, and especially for those attending Catholic schools. The studies found that the students from private schools achieved more, even after taking into account pre-existing differences between the public and private students that could explain their achievement differences. (For example, IQ scores are positively correlated with social class, and wealthier families can better afford private school; even within social classes, parents may be more likely to invest money in the education of more capable students.) The better achievement of the students in private schools was especially clear in comparisons of juniors and seniors (Entwisle, 1990). Charter schools have not been in place long enough for researchers to know whether students achieve more in them than in conventional public schools.

Social scientists have different theories about the root causes of the achievement advantage associated with private schooling. According to Coleman, the chief reason for the advantages enjoyed by Catholic school students has to do with the close links between their schools and families. He has argued that a Catholic school is a part of a community, in which parents, teachers, and students all share similar values and attitudes. Strong communities, whether based in neighborhoods or schools, generate what Coleman calls **social capital**—interpersonal resources that, like financial capital, give "richer" students advantages over poorer ones. Students profit from the social capital associated with attending a Catholic school, for example, because the lessons taught in school are reinforced at home, at church, and in the neighborhood and because the links between home and school are strong (Teachman et al., 1996). In addition, private schools are typically more orderly and more disciplined, and they assign more homework (Coleman et al., 1982). Other researchers also have suggested that the curricula and tracking practices of private and public schools are very different (e.g., Lee & Bryk, 1988). Students at Catholic schools, for example, take more academic courses in school and are less likely to be tracked into general or vocational classes, even if their prior records are not strong. Given the negative effects of being placed in lower tracks, it makes sense that schools that have less tracking will have overall higher levels of achievement (Gamoran, 1987).

RECAP

In an effort to understand better how various types of school environments influence adolescent achievement, researchers have compared students in segregated versus desegregated schools and in private versus public ones. In general, the effects of desegregation on student achievement are very modest, and there appear to be advantages for students who attend Catholic, but not necessarily all types of private, schools.

Food for Thought

How do you feel about vouchers? about charter schools?

THE IMPORTANCE OF SCHOOL CLIMATE

Thus far, we have seen that certain elements of the school's social organization—size, age grouping, tracking, and so forth—can affect students' behavior and achievement. But these factors are important mainly because they influence what takes place in classrooms and in other school settings. Indeed, most social scientists and educators now agree that the school-related factors which are most important in influencing learning and psychosocial development during adolescence concern the more immediate environment of the school and classroom. In good schools, the classroom environments encourage dialogue between teachers and students and among students, and learning is emphasized over memorization (Newmann et al., 1996). Various aspects of the **school climate** have important effects on youngsters' learning and achievement (Rutter, 1983). Specifically, the way teachers interact with students, the way classroom time is used, and the sorts of standards and expectations that teachers hold for their students are all more important than the size of the school, the way that age groups are combined, and the racial composition of the school. One reason that tracking makes a difference, for example, is that classes in different tracks have very different climates.

What sort of climate brings out the best in students? Considered together, the results of several studies indicate that the same factors which influence positive adolescent adjustment at home appear to be important at school. Specifically, students achieve and

are engaged more in school more when they attend schools that are *responsive* and *demanding*. Moreover, academic functioning and psychological adjustment affect each other, so that a positive school climate—where relationships between students and teachers are positive, teachers are supportive, and teachers are demanding—enhances adolescents' psychological well-being, as well as their achievement (Blum & Rinehart, 2000; Phillips, 1997; Roeser & Eccles, 1998; Roeser, Eccles, & Sameroff, 1999; Rowan, Chiang, & Miller, 1997).

Generally speaking, both students and teachers are more satisfied in classes that combine a moderate degree of structure with high student involvement and high teacher support. In these classes, teachers encourage their students' participation but do not let the class get out of control. Classes that are too task-oriented—particularly when they also emphasize teacher control—tend to make students feel anxious, uninterested, and unhappy (Moos, 1978). The pattern of classroom variables that is associated with positive student behavior and attitudes, then, is reminiscent of the *authoritative* family environment (see chapter 4). Similarly, an overemphasis on control in the classroom in the absence of support is reminiscent of the *authoritarian* family, whereas a lack of clarity and organization is reminiscent of both the *indulgent* family and the *indifferent family*—and these styles may affect adolescents detrimentally. Students do best when their teachers spend a high proportion of time on lessons (rather than on setting up equipment or dealing with discipline problems) and when teachers begin and end lessons on time, provide clear feedback to students about what is expected of them and about their performance, and give ample praise to students when they perform well (Rutter, 1983). A good high school teacher, in other words, bears a striking resemblance to a good parent (Wentzel, 1997).

Students in schools in which teachers are supportive but firm and maintain high, well-defined standards for behavior and academic work have stronger bonds to their school and more positive achievement motives; these beliefs and emotions, in turn, lead to fewer problems, better attendance, lower rates of delinquency, and higher scores on tests of achievement (see figure 6.3) (Roeser et al., 1996). This pattern is remarkably similar to that uncovered in studies comparing public and private high schools (Coleman et al., 1982). In these studies, too, the students' achievement was higher in schools that were somewhat more structured and demanding—no matter whether the school was public or private.

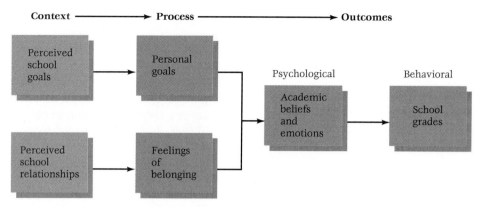

Figure 6.3   *A positive school climate fosters students' feelings of belonging and strengthens their feelings of academic efficacy. These feelings, in turn, lead to better school performance.* (Roeser et al., 1996)

Unfortunately, many students attend schools in which serious disruption—even violence—is an all too prevalent feature of the school climate (Noguera, 1995; Vaughan et al., 1996). According to a national survey of secondary school students in American public schools, one out of every four students has been a victim of violence in or around school, and one out of six is worried about being physically attacked or hurt while in school. Nearly one-third of the boys surveyed reported having carried a weapon to school (Everett & Price, 1995). Fifty years ago, teachers expressed concerns about such disciplinary problems as students chewing gum, talking out of turn, and making noise; today, when teachers are surveyed about disciplinary problems in their schools, they list such things as rape, robbery, and assault (Toch, 1993). Some writers contend that the new, get-tough approach to violence prevention in schools has only made the situation worse and that school violence is more effectively reduced through programs that attempt to create a more humane climate (Noguera, 1995).

In addition to research on school climate, several studies also point to the importance of teachers' expectations of students. When teachers expect more of their students, the students actually learn more; when teachers expect less, students learn less. This phenomenon is known as the **self-fulfilling prophecy** (Rosenthal & Jacobson, 1968) (see the accompanying box on pages 218–219). The self-fulfilling prophecy appears to be an especially strong influence on the school performance of weaker students, both with respect to the positive impact of high teacher expectations and to the negative impact of low expectations (Madon, Jussim, & Eccles, 1997; Rowan et al., 1997).

Because teachers' expectations influence student performance, it is important to understand where these expectations come from. Unfortunately, research suggests that teachers are likely to base their expectations in part on students' ethnic and socioeconomic backgrounds. In much the same way that these factors may influence tracking decisions, they may consciously and unconsciously shape teachers' expectations, which, in turn, affect students' learning. Thus, for example, teachers may call on poor or minority students less often than they call on affluent or white students—conveying a not-so-subtle message about whose responses the teacher believes are more worthy of class attention (Good & Brophy, 1984). It is not difficult to see how years of exposure to this sort of treatment can adversely affect a student's self-concept and interest in school. Indeed, teachers' biases may make it difficult for students from lower socioeconomic groups to attain a level of academic accomplishment that would permit upward mobility.

Several writers have suggested that, if we want to understand the impact of classroom climate on student achievement, we need to understand better how to enhance **student engagement**—the extent to which students are psychologically committed to learning and mastering the material, rather than simply completing the assigned work (Newmann, 1992; Newmann et al., 1996; Steinberg et al., 1996). Students frequently say they are bored while in school, a complaint that is especially strong among high school students, who find school far more boring than do middle school students. As you can see in figure 6.4, students are bored for most of the time on weekdays between 8 A.M. and 3 P.M., and the improvement in their mood seems to have more to do with the school day ending than with any special activity that takes place in the evening. Many experts

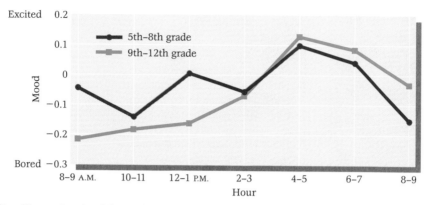

Figure 6.4 *Studies of fluctuations in adolescents' mood over the course of the day show that students—especially high school students—feel bored most of the time they are in school. (Note: Times are rounded to the nearest hour.)* (Larson & Richards, 1998)

believe that the make-work, routinized, rigid structure of most classrooms, in which teachers lecture at students, rather than engage them in discussion, alienates most students from school and undermines their desire to achieve. As one student explains,

> What do I like least about school? Basically, it's boring. Like English. What we do in there—we're supposed to read something, and then maybe do something in your notebook, when you could do everything at home. So I don't really have to show up. So, I'd say that class could be about 10 minutes long. (Brown, Lamborn, & Newmann, 1992)

The notion that many students feel disengaged from school—unchallenged and bored—has been borne out in numerous studies of contemporary American students (e.g., Owen, 1995; Steinberg, 1996). According to a recent study, entitled *Getting By: What American Teenagers Really Think About Their Schools,*

> Students routinely admitted—some with bravado and some with chagrin—that they calibrate their efforts, often meticulously, to do only as much as it takes to get the grade they can live with. For youngsters aiming for private colleges or elite public universities, this concept of "getting by" implies a certain grade-point average.... Other youngsters ... seem satisfied with any passing grade.... [S]tudents from across the country repeatedly said that they could "earn" acceptable grades, pass their courses, and receive a diploma, all while investing minimal effort in their school work.... [A]lmost two-thirds of teens across the country (65%) say they could do better in school if they tried harder. (Public Agenda, 1997, p. 20)

Think back to your own high school experience. What distinguished the good classes from the tedious ones? Newmann (1992) suggests a number of specific factors that contribute to student engagement. First, teachers need to provide opportunities for students to genuinely display their competencies. Second, schools should try to facilitate students' feelings of belonging to their school. Finally, and most important, teachers should assign work that is "authentic" —work that is interesting, fun, and relevant to the real world. There is nothing more alienating to a student than being asked to perform tasks that are boring, colorless, and irrelevant.

Teachers and school personnel, of course, are not the only influences on adolescents' behavior in school. Several writers have noted that the peer group's values and norms also exert an important influence, especially in high school (Bishop, 1999; Steinberg et al., 1996). In *The Adolescent Society* (1961), for example, James Coleman found that high schools vary a great deal in the extent to which the prevailing peer culture emphasizes academic success as a route toward status and popularity. In schools in which academic success is not valued by the student body, students are less likely to achieve grades that are consonant with their tested ability. In other words, a bright student who attends a school in which getting good grades is frowned upon by other students will actually get lower grades than he or she would in a school in which scholastic success is generally admired.

As noted in chapter 5, however, cliques and crowds differ enormously in the extent to which they encourage or discourage academic success (Clasen & Brown, 1985). It is therefore misleading to generalize about the impact of peer groups on adolescents' engagement in school without knowing more about the specific peer group in question. Some peer groups (e.g., the "brains") may place a great deal of pressure on their

Teacher Expectations and Student Performance

Although researchers have documented a link between teachers' expectations for their students and their students' performance, it is not clear whether this connection exists because teacher expectations create self-fulfilling prophecies that ultimately influence student achievement, or, instead, because teachers' expectations are genuinely accurate reflections of students' ability. One study of nearly 2,000 early adolescents in Michigan attempted to disentangle these two explanations.

Psychologists Lee Jussim and Jacquelynne Eccles (1992) gathered information from teachers and stu-

dents at several points in time in order to look at the over-time relation between teacher expectations and student performance. A longitudinal design, in which the same students were followed over time, was necessary for this research, because a cross-sectional study, in which one might examine the correlation at one point in time between teacher expectations and student performance, would not reveal which came first (that is, whether expectations preceded performance or performance preceded expectations). Because the researchers had information about student achievement both before and after the assessment of

members to succeed in school and may engage in behaviors (e.g., studying together) that promote academic success. Other groups, in contrast, may actively discourage scholastic efforts and success. An especially telling example of this is seen in a now-classic ethnographic study of African American male peer groups in an inner-city school (Fordham & Ogbu, 1986). In the peer groups studied, pressure was put on the group members not to achieve, because succeeding in school was seen as "acting white" and breaking from the group's ethnic identity. Thus, the students with high aspirations found themselves having to choose between succeeding in school and keeping their friends, a position that few adolescents of any race or ethnicity would want to find themselves in.

Other researchers have focused on adolescents' experiences outside of school—at home, at work, and in extracurricular activities—and on the impact of those experiences on their school achievement and engagement. This research demonstrates that the impact of school on adolescent achievement cannot be understood in isolation. Studies show, for example, that students whose parents are involved in school activities (such as parent-teacher conferences and "back-to-school" nights), who encourage and emphasize academic success, and who use authoritative parenting practices (see chapter 4) do better than their peers in secondary school (Dornbusch, Ritter, Liederman,

Roberts, & Fraleigh, 1987; Seginer, 1983; Steinberg, Lamborn, Dornbusch, & Darling, 1992; Stevenson & Baker, 1987). In chapter 7, we will look more closely at the effects of employment and extracurricular participation on school achievement; suffice it to say here that students who overextend themselves on the job or the playing field may inadvertently jeopardize their school performance (Brown et al., 1992; Steinberg & Dornbusch, 1991).

RECAP

Researchers agree that the climate of the school is more important than its organization or structure. Effective teachers are like authoritative parents—they are warm, firm, and fair—and they have high expectations for student performance. Students are also more likely to be engaged in school when they have opportunities for developing their competencies, when they feel attached to the school as an institution, and when they are engaged in authentic work, rather than make-work. Studies also show that students perform better in school when their peers value academic achievement and when their involvement in activities that compete with school is kept to a minimum. Unfortunately, many studies of American high school students indicate that they find school boring and undemanding.

teacher expectations, they were able to look at both possible pathways.

Data about student achievement were gathered at the end of fifth grade and at the beginning of sixth grade and, again, at the end of sixth grade and the beginning of seventh grade. Data about teacher expectations were gathered during October of the students' sixth grade. If teachers' expectations are accurate, the researchers argued, there should be a correlation between student achievement before sixth grade and teacher expectations in October. If teachers' expectations really influence students' achievement, the researchers reasoned, the October expectations should predict student performance later in the year, even after taking into account student performance before teacher expectations were measured.

The researchers found support for both possibilities. The teachers' expectations were accurate, in that student achievement in the fifth grade predicted both teacher expectations in the sixth grade and student achievement in the sixth grade. However, these very expectations, in turn, further influenced student performance, because teacher expectations in October predicted whether and how much student achievement changed over the course of the year. Which pathway was more powerful? Based on the size of the various correlations they computed, the researchers concluded that about 80 percent of the connection between teacher expectations and student achievement results from teachers' having accurate perceptions, whereas about 20 percent is an effect of the self-fulfilling prophecy. The self-fulfilling prophecy

appears to be somewhat stronger for academically weaker students, whose performance is more tied to teacher expectations (Madon et al., 1997).

Even though the self-fulfilling prophecy effect is relatively small, it may be quite powerful, as the researchers point out, when accumulated over years of schooling. If teachers' expectations are unfairly based on characteristics such as students' gender, ethnicity, or socioeconomic background, the over-time effect of having teachers with low expectations may be quite substantial.

Source: Jussim, L., & Eccles, J. (1992). Teacher expectations II: Construction and reflection of student achievement. *Journal of Personality and Social Psychology, 63,* 947–961.

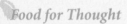

Food for Thought

Describe the elements of a school climate that is favorable to learning. Given the consistency with which these factors appear in research on good schools, why do you think classrooms in which students feel genuinely engaged are so rare?

BEYOND HIGH SCHOOL

The College-Bound

The early part of the twentieth century was an important time in the development not only of secondary schools but also of postsecondary educational institutions in the United States. Although colleges and, to a lesser extent, universities had existed for some time previously, not until the latter part of the nineteenth century did diversity in institutions of higher education begin to develop. Early postsecondary institutions were typically small, private liberal arts academies, often with a strong theological emphasis. However, during a relatively brief period bridging the nineteenth and twentieth centuries, these colleges were joined by a host

of other types of institutions, including large private universities, technical colleges, professional schools, publicly financed state universities, land-grant colleges, urban universities, and two-year community colleges (Brubacher & Rudy, 1976).

Although postsecondary educational institutions multiplied and became more varied during the early part of the twentieth century, enrollment in college was still a privilege enjoyed by very few young people. In 1900, only 4 percent of the 18- to 21-year-old population was enrolled in college; by 1930, the proportion had grown to only 12 percent. Even as recently as 1950, fewer than one in five young people were enrolled in college (Church, 1976). During the first half of the twentieth century, then, colleges and universities were not prominent in the lives of most American youth.

How different the state of affairs is today. Paralleling the rise of secondary education between 1920 and 1940, postsecondary education grew dramatically between 1950 and 1970. By 1960, one-third of all young people were entering college directly after high school graduation. College enrollments, which numbered about 1 million in 1930, had risen to more than 3 million by 1960 and to nearly 8.5 million by 1970. Today, two-thirds of young people who are high school graduates enroll in college immediately after graduation (National Center for Education Statistics, 1999b). Although there were large increases in the enrollment of

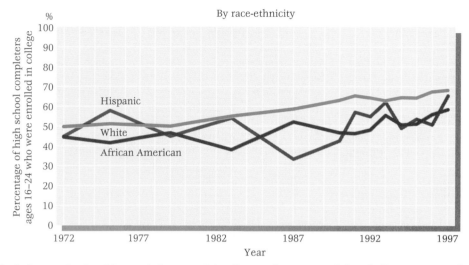

Figure 6.5   In the last two decades of the twentieth century, U.S. college enrollments expanded markedly. By 1997, two-thirds of all high school graduates were enrolling in college in the fall following high school graduation. (National Center for Education Statistics, 1999a)

minority youth during the 1970s, the proportion of minority youth enrolled in higher education fell during the early 1980s, primarily because of reductions in the availability of financial aid (Baker & Velez, 1996). The proportion of African American and Hispanic high school graduates enrolled in college has increased somewhat in recent years, however (National Center for Education Statistics, 1999b) (see figure 6.5).

If there are two dominant characteristics that distinguish the development of postsecondary education in contemporary America from that in other parts of the world, they are diversity and accessibility (Brubacher & Rudy, 1976). In countries other than the United States, postsecondary education is likely to be monopolized by monolithic public universities, and fewer adolescents continue their formal education beyond high school (President's Science Advisory Committee, 1974). Individuals are often separated into college- and noncollege-bound tracks early in adolescence, typically on the basis of standardized national examinations. In fact, rather than housing all high school students in comprehensive high schools such as those found in the United States, many European nations separate students during early adolescence into schools for college-bound youngsters and schools designed to provide vocational and technical education.

Although the accessibility and diversity of its postsecondary educational institutions have been commended by many, the American system of higher education has not been without its critics (Brubacher & Rudy, 1976). Some observers have suggested that edu-

cational diversity has been gained at the expense of quality. With so many different options and electives for young people to choose among, it has been hard for colleges to ensure that all students receive a high-quality education. Others have pointed out that it is difficult for many young people to obtain adequate information about the range of alternatives open to them and that students are often poorly matched with the colleges they enter (Boyer, 1986). The large enrollments of high schools make it difficult for school counselors to give each student individualized advice.

In some respects, the transition from high school to college parallels the transition from elementary to secondary school. For many students, going to college means entering an even larger, more formidable, and more impersonal environment. For some, the transition may coincide with other life changes, such as leaving home, breaking off or beginning an important relationship, and having to manage one's own residence or finances for the first time.

As a consequence of all of these factors, although many more young people enroll in college today than in previous years, a very large number do not graduate. Perhaps as a consequence of increasing accessibility, poor matching, and a lack of "consumer" knowledge among college applicants, rates of college attrition are high: 3 out of every 10 students who enter college in the United States leave after one year. Of the students who leave after one year, about half eventually finish their degree program, either returning to that particular college or transferring to another. Half, however, never finish. In other words, although a great deal has been done to make college entrance more likely, rates of college graduation lag far behind rates of enrollment.

The Forgotten Half

The problems associated with moving from high school to college pale in comparison with the problems associated with not going to college at all. In general, college graduates earn substantially more income over their lifetimes than do individuals who attend college but do not graduate, and these individuals in turn earn much more than students who do not attend college at all (William T. Grant Foundation, 1988). Individuals who drop out of high school before graduation suffer a wide range of problems, which we will examine in detail in chapter 13.

One of the unfortunate by-products of making postsecondary education so accessible—and so expected—is that education policy-makers have turned their backs on individuals who do not graduate from college, even though they compose about half of the adolescent population—approximately 20 million individuals (William T. Grant Foundation, 1988). This so-called **Forgotten Half** was the subject of a lengthy and detailed study conducted in the late 1980s by a prestigious national commission.

The report concluded that American secondary schools are geared almost exclusively toward college-bound youngsters. Opportunities for learning and for higher-order thinking are much greater in college-prep classes than in the general or vocational tracks. In addition to this, the commission noted that students who are not headed for college—some by choice, others by unavoidable circumstance—find that their high schools have not prepared them at all for the world of work. Even those who complete school and earn a diploma—who have done what they were supposed to do as adolescents —may have a hard time finding employment and a nearly impossible time finding a satisfying, well-paying job. As a consequence, many individuals who make up the Forgotten Half spend their early adult years floundering between periods of part-time work, underemployment (working at a job that is less challenging than one would like), and unemployment. By the time they are 25 or so, most have found steady, if low-paying, employment. But they may have spent six or seven years living very close to the edge, if not in genuine poverty.

One important factor contributing to the difficulties faced by of the Forgotten Half has been the change in the world of work: As manufacturing jobs began to be re-placed by minimum-wage service jobs during the second half of the twentieth century, the chances of making a decent living without college experience worsened appreciably. Today, many young adults without college experience must try to make ends meet on minimum-wage jobs—jobs that offer little in the way of promotion or advancement. The economic problems faced by non-college-bound youth have been compounded by the escalating costs of such essentials as housing and health care.

Given the high dropout rate already characteristic of most colleges, the answers to the problems of the Forgotten Half does not seem to be simply to encourage more individuals to continue their education past high school. Obviously, for those who want postsecondary education, every attempt should be made to see that they can obtain and afford it. But what about the adolescents who just are not interested in a college degree? How can these individuals be helped?

Experts believe that one potential answer involves strengthening the links between the worlds of school and work during high school, as we discussed in chapter 3. In most other industrialized countries, non-college-bound youth begin apprenticeships during their last two years of compulsory school, so that, by the time they have completed their formal schooling, they are well trained to take on skilled jobs (Hamilton, 1990). Instead of just dumping such adolescents into the labor force at graduation, as we do in America, schools and communities provide training, career counseling, and job placement services throughout high school. In most contemporary American high schools, counseling is geared toward helping college-bound students continue their education. Some critics have suggested that we should spend just as much time helping the other 50 percent of the adolescents make their transition into adulthood as smooth as possible.

RECAP

About two-thirds of all American adolescents go on to education beyond high school, but many students drop out after their first year of postsecondary education, probably because of a mismatch between their needs and the school environment. More worrisome, perhaps, is the experience of adolescents who do not attend college. Many social critics believe that high schools as they are presently structured do not serve noncollege-bound adolescents very well. As a result, half of the country's adolescents—the so-called Forgotten Half—leave high school without adequate preparation for the world of work they hope to enter.

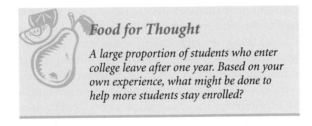

SCHOOLS AND ADOLESCENT DEVELOPMENT

Whatever the shortcomings of schools may be, staying in school is preferable to dropping out, not only in terms of earnings but in terms of cognitive development as well. One study contrasted the performance of dropouts and graduates on a battery of standardized tests of achievement administered during late adolescence (Alexander, Natriello, & Pallas, 1985). The study took into account the differences in achievement levels that existed before the dropouts had left school (two years before the assessment was conducted), because dropouts are more likely than graduates to show achievement problems early in their education. Compared with the dropouts, adolescents who stayed in school gained far more intellectually over the two-year interval in a variety of content areas. More important, the results showed that the adverse effects of dropping out were most intense among socioeconomically disadvantaged students. Paradoxically, then, the students who are most likely to leave school prior to graduation may be most harmed by doing so.

One other way of assessing the contribution of schools to adolescents' intellectual development is by comparing early adolescents' intellectual gains during the school year with their gains during the summer. Several studies have done just this (e.g., Cooper, Charlton, Valentine, & Muhlenbruck, 2000). Using information about the academic progress of students measured at three points in time—the beginning of the school year, the end of the school year, and the beginning of the next year—researchers are able to see how the academic progress of students during the summer compared with their academic progress during the school session. Among students from higher social classes, rates of academic progress during the school year and during the summer are comparable. Among disadvantaged students, however, the pattern is different. Although rates of progress during the school year are more or less equal to those of higher-SES students, during the summer months disadvantaged students' scores decline. In other words, if it were not for the effects of school on cognitive development, the discrepancy between affluent and poor youngsters' achievement scores would be much greater than it currently is. One benefit of summer school for disadvantaged students is that it diminishes the decline in achievement that would otherwise occur between the spring and fall semesters (Cooper et al., 2000) (see figure 6.6).

Far less is known about the impact of schools on the psychosocial development of adolescents. Some

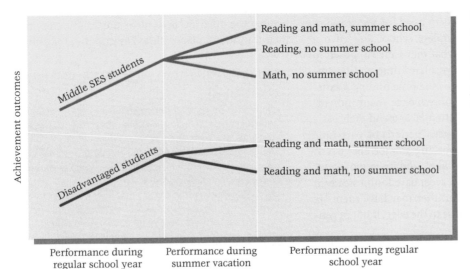

Figure 6.6 Summer school for disadvantaged students may prevent the achievement gap between affluent and poor students from widening. (Cooper et al., 2000)

observers have noted that most schools are not structured to promote psychosocial development, with their excessive focus on conformity and obedience and their lack of encouragement for creativity, independence, and self-reliance (Friedenberg, 1967). This certainly comes through loud and clear when adolescents are asked about their classroom experiences. But there are very many good schools, in which students not only learn the academic material taught in classes but also learn about themselves, their relationships with others, and their society. Schools differ from each other, and it is difficult to generalize about the impact of schools on adolescent development without knowing more about the particular school in question.

It is also important to recognize that, despite adults' intentions and objectives, students do not view school solely in terms of its academic agenda. In one study, the researchers asked a sample of seventh- through twelfth-graders to list the best and worst things about school. The best things? "Being with my friends" and "meeting new people." The worst? Homework, tests, and the school's restrictive atmosphere (Brown et al., 1992). Adults may evaluate schools in terms of their contribution to adolescents' cognitive and career development, but for the typical adolescent, school is the main setting for socializing. When we ask about the consequences of leaving school early, we must take into account the impact this has on the individual's social, as well as cognitive, development.

Studies also show that students' experiences within a school can vary widely according to the track they are in, the peer group they belong to, and the extracurricular activities in which they participate. It seems safe to say that academically talented and economically advantaged students have a more positive experience in school than do their less capable or less affluent counterparts—positive not only with respect to what they learn in class but also with respect to the impact of school on their feelings about themselves as individuals. Their teachers pay more attention to them, they are more likely to hold positions of leadership in extracurricular organizations, and they are more likely to experience classes that are engaging and challenging. In other words, the structure of a school—its size, its tracking policy, and its curricula—provides different intellectual and psychosocial opportunities for students who occupy different places within that structure. Not surprisingly, a study of Swedish adolescents found a great deal of variability in students' feeling about school: About 25 percent enjoyed school a great deal, about 25 percent detested school (and felt that their friends in school were their only salvation), and the remainder felt ambivalent (Andersson, 1994). The best answer to the question "How do schools affect adolescent development?" then, is another question: "Which schools, which adolescents, and in what respects?"

Web Researcher   What is the average class size in elementary schools, high schools, liberal arts colleges, and large universities? How many students do teachers in each of these institutions see in a week? How much time do they spend with each student? How might these differences relate to the goals and means of instruction, the types of assignments teachers give, and students' experience in the classroom? Go to www.mhhe.com/steinberg6 for further information.

KEY TERMS

charter schools

comprehensive high school

education vouchers

Forgotten Half

gifted students

higher-order thinking

junior high school

learning disability

mainstreaming

middle school

school climate

secondary education

self-fulfilling prophecy

social capital

student engagement

tracking

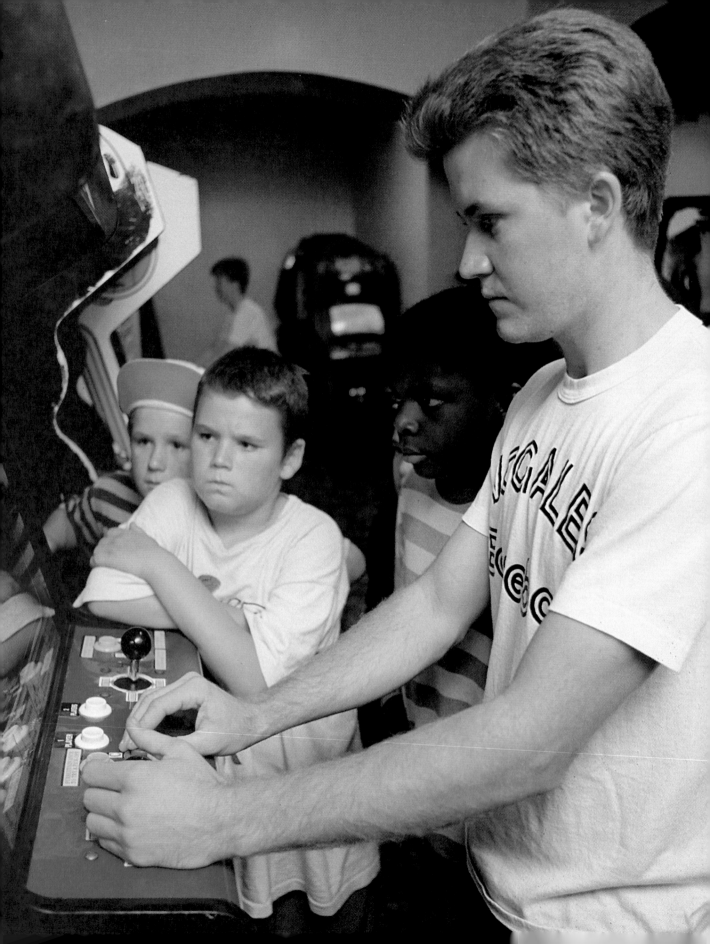

Chapter 7

Work and Leisure

There is no question that the family, the peer group, and the school exert a profound influence on the development and behavior of young people. Yet it may surprise you to learn that today's teenagers spend more time in leisure activities than they do in the "productive" activities of school, more time alone than with members of their family, about four times the number of hours each week on a part-time job as on homework, and considerably more time "wired" to music, the Internet, or television than "tuned into" the classroom (Carnegie Council on Adolescent Development, 1992; Csikszentmihalyi & Larson, 1984; Roberts, Foehr, Rideout, & Brodie, 1999). In this chapter, we will look at these other important contexts of adolescence—the contexts of work and leisure.

Social scientists have only recently begun to study systematically the ways in which work and leisure influence adolescent development (Brown & Cantor, 2000; Larson & Verma, 1999; Roberts et al., 1999; Steinberg & Cauffman, 1995). Perhaps because we historically have considered school to be the most important activity of adolescence in contemporary society, we have paid far less attention to what adolescents do in their spare time—even though their spare time occupies more of their waking hours than does their time in school. As you know, however, one of the hallmarks of life in industrialized society is that adolescents have considerable amounts of time and money to devote to activities of their choosing. Among the most popular are working at a part-time job, participating in an after-school extracurricular activity, shopping and hanging out with friends, and enjoying one or more of the mass media, including television, radio, movies, recorded music and video, video games, and, increasingly, the Internet. ●

WORK AND LEISURE IN CONTEMPORARY SOCIETY

The significant level of discretionary, or free, time in the lives of contemporary adolescents has several origins. Ironically, one of the most important contributors was the development of compulsory schooling. Prior to this, adolescents were expected to work full-time, and most maintained schedules comparable to those of adults, working long hours each week. With the spread of high schools during the early decades of the twentieth century, however, adolescents were, in effect, barred from the labor force; the part-time jobs familiar to us today simply did not exist in large numbers, making after-school employment relatively rare. One indirect effect of compulsory high school, then, was to increase the amount of free time available to young people—time that previously would have been occupied by work. Indeed, adults were so worried about the free time available to adolescents that they began to organize various youth clubs and activities—such as the Boy Scouts and organized sports—in order to occupy their "idle hands" (Hine, 1999; Modell & Goodman, 1990). In some respects, organized leisure became an institutionalized part of adolescence as a supplement to school and a replacement for full-time employment.

A second influence on the rise of free time for adolescents in contemporary society was the increased affluence of Americans following World War II. As noted in Chapter 3, the invention of the "teenager"—and, more important, the discovery of the teenager by those in media advertising and marketing—changed the nature of adolescence in modern society. As adolescents gained more autonomy, they came to be recognized as consumers with plenty of discretionary income, an accurate image that persists today (Zollo, 1999). This week, notice the commercials and advertisements aimed at teenagers on television shows, in magazines, on radio, or on the Internet. You'll see that much of the advertising targeted toward young people concerns leisure expenditures: music, movies, fast food, cosmetics, and athletic equipment.

How much time do adolescents spend in various leisure activities? According to one study, in which adolescents were asked to monitor their time use with electronic pagers, the typical American middle-class adolescent early adolescent spends about 29 percent of his or her waking hours in productive activities, such as attending class and studying; about 24 percent in maintenance activities, such as grooming, eating, and running errands; and about 46 percent in leisure activities, such as socializing, watching TV, and playing sports (Larson et al., 1999) (see figure 7.1). As you can see, inner-city African American teenagers spend relatively less time in productive activities (especially in school-related activities) and relatively more time in leisure (especially watching television).

American adolescents spend far more time on leisure, and far less time in productive activities, than their counterparts in other countries. American students' use of their time out of school for school-related activities is especially low. For instance, the average American high school student spends fewer than five hours per week on homework; in Asian countries, such as India, Taiwan, and Japan, the average is between four

**Suburban, middle-class
white teenagers**

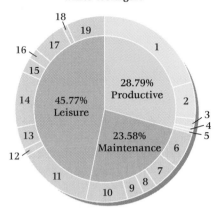

**Urban, poor
African American teenagers**

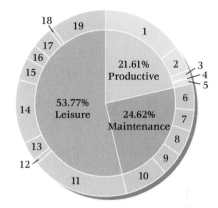

1 Classwork 19.92%	1 Classwork 14.74%
2 Homework 6.23%	2 Homework 4.48%
3 Extracurricular activities (includes school assemblies) 1.58%	3 Extracurricular activities (includes school assemblies) 1.13%
4 Working for pay (includes babysitting) 0.56%	4 Working for pay (includes babysitting) 0.27%
5 Religious activities 0.49%	5 Religious activities 0.99%
6 Eating 6.19%	6 Eating 4.53%
7 Transportation (includes walking) 4.63%	7 Transportation (includes walking) 3.76%
8 Resting 2.52%	8 Resting 4.46%
9 Chores and errands 2.92%	9 Chores and errands 3.99%
10 Personal maintenance 7.33%	10 Personal maintenance 7.89%
11 Television viewing 13.00%	11 Television viewing 17.53%
12 Music listening 1.27%	12 Music listening 0.83%
13 Creative activities 3.82%	13 Creative activities 3.34%
14 Talking 9.58%	14 Talking 11.12%
15 Playing 2.62%	15 Playing 3.97%
16 Playing games 1.83%	16 Playing games 2.55%
17 Playing sports (includes exercise, swimming, and other physical activities) 5.96%	17 Playing sports (includes exercise, swimming, and other physical activities) 3.73%
18 Public leisure (includes leisure shopping, attending a movie, outings) 0.89%	18 Public leisure (includes leisure shopping, attending a movie, outings) 0.77%
19 Idling (includes doing nothing, thinking, waiting) 6.79%	19 Idling (includes doing nothing, thinking, waiting) 9.94%

Figure 7.1   How suburban and urban adolescents spend their time. (Larson et al., 1999)

and five hours per *day* (Larson & Verma, 1999). And European and Asian adolescents spend almost three times more hours each week reading for pleasure than American adolescents (Larson & Verma, 1999). In contrast, American teenagers spend relatively more time playing sports, socializing with friends, caring for their physical appearance, and working in after-school jobs (Alasker & Flammer, 1999; Flammer, Alasker, & Noack, 1999; Larson & Verma, 1999).

What is the effect of all this free time on adolescents' behavior and development? Are they learning about the real world from their part-time jobs? Are their extracurricular activities as character building as adults believe they are? Are they being driven toward sex and violence by the mass media? Are teenagers really affected by the lyrics of rock music, the images of MTV,

and the brutality of many video games? These are some of the questions we will examine in this chapter. We will begin with one of the most controversial issues in the study of contemporary adolescents: how teenagers are affected by after-school employment.

RECAP

The rise of compulsory schooling and the affluence of the adolescent population have contributed to the increased importance of both part-time employment and leisure activities in the lives of contemporary adolescents. Having large amounts of free time is one hallmark of adolescence in modern society, although the ways in which adolescents use their free time vary considerably around the world.

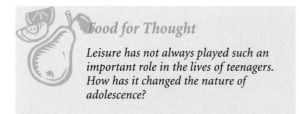

Food for Thought

Leisure has not always played such an important role in the lives of teenagers. How has it changed the nature of adolescence?

ADOLESCENTS AND WORK

Today, in the United States, it is commonplace to see teenagers working in restaurants and retail stores. Indeed, almost 80 percent of today's high school students will have worked before graduating (Steinberg & Cauffman, 1995). However, although working while attending high school may currently be the norm, only in the past three decades has part-time employment become widespread among American adolescents. In fact, the employment of students in present day America represents an important break from past eras, in which going to school and working were mutually exclusive activities.

School and Work in the Early Twentieth Century

Before 1925—when continuing on in high school was the exception, not the rule—most teenagers entered the workforce by the time they turned 15 years old. Teenagers from all but the most affluent families left school between the ages of 12 and 15 and became full-time workers (Horan & Hargis, 1991; Modell, Furstenberg, & Hershberg, 1976). Adolescents were either students or workers, but not both.

During the second quarter of the twentieth century, however, school began to replace the workplace as the

▲ *In previous eras, adolescents played an important role in farming. Early work experience of this sort readied young people for the work they would perform during adulthood.* (Bettmann)

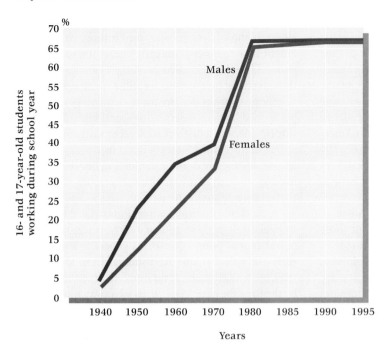

Figure 7.2 The proportion of U.S. high school students with jobs rose dramatically between 1940 and 1980. For the past 20 years, most U.S. high school students have held part-time jobs during the school year.

setting in which most adolescents spent their weekdays. As secondary education became more widespread among the social and economic segments of American society, more youngsters remained in school well into middle and late adolescence, and fewer elected to work. Compulsory education laws were passed in most states that required youngsters to remain in school until at least the age of 16. Part-time jobs were not plentiful, and a variety of child labor laws were enacted to restrict youngsters' employment (Kett, 1977). As a result of these social and legislative changes, the employment of American teenagers in the formal labor force declined steadily during the first four decades of the twentieth century. In 1940, for example, only 5 percent of 16- and 17-year-old male high school students worked during the school year. Less than 2 percent of the female students of this age were employed (U.S Bureau of the Census, 1940).

The Emergence of the Student-Worker

The situation began to change between 1940 and 1950. Following the end of World War II, the sectors of the American economy that needed large numbers of part-time employees expanded rapidly (Ginzberg, 1977). More than three out of every five new jobs cre-

ated between 1950 and 1977 were in retail trade or services, where many jobs are part-time. Employers, particularly in businesses such as fast-food restaurants, needed workers who were willing to work part-time for relatively low wages and for short work shifts. Many employers looked to teenagers to fill these jobs.

As shown in figure 7.2, the proportion of high school students holding part-time jobs rose dramatically between 1940 and 1980. In 1980, about two-thirds of all high school seniors and about half of all high school sophomores held part-time jobs during the school year (Lewin-Epstein, 1981). More recent estimates indicate that the proportion of working high school students has not changed appreciably since that time (Carr, Wright, & Brody, 1996; Mortimer & Johnson, 1998). By current estimates, at any one time during the school year, well over 6 million American high school students are working.

When you think of the typical working teenager, what image comes to mind—an adolescent from a poor family who relies on the teenager's income to make ends meet? Although in the past it was young people from less affluent families who were more likely to work, today the opposite is true (Keithly & Deseran, 1995; McNeal, 1997; Schoenhals, Tienda, & Schneider, 1998). Working during high school is slightly more common among middle- and upper-middle-class teenagers than among poor youth. Experts believe that this is because affluent youngsters have an easier time finding employment. Jobs in the adolescent workplace are more likely to be located in suburban areas, where the more affluent families reside. Working is also more common among white than among nonwhite students, with employment rates being lowest for African American youth. Male and female adolescents are equally likely to be employed, although they often work in very different types of jobs (McNeal, 1997; Steinberg & Cauffman, 1995).

Not only do more high school students work in contemporary society than in previous eras, but those who do are working for considerably more hours than adolescents have in the past (Greenberger & Steinberg, 1986; National Research Council, 1998). The average high school sophomore puts in close to 15 hours per week at a job, and the average senior works about 20 hours per week (Bachman et al., 1986; Barton, 1989; Lewin-Epstein, 1981; Steinberg & Cauffman, 1995). Considering that the average school day runs for about 6 hours, today's typical working adolescent is busy with school or work commitments for close to 50 hours a week.

Although youngsters in contemporary America do not enter the formal labor force until the age of 15 or 16, many individuals have worked on an informal basis during childhood, when most boys and girls are assigned chores around the house; this is especially common in less industrialized societies and, among industrialized nations, more common in Western than Asian countries (Larson & Verma, 1999; White & Brinkerhoff, 1981). By early adolescence, many youngsters have begun to take on informal employment outside the home for other family members or neighbors. Baby-sitting is a common source of income for many young adolescent girls, whereas gardening and lawn work are common among young adolescent boys (Greenberger & Steinberg, 1983; McNeal, 1997).

Teenage Employment in the United States and Other Nations

The extent and nature of teenage employment vary considerably from country to country. In most nonindustrialized societies, work life and family life are not as distinct as they are in contemporary America, and youngsters are typically integrated into the world of

work before they reach adolescence (Whiting & Whiting, 1975). If the society subsists on farming, children are taught how to farm at an early age. If the society subsists on hunting, children are taught how to hunt. Although young people who are still acquiring work skills may be given tasks that are more elementary than those performed by their elders, adolescents and adults work side by side, and a distinct adolescent workplace—such as that in the United States—is not usually found. Contemporary society draws a distinction between schooling and work; in many traditional societies, the two activities are essentially the same.

In developing nations, where industrialization is still in a relatively early stage and a large percentage of the population is poor, adolescents generally leave school early—at least by American standards. In these countries, most adolescents enter into full-time employment by the time they are 15 or 16, in jobs similar to the ones they will hold as adults. Very often, adolescents work for their families. The pattern in these countries closely resembles the United States during an earlier stage in its industrialization: school for adolescents of the extremely affluent and work for most other teenagers (Larson & Verma, 1999).

Other comparably industrialized countries provide the most interesting contrast with the United States. In other industrialized countries, adolescents are likely to defer employment until their education is completed. Thus, whereas about three-quarters of American high school juniors hold jobs during the school year, only one-quarter of Japanese and Taiwanese juniors do (Larson & Verma, 1999). Paid employment during the school year is even rarer in most European countries and virtually nonexistent in many, such as France, Hungary, Russia, and Switzerland (Alasker & Flammer, 1999; Flammer et al., 1999). In other industrialized countries, then, young people generally move from school directly into full-time employment without an intervening period of formal part-time work. In the United States, in contrast, it is more common for youngsters to move from full-time school with no formal employment (during early adolescence) to a combination of school and part-time work (during middle and late adolescence) to full-time work (during late adolescence or early adulthood).

Although European adolescents are less likely than their American counterparts to hold paying part-time jobs during the school year, they are more likely to work in school-sponsored or government-sponsored apprenticeships (Hamilton, 1990; Hamilton & Lempert, 1996; Kantor, 1994). In many countries, such as Germany, these apprenticeships play an extremely important role in preparing adolescents for the transition into adult employment, especially for students who are not bound for college. It is important to remember as you read this chapter that the studies of teen employment in the United States are typically studies of students who are working in part-time jobs that have little to do with the careers they hope to pursue after they complete their education. In contrast, in Europe, students' work experience is much more continuous with the roles they will enter as adults (Hamilton & Hurrelmann, 1994).

How can we account for these differences between the United States and other industrialized countries? First, part-time employment opportunities are not as readily available elsewhere as they are in America. Fast-food restaurants, although increasingly popular in other countries, are not seen on every major street. Second, the scheduling of part-time jobs in other countries is not well suited to the daily routines of students. In Europe, for example, the school day lasts well into the late afternoon, and relatively few shops are open in the evenings. In the United States, many adolescents leave school early in the afternoon and go straight to their part-time jobs, where they work until 9 or 10 o'clock in the evening. Third, in most other industrialized countries, the employment of children is associated with being poor, and there is a strong stigma attached to having one's children work. Many middle-class parents do not feel that it is appropriate for their children to have jobs while attending school. Fourth, schools in countries other than the United States demand much more out-of-school time (Steinberg, 1996). Finally, as noted in chapter 6, American schools have not done a very good job of anticipating the needs of adolescents who do not intend to go to college. As a result, formal apprenticeship programs, such as those found in most other industrialized countries, are quite rare in the United States; one of the only ways for American adolescents to gain work experience is through part-time jobs. The school-to-work transition is far more systematic, and far more effective, in most European countries than in the United States (Hamilton & Hurrelmann, 1994; Rosenbaum, 1996). Although having a part-time job while in high school has a positive impact on employment in young adulthood, the effect is very, very small, and it comes at a price (Carr et al., 1996).

RECAP

Today, most American teenagers hold part-time jobs during the school year, and many work more than 20 hours weekly. This is an important departure from the recent past, when it was unlikely for students to work. This is also a departure from the case in most other industrialized countries, where student employment is quite rare. Students in other countries are more likely to gain work experience through structured apprenticeship programs in career-related jobs.

Food for Thought

Student employment is far more common in the United States than elsewhere. Does this have a great effect on the nature of adolescence in these different contexts?

The Adolescent Workplace Today

● **Common Adolescent Jobs**   The range of jobs open to American adolescents who wish to work in the formal labor force is rather limited, and surveys indicate that the proportion of adolescents who hold challenging or interesting jobs is very, very small. Most studies of contemporary youth indicate that the vast majority are employed in the retail and service industries, although, as one would expect, there are important differences according to region, age, and gender. In general, older working students are more likely to hold formal jobs (e.g., retail or food-service work) than are younger working students, who are more likely to hold informal jobs (e.g., baby-sitting, yard work) (Greenberger & Steinberg, 1986; Mortimer, Finch, Shanahan, & Ryu, 1992; Schneider & Shouse, 1991). As expected, working teenagers who live in rural areas are more likely to be employed in agricultural occupations than are their urban or suburban counterparts. Also, boys are more likely to work in manual labor than are girls, who are more likely than boys to work in service positions (see the accompanying box) (Greenberger & Steinberg, 1986; McNeal, 1997).

These differences notwithstanding, it is important to recognize that a very small number of different sorts of jobs accounts for a very large proportion of today's student workers. According to data from government

Leisure, Work, and Sex-Role Socialization

Many work and leisure activities—especially those organized and controlled by adults—are designed to socialize adolescents into adult roles, including, quite often, traditional sex roles. For example, virtually all forms of mass media, from television and film to magazines and video games, are targeted separately at boys or girls. Studies show that traditional sex-role socialization takes place in extracurricular and work settings as well.

Sociologist Donna Eder (Eder & Kinney, 1995; Eder & Parker, 1987), for example, has studied sex-role socialization in high school extracurricular activities. In an extensive ethnographic study of a secondary school, she and her colleagues examined how different extracurricular activities were viewed within the school, and they studied the values that were communicated to adolescents through those activities.

In the school they studied, as in many others, athletics were the chief route to popularity and status for boys. But which values were communicated through team sports? An analysis of interactions during practice and during other free periods (e.g., lunch time) revealed that the culture of boys' athletics emphasized achievement, toughness, dominance, and competition—all traits that society has traditionally valued in the socialization of adult males. Consider, for example, the following observation taken from the researchers' field notes during football practice:

A player came up to a coach as practice was just beginning and complained that another player was starting a fight with him. The coach seemed aggravated at having to deal with this and told him to "knock his socks off in practice." This player was

▲ *Many of the articles and advertisements contained in magazines read by adolescent girls convey the message that physical beauty is the road to true happiness.* (Michael Newman/PhotoEdit)

not particularly satisfied with the suggestion but realized that was all he could get from Coach James. (Eder & Parker, 1987, p. 205)

In contrast, although aggression and competitiveness were valued within girls' sports, athletics were not a route toward popularity or status for the girls in the school; as a consequence, these traits were less likely to be socialized among the girls. For instance, on days when "big" games were to be played by the boys' teams, team members wore their athletic jerseys to school, so that they would be recognized by their peers. On days when the girls' teams had "big" games, however, the team members did not wear their jerseys. One reason was that being a member of an athletic team detracted from a girl's popularity (Eder & Kinney, 1995).

The main route toward popularity for the girls in this school was through cheerleading. Are the traits that were valued in this activity the ones traditionally stressed in the socialization of adult women? Consider the following observation recorded during cheerleading tryouts:

At one point, Mrs. Tolson started to tell them what they were going to be judged on, saying they would get 10 points (out of 50) for a "sparkle," which was their smile, personality, bubbliness, appearance, attractiveness—not that all cheerleaders had to be attractive, but it was important to have a clean appearance, not to be sloppy, have messy or greasy hair, because that doesn't look like a cheerleader. (Eder & Parker, 1987, p. 207)

These traits—appearance, neatness, and "bubbliness"—are all characteristics traditionally socialized in women. In essence, the popularity accorded the male athletes rewarded the boys for behaving in ways stereotypical for men, whereas the popularity accorded the female cheerleaders rewarded the girls for behaving in ways stereotypical for women.

You may be thinking that this difference in emphasis makes perfect sense, because football requires aggression and toughness and cheerleading requires "sparkle." However, as the researchers point out, it is "interesting that neatly combed hair was emphasized [in cheerleading tryouts], given the physical nature of this activity, which includes cartwheels and backflips. It is also interesting to compare the focus on neatness during cheerleading with the absence of this concern during male and female athletics" (Eder & Parker, 1987, p. 207). According to these researchers, an important reason for the difference between the emphases of football and cheerleading concerns the function of extracurricular activities in the socialization of male and female gender roles. Along similar lines, male and female athletes are more likely to be admired when they participate in "sex-appropriate" sports (Holland & Andre, 1994).

Interestingly, participation in athletics (until recently, a male-dominated activity) enhances the science achievement of high school girls, whereas participation in cheerleading (still today a female-dominated activity) hampers it. In contrast, boys' science achievement is unaffected by their athletic participation (Hanson & Kraus, 1998). One reason for this pattern of findings may be that female athletes acquire certain traits through athletic participation—independence, competition, and aggression—which help them compete in academic disciplines that have historically been dominated by males. High school boys, presumably, have many opportunities in addition to sports to develop these characteristics, since they are often socialized in males from an early age.

Similar results have emerged from analyses of the leading magazines aimed at adolescent girls (Brumberg, 1997; Evans, Rutberg, Sather, & Turner, 1991). Most articles in these magazines focus on dating and heterosexual relationships, and most emphasize the importance of physical attractiveness for young women. According to researchers, the articles and advertisements contained in these magazines convey a clear message that attracting males by being physically beautiful is the road to true happiness for women. In contrast, little space in magazines aimed at teenage girls is devoted to issues of education, to self-improvement in other than physical ways, and to matters of ethics. As in cheerleading, the emphasis in teen magazines aimed at girls is on cultivating that superficial "sparkle." Another analysis, of the fiction appearing in *Seventeen* magazine, found that, in most of the stories, the main character did not solve her own problems but, instead, depended on someone else to solve them for her. In these stories, as well, occupations were portrayed in traditionally sex-stereotyped terms (Pierce, 1993).

There are important differences between boys' and girls' work experiences as adolescents, too. As you may know, it is well documented that men and women typically work in different types of jobs and that men generally are paid higher wages—even when they do the same work as women. This disparity has been an important concern to many people, who feel that such sex differences in patterns of work are unfair and maintain economic inequities between the sexes. Are the same sorts of disparities found in teenagers' jobs? The answer seems to be yes (Greenberger & Steinberg, 1983; Lewin-Epstein, 1981).

Boys and girls are equally likely to be employed during the school year, but, generally speaking, they work at very different jobs (Greenberger & Steinberg, 1983; McNeal, 1997). Boys are more likely to work as manual laborers, skilled laborers, gardeners, busboys, janitors, and newspaper deliverers. Girls are more likely to be employed as food servers, house cleaners, and baby-sitters. Moreover, boys almost never work as secretaries, receptionists, baby-sitters, nurses' aides, or house cleaners, and girls almost never work as busgirls, dishwashers, gardeners, manual laborers, janitors, or newspaper deliverers. A study of more than 3,000 adolescents in southern California revealed that boys work longer hours than girls and that "boys'" jobs pay better than "girls'" jobs (Greenberger & Steinberg, 1983). Early work experience, like experience in extracurricular activities, reinforces and readies adolescent boys and girls for the sex roles they are likely to encounter as adults.

surveys, nearly 60 percent of employed eighth-graders work in one of two jobs: baby-sitting and lawn work (Schneider & Shouse, 1991). And job opportunities appear to be just as restricted for older workers: Restaurant work (such as a counter worker in a fast-food restaurant) and retail sales work (such as a cashier in a clothing store) account for nearly 60 percent of all working students (Steinberg, Fegley, & Dornbusch, 1993). Very few teenagers are employed on farms or in factories anymore (Charner & Fraser, 1987).

● **The Adolescent Work Environment**   What do adolescents learn on the job? In one series of studies of adolescents who work, a team of researchers examined teenagers' work environments (Greenberger & Steinberg, 1981; Greenberger, Steinberg, & Ruggiero, 1982). Most of the workers studied were employed in five types of work: food service (e.g., fast-food counter worker); clerical (e.g., file clerk in an office); retail (e.g., cashier in a store); manual labor (e.g., gardener); and skilled labor (e.g., assistant automobile mechanic). Using an elaborate coding system to record on-the-job activities, the researchers observed what went on in the work settings. They recorded the tasks that the adolescents performed (for example, "cleans table"), the things they said (for instance, "May I help you?"), and the people with whom they interacted (such as an adult customer). They also interviewed the adolescent workers and had them complete a series of questionnaires about their experiences at work.

The results of the studies were surprising. Unlike adolescents in traditional societies, whose work typically brings them into extensive contact with adults, the young people who were observed in these studies spent as much time on the job interacting with other adolescents as they did with their elders. In the typical fast-food restaurant, for example, nearly all the workers were teenagers, the supervisor was usually not much older, and the customers were often young people. Few of the teenage workers surveyed reported having formed close relationships with adults at work. They were unlikely to see their adult supervisors or co-workers outside of work; they felt reluctant to go to the adults at work with personal problems; and generally they reported feeling less close to adults at work than to other people in their lives (Greenberger & Steinberg, 1981).

The studies also indicated that most teenagers' jobs are pretty dreary. Few jobs permit adolescents to behave independently or make decisions; adolescents receive little instruction from their supervisors, and they are rarely required to use the skills they have been taught in school (Greenberger & Steinberg, 1986). With occasional exceptions, most teenagers' jobs are repetitive, monotonous, and unlikely to be intellectually stimulating. Some are even highly stressful, requiring that youngsters work under intense time pressure without much letup and exposing teen workers to injury and accidents (Greenberger & Steinberg, 1986; National Research Council, 1998). Not all jobs are this tedious or dangerous, of course, and some researchers have argued that adolescents in better jobs—jobs in which adolescents can learn genuinely useful skills, for example—benefit more from employment as a result (Mortimer, Pimentel, Ryu, Nash, & Lee, 1996; Schulenberg & Bachman, 1993). The proportion of adolescents who hold "good" jobs—jobs in which there is ample opportunity to learn new or higher-level skills, is quite small, however.

RECAP

Most employed U.S. adolescents work in retail jobs or in restaurants. Studies suggest that the work they do is highly routine and uninteresting and that male and female adolescents work in very different jobs.

 Food for Thought

What sorts of skills are required to perform the jobs typically held by adolescents, and what sorts of skills might develop as a result of work experience?

Working and Adolescent Development

● **The Development of Responsibility**   Most people believe that working builds character, teaches adolescents about the real world, and helps young people prepare for adulthood; however, these assumptions are not entirely supported by research. Indeed, studies indicate that the benefits of working during adolescence have probably been overstated and, moreover, that intensive employment during the school year may even have some costs to young people's development and schooling.

Studies of contemporary youth, for example, generally do not support the view that holding a job makes adolescents become more personally responsible (Mortimer & Johnson, 1998; Steinberg et al., 1993; Wright, Cullen, & Williams, 1997). Although working may help adolescents become more responsible when their work makes a genuine contribution to their family's welfare, as it often did during the Great Depression (Elder, 1974), this condition does not characterize the situation of most contemporary middle-class adolescents, who work mainly to earn their own spending money.

Moreover, adolescents who have jobs are more likely to express cynical attitudes toward work and to endorse unethical business practices. For example, workers are more likely than nonworkers to agree with such statements as "People who work harder at their jobs than they have to are a little crazy" and "In my opinion, it's all right for workers who are paid a low salary to take little things" (Steinberg, Greenberger, Garduque, Ruggiero, & Vaux, 1982). One study found high rates of misconduct among adolescent workers (e.g., stealing from employers, lying about the number of hours worked), even in the early months of their first jobs (Ruggiero, Greenberger, & Steinberg, 1982). And adolescents who work long hours (20 or more hours weekly) are less satisfied with their lives than are adolescents who work fewer hours (Fine, Mortimer, & Roberts, 1990).

What can we make of these findings? Why would working make youngsters more cynical about work and less satisfied with their lives? Perhaps the answer has something to do with the nature of the work most adolescents perform. Think for a moment about the job environment of most teenagers—or perhaps even the environment you worked in as a teenager, if you had a job. The work generally is dull, monotonous, and often stressful. Even if you have never worked in such a job, you can certainly imagine that working under these conditions can make people feel cynical and protective of their own interests.

• **Money and Its Management**   One aspect of responsibility that working is be-

lieved to affect is money management. Because the average working teenager earns around $400 each month, holding a job may provide many opportunities for learning how to budget, save, and use money responsibly. Although about half of all adolescents are given an allowance by their parents (most often, these are younger adolescents who are not employed), parents appear to exert more control over purchases made from allowances than they do over purchases made from job earnings (Greenberger & Steinberg, 1986; Miller & Yung, 1990).

Research indicates, however, that few teenagers exercise a great deal of responsibility when it comes to managing their earnings. Most working teenagers spend most of their earnings on their own needs and activities (Johnston, Bachman, & O'Malley, 1982). Few adolescents who work save a large percentage of their income for their education, and fewer still use their earnings to help their families with household expenses. Instead, the picture of the contemporary working teenager that emerges from these studies is one of self-indulgent materialism. Wages are spent on designer clothing, expensive stereo equipment, movies, and eating out (Steinberg et al., 1993). A fair proportion of the earnings are spent on drugs and

▲ Few adolescents who work save a large percentage of their income for their education, and fewer still use their earnings to help their families with household expenses. More often than not, wages are spent on clothing, cars, entertainment, and fast food. (Felicia Martinez/PhotoEdit)

alcohol (Greenberger & Steinberg, 1986). According to one social scientist, today's working teenagers may suffer from **premature affluence**—"affluence because [$400] or more per month represents a lot of 'spending money' for a high school student, and premature because many of these individuals will not be able to sustain that level of discretionary spending once they take on the burden of paying for their own necessities" (Bachman, 1983, p. 65).

What are some of the effects of premature affluence? Some of the consequences may be increased cynicism about the value of hard work and a lack of interest in working harder than is absolutely necessary, increased interest in buying drugs and alcohol, and the tendency to develop more materialistic attitudes (Greenberger & Steinberg, 1986; Mihalic & Elliot, 1997). Ironically, the very experience that many adults believe builds character may, in reality, teach adolescents undesirable lessons about work and the meaning of money.

● **Work and Deviance**   Some studies have examined the time-honored belief that having a job deters youngsters from delinquent and criminal activity—that keeping teenagers busy with work will keep them out of trouble. Contrary to popular belief, however, employment during adolescence does not deter delinquent activity (Steinberg & Cauffman, 1995). Indeed, several studies suggest that working may actually be associated with *increases* in deviance, including aggression; increases in school misconduct; and increases in minor delinquency, including engaging in petty theft, joyriding, carrying a weapon, and buying stolen goods (Gottfredson, 1985; Wright et al., 1997).

Many studies also have found that drug and alcohol use is higher among workers than nonworkers, especially among students who work long hours (e.g., Bachman & Schulenberg, 1993; Elliott & Wofford, 1991; Greenberger, Steinberg, & Vaux, 1981; Mihalic & Elliott, 1997; Mortimer & Johnson, 1998; Steinberg et al., 1993). Although some writers have proposed that adolescents who are already inclined toward using drugs and alcohol are more likely to choose to work long hours (e.g., Bachman & Schulenberg, 1993), more recent analyses suggest that this is not, in fact, the case. Rather, increases in work hours precede increases in drug and alcohol use (Mortimer et al., 1993; Steinberg et al., 1993). The impact of extensive employment on adolescent drug and alcohol use probably reflects the fact that adolescents who work long hours have more discretionary income and, hence, greater opportunity

to purchase drugs and alcohol. In addition, drug and alcohol use is higher among adolescents who work under conditions of high job stress than it is among their peers who work for comparable amounts of time and money but under less stressful conditions (Greenberger et al., 1981). Whatever the reason, the impact of school-year employment on drug and alcohol use persists over time; individuals who worked long hours as teenagers drink and use drugs more in their late twenties than do their peers who worked less or not at all (Mihalic & Elliott, 1997).

● **Work and Its Impact on School**   Many experts now believe that working more than 20 hours a week may jeopardize adolescents' schooling (National Research Council, 1998). Youngsters who work long hours are absent from school more often, are less likely to participate in extracurricular activities, report enjoying school less, spend less time on their homework, and earn lower grades. These results occur both because youngsters who are less interested in school choose to work longer hours and because working long hours leads to disengagement from school—meaning, in effect, that intensive employment during the school year most threatens the school performance of the students who can least afford to have their grades decline (Mihalic & Elliott, 1997; Schoenhals et al., 1998; Steinberg & Cauffman, 1995). There is no evidence that summer employment, even when it is for long hours, affects school performance, however, suggesting that the negative impact of working on school performance may be due to the time demands of having a job while going to school (Oettinger, 1999).

Working long hours also seems to lead to increased absenteeism and decreased time spent on homework and school activities. In addition, intensive involvement in a part-time job early in a student's education—during sophomore year in high school, for example—may actually increase the likelihood of dropping out of school, although this does not seem to be true among students in informal jobs, such as baby-sitting or yardwork (Carr et al., 1996; Damico, 1984; McNeal, 1997). Moreover, students who work a good deal have less ambitious plans for further education while in high school, and they complete fewer years of college (Mortimer & Finch, 1986).

Although the impact that working has on students' grades and achievement test scores is small (Barton, 1989), several studies indicate that extensive employment during the school year may take its toll on students in ways that are not revealed by looking only at grade-point averages. Students who work a great deal, for example, report paying less attention in class, exerting less effort on their studies, and skipping class more frequently (Steinberg & Dornbusch, 1991). Additionally, when students work a great deal, they often develop strategies for protecting their grade-point averages. These strategies include taking easier courses, cutting corners on homework assignments, copying homework from friends, and cheating (Greenberger & Steinberg, 1986; McNeil, 1984; Steinberg & Dornbusch, 1991). Teachers express concern about the excessive involvement of students in after-school jobs (Bills, Helms, & Ozcan, 1995), and some teachers may respond to an influx of students into the workplace by lowering classroom expectations, assigning less homework, and using class time for students to complete assignments that otherwise would be done outside of school (Bills et al., 1995; McNeil, 1984).

▲ *Participation in extracurricular activities, such as working on the school yearbook, is less frequent among students who work long hours at a part-time job.* (Tony Freeman/PhotoEdit)

Food for Thought

To what extent are the findings from research on adolescent employment counterintuitive? Why or why not?

Youth Unemployment

Although the employment of teenagers has become commonplace in contemporary America, some young people who wish to work are unable to find jobs. In general, however, youth unemployment is not very widespread, once the proportion of young people who are in school is taken into account (i.e., most adolescents who are not working are enrolled in school). According to the U.S. Bureau of the Census (1999), in 1998, for example, slightly more than half of all 16- to 24-year-olds were enrolled in school (either in high school or college); of the remaining half who were not in school, nearly 75 percent were employed. Overall, then, only a small percentage of 16- to 24-year-olds—about 12 percent—are neither in school nor employed, and many of these may be young parents who are at home full-time and not actively seeking work. Only 3 percent of young people are not enrolled in school, actively looking for work, and unemployed. Moreover, young people who are out of school and out of work are typically unemployed for only short periods of time. Most unemployed youth are high school dropouts. Although high school dropouts constitute only about 14 percent of the population of 18- to 21-year-olds, they account for about half of the unemployed people in this age bracket.

Minority youth are far more likely to experience unemployment than are white youth. Among the reasons for this are the relatively higher proportion of minority youth who drop out of high school (dropout rates are especially high among Hispanic American youth) and the relatively lower proportion of minority high school graduates who attend college. In 1998, for example, 60 percent of all white youth between the ages of 18 and 21 were in school, compared with 50 percent of all African American youth and only 30 percent of Hispanic youth (U.S. Bureau of the Census, 1999). And, whereas 8 percent of white 16- to 19-year-olds were both out of school and out of work, nearly twice the percentage of African American and Hispanic youth were (Federal Interagency Forum on Child and Family Statistics, 1997).

Most studies show that unemployment during adolescence and young adulthood results primarily from a combination of economic and social factors, rather than from a lack of motivation on the part of unemployed individuals (Freeman & Wise, 1982). Perhaps more important, the consequences of unemployment during adolescence and young adulthood appear to be worse in the short term than in the long term. Most people who have been unemployed as teenagers are eventually able to secure stable full-time employment. Youth unemployment is a problem among individuals not in school, mostly because it is associated with higher rates of crime, drug abuse, and violence (Freeman & Wise, 1982).

Many approaches have been taken over the years in trying to solve the youth unemployment problem. One set of proposals comes out of concern for the Forgotten Half—the nearly 50 percent of all adolescents who do not go on to college. As noted in chapter 6, American secondary schools do little to prepare noncollege-bound youngsters for the world of work. These youngsters, of course, are far more likely to experience unemployment. Many experts, therefore, believe that the youth unemployment problem is attributable mainly to the lack of clear linkages between school and work. They point out that there are so many gaps in the transition from school to work that it is easy for students who are not in school—and who are carried along by inertia—to fall into periods of unemployment.

Several suggestions have been made to combat this problem (Rosenbaum, 1996). Many commentators have argued that expanding opportunities for community service will help integrate adolescents into the community, will enhance their feelings of confidence and responsibility, and will put them in touch with adult role models. Studies of **service learning** (non-paid programs, sometimes connected with school, that place adolescents in volunteer positions in the community) indicate that some volunteer experiences may enhance adolescents' self-esteem and feelings of efficacy, impart academic and career skills, enhance community involvement, improve mental health, and deter problem behavior; these positive results are most likely to occur in programs in which adolescents have good relationships with their supervisors, are given sufficient autonomy, and have adequate time to reflect on and learn from their experience (Johnson, Beebe, Mortimer, & Snyder, 1998; Stukas, Clary, & Snyder, 1999).

A second suggestion is that communities improve their services for young people and strengthen youth organizations. In Europe, for example, local communities provide much better employment services for youth—including job placement—than is the case in the United States. Such services would also help with career counseling, college counseling, summer employment, and placement in volunteer activities. In most American high schools, guidance counselors are so busy counseling students for college that they rarely pay attention to noncollege-bound students.

Finally, it has been proposed that American schools experiment with apprenticeship programs modeled after those found in Europe (Hamilton, 1990; Hamilton & Hurrelmann, 1994). These programs would introduce young people to the world of work early in high school and would gradually move them from full-time school into a mixture of school and work and finally into full-time employment. Instead of working in the dead-end jobs of the adolescent workplace, teenagers would combine schooling and on-the-job training with employers who are likely to offer them full-time, career-oriented jobs after graduation. However, although these programs have been successful abroad, many scholars have questioned whether they can be exported successfully to the United States (Kantor, 1994).

What about the substantial proportion of adolescents who do not graduate from high school, who, as you have seen, are at the greatest risk of experiencing unemployment? To date, many types of interventions have been tried, but few have succeeded (Smith, 1993). Despite about 30 years of government programs designed to train unemployed youth and place them in the labor force, most evaluations of these efforts find that high school dropouts who participate in such programs are no more likely to find full-time employment than are dropouts who do not participate in the programs (Foster, 1995). This is quite disconcerting, since the programs that were evaluated have tried a wide array of approaches, including work experience, job training, job placement, and instruction in labor market skills (such as interviewing and job seeking). In light of this evidence, most experts believe that efforts should be redirected away from work experience programs and, instead, concentrated on helping youngsters who are at-risk for dropping out of school stay in school (Foster, 1995; Kantor, 1994).

RECAP

Although extensive part-time employment during the school year may be a problem among working- and middle-class adolescents, many social commentators have worried about the high rate of youth unemployment, especially among poor, minority youth who have dropped out of high school, but also among high school graduates who do not attend college. Among the suggestions offered for combating youth unemployment are increasing adolescents' opportunities for community service, strengthening counseling and career services for high school students, encouraging the development of apprenticeship programs such as those found in Europe, and, above all, encouraging all adolescents to complete high school.

Food for Thought

Discuss the extent, causes, and consequences of youth unemployment. What sorts of efforts have been successful in combating youth unemployment, and what sorts have failed? If you were a policymaker, what approach would you take?

ADOLESCENTS AND LEISURE

The average American middle-class teenager feels bored more than 25 percent of the time, and some complain of boredom more than 50 percent of the time (Larson & Richards, 1991). As one expert noted, "The litany of explanations for this boredom—'algebra

sucks,' 'I'm always bored on Sunday,' 'there's nothing to do,' 'the Odyssey is boring'—reads like a script from Bart Simpson" (Larson, 2000, p. 170).

One context in which boredom is seldom reported by teenagers is leisure, however. Leisure occupies more of the typical adolescent's waking hours (between 40 and 50 percent) than do school and work combined (between 35 and 40 percent) (Larson, 2000). Leisure activities include socializing with friends, playing sports and games, watching television and listening to music, surfing the Internet, playing video games, practicing a musical instrument, shopping, working on hobbies, and just plain "chilling."

One important difference between leisure and other activities is that adolescents choose their leisure activities, whereas their time at school and work is dictated by others (teachers, supervisors, etc.). Perhaps as a consequence, studies show that adolescents report being in a better mood during leisure activities than during school or work (Csikszentmihalyi & Larson, 1984). According to one study, in which adolescents' moods were monitored using the Experience Sampling Method (see the accompanying box), leisure activities that are both structured and voluntary—such as sports, hobbies, artistic activities, and clubs—seem to carry special benefits for adolescents' psychological well-being (Larson, 2000). As figure 7.3 indicates, when adolescents are in school, they report moderate levels of concentration but very low levels of motivation or interest in what they are doing, consistent with other studies indicating that most American teenagers do not find high school engaging (e.g., Steinberg et al., 1996). When they are with friends, teenagers report moderate levels of motivation and interest but low levels of concentration. It is only when adolescents are playing sports or involved in the arts, a hobby, or an extracurricular organization that they report high levels of *both* concentration and interest. While they are in unstructured leisure activities, such as watching TV, adolescents tend to show the same pattern of moderate interest but low concentration that they report when they are socializing with friends.

Adults have mixed feelings about adolescents' leisure. On the positive side, adults take pride in watching teenagers' organized sports and creative activities and believe that these productive uses of leisure help build character and teach important skills, such as teamwork and perseverance (consider, for example, all the movies you have seen about the character-building benefits of team sports). On the other hand, adults view many adolescent leisure activities as

The Scientific Study of Adolescence

The Experience Sampling Method

Many of the questions that psychologists who study adolescence are interested in are difficult to answer through the conventional methodologies of observational or questionnaire research. Questions concerning adolescents' emotional states, for instance, are especially tricky, because individuals' emotions change during the day and may not be, at the time of a researcher's assessment, reflective of their moods at other points in the day. Suppose a researcher wanted to know how adolescents' moods were affected by various activities—such as attending school, watching television, and having dinner with the family. Although it would be possible to interview respondents and ask them to recall their moods at different points in the day, the researcher cannot be sure whether their recollections are entirely accurate.

One of the most interesting innovations to shape the scientific study of adolescence was designed to overcome this and other sorts of methodological problems. Using the **Experience Sampling Method (ESM),** researchers can collect much more detailed information about adolescents' experiences over the course of the day, and scientists using this method have illuminated many aspects of the adolescent experience. The ESM has been used to chart adolescents' moods, to monitor their social relationships, and to catalog their activities in far greater detail than has been previously available.

The use of the ESM in the study of adolescent development was pioneered by psychologist Reed Larson and his colleagues (Larson & Lampman-Petraitis, 1989; Larson & Richards, 1989, 1991). In studies using this method, adolescents "carry electronic pagers and report on their activities, companionship, and internal states at random times when signaled by the pagers" (Larson & Richards, 1991). In one study, for example, Larson had nearly 500 adolescents between the ages of 9 and 15 carry pagers and booklets of self-report forms for one week and asked the adolescents to fill out a form each time they were signaled. The form contained a series of questions about companionship ("Who were you with [or talking to on the phone]?"), location ("Where were you?"), activity ("What were you doing?"), and affect (the adolescents used a checklist to report their moods). The adolescents were paged seven times each day, once within every two-hour block between 7:30 A.M. and 9:30 P.M. By examining the adolescents' many reports, the researchers were able to chart changes in activities, companionship, and mood over the course of the week and to relate variations in activity, companionship, and mood to one another. Thus, the method permitted the researchers to ask how activities, companionship, and mood varied as a function of age; how mood varied as a function of what the adolescent was doing; and how both activity and mood varied as a

---

wasted time or, worse, as preludes to trouble: They worry about groups of teenagers cruising the mall, they poke fun at groups of girls sequestered in front of a mirror trying on an array of cosmetics, and they cringe at images of adolescents surfing chat rooms on the Internet or plugged into their personal stereos, mindlessly starting off into space.

This mixed view of adolescent leisure reflects an interesting paradox about the nature of adolescence in modern society. Because industrialized society has allowed adolescents a good deal of free time, adults expect them to use it productively. However, by definition, leisure is supposed to be time that can be used for purposes other than production. As you will read in chapter 8, some theorists of adolescence believe that the existence of large blocks of uncommitted time is one feature of adolescence in modern society that has the potential to contribute in positive ways to young people's development (e.g., Erikson, 1968).

Nevertheless, it seems difficult for adults to resist the temptation to worry that leisure activities are displacing the more "important" tasks of adolescence,

function of whom the adolescent was with.

Two of the questions asked in the study were how adolescents' moods varied as a function of whom they were with (parents, peers, or no one) and whether the connection between mood and companionship changed with age. The results are presented in the accompanying figure. As you can see, adolescents' moods are generally most positive when they are with their friends and least positive when they are alone; their moods when with their families fall somewhere in between. More interesting, perhaps, is that, between grades 5 and 9, adolescents' moods while with friends become more positive, whereas their moods while with their family follow a **curvilinear pattern,** which either can be U-shaped or can look like an inverted U. That is, their moods while

with their family become more negative between elementary and middle school (i.e., between grades 5 and 7) and then rise between middle school and high school (between grades 8 and 9). As Larson and Richards point out, this dip parallels findings from other research on famil.y relations (see chapter 4), which points to early adolescence as a time of somewhat heightened strain in the parent-child relationship.

The data about these adolescents' moods when they are alone are somewhat surprising. Given the fact that adolescents spend increasingly more time alone as they get older, one might expect solitude to be associated with more positive—not more negative—affect. Although the researchers could not explain this finding easily, one hypothesis is that, when alone, adolescents spend a good deal of their time thinking about them-

selves and working through the events of the day (Larson, 1990). Some of the time alone is spent listening to music, and some of the music adolescents listen to may have sad or depressing themes (unrequited love, broken relationships, etc.). Interestingly, other studies using the ESM (e.g., Csikszentmihalyi & Larson, 1984) find that adolescents feel better after being alone and that, with age, solitude tends to become associated with more positive feelings (Larson, 1990, 1997). Together, these findings suggest that periods of solitude are associated with negative mood in the short term but with positive mood in the long term.

Source: Larson, R., & Richards, M. (1991). Daily companionship in late childhood and early adolescence: Changing developmental contexts. *Child Development, 62,* 284–300.

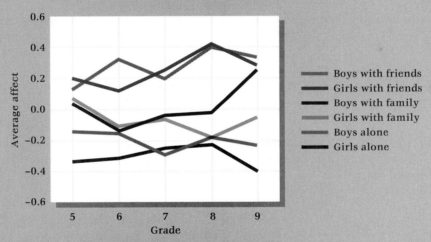

▲ *Average affect reported by girls and boys at different ages when alone, with friends, and with family.* (Larson & Richards, 1991)

such as school. Interestingly, however, studies show that intensive involvement in the productive activity of part-time work has a more consistently negative impact on school performance than does comparable involvement in extracurricular activities (Lamborn, Mounts, Brown, & Steinberg, 1992; Mahoney & Cairns, 1997; McNeal, 1995). And, although adults believe that television viewing has a negative effect on adolescents' academic performance, it is more likely that poor school performance leads to increased television viewing than the reverse. More often displaced by

television viewing than schoolwork are more marginal activities, such as daydreaming or goofing off, or other forms of entertainment, such as listening to music and going to movies (Larson & Verma, 1999, p. 718).

By valuing adolescents' leisure only when it is free time that is used productively, adults may misunderstand the important functions that leisure serves in the psychosocial development of the young person. For example, studies show that a moderate amount of solitude (during which daydreaming is a central activity) is positively related to high school students' psychological

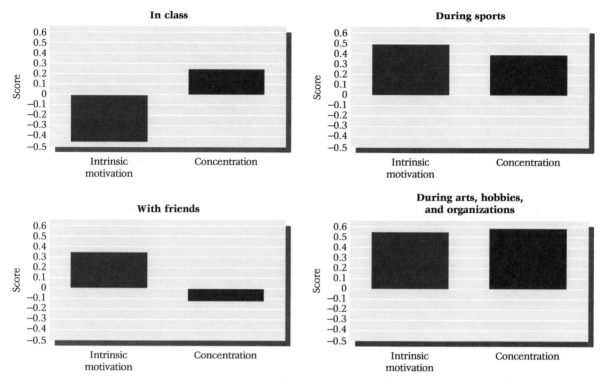

Figure 7.3   *Adolescents' state of mind is more positive when they are in structured leisure activities than when they are in class or with friends.* (Larson, 2000)

well-being (Csikszentmihalyi & Larson, 1984; Larson, 1997). Leisure plays an important role in helping young people to develop a sense of themselves, to explore their relationships with each other, and to learn about the society around them.

Participation in Extracurricular Activities

For many adolescents around the world, school-sponsored extracurricular activities provide the context for much of their leisure activity (Stevenson, 1994). According to surveys, about two-thirds of American high school students participate in one or more extracurricular activities, although the participation rate varies greatly from school to school. The most popular type of extracurricular activities in the United States are athletics, in which nearly half of all adolescents participate. The other two sets of activities in which many adolescents participate are those related to music (such as band, chorus, orchestra, and glee club; about one-fourth of all adolescent students participate in these) and those related to academic or occupational interests (such as science clubs, language clubs, and clubs oriented toward certain careers; about one-fifth participate in these) (Berk, 1992).

Participation in extracurricular activities is influenced by a number of factors. In general, participation is somewhat more prevalent among adolescents from middle-class families, among students who earn better grades, and among students from smaller schools and smaller, more rural, communities, where school activities often play a relatively more central role in the lives of both adults and adolescents (e.g., where an entire community may turn out for a school's Friday night basketball or football game). African American students are somewhat more likely to participate than white students, and, although boys are more likely than girls to participate in athletic activities, the reverse is true for nonathletic activities (Berk, 1992). Adolescents whose parents are themselves involved in the community or reinforce their child's interests are also more likely to participate (Fletcher, Elder, & Mekos, 2000).

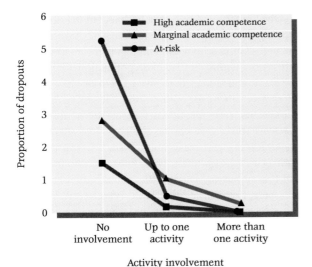

Figure 7.4   Participation in athletic extracurricular activities benefits less competent students more than their academically talented counterparts. (McNeal, 1995)

Researchers have spent considerable time studying the impact of extracurricular participation on adolescent development, but it has been difficult to draw any firm conclusions, because few studies separate cause from effect. For example, although researchers generally find that participants have higher self-esteem than nonparticipants, it isn't clear whether students with high self-esteem are more likely to go out for extracurricular activities to begin with, or whether participation makes students feel better about themselves (Spreitzer, 1994). The few studies that have tried to get at cause and effect, however, by tracking students over time, suggest that participation in an extracurricular activity—especially in athletics or fine arts—seems to improve students' performance in school; to reduce the likelihood of dropping out; to deter delinquency, drug use, and other types of risk taking; and to enhance students' psychological well-being and social status (Eder & Kinney, 1995; Mahoney & Cairns, 1997; McNeal, 1995; Savage & Holcomb, 1999); the one exception is that involvement in team sports, which, although educationally positive, appears to be associated with an increase in alcohol use (Eccles & Barber, 1999; Savage & Holcomb, 1999). Participation in extracurricular activities appears especially beneficial to adolescents whose network of friends also participates in the same activity—an indicator, perhaps, of membership in a peer group that is involved in prosocial activities that revolve around the school (Mahoney, 2000).

As figure 7.4 illustrates, the benefits of athletic participation to academic performance—a so-called spillover effect—are found mainly among adolescents who are poorer students (Mahoney & Cairns, 1997). Extracurricular activities also may provide greater opportunities for cross-racial friendship than does the regular school day, and African American adolescents in integrated schools who participate in extracurricular activities especially show better mental health as a result. Extracurricular participation in high school also seems to be linked to extracurricular participation in college and to community involvement in adulthood—people who are "do-ers" as adolescents tend to remain so in young and middle adulthood.

Researchers speculate that the generally positive impact of extracurricular participation is because extracurricular activities increase students' contact with teachers and other school personnel, who may reinforce the value of school (as when a coach or an advisor counsels a student about plans for college) and because participation itself may improve students' confidence and self-image. Some educators believe that extracurricular participation also helps bond students to their school, especially in the case of adolescents who are not achieving much academically; for many of them, their extracurricular activity is what keeps them going to school each day (Berk, 1992; Mahoney & Cairns, 1997).

One serious caution has been raised about adolescents' participation in athletics, however. As extracurricular sports have become more competitive, the number of young people injured during these activities has risen substantially. According to some estimates, around 25 percent of all adolescent athletes are injured while playing organized sports (Overbaugh & Allen, 1994). There is a clear need for more rigorous injury prevention education among athletes, coaches, and parents (Dalton, 1992).

RECAP

Leisure occupies more of an adolescent's time than do school and work combined. Although adults are prone to see leisure as wasted time, leisure serves a number of important functions during adolescence. It socializes adolescents for adult roles and, in the case of participation in school-sponsored extracurricular activities, may enhance adolescents' well-being and strengthen their attachment to school.

After-School Activities and Adolescent Development

The changes in patterns of school, work, and family life discussed in chapters 4, 5, and 6 have resulted in a large number of young people—between 2 million and 6 million school-age youngsters—who are not supervised by their parents after school. Whereas some of these youngsters are involved in school- or community-based programs that provide adult supervision, others spend their after-school hours away from adults, in their homes, with friends, or simply hanging out in neighborhoods and shopping malls (Carnegie Council on Adolescent Development, 1992). Affluent, suburban, and white children are most likely to be home unsupervised, and poor, minority, and urban and rural children are least likely (U.S. Bureau of the Census, 1994).

Psychologists have debated whether latchkey youth are profiting from these opportunities for self-management (e.g., Rodman, Pratto, & Nelson, 1988) or potentially are heading for trouble (Richardson, Radziszewska, Dent, & Hay, 1993; Richardson et al., 1989). In general, most studies show that children who care for themselves after school are not different from their peers when it comes to psychological development, school achievement, and self-conceptions (e.g., Galambos & Garbarino, 1985; Vandell & Corasaniti, 1988). These studies argue against the view that having to care for oneself contributes in positive ways to the development of self-reliance and personal responsibility. In addition, several studies, including a study of nearly 4,000 youngsters from a variety of ethnic backgrounds (Richardson et al., 1993), suggest that children in self-care are more socially isolated, more depressed, more likely to be involved in problem behavior, and more likely use more drugs and alcohol than are children who are supervised after school by adults (Carnegie Council on Adolescent Development, 1992; Galambos & Maggs, 1991; Richardson et al., 1989, 1993; Steinberg, 1986). Together, these studies seem to suggest that latchkey arrangements may have more costs than benefits.

One limitation of studies of latchkey youth is that they typically lump together all children who take care of themselves after school, even though there are important differences *within* the latchkey population (Steinberg, 1986). Several studies that have recognized these differences have shown, for example, that the setting in which adolescents care for themselves makes a difference: Latchkey youngsters who go straight home after school are far less likely to engage in problem behavior than are their peers who go to a friend's house or who just hang out (Galambos & Maggs, 1991; Richardson et al., 1993; Steinberg, 1986). In addition, latchkey youngsters who are raised by authoritative parents and who are monitored by their parents from a distance—via telephone check-ins, for example—are no more susceptible to problem behavior than are children whose parents are home with them (Galambos & Maggs, 1991; Steinberg, 1986; Vandell & Ramanan, 1991).

Several recent studies indicate, however, that spending time after school with friends in unsupervised settings is more problematic under some circumstances than under others. One study found, for example, that it was not simply spending unsupervised time with peers that increased an adolescent's likelihood of alcohol and drug use, but it was the combination of having low supervision, having friends who liked to party and use drugs, and being an adolescent who was especially susceptible to peer pressure that was most damaging (Caldwell & Darling, 1999). In another study, the researchers examined rates of problem behavior among seventh-graders as a function of three factors: (1) whether they spent their after-school time in unsupervised settings; (2) whether they had parents who monitored their activities and whereabouts; and (3) whether they lived in a neighborhood that was considered safe (Pettit, Bates, Dodge, & Meece, 1999). In all groups, being closely monitored by one's parents was a deterrent against problem behavior. And, not surprisingly, adolescents who reported spending a lot of after-school time with peers in unsupervised settings were more likely to show problem behavior one year later than were other teenagers. But the negative effects of low parental monitoring and unsupervised peer group activity were far more important for teenagers living in unsafe neighborhoods. Indeed, in safe neighborhoods, the adolescents who spent time in unsupervised peer activities were not at greater risk for developing problems, even if they were not monitored closely by their parents (see figure 7.5). This study serves as reminder of the importance of looking at the broader context in which adolescents live in order to understand fully how they are affected by parents, peers, and other influences.

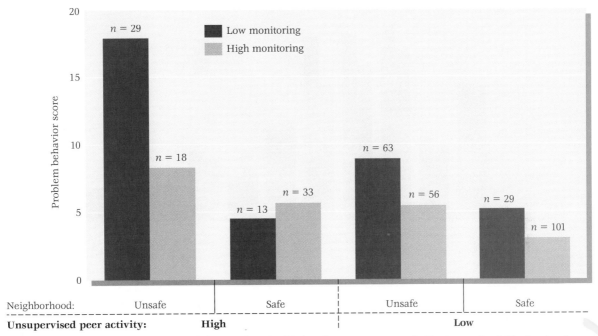

Figure 7.5   The greatest risk for problem behavior after school is found among teenagers who live in unsafe neighborhoods, who spend a lot of time in unsupervised activity with peers, and who are poorly monitored by their parents. Although hanging out with friends is thought to place adolescents at risk for antisocial behavior, unsupervised time with peers is not a risk factor when adolescents live in safe communities and are monitored by their parents. (Pettit et al., 1999)

Together, these studies suggest that self-care after school does not hold great benefits for youngsters and, under some conditions, causes problems if adolescents' parents do not promote the development of responsible behavior when they are with their child. What should parents who have no choice but to leave their youngsters in self-care do? Experts advise parents to provide clear instructions about the child's after-school activities and whereabouts, asking the child to check in with an adult as soon as he or she gets home and teaching the child how to handle emergencies, should they arise (Steinberg & Levine, 1991).

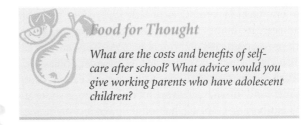

Food for Thought

What are the costs and benefits of self-care after school? What advice would you give working parents who have adolescent children?

Leisure and the Mass Media

Leisure activities play an important role in exposing adolescents to elements of the popular culture in general, and to elements of the youth culture in particular. Indeed, it is in this respect that adolescent leisure activity has generated the most controversy.

Several years ago, a major study on media usage among American children and adolescents was conducted, in which a nationally representative sample of more than 2,000 students were surveyed (Roberts, Foehr, Rideout, & Brodie, 1999). The results were absolutely staggering, in several respects. First, the availability of media in young people's homes was far greater than anyone had imagined. For example, although it is not surprising

RECAP

Between 2 million and 6 million school-age American youngsters are not supervised by their parents after school. Studies suggest that self-care after school does not hold great benefits for youngsters and, in fact, causes problems if adolescents are unsupervised with their friends and if adolescents' parents do not promote the development of responsible behavior when they are with their child.

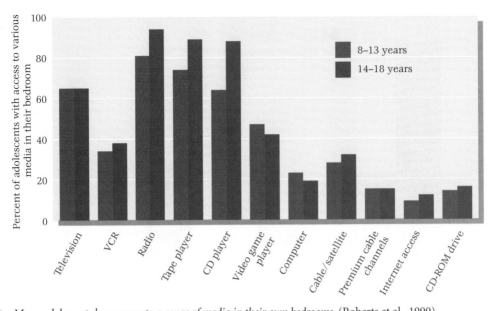

Figure 7.6   *Many adolescents have access to a range of media in their own bedrooms.* (Roberts et al., 1999)

to learn that 99 percent of all American adolescents live in homes with a television, the survey indicated that the proportion of homes with a VCR or CD player is nearly as high (98 percent and 94 percent, respectively), and the vast majority of teenagers' homes have a video game player (82 percent), cable or satellite TV (74 percent), and a computer (73 percent). As of early 1999, about half of all adolescents' homes had Internet access. With the exceptions of computers and Internet access, very few differences in media availability were found among adolescents from different social classes. As you would expect, computers and Internet access are more common in more affluent homes; even still, half of all lower-income homes had a computer, and one-quarter of them had Internet access. Most adolescents have access to many of these media *in their own bedrooms*, as figure 7.6 indicates. Thus, the context in which many adolescents view TV, listen to music, and play video games is one that makes parental monitoring very difficult.

Second, television, in particular, is ever-present in adolescents' homes. Nearly 70 percent of adolescents live in homes with three or more televisions. Two-thirds of adolescents report that the TV is on during meals. Half of all adolescents live in what might be called a "constant television environment," in which the television remains on throughout the day, regardless of whether anyone is watching it. Television is especially pervasive in African American homes, which on average have more televisions and more televisions in adolescents' bedrooms, and in

which the television is more likely to be on during meals or on constantly.

Third, adolescents' total media exposure—the amount of time they spend each day using one of the mass media—is extremely high. The average adolescent spends nearly seven hours each day using one or more media, and this includes time spent using different media simultaneously (e.g., in the study, one hour watching TV while surfing the Internet was recorded as one hour of media use). Between 40 and 50 percent of adolescents use the media more than seven hours daily. Among high school students, most of this time is spent watching TV (three hours per day), followed by CDs and tapes (more than an hour each day), and the radio (about an hour each day). Reading occupies far less time—about a half-hour, on average—and only about one-third of high school students read more than 30 minutes each day (this includes books, magazines, and newspapers, but not homework). Although adults have become increasingly concerned about teenagers' exposure to the Internet, the amount of time they spend on the computer for leisure (about 30 minutes daily) is far less than the amount of time they spend watching television, and substantially more time is spent playing video games than computer games. Generally speaking, exposure to video media (TV, VCR, movies, video games) follows an inverted U-shaped curve as individuals age, with more frequent use during preadolescence and adolescence than before or after. Exposure to musical media follows a different pattern with age—it increases linearly throughout childhood and adolescence.

According to psychologist Reed Larson (1994), one of the reasons that television viewing declines during adolescence, and listening to music increases, is that television viewing is far less satisfying to the adolescent as far as his or her developmental needs are concerned. Television, Larson argues, is created by adults for a general audience, whereas many types of popular music (e.g., rap, heavy metal) are created specifically for adolescents. Not surprisingly, studies of teenagers' emotional states indicate that they often feel vacant while watching television but are more aroused (either positively or negatively) while listening to music (Larson, 1994; Thompson & Larson, 1995). Not surprisingly, nearly two-thirds of high school students say that, when they are watching TV, they are very often just killing time (Roberts et al., 1999).

In addition, Larson finds that television tends to link adolescents with their families (in part because adolescents, especially young adolescents, often watch television with other family members), whereas listening to music is often a solitary activity. (Watching television with parents becomes less frequent during adolescence, however [Roberts et al., 1999].) Indeed, the typical teenager spends 13 percent of waking hours in the bedroom—second only to time spent at school—and much of that time is spent listening to music (J. Brown, 1994). Over the course of adolescence, there is a substantial increase in the amount of time adolescents spend alone, although this increase is greater for boys than for girls (Larson & Richards, 1991; Wong & Csikzentmihalyi, 1991) (review the box on pages 240–241). Solitude, with or without music or television in the background, can actually be a positive contributor to adolescents' mental health (Larson, 1995, 1997; Steele & Brown, 1995; Thompson & Larson, 1995).

Given the fact that adolescents spend so much time watching television, listening to music, and playing video games, it is reasonable to ask what they are watching, listening to, and playing. By far, the most popular television shows among teenagers are comedies (half of the teenagers surveyed had watched a TV comedy the previous day), followed by dramatic shows (26 percent), movies (21 percent), and sports (19 percent). Music videos, talk shows, and reality programs, all of which have content that often concerns adults, are far less popular. Generally, there are few substantial social class or ethnic differences in the types of shows adolescents watch, although there is one huge sex difference: Boys are four times more likely than girls to watch sports. And, as anyone who has been to a movie theater lately knows, action movies and comedies top the list of teenagers' film preferences.

With respect to music, rap and hip-hop lead the list, at least they did in 1999 (53 percent), followed by alternative rock (42 percent), hard rock or heavy metal (19 percent), and country and western (14 percent). There are strong ethnic differences in music preferences, with rap and hip-hop the overwhelming choices of African American and Hispanic youth. Rap and hip-hop are very popular among white youth, too, but not as popular as alternative rock. Sports (50 percent), action (45 percent), and adventure (34 percent) are the most popular types of video games.

The 1999 media usage survey discussed in the preceding pages was one of the first efforts to collect information from a representative sample of youth on their use of the Internet. Although researchers still know next to nothing about the role of the Internet in adolescent development, there was little in the survey that was alarming about adolescents' visits to chat rooms and websites. The most frequently visited chat rooms and sites were those about entertainment (celebrities, TV shows, movies, music), sports, and relationships and lifestyles (especially among older teenagers). The frequent use of websites and chat rooms about relationships indicates that many teenagers are using the Internet to get and give advice on a range of personal matters. The extent to which this is helpful (because it allows the adolescent to connect with others who have similar concerns) or harmful (because the advice and information provided may be erroneous, misguided, or even dangerous) is not known.

Given the considerable amount of time adolescents spend in the presence of mass media, it is not surprising to find that the impact of the media on teenagers' behavior and development has been the subject of much debate. Unfortunately, little of the debate is grounded in scientific research. Although some adults have expressed worry that the sexually explicit lyrics of rock music and the aggressive images of MTV corrupt the values of young people (e.g., Gore, 1987), the evidence that teenagers are influenced in any dramatic way by what they listen to or watch is very slim (Fine et al., 1990).

One tremendous problem in interpreting studies of media use and adolescent development is that it is extremely difficult to disentangle cause from effect, because adolescents *choose* which mass media they are exposed to (Arnett, 1995; Arnett, Larson, & Offer, 1995). Although it has been speculated that violent film images and heavy metal music provoke aggression, for example, it is just as likely, if not more so, that aggressive adolescents are more prone to choose to watch violent images (Arnett, 1996; Roe, 1995). Similarly, sexual behavior may be correlated with listening to "sexy" music, but it is impossible to say which causes which.

For example, although the major study of media use conducted by Roberts and colleagues found that the adolescents who watched a lot of television and movies were significantly more troubled (bored, unhappy, and in trouble at home or school) than the adolescents who watched less often, it is not known whether large doses of mass media *cause* problems or, more plausibly, that adolescents with more problems watch more TV, perhaps as a way of distracting themselves from their troubles. Similarly, although the study found that the students who watched relatively more TV and videos and listened to relatively more music earned lower grades in school than their peers, it is impossible to say whether high media use *leads to* poor school performance (e.g., the old idea that TV "rots the brain"), *results from* poor school performance (e.g., that students who are discouraged by their grades in school use TV and music to distract themselves), or is correlated with poor school performance because of another factor (e.g., adolescents with poor family relationships both watch a lot of TV and do badly in school).

These chicken-and-egg problems notwithstanding, there are a few generalizations about media usage and adolescent development that have enough evidence, however indirect, to generate some consensus among experts in the area. Most of the relevant research has focused on television (as a consequence, virtually nothing is known about the impact of other media on development), and the bulk of the research has focused on the three topics about which adults are most concerned (some might say obsessed): sex, violence, and drugs. Although little is certain about the long-term effects of adolescents' exposure to sex, violence, and drug use in the media, there is no question that the exposure is considerable.

One analysis of teenagers' top 10 favorite television programs found, for example, that more than one-quarter of all the interactions between the individuals on the shows contained sexual content (Ward, 1995). In some shows, among the most popular, more than half of all interactions between individuals contained sexual content. The most common messages concerned men seeing women as sex objects ("Look at the body on that chick"; "In case she's a dog, I can fake a heart attack"); sex being viewed as a defining aspect of masculinity ("I slept with 10 girls last week"; "Oh, that's one afternoon

for me"); sex as a competition ("You're supposed to be keeping score, not trying to score"); and sex as fun and exciting ("It's so romantic, all that passion, when you have to make love every minute of the day"). Similar messages are carried in most MTV videos, in which men are shown as aggressive and dominant and women are seen as the subservient objects of men's sexual advances (Brown & Witherspoon, in press).

Adolescents are also exposed to a great deal of violent imagery on television and in movies. More than 60 percent of television programming contains violence; as a consequence, young people see an estimated 10,000 acts of mass media violence each year, and more than one-fourth of all violent incidents on television involve guns. A recent analysis of MTV programming indicated that more than one-fifth portrayed overt violence, that one-fifth of rap videos contained violence, and that weapon carrying appeared in one-quarter of all MTV videos (Strasburger & Donnerstein, 1999). Precise estimates of the amount of violent imagery in the most popular video games or other visual media are not available, but concerns have been raised over the impact of playing violent video games on young people's behavior and attitudes (Cantor, 2000).

Finally, many analyses have shown that alcohol and tobacco use are ubiquitous in the mass media to which adolescents are exposed. As one team of experts recently noted, "Alcohol, tobacco, or illicit drugs are present in 70% of prime time network dramatic programs, 38 out of 40 top-grossing movies, and half of all music videos" (Strasburger & Donnerstein, 1999, pp. 129–130). Nearly 10 percent of the commercials that young people see on television are for beer or wine—for every public service announcement discouraging alcohol use, teenagers will view 25 to 50 ads for beer or wine. And alcohol and tobacco companies have an increasing presence on the Internet, sponsoring numerous websites and specially designed chat rooms (Strasburger & Donnerstein, 1999).

Studies that unequivocally demonstrate that exposure to messages about sex, violence, and drugs causes changes in adolescents' behavior are harder to find. The strongest evidence is in the area of violence, where numerous studies have shown that repeated exposure to violent imagery leads to aggressive behavior in children and youth. It is important to note, however, that the bulk of the evidence comes from studies of aggressive behavior, rather than serious violence, and that other factors, such as experiences in the family or community, likely play a far greater role in serious violence than does media exposure. Despite claims about the role of violent media in the genesis of school violence, no study has ever shown that viewing gun use on television or in video games causes gun use in real life (Strasburger & Donnerstein, 1999). Nevertheless, exposure to violence has been linked to increased fear, heightened tolerance of violence, and greater desensitization to the effects of violence on others (Cantor, 2000).

Data linking exposure to messages about sex and drugs to actual sexual activity and drug use are considerably weaker than those concerning violence (Strasburger & Donnerstein, 1999). However, although researchers are not sure that exposure to messages about sex and drugs alters adolescents' *behavior,* repeated exposure likely affects their beliefs. For example, adolescents who watch a lot of music videos have more tolerant attitudes toward sexual harassment (Strouse, Goodwin, & Roscoe, 1994). Along similar lines, one study found that college students who frequently watched soap operas (which have a high sexual content) gave higher estimates than nonviewers did of the number of real-life extramarital affairs, children born out of wedlock, and divorces. Another found that high school students who believed that television characters enjoy highly satisfying sex were less likely themselves to feel that sex is satisfying, presumably because the images they had seen on television had set up false expectations (Roberts, 1993). Similarly, prolonged exposure to pornography leads to exaggerated beliefs about the extent of sexual activity in the real world (Zillman, 2000). And studies of exposure to ads for alcohol and tobacco have shown that they are effective in changing teenagers' attitudes about drinking and smoking and in the development of brand recognition (Brown & Witherspoon, in press).

Others have noted that many of the messages communicated to adolescents about the world are simply inaccurate. One analysis of the content of popular television shows about families, for example, found that the portrayal of families on television was markedly different from reality. On these shows, nonconventional families (single-parent homes, families with adopted children, families composed of children and nonparental guardians) were greatly overrepresented on television and that men were depicted as being much more involved in family roles than is generally the case. Difficult issues such as poverty, family conflict, divorce, and stress were generally sidestepped (Moore, 1992). Daytime soap operas, which are especially popular among adolescents, often present single mothers as having far more comfortable lives than is actually the case (Larson, 1996). Another analysis, of the presenta-

tion of work on television, found that television shows overrepresent and glamorize more prestigious, exciting, and adventurous jobs (e.g., lawyers, doctors, entertainers). Interestingly, adolescents who watch a great deal of television are more likely to aspire to such jobs and to believe that such jobs are easy and lucrative and permit one to take long vacations (Signorelli, 1993).

It is important to note that discussions of media effects often fail to distinguish between what adolescents actually perceive and remember and what *adults believe* adolescents see and remember. After all, the media are not simply viewed or heard—they are interpreted. Studies of violent video games, for example, find that adolescents, college students, and parents rate the same games very differently (Funk, Flores, Buchman, & Germann, 1999). Adolescents are not exposed to the mass media as blank slates; rather, they bring pre-existing values, beliefs, and expectations to the experience of watching or listening, and these pre-existing states influence what they perceive and remember (Leming, 1987). For instance, one extensive study of girls' responses to sexual media content found that some of the girls were disinterested in sexual media, others were intrigued, and still others resisted the sexual imagery to the point of criticizing it. When asked to comment on what she had been watching on television, for example, a disinterested girl wrote,

> I was watching Moonlighting [a TV show popular during the 1980s] tonight. . . . Maddie takes off her clothes (you don't see anything) and says, "Sam, I can't marry you because I love David, but for tonite, hold me. Make love to me." I thought it was kind of gross. (Brown, White, & Nikopoulou, 1993, p. 182)

This lack of interest in sexual matters was not seen among all other girls, however, some of whom were intrigued with the sexual content of media messages, if still somewhat confused. One such girl had written the following about a popular song:

> This song was about sex. This song was saying basically "Come over to my house so we can do it!" This represents sex as being O.K. Later I heard "Let's Wait Awhile" by Janet Jackson. Which basically says, "Let's not rush into it." It's kind of hard as a teenager to decide which is right. The guy who was talking about it as being good seemed happy with a carefree sound. Janet sounded sad and depressed. Even though I know it's better "to wait awhile" the other song was more appealing. It seemed harmless. They talk about it like, "come over and have ice cream." . . . I really know which way is the right way but sometimes the way the media talks about it you really begin to wonder. (p. 187)

Finally, some of the girls in the study actively resisted, even criticized, the sexual messages conveyed in the popular media. One commented on the movie *Top Gun*:

> Everyone went to see it because of Tom Cruise, they didn't go see it because it was a movie. They came back saying Tom Cruise looked so good and when I asked what it was about, they said, "Oh, flying or something." I didn't like it because of the relationship. They were just using each other at different times for different things. (p. 192)

Of a magazine ad for perfume, the same girl wrote,

> This is a very BAD sketch of part of an ad for Obsession by Calvin Klein—the whole idea portrayed is SEX, SEX, SEX—people are so goddamned hypocritical. They go all out against pornography and probably some of them buy this perfume. (p. 189)

RECAP

Much of adolescents' leisure time involves one or more of the mass media. Indeed, the average adolescent is exposed to the mass media about seven hours daily, with television being the most used medium. Whereas television viewing declines during adolescence, the use of music media, movies, and print media increases. Although adults have worried about the corrupting influence of media such as television and rock music, it has been difficult to document such alleged effects. Nevertheless, many observers of the adolescent scene are concerned about the high level of adolescents' exposure to messages about sex, violence, and drug use through the mass media.

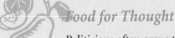

Food for Thought

Politicians often argue that adolescents' development is being adversely affected by the mass media. How do you respond to these claims?

Leisure and the Economy

A final, and very important, function of adolescent leisure activity is economic. Both the size of the adolescent population and the fact that adolescents save less than any other age group make young people an attractive target for a variety of businesses (Fine et al., 1990; Zollo, 1999). In 1999, teenagers spent $105 billion of their own money and an additional $48 billion of their family's money (Teen Research Unlimited, 1999). The average adolescent has nearly $400 per month in spending money and spends nearly all of it (girls spend slightly more each month than boys). Not surprisingly, virtually all of adolescents' money is spent on purchases related to leisure activities. According to surveys, girls spend money on clothes, food, and cosmetics, in that order; boys use their money for food, clothes, and savings for big-ticket items, such as cars and stereo equipment (Meyer, 1994).

One can certainly debate the merits of cultivating such strong consumer urges among the young and impressionable (see Greenberger & Steinberg, 1986). But it is important to recognize that the segments of our economy that are devoted to leisure and recreation depend on the adolescent market. Among the most important industries are those connected with movies, music, sports, and television. Teenagers make up a large, and therefore influential, segment of the consumers of these products—as a glance at the local movie or television listings or a trip through a music store will readily attest.

Students of adolescent consumerism have been quick to point out the strong influence that teenagers have on each other when it comes to purchases. It is important to point out, however, that the influence of the adolescent market extends well beyond the youth cohort—as evidenced by the uncanny predictability with which adult tastes in clothing and music often follow those of teenagers, albeit in a toned-down fashion. Teengers often have considerable influence over their parents' purchases, which gives added incentive for advertisers to market products with young people's tastes in mind (Valkenburg, 2000). Interestingly, the power of adolescents as consumers has increased in recent decades, owing to the growth in the proportion of single-parent and dual-worker households. In many such homes, adolescents influence both day-to-day and major purchases—in part, because adolescents themselves may do a fair amount of the family's shopping (Graham, 1988).

Web Researcher Financially strapped school districts are being forced to make tough decisions about how their budgets are spent. Some people argue that extracurricular activities are a frill that should be cut. Build a case for making extracurricular activities a central part of the educational experience. What do they do for adolescents? Whom do they benefit? How would you structure them to best support the school's academic program? Go to www.mhhe.com/steinberg6 for further information.

KEY TERMS

curvilinear pattern
Experience Sampling Method (ESM)
premature affluence
service learning

III

Psychosocial Development During Adolescence

Chapter 8

Identity

What am I like as a person? You're probably not going to understand. I'm complicated! With my really close friends, I am very tolerant. I mean, I'm understanding and caring. With a *group* of friends, I'm rowdier. I'm also usually friendly and cheerful but I can get pretty obnoxious and intolerant if I don't like how they're acting. I'd *like* to be friendly and tolerant all of the time, that's the kind of person I *want* to be, and I'm disappointed when I'm not. At school, I'm serious, even studious every now and then, but on the other hand I'm a goof-off too, because if you're *too* studious, you won't be popular. So I go back and forth, which means I don't do all that well in terms of my grades. But that causes problems at home, where I'm pretty anxious when I'm around my parents. They expect me to get all A's, and get pretty annoyed with me when report cards come out. I care what they think about me, and so then I get down on myself, but it's not fair! I mean, I worry about how I probably *should* get better grades, but I'd be mortified in the eyes of my friends if I did too well. So I'm usually pretty stressed-out at home, or sarcastic, since my parents are always on my case. But I really don't understand how I can switch so fast. I mean, how can I be cheerful with my friends, then coming home and feeling anxious, and then getting frustrated and sarcastic with my parents. Which one is the *real* me? I have the same question when I'm around boys. Sometimes I feel phony. Say I think some guy might be interested in asking me out. I try to act different, like Madonna. I'll be a real extrovert, fun-loving and even flirtatious, and think I am really good-looking. And then *everybody,* I mean everybody else is looking at me like they think I'm totally weird! *They* don't act like they think I'm attractive, so I end up thinking I look terrible. I just hate myself when that happens. Because it gets worse! Then I get self-conscious and embarrassed and become radically introverted, and I don't know who I really am! Am I just acting like an extrovert, am I just trying to impress them, when really I'm an introvert? But I don't really care what they think anyway. I mean, I don't *want* to care, that is. I just want to know what my close friends think. I can be my true self with my close friends. I can't be my real self with my parents. They don't understand me. What do *they* know about what it's like to be a teenager? They treat me like I'm still a kid. At least at school people treat you more like you're an adult. That gets confusing, though. I mean, which am I, a kid or an adult? . . . I have a part-time job and the people there treat me like an adult. I want to make them approve of me, so I'm very responsible at work. . . . But then I go out with my friends and I get pretty crazy and irresponsible. So which am I, responsible or irresponsible? How can the same person be both? . . . So I think a lot about who is the real me, and sometimes I try to figure it out when I write in my diary, but I can't resolve it. There are days when I wish I could just become immune to myself! (Harter, 1999, pp. 67–68)

As you may recall from your own adolescence, there are few experiences that can be as trying—or as exhilarating—as questioning who you really are and, more important, who you would like to be. Some, but not all, adolescents share the feelings of self-consciousness and confusion expressed in the preceding statement, by a 15-year-old girl. For these young people, adolescence is a time of identity crisis. For other adolescents, though, this period is one of more gradual and more subtle change.

Because changes—whether gradual or abrupt—take place during adolescence in the way young people view and feel about themselves, the study of identity development has been a major focus of research and theory on adolescents. In this chapter, we will examine whether adolescence is indeed a time of major changes in identity and how the course of adolescent identity development is shaped by the nature of life in contemporary society. •

IDENTITY AS AN ADOLESCENT ISSUE

Changes in the way in which we see and feel about ourselves occur throughout the life cycle. You have probably heard and read about the so-called midlife crisis, for example—an identity crisis thought to occur during middle age. And certainly there are important changes in self-conceptions and in self-image throughout childhood. When a group of 4-year-olds and a group of 10-year-olds are asked to describe themselves, the older children provide a far more complex self-portrait. Whereas young children restrict their descriptions to lists of what they own or what they like to do, older children are more likely to tell you also about their personality.

If, in fact, changes in identity occur throughout the life cycle, why have researchers who are interested in identity development paid so much attention to adolescence? One reason is that the changes in identity that take place during adolescence involve the first substantial reorganization and restructuring of the individual's sense of self at a time when he or she has the intellectual capability to appreciate fully just how significant the changes are. Although important changes in identity certainly occur during childhood, the adolescent is far more self-conscious about these changes and feels them much more acutely.

▲ *For some young people, like those portrayed in the television show* Dawson's Creek, *adolescence is a time of identity crisis. For other adolescents, the period is one of more gradual and subtle change.* (Photofest)

Another reason for the attention that researchers and theorists have given the study of identity development during adolescence concerns the fundamental biological, cognitive, and social changes characteristic of the period. Puberty, as we saw in chapter 1, brings with it dramatic changes in physical appearance and alters the adolescent's self-conceptions and relationships with others. It is not hard to see why puberty plays an important role in provoking identity development during adolescence. When you change the way you look— when you have your hair cut in a different way, lose a great deal of weight, or dramatically change the way you dress—you sometimes feel as though your personality has changed, too. During puberty, when adolescents are changing so dramatically on the outside, they understandably have questions about changes that are

taking place on the inside. For the adolescent, undergoing the physical changes of puberty may prompt fluctuations in the self-image and a reevaluation of who he or she really is.

Just as the broadening of intellectual capabilities during early adolescence provides new ways of thinking about problems, values, and interpersonal relationships, it also permits adolescents to think about themselves in new ways. We saw in chapter 2 that it is not until adolescence that the young person is able to think in systematic ways about hypothetical and future events. For this reason, it is not until adolescence that individuals typically begin to wonder "Who will I become?" "What possible identities are open to me?" or "What am I really like?" Because the preadolescent child's thinking is concrete, it is difficult for him or her to think seriously about being a different person. But the changes in thinking that take place during adolescence open up a whole new world of alternatives.

Finally, we saw in chapter 3 that the changes in social roles that occur at adolescence open up a new array of choices and decisions for the young person that were not concerns previously. In contemporary society, adolescence is a time of important decisions about work, marriage, and the future. Facing these decisions about our place in society does more than provoke questions about who we are and where we are headed—it necessitates the questions. At this point in the life cycle, young people must make important choices about their careers and their commitments to other people, and thinking about these questions prompts them to ask more questions about themselves: "What do I *really* want out of life?" "What things are important to me?" "What kind of person would I *really* like to be?" Questions about the future, which inevitably arise as the adolescent prepares for adulthood, raise questions about identity.

Identity development is complex and multifaceted. Actually, it is better understood as a series of interrelated developments—rather than one single development—that all involve changes in the way we view ourselves in relation to others and in relation to the broader society in which we live. Generally speaking, researchers and theorists have taken three approaches to the question of how the individual's sense of identity changes over the course of adolescence. Each approach, examined in detail in this chapter, focuses on a different aspect of identity development.

The first approach emphasizes changes in *self-conceptions*—the ideas that individuals have of themselves as regards various traits and attributes. An entirely different approach focuses on adolescents' *self-esteem,* or self-image—how positively or negatively individuals feel about themselves. Finally, a third approach emphasizes changes in the *sense of identity*—the sense of who one is, where one has come from, and where one is going.

RECAP

Although changes in the way we see and feel about ourselves occur throughout the life cycle, the study of identity development has been a prominent issue in the field of adolescent development in particular. One reason for this attention concerns the impact of the biological, cognitive, and social definitional changes of adolescence on the young person's ability to engage in self-examination, as well as on his or her interest in doing so. Researchers have traditionally distinguished among three aspects of identity development in adolescence: changes in self-conceptions, changes in self-esteem, and changes in the sense of identity.

CHANGES IN SELF-CONCEPTIONS

During adolescence, important shifts occur in the way individuals think about and characterize themselves—that is, in their **self-conceptions.** As individuals mature intellectually and undergo the sorts of cognitive changes described in chapter 2, they come to conceive of themselves in more sophisticated and more differentiated ways. As we saw in that chapter, adolescents are much more capable than children of thinking about abstract concepts and considerably more proficient in processing large amounts of information. These intellectual advantages affect the way in which individuals characterize themselves. Compared with children, who tend to describe themselves in relatively simple, concrete terms, adolescents are more likely to use complex, abstract, and psychological self-characterizations (Harter, 1999).

Self-conceptions change in structure as well as in content during the transition from childhood into and through adolescence. Structurally, self-conceptions become more differentiated and better organized (Byrne & Shavelson, 1996; Marsh, 1989; Montemayor & Eisen, 1977).

Let's first consider the idea that self-conceptions become more differentiated. In answer to the question "Who am I?" adolescents are more likely than children to link traits and attributes that describe themselves to specific situations, rather than to use them as global characterizations. Whereas a preadolescent child might say, "I am nice" or "I am friendly" and not specify when or under what conditions, an adolescent is more likely to say, "I am nice *if* I am in a good mood" or "I am friendly *when* I am with people I have met before." The realization that one's personality is expressed in different ways in different situations is one example of the increased differentiation that characterizes the self-conceptions of youngsters as they mature toward adulthood.

There is another way in which self-conceptions become more highly differentiated at adolescence. As opposed to characterizations provided by children, adolescents' self-descriptions take into account *who* is doing the describing (Harter, 1999). Teenagers differentiate between their own opinions of themselves and the views of others. Suppose you were to ask a group of youngsters to describe how they behave when they are with other people. Instead of saying, "I am shy" or "I am outgoing," an adolescent would be more likely to say, "People think I'm not at all shy, but, most of the time, I'm really nervous about meeting other kids for the first time." Adolescents also recognize that they may come across differently to different people, another type of differentiation in self-conceptions that does not appear until this point in time: "My parents think I'm quiet, but my friends know I really like to party a lot."

With this shift toward increased differentiation in self-conceptions comes better organization and integration (Harter, 1999; Marsh, 1989a). When children are asked to describe themselves, the traits and attributes they list remain somewhat disparate, like items haphazardly placed on a grocery list. Adolescents, however, are likely to organize and integrate various aspects of their self-conception into a more logical, coherent whole. Whereas a younger child may list a sequence of several traits that appear to be contradictory ("I am friendly. I am shy."), an adolescent will attempt to organize apparently discrepant bits of information into more highly organized statements ("I am shy when I first meet people, but, after I get to know them, I am usually pretty friendly.")

Although it does not appear that self-conceptions become even more differentiated after early adolescence (Marsh, 1989a), the movement toward more abstract and more psychological self-conceptions continues well into the high school years, as the 15-year-old's self-description at the beginning of this chapter clearly indicates. Interestingly, however, the increased abstraction and psychological complexity of self-conceptions may present some difficulties for middle adolescents, who may be able to recognize—but not yet quite understand or reconcile—inconsistencies and contradictions in their personalities. The proportion of adolescents who give opposite traits in self-descriptions, who feel conflicts over such discrepancies, and who feel confused over such discrepancies increases markedly between the seventh and ninth grades, and then it declines somewhat after (Harter & Monsour, 1992). For example, one 15-year-old girl, when asked about her contention that she was happy with friends but depressed with her family, said, "I really think of myself as a happy person, and I want to be that way with everyone because I think that's my true self, but I get depressed with my family and it bugs me because that's not what I want to be like" (Harter & Monsour, 1992, p. 253).

In one study, when asked to reflect on contradictions in their personalities, early, middle, and late adolescents responded in very different ways, as in the following examples (cited in Harter, 1990, p. 358):

> I guess I just think about one thing about myself at a time and don't think about the other until the next day. (*early adolescent*)

> I really think I am a happy person and I want to be that way with everyone, but I get depressed with my family and it really bugs me because that's not what I want to be like. (*middle adolescent*)

> You can be shy on a date, and then outgoing with friends because you are just different with different people; you can't always be the same person and probably shouldn't be. (*late adolescent*)

In another series of studies, psychologist Susan Harter (1999) and her colleagues asked adolescents to characterize their personalities by listing the traits they thought characterized themselves in various settings. The adolescents were also asked to identify opposite traits, either within or across settings, by connecting them with a line and to indicate opposite traits that *clashed* with each other by drawing arrowheads on the line. Figure 8.1 shows the diagram constructed by one 15-year-old girl.

Although the recognition that one's personality is multifaceted—even contradictory—may initially cause some distress, in the long run it probably has a number of advantages. Indeed, some psychologists have suggested that the development of a more complicated view of oneself is one way that individuals cope with the recognition of their faults and weaknesses, a recognition that comes with the increased self-awareness of adolescence ("I'm not really a nasty person; I just act mean when people tease me"). Consistent with this, adolescents who have more complex self-conceptions are less likely to be depressed (Evans, 1993; Jordan & Cole, 1996). One additional advantage of having a more differentiated self-conception is that the adolescent is now able to distinguish among his or her actual self (who the adolescent really is), ideal self (who the adolescent would like to be), and feared self (who the adolescent most dreads becoming). According to one view, being able to make these distinctions provides a motive for the adolescent to improve—either to bring his or her actual self more into line with the ideal self or to strive to become one's ideal self and avoid becoming one's feared self (Markus & Nurius, 1986; Oyserman & Markus, 1990). One important aspect of having a healthy self-conception is having an ideal self to balance a feared self. One study found, for example, that delinquent adolescents are less likely than nondelinquent youth to have this sort of balanced view; although delinquent adolescents might dread becoming criminals, for instance, they may not have a positive hoped-for self (e.g., to be successfully employed) to balance this fear (Oyserman & Markus, 1990). Interestingly, adolescents tend to imagine more similarity between their present and future selves than they say exists between their past and present selves (Hart, Fegley, & Brengelman, 1993).

Another interesting consequence of adolescents' recognition that they are not always consistent in their personalities relates to their ability to distinguish between their true and false selves (i.e., their authentic and inauthentic selves). Adolescents are most likely to behave inauthentically in romantic and dating situations and with classmates, and they are least likely to put on a false front with close friends. Interestingly, false-self behavior—acting in a way that one knows is inauthentic—occurs less often with parents than with dates, but more often with parents than with close friends (Harter, 1990). Although adolescents sometimes say that they dislike false-self behavior, they also say that there are times in which it is acceptable, such as when one is trying to impress another person or trying to hide an aspect of his or her personality that others do not like. You can well imagine how the ability to put on a false front would come in handy on a date, at school, or with one's parents.

Adolescents differ, of course, in the degree to which they present false fronts and in their reasons for doing so. In general, adolescents who report less emotional support from parents and peers, those who have low self-esteem, and those who are relatively more depressed and hopeless than their peers are more likely to engage in false-self behavior. Whereas some adolescents engage

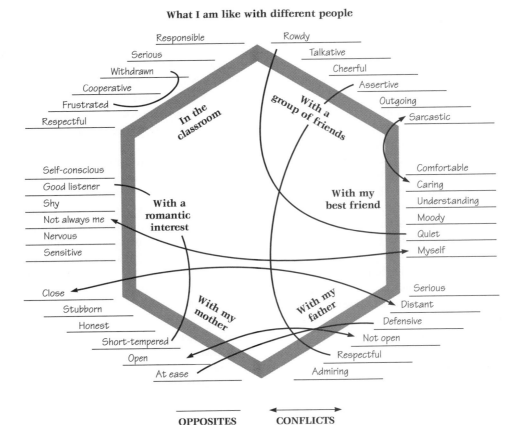

Figure 8.1   *The multiple selves of a 15-year-old girl. Some opposing traits are experienced as clashing with each other (indicated by lines with arrowheads), whereas others are not.* (Harter, 1999)

in false-self behavior because they are low in self-esteem, others experience a drop in self-esteem because they knowingly put on a false front. Depression and hopelessness are highest among adolescents who engage in false-self behavior because they genuinely devalue their true selves, in contrast to those who put on a false front because they want to please others or because they are experimenting with different personalities (Harter, Marold, Whitesell, & Cobbs, 1996).

Understanding how self-conceptions change during adolescence helps explain why identity issues begin to take on so much importance at this time in the life span. As self-conceptions become more abstract and as individuals become more able to see themselves in psychological terms, young people become more interested in understanding their own personalities and why they behave the way they do. The distress caused by recognizing one's inconsistencies may spur identity development. You may recall having wondered as a teenager about your personality development, about the influences that shaped your character, and about how your

personality had changed over time. "Am I more like my father or like my mother? Why do my sister and I seem so different? Will I always be so shy?" Although these sorts of questions may seem commonplace to you now, in all likelihood you did not think about these things until adolescence, when your own self-conceptions became more abstract and more sophisticated.

RECAP

During the transition into adolescence, self-conceptions become increasingly complex, abstract, and psychological. In addition, adolescents' self-conceptions are more differentiated and better organized than those of children. Although having more complex self-conceptions initially may be unsettling to the adolescent, it ultimately provides for a more sophisticated and more accurate view of oneself. In addition, adolescents are able to distinguish between their actual and their imagined selves, as well as between their authentic and false selves.

Food for Thought

False-self behavior occurs less often with parents than with dates but more often with parents than with close friends. How do you explain this?

Dimensions of Personality in Adolescence

Whereas many researchers have studied adolescent personality development by examining young people's views of themselves, others have attempted to assess personality by administering standardized inventories designed to assess the most important aspects of personality. Most personality researchers now approach the study of personality using the **Five-Factor Model** (McCrae & John, 1992), which is based on the observation that there are five critical personality dimensions, often referred to as the **Big Five:** *extraversion* (how outgoing and energetic a person is), *agreeableness* (how kind or sympathetic someone is), *conscientiousness* (how responsible and organized someone is), *neuroticism* (how anxious or tense someone is), and *openness to experience* (how curious and imaginative someone is). Although the Five-Factor Model was developed through research on adults, it has been applied successfully to adolescents as well (Caspi, 1997). For example, delinquent adolescents are more likely than their peers to score high on the extraversion dimension and low on the agreeableness and conscientiousness dimensions, whereas adolescents who are high achievers in school score high on the conscientiousness and openness dimensions (John, Caspi, Robins, Moffitt, & Stouthamer-Loeber, 1994). In general, the structure of personality appears comparable across groups of adolescents from different ethnic backgrounds (Markstrom-Adams & Adams, 1995; Rowe, Vazsonyi, & Flannery, 1994).

Researchers point to both genetic and environmental influences on individual differences in personality traits (e.g., Rose, 1988). Individuals may inherit temperamental predispositions (such as a high activity level or an inclination to be sociable), which are observable early in life, and these predispositions may harden and become organized into personality traits partially in response to the environment (Gest, 1997; John et al., 1994). Thus, an active, sociable child who enjoys interacting with others may be rewarded for doing so and, over time, may become extraverted. Longitudinal studies show that both temperament and personality be-

come increasingly stable as we grow older, in part because we tend to spend time in environments that reward and reinforce the traits that draw us to these settings (Guerin & Gottfried, in press).

In sum, there is a good deal of evidence that many core personality traits, such as impulsivity and timidity, are quite stable between childhood and adolescence and between adolescence and young adulthood. Although the external manifestations of these traits may change with age (for example, anxiety may appear as bed wetting in early childhood but as nervous talkativeness in adolescence), basic, underlying traits are quite stable over time. For example, studies show that individuals who displayed relatively higher levels of aggression in preadolescence, temper tantrums during childhood, or negative emotions during infancy are more likely to behave aggressively as adolescents (Cairns, Cairns, & Neckerman, 1989; Caspi, Elder, & Bem, 1987; Caspi, Henry, McGee, Moffitt, & Silva, 1995; Hart, Hofmann, Edelstein, & Keller, 1997; Lerner, Hertzog, Hooker, Hassibi, & Thomas, 1988). Similarly, individuals who have difficulty controlling their impulses as preschoolers are more likely to be impulsive, aggressive, and danger-seeking as adolescents and young adults, whereas young children who are inhibited or sluggish tend to be relatively more timid, anxious, and shy as teenagers. Not surprisingly, then, individuals who are judged to be well adjusted in early and middle childhood tend to be resilient and competent in adolescence (Caspi & Silva, 1995; Caspi, et al., 1995; Gest, 1997; Gjerde, 1995; Hart, Hofmann, Edelstein, & Keller, 1997; Hart, Keller, Edelstein, & Hoffmann, 1998).

RECAP

There are five basic personality dimensions in adolescence and adulthood, often referred to as the Big Five: extraversion, agreeableness, conscientiousness, neuroticism, and openness to experience. In general, these traits are influenced by a combination of genetic and environmental factors and are highly stable over time. Longitudinal studies show strong links between early temperament and adolescent personality.

Food for Thought

What are the basic dimensions of personality in adolescence? Why is there continuity in personality over childhood and adolescence?

CHANGES IN SELF-ESTEEM

As noted in the Introduction to this book, ever since G. Stanley Hall initially suggested that adolescence is a time of storm and stress, researchers and theorists have asked whether adolescence is a more difficult time for the developing person than are earlier or later periods in the life span. For many years, in fact, the idea that adolescence is inherently stressful for the individual was accepted without question. One of the manifestations assumed to result from the stress of adolescence involves problems in the adolescent's **self-esteem**—how the individual feels about himself or herself.

Despite these popular stereotypes, research has not supported the view that adolescence is a time of tumultuous upheaval in personality, however; nor is adolescence the time of "rebirth" that philosophers once cast it as being—far from it. Indeed, as one team of researchers put it, "The person who enters adolescence is basically the same as that who exits it" (Dusek & Flaherty, 1981, p. 39).

Adolescents' feelings about themselves, nevertheless, may fluctuate from day to day, particularly during the very early adolescent years (late elementary school and junior high school). From about eighth grade on, however, self-esteem remains highly stable; in other words, individuals with high self-esteem as children are likely to have high self-esteem as adolescents. Nor is there any apparent loss of self-esteem during adolescence. If anything, over the course of middle and late adolescence, and between late adolescence and young adulthood, self-esteem either remains at about the same level or increases (Block & Robins, 1993; Harter, 1997; Nottelmann, 1987; O'Malley & Bachman, 1983; Rosenberg, 1986; Savin-Williams & Demo, 1984). In general, self-esteem tends to become increasingly more stable with age, suggesting that adolescents' feelings about themselves gradually consolidate over time and become less likely to fluctuate in response to various experiences (Alasker & Olweus, 1992).

Although the storm-and-stress view of adolescence is not supported in studies of adolescent self-esteem, there is some evidence that, for a brief and temporary period during early adolescence, minor problems in self-image may arise. About 30 years ago, Roberta Simmons and her colleagues conducted a series of now-classic studies that shed light on when and why these problems in self-image are likely to occur. These researchers (Simmons, Rosenberg, & Rosenberg, 1973) used an extensive questionnaire to assess three aspects of adolescents' self-image: their self-esteem (how positively or negatively they feel about themselves), their **self-consciousness** (how much they worry about their self-image), and their **self-image sta-**

bility (how much they feel that their self-image changes from day to day). They hypothesized that young adolescents would show the lowest levels of self-esteem, the highest levels of self-consciousness, and the shakiest self-image.

Consistent with their expectations, these researchers found that fluctuations in the self-image are most likely to occur between the ages of 12 and 14. Compared with older adolescents (15 years and older) and with preadolescents (8 to 11 years old), early adolescents have lower self-esteem, are more self-conscious, and have a more unstable self-image than other youngsters. Younger adolescents are also more prone to feel shame than older individuals, which may result from, and contribute to, their heightened self-consciousness (Reimer, 1996a, 1996b). Generally speaking, the small but reliable differences between the preadolescents and the early adolescents are greater than those between the younger and the older adolescents, which indicates that the most marked fluctuations in self-image occur during the transition into adolescence, rather than over the course of adolescence itself (Simmons, Rosenberg, & Rosenberg, 1973).

How can we reconcile these findings about fluctuations in self-esteem with studies indicating that self-esteem is quite stable during adolescence? According to sociologist Morris Rosenberg (1986), it is important to differentiate between two aspects of self-perceptions in looking at studies of self-esteem. **Barometric self-esteem** is the extent to which our feelings about ourselves shift and fluctuate rapidly, from moment to moment. Perhaps you can remember times as a teenager—or even as an adult—when you entered a room full of people and were feeling confident, but you suddenly felt nervous and insecure—only to engage in a pleasant interaction with someone an hour later and feel confident once again. You were experiencing fluctuations in your barometric self-esteem. **Baseline self-esteem,** in contrast, is less transitory and less likely to fluctuate from moment to moment. This aspect of self-image is relatively stable over time and is unlikely to be easily shifted by immediate experiences. Even if you feel momentarily insecure when entering a room full of unfamiliar people, your integral, or baseline, self-esteem has not shifted. Indeed, individuals with high baseline self-esteem readily dismiss transient feelings of insecurity as having more to do with the situation than with themselves.

Studies that report very high stability in self-esteem during adolescence are likely tapping the individual's baseline self-esteem, which is unlikely to change dramatically over time. This may be because the determinants of baseline self-esteem are themselves relatively stable factors, such as social class (middle-class adolescents have higher self-esteem than do less affluent peers); sex (boys have higher self-esteem than girls); birth order (oldest or only children have higher self-esteem); and academic ability (more able adolescents have higher self-esteem) (Bachman & O'Malley, 1986; Jackson, Hodge, & Ingram, 1994; Savin-Williams & Demo, 1983). In contrast, studies that show fluctuation and volatility in self-image during early adolescence are probably focusing on the barometric self-image, which, by definition, is more likely to fluctuate.

It seems safe to say, therefore, that, although individuals' baseline self-image does not change markedly during adolescence, early adolescence is a time of increased volatility in the barometric self-image (Rosenberg, 1986). In other words, young adolescents are more likely than children and older adolescents to experience moment-to-moment shifts in self-esteem. Interestingly, the extent to which an individual's barometric self-esteem is volatile is itself a fairly stable trait; that is, young adolescents whose self-image fluctuates a lot from moment to moment are likely to develop into older adolescents who experience the same thing (Savin-Williams & Demo, 1983).

Although an individual's baseline self-image is probably a better overall indicator of how the person feels about himself or herself, fluctuations in barometric self-image can be distressing and uncomfortable—as most of us know well (Rosenberg, 1986). Consistent with this, studies indicate that young adolescents report higher levels of depression than do preadolescents and older teenagers (Simmons, Rosenberg, & Rosenberg, 1973). Moreover, young adolescents with the most volatile self-image report the highest levels of anxiety, tension, psychosomatic symptoms, and irritability (Rosenberg, 1986). This is especially likely among adolescents who have a great deal of stress in their day-to-day lives (Tevendale, DuBois, Lopez, & Prindiville, 1997). In other words, having a volatile self-image may make individuals especially vulnerable to the effects of stress.

Volatility in barometric self-image during early adolescence probably reflects several interrelated factors. First, the sort of egocentrism that is common in early adolescence, discussed in chapter 2, may make the young adolescent painfully aware of others' reactions to his or her behavior. Second, as individuals become more socially active, they begin to learn that people play games when they interact; consequently, they learn that it is not always possible to tell what people are thinking on the basis of how they act or what they say. This ambiguity may leave the young adolescent—who is relatively unskilled at this sort of "impression management"—puzzled and un-

comfortable about how he or she is really viewed by others. Finally, because of the increased importance of peers in early adolescence, young adolescents are especially interested in their peers' opinions of them. For the first time, they may have to come to terms with contradictions between the messages they get from their parents ("I think that hairstyle makes you even *more* beautiful") and the messages they get from their peers ("You'd better wear a hat until your hair grows back"). Hearing contradictory messages probably generates a certain degree of uncertainty about oneself (Rosenberg, 1986).

Some researchers have argued that the question of whether self-esteem is stable during adolescence is a poor one. According to several studies (Deihl, Vicary, & Deike, 1997; Hirsch & DuBois, 1991; Zimmerman, Copeland, Shope, & Dielman, 1997), some adolescents show very high stability in self-esteem over time, whereas others do not. In one study, the researchers identified four dramatically different self-esteem trajectories followed by youngsters during the transition into junior high school (see figure 8.2). Approximately one-third of the adolescents were classified as consistently high in self-esteem, and approximately one-sixth were classified as chronically low. Half the sample, however, showed impressive patterns of change over just a two-year period: About one-fifth were categorized as steeply declining, and nearly one-third showed a small but significant increase

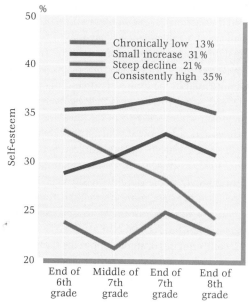

Figure 8.2   Research indicates that individuals follow four types of self-esteem trajectories during early adolescence. (Adapted from Hirsch & DuBois, 1991)

▲ *Today, most researchers believe that self-esteem is multidimensional and that young people evaluate themselves along several dimensions simultaneously. As a consequence, it is possible for an adolescent to have high self-esteem when it comes to athletic abilities but low self-esteem when it comes to academics.*
(Larry S. Voight/Photo Researchers)

in self-esteem. This pattern is reminiscent of one we encountered in chapter 2, in which we saw that, while most of the youngsters in one study demonstrated stability in IQ scores over time, a substantial minority showed marked fluctuations. These studies remind us that focusing only on general tendencies may mask important individual differences in developmental trajectories. Studies indicate that boys may be disproportionately overrepresented in the group of adolescents whose self-esteem increases, whereas girls may be overrepresented in the group whose self-esteem declines—even though most boys and girls show stability, rather than dramatic change, in self-esteem during adolescence (Block & Robins, 1993; Koenig, 1995; Zimmerman et al., 1997). Not surprisingly, adolescents with stronger family and peer relationships are more likely than their peers to maintain positive self-esteem or to develop enhanced self-esteem over time (Deihl et al., 1997).

A second criticism of studies about the stability of self-esteem in adolescence questions the validity of examining self-esteem in such a global, or general, sense. Although most research on adolescent self-esteem has focused on teenagers' overall feelings about themselves, most researchers today believe that young people evaluate themselves both globally (which may be a good indicator of

general psychological well-being) and along several distinct dimensions, such as academics, athletics, appearance, social relationships, and moral conduct (which may indicate specific areas of strength and weakness) (Andrews, Hops, Davis, & Duncan, 1995; Cauce, 1987; DuBois, Felner, Brand, Phillips, & Lease, 1996; Harter, 1999; Graziano, Jensen-Campbell, & Finch 1997; Lau, 1990; Masten et al., 1995; Owens, 1994; Rosenberg, Schooler, Schoenbach, & Rosenberg, 1995). As a consequence, it is possible for an adolescent to have high self-esteem when it comes to academic abilities, low self-esteem when it comes to athletics, and moderate self-esteem when it comes to physical appearance, social relationships, or moral conduct. The following passage, taken from a study of adolescent self-esteem by Susan Harter (1990), is fairly typical:

How much do I *like* the kind of person I am? Well, I like some things about me, but I don't like others. I'm glad that I'm popular since it's really important to me to have friends. But in school I don't do as well as the really smart kids. That's OK, because if you're too smart you'll lose your friends. So being smart is just not that important. Except to my parents. I feel like I'm letting them down when I don't do as well as they want. But what's really important to me is how I look. If I like the way I look, then I really like the kind of person I am. Don't get me wrong. I mean, I don't exactly look like Madonna even though I try to act like her. But compared to the other girls in my school, I'm sort of good-looking. There's another thing about how much I like the kind of person I am. It matters what other people think, especially the other kids at school. It matters whether they like you. I care about what my parents think about me too. I've also changed. It started when I went to junior high school. I got really depressed. I thought it was going to be so great, like I'd feel so grown-up, and then I saw all of these new, older kids who really had it together and I didn't. So I felt terrible. There was this one day when I hated the way I looked, and I didn't get invited to this really important party, and then I got an awful report card, so for a couple of days I thought it would be best to just end it all. I mean, why bother getting up the next morning? What's the point? Who cares? I was letting my parents down, I wasn't good-looking anymore, and I wasn't that popular after all, and things were never going to get better. I talked to Sheryl, my best friend, and that helped

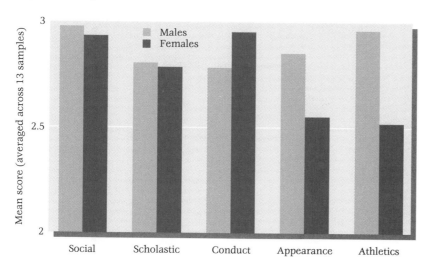

Figure 8.3 Sex differences in various domains of self-esteem. (Harter, 1999)

measurement of level of self esteem in student

some, but what does she really know? I mean, she's my best friend, so of course she likes me! I mean, her opinion doesn't really count. It's what all the other kids think and want that counts. It was a lot easier for my brother. He got involved in this gang and just decided that what they thought was what was really important, and he stopped caring about the kids in school, or my parents, or even society. That's what he did, and he likes himself fine. But I really don't, not right now. (pp. 364–365)

Even within the broad domains of self-esteem (academics, athletics, social relationships, etc.) adolescents may have quite differentiated views of themselves. Studies show, for example, that adolescents' evaluations of themselves within the context of their relationships with their parents may be very different from the way they see themselves in the context of their relationships with teachers, which in turn may differ from their evaluations of themselves in the context of their friendships with peers (Harter, Waters, & Whitesell, 1998). Moreover, adolescents' social self-esteem may vary depending on whether they are thinking about their friendships or their romantic relationships (Connolly & Konarski, 1994). Therefore, it may be misleading to characterize an adolescent's social self-esteem as low or high without specifying the context of the relationship.

Do some aspects of self-esteem contribute more to an adolescent's overall self-image than others? The answer appears to be yes. In general, adolescents' physical self-esteem—how they feel about their appearance—is the most important predictor of overall self-esteem, followed by self-esteem about relationships with peers (Harter, 1999). Less important are self-esteem about academic ability, athletic ability, and moral conduct. Interestingly,

although researchers find that adolescents' physical self-esteem is the best predictor of their overall self-esteem, adolescents, when asked, say that their physical appearance is one of the *least* important contributors to how they feel about themselves. This suggests that adolescents are unaware of the degree to which their self-worth is based on their feelings about their appearance (DuBois, Tevendale, Burk-Braxton, Swenson, & Hardesty, 2000). It is important to note both that physical self-esteem is a more important influence on overall self-esteem among girls than among boys (Harter, 1990; Usmiani & Daniluk, 1997) and that girls' physical self-esteem is, on average, lower than boys' (see figure 8.3) (Harter, 1999). Together, these findings help explain why there are sex differences in the extent to which adolescents experience self-image difficulties and depression (see chapter 13).

RECAP

Researchers have differed in their approach to the study of self-esteem. Whereas some have studied adolescents' general, or global, feelings about themselves, others have stressed the multidimensional nature of self-esteem. Research into changes in self-image during adolescence has helped paint a new picture of adolescence as a developmental period. In contrast to views that prevailed 30 years ago, adolescence is now viewed as a time of gradual rather than tumultuous change in the individual's self-image. For most individuals, global self-esteem is quite stable during adolescence and, contrary to popular belief, increases slightly. During early adolescence, however, individuals' self-image may fluctuate more than during other periods.

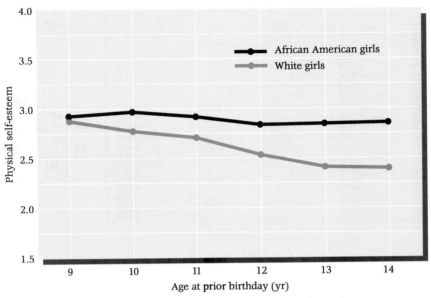

Figure 8.4   *Race differences in patterns of change in physical self-esteem.* (Brown et al., 1998)

Food for Thought

Does the concept of barometric self-esteem make sense to you? What do you think makes barometric self-esteem more volatile in some individuals than in others? Is it possible to have high baseline self-esteem but very volatile barometric self-esteem?

Sex, Class, and Ethnic Differences in Self-esteem

Not all adolescents undergo the same degree of fluctuation in self-esteem; nor are all adolescents' levels of self-esteem comparable. Several studies have shown that early adolescent girls, especially white girls, are more vulnerable to disturbances in self-image than is any other group of youngsters. Specifically, their self-esteem is lower, their degree of self-consciousness higher, and their self-image shakier than is the case for boys (Harter, 1999; Kling, Hyde, Showers, & Buswell, 1999; Simmons & Rosenberg, 1975). They are more likely to say negative things about themselves, to feel insecure about their abilities, and to worry about whether other people like being with them. Studies of African American girls, however, do not find the same sort of self-esteem

vulnerability, in part because they do not experience the same drop in body image during puberty as white girls (see figure 8.4) (Brown et al., 1998).

Why would girls have greater difficulty than boys during early adolescence? The answer may be related to the special significance of physical self-esteem and self-esteem about acceptance by peers. Young girls seem to worry a great deal about their looks and about dating and being popular in school, yet they are also worried about doing well academically. Boys and older adolescents care about these things, of course, but they have a more casual, less worried attitude. Adolescent girls may feel caught in bind between pressures to do well academically and pressures to do well socially, especially as they move into secondary school. As we saw in chapter 5, getting good grades in school is at the bottom of the list of attributes that adolescent girls feel are important for being accepted into the leading crowd (Coleman, 1961). Several studies have shown that adolescents who worry a lot about being popular are most likely to feel self-conscious and are most likely to have unstable views of themselves (Simmons & Rosenberg, 1975). Because young girls appear to be more concerned than boys about physical attractiveness, dating, and peer acceptance, they may experience a greater number of self-image problems. Because African American girls do not feel as negatively about their appearance as white and Latina girls, African American girls have higher overall self-esteem and show less of a decline in self-esteem over adolescence than do white and Latina girls (Gray-Little & Hafdahl, 2000; Malanchuk & Eccles, 1999; Prosser & Carlson, 1999).

Studies also indicate that an adolescent's social class—as indexed by his or her parents' occupations, education, and income—is an important determinant of self-esteem, especially as the individual moves into middle and later adolescence. In general, middle-class youngsters have higher self-esteem than their less affluent peers, and this discrepancy grows greater over the course of adolescence. One explanation for this is that middle-class youngsters do better in school than their less affluent peers, and this success leads to enhanced self-esteem (Demo & Savin-Williams, 1983).

Most research on ethnic differences in self-esteem has focused on African American youngsters. Although early studies suggested that African American children suffer from a poor self-image, more recent research indicates that the self-esteem of African American adolescents is comparable to, or greater than, that of their majority peers (Gray-Little & Hafdahl, 2000). A number of researchers have asked why this is, given the prevalence of prejudice in American society and the generally disadvantaged position of African Americans in the workplace and in school, two institutions where individuals' performance is believed to influence their self-image. Three main explanations for the relatively high self-esteem of African American adolescents have been offered.

First, some writers have argued that, despite their encounters with racism and prejudice, African American teenagers benefit from the support and positive feedback of adults in the African American community, especially in the family (Barnes, 1980). This is not surprising, given the wealth of research showing that the approval of significant others is an especially powerful influence on adolescents' self-esteem—much more so than the opinion of the broader society (e.g., Felson & Zielinski, 1989; Gray-Little & Hafdahl, 2000; Luster & McAdoo, 1995; Robinson, 1995). Second, other researchers suggest that all teenagers—minority and otherwise—tend to shift their priorities over time, so that they come to value the activities at which they excel. In doing so, adolescents are able to protect their self-esteem by focusing on areas of strength instead of weakness. For example, a boy who is an outstanding student but who feels physically unattractive and has not been doing well in sports will likely derive positive self-esteem from his school achievement and not restrict his self-evaluation to his looks or performance on the playing field (Luster & McAdoo, 1995). Finally, several

writers have suggested that the very strong sense of ethnic identity among African American adolescents enhances their overall self-esteem (Gray-Little & Hafdahl, 2000).

The context in which adolescents develop has a substantial impact on self-image, however. Some research indicates, for example, that high school–age youngsters who live in a social environment or go to a school in which their ethnic or socioeconomic group is in the minority are more likely to have self-image problems than those who are in the majority (Rosenberg, 1975). This seems to be true with regard to religion, socioeconomic status, race, and household composition. African American teenagers, for example, have a higher opinion of themselves when they go to schools in which African American students are a majority than when they attend predominantly white schools, where they may feel out of place and under pressure to play down their cultural heritage. By the same token, Jewish adolescents have higher self-esteem in schools in which there are many other Jewish students than in schools in which Jews compose a small minority of the student body. Similarly, levels of maladjustment are higher among both Hispanic and non-Hispanic youngsters when they are in the minority in their school (Kaufman, Gregory, & Stephan, 1990).

Interestingly, studies of differences in self-esteem within families indicate that self-esteem actually may have some genetic determinants (McGuire, Neiderhiser, Reiss, Hetherington, & Plomin, 1994). Thus, at least some of the factors that influence how we evaluate ourselves are biological, and parents influence their children's self-esteem through the genes they pass on as well as through the environment they provide.

Antecedents and Consequences of High Self-esteem

Several researchers have examined the link between self-esteem and adolescent behavior, in an attempt to see whether certain sorts of experiences contribute—either positively or negatively—to adolescents' feelings about themselves. Others have posed the question in reverse: Does having high (or low) self-esteem lead adolescents to behave in particular ways?

Regarding the question of whether experience contributes to self-esteem, studies find that self-esteem is enhanced by having the approval of others, especially of parents and peers, and by having success in school (Bachman & O'Malley, 1986; Bohrnstedt & Felson, 1983; Hoge, Smit, & Hanson, 1990; Liu, Kaplan, & Risser, 1992; Luster

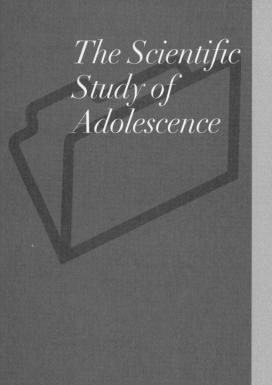

The Scientific Study of Adolescence

Ethnic Differences in Self-esteem: Studying Means Versus Studying Correlations

Social scientists who study adolescence often rely on two very different types of statistical tests to draw conclusions about adolescent development. One set of tests searches for *mean differences* in a variable of interest between one or more groups: Do boys have higher self-esteem than girls? Do adolescents who attend coeducational schools have more positive self-esteem than their peers who attend single-sex schools? Do 8-year-olds score higher on measures of self-esteem than 11-year-olds? All these questions ask whether the mean score of a certain group (boys, students from coed schools, 8-year-olds) is significantly different from the mean score of a comparison group (girls, students from single-sex schools, 11-year-olds).

Usually, social scientists compare mean scores using a statistical procedure called the **analysis of variance (ANOVA)**, which tests whether the differences between people from different groups are greater than the differences among people within each group. Typically, the variable used to create the groups is referred to as the **independent variable** and the vari-

able on which the groups are compared as the **dependent variable** (because scores on this variable are assumed to "depend" on what group a person is in). In the three examples in the previous paragraph, self-esteem is always the dependent variable, whereas the independent variables are sex, type of school, and age.

A different sort of test is used to answer questions about whether scores on two variables are correlated with each other. Does higher self-esteem go hand in hand with academic achievement? Is there a link between parental warmth and adolescent self-esteem? Is low self-esteem predictive of involvement in delinquent activity? In each of these cases, we want to know whether variations in the value of one score are systematically linked to variations in the value of the other score and, if so, how strong the link is. Typically, a researcher who is interested in a question of this sort computes a **correlation coefficient** (which can range from 1.0 to -1.0) and then tests whether the correlation is significantly different from 0. The larger the correlation (that

& McAdoo, 1995; Robinson, 1995). These correlates of high self-esteem have been found in virtually all ethnic and cultural groups, although the self-esteem of Asian American youngsters seems especially influenced by their academic success (e.g., Szesulski, Martinez, & Reyes, 1994). Adolescents whose self-esteem is too wrapped up in the approval of others —especially the approval of peers—may be at risk for developing self-image problems, however, since peer acceptance may fluctuate over time, leading to temporary drops in self-esteem (Harter, Stocker, & Robinson, 1996). Consistent with this, adolescents who tend to derive their self-esteem from peers, rather than teachers or parents, show more behavioral problems and poorer school achievement (DuBois, Bull, Sherman, & Roberts, 1998; DuBois, Felner, Brand, & George, 1999).

How does having high self-esteem influence adolescents' adjustment and behavior? Although it once was believed that enhanced self-esteem leads to school success, there actually is little evidence for this and a good deal of evidence for the reverse (e.g., Liu et al., 1992; Rosenberg, Schooler, & Schoenbach, 1989). That is, academic success leads to improvements in the way that adolescents feel about themselves, not the other way around. These findings cast doubt on the logic behind programs designed to raise teenagers' school performance by increasing their self-esteem. High self-esteem does enhance adolescents' *well-being*, however, whereas low self-esteem may lead to involvement in deviant activity, psychological distress, and victimization (Andrews, Alpert, Hops, & Davis, 1996; DuBois & Tevendale, 1999; Egan & Perry, 1998; Liu et al., 1992; Rosenberg et al., 1989).

is, the closer the correlation is to 1.0 or −1.0), the stronger the link. A correlation close to 0 indicates that the scores on the two variables are unrelated.

It is important to understand the differences between the kinds of questions these two approaches are designed to answer and the kinds of conclusions one can draw from each sort of test. One illustration comes from the study of ethnic differences in self-esteem. According to many studies, African American adolescents report higher self-esteem than their white peers (Harter, 1990). As explained in this chapter, one common explanation for this finding is that African American adolescents receive especially high levels of support from immediate and extended family members and that this support contributes positively to youngsters' self-image. Studies documenting the higher self-esteem of African American adolescents typically rely on analysis of variance to examine the data. This test asks whether the difference in self-esteem *between* the ethnic groups studied is significantly greater than differences in self-esteem *within* the groups.

The test of the difference between the two means does not tell us whether the *correlates* of self-esteem among African American and white adolescents are different, however. In order to examine this question, one would need to look at the relation between self-esteem and another variable—family support, for example—and compare the two correlation coefficients to see if they are significantly different from each other. Unfortunately, social scientists use this technique much less often than they should in the study of ethnic differences in development, focusing instead on mean differences between ethnic groups.

One exception to the typical approach was reported in an article by David Rowe and his colleagues (Rowe, Vazsonyi, & Flannery, 1994), entitled "No More Than Skin Deep: Ethnic and Racial Similarity in Developmental Processes." Instead of asking whether there are ethnic differences in mean levels of various psychological traits (including self-esteem), Rowe asked whether the pattern of relations among various psychological variables (e.g., self-esteem, school achievement, self-efficacy, parental warmth, and drug use) is comparable across ethnic groups. (This study included Hispanic American, Asian American, African American, and white youngsters.) In order to investigate this, he divided samples of adolescents into ethnic groups and then calculated the correlations among the variables separately within each group. Rowe then tested to see whether the observed patterns of relations were different from one ethnic group to another.

The analyses showed quite clearly that the correlations were not different. That is, although there may have been mean differences in the ethnic groups' scores on some of the variables of interest (e.g., Asian Americans tend to have higher school achievement, and white adolescents tend to use more drugs), there were no differences in the relations among these variables (e.g., in all ethnic groups, school achievement was negatively correlated with drug use and positively correlated with parental warmth).

The answer to the question "Are there ethnic differences in self-esteem?" is a complicated one. Yes, there are differences, in that adolescents from different ethnic groups report different levels of self-esteem. However, no, there are not, in that the predictors of self-esteem—doing well in school, having parents who love you, and having friends who support you—seem to be the same among adolescents of all ethnicities.

Source: Rowe, D., Vazsonyi, A., & Flannery, D. (1994). No more than skin deep: Ethnic and racial similarity in developmental processes. *Psychological Review, 101*, 396–413.

The relation between low self-esteem and emotional and behavior problems is complicated (Cole, Peeke, Dolezal, Murray, & Canzoniero, 1999). Low self-esteem is one of several symptoms of depression, but it is not clear whether depression leads to low self-esteem or vice versa. The answer, it seems, depends on the individual. For about half of all adolescents, having low self-esteem leads to depression and other forms of emotional distress. For the other half, however, the reverse is true (Harter, 1999). Interestingly, although low self-esteem initially may draw some adolescents toward delinquency, involvement with delinquent peers actually may lead to an *increase* in self-esteem, perhaps because involvement in delinquency gets teenagers approval from certain peers (Dishion, Andrews, & Crosby, 1995; Jang & Thornberry, 1998; Rosenberg et al., 1989).

RECAP

Generally speaking, males, middle-class adolescents, and African American adolescents have higher self-esteem than females, less affluent youth, and white adolescents. Across all demographic groups, high self-esteem is related to parental approval, peer support, and success in school. Although it is difficult to disentangle cause from effect, high self-esteem is associated with better mental health, whereas low self-esteem is correlated with a number of emotional and behavior problems.

▲ *Youngsters who attend schools in which they are in the racial minority may suffer greater self-esteem problems than their peers who attend schools in which they are in the majority. Although desegregation may have a positive impact on minority youngsters' academic achievement, this benefit may be counterbalanced by the apparently negative impact of desegregation on minority youngsters' self-image.* (Rick Smolan/ Stock, Boston)

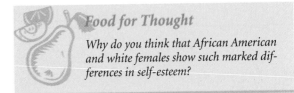

Food for Thought

Why do you think that African American and white females show such marked differences in self-esteem?

THE ADOLESCENT IDENTITY CRISIS

Many of the twentieth century's most important novels, from James Joyce's *Portrait of the Artist as a Young Man* to J. D. Salinger's *The Catcher in the Rye*, revolve around an adolescent's identity crisis. Indeed, the coming of age novel is a classic literary genre. One of the most wonderful and memorable stories of an adolescent's struggle to find her identity is told in Carson McCullers's novel *The Member of the Wedding*. Set in the South during the mid-1940s, the story revolves around the identity devel-opment of Frankie Addams, a 12-year-old girl who has her first encounter that summer with the sort of self-examination and introspection that we have come to associate with the adolescent years. The following is Frankie speaking to her confidante, Berenice:

> Listen. . . . What I've been trying to say is this. Doesn't it strike you as strange that I am I, and you are you? I am F. Jasmine Addams. And you are Berenice Sadie Brown. And we can look at each other, and touch each other, and stay together year in and year out in the same room. Yet always I am I, and you are you. And I can't ever be any-thing else but me, and you can't ever be anything else but you. Have you ever thought of that? And does it seem to you strange? (McCullers, 1946, p. 109)

If you were asked to write a novel about your own identity development, what sorts of things would you mention? Perhaps you would talk about the develop-ment of a sense of purpose, or the clarification of your long-term plans and values, or the growing feeling of knowing who you really are and where you are headed.

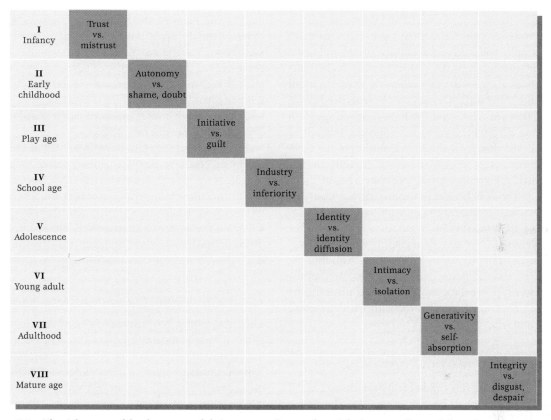

Figure 8.5   The eight stages of development and their corresponding psychosocial crises, according to Erikson (1959).

If these are the sorts of things that come to mind when you think about identity development in adolescence, you are thinking about an aspect of development that psychologists refer to as the **sense of identity.** The dominant view in the study of adolescent identity development emphasizes precisely these aspects of psychosocial development, and the theorist whose work has been most influential in this area is Erik Erikson.

Erikson's Theoretical Framework

Erikson's (1959, 1963, 1968) theory developed out of his clinical and cross-cultural observations of young people at various stages of development. He viewed the developing person as moving through a series of eight psychosocial crises over the course of the life span. Each crisis, although present in one form or another at all ages, takes on special significance at a given period of the life cycle because biological and social forces interact to bring the crisis into prominence. Erikson believed that the establishment of a coherent sense of identity is the chief psychosocial crisis of adolescence.

In Erikson's model, each psychosocial crisis defines an age, or stage, of the life span (see figure 8.5). Each crisis is a sort of challenge that the individual must resolve. The crises are normative, in the sense that they are an inevitable part of being alive and growing older. Erikson described each of the eight crises as a continuum with positive and negative poles. In infancy, for example, the crisis is labeled "trust versus mistrust." By this, Erikson meant that, during infancy, a child must be able to establish a feeling of trust, or security, with his or her caregivers.

Resolving each crisis, though, does not entail coming through the crisis either entirely positively or entirely negatively, nor does it mean resolving the issue once and for all. "It is instead a matter of tipping the balance more in one direction (i.e., toward one end of the continuum) than in another" (Gallatin, 1975, p. 175). In other words, it is important that the infant come through the first stage of development feeling more secure than insecure.

In Erikson's view, each crisis builds on the previous ones. Specifically, the successful resolution of each challenge depends on the healthy resolution of the challenges that have preceded it. An infant who has not successfully resolved the crisis of trust versus mistrust, for example, will have a difficult time with the crises encountered through the rest of the life cycle. Such individuals may always be somewhat hesitant about becoming close with other people because, deep down inside, they fear that others will let them down. With respect to adolescent identity development, then, Erikson believed that the successful resolution of the crisis of "identity versus identity diffusion" depends on how the individual has resolved the previous crises of childhood. Without a healthy sense of trust, autonomy, initiative, and industry, it is difficult to establish a coherent sense of identity. Moreover, the way in which the adolescent resolves the crisis of identity will have an impact on his or her struggle with the crises of adulthood. Far from seeing adolescence as a separate period of the life cycle, Erikson believed that what takes place during adolescence is much intertwined with what has come before and what will follow.

Identity Versus Identity Diffusion

Before adolescence, the child's identity is like patches of fabric that have not yet been sewn together. But by the end of adolescence, these patches will have been woven into a patchwork quilt that is unique to the individual. This process of integration is at the center of the fifth psychosocial crisis described by Erikson: the crisis of **identity versus identity diffusion.** As Erikson described it, "From among all possible and imaginable relations, [the young person] must make a series of ever-narrowing selections of personal, occupational, sexual, and ideological commitments" (1968, p. 245). The maturational and social forces that converge at adolescence force young people to reflect on their place in society, on the ways that others view them, and on their options for the future. Achieving a balanced and coherent sense of identity is an intellectually and emotionally taxing process. According to Erikson, it is not until adolescence that one even has the mental or psychological capacity to tackle this task.

The key to resolving the crisis of identity versus identity diffusion, argued Erikson, lies in the adolescent's interactions with others. Through responding to the reactions of people who matter, the adolescent selects from among the many elements that could conceivably become a part of his or her adult identity. The other people with whom the young person interacts serve as a mirror that reflects back to the adolescent information about who he or she is and who he or she

ought to be. As such, the responses of these important others shape the adolescent's developing sense of identity. Through others' reactions, we learn whether we are competent or clumsy, attractive or ugly, socially adept or tactless. Perhaps more important—especially when our sense of identity is still forming—we learn from others what it is we do that we ought to keep doing, and what it is we do that we ought not to do.

Forging an identity, therefore, is a social as well as a mental process. Erikson placed a great deal of weight on the role of the young person's society (and, especially, on the individuals who have influence over the adolescent) in shaping the adolescent's sense of self. The adolescent's identity is the result of a mutual recognition between the young person and society: The adolescent forges an identity, but at the same time society identifies the adolescent.

The Social Context of Identity Development

The social context in which the adolescent attempts to establish a sense of identity exerts a tremendous impact on the nature and outcome of the process. Clearly, if adolescents' identities are forged out of a recognition on the part of society, society will play an important role in determining which sorts of identities are possible alternatives; of the identities that are genuine options, society will influence which are desirable and which are not.

As a consequence, the course of identity development varies in different cultures, among different subcultures within the same society, and over historical eras (Kroger, 1993). For example, the career options open to women in contemporary American society have changed dramatically in the past 30 years; consequently, so has the nature of adolescent girls' identity development. In the past, most young women assumed that their adult identity would be tied exclusively to marriage and family life. But today far more alternative identities are open to women. As a result, the process of choosing from among alternatives has become more complicated than it once was.

The social context in which an adolescent develops also determines, to a large extent, whether the youngster's search for self-definition will take the form of a full-blown crisis or a more manageable challenge. Generally speaking, the more alternatives available to the young person and the more arenas in which decisions must be made, the more difficult establishing a sense of identity will be. Growing up in contemporary America, where adolescents have a range of careers to decide among, for example, is far more likely to provoke an occupational identity crisis than is growing up in a small agrarian community in which each young person continues farming the family's land. The rapid rate of social change in most of the industrialized world has raised new and more complicated sets of questions for young people to consider—questions not only about occupational plans but also about values, lifestyles, and commitments to other people. No longer are all young people expected to follow the same narrow path into adulthood: marriage and children for all, work for men, and homemaking for women. Today, both male and female adolescents must ask themselves if they want to remain single, live with someone, or marry; if and when they want to have children, and how they plan to incorporate these choices into their career plans. Consequently, the likelihood of going through a prolonged and difficult identity crisis is probably greater today than it has ever been.

● **The Psychosocial Moratorium**   According to Erikson, the complications inherent in identity development in modern society have created the need for a **psychosocial moratorium**—a timeout during adolescence from the sorts of excessive responsibilities and obligations that might restrict the young person's pursuit of self-discovery. Adolescents in contemporary America are given a moratorium of sorts by being encouraged to remain in school for a long time, where they can think seriously about their plans for the future without making irrevocable decisions.

During the psychosocial moratorium, the adolescent can experiment with various roles and identities, in a context that permits and encourages this sort of exploration. The experimentation involves trying on various postures, personalities, and ways of behaving—sometimes to the consternation of the adolescent's parents, who may wonder why their child's personality seems so changeable. One week, an adolescent girl will spend hours putting on makeup; the next week, she will insist to her parents that she is tired of caring so much about the way she looks. An adolescent boy will come home one day with a shaved head and pierced ear, and a few weeks later he will discard this image for that of a serious student. Sometimes, parents describe their teenage children as going through phases. Much of this behavior is actually normal experimentation with roles and personalities.

Having the time to experiment with roles is an important prelude to establishing a coherent sense of identity. But role experimentation can take place only in an environment that allows and encourages it (Gallatin, 1975). Without a period of moratorium, a full and thorough exploration of the options and alternatives available to the young person cannot occur, and

▲ *Role experimentation during adolescence often involves trying different looks, images, and patterns of behavior. According to theorists such as Erik Erikson, having time to experiment with roles in an important prelude to establishing a coherent sense of identity.* (Judy Gelles/Stock Boston)

identity development will be somewhat impeded. In other words, according to Erikson, adolescents must *grow* into an adult identity—they should not be forced into one prematurely.

It is clear, however, that the sort of moratorium Erikson described is an ideal; indeed, some might even consider it to be a luxury of the affluent. Many young people—perhaps even most—do not have the economic freedom to enjoy a long delay before taking on the responsibilities of adult life. For many youngsters, alternatives are not open in any realistic sense, and introspection only interferes with the more pressing task of survival.

Does the 17-year-old who must drop out of school to work a full-time factory job go through life without a sense of identity? Do youngsters who cannot afford a psychosocial moratorium fail to resolve the crisis of identity versus identity diffusion? Certainly not; however, from an Eriksonian point of view, the absence of a psychosocial moratorium in some adolescents' lives—either because of restrictions they place on themselves or restrictions placed on them by others or because of their life circumstances—is truly lamentable. The price these youngsters pay is not in failing to develop a sense of identity but in lost potential. You may know people whose parents have forced them into prematurely choosing a certain career or who have had to drop out of college and take a job they really did not want because of financial pressures. According to Erikson, without a chance to explore, to experiment, and to choose among options for the future, these young people may not realize all that they are capable of becoming. In theory, these individuals should encounter difficulties in resolving the subsequent crises of intimacy, generativity, and integrity.

Resolving the Identity Crisis

Is establishing a sense of identity a consciously felt achievement? According to Erikson, it is. It is experienced as a sense of well-being, a feeling of "being at home in one's body," a sense of knowing where one is going, and an inner assuredness of recognition from those who count. It is a sense of sameness through time—a feeling of continuity between the past and the future.

Establishing a coherent sense of identity is a lengthy process. Most writers on adolescence and youth believe that identity exploration continues well into young adulthood. However, rather than thinking of the adolescent as going through an identity crisis, it probably makes more sense to view the phenomenon as a series of crises that may concern various aspects of the young person's identity and that may surface—and resurface—at various points in time throughout the adolescent and young adult years. As Erikson wrote, "a sense of identity is never gained nor maintained once and for all" (1959, p. 118). Indeed, during adolescence, the feeling of well-being associated with establishing a sense of identity is often fleeting. Ultimately, however, the identity crisis of adolescence, when successfully resolved, culminates in a series of basic life commitments: occupational, ideological, social, religious, ethical, and sexual (Bourne, 1978a).

> **RECAP**
> *The predominant influence on the study of identity development in adolescence comes from the work of Erik Erikson. Erikson suggested that the major psychosocial issue of adolescence revolves around the identity crisis—coming to terms with who one is and where one is headed. In order to resolve this crisis successfully, the young person needs some time out from excessive responsibilities—a psychosocial moratorium—in order to engage in identity exploration and experimentation.*

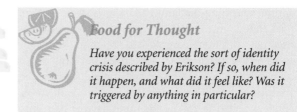

Food for Thought

Have you experienced the sort of identity crisis described by Erikson? If so, when did it happen, and what did it feel like? Was it triggered by anything in particular?

Problems in Identity Development

Given the wide variations in developmental histories that individuals bring to adolescence and the wide variations in the environments in which adolescence is experienced, it is not surprising to find differences in the ways in which individuals approach and resolve the crisis of identity versus identity diffusion. Problems in identity development can result when an individual has not successfully resolved earlier crises or when the adolescent is in an environment that does not provide the necessary period of moratorium. Three sorts of problems received special attention from Erikson. They are labeled identity diffusion, identity foreclosure, and negative identity.

● **Identity Diffusion**   **Identity diffusion** (sometimes called **identity confusion**) is characterized by an incoherent, disjointed, incomplete sense of self. Identity diffusion can vary in degree from a mild state of not quite knowing who you are while in the midst of an identity crisis to a more severe, psychopathological condition that persists beyond a normal period of exploration. It is marked by disruptions in the individual's sense of time (some things seem to happen much faster than they really do, whereas others seem to take forever), excessive self-consciousness, to the point that it is difficult to make decisions, problems in work and achievement-related activities; difficulties in forming intimate relationships with others; and concerns over sexuality. Identity confusion is reflected not only in problems of identity but also in the areas of autonomy, intimacy, sexuality, and achievement.

A classic example of an adolescent in the throes of identity diffusion is Holden Caulfield in the 1951 novel *The Catcher in the Rye.* He has flunked out of several prep schools, has severed most of his friendships, and has no sense of where he is headed. At one point in the book, for example, while walking up Fifth Avenue in New York City, Holden says, "Every time I came to the end of a block and stepped off the goddam curb, I had this feeling that I'd never get to the other side of the street. I thought I'd just go down, down, and nobody'd ever see me again. Boy, did it scare me" (Salinger, 1951/1964, pp. 197–198).

● **Identity Foreclosure**   Some young people bypass—either willingly or unwillingly—the period of exploration and experimentation that precedes the establishment of a healthy sense of identity. Instead of considering a range of alternatives, these adolescents prematurely commit themselves to a role, or series of roles, and settle on a certain identification as a final identity. In essence, these individuals are not given—or do not take advantage of—a psychosocial moratorium. For example, a college freshman who made up her mind about becoming a doctor at the age of 13 may enroll in a rigid pre-med curriculum without considering other career possibilities. This circumvention of the identity crisis is called **identity foreclosure.**

Typically, the roles adopted in the process of identity foreclosure revolve around the goals set for the young person by parents or other authority figures. The adolescent may be led into these roles directly or may be forced into them indirectly by being denied a true period of psychosocial moratorium. Perhaps the parents of the would-be doctor have arranged their child's school schedule and summer vacations so that all of his or her spare time is spent taking extra science courses. No time is left for role experimentation or introspection. Individuals who have bypassed the identity crisis have made commitments, but they have not gone through a period of experimentation before making them. Identity foreclosure can be viewed, then, as a kind of interruption of the identity development process, an interruption that interferes with the individual's discovery of his or her full range of potentials.

● **Negative Identity**   Occasionally, adolescents appear to select identities that are obviously undesirable to their parents and their community. The examples are familiar: the daughter of the local police chief who repeatedly gets into trouble with the law; the son of prestigious and successful parents who refuses to go to college; the child of a devoutly religious family who insists that he or she is a confirmed atheist. Because the establishment of a healthy sense of identity is so intimately tied to the recognition of the adolescent by those who count in his or her life, the adoption of a so-called **negative identity** is a sign that problems in identity development have arisen. The adolescent who adopts a negative identity, to be sure, is recognized by those around him or her, but not in a way that fosters healthy development.

Usually, selecting a negative identity is an attempt to forge a sense of self-definition in an environment that has made it difficult for the young person to establish an acceptable identity. This appears to be especially likely when, after repeatedly trying and failing to receive positive recognition from those who are important in their lives, adolescents turn to a different, perhaps more successful, route to being noticed—adopting a negative identity. Consider this example: The son of successful parents is a good student but not quite good enough to please his excessively demanding parents. He feels he is a nobody in his parents' eyes, so the boy drops out of school to play guitar in a band—something his parents vehemently oppose. To paraphrase Erikson, this adolescent, like most youngsters, would rather be somebody "bad" than nobody at all. Some observers of the adolescent scene have suggested that a form of graffiti writing popular in the 1980s and early 1990s known as "tagging"—writing one's nickname on city walls—can be understood as a display of negative identity by adolescents for whom traditional channels of achievement are closed (Ferrell, 1995).

> **RECAP**
> *Some adolescents have difficulty in successfully resolving the identity crisis. Among the three most common problems described by Erikson are identity diffusion, identity foreclosure, and negative identity. Problems in identity development can result when an individual has not successfully resolved earlier crises or when the adolescent is in an environment that does not provide the necessary period of psychosocial moratorium.*

> *Food for Thought*
>
> *The broader context in which adolescents develop affects the nature of their identity development. Are there any aspects of today's environment that might make the resolution of the identity crisis especially more difficult?*

RESEARCH ON IDENTITY DEVELOPMENT

Determining an Adolescent's Identity Status

The term *identity status* refers to the point in the identity development process that characterizes an adolescent at a given time. In order to determine an individual's identity status, most researchers have used an approach developed by James Marcia (1966, 1976), which focuses on identity exploration in three areas—occupation, ideology (values and beliefs), and interpersonal relations.

The Sexes

Are There Sex Differences in the Route to a Sense of Identity?

Many writers have argued that male and female adolescents approach the crisis of identity from different perspectives and resolve it through different means. Some theorists have gone so far as to say that, although Erikson's framework (which places the crisis of identity development earlier than the crisis of intimacy) is a reasonable model of psychosocial development for males, it does not adequately account for development among girls (Gallatin, 1975). They argue that girls are much more interpersonally oriented than boys and that, as a consequence, girls are likely to face the challenge of intimacy before they deal with the crisis of identity—or, at the very least, that girls pursue their sense of identity through their relationships with others. Girls learn about themselves, it is argued, in the context of friendships and close relationships, whereas boys forge a sense of identity by being autonomous and independent (Douvan & Adelson, 1966).

There is undoubtedly some truth to the idea that males and females approach and resolve the psychosocial issues of adolescence differently; how could they help but do so, given the strong pressures on them to adhere to two different sets of behavioral standards? But linking male identity development to autonomy and independence and female identity development to intimacy and other interpersonal pursuits is no longer as useful as it once was. Although one classic study of adolescents that was conducted during the early 1960s (Douvan & Adelson, 1966) concluded that "there is not one adolescent crisis, but two major and clearly distinctive ones—the masculine and the feminine" (p. 350), research during the 1980s and 1990s pointed to similarities, rather than differences, in the ways in which males and females struggle with the task of self-definition (Adams & Fitch, 1982; Archer, 1989;

Based on responses to an interview or a questionnaire, individuals are rated on two dimensions: (1) the degree to which they have made commitments and (2) the degree to which they have engaged in a sustained search in the process (see figure 8.6). On the basis of these ratings, the researchers assign young people to one of four categories: identity achievement (the individual has established a coherent sense of identity—that is, has made commitments after a period of crisis and experimentation); moratorium (the individual is in the midst of a period of crisis and experimentation); identity foreclosure (the individual has made commitments but without a period of crisis or experimentation); and identity diffusion (the individual does not have firm commitments and is not currently trying to make them). Within each of these categories, it is also possible to draw somewhat finer distinctions—for example, between foreclosed individuals whose foreclosure seems temporary and those whose foreclosure appears "firm" (Kroger, 1995).

Generally speaking, research using this approach has supported many aspects of Erikson's theory (for a recent

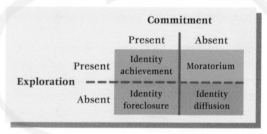

Figure 8.6 *Identity status categories derived from Marcia's (1966) measure.*

discussion, see Berzonsky & Adams, 1999; Meeus, Iedema, & Vollenbergh, 1999; Van Hoof, 1999; Waterman, 1999a, 1999b). The strongest support for the theory comes from studies that show a pattern of correlations between various traits and the different identity statuses that are consistent with predictions based on Erikson's model. As one would expect, for example, identity achievers are psychologically healthier than other individuals on a variety of measures: They score highest on measures of achievement motivation, moral reasoning,

Grotevant & Thorbecke, 1982). Were the early descriptions of sex differences in identity development erroneous, or were these more recent studies off the mark?

In answering this question, we must bear in mind that sex differences—or, for that matter, similarities—in identity development can be understood only against the backdrop of the social context in which development takes place. Assessing the studies in a historical context sheds some light on the controversy. For many adolescent girls, particularly 25 or 30 years ago, the roles of adulthood open to them were primarily interpersonal in nature, so it comes as no surprise that the crisis of identity manifested itself for these young women through their relationships with others. After all, in Erikson's model, identity is pursued with one eye toward the future. However, today, as new generations of adolescent girls face a society that presents them with greater and more diverse options for the future, especially in terms of occupation, their identity explorations are likely to extend further into the realms of autonomy and independence than they did in the past.

Changes in the broader social context of adolescence have continued to minimize sex differences in the process of identity development. For instance, whereas a review of research conducted during the 1960s and 1970s concluded that adolescent males move through the process of identity development faster than females (Marcia, 1980), more recent studies suggest that this is no longer the case (Archer, 1989). If young women in the past took more time resolving the crisis of identity than young men did, perhaps it was because the options open to women in society at that time were more confusing, more complicated, and more rapidly changing than they were for men. The length of a moratorium needed to experiment with enough roles is linked to the complexity of the choices the young person faces.

This is not to say that the outcomes of the identity development process are the same for males and females, however, or that the similarities that may characterize identity development during adolescence persist into adulthood. Society has still not fully come to terms with women's interest in careers; consequently, the task of integrating occupational and interpersonal commitments into a coherent and satisfying sense of self is likely to be more difficult for women than men. Accordingly, even though boys and girls may go through similar struggles in establishing a sense of identity in adolescence, the consequences of resolving the crisis may have clearer and more immediate advantages for men than for women. Thus, for example, achieving a coherent sense of identity during adolescence is a strong predictor of life satisfaction and of marriage as an adult for men, but for women it predicts neither (Kahn, Zimmerman, Csikszentmihalyi, & Getzels, 1985). Whatever similarities exist between boys and girls in their search for identity as adolescents, the structure of adult experience introduces important differences into the outcome.

intimacy with peers, reflectiveness, and career maturity. Individuals in the moratorium category score highest on measures of anxiety, show the highest levels of conflict over issues of authority, and are themselves the least rigid and least authoritarian. Individuals classified as being in the foreclosure group have been shown to be the most authoritarian and most prejudiced and to have the highest need for social approval, the lowest level of autonomy, and the greatest closeness to their parents. Individuals in a state of identity diffusion display the highest level of psychological and interpersonal problems: They are the most socially withdrawn and show the lowest level of intimacy with peers (Adams, Gullotta, & Montemayor, 1992; Fulton, 1997; Meeus, 1996; Wallace-Broscious, Serafica, & Osipow, 1994).

More evidence of this sort comes from a study that attempted to link classifications based on a measure of identity development with scores on the personality dimensions tapped within the Five-Factor Model of personality (Clancy & Dollinger, 1993). As expected, adolescents who were classified as identity achievers were higher in extraversion and less neurotic than other adolescents; foreclosed adolescents were less open; and diffused adolescents were more neurotic, less open, and less agreeable. It was not clear from this study whether different personality constellations led to different patterns of identity development or, alternatively, whether different patterns of identity development influenced subsequent personality. Given what is known about the childhood antecedents of personality traits, however, it would seem that the former explanation (that personality affects identity development) is more likely than the latter.

What sorts of parenting practices are associated with these different identity statuses? Generally speaking, individuals whose identity development is healthy are more likely to come from homes characterized by warm, but not excessively constraining, relations (Grotevant & Cooper, 1986; Perosa, Perosa, & Tam, 1996). As we saw in chapter 4, individuals who grow up in these environments are encouraged to assert their individuality but to remain connected to their families at the same time. Typically, the absence of parental warmth is associated with problems in making commitments—the most extreme case being identity diffusion—whereas the absence of parental encouragement of individuality is associated with problems in engaging in extensive exploration (Campbell, Adams, & Dobson, 1984).

Studying Identity Development over Time

In order to examine the development of a sense of identity, researchers have done both cross-sectional studies (comparing individuals of different ages) and longitudinal studies (following the same individuals over a period of time). It is in this area of work that questions have been raised about the accuracy of the identity status model. Perhaps the most significant finding to emerge from this line of research is that establishing a coherent sense of identity generally does not occur much before age 18—not earlier in adolescence, as originally hypothesized (Marcia, 1980). In general, when comparisons are made among groups of youngsters of different ages over the span from ages 12 to 24, differences in identity status are most frequently observed between groups in the 18- to 21-year-old range. Few consistent differences emerge in comparisons of teenagers in the middle adolescent years, suggesting that, although self-examination may take place throughout adolescence, the consolidation of a coherent sense of identity does not begin until very late in the period (Adams & Jones, 1983; Archer, 1982). The late teens and early twenties appear to be the critical times for the crystallization of a sense of identity.

The movement toward identity achievement that occurs between ages 18 and 21 among college students appears to be primarily in the area of occupational commitments. Alan Waterman and his associates (Waterman, Geary, & Waterman, 1974; Waterman & Goldman, 1976; Waterman & Waterman, 1971), who followed samples of college students for several years, found that during the college years vocational plans solidify but that religious and political commitments are not as clearly established. More specifically, individuals emerge from college with more clearly defined occupational plans but no firm religious or political commitments (Waterman, 1982). In fact, college seems to undermine students' traditional religious beliefs—the beliefs that they acquired from their parents—without replacing them with others. Students who enter college as devout Catholics, for example, may graduate having lost some of their commitment to Catholicism but without having developed any new religious commitments. This pattern may not hold for adolescents from all religious groups, however. One study of Mormon adolescents, for example, found that these youngsters were much more likely than their peers to

maintain a strong—even foreclosed—commitment to their religious upbringing (Markstrom-Adams, Hofstra, & Dougher, in press).

A study by Raymond Montemayor and his colleagues supports the idea that the freshman year of college may be an important time in the process of identity development. A group of students was assessed before entering college and again toward the end of the freshman year. Before entering college, half of the adolescents were judged to be in a state of identity diffusion, and 40 percent were judged to be in a state of moratorium—consistent with the notion that the identity crisis is unlikely to be resolved during high school. Another 8 percent were in the identity achievment status, and the rest were judged to be foreclosed. What happened to these individuals as college freshmen? Over the first year of college, the most common pathway was either remaining diffused or in a state of moratorium or moving from one of the committed statuses (identity achievement or identity foreclosure) to one of the noncommitted statuses (diffusion or moratorium). In other words, although freshman year may "shake up some students and cause them to reexamine previously held commitments, students who are uncertain to begin with . . . remain so. . . . The freshman year appears to produce uncertainty in many students but does not help to resolve it" (Montemayor, Brown, & Adams, 1985, p. 7). For many young people, college may prolong the psychosocial moratorium, especially in matters of political and religious beliefs.

Shifts in Identity Status

As you will recall, Erikson theorized that the sense of identity that is developed during adolescence is constantly lost and regained, that the identity challenge is not resolved once and for all at one point in time. If, according to Erikson's model, identity crises surface and resurface throughout the life cycle, we ought to find that individuals move from one identity status to another, particularly during the adolescent and young adult years.

This appears to be precisely the case. In a four-year study of Dutch youth between the ages of 12 and 14, for example, nearly 60 percent of the individuals classified as diffused with respect to their educational and occupational identity were no longer classified that way four years later, and nearly 75 percent of the individuals who were in the midst of a moratorium at the beginning of the study were no longer in this category at the later assessment (Meeus et al., 1999). Nearly two-thirds of the individuals who had apparently foreclosed the identity development process were in the midst of an identity crisis four years later, suggesting that foreclosure is a temporary stage, at least for some adolescents (see figure 8.7). Other longitudinal studies of adolescents have revealed similar findings (Adams & Fitch, 1982; Waterman et al., 1974; Waterman and Goldman, 1976).

Much of this shifting is understandable and perfectly consistent with Erikson's view of adolescent identity development. But how can we account for the fact that, in the same longitudinal studies, a large proportion of the identity achievement group *also* shifted status over the course of the study? In the Dutch study, for example, half of the adolescents who were classified as identity achieved at the first assessment were not classified this way four years later. How do we explain the fact that some individuals who at one point had apparently resolved their identity crisis actually had not resolved it—at least, not in any final sense? According to some writers, these sorts of regressions to a less mature identity status are part of the normal process through which individuals ultimately establish a coherent sense of self (Kroger, 1996). That is, we should not view the achievement of a sense of identity in adolescence as a final state but, rather, as a step on a long road toward the establishment of a mature sense of self.

Because little research has focused on the *processes* through which identity development occurs, the factors associated with changing from one identity status to another are not well understood (Kroger & Green, 1996; LaVoie, 1994). Indeed, it is fair to say that psychologists are much better at describing the various stages that adolescents move through over the course of their identity development than at understanding why or how individuals' sense of identity changes when it does. The little research that has been done on this subject indicates that turning points in the development of a sense of identity are provoked both by internal factors—discontent with one's life, for example—and by specific life events or changes in life circumstances, such as making the transition into or out of high school (Kalakoski & Nurmi, 1998; Kroger & Green, 1996).

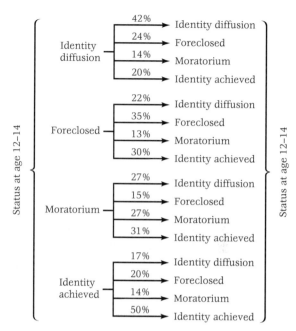

Figure 8.7   Changes in identity status over a four-year period. (Adapted from Meuus, Iedema, Helsen, & Vollebergh, 1999)

> ### Food for Thought
>
> Explain how identity development is studied empirically. Why do you think that research indicates that most identity development occurs in late adolescence or early adulthood, rather than in early or middle adolescence?

THE DEVELOPMENT OF ETHNIC IDENTITY

For all individuals, but especially for those who are not part of the white majority, integrating a sense of **ethnic identity** into an overall sense of personal identity is likely to be an important task of late adolescence, perhaps as important as establishing a coherent occupational, ideological, or interpersonal identity (Phinney & Alipuria, 1987). Over the past decade, an extensive literature has been amassed on the process through which ethnic identity develops, as well as on the implications of having a strong versus weak sense of ethnic identity

> ### RECAP
>
> Research on identity development from Erikson's theoretical perspective has generally supported his model. Most studies indicate, however, that the major developments in this domain occur in late adolescence and young adulthood, rather than earlier during the adolescent decade.

for adolescent adjustment and behavior. Ethnic identity has been studied in samples of African American, Hispanic American, Native American, Asian American, and white youth (Gil, Vega, & Dimas, 1994; Marshall, 1995; Martinez & Dukes, 1997; Phinney, Cantu, & Kurtz, 1997; Phinney & Chavria, 1995; Phinney & Devich-Navarro, 1997; Plummer, 1995; Roberts et al., 1999; Spencer & Markstrom-Adams, 1990; Stevenson, 1998; Vega, Khoury, Zimmerman, Gil, & Warheit, 1995; Zimmerman, Ramirez-Valles, Washienko, Walter, & Dyer, 1996). Although white American youth in general have a weaker sense of ethnic identity than their non-white peers, many white adolescents nevertheless identify strongly with a particular ethnic group (e.g., German, Irish, Italian, or Jewish) and derive part of their overall sense of self from this identification (Martinez & Dukes, 1997; Roberts et al., 1999).

The Process of Ethnic Identity Development

According to several writers (Cross, 1978; Kim, 1981, cited in Phinney & Alipuria, 1987), the process of ethnic identity development follows in some respects the process of identity development in general, with an unquestioning view of oneself being displaced or upset by a crisis. Following the crisis, the individual may become immersed in his or her own ethnic group and may turn against the white majority culture. Eventually, as the value and importance of having a strong ethnic identity become clear, the individual establishes a more coherent sense of personal identity that includes this ethnic identity, and, with growing confidence, he or she attempts to help others deal with their own struggles with ethnic identity.

Some research indicates that moving through the early stages of ethnic identity development may be speeded up somewhat when parents take a more deliberate approach to racial, or ethnic, socialization (Marshall, 1994; Quintana, Castaneda-English, & Ybarra, 1999). **Racial socialization** is the process through which parents attempt to teach their children about their ethnic identity and about the special experiences they may encounter within the broader society, given their ethnic background (Stevenson, Reed, Bodison, & Bishop, 1997; Thornton, Chatters, Taylor, & Allen, 1990). According to one model, racial socialization in minority families focuses on three themes: (1) understanding one's culture, (2) getting along in mainsteam society, and (3) dealing with racism (Boykin & Toms, 1985). Although racial socialization by parents may speed up the process of ethnic identity development, it does not appear to lead adolescents to an ultimately stronger sense of ethnic identity (DeBerry, Scarr, & Weinberg, 1996; Marshall, 1995; Phinney & Chavira, 1995). Interestingly, having positive attitudes about one's own ethnic group is correlated with having positive attitudes about adolescents from *other* ethnic groups, suggesting that racial socialization may enhance, rather than upset, interracial relations (Phinney, Ferguson, & Tate, 1997).

Do members of ethnic minorities have more difficulty than white adolescents in resolving the identity crisis? Researchers are just now beginning to examine this question, and the answer is still not known. The little research that has been done suggests more similarities than differences in the process through which ethnic identity development occurs. One difference, though, appears to be quite important, if perhaps not very surprising: Having a strong ethnic identity is consistently associated with higher self-esteem and stronger self-efficacy among minority youngsters, whereas the

▲ *Having a strong sense of ethnic identity is an important part of the adolescent's psychosocial development, especially among young people who are in the minority within their society.* (Rogers/Monkmeyer)

Identification with majority group	Identification with ethnic group	
	Strong	Weak
Strong	Bicultural	Assimilated
Weak	Separated	Marginal

Figure 8.8   *A two-dimensional model of identification with two cultures.* (Phinney 1990)

link between ethnic identity and mental health is weaker among white youth (Blash & Unger, 1992; DeBerry et al., 1996; Deyhle, 1995; Martinez & Dukes, 1997; McCreary, Slavin, & Berry, 1996; Phinney & Alipuria, 1987; Reviere & Bakeman, 1992; Smith, 1996; Verkuyten, 1995). It would seem, therefore, that establishing a sense of ethnic identity is more important to individuals who are part of an ethnic minority than for those who are part of a majority (Gray-Little & Hafdahl, 2000). Indeed, among white American adolescents, having a strong sense of ethnic identity is highly correlated with identifying oneself as American (Phinney, Cantu, & Kurtz, 1997).

As many writers have noted, the task of developing a coherent sense of identity is much more complicated for minority adolescents than for their majority counterparts (Gray-Little & Hafdahl, 2000; Spencer & Dornbusch, 1990; Stevenson et al., 1997). Because identity development is profoundly influenced by the social context in which the adolescent lives, the development of the minority adolescent must be understood in relation to the specific context that nonmajority youngsters face in contemporary society (Garcia Coll et al., 1996). All too often, this context includes racial stereotypes, discrimination, and mixed messages about the costs and benefits of identifying too closely with the majority culture. Not surprisingly, a number of studies suggest that the incidence of identity foreclosure is more prevalent among minority youth (e.g., Hauser & Kasendorf, 1983).

Alternative Orientations to Ethnic Identity

According to psychologist Jean Phinney and her colleagues (e.g., Phinney, Devich-Navarro, DuPont, Estrada, & Onwughala, 1994), minority youth have four possibilities open to them for dealing with their ethnicity: *assimilation* (i.e., trying to adopt the majority culture's norms and standards while rejecting those of one's own group);

marginality (i.e., living within the majority culture but feeling estranged and outcast); *separation* (i.e., associating only with members of one's own culture and rejecting the majority culture); and *biculturalism* (i.e., maintaining ties to both the majority and the minority cultures) (see figure 8.8). In the past, minority youth were encouraged by the majority society to assimilate as much as possible. Assimilation, however, has not proven to be as simple as many nonminority individuals imagine (Gil et al., 1994). First, although minority youth are told to assimilate, they may be tacitly excluded from the majority society on the basis of their physical appearance or language (Vega et al., 1995). This leads to a situation of marginality, in which the minority adolescent is on the edge of majority society but is never really accepted as a full-status member.

Second, minority youth who do attempt to assimilate are often scorned by their own communities for trying to "act white"—as captured in the array of pejorative terms minority youth have for their friends who have tried too hard to assimilate: Asian Americans who act white are "bananas"; Hispanic Americans are "coconuts"; and African Americans are "Oreos" (Spencer & Dornbusch, 1990, p. 132). Partly in reaction to this, many minority youth adopt a strategy of separation. This seems especially common among African American adolescents, who may be the victims of especially intense discrimination and prejudice (Phinney et al., 1994).

Some writers argue that a more viable, and psychologically healthier, alternative to assimilation or separation is **biculturalism.** Bicultural adolescents "shuttle successfully between their primary or familial culture and the dominant culture" (Spencer & Dornbusch, 1990, p. 133). Several writers (e.g., Phinney & Devich-Navarro, 1997) have proposed a flexibility model, in which minority youth have open to them the norms of both cultures, or "multiple worlds," and select between them, depending on the situation, a process called

code switching. At a majority-controlled school, for example, it may be more adaptive to "act white" when being evaluated by white teachers but also more adaptive to conform with the minority group's own norms and standards when in one's neighborhood. Although code switching may be strategic, it may have a psychological price if it leads to adolescents' feeling that their identity is fragmented (Hemmings, 1998).

One study compared the ethnic identity orientations of Asian American, African American, Hispanic, and white adolescents (Rotherham-Borus, 1990). As expected, the white youngsters were more likely to characterize themselves as assimilated (or "mainstream") than were the minority students, who were more likely to characterize themselves as bicultural than as either mainstream or embedded solely within their ethnic group. In this, and other studies, African American and Puerto Rican adolescents were relatively more likely to be ethnically embedded, whereas Mexican American and Asian American adolescents were more likely to be bicultural (e.g., Phinney, DuPont, Espinosa, Revill, & Sanders, 1994). More interesting, however, was the finding that, although adolescents' ethnic attitudes differed among the mainstream, bicultural, and strong ethnic groups, their mental health did not. The adolescents with all three orientations had equal self-esteem, grades in school, and feeling of social competence. Similar findings were reported in a study that further separated bicultural adolescents into groups that differed in the ways they expressed their bicultural orientation (e.g., having a strong American identity with recognition of one's ethnic heritage versus having a strong ethnic orientation with recognition of one's American citizenship); in this study, bicultural adolescents with different types of orientations scored similarly on measures of personality and adjustment (Phinney et al., 1994). In general, then, positive mental health among ethic minority adolescents is associated with having strong positive feelings about one's own ethnic group, but not with separation from the mainstream culture (Birman, 1998; DeBerry et al., 1996; Gil et al., 1994).

Several researchers have focused on the special situation of ethnic minority youth who are recent immigrants to a new culture (e.g., Gil et al., 1994; Rumbaut & Cornelius, 1995). Interestingly foreign-born ethnic minority adolescents tend to express more positive feelings about mainstream American ideals than do their counterparts whose families have been in the United States longer, and foreign-born ethnic minority youth are less likely to be involved in delinquent behavior, perform better in school,

and are less likely to have physical, emotional, and behavior problems than are their more acculturated peers (Rumbaut 1997; Vega et al., 1995). One interpretation of this is that ethnic minority immigrants arrive in America idealistic about the "melting pot" society, only to discover they are objects of prejudice and discrimination. This realization may prompt a strengthening of ethnic identity, a desire for separatism, cynicism about endorsing mainstream American values, and increased conflict in the adolescent's family (Phinney, DuPont, Espinosa, Revill, & Sanders, 1994; Samaniego & Gonzales, 1999).

RECAP

Several researchers have turned their attention to the study of identity development among ethnic minority youth and, in particular, to the study of ethnic identity. Although adolescents from ethnic minorities benefit from having a strong ethnic identity, there are a variety of ways in which this can be positively expressed. Many experts believe that an especially successful approach is a flexible type of biculturalism, in which minority youth have open to them the norms of both the majority and the minority cultures and they select from among them, depending on the situation.

Food for Thought

How strong is your own sense of ethnic identity? Have there been points in your life when it was especially important?

GENDER-ROLE DEVELOPMENT

Gender is a critical component of one's identity. From birth, boys and girls are socialized to behave in "sex-appropriate" ways—that is, to conform to society's standards for acceptable masculine and acceptable feminine behavior. In American society, strong gender-role stereotypes prevail among children, adolescents, and adults. Traits such as logical, independent, ambitious, and aggressive are considered masculine; and traits such as gentle, sociable, empathic, and tender are considered feminine (Broverman, Vogel, Broverman, Clarkson, & Rosenkrantz, 1972).

Individuals vary in their degrees of masculinity and femininity. Some are decidedly more masculine than feminine, and others are decidedly more feminine than masculine. But some people have a high degree of both masculinity and femininity. For instance, some people are both highly ambitious (a trait usually considered masculine) and highly sensitive (a trait usually considered feminine). Individuals who are both highly masculine and highly feminine are said to be high in **androgyny** (Bem, 1975).

Many researchers have been interested in the relation between gender-role stereotypes and adolescent identity development. Are teenagers, for example, pressured more than children to behave in stereotypically masculine or feminine ways? If so, to what extent does a person's compliance with prevailing gender-role stereotypes affect his or her self-image?

Gender-Role Socialization During Adolescence

There is some thought that pressures to behave in sex-appropriate ways intensify during adolescence, especially for girls (Crouter, Manke, & McHale, 1995; Huston & Alvarez, 1990). This idea, called the **gender intensification hypothesis** (Hill & Lynch, 1983), is that many of the sex differences observed between adolescent boys and girls result from an acceleration in their socialization to act in stereotypically masculine or feminine ways. Even though individuals' *beliefs* about gender roles may become more flexible as they move through adolescence, social pressures may drive teenagers toward more gender-stereotypic behavior (Alfieri, Ruble, & Higgins, 1996; Katz & Ksansnak, 1994). For example, at adolescence, achievement behavior becomes more gender-stereotyped, with girls beginning to disengage from math and science (Hill & Lynch, 1983). And, over the course of adolescence, boys become less emotionally expressive, whereas girls become more so (Polce-Lynch, Myers, Kilmartin, Forssmann-Falck, & Kliewer, 1998).

One study found that sex differences in gender-role attitudes and in the expression of masculinity do, in fact, increase in early adolescence, although these increases seem more tied to chronological age than to the onset of puberty (Galambos, Almeida, & Petersen, 1990). The entry into early adolescence may mark the emergence of new behaviors, which in turn may elicit more sex-differentiated behavior. As teenagers begin to date, for example, it may become more important for them to act in ways that are consistent with gender-role expectations and that meet with approval in the peer group. Boys who do not act masculine enough and girls who do not act feminine

enough may be less popular and less accepted by their same- and opposite-sex peers. Studies suggest that gender role intensification is more likely to occur in families in which the adolescent has a younger, opposite-sex sibling (Crouter et al., 1995).

In many respects, gender-role identity—already an important part of the self-concept during childhood—may become an even more important aspect of identity during adolescence. As we will see in chapters 10, 11, and 12, which examine intimacy, sexuality, and achievement, the intensification of gender-role socialization during adolescence has important implications for understanding sex differences in a range of issues. For example, girls' achievement in high school may be lower than boys' because doing well in school is not perceived as appropriately feminine, so girls who earn high grades may pay a price in popularity.

According to psychologists Carol Gilligan (Gilligan, Lyons, & Hanmer, 1990) and Annie Rogers (1993), who have argued that adolescence is a critical turning point in female psychological development, the mixed messages that adolescent girls receive about desirable behavior are confusing and not easily reconciled. Girls, they argue, arrive at adolescence more likely than boys to prize intimacy and interpersonal communication. Throughout childhood, they have been rewarded for this more relational orientation. At adolescence, however, social cognitive abilities grow, and girls begin to realize that the very traits they have been socialized for are not valued in the broader, male-dominated society. As a consequence, girls feel caught between what they have been told is correct for their gender (e.g., caring and nurturance) and what they can see is valued by society at large (e.g., assertiveness and independence). Overwhelmed by ambivalence, many girls become less confident—they lose their "voice" (Gilligan, 1993). This does not appear to happen to all girls but is more likely to happen to those with an especially feminine gender-role identity (Harter, Waters, Whitesell, & Kastelic, 1998). As you will read in chapter 13, some theorists believe that this conflict may contribute to the greater prevalence of depression among females than males, both in adolescence and in adulthood.

Other feminist theorists, such as Jean Baker Miller (1986), have argued that the very ways in which psychologists have defined mental health have forced a very one-sided view of psychological development. By defining competence as assertive, independent behavior (even the term "identity achieved" has an assertive ring to it), psychologists may have overlooked the importance of understanding how adolescents' psychological growth is facilitated through the formation of relationships with others. These theorists argue that the study of female adolescent development will reveal different pathways to competence for adolescents in general.

Masculinity, Femininity, and Androgyny

If gender-role socialization becomes more intense during adolescence, we would expect to find that conformity to gender-role expectations is an important influence on the adolescent's self-image. Do more feminine girls and more masculine boys feel better about themselves than do their peers, or are both boys and girls better off being somewhat androgynous—as some psychologists suggest (Bem, 1975; Spence & Helmreich, 1978)?

Recent research on gender-role identity during adolescence suggests that the answer to this question may differ for males and females. The relative benefits of androgyny to youngsters' self-image are likely to be greater for girls than for boys. This is because it is specifically the masculine component of androgyny that is associated with better mental health in adolescence (Markstrom-Adams, 1989). Interestingly, this is not the case during childhood, when aspects of both masculinity and femininity are linked to well-being for both sexes (Allgood-Merten & Stockard, 1991), or during young adulthood, when femininity, as well as masculinity, is predictive of well-being among young women (Stein, Newcomb, & Bentler, 1992).

Although masculinity is predictive of mental health among adolescent males and females, androgynous girls feel better about themselves than either very masculine or very feminine girls. Masculine boys, though—not androgynous boys—show the highest levels of self-acceptance, a finding that has emerged in studies of both Western and non-Western youth (Frome & Eccles, 1996; Lau, 1989; Orr & Ben-Eliahu, 1993). This may be because peer acceptance during adolescence is highest for androgynous girls and masculine boys (Massad, 1981). These findings suggest that it is easier for girls to behave sometimes in masculine ways during adolescence than it is for boys to act occasionally in feminine ways. Consistent with research on younger children (Lynn, 1966), during adolescence—at least in contemporary American society—males who do not conform to traditionally masculine gender-role norms are judged to be more deviant than are females whose behavior departs from exclusively feminine roles. Interestingly, however, boys who have a more traditionally masculine orientation, while higher in self-acceptance than other boys, are more likely

▲ *Although masculinity is predictive of mental health for both adolescent males and females, androgynous girls feel better about themselves than either very masculine or very feminine girls. Masculine boys—not androgynous boys—show the highest levels of self-acceptance.* (Michael Newman/PhotoEdit)

to be involved in various types of problem behavior— perhaps because part of being masculine in contemporary society involves being "macho" enough to experiment with delinquency, drugs, and unprotected sex (Pleck, Sonenstein, & Ku, 1994) or because boys who live in difficult environments, where problem behavior is prevalent, adopt a more macho posture for survival in the community (Cunningham, 1999).

Given that pressures to conform with gender-role norms increase more for girls than for boys during adolescence, why is it that boys suffer greater self-image problems when they deviate from what is viewed as appropriate for their gender? The answer is that, although girls may be pressured to adopt (or maintain) certain feminine traits during adolescence, they are not necessarily pressured to relinquish all elements of masculinity. In contrast, boys are socialized from a very early age not to adopt feminine traits and are judged deviant if they show signs of femininity. In other words, girls can be highly pressured during adolescence to behave in feminine ways without necessarily being punished or labeled as deviant for exhibiting some masculine traits at the same time; thus, for girls, androgyny is a viable alternative to exclusive femininity. Girls may feel increasingly pressured to dress nicely and to wear makeup when they reach adolescence, but they are not pressured to give up athletics or other typically masculine interests. But boys, from childhood on, are pressured not to behave in feminine ways—even if the femininity is in the context of androgyny. Their gender-role socialization does not intensify during adolescence as much as it does for girls because it is so intense to begin with.

RECAP

An important aspect of adolescent identity is the development of gender identity. Research suggests that, although individuals grow more flexible over adolescence in the way that they think about gender roles, adolescents may feel especially strong pressure to adhere to stereotypic gender roles. In general, among both males and females, many traits traditionally labeled as masculine are associated in adolescence—but not in childhood or young adulthood—with better adjustment and greater peer acceptance. As a result, androgynous females and masculine males report higher self-esteem than their peers do.

Food for Thought

Explain the gender intensification hypothesis. In your opinion, why are pressures to adhere to sex-role stereotypic behavior so strong in early adolescence?

KEY TERMS

analysis of variance (ANOVA)

androgyny

barometric self-esteem

baseline self-esteem

biculturalism

Big Five

code switching

correlation coefficient

dependent variable

ethnic identity

false-self behavior

Five-Factor Model

gender intensification hypothesis

identity diffusion (identity confusion)

identity foreclosure

identity versus identity diffusion

independent variable

negative identity

psychosocial moratorium

racial socialization

self-conceptions

self-consciousness

self-esteem

self-image stability

sense of identity

Web Researcher Track down websites that provide information on raising adolescents' self-esteem. What do they think gives adolescents high (or low) self-esteem? Do they say the same things about the self-esteem of boys and girls? Given the information in the text, do you think the information they provide about the self-esteem of boys and girls is accurate? Evaluate how effective you think their advice will be in raising self-esteem and under what conditions their interventions are most likely to succeed. Go to www.mhhe.com/steinberg6 for further information.

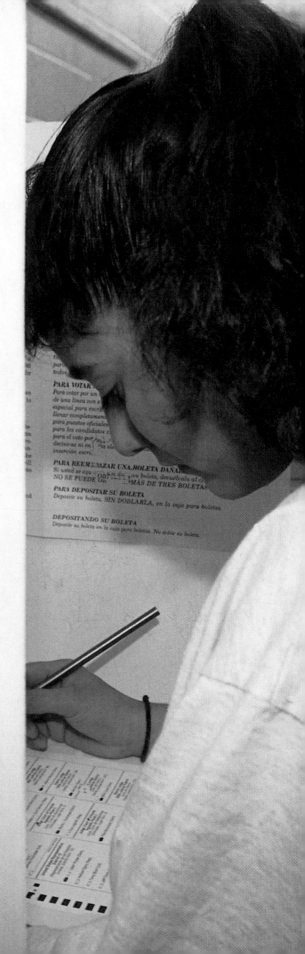

Chapter 9

Autonomy

You are about to leave the house:
"Where are you going?"
"Out."
"Out where?"
"Just out."
"Who are you going with?"
"A friend."
"Which friend?"
"Mom, just a friend, okay? Do you have to know everything?"
"I don't have to know everything. I just want to know who you're going out with."
"Debby, okay?"
"Do I know Debby?"
"She's just a friend, okay?"
"Well, where are you going?"
"Out."

Source: Delia Ephron, *Teenage Romance, or How to Die of Embarrassment* (New York: Viking, 1981).

For most adolescents, establishing a sense of autonomy is as important a part of becoming an adult as is establishing a sense of identity. Becoming an autonomous person—a self-governing person—is one of the fundamental development tasks of the adolescent years.

Although we often use the words *autonomy* and *independence* interchangeably, in the study of adolescence they mean slightly different things. *Independence* generally refers to individuals' capacity to behave on their own. The growth of independence is surely a part of becoming autonomous during adolescence, but, as you will see in this chapter, *autonomy* has emotional and cognitive as well as behavioral components.

During adolescence, there is a movement away from the dependency typical of childhood toward the autonomy typical of adulthood. But the growth of autonomy during adolescence is often misunderstood. Autonomy is often confused with rebellion, and becoming an independent person is often equated with breaking away from the family. This perspective on autonomy goes hand in hand with the idea that adolescence is inevitably a time of stress and turmoil. But the view that adolescence is a period of storm and stress has been questioned repeatedly by scientific research. The same sort of rethinking has taken place with regard to the development of autonomy. Rather than viewing adolescence as a time of spectacular and active rebellion, researchers now see the growth of autonomy during adolescence as gradual, progressive, and—although important—relatively undramatic.

Because today's adolescents spend so much time away from the direct supervision of adults, either by themselves or with their peers, learning how to govern their own behavior in a responsible fashion is a crucial task for contemporary youth. With increasing numbers of single-parent and two-career households, more young people are expected to supervise themselves for a good part of the day (Carnegie Council on Adolescent Development, 1992). Many young people feel pressured—by parents, by friends, and by the media—to grow up quickly and to act as adults at an earlier age (Elkind, 1982). One 13-year-old must make plane reservations to fly back and forth between his separated parents' homes. Another is pregnant and, afraid to tell her parents, must seek counseling on her own. A third is expected to take care of his younger siblings each afternoon because both of his parents work. In many regards, the demands on young people to behave independently are greater today than ever before.

There is a curious paradox in all of this, however. At the same time that adolescents have been asked to become more autonomous psychologically and socially, they have become less autonomous economically. Because of the extension of schooling well into the young adult years for most individuals, financial independence may not come until long after psychological independence has been established. Many young people who are emotionally independent find it frustrating to discover that they have to abide by their parents' rules as long as they are being supported economically. They may feel that the ability to make their own decisions has nothing to do with financial dependence. A 16-year-old who drives, has a part-time job, and has a serious relationship with his girlfriend, for example, may be independent in these respects, but he is nonetheless still dependent on his parents for food and shelter. His parents may feel that, as long as their son lives in their home, they should decide how late he can stay out at night. The adolescent may feel that his parents have no right to tell him when he can come and go. This sort of difference of opinion can be a major source of problems and confusion for teenagers and their parents, particularly when they have difficulty agreeing on a level of independence for the adolescent. Disagreements over autonomy-related concerns are at the top of the list of things that provoke quarrels between adolescents and parents (Holmbeck & O'Donnell, 1991; Montemayor, 1986; Steinberg, 2001). ●

▲ *The demands on young people to behave independently are greater today than ever before. This adolescent is expected to supervise her younger brother each day after school.* (Michael Newman/PhotoEdit)

AUTONOMY AS AN ADOLESCENT ISSUE

Like identity, autonomy is a psychosocial concern that surfaces and resurfaces during the entire life cycle. The development of independent behavior begins long before puberty. Erik Erikson (1963), whose ideas we examined in chapter 8, believed that autonomy is the central issue of toddlerhood, just as identity is the central issue of adolescence. Young children, he observed, try to establish an initial sense of autonomy when they begin to explore their surroundings on their own and assert their desire to do as they please. If you spend any time with 3-year-olds, you know that one of their favorite expressions is "no!" In some regards, the early adolescent's behavior that is captured in the excerpt at the beginning of this chapter is quite similar. The toddler who insists on saying "no!" and the young adolescent who

insists on keeping her whereabouts secret are both demonstrating their growing sense of independence and autonomy.

Although childhood and adolescence are important periods for the development of autonomy, it is a mistake to suggest that issues of autonomy are resolved once and for all upon reaching young adulthood. Questions about our ability to function independently arise whenever we find ourselves in positions that demand a new degree of self-reliance. Following a divorce, for example, someone who has depended on a spouse over the years for economic support, guidance, or nurturance must find a way to function more autonomously and more independently. During late adulthood, autonomy may become a significant concern of the individual who suddenly finds it necessary to depend on others for assistance and support.

If establishing and maintaining a healthy sense of autonomy is a lifelong concern, why has it attracted so much attention among scholars interested in adolescence? When we look at the development of autonomy in relation to the biological, cognitive, and social changes of adolescence, it is easy to see why. Consider first the impact of puberty. Some theorists (for example, A. Freud [1958]) have suggested that the physical changes of early adolescence trigger changes in the young person's emotional relationships at home (Holmbeck, 1996). Adolescents' interest in turning away from parents and toward peers for emotional support—a development that is part of establishing adult independence—may be sparked by their emerging interest in sexual relationships and by their concerns over such things as dating and intimate friendships. In some senses, puberty drives the adolescent away from exclusive emotional dependence on the family. Furthermore, the changes in stature and physical appearance occurring at puberty may provoke changes in how much autonomy the young person is granted by parents and teachers. Youngsters who simply look more mature may be given more responsibility by the adults around them.

The cognitive changes of adolescence also play an important role in the development of autonomy. Part of being autonomous involves being able to make our own decisions. When we turn to others for advice, we often receive conflicting opinions. For example, if you are deciding between staying home to study for an exam and going out to a party, your professor and the person throwing the party would probably give you different advice. As an adult, you are able to see that each individual's perspective influences his or her advice. The ability to see this, however, calls for a level of intellectual abstraction that is not available until adolescence. Being able to take into account other people's perspectives, to reason in more sophisticated ways, and to foresee the consequences of alternative courses of action all help the young person weigh the opinions and suggestions of others more effectively and reach his or her independent decisions. The cognitive changes of adolescence also provide the logical foundation for changes in the young person's thinking about social, moral, and ethical problems. These changes in thinking are important prerequisites to the development of a system of values that is based on the individual's own sense of right and wrong and not merely on rules and regulations handed down by parents or other authority figures (Mazor & Enright, 1988; Mazor, Shamir, & Ben-Mosche, 1990).

Finally, changes in social roles and activities during adolescence are bound to raise concerns related to independence, as the adolescent moves into new positions that demand increasing degrees of responsibility and self-reliance. Being able to work, to marry, to drive, to drink, and to vote—to name just a few activities that are first permitted during adolescence—all require the ability to manage oneself responsibly in the absence of monitoring by parents or teachers. Becoming involved in new roles and taking on new responsibilities place the adolescent in situations that require and stimulate the development of independent decision-making abilities and the clarification of personal values. A teenager might not really think much about the responsibilities associated with taking a job, for example, until he or she actually ends up in one. Choosing whether to drink does not become an important question until the adolescent begins to approach the legal drinking age. And deciding what one's political beliefs are becomes a more pressing concern when the young person realizes that he or she will soon have the right to vote.

We have talked a great deal thus far about the need to develop a sense of autonomy during adolescence. But what does it really mean to be an autonomous or independent person? One way to approach this question is to begin by thinking about the people whom you would describe as independent. Why do they seem so? Is it because they are able to rely on themselves rather than depending excessively on others for support or guidance? Is it because they can make their own decisions and follow them through, withstanding pressures to go against what they know is right? Or is it perhaps because they are independent thinkers—people who have strong principles and values that they won't compromise?

Each of these characterizations is a reasonable enough description of what it means to be independent, yet each describes a different sort of independence. The first characterization involves what psychologists call **emotional autonomy**—the aspect of independence that is related to changes in the individual's close relationships, especially with parents. The second characterization corresponds to what is sometimes called **behavioral autonomy**—the capacity to make independent decisions and follow through with them. The third characterization involves an aspect of independence referred to as **value autonomy,** which is more than simply being able to resist pressures to go along with the demands of others; it means having a set of principles about right and wrong, about what is important and what is not. Throughout this chapter, we will examine these three aspects of autonomy (Douvan & Adelson, 1966).

> ### RECAP
>
> *Although the development of autonomy is an important psychosocial issue throughout the life span, it is especially salient during adolescence because of the physical, cognitive, and social changes of the period. Psychologists generally differentiate among three types of autonomy in adolescence: emotional autonomy, which is emotional independence in relationships with others, especially parents; behavioral autonomy, which is the development of independent decision-making abilities; and value autonomy, which concerns the development of independent beliefs.*

> ### Food for Thought
>
> *Many psychologists contend that the two periods of life during which autonomy is an especially salient issue are early adolescence and toddlerhood. What do these periods share that might account for the importance of autonomy during each?*

THE DEVELOPMENT OF EMOTIONAL AUTONOMY

The relationship between children and their parents changes repeatedly over the course of the life cycle. Changes in the expression of affection, the distribution of power, and patterns of verbal interaction, to give a few examples, are likely to occur whenever important transformations take place in the child's or the parents' competencies, concerns, and social roles.

By the end of adolescence, individuals are far less emotionally dependent on their parents than they were as children. This can be seen in several ways. First, older adolescents do not generally rush to their parents whenever they are upset, worried, or in need of assistance. Second, they do not see their parents as all-knowing or all-powerful. Third, adolescents often have a great deal of emotional energy wrapped up in relation-ships outside the family; in fact, they may feel more attached to a boyfriend or a girlfriend than to their parents. And, finally, older adolescents are able to see and interact with their parents as people—not just as their parents. Many parents find, for example, that they can confide in their adolescent children, something that was not possible when their children were younger, or that their adolescent children can easily sympathize with them when they have had a hard day at work. These sorts of changes in the adolescent-parent relationship all reflect the development of emotional autonomy (Steinberg, 1990).

Emotional Autonomy and Detachment

Early writings about emotional autonomy were influenced by psychoanalytic thinkers such as Anna Freud (1958), who argued that the physical changes of puberty cause substantial disruption and conflict inside the family system. The reason, Freud believed, is that intrapsychic conflicts that have been repressed since early childhood are reawakened at early adolescence by the resurgence of sexual impulses. (These conflicts revolve around the young child's unconscious attraction toward the parent of the opposite sex and ambivalent feelings toward the parent of the same sex.) The reawakened conflicts are expressed as increased tension among family members, arguments, and a certain degree of discomfort around the house. As a consequence of this tension, early adolescents are driven to separate themselves, at least emotionally, from their parents, and they turn their emotional energies to relationships with peers—in particular, peers of the opposite sex. Psychoanalytic theorists call this process of separation **detachment,** because to them it appears as though the early adolescent is attempting to sever the *attachments* that have been formed during infancy and strengthened throughout childhood.

Detachment and the accompanying storm and stress inside the family were viewed by Freud and her followers as normal, healthy, and inevitable aspects of emotional

▲ In contrast to the view that adolescent-parent tension is the norm, every major study done to date of teenagers' relations with their parents has shown that most families get along quite well during the adolescent years. (Myrleen Ferguson/PhotoEdit)

development during adolescence. In fact, Freud believed that the absence of conflict between an adolescent and his or her parents signifies that the young person is having problems growing up. This view is compatible with the idea that adolescence is an inherently tumultuous time—a perspective that, as you know, dominated ideas about adolescence for many, many years.

Studies of adolescents' family relationships have not supported Freud's idea, however. In contrast to predictions that high levels of adolescent-parent tension are the norm, that adolescents detach themselves from relationships with their parents, and that adolescents are driven out of the household by unbearable levels of family conflict, every major study done to date of teenagers' relations with their parents has shown that most families get along quite well during the adolescent years (Steinberg, 2001). Although parents and adolescents may bicker more often than they did during earlier periods of development, there is no evidence that this bickering significantly diminishes closeness between parents and teenagers (Grotevant, 1997; Hill & Holmbeck, 1986). For example, one team of researchers who asked adolescents and children of different ages to rate how close they were to their parents, found that the 19-year-old college students reported being just as close as the fourth-graders (Hunter & Youniss, 1982).

The psychic and interpersonal tension believed to arise at puberty does not show up in markedly strained family relationships. Although adolescents and their parents undoubtedly modify their relationships during adolescence, their emotional bonds are by no means severed. This is an important distinction, for it means that emotional autonomy during adolescence involves a *transformation,* not a breaking off of family relationships (Guisinger & Blatt, 1994). In other words, adolescents can become emotionally autonomous from their parents without becoming detached from them (Collins, 1990; Grotevant, 1997; Steinberg, 1990).

Emotional Autonomy and Individuation

As an alternative to the classic psychoanalytic perspective on adolescent detachment, some theorists have suggested that the development of emotional autonomy be looked at in terms of the adolescent's developing sense of **individuation.** One such theorist is noted psychoanalyst Peter Blos. According to him, "Individuation implies that the growing person takes increasing responsibility for what he does and what he is, rather than depositing this responsibility on the shoulders of those under whose influence and tutelage he has grown up" (1967, p. 168). The process of individuation, which begins during infancy and continues well into late adolescence, involves a gradual, progressive sharpening of one's sense of self as autonomous, competent, and separate from one's parents. Individuation, therefore, has a great deal to do with the development of a sense of identity, in that it involves changes in how we come to see and feel about ourselves.

Individuation does not involve stress and turmoil. Rather, individuation entails relinquishing childish dependencies on parents in favor of more mature, more responsible, and less dependent relationships. Adolescents who have been successful in establishing a sense of individuation can accept responsibility for their choices

and actions instead of looking to their parents to do it for them (Josselson, 1980). For example, rather than rebelling against her parents' midnight curfew by deliberately staying out later, a girl who has a healthy sense of individuation might take her parents aside before going out and say, "This party tonight may last longer than midnight. If it does, I'd like to stay a bit longer. Suppose I call you at eleven o'clock and let you know when I'll be home. That way, you won't worry as much if I come home a little later."

Studies of the growth of emotional autonomy indicate that the development of emotional autonomy is a long process, beginning early in adolescence and continuing well into young adulthood. In one study (Steinberg & Silverberg, 1986), a questionnaire measuring four aspects of emotional autonomy was administered to a sample of 10- to 15-year-olds. The four components were (1) the extent to which the adolescents' *deidealized* their parents ("My parents sometimes make mistakes"); (2) the extent to which the adolescents were able to *see their parents as people* ("My parents act differently with their own friends than they do with me"); (3) *nondependency,* or the degree to which the adolescents depended on themselves, rather than on their parents, for assistance ("When I've done something wrong, I don't always depend on my parents to straighten things out"); and (4) the degree to which the adolescents felt *individuated* within the relationship with their parents ("There are some things about me that my parents do not know"). As you can see in figure 9.1, the scores on three of the four scales—all except "perceives parents as people"—increased over the age period studied.

Similar findings have emerged in other studies. In one, for example, the researchers found that, as the adolescents aged, the number of their friends whom their parents knew declined significantly, reflecting greater individuation and privacy on the part of the adolescent (Feiring & Lewis, 1993). In another study, in which adolescents were interviewed about their family relationships, the researchers found that the older adolescents were also more likely to de-idealize their parents. For example, one adolescent said this about his father: "I used to listen to everything. I thought he was always right. Now I have my own opinions. They may be wrong, but they're mine and I like to say them" (Smoller & Youniss, 1985, p. 8). A third study, which examined adolescent boys' reports of homesickness during summer camp, found that homesickness—which was experienced by youngsters as anxiety and

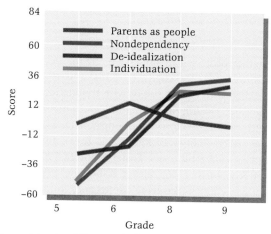

Figure 9.1   Age differences in four aspects of emotional autonomy. (Steinberg & Silverberg, 1986)

depression—became less prevalent during middle adolescence than it had been in early adolescence or preadolescence (Thurber, 1995). Finally, one study found that adolescents were less willing to express negative emotions in front of their parents—anger and sadness—during early adolescence than before or after, perhaps because keeping some emotional distance from one's parents is a part of the individuation process (Zeman & Shipman, 1997).

Psychologists believe that **de-idealization** may be one of the first aspects of emotional autonomy to develop, because adolescents may shed their childish images of their parents before replacing them with more mature ones. Although middle adolescents are less likely than young adolescents to hold on to idealized pictures of their parents, when it comes to seeing their parents as individuals, 15-year-olds are no more emotionally autonomous than are 10-year-olds. Even during the high school years, adolescents appear to have some difficulty in seeing their parents as individuals beyond their roles as parents. This aspect of emotional autonomy may not develop until much later—perhaps not until young adulthood (Smollar & Youniss, 1985; White, Speisman, & Costos, 1983). This aspect of emotional autonomy appears to develop later in adolescents' relations with their fathers than with their mothers, because fathers seem to interact less often with their adolescents in ways that permit them to be seen as individuals (Youniss & Smollar, 1985).

Interestingly, and in contrast to the old view that adolescents need to sever their ties with their parents in order to grow up healthily, a number of studies find

that the development of emotional autonomy, and individuation in particular, may have different psychological effects on the adolescent, depending on whether his or her parent-child relationship is a close one. Adolescents who become emotionally autonomous, but who also feel distant or detached from their parents, score poorly on measures of psychological adjustment, whereas adolescents who demonstrate the same degree of emotional autonomy, but who still feel close and attached to their parents, are psychologically healthier than their peers (Allen, Hauser, O'Connor, Bell, & Eickholt, 1996; Chen & Dornbusch, 1998; Fuhrman & Holmbeck, 1995; Lamborn & Steinberg, 1993; Ryan & Lynch, 1989). In essence, whereas detachment has negative effects on adolescents' mental health, individuation has positive ones.

Several writers have explored the ways in which the process of developing autonomy may differ for adolescents whose parents have divorced (Feldman & Quatman, 1988; Sessa & Steinberg, 1991; Wallerstein & Kelly, 1974; Weiss, 1979). These writers argue that having divorced parents prompts the adolescent to grow up faster—to de-idealize parents at an earlier age. As a consequence, adolescents from divorced homes may begin the process of individuation somewhat earlier than their peers. Whether this has positive or negative consequences, however, is not known.

What triggers the process of individuation? Two models have been suggested. According to several researchers, puberty is the main catalyst (e.g., Bulcroff, 1991; Holmbeck, 1996; Steinberg, 1989). Changes in the adolescent's physical appearance provoke changes in the way that adolescents are viewed—by themselves and by their parents—which, in turn, provoke changes in parent-child interaction. As we saw in chapter 4, shortly after puberty most families experience an increase in bickering and squabbling. Some writers have suggested that this increase in conflict helps adolescents see their parents in a different light and develop a sense of individuation (Cooper, 1988; Holmbeck & Hill, 1991; Steinberg, 1990).

Other authors believe that adolescents' movement toward higher levels of individuation is stimulated by their social-cognitive development (Collins, 1990; Smetana, 1988b). As you read in chapter 2, social cognition is the thinking we do about ourselves and our relationships with others. The development of emotional autonomy in adolescence may be provoked by young people's development of more sophisticated understandings of themselves and their parents. Prior to adolescence, individuals accept their parents' views of themselves as accurate (e.g., "My parents think I am a good girl, so I must be"). However, as individuals develop more differentiated self-conceptions in early and middle adolescence (recall the discussion of this in chapter 8), they come to see that their parents' view is but one of many—and one that may not be entirely accurate ("My parents think I am a good girl, but they don't know what I am *really* like"). By late adolescence, individuals are able to see that these apparent discrepancies between their self-conceptions and their parents' views are perfectly understandable ("There are sides of me that have been influenced by my parents and sides of me that have not") (see Mazor & Enright, 1988).

This is not to suggest that the process of individuation is always a smooth one. Some writers have suggested that, as adolescents begin to de-idealize their parents, they may begin to feel both more autonomous and more insecure—what one research team labeled a "double-edged sword" (Frank, Pirsch, & Wright, 1990). That is, even though our childish images of our parents as being all-knowing and all-powerful may be inaccurate, they still provide a degree of emotional comfort. Leaving such images behind can be both liberating and frightening. Indeed, some researchers have found that emotional autonomy is associated not only with insecurity for the adolescent but also with increased feelings of rejection for the parents (Ryan & Lynch, 1989; Steinberg & Steinberg, 1994).

RECAP

Formerly, adolescence was viewed as a time during which individuals need to break away from and rebel against their parents. More recent research indicates, however, that the growth of emotional autonomy is typically more peaceful and less tumultuous. Instead of emphasizing the young person's need for detachment, therefore, contemporary psychologists stress the process of individuation, which is set in motion in early adolescence by the physical and cognitive changes of the period. One of the first signs of individuation may be adolescents' de-idealization of their parents.

Food for Thought

Do you recall going through a period of time during which you de-idealized your parents? How did this affect your relationship?

Emotional Autonomy and Parenting Practices

Whether provoked by puberty or by the development of more advanced cognitive skills, and whether approached with confidence or with trepidation, one fact is certain: Healthy individuation and positive mental health are fostered by close, not distant, family relationships (Allen, Hauser, Eickholt, Bell, & O'Connor, 1994; Bomar & Sabatelli, 1996; Foster & Ritter, 1995; Grotevant & Cooper, 1986; Keener & Boykin, 1996). Tense family relationships during adolescence indicate problems, not positive development (Fuhrman & Holmbeck, 1995). Researchers have found, for example, that adolescents who feel the most autonomous—that is, those who are most likely to feel that they have been granted enough freedom by their parents—are not the ones who have severed relationships at home. In fact, just the opposite is the case: Autonomous adolescents report that they are quite close to their parents, enjoy doing things with their families, have few conflicts with their mothers and fathers, feel free to turn to their parents for advice, and say they would like to be like their parents (Kandel & Lesser, 1972). Rebellion, negativism, and excessive involvement in the peer group are more common among psychologically immature adolescents than among mature ones (Josselson, Greenberger, & McConochie, 1977a, 1977b). Even during the college years, students who live away from home (which is, in its own way, a type of autonomy)—as opposed to remaining in their parents' home and commuting to school—report more affection for their parents, better communication, and higher levels of satisfaction in the relationship (Holmbeck, Durbin, & Kung, 1995; Sullivan & Sullivan, 1980). Strained family relationships appear to be associated with a lack of autonomy during adolescence, rather than with its presence (Bomar & Sabatelli, 1996). At the same time, adolescents whose parents are close to the point of being intrusive or overprotective may have difficulty individuating from them, which may lead to depression, anxiety, and diminished social competence (Allen & McElhancy, 2000; Holmbeck et al., 2000). Overprotectiveness may be especially harmful for adolescents who are less competent to begin with (Thompson & Zuroff, 1999).

Psychologists now know that emotional autonomy develops best under conditions that encourage both individuation and emotional closeness. The need for parents to strike the right balance can be seen quite clearly in the work of Stuart Hauser and Joseph Allen, who have studied videotapes of parents and adolescents in discussion and have examined whether certain types of interaction are more or less facilitative of healthy adolescent development (Allen & McElhaney, 2000; Allen et al., 1994a, 1996; Hauser, Powers, & Noam, 1991; Hauser & Safyer, 1994). The tapes were coded for two specific types of behavior: *enabling behavior* and *constraining behavior*. Parents who use a lot of enabling behavior accept their adolescent while helping the teenager develop and state his or her own ideas through questions, explanations, and the tolerance of differences of opinion. In contrast, parents who use constraining behavior have difficulty accepting their child's individuality and react to expressions of independent thinking with remarks that are distracting, judgmental, or devaluing. After hearing an adolescent's opinion that differs from his own, for example, an enabling father might ask for more clarification or might genuinely probe the adolescent's logic, whereas a constraining father might cut off further discussion by saying that the adolescent is wrong or ignorant.

Not surprisingly, researchers have found that adolescents whose parents use a great deal of enabling and relatively little constraining behavior are more likely to develop in healthy ways: They are more individuated and score higher on measures of identity development and psychosocial competence. This is in line with other research, showing that healthy identity development is more likely to occur within families in which adolescents are encouraged both to be connected to their parents and to express their own individuality (Cooper, Grotevant, & Condon, 1983; Grotevant & Cooper, 1986) and that adolescents fare best when their relationships at home strike the right balance between autonomy and connectedness (Hodges, Finnegan, & Perry, 1999). Adolescents who grow up in families that inhibit individuation are more likely to report feeling anxious and depressed, whereas adolescents from families with low levels of closeness are more likely to display behavior problems, such as poor impulse control (Allen et al., 1994b; Pavlidis & McCauley, 1995).

As we saw in chapter 4, adolescents' development is affected differently by different styles of parenting. In particular, independence, responsibility, and self-esteem are all fostered by parents who are authoritative (friendly, fair, and firm), rather than authoritarian (excessively harsh), indulgent (excessively lenient), or indifferent (excessively aloof to the point of neglectful). Let us now look more closely at these findings in light of what we know about the development of emotional autonomy.

In authoritative families, guidelines are established for the adolescent's behavior, and standards are upheld, but they are flexible and open to discussion. Moreover, these standards and guidelines are explained and implemented in an atmosphere of closeness, concern, and fairness. Although parents may have the final say when it comes to their child's behavior, the decision that is reached usually comes after consultation and discussion—with the child included. In discussing an adolescent's curfew, for example, authoritative parents sit down with their child and explain how they arrived at their decision and why they picked the hour they did. They also ask the adolescent for his or her suggestions and consider them carefully in making a final decision.

It is not difficult to see why the sort of give-and-take that is found in authoritative families is well suited to the child's transition into adolescence. Because standards and guidelines are flexible and adequately explained, it is not hard for the family to adjust and modify them as the child matures emotionally and intellectually (Smetana & Asquith, 1994). Gradual changes in family relations that permit the young person more independence and encourage more responsibility but that do not threaten the emotional bond between parent and child—in other words, changes that promote increasing emotional autonomy—are relatively easy to make for a family that has been flexible and has been making these sorts of modifications in family relationships all along (Baumrind, 1978; Vuchinich, Angeletti, & Gatherum, 1996).

In authoritarian households, where rules are rigidly enforced and seldom explained to the child, adjusting to adolescence is more difficult for the family. Authoritarian parents may see the child's increasing emotional independence as rebellious or disrespectful, and they may resist their adolescent's growing need for independence, rather than reacting to it openly. Authoritarian parents, on seeing that their daughter is becoming interested in boys, may implement a rigid curfew in order to restrict her social life. Instead of encouraging autonomy, authoritarian parents may inadvertently maintain the dependencies of childhood by failing to give their child sufficient practice in making decisions and being responsible for his or her actions. In essence, authoritarian parenting may interfere with adolescent individuation.

When closeness is absent as well, the problems are compounded. In families in which excessive parental control is accompanied by extreme coldness and punitiveness, the adolescent may rebel against the parents' standards explicitly, in an attempt to assert his or her independence in a visible and demonstrable fashion

(Hill & Holmbeck, 1986). Adolescents whose parents refuse to grant reasonable curfews are the teens who typically stay out the latest. Such rebellion is not indicative of genuine emotional autonomy, though; it is more likely to be a demonstration of the adolescent's frustration with his or her parents' rigidity and lack of understanding. And, when adolescents attempt to establish emotional autonomy within the context of a cold or hostile family, the effects on the young person's mental health are likely to be negative (Lamborn & Steinberg, 1993). Indeed, adolescents from hostile or stressful family environments may do best when they actively detach themselves from their parents (Fuhrman & Holmbeck, 1995).

In both indulgent families and indifferent families, a different sort of problem arises. These kinds of parents do not provide sufficient guidance for their children; as a result, youngsters who are raised permissively do not acquire adequate standards for behavior. Someone who has never had to abide by his or her parents' rules as a child faces tremendous difficulty learning how to comply with rules as an adult. In the absence of parents' guidance and rules, permissively reared teenagers often turn to their peers for advice and emotional support—a practice that can be problematic when the peers are themselves still relatively young and inexperienced. Not surprisingly, adolescents whose parents have failed to provide sufficient guidance are likely to become psychologically dependent on their friends—emotionally detached from their parents, perhaps, but not genuinely autonomous (Devereux, 1970). The problems of parental permissiveness are exacerbated by a lack of closeness, as is the case in indifferent families.

Some parents who have raised their children permissively until adolescence are caught by surprise by the consequences of not having been stricter earlier on. The greater orientation toward the peer group of permissively raised adolescents may involve the young person in behavior that his or her parents disapprove of. As a consequence, some parents who have been permissive throughout a youngster's childhood shift gears when he or she enters adolescence and become autocratic, as a means of controlling the youngster over whom they feel they have lost control. For instance, parents who have never placed any restrictions on their daughter's afternoon activities during elementary school suddenly begin monitoring her teenage social life once she enters junior high school. Shifts like these can be extremely hard on adolescents—just at the time when they are seeking greater autonomy, their parents become more restrictive. Having become ac-customed to relative leniency, adolescents whose parents change the rules in the middle of the game may find it difficult to accept standards that are being strictly enforced for the first time.

Food for Thought

What should parents do to help facilitate the development of healthy emotional autonomy? What are the problems associated with too little closeness? with too much overprotectiveness?

THE DEVELOPMENT OF BEHAVIORAL AUTONOMY

One of the most popular misconceptions about adolescent development is that adolescents demonstrate autonomy by rebelling against the wishes of their parents. However, in many instances, rebelling against one's parents or other authorities is done not out of independence but out of a desire to conform to one's peers. During early adolescence, in fact, individuals become more emotionally autonomous from their parents but *less* autonomous from their friends (Steinberg & Silverberg, 1986). Merely substituting one source of influence (the peer group) for another (the family), though, is hardly evidence of growth toward independence. After all, excessive adherence to the pressures of one's friends is no more autonomous than is excessive adherence to the pressures of one's parents. Moreover, rebellion is associated with immaturity, not with healthy development. Just what is meant, then, by behavioral autonomy?

All individuals—at all ages—are susceptible to the pressures of those around them. The opinions and advice of others, especially people whose knowledge and judgment they respect, are, and should be, important influences on their choices and decisions. Surely, then, we would not want to say that the behaviorally autonomous adolescent is entirely free from the influence of others. Rather, an individual who is behaviorally autonomous is able to turn to others for advice when it is appropriate, can weigh alternative courses of action based on his or her own judgment and the suggestions of others, and can reach an independent conclusion about how to behave (Hill & Holmbeck, 1986). Let's look more closely at why and how changes in behavioral autonomy occur during adolescence. Researchers have looked at this in three domains: changes in decision-making abilities, changes in susceptibility to the influence of others, and changes in feelings of self-reliance.

Changes in Decision-Making Abilities

The more sophisticated reasoning processes used by the adolescent permit him or her to hold multiple viewpoints in mind simultaneously, allowing comparisons among the viewpoints—an ability that is crucial for weighing the opinions and advice of others. In addition, because adolescents are better able than children to think in hypothetical terms, they are more likely to consider the possible long-term consequences of choosing one course of action over another. And the enhanced role-taking capabilities of adolescence permit the teenager to consider another person's opinion while taking into account that person's perspective. This is important in determining whether someone who gives advice has special areas of expertise, particular biases, or vested interests that one should keep in mind. Together, these cognitive changes result in improved decision-making skills and, consequently, in the individual's greater ability to behave independently.

A study by Catherine Lewis (1981b) sheds a good deal of light on these issues. She presented more than 100 adolescents ranging in age from 12 to 18 with a series of problems that they were to help another teenager solve. The problems concerned such things as becoming involved in various risky situations, revising an opinion of someone who had previously been respected, or reconciling different pieces of advice from two "experts." One of the problems, for example, focused on a teenager's indecision about whether to have cosmetic surgery.

Lewis looked at the adolescents' responses along five dimensions: whether they were aware of risks; whether they were aware of likely future consequences; whether parents, peers, or outside specialists were recom-

mended as consultants; whether attitudes were revised in light of new information; and whether the adolescents recognized and cautioned against the vested interests of people giving advice. The adolescents were grouped by grade level, with seventh- and eighth-graders forming one group, tenth-graders a second group, and twelfth-graders a third group. The results of the study are shown in figure 9.2.

The age groups differed along four of the five dimensions studied, with the older adolescents demonstrating more sophisticated decision-making abilities. The older adolescents were more likely to be aware of risks, more likely to consider future consequences, more likely to turn to an independent specialist as a consultant, and more likely to realize when vested interests existed and to raise cautions about accepting advice from people who might be biased. A recent study of adolescents' and adults' decision making, using a similar methodology, found comparable results: Compared with adolescents, adults are more likely to consider the risks and benefits associated with the decisions they make, and they are more likely to suggest seeking the advice of an independent specialist (Halpern-Felsher & Cauffman, in press).

In other words, decision-making abilities improve over the course of the adolescent years, with gains continuing well into the later years of high school and into adulthood. These developments provide the cognitive tools for behavioral autonomy: being able to look ahead and assess the risks and likely outcomes of alternative choices, being able to recognize the value of turning to an independent expert, and being able to see that someone's advice may be tainted by his or her own interests.

The recognition that individuals' decision-making skills improve over the course of adolescence has prompted numerous debates about young people's abilities to make decisions in the real world. However, this is an area in which the evidence is sufficiently fuzzy to make drawing firm conclusions very difficult. Older adolescents (those 16 and up) reason in ways that are significantly more sophisticated than younger adolescents. Youth advocates have argued, on the basis of this, that older adolescents should have the right to seek healthcare services (including abortions and contraception) without parental knowledge or consent (Blum, Resnick, & Stark, 1990; Gardner, Scherer, & Tester, 1989; Melton, 1990; Scherer & Gardner, 1990). But the same evidence has been used to justify trying adolescent offenders as adults, on the grounds that their decision making is not

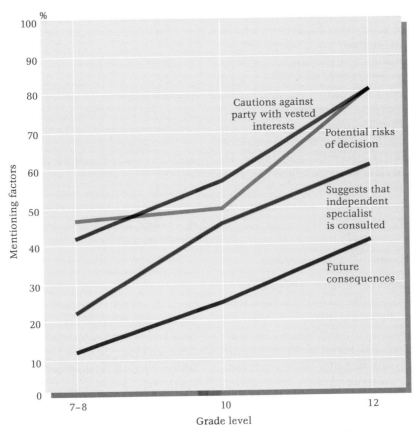

Figure 9.2   Decision-making abilities improve during adolescence. (Derived from Lewis, 1981b)

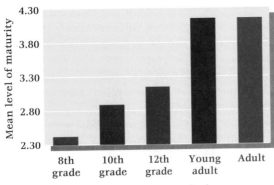

Figure 9.3   Age differences in maturity of judgment.
(Cauffman & Steinberg, 2000)

all that different (Grisso & Schwartz, 2000). At the same time, because there appears to be continued improvement in decision-making competence beyond adolescence, individuals who are opposed to trying juvenile offenders as adults use *this* evidence to argue in favor of

keeping adolescents in the juvenile justice system. The fact of the matter is that, although experts agree that adolescents' decision-making tools improve with age, there is little consensus about whether the improvement is sufficient to permit adolescents to be treated as adults, or at what age the boundary should be drawn (Steinberg & Cauffman, 2000). As a consequence, laws governing adolescents' independent health-care behavior as well as their criminal prosecution are inconsistent and highly variable from state to state (Fagan & Zimring, 2000; Gittler, Quigley-Rick, & Saks, 1990).

A recent study of age differences in maturity and decision making indicates both that there are significant improvements in these capabilities over the adolescent years and that there is tremendous variability within groups of individuals of the same chronological age (Cauffman & Steinberg, 2000) (see figure 9.3). Thus, although it is probably correct to assume that the "average" 15-year-old is not as competent a decision maker as the "average" 20-year-old, there are many 15-year-olds who are capable of mature decision making and many 20-year-olds who are quite irresponsible. The dilemma for policymakers, then, is to try to find a way to create laws that take chronological age into account but that allow for exceptions to be made for individuals whose behavior and judgment are not typical for people their age.

RECAP

One of the main ways in which the development of behavioral autonomy during adolescence is evident is in the growth of decision-making abilities. As individuals mature, they become better able to seek out and weigh the advice of individuals with various degrees of expertise and to use this information in making independent decisions. One controversy that has been debated is whether adolescents' decision-making abilities are mature enough to warrant their treatment as adults under the law.

Food for Thought

Based on what you have read about changes in decision-making abilities in adolescence, should adolescents be treated as adults under the law? If you were a lawmaker, where would you draw the line for issues concerning access to health care? for issues concerning criminal activity? Would you favor laws holding parents legally responsible for the behavior of their teenagers?

Changes in Susceptibility to Influence

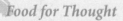

As the adolescent comes to spend more time outside the family, the opinions and advice of others—not only peers but adults as well—become more important. At a certain point, for example, adolescents seek the advice of friends, rather than of their parents, concerning how to dress. They may turn to a teacher or guidance counselor for advice about what courses to take in school, instead of bringing such questions home. Understandably, a variety of situations arise in which adolescents feel that their parents' advice is less valid than the opinions of others.

There also are issues that might be talked over with more than one person. For example, a teenage girl who is trying to decide whether to take a part-time job after school might discuss the pros and cons with her parents, but she might also turn to friends and ask for their advice. When friends and parents disagree, adolescents must reconcile the differences of opinion and reach their own, independent conclusions.

In situations in which parents and peers give conflicting advice, do teenagers tend to follow one group more often than the other? Adolescents are often portrayed as being extremely susceptible to the influence of **peer pressure**—more so than children or young adults—and as stubbornly resistant to the influence of their parents. But is peer pressure really more potent during adolescence than during other times in the life cycle?

Researchers have studied conformity and peer pressure during adolescence by putting adolescents in situations in which they must choose either between the pressures of their parents and the pressures of their peers or between their own wishes and those of others—typically, parents or friends. For example, an adolescent boy might be told to imagine that he and his friends discover something that looks suspicious on the way home from school. His friends tell him that they should keep it a secret. But the adolescent tells his mother about it, and she advises him to report it to the police. He then would be asked by the researcher to say what he would do.

In general, studies that contrast parents' and peers' influences indicate that, in some situations, peers' opinions are more influential; in other situations, parents' opinions are more influential. Specifically, adolescents are more likely to conform to their peers' opinions when it comes to short-term, day-to-day, and social matters—styles of dress, tastes in music, choices among leisure activities, and so on. This is particularly true during junior high school and the early years of high school. When it comes to long-term questions concerning educational and occupational plans, however, or to questions of values, religious beliefs, and ethics, teenagers are primarily influenced by their parents (Brittain, 1963; Young & Ferguson, 1979). Some studies also have looked at adolescents' willingness to seek advice from adults outside their family. These studies indicate that, in situations calling for objective information (such as facts about getting admitted to a particular college) rather than opinion (such as whether the college is supposed to be a friendly place), teenagers are likely to turn to outside experts, such as their teachers (Young & Ferguson, 1979).

Similar findings emerge from studies of the consultants to whom adolescents turn when they have problems (Morrison, Laughlin, Miguel, Smith, & Widaman,

▲ *Adolescents are more likely to conform to their peers' opinions when it comes to short-term, day-to-day, and social matters, such as styles of dress. However, when it comes to long-term questions or issues concerning basic values, parents remain more influential than peers.* (Spencer Grant/PhotoEdit)

1997; Wintre, Hicks, McVey, & Fox, 1988). In general, when the adolescent's problem centers on a relationship with a friend, he or she chooses to turn to a peer, a preference that becomes stronger with age. But adolescents' willingness to turn to an adult for advice with problems—especially problems that involve adolescents and their parents—remains very strong and increases as individuals move toward late adolescence. This suggests that older adolescents are quite willing to turn to adult experts whose advice they consider valuable.

Considered together, these findings are consistent with some of the findings regarding changes in adolescents' decision-making abilities. With age, adolescents become increasingly likely to turn to experts for advice. On social matters, the experts are friends; on issues requiring specific objective information, teachers and other adults likely to have the necessary knowledge are the authorities; and, on questions of values, ethics, and plans, parents remain the advisors of choice. More important, the results of these studies

indicate that peer pressure—or, for that matter, parental pressure—is likely to be ineffective in some situations and powerful in others. In short, adolescents turn for advice to different people in different situations (Finken & Jacobs, 1996).

It is clear, nevertheless, that youngsters' views of adult authority change over the course of adolescence. Preadolescents, for example, are more likely to believe that parents and teachers have authority over a wide range of decisions, that the rules made by adults are important and legitimate, and that breaking these rules—even in the interest of preserving a relationship with a friend—is wrong. As most parents and teachers can attest, however, over time adolescents become more questioning of adult authority, more likely to see some issues as personal (and out of the jurisdiction of adults), and more likely to allow their friendships with peers to be important determinants of their decision making (Smetana & Bitz, 1996; Tisak, Tisak, & Rogers, 1994).

Studies that contrast the influence of peers and adults do not really reveal all there is to know about peer pressure, however, because most peer pressure operates when adults are absent from the scene—when adolescents are at a party, on the way home from school, or on a date. In order to get closer to this issue, researchers have studied how adolescents respond when placed between the pressure of their friends and their *own* opinions of what to do. For example, an adolescent boy might be asked whether he would go along with his friends' pressure to vandalize some property, even though he does not want to do so (Berndt, 1979).

In general, most studies using this approach show that conformity to peers is higher during early and middle adolescence than during preadolescence and later adolescence (Berndt, 1979; Brown, 1990; Krosnick & Judd, 1982; Steinberg & Silverberg, 1986). This is especially true when the behavior in question is antisocial—such as cheating, stealing, or trespassing—and it is especially true for boys. These findings are in line with studies of delinquent acts, which are often committed by boys in groups and is more common during middle adolescence (Berndt, 1979). Susceptibility to antisocial peer pressure is also higher among relatively more acculturated Hispanic adolescents than their less acculturated peers, consistent with research showing higher rates of delinquency among more acculturated adolescents (Wall, Power, & Arbiona, 1993). Several studies indicate that, compared with their more autonomous friends, adolescents who are more susceptible to peer pressure to engage in delinquent activity actually are more likely to misbehave (Brown, Clasen, & Eicher, 1986).

Although conformity to peer pressure is greater during early adolescence than before or after, it is not exactly clear just why this is so. One interpretation is that adolescents are more susceptible to peer influence during this time because of their heightened orientation toward the peer group. Because they care more about what their friends think of them, they are more likely to go along with the crowd to avoid being rejected (Brown et al., 1986). It is possible that this heightened conformity to peer pressure during early adolescence is a sign of a sort of emotional "way station" between becoming emotionally autonomous from parents and becoming a genuinely autonomous person (Steinberg & Silverberg, 1986). In other words, the adolescent may become emotionally autonomous from parents before he or she is emotionally ready for this degree of independence and may turn to peers to fill this void. Each of these accounts suggests that susceptibility to peer pressure increases as youngsters move into early adolescence, peaks at around age 14, and declines thereafter (Brown et al., 1986; Steinberg & Silverberg, 1986).

A different version of the same story focuses on changes in the sheer *strength* of peer pressure. It may be, for instance, that individuals' susceptibility to peer pressure remains constant over adolescence but that the peer pressure itself strengthens and then weakens over the period. Early adolescent peer groups may exert more pressure on their members to conform than do groups of younger or older individuals, and the pressure may be strong enough to make even the most autonomous teenagers comply. Although this is an attractive alternative explanation—particularly to adolescents who appeal to their parents by saying, "No one will talk to me if I don't do it!"—studies have not borne it out. In fact, it appears that peer pressure to misbehave increases steadily throughout adolescence, beyond the age at which it would be expected to diminish (Brown et al., 1986).

When we put together the research about peer pressure, peer conformity, and parental conformity, the following picture emerges. During childhood, boys and girls are highly oriented toward their parents and far less oriented toward their peers; peer pressure is not especially strong. As they approach adolescence, children become somewhat less oriented

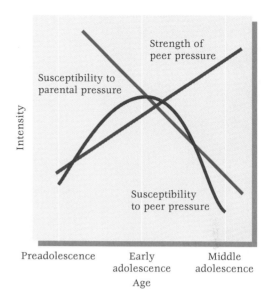

Figure 9.4   *During adolescence, susceptibility to peer pressure increases and then falls, while susceptibility to parental pressure decreases. Perceptions of the strength of peer pressure increase throughout the period.*

toward their parents and more oriented toward their peers, and peer pressure begins to escalate. As a result, during preadolescence, there is little net gain in behavioral autonomy—overall levels of conformity do not change, but the source of influence shifts. During early adolescence, conformity to parents continues to decline, and both conformity to peers and peer pressure continue to rise—again, there is little change in overall behavioral autonomy. It is not until middle and late adolescence, therefore, that genuine increases in behavioral autonomy occur, for it is during this time period (between the ninth and twelfth grades) that conformity both to parents and to peers declines, even though peer pressure continues to increase (see figure 9.4).

Within a group of teenagers of the same age, of course, there are some who are highly autonomous, others who are easily influenced by their peers, others who are oriented toward their parents, and still others who are swayed by both peers and parents, depending on the situation. In general, autonomous youngsters and adult-oriented youngsters are likely to have come from homes in which their parents were warm and moderately controlling—the typical authoritative household. Peer-oriented children, especially when in antisocial situations, are likely to have parents who were less nurturant and either extremely controlling or extremely permissive. Like

The Scientific Study of Adolescence

Parent-Child Relations and Adolescents' Peer Orientation

Most social scientists interested in adolescent development study young people in one setting at a time. Researchers look at family relations or at peer relations, at school or at work, at home or in the community. Increasingly, however, researchers have begun to acknowledge the linkages among the contexts of adolescence, and they are beginning to ask questions about the nature of these connections. Instead of asking how adolescents are affected in the home environment, for example, studies might ask how events in the home environment affect events in the peer group.

This change in orientation reflects, in part, the increased importance of a perspective called the **ecology of human development.** From this perspective, one focuses not only on the developing individual but also on the interrelations between the individual and his or her contexts and on the interconnections among the contexts themselves. The most important proponent of this view has been psychologist Urie Bronfenbrenner (1979, 1989). According to Bronfenbrenner, the ecol-

ogy of adolescent development can be thought of as having four distinct levels: each of the immediate settings in which adolescents live (e.g., the family, the school), which he calls **micro-systems;** the system of relations between these immediate settings (e.g., the family–peer group link, the home-school link), which he calls the **meso-system;** the settings that do not contain the adolescent but that affect him or her indirectly (e.g., the parent's workplace), which he calls the **exo-system;** and the broader context of culture and historical time (e.g., the country and era in which an adolescent lives), which he calls the **macro-system.** Most research on adolescent development has focused on either one or more micro-systems or the macro-system, and far less attention has been paid to the meso-system and to the exo-system.

Several illustrations of a study of adolescent development at the level of the meso-system are found in the literature on adolescent peer orientation (e.g., Mounts & Steinberg, 1995). In one such study, psychologists Andrew Fuligni and Jacquelynne Eccles (1993)

emotional autonomy, then, behavioral autonomy appears to be associated with authoritative, rather than with permissive, autocratic, or neglectful, parenting (Devereux, 1970) (see accompanying box).

One study indicates that the situation may be somewhat more complicated than this, however. It turns out that the impact of having authoritative parents on adolescents' susceptibility to peer pressure depends on the nature of the peer pressure in question. Adolescents from authoritative homes are less susceptible to antisocial peer pressure, but they may be more susceptible to the influence of positive peers. Adolescents from authoritative homes are, for example, less likely than other teenagers to be influenced by having drug-using friends, but they are *more* likely than their peers to be influenced by having friends who perform well in school (Mounts & Steinberg, 1995). Adolescents from single-parent families, as well as those with less sup-

portive or involved parents, appear relatively more susceptible to antisocial peer pressure (Farrell & White, 1998; Wong, Crosnoe, Laird, & Dornbusch, in press).

Although it is tempting to conclude from these studies that authoritative parenting fosters the development of responsible autonomy, we must be careful about drawing this conclusion, since the direction of effects could work just as plausibly the other way around. Perhaps responsible, independent children elicit warm and democratic behavior from their parents, whereas less autonomous youngsters invoke harsher discipline or parental nonchalance. In all likelihood, both processes are at work—children are affected by their parents, and parents are affected by their children. Authoritative parenting probably leads to adolescent autonomy, which in turn leads to more authoritative parenting.

Interestingly, the development of behavioral autonomy varies across cultures because of differences in the

examined whether the ways in which adolescents are treated by their parents affect the ways in which they behave with their friends—a meso-system question, in Bronfenbrenner's model, because it focuses on the link between two settings (the home and the peer group). The researchers hypothesized that authoritatively reared adolescents should be less peer oriented than other young people, because adolescents in authoritative homes have more opportunities to practice independent decision making. This practice, the researchers reasoned, should translate into greater independence outside the home environment.

Fuligni and Eccles administered a series of questionnaires to young adolescents over a one-year period. The questionnaires measured such family variables as parental strictness and decision-making opportunity and such peer-group variables as peer advice seeking and peer orientation. The researchers found that the adolescents who were the most strongly peer oriented—both in terms of healthy advice seeking and in terms of less healthy, excessive peer orientation—were more likely to come from families in which they were granted few opportunities for decision making and in which parents

were especially strict. Moreover, the adolescents whose parents became even more authoritarian (i.e., stricter and less likely to permit the adolescent to make decisions) over the one-year period were the most peer oriented of all (see the accompanying figure).

Although many parents clamp down on their teenagers' independence out of fear that not doing so will allow them to fall under the "evil" influence of the peer group, this strategy often

backfires. Evidently, having one's parents limit one's autonomy at just the time when more independence is desired and expected makes adolescents turn away from the family and toward their friends.

Source: Fuligni, A., & Eccles, J. (1993). Perceived parent-child relationships and early adolescents' orientation toward peers. *Developmental Psychology, 29,* 622–632.

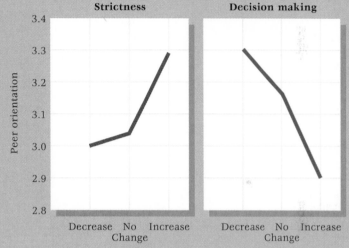

▲ *Effects of changes in parental strictness and family decision making on adolescents' orientation toward their peers.* (Fuligni & Eccles, 1993)

age expectations that adolescents and parents have for independent behavior. Psychologist Shirley Feldman and her colleagues have examined this issue by asking parents and adolescents from both Asian and Anglo cultural groups to fill out a "teen timetable"—a questionnaire that asks at what age one would expect an adolescent to be permitted to engage in various behaviors that signal autonomy (e. g., "spend money however you want," "go out on dates," "go to rock concerts with friends") (Feldman & Wood, 1994). In general, she has found that Anglo adolescents and their parents living in the United States, Australia, or Hong Kong have earlier expectations for adolescent autonomy than do Asian adolescents and parents from these same countries (Feldman & Quatman, 1988; Rosenthal & Feldman, 1991). Because of this, adolescents from Asian families may be less likely to seek autonomy from their parents than are their Anglo counterparts. Perhaps because of this, whereas individuation

tends to be associated with higher self-esteem among American youth, it is associated with lower self-esteem among Asian adolescents (Chun & MacDermid, 1997). In general, though, adolescents' mental health is best when their desires for autonomy match their expectations for what their parents would grant (Juang, Lerner, McKinney, & von Eye, 1999).

Surprisingly, in these studies, there were neither sex nor birth-order differences in age expectations for autonomy—contrary to the popular beliefs that boys expect more autonomy than girls and that later-born adolescents are granted earlier freedom because their older siblings have paved the way. There are sex differences in the extent to which parents *grant* autonomy, however, with parents more controlling of early adolescent daughters than sons. These sex differences appear to be most pronounced within African American households, where, compared with other ethnic groups, boys

▲ *Conformity to peers—especially in situations involving antisocial or delinquent behavior—is higher during early and middle adolescence than during other points in the life span. According to some theorists, some forms of delinquency may result from youngsters' heightened susceptibility to the influence of their friends.* (Joel Gordon)

are given relatively more freedom but girls are given less (Bulcroft, Carmody, & Bulcroft, 1996).

Interestingly, the autonomy-granting timetable of families who have emigrated from a culture that is relatively slower to grant adolescents autonomy to a culture where autonomy is granted sooner falls somewhere between the two extremes; this has been found in studies both of Chinese immigrants in the United States and Australia (Rosenthal & Feldman, 1990) and of East German immigrants in the former West Germany (Silbereisen & Schmitt-Rodermund, 1994). It is also the case that adolescents who feel older seek more independence than their same-aged peers who feel younger (Galambos, Kolaric, & Maggs, 1994).

Changes in Feelings of Self-reliance

A third approach to the study of behavioral autonomy focuses on adolescents' own judgments of how au-

tonomous they are. When adolescents of various ages are asked to complete standardized tests of self-reliance, for example, the results show that subjective feelings of autonomy increase steadily over the adolescent years and, contrary to stereotypes, that adolescent girls report feeling more self-reliant than adolescent boys do (Greenberger, 1982; Steinberg & Silverberg, 1986). This is especially interesting in light of the findings concerning susceptibility to peer pressure, since it indicates that adolescents may describe themselves as gaining in self-reliance during a period when their susceptibility to peer pressure may be increasing (see figure 9.5). Although adults may view adolescents' giving in to peer pressure as a sign of diminished autonomy, adolescents may not see their own behavior in this light. Not surprisingly, adolescents who have a stronger sense of self-reliance report higher self-esteem and fewer behavior problems (Owens, Mortimer, & Finch, 1996; Wolfe & Truxillo, 1996).

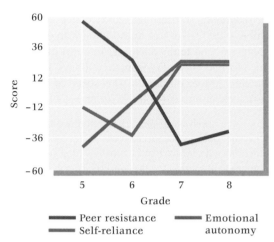

Figure 9.5   *Age differences in three types of autonomy.*
(Steinberg & Silverberg, 1986)

RECAP

Although adolescence is, in general, a time of advances in decision-making abilities, there is a temporary period, during early adolescence, when individuals are particularly susceptible to peer pressure, especially on issues concerning day-to-day activities. Susceptibility to peer pressure increases between childhood and early adolescence, and then it decreases over the high school years. Generally speaking, adolescents whose parents are extremely authoritarian or extremely permissive are the most easily influenced by their friends, especially in antisocial situations.

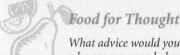

Food for Thought

What advice would you give to parents who are concerned about adolescent peer pressure?

THE DEVELOPMENT OF VALUE AUTONOMY

The development of value autonomy entails changes in the adolescent's conceptions of moral, political, ideological, and religious issues. Three aspects of the development of value autonomy during adolescence are especially interesting. First, adolescents become increasingly *abstract* in the way they think about these sorts of issues. Consider the example of an 18-year-old who is deciding whether to participate in a disruptive demonstration at his state capital against policies that he believes indirectly support the interests of environmental polluters. Instead of looking at the situation only in terms of the specifics of discrimination, he might think about the implications of knowingly violating the law in general. Second, during adolescence, beliefs become increasingly *rooted in general principles* that have an ideological basis. Thus, an 18-year-old might say that demonstrating against discrimination is acceptable because protecting the environment is more important than living in accord with the law, so breaking a law is legitimate when the status quo leads to environmental degradation. Finally, beliefs become increasingly *founded in the young person's own values* and not merely in a system of values passed on by parents or other authority figures. Thus, an 18-year-old may look at the issue of environmental protection in terms of what he himself believes, rather than in terms of what his parents have told him to do.

Much of the growth in value autonomy can be traced to the cognitive changes characteristic of the period. With the adolescent's enhanced reasoning capabilities and the further development of hypothetical thinking come a heightened interest in ideological and philosophical matters and a more sophisticated way of looking at them. The ability to consider alternative possibilities and to engage in thinking about thinking allows for the exploration of various value systems, political ideologies, personal ethics, and religious beliefs.

However, the growth of value autonomy is encouraged by the development of emotional and behavioral independence as well. There is some evidence that the development of value autonomy occurs later (between ages 18 and 20) than does the development of emotional or behavioral autonomy, which takes place during early and middle adolescence. As young people gain increasing distance from the emotional dependencies of childhood, they rely less on their parents' beliefs and values. The establishment of emotional autonomy provides adolescents with the ability to look at their parents' views more objectively. When young people no longer see their parents as omnipotent and infallible authorities, they may seriously reevaluate the ideas and values that they accepted without question as children. Not surprisingly, individuals with a stronger sense of value autonomy show more maturity in other psychological domains as well, such as in the realms of identity development and self-awareness (Hart & Chmeil, 1992; Hart & Fegley, 1995).

As adolescents begin to test the waters of independence behaviorally, they may experience a variety of cognitive conflicts caused by having to compare the advice of parents and friends and having to deal with competing pressures to behave in given ways. These conflicts may prompt the young person to consider, in more serious and thoughtful terms, what it is that he or she really believes. This struggle to clarify values, provoked in part by the exercise of behavioral autonomy, is a large part of the process of developing a sense of value autonomy. The development of value autonomy has been studied with regard to adolescents' beliefs about morality, politics, and religion.

Moral Development During Adolescence

Moral development has been the most widely studied aspect of value autonomy during adolescence. The study of moral development involves both moral reasoning (how individuals think about moral dilemmas) and moral behavior (how they behave in situations that call for moral judgments). Related to this is the study of prosocial behavior, the behaviors in which individuals engage to help others.

● **Moral Reasoning** The dominant theoretical viewpoint for some time now in the study of moral reasoning has been a perspective that is grounded in Piaget's theory of cognitive development. As you will recall from the discussion in chapter 2 of changes in thinking processes during adolescence, the emphasis within the Piagetian view, or the cognitive-developmental perspective, is on changes in the structure and organization of thought, rather than on changes in its content. Theories of morality that stem from the cognitive-developmental viewpoint similarly emphasize shifts in the type of reasoning that individuals use in making moral decisions, rather than changes in the content of the decisions they reach or the actions they take as a result. Although the initial formulation of the cognitive-developmental perspective on morality was presented by Piaget himself, the theory was subsequently expanded by Lawrence Kohlberg, and it is Kohlberg's work that is more relevant to the study of moral development during adolescence (Eisenberg & Fabes, 1998; Turiel, 1998).

Researchers assess individuals' levels of moral reasoning by examining their responses to a series of hypothetical moral dilemmas about difficult, real-world situations. These dilemmas are presented either in an interview—in which case, the adolescents' responses are recorded, transcribed, and coded (Colby & Kohlberg, 1987)—or in a questionnaire, in which adolescents respond to the dilemmas in a sort of multiple-choice format (Rest, Davison, & Robbins, 1978). The following are examples of the sorts of dilemmas researchers have used (Colby & Kohlberg, 1987).

Judy was a twelve-year-old girl. Her mother promised her that she could go to a special rock concert coming to their town if she saved up from baby-sitting and lunch money to buy a ticket to the concert. She managed to save up the fifteen dollars the ticket cost plus another five dollars. But then her mother changed her mind and told Judy that she had to spend the money on new clothes for school. Judy was disappointed and decided to go to the concert anyway. She bought a ticket and told her mother that she had only been able to save five dollars. That Saturday she went to the performance and told her mother she was spending the day with a friend. A week passed without her mother finding out. Judy then told her older sister, Louise, that she had gone to the performance and had lied to her mother about it. Louise wonders whether to tell their mother what Judy did.

Should Louise, the older sister, tell their mother that Judy lied about the money or should she keep quiet?

Two young men, brothers, had got into serious trouble. They were secretly leaving town in a hurry and needed money. Karl, the older one, broke into a store and stole a thousand dollars. Bob, the younger one, went to a retired old man who was known to help people in town. He told the man that he was very sick and that he needed a thousand dollars to pay for an operation. Bob asked the old man to lend him the money and promised that he would pay him back when he recovered. Really Bob wasn't sick at all, and he had no intention of paying the man back. Although the old man didn't know Bob very well, he lent him the money. So Bob and Karl skipped town, each with a thousand dollars.

Which is worse, stealing like Karl or cheating like Bob?

Perhaps Kohlberg's most well-known dilemma involved a man who had to choose between stealing a drug to save his wife or letting his wife remain ill:

In Europe, a woman was near death from a very bad disease, a special kind of cancer. There was one drug that the doctors thought might save her. It was a form of radium that a druggist in the same town had recently discovered. The drug was expensive to make, but the druggist was charging ten times what the drug cost him to make. He paid $200 for the radium and charged $2,000 for a small dose of the drug. The sick woman's husband, Heinz, went to everyone he knew to borrow the money, but he could only get together about $1,000, which was half of what it cost. He told the druggist that his wife was dying, and asked him to sell it cheaper or let him pay later. But the druggist said, "No, I discovered the drug and I'm going to make money from it." Heinz got desperate and broke into the man's store to steal the drug for his wife. Should the husband have done that? Was it right or wrong?

▲ *The ways in which individuals think about moral dilemmas change during adolescence.* (Tom McCarthy/Unicorn Stock Photos)

According to Kohlberg, whether or not you think that Heinz should have stolen the drug, or that Louise should tell her mother, or that cheating someone is worse than stealing from a store is less important than the reasoning behind your answers. Kohlberg theorized that individuals' reasoning about moral issues becomes more sophisticated with development. Specifically, Kohlberg suggested that there are three levels of moral reasoning: **preconventional moral reasoning,** which is dominant during most of childhood; **conventional moral reasoning,** which is usually dominant during late childhood and early adolescence; and **postconventional moral reasoning** (sometimes called principled moral reasoning), which emerges sometime during the adolescent or young adult years.

Preconventional reasoning is characterized by reference to external and physical events. Preconventional moral decisions are not based on society's standards, rules, or conventions (hence the label *pre*conventional). Children at this stage approach moral dilemmas in ways that focus on the rewards and punishments associated with various courses of action. One preconventional child might say that Heinz should not have stolen the drug because he could have gotten caught and sent to jail. Another might say that Heinz was right to steal the drug because people would have been angry with him if he had let his wife die. In either case, the chief concern to the preconventional thinker is what would happen to Heinz as a result of his choice.

Conventional reasoning about moral issues focuses not so much on tangible rewards and punishments but on how an individual will be judged by others for behaving in a certain way. In conventional moral reasoning, special importance is given to the roles people are expected to play and to society's rules, social institutions, and conventions. One behaves properly because, in so doing, one receives the approval of others and helps maintain the social order. The correctness of society's rules is not questioned, however—one does one's duty by upholding and respecting the social order. A conventional thinker might say that Heinz should not have stolen the drug because stealing is against the law. But another might counter that Heinz was right to steal the drug because it is what a good husband is expected to do. According to most studies of moral reasoning, most adolescents and adults think primarily in conventional terms—they evaluate moral decisions in terms of a set of rules that people are supposed to abide by.

Postconventional reasoning is relatively rare. At this level of reasoning, society's rules and conventions are seen as relative and subjective, rather than as absolute and definitive. One may have a moral duty to abide by society's standards for behavior—but only insofar as those standards support and serve moral ends. Thus, occasions arise in which conventions ought to be questioned and when more important principles—such as justice, fairness, and the sanctity of human life—take precedence over established social norms. For instance, a postconventional response might be that Heinz should not have stolen the drug because, in doing so, he violated an implicit

Do Men and Women Speak About Moral Problems "In a Different Voice"? Probably Not, After All

Few theories have generated as much controversy among psychologists as Lawrence Kohlberg's theory of the development of moral reasoning. In particular, critics have argued that his view of what constitutes "more advanced" moral reasoning is based on Western conceptions of morality and is oriented to how men typically view moral problems (Turiel, 1997).

Feminist scholars, in particular, have argued that Kohlberg's model underrepresents an equally valid approach to morality that women happen to use more often. The most compelling argument in this spirit was made by psychologist Carol Gilligan in her widely cited book *In a Different Voice* (1982). Gilligan's perspective on female adolescent development and, in particular, her argument that the reasoning, moral orientation, and concerns of adolescent girls are dramatically different from those of boys has spawned a tremendous outpouring of work—some might say, an industry—on the special psychological vulnerability of adolescent girls. Although Gilligan's work has been popular with the general public, the scientific community has been less enamored with it (e.g., Sommers, 2000). Indeed, it is fair to say that Gilligan's work has provoked even more controversy than Kohlberg's.

Gilligan argues that Kohlberg's scheme places too much emphasis on what she calls a **justice orientation** to moral problems. The justice orientation holds out as its ideal a morality of reciprocity and equal respect. From this perspective—or "voice," as Gilligan calls it—the most important consideration in resolving a moral dilemma is whether the individuals involved are treated fairly by the ultimate decision.

An equally valid alternative to the justice orientation, says Gilligan, is a **care orientation.** From this perspective, the ideal is a morality of attention to others and responsiveness to human need. As opposed to the justice orientation, which is rooted in the premise that moral decisions are best made from a detached position of objectivity ("rules are rules," "fair is fair"), the care orientation is rooted in the belief that our moral decisions should be shaped by our attachments and our responsiveness to others.

An example may help to clarify the distinction. In responding to the Heinz dilemma, discussed on pages 306–308, individuals with a justice orientation cast the problem as a conflict between Heinz's desire to save his wife and the druggist's right to engage in his business—a conflict between the abstract values of life and property. Individuals with a care orientation, in contrast, see the dilemma in entirely different terms: as a dilemma of responsiveness. The question is not whether the druggist has a right to personal property that outweighs other rights but, rather, why the druggist is not being responsive to the needs of another person. Rather than seeing society as functioning with a system of rules or abstract principles, individuals with a care orientation view society as functioning through the interconnection of human relationships.

Theories of morality and of human development in general, argues Gilligan, have emphasized the sort of intellectual, individualistic, and detached reasoning characteristic of the justice orientation as the index of mental health and have

agreement among members of society—an agreement that gives each person the freedom to pursue his or her livelihood. However, another principled thinker might respond that Heinz was right to steal the drug because someone's life was at stake and because preserving human life is more important than preserving individual freedoms. Whereas conventional thinking is oriented toward society's rules,

given short shrift to emotional and interpersonal concerns. Gilligan criticizes most theories of psychological adjustment for holding up as the pinnacle of psychological health the individual who can function independently, rather than the person who can function *interdependently*. This is seen not only in models of development but also in the way in which children are socialized to emphasize competition over cooperation ("Winning isn't everything, it's the only thing") and in assertiveness over concern for others ("Nice guys finish last"). In Kohlberg's theory, this bias toward detached individualism is reflected in the elevation to the highest level of morality of a view that places abstract principles of individual rights over all other considerations. In her book, Gilligan presents evidence that women are likely to approach moral problems from a care orientation, rather than from the justice orientation idealized in Kohlberg's theory.

Gilligan's perspective has been widly popular, yet, despite the appeal of her view, there is virtually no empirical evidence to support Gilligan's contention that there are substantial sex differences in the ways adolescents approach moral problems (Sommers, 2000; Turiel, 1997). Many studies have found that men and women approach moral problems from the perspectives of justice and caring, depending on the problem, and explicit examinations of sex differences in how individuals respond to moral dilemmas generally do not find that males and females differ (Turiel, 1997; Walker, deVries, & Trevethan, 1987).

How could Gilligan's conclusions be so different from those obtained in subsequent work? One reason is that Gilligan did not study males in the research that led to *In a Different Voice*. As a consequence, it is not clear whether the observations she drew from this work

reflected the particular moral development of women, as she contended, or the moral development of the subjects in her study who responded to the hypothetical dilemmas she happened to use. That is, it is not known how men would have responded had they been included in Gilligan's research and presented with the same dilemmas.

A more recent study by Susan Harter and her colleagues (Harter et al., 1998) helps clarify matters a bit. One of Gilligan's contentions has been that, at adolescence, many girls feel a "loss of voice"—a suppression of their thoughts and opinions. "Gilligan argued," Harter explains, "that teenage girls quickly perceive that the desirable stereotype is being nice, polite, pleasing to others, unassertive, and quiet" (Harter et al., 1998, p. 892). This assertion formed the basis for the best-selling book *Reviving Ophelia* (Pipher, 1994), which argues that the loss of voice at early adolescence leads many teenage girls to be confused and troubled.

In Harter's studies of "level of voice" among male and female adolescents, she did not find the sex differences hypothesized by Gilligan, nor did she find that the females' voice declined over the course of adolescence. Harter did find, however, that the adolescents' gender-role orientation and the social support they received from others were predictive of loss of voice. The girls with a highly feminine gender role orientation and both boys and girls who felt that significant others in their lives did not take their opinions seriously suffered the loss of voice Gilligan had described. But the androgynous girls, and the adolescents who felt that others supported their having strong opinions, suffered no such loss. If Harter had included just girls in her study and had not examined variables other than gender, she might have drawn the same questionable conclusions that Gilligan drew.

Critics of Gilligan's work have also challenged many of her other assertions, including the widely believed (but empirically unsupported) contentions that girls are more confused and more troubled than boys, that girls have more difficulty finding their voice, and that girls are more likely to be short-changed by schools and other institutions. Indeed, some critics (e.g., Sommers, 2000) have argued that, in many respects (school problems, academic failure, trouble with the law, drug and alcohol abuse), adolescent boys are doing far worse than adolescent girls.

Although many of Gilligan's propositions have not received empirical support, her work has been an important stimulus in discussions about how we should judge moral development. Even if there are not sex differences in moral reasoning, Gilligan's work suggests that there are two distinct voices to be heard in moral debates. By helping children hear and speak with both voices, we may encourage the development of more complete—and more moral—people. Indeed, some writers (e.g., Keller, Edelstein, Schmid, Fang, & Fang, 1998; Miller & Bersoff, 1995) have suggested that the "tension" believed to exist between the two voices—the abstract and impersonal voice (i.e., the justice orientation) versus the personal and interpersonal voice (i.e., the care orientation)—is a tension that is particular to Western societies. In other cultures, behaving morally within relationships is seen not as a matter of interpersonal obligation but as a part of one's more general duty as a member of society (Turiel, 1997).

Nevertheless, it is interesting to ponder why Gilligan's theory has generated so much popular enthusiasm, despite its lack of acceptance among social scientists. Sometimes, it seems, what we want to think is true is more powerful than what the data really reveal.

postconventional thinking is founded on more broadly based, abstract principles. For this reason, it is the development of postconventional reasoning that is especially relevant to the discussion of value autonomy.

Kohlberg's theory and its derivatives (for example, Gilligan [1982]) have generated a wealth of research and have dominated the study of moral development during adolescence, although the theory has been criticized for emphasizing a type of morality that tends to be favored by Western cultures and by males. An important alternative to Kohlberg's model was proposed in the late 1970s by psychologist Carol Gilligan (1982), who argued that Kohlberg's view of morality places too much emphasis on a type of moral orientation characteristically used by men. (Gilligan's perspective is discussed in the accompanying box.) Although many recent studies have questioned the validity of Gilligan's assertions about gender differences in moral reasoning (Turiel, 1997), her point of view remains extraordinarily influential.

Studies have confirmed Kohlberg's suggestion that moral reasoning becomes more principled over the course of childhood and adolescence (Turiel, 1997). Moreover, development appears to proceed through the sequence described in Kohlberg's theory (Colby, Kohlberg, Gibbs, & Lieberman, 1983). Preconventional reasoning dominates the responses of children; conventional responses begin to appear during preadolescence and continue into middle adolescence; and postconventional reasoning does not appear until late adolescence.

As is the case with formal operational thought, the most advanced stage of reasoning described by Piaget (see chapter 2), not all individuals develop the capacity to engage in postconventional moral reasoning. Advanced levels of moral reasoning are more common among children raised in authoritative families in which parents encourage their child to participate in family discussions, in which the level of conflict in family discussions is neither extremely low nor extremely high, and in which parents expose the adolescent to moral arguments that are fashioned at a higher stage than his or her own (Boyes & Allen, 1993; Haan, Smith, & Block, 1968; Holstein, 1972; Speicher, 1994; Walker & Taylor, 1991b). According to Kohlberg's theory, development into higher stages of moral reasoning occurs when the adolescent is developmentally ready—when his or her reasoning is predominantly at one stage but partially at the next higher one—and when he or she is exposed to the more advanced type of reasoning by other people, such as parents (Walker & Taylor, 1991a).

Although not all individuals enter a stage of postconventional reasoning during adolescence, they do begin to place greater emphasis on abstract values and moral principles during the adolescent years (Rest et al., 1978). Moreover, if you present individuals of different ages with other people's moral arguments, older individuals are drawn to arguments that, in Kohlberg's

framework, are more advanced. Thus, the appeal of postconventional moral reasoning increases over the course of adolescence, whereas the appeals of preconventional and of conventional reasoning both decline. Interestingly, the appeal of postconventional thinking appears to increase both with age and with schooling; most adults reach a plateau in moral reasoning after completing their formal education.

● **Moral Reasoning and Moral Behavior**   It is one thing to reason about hypothetical moral problems in an advanced way, but it is another thing to *behave* consistently with one's reasoning. After all, it is common for people to say one thing (e.g., "cheating on a test is immoral") but do another (sneak a peek at a classmate's test when running out of time during an exam). Some critics have argued that, although Kohlberg's theory may provide a window on how people think about abstract and hypothetical dilemmas—or about life-and-death situations, as in the Heinz story—it does not tell us very much about the ways people reason about day-to-day problems or the ways people behave when they find themselves in situations that might evoke moral considerations.

As it turns out, research on Kohlberg's theory has answered these criticisms fairly well. As for the first of these concerns, for example, research indicates that people reason about life-and-death dilemmas in ways parallel to their reasoning about the moral dilemmas that they actually encounter in their everyday life (Walker et al., 1987). And, as for the second of these concerns, many studies indicate that individuals' behavior is indeed related to the way in which they reason about hypothetical moral dilemmas. Although individuals do not always behave in ways consistent with their moral reasoning, on average, individuals who reason at higher stages behave in more moral ways. For example, individuals who are capable of reasoning at higher stages of moral thought are less likely to commit antisocial acts, less likely to cheat, less likely to conform to the pressures of others, more likely to engage in political protests, and more likely to assist others in need of help (Rest, 1983).

● **Prosocial Moral Reasoning**   Although most research on moral reasoning has focused on what adolescents do under circumstances in which a law might be broken or a rule violated, researchers have increasingly turned their attention to the study of moral reasoning in prosocial situations. In general, the ways in which individuals think about prosocial phenomena, such as honesty and kindness, become more sophisticated during late adolescence (Eisenberg & Fabes, 1998; Killen & Turiel, 1998). In addition, studies find important differences among adolescents in their **prosocial moral reasoning,** and these differences are correlated both with actual prosocial behavior and with attitudes toward helping others (Eisenberg & Fabes, 1998). For example, studies of exemplary youth—adolescents who have volunteered considerable amounts of time in service activities—show that these adolescents score higher than their peers on measures of moral reasoning (Hart & Fegley, 1995; Yates & Youniss, 1996). Individuals who score high on measures of prosocial moral reasoning have been shown also to be more sympathetic and empathic (Eisenberg, Carlo, Murphy, & Van Court, 1995). In general, female adolescents score higher on measures of prosocial moral reasoning than do male adolescents (Carlo, Kollev, Eisenberg, Da Silva, Frohlick, 1996; Eisenberg et al., 1995).

Of course, moral behavior and moral reasoning do not *always* go hand in hand. Most of us have found ourselves in situations where we have behaved less morally than we would have liked to act. According to one writer, however, we would not expect that moral behavior would follow exactly from moral reasoning, because other factors enter into moral decision making that complicate matters (Rest, 1983). In tests measuring moral reasoning, assessments are made in a social vacuum, but such vacuums rarely exist in the real world. For example, you may realize in the abstract that complying with highway speed limits is important because such limits prevent accidents, and you may obey these limits most of the time when you drive. But you may have found yourself in a situation in which you weighed your need to get somewhere in a hurry (perhaps you were late for an important job interview) against your moral belief in the importance of obeying speeding laws, and you decided that in this instance you would behave in a way inconsistent with your belief. Situational factors influence moral choices, and they influence moral reasoning. When individuals perceive that they will be severely hurt by behaving in a morally advanced way (for example, if standing up for someone will lead to severe punishment), they are less likely to reason at a higher moral level (Sobesky, 1983). Moral reasoning is an important influence on moral behavior, but it cannot be considered out of context.

RECAP

Most of the research to date on the development of value autonomy has focused on moral development in particular. According to Lawrence Kohlberg's theory, which is the dominant perspective on the development of moral reasoning, adolescence is a time of potential shifting from a morality that defines right and wrong in terms of society's rules to one that defines right and wrong on the basis of one's own basic moral principles. This shift does not tend to occur until late in adolescence, however, suggesting that the development of value autonomy occurs later than the development of either emotional or behavioral autonomy. One important critic of Kohlberg's theory has been Carol Gilligan, who has argued that Kohlberg's theory, like most developmental theories, overemphasizes traditional conceptions of morality (which emphasize justice) and underemphasizes conceptions that are more likely to be espoused by females (which emphasize care). Although Gilligan's views about sex differences in moral development have attracted a good deal of popular attention, scientific studies have not supported many of her assertions.

Food for Thought

Should schools attempt to facilitate adolescents' moral development as a part of their curriculum? If so, what sorts of activities would be most useful?

Political Thinking During Adolescence

Less is known about the development of political thinking during adolescence than about moral development, but research on this topic is generally consistent with the view that beliefs become more principled, more abstract, and more independent during the adolescent years. This pattern is linked in part to the general cognitive development of the adolescent and in part to the growth of specific expertise as the adolescent is exposed to more political information and ideas (Torney-Purta, 1992).

Political thinking changes during adolescence in three important ways (Adelson, 1972; Torney-Purta, 1990). First, it becomes more abstract. For example, in response to the question "What is the purpose of laws?" 12- and 13-year-olds are likely to reply with concrete answers—"So people don't kill or steal," "So people don't get hurt," and so on. Older adolescents, in contrast, are likely to respond with more abstract and more

▲ *Whereas younger adolescents believe in autocratic rule and support existing laws, older adolescents are more likely to challenge authority and argue that laws should be reexamined. These Los Angeles students are protesting cuts in educational funding.* (D. Young-Wolfe/PhotoEdit)

general statements—"To ensure safety and enforce the government" and "They are basically guidelines for people. I mean, like this is wrong and this is right and to help them understand" (Adelson, 1972, p. 108). Individuals' understanding of various rights—for example, their beliefs about whether children and adolescents have the right to have some control over their lives—becomes more abstract with age as well (Ruck, Abramovitch, & Keating, 1998). Additionally, with age, individuals are more likely to judge the appropriateness of having certain rights (e.g., freedom of speech) in light of characteristics of the individual (e.g., whether the individual is mature enough to act responsibly) and the context within which the right is expressed (e.g., whether the authority who is regulating one's speech is a parent or a government official) (Helwig, 1997).

Second, political thinking during adolescence becomes less authoritarian and less rigid (Flanagan & Galay, 1995). Young adolescents are inclined toward obedience, authority, and an uncritical, trusting, and acquiescent stance toward government. For example, when asked what might be done in response to a law that is not working out as planned, the young adolescent will "propose that it be enforced more rigorously." An older teenager may suggest, instead, that the law needs reexamination and perhaps amendment. In contrast to older adoles-

cents, younger adolescents are "more likely to favor one-man rule as [opposed to] representative democracy; . . . [show] little sensitivity to individual or minority rights; [and are] indifferent to the claims of personal freedom" (Adelson, 1972, p. 108).

Of special significance is the development during late adolescence of a roughly coherent and consistent set of attitudes—a sort of ideology—that does not appear before this point. This ideology is "more or less organized in reference to a more encompassing . . . set of political principles" (Adelson, 1972, p. 121). These principles may concern a wide range of issues, including civil liberties, freedom of speech, and social equality (Flanagan & Galay, 1995; Helwig, 1995). As is the case among adults, adolescents' views about political matters—views about such things as the reasons for unemployment, poverty, or homelessness, for example—are strongly linked to their social upbringing. Adolescents from higher social classes tend to attribute unemployment, poverty, and homelessness to societal factors ("people are unemployed because companies are moving a lot of jobs to Mexico"), whereas adolescents from lower-class backgrounds are more likely to attribute these problems to individual factors ("people are poor because they have problems managing money") (Flanagan & Tucker, 1999).

Shifts in all three of these directions—increasing abstraction, decreasing authoritarianism, and increasing the use of principles—are similar to the shifts observed in studies of moral development, and they support the idea that value autonomy begins to emerge during the late adolescent years. The movement away from authoritarianism, obedience, and unquestioning acceptance of the rulings of authority is especially interesting because it suggests, further, that an important psychological concern for adolescents revolves around questioning the values and beliefs emanating from parents and other authority figures and trying to establish one's own priorities.

As is the case with moral development, there may be gaps between adolescents' political thinking in hypothetical situations and their political attitudes and behavior. In general, the most important influences on the political behavior of young people tends to be the social context in which they come of age (Torney-Purta, 1990). This context includes the adolescent's immediate community as well as the larger social and historical environment. Thus, for example, minority adolescents, especially those living in environments in which there are limited economic opportunities, tend to be more cynical about politics than their white counterparts. Similarly, a study of German youth indicates that adolescents are more likely to develop right-wing (excessively authoritarian) attitudes when they are raised by authoritarian parents within a broader context that promotes antiforeigner and antidemocratic attitudes (Noack, Kracke, & Hofer, 1994).

Finally, studies of adolescents' political attitudes over historical periods show quite clearly that young people's political attitudes and levels of political participation (voting, demonstrating, letter writing, etc.)—like those of adults—fluctuate and change in relation to current events (Torney-Purta, 1990). Although we stereotypically think of late adolescence as a time of intense political activism, perhaps because of the high level of American student activism in the 1960s, this image hardly characterizes contemporary youth. Recent surveys indicate a significantly lower interest among American youth in political matters than was the case in previous eras. For example, the percentage of college freshmen who believe that it is important to keep up with political affairs declined by the end of the twentieth century to about 25 percent, down from nearly 60 percent in the mid-1960s. Similarly, whereas only 14 percent of contemporary freshmen say they frequently discuss politics, the figure was twice this in the late 1960s. Parallel declines are seen in adolescents' interest in civic affairs, suggesting that contemporary college students are among the most politically apathetic students seen in the United States in the past 15 years. Fewer than 60 percent are committed to "helping others who are in difficulty." Only around a third of freshmen feel it is very important or essential for them to "influence social values," aspire to be a community leader, or feel a strong commitment to promote racial understanding. Fewer than one-fifth are committed to helping clean up the environment. In general, college students have become increasingly politically conservative over the past several decades, with relatively more students, for example, in favor of capital punishment, opposed to casual sex, and against keeping abortion legal (UCLA Higher Education Research Institute, 1999, 2000).

Religious Beliefs During Adolescence

Religious beliefs, like moral and political beliefs, also become more abstract, more principled, and more independent during the adolescent years. Specifically, adolescents' beliefs become more oriented toward spiritual and ideological matters and less oriented toward rituals, practices, and the strict observance of religious customs. For example, although 87 percent of all adolescents pray, and 95 percent believe in God, 60 percent of all young people feel that organized religion does not play a very important role in their lives (Farel, 1982; Gallup & Bezilla, 1992). Compared with children, adolescents place more emphasis on the internal aspects of religious commitment (such as what an individual believes) and less on the external manifestations (such as whether an individual goes to church) (Elkind, 1978).

Generally speaking, the stated importance of religion—and especially of participation in an organized religion—declines somewhat during the adolescent years. More high school students than older adolescents attend church regularly, and, not surprisingly, more of younger adolescents state that religion is important to them (Benson, Donahue, & Erickson, 1989; Johnston, O'Malley, & Bachman, 1986). In addition, church attendance and religious observation are more common among rural youth and, especially, among rural youth from farm families (King, Elder, & Whitbeck, 1997). Interestingly, several studies have indicated that the decline in the importance of religion during late adolescence appears to be more noteworthy among college than noncollege youth (Yankelovich, 1974), suggesting that college attendance plays a part in shaping (or, as the case may be, in *un*shaping) young people's religious beliefs. As we saw in chapter 8, studies of identity development during the college years have indicated that, over the course of college, students' traditional religious commitments are shaken but are not replaced with alternative beliefs (Waterman, 1982). Late adolescence appears to be a time when individuals reexamine and reevaluate many of the beliefs and values they grew up with.

Although some parents may interpret this transformation as indicating a sort of rebellion against the family's values, the development of religious thinking during late adolescence might be better understood as part of the overall development of value autonomy. As the adolescent develops a stronger sense of independence, he or she may leave behind the unquestioning conventionality of earlier religious behavior as a first step toward finding a truly personal faith. According to one writer, an adolescent who continues to comply with his or her religious beliefs without ever questioning them may actually be showing signs of immature conformity or identity foreclosure, rather than spiritual maturity (Hill, 1986).

Although individuals generally become less involved in formal religion during the adolescent years, there are differences among adolescents in their degree of religiosity. Approximately 35 percent of high school seniors report weekly attendance at religious services; another 30 percent report that religion is "very important" to them, even though they do not worship regularly; and about 10 percent report no religious preference at all. The remaining 25 percent report having a religious preference but do not feel that religion is very important to them (Johnston et al., 1986). Some, but not all, research suggests that religious adolescents are less depressed than other adolescents, significantly less likely than their peers to engage in premarital sexual intercourse, and somewhat less likely to engage in deviant or delinquent behavior, such as drug use (Benson et al., 1989; Donahue, 1994; Litchfield, Thomas, & Li, 1997; Wright, Frost, & Wisecarver, 1993). Not only does religious participation affect other aspects of adolescent behavior, but certain behaviors themselves also affect religious participation. For example, more frequent sexual activity leads to less frequent church attendance, just as the reverse is true (Thornton & Camburn, 1989).

All in all, studies of the development of religious beliefs during adolescence indicate many parallels with the development of moral and political reasoning. According to a widely cited stage theory of religious development, during late adolescence individuals enter into a stage in which they begin to form a system of personal religious beliefs, rather than relying solely on the teachings of their parents (Fowler, 1981). This is reminiscent, of course, of the adolescent's transition to principled moral reasoning or to the development in middle to late adolescence of a coherent political ideology. In all likelihood, developments in all three domains—moral, political, and religious—probably reflect the underlying growth of cognitive abilities and the shift from concrete to abstract reasoning that characterizes the adolescent transition. As you now understand, this fundamental shift in cognitive ability affects adolescents' thinking across a wide variety of topics.

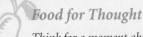

Food for Thought

Think for a moment about general trends in cognitive development, social cognitive development, moral development, and the development of political and religious beliefs. What parallels can you identify?

A CONCLUDING NOTE

Popular theories of adolescent development in Western societies have tended to emphasize the goals of self-definition (i.e., identity) and independent functioning (i.e., autonomy) (Baumeister & Tice, 1986). It is important to keep in mind, however, that healthy adolescent development involves not only the ability to be a successful individual but also the ability to maintain healthy and satisfying attachments with others. Put another way, experts think of positive psychological development in terms of the adolescent's capacity to function both independently and interdependently (Ford, 1987; Greenberger & Sorensen, 1974; Killen & Nucci, 1995; Raeff, 1997).

These dual goals—what some writers have called *agency* (acting autonomously) and *communion* (connecting with others) (e.g., Bakan, 1972)—define the psychosocial agenda during adolescence. In this chapter, about autonomy, and in chapter 8, about identity, we emphasized the development of agency. In chapters 10 and 11, covering intimacy and sexuality, we will focus on communion.

Web Researcher Children and adolescents are treated differently in the criminal justice system than adults are. What are some of the differences between the juvenile justice system and the adult criminal system in your state, and where do those differences come from? Under what conditions are youth moved from one system to the other? Given what you know about adolescent cognitive and social development, write a set of guidelines that would help law enforcement officials decide which system a particular youth would be referred to. Go to www.mhhe.com/steinberg6 for further information.

KEY TERMS

behavioral autonomy

care orientation

conventional moral reasoning

de-idealization

detachment

ecology of human development

emotional autonomy

exo-system

individuation

justice orientation

macro-system

meso-system

micro-systems

peer pressure

postconventional moral reasoning

preconventional moral reasoning

prosocial moral reasoning

value autonomy

Chapter 10

Intimacy

One of the most remarkable things about adolescence is the way in which close relationships change during these years. Think about the friendships you had as a child and compare them with those you had as a teenager. Think about the boyfriends or girlfriends that children have and the boyfriends or girlfriends of adolescents. And think about relationships between parents and their children and about how these relationships change during adolescence. In all three cases, adolescents' relationships are closer, more personal, more involved, and more emotionally charged. During adolescence, in short, relationships become more intimate.

At the outset, it is necessary to draw a distinction between *intimacy* and *sexuality*. The concept of intimacy—at least as it is used in the study of adolescence—does not have a sexual or physical connotation. Rather, an intimate relationship is an emotional attachment between two people that is characterized by concern for each other's well-being; a willingness to disclose private, and occasionally sensitive, topics; and a sharing of interests and activities. Two individuals can, therefore, have an intimate relationship without having a sexual one. And, by the same token, two people can have a sexual relationship without being especially intimate.

The development of intimacy during adolescence involves changes in the adolescent's *need* for intimacy, changes in the *capacity* to have intimate relationships, and changes in the extent to which and the way in which this capacity to be intimate is *expressed*. Although the development of intimacy during adolescence is almost always studied in relation to friendships with peers, adolescents' intimate relationships are by no means limited to other teenagers. Parents often have intimate relationships with their adolescents, especially when their children have reached a sufficient level of maturity. Siblings, even with many years between them, are often close confidants. Sometimes young people even form intimate relationships with adults who are not in their immediate family.

Obviously, one of the central issues in the study of intimacy during adolescence is the onset of dating. Although the young person's initiation into opposite-sex relationships is undoubtedly important, it is not the only noteworthy change that occurs in close relationships during adolescence. Adolescence is also an important time for changes in what we look for in friends, in our capacity to be intimate with people of both sexes, and in the way we express our closeness with friends. •

INTIMACY AS AN ADOLESCENT ISSUE

Intimacy is an important concern throughout most of the life span. Friends and confidants provide support when we are feeling emotionally vulnerable, assistance when we need it, and companionship in a variety of activities and contexts (Weiss, 1974). During childhood, not having friends is associated with a range of psychological and social problems (Hartup, 1992). And, during adulthood, having at least one intimate friendship is beneficial to an individual's health: People who have others to turn to for emotional support are less likely to suffer from psychological and physical disorders (Myers, Lindenthal, & Pepper, 1975). Without question, close relationships are extremely important to people of all ages. Why, then, is the development of intimacy especially important during adolescence?

One reason is that it is not until adolescence that truly intimate relationships—relationships characterized by openness, honesty, self-disclosure, and trust—first emerge. Although children certainly have important friendships, their relationships are different from those formed during adolescence. Children's friendships are activity oriented—for example; they are built around games and shared pastimes. To a child, a friend is someone who likes to do the same things he or she does. But teenagers' close friendships are more likely to have a strong emotional foundation; they are built on the sorts of bonds that form between people who care about and know and understand each other in a special way (Newcomb & Bagwell, 1995).

Another reason for the importance of intimacy during adolescence concerns the changing nature of the adolescent's social world: during early adolescence, the increasing importance of peers in general and, during middle and late adolescence, the increasing importance of opposite-sex peers in particular (Furman, Brown, & Feiring, 1999). In chapter 9, we looked at the young person's growing orientation toward peers as part of the development of emotional autonomy. In this chapter, we will look at changes in adolescent peer relations again but in a different light—as part of the development of intimacy.

Why do such important changes take place in close relationships during adolescence? Several theorists have answered this question by pointing to significant links between the development of intimacy during adolescence and the biological, cognitive, and social changes of the period (Berndt, 1982; Savin-Williams & Berndt, 1990). Puberty and its attendant changes in sexual

▲ *Children's friendships center around shared activities. Not until adolescence are friendships based on the sorts of bonds that are formed between individuals who care about, know, and understand each other in a special way.* (David Wells/ Image Works)

impulses often raise new issues and concerns requiring serious, intimate discussion. Some young people feel hesitant to discuss sex and dating with their parents, so they turn instead to relationships outside the family. But sexual maturation may also provoke intimacy between adolescents and their parents, as when young people turn to their mothers or fathers for advice, information, and guidance (Kandel & Lesser, 1972).

Advances in thinking—especially in the realm of social cognition—are also related to the development of intimacy during adolescence (Hill & Palmquist, 1978). The growth of social cognition during adolescence, as we saw in chapter 2, is reflected in the young person's more sophisticated conceptions of social relationships and in improvements in interpersonal understanding and communication. These changes permit adolescents to establish and maintain far more mature relationships that are characterized by higher levels of empathy, self-disclosure, and responsiveness to each other's thoughts and feelings. The

limitations in preadolescents' ability to look at things from another person's point of view may make intimate interpersonal relationships a cognitive impossibility (Beardslee, Schultz, & Selman, 1987; Selman, 1980). It is hard to be an intimate friend to someone when you are unable to empathize with that person. Improvements in social competence and gains in intimacy during adolescence, therefore, are partly attributable to improvements in social cognition (Ford, 1982).

We can also point to changes in the adolescent's social roles as potentially affecting the development of intimacy. Perhaps most simply, the behavioral independence that often accompanies the transition from childhood into adolescence provides greater opportunities for adolescents to be alone with their friends, engaged in intimate discussion. Adolescents spend more time talking to their friends than in any other activity (Csikszentimihalyi & Larson, 1984). Moreover, the recognition of adolescents as "near adults" may prompt their parents and other adults to confide in them and turn to them for support. Shared experiences, such as working, as well as the development of emotional autonomy, may help give young people and their parents more of a basis for friendship and communication (Youniss & Smollar, 1985). Finally, changes in the structure of schools during early adolescence—often giving younger teenagers more contact with older ones—may promote new types of peer relationships (Blyth, Hill, & Smyth, 1981).

During the course of preadolescence and adolescence, relationships are gradually transformed from the friendly but activity-oriented friendships of childhood to the more self-conscious, more analytical, and more intimate relationships of adulthood. In the section "Theoretical Perspectives on Adolescent Intimacy," we will examine why and how this transformation occurs.

RECAP

Most writers draw a distinction between intimacy and sexuality. In adolescence, the development of intimacy is the development of relationships characterized by self-disclosure, trust, and concern. There are a number of reasons that intimacy becomes an important psychosocial concern in adolescence. Chief among them are the changes of puberty, which draw young people together around common concerns; the cognitive changes of the period, which allow for a more sophisticated understanding of relationships; and the social changes of the period, which provide for more opportunities for adolescents to be alone with each other.

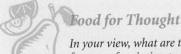

Food for Thought

In your view, what are the defining features of an intimate relationship? Do you agree with the assertion that genuine intimacy in relationships does not appear before adolescence?

THEORETICAL PERSPECTIVES ON ADOLESCENT INTIMACY

The most important theoretical perspectives on the development of intimacy during adolescence are those of Harry Stack Sullivan (1953b), Erik Erikson (1968), and, more recently, a group of writers who have studied attachment relationships in adolescence, using models that initially had been developed for the study of attachment in infancy (e.g., Allen & Land, in press; Greenberg, Siegel, & Leitch, 1983; Kobak & Sceery, 1988; Rice, 1990). Let's look at each of these views in turn.

Sullivan's Theory of Interpersonal Development

Like Erikson, whose theory of adolescent identity development was discussed at length in chapter 8, Sullivan took a far less biological view of development than

other psychoanalytic thinkers, such as Anna Freud, had taken. Instead, Sullivan emphasized the social aspects of growth, suggesting that psychological development can be best understood when looked at in interpersonal terms. Specifically, Sullivan's theory focuses on transformations in the adolescent's relationships with others. In particular, the challenges of adolescence (and, indeed, according to Sullivan, of the entire life cycle) revolve around trying to satisfy our changing interpersonal needs (Buhrmester, 1996).

As the child develops, different interpersonal needs surface that lead either to feelings of security (when the needs are satisfied) or to feelings of anxiety (when the needs are frustrated). Sullivan charted a developmental progression of needs, beginning in infancy and continuing through adolescence (see table 10.1): the *needs for contact and for tenderness* (infancy), the *need for adult participation* (early childhood), the *needs for peers and for peer acceptance* (middle childhood), the **need for intimacy** (preadolescence), the **need for sexual contact** and the **need for intimacy with a peer of the opposite sex** (early adolescence), and the **need for integration into adult society** (late adolescence) (Sullivan, 1953a). These changing interpersonal needs define the course of interpersonal development through different phases of the life span. During middle childhood, for example, youngsters need to be accepted into peer groups, or else they feel rejected and ostracized.

In Sullivan's view, the security that is derived from having satisfying relationships with others is the glue that holds one's sense of self together. Identity and self-

Table 10.1   Interpersonal needs associated with different developmental eras: Sullivan's theory

Developmental Epochs	Interpersonal Needs
Infancy (0 to 2–3 yrs.)	Need for contact with people, need for tenderness from the mothering one
Early childhood (2–3 to 6–7 yrs.)	Need for adult participation in the child's play
Middle childhood (6–7 to 8–10 yrs.)	Need for peer playmates, need for acceptance into peer society groups
Preadolescence (8–10 to 12–14 yrs.)	Need for intimacy and consensual validation in same-sex chumships
Early adolescence (12–14 to 17–18 yrs.)	Need for sexual contact, need for intimacy with an opposite-sex peer
Late adolescence (17–18 yrs. to adult)	Need for integration into adult society

Source: Sullivan, 1953a.

esteem are gradually built up through interpersonal relationships. Like Erikson, Sullivan viewed psychosocial development as cumulative: The frustrations and satisfactions we experience during earlier periods affect our later relationships and developing sense of identity. The child who as an infant has his or her need for contact or tenderness frustrated will approach interpersonal relationships in subsequent eras with greater anxiety, a more intense need for security, and a shakier sense of self.

When important interpersonal transitions arise (for example, during childhood, when the social world is broadened to include significant relationships with peers), having a solid foundation of security in past relationships will aid in the successful negotiation of the transition. An individual who is very anxious about forming relationships with others is likely to have trouble forming new types of relationships, because they threaten an already shaky sense of security. A child who does not have a strong sense of security may have many friends in elementary school but may be too afraid to form intimate friendships on reaching preadolescence. He or she may try to continue having friendships like those of childhood—friendships that focus on playing games, for example, rather than talking—long after friends have outgrown getting together to "play." As a result, that youngster may be rejected by peers and may feel lonely and isolated.

● **Sullivan's View of Interpersonal Development during Adolescence.**   Looking back at the progression of interpersonal needs that Sullivan mapped out, we see that he distinguished between intimacy and sexuality and, perhaps more important, that he suggested that the need for intimacy—which surfaces during preadolescence—precedes the development of heterosexual relationships, which do not emerge until adolescence. In other words, Sullivan believed that the capacity for intimacy first develops before adolescence and in the context of same-sex, not opposite-sex, relationships. One of the main challenges of adolescence, according to Sullivan, is making the transition from the nonsexual, intimate, same-sex friendships of preadolescence to the sexual, intimate, opposite-sex friendships of late adolescence.

Sullivan divided the years between childhood and adulthood into three periods: *preadolescence, early adolescence,* and *late adolescence.* During preadolescence, children begin to focus their attention on relationships with a few close friends, generally of the same sex. It is through these friendships—"chumships," as Sullivan called them—that the need for intimacy is first satisfied. With chums, the young person learns to disclose and receive intimate, private information and to build close, mutual friendships based on honesty, loyalty, and trust. Sullivan believed that these relationships can even have a corrective influence, helping repair interpersonal problems that might have developed during childhood. A good preadolescent friend, for example, can help one overcome feelings of insecurity that have developed as a result of poor family relationships.

Not all youngsters feel secure enough as preadolescents, however, to forge these more mature, intimate friendships. The feelings of insecurity are so strong for some that anxiety holds them back. As a result, some youngsters never fully develop the capacity to be intimate with others, a limitation that takes its toll on relationships throughout adolescence and adulthood. In other words, Sullivan felt that forming intimate friendships during preadolescence is a necessary precondition to forming close relationships as an adolescent or a young adult.

According to Sullivan, the preadolescent era comes to an end with the onset of puberty. Early adolescence is marked by the emergence of sexuality, in the form of a biologically based, powerful sex drive. As a consequence of this development, a change in the preferred "target" of the adolescent's need for intimacy takes place. He or she must begin to make a shift from intimate relationships with members of the same sex to intimate relationships with members of the opposite sex. It is important to note that, during the historical epoch when Sullivan was writing, homosexuality was considered abnormal, and, like other writers of his era, Sullivan equated normal sexual development with the development of heterosexual relationships. Social scientists no longer hold this view, however, and most would say that the crucial challenge is not the movement from same-sex to opposite-sex relationships but, rather, the transition from nonromantic friendships to romantic relationships.

Like all interpersonal transitions, the movement from nonromantic to romantic relationships can be fraught with anxiety. For adolescents who do not have a healthy sense of security, it can be scary to leave the safety of nonsexual friendships and venture into the world of dating and sexuality.

The chief challenge of adolescence, according to Sullivan, is to integrate the individual's established need for intimacy with the emerging need for sexual contact in a way that does not engender an excessive degree of anxiety. Just as Erikson viewed adolescence as a time of experimentation with various identities, Sullivan saw adolescence as a time of experimentation with various types of interpersonal relationships. Some adolescents choose to date many people to try to find out what they are looking for in a relationship with someone else. Others get involved very deeply with a boyfriend or girlfriend in a relationship that lasts throughout their adolescence. Others may have a series of serious relationships. And still others keep intimacy and sexuality separate. They may develop close platonic relationships with opposite-sex peers, for example, or they may have sexual relationships without getting very intimate with their sex partners. And, just as Erikson viewed role experimentation as a healthy part of the adolescent's search for identity, Sullivan viewed the adolescent's experimentation with various types of relationships as a normal way of handling new feelings, new fears, and new interpersonal needs. For many young people, experimentation with sex and intimacy continues well into late adolescence.

If the interpersonal tasks of adolescence have been negotiated successfully, the young person enters late adolescence able to be intimate, able to enjoy sex, and, most critical, able to experience intimacy and sexuality in the same relationship. This accomplished, the adolescent turns to the interpersonal needs of late adolescence: carving a niche in adult society. This latter task, in some senses, is reminiscent of the adolescent identity crisis described by Erikson.

RECAP

The three main theoretical approaches to the study of intimacy in adolescence are those of Sullivan, Erikson, and the attachment theorists. According to Sullivan, the need for intimacy emerges in preadolescence and is typically satisfied through same-sex friendships. During adolescence, this need is integrated with sexual impulses and desires, and the focus of the adolescent's interpersonal concerns are redirected toward romantic relationships with peers. According to Sullivan, the chief challenge of adolescence is to integrate an already established need for intimacy with the emerging need for sexual contact in a way that does not engender an excessive degree of anxiety.

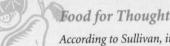

Food for Thought

According to Sullivan, intimacy first develops in same-sex friendships. Given the differences in the ways that males and females are socialized, how might we expect male and female versions of intimacy to differ?

▲ *Generally, intimacy develops first within same-sex friendships. Only later in adolescence are emotionally intimate relationships between males and females common.* (Spencer Grant/Picture Cube)

Erikson's View of Intimacy

Erik Erikson (1968) argued that development during the adolescent and young adult years revolves around two psychosocial crises: the crisis of identity versus identity diffusion, prominent during adolescence (see chapter 8), and the crisis of **intimacy versus isolation,** prominent during early adulthood. Erikson's ideas about the subject of intimacy were far less developed than his ideas about the issue of identity. Nonetheless, his view of the relation *between* intimacy and identity is important to understand and provides somewhat of a contrast to Sullivan's perspective.

Erikson believed that, in a truly intimate relationship, two individuals' identities become fused in such a way that neither person's identity is lost. Together, two people who are in love form a couple that has its own life, its own future, and its own identity, yet the partners do not lose their own sense of individuality. When two people marry, for example, becoming a part of a couple becomes an important part of each person's identity, but it doesn't erase the sense of self that each person had before the marriage.

It follows, Erikson reasoned, that adolescents must establish a sense of identity before they are capable of real intimacy. Without a secure sense of identity, people are afraid and unwilling to make serious commitments to others: They fear that they will lose their identity in the relationship. A young woman who is struggling to establish an occupational identity, for example, may feel that getting seriously involved with someone may impede her progress toward discovering who she really is as an individual.

Relationships between individuals who have not yet established a sense of identity may look intimate, but generally they are not. Adolescents who throw themselves into going steady often display a sort of "pseudo-intimacy." On the surface, their relationship may seem to be close, but a more careful examination usually reveals a sort of shallow, superficial intimacy. The couple may proclaim their faith in each other, for instance, but deep down they may be mistrustful or afraid to voice their concerns. They may say that they are open with each other, but they may not disclose what they are really feeling, for fear of losing the relationship. They may say that they will stay together for ever, but they have trouble making any concrete plans for the future that include each other. According to Erikson, this type of pseudointimacy is to be expected during adolescence. After all, it is difficult to commit yourself to someone else before you yourself know who you are.

● **Erikson and Sullivan: Conflicting Views?**   It may appear that there is a disagreement between Erikson and Sullivan about the relation between intimacy and identity. Sullivan viewed the development of intimacy as occurring primarily during preadolescence. He suggested that the development of the capacity for intimacy is a precedent to the development of a coherent sense of identity, which does not occur until late adolescence. Erikson, on the other hand, argued that the establishment of a coherent sense of identity necessarily occurs prior to the development of intimacy, since one must have a clear sense of who one is in order to avoid becoming lost in a relationship with someone else. What are we to make of this difference? Which comes first, the development of identity or the development of intimacy?

A number of studies have attempted to answer this question by assessing individuals on separate measures of identity and intimacy and examining the relation between the two scores (e.g., Dyk & Adams, 1990; Levitz-Jones & Orlofsky, 1985; Orlofsky, Marcia, & Lesser, 1973). If Erikson's view is correct, only individuals who have achieved a sense of identity should score high in intimacy, and no individuals who are high in intimacy should be low in identity. If Sullivan's view is correct, only individuals who have achieved intimacy in their relationships should score high in identity, and no individuals who score high in identity should score low in intimacy.

Unfortunately, none of the studies of the relation between identity and intimacy provide clear support for one theory over the other. Although scores on measures of identity and intimacy are generally correlated (that is, individuals who have a coherent sense of identity are more likely to have intimate interpersonal relationships, and vice versa), it has been difficult to determine whether development in one domain actually leads to development in another. Rather, it seems that individuals follow different developmental routes, with some establishing a sense of identity first and then advancing in the realm of intimacy, and others following the reverse pattern.

One hypothesis along these lines concerns sex differences in patterns of psychological development. Many theorists have argued that intimacy is a far more fundamental concern for adolescent girls than for adolescent boys and that the psychosocial crises of identity and intimacy may even be merged for female adolescents (Josselson, Greenberger, & McConochie, 1977b). For adolescent boys—actually, for males at all ages—intimacy is perhaps a more distant concern that is less important in the process of self-definition (Maccoby, 1990). In essence, Sullivan's view may be more applicable to girls, whereas Erikson's may be more applicable to boys (Bakken & Romig, 1992; Dyk & Adams, 1990). Even within gender groups, however, there is considerable variation in how individuals approach and integrate the developmental tasks of identity and intimacy.

Rather than debating which comes first—identity (in some senses, the development of *individuality*) or intimacy (in some senses, the development of *connectedness*)—it seems more sensible to suggest that the development of intimacy and the development of identity go hand in hand throughout adolescence, with changes in one realm of psychosocial development affecting changes in the other. One reason for the apparent disagreement between Erikson and Sullivan is that the two theorists focus on different aspects of intimacy. Whereas

Sullivan's concern was primarily with the adolescent's need and *capacity* for intimacy (hence, his focus on early adolescence), Erikson's was with the *expression* of intimacy and commitment (hence, his focus on late adolescence). Close relationships are used as a safe context in which adolescents confront difficult questions of identity, yet, at the same time, the development of an increasingly coherent and secure sense of self provides the foundation on which adolescents build and strengthen intimate relationships with others.

RECAP

In Erikson's theory, the psychosocial crisis of late adolescence is labeled intimacy versus isolation. According to this viewpoint, individuals must first develop a coherent sense of identity before they are able to develop genuinely intimate relationships with others. This position contrasts somewhat with that of Sullivan, who argues that the development of intimacy precedes the development of a coherent sense of self. Most contemporary writers view the development of identity and the development of intimacy as complementary, not competing, tasks.

Food for Thought

How does Erikson's view of the development of intimacy differ from Sullivan's? Some writers have proposed that Sullivan's theory seems more appropriate to understanding female development, whereas Erikson's may be more applicable to males. What do you think?

Attachment in Adolescence

In more recent years, a perspective on intimacy during adolescence has emerged that draws on theories of the development of the attachment relationship during infancy (e.g., Ainsworth, Blehar, Waters, & Wall, 1978; Bowlby, 1969; Sroufe, 1979). In these theories of infant development, an **attachment** is defined as a strong and enduring emotional bond. Virtually all infants form attachment relationships with their mothers (and most do with their fathers and other caregivers, as well), but not all infants have attachment relationships of the same quality. Psychologists differentiate among three types of attachment: **secure attachment, anxious-avoidant attachment,** and **anxious-resistant attachment.** A secure attachment between infant and caregiver is characterized by trust, an

anxious-avoidant attachment is characterized by indifference on the part of the infant toward the caregiver, and an anxious-resistant attachment is characterized by ambivalence. The security of the early attachment relationship is important, because studies show that infants who have had a secure attachment are more likely to grow into psychologically healthy and socially skilled children (Matas, Arend, & Sroufe, 1978).

Many theorists who study adolescent development believe that the nature of the individual's attachment relationships during infancy continues to have an influence on his or her capacity to form satisfying intimate relationships during adolescence and adulthood, for two reasons. First, some theorists have argued that the initial attachment relationship forms the basis of a more general model of interpersonal relationships used throughout life. This so-called **internal working model** determines in large measure whether we feel trusting or apprehensive in relationships with others and whether we see ourselves as worthy of others' affection. We might think of an internal working model as a set of beliefs and expectations that we draw on in forming close relationships with others. According to the theory, individuals who had enjoyed a secure attachment relationship during infancy have a more positive and healthy internal working model of relationships during adolescence, whereas individuals who had been anxiously attached as infants have a less positive model (e.g., Kobak & Sceery, 1988). A number of writers have suggested that individuals who emerge from infancy with an insecure attachment relationship will be more sensitive to being rejected by others in later romantic encounters (Downey, Bonica, & Rincón, 1999). Along similar lines, children who have been physically abused by their parents behave less intimately with their friends than do nonabused children (Parker & Herrera, 1996).

A second reason for the continued importance of early attachment relationships during adolescence is cumulative (Kerns, 1996). A number of studies that have followed infants well into the childhood years show that anxiously attached infants are more likely to develop psychological and social problems during childhood and adolescence, including poor peer relationships (e.g., Erickson, Sroufe, & Egeland, 1985; Lewis, Feiring, McGuffog, & Jaskir, 1984; Renken, Egeland, Marvinney, Mangelsdorf, & Sroufe, 1989; Weinfeld, Ogawa, & Sroufe, 1997). It has been hypothesized that these problems in peer relations during childhood affect the development of social competence during adolescence—in essence, forming a link between early experience and later social relations. Additionally, several studies indicate that the benefits of positive relations with peers extend beyond adolescence: Individuals who establish healthy intimate relationships with age-mates during adolescence are more psychologically healthy and more satisfied with their lives as middle-aged adults (Hightower, 1990; Willits, 1988). Together, these studies suggest an orientation toward the study of intimate relationships that examines the development of close relationships over the entire life span, as emphasized in the theoretical models of both Erikson and Sullivan.

Of course, it is possible for interpersonal development to be cumulative without the root cause of this continuity being the individual's internal working model. For example, individuals who have positive peer relationships in childhood may simply learn how to get along better with others, and this may lead to more positive peer relationships in adolescence, which in turn may lead to better relationships in adulthood. How strong is the *specific* link between infant attachment and the quality of interpersonal relationships in adolescence and young adulthood? Do individuals who were securely attached as infants have more positive working models of relationships as adolescents or young adults? The few studies of attachment that have followed individuals from infancy through adolescence have yielded conflicting results, with some showing considerable continuity from infancy through adolescence (e.g., Hamilton, 2000; Waters, Merrick, Treboux, Crowell, & Albersheim, 2000) but others showing no continuity whatsoever (Lewis, Feiring, & Rosenthal, 2000; Weinfeld, Sroufe, & Egelund, 2000). Some researchers have suggested that individuals' security of attachment remains stable only in the absence of major life events that could upset the course of interpersonal development (e.g., loss of a parent, parental divorce) and that the lack of continuity observed in some studies is due to the importance of intervening events (Beckwith, Cohen, & Hamilton, 1999; Weinfeld et al., 2000). Others, however, argue that the significance of early attachment for later relationships is far outweighed by the importance of the experiences one has in childhood and the context in which the individual lives as an adolescent (Lewis et al., 2000).

In addition to using the three-way attachment classification scheme to study the links among infancy, childhood, and adolescence, attachment theorists have also applied similar classifications to the study of adolescents attachments to others (e.g., Allen & Land, in press; Allen et al., 1998; Armsden & Greenberg, 1987; Greenberg et al., 1983; Kenny, 1987), as well as to adolescents' internal working models (Kobak, Cole, Ferenz-Gillies, Fleming, & Gamble, 1993; Kobak & Sceery, 1988). In some of these studies, adolescents' current relationships with parents and peers are assessed, whereas in other studies adolescents are asked to recount their

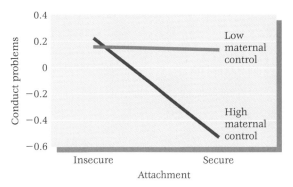

Figure 10.1   *Maternal control has different effects on adolescent behavior, depending on the security of the adolescent's working model.* (Allen et al., 2000)

childhood experiences through the use of a procedure called the **Adult Attachment Interview** (see the accompanying box). In general, individuals who have secure attachments during adolescence (or who describe their earlier attachments as having been secure) are more socially competent and better adjusted than their insecure peers (Allen et al., 1998, Benson, Harris, & Rogers, 1992; Black & McCartney, 1997; Cooper, Shaver, & Collins, 1998; Finnegan & Perry, 1993; Jacobsen & Hofmann, 1997; Kerns, 1994; Kobak & Cole, 1994; Lieberman, Doyle, & Markiewicz, 1999; Rice, 1990). Interestingly, elements of authoritative parenting that seem to protect against problem behavior in adolescence may be far more effective when the adolescent is securely attached. As figure 10.1 indicates, for example, maternal control and supervision seem to deter conduct problems among adolescents who are securely, but not insecurely, attached.

RECAP

According to attachment theorists, intimacy during adolescence must be examined in relation to the individual's history of close relationships and, in particular, of the individual's infant attachments. There is evidence that individuals who enjoyed a secure attachment to their caregiver during infancy are more competent with peers in childhood, as well as some evidence that they develop a healthier or more secure internal working model of relationships, which is thought to permit the individual to enter into more satisfying intimate relationships during adolescence and adulthood. At the same time, however, there is evidence that intervening experiences as well as the adolescent's current life situation influence the development of intimate relationships in important ways, often undoing the effects of earlier attachment.

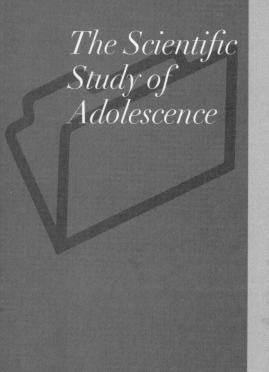

Characterizing Adolescent Attachment Using the Q-Sort Procedure

Once limited to research on infants, the study of attachment has now established a strong presence in research on adolescents. However, whereas infants' attachments to their parents are studied by observing babies interacting with their caregivers, adolescents' attachments are usually studied by interviewing young people about their early family relationships. The Adult Attachment Interview, developed by psychologist Mary Main and her colleagues (Main, Kaplan, & Cassidy, 1985), is designed to yield insight into the individual's internal working model of himself or herself in relation to others. An individual's internal working model during adolescence or adulthood is presumed to have been influenced significantly by his or her early attachment experiences.

Gathering information through interviews can provide rich, detailed insight into an individual's life, and interviewing is often preferable to collecting data through questionnaires or observations, especially when one is interested in the person's subjective recollections. But analyzing information that is collected through an interview can be extremely difficult and time-consuming: Interviews usually are transcribed and then coded before being used in research. Fortunately, there is an extremely useful method for analyzing interviews or, for that matter, any data for which you would like to have raters give their evaluations, such as a videotaped observation.

This method, called a **Q-Sort,** asks raters to read the interview transcript and then to sort a certain number of cards with statements potentially describing the interview into piles ranging from "extremely characteristic" to "extremely uncharacteristic" of the interview content. What is different in the Q-Sort from other rating procedures is that raters are forced to place a specific number of items in each pile. Sometimes, raters must place equal numbers of items in each pile, but more often they are asked to make the piles form a bell curve by placing more items in the

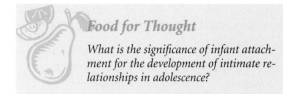

Food for Thought

What is the significance of infant attachment for the development of intimate relationships in adolescence?

THE DEVELOPMENT OF INTIMACY IN ADOLESCENCE

Changes in the Nature of Friendship

"How do you know that someone is your best friend?" When this question is posed to children and adolescents of different ages, younger and older respondents give different sorts of answers. Consider, for example, the following two responses—the first from a kindergarten child, the second from a sixth-grader (Berndt, 1981, p. 180):

Kindergarten child: I sleep over at his house sometimes. When he's playing ball with his friends, he'll let me play. When I slept over, he let me get in front of him in four-squares [a playground game]. He likes me.

Sixth-grader: If you can tell each other things that you don't like about each other. If you get into a fight with someone else, they'd stick up for you. If you can tell them your phone number and they don't give you crank calls. If they don't act mean to you when other kids are around.

These two examples illustrate the most important trend in the development of children's conceptions of friendship: It is not until early adolescence that such features as self-disclosure and loyalty are mentioned as important dimensions of friendship. Psychologist Thomas Berndt (1981), for example, compared how kindergarten children, third-graders, and sixth-graders responded to questions about their conceptions of close friendship. The children's

middle piles than in the outer piles. This procedure makes it impossible for a rater to overuse one of the categories (e.g., by placing most of the items in the pile marked "somewhat characteristic"), which frequently happens if raters are not instructed otherwise.

Psychologist Roger Kobak has developed a Q-Sort specifically for rating adolescents' responses to the Adult Attachment Interview (Kobak et al., 1993). In his studies, raters read the interview transcripts and then sort 100 items potentially describing the respondent into nine piles, using a forced bell-curve distribution. The distribution of items obtained for an individual's interview are then compared with what experts say that different prototypic profiles should look like. On the basis of the similarities between an adolescent's Q-Sort and those suggested by the experts, adolescents are characterized as *secure* (e.g., among the most characteristic items are "Is generally trusting in his or her relationships" and "Is generous, forgiving of faults in self and parents"); *dismissing* (e.g., "Demeans or plays down the need to rely on others" and "Seems detached or uninfluenced by childhood experiences"); or *preoccupied* (e.g., "Relies on others in a frustrated or dissatisfied way" and "Is confused or overwhelmed with information about relationships").

Kobak, as well as many other researchers, has found that secure, dismissing, and preoccupied adolescents differ in interesting ways. Compared with dismissing or preoccupied adolescents, for example, secure adolescents interact with their mothers with less unhealthy anger and more appropriate assertiveness, suggesting that they may experience fewer difficulties in establishing emotional autonomy (Kobak et al., 1993). In a study of college students, a lack of security was associated with depression (especially among preoccupied women) and with higher rates of eating disorders (especially among dismissing women) (Kobak & Cole, 1994; Kobak, Sudler, & Gamble, 1992). Other research has indicated that individuals with dismissive or preoccupied attachment profiles are more likely to show a range of emotional and behavior problems in adolescence, including depression, anxiety, conduct problems, and delinquency (Allen et al., 1998). Individuals who are judged to be secure also have more stable romantic relationships than their insecure counterparts (Davis & Kirkpatrick, 1994).

On a final note, in one of his studies (Dozier & Kobak, 1992), Kobak used a fascinating approach to make sure that the individuals who were classified as dismissing based on their interview responses were actually insecure and were genuinely avoiding the subject of relationships during the interview, rather than simply being forgetful. The researchers measured the individuals' physiological responses both before and during the interview, using standard measures such as skin conductance. Elevations in skin conductance have been shown in previous research to occur when individuals are being deceptive and when they deliberately attempt to inhibit their emotions in the presence of emotionally powerful or disturbing material. Kobak found that the individuals who were classified as dismissing showed marked increases in skin conductance when asked to recall experiences of separation and rejection by their parents.

Source: Dozier, M., & Kobak, R. (1992). Psychophysiology in attachment interviews: Converging evidence for deactivating strategies. *Child Development, 63,* 1473–1480.

responses were classified into one of eight categories, including play or association ("He calls me all the time"), prosocial behavior ("She helps me do things"), intimacy or trust ("I can tell her secrets"), and loyal support ("He'll stick up for me when I'm in a fight"). In general, responses mentioning prosocial behavior and association were equally frequent across all age groups—in fact, they were among the most frequent types of responses at all ages. But answers mentioning intimacy and loyalty, which were virtually absent among the kindergarten students, increased dramatically between the third and sixth grades.

A similar study revealed comparable results (Bigelow & LaGaipa, 1975). Not until seventh grade did the individuals mention intimacy, and not until this time did the children mention "common interests" or "similar attitudes and values" (see figure 10.2). As in Berndt's study, the researchers found that responses mentioning prosocial behavior and common activities were high at all age levels. In other words, it may be important to differentiate between companionship, which appears much before adolescence, and intimacy, which may not emerge until considerably later (Buhrmester & Furman, 1987).

That conceptions of friendship come to place greater weight on such dimensions as intimacy, loyalty, and shared values and attitudes during early adolescence is consistent with Sullivan's theory (Savin-Williams & Berndt, 1990). As adolescents' needs for intimacy increase, so might the emphasis they place on intimacy as an important component of friendship. The findings are also consistent with what is known about other cognitive changes characteristic of early adolescence. As we saw in chapter 2, adolescents have greater facility than children in thinking about abstract concepts, such as intimacy and loyalty. And adolescents' judgments of others are more sophisticated, more psychological, and less tied to concrete attributes than are those of children.

Several studies indicate that the importance of intimacy as a defining feature of close friendship continues to increase throughout early and middle adolescence (Berndt & Perry, 1990; McNelles & Connolly, 1999;

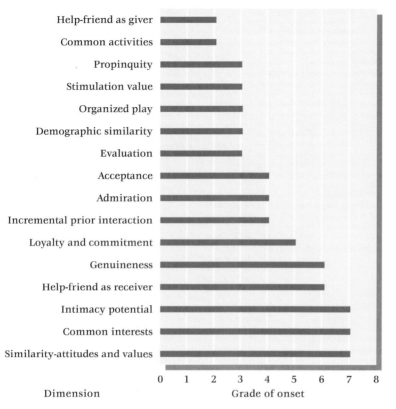

Help-friend as giver
Common activities
Propinquity
Stimulation value
Organized play
Demographic similarity
Evaluation
Acceptance
Admiration
Incremental prior interaction
Loyalty and commitment
Genuineness
Help-friend as receiver
Intimacy potential
Common interests
Similarity-attitudes and values

0 1 2 3 4 5 6 7 8

Dimension   Grade of onset

Figure 10.2   Children and adolescents have different conceptions of friendship. Some sorts of conceptions do not appear until the fifth or sixth grade. (Derived from Bigelow & LaGaipa, 1975)

Phillipsen, 1999). But an interesting pattern of change occurs around age 14. During middle adolescence (between ages 13 and 15), particularly for girls, concerns about loyalty and anxieties over rejection become more pronounced and may temporarily overshadow concerns about intimate self-disclosure (Berndt & Perry, 1990; Douvan & Adelson, 1966). Girls, in particular, show a pronounced increase in jealousy over their friends' friends during early adolescence (Parker, Low, & Wargo, 1999). As two writers explain,

> The girls in this age group [ages 14 to 16] are unique in some respects, that is, different from both older and younger girls. What stands out in their interviews is the stress placed on security in friendships. They want the friend to be loyal, trustworthy, and a reliable source of support in any emotional crisis. She should not be the sort of person who will abandon you or who gossips about you behind your back. . . . With so much invested in the friendship, it is no wonder that the girl is so dependent on it. . . . The girl is likely to feel like the [patient] in that famous *New Yorker* cartoon, who, getting up from the couch, takes a pistol from her purse and says [to her psychoanalyst]: "You've done me a world of good, Doctor, but you know too much." (Douvan & Adelson, 1966, pp. 188–189)

How might Sullivan have explained this pattern? Why might loyalty become such a pressing concern for girls during the middle adolescent years? One possible answer is that, at that age, girls may feel more anxious about their relationships because they are beginning to make the transition into opposite-sex relationships. These transitions, as Sullivan noted, can sometimes make us feel insecure. Perhaps it is anxiety over dating and heightened feelings of insecurity that cause adolescent girls temporarily to place a great deal of emphasis on the trust and loyalty of their close friends. Indeed, close friends who have highly intimate and exclusive relationships with each other often behave more aggressively *within* the friendship than they do toward peers who are not their close friends (Grotpeter & Crick, 1996).

Adolescents' close friendships also are distinguished from their casual friendships in the types of conflicts they have and in the ways their conflicts are resolved (Laursen, 1995, 1996; Raffaeli, 1997; Whitesell & Harter, 1996). Although conflicts between adolescents and their close friends are less frequent than they are between adolescents and other peers, arguments with close friends are more emotional (i.e., lots of anger and hurt feelings). More important, though, conflict between close friends is more likely to provoke efforts to restore the relationship than is conflict between classmates who are not close friends.

There are interesting sex differences in the nature of conflicts between close friends during adolescence. Boys' conflicts with their friends are briefer, are typically over issues of power and control (e.g., whose turn it is in a game), are more likely to escalate into physical aggression, and are resolved without any explicit effort to do so, often by just "letting things slide." Girls' conflicts, in contrast, are longer, are typically about a form of betrayal in the relationship (e.g., breaking a confidence or ignoring the other person), and are resolved when one of the friends apologizes to the other (Raffaeli, 1997).

Changes in the Display of Intimacy

In addition to placing greater emphasis on intimacy and loyalty in defining friendship than children do, teenagers are more likely to display intimacy in their relationships. For example, one team of researchers examined age differences in the degree to which youngsters had intimate knowledge about their best friends (Diaz & Berndt, 1982). Although the fourth- and eighth-graders had comparable degrees of knowledge about nonintimate characteristics of their best friends (such as the friend's telephone number or birth date), the eighth-graders knew significantly more things about their friends that could be classified as intimate (such as what their friends worry about or what they are proud of) (see also Jones & Dembo, 1989). Along similar lines, another study showed that, between the fifth and eleventh grades, increasingly more adolescents agree with such statements as "I know how [my friend] feels about things without his [or her] telling me" and "I feel free to talk to [my friend] about almost everything" (Sharabany, Gershoni, & Hofman, 1981). Consistent with Sullivan's viewpoint, then, during preadolescence and early adolescence, youngsters' friendships become more personal.

Individuals also become more responsive to close friends, less controlling, and more tolerant of their friends' individuality during adolescence (Berndt, 1982; Berndt & Perry, 1990; Estrada, 1995; Keller, Edelstein, Schmid, Fang, & Fang, 1998; Newcomb & Bagwell, 1995; Shulman, Laursen, Kalman, & Karpovsky, 1997). This can be interpreted as another indicator of their increased capacity for intimacy. Before preadolescence, for example, children are actually less likely to help and share with their friends than with other classmates (perhaps because children are more competitive with their friends than with

other youngsters and do not want to feel inferior). By about fourth grade, children treat their friends and other classmates similarly when it comes to sharing and cooperation. However, by the time they have reached eighth grade, one team of researchers found, friends are "more generous and more helpful toward each other than toward other classmates" (Berndt, 1982, p. 1452). Interestingly, adolescents are also *physically and physiologically* responsive to their friends: Studies show that the behaviors and emotional states of pairs of friends are more frequently synchronized, or "on the same wavelength," than are those of acquaintances, even when the friends and acquaintances are engaged in the same task (Field et al., 1992). Evidently, there is something genuine about chemistry between close friends.

Finally, during the course of adolescence, individuals become more interpersonally sensitive—they show greater levels of empathy and social understanding—in situations in which they are helping or comforting others. Compared with children, adolescents are more likely to understand and acknowledge how their friends feel when those friends are having problems. For instance, one researcher asked children and adolescents how they would help a younger friend who had been scared by a horror movie on television. The children were more likely to deny their friend's feelings, whereas the adolescents were more likely to respond sensitively and supportively (Burleson, 1982). Indeed, over the course of adolescence, individuals' attempts to help their friends with personal problems of all sorts become more centered around providing support for the troubled friends and less aimed at mere distraction (Denton & Zarbatany, 1996).

RECAP

Research on the development of intimacy in adolescence points to changes in individuals' conceptions about friendship and in the display of intimacy. With development, adolescents place more emphasis on trust and loyalty as defining features of friendship, they become more self-disclosing in their relationships, and they become more responsive to their friends.

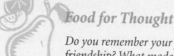

Food for Thought

Do you remember your first intimate friendship? What made the relationship different from other friendships that you had previously had?

Are There Sex Differences in Intimacy?

When asked to name the people who are most important to them, adolescent girls—particularly in the middle adolescent years—list more friends than boys do, and girls are more likely to mention intimacy as a defining aspect of close friendship. In interviews, adolescent girls express greater interest in their close friendships, talk more frequently about their intimate conversations with friends, express greater concern about their friends' faithfulness and greater anxiety over rejection, and place greater emphasis on emotional closeness in their evaluation of romantic partners (Berndt, 1982; Feiring, 1996; Feiring & Lewis, 1991). Girls are more likely than boys to make distinctions in the way they treat intimate and nonintimate friends, and girls appear to prefer to keep their friendships more exclusive, being less willing to include other classmates in their cliques' activities (Berndt, 1982; Bukowski et al., 1993b). Intimacy with same-sex friends increases markedly between childhood and early adolescence among girls but does not show a similar increase among boys. Indeed, when self-disclosure is taken as the measure of intimacy, it is clear that boys' friendships with other boys do not approach girls' friendships with other girls until late in adolescence, if at all (Buhrmester & Furman, 1987; Savin-Williams & Berndt, 1990). Girls also appear to develop intimate relationships with boys earlier than boys do with girls (see the accompanying figure). And girls appear to be more sensitive and empathic than boys, especially when comforting friends who are distressed (Berndt, 1982; Blyth, Hill, & Thiel, 1982; Burleson, 1982; Eisenberg, Miller, Shell, McNalley, & Shea, 1991; Sharabany et al., 1981). In these very numerous—and very important—respects, the expression of intimacy certainly appears to be more advanced among adolescent girls than among boys (Buhrmester, 1996).

On some measures, however, adolescent boys and girls show similar degrees of intimacy in their interpersonal relationships. Although girls are more likely to mention self-disclosure when asked to define close friendship, boys and girls report similar levels of *actual* self-disclosure in their same-sex friendships and have equivalent degrees of intimate knowledge about their best friends (Diaz & Berndt, 1982; Sharabany et al., 1981). In group situations, boys and girls are equally likely to help their friends (Zeldin, Small, & Savin-Williams, 1982). Boys and girls report comparable levels of intimacy with their mothers, and most adolescents feel closer to their mothers than to their fathers; however, boys report greater intimacy with fathers than girls do (Kandel & Lesser, 1972; Youniss & Smollar, 1985).

On the face of it, it appears that intimacy is a more conscious concern for adolescent girls than for boys. But this does not mean that intimacy is absent from boys' relationships. "Boys may spend less time in conversations about

Changes in the Targets of Intimacy

According to Sullivan, adolescence is a time of noteworthy changes in the targets of intimate behavior. During preadolescence and early adolescence, intimacy with peers is hypothesized to replace intimacy with parents, and, during late adolescence, intimacy with peers of the opposite sex is thought to take the place of intimacy with same-sex friends. Actually, this view appears to be only somewhat accurate. New targets of intimacy do not *replace* old ones. Rather, new targets are *added to* old ones.

● **Parents and Peers as Targets of Intimacy**   Two conclusions emerge repeatedly in studies of adolescents' intimacy with parents and peers, at least in the contemporary United States. First, from early adolescence on, teenagers describe their relationships with their best friends and romantic partners as more intimate than those with their mother or father (Beaumont, 1996; Hunter & Youniss, 1982; Rice & Mulkeen, 1995). Second, although there is sometimes a slight drop in intimacy between adolescents and parents sometime during adolescence, the decline reverses as young people

their emotions and ideas than girls, but they may [nevertheless] acquire a deep understanding of each other by spending time together" (Berndt, 1982, p. 1450). It is important to recognize, therefore, that boys and girls have different types of friendships. Consequently, they express intimacy in somewhat different ways. In general, boys' friendships are more oriented toward shared activities than toward the explicit satisfaction of emotional needs—as is often the case in girls' friendships, and the development of intimacy between adolescent males may be a quieter, more subtle phenomenon.

Many theorists have suggested that these sex differences in intimacy are the result of different patterns of socialization, with females being more strongly encouraged to develop and express intimacy—especially verbal intimacy—than males. Consistent with this, research shows that an individual's sex role (how masculine, feminine, or androgynous he or she is) is a better predictor of the person's capacity for intimate friendship than is his or her sex (Jones & Costin, 1993). For instance, androgynous males (males who are both masculine and feminine) report levels of intimacy in their friendships that are comparable to females' levels of intimacy (Jones & Dembo, 1989).

Other factors could be at work, however, that lead to the greater expression of certain types of intimacy between females than between males. Social pressures on males and females during adolescence are quite different and may lead to differences in expressions of intimacy in certain types of relationships. For instance, theorists have noted that **homophobia**—the fear of homosexuality—is stronger among adolescent males than among adolescent females and leads to suppressed intimacy in relationships between boys (Kite, 1984). One reason that male adolescents may not be as intimate in their friendships as female adolescents may be that boys are nervous that expressions of intimacy—even without sexual contact—will be taken as a sign of their sexual orientation.

Although much research to date has led to the conclusion that girls experience more intimacy in their relationships than boys do (Buhrmester, 1996; Maccoby, 1990), it is important to bear in mind that these studies have been based mainly on samples of white youngsters. Several studies of nonwhite youth, however, suggest that there may not be sex differences in intimacy in some ethnic groups. In particular, African American males report as much intimacy in their friendships as do African American females, and sex differences in intimacy among Mexican American adolescents appear far less consistently than they do among their white counterparts (DuBois & Hirsch, 1990; Jones, Costin, & Ricard, 1994). Sanctions against intimate disclosure may be especially strong among white males, but they may be far less so among their minority counterparts.

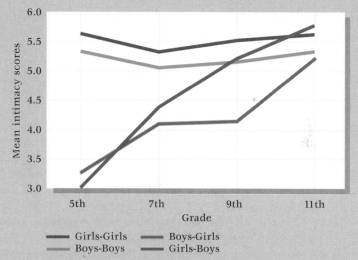

▲ Age differences in reported intimacy in same- and opposite-sex relationships. In general, intimacy is reported by girls at an earlier age than by boys. (Adapted from Sharabany et al., 1981)

move toward young adulthood. Consider, for example, the results of a study of age differences in intimate self-disclosure with parents, friends, and romantic partners over the course of childhood and young adulthood (Buhrmester, 1996). As figure 10.3 indicates, intimacy between individuals and their parents declines between the fifth and tenth grades but increases between tenth grade and young adulthood. Intimacy with friends increases steadily throughout adolescence, although most dramatically during the early adolescent years. Intimacy with romantic partners also increases steadily throughout adolescence; however, in this case, the most dramatic increase takes place during the late high school years.

It seems safe to say that, although peers become relatively more important during adolescence as confidants and sources of emotional support, by no means do parents become *un*important. Findings consistent with these were obtained when nearly 2,500 students in a large midwestern school district were asked to list the important people in their lives—people they cared about, went to for advice, or did things with (Blyth,

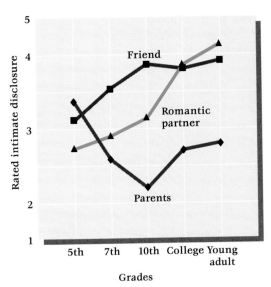

Figure 10.3 *Age differences in self-disclosure to parents, friends, and romantic partners.* (Buhrmester, 1996)

Hill, & Thiel, 1982). The number of peers listed increased over the course of the age range studied (from grades 7 through 10). But no changes were found across the same age range in the percentage of adolescents listing their mothers or fathers—in each grade, for both boys and girls, about 93 percent of the adolescents who were sampled listed their parents. Moreover, studies indicate that adolescents who spend a good deal of time with their parents also spend a good deal of time with their friends. Thus, rather than drawing distinctions between parent-oriented and peer-oriented adolescents, it may make more sense to distinguish between adolescents who have a lot of social contact (with both family and friends) and those who are socially isolated or lonely (Fallon & Bowles, 1997).

Studies of adolescents' preferences for social support similarly show that the likelihood of turning to a peer during a time of trouble increases during adolescence but that the likelihood of turning to a parent remains constant (Kneisel, 1987). In a study of African American, Hispanic American, and European American youth, the researchers found that, between ages 7 and 14, the amount of support received from one's immediate family remained fairly constant, whereas the amount of support received from friends increased—a pattern seen in all three ethnic groups (Levitt, Guacci-Franci, & Levitt, 1993). In other words, even though adolescents begin to see their friends as increasingly important sources of emotional support, they do not cease need-

ing or using their parents for the same purpose. What seems to occur, instead, is that adolescents develop preferences for social support that vary as a function of the topic matter (see figure 10.4). Interestingly, adolescents may feel freer to express anger during arguments with family members than during arguments with friends, presumably because anger may lead to the end of a friendship but not to the end of a family relationship (Laursen, 1993).

Patterns of adolescents' relationships with parents and peers vary across cultures, however, and it may be misleading to generalize the results of studies of U.S. teenagers to other countries. One comparison of adolescents from Canada, Belgium, and Italy, for example, found that the Italian adolescents were closer to their family than to their friends, whereas the Canadian adolescents were closer to their friends (Claes, 1998). It may also be wrong to assume, for example, that American youngsters are more peer oriented than their counterparts in other cultures. In fact, one study found that the Japanese adolescents (Japanese boys, in particular) were *less* likely than the American adolescents to list their parents—and were more likely to list their peers—as significant others (Darling, Hamilton, & Matsuda, 1990). Another study, of Dutch youth, found that parent-adolescent relationships were least positive during *late* adolescence, not early adolescence, as has been found in U.S. samples (van Wel, 1994).

There are also some differences among ethnic groups within the United States in the expression of intimacy between adolescents and parents, although some of these differences may have more to do with recency of immigration into the United States than with ethnicity per se. One recent study of late adolescents found, for example, that Vietnamese American and Chinese American individuals felt less comfortable talking to their parents about such intimate matters as sex or dating than did Filipino Americans and Mexican Americans, who in turn felt less comfortable than European Americans. The researchers speculated that these differences reflected ethnic differences in norms of formality in family relationships, especially in relationships between adolescents and their fathers (Cooper, Baker, Polichar, & Welsh, 1994). Other studies indicate that ethnic minority American adolescents are more likely to believe that it is important to respect, assist, and support their family than are white adolescents (Fuligni, Tseng, & Lam, 1999), although ethnic differences in adolescents'

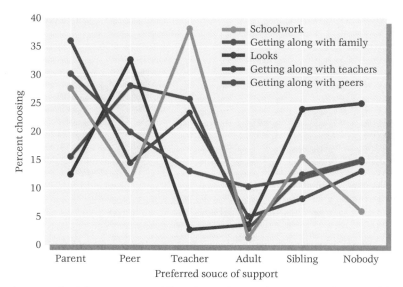

Figure 10.4   Preferred sources of social support among Hispanic American students vary as a function of their area of concern.
(Morrison, Laughlin, Miguel, Smith, & Widaman, 1997)

beliefs and *expectations* appear to be more substantial than ethnic differences in how adolescents and their parents actually interact. Indeed, with the exception of families who are recent immigrants to the United States, relations between American adolescents and their parents look surprisingly similar across ethnic groups (Fuligni, 1998).

There are important differences between adolescents' relationships with mothers versus fathers, as well. In general, adolescents interact much more often with, are closer to, and argue more with their mothers than with their fathers, and this is seen among males as well as females and across a variety of cultures (Claes, 1998; Cooper, 1994; Fuligni, 1998). Of their two parents, adolescents see their mothers as being more understanding, more accepting, and more willing to negotiate; they view their mothers as less judgmental, less guarded, and less defensive (see figure 10.5). The difference between perceptions of mothers and perceptions of fathers is especially large for girls: As a rule, the mother-daughter relationship tends to be the closest and the father-daughter relationship the least intimate, with mother-son and father-son relationships falling in between (Monck, 1991; Noller & Callan, 1990; Rice & Mulkeen, 1995; Youniss & Smollar, 1985).

All in all, then, an important transition in intimate relationships appears to take place sometime between the fifth and eighth grades. During this period, peers become the most important source of companionship and intimate self-disclosure—surpassing parents and, interestingly, other family members, such as siblings (Buhrmester & Furman, 1987; Larson & Richards, 1991). Peers may become increasingly important as targets of intimacy not simply because they are similar in age but also because they do not share the same family with the adolescent. As adolescents begin the process of individuation, they may need to seek intimacy outside the family as a means of establishing an identity beyond their family role.

Adolescents also have very different sorts of intimate relationships with parents and peers, and these differences point to different ways in which mothers, fathers, and friends contribute to the social development of the young person. Even in close families, parent-adolescent relations are characterized by an imbalance of power, with parents as nurturers, advice givers, and explainers to whom adolescents turn because of their experience and expertise. Adolescents' interactions with their friends, in contrast, are more mutual and more balanced and are more likely to provide adolescents with opportunities to express alternative views and engage in an equal exchange of feelings and beliefs (Hunter, 1984). Rather than viewing one type of relationship as more or less intimate than the other, it seems wiser to say that both types of intimacy are important, for each influences a different aspect of the adolescent's developing character in important ways. Intimacy with parents provides opportunities to learn from someone

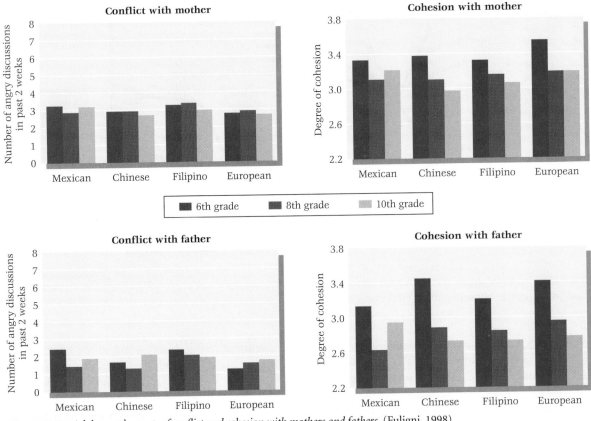

Figure 10.5   *Adolescents' reports of conflict and cohesion with mothers and fathers.* (Fuligni, 1998)

older and wiser; intimacy with friends provides opportunities to share experiences with someone who has a similar perspective and degree of expertise.

The different functions of intimacy with parents and peers are illustrated in a study of social support during a transition into a new school (Dunn, Putallaz, Sheppard, & Lindstrom, 1987). As you recall from chapter 6, changing schools during adolescence can sometimes be stressful, and **social support**—emotional assistance from others—can help buffer adolescents against the potential negative effects of stress (Hauser & Bowlds, 1990). The study found that support from family members was more predictive of adaptation to the demands of the new school, as indexed by grades and attendance, but that support from peers was more predictive of low psychological distress, as indexed by measures of depression and anxiety. The absence of peer support was especially critical for boys. One reason is that girls may be more likely than boys to seek out other sources of support when their peers do not provide it. Although more research on the nature and ef-

fects of social support among minority adolescents is needed, at least one study indicates that parental support is more strongly related to self-esteem among white than among African American adolescents (Levitt et al., 1993).

Studies show that a lack of support from parents *or* from friends in school is associated with low self-worth and poorer social adjustment in early adolescence. Social support from one source (e.g., the family) can be especially important when other sources of support (e.g., friends) are lacking (Ohannessian, Lerner, Lerner, & von Eye, 1994). One study found, for example, that having support from one's family was more important for the healthy adjustment of adolescents who did not have a close friend, whereas support from friends was more crucial among adolescents whose family relationships were strained (Gauze, Bukowski, Aquan-Assee, & Sippola, 1996). Having support from parents, siblings, or nonschool friends does not *fully* compensate for a lack of support from classmates, though, and having support from siblings, classmates, or others does not fully compensate for a lack of support from parents (East & Rook, 1992; Gore & Aseltine, 1995). In other words, optimal social development during adolescence may require healthy relationships *both* with parents and with peers (Barber & Olsen, 1997; Eccles, Early, Frasier, Belansky, & McCarthy, 1997).

Studies of the differential uses of parents and peers as sources of support indicate that adolescents' choices of whom to turn to is likely to be highly dependent on the specific issue at hand, which explains, in part, why adolescents may need support both from parents and from peers (Boldero & Fallon, 1995; Morrison, Laughlin, Miguel, Smith, & Widaman, 1997). One study asked adolescents whom they would turn to if they had a substance-abuse problem; the respondents could name as many different people as desired (Windle, Miller-Tutzauer, & Barnes, 1991). Among the early adolescents surveyed, only 43 percent listed their parents among the people they would turn to for help, whereas 60 percent listed friends; among the middle adolescents, the proportions were 39 percent and 70 percent, respectively. More interestingly, 10 percent of all the early adolescents and almost that proportion of the middle adolescents said that they would turn to no one at all—a far more common response among boys than girls. There also were interesting ethnic differences in adolescents' responses, with African American and Hispanic youngsters being *twice* as likely as white adolescents to report being socially isolated (i.e., having no one to turn to).

In general, the results of research on changes in intimacy with parents and peers as an individual ages are similar to the findings discussed in chapter 9, regarding autonomy: Although the importance of peer relationships undoubtedly increases during adolescence, the significance of family relationships does not decline so much as it narrows in focus. Parents do not cease to be important sources of influence or, as we see here, targets of intimacy. Throughout adolescence, parents and adolescents remain close; parents—especially mothers—remain important confidants, and both mothers and fathers continue to be significant influences on the young person's behavior and decisions. Indeed, even in adolescence being close to one's parents has a more positive impact on psychological health than does being close to one's friends (Greenberg, Siegel, & Leitch, 1983), and studies show that the quality of the relation-

▲ *In general, adolescents interact much more often with their mothers than with their fathers, and this is true for males as well as females. Adolescents see their mothers as more understanding, accepting, and willing to negotiate and less judgmental, guarded, and defensive.* (Nancy Raymond/The Image Works)

ship adolescents have with their parents may have an influence on the quality of the relationship they have with close friends (Cooper, Carlson, Keller, Koch, & Spradling, 1993; Gold & Yanof, 1985). Increasingly, psychologists are coming to see family relationships and peer relationships as influencing, rather than competing with, each other (Fallon & Bowles, 1997; Gavin & Furman, 1996). Nevertheless, it seems clear that peers take on an increasingly important role in the individual's social life over the course of adolescence. Although peers do not replace parents, they clearly contribute to the adolescent's social development in a unique and beneficial way.

● **Other Individuals as Targets of Intimacy**   Comparatively little is known about intimacy in adolescents' relationships with siblings, with members of their extended family, and with nonfamilial adults, such as teachers and coaches. Only about 10 percent of the adolescents who have a brother or a sister fail to list a sibling as an important person in their life. Furthermore, more than two-thirds of adolescents with brothers or sisters list all of their siblings as significant (Blyth et al., 1982). Adolescents typically rate their relationship with their "favorite" brother or sister as having about the same level of intimacy as their relationship with their best friend (Greenberger, Steinberg, Vaux, & McAuliffe, 1980). When researchers do not specify that the sibling be a "favorite" brother or sister, however, the relationship is usually described as less intimate than the adolescent's relationship with parents or friends (Buhrmester & Furman, 1987). Adolescents fight more with brothers and sisters than they do with close friends, and their arguments with siblings tend to be resolved less by giving in or by letting things slide than through the intervention of others, presumably parents (Raffaelli, 1997).

When teenagers are asked to list the significant people in their lives, approximately 80 percent list at least one member of their extended family (grandparents, aunts, uncles, and cousins), with extended family members constituting about one-fifth of all people listed as important (Blyth, Hill, & Thiel, 1982). Contact with extended family is infrequent for many adolescents, however, because extended family members often live outside the adolescent's immediate area (Feiring & Lewis, 1991). One might suspect, therefore, that, although adolescents consider grandparents, aunts, uncles, and cousins to be important, these relatives rarely serve as targets of intimacy. There appears to be a slight increase in intimacy with extended family members during childhood, but an especially steep drop-off in intimacy with grandparents and other extended family members occurs between childhood and adolescence (Buhrmester & Furman, 1987; Creasey & Kaliher, 1994; Levitt et al., 1993).

Although a decline in intimacy with grandparents is often observed during adolescence, this may not be as common among adolescents who are living with a divorced mother (Clingempeel, Colyar, Brand, & Hetherington, 1992). Indeed, divorce may be associated with increased contact between adolescents and their grandparents, especially between the adolescent and his or her maternal grandfather. Interestingly, puberty seems to increase the intimacy between adolescent boys from divorced homes and their grandfathers (perhaps to compensate for diminished contact with their father), whereas it seems to distance adolescent girls from their grandfathers (perhaps because of discomfort about the girl's sexuality).

Researchers also have asked whether relationships between adolescents and nonfamilial adults in their schools, work places, or neighborhoods can play a significant role in teenagers' lives (Greenberger, Chen, & Beam, 1998; Munsch, Liang, & DeSecottier, 1996). Close friendships may develop naturally between adolescents and their teachers or work supervisors or can be cultivated through community organizations, such as Big Brother, Big Sister, or similar programs designed to pair young people—especially those under stress—with supportive and caring adults. One study of Latina adolescent mothers found, for example, that those who had mentors reported significantly better mental health than their peers who did not (Rhodes, Contreras, & Mangelsdorf, 1994). The benefits of having a Big Brother or Big Sister may be especially significant among adolescents with more difficulties at home, such as those living in foster care (Rhodes, Haight, & Briggs, 1999). Not all close relationships with nonparental adults are beneficial to adolescents' development, however: Adolescent boys who have close friendships with young adult men are more likely to engage in antisocial behavior when they perceive their older friends as likely to condone or commit antisocial acts themselves (Greenberger et al., 1998).

> **RECAP**
>
> *Adolescence is a time during which adolescents broaden their circle of confidants. In general, new types of relationships are added to the adolescent's social world without replacing previous ones. Whereas in childhood the primary targets of intimacy are parents and, to a lesser extent, siblings, beginning in preadolescence the network of intimates widens to include peers as well as family members.*

> *Food for Thought*
>
> *Do you think changes in family life—divorce, remarriage, parental employment, and so on—have affected the nature of the development of intimacy in adolescence? Why or why not?*

Friendships with the Other Sex

It is not until late adolescence that intimate friendships with opposite-sex peers begin to be important. Consistent with Sullivan's theory, studies of preadolescents and young teenagers point to very strong sex segregation in adolescents' friendships, with boys rarely reporting friendships with girls, and girls rarely reporting friendships with boys (Hallinan, 1981). Indeed, gender is the single most important determinant of friendship during preadolescence, playing a considerably more powerful role than, for example, race or socioeconomic background (Schofield, 1981). (Age is also an important determinant of preadolescents' friendships, but it is difficult to study, since the organization of most elementary schools—at least in the United States—makes it hard for children to develop friendships with older and younger peers.)

The schism between boys and girls during early adolescence results from various factors. First, despite whatever changes may have taken place in American society with regard to sex-role socialization during the past 25 years, it is still the case that preadolescent and early adolescent boys and girls have different interests, engage in different sorts of peer activities, and perceive themselves to be different from each other (Schofield, 1981). In one study, for example, an interviewer asked a young adolescent boy why boys and girls sit separately in the school lunchroom. "So they can talk," the boy replied. "The boys talk about football and sports and the girls talk about whatever they talk about" (Schofield, 1981, p. 68). The sex cleavage in adolescent friendships results more from adolescents' preferring members of the same sex—and the activities they engage in—than from their actually disliking members of the opposite sex, although boys express more positive feelings about their female classmates than vice versa (Bukowski, Gauze, Hoza, & Newcomb, 1993; Bukowski, Sippola, & Hoza, 1999).

Perhaps a more interesting reason for the low frequency of cross-sex friendships during early adolescence is the concern of some adolescents that contact with members of the opposite sex will be interpreted as a sign of romantic involvement (Schofield, 1981). As one girl put it, "If you talk with boys they [other girls] say that you're almost going with him." Another girl from the same class remarked that boys and girls rarely work together on class projects "because people like to work with their friends. . . . When you're working on a project . . . your friend has to call and come over to your house. If it's a boy, it can be complicated" (Schofield, 1981, p. 69).

The discomfort that younger adolescents feel about cross-sex relationships is vividly illustrated in the following observation of three preadolescent boys in an amusement park:

> The boys seem very interested in the girls they see, and there is considerable whispering and teasing about them. Tom had received a small coin bank as a prize which he decides that he no longer wishes to keep. At this time we are standing in line for a roller coaster directly behind

three girls—apparently a year or two older than these twelve-year-olds—one of whom is wearing a hooded jacket. Frank tells Tom to take the bank and "stuff it in her hood," which Tom does to the annoyance of his victim. When she turns around, Tom and Hardy tell her that Frank did it, and of course Frank denies this, blaming Tom. The girls tell the boys to shut up and leave them alone. As things work out, Hardy has to sit with one of these girls on the ride and he clearly appears embarrassed, while Tom and Frank are vastly amused. After the ride Tom and Frank claim that they saw Hardy holding her. Frank said that he saw them holding hands, and Tom said: "He was trying to go up her shirt." Hardy vehemently denies these claims. A short while later we meet these girls again, and Frank turns to Hardy, saying "Here's your honey." The girl retorts as she walks away, "Oh, stifle it." (Fine, 1981, p. 43)

Friendly interactions between early adolescent boys and girls, when they do occur, typically involve "overacting attraction or romantic interest in such a pronounced or playful way that the indication of interest can be written off as teasing or fooling around" (Schofield, 1981, p. 71).

The transitional period—between same-sex nonsexual relationships and opposite-sex sexual ones—appears to be a somewhat trying time for adolescents. This period usually coincides with the peer group's shift from same-sex cliques to mixed-sex crowds, which we examined in chapter 5. The interpersonal strains and anxieties inherent in the transition show up in the high levels of teasing, joking around, and overt discomfort young adolescents so often display in situations that are a little too close to being romantic or sexual. As one researcher put it, intimacy between boys and girls before middle adolescence appears to be "impeded at least partly because . . . children are aware that they are approaching the age when they may begin to become deeply involved with each other in a romantic or sexual way" (Schofield, 1981, pp. 69–70).

These observations support Sullivan's claim that intimacy between adolescent boys and girls is relatively slow to develop and generally is tinged with an air of sexuality. Contrary to his notion that cross-sex intimacy comes to replace intimacy with peers of the same sex, however, researchers have found that intimate relationships between adolescents of the same sex continue to develop throughout adolescence. They clearly are not displaced by the eventual emergence of intimacy between adolescent males and females (Connolly & Johnson, 1993; Sharabany et al., 1981). Although researchers find that the likelihood of opposite-sex peers' appearing on adolescents' lists of people who are important to them increases

▲ *As mixed-sex relationships begin to develop, adolescents may mask their anxieties by teasing and joking around with members of the opposite sex.* (Glass/Monkmeyer)

during early and middle adolescence, and although the amount of time adolescents spend with opposite-sex peers increases as well, the number of same-sex peers listed also increases or remains constant, and time spent with same-sex peers does not decline (Blyth et al., 1982; Feiring & Lewis, 1991; Richards, Crowe, Larson, & Swarr, 1998; Zimmer-Gembeck, 1999). There are substantial individual differences in patterns of time allocation to same- and opposite-sex relationships, however; some adolescents shift their energy from same-sex friends to opposite-sex relationships early and abruptly; others do so gradually, over the course of high school; and others do not shift their focus during high school at all (Zimmer-Gembeck, 1999).

Although intimacy between the sexes increases during early adolescence (Buhrmester & Furman, 1987), many adolescents do not list a single opposite-sex peer as a significant person in their lives. In middle school, only 8 percent of adolescents' friendships are with members of the opposite sex; by high school, this figure has risen to only 13 percent (Degirmencioglu & Urberg, 1994). When females do include opposite-sex peers, the boys they list are often older and often from another school; when boys list girls as important friends, they generally are of the same age or younger (Blyth et al., 1982). Consistent with this, the increase in time spent

with opposite-sex peers that occurs in adolescence takes place much earlier among girls than boys—by the time they are in eleventh grade, girls are spending 10 hours each week alone with a boy, compared with only 5 hours per week spent by boys alone with a girl. Young adolescents of both genders spend a lot of time *thinking* about the opposite sex, but relatively little time with them. Interestingly, as adolescents get older, the time they spend thinking about the opposite sex tends to be increasingly associated with negative mood states, perhaps because the fantasies about the opposite sex experienced in early adolescence come to be replaced by more realistic feelings of longing for romantic companionship (Richards et al., 1998).

Although the emergence of close opposite-sex friendships in early adolescence is not explicitly in the context of romance, it likely sets the stage for later romantic experiences. The pattern of age differences in opposite-sex friendships, for example, is consistent with what is known about age differences between dating partners in early and middle adolescence, with boys generally older than their girlfriends, rather than the reverse (Montgomery & Sorell, 1998). In addition, adolescents who have more opposite-sex friends than their peers early in adolescence tend to enter into romantic relationships at an earlier age and tend to have longer romantic relationships (Feiring, 1999a). This could be due to many factors, including the adolescent's use of the pool of opposite-sex friends to rehearse for later romantic relationships and to develop a social network that is used to meet potential dates later on (Connolly & Goldberg, 1999; Darling, Dowdy, Van Horn, & Caldwell, 1999). In any case, however, it is clear that even preadolescents as young as 9 differentiate between cross-sex relationships that are friendships and those that are romantic (Connolly, Craig, Goldberg, & Pepler, 1999).

Not all relationships between males and females in adolescence are romantic, of course, and having close opposite-sex friendships is a common experience among contemporary youth (Kuttler, La Greca, & Prinstein, 1999). Very little is known about the nature or significance of these friendships, however (Sippola, 1999). It appears that two very different types of adolescents have close opposite-sex friends—adolescents who are socially competent and highly popular with peers of the same sex, and adolescents who are socially incompetent and highly unpopular with same-sex peers (Bukowski et al., 1999; Degirmencioglu & Urberg, 1994; Feiring & Lewis, 1991). Among boys, having an opposite-sex friend serves as a back-up system for individuals who do not have same-sex friends, leading to more positive mental health than is seen among boys without friends. Among girls, however, this is not the case; for a girl with no close same-sex friends, "there is no advantage, or perhaps there is even a disadvantage, to having a friendship with a boy" (Bukowski et al., 1999, p. 457). This is consistent with other data suggesting that boys have more to gain from friendships with girls than vice versa; having an intimate relationship with an opposite-sex peer is more strongly related to boys' general level of interpersonal intimacy than it is to girls' (Buhrmester & Furman, 1987). These findings are not surprising, given that adolescents' friendships with girls (regardless of whether they themselves are male or female) tend to be more intimate and supportive than friendships with boys (Kuttler et al., 1999).

▲ *The capacity for intimacy, which initially develops out of same-sex friendships, eventually is brought into opposite-sex relationships. Relationships between boyfriends and girlfriends more often than not are contexts in which intimacy is expressed rather than learned.* (Richard Hutchings/Photo Researchers)

RECAP

Although many adolescents have nonromantic friendships with opposite-sex peers, relatively little is known about the nature or significance of these relationships. What little research there is suggests that opposite-sex relationships help set the stage for the emergence of romantic relationships later on. In addition, there is some evidence that boys profit psychologically from opposite-sex friendships more than girls do.

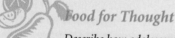

Food for Thought

Describe how adolescents' friendships with members of the opposite sex change with development. What is the link, if any, between opposite-sex friendships and romantic relationships?

DATING AND ROMANCE

Opposite-sex relationships during middle and late adolescence may play an important role in furthering the development of intimacy, although there are surprisingly few studies of how adolescents are affected by their boyfriends or girlfriends. Only recently have social scientists begun writing systematically about adolescents' romantic relationships, and most of what has been written is theoretical, rather than data-based (Furman et al., 1999).

Most starting points in discussions of adolescent romance begin with Sullivan's theory of interpersonal

development. As you may recall, Sullivan believed that establishing intimate relationships with peers of the opposite sex is the chief developmental task of middle and late adolescence. The capacity for intimacy, which initially develops out of same-sex friendships, eventually is brought into romantic relationships, which, for most adolescents, are with members of the opposite sex. In some senses, then, Sullivan viewed relationships between romantic partners as a context in which intimacy is *expressed* rather than learned.

This view may be more accurate for females than for males, however (Feiring, 1999a). In American society, boys are not encouraged to develop the capacity to be emotionally expressive, particularly in their relationships with other males. During middle adolescence, girls may be better than boys at certain types of intimacy—self-disclosure and interpersonal understanding, for example. Girls, therefore, are more likely than boys, on entering a relationship, to be capable of being intimate and eager for emotional closeness. Some studies of early sexual relationships confirm this idea: For adolescent girls more than boys, early sexual relationships are far more likely to involve love, emotional involvement, and intimacy (Shulman & Scharf, 2000).

For this reason, some writers have suggested that girls play an important role in teaching boys how to be more open, more sensitive, and more caring (Simon & Gagnon, 1969). In other words, whereas for girls cross-sex relationships may provide a context for further *expression* of intimacy, for boys they may provide a context for the further *development* of intimacy. This notion is consistent with the finding that opposite-sex relationships play a more important role in the development of intimacy among boys than among girls, who, on average, develop and experience intimacy earlier with same-sex friends than boys do (Buhrmester & Furman, 1987).

There is a big difference between the sort of learning that takes place in a long-term, intimate relationship between two people and the lessons that are learned through casual dating, however. Dating is a well-established social institution in American adolescent life. Today, the average adolescent begins dating around age 13, although nearly half of all adolescents have at least one date before they turn 12. By the age of 16, more than 90 percent of adolescents of both sexes have had at least one date, and, during the later years of high school, more than half of all students average one or more dates weekly. Only 15 percent of high school students date less than once a month (Feiring, 1993). By age 18, virtually all adolescents have dated once, and three-fourths have had a steady relationship (Neemann, Hubbard, & Masten, 1995).

Although early maturers begin dating somewhat earlier than late maturers (Neemann et al., 1995), age norms within the adolescents' school are more important in determining the age at which dating begins than is the adolescent's level of physical development. In other words, a physically immature 14-year-old who goes to school where it is expected that 14-year-olds date is more likely to date than is a physically mature 14-year-old who lives in a community where dating is typically delayed until 16 (Dornbusch et al., 1981). *Sexual* activity, however, as we will see in chapter 11, is more strongly influenced by biological development (Udry, Billy, Morris, Gruff, & Raj, 1985). Dating also begins earlier among adolescents who have older siblings, as well as among those with single mothers, especially if their mother is sexually active herself (Neeman et al., 1995).

"Dating" can mean a variety of things, of course, from group activities that bring males and females together (without much actual contact between the sexes) to group dates, in which a group of boys and girls go out jointly (and spend part of the time in couples and

part of the time in large groups) to casual dating in couples to serious involvement with a steady boyfriend or girlfriend. Generally speaking, casual socializing with opposite-sex peers and experiences in a mixed-sex social network generally occur before the development of romantic relationships (Connolly & Goldberg, 1999). As a consequence, more adolescents have experience in mixed-sex group activities, such as parties and dances, than in dating, and more have experience in dating than in having a serious boyfriend or girlfriend (Tobin-Richards, 1985).

Dating serves many purposes in adolescence, only one of which is the development of intimacy. Indeed, it is not until late adolescence that dating relationships begin to be characterized by a level of emotional depth and maturity that can be described as intimate, and it is not until late adolescence that individuals develop genuinely deep attachments to individuals other than their parents (Douvan & Adelson, 1966; Furman & Simon, 1999; Hazan, 1994). Over the course of adolescence, the importance of one's romantic partner—relative to other relationships—increases, and, by college, individuals typically name their romantic partner first on a list of significant others (up from fourth in grade 7 and third in grade 10) (Buhrmester, 1996; Furman & Wehner, 1994).

Prior to middle or late adolescence, therefore, dating may be less important for the development of intimacy than it is for other purposes, including establishing emotional and behavioral autonomy from parents (Dowdy & Kliewer, 1998; Gray & Steinberg, 1999), furthering the development of gender identity (Feiring, 1999a), learning about oneself as a romantic partner (Furman & Simon, 1999), and establishing and maintaining status and popularity in the peer group (Brown, 1999). For these reasons, adolescents' choices of dating partners may have more to do with how they will be seen by others (e.g., "grown up," "macho," "popular") than with the actual quality of the relationship.

The development of intimacy and more sophisticated social cognitive abilities is paralleled by changes in the ways adolescents think about, and behave within, romantic relationships. The evolution of romance in the adolescent's life proceeds through four phases (Brown, 1999; Connolly & Goldberg, 1999). During the *infatuation* phase, adolescents first discover an interest in socializing with potential romantic and sexual partners. The focus of activity during this phase is primarily on learning about oneself, as adolescents broaden their self-conceptions to include seeing themselves as a potential romantic partner for someone else. Actual romantic relationships tend to be short-lived and frequently based on superficial infatuations. During the *status* phase, the main purpose of romantic activity involves "establishing, improving, or maintaining peer group status. Dating the 'wrong' person or conducting romantic relationships in the 'wrong' way can seriously damage one's standing in the group. . . . This makes it difficult to sustain relationships that are too heavily focused inward, on the quality of the interaction or needs of the couple" (Brown, 1999, p. 297). During the *intimate* phase, adolescents begin to establish true and meaningful attachments to romantic partners. Although adolescents are still learning about themselves as romantic and sexual partners and are still aware of the way that their peers view their romantic relationships, they are now sufficiently involved in the emotional side of romance for this to overshadow the personal and status concerns that dominated the earlier phases of romantic involvement. Relationships become a source of passion and preoccupation—recalling the themes expressed in popular love songs that appeal to teenagers. Finally, during the *bonding* phase, concerns about commitment begin to move to the forefront, as adolescents begin to think about the long-term survival and growth of their romantic attachments. It is not so much that adolescents in this phase are contemplating marriage—in contemporary society, this typically does not occur until individuals are in their mid- or late twenties. However, as conceptions of romance develop, adolescents come to value commitment and caring as features of relationships that are as, if not more, important than passion and pleasure (Brown, 1999).

There is a similar developmental progression in what adolescents look for in a romantic partner, although there are important sex differences in this area. During middle adolescence, boys are more likely to mention physical attractiveness, and girls are more likely to mention interpersonal qualities, such as support or intimacy. By late adolescence, however, both sexes emphasize interpersonal qualities, and the ingredients of a satisfying relationship are very similar for males and females (and quite similar to those mentioned by adults): passion, communication, commitment, emotional support, and togetherness (Connolly et al., 1999; Feiring, 1996; Levesque, 1993). Interestingly, adolescents' satisfaction with their romantic relationships is not as negatively affected by such qualities as conflict or possessiveness as is the case among adults (Levesque, 1993).

There is some evidence that, especially for girls, it may be important to differentiate between group versus couple activities in examining the impact of dating on adolescents' psychological development. Participating in mixed-sex activity in group situations—going to parties or dances, for example—may have a positive impact on the psychological well-being of young adolescent girls, whereas serious dating in couples may have a more negative effect (Tobin-Richards, 1985). The reasons for this are not entirely clear, but researchers believe that pressures on girls to engage in sexual activity when they are out alone on dates or involved with a steady boyfriend likely have a negative impact on their mental health (Simmons & Blyth, 1987), and studies show that sexual coercion is common during the high school years (McMaster, Connolly, & Craig, 1997; Patton & Mannison, 1995). Although boys may feel peer pressure to become sexually active, this may be a very different sort of pressure—with very different consequences—from what girls feel. Because boys generally begin dating at a later age than girls—and date people who are younger, rather than older—beginning to date in couples may be less anxiety provoking for boys, who have the advantage of a few additional years of "maturity."

Given the generally high level of superficiality operating in most adolescents' dating relationships, it comes as no surprise that early and intensive dating—for example, becoming seriously involved before age 15—has a somewhat stunting effect on psychosocial development (Neemann et al., 1995). This is probably true for both sexes, but researchers have focused primarily on girls, because boys are less likely to begin serious dating quite so early. Compared with their peers, girls who begin serious dating early are less mature socially, less imaginative, less oriented toward achievement, less happy with who they are, and more superficial (Douvan & Adelson, 1966; McDonald & McKinney, 1994; Neemann et al., 1995). (Interestingly, in one study, the most frequently mentioned negative aspect of romantic relationships was "too much commitment" [Feiring, 1996].) In addition, adolescents of different ages date for different reasons—younger adolescents are more likely than older ones to date because it enhances their own status (Roscoe, Dian, & Brooks, 1987).

This is not to say that dating is not a valuable interpersonal experience for the adolescent, only that dating may have different effects in early adolescence than in middle and late adolescence (Neemann et al., 1995). Although early involvement in serious romance has its costs, adolescent girls who do not date at all show signs of retarded social development, excessive dependency on their parents, and feelings of insecurity (Douvan & Adelson, 1966), and adolescents who date and go to parties regularly are more popular, have a stronger self-image, and report greater acceptance by their friends (Connolly & Johnson, 1993; Long, 1989; Tobin-Richards, 1985). It is not clear, of course, whether a moderate degree of dating leads to higher levels of social development or whether more socially advanced and confident adolescents are simply more likely to date and go to parties. Nonetheless, it does seem that for girls, in particular, early and intensive involvement with a boyfriend may do more harm than good. All in all, a moderate degree of dating—and delaying serious involvement until middle adolescence—appears to be the most potentially valuable pattern. Perhaps adolescents need more time to develop the capacity to be intimate through same-sex friendships and less pressured group activities before they enter intensively into the more highly ritualized and not very intimate relationships that are encouraged through dating.

Regardless of the impact that dating does or does not have on the adolescent's psychosocial development, studies show that romance has a powerful impact on the adolescent's emotional state. According to several studies, adolescents' real and fantasized relationships trigger more of their strong emotional feelings during the course of a day (one-third of girls' strong feelings and one-quarter of boys') than do family, school, or friends. Not surprisingly, the proportion of strong emotions attributed to romantic relationships increases dramatically between preadolescence and early adolescence, as well as between early and middle adolescence. And, although most adolescents' feelings about their romantic relationships are positive, a substantial minority of their feelings—more than 40 percent, in fact—are negative, involving feelings of anxiety, anger, jealousy, and depression (Larson, Clore, & Wood, 1999).

Adolescents behave in a variety of ways within dating relationships, and these patterns of behavior are shaped by "scripts" for how males and females are expected to behave—scripts that are learned at home and from the mass media (Feiring, 1999; Gray & Steinberg, 1999; Larson, Clore, & Wood, 1999). One study, for example, looked at the relationship among the type of conflict behavior that adolescents saw their parents engage in, the level of conflict they experienced with their parents, and the type of conflict behavior the adolescents engaged in with their dating partners (Martin, 1990). In general, the adolescents' ways of dealing with conflict in their romantic relationships were linked to the models they

had been exposed to at home, especially among daughters. For example, the girls who had witnessed a great deal of conflict between their parents reported higher levels of verbal aggression, physical aggression, and relationship difficulties with their boyfriends. This study, along with those of adolescent attachment, suggest that variations in adolescents' romantic relationships have their origins—at least in part—in the adolescents' family experiences. Indeed, at least some research indicates that individuals' early experiences in the family, in interaction with their cumulative experiences with peers during childhood and preadolescence, affect the nature and quality of their romantic relationships in adolescence (Collins & Sroufe, 1999).

Although the progression through the infatuation, status, intimate, and bonding phases of dating and romance may characterize the development of most adolescents, a number of writers interested in the experiences of gay, lesbian, and bisexual adolescents have pointed out that this picture may be less applicable to **sexual-minority youth**—adolescents who are not exclusively heterosexual (Diamond, Savin-Williams, & Dubé, 1999). Although great strides have been made in increasing the public's tolerance and understanding of homosexuality, stigmas and stereotypes still make the development of intimate relationships—whether nonsexual friendships, dating relationships, or sexual relationships—a far more complicated matter among sexual-minority youth than among their heterosexual peers. For example, because few sexual-minority youth have the freedom to express publicly their romantic and sexual interests in members of the same sex, they often find it difficult, if not impossible, to engage in many of the social and interpersonal activities that their heterosexual friends are permitted to enjoy. Thus, many sexual-minority youth end up pursuing sexual activity *outside* the context of a dating relationship, because the prejudices and harassment of others may preclude any public display of romantic intimacy with a same-sex partner. At the same time, for sexual-minority youth who are even somewhat open about their sexual identity, the development of close, nonsexual friendships with same-sex peers may be hampered by the suspicions and homophobia of others. As one group of writers explain the special predicament faced by sexual-minority adolescents, "A sexual-minority adolescent may already be privately plagued by the sense that he or she is profoundly different from other youths. To have this differentness acknowledged and perhaps ridiculed by peers may prove intolerable" (Diamond et al., 1999).

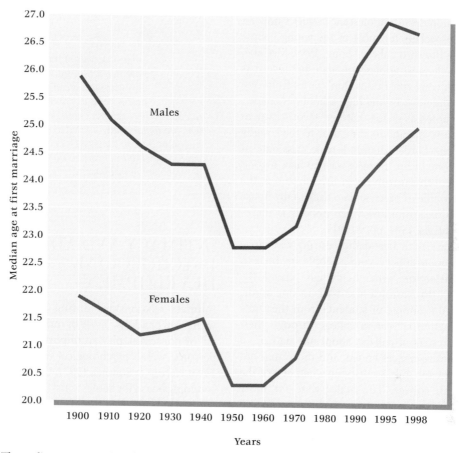

Figure 10.6   The median age at marriage declined from 1900 through the mid-1950s but increased markedly during the second half of the twentieth century.

Dating plays a very different role in adolescents' lives today than it did in previous times (Gordon & Miller, 1984). In earlier eras, dating during adolescence was not so much a recreational activity (as it is today) as it was a part of the process of courtship and mate selection. Individuals dated in order to ready themselves for marriage, and unmarried individuals played the field—under the watchful eyes of chaperones—for a relatively long period before settling down (Montgomery, 1996). You may be surprised to learn that, at the turn of the twentieth century, most individuals did not marry until their midtwenties (Modell & Goodman, 1990). The first half of that century saw a gradual decline in the age of marriage, however; as a result, individuals began dating more seriously at an earlier age (see figure 10.6). By the mid-1950s, the average age at first marriage in the United States had fallen to 20 among women and 22 among men—which means that substantial numbers of individ-

uals were marrying during their late adolescent years and courting during high school.

The function of dating changed, however, in the mid-1950s, as individuals began to marry later and later—a trend that continues today. Now, the average age at which people marry is considerably later than it was 45 years ago—about 25 for women and 27 for men (U.S. Bureau of the Census, 1999b). This, of course, gives high school dating a whole new meaning, since it is clearly divorced from its function in mate selection. Adults continue to regulate and monitor adolescent dating, in order to prevent rash or impulsive commitments to early marriage (Laursen & Jensen-Campbell, 1999), but it is clear that, in the minds of most young people, high school dating has little to do with courtship or marriage.

One sign of this change in the function of dating is that, over the past two decades, dating appears to have become more informal, less competitive, and less rigidly structured by traditional sex-role stereotypes

(Miller & Gordon, 1986). Adolescent dating is now an end in itself, especially for most of the young people who are headed toward college (Long, 1989; McCabe, 1984). All in all, most adolescents date because it is fun—although what constitutes "fun" varies from one adolescent to the next: In one high school newspaper, one girl was quoted as saying that her "favorite way to have a good time is going to church or to Bible study and praising the Lord," whereas a male classmate of hers said that one of his "favorite ways to have a good time is to go out to eat with my girlfriend, stop at the store to get a couple of beers, and go back to my house to make sweet, beautiful love when nobody is there" (*Glenbard East Echo,* 1984, pp. 90–91).

As is the case with friendships during the move from high school to college, young people are likely to report dissatisfaction with their high school romances during this transition as well. In one study, which followed a sample of students from the summer before their first year in college through their first three semesters of college, about one-half of all the high school romances ended, and those that did not end became much less satisfying when one of the partners began college. The males were far more likely than the females to report feeling lonely and dissatisfied with their older relationships (Shaver, Furman, & Buhrmester, 1985).

RECAP

Despite the fact that almost all adolescents date by the time they are 16, far less is known about the nature and consequences of romantic relationships during adolescence than about adolescent friendships. Because the age at which individuals marry has become considerably later over the past half-century, dating during adolescence has lost its significance for courtship. In general, social activities with the opposite sex begin in early adolescence as group activities that bring males and females together, proceed to casual dating in couples, and, later in adolescence, progress to serious involvement with a steady romantic partner. Paralleling these changes in the context of dating are changes in the nature and function of dating. As adolescents develop, dating shifts from being oriented around affiliation, to status, intimacy, and finally bonding. Although early intense dating may have adverse effects on adolescents' mental health and behavior, a moderate degree of dating, without any serious involvement until late in adolescence, is associated with better mental health and well-being than no dating at all.

Food for Thought

Some observers of the adolescent scene have noted that traditional, one-on-one dating is far less common today than in past generations and that relatively more interaction between males and females, even those who are romantically interested in each other, occurs in groups than in couples. Does this sound correct to you? If so, what implications does it have for the development of intimacy?

INTIMACY AND ADOLESCENT PSYCHOSOCIAL DEVELOPMENT

Intimate relationships during adolescence, whether with peers or adults, inside or outside the family, or sexual or nonsexual, play an important role in the young person's overall psychological development (Hartup, 1993; Hartup & Stevens, 1997). Close friends serve as a sounding board for adolescents' fantasies and questions about the future. Adolescents often talk to their friends about the careers they hope to follow, the people they hope to get involved with, and the life they expect to lead after they leave home. Friends provide advice on a range of identity-related matters—from how to act in various situations to what sorts of occupational and educational paths to pursue. At least one study finds that having an intimate friendship is more central to adolescents' mental health than it is to children's (Buhrmester, 1990). It also has been found that intimacy with same-sex friends and intimacy with romantic partners make distinct contributions to adolescents' self-esteem (Connolly & Konarski, 1994). Not surprisingly, adolescents who report having at least one close friendship report higher levels of self-esteem than their peers who do not, although it is not known whether intimacy enhances mental health, mental health facilitates intimacy, or most likely both (Savin-Williams & Berndt, 1990).

These positive aspects of close relationships notwithstanding, it is important to recognize that intimate relationships can have negative as well as beneficial effects on the young person's development. According to one theorist, frequent conversations with friends about personal problems and difficulties may lead to too much introspection and self-consciousness in the young person (Mechanic, 1983). Adolescent friendships may be beneficial precisely because they are not like those envisioned by Sullivan, but because they involve young people in exciting activities that distract them from being preoccupied with themselves (Savin-Williams & Berndt, 1990).

We should also keep in mind that the effects of having an intimate friendship with someone depend on who that someone is and what takes place in the relationship; being popular is less important than genuinely having friends, and having friends is less important than having *good friendships* (Asher, Parker, & Walker, 1996; Berndt, 1996; Hartup & Stevens, 1997; Keefe & Berndt, 1996). Not all friendships are consistently good friendships, however; friendships often provide positive things such as self-disclosure, intimacy, and companionship, but they also may give rise to insecurity, conflict, jealousy, and mistrust (Rubin, 1980). And, as we saw in chapter 5, adolescents who are intimate with peers who have antisocial values or habits are themselves more likely to develop similar patterns of behavior. It is easy to forget, but it goes without saying, that not all close relationships foster positive developmental outcomes.

Nevertheless, studies consistently show that individuals with satisfying close friendships fare better than those without them, not only in adolescence, but in adulthood as well. Adolescence is an especially important time in the development of close relationships because many of the capacities and capabilities that permit intimacy in adult relationships make their first appearance in adolescence.

RECAP

Adolescents who have intimate friendships typically have better mental health than peers who do not. It is not known which comes first, however—intimacy or psychological health. Although it seems likely that intimacy, and the social support it provides, enhances adolescents' well-being, it is also likely that psychologically healthy adolescents are better able to make and maintain close relationships with others. Nonetheless, experts agree that close peer relationships are an essential part of healthy social development during adolescence.

Food for Thought

Discuss the ways in which friends both enhance and harm adolescents' mental health. Which is more important to adolescent mental health, having many friends (e.g., being popular) or having a close friend? In your opinion, is this the case?

Web Researcher Intimacy and autonomy are both important adolescent needs. But they sound as if they are antithetical to one another. Examine several websites that give adolescents advice about handling close personal relationships. How do these two themes play themselves out in this context? Is the same advice given to boys as to girls? About same-sex and opposite-sex relationships? Go to www.mhhe.com/steinberg6 for further information.

KEY TERMS

Adult Attachment Interview

anxious-avoidant attachment

anxious-resistant attachment

attachment

homophobia

internal working model

intimacy versus isolation

need for integration into adult society

need for intimacy

need for intimacy with a peer of the opposite sex

need for sexual contact

Q-Sort

secure attachment

sexual-minority youth

social support

Chapter 11

Sexuality

Have teenagers' attitudes toward sex changed in recent decades? Should society be worried about sexual activity among young adolescents, or is teenage sex no more troublesome than many of the other adultlike activities that young people engage in? Does sex education prevent unwanted pregnancies, or does it encourage young people to begin sexual activity earlier? Should adolescents have access to contraceptives, and, if so, should their parents be told? Have adolescents changed their sexual behavior in response to the threat of AIDS?

In this chapter, we will examine adolescent sexuality in contemporary society with an eye toward dedramatizing and demystifying an aspect of adolescent behavior that has received a great deal more media attention than systematic research investigation. In order to present a more accurate picture of adolescent sexuality, we will need to step back and look at sexual behavior and development during adolescence in context—in the context of society and how it has changed and in the context of adolescence as a period in the life cycle and how it has changed. •

SEXUALITY AS AN ADOLESCENT ISSUE

Like other aspects of psychosocial development, sexuality is not an entirely new issue that surfaces for the first time during adolescence. Young children are curious about their sex organs and at a very early age derive pleasure (if not what adults would label orgasm) from genital stimulation—as both Sigmund Freud and famous sex researcher Alfred Kinsey pointed out long ago (Kinsey, Pomeroy, & Martin, 1948). And, of course, sexual activity and sexual development continue long after adolescence. Although sexual development may be more dramatic and more obvious before adulthood, it by no means ceases at the end of adolescence.

Nonetheless, most of us would agree that adolescence is a fundamentally important time—if not the most important time in the life cycle—for the development of sexuality. There are several reasons for this. Perhaps most obvious is the link between adolescent sexuality and puberty. There is an increase in the sex drive in early adolescence as a result of hormonal changes (Udry, 1987). Moreover, it is not until puberty that individuals become capable of sexual reproduction. Before puberty, children are certainly capable of kissing, petting, masturbating, and even having sexual intercourse. But it is not until pu-

berty that males can ejaculate semen and females begin to ovulate, and the fact that pregnancy is a possible outcome of sexual activity changes the nature and meaning of sexual behavior markedly—for the adolescent and for others. What had previously been innocuous sex play becomes serious business when pregnancy is a genuine possibility. Finally, as we saw in chapter 1, not until puberty do individuals develop the secondary sex characteristics that serve as a basis for sexual attraction and as dramatic indicators that the young person is no longer physically a child.

However, the increased importance of sexuality at adolescence is not solely a result of puberty. The cognitive changes of adolescence play a part in the changed nature of sexuality as well. One obvious difference between the sexual play of children and the sexual activity of adolescents is that children are not especially introspective or reflective about sexual behavior. Sex during adolescence is the subject of sometimes painful conjecture ("Will she or won't she?"), decision making ("Should I or shouldn't I?"), hypothetical thinking ("What if he wants to do it tonight?"), and self-conscious concern ("Am I good-looking enough?"). As we saw in chapter 10, one of the chief tasks of adolescence is to figure out how to deal with sexual desires and how to incorporate sex successfully and appropriately into social relationships. Much of this task is cognitive, and much of it is made possible by the expansion of intellectual abilities that takes place during the period.

In addition to how the physical changes of puberty and the growth of sophisticated thinking capabilities influence sexuality during adolescence, the new social meaning given to sexual and dating behavior at this time in the life cycle makes sexuality an especially important psychosocial concern. The main influences on adolescents' sexual behavior are social, not biological.

You may have played "doctor" with your friends when you were a little child, but—as you well know—the game meant something quite different then from what it would if you were to play it now. Although younger children may engage in sex play, and although even infants may experience sexual arousal, it is not until adolescence that sexual activity begins to take on the social meaning it will continue to have throughout adulthood. With all due respect to Freud and Kinsey, one must place the sex play of children in proper perspective. Indeed, Sullivan (1953b), whom you read about in chapter 10, believed that sex play before adolescence has more to do with simple curiosity than with true sexuality. Adolescence is a turning point in the

▲ *Although sexuality is undoubtedly an important psychosocial issue during adolescence, sexual concerns do not surface for the first time at this stage in the life span. It is normal for children to be curious about sex and about their sex organs at an early age.* (Fredrick D. Bodin/Stock, Boston)

development of sexuality because it marks the onset of deliberate, sexually motivated behavior that is recognized, both by oneself and by others, as primarily and explicitly sexual.

According to two experts, there are four distinct developmental challenges concerning sexuality in adolescence (Brooks-Gunn & Paikoff, 1993). First, the adolescent needs to feel comfortable with his or her maturing body—its shape, size, and attractiveness. Second, the individual should accept having feelings of sexual arousal as normal and appropriate. Third, healthy sexual development in adolescence involves feeling comfortable about choosing to engage in—or choosing not to engage in—various sexual activities; that is, healthy sexual development involves understanding that sex is a voluntary activity for onself and for one's partner. Fi-

nally, healthy sexual development, at least for those who are sexually active, includes understanding and practicing safe sex—sex that avoids pregnancy and sexually transmitted infections.

RECAP

Adolescence is a fundamentally important time in the life cycle for the development of sexuality, reflecting the physical and hormonal changes of puberty, the increased capacity for the individual to understand and think about sexual feelings, and the new social meaning given to sexual behavior by society and its institutions. Four developmental challenges of adolescence are accepting one's changing body, accepting one's feelings of sexual arousal, understanding that sexual activity is voluntary, and practicing safe sex.

Food for Thought

What role, if any, should school-based sex education play in the promotion of healthy sexuality?

HOW SEXUALLY PERMISSIVE IS CONTEMPORARY SOCIETY?

It is impossible to understand sexuality as a psychosocial phenomenon without taking into account the social milieu in which adolescents learn about and first experience sexuality. Although we tend to think of sex as something that adolescents are inevitably anxious or concerned about, it is no more true to suggest that sexuality is always riddled with problems during adolescence than it is to say that all adolescents have problems in establishing a sense of identity or in developing a sense of autonomy. Like any other aspect of psychosocial growth, the development of sexuality is determined largely by its context. Of particular importance is the way in which adolescents and children are exposed to and educated about sexuality—a process called **sexual socialization.**

When did you first learn about sex? How much were you exposed to as a child? Was it something that was treated casually around your house or something that had an air of mystery to it? Was your transition into adult sexual activity gradual or abrupt?

The passage of adolescents into adulthood is believed to be easier and less stressful when transitions between the two eras are gradual, or continuous (Benedict, 1934). One aspect of the adolescent passage that anthropologists have examined extensively from this perspective is the transition of young people into adult sexual roles. In *Patterns of Culture* (1934), Ruth Benedict observed that anxiety about sex—which was thought to be common among teenagers in contemporary society—was absent in many traditional cultures. Margaret Mead's (1928/1978) observations of young people in Samoa and New Guinea provided evidence that sexual development during adolescence is calm, not stressful, in societies where sexual experimentation is treated openly and casually during childhood and where special attention is not drawn to the adolescent's changed sexual status.

Think about some of the things you learned gradually and casually as a child—learning your way around the kitchen, for example—and imagine how different things would have been had this learning been handled the way most families handle sexual socialization. Suppose that early in your childhood your parents had treated cooking food as though the activity had special, mysterious significance. Suppose that you had never been permitted to see anyone actually cooking food, that you had been prohibited from seeing movies in which people cooked food, and that you had been ex-

cluded from any discussions of cooking. Nevertheless, imagine that you knew that *something* went on in the kitchen and that there was a special activity that adults did there that you would be permitted, even expected, to do when you grew up. Perhaps you even overheard other kids at school talking about cooking, but you still weren't sure just what the activity was or what one was supposed to do (or not do). Imagine how confused, ambivalent, and anxious you would feel. In some respects, this is how many families in contemporary society handle sexual socialization. By being so secretive about sex when children are young and so worried about it when they are adolescents, Mead and Benedict argued, contemporary societies may have turned sexuality into a problem for young people.

Mead's and Benedict's observations of sexual socialization in traditional societies also indicated that cultures vary considerably in the ways in which they handle the sexual development of children and adolescents. Their observations were further borne out in *Patterns of Sexual Behavior* (Ford & Beach, 1951), perhaps the most extensive study to date of sexual behavior in different cultural contexts. In this enormous undertaking, the authors catalogued the sexual socialization and activity of children and adolescents in more than 200 societies. Drawing on hundreds of studies undertaken by cultural anthropologists over the years, Ford and Beach categorized societies into three groups: restrictive societies, semirestrictive societies, and permissive societies.

Sexual Socialization in Restrictive Societies

In **restrictive societies,** the adolescent's transition into adult sexual activity is highly discontinuous. Pressure is exerted on youngsters to refrain from sexual activity until they either have undergone a formal rite of passage or have married. In many restrictive societies, adolescents pursue sex in secrecy. Within the broad category of restrictive societies, of course, are wide variations in the degree of restrictiveness and in the methods used to discourage sexual activity before marriage. For example, in some societies, the

▲ *In restrictive societies, sexual activity before marriage is explicitly discouraged.*
(Nickelsberg/Gamma-Liaison)

sexual activity of young people is controlled by separating the sexes throughout childhood and adolescence. Boys and girls are not permitted to play together and never associate with each other in the absence of chaperons before marriage. In other societies, sexual activity before the attainment of adult status is restricted through the physical punishment and public shaming of sexually active youngsters (Ford & Beach, 1951).

Sexual Socialization in Semirestrictive Societies

In **semirestrictive societies,** "adult attitudes toward . . . premarital affairs in adolescents are characterized by formal prohibitions that are . . . not very serious and in fact are not enforced" (Ford & Beach, 1951, p. 187). For example, sexual activity among youngsters may be formally prohibited, but children playing together may imitate the sexual behavior of their elders, and, unless this play is brought explicitly to the attention of adults, little is done about it. In other semirestrictive societies, "premarital promiscuity is common, and the parents do not object as long as the love affairs are kept secret" (Ford & Beach, 1951, p. 187). It is premarital pregnancy, rather than premarital sex, that is objectionable, and unmarried adolescents whose sexual activity has resulted in pregnancy are often forced to marry.

We are frequently told that contemporary America is excessively permissive when it comes to sex; however, by world standards, the sexual socialization of children and adolescents in the United States and other industrialized societies generally has followed either a restrictive or a semirestrictive pattern, depending on the historical period and social group in question. At the time of the publication of *Patterns of Sexual Behavior* more than five decades ago, Ford and Beach classified the United States as restrictive. And some (although clearly a minority) would argue that this classification is still valid today. For the most part, for example, American children are likely to be discouraged from—or even punished for—masturbation, sexual exploration is frowned on, and sex play is discouraged. Adults rarely mention sexual matters in the presence of children, and there are regulations prohibiting children from being exposed to sexual activity on television or in the movies. Adults openly try to discourage young people—especially young women—from becoming sexually active by lecturing to them about the virtues of virginity, by not openly discussing matters of sex and pregnancy, and by making it difficult for young people to obtain contraception.

At the same time, however, some aspects of sexual socialization place contemporary America more in the semirestrictive category. Adolescent boys and girls are not typically segregated, boys and girls usually date without chaperons present, and premarital sex is not generally punished with public humiliation. Adolescents are encouraged to date, even though adults know that dating provides a context for sexual activity. And it does seem at times as though we attempt only halfheartedly to enforce prohibitions against premarital sexual activity. Many parents are well aware that young people are sexually active, and they prefer to look the other way, rather than restrict children's activities.

Sexual Socialization in Permissive Societies

In **permissive societies,** the transition of young people into adult sexual activity is highly continuous and usually begins in childhood. Whether contemporary America is restrictive or semirestrictive may be subject to debate, and religious conservatives may bemoan the lack of morals among the young, but by no stretch of the imagination is the United States a sexually permissive society—at least in comparison with many of the cultures described by Ford and Beach. Consider, for example, the following descriptions of sexual socialization in some of the societies they categorized as permissive:

> Among the Pukapukans of Polynesia, where parents simply ignore the sexual activities of young children, boys and girls masturbate freely and openly in public.
>
> Lesu children playing on the beach give imitations of adult sexual intercourse, and adults in this society regard this to be a natural and normal game.
>
> Young Trobriand children engage in a variety of sexual activities. In the absence of adult control, typical forms of amusement for Trobriand girls and boys include manual and oral stimulation of the genitals and simulated coitus. Sexual life begins in earnest among the Trobrianders at six to eight years for girls, ten to twelve for boys. Both sexes receive explicit instruction from older companions whom they imitate in sex activities. . . . At any time a couple may retire to the bush, the bachelor's hut, an isolated yam house, or any other convenient place and there engage in prolonged sexual play with full approval of their parents. (Ford & Beach, 1951, pp. 188–191)

SEXUAL ATTITUDES AMONG ADOLESCENTS

Most social scientists agree that American adolescents' attitudes toward sex—and toward premarital sex in particular—became more liberal during the late 1960s and 1970s and have become only slightly more conservative since then (Chilman, 1986; UCLA Higher Education Research Institute, 1999, 2000). But the meaning of this change in attitudes is often misunderstood. Three points must be kept in mind. First, although it is certainly true that teenagers became more tolerant of sexual relations before marriage, it is also true that adults themselves became more permissive of premarital sex during the same time period (Clayton & Bokemeier, 1980). In other words, during the 1960s and 1970s, American society as a whole—not simply young people—changed its views toward sex.

Second, the changes in attitudes toward premarital sex among adolescents during the late 1960s and early 1970s, and the trend toward greater conservatism during the 1980s and 1990s, cannot be understood apart from many other attitudinal changes that took place during these decades. Although attitudes toward premarital sex changed, many other attitudes also shifted (for example, attitudes toward racial equality, women's rights, and abortion). Trends in sexual attitudes are best understood as a part of a larger attitudinal shift. Not surprisingly, therefore, there are substantial cross-cultural differences in adolescents' attitudes toward sex, even among industrialized societies; one study found, for example, that American college students are more accepting of premarital sex than their Russian or Japanese counterparts (Sprecher & Hatfield, 1996).

Third, although adolescents became more permissive of premarital intercourse, they did not become proponents of promiscuity, "free love," or casual sex (Alan Guttmacher Institute, 1994). Being emotionally involved, rather than being legally married, became the important criterion for judging the acceptability of sexual involvement. It is important to keep in mind, however, that adolescents as a group are as varied in their attitudes toward sex as adults are (Katchadourian, 1990).

Although young people have become more permissive over the past three decades, adolescents clearly do not favor sexual promiscuity or sexual exploitation. Surveys indicate that most American and European adolescents believe that openness, honesty, and fidelity are important elements of a sexual relationship (Alan Guttmacher Insti-

tute, 1994; Arnett, in press). Although an adolescent may have a series of sexual partners over a period of time, he or she is likely to be monogamous within each relationship, a pattern known as **serial monogamy.**

Another important trend in young people's changing attitudes toward sex has been the decline in popularity of the double standard. In past eras, many people believed that premarital sex is permissible for men but not for women. But most adolescents believe that males and females should follow the same standards for premarital sexual behavior (Ferrell, Tolone, & Walsh, 1977; King, Balswick, & Robinson, 1977). This shift toward a single standard of sexual conduct, which began during the late 1960s and accelerated during the early 1970s, was related, no doubt, to other large-scale attitudinal shifts in matters related to women's rights and sexual equality. Although the double standard has waned, it has not disappeared: Aggressive sexual behavior is still more accepted among adolescent males than females, especially in the context of early sexual activity (Goodchilds & Zellman, 1984; Sprecher & Hatfield, 1996).

It appears, then, that what has taken place—not only in sexual values and attitudes but across a range of topics—has been a shift away from conformity to institutionalized norms and toward a perspective that places greater emphasis on the individual's personal judgment and values (Conger, 1975). Television sitcoms and parents' concerns to the contrary, today's adolescents are neither preoccupied with sex nor anxious about it. Indeed, being sexually active during adolescence—and being comfortable about it—has become part of the normal adolescent experience.

RECAP

Although many people think of contemporary industrialized society as being sexually permissive, there are plenty of societies around the world that are far more lenient about sex. By most indications, Americans' attitudes toward adolescent sex are neither restrictive nor permissive—but semirestrictive. Important changes in attitudes toward adolescent premarital sex occurred during the 1960s and 1970s and have continued since that time. Most teenagers today believe that it is acceptable to have intercourse before marriage as long as it takes place within the context of a loving, intimate relationship. Another important trend in young people's changing attitudes toward sex has been the decline in acceptance of the double standard.

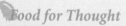

Food for Thought

Provide some illustrations of the differences between sexual socialization in restrictive, semirestrictive, and permissive societies. In light of what you've read, how would you characterize the context in which you grew up?

TRENDS IN SEXUAL ACTIVITY DURING ADOLESCENCE

Because of the controversies surrounding premarital intercourse, most of the research conducted into the sexual behavior of adolescents has focused on this single activity. Although this is undoubtedly an important topic of concern, it is also wise to remember that a good deal of the sexual activity of adolescents—even sexually experienced adolescents—involves activities other than sexual intercourse, such as making out or "hooking up." Moreover, because most individuals do not begin their sexual experiences with intercourse but progress toward it through stages of gradually increasing intimacy, it is important to view intercourse as one activity in a long progression, rather than as an isolated behavior (Brooks-Gunn & Paikoff, 1993).

The Stages of Sexual Activity

Most adolescents' first experience with sex falls into the category of **autoerotic behavior**—sexual behavior that is experienced alone (Katchadourian, 1990). The most common autoerotic activities reported by adolescents are having erotic fantasies (about three-quarters of all teenagers report having sexual fantasies, mainly about television figures or movie stars) and masturbation (reported by about half of all adolescent boys and one-fourth of all adolescent girls) (Koch, 1993). In addition, many boys have wet dreams, or nocturnal orgasms, during adolescence, although they generally are infrequent (Katchadourian, 1990).

By the time most adolescents have reached high school, they have "crossed the line from autoerotic to sociosexual behaviors" (Katchadourian, 1990, p. 335). **Sociosexual behaviors** are those involving another person. Interestingly, the developmental progression of sexual behaviors, from less intimate to more intimate, has not changed very much over the past 40 years, and the se-

quence in which males and females engage in various sexual activities is remarkably similar. Kissing and touching above the waist occur earlier than genital touching through clothing, which occurs before direct genital contact, which in turn occurs earlier than intercourse or oral sex (Rosenthal & Smith, 1997). There is some evidence that teenagers are engaging in oral sex at an earlier age today than in the past, and among adolescents oral sex is actually more common than intercourse (Newcomer & Udry, 1985). Although boys engage in these activities at a somewhat earlier age than girls, the similarities in age of first experience and in prevalence are far more striking than the differences between genders. Studies also show that the timing and tempo of involvement in various sexual activities are comparable among adolescents with, and without, chronic disease or disability (Suris, Resnick, Cassuto, & Blum, 1996).

There is some evidence that the orderly progression of sexual activity is more common among white adolescents than among African Americans, however (Smith & Udry, 1985). White adolescents are likely to follow a more predictable pattern that includes more petting and takes longer to move toward intercourse. African Americans, in contrast, are more likely to move toward intercourse at an earlier age and without as many intervening steps (Brewster, 1994). This difference has an important implication for our understanding of adolescent pregnancy. Virtually all adolescents who are virgins find themselves unprepared for contraception when they begin making out, but the more gradual progression of sexual activity among whites is less likely to be affected by this lack of preparation than is the case among African Americans. A faster progression of sexual activity may place young African American adolescents at relatively greater risk for pregnancy. It is also the case that the expected timetable for progressive sexual activities is faster among adolescents who expect a relatively faster timetable for achieving autonomy from parents and experimenting with drugs and alcohol, suggesting that earlier involvement in sex may be part of a larger pattern of earlier involvement in "adult" activities (Rosenthal & Smith, 1997).

Premarital Intercourse During Adolescence

Estimates of the prevalence of premarital intercourse among contemporary adolescents vary considerably from study to study, depending on the nature of the sample surveyed, the year and region in which the study was

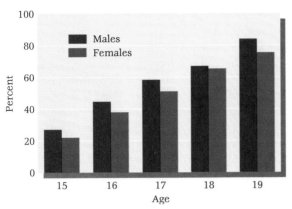

Figure 11.1   Percentages of sexually experienced American males and females in 1995, according to data from The National Survey of Family Growth and The National Survey of Adolescent Males.

undertaken, and the reliability of the data gathered. Some studies suggest that adolescents do not always report their sexual activity honestly or accurately, with males tending to overstate their level of activity and females tending to understate it (Alexander, Somerfield, Ensminger, Johnson, & Kim, 1993; Newcomer & Udry, 1988). Nevertheless, the following paragraphs summarize what social scientists have concluded from recent surveys.

Although regional and ethnic variations make it difficult—if not misleading—to generalize about the average age at which American adolescents initiate sexual intercourse, national surveys of young people indicate that far more adolescents are sexually active at an earlier age today than several decades ago, although there has been a slight decrease in the proportion of sexually experienced teenagers in the past few years (Singh & Darroch, 1999; Sonenstein, Ku, Lindberg, Turner, & Pleck, 1998). The best estimates are that, by age 15, about one-fourth of American adolescents have had heterosexual vaginal intercourse (these estimates, which are based on large national surveys, do not include same-sex intercourse or other types of sex, such as oral or anal sex). By age 18, the percentage of adolescents who have had intercourse has risen to about 67 percent (see figure 11.1) (Abma, Chandra, Mosher, Peterson, & Piccinino, 1997; Sonenstein et al., 1998). Whatever one feels about these figures, one conclusion is inescapable: Sexual intercourse during high school is now a part of the normative experience of adolescence in the United States.

There are substantial ethnic differences in age of sexual initiation, especially among males (Warren et al., 1998). Among African American males, the average age

of first intercourse is 15; among white and Hispanic males, it is 16.5; and, among Asian American males, it is 18 (Upchurch, Levy-Storms, Sucoff, & Aneshensel, 1998). Ethnic differences in the age of sexual initiation are far smaller among females, although Hispanic and Asian American females generally have their first sexual intercourse at a later age than is the case among their African American and white counterparts. One reason for the relatively high rate of early sexual activity of African American males is the higher proportion of African American youth who grow up in single-parent homes and in poor neighborhoods, both of which are correlated with early sexual activity (Brewster, 1994; Lauritsen, 1994). In general, Mexican American youngsters who were born in Mexico are less likely to be sexually active at an early age than are their counterparts who are American-born, reflecting differences in norms between the two countries (Aneshensel, Becerra, Fielder, & Schuler, 1990). Studies also indicate that, among all ethnic groups, rates of sexual activity are higher among economically disadvantaged youth, although the gap in rates of sexual activity between rich and poor is substantially narrower now than it was a decade ago, again pointing to the increasingly normative nature of sexual intercourse among American teenagers (Singh & Darroch, 1999). Interestingly, early sexual activity is more common among African American youth attending all-black schools than among their peers in integrated schools (Furstenberg, Morgan, & Allison, 1987), indicating the importance of the social context in which teenagers live as an influence on their sexual behavior. Adolescents in the United States initiate sex at a slightly younger age than do teenagers in other industrialized countries, as figure 11.2 indicates.

It is important to note that many girls' first sexual experience is not voluntary. This is especially frequent among girls who have sex for the first time when they are 13 or younger; one-fourth report that their first intercourse was against their will, in contrast to 10 percent of women whose first intercourse was after the age of 18. Moreover, many other young women who report that they had sex voluntarily the first time nevertheless report that they did not really want to have sex. Young girls whose first partner was seven or more years older were twice as likely as others to report having had voluntary but unwanted intercourse (Abma, Driscoll, & Moore, 1998).

According to national surveys, most high school students who have had sex at least once are sexually active on a regular basis (Singh & Darroch, 1999). This does

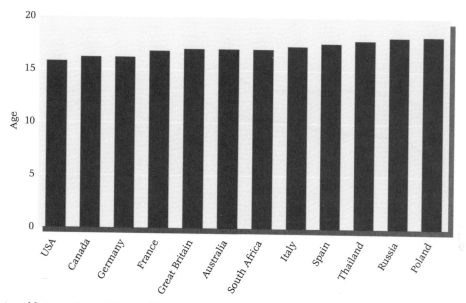

Figure 11.2   *Age of first experience with sexual intercourse, as of 1997.* (Stetsenko, in press)

not mean that they are promiscuous, however; most teenagers who have had intercourse have had only one sexual partner, about 20 percent have had four or more different partners, and about 10 percent have had sex with six or more partners (Miller & Moore, 1990; *Washington Post*, 1994). As with other aspects of sexual behavior, there are ethnic and gender variations in the number of sexual partners adolescents report having had: African American males are more than twice as likely as white males to have had six or more partners; African American females and white females are about equally likely to have had multiple partners, however (Miller & Moore, 1990).

Changes in Patterns of Adolescent Premarital Intercourse over Time

Attitudes toward premarital intercourse during adolescence became more liberal during the mid-1960s and became especially so during the early 1970s. Not surprisingly, accompanying this shift in attitudes was an equally noteworthy shift in the prevalence of adolescent premarital sex. The major changes have not been in behaviors such as making out but in the incidence and prevalence of intercourse among teenagers (Alan Guttmacher Institute, 1994). Presumably, teenagers have long distinguished between intercourse and other sexual activities in their values and

actions, and what has shifted during the past three decades has been their stance specifically toward intercourse.

Three trends are of special interest. First, as figure 11.3 indicates, the overall percentage of American adolescents who have engaged in premarital sex accelerated markedly during the early 1970s, stabilized somewhat during the early 1980s, increased again during the late 1980s, and stabilized throughout the 1990s (Alan Guttmacher Institute, 1994; Singh & Darroch, 1999; Sonenstein et al., 1998). For example, the proportion of high school youth who have had premarital intercourse rose from about 20 percent before the mid-1960s to about 35 percent during the early 1970s to approximately 50 percent in the late 1970s to slightly more than 50 percent today (Hayes, 1987; Katchadourian, 1990; Miller, Forehand & Kotchick, 1999; Singh & Darroch, 1999).

Second, the proportion of individuals who have sexual intercourse *early* in adolescence is substantial. Although the median age at which adolescents first engage in intercourse has remained between 16 and 17, on average, for the past three decades, between one-third and one-fourth of all contemporary American adolescents are sexually active by 15, and more than 15 percent are sexually active by 13 (Blum & Rinehart, 2000; Miller et al., 1997). Among 14- and 15-year-olds who have not had sex, fears of pregnancy and disease (including HIV/AIDS) are the most common reasons for abstaining (Blinn-Pike, 1999). These figures on sexual

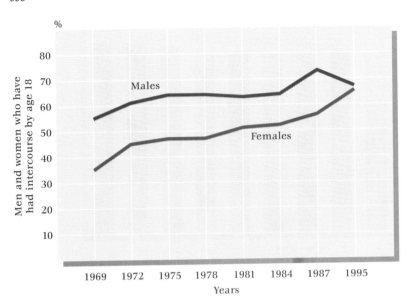

Figure 11.3   *Historical changes in the percentage of 18-year-old males and females who have experienced sexual intercourse.* (Alan Guttmacher Institute, 1994; Singh & Darroch, 1999; Sonenstein, 1998)

activity among younger adolescents are noteworthy because younger individuals are more likely to have unprotected sex and to expose themselves to the risks of pregnancy and sexually transmitted infections (Dittus, Jaccard, & Gordon, 1997). In addition, the fact that a large number of adolescents are sexually active before high school is important to consider in discussions of sex education, because they indicate that programs that do not begin until the later years of high school are probably too late for a substantial number of young people.

Finally, the greatest increase in the prevalence of premarital intercourse has been among females. Before 1965, there were substantial gaps between the proportions of sexually active boys and girls. Since about 1965, the proportion of sexually experienced high school males has nearly tripled, but the proportion of sexually experienced high school females is nearly five times higher today than 35 years ago. Among college students, the proportion of males who have had premarital intercourse has increased by 60 percent since 1965; among females, the increase has been greater than 300 percent. Sex differences in the rates of premarital intercourse today—among high school or college youth—are not large at all (Singh & Darroch, 1999; Sonenstein et al., 1998).

Whether adults approve or not, then, sexual activity has become a part of the normal American teenager's life. And, although many parents, educators, and other adults are alarmed and concerned about sexual activity among the young, for most ado-

lescents, sexual involvement is accompanied by affection, emotional involvement, and commitment to a relationship. By no stretch of the imagination can most of today's young people be described as promiscuous or morally lax in matters of sex.

Although it is interesting to speculate on the causes of these changes in adolescents' sexual behavior—the increased availability of the birth control pill, the overall liberalization of social attitudes, and the earlier age of puberty have all been suggested—the more pressing issue is how society ought to react to the changed nature of sex during adolescence. Premarital intercourse is not limited to males, to minority youngsters, or to adolescents with emotional problems. It is a part of life for the *average* teenager. Many experts contend that the longer we ignore this—by failing to provide adequate sex education, by limiting the accessibility of effective contraception, and by not dealing with the issue squarely—the more difficulties society, and young people in particular, will face.

RECAP

Sexual intercourse, once delayed until early adulthood, is clearly now a part of the typical adolescent's experience, regardless of the young person's ethnic or socioeconomic background. More than half of all teenagers have sexual intercourse before graduating from high school, and two-thirds have intercourse before turning 19.

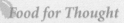

Food for Thought

Today's teenagers are growing up within a context in which sexual intercourse before high school graduation is considered normative in many segments of society. Has this changed the nature of adolescence in any profound ways?

THE SEXUALLY ACTIVE ADOLESCENT

Psychological and Social Characteristics of Sexually Active Adolescents

For many years, researchers studied the psychological and social characteristics of adolescents who engaged in premarital sex with the assumption that sexually active teenagers were more troubled than their peers. This view has been replaced as sexual activity has become more prevalent.

Indeed, numerous studies show that sexual activity during adolescence is decidedly *not* associated with psychological disturbance. Several studies, for example, have shown that adolescents who become sexually active earlier than their peers have levels of self-esteem and life satisfaction similar to the levels of other adolescents (Billy, Landale, Grady, & Zimmerle, 1988; Bingham & Crockett, 1996; Jessor, Costa, Jessor, & Donovan, 1983). Another study indicated that unmarried girls who become pregnant are more likely to have high self-esteem and strong feelings of efficacy, rather than the reverse (Robbins, Kaplan, & Martin, 1985). Losing one's virginity, even in early adolescence, does not have negative psychological repercussions, either in the short or long term (Bingham & Crockett, 1996; Langer, Zimmerman, & Katz, 1995). Thus, both the prejudice that only "troubled" adolescents have sex and the belief that sexual activity during adolescence leads to later psychological disturbance are false.

It does seem to be the case, however, that *early* sexual activity (i.e., having intercourse before age 16) is associated with a more general attitudinal and behavioral profile that includes experimentation with drugs and alcohol, a low level of religious involvement, a tolerance of deviant behavior, a lower interest in academic achievement, and a higher orientation toward independence

(Brewster, Cooksey, Guilkey, & Rindfuss, 1998; Costa, Jessor, Donovan, & Fortenberry, 1995; Miller & Moore, 1990; Rosenthal, Smith, & Visser, 1999). Although many studies have found this link between early sexual activity and minor deviance, the nature of the causal chain is not entirely clear. Some studies show that involvement in minor deviance (especially alcohol and drug use, but aggression as well) precedes early involvement with sex (Capaldi, Crosby, & Stoolmiller, 1996; Miller-Johnson et al., 1996; Mott, Fondell, Hu, Kowaleski-Jones, & Menaghan, 1996; Rosenbaum & Kandel, 1990; Tubman, Windle, & Windle, 1996; Underwood, Kupersmidt, & Coie, 1996). Others show that deviance follows earlier sexual activity (Elliott & Morse, 1989). And still others suggest that experimentation with deviant activity and early sex occur simultaneously and may reflect a common underlying factor (e.g., Bingham & Crockett, 1996; Dorius, Heaton, & Steffen, 1993; Orr, Beiter, & Ingersoll, 1991; Rowe, Rodgers, Meseck-Bushey, & St. John, 1989). As you will read in chapter 13, many experts believe that a more general inclination toward problem behavior is behind an overarching pattern that combines minor delinquency, precocious or promiscuous sex, disengagement from school, and drug and alcohol use (Costa et al., 1995; Rosenthal et al., 1999; Valois, Oeltmann, Waller, & Hussey, 1999). It is important to bear in mind, however, that studies of adolescents who become sexually active *after age 16* do not find major differences between these youth and their virginal counterparts. One consistent finding that has emerged from research, however, is that young adolescents who are sexually active are less likely than older teenagers to protect themselves against pregnancy and sexually transmitted infections.

Researchers also have asked whether adolescents who become sexually active earlier than their peers have family histories that are different from those of other adolescents. Studies generally have not supported the widely held view that vigilant monitoring by parents and open communication between parents and children have a strong impact on adolescent sexual behavior (Casper, 1990; Moore, Peterson, & Furstenberg, 1986; Newcomer & Udry, 1984; Taris & Semin, 1997; but see Small & Luster, 1994). Adolescents whose parents keep close tabs on them or who discuss sex with them are neither more nor less likely to be sexually active (Miller & Moore, 1990). One factor that is consistently related to the age at which adolescents initiate sex is physical maturation; adolescents who mature earlier are also likely to have sex earlier (Miller, Norton, Fan, & Christopherson, 1998) (see the accompanying box).

Risk Factors for Sexual Activity

If you keep up with reports on health in the popular media, you have probably heard the term *risk factor* used in discussions of heart disease or cancer. A **risk factor** is an individual or environmental hazard that increases a person's vulnerability to a negative outcome, such as a disease (Werner & Smith, 1982). The presence of a risk factor does not guarantee that the negative outcome will occur, but it increases the probability of the outcome. Thus, someone who smokes cigarettes (a risk factor for lung cancer) will not necessarily develop lung cancer, but the smoker has a higher probability of doing so than a nonsmoker does, all other factors being equal. Risk factors also operate in a cumulative fashion: Individuals who have several risk factors have a greater probability of developing the outcome than do those with only one of the risk factors. For instance, someone with multiple risk factors for cancer (e.g., cigarette smoking, a familial history of cancer, and a high-fat diet) has a much greater probability of developing the disease than does a person with only one of the risk factors.

Social scientists have applied cumulative risk factor models to the study of adolescent behavior, asking, for example, which adolescents are at risk for developing substance-abuse problems or for contracting AIDS. Such models can be extremely informative when the outcome in question has multiple causes. Instead of searching for *the* cause of drug use, a researcher might acknowledge that drug use is multiply determined and might ask, instead, how a diverse set of potential causes work together. In so doing, the researcher may be able to discover which adolescents are most at risk for developing the problem (that is, which adolescents have the most risk factors); then preventive interventions can be designed and aimed specifically at the most vulnerable population.

An illustration of this approach comes from a study of adolescent sexual activity by human ecologists Stephen Small and Tom Luster (Luster & Small, 1994; Perkins, Luster, Villarruel, & Small, 1998; Small & Luster, 1994). **Human ecology** is a branch of social science that is devoted to studying development in context. Small and Luster began their investigation by acknowledging that adolescent sexual activity is multiply determined and is influenced by factors at the individual, familial, and extrafamilial levels (see the accompanying figure). Previous research had shown, for example, that drug use (an individual factor), household composition (a familial factor), and peer norms (an extrafamilial factor) all contribute independently to an adolescent's sexual behavior. But how do these factors operate together? Is an adolescent who uses drugs *and* who comes from a divorced home more at risk for involvement in sexual activity than one who uses drugs *or* who comes from a divorced home?

Small and Luster surveyed a sample of approximately 2,200 adolescents and collected information about their sexual behavior (that is, whether they were sexually experienced or not) and about 14 factors that were hypothesized to place adolescents at risk for involvement in sexual activity. Among the factors studied were alcohol use, school performance, having a steady boyfriend or girlfriend, parental values, and self-esteem. The researchers then looked at the relation between each of the potential risk factors and sexual activity to see which risk factors were independent predictors of sexual activity. Among the most important predictors of sexual activity were having a steady boyfriend or girlfriend, using alcohol regularly, having parents with permissive values about sex, and being worried about one's future occupational chances. These variables had been found in previous studies to be predictive of adolescent sexual activity. Small and Luster found—also consistent with earlier research (e.g., Lauritsen, 1994; O'Beirne, 1994)—more predictors of girls' sexual activity than of boys'; for instance, not having parental support was a risk factor for females but not for males.

Once the risk factors were identified, Small and Luster gave each adolescent a score of 1 for each factor that was present in his or her life. They then looked to see whether the adolescents with higher scores were indeed more likely to be sexually active. The results are presented in the accompanying figure.

As you can see, there was a clear relation between adolescents' sexual behavior and the number of risk factors they reported. Among the girls, for example, only 1 percent of those with no risk factors were sexually active, in comparison with 22 percent of those with two risk factors, 50 percent with four risk factors, and 80 percent with eight or more risk factors. Among the boys, 15 percent of those with no risk factors were sexually active, as opposed to 39 percent of those with one risk factor, 55 percent with two risk factors, and 93 percent with five or more risk factors. The graph shows quite clearly that the percentage of sexually experienced adolescents rose steadily as a function of the number of risk factors present.

In a subsequent study of more than 15,000 adolescents (Perkins et al., 1998), the researchers asked whether the risk factors identified in studies of white adolescents also predict sexual activity among African American and Latino youth. They found that the very same set of factors cut across ethnic groups. Specifically, sexual activity was more likely among adolescents who used alcohol, who had been physically or sexually abused, who performed poorly in school, who had antisocial friends, who attended unsupportive and discouraging schools, and who were left alone at home for five or more hours each day.

What are the implications of these findings? According to the researchers, the most important implication is that efforts aimed at preventing adolescent sexual activity must focus on more than one factor. In their words, "programs should try to reduce the number of risk factors adolescents are exposed to at various levels of the human ecology, and they need to try to help teens deal successfully with the risks they are exposed to" (Small & Luster, 1994, p. 191).

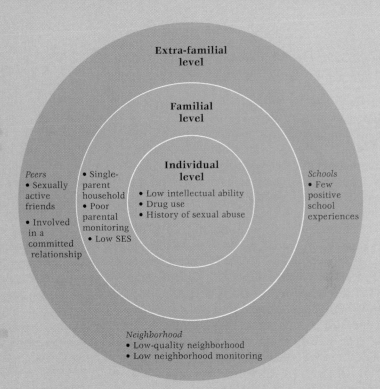

▲ *An ecological model of selected risk factors for adolescent sexual activity.* (Small & Luster, 1994)

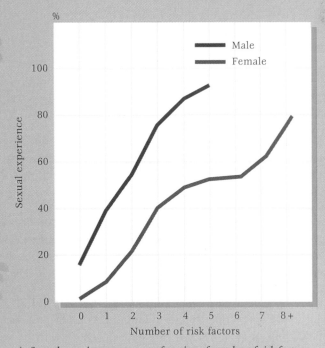

▲ *Sexual experience status as a function of number of risk factors.*

Source: Small, S., & Luster, T. (1994). Adolescent sexual activity: An ecological, risk-factor approach. *Journal of Marriage and the Family, 56,* 181–192.

Parental and Peer Influences on Adolescents' Sexual Activity

The study of parent-adolescent communication about sex has increased rapidly over the past decade, although it is quite clear from this research that the conclusions one draws about the nature and impact of these conversations depend entirely on whom you ask. Many more parents report communicating with their adolescent about sex than vice versa. Other discrepancies abound as well: Parents underestimate their adolescents' sexual activity and unrealistically assume that, if they disapprove of sexual activity, their adolescent is likely not sexually active; on the other hand, sexually active adolescents underestimate their parents' disapproval of sexual activity (Jaccard, Dittus, & Gordon, 1998). In addition, parents often say that they have communicated about a particular topic (e.g., AIDS) when their teenager says they have not (Miller, Kotchick, Dorsey, Forehand, & Ham, 1998). Generally speaking, teenagers are more likely to talk about sex with mothers than fathers and rate their mothers as better sex educators (DiIorio, Kelley, & Hockenberry-Eaton, 1999; Feldman & Rosenthal, 2000; Rosenthal & Feldman, 1999). Most discussions about sex between parents and teenagers focus on issues of safety (AIDS, condom use), rather than issues of sexual behavior or relationships (DiIorio et al., 1999; Miller et al., 1998). And, despite the progressive image of countries such as the Netherlands, studies indicate that parent-adolescent communication about sex is no more open in Europe than in the United States (Arnett, in press). Across cultures, however, adolescents are more likely to be well educated about sex when their conversations with their parents are genuinely interactive, rather than dominated by their parents (Lefkowitz, Romo, Corona, Au, & Sigman, 2000).

The effect of parent-child communication about sex on adolescent sexual behavior depends on who is doing the communicating and what is being communicated. Overall, most studies find that the impact of parent-adolescent communication on the likelihood of the adolescent being sexually active is very small (Casper, 1990; Paikoff et al., 1997), although parent-child communication about contraception does appear to lower the rate of *risky* sex (Holtzman & Rubinson, 1995; Luster & Small, 1994; Miller et al., 1999; Rodgers, 1999; Whitaker, Miller, May, & Levin, 1999), especially if the discussions take place before the adolescent becomes sexually active (Miller, Levin, Whitaker, & Xu, 1998).

Not surprisingly, parental attitudes may make a difference in the impact of parent-adolescent discussion on sexual activity, especially for girls: Among girls with liberal parents, talking about sex is associated with more sexual activity; this is not true among girls with parents who disapprove of premarital sex, however (Fisher, 1989; Jaccard, Dittus, & Gordon, 1996). Thus, despite many parents' optimistic beliefs that they can deter their adolescent's sexual activity by talking about it, and, despite other parents' fears that talking about sex will have the unintended effect of encouraging their teenager's sexual behavior, studies show that parent-adolescent communication about sex has surprisingly little impact on rates of sexual activity, one way or the other. Having an opportunity to have sex (e.g., being in a steady relationship or dating frequently), having sexually active friends, and using alcohol and drugs are far more important predictors of early sexual initiation among teenagers than are family factors (Black, Ricardo, & Stanton, 1997; Miller et al., 1997; Whitbeck, Yoder, Hoyt, & Conger, 1999).

One family factor that does appear to predict adolescent sexual involvement, however—especially among girls—is household composition. Researchers consistently find that adolescents whose parents are in the process of divorcing, as well as girls who live in single-parent households—regardless of when (or if) a divorce took place—are more likely to be sexually active earlier than their peers (Brewster, 1994; Crockett & Bingham, 1994; Flewelling & Bauman, 1990; Lauritsen, 1994; Miller et al., 1997; Murry, 1996; Newcomer & Udry, 1987). One hypothesis, consistent with what we saw about the family in chapter 4, is that parental divorce temporarily disrupts the adolescent's behavior, leading him or her into early involvement with drugs, alcohol, and minor delinquency, which, according to some studies, increases the likelihood of sex.

Why should growing up in a single-parent home affect girls' sexual behavior more than that of boys? At least three possibilities exist. One is that social influences on girls' sexual behavior are in general stronger and more varied than are the influences on boys' behavior (Whitbeck, Simons, & Kao, 1994). Boys' parents may not attempt to exert great control over their sexual activity, regardless of whether the household has one parent or two. Consequently, boys from one- and two-parent homes may be equally likely to be sexually active. Girls' sexual behavior, in contrast, may be more subject to parents' controls. Single-parent homes are typically more permissive than two-parent homes (Dornbusch et al., 1985), and this difference in control may be enough to make a difference in girls' sexual activity.

A second possibility is that many single-parent mothers date and, in so doing, may inadvertently be role models of sexual activity to their adolescents (Miller & Moore, 1990; Whitbeck et al., 1994). Other research shows, for example, that adolescents whose mothers were sexually active at an early age are themselves more likely to begin having sex early (Mott et al., 1996). To the extent that this modeling effect is stronger between parents and children of the same sex, we would expect to find a more powerful effect of growing up with a single mother on the sexual behavior of daughters than sons.

Still a third possibility is that girls are more likely than boys to respond to problems at home by turning outside the family for alternative sources of warmth and support. If their family environment is not satisfying, girls (whether in divorced homes or not) may be more likely than boys to seek the affection and attention of a romantic partner (Whitbeck, Hoyt, Miller, & Kao, 1992).

Other studies have examined the influence of people other than parents on adolescents' sexual behavior—in particular, the influence of peers and siblings. Generally speaking, adolescents are more likely to be sexually active when their peers are (DiBlasio & Benda, 1992; East, Felice, & Morgan, 1993; Udry, 1987); when they *believe* that their friends are sexually active, whether or not their friends actually are (Brooks-Gunn & Furstenberg, 1989); and when they have older siblings who model more sexually advanced behavior (East et al., 1993; Rodgers & Rowe, 1988; Widmer, 1997). Conversely, regular church attendance is associated with delayed sexual activity only among adolescents whose friends attend the same church (Mott et al., 1996). There are age and ethnic differences in the relative importance of parental and peer influence, however. As one would expect, peers become increasingly more influential with age (Treboux & Busch-Rossnagel, 1990). In addition, African American adolescents report relatively less familial influence over their sexual behavior than do white adolescents, and Hispanic adolescents report relatively more (Scott & Owen, 1990).

Peer influences on adolescents' sexual activity appear to operate in two different, but compatible, ways. First, when an adolescent's peers are sexually active, they establish a normative standard that having sex is acceptable (Dornbusch et al., 1981; Furstenberg et al., 1987; Miller & Moore, 1990; Stack, 1994). Interestingly, one of the reasons that minor drug use may lead to earlier involvement in sexual activity is that drug use may lead an adolescent to form friendships with a different group of friends, a group that is sexually more permissive (Whitbeck, Conger, Simons, & Kao, 1993). Consistent with this, adolescents' initiation of sexual activity varies from neighborhood to neighborhood, with earlier sexual activity more likely in relatively more disorganized neighborhoods, where adults have little control over teenagers and where peer groups are relatively more powerful (Upchurch, Aneshensel, Sucoff, & Levy-Storms, 1999).

Second, peers influence each other's sexual behavior directly, either through communication among friends ("You haven't done it yet! What's the matter with you?") or, more commonly, between potential sex partners. Along these lines, several studies show that sexual activity spreads within a community of adolescents much like an epidemic, with sexually experienced adolescents initiating their less experienced partners into increasingly more advanced sex (Rodgers & Rowe, 1993). Once they become sexually experienced, previously inexperienced adolescents then "infect" other adolescents in turn. Over time, then, the percentage of sexually experienced adolescents within a community grows and grows.

Finally, several studies have examined the role of the broader environment in influencing adolescent sexual behavior. Adolescents growing up in poor neighborhoods, for example, are more likely to engage in early sexual activity than are adolescents from more affluent communities (Billy, Brewster, & Grady, 1994; Brewster, Billy, & Grady, 1993; Brooks-Gunn, Duncan, Klebanov, & Sealand, 1993; Crane, 1991). When adolescents grow up in poverty, they may see little hope for the future, and they therefore may be more likely to risk their occupational and economic future by becoming sexually active (Benda & Corwyn, 1998; Lauritsen, 1994; Murry, 1994). To a young person who believes that the chances of getting a good job are slim, an early pregnancy does not seem as costly as it might seem to someone who hopes to complete high school, attend college, and secure a good job. Studies also show that adolescents who watch a lot of sexually oriented television are themselves more likely to be sexually active, although it is not clear whether television viewing leads to sexual activity or vice versa (Brown & Newcomer, 1991).

RECAP

Sexual activity during adolescence does not carry the psychological risks that many adults associate with it. In general, adolescents who are sexually active have psychological profiles that are similar to, rather than different from, those of their nonactive peers. There is evidence, however, that early sexual activity (having intercourse before age 16) is more common among teenagers growing up in single-parent households and is associated with higher rates of problem behaviors, such as drug and alcohol use. Adolescent sexual behavior is influenced not only by the family but also by peers, siblings, and forces in the broader community.

Food for Thought

In your opinion, why are the psychological correlates of early sexual intercourse different from the correlates of sexual intercourse when it is delayed until the last years of high school? Would you be in favor of sex education courses whose focus is on persuading adolescents to wait until they are 16 before having intercourse?

Sex Differences in the Meaning of Sex

Any discussion of the psychosocial significance of sexual experience during adolescence must be sensitive to the very substantial sex differences in the way in which early sexual activity is experienced. Despite the convergence of males' and females' rates of sexual activity, the early sexual experiences of adolescent boys and girls are usually very different and, as a consequence, are imbued with very different *meanings* (Brooks-Gunn & Paikoff, 1993). In other words, the sexual behavior of males and females may be similar, but the sexual socialization of males and females is quite different.

The typical adolescent boy's first sexual experience is in early adolescence, through masturbation (Gagnon, 1972). At the outset, then, the sexual socialization of the adolescent boy typically places sex outside of an interpersonal context. Before adolescent boys begin dating, they have generally already experienced orgasm and know how to arouse themselves sexually. For males, the development of sexuality during adolescence revolves around efforts to integrate the capacity to form close relationships into an already existing sense of sexual capability.

However, at the time of first intercourse, boys are likely to keep matters of sex and intimacy separate. Boys often have as their first partner someone they describe as a "casual date" (Carns, 1973). Generally, it is the male partner of a couple who is likely to initiate sex, and, interestingly, the typical male reports more love for a woman who lost her virginity with him than for a woman who lost her virginity with a previous partner. His own loss of virginity, however, has no impact on his feelings of affection in a relationship (Peplau, Rubin, & Hill, 1977). These findings suggest that the early sexual experiences of males are often interpreted not in terms of intimacy and emotional involvement but in terms of recreation (Hendrick & Hendrick, 1994). Consistent with this, boys are more likely than girls to mention sexual arousal as a reason for having sex (Eyre & Millstein, 1999). And males typically report that the people to whom they describe their first sexual liaison—generally, male peers—are overwhelmingly approving (Carns, 1973; Miller & Simon, 1980). It is little surprise, when looked at in light of these findings, that the most common immediate reactions among adolescent males to having intercourse for the first time are excitement, satisfaction, exhilaration, and happiness (Gordon & Gilgun, 1987; Oswald, Bahne, & Feder, 1994; Sorensen, 1973).

The typical girl's first experience is likely to be very different and likely to leave her feeling very differently as well. Although most adolescent girls masturbate, masturbation is a far less prevalent activity among girls than among boys, and it is far less regularly practiced. Thus, the typical adolescent girl, in contrast to the typical boy, is more likely to experience sex for the first time with another person. For her, the development of sexuality involves the integration of sexual activity into an existing capacity for intimacy and emotional involvement. The girl's sexual script is one that, from the outset, hinges sex with romance, love, friendship, and intimacy (Aitken & Chaplin, 1990; Hendrick & Hendrick, 1994).

Boys and girls also encounter very different social attitudes about sex: Society still is much more discouraging of sexual activity outside the context of emotional involvement among adolescent girls than boys (Goodchilds & Zellman, 1984; Gordon & Gilgun, 1987). Because of the possibility of pregnancy, the potential adverse consequences of premarital sexual activity are far more serious for girls than for boys. For this reason, society monitors the sexual activity of girls more carefully, and girls are more likely to be encouraged to approach sex cautiously (Rosenthal, 1994). Girls' feelings of sexual desire—which may be just as strong as boys'—are "tempered by their knowledge that girls are not supposed to be sexual or that if they are, they will be marked as bad and unlovable" (Tolman, 1993, p. 4). Girls have an easier time saying "no" to unwanted sex than boys do (Zimmerman, Sprecher, Langer, & Holloway, 1995).

Not surprisingly, then, at the time of first intercourse, the adolescent girl's first sexual partner is likely to be a person she describes as someone she was "in love with" at the time (Kallen & Stephenson, 1982). There is a social meaning to losing one's virginity that is still today very different for young women and for young men, and women typically report feeling more love for a man if he was their first sexual partner (Peplau et al., 1977). After having intercourse for the first time, the typical adolescent girl is more likely to encounter disapproval or mixed feelings on the part of others in whom she confides (generally speaking, peers) than is the typical boy (Carns, 1973). And she is likely to report feeling afraid, guilty, and worried, as well as happy or excited about the experience (Gordon & Gilgun, 1987; Oswald et al., 1994; Sorensen, 1973). For the adolescent girl, then, early sexual experience is tied more to emotional involvement and, more often than not, is complicated by fears of becoming pregnant (Gordon & Gilgun, 1987). Although young women are more likely today than they were 20 years ago to admit to their friends that they have lost their virginity soon after the event has occurred, boys still are more likely than girls to tell their friends soon after having intercourse for the first time because it is easier to do so when the act has not been accompanied by emotional involvement (Kallen & Stephenson, 1982).

▲ *There are substantial sex differences in the way in which early sexual activity is experienced psychologically. For adolescent boys, early sexual relationships are often brief, impersonal, and associated with a sense of achievement.* (B. Daemmrich/ The Image Works)

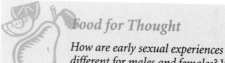

Food for Thought

How are early sexual experiences different for males and females? What societal factors contribute to these differences? What biological factors contribute to them?

RECAP

Any discussion of the psychological aspects of adolescent sexuality must differentiate between the experiences of males and females. Early sexuality for males is tinged with elements of recreation, whereas for females it is linked more to feelings of intimacy and closeness. Because of the risks of pregnancy, adolescent girls are more likely than boys to be socialized to view sex with caution and are therefore more likely to feel ambivalent, rather than uniformly positive, about engaging in sex.

Homosexuality During Adolescence

Much discussion about homosexuality during adolescence is muddied with confusion and misinformation about the nature and antecedents of homosexuality. In attempting to separate fact from myth, we need to keep in mind several important distinctions.

First, there is an important distinction between engaging in homosexual activity or having homosexual feelings, on the one hand, and having an exclusive, enduring preference for sexual activity with people of the same sex, on the other. It is not uncommon, for example, for young adolescents to engage in sex play with members of the same sex or to have questions about the nature of their feelings for same-sex peers. Indeed, one classic study of sexual behavior in the United States indicated that, by age 16, over 20 percent of the adolescent boys studied had

The Influences of Hormones and Friends on Adolescent Sexual Behavior

Increased interest in sex at adolescence is likely to have both biological and social causes. Specifically, adolescents are thought to become interested in sex in part because of increases in sex hormones at puberty and in part because sexual activity becomes accepted—even encouraged—in their peer group. But is one set of factors more important than the other? A series of studies, by J. Richard Udry and his colleagues (Smith, Udry, & Morris, 1985; Udry, 1987; Udry, Talbert, & Morris, 1986), suggests that a fuller understanding of adolescent sexual behavior necessitates looking at biological and social influences in interaction, rather than at either set of influences alone. However, the way in which hormones and friends interact to influence sexual behavior appears to be different for males than for females.

According to Udry's studies, boys' and girls' initial interest in sex is influenced primarily by the surge in certain hormones—**testosterone,** to be specific—at puberty. Adolescents with higher levels of **androgens** (testosterone is an androgen) are more likely than their peers to report masturbating, thinking about sex, and planning to have sexual intercourse within the next year. This hormonal change appears to increase adolescents' interest in sex and in their arousal when exposed to sexual stimuli.

Motivation to have sex is one thing; becoming sexually active is another. How important is the rise in testosterone levels at puberty in determining the onset of sexual intercourse? The answer appears to differ in boys and girls. Among boys, but not girls, the increased level of androgens is directly related to the likelihood of their being sexually active. Younger boys who are more mature biologically are more likely to be sexually active than older boys whose hormone levels are lower. Boys' sexual behavior is not entirely dependent on their hormone levels, however. Boys who are more popular with girls in their school are more likely to initiate sex early than are boys who are less popular with girls.

engaged in homosexual activity to the point of orgasm (Kinsey et al., 1948), although more recent surveys indicate that these estimates may have been erroneously high (Michael et al., 1994). However, even though a large number of adolescents have such homosexual experiences, nearly all young people—well over 90 percent, in fact—develop an exclusive preference for heterosexual relationships by the end of adolescence (Michael et al., 1994). And, contrary to myths about the increasing prevalence of homosexuality in contemporary American society, the proportion has remained at or near this level since the mid-1940s, when researchers began studying the phenomenon (Hunt, 1974).

A second distinction to be made is the one between homosexuality as an exclusive preference and homosexuality as an interest that may exist simultaneously with strong heterosexual interests (Diamond, Savin-Williams, & Dubé, 1999). Many people mistakenly view sexual orientation as an "either-or" attribute, with individuals being either exclusively heterosexual or exclusively homosexual.

In fact, however, of the 8 percent of Americans who do not develop an exclusive preference for heterosexual relationships, only one-third are exclusively homosexual in their orientation. Nearly twice as many describe themselves as bisexual—having both heterosexual and homosexual interests. Surveys indicate that only about 3 percent of males and 1 percent of females are exclusively homosexual (Michael et al., 1994).

Finally, a great deal of confusion about homosexuality results because people tend to confuse **sexual orientation** (the extent to which someone is oriented toward heterosexual activity, homosexual activity, or both), **sex-role behavior** (the extent to which an individual behaves in traditionally "masculine" or "feminine" ways), and **gender identity** (the gender that an individual believes he or she is psychologically). There is no connection between an adolescent's sexual orientation and his or her sex-role behavior. Individuals with strong, or even exclusive, preferences for homosexual relationships exhibit the same range of masculine and feminine behaviors that is seen

Although there is also some evidence that boys whose friends are sexually active are themselves more likely to be involved in sex, this seems to do more with the influence of hormones than with the influence of friends: Boys tend to have friends who are at a similar level of pubertal development and who therefore are likely to have similar testosterone levels and rates of sexual activity. All in all, the evidence provided in Udry's studies indicates a very strong biological influence on the sexual behavior of adolescent boys.

As you know from the discussion in chapter 1 concerning biological development during adolescence, androgens, including testosterone, contribute to increases in boys' sex drive as well as to the development of secondary sex characteristics, such as facial hair. Because of this, it is difficult to determine whether increases in androgens lead to increased sexual activity because of the increased sex drive (which may make boys with higher testosterone levels want to have sex more) or because of changes in their physical appearance (which may make them more attractive to girls). In girls, however, although androgens are responsible for increases in the sex drive, a different set of hormones—**estrogens**—is primarily responsible for changes in appearance, including breast development, and for changes in females' receptivity to males' sexual advances. Because of this, it is possible to study whether the increased interest in sex among girls after puberty is more influenced by increases in their sex drive or by changes in their receptivity and physical appearance (both of which, presumably, influence their sexual attractiveness to boys). Thus far, the answer appears to point mostly to the impact of estrogen on girls' receptivity to boys' sexual overtures (Udry, Halpern, & Campbell, 1991).

Despite these effects of hormones on girls' sexual behavior, though, numerous studies show that social factors are far more important in influencing girls' involvement in sexual intercourse than boys', especially among white girls (Crockett, Bingham, Chopak, & Vicary, 1996; Udry & Billy, 1987). Although increases in androgens lead to increased interest in sex among girls, whether this interest is translated into behavior depends on the social environment. Among girls with high levels of androgens, those who have sexually permissive attitudes and friends who are sexually active are more likely to engage in intercourse. But girls whose social environment is less encouraging of sex—even girls with high levels of androgens—are unlikely to be sexually active. In other words, whereas hormones seem to have a direct and powerful effect on the sexual behavior of boys, the impact of hormones on the sexual behavior of girls seems to depend on the social context in which they live.

To what can we attribute this sex difference? Udry hypothesizes that boys develop in an environment that is more uniformly tolerant and encouraging of sexual behavior than girls do. In this environment, all that boys need to become sexually active is the jolt that the increase in androgens provides. For girls, however, the environment is more varied. Some girls develop within a context that permits or even encourages sexual activity; others do not.

Although the increase in androgens also provides a jolt to the sexual motivation of the adolescent girl, if she develops within a context that places social controls on sexual activity, this hormonal awakening will not be translated into sexual experience.

among individuals with strong or exclusive heterosexual interests. In other words, exclusively gay men (like exclusively heterosexual men) may act in very masculine, very feminine, or both masculine and feminine ways; the same holds true for exclusively lesbian and exclusively heterosexual women. Along similar lines, individuals with homosexual interests are generally not confused about their gender identity—or, at least, they are no more confused than are individuals with heterosexual interests.

Studies of the antecedents of homosexuality generally have focused on two sets of factors: biological influences, such as hormones, and social influences, such as the parent-child relationship. More is known about the development of homosexuality among men than among women—the prevalence of homosexuality is much greater among men than among women—but the weight of the evidence thus far suggests that an adolescent's sexual orientation is likely to be shaped by a complex interaction of social and biological influences (Bem, 1996; Green, 1980, 1987; Paul, 1993; Savin-Williams, 1988).

Support for the contention that homosexuality is determined at least partly by biological factors comes from two sources. You may recall that, in chapter 1, we drew a distinction between the organizational and the activational roles of hormones on behavior. The hormonal changes of puberty activate sexual behavior, but the particular pattern of sexual behavior that is activated may depend on the way in which hormonal pathways in the brain were organized early in life. There is suggestive evidence that gay and lesbian adults were exposed prenatally to certain hormones that, in theory, could affect sexual orientation through their effects on early brain organization (Meyer-Bahlburg et al., 1995; Savin-Williams, 1988). Second, there is some evidence that homosexuality has a strong genetic component, since sexual orientation is more likely to be similar among close relatives than distant relatives and between identical twins than fraternal twins (Savin-Williams, 1988). Although environmental explanations for this similarity cannot be ruled out, chances are that at least

▲ *There is no connection between an adolescent's sexual preference and his or her sex-role behavior. Individuals with strong, or even exclusive, preferences for homosexual relationships exhibit the same range of masculine and feminine behaviors seen among individuals with strong or exclusive heterosexual interests.* (Paula Lerner/Woodfin Camp)

some of the predisposition to develop a homosexual orientation is inherited.

One theory of biological-environmental interaction, proposed by psychologist Daryl Bem (1996), is that early biological predispositions may channel some youngsters into patterns of play and social relationships that can lead to the development of homosexuality (see figure 11.4). Studies suggest that sex hormones influence preferences for aggressive activities, which, consequently, may be related to preferences for stereotypic masculine or feminine behavior. Thus, for example, boys who are biologically predisposed toward timidity may avoid rough play as young children, may come to prefer activities that are more typical of young girls, and may gradually develop the feeling that they are different from other boys. Bem has argued that we become sexually attracted to those

whom we perceive as "exotic" and that, for young boys who grow accustomed to playing with girls, the people they come to see as exotic, and therefore erotic, are other boys. Critics of Bem's theory have noted that it does not adequately explain the development of sexual orientation among females, since the consequences of having early preferences for the activities and peers of the opposite sex are not the same for girls as they are for boys (Peplau, Garnets, Spalding, Conley, & Veniegas, 1998). In response, Bem (1998) has countered that the proportions of gay men and lesbians who report having felt different from their same-sex peers during childhood are identical.

These early behavioral preferences for activities of the opposite sex also may affect the parent-child relationship in ways that increase the likelihood of an individual's developing a homosexual orientation. Several studies suggest that a higher proportion of homosexuals than heterosexuals had problems in their early family relationships and, specifically, in their relationship with their father. The stereotype of the homosexual's father as cold and distant once was rejected as an artifact of popular stereotype and poor research designs. But more carefully designed studies have offered at least partial confirmation of this notion. Both gay and lesbian adults are more likely than heterosexuals to describe their fathers as distant and rejecting. Whereas gay men are more likely than heterosexuals to report having had close and generally positive relationships with their mothers, lesbians are more likely than heterosexuals to describe their mothers as cold and unpleasant (Bell, Weinberg, & Hammersmith, 1981).

Although these studies point to certain factors that appear more often than not in the early histories of homosexuals, the research evidence does not indicate that all individuals who show patterns of gender nonconformity or who have distant relations with their fathers inevitably become homosexual (Golombock & Tasker, 1996). Nor does research show that all homosexuals have identical developmental histories. For example, although it is true that homosexuals are more likely than heterosexuals to describe their parents in negative terms, not all gay and lesbian individuals feel this way. Indeed, only about half do, suggesting that a large number of homosexuals had quite positive family relationships growing up. And, of course, many heterosexuals describe their parents in exceedingly negative terms. Similarly, although most boys with persistently feminine behavior preferences may grow up to be gay, a substantial number of boys with these preferences do not.

Several writers have described the process through which gay, lesbian, and bisexual individuals discover, come to terms with, and disclose their sexual-minority identity (Diamond, 1998; Dubé & Savin-Williams, 1999; Savin-Williams, 1998). Although the traditional model of this progression—feeling different as a child, engaging in gender-atypical behavior, being attracted to the same sex, being disinterested in the opposite sex, realizing one's sexual attraction to others of the same sex, and consciously questioning one's sexual identity—describes the experience of many sexual-minority adolescents, it is by no means universal. Indeed, some writers have suggested that this may be more applicable to the development of white gay men than to lesbians, bisexual adolescents, and ethnic minority gay men (Diamond, 1998; Dubé & Savin-Williams, 1999). There is also evidence that females' sexual orientation may be more fluid than males', which some have taken as evidence that homosexuality has a stronger biological component among men and a stronger volitional component among women (Bem, 1998; Diamond, 1998).

Regardless of its origins, homosexuality is not considered by mental health experts to be a form of psychopathology, an indicator of an underlying psychological disturbance, or a condition warranting psychological treatment. Perhaps as we begin to understand more about the interplay among biological and social factors that contribute to the development of a homosexual orientation, our attitudes toward homosexuality will change for the better. Indeed, as one expert noted, "Society tends to treat . . . homosexuals as if they had a choice about their sexual orientation, when in fact they have no more choice about how they develop than heterosexuals do" (Marmor, quoted in Brody, 1987, p. 17).

Indeed, prejudice and ignorance about homosexuality may cause significant psychological distress for gay and lesbian adolescents, especially if they encounter hostility from those around them. As you know by now, the developmental tasks in the domains of identity, intimacy, and sexuality present formidable challenges for many teenagers. These challenges may be exacerbated for sexual-minority adolescents, who may be forced to resolve these issues without the same degree of social support as their heterosexual peers. Indeed, reviews of the literature have found that a very substantial number of gay, lesbian, and bisexual adolescents were harassed, physically abused, or verbally abused by peers or adults while growing up (Hershberger & D'Augelli, 1995; Pilkington & D'Augelli, 1995; Savin-Williams, 1994; Telljohann & Price, 1993). Abuse of this sort may account for the relatively higher rates of suicide, substance abuse, running away from home, and school difficulties reported by gay and lesbian adolescents (Faulkner & Cranston, 1998;

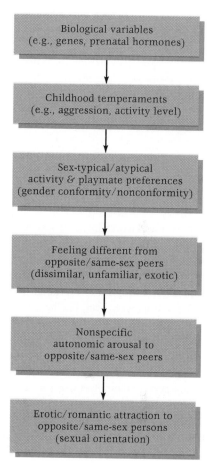

Figure 11.4 *Sexual orientation is believed to be influenced by a complex interplay of biological and environmental factors.* (Bem, 1996)

Hershberger, Pilkington, & D'Augelli, 1997; Rosario, Rotheram-Borus, & Reid, 1996; Rotheram-Borus, Hunter, & Rosario, 1994; Safren & Heimberg, 1999; Savin-Williams, 1994).

RECAP

Approximately 8 percent of the adolescent and young adult population is either partially or exclusively gay or lesbian. Current theories of the origins of homosexuality suggest a complex interaction of genetic and environmental influences. Experts agree that homosexuality is not a form of psychopathology, an indicator of an underlying psychological disturbance, or a condition warranting psychological treatment. Indeed, many difficulties experienced by sexual minority youth result from their being harassed by peers and adults.

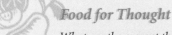

Food for Thought

What are the current theories about the relative contributions of biology and environment to the development of sexual orientation? Should social scientists be concerned about the antecedents of homosexuality?

Sexual Harassment, Rape, and Sexual Abuse During Adolescence

Although most research on adolescent sexual activity has focused on voluntary sexual behavior between consenting individuals, there is growing public awareness that a large proportion of teenagers are sexually harassed, and that a significant minority are forced to have sex against their will (Lee, Croninger, Linn, & Chen, 1996; Lewin, 1997; Moore, Nord, & Peterson, 1989; Stein, 1995; Vicary, Klingaman, & Harkness, 1995). This latter group includes adolescents who have been the victims of forcible rape by a stranger, sexual abuse within the family, or date rape—when a young person, typically a woman, is forced by a date to have sex against her will.

Recent studies indicate that sexual harassment is widespread within American public schools (Lee et al., 1996; Loredo, Reid, & Deaux, 1995; Stein, 1995). In one study of a nationally representative sample of middle and secondary school students, more than 80 percent of the girls and 60 percent of the boys reported having received unwanted sexual attention while in school (Lee et al., 1996) (see figure 11.5). Because most of those who had been sexually harassed had themselves harassed others, and because many incidents occurred within full view of teachers and other school personnel, numerous experts have suggested the need for wholesale changes in the moral and ethical climate of secondary schools (Lee et al., 1996; Stein, 1995). One evaluation of a school-based program called Safe Dates found significant reductions in psychological abuse and sexual violence in schools in which the program was implemented (Foshee et al., 1998). Other research, on the histories of individuals who commit dating violence, indicates that perpetrators themselves are likely to have been exposed to physical punishment and abuse at home (Capaldi & Clark, 1998; Simons, Lin, & Gordon, 1998; Wolfe, Wekerle, Reitzel-Jaffe, & Lefebvre, 1998).

Because both perpetrators and victims of sexual as-

saults are often reluctant to admit their experience, it is difficult to obtain accurate estimates of the numbers of adolescents who have been sexually victimized. It is known, however, that adolescent victims of sexual abuse are disproportionately female and poor (Cappelleri, Eckenrode, & Powers, 1993). According to several studies, however, more than 10 percent of white females, and more than 5 percent of African American females, report having had nonvoluntary sexual intercourse before age 18 (Luster & Small, 1997; Moore et al., 1989). In those studies, the women who were most likely to have been raped during adolescence were those who lived apart from their parents before age 16; who were physically, emotionally, or mentally limited; who were raised at or below the poverty level; or whose parents abused alcohol or used other drugs. Indeed, two-thirds of all the women who had three or more of these risk factors were raped as adolescents. In contrast to popular perception, adolescents are abused (sexually, physically, and emotionally) and neglected at a higher rate than are younger children (Cappelleri et al., 1993).

The figures on sexual abuse do not include adolescents who have been forced to engage in sexual activity other than intercourse and, as such, clearly underestimate the proportion of teenagers who have been sexually abused. Other estimates, which include all forms of nonvoluntary sex, however, suggest that about 25 percent of all females and close to 10 percent of all males were victimized sexually before reaching adulthood (Camarena & Sarigiani, 1994; Lewin, 1997; Nagy, Adcock, & Nagy, 1994).

Several studies have examined the psychological consequences of having been the victim of sexual abuse during adolescence. Adolescents who have been sexually abused show higher than average rates of poor self-esteem, academic difficulties, anxiety, fear, and depression (Calverley, Fischer, & Ayoub, 1994; Nagy, DiClimente, & Adcock, 1995; Trickett, McBride-Chang, & Putnam, 1994; Williamson, Borduin, & Howe, 1991); are more likely to engage in risky behavior (Hibbard, Ingersoll, & Orr, 1990; Nagy, Adcock, & Nagy, 1994; Whitbeck, Hoyt, & Ackley, 1997; Widom & Kuhns, 1996); and are more likely to have multiple sexual partners and to become pregnant as teenagers (Butler & Burton, 1990; Stock, Bell, Boyer, & Connell, 1997). There is also some evidence that sexual abuse prior to adolescence may lead to precocious (i.e., very early) puberty (Herman-Giddens, Sandler, & Friedman, 1988).

At the same time, it is worth noting that there are substantial differences among individuals in the

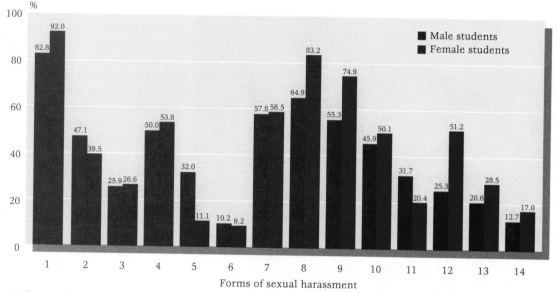

1. Made sexual comments, jokes, gestures, or looks
2. Showed you sexual pictures, photographs, messages, etc.
3. Wrote sexual messages about you on bathroom walls, etc.
4. Spread sexual rumors about you
5. Said you were gay or lesbian
6. Spied on you as you dressed or showered at school
7. Flashed or mooned you
8. Touched, grabbed, or pinched you in a sexual way
9. Intentionally brushed up against you in a sexual way
10. Pulled at your clothing in a sexual way
11. Pulled your clothing off or down
12. Blocked your way or cornered you in a sexual way
13. Forced you to kiss him/her
14. Forced you to do something sexual, other than kissing

Figure 11.5   The percentage of male and female students having ever experienced various forms of sexual harassment. (Lee et al., 1996)

extent to which they show problems as a result of having been sexually abused and in the form those problems take (Bauserman & Rind, 1997; Luster & Small, 1997). Generally speaking, individuals who have been both sexually and physically abused fare worse than those who experience only sexual abuse. Adolescents who have been sexually abused also fare better psychologically if they have parents who are authoritative (firm and supportive) and if they are successful in school (Luster & Small, 1997).

Food for Thought

If you were asked to devise a sexual harassment policy for a high school, what would be the main elements of your policy? Should policies governing adolescents' conduct in school be the same as those governing adults' conduct in the workplace?

RECAP

Most teenagers report having been sexually harassed in school, and a significant minority of young people, mainly females, are forced to have sex against their will. Living apart from one's parents, having physical or psychological problems, being raised in poverty, and having parents who abuse alcohol or other drugs are all risk factors for sexual abuse. Adolescents who have been sexually abused show higher than average rates of poor self-esteem, academic difficulties, anxiety, fear, and depression; are more likely to engage in risky behavior; and are more likely to become pregnant as teenagers.

Contraceptive Use

One reason for adults' great concern about adolescents' sexual activity is the failure of many sexually active young people to use contraception regularly. Among late adolescent males, 40 percent report using either no contraception or an ineffective method (e.g., withdrawing before ejaculating) the first time they had sex (Miller & Moore, 1990). Only half of all young women report having used birth control regularly during their first year of having intercourse, and nearly one-sixth of all 15- to 19-year-old sexually active women report never having used any contraception at all (Chilman,

▲ One of the reasons for adults' great concern about adolescents' sexual activity is the failure of many sexually active young people to use birth control measures regularly. Forty percent of late adolescent males report having used either no contraception or an ineffective method the first time they had sex. (Goodwin/Monkmeyer)

all teenagers and young adults did not use a condom the last time they had sex (Coleman, 1999).

Among adolescents who do use contraception, the most popular method by far is the birth control pill, which is used by approximately 60 percent of sexually active teenage girls, followed by condoms, which are used by between one-third and one-half of teenagers as their primary means of preventing pregnancy. About 20 percent of girls who are on the pill report that their partner uses a condom as well (Santelli et al., 1997). Withdrawal, a highly ineffective method of preventing pregnancy, unfortunately is still used by a large number of teenagers, as is the rhythm method—a method of birth control that requires more regular menstrual cycling than many teenagers have and more careful monitoring of menstrual cycling than most teenagers are capable of. Other methods, such as the intrauterine device (IUD), are not widely used by teenagers (Hayes,

1990; Hayes, 1987). Studies indicate that between 20 and 30 percent of young people had not used contraception the last time they had sex (Coleman, 1999; Miller & Moore, 1990). About 40 percent of sexually active teenagers report using birth control sporadically. Only one-third of sexually active adolescents always use birth control (Hayes, 1987). It is estimated that, in the United States alone, 1.65 million pregnancies to adolescent women are averted each year as a result of contraception (Kahn, Brindis, & Glei, 1999).

Although these figures are worrisome, there has been a clear improvement in adolescent contraceptive behavior during the past 25 years. In 1976, for example, nearly two-thirds of sexually active young women reported that they had not used contraception during their first intercourse (as opposed to about one-fourth today), and more than 35 percent reported never using birth control (as opposed to about 15 percent today) (Kahn, Brindis, & Glei, 1999). During the late 1980s, partly in response to the threat of AIDS, condom use among older teenagers more than doubled (Miller & Moore, 1990). Even today, however, surveys indicate that about half of

1987). Studies also show that a large proportion of condom users do not use condoms correctly (e.g., putting the condom on before first entry and holding onto the condom while withdrawing) (Oakley & Bogue, 1995).

Why do so few adolescents use contraception regularly and effectively? Social scientists point to several factors. First, for a sizable minority of adolescents, contraceptives are not readily available—or, if they are, young people may not know where to get them. Approximately 15 percent of adolescent girls and 25 percent of adolescent boys reported that they did not use contraceptives when they had sex for the first time because they could not get them (Hayes, 1987). This is likely to be an especially important barrier for younger adolescents, who may feel uncomfortable discussing their sexual activity with parents or other adults, whose help or consent may be necessary in order to obtain birth control. Having ready access to a free, confidential family planning service that does not require parents' consent is a strong predictor of whether adolescents will use contraceptives at all or will use them consistently (Brooks-Gunn & Furstenberg, 1989; Mauldon & Luker,

1996). It is also the case that adolescents who are conscious about their health generally are more likely to use contraception, suggesting that it may be useful to incorporate education about contraception into broader health promotion efforts (Fortenberry, Costa, Jessor, & Donovan, 1997).

Second, many young people are insufficiently educated about sex, contraception, and pregnancy (Trussell, 1989), although knowledge alone does not seem to be sufficient to promote contraceptive use; individuals must be motivated to use contraception as well as know why they need to (Sheeran, Abraham, & Orbell, 1999). Nevertheless, many young people do not fully understand that the likelihood of pregnancy varies over the course of a woman's menstrual cycle, and more than half mistakenly believe that it is during menstruation that the risk of pregnancy is greatest (Zelnick & Kantner, 1973). At the time of first intercourse, about one-third of all teenagers who do not use contraception fail to do so because they don't know about contraception or don't think about using contraceptives (Hayes, 1987). Among sexually active teenagers, 20 percent of all girls and more than 40 percent of all boys usually "just trust to luck" that pregnancy will not result from intercourse (Sorensen, 1973). Consistent with this, adolescents who have pregnancy tests but who learn that they are not pregnant—that is, those who believe that they *are* lucky—are less likely to use contraceptives regularly during subsequent months (Zabin, Sedivy, & Emerson, 1994). Unfortunately, few sexually active adolescents who fail to use contraception remain lucky for very long.

Psychological factors also play a role in adolescents' failure to use contraception. Many young people do not recognize the seriousness of pregnancy and take the possibility lightly (Hayes, 1987). More than 25 percent of nonusers of contraception report that they or their partners simply do not want to use birth control. From a cognitive perspective, the limited ability of young adolescents to engage in long-term hypothetical thinking, and their occasionally egocentric tendency to believe that they are immune from the forces that affect others, may impede their consideration of pregnancy or a sexually transmitted infection as a likely outcome of sexual activity. Perhaps most important, many adolescents fail to use birth control because doing so would be tantamount to admitting that they are planfully and willingly sexually active (Miller & Moore, 1990). Going on the pill or purchasing a condom requires an adolescent to acknowledge that he or she is having sexual relations. For many young people,

this is an extremely difficult admission to make. This may be especially true for young women who feel ambivalent and guilty about sleeping with someone for the first time. And many teenagers do not anticipate having intercourse (Trussell, 1989). Consistent with this, studies show that one of the best predictors of condom use is the individual's intent to use a condom and willingness to communicate about it with his or her partner (Sheeran et al., 1999; Tschann & Adler, 1997). Interventions designed to strengthen adolescents' intentions, and not just increase their knowledge, have been shown to be effective in promoting condom use, even within high-risk populations (Jemmott, Jemmott, Fong, & McCaffree, 1999).

Given all these reasons, it comes as no surprise to learn that one of the best predictors of contraceptive use is the adolescent's age: Younger teenagers are less informed, more guilty about having sex, less likely to be able to discuss contraception with their partner, and less able to see and understand the potential negative consequences of an unwanted pregnancy (Miller & Moore, 1990; Sheeran et al., 1999). Relatively younger women are even less likely to use contraception if their sexual partner is older (Glei, 1999; Miller, Clark, & Moore, 1997). It is also important for adolescents to understand the need to use contraception every time they have sex. A very large proportion of teenagers who have had sex with contraception have also had sex *without* contraception (Arnett & Balle-Jensen, 1993; Gillmore, Morrison, Lowery, & Baker, 1994).

One study illustrates the role that emotional factors play in influencing contraceptive use. Individuals who feel very guilty about having sex are less likely to be sexually active; however, when they are, they are also less inclined to use effective contraception—perhaps because their guilt inhibits their ability to plan for sex (Gerrard, 1987). When sexual standards become more permissive, many individuals who would otherwise feel guilty about having sex are drawn into sexual relationships. Unfortunately, their feelings of guilt are not changed by the aura of permissiveness, and, as a consequence, they have sex without using effective contraception. Along these lines, studies indicate that religious adolescents are less likely to be sexually active but also are less likely to use birth control if they do have sex (Studer & Thornton, 1987). Sexually active adolescents who are less impulsive and more conventional are more likely to use contraceptives than their peers, however (Costa et al., 1996; DiClimente et al., 1996; Serovich & Greene, 1997).

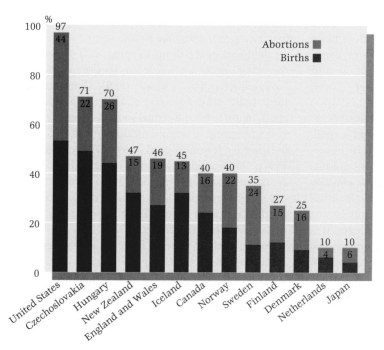

More interesting, perhaps, is research indicating that the rate of adolescent pregnancy is substantially higher in the United States than in other industrialized countries—despite the fact that the rate of teenage sexual activity in the United States is comparable to that in other countries (Jones et al., 1987) (see figure 11.6). For numerous reasons, American teenagers are less likely than their counterparts in other industrialized countries to use contraception regularly and effectively (Arnett & Balle-Jensen, 1993). According to one widely cited study, this is because nonmarital sex is portrayed in the United States as "romantic, exciting, and titillating . . . [while] at the same time, young people get the message that good girls should say no" (Jones et al., 1987, p. 239). As yet another expert wrote, "Sex saturates American life—in television programs, movies, and advertisements—yet the media generally fail to communicate responsible attitudes toward sex, with birth control remaining a taboo subject" (Westoff, 1988, p. 254). One result of this set of mixed messages is that the rates of both teenage childbearing and teenage abortion are substantially higher here than in many industrialized nations (Westoff, 1988).

This evidence suggests that there is a great deal that adults can do to improve the contraceptive behavior of adolescents. First, adults can see that contraceptives are made accessible to the young people who feel they need them. Second, adults can provide sex education at an early enough age to instruct young people in the fundamentals of contraceptive use before, rather than after, adolescents have become sexually active; such education should be aimed at strengthening adolescents' intentions to use contraception, not just their contraceptive knowledge. Third, parents and teachers can make adolescents feel more free to talk about their sexual interests and concerns, so that young people will be more apt to look at their own behavior seriously and thoughtfully. Finally, the mass media need to portray sex in a more responsible fashion, showing contraception use along with sexual activity. When, for instance, was the last time you saw a couple in a film or on television interrupt sex in order to discuss birth control?

AIDS and Other Sexually Transmitted Infections

Helping youngsters understand sex, pregnancy, and contraception is an important goal of sex education programs for adolescents. Helping them avoid the risks of **sexually transmitted infections,** or **STIs,** is another. Once called venereal diseases or sexually transmitted diseases (STDs), STIs are caused by viruses, bacteria, and parasites that are transmitted through sexual contact (Mahoney, 1983). Several million adolescents contract a sexually transmitted infection each year, and one in four teenagers contracts a sexually transmitted infection be-fore graduating from high school (Gans, 1990; Luster & Small, 1994). Some of the most common STIs among adolescents are **gonorrhea** and **chlamydia** (both caused by bacteria) and **herpes** and the infection associated with the **human papilloma virus** (both caused by viruses) (Slap & Jablow, 1994). These infections pose a significant health risk to young people, because they are associated with increased rates of cancer and infertility.

During the 1980s, a new and far more serious STI commanded the world's attention: **AIDS, or acquired immune deficiency syndrome.** AIDS is transmitted through bodily fluids, especially semen, during sexual intercourse and through blood when drug users share needles. Before information was available about the transmission of AIDS, some individuals were infected through blood transfusions in hospitals. Now hospitals routinely screen blood for the AIDS virus—**HIV, or human immunodeficiency virus**—and this means of transmission is extremely rare today.

AIDS itself has no symptoms, but HIV attacks the body's immune system, interfering with the body's ability to defend itself against life-threatening diseases, such as pneumonia and cancer. About 25 percent of all individu-als who are infected with the virus develop complications within five years; about half of all people in the United States known to have AIDS have died as a result.

Although the incidence of AIDS in the United States was initially concentrated within two groups, gay men and drug users who use needles, surveys indicate that the transmission of AIDS through heterosexual activity is currently a clear danger within the adolescent community, particularly among inner-city minority youngsters (D'Angelo, Getson, Luban, & Gayle, 1991), among homeless youth (Rotheram-Borus, Koopman, & Ehrhardt, 1991), and among high school dropouts (St. Louis et al., 1991). Among HIV-infected females, the major source of infection is heterosexual intercourse (Futterman, Hein, Reuben, Dell, & Shaffer, 1993). Be-cause there is a long period of time between HIV infec-tion and the actual manifestation of illness, however—sometimes, as long as 10 years—many more adolescents are likely to be asymptomatic carriers of the HIV virus who may develop AIDS in young adulthood (Hein, 1988a). You should be aware that HIV infection is not limited to poor, inner-city adolescents, however: In 1990, it was estimated that 1 in 500 college students (and 1 in 200 male college students) would test HIV-positive (Gayle et al., 1990). Studies of adolescents' behavior and beliefs indicate that heterosexual, bisexual, and homo-

sexual youth are all at high risk for HIV infection (Rotheram-Borus, Marelich, & Srinivasan, 1999).

The chances of contracting HIV are greatest among individuals who use drugs, have unprotected sex, have many sexual partners, have been sexually abused, and al-ready have another sexually transmitted infection (such as gonorrhea) (Hein, Dell, Futterman, Rotheram-Borus, & Shaffer, 1995; Lowry et al., 1994). Because these risk fac-tors are more common among young people than adults, the risk of HIV infection among adolescents is substan-tial. Accordingly, in recent years numerous efforts have been made to develop AIDS education programs specifi-cally aimed at teenagers (e.g., Fang, Stanton, Feigelman, & Baldwin, 1998; Hausser & Michaud, 1994; Jemmott et al., 1999; St. Lawrence, 1993). Unfortunately, despite the exis-tence of many programs designed to reduce the preva-lence of HIV infection among adolescents, many young people, especially minority youth, remain confused and misinformed about AIDS (DiClemente, Boyer, & Morales, 1988; Goodman & Cohall, 1989; Stevenson, Davis, Weber, Weiman, & Abdul-Kabir, 1995).

Most experts believe that, short of abstinence, the best way for teenagers to protect themselves against contract-ing HIV and many other STIs is by using condoms during sex. Educating young people about the risk factors associ-ated with AIDS is important, because studies show that adolescents who believe that they are at risk for HIV in-fection, and who are motivated to avoid the risk, are more likely to take precautions during intercourse (DiClemente et al., 1992; Hausser & Michaud, 1994; Jemmott et al., 1999; Orr & Langefeld, 1993; Rotheram-Borus & Koop-man, 1991). Increasing adolescents' perceptions of vul-nerability to HIV infection is not sufficient to motivate them to use condoms, however (Gerrard, Gibbons, & Bushman, 1996). Even adolescents who know they are vulnerable to infection are less likely to protect themselves when they feel negatively about using condoms, when they themselves are positively inclined toward risk taking, and when their friends are actively engaged in risky sex (St. Lawrence, Brasfield, Jefferson, Allyene, & Shirley, 1994; Romer et al., 1994; Serovich & Greene, 1997; Shoop & Davidson, 1994). It is important to remember that ado-lescents' sexual behavior is as much, if not more, influ-enced by their perceptions of benefits (e.g., the fun of having different partners) as it is by their perceptions of costs (e.g., the risks of having different partners) (Levin-son, Jaccard, & Beamer, 1995). In short, although most adolescents are aware of the risk of HIV infection, and although few conceive of themselves as immortal, it has been difficult to convince teenagers to translate this knowledge into safer behavior (Gerrard et al., 1996; Langer, Tubman, & Duncan, 1998). As one team of authors concluded, "dissemination of information, in and of itself, is unlikely to deter the spread of AIDS significantly" (Shayne & Kaplan, 1988, p. 199). More promising strategies emphasize adolescents' motives and social relations, rather than their knowledge (Fang et al., 1998; Jemmott et al., 1999).

RECAP

Adolescents are infamously poor users of contraception, especially in the United States. Most experts agree that the reasons so few adolescents use birth control regularly are that contraceptives are not as accessible as they might be, that adolescents are insufficiently educated about pregnancy and contraception, that adolescents seldom anticipate having intercourse until they become sexually active on a regular basis, and that using birth control requires the sort of long-term planning that many young people are reluctant or unable to engage in. Several million adolescents contract a sexually transmitted infection each year, and one in four teenagers contracts a sexually transmitted infection before graduating from high school. Although most adolescents are now aware of the risk of HIV infection, it has been difficult to convince teenagers to translate this knowledge into safer behavior. Programs that simply advocate abstinence have not been successful, and information alone appears to do little to change adolescents' sexual behavior.

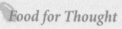

Food for Thought

Explain why adolescents are not, for the most part, reliable users of contraception. Based on the research, what sorts of interventions do you think hold the most promise for increasing contraceptive use among teenagers?

TEENAGE PREGNANCY AND CHILDBEARING

The Nature and Extent of the Problem

Given the high rate of sexual activity and poor record of contraceptive use among contemporary adolescents, it comes as little surprise that many young women become pregnant before the end of adolescence. Each year, approximately 1 million American adolescents become pregnant—the highest rate of teen pregnancy in the industrialized world (review figure 11.6). The rate of teenage births in the United States is twice as high as in Great Britain (which has the second highest teen birth rate), 4 times greater than in Spain or Sweden, 7 times greater than in Denmark and the Netherlands, and 15 times greater than in Japan (Coley & Chase-Lansdale, 1998).

Statistics indicate that nearly one-fourth of young American women experience pregnancy before the age of 18, and the number increases to about 45 percent before the age of 21. Among African American youth, over 40 percent experience pregnancy by age 18, and nearly two-thirds by age 21. These rates are actually slightly lower than they were in the 1970s, not because rates of sexual activity have declined but primarily because of more effective contraceptive use among sexually active teenagers (Furstenberg, Brooks-Gunn, & Chase-Lansdale, 1989; Mosher & Bachrach, 1996). In 1988, however, the rate of teenage childbearing increased, either because of increased sexual activity, decreased use of contraceptives, decreased access to abortion, or a combination of these factors (Barringer, 1990). Indeed, between 1983 and 1993, the rate of childbearing among unwed women (most of whom were teenagers or young adults) soared by 70 percent (Holmes, 1994). During the 1990s, the rate of teenage childbearing declined once again (Coley & Chase-Lansdale, 1998).

It is important to keep in mind that only about half of all adolescent pregnancies result in childbirth. About 40 percent of all teenage pregnancies are aborted, and slightly more than 10 percent end in miscarriage. Among women who carry their pregancy full-term, the vast majority—over 90 percent—keep and raise the infant, whereas 1 in 10 chooses to have the child adopted. Thus, of the approximately 1 million pregnancies recorded among teenage girls each year, approximately half end in abortion or miscarriage, about 45 percent result in the birth of an infant who will be raised by his or her mother (with or without the help of a spouse or other family members), and about 5 percent result in the birth of an infant put up for adoption (Coley & Chase-Lansdale, 1998; Hayes, 1987).

It is important to distinguish between pregnancies and actual births—a distinction that seems often to get lost in debates over the consequences of teenage pregnancy. Because of the many pregnant adolescents choosing abortion, the birthrate among teenagers is far lower than it would otherwise be, and it may surprise you to learn that the birthrate among adolescents today is considerably lower than it was in previous eras. Contrary to the popular idea that teenage childbearing has reached epidemic proportions in this country is the truth of the matter: Relatively more women gave birth to an infant before reaching adulthood in previous decades than today—by a large margin. For example, in 1955, the rate of childbearing among women between the ages of 15 and 19 was 90 births per 1,000 women. In 1999, by contrast, it was fewer than 50 births per 1,000 women (Centers for Disease Control, 2000a).

If teenage childbearing is less prevalent today than in earlier eras, why does the issue receive so much attention in the popular press? First, although the rate of childbearing may be lower today than before, the proportion of teenage childbearing that occurs out of wedlock is much higher. In earlier eras, adolescents who became pregnant were much more likely to marry before the child was born. Their pregnancy and childbearing did not cause as much concern, because they were "legitimized" by marriage. One source estimates that half of all adolescent women who married during the late 1950s were pregnant at the time of marriage (Furstenberg, Brooks-Gunn, & Morgan, 1987). As recently as 1955, out-of-wedlock births accounted for only about 14 percent of all births to young women. However, by 1995, this figure had skyrocketed to 75 percent (Coley & Chase-Lansdale, 1998).

Society is now more tolerant of single parenthood and of nonmarital pregnancy than it was 50 years ago, and many more women choose this option today than did so in the past. Nonetheless, one reason for the special concern about teenage childbearing in the popular press is that such a high proportion of it occurs outside of marriage. Whether this should be a concern, however—setting issues of morality aside for the moment—is still hotly debated. Indeed, there is some evidence that the fates of a large group of adolescent mothers are worsened, not bettered, by marrying the father of their child.

A second reason for widespread concern is that rates of teenage childbearing vary markedly across ethnic and socioeconomic groups. Middle-class women are far more likely to abort their pregnancies than are poor women, and, as a consequence, the problem of teenage childbearing is densely concentrated among economically disadvantaged youth (Miller & Moore, 1990; Russell, 1994). Part of the controversy surrounding teenage childbearing is linked to the American public's concern about the large number of teenage mothers who spend extended periods

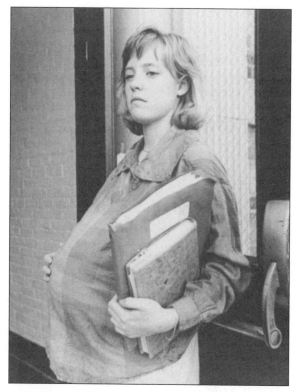

▲ *Nearly one-fourth of American young women become pregnant before their 18th birthday. About half of these pregnancies result in the birth of a baby.* (Gale Zucker/Stock, Boston)

of time on welfare—more than half of all welfare funding in the United States is spent on families caused by teenage births (Coley & Chase-Lansdale, 1998). And, because minority adolescents are more likely to grow up poor, teenage childbearing is especially high in nonwhite communities. Among white adolescents, nearly two-thirds of all births occur outside of marriage, but a large proportion of these births occur within the context of cohabitation; among African American adolescents, the percentage of out-of-wedlock childbirths is close to 100, and relatively few of these occur among cohabiting couples (Manning & Landale, 1996; Schellenbach, Whitman, & Borkowski, 1992). The rate for Hispanic teenagers falls somewhere in between; interestingly, young Mexican American women are more likely to bear their first child within marriage, whereas young Puerto Rican women are more likely to bear children out of wedlock but within the context of cohabitation, suggesting that cultural attitudes toward marriage and cohabitation influence the context of childbearing in important ways (Darabi & Ortiz, 1987; East & Blaustein, 1995; Manning & Landale, 1996).

Because minority youth are more likely to experience problems such as school failure or unemployment, early childbearing is likely to take place in the context of limited social and economic resources. Indeed, the main reason for the high rate of nonmarital childbearing among African Americans is the higher proportion of adolescents growing up in single-parent homes (Bumpass & McLanahan, 1987), which experience more stress. In addition, many poor African American young women believe that it is perfectly normal to become a mother while still a teenager and to become a grandmother before turning 40 (Perez-Febles, Allison, & Burton, 1999), norms that may be handed down from one generation to the next (Hardy, Astone, Brooks-Gunn, Shapiro, & Miller, 1998).

Contributing Factors

Many myths permeate discussions of the causes of adolescent pregnancy and complicate what is actually a fairly simple matter. The most important differences between young women who do and do not become pregnant during adolescence are in their sexual activity and contraceptive use. Sexual activity among American young people is high, and contraceptive use is sporadic and inadequate. Although there is some evidence that African American and Hispanic teenagers are more likely than white teenagers to say they intend to have a baby at an early age, the large racial difference in teenage childbearing is due mainly to racial differences in *unintended* pregnancies (Mosher & Bachrach, 1996; Trent & Crowder, 1997).

Deep down inside, though, do adolescents who become pregnant actually want to have a baby? This has been an extremely difficult question for social scientists to answer. According to national surveys, 85 percent of births to women aged 15 to 19 are unintended—that is, unwanted or mistimed—a figure suggesting that the vast majority of adolescent mothers did not become pregnant intentionally. Yet studies that plumb the issue a bit deeper find that many young women who say they do not want to become pregnant are actually ambivalent, not unequivocally negative, about the prospect of having a child. More important, those who are ambivalent about childbearing are less likely to use contraception effectively (Zabin, Astone, & Emerson, 1993). Thus, it seems safe to say that, whereas the vast majority of sexually active teenagers do not actively wish to become pregnant, a significant minority feel less troubled by the prospect of early parenthood than do their peers, and that these youngsters are more likely to risk pregnancy by having unprotected sex. Risky sex may be part of a larger constellation of risk behaviors, including delinquency and ex-

perimentation with drugs and alcohol (Scaramella, Conger, Simons, & Whitbeck, 1998). As one team of authors wrote, "Adolescent childbearing is more an unintended result of risky behaviors than a result of rational choice" (Trent & Crowder, 1997, p. 532). Research also indicates that the younger sisters of adolescent mothers may be more likely to become adolescent parents themselves, in part because their older sister may communicate some acceptance of early motherhood (East, 1996a, 1996b; East & Felice, 1992).

There are important differences between pregnant teenagers who do, and do not, seek abortion. Although studies show that teenagers can make well-reasoned decisions about abortion, this option is not chosen equally often within all segments of the adolescent population: Unplanned pregnancies are much more likely to be terminated by abortion among young women who are academically successful and ambitious; who come from middle- or upper-class families; whose parents are well educated; and whose significant others support the decision to terminate the pregnancy (Hayes, 1987; Miller & Moore, 1990). An important factor accounting for the racial and socioeconomic differences in adolescent childbearing, therefore, is that white and middle-class adolescent women perceive themselves as having more to lose—economically and in terms of their careers—by having a child so early in life than do their minority and poor counterparts. It has also been suggested that, because teenage childbearing is so prevalent in the African American community, it is more accepted by adults and more acceptable to teenagers (Coley & Chase-Lansdale, 1998). Consistent with this, research shows strong neighborhood influences on teenage childbearing: Among urban African American adolescents, childbearing is more common in segregated neighborhoods than in integrated ones (Sucoff & Upchurch, 1998).

Several studies have examined whether teenagers who choose to abort an unwanted pregnancy are harmed psychologically by the experience. The consensus among experts is that they are not (Hayes, 1987). Indeed, one study indicates that pregnant teenagers who abort their pregnancy are significantly better off two years later, psychologically as well as socially and economically, than comparable women who choose to give birth to their child (Zabin, Hirsch, & Emerson, 1989). In that study, among the most important differences between the groups was that the young women who had terminated their pregnancy by abortion were less likely over the following two years to experience a subsequent pregnancy and were more likely to practice contraception. Given the apparent psychological and economic benefits of terminating an unwanted adolescent pregnancy, it is easy to understand why many social scientists have questioned the wisdom of recent court decisions designed to restrict adolescents' access to abortion services (Blum, Resnick, & Stark, 1990). Although some studies show that laws requiring parental notification or limiting access to legal abortion do, in fact, result in fewer terminated pregnancies among pregnant adolescents (Joyce & Mocan, 1990; Rogers, Boruch, Stoms, & DeMoya, 1991), not all studies reach the same conclusion (e.g., Henshaw, 1995).

Less research has examined pregnant adolescents who choose adoption. In general, formal adoption, like abortion, is selected by adolescents from more affluent backgrounds and with higher educational aspirations (Donnelly & Voydanoff, 1996). However, informal adoption—in particular, having one's child raised by one's own mother—is widely practiced within the poor, African American community (Resnick, Blum, Bose, Smith, & Toogood, 1990; Sandven & Resnick, 1990). Like adolescents who choose to abort their pregnancy, those who choose to have their infant adopted (formally or informally) show no negative psychological effects of the decision. In fact, in terms of occupational and educational attainment, adolescents who select adoption are better off than those who choose to rear their child (Donnelly & Voydanoff, 1996; Kalmuss, Namerow, & Bauer, 1992; Sandven & Resnick, 1990). Unfortunately, many adolescents are ill-informed about adoption procedures, and this lack of information likely makes adoption a relatively less frequent choice among pregnant teenagers (Daly, 1994).

The Role of the Father

A number of studies have focused on the male partners of pregnant adolescents. In general, research indicates that these males share a number of distinguishing characteristics that differentiate them from their peers who do not impregnate adolescent girls. Most important is the fact that they are more likely than their peers to have problems with self-esteem, school, work, drugs and alcohol, and the law and are more likely to have fathered a child previously (Dearden, Hale, & Woolley, 1995; Fagot, Pears, Capaldi, Crosby, & Leve, 1998; Hardy, Duggan, Masnyk, & Pearson, 1989; Males & Chew, 1996; Pirog-Good, 1995; Spingarn & DuRant, 1996; Thornberry, Smith, & Howard, 1997). Although much has been made in the popular media about the age gap between teenage mothers and the men who fathered their children, the proportion of teenage births fathered by adult men (i.e., 20 years or older) actually has declined over the

past 40 years, and the age difference between teenage mothers (most of whom are 18 or 19) and their sexual partners is generally about 2 or 3 years—a gap not substantially different from the age gap between husbands and wives in the general population (Elo, King, & Furstenberg, 1999). Regardless of the age difference between mother and father, however, the higher rates of problem behavior among the male partners of pregnant adolescents help explain why marriage may not be the best response to pregnancy for teenage women.

Although many of their problems precede the pregnancy, young men's educational development and mental health are hurt by fathering a child early in life, even if they do not marry the child's mother (Buchanan & Robbins, 1990; Furstenberg et al., 1989; Nock, 1998; Vera Institute of Justice, 1990). Men who impregnate adolescents are more likely to drop out of school and to report feeling anxious and depressed as young adults than are their peers. The adverse effects of teenage fatherhood appear to be greater among white and Hispanic men than among African American men, however, perhaps because teenage fatherhood is more disruptive and is seen as less acceptable within the white and Hispanic communities (Buchanan & Robbins, 1990). In general, however, teenage fathers receive little in the way of supportive services or assistance in becoming responsible parents (Kisela & Sturmer, 1993).

The Consequences for Mother and Child

Because teenage childbearing tends to go hand in hand with a variety of problems—the most critical of which is poverty—it is extremely difficult to know whether any problems of teenage mothers or their children result from the mother's young age or from other, correlated factors. Separating the effects of early childbearing from poverty is a matter of more than theoretical importance: If early childbearing is, in fact, a problem in and of itself, it is important to direct preventive programs at deterring adolescent pregnancy (either by discouraging sexual activity or by encouraging effective contraceptive use) and childbearing (by encouraging adoption and abortion). However, if poverty, not the mother's age, is the key, an entirely different set of strategies is called for, aimed not at youngsters' sexual behavior but at all individuals' economic circumstances. It is extremely important, therefore, to ask whether and in what ways a mother's age at the time she gives birth affects her and her child's well-being.

The prevailing wisdom until fairly recently was that children born to teenage mothers are at great risk for a range of health and behavior problems in the short and long term, including low birth weight, conduct problems, hyperactivity, and achievement difficulties. Newer and more sophisticated studies, however, temper this conclusion. These studies indicate that many of the problems that are believed to plague children born to adolescent mothers result primarily from the environment of poverty and single parenthood in which these children are raised, rather than from the mother's age (e.g., Moore & Snyder, 1991; Schellenbach et al., 1992; Wasserman, Rauh, Brunelli, Garcia-Castro, & Necos, 1990). In general, infants born to middle-class adolescents differ little from their counterparts born to older mothers, and infants born to poor adolescents are similar to children born to equally poor adults. One important exception to this general similarity between the children of adolescents and the children of adult mothers is that adolescent mothers—even of similar socioeconomic origin—may perceive their babies as being especially difficult and may interact with their infants less often in ways that are known to be beneficial to the child's cognitive and social development (Coley & Chase-Lansdale, 1998; Furstenberg et al., 1989; Miller & Moore, 1990; Schellenbach et al., 1992; Sommer et al., 1993). To what extent this directly jeopardizes the child's development is not known with any certainty, although studies suggest that children born to adolescent mothers are more likely to have school problems, more likely to be involved in misbehavior and delinquent activity, and more likely themselves to be sexually active at an early age (Coley & Chase-Lansdale, 1998; Conseur & Rivara, 1997; Furstenberg et al., 1987). In general, therefore, and for reasons that are not known, the cognitive and psychosocial problems of children born to adolescent mothers are increasingly more apparent with age. There is also some evidence that children of adolescent mothers may be at greater risk for abuse and neglect (Stier, Leventhal, Berg, Johnson, & Mezger, 1993). Not surprisingly, adolescent mothers who were relatively more intelligent and better adjusted before the birth of their infant have greater parenting skills later (Mylod, Whitman, & Borkowski, 1997; O'Callaghan, Borkowski, Whitman, Maxwell, & Keogh, 1999).

Many of the problem behaviors seen among children of adolescent mothers are prevalent among poor children growing up in single-parent homes. Because adolescent mothers are more likely than adult mothers to be both unmarried and poor, their children are at greater risk of developing a variety of psychological and social problems. In other words, the greater incidence of problems among offspring of adolescent mothers may reflect the overall environment in which their children grow up, rather than the ways in which they are raised by their mothers. Although we can in theory separate the effects of poverty on children from the effects of adolescent childbearing, in reality the two usually go together, and the result is that children born to adolescent mothers are more likely than other children to suffer the effects both of malnutrition—in the womb as well as in the world—and of environmental deprivation.

Studies of the long-term consequences of adolescent parenthood indicate that there may be problems associated with it that directly involve the teenage mother, however (Furstenberg et al., 1989). In general, women who bear children early suffer disruptions in their educational and occupational careers (Ahn, 1994; Hayes, 1987; Klepinger, Lundberg, & Plotnick, 1995). Not only are adolescent mothers more likely to come from a poor background and to have a greater history of academic difficulties, but they are also more likely to remain poor than are their equally disadvantaged peers who delay childbearing until after their schooling is completed (Hoffman, Foster, & Furstenberg, 1993; Moore et al., 1993; Richardson, 1996). It is important to bear in mind, however, that many adolescent mothers were poor students *before* becoming pregnant, and the limited educational attainment of teenage mothers is at least partly due to factors that were in play long before the pregnancy (Fergusson & Woodward, 2000; Hoffman et al., 1993; Miller-Johnson et al., 1999; Roenkae & Pulkkinen, 1998). In short, poverty and low achievement are both causes *and* consequences of early childbearing.

The news is not always bad, however, and having a child early in life does not cast in concrete a life of poverty and misery for the mother and her youngster. Studies show that there is considerable diversity among teenage mothers in the routes that their adult lives take (Ahn, 1994; Coley & Chase-Lansdale, 1998). Some research suggests that the long-term consequences of early childbearing may not be as negative among African Americans as among whites or Hispanics, especially among African Americans living in communities in which early childbearing is accepted as normative (Moore et al., 1993; Smith & Zabin, 1993).

In general, young mothers who remain in, or return to, high school and delay subsequent childbearing fare a great deal better over the long run—as do their children—than do their counterparts who drop out of school or have more children relatively early on (Furstenberg et al., 1987; Leadbeater, 1996; Upchurch & McCarthy, 1990). Marriage tends to be a high-risk strategy (Furstenberg, Brooks-Gunn, & Morgan, 1987). In some cases, when a stable relationship is formed and economic resources are available, marriage improves the mother's and the child's chances for life success; this seems to be especially true for women who marry somewhat later. In other cases, however, a hasty decision to marry in the absence of a stable relationship and economic security actually worsens many other problems (Teti & Lamb, 1989).

Teenage Pregnancy Prevention and Intervention Programs

Although there are stories of young women whose lives are not devastated by early childbearing, in general, studies suggest that there are not many such successes. The statement, more than 30 years old, that "the girl who has an illegitimate child at the age of 16 suddenly has 90 percent of her life's script written for her" (Campbell, 1968, p. 238) is still more often than not true today. In general, the successes are young women who have avoided dire poverty, rather than those who have achieved great economic success. Although the picture of adolescent parenthood appears less uniform or dire than typically painted in the popular press, there is still consensus among experts that it is important to try to prevent teenage pregnancy and childbearing. Unfortunately, this task is more easily said than done. To date, few strategies have proven effective on a large scale.

The first line of teenage pregnancy prevention has been classroom-based sex education. Today, many adolescents receive classroom instruction about sex—whether through high school health classes, biology classes, classes designated exclusively for the purpose of sex education, or educational programs administered through youth or religious organizations. Such classes and programs, if they are available, are likely to be targeted at adolescents rather than at children and preadolescents (Kirkendall, 1981).

Most evaluations of formal sex education programs administered through schools have shown them to have no effect on adolescents' sexual activity but small effects on their contraceptive behavior (Franklin, Grant, Corcoran, Miller, & Bultman, 1997). The consensus among experts has been that most traditional sex education programs fail because they emphasize the biological over the emotional aspects of sex (and thus do not prepare adolescents for making decisions about sexual involvement); because they come too late in high school (and thus do not reach adolescents before they become sexually active); and because they focus primarily on changing students' knowledge rather than their behavior

(and thus do not directly affect patterns of sexual activity or contraceptive use).

During the mid-1980s, the emphasis in sex education shifted from encouraging "responsible" sex to encouraging sexual abstinence, an emphasis that still prevails in many school districts (Landry, Kaeser, & Richards, 1999). In addition to sessions about sexual decision making and values and exercises designed to enhance students' self-esteem, such programs taught adolescents to "just say no" to sexual intercourse. It was hoped that, by encouraging sexual abstinence, these programs would also have the effect of reducing teenage pregnancy. Unfortunately, careful evaluations of these programs have shown that they are not usually successful, either in changing adolescents' sexual behavior or in reducing rates of nonmarital pregnancy (Christopher, 1995; Christopher & Roosa, 1990; Kirby, Korpi, Barth, & Cagampang, 1997; Roosa & Christopher, 1990).

Does anything work? One approach that experts are cautiously optimistic about involves a combination of school-based sex education and community-based health clinics through which adolescents can receive information about sex and pregnancy, as well as contraception. Some evaluations indicate that this combination of sex education and clinic may diminish the rate of teen pregnancy, even within inner-city communities characterized by high rates of adolescent pregnancy and childbearing (Christopher, 1995; Frost & Forrest, 1995; Koo, Dunteman, George, Green, & Vincent, 1994; Tiezzi, Lipshutz, Wrobleski, Vaughan, & McCarthy, 1997). Unfortunately, as you might suspect, many parents have objected to such programs in their community, fearing that they will stimulate teenage sexual activity. However, most studies indicate that these fears—however intuitively reasonable—are unwarranted; in general, condom-distribution programs increase adolescents' condom use but have little impact on the rate of sexual activity (Christopher, 1995; Furstenberg, Geitz, Teitler, & Weiss, 1997; Guttmacher et al., 1997; Hausser & Michaud, 1994; Richardson, 1997; Schuster, Bell, Berry, & Kanouse, 1998; Sellers, McGraw, & McKinlay, 1994; Wolk & Rosenbaum, 1995).

At the same time, it is clear that programs that provide family planning services to adolescents are unlikely, on their own, to be a successful solution to the problems of teenage pregnancy and sexually transmitted infection. Even the best programs affect the sexual behavior only of teenagers who actually use the services (Brindis, Starbuck-Morales, Wolfe, & McCarter, 1994; Christopher, 1995; Erikson, 1994; Hughes, Furstenberg, & Teitler, 1995). As a consequence, many communities that

▲ *Sex education courses that focus on increasing youngsters'
knowledge about sex, contraception, and pregnancy should begin early and should be combined with courses designed to
teach decision-making skills and interpersonal assertiveness.*
(Michael Newman/PhotoEdit)

implement these sorts of prevention programs do not
find overall declines in rates of teen pregnancy (Christopher, 1995). Clearly, effective prevention programs must
find ways to motivate sexually active adolescents to make
use of whatever health-care services are provided. One
program, for example, had success by combining service
learning with classroom discussions about life options
(Allen, Philliber, Herrling, & Kuperminc, 1997).

Research on the consequences of adolescent childbearing also suggests that many of the negative effects of
having children early can be prevented or at least mini-
mized by lessening the disruptive economic impact of
teenage parenthood on young women's lives (Sandfort &
Hill, 1996). What is known about the factors that work
toward this end? First, it is clear that marrying the father
of the child may place the adolescent mother at greater
risk if the father is not capable of economically supporting himself, much less his family. Studies show, in contrast, that, if the father is able to find a good job and remains employed, he can be an important source of
psychological and economic support and a healthy influence on the mother and child. Given the characteristic
problems of male partners of adolescent mothers, however, it is all too likely that marriage will diminish, rather
than enhance, an adolescent mother's economic circumstances. In addition, marriage places the adolescent
mother at greater risk of having another child relatively

soon, which further jeopardizes her already precarious
economic situation. One of the factors most likely to
worsen the problems of teenage mothers is having yet another child (Apfel & Seitz, 1997; Furstenberg et al., 1987;
Kalmuss & Namerow, 1994). Moreover, teenage marriage
is very likely to end in divorce, which itself is an additional
stressor on the mother and child.

Adolescent mothers, therefore, cannot always look to
the father of the child to help break the cycle of poverty
that afflicts young parents. However, they can, in many
cases, look to their own parents for support, and this may
be an effective strategy for some (Stevens, 1988). Teenage
mothers who move in with their own family *for a short
time*—a practice far more common among African
Americans than among Hispanic or white adolescents—
are more likely to enjoy educational and occupational
success than are their counterparts who live on their own,
studies show (Miller & Moore, 1990; Roye & Balk, 1996;
Trent & Harlan, 1994). The family's help allows the young
mother to return to school or find employment. Without
this help, many young mothers must drop out of school
and find and pay for child care, which often is more costly
than the income their low-paying jobs generate. Without
a high school diploma, these women have little chance of
improving their economic situation and, consequently, of
improving the opportunities for their child.

Although having the support of one's own family is
important for adolescent mothers' development and
well-being, actually living with one's family of origin after
having a baby is not uniformly beneficial, as several studies of three-generational African American families show.
On the negative side, when adolescent mothers live with
their own mother, the living arrangement may undermine the development of their own parenting skills and
increase their risk of getting pregnant again (Chase-Lansdale, Brooks-Gunn, & Zamsky, 1994; Gillmore, Lewis,
Lohr, Spencer, & White, 1997; Spieker & Bensley, 1994),
and problems in the relationship between the adolescent
and her mother can adversely affect the teen parent's
mental health (Davis & Rhodes, 1994; East & Felice, 1996;
Musick, 1994). On the positive side, living with one's
mother is associated with continued schooling, which
confers long-term economic advantages (Spieker & Bensley, 1994). Interestingly, several studies have found that
support from the adolescent mother's father, in addition
to that of her child's father, may be especially beneficial
(Davis, Rhodes, & Hamilton-Leaks, 1997; Oyserman,
Radin, & Benn, 1993). One fact is certain, though: Adolescent mothers who receive social support fare better, are
better parents, and have healthier children than do adolescent mothers who lack support (Barratt, Roach,

Morgan, & Colbert, 1996; Leadbeater & Bishop, 1994; Roye & Balk, 1996). Studies suggest that a lack of support is an especially dire problem among poor Hispanic adolescent mothers (Wasserman et al., 1990). Together, these and other studies suggest that the best arrangement for a teenage mother may be to live independently from her own parents but to be able to rely on them for emotional support and child care (Coley & Chase-Lansdale, 1998).

Because it is so important for young mothers to have an adequate income and the chance for adequate employment, many policymakers have called for changes in the ways that schools and other social institutions treat pregnant students and for changes in the provision of day care (Sandfort & Hill, 1996; Seitz & Apfel, 1993, 1994). Among the most important are adaptations in school schedules and the development of school-based child-care centers, so that pregnant students can remain in school after the birth of their child; the expansion of subsidized child care for young mothers who are out of school, so that the economic benefits of having a job are not outweighed by the costs of suitable child care during the workday; and the expansion of family planning services for adolescent mothers, so that they can prevent yet another pregnancy. Unfortunately, evaluations of programs aimed at enhancing teen mothers' employability, decreasing their reliance on welfare, or preventing their subsequent pregnancies have been largely disappointing (Coley & Chase-Lansdale, 1998), although there have been occasional successes reported in the literature (e.g., Solomon & Liefeld, 1998).

Food for Thought

Describe trends in teenage childbearing over the past 50 years. Does the public's concern over teenage childbearing match the data? Why or why not?

Web Researcher Check out one or more websites aimed at gay, lesbian, or bisexual teenagers. What seem to be the dominant issues and concerns? Go to www.mhhe.com/steinberg6 for further information.

KEY TERMS

AIDS (acquired immune deficiency syndrome)

androgens

autoerotic behavior

chlamydia

gender identity

gonorrhea

herpes

HIV (human immunodeficiency virus)

human ecology

human papilloma virus

permissive societies

restrictive societies

risk factor

semirestrictive societies

serial monogamy

sex-role behavior

sexual orientation

sexual socialization

sexually transmitted infections (STIs)

sociosexual behaviors

testosterone

RECAP

Preventing teenage pregnancy has been extremely difficult, and most sex education programs developed during the past two decades have failed in this respect. There are approximately 1 million teenage pregnancies each year in the United States, about half of which are carried full-term. Research indicates that teenagers are not harmed psychologically by aborting their pregnancy or by placing their infant up for adoption, but studies of the consequences of teenage childbearing indicates that the short- and long-term problems for the teenage mother may be considerable. Although there are occasional success stories, teenage parents are more likely than their peers to experience disruptions in their educational and occupational development. Studies clearly show that adolescent mothers who have social support from family or friends and who are able to complete high school fare far better than those who do not.

Chapter 12

Achievement

Because adolescence typically is a time of preparation for the roles of adulthood, considerable attention has been paid to the development and expression of achievement during these years. Broadly defined, **achievement** concerns the development of motives, capabilities, interests, and behavior that have to do with performance in evaluative situations. More specifically, the study of achievement during adolescence has focused on young people's performance in educational settings and on their hopes and plans for future scholastic and occupational careers. Since most young people form their first realistic educational and vocational plans during adolescence, researchers have long been interested in the factors that appear to play the greatest role in influencing individuals' futures.

Achievement is a particularly important consideration in the study of adolescence in contemporary society. Industrialized societies place an extraordinary emphasis on achievement, competition, and success—more so than on cooperation, for example, or on the development of satisfying interpersonal relationships (McClelland, 1961). During childhood and adolescence, youngsters are continually tested to determine how they stand scholastically in relation to their peers. In most industrialized societies, the amount of education a person has completed and the job he or she holds—two of the most important indicators of achievement—provide a basis for individuals' self-conceptions and their image in the eyes of others (Featherman, 1980).

A second reason for the importance of achievement in the study of adolescence in contemporary society concerns the range and rapidly changing nature of the choices faced by today's young people. Unlike youth in most traditional cultures, adolescents in modern societies are confronted with a phenomenally wide array of difficult occupational and educational decisions before they turn 25. Beyond such fundamental questions as what type of career to follow and whether to continue with schooling after high school, there are other difficult issues to ponder: what specific sorts of jobs should be pursued within a particular career path, what kind of educational preparation would be most appropriate, and how entry into the labor force is best negotiated. For the college student contemplating a career in business, for instance, is it better to major in business administration, or is it better to follow a liberal arts course of study? How early is it necessary to decide which aspects of business to specialize in? Is it necessary to go to graduate school, or do employers prefer applicants with

work experience in place of an advanced degree? These are all difficult questions to answer. And they are made more difficult because the nature of education and work changes so rapidly in contemporary society.

Finally, achievement is a particularly important issue in the study of adolescence in contemporary society because of wide variation in levels of educational and occupational success. By the end of high school, many adolescents have demonstrated a high enough level of academic achievement to enter selective colleges and universities, yet a sizable number of their peers enter adulthood unable even to read a newspaper or understand a bus schedule. Although most adolescents today complete high school and go on to college, a substantial number leave high school before graduating. Similar disparities exist in the occupational achievements of young people: Most youth make the transition from school to work without a great deal of difficulty, but a significant number experience long bouts of unemployment. Even within the population of young people who enter the labor force, there is considerable variation in earnings and in occupational status. Many important questions in the study of adolescent achievement, therefore, concern factors that distinguish between young people who are successful—however success is defined—and those who are not. •

ACHIEVEMENT AS AN ADOLESCENT ISSUE

In contemporary society, achievement is a lifelong concern. Educational institutions—even for young children—stress performance, competition, and success on tests of knowledge and ability. Concerns over achievement continue throughout adulthood as well. Like their younger counterparts, most adults place a premium on success. Work and occupational attainment play an important role in shaping the adult's values, self-concept, and self-esteem (Featherman, 1980). Development in the realm of achievement neither begins nor ends during adolescence.

Achievement during the adolescent years, though, merits special attention for several reasons (Masten et al., 1995). First, the fact that adolescence is a time of preparation for adult work roles raises questions about the nature of the preparation that young people receive and the processes through which they sort themselves (or are sorted) into the occupational roles that may influence the remainder of their lives. Many of the factors that narrow an individual's educational options and vocational alternatives are prominent during the high school and college years, and it is important to ask how such options are defined and at what age educational and occupational decisions are made.

Second, although differences in school performance and achievement are apparent as early as the first grade, not until adolescence do individuals begin to appreciate fully the implications of these differences for immediate and future success. During childhood, for example, children's occupational plans are made, to a large extent, on the basis of fantasy and passing interests, without any realistic assessment of their practicality or feasibility. Not until adolescence do individuals begin to evaluate their occupational choices in light of their talents, abilities, and opportunities and the performance of those around them. For example, high-achieving students who attend schools in which average achievement levels are high do not feel as good about themselves as their high-achieving counterparts in schools with lower average achievement levels (Marsh, Kong, & Hau, 2000).

Third, it is clear that the educational and occupational decisions made during adolescence are more numerous, and that the consequences of such decisions are more serious, than the decisions characteristic of childhood. For example, in most elementary schools, although children may be grouped by ability—groupings that have implications for subsequent achievement—they generally are all exposed to fairly similar curricula and have few opportunities to veer from the educational program established by their school system. In high school, however, students can select how much science and math they want to take, whether they wish to study a foreign language, whether they want to pursue an academic or a vocational track—even whether they want to remain in school once they have reached the legal age for leaving school. Moreover, it is during adolescence that most individuals decide whether they want to pursue postsecondary education or enter a full-time job directly from high school. All these decisions have important implications for the sort of choices and plans the adolescent will make in the future, which in turn will influence his or her earnings, lifestyle, identity, and subsequent psychosocial development.

It is neither surprising nor coincidental that many achievement-related issues surface for the first time during adolescence. One major reason for this relates to the social transition of adolescence. In virtually all societies, adolescence is the period when important educational and occupational decisions are made, and society has

structured its educational and work institutions accordingly. In the United States, for example, it is not until adolescence that individuals attain the status necessary to decide whether they will continue or end their formal education. And it is not until adolescence that people are allowed to enter the labor force in an official capacity, since child labour regulations typically prohibit the employment of youngsters under the age of 14 or so. The transition from school to work—one of the central issues in the study of achievement during adolescence—is a socially defined transition, a passage that society has determined will be negotiated during adolescence.

The special significance of achievement in adolescence does not derive solely from the transitional nature of the period, however. The intellectual changes of the period are important as well. Not until adolescence are individuals cognitively capable of seeing the long-term consequences of educational and occupational choices or of realistically considering the range of scholastic and work possibilities open to them. Thus, a second reason for the prominence of achievement-related issues during adolescence relates to the advent of more sophisticated forms of thinking. The ability to think in hypothetical terms, for example, raises new achievement concerns for the individual ("Should I go to college after I graduate, or should I work for a while?"); it also permits the young person to think through such questions in a logical and systematic fashion ("If I decide to go to college, then . . . ").

Finally, the emergence of many achievement concerns during adolescence is tied to the biological changes of puberty. As noted in chapter 2, not until early adolescence do sex differences in achievement test performance begin to emerge, with boys scoring higher on tests of mathematics and girls outscoring boys on tests of verbal skills. Sex differences in achievement-related motives and beliefs appear around puberty as well. These sex differences are related primarily to the differential responses that boys and girls receive from others as a result of changes in their appearance at puberty and as a result of differences in how adolescent boys and girls view themselves. Boys may be encouraged to pursue coursework (and, by implication, careers) in math and science, whereas girls may be encouraged to study the arts and humanities. This differential treatment may have important implications for sex differences in educational and occupational attainment.

In this chapter, we will look at the nature of achievement during the adolescent years. As you will see, the extent to which an adolescent is successful in school and in preparing for work is influenced by a complex array of personal and environmental factors. In addition, we will find that development in the realm of achievement is cumulative, in that youngsters who are successful early are likely to reap the benefits of the educational system, to continue to succeed in school, and to complete more years of education than their peers. This success, in turn, gives them an advantage in the labor market, since the prestige and status of individuals' entry-level jobs are largely dependent on their educational background.

If there is a theme to this chapter, it is that, at least with respect to achievement during adolescence, the rich get richer, and the poor get poorer. More often than not, personal and environmental influences on achievement complement rather than correct each other, in the sense that individuals who bring personal advantages to the world of achievement—talent, a motive to succeed, high aspirations for the future—are also likely to grow up in an environment that supports and maintains achievement success. We will begin with a look at one set of factors that may differentiate the "rich" from the "poor" early in their schooling—long before adolescence, in fact: their motives to succeed and their beliefs about the causes of their successes and failures.

RECAP

Achievement is an important issue during adolescence because society typically designates adolescence as a time for preparation for adult work roles; because individuals now can understand the long-term implications of their educational and career decisions; and because, during adolescence, schools begin making distinctions among individuals that potentially have profound effects on their long-term occupational development. Because educational and occupational achievement are so cumulative, during adolescence the rich tend to get richer, whereas the poor get poorer.

Food for Thought

Adults disagree about the extent to which achievement is made an especially salient issue among adolescents. Some contend that we place too much pressure on teenagers to succeed in school. Others argue that we do not place enough. What's your view?

ACHIEVEMENT MOTIVES AND BELIEFS

The Motive to Achieve

One of the oldest notions in the study of achievement is that individuals differ in the extent to which they strive for success and that this differential striving—which can be measured independently of sheer ability—helps account for different degrees of actual achievement. Two students may both score 100 on an intelligence test; however, if one student simply tries much harder than the other to do well in school, their actual grades may differ. The extent to which an individual strives for success is referred to as his or her **need for achievement** (McClelland, Atkinson, Clark, & Lowell, 1953). Need for achievement is an intrinsically motivated desire to perform well that operates even in the absence of external rewards for success. A student who works very hard on an assignment that is not going to be graded probably has a very strong need for achievement. All other factors being equal, a student who tries hard to succeed in school is, in fact, more likely to succeed than one who tries less (Wentzel, 1989).

Generally, researchers have found that adolescents who have a strong need for achievement come from families in which parents have set high performance standards, have rewarded achievement success during childhood, and have encouraged autonomy and independence (Rosen & D'Andrade, 1959; Winterbottom, 1958). Equally important, however, this training for achievement and independence generally takes place in the context of warm parent-child relationships, in which the child forms close identifications with his or her parents (Shaw & White, 1965). Put most succinctly, authoritative parenting, coupled with parents' encouragement of success, is likely to lead to the development of a strong need for achievement.

One psychological factor that interacts with an adolescent's need for achievement is a related and, in some senses, complementary motive—**fear of failure.** Fear of failure, which is often manifested in feelings of anxiety during tests or in other evaluative situations, can interfere with successful performance. Generally speaking, when the achievement situation involves an easy task, and when a little anxiety helps focus attention (if, for example, the task is boring), a moderate amount of fear of failure may improve performance by increasing one's concentration. Usually, however, the anxiety generated by a strong fear of failure interferes with successful performance. This is often the case in situations in which the task involves learning something new or solving a complex problem—like many tasks faced by adolescents in school settings. Many individuals with a high fear of failure come from family environments in which parents have set unrealistically high standards for their children's achievement and react very negatively to failure (rather than simply reacting positively to success) (Spielberger, 1966).

An adolescent's need for achievement and his or her fear of failure work together simultaneously to pull the individual toward, and repel the individual from, achievement situations. Individuals with a relatively strong need for achievement and a relatively weak fear of failure are more likely to achievely approach challenging achievement situations—by taking more difficult classes, for example—and to look forward to them. In contrast, those whose fear of failure is relatively intense and whose need for achievement is relatively weak will dread challenging situations and will do what they can to avoid them. Many students who have trouble persisting at tasks and who fear failure become **underachievers**—students whose grades are far lower than one would expect, based on their intellectual ability.

It is important to distinguish between students whose underachievement is due mainly to anxiety and those who underperform for other reasons, however (Midgley, Arunkumar, & Urdan, 1996; Midgley & Urdan, 1995). Some students, for example, *want* to appear uninterested in school because in some contexts this presentation may garner more respect and admiration from peers than academic success. Others want to make sure that they have an excuse for poor performance other than a lack of ability (Nurmi, Onatsu, & Haavisto, 1995). Still others may diminish the importance of academics as a response to poor performance (Gibbons, Benbow, & Gerrard, 1994). These students may use various self-handicapping strategies—such as fooling around in class, waiting until the last minute to study for an exam, and turning in incomplete homework—as a way of self-protection ("I failed the test because I didn't try hard, not because I'm stupid") or self-presentation ("I'm too cool to care about doing well in school"). A number of writers have drawn special attention to the use of self-handicapping strategies among ethnic minority youth, who may disengage from school because they perceive their long-term prospects as limited by discrimination and prejudice (Mickelson, 1990; Taylor, Casten, Flickinger, Roberts, & Fulmore, 1994).

The Importance of Beliefs

In recent years, researchers have questioned the usefulness of asserting the existence of global achievement-related motives that are expressed equally in a variety of situations. The relation between an individual's internal needs and his or her actual effort and performance varies in different situations. Someone who has a strong need for achievement might express this need to different degrees in academic and in social situations—or even in different sorts of academic and different sorts of social situations—depending on past experiences and the individual's perception of the specific situation. Because of this, individuals' actual performance in achievement situations may not be strongly related to their general achievement motives. Some students who want very much to succeed, for example, are susceptible to feelings of anxiety and helplessness in performance settings.

Newer research indicates that adolescents make judgments about their likelihood of succeeding or failing and that they exert different degrees of effort accordingly. For example, adolescents' choices of what

▲ *Individuals who are intrinsically motivated strive to achieve because of the pleasure they get out of mastering the material.* (Spencer Grant/Stock, Boston)

Patterns of Achievement in Adolescent Boys and Girls

We noted in chapter 2 that sex differences in cognitive skills during adolescence are trivial. On standardized tests of intellectual abilities, girls and boys perform at about the same level, and, when sex differences are observed, they are small—too small, indeed, to make a meaningful difference in adolescents' school performance. Despite this absence of sex differences in ability, though, girls in general are less likely than boys to pursue advanced courses in math and science, and the girls who do so are more likely to drop out before finishing (Hanson, 1996; Stumpf & Stanley, 1996). Studies of college students show that women are underrepresented among graduates whose degrees are in math, engineering, and the physical sciences are overrepresented among graduates whose degrees are in the humanities and education (Smith, 1992). Because high school preparation undoubtedly influences college course choices—which, in turn, affect career choices—educators have been interested in understanding why sex differences in math and science achievement emerge during adolescence. If adolescent girls and adolescent boys have equal ability, why do they show different patterns of math and science course selection and achievement during high school?

Social scientists have offered several explanations. The first concerns sex differences in the social consequences of succeeding in school and, particularly, of succeeding in math and science. Most notably, fear of success may be more prevalent among females than among males during early and middle adolescence than during childhood or adulthood (Butler & Nissan, 1975; Hoffman, 1977; Ishiyama & Chabassol, 1985). This finding and other research on achievement-related conflicts among adolescent girls (e.g., Rosen & Aneshensel, 1975) suggest that the social world of adolescent peer groups make it difficult for adolescent girls to integrate positive feelings toward achievement—especially toward achievement in stereotypically masculine subject areas—into their sense of identity (Bornholt, Goodnow, & Cooney, 1994; Douvan & Adelson, 1996). This may be an especially salient factor in classrooms in which students' performance is public, as in science classes with a strong hands-on component (Jovanovic & King, 1998).

Of special importance for girls is the relation among academic achievement, the development of a feminine identity, and social relations with boys. As psychologists Judith Bardwick and Elizabeth Douvan (1981) explained two decades ago, "Until adolescence the idea of equal capacity, opportunity, and life style [for men and women] is held out to [girls]. But sometime in adolescence the message becomes clear that one had better not do too well, that competition is aggressive and unfeminine, that deviation threatens the heterosexual relationship" (p. 152). In other words, adolescent girls may not fear success per se, but they may be wary of other consequences—not necessarily negative consequences, but often merely *complicated* consequences—that may befall them as a result of their achievement. During adolescence, when concerns over dating and socializing may be paramount, and when the sense of self is shaky and the view of the future cloudy, achievement in math and science may carry a different connotation for girls than for boys.

A second account focuses on sex differences in attitudes, especially toward mathematics (Catsambis, 1994). Although girls and boys are equally likely to report liking math, girls are less likely than boys to believe that taking math classes will be useful to their future careers, and, by high school, there are clear sex differences in course selection and preference (Kavrell & Petersen, 1984; Klebanov & Brooks-Gunn, 1992). As a result, girls may place less value on achievement in math classes, may have poorer self-conceptions about their math abilities, and may be less inclined to continue a math curriculum and more inclined to drop out of advanced math classes (Marsh & Yeung, 1998; Smith, 1992). In other words, sex differences in career expectations may influence early attitudes toward math classes, which, in turn, influence attainment in math. Unfortunately, to the extent that young adolescent girls opt out of advanced math classes, they limit their chances of moving into occupations that require preparation in math—including careers in science and engineering—and thus contribute to perpetuating occupational sex stereotypes.

Interestingly, the findings that boys are more positive about math and science than girls are and that girls are more positive about language arts than boys are are not limited to the United States, as the accompanying figure illustrates. There is some evidence that these trends are changing, however, because improvements in girls' achievement—across all subject areas—are closing the achievement gap, even in subjects traditionally dominated by males. Indeed, observations that boys are not doing as well as girls in school, that boys are disciplined more in school than are girls, and that boys are more likely to perceive their schools and teachers as unfair (Nichols & Good, 1998) are now prompting numerous writers to express concern about the achievement problems of boys (Marsh & Yeung, 1998; Sommers, 2000).

Psychologist Jacquelynne Eccles and her colleagues have argued that sex differences in course selection may be related to sex differences in achievement attributions and beliefs. Parents, in particular, may pass on different expectations about math and science achievement to sons and daughters, and they may tacitly accept their children's sex-stereotyped preferences for course selection, regardless of similarities in sons' and daughters' actual abilities (Muller, 1998). Parents of sons are more likely to believe that their child's success in math reflects his intrinsic ability, whereas parents of daughters are more likely to attribute their child's math success to hard work. Parents of sons are also more likely than parents of daughters to think that

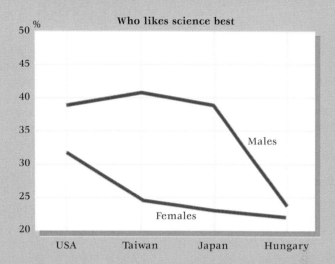

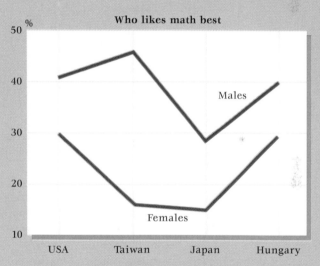

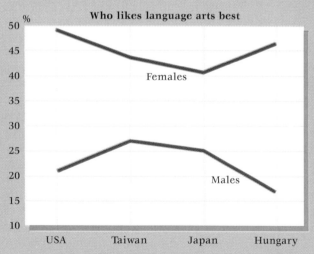

▲ Cross-cultural differences in males' and females' favorite classes. (Evans, 1992)

taking advanced math courses is important (Parsons, Adler, & Kaczala, 1982). To make matters worse, studies indicate that school counselors and teachers also endorse views that support math achievement among boys but discourage it among girls (Kavrell & Petersen, 1984). Studies indicate that sexist attitudes toward adolescents' math and science ability exist within all-female, all-male, and coeducational schools (Lee, Marks, & Byrd, 1994).

Overall, then, research indicates that parents' beliefs about their child's abilities—which are, in part, determined by the parents' own stereotypes about gender—influence the child's academic self-conceptions, which in turn influence performance in school (Eccles, 1993; Jacobs, 1991; Jacobs & Eccles, 1992) (see the accompanying figure). This seems to be especially important during the middle-school years, when adolescents' self-conceptions are relatively more malleable and perhaps more susceptible to their parents' influences (Klebanov & Brooks-Gunn, 1992).

Grades in school decline during early adolescence, among both boys and girls. This decline has been attributed to harder grading practices by teachers (Kavrell & Petersen, 1984) and to the declining importance of achievement to adolescents as they approach high school (Elmen, 1991). But the decline in grades in math and science may evoke very different responses in boys and girls. Boys, who have been told that they are good at math and science and that these subjects are important, may simply try harder to do better. Girls, who receive less support for achievement in math and science both from adults (who may inadvertently socialize them to believe that these subjects are difficult and not very useful) and peers (who may convey the message that success in these subjects is not attractive), may respond by avoiding math and science entirely. This response is easy to understand: By the time an adolescent girl has reached the point in high school that she is able to choose among electives, she has been socialized to believe that math and science are difficult, that these classes are not especially worthwhile, and that success in them is inconsistent with being popular and attractive.

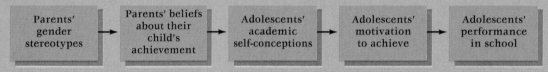

▲ *How parents contribute to sex differences in math and science achievement.* (Adapted from Eccles, 1993)

classes to take in school are influenced by their beliefs about their abilities. Students who believe that they are good at math, for instance, will take more, and more difficult, math courses than their peers. However, because course selection influences subsequent achievement (students who take more challenging math perform better on math tests) and achievement, in turn, influences students' beliefs about their abilities (students who do well on math examinations come to see themselves as better math students), a cycle is set in motion in which students' beliefs and their abilities and actual achievement have a reciprocal influence on each other (Marsh & Yeung, 1997).

A number of studies indicate that student' beliefs about their abilities exert a strong influence on their motivation and effort, which in turn influences their scholastic performance (Harter, Whitesell, & Kowalski, 1991; Little, Oettingen, Stensenko, & Baltes, 1995; Mac Iver, Stipek, & Daniels, 1991; Marsh, 1990; Pintrich, Roeser, & De Groot, 1994). In order to understand this process, it is necessary to draw a distinction between **intrinsic motivation** and **extrinsic motivation.** Individuals who are intrinsically motivated strive to achieve because of the pleasure they get out of learning and mastering the material. Individuals who are extrinsically motivated strive to achieve because of the rewards they get for performing well and the punishments they receive for performing poorly. Early theories of achievement motivation did not draw this distinction and, as a consequence, may have grouped together students who—although highly motivated to do well in achievement situations—may have been motivated for very different reasons.

We all know individuals who are genuinely interested in what they learn in school, and we know others whose main concern is really just their grade-point average. These two approaches to achievement have very different psychological consequences for the individual adolescent. Adolescents who believe that they are competent are more likely to be intrinsically motivated and are more likely to maintain their efforts to do well in school (Pintrich et al., 1994). In contrast, adolescents who have doubts about their abilities are more likely to be extrinsically motivated and to be more susceptible to feelings of anxiety and hesitation in the face of challenge. That is, although extrinsically motivated adolescents want to do well in school, the source of their motivations puts them on shaky ground.

It is known that adults—parents and teachers, for instance—can affect adolescents' *degree* of achievement motivation. Adults also affect the extent to which an adolescent's achievement motives are intrinsic or extrinsic. When adults attempt to control an adolescent's achievement behavior through rewarding good grades (e.g., by giving prizes or money), punishing bad grades (e.g., by restricting privileges), or excessively supervising their performance (e.g., by constantly checking their homework), adolescents are more likely to develop an extrinsic orientation and, as a result, are less likely to do well in school. In contrast, adolescents whose parents encourage their autonomy, provide a cognitively stimulating home environment, and are supportive of school success (without rewarding it concretely) tend to perform better in the classroom (Deci & Ryan, 1985; Ginsburg & Bronstein, 1993; Gottfried, Fleming, & Gottfried, 1998). Girls, especially, are negatively affected by overcontrolling parents and teachers, perhaps because girls tend to be more susceptible to adult influence than boys are (Boggiano, Main, & Katz, 1991). Research also suggests that low-achieving students are more affected—for better or for worse—by their teachers' expectations than are high-achieving students (Madon, Jussim, & Eccles, 1997).

Other studies suggest that the way an adolescent views intelligence in general also enters into the achievement equation (Stipek & Gralinski, 1996).

Table 12.1   How researchers measure cognitive stimulation in the home environment

Instruments and items
Home observation for the measurement of the environment
Family has a television, and it is used judiciously, not left on continuously.
Family encourages child to develop or sustain hobbies.
Child is regularly included in family's recreational hobby.
Family provides lessons or organizational membership to support child's talents.
Child has ready access to at least two pieces of playground equipment in the immediate vicinity.
Child has ready access to a library card, and family arranges for child to go to library once a month.
Family member has taken child, or arranged for child to go to a scientific, historical, or art museum within the past year.
Family member has taken child, or arranged for child to take a trip on a plane, train, or bus, within the past year.
Home environment survey
Does your child have access to a real musical instrument?
Does your child have his or her own subscription to a magazine or book club?
Is your child receiving private lessons?
How many different magazines or journals does your family receive at home each month?
Is there a personal computer at home that the child has had experience working with?
How much education do you expect your child to achieve?
Family environment scale
We often talk about political and social problems.
We rarely go to lectures, plays, or concerts.*
Learning about new and different things is very important in our family.
We are not that interested in cultural activities.*
We rarely have intellectual discussions.*
Someone in our family plays a musical instrument.
Family members often go to the library.
Watching TV is more important than reading in our family.*
Family members really like music, art, and literature.

* Item is reverse scored.
Source: Gottfried, Fleming, and Gottfried 1998.

Three factors interact to predict a student's behavior: whether the student believes that intelligence is fixed or malleable; whether the student is oriented more toward extrinsic rewards (performance) or more toward intrinsic rewards (mastery); and whether the student is confident about his or her abilities, or, as some theorists have put it, has a strong sense of **self-efficacy** (Bandura, Barbaranelli, Caprara, & Pastorelli, 1996).

Students who believe that intelligence is fixed tend to be oriented toward their performance and are greatly affected by their degree of confidence (Stipek & Gralinski, 1996). If they are confident about their abilities, they tend to work hard and seek out challenges. If they are insecure, however, they tend to give up easily and feel helpless. Students who believe that intelligence is malleable, in contrast, approach achievement situations from a different perspective. These students are more likely to have learning goals than performance goals; for them, satisfaction comes from mastering the material, not simply from gaining a good evaluation. Students who have this orientation are far less affected by their level of confidence, because they are less concerned about their performance. Whether assured or insecure, these students exert effort and seek out challenges, because they are motivated by learning rather than by performing (Purdie, Hattie, & Douglas, 1996).

When conditions change such that performance becomes more important than learning, students' motives and beliefs change as a result. You have probably experienced this when you have enrolled in a course in which the instructor stressed grades, rather than mastery of the material. This sort of emphasis brings out the worst in students—literally. Performance goals make students more extrinsically motivated, more insecure about their abilities, more hesitant to challenge themselves, and less likely to ask for help to improve their performance (Newman & Schwager, 1995).

One of the most interesting applications of this perspective on achievement has been in studies of changes in adolescents' academic motivation during the transition from elementary school to junior high school (Eccles et al., 1993). It has been widely reported that students' motivation and school performance decline when they move into secondary school (Elmen, 1991; Wigfield, Eccles, Mac Iver, Reuman, & Midgley, 1991; Yoon, Eccles, Wigfield, & Barber, 1996). Why might this be? Among the other important changes that take place during this school transition (see chapter 6) is a shift, by teachers, toward a more performance-oriented style of instruction and evaluation. During secondary

school, students discover that more of an emphasis is placed on grades than had been the case in elementary school. This shift in emphasis undermines many students' intrinsic motivation and their self-confidence, which diminishes their performance. In addition, studies find that individuals' beliefs about intelligence change as they move into and through adolescence, with older students more likely to view intelligence as stable (Ablard & Mills, 1996).

These newer models of the psychological aspects of achievement during adolescence suggest that, across all ethnic groups, students' beliefs (about the nature of ability in general and the nature of their ability in particular) influence their motivation, which in turn influences their performance (Bandura et al., 1996; Gordon, 1995). One additional factor involves the way in which students interpret their successes and failures. Researchers who are interested in **achievement attributions** (Dweck & Wortman, 1980) have studied how the attributions that individuals make for their success or failure influence their performance. According to these theorists, individuals attribute their performance to a combination of four factors: ability, effort, task difficulty, and luck. When individuals succeed and attribute their success to internal causes, such as their ability or effort, they are more likely to approach future tasks confidently and with self-assurance. If, however, individuals attribute their success to external factors outside their control, such as being lucky or having an easy task, they are more likely to remain unsure of their abilities. Not surprisingly, scholastically successful individuals, who tend to be high in achievement motivation, are likely to attribute their successes to internal causes (Carr, Borkowski, & Maxwell, 1991; Powers & Wagner, 1984; Vispoel & Austin, 1995).

The way in which youngsters interpret their failures is also important in influencing their subsequent behavior. Some youngsters try harder in the face of failure, whereas others withdraw and exert less effort. According to psychologist Carol Dweck (Dweck & Light, 1980), when individuals attribute their failures to a lack of effort, they are more likely to try harder on future tasks. But individuals who attribute their failure to factors that they feel cannot be changed (bad luck, lack of intelligence, difficult material) are more likely to feel helpless and to exert less effort in subsequent situations.

Suppose, for instance, a student takes the SAT and receives a combined score of 1000. He then is told by his guidance counselor that the SAT is a measure of intelligence and that his score reflects how smart he is. The counselor tells the student that he can retake the test if he wants to but that he should not expect to score much higher than 1000. Now imagine a different student, who also scored 1000 on the test. She is told by her guidance counselor that effort has a great deal to do with scores on the SAT and that she can raise her score by trying harder. In all likelihood, the next time these students take the test, the first student will not try as hard as the second student will, because the first student is more likely to feel helpless.

Students who are led to believe that their efforts do not make a difference—by being told, for example, that they are stupid or that the work is too difficult for them—develop **learned helplessness:** the belief that failure is inevitable (Dweck & Light, 1980). As a result of learned helplessness, some students try less hard than their peers, and they do not do as well as they might. Research on adolescents' attributions for success and failure suggests that, instead of dismissing low-achieving students as having "low needs for achievement" or "low intelligence," teachers and other school personnel can help students achieve more by helping them learn to attribute their performance to factors that are under their own control (Hudley, 1997; Wilson & Linville, 1985).

RECAP

Early theories of the development of achievement stressed individual differences in achievement motivation: Some individuals were believed to have a stronger need for achievement than others, and individuals were thought to differ as well in the extent to which they are afraid of failure. Although it is surely true that adolescents who strive for success expend more effort in school and achieve more there, contemporary theories tend to stress the interaction of motives, beliefs, attributions, and goals as influencing adolescents' achievement orientation. Adolescents who believe that ability is malleable (rather than fixed); who are motivated by intrinsic, rather than extrinsic, rewards; who are confident about their abilities; and who attribute their successes and failures to effort (rather than to ability or luck) achieve more in school than their peers.

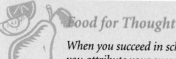

Food for Thought

When you succeed in school, to what do you attribute your success? When you fail, how do you explain your failure?

ENVIRONMENTAL INFLUENCES ON ACHIEVEMENT

Ability, beliefs, and motivation may play a large role in influencing individual performance, but opportunity and situational factors also have a great deal to do with achievement (Eccles, Wigfield, & Schiefele, 1998). Many of the differences in academic or occupational achievement that are observed among adolescents result not from differences in adolescents' abilities, motives, or beliefs but from differences in the environments where abilities and motives are expressed.

School environments differ markedly—in physical facilities, in opportunities for pursuing academically enriched programs, and in classroom atmospheres. For example, students are more engaged and achieve more in schools that are more personal, less departmentalized, and less rigidly tracked and in which team-teaching is used more frequently (Gamoran, 1992; Lee & Smith, 1993). Unfortunately, many school districts, plagued with shrinking tax bases, are characterized by decaying school buildings, outdated equipment, and textbook shortages. In some schools, the problems of crime and discipline have grown so overwhelming that attention to these matters has taken precedence over learning and instruction. Many young people who genuinely want to succeed are impeded not by a lack of talent or motivation but by a school environment that makes academic success virtually impossible. Students who attend schools with a high concentration of poor, minority students are especially disadvantaged, as are students who attend schools with a high proportion of students from single-parent families (Bankston & Caldas, 1996, 1998; Pong, 1997, 1998).

The school, of course, is not the only environment that makes a difference in adolescents' achievement, and few would argue that schools should accept full responsibility for adolescents who do not succeed at a level consonant with their abilities. If anything, the evidence suggests that important aspects of the home environment are better predictors of adolescents' academic achievement (Coleman et al., 1966; Steinberg, 1996).

The Influence of the Home Environment

Researchers have focused on three ways in which the adolescent's home may influence his or her level of achievement. First, as you now know from studies of parental influences on sex differences in achievement, adolescents' achievement is directly related to the level of achievement that their parents expect them to attain. Adolescents whose parents expect them to go to college are more likely to do so than are adolescents of equal ability whose parents expect less of them (Featherman, 1980). Parental encouragement of academic success may be manifested in a number of ways, all of which have been shown to be beneficial to adolescents' school performance.

First, parents who encourage school success set higher standards for their child's school performance and homework completion and have higher aspirations for their child, which in turn contributes to school success (Entwisle & Hayduk, 1988; Natriello & McDill, 1986; Patrikakou, 1996; Wilson & Wilson, 1992). Second, parents who encourage school success support values that are consistent with doing well in school, and they structure the home environment to support academic pursuits, so that the messages children receive from their teachers are echoed at home (Hanson & Ginsburg, 1988; Kurdek & Sinclair, 1988; Sui-Chu & Willms, 1996). Third, parents who encourage success are likely to be more involved in their child's education—more likely to attend school programs, to help in course selection, to maintain interest in school activities and assignments, and the like—all of which contribute to students' success (Astone & McLanahan, 1991; Baker & Stevenson, 1986; Bogenschneider, 1997; Grolnick & Slowiaczek, 1994; Hoover-Dempsey & Sandler, 1995; Muller, 1998; Steinberg, Lamborn, Dornbusch, & Darling, 1992; Stevenson & Baker, 1987). Parental involvement in schooling may make academics seem both more important and more conquerable to the adolescent, which may enhance the young person's academic self-conceptions (Grolnick & Slowiaczek, 1994). In contrast, parental disengagement from school may make students themselves more likely to disengage and do poorly (Roeser, Lord, & Eccles, 1994). Interestingly, parental involvement in schooling has a more substantial effect when the adolescent attends a school in which a large proportion of *other* students' parents are involved as well (Darling & Steinberg, 1997; Pong, 1998).

Studies also have shown that authoritative parenting—parenting that is warm, firm, and fair—is linked to school success during adolescence, as indexed by better performance, better attendance, higher expectations, more positive academic self-conceptions, and stronger engagement in the classroom (Bronstein et al., 1996; Corville-Smith, Ryan, Adams, & Dalicandro, 1998; Deslandes, Potvin, & LeClerc, 1999; Dornbusch, Ritter, Liederman, Roberts, & Fraleigh, 1987; Steinberg,

Lamborn, Darling, Mounts, & Dornbusch, 1994; Wentzel, 1998). In contrast, parenting that is especially punitive, harsh, strict, or inept is associated with lower school engagement and diminished achievement (DeBaryshe, Patterson, & Capaldi, 1993; Melby & Conger, 1996). In one study, for example, sociologist Sanford Dornbusch and his colleagues (Dornbusch et al., 1987) demonstrated that adolescents whose parents were authoritative consistently performed better in school than did peers whose parents were indulgent or authoritarian. Interestingly, the poorest school performance was observed among adolescents whose parents were inconsistent in their child rearing. That is, even though adolescents whose parents were autocratic received lower grades than did students whose parents were authoritative, adolescents whose parents used a mixture of authoritarian and indulgent techniques performed even worse. Interestingly, extreme parental permissiveness, not authoritarianism, is associated with higher rates of dropping out of school (Rumberger, Ghatak, Poulos, Ritter, & Dornbusch, 1990). Positive parenting has been shown as well to help adolescents adjust to middle school (Bronstein et al., 1998) and to help poorly performing early adolescents turn their academic performance around in high school (Catterall, 1998).

Why do adolescents achieve more in school when they come from authoritative homes? One reason is that authoritative parenting promotes the development of a healthy achievement orientation—including an emphasis on intrinsic motivation—which in turn facilitates adolescent school performance (Bronstein, Ginsburg, & Herrera-Leavitt, 2000; DeBaryshe et al., 1993; Lamborn, Mounts, Steinberg, & Dornbusch, 1991; Steinberg, Elmen, & Mounts, 1989). This is, in part, because authoritative parents are more likely to hold healthier beliefs about their child's achievement and less likely to be overly controlling—two factors that strengthen adolescents' work orientation and intrinsic motivation (Arbeton, Eccles, & Harold, 1994; Grolnick & Slowiaczek, 1994). Having a strong work orientation enhances achievement both directly and indirectly, through the positive impression it makes on teachers (Farkas, Grobe, & Shuan, 1990). In general, these findings are in line with a good deal of research suggesting that consistent, authoritative parenting is associated with a wide array of benefits to the adolescent, including higher achievement motivation, greater self-esteem, and enhanced competence (Maccoby & Martin, 1983; Wentzel, 1994a). Authoritative parents also tend to be more involved in school, which benefits adolescents through that pathway (Paulson, 1994;

Steinberg, Dornbusch, & Brown, 1992). It is also the case that students perform better when the values and expectations they encounter at home are consistent with those they encounter in school (Arunkumar, Midgley, & Urdan, 1999).

Finally, studies have shown that the quality of an adolescent's home environment—as measured simply in terms of the presence of such items as a television set, a dictionary, an encyclopedia, a newspaper, a vacuum cleaner, and other indicators of family income—is more strongly correlated with youngsters' level of academic achievement than is the quality of the physical facility of the school they attend, the background and training of their teachers, or the level of teachers' salaries paid by the school district (Armor, 1972). A number of researchers have also shown that the extent to which the adolescent's parents provide the youngster with **cultural capital**—

▲ Adolescents who attend schools in which there are ample resources—such as computers—have a distinct advantage over their peers who attend schools in impoverished communities. (Spencer Grant/The Picture Cube)

by exposing the adolescent to art, music, literature, and so forth—exerts a positive impact on achievement, above and beyond the effects of the parents' own level of education (Buechel & Duncan, 1998; DiMaggio, 1982; Roscigno & Ainsworth-Darnell, 1999).

Interestingly, evidence on the heritability of school achievement suggests that, although intelligence and cognitive achievement have strong genetic components, school performance is highly influenced by environmental factors, both inside and outside the family (Teachman, 1997). With this in mind, it is important to realize that a disheartening numbr of young people in this country live in overcrowded, inadequate housing and come from families that are under severe economic and social stress—so much so that parental encouragement and involvement are often undermined by neighborhood conditions (Gonzales, Cauce, Friedman, & Mason, 1996). These obstacles to success disproportionately afflict youngsters from minority backgrounds. Put succinctly, many American youngsters do not grow up in an atmosphere that is conductive to academic achievement. Many communities lack what social scientists sometimes call **social capital**—the support, encouragement, and involvement of adults necessary to facilitate youngsters' success in school (Coleman & Hoffer, 1987). Social capital, which is

strengthened when families have strong ties to other families in the community, has been shown to be an important contributor to success in school, above and beyond the contribution of the adolescent's family's income, parents' education, or household composition (Pong, 1997, 1998). Students whose families lack social capital are more likely to have difficulty in school (Teachman, Paasch, & Carver, 1996).

The Influence of Friends

There is also evidence that, in addition to parents, friends influence adolescents' achievement. Indeed, some studies suggest that friends, not parents, are the most salient influences on adolescents' day-to-day school behaviors, such as doing homework and exerting effort in class (Kurdek, Fine, & Sinclair, 1995; Midgley & Urdan, 1995; Steinberg, 1996). When most of us think about the influence of adolescents' peers on achievement, we tend immediately to think of the ways in which peers undermine academic success. However, contrary to the notion that the influence of the peer group is always negative, studies suggest that the impact of friends on adolescents' school performance depends on the academic orientation of the peer group. Having friends who earn high grades and aspire to further

▲ *Having friends who value school can positively affect academic achievement; by the same token, having friends who disparage school success can depress school performance.* (Antman/The Image Works)

education appears to enhance adolescents' achievement, whereas having friends who earn low grades or disparage school success may interfere with it (Natriello & McDill, 1986; Steinberg, 1996). As they move into middle school, adolescents become increasingly worried about their friends' reactions to success in school; one study found, for example, that, by eighth grade, students did not want their classmates to know that they worked hard in school, even though they knew that it would be helpful to convey this impression to their teachers (Juvonen & Murdock, 1995). Adolescents with an extremely high orientation toward peers tend to perform worse in school, on average (Fuligni & Eccles, 1992). Conversely, adolescents who are neglected by their peers often have a stronger academic orientation than relatively more popular students (Luthar & McMahon, 1996; Wentzel & Asher, 1995).

According to one extensive study of friends in school (Epstein, 1983b), students' grades change over time in relation to the grades of their friends. Students with best friends who achieve high grades in school are more likely to show improvements in their own grades than

are students who begin at similar levels of achievement but whose friends are not high achievers. Peers also exert a small but significant influence on each other's college plans. Among low-achieving adolescents, for example, those with high-achieving friends are more likely to plan to continue their education than are those with low-achieving friends.

The potential negative impact of friends on achievement is vividly seen in a widely reported study of African American male peer groups in an inner-city school (Fordham & Ogbu, 1986). These researchers found that the bright students in that school had to live down the "burden of acting white" and face criticism from their peers, who referred to them as "brainiacs." When a small group of these students were placed in an environment in which all their peers were high achievers, the derision and negative labeling did not occur, however.

A number of researchers have begun to study how the influences of parents and peers operate *together* to affect adolescents' achievement (Brown, Mounts, Lamborn, & Steinberg, 1993; Fletcher, Darling, Steinberg, & Dornbusch, 1995; Gonzales et al., 1996; Kurdek et al., 1995;

Steinberg, 1996). These studies show that the family environment has an effect on adolescents' choice of friends, and this in turn can influence school achievement (Brown et al., 1993). In addition, having friends who value school can positively affect academic achievement, even among teenagers who do not come from nonauthoritative homes. By the same token, having friends who disparage school success may offset the benefits of authoritative parenting. Rather than asking whether family or friends influence adolescents' school performance, then, it may make more sense to ask how these two forces—along with the influence of the school itself—work together.

Situational factors can affect occupational attainment as well. In the opinion of some social critics, strong institutional barriers impede the occupational attainment of women and members of ethnic minorities (Ogbu, 1978). These barriers may be especially strong during adolescence, when young people are steered away from some educational and occupational pursuits and toward others—not on the basis of ability or interest but because of gender, socioeconomic background, or ethnicity. As we saw in chapter 6, the ways in which schools determine which students are exposed to which curricula restrict the opportunities of those students who are placed in the slower tracks and perpetuate these students' academic disadvantages. The courses they encounter are likely to be less stimulating and less intellectually enriching than those taken by their peers. And students who are placed in the slower tracks tend to come disproportionately from minority groups and to be economically disadvantaged—partly because their academic test scores warrant remedial placement, but partly as a consequence of their social background (Featherman, 1980).

Thus, although psychological factors play an important role in determining occupational and scholastic success, it is impossible to examine achievement during adolescence thoroughly without taking into account the broader environment in which individuals pursue their educational and occupational careers (Gonzales et al., 1996; Steinberg, 1996). Moreover, distinguishing between motivational and environmental factors is hard; they typically go hand in hand. Living in an environment that offers few opportunities for success induces feelings of learned helplessness, which in turn leads individuals to feel that exerting any effort to succeed is futile. Attending school in an environment where achievement is not encouraged engenders attitudes and beliefs inconsistent with striving for achievement. Rather than viewing achievement during adolescence as being determined by a single factor, such as ability, it is more accurate to say that patterns of achievement are the result of a cumulative process, which includes a long history of experience and socialization in school, in the family, in the peer group, and in the community.

RECAP

In addition to the influence of beliefs, motives, attributions, and goals, individuals' levels of achievement are also affected by the social context in which they develop, including conditions in the school, the family, and the peer group. A good deal of research indicates that adolescents perform better and are more engaged in school when they come from authoritative homes in which their parents are highly involved in their education. In addition, adolescents whose friends support academic achievement perform better in school than do peers whose friends disparage academic achievements.

Food for Thought

What sorts of parent education activities are used in the district in which you live? In view of what is known about the home environments of high-achieving students, how likely are these activities to succeed?

EDUCATIONAL ACHIEVEMENT

Educational achievement is usually defined in one of three ways: **school performance** (the grades students earn in school), **academic achievement** (performance on standardized tests), or **educational attainment** (the number of years of schooling completed). These measures of educational achievement are, not surprisingly, interrelated, but they are less tied to each other than one would expect.

No single factor adequately accounts for differences in adolescents' levels of educational achievement. Generally speaking, intellectual ability—as assessed by IQ tests—is highly correlated with performance on achievement tests (hardly a surprise, since IQ tests and achievement tests are designed to tap similar abilities). Intellectual ability is only moderately correlated with school grades, however, and just mildly correlated with educational attainment (Featherman, 1980).

The truth of the matter is that grades in school—and, to an even greater extent, educational attainment—are influenced by a wider range of factors than simply an adolescent's intellectual abilities. Grades, for example, are influenced by teachers' judgments of students' mastery of the material, and these judgments may be influenced by teachers' evaluations of students' efforts and behaviors in the classroom (Farkas et al., 1990). The number of years of school an adolescent completes is likely to be influenced by his or her family background and living circumstances, as well as by school performance. Two adolescents may have similar grade-point averages; however, if one comes from a poor family and cannot afford to go to college, the two will have different levels of educational attainment (Featherman, 1980). Even as early as elementary school, for example, many inner-city youth have very limited occupational expectations, and these low expectations affect their educational achievement and attainment (Cook et al., 1996).

Regardless of what influences educational attainment, however, it has important implications for subsequent earnings (Ceci & Williams, 1999). The gap in earnings between high school graduates and college graduates is considerable, and this is true across all ethnic groups. When individuals with a college degree enter the labor force, they earn nearly twice as much per hour as do individuals with only a high school diploma (Economic Policy Institute, 1994).

The Importance of Socioeconomic Status

One of the most powerful influences on educational achievement is the socioeconomic status of the adolescent's family. Studies have shown over and over that middle-class adolescents score higher on basic tests of academic skills, earn higher grades in school, and complete more years of schooling than do their working-class and lower-class peers (Featherman, 1980; Sewell & Hauser, 1972). Adolescents who come from lower socioeconomic levels are more likely to score lower than their more advantaged peers on standardized tests of achievement, and youngsters who come from higher socioeconomic levels are more likely to score higher. Similarly, youngsters whose parents have gone to college are more likely to attend college themselves than are those whose parents did not attend college. And youngsters whose parents completed high school are also more likely to attend college than are youngsters whose parents did not complete high school (Johnson, 1975). Although some of the socioeconomic gaps in school achievement have narrowed, and although families influence student achievement through additional pathways as well—by providing cultural and social capital, for example—many disparities in achievement between the social classes remain

strong, and the importance of socioeconomic status in determining educational achievement remains substantial, across all ethnic groups (Kao & Tienda, 1998; Goyette & Xie, 1999; Hanson, 1994; Lucas, 1996; Teachman & Paasch, 1998).

Socioeconomic status, therefore, influences both achievement and attainment and, as a consequence, influences occupational achievement as well. However, you should bear in mind that variations *within* socioeconomic categories are often as substantial as differences *between* categories. Not all youngsters from affluent backgrounds have higher levels of educational achievement than adolescents from poorer families, and many youngsters from economically disadvantaged households go on to receive college and postcollege degrees.

One major reason that family background is related to educational achievement is that children from lower socioeconomic levels are more likely to enter elementary school scoring low on tests of basic academic competence. These initial differences reflect both genetic and environmental factors. Middle-class adults generally have higher IQs than lower-class adults, and this advantage is passed on to middle-class children—both through inheritance and through the benefit that middle-class youngsters receive from growing up under more favorable environmental conditions (Chen, Lee, & Stevenson, 1996; Featherman, 1980; Teachman, 1996). Affluent youngsters receive better health care and better nutrition, for example, both of which contribute to their higher performance on intelligence tests. The disadvantages of poorer youngsters in achievement test scores persist—and may even increase—throughout elementary and secondary school (Coleman et al., 1966; Entwisle & Hayduk, 1988). Because progress in high school depends so heavily on having a solid foundation of basic academic competence, adolescents who enter secondary school without having mastered basic academic skills quickly fall behind. Many leave high school before graduating.

One bit of encouraging news on this front comes from long-term evaluations of interventions designed to improve the academic achievement of very poor youngsters, who, by virtue of their poverty, were at high risk for academic failure (Campbell & Ramey, 1995; Reynolds & Temple, 1998). In these sorts of evaluations, researchers compare groups of adolescents who participated in an intensive educational program during their preschool and elementary school years with matched samples of adolescents who had the preschool intervention only, the elementary school intervention only, or no educational intervention at all. The interventions were targeted at improving the children's school skills and at strengthening the links between parents and their child's school.

The long-term evaluations show that individuals who have participated in preschool interventions (with or without participating in elementary school interventions) perform significantly better in school during adolescence than those who have not (Campbell & Ramey, 1995). In one study, participating in both the preschool *and* elementary programs provided additional advantages over the preschool program alone (Reynolds & Temple, 1998). Interestingly, however, the adolescents who had been in the elementary school program but *not* the preschool program had no advantages over those who had been in no intervention at all (Campbell & Ramey, 1995). These findings suggest that intervention prior to entering first grade is extremely important in preventing long-term academic problems among impoverished youngsters, that extended participation is better than short-term participation, and that the intervention must begin before elementary school to be successful.

One reason for the relatively poorer school performance of disadvantaged youth, therefore, is that these youngsters begin school at a distinct academic disadvantage. A second reason for the disparity is stress, however—both before and during adolescence. Adolescents who come from lower-class backgrounds experience more stressful life events, report more daily hassles, and attend schools with more negative climates (DuBois, Felner, Meares, & Krier, 1994; Felner et al., in press; Gillock & Reyes, 1999; Pungello, Kupersmidt, Burchinal, & Patterson, 1996). Stress has been shown to adversely affect adolescents' mental health, well-being, and school performance (DuBois, Felner, Brand, Adan, & Evans, 1992; Felner et al., in press) (see the accompanying box).

Some studies also suggest that parents from higher social classes are more likely to be involved in their adolescent's education, especially through formal parent-teacher organizations, such as the PTA or PTO (Stevenson & Baker, 1987). Middle- and upper-middle-class parents also are more likely to have information about their child's school, to be responsive to their child's school problems, and to help select more rigorous courses for their child to take (Baker & Stevenson, 1986). Because adolescents whose parents are involved in their schooling perform better than adolescents whose parents are not involved, youngsters from higher social classes may achieve more in school than do their less advantaged peers (Lee & Croninger, 1994; Stevenson & Baker, 1987). In addition, parents with greater economic resources are able to provide their children with more cul-

tural capital, which is an important contributor to school success (Roscigno & Ainsworth-Darnell, 1999).

Socioeconomic differences in school achievement obviously reflect the cumulative and combined effects of a variety of influences, and it is simplistic to explain class differences in achievement without considering these factors simultaneously. What is perhaps more interesting—and more worthy of scientific study—is to ask what it is about the many youngsters from economically disadvantaged backgrounds who are successful that accounts for their overcoming the tremendous odds against them. Put concretely, the successful college student who has come from an environment of severe economic disadvantage has had to overcome incredible barriers.

Although more research on successful students from poor backgrounds is sorely needed, several findings suggest that what might be most important is social support for academic achievement: the presence of warm and encouraging parents who raise their children authoritatively, take an interest in their children's academic progress, and hold high aspirations for their children's educational attainment and the availability of peers who support and encourage academic success (Brody, Stoneman, & Flor, 1995; Gregory, 1995; Simpson, 1962; Steinberg, 1996; Sui-Chu & Willms, 1996). In other words, positive relations at home and the encouragement of significant others can, in some circumstances, overcome the negative influence of socioeconomic disadvantage.

RECAP

Socioeconomic status is an extremely powerful influence on educational achievement. Generally, adolescents from higher social classes perform better in school and complete more years of schooling than do their less advantaged counterparts. One reason for this difference is that the home environment of more affluent adolescents is more supportive of school success: Middle-class adolescents are better nourished, more consistently encouraged, and less exposed to stress than are their less affluent peers.

Food for Thought

Why does socioeconomic status have such a profound impact on student achievement? In light of this, what would you suggest as policies or practices to raise the achievement of poor youth?

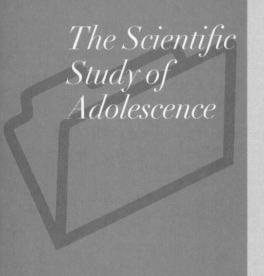

Stress as the Link Between Socioeconomic Status and Achievement

Social scientists have long known that, on average, adolescents from lower-class families achieve less in school and complete fewer years of schooling than do their counterparts from middle-class homes. This achievement gap has been attributed to differences in the early family environments of poor and well-to-do youngsters, to differences in their parents' expectations and aspirations, and to differences in the youngsters' academic capabilities. New studies on this topic demonstrate, however, that yet another factor—stress—may play an important role in explaining socioeconomic differences in educational achievement.

Psychologist Robert Felner (Felner et al., 1995) and his colleagues (DuBois, 1994) studied a sample of African American and white young adolescents living in a poor rural community. One-third of the parents in the sample were employed in unskilled occupations, and more than one-third of the parents studied did not graduate from high school. Thus, in terms of two of the most widely used indexes of social class—occupation and education—the sample had a high proportion of lower-class families. The study is especially interesting because it focuses on the rural poor—most of what is known about adolescent development in poverty comes from studies of inner-city families (McLoyd, 1990).

As in previous studies, Felner found that the youngsters from the lower-class homes (whether defined by parental education or by occupation) performed more poorly in school and on tests of achievement than did their counterparts from higher-class homes. Interestingly,

the adolescents' achievement was affected by *both* parental education and occupation, indicating that each component of social class contributes to achievement independently. The negative effects of low socioeconomic status on achievement were apparent among both African American and white youngsters. Once this pattern was established, Felner than asked *why* this is so.

Psychologists use the term **mediating variable** to refer to a variable that helps explain the link between an independent variable, such as social class, and scores on a dependent variable, such as educational achievement. In Felner's study, the researchers hypothesized that stress is a mediating variable that links social class and school achievement. They looked at several types of stressors, including **stressful life events** (such as the death of a loved one), daily hassles (such as having nagging parents), family conflict, and an alienating school climate.

In order to establish that a mediating variable is, in fact, at work, a researcher attempts to demonstrate four things: (1) that scores on the dependent variable are linked to scores on the independent variable (in this case, educational achievement and social class); (2) that scores on the mediating variable are linked to the independent variable (e.g., that stress is related to social class); (3) that scores on the dependent variable are also linked to the mediating variable (e.g., that educational achievement is linked to stress); and (4) that the link between the independent variable and the dependent variable is

Ethnic Differences in Educational Achievement

Among the most controversial—and intriguing—findings in research on adolescents' achievement are those concerning ethnic differences in school success. On average, the educational achievement of African American and Hispanic American students—virtually however indexed—lags behind that of white students, and all three groups achieve less in school than do Asian American students. Although some of these differences can be attributed to socioeconomic differences among these ethnic groups, the group disparities persist even after socioeconomic factors are taken into account

significantly weakened when the mediating variable is taken into account (in this case, that once stress is taken into account, the link between social class and educational achievement will diminish) (see the accompanying figure).

Felner first established that educational achievement is, in fact, linked to social class, satisfying the first condition listed in the preceding paragraph. He then examined whether the scores on the measures of stress used in the research were in fact correlated with social class and found that they were: The students from lower-class homes were more likely to be exposed to stress than were their more advantaged counterparts. This satisfied the second condition. Next, Felner looked to see whether the third condition was met, by examining the relation between stress and achievement. Sure enough, the researchers found that the scores on most of the indexes of stress were significantly correlated with students' school performance and with math and reading achievement test scores. Students who had experienced more negative life events or daily hassles, for example, earned lower grades, were absent from school more often, and scored lower on standardized tests of achievement. The pattern of correlations satisfied the third condition.

Finally, Felner turned to the fourth condition—that taking stress into account would diminish the link between social class and educational achievement. In order to do this, the researchers reexamined the link between social class and achievement after controlling for stress. There are a number of ways of doing this statistically, but, in essence, what the researchers did was to ask whether individuals from different social classes who report *the same amount of stress* still have different achievement scores. If they do, this means that stress did not account for the social class differences in achievement. If they do not, however, this indicates that stress is a significant mediating variable.

As the researchers hypothesized, once they took stress into account, the social class differences in school grades and in math achievement disappeared. This indicated that stress is a significant mediating variable linking social class and these two outcomes. In the case of reading scores, however, the researchers found that the link between social class and achievement remained significant, even after taking stress into account. This finding suggested that something other than stress—not measured in this study—accounts for the link between social class and reading achievement.

In many social science studies comparing groups of adolescents—for example, males and females, poor and affluent youth, or African Americans and whites—the researcher is content merely to document that the groups differ on an outcome of interest, such as achievement. Although this sort of research can be a good starting point, it rarely adds much to the understanding of adolescent development, since the studies invariably leave open the question of *why* the difference exists. Without understanding the underlying processes that have led to group differences, it is difficult, if not impossible, to design programs to influence patterns of development, if that is a researcher's ultimate goal. Thus, if we are interested in helping lower-class youngsters achieve more in school, we need to know not only that they do, in fact, achieve less than their more affluent peers but also the reasons for the difference. Felner's research suggests that at least one step we can take involves reducing the amount of stress in poor adolescents' lives.

Source: Felner et al. (1995). Poverty and educational disadvantage: Environmental mediators of socioemotional and academic achievement in early adolescence. *Child Development, 66*, 774–792.

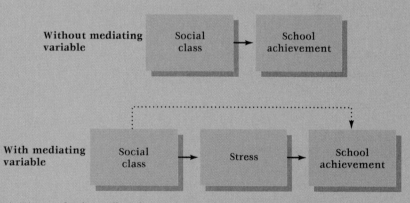

▲ *Direct and indirect effect of social class on educational achievement. Part of the effect results from stress.* (Felner et al., 1995)

(Brandon, 1991; Call & McNall, 1992; Chen & Stevenson, 1995; Fejgin, 1995; Goyette & Xie, 1999; Hedges & Nowell, 1999; Humphries, 1988; Mickelson, 1990; Steinberg et al., 1992; Sue & Okazaki, 1990; Warren, 1996). The academic superiority of Asian American students tends to emerge during the transition into junior high school—when most other students' grades typically decline (Fuligni, 1994). What has been most intriguing to social scientists is the observation that African American and Hispanic American students have educational aspirations and attitudes that are similar to those of Asian American and white students but significantly poorer academic skills, habits, and behavior (Ainsworth-Darnell & Downey, 1998). If African

▲ *Adolescents whose parents are involved in their schooling perform better than adolescents whose parents are not. Parents from higher social classes are more likely to be involved in their adolescents' education.* (Michael Newman/PhotoEdit)

American and Hispanic American students ostensibly have the same long-term goals as other students, why do they not behave in similar ways? Although some of the reason has to do with socioeconomic differences between ethnic groups, this "attitude-achievement paradox" persists even after social class is taken into account (Mickelson, 1990).

Several theories have been advanced to explain the paradox. One set of theories involves the perceptions that adolescents have about the likely payoff of hard work in school. Some writers, for instance, have argued that, even though minority youth have high aspirations in the abstract, many do not believe that educational success will have substantial occupational payoff for them, because of a prejudicially imposed job ceiling on the career development of African American, Hispanic American, and Native American individuals (Mickelson, 1990; Ogbu, 1974). Although intuitively appealing, this theory has not received much empirical support. It is true that adolescents who believe they have been victims of discrimination, or who believe that their opportunities for occupational success are unfairly constrained by society, achieve less in school than do peers who do not hold this belief (Taylor et al., 1994; Wood & Clay, 1996). It is not true, however, that African American or Hispanic American youngsters are more likely to believe that their opportu-

nities for success are blocked (Ainsworth-Darnell & Downey, 1998; Kao & Tienda, 1998; Steinberg, Dornbusch, & Brown, 1992). Indeed, several studies indicate that African American and Hispanic American youth may actually have more optimistic beliefs and positive feelings about school than other students (e.g., Ainsworth-Darnell & Downey, 1998; Voelkl, 1997).

If anything, it may be adolescents' fear of failure, rather than their desire (or lack of desire) to succeed that matters most (Steinberg et al., 1992). Asian American youngsters not only believe in the value of school success but also are very anxious about the possible negative repercussions of not doing well in school, both in terms of occupational success and in terms of their parents' disappointment (Chung & Walkey, 1989; Eaton & Dembo, 1997; Steinberg, 1996). Moreover, many Asian American youth believe that the *only* way they can succeed in mainstream American society is through educational achievement (Sue & Okazaki, 1990). Interestingly, Asian American students' sense of obligation to their parents—a factor frequently suggested as a reason for their high rates of school success—does not seem to play a very important role in predicting school achievement. In addition, being expected to assist one's family with household chores and other family work—something that is especially salient in Asian American and Hispanic American households—

has a negative impact on school performance (Fuligni et al., 1999). As one team of researchers explained,

> One Mexican youth . . . , when asked to describe the thoughts of a girl in a picture who is holding school books while watching her parents labor in the fields, said: ". . . she is watching her parents working so hard . . . she feels like they have a big problem. She tries to help her parents, but she has to study. In the end, she tries to help them." . . . Education remains important to these youths, but the families may face more pressing needs that demand the students' attention. These periodic compromises, in turn, may cumulatively erode the students' progress at school over time. (Fuligni et al., 1999, p. 104)

An alternative view stresses differences in ethnic groups' beliefs about ability. Recall that adolescents who believe that intelligence is malleable are more likely to be intrinsically motivated, mastery oriented, and, as a consequence, academically successful. It is therefore interesting to note that Asian cultures tend to place more emphasis on effort than on ability in explaining school success and are more likely to believe that all students have the capacity to succeed (Hess, Chih-Mei, & McDevitt, 1987; Holloway, 1988; Stevenson & Stigler, 1992). It is also important to note that Asian students—both in the United States and in Asia—spend significantly more time each week on homework and other school-related activities, and significantly less time socializing and watching television, than do other youth, as figure 12.1 clearly illustrates (Caplan, Choy, & Whitmore, 1992; Fuligni & Stevenson, 1997; Steinberg, 1996). You may be interested to know that, contrary to popular belief, Asian students do not pay a price for their superior achievement in terms of increased anxiety, depression, stress, or social competence; the suicide rate among American teenagers is substantially higher than it is among Japanese youth, for example (Chen, Rubin, & Li, 1997; Crystal et al., 1994; King, Akiyama, & Elling, 1996). And Asian students' moods while studying are significantly more positive than those of other students (Asakawa & Csikszentmihalyi, 1998).

Of course, as is the case with research on socioeconomic differences in educational achievement, research on ethnic differences indicates that there are large and important variations *within* as well as between ethnic groups. First, there are differences in educational achievement among youngsters from different countries of origin who may be classified together into the same larger ethnic group (e.g., although both groups are classified as Asian, Chinese American adolescents have much higher academic achievement than Filipino Americans; similarly, there are large differences in academic achieve-

ment among Puerto Rican, Cuban American, and Mexican American adolescents, all of whom are classified as Hispanic) (Blair & Qian, 1998; Kao, 1995; Portes & MacLeod, 1996; Velez, 1989; Wojtkiewicz & Donato, 1995). Second, studies of ethnic minority youngsters show that recent immigrants tend to achieve more in school than do American-born minority youngsters, suggesting that part of becoming acculturated to American society—at least among teenagers—is learning to devalue academic success (Fuligni, 1997; Kao, 1999; Kao & Tienda, 1995; Steinberg, 1996). Third, and most important, studies indicate that, within all ethnic groups, students achieve more when they feel a sense of belonging to their school, when they see the connection between academic accomplishment and future success, when their friends and parents value and support educational achievement, and when their parents are effective monitors of their children's behavior and schooling (Alva, 1993; Chen & Stevenson, 1995; Chen et al., 1996; Connell, Spencer, & Aber, 1994; Ford & Harris, 1996; Goodenow, 1992; Luthar, 1994; Murdock, 1994; Reyes & Jason, 1993; Steinberg et al., 1996).

RECAP

Studies indicate that there are ethnic differences in educational achievement above and beyond those attributable to socioeconomic status. In general, Asian American adolescents outperform white students, who in turn do better in school than African American, Hispanic American, and Native American students. One reason for the superior performance of Asian American students is that they are more likely to hold beliefs about achievement that are predictive of success in school. In contrast, parents and teachers in African American, Hispanic American, and Native American communities are more likely to communicate the message that, although education is important, there is little that minority individuals can do to succeed within a discriminatory society. These different messages may lead students from different backgrounds to devote different degrees of effort to their studies.

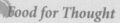

Food for Thought

Many immigrant adolescents in the United States achieve more in school than their counterparts from the same ethnic group who were born in America. How do you account for this?

Figure 12.1   Cross-cultural differences in the time adolescents spend studying and reading. (Fuligni & Stevenson, 1995)

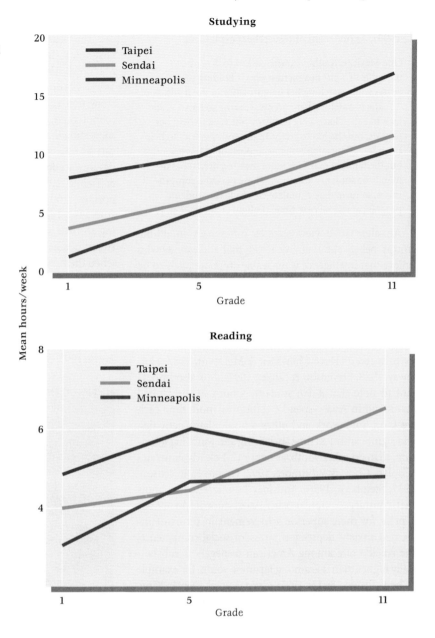

Changes in Educational Achievement over Time

As noted in chapter 6, more students are going on to postsecondary education today than ever before. In other words, levels of educational attainment in the United States have risen substantially over the past six decades. For example, whereas in 1937 only 15 percent of the students enrolled in the fifth grade eventually entered college, by 1982, this figure had risen to well over

50 percent. Today, more than two-thirds of all high school graduates enroll in postsecondary programs immediately after finishing high school (National Center for Education Statistics, 1999a).

Although ethnic differences in educational attainment have narrowed over the past 40 years, there remain substantial gaps in attainment between white and nonwhite individuals, and, especially, between white and Hispanic American individuals, as figure 12.2 illustrates. Thus, whereas about 25 percent of all white adults aged 25 and

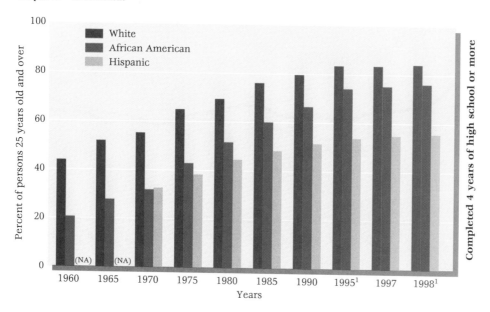

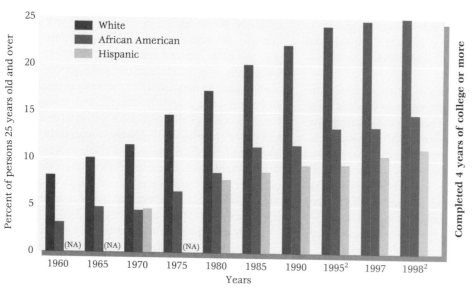

Figure 12.2   Ethnic differences in educational attainment in the United States, 1960–1998. (U.S. Census Bureau, 1999)

NA Not available. [1]High school graduate or more. [2]College graduate or more.
Note: Persons of Hispanic origin may be of any race.

over are college graduates, only 15 percent of African American adults and only 11 percent of Hispanic American adults are. Discrepancies in rates of high school graduation, although not as large, are nonetheless significant —84 percent of white adults 25 and over have completed high school, compared with 76 percent of African American adults and only 56 percent of Hispanic American adults (U.S. Bureau of the Census, 1999b).

Equally worrisome is that fact that trends in academic *achievement* (what students know) have not paralleled

trends in educational *attainment* (the number of years of schooling they have completed). Although more students are staying in school longer, they are not necessarily learning more. For example, as figure 12.3 indicates, between 1970 and 1980, average scores on the Scholastic Assessment Test (SAT) declined by about 35 points on the verbal test and 20 points on the math test. Scores remained more or less flat between 1980 and 1990 and have risen only very slightly since then (National Center for Education Statistics, 1999). Moreover, the gap in SAT scores

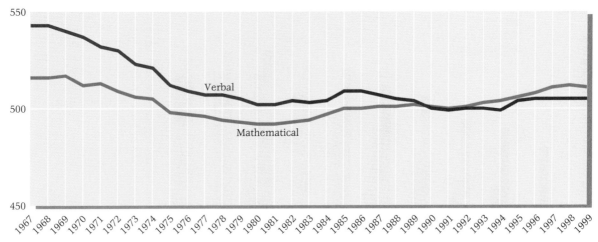

Figure 12.3   *SAT scores declined between 1970 and 1980, rose for a few years, and then declined between 1985 and 1990. Scores have increased slightly in recent years.* (National Center for Education Statistics, 1999)

between African American and Hispanic American students, on the one hand, and Asian American and white students, on the other, remains substantial, on the order of 100 points on the math SAT and 60 points on the verbal SAT (O'Neill, 1997).

The relatively poor showing of American adolescents on standardized tests of achievement was carefully documented in a series of reports based on the **National Assessment of Educational Progress (NAEP)** (National Assessment of Educational Progress, 1999). This national assessment of student achievement is conducted by the federal government, in order to track trends in educational achievement over time. Because the NAEP tests have been administered regularly over the past 30 years, it is possible to compare the achievement levels of today's adolescents with their counterparts three decades ago.

According to recent NAEP reports, adolescent achievement in reading, math, and science has not improved significantly over the past 30 years, despite massive national efforts at educational reform (see figure 12.4). Among 17-year-olds, for example, students in 1999 scored no better than their counterparts did in the early 1970s in reading, about 1 percent better than their counterparts did in math, and about 3 percent *worse* than their counterparts did in science. Among 13-year-olds, reading scores in 1999 were better than they had been in the 1970s, but not any better than they had been in 1980, and science scores showed no improvement between 1970 and 1999. The only bit of good news was in math scores among 13-year-olds: Scores have improved steadily since the 1970s (National Assessment of Educational Progress, 1999).

Perhaps more important, most analyses of the NAEP data indicate that the modest gains in achievement that

have occurred during the past decade or so have been in relatively simple skills. In reading and writing, for example, although more than half of all American 13-year-olds today can read well enough to be able to search for specific information and can make generalizations from reading material, only 10 percent can understand and summarize relatively complicated information. Fewer than half of all students are able to write a simple report (e.g., on a book or television show) at their grade level, and fewer than one-third are able to write a persuasive essay. Only 2 percent of eleventh-graders, and only 1 percent of eighth-graders, are able to write a reasonably sophisticated report that is able to interest and inform a reader (Mullis et al., 1994).

Levels of achievement in math and science show a similar pattern. Thus, whereas virtually all 17-year-olds can add, subtract, multiply, and divide using whole numbers, only half can perform computations with decimals, fractions, and percentages and solve simple equations, and only 6 percent can use basic algebra. Nearly all 17-year-olds have some simple knowledge about plants and animals, but only 40 percent have any detailed knowledge of science, and only 7 percent can use scientific knowledge to draw conclusions. As one writer put it, virtually all adolescents can "read, write, add, subtract and count their change. But as one moves up the scale toward slightly more complicated tasks, success falls off rapidly" (Manegold, 1994, p. A14).

As is the case in rates of high school graduation and SAT scores, the gap in achievement between white and minority youngsters narrowed during the 1970s, but a wide disparity still exists. The achievement gap did not shrink at all during the 1980s and, if anything, widened

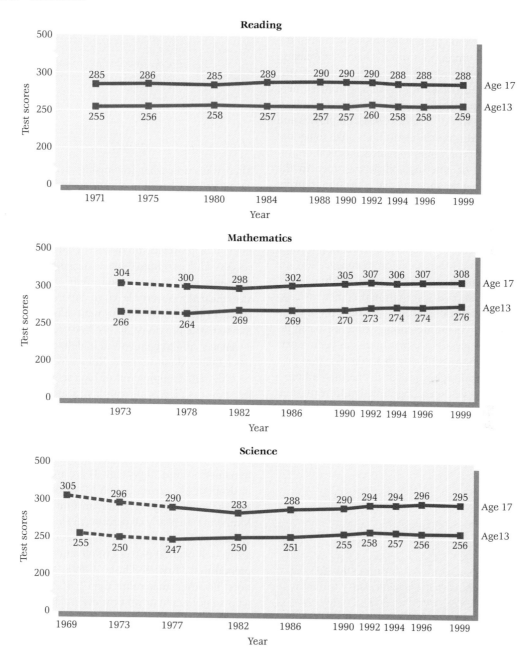

Note: Dashed lines represent extrapolated data.

Figure 12.4   *Over-time changes in adolescents' scores on standardized tests of achievement.* (National Assessment of Educational Progress, 1999)

during the 1990s (Education Trust, 1996; National Assessment of Educational Progress, 1999). According to NAEP data, across virtually all subject areas, the average African American or Hispanic American high school senior is performing at a level comparable to the average white *eighth-grader* (Stedman, 1998).

There is no reason to be sanguine about the performance of white students, however—since the 1970s, their achievement test scores have remained stagnant, and U.S. scores on standardized tests of math and science are mediocre in comparison with the scores of other industrialized countries, as figure 12.5 indicates

(Stedman, 1998; Stevenson & Lee, 1998; TIMSS, 1997). This is true even though spending on education in the United States is among the world's highest (Walberg, 1998). Especially distressing have been studies of students in advanced classes from various countries; here the best U.S. students fare worse than their counterparts all over the world (Bronner, 1998). Employers and postsecondary educational institutions alike today devote vast amounts of money to remedial education. Indeed, one-third of entering college freshmen in the United States now require remedial education in order to do college-level work, and one-third of American corporations report that they have trouble finding skilled employees (Steinberg, 1998).

If more American students are remaining in high school, and so many are going on to college, why are their achievement test scores so low according to absolute, historical, and international standards? Experts suggest several reasons—among them, that teachers are not spending enough time on basic instruction in the classroom; that there has been a pervasive decline in the difficulty of textbooks; that parents are not encouraging academic pursuits at home; that students are not spending sufficient time on their studies outside of school; and that students know that, thanks to "grade inflation," they can earn good grades without working very hard (Hayes, Wolfer, & Wolfe, 1996; Owen, 1995; Public Agenda, 1997; Steinberg, 1998).

Food for Thought

Are the trends in American student achievement something to worry about?

High School Dropouts

There was a time when leaving high school before graduating did not have the dire consequences that it does today. With changes in the labor force, however, have come changes in the educational requirements for entry into the world of work. Today, educational attainment is a powerful predictor of adult occupational success and earnings. Not surprisingly, high school dropouts are far more likely than graduates to live at or near the poverty level, to experience unemployment, to depend on government-subsidized income-maintenance programs, to become pregnant while still a teenager, and to be involved in delinquent and criminal activity (Manlove, 1998; Rumberger, 1995).

Although dropping out of high school is less prevalent now than it was 40 years ago, a substantial number of today's adolescents leave school before graduating. The national dropout rate declined from more than 30 percent in 1960 to 20 percent in 1970, but the rate began to increase in the late 1970s, and since then it has remained around 25 percent. There are huge variations in dropout rates from region to region, however, with average rates varying from around 10 percent (in Minnesota) to nearly 40 percent (in Florida) (Fitzpatrick & Yoels, 1992; Rumberger, 1995); indeed, in some urban areas, well over 50 percent of all students leave school prematurely (Bryk & Thum, 1989). It is important to note, however, that more than half of all youngsters who do not graduate on time eventually complete their high school education by returning to school or by getting a General Education Development (GED) degree. Only 12 percent of individuals have not completed a high school degree by age 24 (National Center on Education Statistics, 1999).

When dropout rates are examined for different ethnic groups, we find that African American youngsters drop out of high school at a rate only slightly greater than white youngsters (both are near the national average) but that Hispanic American youngsters drop out at more than twice the rate of other youth (Rumberger, 1995). One reason for this is the large proportion of Hispanic American youth who

RECAP

The low level of educational achievement among American youth—and among African American and Hispanic American youth, in particular—has been a national concern for some time. Although some gains in scores on standardized tests of achievement were reported during the mid-1980s, test scores have not improved since that time, and the ground that was lost in the late 1960s and early 1970s has not been recovered. In addition, American students fare poorly in international comparisons. Among the reasons given for the poor achievement of American students are that teachers are not spending enough time on basic instruction, that textbooks have become much less challenging, that parents are not encouraging academic pursuits at home, that adolescents are not spending sufficient time on their studies outside of school, and that students know they can earn good grades without working very hard.

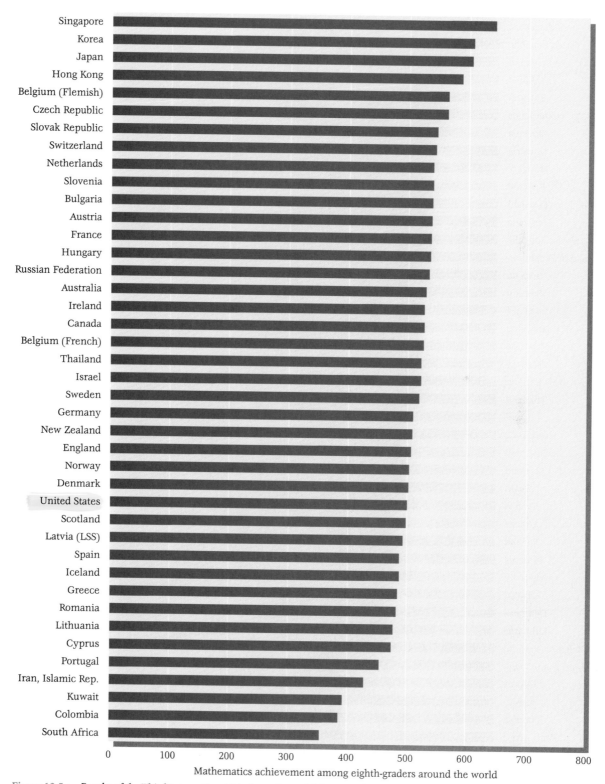

Figure 12.5a   *Results of the Third International Mathematics and Science Study.*

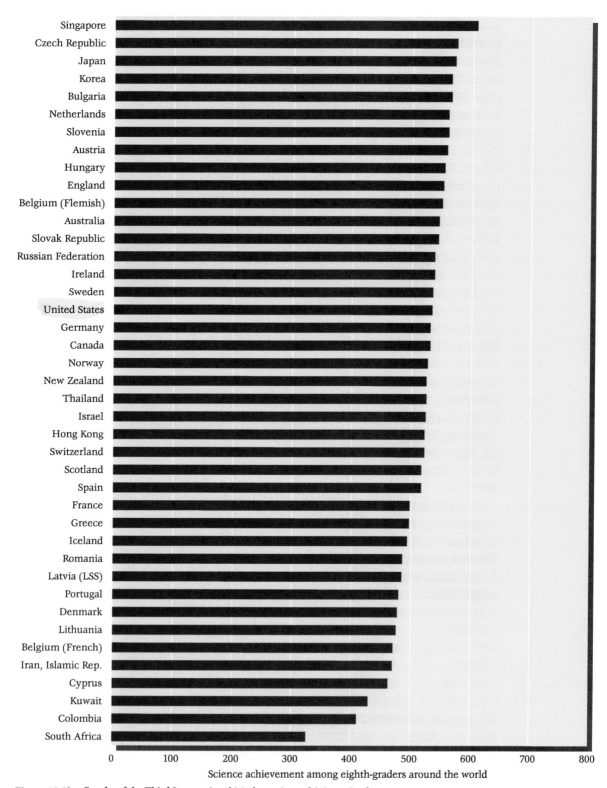

Figure 12.5b　Results of the Third International Mathematics and Science Study.

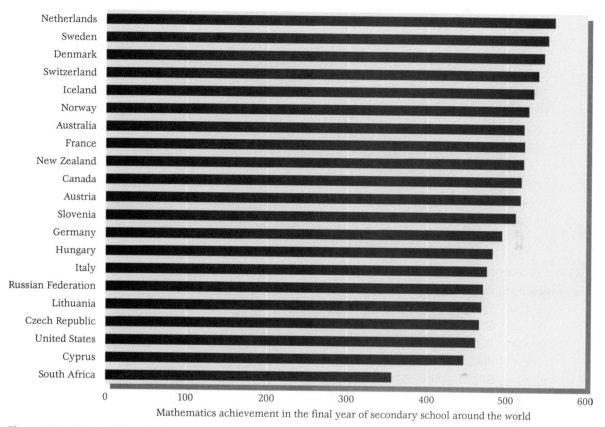

Figure 12.5c   Results of the Third International Mathematics and Science Study.

are not English-speaking; among Hispanic American youth, a lack of proficiency in English is a major determinant of dropping out (Singh & Hernandez-Gantes, 1996; Stanton-Salazar & Dornbusch, 1995; Steinberg, Blinde, & Chan, 1984).

Given the findings on educational achievement, the research evidence on the other correlates of dropping out comes as no surprise. In addition to the prevalence of dropping out among Hispanic American youngsters and among youngsters who are not fluent in English, adolescents who leave high school before graduating are more likely to come from lower socioeconomic levels, poor communities, large families, single-parent families, nondemanding families, and households where little reading material is available. In short, adolescents who drop out of school are more likely to come from backgrounds with limited financial, social, and cultural capital (Entwisle, 1990; Pong & Ju, 2000; Rumberger, 1995; Zimiles & Lee, 1991).

Coupled with this disadvantage in background, adolescents who drop out of high school also are

more likely to have a history of poor school performance, low school involvement, multiple changes in schools, poor performance on standardized tests of achievement and intelligence, negative school experiences, and a variety of behavior problems, such as excessive aggression (Cairns, Cairns, & Neckerman, 1989; Jordan, Lara, & McPartland, 1996; Kasen, Cohen, & Brook, 1998; Rumberger & Larson, 1998). Many high school dropouts have had to repeat one or more grades in elementary school; indeed, having been held back is one of the strongest predictors of dropping out (Janosz, LeBlanc, Boulerice, & Tremblay, 1997; Roderick, 1994; Rumberger, 1995). Students who ultimately drop out of school generally have an especially difficult time during the transition into high school, when their grades decline dramatically (Roderick, 1991).

The picture that emerges, then, is that dropping out of high school is not so much a discrete decision that is made during the adolescent years but, like other aspects of adolescent achievement, the culmination

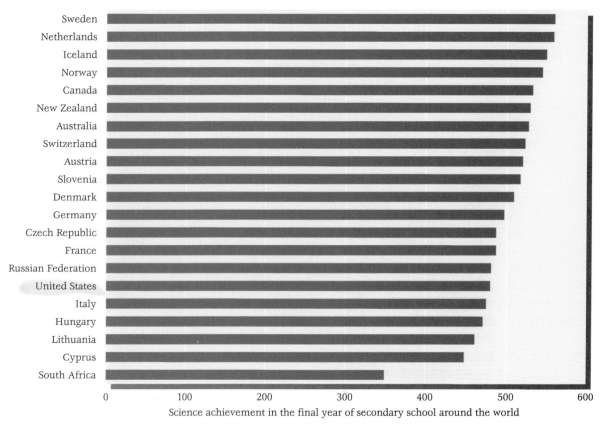

Figure 12.5d   Results of the Third International Mathematics and Science Study.

of a long process (Garnier, Stein, & Jacobs, 1997). Specific factors may instigate a student's final decision to leave school—a suspension for misbehavior, a failed course, an unintended pregnancy, the lure of a job—but, by and large, dropping out is a process characterized by a history of repeated academic failure and increasing alienation from school (Jordan et al., 1996). Although programs designed to enhance adolescents' academic skills have been largely unsuccessful in preventing dropping out, one approach that has met with success has focused on involving at-risk adolescents in service learning and in guided discussions of their life options (Allen, Philliber, Herrling, & Kuperminc, 1997).

Although most research on the causes of dropping out has focused on the characteristics of adolescents who leave school prematurely, a number of studies have focused on the schools that dropouts leave (Roderick & Camburn, 1999; Rumberger & Thomas, 2000). In general, dropping out is less likely from schools where the environment is orderly, where academic pursuits are emphasized, and where the faculty is supportive and committed (Connell, Halpern-Felsher, Clifford, Crichlow, & Usinger, 1995). In addition, dropout rates are higher in larger schools that group students according to ability and that fail a relatively high proportion of students in the early years of high school (Bryk & Thum, 1989; Roderick & Camburn, 1999). Consistent with this, some research suggests that dropout rates are reduced in some cases by permitting students who are having educational difficulties to change schools, rather than leaving school altogether (Lee & Burkam, 1992). Although some educators have expressed concern about the recent trend toward toughening graduation requirements and ending "social promotion"—the practice of promoting students from one grade to the next on the basis of age rather than actual achievement—evaluations of such policies show that they do not increase the rate of dropping out (Bishop, in press; Hoffer, 1997).

RECAP

About 25 percent of adolescents leave high school before graduating, although a substantial number return to school in young adulthood and earn their diploma at a later date. There are wide ethnic and regional differences in dropout rates, however, and dropping out of school is an especially serious problem among Hispanic American youth. Dropouts are more likely than their peers to come from economically disadvantaged backgrounds, to come from single-parent homes, and to have a poor record of educational achievement throughout their school years. Dropping out is not so much a decision that is made during adolescence as it is the culmination of a long process that begins early on. Studies also suggest that the schools from which students drop out are larger, more disorderly, and less focused on academics than are other schools.

Food for Thought

Based on what we know about the causes and consequences of dropping out, what steps should be taken to reduce the dropout rate?

OCCUPATIONAL ACHIEVEMENT

During early and middle adolescence, school is the setting in which achievement is most often expressed. During late adolescence, at least for some individuals, the focus shifts to the world of work and careers. Although we often think of school and work as separate domains, achievement is one aspect of psychosocial development during adolescence that links them together. Rather than thinking of educational achievement and occupational achievement as separate, it is more useful to think of them as different manifestations of the same basic psychosocial phenomenon.

The number of years of schooling an individual completes is the single best indicator of his or her eventual occupational success (Arum & Hout, 1998). It is not simply that adolescents benefit in the labor force by having a high school diploma or a college degree. Although these credentials matter, research shows that each year of education—even without graduating—adds significantly to occupational success. In other words, individuals who have completed three years of college earn more money, on average, than individuals

who have completed only one year, even though neither group has a college degree in hand. You may be surprised to learn, however, that *grades* in high school and college are virtually unrelated to occupational success. A few years after graduation, *A* students and *C* students hold similarly prestigious jobs and earn comparable amounts of money (Garbarino & Asp, 1981).

Researchers who are interested in occupational achievement during adolescence have examined several issues, including the ways in which young people make decisions about their careers and the influences on their occupational aspirations and expectations. We will begin with a look at the development of adolescents' occupational plans.

The Development of Occupational Plans

The development of occupational plans during adolescence can be viewed in many respects as paralleling, or even as part of, the identity development process. As with developing a coherent sense of identity, the development of occupational plans follows a sequence that involves an examination of one's traits, abilities, and interests; a period of experimentation with different work roles; and an integration of influences from one's past (primarily, identification with familial role models) with one's hopes for the future. And, as is also the case with identity development, occupational role development is profoundly influenced by the social environment in which it takes place.

For more than 30 years, the dominant theoretical viewpoint in the study of the development of occupational plans has been that of Donald Super (1967). Super suggests that occupational plans develop in stages, with adolescence as an important time for the crystallization of plans that are more realistic, less based on fantasy, and more grounded in the adolescent's assessment of his or her talents. Before adolescence, individuals express occupational interests, but these are much like fantasies and have little to do with the plans they will eventually make. When children are asked what they want to be when they grow up, they are likely to respond with occupations that are exciting, glamorous, or familiar—a teacher, a police officer, a baseball player, or a movie star.

However, with the advent of more sophisticated thinking capabilities during early adolescence and as the economic and practical realities of adulthood become imminent, young people begin to consider career alternatives in a more systematic fashion. They plan educational and work activities to suit their career interests, and they evaluate career decisions in terms of long- as well as short-term consequences. Instead of merely being attracted to glamorous or exciting jobs, adolescents think about such mundane realities as the need to earn a living.

According to Super, between ages 14 and 18, individuals first begin to crystallize a vocational preference. During this period of **crystallization,** individuals begin to formulate ideas about appropriate work and begin to develop the occupational self-conceptions that will guide subsequent educational decisions. Although adolescents may not settle on a particular career at this point, they do begin to narrow their choices according to their interests, values, and abilities. One adolescent may decide that she wants a career in which she works with people. Another may decide that he wants a career in which he can earn a great deal of money. A third may think about a career in science. During this period, the adolescent begins to seek out information on his or her tentative choice and to make plans for the future (Osipow, 1973). The process is reminiscent of the sort of role experimentation described by Erik Erikson (1968) in his theory of adolescent identity development (see chapter 8). In both cases, during middle adolescence, alternative identities are considered and evaluated on the basis of exploration, experimentation, and self-examination (Crites, 1989).

Following the period of crystallization is a period of **specification,** occurring roughly between the ages of 18 and 21. During this period, the young person recognizes the need to specify his or her vocational interests and begins to seek appropriate information to accomplish this. In many regards, a similar process is followed during the stage of specification as during the stage of crystallization: Alternatives are considered, information is sought, decisions are made, and preferences are consolidated. The chief difference, however, is that, during the period of specification, more narrowly defined career pursuits within a general career category are considered (rather than general career categories themselves). For example, during the period of crystallization, a young person may decide to pursue a career in the field of mental health, without being able to specify a vocational preference within this general category. During the specification stage, he or she might begin to consider and compare a variety of careers within the mental health profession—social work, educational counseling, clinical psychology, psychiatry, and so on—and make choices among them.

Although the chronological ages given in Super's theory must be taken as only rough guidelines, his perspective is an influential one, and it has shaped the way in which career counselors advise young people. Perhaps most important, Super's perspective reminds us that vocational development comes relatively late during adolescence and that a good deal of growth in this arena takes place during the young adult years. This has become increasingly true in contemporary society, as more and more young people have chosen to continue their education in college and postpone their entrance into a career until their midtwenties. Changes in the broader environment in which adolescents develop—in this case, changes in the accessibility of higher education—can exert a powerful influence on the developmental course of occupational planning.

Influences on Occupational Choices

What makes one individual choose to become an attorney and another decide to be a teacher? Why do some students pursue careers in psychology, whereas others major in computer science? Researchers have long been interested in the reasons that individuals end up in certain careers. Although Super's developmental theory has helped us understand the general stages of career planning, it does not shed light on why certain careers appeal to some individuals but not to others. In other words, Super's theory focuses on how and when individuals make career choices, rather than on why they make the career choices they do.

● **The Role of Personality**   Many theorists who are interested in why people enter various occupational fields have examined the role of personality factors—traits, interests, and values—in the process of career selection. They believe that individuals select careers that match, in one way or another, certain elements of their personality. Perhaps the most widely cited perspective of this sort is that of John Holland (1985).

After years of extensive analysis of jobs and the people who select them, Holland determined that career choices can be viewed as a reflection of basic personality styles. Certain occupational environments are well suited to individuals with certain personalities, and others are not. Successful career choice, in Holland's model, entails the matching of a particular personality type—a given set of interests and personality characteristics—with a vocation that allows the expression of these traits. By answering questions on a standardized personality inventory, an individual can determine which basic personality dimensions are characteristic of himself or herself and can then examine directories in which occupations have been classified according to the same typology.

After completing Holland's personality inventory—called the **Self-Directed Search**—an individual better understands his or her vocational profile (which of the personality dimensions are dominant and which are less important). Because different occupations typically offer different degrees of opportunity to express different traits, a good career choice in Holland's view is one that provides the best fit between a person's personality and a vocation's characteristics. Someone who is artistic, social, and enterprising, for example, is better suited to a career in acting than in accounting. Other theoretical frameworks focusing on the fit between individual personality characteristics and work environments are popular as well.

There are important limitations to theories of career choice that are based solely on personality traits, however. First, it is clear that interests and abilities are not fixed during adolescence and young adulthood (Mortimer & Lorence, 1979). They continue to develop and change during the adult years. Indeed, one of the most important influences on personality development during adulthood is work itself. Thus, through working in a job that emphasizes certain personality characteristics, requires certain abilities, or reinforces certain values, individuals begin to change in these directions. Consequently, a job that may seem like a bad match during early adulthood may, over time, become a good match, as the adult employee grows and changes in response to the work environment. For example, an individual may not be especially interested in social interactions but may, because of a tight job market, end up in a teaching position after graduating from college. Over time, the more he or she interacts with students, the more appealing the interpersonal aspects of the job may become. Eventually, this person may come to feel that having opportunities for social interaction on the job is very important.

A second problem with theories of career choice that emphasize personality dimensions is that they may underestimate the importance of other factors that influence and shape vocational decisions. Many career decisions are influenced more by individuals' beliefs about what sorts of jobs are "appropriate" for them than by interests and preferences. It is all well and good, for example, for an adolescent to discover that he or she

is well suited for a career in medicine, but the realization is of little value if the young person's family cannot afford the cost of college or medical school. An adolescent girl may discover, through taking a vocational preference inventory, that she is well suited for work in the area of construction or building, but she may find that her parents, peers, teachers, and potential employers all discourage her from following this avenue of employment. Put most simply, career choices are not made solely on the basis of individual preference; they are the result of an interaction among individual preference, social influence, and important forces in the broader social environment. It is to these influences and forces that we will now turn.

● **The Influence of Parents and Peers**   Adolescents' occupational ambitions and achievements are highly correlated with the ambitions and achievements of those around them (Duncan, Featherman, & Duncan, 1972). Youngsters from middle-class families are more likely than their less advantaged peers to aspire to and enter middle-class occupations. In addition, apart from their own socioeconomic status, youngsters who have many friends from middle-class backgrounds are more likely than those who have many friends from lower socioeconomic levels to aspire to high-status occupations (Simpson, 1962).

A variety of explanations have been offered for the fit between adolescents' ambitions and the socioeconomic status of those around them. First, and perhaps most important, **occupational attainment**—the prestige or status an individual achieves in the world of work—depends strongly on educational attainment (Alexander & Eckland, 1975). Educational attainment is greatly influenced by socioeconomic status. Thus, because middle-class adolescents are likely to complete more years of schooling than their lower-class peers, economically advantaged adolescents are more likely to seek and enter higher-status occupations.

Second, middle-class parents are more likely to raise their children in ways that foster the development of strong needs for achievement (Rosen, 1956) and interest in career exploration (Grotevant & Cooper, 1988). The development of achievement motivation, which has an impact on school performance, also has an impact on youngsters' occupational ambitions—both directly (in that individuals with strong needs for achievement will express these needs by aspiring to occupations that provide opportunities to achieve status or wealth) and indirectly, through the effects of achievement motivation on academic achievement (in that youngsters who are successful in school are likely to be encouraged to seek higher-status occupations and engage in identity exploration).

Third, the same opportunities that favor economically advantaged youngsters in the world of education—better facilities, more opportunities for enrichment, and greater accessibility of higher education—also favor middle-class youngsters in the world of work. Because their parents, for example, are more likely to work in positions of power and leadership, middle-class youngsters often have important family connections and sources of information about the world of work that are less available to youngsters from poorer families. In addition, coming from a family that is economically well off may provide an adolescent with more time to explore career options and to wait for an especially desirable position, rather than having to take the first job that becomes available, out of economic necessity.

Fourth, parents, siblings, and other important sources of influence serve as models for adolescents' occupational choices (Barber & Eccles, 1992; Grotevant & Cooper, 1988). Although some young people establish career choices through the explicit rejection of their parents' careers, the weight of the evidence suggests that adolescents' and parents' vocations are more similar than different, particularly when the adolescents' family relationships have been warm and close and when strong identifications have formed. As we saw in our discussion of mothers' employment in chapter 4, adolescents are especially influenced by the work roles of the parent of the same sex. This finding has become increasingly important as growing numbers of women enter the labor force and hold high-status occupations. Daughters of women who are happily employed outside the home are far more likely themselves to seek careers in addition to marriage and family responsibilities than are adolescent girls whose mothers are not employed (Leslie, 1986). Young women whose mothers occupy high-status occupations are more likely to do so themselves when they enter the labor force (Hoffman, 1974). And both sons and daughters are less likely to have sex-stereotyped attitudes about work and more likely to prefer a dual-career arrangement if they come from dual-career families themselves (Barber & Eccles, 1992).

Finally, parents—and, to a lesser extent, peers—influence adolescents' occupational plans by establishing a value context in which certain occupational choices are encouraged and others are discouraged. According to sociologist Melvin Kohn (1977), middle-class fami-

▲ *Although some young people establish career choices by rejecting their parents' occupations, most adolescents select careers that are similar to, rather than different from, those of their parents. Parents-child similarity in occupational choices is greatest in families with warm, close relationships.* (John Griffin/The Image Works)

lies and middle-class schools encourage children to value autonomy, self-direction, and independence—three features that are more likely to be found in middle-class than in working-class jobs. The children are told, implicitly and explicitly, how important it is to have freedom, power, and status. Adolescents who have been raised to value attributes that are characteristic of middle-class jobs will, not surprisingly, seek those attributes when they plan their careers. They will look for jobs that offer independence and power. In working-class families, in contrast, children are more likely to be raised to value obedience and conformity—two characteristics that are highly valued in most working-class jobs. For youngsters from this socioeconomic background, jobs that appeal to these values will be relatively more attractive. They will have been raised to value such things as job security and not having to worry too much about making high-pressured decisions. Indeed, to many working-class youngsters, the high-stress world of the business executive is not at all an attractive career possibility.

- **The Broader Context of Occupational Choice** Adolescents' occupational choices are made, of course, in a broader context that profoundly influences the nature of their plans. At different times, different employment opportunities arise, and young people—particularly by the time they reach the end of their formal schooling—are often very aware of the prospects for employment in various fields. Indeed, one recent study of inner-city youngsters found that many had developed ideas about their future job prospects by the time they were in *second grade* (Cook et al., 1996). Understandably, young people often tailor their plans in response to what they perceive as the needs and future demands of the labor market, as well as the acceptability of given occupational choices within their community. One study found, for example, that many rural adolescents experience great conflicts between wanting to pursue a career that would take them away from their rural community and wanting to remain close to their roots (Hektner, 1994).

Unfortunately, adolescents also tailor their plans based on their beliefs about which jobs are "acceptable" for individuals of a particular social class, ethnicity, or gender. Despite the liberalization in sex-role stereotypes that has occurred during the past 30 years, for example, adolescent girls' vocational choices still tend to be concentrated among jobs that have historically been occupied by women, such as secretarial work, teaching, and nursing, and they are more oriented toward occupations that involve working with people and that allow the expression of compassion and altruism (Beutel & Marini, 1995; Marini, Fan, Finley, & Beutel, 1996). In contrast, relatively fewer adolescent girls plan to enter jobs where the main tasks involve working with things, rather than people, as is the case in science and engineering (Jozefowicz, Barber, Eccles, & Mollasis, 1994).

Moreover, many more adolescent girls than boys express concern about having to balance family and work demands in adulthood, and this further affects their occupational decision making, since they may be reluctant to pursue careers that they believe will interfere with family life (Astin, 1984). This task may vary between daughters who grow up in divorced versus nondivorced households, since they probably have been exposed to very different models of how to balance work and family obligations (Barber & Eccles, 1992).

One problem faced by all young people in making career plans is obtaining accurate information about the labor market needs of the future and the appropriate means of pursuing positions in various fields. Most young people do not have educational plans that are consistent with the educational requirements of the jobs they hope to enter. In one study, even among the high school seniors who perceived themselves as having "considerable" knowledge of the fields they planned to enter, approximately one-fifth were planning on too little education, and nearly one-third were planning too much education, given the requirements of the careers to which they aspired (Grotevant & Durrett, 1980). One goal of career educators is to help adolescents make more informed choices about their careers and to free them from the stereotypes that constrain their choices.

> ### RECAP
> *Adolescence is a time for the development of realistic occupational plans. In general, research indicates that adolescents' career choices are influenced by a number of factors, including their personality, their social background, and their perceptions of the labor market and their potential place within it. As is the case with educational achievement, occupational achievement is strongly influenced by socioeconomic status.*

> ### Food for Thought
> *Think about your own occupational development. What factors have most influenced your choices?*

Web Researcher On average, people who complete more years of schooling earn more money. However, the relationship between education and income differs for men and women and for people of different ethnic backgrounds. Summarize the major patterns you see. Are these differences becoming smaller over time, staying the same, or increasing? Is the pattern the same for people with more and less education? Discuss the implications of your findings in terms of their potential effects on adolescents' decisions to remain in school. Go to **www.mhhe.com/steinberg6** for further information.

KEY TERMS

academic achievement

achievement

achievement attributions

crystallization

cultural capital

educational attainment

extrinsic motivation

fear of failure

intrinsic motivation

learned helplessness

mediating variable

National Assessment of Educational Progress (NAEP)

need for achievement

occupational attainment

school performance

Self-Directed Search

self-efficacy

social capital

specification

stressful life events

underachievers

Chapter 13

Psychosocial Problems in Adolescence

Although the vast majority of young people move through the adolescent years without experiencing major difficulty, some encounter serious psychological and behavior problems that disrupt not only their lives but also the lives of those around them. Problems such as substance abuse, depression and suicide, and crime and delinquency—although certainly not the norm during adolescence—do affect a worrisome number of teenagers. Moreover, these problems indirectly touch the lives of all of us, either through the personal contact we have with a troubled young person or indirectly, through increased taxes for community services or heightened anxiety about the safety of our neighborhoods.

In chapters 1–12, which examined the normative aspects of adolescent development, the more problematic aspects of adolescent behavior and development were deliberately deemphasized, in order to dispel the erroneous stereotype of adolescence as an inherently troubled time. As you now know, most individuals emerge from adolescence with positive feelings about themselves and their parents; with the ability to form, maintain, and enjoy close relationships with same- and opposite-sex peers; and with the basic capabilities needed to take advantage of a range of educational and occupational opportunities. Most settle into adulthood relatively smoothly and begin establishing their work and family careers with little serious difficulty. Although the transition into adulthood may appear forbidding to the young adolescent approaching many weighty decisions about the future, statistics tell us that, for a remarkably high proportion of youth, the transition is relatively peaceful. Yes, it is true that one in five adolescent girls gets pregnant before she is 18, but it is also true that four in five do not. Although 20 percent of students do not complete high school by the societally expected age, 80 percent do, and more than half of the young people who leave school prematurely later receive a high school diploma. And, despite popular media portrayals otherwise, most ethnic minority youth are not poorly adjusted (Barbarin, 1993; McDermott & Spencer, 1997). We should not gloss over the fact that many healthy adolescents at one time or another experience bouts of self-doubt, periods of family squabbling, academic or vocational setbacks, and broken hearts. But it is important to keep in mind, as we look at psychosocial problems during adolescence, that there is an important distinction between the normative, and usually transitory, difficulties that are encountered by many young people—and by many adults, for that matter—and the serious psychosocial problems that are experienced by a relatively small minority of youth. ●

SOME GENERAL PRINCIPLES ABOUT PROBLEMS IN ADOLESCENCE

The mass media like nothing more than to paint extreme pictures of the world in which we live. One way in which this exaggerated view of the world is most obvious is in the presentation of teenage problem behavior. Rarely are portrayals of behavioral disorder, psychological distress, drug use, or delinquency accurate: On television, one experiment with marijuana inevitably leads to drug addiction and school failure. A breakup with a boyfriend is followed by a suicide attempt. An after-school prank develops into a life of crime. A couple's passionate necking session on the beach fades into a commercial, and, when the program returns, the adolescent girl is on her way to a life of single parenthood and welfare dependency. Those of you for whom adolescence was not that long ago know that these "facts" about adolescent problem behavior are rarely true. But we are so often bombarded with images of young people in trouble that it is easy for us to get fooled into believing that "adolescence" equals "problems."

One of the purposes of this chapter is to put these problems in perspective. It is therefore helpful, before we look at several specific sorts of problems in detail, to lay out some general principles about adolescent psychosocial problems that apply to a range of issues.

First, *we need to distinguish between occasional experimentation and enduring patterns of dangerous or troublesome behavior.* Research shows that rates of occasional, usually harmless, experimentation far exceed rates of enduring problems. For example, most adolescents experiment with alcohol sometime before high school graduation, and most will have been drunk at least once; however, relatively few teenagers will develop drinking problems or will permit alcohol to adversely affect their school or personal relationships. Similarly, although the vast majority of teenagers do *something* during adolescence that is against the law, very few of these young people develop criminal careers.

▲ *It is important to differentiate between occasional experimentation and enduring patterns of troublesome behavior.* (A. Farnsworth/The Image Works)

Second, *we need to distinguish between problems that have their origins and onset during adolescence and those that have their roots during earlier periods of development.* It is true, for example, that some teenagers fall into patterns of criminal or delinquent behavior during adolescence, and for this reason we tend to associate delinquency with the adolescent years. But studies suggest that most teenagers who have recurrent problems with the law had problems at home and at school at an early age; in some samples of delinquents, the problems were evident as early as preschool (Moffitt, 1993). Many individuals who develop depression during adolescence suffered from other types of psychological distress, such as excessive anxiety, as children. In other words, simply because a problem is *displayed* during adolescence does not mean that it is a problem *of* adolescence.

Third, *it is important to remember that many, although not all, of the problems experienced by adolescents are relatively transitory and are resolved by the beginning of adulthood, with few long-term repercussions in most*

cases. Substance abuse, delinquency, and unemployment are three good examples of problems that tend to follow this pattern: Rates of drug and alcohol use, unemployment, and delinquency are all higher within the adolescent and youth population than in the adult population, but most individuals who have abused drugs and alcohol, have been unemployed, or have committed delinquent acts as teenagers grow up to be sober, employed, law-abiding adults. Individuals for whom problem behavior persists into adulthood are likely to have had a problematic childhood as well as a problematic adolescence. The fact that some of the problems of adolescence seem to disappear on their own with time does not make their prevalence during adolescence any less significant, but it should be kept in mind when rhetoric is hurled back and forth about the "inevitable" decline of civilization at the hands of contemporary youth.

Finally, as should be evident, *problem behavior during adolescence is virtually never a direct consequence of going through the normative changes of adolescence itself.* Popular theories about "raging hormones" causing oppositional or deviant behavior have no scientific support whatsoever, for example, nor do the widely held beliefs that problem behaviors are manifestations of an inherent need to rebel against authority and that bizarre behavior results from having an identity crisis. The hormonal changes of puberty have only a modest direct effect on adolescent behavior; rebellion during adolescence is atypical, not normal; and few adolescents experience a tumultuous identity crisis. When a young person exhibits a serious psychosocial problem, such as depression, the worst possible interpretation is that it is a normal part of growing up. It is more likely to be a sign that something is wrong.

RECAP

Although the vast majority of individuals do not develop serious psychological or social problems during the adolescent years, a significant minority do. In thinking about problem behavior during adolescence, it is important to distinguish between experimentation and enduring patterns of behavior, between problems that have their origins during adolescence and those that do not, and between problems that are transitory and those that persist into adulthood. Most serious problem behavior during adolescence is almost never a direct consequence of going through the normative changes of adolescence itself.

PSYCHOSOCIAL PROBLEMS: THEIR NATURE AND CO-VARIATION

Clinical practitioners (psychologists, psychiatrists, social workers, and counselors) and other experts on the development and treatment of psychosocial problems during adolescence typically distinguish among three broad categories of problems: substance abuse, internalizing disorders, and externalizing disorders (Achenbach & Edelbrock, 1987). **Substance abuse** is the maladaptive use of drugs, including legal drugs such as alcohol and nicotine; illegal drugs such as marijuana, cocaine, and LSD; and prescription drugs such as stimulants and sedatives. **Internalizing disorders** are those in which the young person's problems are turned inward and are manifested in emotional and cognitive distress, such as depression, anxiety, or phobia. **Externalizing disorders** are those in which the young person's problems are turned outward and are manifested in behavior problems (some writers use the expression "acting out" to refer to this set of problems). Common externalizing problems during adolescence are delinquency, antisocial aggression, and truancy. Some adolescents also have problems that do not fit neatly into one of these three categories, such as academic problems (e.g., low motivation, poor attention) or peer problems (e.g., low popularity, poor social skills) (Wångby, Bergman, & Magnusson, 1999).

Although we often think of adolescent substance abuse as an externalizing disorder, more recent research indicates that it is just as likely to accompany depression and other internalizing disorders as it is to be a part of acting out behavior. We are simply more likely to be aware of substance-abuse problems when they are seen among adolescents who are antisocial (e.g., a rowdy group of drunk, delinquent youth) than when they occur in the context of internalizing problems (e.g., a depressed teenager who drinks herself to sleep

each night). Because substance-abuse problems co-occur, or are **comorbid** with, both externalizing and internalizing problems, and because many adolescents who experiment with drugs have neither internalizing nor externalizing problems, it makes more sense to discuss substance abuse as a separate category of problem behavior rather than as a subcategory of either internalizing or externalizing behavior.

Although the distinction between internalizing disorders and externalizing disorders is useful for organizing information about psychosocial problems during adolescence, it is important to bear in mind that some adolescents experience problems in both domains simultaneously. That is, some adolescents who engage in delinquency also suffer from depression (Cantwell & Baker, 1991; Capaldi, 1991, 1992; Garnefski & Diekstra, 1997; Hinden, Compas, Howell, & Achenbach, 1997). And many depressed or anxious adolescents, as well as many antisocial adolescents, also abuse drugs and alcohol (Aseltine, Gore, & Colten, 1998; Donovan & Jessor, 1985; Garnefski & Diekstra, 1997; Henry et al., 1993; Kandel, Raveis, & Davies, 1991; Patton et al., 1998). Many researchers believe that it is important to distinguish among adolescents who exhibit one specific problem without any others (e.g., depressed adolescents who do not have other internalizing or externalizing problems); adolescents who exhibit more than one problem within the same general category (e.g., violent delinquent youth or anxious-depressed youth); and adolescents who exhibit both internalizing and externalizing problems (e.g., depressed delinquents). These adolescents may have followed very different pathways to deviance and may require very different types of treatment (Capaldi, 1991, 1992; Colten, Gore, & Aseltine, 1991; Ensminger, 1990; McCord, 1990). In general, studies show that multiproblem teenagers have had far worse family experiences than those with one problem (Aseltine et al., 1998; Capaldi, 1992; Ge, Best, Conger, & Simons, 1994).

Problem Behavior Syndrome

One of the reasons it is helpful to differentiate between internalizing and externalizing disorders is that the specific problems *within* each broad category are often highly intercorrelated. Delinquency is often associated with problems such as truancy, defiance, sexual promiscuity, academic difficulties, and violence (Donovan & Jessor, 1985; Elliott, Huizinga, & Menard, 1989; Farrell, Danish, & Howard, 1992; Gillmore et al., 1991; Jenkins, 1995; Luster & Small, 1994; McGee & Newcomb, 1992;

Morris et al., 1995; Newcomb & Bentler, 1989; Osgood, Johnston, O'Malley, & Bachman, 1988; Resnick & Blum, 1994). All these problems are different manifestations of a lack of impulse control, and adolescents who engage in these behaviors are often described as "undercontrolled" (Robins, John, Caspi, Moffitt, & Stouthamer-Loeber, 1996).

Researchers have devoted a great deal of attention to studying the co-variation among externalizing problems during adolescence—and the comorbidity of externalizing and substance-abuse problems in particular—and a number of theories about the origins of what some experts call **problem behavior syndrome** have been proposed. The most widely cited perspective comes from the work of social psychologist Richard Jessor and his colleagues (Donovan & Jessor, 1985; Jessor & Jessor, 1977). According to Jessor, the underlying cause of externalizing problems during adolescence is *unconventionality* in both the adolescent's personality and social environment (Donovan & Jessor, 1985; Menard & Huizinga, 1994). Unconventional individuals are tolerant of deviance in general, are not highly connected to school or to religious institutions, and are very liberal in their social views. Unconventional environments are those in which a large number of individuals share these attitudes. Unconventional individuals are more likely to engage in a wide variety of **risk-taking behavior,** including experimentation with illegal drugs, sex without contraception, delinquent activity, and even risky driving (Brack, Brack, & Orr, 1996; Fergusson & Lynskey, 1996; Jakobsen, Rise, Aas, & Anderssen, 1997; Jessor, 1987; Spingarn & DuRant, 1996). One reason that so many behavior problems appear to go hand in hand is that unconventional individuals in unconventional environments are likely to engage in all sorts of risky activities.

Although Jessor's theory does not specifically hypothesize what the origins of unconventionality are, a number of possibilities have been proposed. One set of theories, for example, emphasizes the biological underpinnings of risk taking and of unconventionality and argues that a predisposition toward deviance may actually be inherited (e.g., Mednick, Gabrielli, & Hitchings, 1987; Rowe, Rodgers, Meseck-Bushey, & St. John, 1989). A second view stresses biologically based differences (either inherited or acquired through experience)

▲ *According to one theory, the underlying cause of behavior problems in adolescence is unconventionality. Unconventional individuals, who are tolerant of deviance in general, not highly connected to school or to religious institutions, and very liberal in their social views are more likely to engage in a wide variety of risk-taking behavior, including experimentation with illegal drugs. This pattern is referred to as problem behavior syndrome.* (Graphix/Gamma Liason)

among individuals in arousal and sensation seeking (e.g., Zuckerman, 1983). Yet a third viewpoint emphasizes the early family context in which deviance-prone children are reared and presents problem behavior as a sort of adaptive response to a hostile environment (Belsky, Steinberg, & Draper, 1991).

An alternative to the view that there is an underlying trait has been proposed by sociologist Denise Kandel. Kandel and her associates argue that different types of deviance have distinctly different origins but that involvement in a given problem behavior may itself lead to involvement in a second one. For example, the use of illicit drugs other than marijuana (e.g., cocaine, heroin) increases the chances that an adolescent will become premaritally pregnant (Elliott & Morse, 1989; Yamaguchi & Kandel, 1987) or suicidal (Kandel et al., 1991). Thus, problem behaviors may cluster together not mainly because of an underlying trait, such as unconventionality, but because some activities—drug use, in particular—lead to involvement in other problem behaviors (Allen, Leadbeater, & Aber, 1994).

According to a third view, **social control theory** (Gottfredson & Hirschi, 1990; Hawdon, 1996; Hirschi, 1969; Osgood, Wilson, O'Malley, Bachman, & Johnston,

1996), individuals who do not have strong bonds to society's institutions—such as the family, the school, or the workplace—are likely to deviate and behave unconventionally in a variety of ways. This view suggests that the apparent clustering of various problem behaviors may stem not from a problem "in" the person (such as inherent unconventionality or a biological predisposition toward risky behavior) but from an underlying weakness in the attachment of certain youngsters to society. This underlying problem leads to the development of an unconventional attitude, to membership in an unconventional peer group, or to involvement in one or several problem behaviors that may set a chain of problem activities in motion. Social control theory helps explain why behavior problems are not just clustered together but are also far more prevalent among poor, inner-city, minority youngsters.

Finally, a number of researchers stress that we should be careful about overstating the case for a single problem behavior "syndrome" (McCord, 1990; Osgood et al., 1988; Resnicow, Ross-Gaddy, & Vaughan, 1995). They note that, although engaging in one type of behavior problem increases the likelihood of engaging in another, the overlap among behavior problems is far from perfect. Indeed, in one study, it was found that the vast majority of delinquents are *not* serious drug users (Elliott et al., 1989). Other studies suggest that it is important to differentiate between engaging in problem behavior that adults disapprove of but that many adolescents consider normative (e.g., smoking, drinking, having sex) and problem behavior that both adults and adolescents view as serious (e.g., violent crime) (Basen-Engquist, Edmundson, & Parcel, 1996). Such evidence makes it difficult to embrace a theory that identifies a single cause of problem behavior. Like other types of behavior, problem behavior has multiple and complex causes that vary from one individual to the next. It may be just as erroneous to generalize about the troubled adolescent as it is to generalize about young people overall.

The clustering of various problem behaviors is seen more often in some populations than others. Generally, it is seen more often in studies of adolescents than in studies of children or young adults (Gillmore et al., 1991; McGee & Newcomb, 1992). In addition, some studies find that disengagement from school and early sexual intercourse—two of the factors that often are correlated with other externalizing problems, such as delinquency—may not be part of a problematic syndrome among inner-city African American youth or Native Americans (Ensminger, 1990; Mitchell & O'Nell,

1998; Neumark-Sztainer et al., 1996; Resnicow, Ross-Gaddy, & Vaughan, 1995; Rotheram-Borus, Rosario, Van Rossem, Reid, & Gillis, 1995; Stanton et al., 1993). Therefore, it may be erroneous to view certain behaviors, such as precocious sexual activity, as indicative of underlying problems in certain communities.

Comorbidity of Internalizing Problems

Although co-variation among internalizing problems has been less extensively studied than co-variation among externalizing problems, it appears that there is also a good deal of comorbidity in internalizing disorders, which tend to have in common the subjective state of distress. For example, depressed adolescents are more likely to experience anxiety, panic, phobia, obsessional thinking, suicidal ideation, eating disorders, and various psychosomatic disturbances (i.e., physical problems that have psychological causes) (Attie & Brooks-Gunn, 1989; Brady & Kendall, 1992; Cantwell & Baker, 1991; Colten et al., 1991; Gerhardt, Compas, Connor, & Achenbach, 1999; Hinden et al., 1997; Kandel et al., 1991; Petersen et al., 1993).

Just as various externalizing problems are hypothesized to reflect an underlying antisocial syndrome, various indicators of internalizing problems may be thought of as different manifestations of a common underlying factor. This factor is often referred to as **negative affectivity** (Lonigan, Carey, & Finch, 1994; Watson & Kendall, 1989). Individuals who are high in negative affectivity—who become distressed easily—are at greater risk for depression, anxiety disorders, and a range of internalizing problems. As is the case with the underpinnings of externalizing problems, the underpinnings of internalizing problems are believed to have both biological and environmental origins, including high levels of biological reactivity to stress (Katainen, Raeikkoenen, & Keltikangas-Jaervinen, 1998; Susman, Dorn, Inoff-Germain, Nottelmann, & Chrousos, 1997). These common underpinnings contribute to a certain degree of stability in predispositions toward internalizing problems over time (Bardone, Moffitt, Caspi, Dickson, & Silva, 1996).

In this chapter, we will examine the nature, prevalence, consequences, and amelioration of the three sets of problems often seen during adolescence: substance use and abuse; antisocial behavior, violence, and other externalizing problems; and depression, suicide, and other internalizing problems. In each case, we will ask three central questions: How many, and which, young people have problems in this domain? What do we know about the factors that contribute to problems in this area? And, finally, what approaches to prevention and intervention appear to have the most promise? Following our discussions of substance use and abuse, externalizing disorders, and internalizing disorders, we examine stress and coping during adolescence.

RECAP

Psychologists and other mental health experts interested in adolescence distinguish among three categories of problems in adolescence: substance abuse, internalizing problems, and externalizing problems. There is a great deal of co-variation, or comorbidity, among various psychosocial problems during adolescence within these broad categories. Adolescents who engage in delinquency, for example, are more likely than their peers to be truant, to engage in precocious sexual behavior, and to commit acts of aggression—a pattern that has been termed problem behavior syndrome. Similarly, adolescents who are high in negative affectivity are more likely to suffer from depression, to feel anxious, and to report other symptoms of distress.

Food for Thought

How should the recognition that there is considerable comorbidity of problems in adolescence change approaches to prevention and intervention?

SUBSTANCE USE AND ABUSE IN ADOLESCENCE

Our society sends young people mixed messages about drugs and alcohol. Television programs aimed at preadolescents urge viewers to "just say no," but the televised football games and adult situation comedies that many of these viewers watch tell them, no less subtly, that having a good time with friends is virtually impossible without something alcoholic to drink. Many celebrities who are idolized by teenagers speak out against cocaine and marijuana, but many equally famous stars admit to using the same drugs. Tobacco companies spend enormous amounts of money marketing cigarettes to teenagers through advertising (Biener & Siegel, 2000). In MTV and other videos, tobacco and alcohol use is common and often linked to sex, and more often than not, the lead performer is the individual doing the drinking and smoking (DuRant et al., 1997).

The mixed signals sent to young people about drugs reflect, no doubt, the inconsistent way that we view these substances as a society: Some drugs (such as alcohol and Prozac) are fine, as long as they are not abused, but others (such as cocaine and ecstasy) are not; some drinking (enough to relax at a party) is socially appropriate, but too much (enough to impair an automobile driver) is not; some people (those over 21) are old enough to handle drugs, but others (those under 21) are not. It is easy to see why teenagers do not follow the dictates of their elders when it comes to alcohol and other drugs. How then, should we view substance use and abuse among teenagers, when our backdrop is a society that much of the time tolerates, if not actively encourages, adults to use these same substances?

As with most of the problem behaviors that are common during adolescence, discussions of teenage substance use are often filled more with rhetoric than with reality. The popular stereotype of contemporary young people is that they use and abuse a wide range of drugs more than their counterparts did previously, that the main reason adolescents use drugs is peer pressure, and that the "epidemic" level of substance use among American teenagers is behind many of the other problems associated with this age group—including academic underachievement, early pregnancy, suicide, and crime. The simplicity of these assertions is certainly tempting—after all, what could be more reassuring than to identify the "real" culprit (drugs) and the "real" causes (peers) of all the maladies of young people? And what could be even more comforting than the belief that, if we simply teach young people to "say no" to their peers, these problems will all disappear?

Unfortunately, what we would like to believe about adolescent drug use is not necessarily identical to what the facts are. Although there are grains of truth in many of the popular claims about the causes, nature, and consequences of teenage substance use and abuse, there are many widely held misconceptions about this subject, too.

The Prevalence of Substance Use and Abuse in Adolescence

Each year since 1975, a group of researchers from the University of Michigan has surveyed a nationally representative sample of about 15,000 American high school seniors on several aspects of their lifestyle and values, including their use and abuse of a variety of drugs.

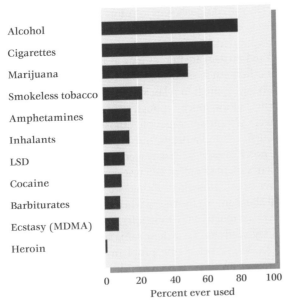

Alcohol
Cigarettes
Marijuana
Smokeless tobacco
Amphetamines
Inhalants
LSD
Cocaine
Barbiturates
Ecstasy (MDMA)
Heroin

0   20   40   60   80   100
Percent ever used

Figure 13.1   Percentages of American high school seniors who have ever used various drugs. (Johnston et al., 1999)

Beginning in 1991, comparable samples of eighth- and tenth-graders were added to the annual survey. Because of the size and representativeness of the sample of respondents, this survey, called **Monitoring the Future** (Johnston, Bachman, & O'Malley, 1999), is an excellent source of information about patterns of adolescent drug and alcohol use, at least among young people who have not dropped out of school (the latest survey results can be accessed at the Monitoring the Future website. See www.mhhe.com/steinberg6 for further details.

The surveys consistently indicate that the two major legal drugs—alcohol and nicotine—are by far the most commonly used and abused substances, both in terms of prevalence (the percentage of teenagers who have ever used the drug) and in terms of recency of use (the percentage of teenagers who have used the drug within the past month). Eight out of 10 teenagers have tried alcohol, and two-thirds have tried cigarettes. Nearly half of all seniors have tried marijuana, more than one-third have smoked marijuana at least once within the past year, and nearly one-fourth have smoked marijuana within the past 30 days. After marijuana, however, the percentage of young people who have tried various other drugs drops precipitously, and only about 10 percent of teenagers have used an illicit drug other than marijuana within the past month (Johnston et al., 1999). And, notwithstanding all the media attention

given to cocaine, far fewer high school seniors have tried cocaine than have tried smokeless tobacco, amphetamines, or inhalants (see figure 13.1). In general, although alcohol and tobacco use among adolescents in most other industrialized countries is comparable to that in the United States, illicit drug use by adolescents is less prevalent abroad (Arnett, in press; Silbereisen, Robins, & Rutter, 1995).

Prevalence statistics, especially those that tap whether an individual has *ever* tried the substance in question, tell little about the nature and extent of drug use from the standpoint of adolescents' health and well-being. It is one thing to have tried alcohol or marijuana, but it is something else to use either of these substances so often that one's life and behavior are markedly affected.

One of the best ways to examine this issue is to look at the percentage of young people who report using various substances daily or nearly daily. When we do so, we find that cigarettes are the only substances used by a substantial number of high school seniors daily (a little more than one-fifth smoke daily) and that, of the remaining drugs, only alcohol and marijuana are used daily by even a modest percentage of teenagers (alcohol is used daily by about 3 percent of seniors; marijuana is used daily by about 6 percent). Although the daily use of alcohol is relatively infrequent among adolescents, about one-third of all seniors, one-fourth of all tenth-graders, and one-sixth of all eighth-graders report having abused alcohol (having had more than five drinks in a row) at least once during the past two weeks (Johnston, Bachman & O'Malley, 1999).

Together, the findings from these surveys cast doubt on some of the most fervently held stereotypes about adolescent drug use. It is true that many adolescents smoke cigarettes, which is certainly cause for concern, and that many adolescents who drink do so in excess. But the data also indicate that only a very small proportion of young people have serious drug-dependency problems (which would lead to daily use) or use hard drugs at all. Moreover, it is very unlikely that drug and alcohol use lurk behind the wide assortment of adolescent problems for which they are so frequently blamed. Rather, the pattern suggests that most adolescents have experimented with alcohol and marijuana, that many have used one or both of these drugs regularly, that alcohol is clearly the drug of choice among teenagers (a substantial minority of whom drink to excess), and that most teenagers have not experimented with other drugs. From a health and safety standpoint, therefore, education about alcohol and tobacco use and abuse is

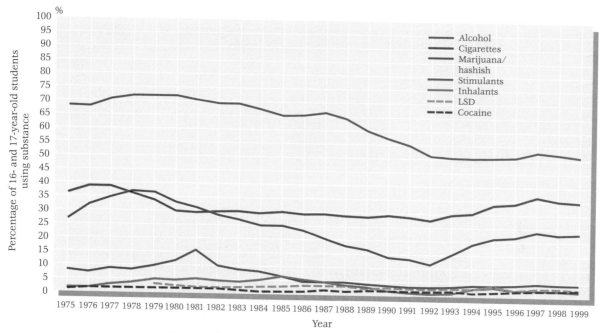

Figure 13.2 *Over-time trends in the proportion of high school seniors who report having used various drugs in the 30 days preceding the survey.* (Johnston, Bachman & O'Malley, 1999)

more urgently needed and may potentially affect a larger percentage of young people than education about any other drug type.

The Monitoring the Future study has also been used to chart changes over time in adolescent drug use, and the most recent administrations of the survey have given experts cause for concern. Marijuana use, which had been on a steady decline since the late 1970s, rose quite sharply during the mid-1990s, as did the use of LSD (acid, or "drop"), stimulants (such as speed), and inhalants (paint thinner, glue), and the use of these drugs has not declined appreciably in recent years. Alcohol use, which had been declining steadily since the early 1980s (when more than 70 percent of seniors reported having had alcohol within the past month), has leveled off, with about 50 percent of seniors reporting alcohol use in the past month. And, despite massive antismoking efforts, cigarette use by teenagers has continued to increase since the early 1990s. As astounding as it may seem, given the huge amount of antismoking publicity, more eighth-, tenth-, and twelfth-graders smoke today than were smoking at the beginning of the 1990s (see figure 13.2). The sharp rise in marijuana use, coupled with increases in the use of stimulants and LSD, troubles many observers, because it is reminiscent of the pattern observed

during the mid-1970s, when adolescent drug use was at an all-time high (Treaster, 1994).

Although pundits and political commentators frequently claim to have discovered the "real" reason for changes in rates of adolescent substance use (the recent increase has been blamed on everything from television to family disruption to former President Clinton's own experimentation with marijuana as a teenager), the truth of the matter is that no one knows why rates of adolescent substance use fluctuate over time. Adolescents' drug use fluctuates with changes in their perceptions of how harmful and disapproved drug use is, but scientists have not been able to determine what influences these perceptions, although it is likely that the messages teenagers receive about drugs—from parents, teachers, and the mass media—are important (Bachman, Johnston, & O'Malley, 1998). What is clear, however, is that cohorts of U.S. adolescents born after World War II use more legal and illegal drugs, at an earlier age, than their counterparts who were born in the first half of the twentieth century (Johnson & Gerstein, 1998). Interestingly, the once existent gender gap in drug use, with males more likely to use and abuse drugs, has all but disappeared for alcohol, marijuana, and

Table 13.1   Percentage of 8th graders who have ever used various illicit drugs.

	1991	1992	1993	1994	1995	1996	1997	1998	1999
Any illicit drug	18.7	20.6	22.5	25.7	28.5	31.2	29.4	29.0	28.3
Marijuana	10.2	11.2	12.6	16.7	19.9	23.1	22.6	22.2	22.0
Inhalants	17.6	17.4	19.4	19.9	21.6	21.2	21.0	20.5	19.7
Hallucinogens	3.2	3.8	3.9	4.3	5.2	5.9	5.4	4.9	4.8
Cocaine	2.3	2.9	2.9	3.6	4.2	4.5	4.4	4.6	4.7
Stimulants	10.5	10.8	11.8	12.3	13.1	13.5	12.3	11.3	10.7

Source: Monitoring the Future, 1997.

cigarettes and has narrowed substantially for other drugs as well (Johnson & Gerstein, 1998).

What to make of this mass of numbers, figures, and trends is not entirely clear. Perhaps the most worrisome finding to emerge in recent surveys is that experimentation with drugs begins at an earlier age now than previously, so that the most pressing problem may not be the prevalence of drug use among high school seniors but, instead, early experimentation with drugs among younger teenagers. More adolescents begin smoking cigarettes and drinking alcohol *before* high school than during high school itself (Johnston, O'Malley, & Bachman, 1986; Kosterman, Hawkins, Guo, Catalano, & Abbott, 2000). For example, recent studies show that one-fourth of all eighth-graders report drinking alcohol regularly, that more than 70 percent of adolescents have had alcohol by the age of 14, that nearly 1 in 10 eighth-graders smokes cigarettes daily, and that nearly 10 percent of sixth-graders—11- and 12-year-olds—have consumed five or more drinks consecutively at least once during the previous two weeks (Kosterman et al., 2000; Matza, 1990; Monitoring the Future, 1999).

Recent trends in drug use among young adolescents are very troubling. One-fifth of eighth-graders have tried inhalants, 22 percent have tried marijuana, and nearly 25 percent have been drunk at least once (Monitoring the Future, 1999). And the typical adolescent who smokes cigarettes begins in grade 7 or 8. Cigarettes are also the most persistent of any drugs that are used, with individuals who begin smoking during adolescence more likely to persist than those who begin drinking (Chen & Kandel, 1995). Estimates are that every day 5,000 American adolescents try cigarettes for the first time and 2,000 become established smokers (Gilpin, Choi, Berry, & Pierce, 1999).

The early initiation into drug use among young teenagers and preadolescents is especially disturbing and,

unfortunately, has been on the rise (see table 13.1) (Monitoring the Future, 1999). Many psychologists believe that early experimentation with drugs is more harmful than is experimentation at a later age (Fergusson, Lynskey, & Horwood, 1996). Younger adolescents may lack the maturity of judgment necessary to use drugs in moderation or under safe circumstances, and younger adolescents may face unique developmental challenges, with which drug use interferes (Baumrind & Moselle, 1985). Marijuana use in early adolescence is predictive of numerous problems later on, including dropping out of high school, having unsafe sex, and becoming involved in delinquency (Brook, Balka, & Whiteman, 1999). In addition, there is some evidence that heavy drug use may hurry adolescents through the psychosocial tasks of adolescence, thereby interfering with the normal developmental timetable (Newcomb & Bentler, 1988).

Several national surveys have examined ethnic differences in rates of adolescent drug use and abuse. In general, white adolescents are more likely to use drugs and alcohol than are minority youngsters, especially African American and Asian American youth. Rates of drug use among Hispanic American adolescents are comparable to those of white youngsters, whereas use among Native American adolescents is the highest (Bachman et al., 1991; Beauvais, 1996; Costello et al., 1997; Gfellner, 1994). In general, foreign-born minority youngsters use drugs at a lower rate than do American-born minority youth, suggesting, unfortunately, that part of becoming an American teenager means experimenting with drugs (Vega, Gil, & Zimmerman, 1993). Indeed, the rate of drug use among immigrant adolescents is *half* the rate of use among adolescents from the same ethnic group who were born in the United States (Harris, 1999).

Researchers have also been interested in the sequence through which adolescents experiment with various drugs. In general, young people experiment with beer and wine before cigarettes or hard liquor, which precede marijuana use, which in turn precedes the use of other illicit drugs (cocaine, stimulants, LSD) (Kandel, 1980). However, although experimentation may follow this sequence, this does not mean that alcohol use invariably leads to marijuana use, or that marijuana use necessarily leads to experimentation with harder drugs. In fact, there is little evidence to support the idea that marijuana is an inevitable stepping-stone to hard drug use (much appears to depend on how frequently marijuana is used) (Treaster, 1994).

The fact that there is a fairly standard sequence of drug use, however, suggests that virtually all users of hard drugs have also tried alcohol, cigarettes, and marijuana and, moreover, that one way to prevent adolescents from experimenting with more serious drugs is to stop them from experimenting with alcohol and marijuana. In fact, studies show that adolescents who have not experimented with alcohol or marijuana by the time they are in their twenties are unlikely ever to use these or other drugs (Chen & Kandel, 1995; Kandel & Logan, 1984). For this reason, alcohol and marijuana are considered **gateway drugs,** in the sense that they form a gate through which individuals pass before using harder drugs. Whether an individual passes through the gate, however, is influenced by many other factors beyond his or her previous patterns of drug use.

The Causes and Consequences of Adolescent Substance Use and Abuse

In looking at the causes and consequences of substance use and abuse, it is especially important to keep in mind the distinction between occasional experimentation and regular, problematic use or abuse. Because most adolescents have experimented with alcohol and marijuana, one can speculate that occasional alcohol and marijuana use has become normative among American high school students and, consequently, that there are plenty of normal, healthy young people who have used these drugs at least once.

Several studies, in fact, indicate that adolescents who experiment with alcohol and marijuana are as well adjusted as—if not somewhat better adjusted and more socially skilled than—their peers who abstain completely from alcohol and marijuana (e.g., Baumrind, 1991; Scheier & Botvin, 1998; Shedler & Block, 1990). This substantial body of research shows quite clearly that it is important to differentiate among adolescents who are

frequent drug users (e.g., at least once a week) or hard drug users (i.e., drugs other than alcohol, tobacco, or marijuana); those who experiment with marijuana and alcohol but who do not use them frequently (i.e., no more than once a month); those who abstain out of irrational fear; and those who abstain out of rational choice (Baumrind, 1991; Hughes, Power, & Francis, 1992; Mitchell et al., 1996; Wills, McNamara, Vaccaro, & Hirky, 1996). Experimenters and rational abstainers score higher on measures of psychological adjustment than either frequent users or irrational abstainers. Longer-term follow-up studies also show that moderate alcohol use during adolescence does not have negative long-term effects (Newcomb & Bentler, 1988). Indeed, cigarette use during adolescence has more harmful long-term health consequences than does experimentation with alcohol or marijuana, partly because nicotine is a more addictive drug, whose use is more likely to persist into middle adulthood (Chen & Kandel, 1996; Elders, Perry, Eriksen, & Giovino, 1994; Pierce & Gilpin, 1996).

These results do not mean that occasional experimentation with drugs during adolescence *leads to* better adjustment, of course. In fact, research shows that the psychological advantages observed among adolescents who experimented with alcohol and marijuana were evident when these individuals were younger children (Shedler & Block, 1990). Together, though, the studies suggest that moderate alcohol and marijuana use has become normative among adolescents in contemporary society (however troublesome some adults may find this), that these substances are typically used in social situations, and that better adjusted and more interpersonally competent young people are likely to participate in social activities in which alcohol and other drugs are present (Burda & Vaux, 1988; Scheier & Botvin, 1998; Shedler & Block, 1990). Relative to experimenters, abstainers—and "irrational" abstainers, in particular—tend to be overcontrolled, narrow in their interests, anxious, and inhibited (Shedler & Block, 1990).

Excessive substance use, or, more precisely, substance abuse, is a different matter. Adolescents who are frequent users of alcohol, tobacco, and other drugs score lower on measures of psychological adjustment as teenagers and are more likely to have been maladjusted as children (Shedler & Block, 1990). Indeed, a team of researchers who had followed a sample of individuals from preschool into young adulthood report that, at age 7, the individuals who would later become frequent drug users as adolescents were described as "not getting along well with other children, not showing concern for

▲ *Alcohol and drugs are typically implicated in adolescent automobile crashes, the leading cause of death and disability among American teenagers.* (Bob Daemmrich/Stock, Boston)

moral issues . . . not planful or likely to think ahead, not trustworthy or dependable . . . [and] not self-reliant or confident" (Shedler & Block, 1990, p. 618). As 11-year-olds, these individuals were described as deviant, emotionally labile, stubborn, and inattentive. In other words, drug and alcohol abuse during adolescence is often a symptom of prior psychological disturbance.

Substance abuse during adolescence, whatever its antecedents, is associated with a host of other problems. Young people who abuse alcohol, tobacco, and other drugs are more likely to experience problems at school, experience psychological distress and depression, have physical health problems, engage in unprotected sexual activity, abuse alcohol as young adults, and become involved in dangerous or deviant activities, including crime, delinquency, and truancy (Andersson, Bergman, & Magnusson, 1989; Brener & Collins, 1998; Holmen, Barrett-Connor, Holmen, & Bjermer, 2000; Kandel, Johnson, Bird, & Canino, 1997; Luthar & Cushing, 1997; Newcomb & Bentler, 1989; Wu & Anthony, 1999). These problems are especially severe among adolescents who are involved in drug dealing (Centers & Weist, 1998). Alcohol and other drugs are typically implicated in adolescent automobile crashes, the leading cause of death and disability among American teenagers (Lang, Waller, & Shope, 1996; O'Malley & Johnston, 1999), and in other fatal and non-

fatal accidents, such as drownings, falls, and burns (Irwin, 1986; Wintemute, Kraus, Teret, & Wright, 1987). Adolescent substance abusers also expose themselves to the long-term health risks of excessive drug use that stem from addiction or dependency; in the case of cigarettes, alcohol, and marijuana, these risks are substantial and well documented—among them, cancer, heart disease, and kidney and liver damage.

Which adolescents are most likely to become substance abusers? Generally, four sets of risk factors—psychological, familial, social, and contextual—for substance abuse have been identified, and, the more risk factors that are present for an individual, the more likely he or she is to use and abuse drugs (Hawkins, Catalano, & Miller, 1992; Newcomb & Felix-Ortiz, 1992; Petraitis, Flay, & Miller, 1995). These risk factors have been found across a variety of studies and in samples of adolescents from a wide range of ethnic and socioeconomic backgrounds, with little variation in the potency of risk factors across socioeconomic, ethnic, or gender groups. In other words, the factors that place an adolescent at risk for substance abuse are pretty much the same, regardless of the adolescent's sex, social class, or ethnicity.

The first set of risk factors is *psychological.* Individuals with certain personality characteristics—which typically are present before adolescence—are more likely to develop drug and alcohol problems than are their peers. These characteristics include anger, impulsivity, depression, and academic difficulties (Brook, Whitman, Gordon, & Cohen, 1986; Scheer & Unger, 1998; Shedler & Block, 1990; Wills, Windle, & Cleary, 1998). In addition, individuals who have more tolerant attitudes about drug use (and about deviance in general) are at greater risk for drug abuse (Schulenberg, Wadsworth, O'Malley, Bachman, & Johnston, 1996; Petraitis et al., 1995), as are those who expect alcohol or other drugs to improve their social relationships (Smith & Goldman, 1994; Smith, Goldman, Greenbaum, & Christiansen, 1995). Even as children, for example, individuals who eventually become heavy drinkers as adolescents expect alcohol to have positive effects on them (Dunn & Goldman, 1998).

Individuals with *distant, hostile, or conflicted family relationships* are more likely to develop substance-abuse problems than are their peers who grow up in close, nurturing families (Barnes, Farrell, & Banerjee, 1994; Dishion, Capaldi, & Yoerger, 1999; Flewelling & Bauman, 1990; Kilpatrick et al., 2000; Needle, Su, & Doherty, 1990). Drug-abusing youngsters are also more likely than their peers to have parents who are excessively permissive, uninvolved, neglectful, or rejecting (Barnes, Reifman, Farrel, & Dintcheff, 2000; Baumrind, 1991; Block, Block, & Keyes, 1988; Bogenschneider, Wu, Raffaelli, & Tsay, 1998; Chilcoat, Dishion, & Anthony, 1995; Crowe, Philbin, Richards, & Crawford, 1998; Doherty & Allen, 1994; Shedler & Block, 1990). They are more likely to come from homes in which one or more other family members (parents or siblings) use drugs or are tolerant of drug use (Blackson, Tarter, Loeber, Ammerman, & Windle, 1996; Boyle, Claxton, & Forster, 1997; Brook, Whitman, & Gordon, 1983; Brook, Whitman, Gordon, & Brook, 1984; Duncan, Duncan, & Hops, 1996; Griesler, Kandel, & Davies, 1998; Kandel & Wu, 1995; Newcombe, Huba, & Bentler, 1983; Peterson, Hawkins, Abbott, & Catalano, 1994).

Socially, individuals with substance-abuse problems also are more likely to have friends who use and tolerate the use of drugs, both because they are influenced by these friends and because they are drawn to them (Coombs, Paulson, & Richardson, 1991; Dishion, Capaldi, Spracklen, & Li, 1995; Flannery, Vazsonyi, Torquati, & Fridrich, 1994; Hazard & Lee, 1999; Killen et al., 1997; Rose, Chassin, Presson, & Sherman, 1999; Urberg, Degirmencioglu, & Pilgrim, 1997; Wang, Fitzhugh, Westerfield, & Eddy, 1995). As you read in chapter 5, whether and how often adolescents use drugs are important defining characteristics of peer groups—abstainers tend to have other abstainers as friends, and users tend to be friends with other users. Drug-using adolescents seek drug-using peers, and drug-using peers encourage even more drug use among their friends (Chassin, Presson, Todd, Rose, & Sherman, 1998; Kandel, 1978; Schulenberg et al., 1999; Steinberg, Fletcher, & Darling, 1994).

Finally, adolescents who become substance abusers are more likely to live in a *social context* that makes drug use easier. Important contextual factors are the availability of drugs, the community's norms regarding drug use, the degree to which drug laws are enforced, and the ways in which drug use is presented via the mass media (Allison et al., 1999; Li, Stanton, Black, & Feigelman, 1996; Petraitis et al., 1995; Robinson, Klesges, Zbikowski, & Glaser, 1997). All other factors being equal, adolescents who have easy access to drugs, who believe that there are ample op-

portunities to use drugs, and who are exposed to messages that tolerate or even encourage drug use are more likely to use and abuse drugs.

Researchers have also identified important **protective factors** that decrease the likelihood of adolescents' engaging in substance abuse (Jessor, Van Den Bos, Vanderryn, Costa, & Turbin, 1995). Among the most important protective factors are positive mental health (including high self-esteem and the absence of depressive symptoms), high academic achievement, close family relationships, and involvement in religious activities (Bahr, Maughan, Marcos, & Li, 1998; Flannery, Vazsonyi, & Rowe, 1996; Dekovi, 1999; Jessor, Turbin, & Costa, 1998; Newcomb & Felix-Ortiz, 1992). These protective factors appear to operate over and above the effects of the established risk factors. Moreover, most of the risk and protective factors operate similarly among adolescents from different ethnic groups (Barnes & Farrell, 1992; Flannery, Vazsonyi, Torquati, & Rowe, 1993; Peterson et al., 1994). One of the reasons for the lower rate of drinking among African American youth, for example, is that their parents are less likely to drink and to tolerate adolescent drinking (Peterson et al., 1994).

Because one of the most important risk factors for adolescent substance abuse is having a parent who abuses drugs or alcohol, researchers have looked closely at the psychological development of adolescents with an alcoholic parent. Among the most important studies on this topic is one directed by psychologist Laurie Chassin and her colleagues (Chassin & Barrera, 1993; Chassin, Pillow, Curran, Molina, & Barrera, 1993; Chassin, Rogosch, & Barrera, 1991; Hussong, Curran, & Chassin, 1998). As suspected, adolescents with an alcoholic parent are, on average, more likely to use alcohol and other drugs than other youth (Chassin et al., 1993; Colder, Chassin, Stice, & Curran, 1997). In addition, although virtually all adolescents experiment with alcohol, adolescents with an alcoholic parent move from experimentation to more frequent and heavier drinking and drug use more rapidly (Chassin & Barrera, 1993). At the same time, Chassin's research shows that only a minority of children of alcoholics develop substance-abuse problems of their own—suggesting that parental alcoholism is a risk factor for substance abuse but by no means a guarantee of it.

What differentiates children of alcoholics who develop substance-abuse problems from those who do not? The answer has to do with the extent to which the parents' alcoholism interferes with family functioning. When the alcoholism diminishes parental monitoring, increases family stress, and heightens family conflict, the adolescent is at much greater risk for developing substance-abuse problems, in part because the poor parenting increases the adolescents' involvement in problem behavior overall, which in turn is linked to alcohol and drug use (Chassin et al., 1993; Chassin, Curran, Hussong, & Colder, 1996; Dobkin, Tremblay, & Sacchitelle, 1997; Hussong et al., 1998; Reuter & Conger, 1994). In families where this does not occur, however, the risk is much lower. Not surprisingly, adolescents with an alcoholic parent who continues to abuse alcohol are at much greater risk than those whose alcoholic parent is recovering.

The Prevention and Treatment of Substance Use and Abuse

Efforts to prevent substance use and abuse among teenagers focus on one of three factors: the supply of drugs, the environment in which teenagers may be exposed to drugs, and characteristics of the potential drug user (Newcomb & Bentler, 1989). Although a good deal of government spending and media publicity have been devoted to the first of these approaches—that is, to attempts to control or limit the availability of drugs—the consensus among experts is that it is more realistic to try to change adolescents' motivation to use drugs and the environment in which they live, since it has proven virtually impossible to remove drugs totally from society. In addition, the two most commonly used and abused drugs are both legal—cigarettes and alcohol—and laws prohibiting the sale of these substances to minors are not well enforced (Cummings, Pechacek, & Shopland, 1994; DiFranza, Savageau, & Aisquith, 1996). Research does show, however, that raising the price of alcohol and cigarettes does reduce adolescents' use of them, as does more stringent enforcement of laws regarding the sale of tobacco and alcohol to minors (Biener, Aseltine, Cohen, & Anderka, 1998; Forster et al., 1998; Grossman, Chaloupka, Saffer, & Laixuthai, 1994; Jason, Berk, Schnopp-Wyatt, & Talbot, 1999).

Many types of drug-abuse prevention programs have been tried, either alone or in combination. In programs designed to change an aspect of the adolescent's personality or behavior, drug use is either targeted indirectly, by attempting to enhance adolescents' psychological development in general or by helping adolescents develop alternative activities and interests that will make drug use less likely. The idea behind these sorts of efforts is that adolescents who have high self-esteem or who are gainfully employed, for example, will be less likely to use

drugs. In other programs, the intervention is more directly aimed at preventing drug use. These programs include information-based efforts (in which adolescents are educated about the dangers of drugs), social skills training (in which adolescents are taught how to turn down drugs), and a combination of informational and general psychological intervention (in which adolescents are educated about drug abuse and exposed to a program designed to enhance their self-esteem, for instance) (Newcomb & Bentler, 1989).

Generally speaking, the results of research designed to evaluate these sorts of individual-focused approaches have not been especially encouraging (Dielman, 1994; Leventhal & Keeshan, 1993). Careful evaluations of Project DARE, for example—the most widely implemented drug education program in the United States—show that the program is largely ineffective (Ennett, Tobler, Ringwall, & Flewelling, 1994). Experts are now fairly confident that drug education alone, whether based on rational information or scare tactics, does not prevent drug use. This is reminiscent of research on sex education, which, as we saw in chapter 11, shows that informational programs are not effective on their own. As a rule, educational programs may change individuals' knowledge, but they rarely affect their behavior.

The most encouraging results have been found in programs that do not focus just on the individual adolescent but, rather, combine social competence training with a communitywide intervention aimed not only at adolescents but also at their peers, parents, and teachers (Chou et al., 1998; Dielman, 1994; Kellam & Anthony, 1998; Leventhal & Keeshan, 1993; Siegel & Biener, 2000). These multifaceted efforts have been shown to be effective in reducing adolescents' use of alcohol, cigarettes, and other drugs, especially if the programs begin when the youngsters are preadolescents and continue well into high school (Bruvold, 1993; Dielman, 1994; Ellickson, Bell, & McGuigan, 1993; Flynn et al., 1994; Perry et al., 1996). Overall, most experts agree that efforts designed simply to change the potential adolescent drug user without transforming the environment in which the adolescent lives are not likely to succeed. Despite their intuitive appeal, efforts to help adolescents "just say no" have been remarkably unsuccessful.

One of the problems with all prevention programs is that they often do not distinguish between drug use and drug abuse. It is abuse, not occasional use, that is the serious problem. In the words of two leading researchers,

> Although it is important to delay the onset of regular drug use as long as possible to allow time for the

development of adaptive and effective personal and interpersonal skills, it may be less important to prevent the use of drugs than the abuse, misuse, and problem use of drugs (which place a tremendous burden on the individual and society). It is in this area that prevention programs have been less successful and are in need of continued development. (Newcomb & Bentler, 1989, p. 246)

A similar problem—that is, failing to distinguish between drug use and drug abuse—has plagued treatment efforts aimed at adolescents who are believed to be drug abusers. Indeed, some experts worry that adolescents who are mistakenly enrolled in treatment programs (because their parents have overreacted to the adolescents' normative and probably harmless experimentation with drugs) may end up more alienated and more distressed— and more likely to become drug abusers—as a result of the "treatment." Evaluations of treatment programs for adolescents who are genuine drug abusers suggest that efforts that involve the adolescent's family, not just the teenager, are more likely to be successful (Dielman, 1994; Dishion & Andrews, 1995; St. Pierre, Mark, Kaltreider, & Aikin, 1997; Zavela et al., 1997).

RECAP

Among contemporary adolescents, alcohol and cigarettes are still the drugs of choice, although a substantial number of young people have experimented with marijuana as well. Research indicates a clear need to distinguish between experimentation with alcohol and marijuana (which has not been shown to be harmful) and regular or heavy use (which has). Adolescents who abuse alcohol and other drugs are more likely to come from hostile family environments, to have friends who use drugs, and to have other problems, in school as well as in interpersonal relationships. The most promising interventions for substance-abuse problems in adolescence are those that target the adolescent's social environment as well as the individual.

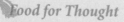

Food for Thought

In your opinion, why have interventions designed to change individuals' knowledge about drug use and its consequences been such failures? How do you explain the fact that many individuals continue to engage in behaviors that they know are dangerous or unhealthy, such as smoking?

ANTISOCIAL BEHAVIOR, VIOLENCE, AND OTHER EXTERNALIZING PROBLEMS

Although social scientists disagree about the causes and treatment of adolescent antisocial behavior—delinquency, crime, aggression, and other conduct problems—there is one point on which there is tremendous agreement: Violations of the law are far more common among adolescents and young adults than among any other age segment of the population. Part of this pattern stems from the fact that certain violations, called status offenses, are by definition limited to minors. **Status offenses**—such as being truant, running away from home, and using alcohol—are behaviors that are not against the law for adults but that nevertheless violate established codes of conduct for juveniles.

Even if we discount status offenses, however, research shows that both **violent crimes** (such as assault, rape, robbery, and murder) and **property crimes** (such as burglary, theft, and arson) increase in frequency between the preadolescent and adolescent years, peak during the high school years, and decline somewhat during young adulthood. Almost one out of every three arrests for serious crimes involves a suspect under 18. Individuals under 18 account for well over one-sixth of all violent crimes in the United States (Federal Bureau of Investigation, 1999) (see figure 13.3).

The Prevalence of Antisocial Behavior During Adolescence

The widely publicized school shootings that occurred in the United States during the late 1990s drew national attention to the problem of youth violence. News accounts of multiple-victim shootings at schools such as Columbine High School made it seem as if adolescent violence, and school violence in particular, were widespread and rising. Many educators and policymakers insisted that schools need to install metal detectors and implement psychological assessment procedures to identify violence-prone students (Federal Bureau of Investigation, 2000). Others called for the elimination of the juvenile justice system, arguing that giving adolescents "adult time for adult crime" would deter adolescents from serious crime (see Reppucci, 1999, for a discussion). Many states began to transfer violent juvenile offenders out of their juvenile justice system and into their adult system (Fagan & Zimring, 2000).

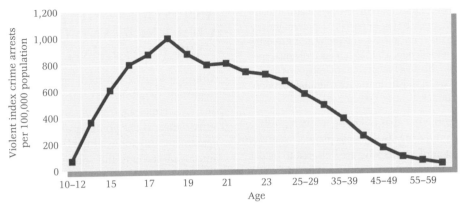

Figure 13.3   Age differences in violent criminal activity. (Federal Bureau of Investigation, 1999)

As is frequently the case when horrifying incidents are widely publicized, an emotional frenzy developed around the issue of school violence that ignored hard facts and common sense (Steinberg, 2000b). It is important, therefore, to look at the statistics on youth crime in the United States before jumping to the conclusion that crime and violence have reached epidemic proportions. Indeed, you may be surprised to learn that school violence is less frequent now than it was in the past, that youth crime is on the decline, and that rates of youth violence have dropped dramatically in recent years.

Between 1950 and 1980, there were steady increases in juvenile arrests in the United States for virtually all classes of misbehavior. In the early 1980s, the rate of youthful criminal activity leveled off, and it has not changed appreciably since then (Zimring, 1998). Because such a large proportion of arrests of juveniles are for property crimes, though, looking at changes in *overall* arrest rates over time can be very misleading, since the overall rate is largely determined by the most commonly committed crimes. The reason the youth crime rate has remained flat is that arrests for property crimes have barely increased over the past two decades.

When we look specifically at *violent crimes*, a different picture emerges. Between 1965 and 1988, and especially after 1984, the arrest rates for the most serious violent crimes—murder, rape, armed robbery, and aggravated assault (an attack on another person for the purpose of inflicting severe injury, typically with a weapon)—increased substantially among young people. In addition, the average age at which individuals were arrested fell during the past several decades, as criminal behavior became increasingly prevalent

among younger boys and girls. In 1994, for example, 35 percent of juveniles arrested were under 15 (Snyder & Sickmund, 1996). These statistics, along with the images of slain students on the evening news, fueled much of the public's concern about youth violence in the United States.

What the news stories about school violence often neglected to note, however, was that, during the mid-1990s, violent crime among young people declined dramatically, contradicting the hyperbolic claims of some that the United States was going to be ravaged by a wave of "superpredators" (Zimring, 1998) (see figure 13.4). Moreover, analyses of data on school shootings indicate that they are extremely rare events—so rare that it is impossible to predict when they are going to occur or who the perpetrators will be (Steinberg, 2000b). During the 1990s, for instance, an average of 12 students were murdered while in school each year (the year in which the Columbine shooting took place was a huge exception to the general trend). When you consider that there are about 50 million elementary and secondary school students in the United States, and about 100,000 schools, you can begin to see just how rare school violence really is (Kachur 1996).

Despite the evidence that violence among young people is not on the rise and that lethal school violence is incredibly rare, the public outcry over Columbine and other school shootings prompted a widespread overhaul of the juvenile justice system in the United States during the 1990s. Increasing numbers of juvenile offenders were transferred to the adult system, where they were tried in adult courts and, if convicted, sentenced to adult prisons. The little research that has been conducted on the impact of transfer into the adult

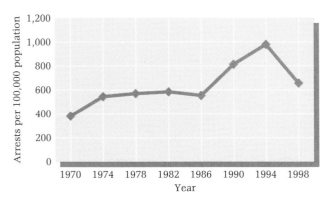

Figure 13.4   Violent crimes committed by individuals aged 15 to 17 in the United States 1970–1998. Violent index crimes include murder, rape, armed robbery, and aggravated assault. (Federal Bureau of Investigation, 1999)

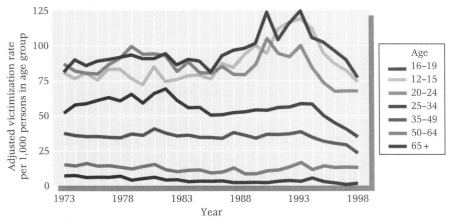

Figure 13.5   Violent crime rates by age of victim. (Federal Bureau of Investigation, 1999)

system suggests that juveniles who are convicted as adults are actually *more,* not less, likely to re-offend after they have been released, however (Bishop & Frazier, 2000). In addition, many social scientists have expressed concern about the likely adverse effects of this practice on juveniles' mental health and development. They have argued that juvenile offenders would be made more troubled and dangerous as a result of their contact with serious adult criminals and have pointed out that secure facilities exist within the juvenile justice system in which dangerous offenders can be housed and rehabilitated (Fagan & Zimring, 2000).

Violent crime among young people is a significant source of worry to adults, of course. But crime is also a significant source of worry to adolescents themselves, who are the age group most likely to be victims of crimes such as theft, robbery, rape, and assault. Indeed, although adolescents under age 18 account for only 10 percent of the population, they constitute nearly one-fourth of all victims of crime (Perkins,

1997). Victims of violent crimes are more likely than are other adolescents to report a wide range of problems, including post-traumatic stress disorder, depressed mood, sleep deprivation, and academic difficulties, and they are more likely themselves to engage in aggression and antisocial behavior (Finkelhor, & Dziuba-Leatherman, 1994; Cooley-Quille & Lorion, 1999; DuRant, Pendergrast, & Cadenhead, 1994; Moses, 1999). Despite recent declines in crime, rates of youth victimization have remained substantially higher than rates of adult victimization (see figure 13.5).

African American and Hispanic American adolescents living in the inner city are disproportionately likely to be the victims of violent crime (Hutson, Anglin, & Pratts, 1994). Indeed, for far too many young adolescents growing up in the inner city, gang violence and victimization are chronic problems. One young adolescent living in a poor Chicago neighborhood told an interviewer

Figure 13.6   *The increase in homicides committed by adolescents during the 1980s and early 1990s was due entirely to an increase in gun-related homicides.* (Federal Bureau of Investigation, 1994)

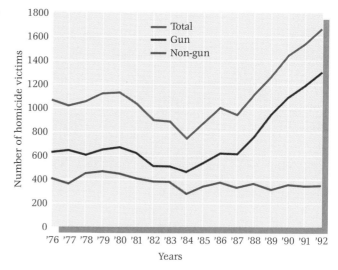

Many people in the night in my building wait for someone to come and visit. Just wait for someone in the building to open the door so they can go in and show them a knife for money and beat them and someone got killed and all the blood was on the floor of the elevator and everybody got scared about going in the night. So they just stay in their houses. (Richards, Suleiman, Sims, & Sedeño, 1994, p. 9)

In light of the escalating rate of violence among inner-city adolescents, researchers have focused special attention on the problem. Most researchers agree that violence and aggression among youth are strongly linked to poverty, for a number of reasons. First, when families live in impoverished neighborhoods, parents are less effective in nurturing and monitoring their children, and this diminished effectiveness leads to increased aggression and crime (Sampson & Laub, 1994). Second, concentrated poverty upsets the social fabric of a neighborhood, making it more difficult for adults and social institutions to provide the guidance and supervision that adolescents need (Sampson, 1992; Sampson & Groves, 1989). Third, in many inner-city communities devastated by unemployment, aggression is used by males to demonstrate their standing and power—characteristics that are typically demonstrated in middle-class communities through occupational success (Wilson & Daley, 1985). Finally, repeated exposure to violence—whether in the home or in the neighborhood—breeds violence itself (DuRant, Cadenhead, Pendergrast, Slavens, & Linder, 1994).

Several analysts have pointed out that much of the increase in violent crime among juveniles is largely due to increases in gun-related crimes. Look at figure 13.6, for example, which presents over-time trends in homicides by juvenile offenders but distinguishes between gun and nongun crimes. As you can see, there has been no increase in the past 20 years in the rate of nongun homicide but a marked increase in the rate of homicides involving guns. Although it is certainly possible that this increase has been due to changes in the nature of adolescents—changes that would make young people more willing to use guns in criminal situations—there is little doubt that the increased availability of guns in young people's neighborhoods is a major contributing factor to the problem (Zimring, 1998). Many inner-city adolescents carry guns in self-defense, but many also carry guns to establish their status, project an image of toughness, and gain power over others. The widespread prevalence of guns in inner-city neighborhoods changes the sorts of interactions that take place when adolescents fight, however, transforming what might have been aggressive disputes into lethal exchanges (Wilkinson & Fagan, 1996).

Most of the data regarding adolescent misbehavior come from official arrest records. Consequently, it is important to keep in mind that the "official" figures about adolescent crime may both *underreport* and *selectively report* rates of misbehavior. Underreporting results from the fact that many adolescents commit offenses that are undetected by authorities or that are handled outside official reporting procedures—for example, when an adolescent who is caught shoplifting is reprimanded by the storekeeper instead of being referred to the police. (Only about one-third of crimes are ever reported to the police [Krisberg, Schwartz, Fishman, Eisikovits, & Guttman, 1986].) Selective reporting results from the fact that lower-class and minority youngsters are more likely both to be arrested and to be treated more harshly than are other youngsters who commit similar offenses, so official statistics may artificially inflate the proportion of crimes committed by poor, minority youth.

An alternative to relying on official records is to ask adolescents directly about their involvement in various criminal or status offenses. Several researchers have done this, promising the respondents anonymity and confidentiality. The results of these surveys have been surprising, to say the least. They do not necessarily provide a more accurate picture of juvenile crime, but they certainly provide a different one. Three conclusions are especially interesting.

First, the surveys indicate that a very large proportion of adolescents—between 60 and 80 percent, depending on the survey sample—have engaged in delinquent behavior at one time or another (Huizinga & Elliot, 1985). Nearly half of all males report being responsible for an assault sometime during adolescence (Zimring, 1998). Although the gender gap in offending has been narrowing at a rapid pace, males nevertheless commit far more delinquent and criminal acts than females, and research on female offending has been very sparse (Hoyt & Scherer, 1998; Kelley, Huizinga, Thornberry, & Loeber, 1997). There is some evidence, however, that violent females may have significantly more mental health problems than violent males, consistent with the notion that gender-inappropriate displays of aggression may be indicative of greater maladjustment (Cauffman, Feldman, Waterman, & Steiner, 1998; Crick, 1997; Ellickson, Saner, & McGuigan, 1997).

Second, in contrast to official records, which portray a disproportionate involvement of minority youth in delinquent activities, the surveys of adolescents themselves indicate that ethnic differences in the prevalence of delinquent and criminal activity are smaller than suspected. According to most surveys of youth, for example, nearly equal proportions of white, African American, and Hispanic American youth admit to having engaged in delinquent activity, and equal proportions admit having committed a serious crime. There are *social class* differences in serious criminal activity, however, and, since minority youth are overrepresented among the poor, they are also overrepresented among those who commit crimes.

▲ Surveys indicate that a very large proportion of adolescents—between 60 and 80 percent, depending on the survey sample—have engaged in delinquent behavior at one time or another. Most of these behaviors are not serious crimes; nevertheless, they are chargeable offenses. (Michael Newman/ PhotoEdit)

Finally, surveys of adolescents indicate that minority youth are far more likely to be arrested and far more likely to be treated harshly by the juvenile justice system (Bridges & Steen, 1998; Feld, 1997; Poe-Yamagata & Jones, 2000). African American adolescents are seven times more likely than white adolescents to be arrested for minor offenses and twice as likely to be arrested for serious crimes. Minority youth in general are more likely to be sent to correctional facilities than are white youth who commit similar offenses (Krisberg et al., 1986). Thus, the reason for the stereotype of the juvenile offender as nonwhite is due, in part, to the higher proportion of arrests in this group, not solely to the higher proportion of delinquent and criminal activity. And, of course, the disproportionate number of nonwhite youth living in poverty contributes to racial differences in criminal activity.

Although studies indicate that most adolescents—regardless of their social background—do something that violates the law at one time or another, the vast majority of teenagers who violate the law do so only once. Thus, although most adolescents have violated the law, a relatively small number of adolescents account for a relatively high proportion of serious criminal activity; one estimate indicates that fewer than 10 percent of adolescents account for about two-thirds of all recorded offenses (Yoshikawa, 1994). It is important, therefore, in thinking about the causes of delinquent behavior, to distinguish between delinquent behavior that is serious and chronic and delinquent behavior that is less worrisome. These two sets of delinquent behavior have very different antecedents (Moffitt, 1993).

The Causes of Antisocial Behavior in Adolescence

In general, the earlier an adolescent's "criminal career" begins—in particular, if it begins before adolescence—the more likely he or she is to become a chronic offender, to commit serious and violent crimes, and to continue committing crimes as an adult (Lahey et al., 1999; Moffitt, 1993; Moffitt, Caspi, Dickson, Silva, & Stanton, 1996; Patterson, Forgatch, Yoerger, & Stoolmiller, 1998; Tolan & Thomas, 1995). The older an adolescent is when the delinquent activity first appears, the less worrisome his or her behavior is likely to become. For purposes of discussion, therefore, it is helpful to distinguish between youngsters who begin misbehaving before adolescence and those whose delinquent activity first appears during adolescence. The causes and the consequences of delinquent behavior that begins during preadolescence are quite different from those of delinquency that begins—and typically ends—during adolescence or young adulthood.

Numerous studies indicate that many youngsters whose problems with the law begin before adolescence are psychologically troubled (Grisso, 1999). Most of these delinquents are male, many are poor, and a disproportionate number come from homes in which divorce has occurred (Piquero & Chung, in press). More important, a large and consistent body of research shows that chronic delinquents typically come from disorganized families with hostile, inept, or neglectful parents who have mistreated their children and have failed to instill in them proper standards of behavior or the psychological foundations of self-control (Cough-

lin & Vuchinich, 1996; Dishion, Patterson, Stoolmiller, & Skinner, 1991; Farrington & West, 1991; Gorman-Smith, Tolan, Loeber, & Henry, 1998; Haapasalo & Tremblay, 1994; Laub & Sampson, 1995; Miller, Cowan, Cowan, Hetherington, & Clingempeel, 1993; McCord, 1996; Moffitt, 1993; O'Donnell, Hawkins, & Abbott, 1995; Patterson, DeGarmo, & Knutson, 2000). There is some evidence that exposure to harsh parenting may adversely affect the developing child's brain chemistry—in particular, the activity of serotonin receptors—increasing the risk of antisocial behavior (Pine et al., 1996).

The idea that family factors may underlie chronic delinquency—because of genetic factors, environmental influences, or both—is supported by observations that preadolescent delinquency tends to run in families. Although studies have shown genetic influences on all types of antisocial behavior, aggression is especially heritable (Deater-Deckard & Plomin, 1999; Eley, Lichtenstein, & Stevenson, 1999; Rutter, 1997). Many adolescents who have been in trouble with the law from an early age have siblings who have had similar problems (Loeber & Stouthamer-Loeber, 1986; Rowe, Rodgers, & Meseck-Bushey, 1992). And, because antisocial behavior in the child typically provokes further parental ineffectiveness and association with other antisocial children, aggressive children often get caught up in a vicious cycle (O'Connor, Deater-Deckard, Fulker, Rutter, & Plomin, 1998; Patterson & Yoerger, 1993; Vuchinich, Bank, & Patterson, 1992). As a consequence, early involvement in antisocial activity tends to escalate and become self-perpetuating over time.

There is also considerable evidence that, apart from family factors, there are individual characteristics that distinguish potential delinquent youngsters from their peers, at a relatively early age. First, and most important, children who become delinquent—especially those who engage in violence—have histories of aggressive and antisocial behavior that were identifiable as early as age 8 (Farrington & West, 1991; Hamalainen & Pulkkinen, 1996; Kupersmidt & Coie, 1990; Loeber et al., 1993; Patterson et al., 1998; Stanger, Achenbach, & Verhulst, 1997; Stattin & Magnusson, 1989).

Second, studies show that many children who become delinquents have problems in self-regulation—they are more impulsive, less able to control their anger, and more likely than their peers to suffer from hyperactivity, or, as it is technically known, **attention deficit/hyperactivity disorder (ADHD)** (Colder & Stice, 1998; Farrington, 1989; Henry, Caspi, Moffitt,

Harrington, & Silva, 1999; Lynam, 1996; McGee, Williams, & Feehan, 1992; Moffitt, 1993; Patterson et al., 2000; Stanger, Achenbach, & McConaughy, 1993; Steiner, Cauffman, & Duxbury, 1999; Thompson, Riggs, Mikulich, & Crowley, 1996; White et al., 1994). ADHD is believed to be primarily biological in origin and is characterized by impulsivity, inattentiveness, restlessness, and inappropriately high levels of activity, especially in learning situations. Although ADHD does not seem to directly cause antisocial behavior, it does elevate the risk for other family and academic problems, which in turn increase the likelihood of an adolescent's developing externalizing problems (Nagin & Tremblay, 1999; Patterson et al., 2000).

Third, children who become delinquent are more likely than their peers to score low in standardized tests of intelligence and to perform poorly in school (Farrington, 1989; Fergusson & Horwood, 1995; Henry et al., 1999; Moffitt & Silva, 1988; White, Moffitt, & Silva, 1989), although the link between low intelligence and chronic delinquency is stronger among white and Hispanic American adolescents than among African American youth (Donnellan, Ge, & Wenk, in press).

Finally, many aggressive adolescents have a history of poor relations with peers; problems with peers is an especially strong predictor of antisocial behavior among boys (Agnew & Brezina, 1997; Coie, Lochman, Terry, & Hyman, 1992; Lewin, Davis, & Hops, 1999; Lyon, Henggeler, & Hall, 1992; Stattin & Magnusson, 1994).

Research by psychologist Kenneth Dodge and his colleagues into the cognitive aspects of antisocial behavior indicates that especially aggressive youngsters are likely to suffer from a tendency toward what has been called a **hostile attributional bias** (Dodge, Price, Bachorowski, & Newman, 1990; Lochman & Dodge, 1994, 1998). Individuals with a hostile attributional bias are more likely than their peers to interpret ambiguous interactions with other children as deliberately hostile and to react aggressively in order to retaliate. What might be viewed by the average adolescent as an innocent and accidental bump on the basketball court might be interpreted as an intentional shove by someone with a biased viewpoint, and it might lead to a fight. Such problematic information processing has been linked to aggression among white, African American, and Hispanic American youngsters alike (Graham, Hudley, & Williams, 1992).

Because aggressiveness, hyperactivity, and intelligence are relatively stable traits over childhood, there is a great deal of continuity in behavior problems over time. Studies that have followed individuals from childhood through adolescence and into adulthood find very high correlations between behavior problems at one point in time and antisocial behavior later in life (Farrington, 1991; Fergusson et al., 1996a; Henry, Caspi, Moffitt, & Silva, 1996; Lahey et al., 1995; Robins, 1986; Ronka & Pulkkinen, 1995). This does not mean that all individuals who show antisocial behavior early necessarily show it later—in fact, most do not (Loeber & Stouthamer-Loeber, 1998). Nevertheless, many antisocial adolescents grow up to be adults who are diagnosed as suffering from antisocial personality disorder and who persist in their delinquent and criminal behavior. This pattern has been called **life-course persistent antisocial behavior.** It is possible, therefore, to identify at a relatively early age individuals who have what might be termed an "antisocial tendency." Contrary to popular belief, there is no evidence that antisocial individuals uniformly have low self-esteem or that raising their self-esteem does anything to diminish their propensity toward misbehavior (McCord, 1990).

Research has shown, however, that is important to differentiate between chronic offenders who are violent and chronic offenders who are not. Psychologist Rolf Loeber and his colleagues have suggested, in fact, that it is especially important to distinguish between the developmental trajectories of aggressive individuals and the trajectories of offenders who engage in more covert antisocial behavior, such as shoplifting or frequent lying (Loeber, Russo, Stouthamer-Loeber, & Lahey, 1994; Loeber & Stouthamer-Loeber, 1998; Nagin & Tremblay, 1999). Whereas chronically violent offenders typically have a childhood history of aggression, chronically nonviolent offenders generally have oppositionalism, or contrariness, rather than aggression, in their past (Loeber & Stouthamer-Loeber, 1998). Aggression, in particular, is a highly stable trait and has more consistent antecedents (e.g., specific types of neuropsychological deficits, especially in the frontal lobe of the brain) than does deviance in general (Seguin, Pihl, Harden, Tremblay, & Boulerice, 1995; Stanger et al., 1997).

In contrast to youngsters who begin their delinquent behaviors before adolescence (and who often continue their antisocial behavior into adulthood), those who begin after adolescence do not always show signs of psychological abnormality or severe family pathology (Moffitt, 1993). Typically, the offenses committed by these youngsters do not develop into serious criminality, and, generally speaking, these individuals do not commit serious violations of the law after adolescence, although they may be more likely to have problems with drugs and alcohol (Nagin, Farrington, & Moffit, 1995). Much of what has been called **adolescence-limited antisocial behavior** occurs in group situations, with peers. In general, individuals who are involved in adolescence-limited antisocial activities have learned the norms and standards of society and are far better socialized than life-course persistent antisocial individuals.

Current research indicates that certain family factors may be associated with adolescence-limited antisocial behavior, however. In particular, there is some evidence that youngsters who fall into this category are less carefully monitored by their parents (Ary et al., 1999; Dornbusch, Carlsmith, Bushwall, Ritter, Hastorf, & Gross, 1985; Forgatch & Stoolmiller, 1994; Patterson & Stouthamer-Loeber, 1984; Steinberg, Lamborn, Darling, Mounts, & Dornbusch, 1994). But there also is evidence that the role of the peer group may be very important, especially in industrialized countries, where peer influence tends to be relatively stronger (Chen, Greenberger, Lester, Dong, & Guo, 1998; Cheung, 1997; Dishion, Andrews, & Crosby, 1995; Heimer & Matsueda, 1994; Keenan, Loeber, Zhang, Stouthamer-Loeber, & Van Kammen, 1995; Tremblay, Mâsse, Vitaro, & Dobkin, 1995). Specifically, studies show that much of this kind of delinquent activity occurs in group situations in which adolescents are pressured by their friends to go along with the group (Zimring, 1998). In chapter 9, you read about studies of age differences in susceptibility to peer pressure, which show that susceptibility increases between preadolescence and middle adolescence and then declines. It comes as no surprise, therefore, to discover that much reported delinquency follows the same pattern: Rates are low during preadolescence, reach a peak during middle adolescence, and drop off as adolescence ends (Berndt, 1979).

A series of studies by psychologist Gerald Patterson and his colleagues (Dishion et al., 1991; Patterson, 1986; Patterson, DeBaryshe, & Ramsey, 1989) indicates how family and peer influences may work together in the development of delinquency. Specifically, these researchers have found that poor parental discipline—discipline that is harsh, inconsistent, and lax—during the early elementary school years leads to the association with deviant or antisocial peers, which in turn leads to delinquent behavior. One of the strongest predictors of delinquency and other forms of problem behavior is the extent to which the adolescent spends unsupervised time in unstructured activities with peers—activities such as hanging out,

driving around, and going to parties (Osgood, Wilson, O'Malley, Bachman, & Johnston, 1996).

Dysfunctional child rearing may contribute to the development of antisocial behavior in two ways. First, adolescents who have distant relationships with their parents are generally more susceptible to peer pressure than other youngsters (Steinberg & Silverberg, 1986). Second, individuals who are raised in dysfunctional ways may develop personality traits that lead children to dislike them—such as aggression—and they may find themselves with few options for friends other than equally disliked and aggressive agemates (Dishion et al., 1991).

● **Runaways** Despite a good deal of attention in the popular media, little systematic research has focused on adolescent runaways. The little research that has been done paints a different picture than is portrayed in most made-for-television melodramas. First, the epidemic of teenage runaways is grossly overstated. Nationally representative samples of adolescents suggest that between 4 and 10 percent of adolescents have *ever* run away from home (running away is more common among poor adolescents) and that fewer than half of all runaways have done so more than once. Second, in contrast to images of teenage runaways traveling across the country, surveys indicate that half of all runaways stay within their community, with relatives or friends. Finally, despite frequent portrayals of "long-lost" runaways, half of all runaways return home within a few days, and from 75 to 80 percent return home within a week. Public concern about runaways is high not because the numbers are large but because of the dangers faced on the streets by the 20 percent who do not return home promptly. These young people are exposed to numerous psychological and physical risks, including prostitution and other criminal behaviors, AIDS and other sexually transmitted infections, victimization, and drug and alcohol abuse (McCarthy & Hagen, 1992; Terrell, 1997; Whitbeck, Hoyt, & Yoder, 1999; Windle, 1989).

Running away from home is typically considered to be another manifestation of externalizing problems in general, along with delinquency, aggression, truancy, and precocious sexuality. Consistent with this view, runaways—and repeat runaways, in particular—are more likely than other adolescents to be delinquent, to drop out of school, and to be aggressive. The antecedents of running away are similar to those for deviance in general: poverty, low scores on intelligence tests, and family conflict (Garbarino, Wilson, & Garbarino, 1986; Windle, 1989).

The Prevention and Treatment of Externalizing Problems in Adolescence

Given the important differences between the causes of life-course persistent antisocial behavior and antisocial behavior that is adolescence-limited, one would expect that these two groups of adolescents would be best served by different sorts of preventive and after-the-fact interventions. In order to lower the rate of chronic antisocial behavior, in particular, experts argue that we need mainly to prevent disruption in early family relationships and to head off early academic problems, through a combination of family support and preschool intervention (Bourduin et al., 1995; Tremblay, Pagani-Kurtz, Mâsse, Vitaro, & Pihl, 1995; Yoshikawa, 1994).

These sorts of preventive strategies are easier proposed than done, however. Our society is hesitant to intervene to prevent family disruption, because we typically wait until we see a sign of trouble in a family before acting. Unfortunately, waiting until after family disruption has occurred before intervening may have little benefit, for research shows that the outlook for delinquents who have begun criminal careers early is not very good. Various attempts at therapy and other sorts of treatment have not, by and large, proven successful. Whereas it is incorrect that nothing works, it is true that even the best programs for treating serious juvenile offenders have very small effects (Lipsey, 1997). This is the case for treatment approaches that use individual psychotherapy, group therapy, and diversion programs designed to remove delinquents from the juvenile justice system (to avoid the harmful effects of being labeled "delinquent") and to provide them with alternative opportunities for productive behavior (McCord, 1990).

Programs that attempt to change delinquents' beliefs about the value of aggression as a means of solving problems and to teach socially acceptable alternatives to aggression have shown some promise (e.g., Farrell & Meyer, 1997; Guerra & Slaby, 1990; Lochman, 1992), but even these programs have been only modestly successful in changing offenders' actual behavior (McCord, 1990). Most chronic delinquents go on to commit serious and violent crimes and to continue criminal behavior into adulthood. There is some evidence that family-based interventions (such as parent training, family therapy, and therapeutic foster care) may be more successful than interventions that focus on the individual adolescent (Chamberlain & Reid, 1998; Henggeler, 1996), but these programs tend to be extremely expensive and time consuming (Bank,

Marlowe, Reid, Patterson, & Weinrott, 1991; Henggeler, Melton, & Smith, 1992). One problem that has been especially difficult to overcome is that interventions that group together high-risk youth may have the unintended effect of *increasing* delinquency, because the interventions themselves may foster friendships among delinquent peers (Poulin, Dishion, & Haas, 1997).

The prognosis for delinquents whose antisocial behavior is adolescence-limited is considerably better. Because they have internalized a basic foundation of norms and moral standards, it is easier to help these youngsters control their own behavior and stop misbehaving. Four types of strategies have been proposed. First, we can help youngsters at the individual level by teaching them how to learn to resist peer pressure and to settle conflicts without resorting to aggression (DuRant et al., 1996). Second, by training parents to monitor their children more effectively, we can minimize the number of opportunities adolescents have to engage in peer-oriented misbehavior (Loeber & Stouthamer-Loeber, 1986). Third, by intervening within classrooms, schools, and neighborhoods, we may be able to alter the broader climate in ways that discourage antisocial behavior and encourage prosocial behavior (Felson, Liska, South, & McNulty, 1994; Hausman, Pierce, & Briggs, 1996; Kellam, Ling, Merisca, Brown, & Ialongo, 1998). Finally, by treating delinquency seriously when it occurs—by making sure that an adolescent knows that misbehavior has definite consequences—we can deter an adolescent from doing the same thing again in the future.

RECAP

Although the juvenile crime rate has declined in recent years, adolescents still account for a disproportionately high number of crimes, including violent crimes. There is tremendous variability among juvenile offenders, however. Research shows, in particular, that it is important to distinguish between life-course persistent offenders—who are more likely than other adolescents to come from distressed families, to have childhood histories of aggressive behavior, to have been diagnosed as hyperactive, and to score low on standardized tests of intelligence and achievement—and adolescence-limited offenders, whose antisocial behavior typically begins and ends during the teenage years. Because few approaches to the treatment of life-course persistent offenders have proven successful, many efforts today in the area of crime and delinquency are being directed at prevention, through early intervention and parent education.

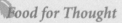

Food for Thought

Explain the distinction between life-course-persistent offenders and adoles-cence-limited offenders. How do these patterns of offending differ with respect to their antecedents, correlates, and prognoses? Should we take this distinction into account when deciding how to treat violent juvenile offenders?

DEPRESSION, SUICIDE, AND OTHER INTERNALIZING PROBLEMS IN ADOLESCENCE

Most individuals emerge from adolescence confident, with a healthy sense of who they are and where they are headed. However, in some instances, the changes and demands of adolescence leave a teenager feeling help-less, confused, and pessimistic about the future. Although minor fluctuations in self-esteem during early adolescence are commonplace—as you read in chapter 8—it is not normal for adolescents (or adults, for that matter) to feel a prolonged or an intense sense of hopelessness or frustration. Such young people are likely to be psychologically depressed and in need of professional help.

The Nature and Prevalence of Adolescent Depression

In its mild form, **depression** is probably the most common psychological disturbance among adolescents (Cicchetti & Toth, 1998; Zahn-Waxler, Klimes-Dougan, & Slattery, in press). Although we typically associate depression with feelings of sadness, there are other symptoms that are important signs of the disturbance, and sadness alone, without any other symptoms, may not indicate depression in the clinical sense of the term. Depression has *emotional symptoms,* including dejection, decreased enjoyment of pleasurable activities, and low self-esteem. It also has *cognitive symptoms,* such as pessimism and hope-lessness. Depression has *motivational symptoms,* as well, including apathy and boredom. Finally, depression usually has *physical symptoms,* such as a loss of appetite, difficulties sleeping, and loss of energy.

Many people use the term *depression* imprecisely, to refer to a wide range of affective problems. Psychologists believe that it is important to distinguish among *depressed mood, depressive syndromes,* and *depressive disorder* (Compas, Ey, & Grant, 1993; Petersen et al., 1993). All individuals experience periods of sadness or depressed mood at one time or another. According to one large-scale survey, more than half of all adolescents occasionally feel sad and hopeless, and more than one-third say they "have nothing to look forward to" (Gans, 1990). According to other surveys, about 25 percent of adolescents regularly feel depressed (Avenevoli & Stein-berg, in press).

Fewer individuals report a pattern of depressive symptoms that includes a wider range of symptoms than sadness alone. At any one point in time, about 5 percent of adolescents have the symptoms of a depressive syndrome, and approximately 3 percent meet the diagnostic criteria for clinical depression (Com-pas et al., 1993; Lewinsohn, Hops, Roberts, Seeley, & Andrews, 1993). Depressed mood, depressive syn-drome, and depressive disorder all become more common over the adolescent period, in part because of the increasing prevalence of stressful events during the adolescent years (Larson & Ham, 1993) and in part because the cognitive changes of adolescence permit the sort of introspection and rumination that often accompanies depression (Avenevoli & Stein-berg, in press; Chen, Mechanic, & Hansell, 1998). Although most adolescents are able to cope with the challenges of the period, some are not.

There is a dramatic increase in the prevalence of depressive feelings around the time of puberty; de-pression is half as common during childhood as it is during adolescence (Avenevoli & Steinberg, in press). Interestingly, whereas depressive feelings are more common among boys than girls prior to adolescence, depressive disorder is much more common among fe-males than males after puberty (see the accompanying box). This sex difference in the prevalence of depres-sive disorder persists throughout most of adulthood, although the size of the sex difference in depression depends on how it is measured and whether the sam-ple is a random sample from the community (in which sex differences in depressed mood tend to be very small) or is composed of people referred for ther-apy (where sex differences in depression are quite large) (Compas et al., 1993; Compas et al., 1997). Ad-ditionally, some studies indicate that there have been historical increases in the prevalence of depression, especially among adolescents, with the rate of depres-sion increasing in each generation (Lewinsohn, Rohde, Seeley, & Fischer, 1993). Several recent studies have indicated that there may be ethnic differences in the prevalence of depression during adolescence, with significantly more Mexican American teenagers reporting depressive symptoms than their white, African American, or Asian American peers, especially within samples of girls (Roberts, Roberts, & Chen, 1997; Siegel, Aneshensel, Taub, Cantwell, & Driscoll, 1998). At this point, it is not known why this is or whether similar patterns are found when the comparison group is drawn from other Hispanic American subpopulations (e.g., Puerto Rican adolescents).

Diagnosing and studying depression among adolescents have been difficult for three, very different, reasons. First, depression during adolescence is often accompanied by other psychosocial or behavior problems, including anxiety, phobia, psychosomatic complaints, and substance abuse (Brady & Kendall, 1992).

Second, many professionals have been tempted to attribute nearly *all* observable difficulties in adolescence to unseen depression. In the past, for example, behaviors such as school phobia and anorexia nervosa were thought to hide the "real" problem—depression. Now, however, it is widely recognized that not all adolescents with behavior problems are necessarily depressed but that depression and other problems are often comorbid (Avenevoli & Steinberg, in press; Cantwell & Baker, 1991; Compas et al., 1993). In cases in which the main problem seems not to be depression, a careful clinician would certainly want to probe to see whether depressive symptoms were present but would not necessarily jump to the conclusion that depression and behavior problems always go hand in hand.

Third, the popular stereotype of adolescents as normally disturbed leads many parents and teachers to fail to recognize genuine psychological problems when they appear. You can probably imagine a parent's description of an adolescent daughter who is critical of herself (which can be an emotional manifestation of depression), unduly negative (a possible cognitive manifestation), bored with everything (a possible motivational manifestation), and not very interested in eating (a possible physical manifestation). It would be easy for this parent to overlook a potentially very real problem and dismiss the daughter's mood and behavior as normal. Obviously, not all instances of self-criticism or apathy reflect psychological disturbance. But a good rule of thumb is that an individual who displays three or more of the signs of depression for two weeks should probably consult a professional (see table 13.2).

▲ *Contrary to myth, adolescents' suicide attempts are rarely impulsive reactions to immediate distress, such as breaking up with someone. Rather, adolescents who attempt to kill themselves usually have made appeals for help and have tried to seek—but have not found—emotional support from family or friends.* (Nancy Hays/Monkmeyer)

Adolescent Suicide

According to national surveys, in any given year, more than 5 percent of American female adolescents and more than 2 percent of males attempt suicide (Blum & Rinehart, 2000). As many as 10 percent of American adolescents have attempted suicide at some point in their life, and a much larger proportion—perhaps as much as 30 percent in the general population and as much as 70 percent in poor communities—have thought about killing themselves (Gans, 1990; Marcenko, Fishman, & Friedman, 1999; Resnick et al., 1997). The suicide rate is especially high among Native American and Alaskan Native adolescents, as well as among adolescents living in rural areas (Blum & Rinehart, 2000; Grossman, Milligan, & Deyo, 1991; Keane, Dick, Bechtold, & Manson, 1996). Fortunately,

Why Are There Sex Differences in Rates of Teenage Depression?

As the accompanying figure indicates, before adolescence boys are somewhat more likely to exhibit depressive symptoms than girls, but after puberty the sex difference in the prevalence of depression reverses. From early adolescence until very late in adulthood, females are much more likely than males to suffer from clinical depression, although females are only slightly more likely than males to report depressed mood (Compas et al., 1997). The increased risk for depression among girls emerges during puberty, rather than at a particular age or grade in school (Angold, Costello, & Worthman, 1998).

Psychologists do not have a certain explanation for the emergence of a sex difference in depressive disorder at adolescence. Although the fact that the emergence of a strong sex differential coincides with puberty suggests a biological explanation, there actually is little evidence that the sex difference in depression is directly attributable to sex differences in hormonal changes (Rutter & Garmezy, 1983). There is some evidence that females are more susceptible than males to genetic influences on depression, such that, even when males and females inherit the same genetic predisposition toward depression from their parents, the predisposition is more likely to be manifested among girls (Jacobson & Rowe, 1999), but it is not known why this is the case. More likely, changes in social relationships around the time of puberty leave girls more vulnerable than boys to some

forms of psychological distress (with some individuals' inheriting a stronger predisposition than others), and depression may be a stereotypically feminine way of manifesting it.

More specifically, social scientists speculate that the emergence of sex differences in depression has something to do with the social role that the adolescent girl finds herself in as she enters the world of boy-girl relationships (Petersen et al., 1993; Wichstrøm, 1999). This role may bring conflict over achievement because of fears that success will be perceived as unattractive, heightened self-consciousness over physical appearance, and increased concern over popularity with peers. Since many of these feelings may provoke helplessness, hopelessness, and anxiety, adolescent girls may be more susceptible to depressive feelings. To make matters worse, pressures on young women to behave in sex-stereotyped ways, which intensify during adolescence (Hill & Lynch, 1983), may lead girls to adopt some behaviors and dispositions—passivity, dependency, and fragility, for example—that they have been socialized to believe are part of the feminine role. Consistent with this, studies show that depression in females is significantly correlated with having a poor body image and with having low scores on measures of masculinity (Allgood-Merten, Lewinsohn, & Hops, 1990; Obeidallah, McHale, & Silbereisen, 1996; Wichstrøm, 1999).

The gender role intensification hypothesis is only one explanation for sex

the vast majority of adolescent suicide attempts— over 98 percent—are not successful. Contrary to myth, adolescents' suicide attempts are rarely impulsive reactions to immediate distress, such as breaking up with a boyfriend or girlfriend. Rather, adolescents who attempt to kill themselves usually have made appeals for help and have tried but have not found emotional support from family or friends.

You may have read that suicide is a leading cause of death among young people, but this is primarily because very few young people die from other causes, such as disease. Although the rate of suicide rises rapidly during the middle adolescent years, it continues to rise throughout adulthood, and suicide is a much more common cause of death among adults than it is among young people (Rutter & Garmezy, 1983; Weiner, 1980). Completed

differences in the prevalence of depression during adolescence. Three other accounts focus on sex differences in the degree to which adolescence is stressful, on sex differences in the ways that boys and girls cope with stress, and on males' and females' vulnerability to various types of stress (Cyranowski & Frank, 2000; Leadbeater, Blatt, & Quinlan, 1995; Nolen-Hoeksema & Girgus, 1994; Rudolph & Hammen, 1999). With respect to the first of these explanations, it is important to note that the link between stress and depression during adolescence is well documented among both males and females; individuals who experience more stress are more vulnerable to depression and other internalizing problems (Petersen et al., 1993). Of interest, then, is evidence that early adolescence is generally a more stressful time for girls than for boys (Allgood-Merten et al., 1990; Petersen et al., 1991; Rudolph & Hammen, 1999). This is because girls are more likely than boys to experience multiple stressors at the same time (e.g., going through puberty while making the transition into junior high school); because girls are likely to experience more stressful life events than boys; and because the bodily changes of puberty, especially when they occur early in adolescence, are more likely to be stressful for girls than for boys—as you saw in chapter 1. In addition, girls are much more likely than boys to have been sexually abused during childhood, which is a very strong risk factor for depression during adolescence (Cutler & Nolen-Hoeksema, 1991).

Second, there is evidence that girls are more likely than boys to react to stress by turning their feelings inward— for instance, by ruminating about the problem and feeling helpless—whereas boys are more likely to respond either by distracting themselves or by turning their feelings outward, in aggressive behavior or in drug and alcohol abuse (Brack et al., 1994; Gjerde, Block, & Block, 1988; Hart & Thompson, 1996; Nolen-Hoeksema & Girgus, 1994; Sethi & Nolen-Hoeksema, 1997). As a result, even when exposed to the same degree of stress, girls are more likely to respond to the stressors by becoming depressed (Angold et al., 1996; Ge, Lorenz, Conger, Elder, & Simons, 1994; Rudolph & Hammen, 1999). This difference in the ways that boys and girls react to stress helps explain why the prevalence of externalizing disorders is higher in boys, whereas the prevalence of internalizing disorders is higher in girls.

The third explanation emphasizes girls' generally greater orientation toward and sensitivity to interpersonal relations. Psychologist Ellen Frank has suggested that gender differences in levels of the hormone **oxytocin** encourages females to invest more in their close relationships but also makes them more vulnerable to the adverse consequences of relational disruptions and interpersonal difficulties (Cyranowski & Frank, 2000). Consistent with this, research indicates that girls are much more likely than boys to develop emotional problems as a result of family discord or problems with peers (Davies & Windle, 1997; Leadbeater, Kuperminc, Blatt, & Hertzog, 1999). Because adolescence is a time of many changes in relationships—in the family, with friends, and with romantic partners—girls' capacity to invest heavily in their relationships with others may be both a strength and a potential vulnerability.

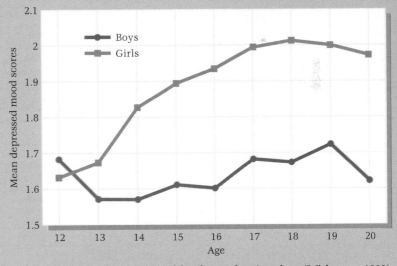

▲ *Depressed mood among males and females as a function of age.* (Wichstrøm, 1999)

suicide is more common among older adults than adolescents and more common among men than women. Attempted suicide, however, is more common during adolescence than during adulthood and is far more common among adolescent girls than boys (Rutter & Garmezy, 1983).

Although the rate of suicide among adults has increased only slightly in recent decades, the adolescent suicide rate has increased alarmingly during the past 45 years—among 15- to 19-year-olds, suicide quadrupled between 1955 and the end of the 1970s, and it increased again during the late 1980s (Garland & Zigler, 1993). More than half a million young Americans attempt suicide each year, and 60 percent of teenagers say that they personally know another teenager who has attempted suicide (Ackerman, 1993).

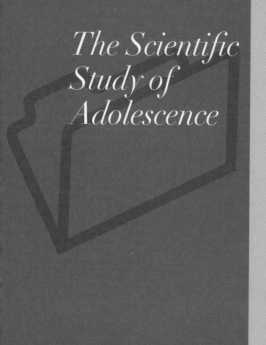

Time-Space Clustering of Teenage Suicide

When the lead singer of the popular grunge-rock band Nirvana, Kurt Cobain, committed suicide in 1994, many parents and teachers worried that his act might provoke a wave of suicide attempts among Cobain's fans. Their fears were founded on the belief that many adolescent suicides occur during outbreaks, or epidemics, when an unusually high number of suicides occur within a limited time period or a small geographic area. When such **cluster suicides** do occur, they typically receive a great deal of publicity in the popular press, which may draw a disproportionate amount of attention to suicide outbreaks. Until recently, social scientists did not actually know whether adolescent suicides occur in clusters with any regularity, or whether we just believe that they do because of the media's attention to them.

An interesting study by epidemiologist Madelyn Gould and her colleagues demonstrates, however, that the clustering of adolescent suicide in time and within location is, in fact, a real phenomenon (Gould, Wallenstein, & Kleinman, 1990). **Epidemiology,** which derives its name from the word *epidemic,* is a branch of medicine devoted to the study of how health problems are spread and distributed within communities. Although we might think of epidemiology as most relevant to the study of physical health problems (such as tracking the spread of a viral infection in a community or monitoring cancer rates across communities as a function of levels of cancer-producing agents in their environments), its tools have been applied to the study of psychological and behavior problems as well. Research into the clustering of adolescent suicides is a case in point.

We know from media reports that some adolescent suicides occur in clusters. But these single case studies (a newspaper report about multiple suicides in a particular high school, for example) do not necessarily indicate that clustering is a genuine phenomenon. The problem in relying on single case studies is that some clusters are bound to

Table 13.2   Diagnostic criteria for mild depressive disorder

1. Depressed or irritable mood for most of the day, for more days than not, for at least one year.
2. The presence, while depressed, of at least two of the following:
   a. Poor appetite or overeating
   b. Insomnia or hypersomnia (sleeping too much)
   c. Low energy or fatigue
   d. Low self-esteem
   e. Poor concentration or difficulty making decisions
   f. Feelings of hopelessness
3. The symptoms cause clinically significant distress or impairment in social, school, or other important areas of functioning.

Source: Diagnostic and statistical manual of the American Psychiatric Association (DSM-IV) Washington, DC. American Psychiatric Association, 1994, p. 349.

A variety of explanations have been given for the increase in suicide among American youth, including pressures to grow up earlier, increasing rates of divorce, less contact with adults, high rates of residential mobility, chronic exposure to violence, and the prospect of facing an unpredictable job market (Bronfenbrenner, 1974; Rutter, 1980). The more recent increase in suicide has been especially pronounced

occur by chance alone. Determining whether adolescent suicides do, indeed, cluster in time and space requires demonstrating that the number of suicides that occur in clusters actually exceeds the number expected by chance.

By analogy, imagine flipping a coin and having heads come up six times in a row. You know that the probability of this happening is exceedingly small. But suppose you knew nothing about coinflipping probabilities and just happened to hit a six-in-a-row sequence on the first six flips you tried. You might easily draw the incorrect conclusion that it was quite common for a coin to land on the same side six times in a row. By the same token, without hard statistical evidence, it might be easy to conclude that adolescent suicides occur in clusters on the basis of undue media attention.

In order to examine the hypothesis that adolescent suicides occur in clusters more than we would expect by chance alone, Gould compiled data about all completed suicides among 15- to 19-year-olds during the period from 1978 to 1984 in the United States, classifying each one by its date and the county in which it occurred. She defined a suicide pair as a cluster if the two suicides occurred in the same county during the same time period. (The researchers examined the data for one-week, two-week, and one-month clustering and found similar results each way.) Since some suicides will occur in the same county within the same time period by chance alone, it was necessary to compare the observed number of suicide clusters in each county with the number that would be expected by chance. If the observed number were significantly greater than the expected number, that would be evidence of a genuine phenomenon.

Gould's analyses showed quite clearly that adolescent suicides cluster more often than would be expected by chance alone. According to her analyses, after taking chance occurrences into account, about 2 percent of adolescent suicides occur in clusters, with considerable variation by state, sampling unit, and year. (This estimate is probably lower than what one would find if one were to examine attempted—rather than completed—suicide, but data about suicide attempts are not collected systematically enough to analyze in this fashion.) Moreover, other analyses showed that the incidence of clustering increases immediately following stories about suicide in the media. Thus, there was legitimate reason for parents and teachers to be concerned about an increase in adolescent suicide attempts following publicity about Kurt Cobain's death.

Epidemiological research on cluster suicides raises concerns about the advisability of publicizing adolescent suicides and suicide attempts. It was initially thought that publicity surrounding suicide would help increase community awareness of the problem and that such news coverage ultimately would lower the suicide rate. Because a number of studies now demonstrate that publicity *increases* the likelihood of further suicide attempts, however, this strategy is being reconsidered. Instead, efforts are more likely to be aimed at diminishing the pressures, drug problems, and family difficulties believed to lead adolescents to consider taking their life.

Source: Gould, M., Wallenstein, S., & Kleinman, M. (1990). Time-space clustering of teenage suicide. *American Journal of Epidemiology, 131,* 71–78.

among African American adolescents, who in general are exposed to more of these risk factors than other teenagers (Summerville & Kaslow, 1993). Suicide is more prevalent, for example, among African Americans who live in areas where the income discrepancy between African Americans and whites is especially pronounced (Burr, Hartman, & Matterson, 1999).

Systematic studies have identified four established sets of risk factors for attempting suicide during adolescence: having a psychiatric problem, especially depression or substance abuse; having a history of suicide in the family; being under stress (especially in the areas of achievement and sexuality); and experiencing parental rejection, family disruption, or extensive family conflict (Blumenthal & Kupfer, 1988; Reifman & Windle, 1995; Rubenstein, Heeren, Housman, Rubin, & Stechler, 1989; Wagner, 1997). Adolescents who have one of these risk factors are significantly more likely to attempt suicide than their peers, and adolescents who have more than one risk factor are dramat-ically more likely to try to kill themselves. It is also the case that adolescents who have attempted suicide once are at risk for attempting it again (Lewinsohn, Rohde, & Seely, 1994).

The Causes of Adolescent Depression and Other Internalizing Disorders

A variety of theories have been proposed to account for the onset of depression and other types of internalizing problems during adolescence, and current consensus is that internalizing problems are likely to result from interacting environmental conditions and individual predispositions, rather than either set of factors alone. Today, most experts endorse a **diathesis-stress model** of depression, which suggests that depression occurs when individuals who are predisposed toward internalizing problems (the term *diathesis* refers to this predisposition) are exposed to chronic or acute stressors that precipitate a depressive reaction (Hilsman & Garber, 1995). Individuals without the diathesis—who are not predisposed toward depression—are able to withstand a great deal of stress, for instance, without developing any psychological problems. Other individuals, who have strong predispositions toward the disorder, may become depressed in the face of stressful circumstances that most of us would consider to be quite normal. Research has focused on both the diathesis and the stress—on identifying individual predispositions toward depression and on identifying the environmental circumstances likely to precipitate the disorder.

Two categories of diatheses, or predispositions, have received the most attention. First, because depression has been found to have a strong genetic component, it is believed that at least some of the diathesis is biological and may be related to problematic patterns of neuroendocrine functioning (*neuroendocrine* refers to hormonal activity in the brain and nervous system). In particular, researchers have focused on the predisposition toward intense problems in the regulation of activity in one or more of the hypothalamic-pituitary axes, including those involving the adrenal, thyroid, gonadal, and somatotropic axes (Brooks-Gunn, Auth, Petersen, & Compas, 2001). Individuals who are prone to intense activation of the hypothalamic-pituitary-adrenocortical (HPA) axis, in particular, are more biologically reactive to stress than are others, and they are more prone to depression and other internalizing disorders.

Other researchers have focused more on the cognitive style of depressed individuals, suggesting that people with tendencies toward hopelessness, pessimism, and self-blame are more likely to interpret events in their lives in ways that lead to the development of depression (Gladstone & Kaslow, 1995; Lewinsohn et al., 1994; Robinson, Garber, & Hilsman, 1995). These sorts of cognitive sets, which may be linked to the ways in which children think they are viewed by parents and, later, by peers, develop during childhood and are thought to play a role in the onset of depression during adolescence (Cole & Jordan, 1995; Cole, Martin, & Powers, 1997; Garber, Weiss, & Shanley, 1993; Nolen-Hoeksema, Girgus, & Seligman, 1992). Because there is evidence that negative cognitions result from, as well as contribute to, depression, it is difficult to say with precision what the cause-and-effect relationship is, however (Cole, Martin, Peeke, Seroczynski, & Hoffman, 1998).

Researchers who have been more concerned with the stress component of the diathesis-stress model—that is, with the environmental influences on depression—have focused on three broad sets of stressors (Aseltine, Gore, & Colten, 1994; Lewinsohn, Gotlib, & Seeley, 1997; Lewinsohn et al., 1994; Petersen et al., 1993). First, depression is more common among adolescents from families characterized by high conflict and low cohesion, and it is higher among adolescents from divorced homes. Second, depression is more prevalent among adolescents who are unpopular or who have poor peer relations. Third, depressed adolescents report more chronic and acute stress than do nondepressed adolescents. These psychosocial factors may both contribute to, and exacerbate, the development of negative cognitive sets (Garber, Robinson, & Valentiner, 1997). By and large, these factors have been found to be linked to depression among adolescents from very different cultures, as a recent comparison of adolescents from the United States and China confirmed (Greenberger, Chen, Tally, & Dong, 2000). There is also evidence that academic difficulties are correlated with depression, especially among adolescents from Asian cultures, where relatively more stress may be placed on achievement (Chan, 1997; Greenberger et al., 2000).

The prevalence of depression rises during adolescence. Can diathesis-stress models of depression account for this increase? For the most part, they can. Biological theorists can point to the hormonal changes of puberty, which are likely to have implications for neuroendocrine activity. Depression and negative affect among both boys and girls are correlated with various hormones known to change at puberty (Angold, Costello, Erkanli, & Worthman, 1999; Nottelman, Inoff-Germain, Susman, & Chrousos, 1990; Paikoff, Brooks-Gunn, & Warren, 1991; Susman et al., 1987). Many studies show that the increase in depression in adolescence is more closely linked to puberty than to age (Hayward, Gotlib, Schraedley, & Litt, 1999), although it is difficult to pinpoint puberty as the cause of the problem, since many other changes typically occur around the same time (e.g., the transition out of elementary school). Cognitive theorists can point to the onset of hypothetical thinking at adolescence, which may result in new (and perhaps potentially more depressing) ways of viewing the world (Keating, 1990). And theorists who emphasize environmental factors draw attention to the new environmental demands of adolescence, such as changing schools, beginning to date, and coping with transformations in family relationships—all of which may lead to heightened stress (Algood-Merten et al., 1990). Thus, there are many good reasons to expect that the prevalence of depression would increase as individuals pass from childhood into adolescence. It is also important to note that individuals who develop internalizing disorders, such as depression and anxiety, in adolescence are at elevated risk to suffer from these problems as adults (Pine, Cohen, Gurley, Brook, & Ma, 1998).

The Prevention and Treatment of Internalizing Problems in Adolescence

The treatment of depression during adolescence is very similar to its treatment at other points in the life span. Clinicians use a wide range of approaches, including biological therapies using antidepressant medication (these address the neuroendocrine problem, if one exists); psychotherapies designed to help depressed adolescents understand the roots of their depression, to increase the degree to which they experience reinforcement in their daily activities, or to change the nature of their cognitive set; and family therapy, which focuses on changing the patterns of family relationships that may be contributing to the adolescent's symptoms (Petersen et al., 1993). Generally speaking, behavioral and cognitive-behavior approaches to psychotherapy with depressed and anxious adolescents are more effective than insight-oriented therapies, and psychotherapy appears to be more effective with female adolescents than with male teenagers (Marcotte, 1997; Silverman et al., 1999; Weisz, Weiss, Han, Granger, & Morton, 1995). With regard to antidepressants, research has confirmed the effectiveness of fluoxetine (Prozac®) in the treatment of depression in adolescence (Brooks-Gunn et al., 2001).

Efforts are also made to prevent adolescent depression, since this strategy may be more effective than delivering treatment to individuals once they have become depressed. **Primary prevention** approaches emphasize teaching all adolescents social competencies and life skills that will help them cope with stress (Weissberg, Caplan, & Harwood, 1991). **Secondary prevention** approaches aim at adolescents who are believed to be at high risk for developing depression, such as teenagers with a depressed parent (who are at risk because of the genetic and environmental risks associated with this) (e.g., Beardslee et al., 1992) and adolescents who are under stress (e.g., Grych & Fincham, 1992).

RECAP

Depression is the most common internalizing disorder of adolescence, afflicting about 3 percent of the adolescent population in its most severe form but 25 percent of adolescents in more minor forms. More remarkably, surveys show that as many as 10 percent of adolescents have attempted suicide. The current consensus is that depression is the result of a set of interacting environmental conditions (especially stress and loss) and individual predispositions, or diatheses. Depression during adolescence is treated through a combination of biological, psychological, and family therapies. Although males are slightly more likely to suffer from depression during childhood, depression is much more common among females after puberty— a sex difference that persists into adulthood. Numerous explanations for the sex difference in depression have been offered, including sex differences in exposure, vulnerability, and response to stress.

Food for Thought

Are you surprised by the fact that 10 percent of all American adolescents have attempted suicide? What can be done to prevent teenage suicide?

STRESS AND COPING IN ADOLESCENCE

Nearly half of all adolescents today report difficulty in coping with stressful situations at home or at school (Gans, 1990). These stressors include major life changes (e.g., changing schools, having someone in the family suddenly become seriously ill); chronically stressful conditions (e.g., poverty, a disabling illness, constant family conflict); and day-to-day hassles (e.g., school exams, arguments with siblings and parents) (Compas, 1987).

Research indicates that stress can affect individuals in different ways (Steinberg & Avenevoli, 2000). For some teenagers, stress can lead to internalized disorders, such as anxiety, depression, headaches, and indigestion—even compromised immune system functioning (Birmaher et al., 1994). For others, the consequences of stress are externalized, in behavior and conduct problems. For others still, the impact of stress is manifested in drug and alcohol abuse. These links between stress and psychosocial problems have been documented in studies of youngsters from all ethnic groups and family backgrounds (Dornbusch, Mont-Reynaud, Ritter, Chen, & Steinberg, 1991) and among youth exposed to both relatively benign stressors (e.g., breaking up with a romantic partner) and relatively severe ones (e.g., exposure to war trauma) (Macksoud & Aber, 1996; Sack, Clarke, & Seeley, 1996).

For some adolescents, however, the very same sources and levels of stress do not seem to be associated with psychological or physical upset at all. Thus, although we tend to think of stress as having negative effects on our well-being, the connection between stress and dysfunction is not clear-cut. Some adolescents show enormous **resilience** in the face of enormous adversity (Masten et al., 1999). What makes some adolescents more vulnerable than others to the effects of stress? Psychologists point to three sets of factors.

First, the effect of any one stressor is exacerbated if it is accompanied by other stressors. Studies show that stress tends to have a multiplicative effect: An adolescent who faces two stressors at the same time (the parents' divorce and a change of schools, for example) is more than twice as likely to experience psychological problems than someone who experiences only one of the same two stressors (Forehand, Biggar, & Kotchick, 1998; Rutter, 1978).

Second, adolescents who have certain resources—either internal (e.g., high self-esteem, healthy identity development, high intelligence, strong feelings of competence) or external (e.g., social support from others)—are less likely to be adversely affected by stress than are their peers (Compas, Hinden, & Gerhardt, 1995; Hauser, 1999; Kliewer & Sandler, 1992; Luthar, 1991; Masten et al., 1999; Wills & Cleary, 1996). Adolescents with close friends and good social skills seem to be better able to handle stressors, such as parental divorce, than are teenagers who lack close friendships or have fewer interpersonal resources. Most important, teenagers who have warm, close family relationships are less likely to be distressed by a stressful experience than are teenagers without such familial support (Weist, Freedman, Paskewitz, Proescher, & Flaherty, 1995). Indeed, a recent report from the extensive National Longitudinal Study of Adolescent Health—a study of more than 90,000 American adolescents—found that the presence of a close parent-adolescent relationship is probably the single most important factor in protecting adolescents from harm (Resnick et al., 1997). The importance of social support as a buffer against the adverse effects of stress has been documented in studies of adolescents around the world, as one recent comparison of American and Russian adolescents clearly indicated (Jose, 1998).

Finally, some adolescents use more effective coping strategies than do others. Specialists who study coping strategies distinguish between strategies that involve taking steps to change the source of the stress (called **primary control strategies**) and those that involve efforts to adapt to the problem (sometimes called **secondary control strategies**) (Weisz, McCabe, & Dennig, 1994). (Researchers in the past [e.g., Lazarus & Folkman (1984)] drew a similar distinction between "problem-focused coping," which is similar to primary control, and "emotion-focused coping," which is similar to secondary control, but many current writers believe that the primary/secondary distinction makes more sense than the problem-focused/emotion-focused one [Compas, Connor, Saltzman, Thomsen, & Wadsworth, in press]). For instance, if you were feeling very worried about an upcoming exam in this course, a primary control strategy would be to form a study group with other students in order to review the material, whereas a secondary control strategy would be to go out to a movie or a party to distract yourself.

There are some situations in which secondary control strategies are quite effective. These tend to be stressful situations that are clearly uncontrollable, such as getting an injection or learning that a loved one has a terminal illness. In these instances, trying to distract and calm oneself may help alleviate some of the stress. But, in general, research shows that adolescents who use primary control strategies are less vulnerable to the detrimental health consequences of stress, especially if the source of the stress is controllable. Adolescents who use primary control strategies are better adjusted, less depressed, and less likely to have behavior problems (Compas, Malcarne, & Fondacaro, 1988; Dumont & Provost, 1999; Ebata & Moos, 1994; Herman-Stahl, Stemmler, & Petersen, 1995; Lee & Larson, 1996; Sandler, Tein, & West, 1994; Windle & Windle, 1996).

> **RECAP**
>
> *For some adolescents, exposure to chronic or severe stress can result in psychological or physical difficulties; however, for others, the very same sources and levels of stress do not seem to be associated with upset at all. In general, the effect of stress is exacerbated if it is accompanied by other stressors, if the adolescent lacks sufficient internal or external resources, or if the adolescent has poorly developed coping skills.*

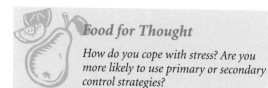

Food for Thought

How do you cope with stress? Are you more likely to use primary or secondary control strategies?

Web Researcher Use the Internet to gather crime statistics on age differences or over-time trends in internalizing problems (such as suicide), and externalizing problems (such as violent behavior) and the use of drugs or alcohol. Go to www.mhhe.com/steinberg6 for further information.

KEY TERMS

adolescence-limited antisocial behavior

attention deficit/hyperactivity disorder (ADHD)

cluster suicides

comorbid

depression

diathesis-stress model

epidemiology

externalizing disorders

gateway drugs

hostile attributional bias

internalizing disorders

life-course-persistent antisocial behavior

Monitoring the Future

negative affectivity

oxytocin

primary control strategies

primary prevention

problem behavior syndrome

property crimes

protective factors

resilience

risk-taking behavior

secondary control strategies

secondary prevention

social control theory

status offenses

substance abuse

violent crimes

Glossary

academic achievement   Achievement that is measured by standardized tests of scholastic ability or knowledge

achievement   The psychosocial domain concerning behaviors and feelings in evaluative situations

achievement attributions   The beliefs one holds about the causes of one's successes and failures

activational role   The process through which changes in hormone levels, especially at puberty, stimulate changes in the adolescent's behavior, appearance, or growth

adolescence   The second decade of human development

adolescence-limited antisocial behavior   Antisocial or delinquent behavior that appears for the first time in adolescence and that does not persist into adulthood (contrast with life-course persistent antisocial behavior)

adolescent growth spurt   The dramatic increase in height and weight that occurs during puberty

adolescent health care   The field of study and health care devoted to understanding the health-care needs of individuals during the second decade of life

adrenarche   The maturation of the adrenal glands that takes place in preadolescence

Adult Attachment Interview   A structured interview used to assess an individual's attachment history and "internal working model" of relationships

age grading   The process of grouping individuals within social institutions on the basis of chronological age

age of majority   The designated age at which an individual is recognized as an adult member of the community

AIDS (acquired immune deficiency syndrome)   A disease, transmitted by means of bodily fluids, that devastates the immune system

analysis of variance (ANOVA)   A statistical technique for comparing two or more groups on a variable of interest

androgens   A class of sex hormones secreted by the gonads, found in both sexes, but in higher levels in males than in females following puberty

androgyny   The combination of both highly masculine and highly feminine traits

anorexia nervosa   An eating disorder found chiefly among young women and characterized by dramatic and severe self-induced weight loss

anxious-avoidant attachment   An insecure attachment between infant and caregiver, characterized by indifference on the part of the infant toward the caregiver

anxious-resistant attachment   An insecure attachment between infant and caregiver, characterized by distress at separation and anger at reunion

asynchronicity of growth   The fact that different parts of the body grow at different rates at puberty, which sometimes results in the appearance of gawkiness or awkwardness during early adolescence

attachment   The strong affectional bond that develops between infant and caregiver

attention deficit/hyperactivity disorder (ADHD)   A biologically based psychological disorder characterized by impulsivity, inattentiveness, and restlessness, often in school situations

authoritarian parents   Parents who use punitive, absolute, and forceful discipline and who place a premium on obedience and conformity

authoritative parents   Parents who use warmth, firm control, and rational, issue-oriented discipline, in which emphasis is placed on the development of self-direction

automatization   The mechanism through which various cognitive processes become automatic, or second nature

autonomy   The psychosocial domain concerning the development and expression of independence

baby boom   The period following World War II, during which the number of infants born was extremely large

Bar (Bas) Mitzvah   In Judaism, the religious ceremony marking the young person's transition to adulthood

barometric self-esteem   The aspect of self-esteem that fluctuates across situations

basal metabolism rate   The minimal amount of energy used by the body during a resting state

baseline self-esteem   The aspect of self-esteem that is relatively stable across situations and over time

behavioral autonomy   The capacity to make independent decisions and follow through with them

behavioral decision theory   An approach to understanding adolescent risk taking, in which behaviors are seen as the outcome of systematic decision-making processes

behavioral genetics   The scientific study of genetic influences on behavior

biculturalism   The successful maintenance of an identification with more than one cultural background

Big Five   In the Five-Factor Model of personality, the five critical dimensions: extraversion, agreeableness, conscientiousness, neuroticism, and openness to experience

454

brother-sister avoidance   The avoidance of any contact or interaction between brothers and sisters from the onset of puberty until one or both persons are married, part of the process of social redefinition at adolescence in many societies

bulimia   An eating disorder found chiefly among young women, characterized primarily by a pattern of binge eating and self-induced vomiting

care orientation   In Gilligan's theory of moral development, a moral orientation that emphasizes responding to others' needs

charter schools   Public schools that have been given the autonomy to establish their own curricula and teaching practices

child protectionists   Individuals who argued, early in the twentieth century, that adolescents need to be kept out of the labor force in order to protect them from the hazards of the workplace

chlamydia   A sexually transmitted infection caused by a bacterium

cliques   Small, tightly knit groups of between 2 and 12 friends, generally of the same sex and age

cluster suicides   Outbreaks of suicides, in which an unusually high number of suicides occur within a limited time period or small geographic area

code switching   Switching between two different cultural groups' norms for behavior, depending on the situation; a strategy often used by ethnic minority adolescents

cofigurative cultures   Cultures in which the socialization of young people is accomplished not only through contact with elders but also through contact between people of the same age

cognitive-developmental view   A perspective on development, based on the work of Piaget, that takes a qualitative, stage-theory approach

cohort   A group of individuals born during the same general historical era

collective efficacy   A community's social capital, derived from its members' common values and goals

comorbid   Co-occurring, as when two or more problems (e.g., drug abuse and depression) are observed in the same individual at the same point in time

competence-performance distinction   The distinction between what individuals are capable of and what they actually do; important in the study of cognitive development

comprehensive high school   An educational institution that evolved during the first half of the twentieth century, offering a varied curriculum and designed to meet the needs of a diverse population of adolescents

concrete operations   The third stage of cognitive development, according to Piaget, spanning the period roughly between age 6 and early adolescence

continuous transitions   Passages into adulthood in which adult roles and statuses are entered into gradually

conventional moral reasoning   According to Kohlberg, the second level of moral development, which develops during late childhood and early adolescence and is characterized by reasoning that is based on the rules and conventions of society

correlation coefficient   A measure of the extent to which two factors are related to one another

cortex   The part of the brain responsible for complex thought and movement

critical thinking   Thinking that is in-depth, analytical, and discriminating

cross-sectional study   A study that compares two or more groups of individuals at one point in time

crowds   Large, loosely organized groups of young people, composed of several cliques and typically organized around a shared activity

crystallization   According to Super, the stage during which individuals, typically between the ages of 14 and 18, first begin to formulate their ideas about appropriate occupations

cultural capital   The resources provided within a family through the exposure of the adolescent to art, music, literature, and other elements of "high culture"

culture-fair tests   Standardized tests that do not, by virtue of their construction, favor one cultural or ethnic group over another

curvilinear pattern   In statistical analyses, a pattern of relation between two variables that resembles a U-shaped or an inverted U-shaped curve

deductive reasoning   A type of logical reasoning, in which one draws logically necessary conclusions from a general set of premises, or givens

de-idealization   The process of no longer idealizing one's parents

delayed phase preference   A pattern of sleep characterized by later sleep and wake times, which often emerges during puberty

demographers   Social scientists who study large-scale changes in the makeup of the population

dependent variable   In a research study, the outcome of interest

depression   A psychological disturbance, characterized by low self-esteem, decreased motivation, sadness, and difficulty finding pleasure in formerly enjoyable activities

detachment   In psychoanalytic theory, the process through which adolescents sever emotional attachments to their parents or other authority figures

diathesis-stress model   A model of psychological disorder, most commonly applied to the study of depression, in which a disorder is seen as the result of an interaction between an existing predisposition (the diathesis) and some sort of environmental stressor

discontinuous transitions   Passages into adulthood in which adult roles and statuses are entered into abruptly

disordered eating   A mild, moderate, or severe disturbance in eating habits and attitudes

divided attention   The process of paying attention to two or more stimuli at the same time

early adolescence   The period spanning roughly ages 11 through 14, corresponding approximately to the junior or middle high school years

ecology of human development   A perspective on development that emphasizes the broad context in which development occurs

education vouchers   Monetary credits, issued by the government, that families can use to purchase schooling

educational attainment   The number of years of schooling completed by an individual

effect size   In research, the actual magnitude (rather than statistical significance) of a finding

endocrine system   The system of the body that produces, circulates, and regulates hormones

epidemiology   The branch of medicine devoted to the study of how health problems are spread and distributed within communities

estrogens   A class of sex hormones secreted by the gonads, found in both sexes but in higher levels in females than in males following puberty

ethnography   A type of research in which individuals are observed in their natural settings

exo-system   In the ecological perspective on human development, the layer of the environment that does not directly contain the developing person but affects the settings in which the person lives

Experience Sampling Method (ESM)   A method for collecting data about adolescents' emotional states, in which individuals are paged and asked to report on their mood and activity

externalizing disorders   Psychosocial problems that are manifested in a turning of the symptoms outward, as in aggression and delinquency

extrinsic motivation   Motivation based on the rewards one will receive for successful performance

extrusion   The practice of separating children from their parents and requiring them to sleep in other households, as part of the process of social redefinition at adolescence in many societies

false-self behavior   Behavior that intentionally presents a false impression to others

fear of failure   Fear of the consequences of failing in achievement situations

feedback loop   A cycle through which two or more bodily functions respond to and regulate each other, such as that formed by the hypothalamus, the pituitary gland, and the gonads

Five-Factor Model   The theory that holds that there are five basic dimensions to personality (see also *Big Five*)

Forgotten Half   The approximately one-half of all American adolescents who do not enroll in college; they have been neglected by researchers and policymakers

formal operations   The fourth stage of cognitive development, according to Piaget, spanning the period from early adolescence through adulthood

functional magnetic resonance imaging (fMRI)   A technique used to produce images of the brain, often while the subject is performing a mental task

gangs   Adolescent peer groups who are organized, in part, around antisocial activity

gateway drugs   Drugs that, when used over time, lead to the use of other, more dangerous substances

gender identity   The aspects of one's sense of self that concern one's masculinity or femininity

gender intensification hypothesis   The idea that pressures to behave in sex-appropriate ways intensify during adolescence

generation gap   The popular phrase for the alleged conflict between young people and adults over values and attitudes

gifted students   Students who are unusually talented in an aspect of intellectual performance

glands   Organs that stimulate particular parts of the body to respond in specific ways to particular hormones

gonads   The glands that secrete sex hormones: in males, the testes; in females, the ovaries

gonorrhea   A sexually transmitted infection caused by a bacterium

health-compromising behaviors   Behaviors that place individuals at risk for health problems

health-enhancing behaviors   Behaviors that lessen individuals' risk for health problems or that increase well-being

herpes   A sexually transmitted infection caused by a virus

higher-order thinking   Thinking that involves analyzing, evaluating, and interpreting information, rather than simply memorizing it

HIV (human immunodeficiency virus)   The virus associated with AIDS

homophobia   The unwarranted fear of homosexuals or homosexuality

hormones   Highly specialized substances secreted by one or more endocrine glands

hostile attributional bias   The tendency to interpret ambiguous interactions with others as deliberately hostile

HPG axis   The neuropsychological pathway that involves the hypothalamus, pituitary gland, and gonads

human ecology   A field of inquiry that focuses on the study of development and behavior in context

human papilloma virus   One of several sexually transmitted infections common among adolescents

hypothalamus   The part of the lower brain stem that controls the functioning of the pituitary gland

iatrogenic effects   Unintended adverse consequences of a treatment or an intervention

identity   The psychosocial domain concerning feelings and thoughts about the self

identity diffusion (identity confusion)   The incoherent, disjointed, incomplete sense of self characteristic of not having successfully resolved the crisis of identity

identity foreclosure   The premature establishment of a sense of identity, before sufficient role experimentation has occurred

identity versus identity diffusion   According to Erikson, the normative crisis characteristic of the fifth stage of psychosocial development, predominant during adolescence

imaginary audience   The belief, often brought on by the heightened self-consciousness of early adolescence, that everyone is watching and evaluating one's behavior

implicit personality theory   The intuitive understanding of human behavior and motivation that emerges during early adolescence

independent variable   In a research study, the variable presumed to influence the outcome of interest

indifferent parents   Parents whose behavior is characterized by low levels of both responsiveness and demandingness

individuation   The progressive sharpening of one's sense of being an autonomous, independent person

inductive reasoning   Reasoning that involves drawing an inference from evidence

indulgent parents   Parents who are characterized by high responsiveness but low demandingness

information-processing perspective   The perspective on cognition that derives from the study of artificial intelligence and attempts to explain cognitive development in terms of the growth of specific components of the thinking process (for example, memory)

initiation ceremony   The formal induction of a young person into adulthood

internal working model   The implicit model of interpersonal relationships that an individual uses through life, believed to be shaped by early attachment experiences

internalizing disorders   Psychosocial problems that are manifested in a turning of the symptoms inward, as in depression and anxiety

intimacy   The psychosocial domain concerning the formation, maintenance, and termination of close relationships

intimacy versus isolation   According to Erikson, the normative crisis characteristic of the sixth psychosocial stage of development, predominant during young adulthood

intrinsic motivation   Motivation based on the pleasure one will experience from mastering a task

inventionists   Theorists who argue that the period of adolescence is mainly a social invention

junior high school   An educational institution, designed during the early era of public secondary education, in which young adolescents are schooled separately from older adolescents

justice orientation   In Gilligan's theory of moral development, a moral orientation that emphasizes fairness and objectivity

juvenile justice system   A separate system of courts and related institutions developed to handle juvenile crime and delinquency

late adolescence   The period spanning roughly ages 18 through 21, corresponding approximately to the college years

learned helplessness   The acquired belief that one is not able to influence events through one's own efforts or actions

learning disability   A difficulty with academic tasks that cannot be traced to an emotional problem or a sensory dysfunction

leptin   The protein produced by fat cells that may play a role in the onset of puberty

life-course persistent antisocial behavior   Antisocial or delinquent behavior that appears prior to adolescence and persists into adulthood (contrast with adolescence-limited antisocial behavior)

limbic system   An area of the brain that plays an important role in emotional experience

longitudinal study   A study following the same group of individuals over time

long-term memory   The ability to recall something from a long time ago

macro-system   In the ecological perspective on human development, the outermost layer of the environment, containing forces such as history and culture

mainstreaming   The integration of adolescents who have educational handicaps into regular classrooms

marginal man   Lewin's term referring to the transitional nature of adolescence—poised on the margin of adulthood

median   In statistics, a measure of a group's average based on the point above and below which half the members of the group have scored

mediating variable   In a research study, a factor presumed to form an intervening link between two variables that are causally connected

menarche   The time of first menstruation, one of the important changes to occur among females during puberty

meso-system   In the ecological perspective on human development, the layer of the environment formed by the intersection of two or more immediate settings, as in the home-school linkage

meta-analysis   A systematic approach to the analysis of a large scientific literature, in which results from different independent studies are pooled

metacognition   The process of thinking about thinking itself

micro-systems   In the ecological perspective on human development, the immediate settings in which adolescents develop, such as the family and the peer group

middle adolescence   The period spanning roughly ages 15 through 18, corresponding approximately to the high school years

middle school   An educational institution housing seventh- and eighth-grade students along with adolescents who are one or two years younger

midlife crisis   The psychological crisis over identity believed to occur between the ages of 35 and 45, the age range of most adolescents' parents

Monitoring the Future   An annual survey of U.S. teenagers, which provides much information on drug use

mutual role taking   In Selman's theory, the stage of social perspective taking during which the young adolescent can be an objective third party and can see how the thoughts and actions of one person can influence those of another

myelination   The process through which brain circuits are insulated with myelin, which improves the efficiency of information processing

National Assessment of Educational Progress (NAEP)   A periodic standardized assessment of achievement sponsored by the U.S. government

need for achievement   The need that influences the extent to which an individual strives for success in evaluative situations

need for integration into adult society   In Sullivan's theory, the interpersonal need that is dominant during late adolescence

need for intimacy   According to Sullivan, the chief interpersonal need of preadolescence

need for sexual contact, need for intimacy with a peer of the opposite sex   According to Sullivan, the chief interpersonal needs of early adolescence

negative affectivity   The presumed underlying cause of internalizing disorders; characterized by high levels of subjective distress

negative identity   An identity that is obviously undesirable in the eyes of significant others and the broader community

nonshared environmental influences   The nongenetic influences in individuals' lives that make them different from people they live with

occupational attainment   A measure of achievement based on the status or prestige of the job an individual holds

organizational role   The process through which early exposure to hormones, especially prenatally, organizes the brain or other organs in anticipation of later changes in behavior or patterns of growth

oxytocin   A hormone believed to influence the formation of close relationships

parental demandingness   According to Baumrind, one of the two important dimensions of parenting; demandingness is the degree to which the parent expects and demands mature, responsible behavior from the child

parental responsiveness   According to Baumrind, one of the two important dimensions of parenting; responsiveness is the degree to which the parent responds to the child's needs in an accepting, supportive manner

participant observation   The research technique in which the researcher "infiltrates" a group of individuals in order to study their behavior and relationships

particularistic norms   Guidelines for behavior that vary from one individual to another; more commonly found in less industrialized societies

peak height velocity   The point at which the adolescent is growing most rapidly

peer groups   Groups of individuals of approximately the same age

peer pressure   The perceived influences of one's agemates or friends to go along with their behavior

permissive societies   Societies in which sexual activity during childhood and adolescence is not greatly restrained

personal fable   An adolescent's belief that he or she is unique and therefore not subject to the rules that govern other people's behavior

pheromones   A class of chemicals, secreted by animals, that stimulate certain behaviors in other members of the species

Piagetian perspective   (See *cognitive-developmental*)

pituitary gland   One of the chief glands responsible for regulating levels of hormones in the body

positron emission tomography (PET)   A technique used to produce images of the brain, often while the subject is performing a mental task; it is more invasive than fMRI

postconventional moral reasoning In Kohlberg's theory, the stage of moral development during which society's rules and conventions are seen as relative and subjective, rather than as authoritative; also called principled moral reasoning

postfigurative cultures Cultures in which the socialization of young people is accomplished almost exclusively through contact between children and their elders

preconventional moral reasoning According to Kohlberg, the first level of moral development, which is typical of children and is characterized by reasoning that is based on the rewards and punishments associated with various courses of action

prefigurative cultures Cultures in which young people socialize their elders, rather than vice versa

prefrontal cortex The part of the brain responsible for many higher-order cognitive skills, such as decision making and planning

premature affluence Having more income than one can manage maturely, especially during adolescence

preoperational period The second stage of cognitive development, according to Piaget, spanning roughly ages 2 through 5

primary control strategies Coping strategies in which one attempts to change the stressor

primary prevention The approach to health promotion that emphasizes teaching all adolescents certain behaviors, values, and information

problem behavior syndrome A pattern of co-variation among various types of externalizing disorders believed to result from an underlying trait of unconventionality

property crimes Crimes that involve property, such as burglary, theft, or vandalism

propositional logic The abstract system of logic that forms the basis for formal operational thinking

prosocial moral reasoning Thinking about prosocial actions, such as cooperation or helping

protective factors Factors that lessen individual vulnerability to harm

psychosocial Referring to aspects of development that are both psychological and social, such as developing a sense of identity or sexuality

psychosocial moratorium A period of time during which individuals are free from excessive obligations and responsibilities and can therefore experiment with different roles and personalities

puberty The biological changes of adolescence

Q-Sort The research procedure in which raters make their evaluations by determining how characteristic each of several descriptors is of the person or thing being evaluated

quinceañera The elaborate "coming-out" celebration for adolescent girls that is practiced in many Latino communities

racial socialization The process through which individuals acquire knowledge, attitudes, and beliefs about their race

reference groups Groups against which an individual compares himself or herself

relational aggression Acts intended to harm another through the manipulation of his or her relationships with others, as in malicious gossip

resilience The ability of the individual to continue to function competently in the face of adversity or stress

restrictive societies Societies in which adolescents are pressured to refrain from sexual activity until they have married or undergone a formal rite of passage into adulthood

risk factor A factor that increases vulnerability to harm

risk-taking behavior Behavior that is pursued simply because it is risky; risk taking is thought to be linked to adolescent problem behavior

rite of passage A ceremony or ritual marking an individual's transition from one social status to another, especially marking the young person's transition into adulthood

scaffolding Structuring a learning situation so that it is just within the reach of the student

scarification The intentional creation of scars on a part or parts of the body, often done as part of an initiation ceremony

school climate The overall atmosphere that pervades a school or classroom

school performance A measure of achievement based on an individual's grades in school

school-based health centers A relatively new approach to the delivery of health-care services to adolescents, which places health-care providers in offices located in or adjacent to schools

school-to-work transition The link between educational institutions and the workplace

secondary control strategies Coping strategies that involve attempts by the individual to adapt to the stressor

secondary education The system of middle schools, junior high schools, and high schools

secondary prevention The approach to health promotion that is specifically aimed at adolescents who are believed to be at high risk for a particular disease or disturbance

secondary sex characteristics The manifestations of sexual maturation at puberty, including the development of breasts, the growth of facial and body hair, and changes in the voice

secular trend The tendency, over the past two centuries, for individuals to be larger in stature and to reach puberty earlier, primarily because of improvements in health and nutrition

secure attachment A healthy attachment between infant and caregiver, characterized by trust

selective attention The process through which individuals focus on one stimulus while tuning out another

self-conceptions   The collection of traits and attributes that individuals use to describe or characterize themselves

self-consciousness   The degree to which an individual is preoccupied with his or her self-image

Self-Directed Search   The personality inventory developed by Holland and used to help individuals better understand their vocational interests

self-efficacy   The sense or belief that one's actions have an effect on the environment

self-esteem   The degree to which individuals feel positively or negatively about themselves

self-fulfilling prophecy   The idea that individuals' behavior is influenced by what others expect of them

self-image stability   The degree to which an individual feels that his or her self-image changes from day to day

semirestrictive societies   Societies in which pressures against adolescent sexual activity exist but are not vigilantly enforced

sensation seeking   Seeking the enjoyment of novel and intense experiences

sense of identity   The extent to which individuals feel secure about who they are and who they are becoming

sensorimotor period   The first stage of cognitive development, according to Piaget, spanning the period roughly between birth and age 2

serial monogamy   Having a series of sexual relationships over time in which one is monogamous within each relationship

service learning   Structured educational experiences that involve volunteering in the community

set point   A physiological level or setting (of a specific hormone, for example) that the body attempts to maintain through a self-regulating system

sex cleavage   The separation of girls and boys into different cliques, common during late childhood and early adolescence

sex-role behavior   Behavior that is consistent with prevailing expectations for how individuals of a given sex are to behave

sexual orientation   An individual's orientation toward same- or opposite-sex sexual partners

sexual socialization   The process through which adolescents are exposed to and educated about sexuality

sexuality   The psychosocial domain concerning the development and expression of sexual feelings

sexually transmitted infections (STIs)   Infections—including gonorrhea, herpes, chlamydia, and AIDS—that are passed on through sexual contact

sexual-minority youth   Gay, lesbian, and bisexual youth

shared environmental influences   Nongenetic influences that make individuals living in the same family similar to each other

significant others   The people most important in an individual's life

social capital   The interpersonal resources available to an adolescent or a family

social class   The social position of an individual or a family in society as determined by wealth, power, reputation, or achievement

social cognition   The aspect of cognition that concerns thinking about other people, about interpersonal relationships, and about social institutions

social control theory   The theory of delinquency that links deviance with the absence of bonds to society's main institutions

social perspective taking   The ability to view events from the perspective of others

social redefinition   The process through which an individual's position or status is redefined by society

social support   The extent to which one receives emotional or instrumental assistance from one's social network

sociosexual behaviors   The aspects of sexual behavior that are merged with social relationships

specification   According to Super, the stage during which individuals, typically between the ages of 18 and 21, first begin to consider narrowly defined occupational pursuits

statistical interaction   In research, when the observed effect of an independent variable (e.g., intelligence) on an outcome (e.g., grades) varies as a function of an additional independent variable (e.g., age)

status offense   A violation of the law that pertains to minors but not to adults

stressful life events   Normative and nonnormative events presumed to increase individuals' susceptibility to psychological distress

student engagement   The extent to which students are psychologically committed to learning and mastering material in school

substance abuse   The misuse of alcohol or other drugs

synaptic pruning   The process through which certain unnecessary brain circuits are eliminated, improving the efficiency of information processing

Tanner stages   A widely used system to describe the five stages of pubertal development

teenager   A term popularized about 50 years ago to refer to young people; it connoted a more frivolous and lighthearted image than the term *adolescent*

temperament   The individual's predisposed style of interacting with the environment, thought to be largely biologically determined and stable over time

testosterone   One of the sex hormones secreted by the gonads, found in both sexes but in higher levels in males than in females

tracking   The grouping of students, according to ability, into levels of classes within the same school grade

underachievers   Individuals whose actual school performance is lower than what would be expected on the basis of objective measures of their aptitude or intelligence

universalistic norms   Guidelines for behavior that apply to all members of a community; more common in industrialized societies

value autonomy   The establishment of an independent set of values and beliefs

violent crimes   Crimes that involve bodily harm, such as assault, homicide, or rape

working memory   The aspect of memory in which information is held for short periods of time while a problem is being solved

youth   Today, a term used to refer to individuals between the ages of 18 and 22; it once referred to individuals between the ages of 12 and 24

youth apprenticeship   A structured, work-based learning experience that places an adolescent under the supervision of a skilled adult

youth culture   The popular culture thought to appeal to and shape the attitudes and behaviors of adolescents and youth

zone of proximal development   In Vygotsky's theory, the level of challenge that is still within the individual's reach but that forces an individual to develop more advanced skills

References

Ablard, K., & Mills, C. (1996). Implicit theories of intelligence and self-perceptions of academically talented adolescents and children. *Journal of Youth and Adolescence, 25,* 137–148.

Abma, J., Chandra, A., Mosher, W., Peterson, L., & Piccinino, L. (1997). Fertility, family planning, and women's health: New data from the 1995 National Survey of Family Growth. National Center for Health Statistics. *Vital Health Statistics, 23*(19).

Abma, J., Driscoll, A., & Moore, K. (1998). Young women's degree of control over first intercourse: An exploratory analysis. *Family Planning Perspectives, 30,* 12–18.

Achenbach, T., & Edelbrock, C. (1987). *The Manual for the Youth Self-Report and Profile.* Burlington: University of Vermont.

Ackerman, G. (1993). A congressional view of youth suicide. *American Psychologist, 48,* 183–184.

Adams, G., & Fitch, S. (1982). Ego stage and identity status development: A cross-sequential analysis. *Journal of Personality and Social Psychology, 43,* 574–583.

Adams, G., Gullotta, T., & Montemayor, R. (Eds.). (1992). *Adolescent identity formation.* Newbury Park, CA: Sage.

Adan, A., & Felner, R. (1995). Ecological congruence and adaptation of minority youth during the transition to college. *Journal of Community Psychology, 23,* 256–269.

Adegoke, A. (1993). The experience of spermarche (the age of onset of sperm emission) among selected adolescent boys in Nigeria. *Journal of Youth and Adolescence, 22,* 201–209.

Adelson, J. (1972). The political imagination of the young adolescent. In J. Kagan & R. Coles (Eds.), *Twelve to sixteen: Early adolescence.* New York: Norton.

Adelson, J. (1979, January). The generalization gap. *Psychology Today,* pp. 33–37.

Adler, N. E., Boyce, T., Chesney, M., Cohen, S., Folkman, S., Kahn, R., & Syme, S. L. (1994). Socioeconomic status and health: The challenge of the gradient. *American Psychologist, 49,* 15–24.

Agnew, R., & Brezina, T. (1997). Relational problems with peers, gender, and delinquency. *Youth and Society, 29,* 84–111.

Agras, W., Schneider, J., Arnow, B., Raeburn, S., & Telch, C. (1989). Cognitive-behavioral and response-prevention treatments for bulimia nervosa. *Journal of Consulting and Clinical Psychology, 57,* 215–221.

Ahn, N. (1994). Teenage childbearing and high school completion: Accounting for individual heterogeneity. *Family Planning Perspectives, 26,* 17–21.

Ainsworth, M., Blehar, M., Waters, E., & Wall, S. (1978). *Patterns of attachment.* Hillsdale, NJ: Erlbaum.

Ainsworth-Darnell, J., & Downey, D. (1998). Assessing the oppositional culture explanation for racial/ethnic differences in school performance. *American Sociological Review, 63,* 536–553.

Aitken, D., & Chaplin, J. (1990). Sex miseducation. *Family Therapy Networker, 14,* 24–25.

Alan Guttmacher Institute. (1994). *Sex and America's teenagers.* New York: Author.

Alasker, F., & Flammer, A. (1999). Time use by adolescents in an international perspective. II: The case of necessary activities. In F. Alasker & A. Flammer (Eds.), *The adolescent experience: European and American adolescents in the 1990s* (pp. 61–83). Hillsdale, NJ: Erlbaum.

Alasker, F., & Olweus, D. (1992). Stability of global self-evaluations in early adolescence: A cohort longitudinal study. *Journal of Research on Adolescence, 1,* 123–145.

Alexander, C., Somerfield, M., Ensminger, M., Johnson, K., & Kim, Y. (1993). Consistency of adolescents' self-report of sexual behavior in a longitudinal study. *Journal of Youth and Adolescence, 22,* 455–471.

Alexander, K., & Cook, M. (1982). Curricula and coursework: A surprise ending to a familiar story. *American Sociological Review, 47,* 626–640.

Alexander, K., & Eckland, B. (1975). School experience and status attainment. In S. Dragastin & G. Elder, Jr. (Eds.), *Adolescence in the life cycle.* Washington, DC: Hemisphere.

Alexander, K., Natriello, G., & Pallas, A. (1985). For whom the cognitive bell tolls: The impact of dropping out on cognitive performance. *American Sociological Review, 50,* 409–420.

Alfieri, T., Ruble, D., & Higgins, E. (1996). Gender stereotypes during adolescence: Developmental changes and the transition to junior high school. *Developmental Psychology, 32,* 1129–1137.

Allen, J., & Land, D. (1999). Attachment in adolescence. In J. Cassidy & P. Shaver (Eds.), *Handbook of attachment theory and research.* New York: Guilford.

Allen, J., & McElhaney, K. (2000, March). *Autonomy in discussions vs. autonomy in decision-making as predictors of developing close friendship competence.* Paper presented at the biennial meetings of the Society for Research on Adolescence, Chicago.

Allen, J., Hauser, S., Bell, K., & O'Connor, T. (1994). Longitudinal assessment of autonomy and relatedness in adolescent-family interactions as predictors of adolescent ego development and self-esteem. *Child Development, 65,* 179–194.

Allen, J., Hauser, S., Eickholt, C., Bell, K., & O'Conner, T. (1994). Autonomy and relatedness in family interactions as predictors of expressions of negative adolescent affect. *Journal of Research on Adolescence, 4,* 535–552.

Allen, J., Hauser, S., O'Connor, T., Bell, K., & Eickholt, C. (1996). The connection of observed hostile family conflict to adolescents' developing autonomy and relatedness with parents. *Development and Psychopathology, 8,* 425–442.

Allen, J., Leadbeater, B., & Aber, J. (1994). The development of problem behavior syndromes in at-risk adolescents. *Development and Psychopathology, 6,* 323–342.

Allen, J., Philliber, S., Herrling, S., & Kuperminc, G. (1997). Preventing teen pregnancy and academic failure: Experimental evaluation of a developmentally based approach. *Child Development, 64,* 729–742.

Allen, R., & Mirabell, J. (1990, May). *Shorter subjective sleep of high school students from early compared to late starting schools.* Paper presented at the second meeting of the Society for Research on Biological Rhythms, Jacksonville, FL.

Allgood-Merten, B., Lewinsohn, P., & Hops, H. (1990). Sex differences and adolescent depression. *Journal of Abnormal Psychology, 99,* 55–63.

Allgood-Merten, B., & Stockard, J. (1991). Sex role identity and self-esteem: A comparison of children and adolescents. *Sex Roles, 25,* 129–140.

Allison, K., Crawford, I., Leone, P., Trickett, E., Perez-Febles, A., Burton, L., & Le Blanc, R. (1999). Adolescent substance use: Preliminary examinations of school and neighborhood context. *American Journal of Community Psychology, 27,* 111–141.

Allison, P., & Furstenberg, F., Jr. (1989). How marital dissolution affects children: Variations by age and sex. *Developmental Psychology, 25,* 540–549.

Almeida, D., & Wethington, E. (1996, March). *Daily spillover between marital and parent-child tension.* Paper presented at the biennial meetings of the Society for Research on Adolescence, Boston.

Alsaker, F. (1995). Is puberty a critical period for socialization? *Journal of Adolescence, 18,* 427–444.

Amato, P., & Booth, A. (1996). A prospective study of divorce and parent-child relationships. *Journal of Marriage and the Family, 58,* 356–365.

Amato, P., & Keith, B. (1991a). Parental divorce and the well-being of children: A meta-analysis. *Psychological Bulletin, 110,* 26–46.

Amato, P., & Keith, B. (1991b). Separation from a parent during childhood and adult socioeconomic attainment. *Social Forces, 70,* 187–206.

Amato, P., & Rezac, S. (1994). Contact with nonresidential parents, interparental conflict, and children's behavior. *Journal of Family Issues, 15,* 191–207.

American Federation of Teachers. (1997). *Reaching the next step.* Washington, DC: Author.

American Psychiatric Association. (1994). *Diagnostic and Statistical Manual of the American Psychiatric Association (DSM-IV).* Washington, DC: Author.

Anastasi, A. (1988). *Psychological testing* (6th ed.). New York: Macmillan.

Anderman, E., & Midgley, C. (1996, March). *Changes in achievement goal orientations after the transition to middle school.* Paper presented at the biennial meetings of the Society for Research on Adolescence, Boston.

Anderson, E. (1992, March). *Consistency of parenting in stepfather families.* Paper presented at the biennial meetings of the Society for Research on Adolescence, Washington.

Anderson, E., Hetherington, E. M., Reiss, D., & Howe, G. (1994). Parents' nonshared treatment of siblings and the development of social competence during adolescence. *Journal of Family Psychology, 8,* 303–320.

Anderson, E., & Starcher, L. (1992, March). *Transformations in sibling relationships during adolescence.* Paper presented at the biennial meetings of the Society for Research on Adolescence, Washington.

Andersson, B. (1994, February). *School as a setting for development—A Swedish example.* Paper presented at the biennial meetings of the Society for Research on Adolescence, San Diego.

Andersson, T., & Magnusson, D. (1990). Biological maturation in adolescence and the development of drinking habits and alcohol abuse among young males: A prospective longitudinal study. *Journal of Youth and Adolescence, 19,* 33–42.

Andrews, J., Alpert, A., Hops, H., & Davis, B. (1996, March). *The relation of competence in middle adolescence to depression and antisocial behavior: A multi-method assessment.* Paper presented at the biennial meetings of the Society for Research on Adolescence, Boston.

Andrews, J., Hops, H., Davis, B., & Duncan, S. (1995, March). *The structure of competence among middle adolescents: A multi-method assessment.* Paper presented at the biennial meetings of the Society for Research in Child Development, Indianapolis, IN.

Aneshensel, C., Becerra, R., Fielder, E., & Schuler, R. (1990). Onset of fertility-related events during adolescence: A prospective comparison of Mexican American and non-Hispanic white females. *American Journal of Public Health, 80,* 959–963.

Angold, A., Costello, E. J., Erkanli, A., & Worthman, C. M. (1999). Pubertal changes in hormone levels and depression in girls. *Psychological Medicine, 29,* 1043–1053.

Angold, A., Costello, E. J., & Worthman, C. (1998). Puberty and depression: The roles of age, pubertal status, and pubertal timing. *Psychological Medicine, 28,* 51–61.

Angold, A., Worthman, C., Costello, E., Stangl, D., Messer, S., & Tweed, D. (1996, March). *Puberty and depression.* Paper presented at the biennial meetings of the Society for Research on Adolescence, Boston.

Apfel, N., & Seitz, V. (1997). The firstborn sons of African American teen mothers: Perspectives on risk and resilience. In S. Luthar, J. Burack, D. Cicchetti, & J. Weisz (Eds.), *Developmental psychopathology: Perspectives on risk and disorder* (pp. 484–506). New York: Cambridge University Press.

Apter, T. (1990). *Altered loves: Mothers and daughters during adolescence.* New York: St. Martin's.

Aquilino, W. (1991). Family structure and home-leaving: A further specification of the relationship. *Journal of Marriage and the Family, 53,* 999–1010.

Arbeton, A., Eccles, J., & Harold, R. (1994, February). *Parents' perceptions of their children's competence: The role of parent attributions.* Paper presented at the biennial meetings of the Society for Research on Adolescence, San Diego.

Archer, S. (1989). Gender differences in identiy development: Issues of process, domain, and timing. *Journal of Adolescence, 12,* 117–138.

Archibald, A., Graber, J., & Brooks-Gunn, J. (1999). Associations among parent-adolescent relationships, pubertal growth, dieting, and body image in young adolescent girls: A short-term longitudinal study. *Journal of Research on Adolescence, 9*(4), 395–415.

Armor, D. (1972). School and family effects on black and white achievement: A reexamination of the USOE data. In F. Mosteller & D. Moynihan (Eds.), *On equality of educational opportunity.* New York: Random House.

Armsden, G., & Greenberg, M. (1987). The inventory of parent and peer attachment: Individual differences and their relationship to psychological well-being in adolescence. *Journal of Youth and Adolescence, 16,* 427–453.

Arnett, J. (1994). Are college students adults? Their conceptions of the transition to adulthood. *Journal of Adult Development, 1,* 213–224.

Arnett, J. (1995). Adolescents' use of media for self-socialization. *Journal of Youth and Adolescence, 24,* 519–533.

Arnett, J. (1996). *Metalheads.* Boulder, CO: Westview Press.

Arnett, J. (1998). Learning to stand alone: The contemporary American transition to adulthood in cultural and historical context. *Human Development, 41,* 295–315.

Arnett, J. (2000). Emerging adulthood: A theory of development from the late teens through the twenties. *American Psychologist, 55,* 469–480.

Arnett, J. (in press). Adolescents in Western countries on the threshold of the 21st century. In B. Brown, R. Larson, & T. Saraswathi (Eds.), *Worlds of adolescence: Global similarities and differences in the experience of adolescence.* NY: Cambridge Univ. Press.

Arnett, J. J. (1999). Adolescent storm and stress, reconsidered. *American Psychologist, 54,* 317–326.

Arnett, J., & Balle-Jensen, L. (1993). Cultural bases of risk behavior: Danish adolescents. *Child Development, 64,* 1842–1855.

Arnett, J., Larson, R., & Offer, S. (1995). Beyond effects: Adolescents as active media users. *Journal of Youth and Adolescence, 24,* 511–518.

Arnett, J., & Taber, S. (1994). Adolescence terminable and interminable: When does adolescence end? *Journal of Youth and Adolescence, 23,* 517–537.

Aro, H., & Taipale, V. (1987). The impact of timing of puberty on psychosomatic symptoms among fourteen- to sixteen-year-old Finnish girls. *Child Development, 58,* 261–268.

Arum, R., & Hout, M. (1998). The early returns: The transition from school to work in the United States. In Y. Shavit & W. Mueller (Eds.), *From school to work: A comparative study of educational qualifications and occupational destinations* (pp. 471–510). Oxford, England: Clarendon Press.

Arunkumar, R., & Midgley, C. (1996, March). *Two different worlds: Home/school dissonance and early adolescent adjustment.* Paper presented at the biennial meetings of the Society for Research on Adolescence, Boston.

Arunkumar, R., Midgley, C., & Urdan, T. (1999). Perceiving high or low home-school dissonance: Longitudinal effects on adolescent emotional and academic well-being. *Journal of Research on Adolescence, 9,* 441–466.

Ary, D., Duncan, T., Biglan, A., Metzler, C., Noell, J., & Smolkowski, K. (1999). Development of adolescent problem behavior. *Journal of Abnormal Child Psychology, 27,* 141–150.

Asakawa, K., & Csikszentmihalyi, M. (1998). The quality of experience of Asian American adolescents in academic activities: An exploration of educational achievement. *Journal of Research on Adolescence, 8,* 241–262.

Aseltine, R., Jr., Gore, S., & Colten, M. (1994). Depression and the social developmental context of adolescence. *Journal of Personality and Social Psychology, 67,* 252–263.

Aseltine, R., Jr., Gore, S., & Colten, M. (1998). The co-occurrence of depression and substance abuse in late adolescence. *Development and Psychopathology, 10,* 549–570.

Asher, S., Parker, J., & Walker, D. (1996). Distinguishing friendship from acceptance: Implications for intervention and assessment. In W. Bukowski, A. Newcomb, & W. Hartup (Eds.), *The company they keep: Friendship in childhood and adolescence* (pp. 366–405). New York: Cambridge University Press.

Asmussen, L., & Larson, R. (1991). The quality of family time among young adolescents in single-parent and married-parent families. *Journal of Marriage and the Family, 53,* 1021–1030.

Astin, H. (1984). The meaning of work in women's lives: A sociopsychological model of career choice and work behavior. *Counseling Psychologist, 12,* 117–126.

Astone, N., & McLanahan, S. (1991). Family structure, parental practices, and high school completion. *American Sociological Review, 56,* 309–320.

Astor, R. (1994). Children's moral reasoning about family and peer violence: The role of provocation and retribution. *Child Development, 65,* 1054–1067.

Attie, I., & Brooks-Gunn, J. (1989). The development of eating problems in adolescent girls: A longitudinal study. *Developmental Psychology, 25,* 70–79.

Avenevoli, S., & Steinberg, L. (2000). The continuity of depression across the adolescent transition. In H. Reese & R. Kail (Eds.), *Advances in child development and behavior.* NY: Academic Press.

Ayalon, H. (1994). Monopolizing knowledge? The ethnic composition and curriculum of Israeli high schools. *Sociology of Education, 67,* 264–278.

Bachman, J. (1983, summer). Premature affluence: Do high school students earn too much? *Economic Outlook USA*, pp. 64–67.

Bachman, J., Bare, D., & Frankie, E. (1986). *Correlates of employment among high school seniors.* Paper available from the Institute for Social Research, University of Michigan, Ann Arbor.

Bachman, J., & O'Malley, P. (1986). Self-concepts, self-esteem, and educational experiences: The frog pond revisited (again). *Journal of Personality and Social Psychology, 50,* 35–46.

Bachman, J., & Schulenberg, J. (1993). How part-time work intensity relates to drug use, problem behavior, time use, and satisfaction among high school seniors: Are these consequences or merely correlates? *Developmental Psychology, 29,* 220–235.

Bachman, J., Johnston, L., & O'Malley, P. (1998). Explaining recent increases in students' marijuana use: Impacts of perceived risks and disapproval, 1976 through 1996. *American Journal of Public Health, 88,* 887–892.

Bachman, J., Wallace, J., Jr., O'Malley, P., Johnston, L., Kurth, C., & Neighbors, H. (1991). Racial/ethnic differences in smoking, drinking, and illicit drug use among American high school seniors, 1976–89. *American Journal of Public Health, 81,* 372–377.

Bagwell, C., Newcomb, A., & Bukowski, W. (1998). Preadolescent friendship and peer rejection as predictors of adult adjustment. *Child Development, 69,* 140–153.

Bahr, S., Maughan, S., Marcos, A., & Li, B. (1998). Family, religiosity, and the risk of adolescent drug use. *Journal of Marriage and the Family, 60,* 979–992.

Bakan, D. (1972). Adolescence in America: From idea to social fact. In J. Kagan & R. Coles (Eds.), *Twelve to sixteen: Early adolescence.* New York: Norton.

Baker, D., & Stevenson, D. (1986). Mothers' strategies for school achievement: Managing the transition to high school. *Sociology of Education, 59,* 156–167.

Baker, L., & Brown, A. (1984). Metacognitive skills and reading. In P. Pearson (Ed.), *Handbook of reading research, Part 2.* New York: Longman.

Baker, M., Milich, R., & Manolis, M. (1996). Peer interactions of dysphoric adolescents. *Journal of Abnormal Child Psychology, 24,* 241–255.

Baker, T., & Velez, W. (1996). *Access to and opportunity in postsecondary education in the United States: A review.* Sociology of Education, Special Issue on Sociology and Educational Policy, 82–101.

Bakken, L., & Romig, C. (1992, March). *The relationship of intimacy and identity development in middle adolescents.* Paper presented at the biennial meetings of the Society for Research on Adolescence, Washington.

Bandura, A., Barbaranelli, C., Caprara, G., & Pastorelli, C. (1996). Multifaceted impact of self-efficacy beliefs on academic functioning. *Child Development, 67,* 1206–1222.

Bandura, A., & Walters, R. (1959). *Adolescent aggression.* New York: Ronald Press.

Bank, L., Marlowe, J., Reid, J., Patterson, G., & Weinrott, M. (1991). A comparative evaluation of parent-training interventions for families of chronic delinquents. *Journal of Abnormal Child Psychology, 19,* 15–33.

Bank, L., Reid, J., & Greenley, K. (1994, February). *Middle childhood predictors of adolescent and early adult aggression.* Paper presented at the biennial meetings of the Society for Research on Adolescence, San Diego.

Bankston, C. III, & Caldas, S. (1996). Majority African American schools and social injustice: The influence of de facto segregation on academic achievement. *Social Forces, 75,* 535–555.

Bankston, C. L. III, & Caldas, S. (1998). Family structure, schoolmates, and racial inequalities in school achievement. *Journal of Marriage and the Family, 60,* 715–723.

Barbarin, O. (1993). Coping and resilience: Exploring the inner lives of African-American children. *Journal of Black Psychology, 19,* 478–492.

Barbarin, O., & Soler, R. (1993). Behavioral, emotional, and academic adjustment in a national probability sample of African-American children. *Journal of Black Psychology, 19,* 423–446.

Barber, B. (1994). Cultural, family, and personal contexts of parent-adolescent conflict. *Journal of Marriage and the Family, 56,* 375–386.

Barber, B., & Eccles, J. (1992). Long-term influence of divorce and single parenting on adolescent family- and work-related values, behaviors, and aspirations. *Psychological Bulletin, 111,* 108–126.

Barber, B., & Olsen, J. (1997). Socialization in context: Connection, regulation, and autonomy in the family, school, neighborhood, and with peers. *Journal of Adolescent Research, 12,* 287–315.

Bardone, A., Moffitt, T., Caspi, A., Dickson, N., & Silva, P. (1996). Adult mental health and social outcomes of adolescent girls with depression and conduct disorder. *Development and Psychopathology, 8,* 811–829.

Bardwick, J., & Douvan, E. (1981). Ambivalence: The socialization of women. In V. Gernick & B. Moran (Eds.), *Women in a sexist society: Studies in power and powerlessness.* New York: Basic Books.

Barenboim, C. (1981). The development of person perception in childhood and adolescence: From behavioral comparisons to psychological constructs to psychological comparisons. *Child Development, 52,* 129–144.

Barker, R., & Gump, P. (1964). *Big school, small school: High school size and student behavior.* Stanford, CA: Stanford University Press.

Barnes, E. (1980). The black community as the source of positive self-concept for black children: A theoretical perspective. In R. Jones (Ed.), *Black psychology* (pp. 106–130). New York: Harper & Row.

Barnes, G., & Farrell, M. (1992). Parental support and control as predictors of adolescent drinking, delinquency, and related problem behaviors. *Journal of Marriage and the Family, 54,* 763–776.

Barnes, G., Farrell, M., & Banerjee, S. (1994). Family influences on alcohol abuse and other problem behaviors among black and white adolescents in a general population sample. *Journal of Research on Adolescence, 4,* 183–201.

Barnes, G., Reifman, A., Farrell, M., & Dintcheff, B. (2000). The effects of parenting on the development of adolescent alcohol misuse: A six-wave latent growth model. *Journal of Marriage and the Family, 62,* 175–186.

Baron, J., & Sternberg, R. (1987). *Teaching thinking skills: Theory and practice.* New York: Freeman.

Barratt, M., Roach, M., Morgan, K., & Colbert, K. (1996). Adjustment to motherhood by single adolescents. *Family Relations, 45,* 209–215.

Barrera, M., Jr., Li, S., & Chassin, L. (1995). Effects of parental alcoholism and life stress on Hispanic and non-Hispanic Caucasian adolescents: A prospective study. *American Journal of Community Psychology, 23,* 479–507.

Barringer, F. (1990, August 17). After long decline, teen births are up. *The New York Times,* p. A14.

Barton, P. (1989). *Earning and learning.* Princeton, NJ: National Assessment of Educational Progress, Educational Testing Service.

Basen-Engquist, K., Edmundson, E., & Parcel, G. (1996). Structure of health risk behavior among high school students. *Journal of Consulting and Clinical Psychology, 64,* 764–775.

Baumeister, R., & Tice, D. (1986). How adolescence became the struggle for self: A historical transformation of psychological development. In J. Suls & A. Greenwald (Eds.), *Psychological perspectives on the self* (Vol. 3, pp. 183–201). Hillsdale, NJ: Erlbaum.

Baumrind, D. (1978). Parental disciplinary patterns and social competence in children. *Youth and Society, 9,* 239–276.

Baumrind, D. (1991). The influence of parenting style on adolescent competence and substance use. *Journal of Early Adolescence, 11,* 56–95.

Baumrind, D., & Moselle, K. (1985). A developmental perspective on adolescent drug abuse. *Advances in Alcohol and Substance Abuse, 4,* 41–67.

Bauserman, R., & Rind, B. (1997). Psychological correlates of male child and adolescent sexual experiences with adults: A review of the nonclinical literature. *Archives of Sexual Behavior, 26,* 105–141.

Bayley, N. (1949). Consistency and variability in the growth of intelligence from birth to eighteen years. *Journal of Genetic Psychology, 75,* 165–196.

Beardslee, W., Hoke, L., Wheelock, I., Rothberg, P., van de Velde, P., & Swatling, S. (1992). Initial findings on preventive interventions for families with parental affective disorders. *American Journal of Psychiatry, 145,* 1335–1340.

Beardslee, W., Schultz, L., & Selman, R. (1987). Level of social-cognitive development, adaptive functioning, and DSM-III diagnoses in adolescent offspring of parents with affective disorders: Implications of the development of the capacity for mutuality. *Developmental Psychology, 23,* 807–815.

Beaumont, S. (1996). Adolescent girls' perceptions of conversations with mothers and friends. *Journal of Adolescent Research, 11,* 325–346.

Beauvais, F. (1996). Trends in drug use among American Indian students and dropouts, 1975 to 1994. *American Journal of Public Health, 86,* 1594–1598.

Beckwith, L., Cohen, S., & Hamilton, C. (1999). Maternal sensitivity during infancy and subsequent life events relate to attachment representation at early adulthood. *Developmental Psychology, 35,* 693–700.

Bell, A., Weinberg, M., & Hammersmith, S. (1981). *Sexual preference: Its development in men and women.* Bloomington: Indiana University Press.

Bell, J., & Bromnick, R. (2000, March). *A grounded approach to understanding modern dilemmas of individuality.* Paper presented at the eighth biennial meeting of the Society for Research on Adolescence, Chicago.

Beller, M., & Gafni, N. (1996). The 1991 international assessment of educational progress in mathematics and sciences: The gender differences perspective. *Journal of Educational Psychology, 88,* 365–377.

Belsky, J., Steinberg, L., & Draper, P. (1991). Childhood experience, interpersonal development, and reproductive strategy: An evolutionary theory of socialization. *Child Development, 62,* 647–670.

Bem, D. (1996). Exotic becomes erotic: A developmental theory of sexual orientation. *Psychological Review, 103,* 320–335.

Bem, S. (1975). Sex-role adaptability: One consequence of psychological androgyny. *Journal of Personality and Social Psychology, 31,* 634–643.

Bence, P. (1992, March). *Patterns of the experience of mood.* Paper presented at the biennial meetings of the Society for Research on Adolescence, Washington.

Benda, B., & Corwyn, R. (1998). Race and gender differences in theories of sexual behavior among rural adolescents residing in AFDC families. *Youth and Society, 30,* 59–88.

Benedict, R. (1934). *Patterns of culture.* Boston: Houghton Mifflin.

Benedikt, R., Wertheim, E., & Love, A. (1998). Eating attitudes and weight-loss attempts in female adolescents and their mothers. *Journal of Youth and Adolescence, 27,* 43–57.

Bennett, S. (1987). *New dimensions in research on class size and academic achievement.* Madison, WI: National Center on Effective Secondary Schools.

Benson, M., Harris, P., & Rogers, C. (1992). Identity consequences of attachment to mothers and fathers among late adolescents. *Journal of Research on Adolescence, 2,* 187–204.

Benson, P., Donahue, M., & Erickson, J. (1989). Adolescence and religion: Review of the literature from 1970–1986. *Research in the Social Scientific Study of Religion, 1,* 153–181.

Berk, L. (1992). The extracurriculum. In P. Jackson (Ed.), *Handbook of research on curriculum.* New York: Macmillan.

Berliner, D., & Biddle, B. (1995). *The manufactured crisis: Myths, fraud, and attack on America's public schools.* Reading, MA: Addison-Wesley.

Berman, B., Winkleby, M., Chesterman, E., & Boyce, T. (1992). After-school child care and self-esteem in school-age children. *Pediatrics, 89,* 654–659.

Bernard, T. (1991). *The cycle of juvenile justice.* New York: Oxford University Press.

Berndt, T. (1979). Developmental changes in conformity to peers and parents. *Developmental Psychology, 15,* 608–616.

Berndt, T. (1981). Relations between social cognition, nonsocial cognition, and social behavior: The case of friendship. In J. Flavell & L. Ross (Eds.), *Social cognitive development: Frontiers and possible futures.* Cambridge, England: Cambridge University Press.

Berndt, T. (1982). The features and effects of friendship in early adolescence. *Child Development, 53,* 1447–1460.

Berndt, T. (1996). Exploring the effects of friendship quality on social development. In W. Bukowski, A. Newcomb, & W. Hartup (Eds.), *The company they keep: Friendship in childhood and adolescence* (pp. 346–365). New York: Cambridge University Press.

Berndt, T., & Keefe, K. (1995). Friends' influence on adolescents' adjustment to school. *Child Development, 66,* 1312–1329.

Berndt, T., & Mekos, D. (1995). Adolescents' perceptions of the stressful and desirable aspects of the transition to junior high. *Journal of Research on Adolescence, 5,* 123–142.

Berndt, T., & Perry, T. (1990). Distinctive features and effects of early adolescent friendships. In R. Montemayor, G. Adams, & T. Gullota (Eds.), *Advances in adolescence research* (Vol. 2, pp. 269–287). Beverly Hills, CA: Sage.

Berzonsky, M., & Adams, G. (1999). Commentary: Reevaluating the identity status paradigm: Still useful after 35 years. *Developmental Review, 19,* 557–590.

Bettis, P. (1996). Urban students, liminality, and the postindustrial context. *Sociology of Education, 69,* 105–125.

Beutel, A., & Marini, M. (1995). Gender and values. *American Sociological Review, 60,* 436–448.

Beyth-Marom, R., Austin, L., Fischoff, B., Palmgren, C., & Jacobs-Quadrel, M. (1993). Perceived consequences of risky behaviors: Adults and adolescents. *Developmental Psychology, 29,* 549–563.

Biafora, F., Jr., Taylor, D., Warheit, G., Zimmerman, R., & Vega, W. (1993). Cultural mistrust and racial awareness among ethnically diverse black adolescent boys. *Journal of Black Psychology, 19,* 266–281.

Biener, L., Aseltine, R., Cohen, B., & Anderka, M. (1998). Reactions of adult and teenaged smokers to the Massachusetts Tobacco Tax. *American Journal of Public Health, 88,* 1389–1391.

Biener, L., & Siegel, M. (2000). Tobacco marketing and adolescent smoking: More support for a casual inference. *American Journal of Public Health, 90,* 407–411.

Bierman, K., & Furman, W. (1984). The effects of social skills training and peer involvement on the social adjustment of preadolescents. *Child Development, 55,* 151–162.

Bierman, K., & Wargo, J. (1995). Predicting the longitudinal course associated with aggressive-rejected, aggressive-nonrejected, and rejected nonaggressive status. *Development and Psychopathology, 7,* 669–682.

Bigelow, B., & LaGaipa, J. (1975). Children's written descriptions of friendship. *Developmental Psychology, 11,* 857–858.

Bills, D., Helms, L., & Ozcan, M. (1995). The impact of student employment on teachers' attitudes and behaviors toward working students. *Youth and Society, 27,* 169–193.

Billy, J., Brewster, K., & Grady, W. (1994). Contextual effects on the sexual behavior of adolescent women. *Journal of Marriage and the Family, 56,* 387–404.

Billy, J., Landale, N., Grady, W., & Zimmerle, D. (1988). Effects of sexual activity on adolescent social and psychological development. *Social Psychology Quarterly, 51,* 190–212.

Bingham, C., & Crockett, L. (1996). Longitudinal adjustment patterns of boys and girls experiencing early, middle, and late sexual intercourse. *Developmental Psychology, 32,* 647–658.

Birmaher, B., Rabin, B., Garcia, M., Jain, U., Whiteside, T., Williamson, D., Al-Shabbout, M., Nelson, B., Dahl, R., & Ryan, N. (1994). Cellular immunity in depressed, conduct disorder, and normal adolescents: Role of adverse life events. *Journal of the American Academy of Child and Adolescent Psychiatry, 33,* 671–678.

Birman, D. (1998). Biculturalism and perceived competence of Latino immigrant adolescents. *American Journal of Community Psychology, 26,* 335–354.

Bishop, D., & Frazier, C. (2000). The consequences of waiver. In J. Fagan & F. Zimring (Eds.), *The changing borders of juvenile justice: Transfer of adolescents to the criminal court.* Chicago: University of Chicago Press.

Bishop, J. (1999). Nerd harrassment, incentives, school priorities and learning. In S. Mayer & P. Peterson (Eds.), *Earning and learning.* Washington, DC: Brookings Institution Press.

Bishop, J. (in press). The role of end-of-course exams and minimum competency exams in standards-based reforms. In D. Ravitch (Ed.), *Brookings papers on educational policy.* Washington, DC: Brookings Institution.

Bjorklund, D. (1997). In search of a metatheory for cognitive development (or, Piaget is dead and I don't feel so good myself). *Child Development, 68,* 144–148.

Black, K., & McCartney, K. (1997). Adolescent females' security with parents predicts the quality of peer interactions. *Social Development, 6,* 91–110.

Black, M., Ricardo, I., & Stanton, B. (1997). Social and psychological factors associated with AIDS risk behaviors among low-income, urban, African American adolescents. *Journal of Research on Adolescence, 7,* 173–195.

Blackson, T., Tarter, R., Loeber, R., Ammerman, R., & Windle, M. (1996). The influence of paternal substance abuse and difficult temperament in fathers and sons on sons' disengagement from family to deviant peers. *Journal of Youth and Adolescence, 25,* 389–418.

Blair, S., & Qian, Z. (1998). Family and Asian students' educational performance: A consideration of diversity. *Journal of Family Issues, 19,* 355–374.

Blash, R., & Unger, D. (1992, March). *Cultural factors and the self-esteem and aspirations of African-American adolescent males.* Paper presented at the biennial meetings of the Society for Research on Adolescence, Washington.

Blinn-Pike, L. (1999). Why abstinent adolescents report they have not had sex: Understanding sexually resilient youth. *Family Relations, 48,* 295–301.

Block, J., Block, J., & Keyes, S. (1988). Longitudinally foretelling drug usage in adolescence: Early childhood personality and environmental precursors. *Child Development, 59,* 336–355.

Block, J., & Robins, R. (1993). A longitudinal study of consistency and change in self-esteem from early adolescence to early adulthood. *Child Development, 64,* 909–923.

Bloom, A. (1987). *The closing of the American mind.* New York: Simon & Schuster.

Blos, P. (1967). The second individuation process of adolescence. In R. Eissler et al. (Eds.), *Psychoanalytic study of the child* (Vol. 15). New York: International Universities Press.

Blos, P. (1979). *The adolescent passage.* New York: International Universities Press.

Blum, R., & Rinehart, P. (2000). *Reducing the risk: Connections that make a difference in the lives of youth.* Minneapolis: Division of General Pediatrics and Adolescent Health, University of Minnesota.

Blum, R., Beuhring, T., Wunderlich, M., & Resnick, M. (1996). Don't ask, they won't tell: The quality of adolescent health screening in five practice settings. *American Journal of Public Health, 86,* 1767–1772.

Blum, R., Resnick, M., & Stark, T. (1990). Factors associated with the use of court bypass by minors to obtain abortions. *Family Planning Perspectives, 22,* 158–160.

Blumenthal, S., & Kupfer, D. (1988). Overview of early detection and treatment strategies for suicidal behavior in young people. *Journal of Youth and Adolescence, 17,* 1–24.

Blyth, D., Hill, J., & Smyth, C. (1981). The influence of older adolescents on younger adolescents: Do grade-level arrangements make a difference in behaviors, attitudes, and experiences? *Journal of Early Adolescence, 1,* 85–110.

Blyth, D., Hill, J., & Thiel, K. (1982). Early adolescents' significant others: Grade and gender differences in perceived relationships with familial and non-familial adults and young people. *Journal of Youth and Adolescence, 11,* 425–450.

Blyth, D., Simmons, R., Bulcroft, R., Felt, D., Van Cleave, E., & Bush, D. (1980). The effects of physical development on self-image and satisfaction with body image for early adolescent males. In F. G. Simmons (Ed.), *Handbook of community and mental health* (Vol. 2). Greenwich, CT: JAI Press.

Blyth, D., Simmons, R., & Zakin, D. (1985). Satisfaction with body image for early adolescent females: The impact of pubertal timing within different school environments. *Journal of Youth and Adolescence, 14,* 227–236.

Bogenschneider, K. (1997). Parental involvement in adolescent schooling: A proximal process with transcontextual validity. *Journal of Marriage and the Family, 59,* 1–16.

Bogenschneider, K., & Steinberg, L. (1994). Maternal employment and adolescent academic achievement: A developmental analysis. *Sociology of Education, 67,* 60–77.

Bogenschneider, K., Wu, M., Raffaelli, M., & Tsay, J. (1998). "Other teens drink, but not my kid": Does parental awareness of adolescent alcohol use protect adolescents from risky consequences? *Journal of Marriage and the Family, 60,* 356–373.

Boggiano, A., Main, D., & Katz, P. (1991). Mastery motivation in boys and girls: The role of intrinsic versus extrinsic motivation. *Sex Roles, 25,* 511–520.

Bohrnstedt, G., & Felson, R. (1983). Explaining the relations among children's actual and perceived performances and self-esteem: A comparison of several causal models. *Journal of Personality and Social Psychology, 45,* 43–56.

Boldero, J., & Fallon, B. (1995). Adolescent help-seeking: What do they get help for and from whom? *Journal of Adolescence, 18,* 193–209.

Bomar, J., & Sabatelli, R. (1996). Family system dynamics, gender, and psychosocial maturity in late adolescence. *Journal of Adolescent Research, 11,* 421–439.

Borduin, C., Mann, B., Cone, L., Henggler, S., Fucci, B., Blaske, D., & Williams, R. (1995). Multisystemic treatment of serious juvenile offenders: Long-term prevention of criminality and violence. *Journal of Consulting and Clinical Psychology, 63,* 569–578.

Bornholt, L., Goodnow, J., & Cooney, G. (1994). Influences of gender stereotypes on adolescents' perceptions of their own achievement. *American Educational Research Journal, 31,* 675–692.

Botstein, L. (1997). *Jefferson's children: Education and the promise of American culture.* New York: Doubleday.

Botvin, M., & Vitaro, F. (1995). The impact of peer relationships on aggression in childhood: Inhibition through coercion or promotion through peer support. In J. McCord (Ed.), *Coercion and punishment in long-term perspectives* (pp. 183–197). New York: Cambridge University Press.

Bourne, E. (1978). The state of research on ego identity: A review and appraisal, Part I. *Journal of Youth and Adolescence, 7,* 223–251.

Bowen, G., & Chapman, M. (1996). Poverty, neighborhood danger, social support, and the individual adaptation among at-risk youth in urban areas. *Journal of Family Issues, 17,* 641–666.

Bowen, N. K., & Bowen, G. L. (1999). Effects of crime and violence in neighborhoods and schools on the school behavior and performance of adolescents. *Journal of Adolescent Research, 14*(3), 319–342.

Bowker, A., Bukowski, W., Hymel, S., & Sippola, L. (2000). Coping with daily hassles in the peer group: Variations as a function of peer experience. *Journal of Research on Adolescence, 10,* 211–243.

Bowlby, J. (1969). *Attachment and loss, Vol. 1: Attachment.* New York: Basic Books.

Boyer, E. (1986, December). Transition from school to college. *Phi Delta Kappan,* pp. 293–297.

Boyes, M., & Allen, S. (1993). Styles of parent-child interaction and moral reasoning in adolescence. *Merrill-Palmer Quarterly, 39,* 551–570.

Boykin, A., & Toms, F. (1985). Black child socialization: A conceptual framework. In H. McAdoo & J. McAdoo (Eds.), *Black children: Social, educational, and parental environments.* Newbury Park, CA: Sage.

Boyle, R., Claxton, A., & Forster, J. (1997). The role of social influences and tobacco availability on adolescent smokeless tobacco use. *Journal of Adolescent Health, 20,* 279–285.

Brack, C., Brack, G., & Orr, D. (1996). Adolescent health promotion: Testing a model using multidimensional scaling. *Journal of Research on Adolescence, 6,* 139–149.

Braddock, J. (1985). School desegregation and black assimilation. *Journal of Social Issues, 41,* 9–22.

Bradley, L., & Bradley, G. (1977). The academic achievement of black students in desegregated schools: A critical review. *Review of Educational Research, 47,* 399–449.

Brady, E., & Kendall, P. (1992). Comorbidity of anxiety and depression in children and adolescents. *Psychological Bulletin, 111,* 244–255.

Branch, C. (1995, August). *Gang bangers: Ethnic variations.* Paper presented at APA, New York.

Brandon, P. (1991). Gender differences in young Asian Americans' educational attainments. *Sex Roles, 25,* 45–62.

Braungart, R. (1980). Youth movements. In J. Adelson (Ed.), *Handbook of adolescent psychology* (pp. 560–597). New York: Wiley.

Bray, J., Berger, S., Tiuch, G., & Boethel, C. (1993, March). *Nonresidential parent-child relationships following divorce and remarriage: A longitudinal perspective.* Paper presented at the biennial meetings of the Society for Research in Child Development, New Orleans.

Brendgen, M., Vitaro, F., & Bukowski, W. (2000). Deviant friends and early adolescents' emotional and behavioral adjustment. *Journal of Research on Adolescence, 10,* 173–189.

Brener, N., & Collins, J. (1998). Co-occurrence of health-risk behaviors among adolescents in the United States. *Journal of Adolescent Health, 22,* 209–213.

Brewster, K. (1994). Race differences in sexual activity among adolescent women: The role of neighborhood characteristics. *American Sociological Review, 59,* 408–424.

Brewster, K., Billy, J., & Grady, W. (1993). Social context and adolescent behavior: The impact of community on the transition to sexual activity. *Social Forces, 71,* 713–740.

Brewster, K., Cooksey, E., Guilkey, D., & Rindfuss, R. (1998). The changing impact of religion on the sexual and contraceptive behavior of adolescent women in the United States. *Journal of Marriage and the Family, 60,* 493–504.

Bridges, G., & Steen, S. (1998). Racial disparities in official assessments of juvenile offenders: Attributional stereotypes as mediating mechanisms. *American Sociological Review, 63,* 554–570.

Brindis, C., Starbuck-Morales, S., Wolfe, A., & McCarter, V. (1994). Characteristics associated with contraceptive use among adolescent females in school-based family planning programs. *Family Planning Perspectives, 26,* 160–164.

Britner, P., Crosby, C., & Jodl, K. (1994, February). *The death penalty as applied to juvenile offenders: Jurors' perceptions of adolescents' criminal responsibility.* Paper presented at the biennial meetings of the Society for Research on Adolescence, San Diego.

Brittain, C. (1963). Adolescent choices and parent/peer cross-pressures. *American Sociological Review, 28,* 385–391.

Brody, G., Moore, K., & Glei, D. (1994). Family processes during adolescence as predictors of parent-young adult attitude similarity: A six-year longitudinal analysis. *Family Relations, 43,* 369–373.

Brody, G., Stoneman, Z., & Burke, M. (1987). Child temperaments, maternal differential treatment, and sibling relationships. *Developmental Psychology, 23,* 354–362.

Brody, G., Stoneman, Z., & Flor, D. (1995). Linking family processes and academic competence among rural African American youths. *Journal of Marriage and the Family, 57,* 567–579.

Brody, G., Stoneman, Z., & Flor, D. (1996). Parental religiosity, family processes, and youth competence in rural, two-parent African-American families. *Developmental Psychology, 32,* 696–706.

Brody, G., Stoneman, Z., Flor, D., & McCrary, C. (1994). Religion's role in organizing family relationships: Family process in rural, two-parent African American families. *Journal of Marriage and the Family, 56,* 878–888.

Brody, G., Stoneman, Z., Flor, D., McCrary, C., Hatings, L., & Conyers, O. (1994). Financial resources, parent psychological functioning, parent co-caregiving, and early adolescent competence in rural two-parent African-American families. *Child Development, 65,* 590–605.

Brody, G., Stoneman, Z., & McCoy, J. (1994). Forecasting sibling relationships in early adolescence from child temperaments and family processes in middle childhood. *Child Development, 65,* 771–784.

Brody, J. (1987, June 3). *Personal health column. The New York Times.*

Bronfenbrenner, U. (1974). The origins of alienation. *Scientific American, 231,* 53–61.

Bronfenbrenner, U. (1979). *The ecology of human development.* Cambridge, MA: Harvard University Press.

Bronfenbrenner, U. (1989). Ecological systems theory. In R. Vasta (Ed.), *Annals of child development* (Vol. 6, pp. 187–249). Greenwich, CT: JAI Press.

Bronfenbrenner, U., & Crouter, N. (1982). Work and family through time and space. In S. Kammerman & C. Hayes (Eds.), *Families that work: Children in a changing world.* Washington, DC: National Academy Press.

Bronner, E. (1998, February 25). U.S. trails the world in math and science. *The New York Times,* p. B10.

Bronstein, P., Duncan, P., & Clauson, J., Abrams, C. L., Yannett, N., Ginsburg, G., & Milne, M. (1998). Preventing middle school adjustment problems for children from lower-income families: A program for aware parenting. *Journal of Applied Developmental Psychology, 19* (1), 129–152.

Bronstein, P., Duncan, P., D'Ari, A., Pieniadz, J., Fitzgerald, M., Abrams, C., Frankowski, B., Franco, O., Hunt, C., & Cha, S. (1996). Family and parenting behaviors predicting middle school adjustment: A longitudinal study. *Family Relations, 45,* 415–426.

Bronstein, P., Ginsburg, G., & Herrera-Leavitt, I. (2000). *Parental predictors of motivational orientation and academic performance in early adolescence: A longitudinal study.* Manuscript submitted for publication. Burlington, VT: Department of Psychology, University of Vermont.

Brook, J., Balka, E., & Whiteman, M. (1999). The risks for late adolescence of early adolescent marijuana use. *American Journal of Public Health, 89,* 1549–1554.

Brook, J., Whitman, M., & Gordon, A. (1983). Stages of drug use in adolescence: Personality, peer, and family correlates. *Developmental Psychology, 19,* 269–277.

Brook, J., Whitman, M., Gordon, A., & Brook, D. (1984). Paternal determinants of female adolescents, marijuana use. *Developmental Psychology, 20,* 1032–1043.

Brook, J., Whitman, M., Gordon, A., & Cohen, P. (1986). Dynamics of childhood and adolescent personality traits and adolescent drug use. *Developmental Psychology, 22,* 403–414.

Brooks-Gunn, J. (1987). Pubertal processes and girls' psychological adaptation. In R. Lerner & T. Fochs (Eds.), *Biological-psychosocial interactions in early adolescence: A life-span perspective* (pp. 123–153). Hillsdale, NJ: Erlbaum.

Brooks-Gunn, J. (1989). Pubertal processes and the early adolescent transition. In W. Damon (Ed.), *Child development today and tomorrow* (pp. 155–176). San Francisco: Jossey-Bass.

Brooks-Gunn, J., & Furstenberg, F., Jr. (1989). Adolescent sexual behavior. *American Psychologist, 44,* 249–257.

Brooks-Gunn, J., & Paikoff, R. (1993). "Sex is a gamble, kissing is a game": Adolescent sexuality and health promotion. In S. Millstein, A. Petersen, & E. Nightingale (Eds.), *Promoting the health of adolescents: New directions for the twenty-first century* (pp. 180–208). New York: Oxford University Press.

Brooks-Gunn, J., & Reiter, E. (1990). The role of pubertal processes. In S. Feldman & G. Elliott (Eds.), *At the threshold: The developing adolescent* (pp. 16–23). Cambridge, MA: Harvard University Press.

Brooks-Gunn, J., & Ruble, D. (1979, April). *The social and psychological meaning of menarche.* Paper presented at the biennial meetings of the Society for Research in Child Development, San Francisco.

Brooks-Gunn, J., & Ruble, D. (1982). The development of menstrual-related beliefs and behaviors during early adolescence. *Child Development, 53,* 1567–1577.

Brooks-Gunn, J., & Warren, M. (1985). The effects of delayed menarche in different contexts: Dance and nondance students. *Journal of Youth and Adolescence, 14,* 285–300.

Brooks-Gunn, J., & Warren, M. (1989). Biological contributions to negative affect in young girls. *Child Development, 60,* 40–55.

Brooks-Gunn, J., Auth, J., Petersen, A., & Compas, B. (2001). In I. Goodyer (Ed.), *The depressed child and adolescent* (2nd ed.) New York: Cambridge University Press, in press.

Brooks-Gunn, J., Duncan, G., Klebanov, P., & Sealand, N. (1993). Do neighborhoods influence child and adolescent development? *American Journal of Sociology, 99,* 353–395.

Brooks-Gunn, J., Graber, J., & Paikoff, R. (1994). Studying links between hormones and negative affect: Models and measures. *Journal of Research on Adolescence, 4,* 469–486.

Brooks-Gunn, J., Newman, D., Holderness, C., & Warren, M. (1994). The experience of breast development and girls' stories about the purchase of a bra. *Journal of Youth and Adolescence, 23,* 539–565.

Broverman, I., Vogel, S., Broverman, D., Clarkson, F., & Rosenkrantz, P. (1972). Sex-role stereotypes: A current appraisal. *Journal of Social Issues, 28,* 59–78.

Brown, A. (1975). The development of memory: Knowing, knowing about knowing, and knowing how to know. In H. Reese (Ed.), *Advances in child development and behavior* (Vol. 10). New York: Academic Press.

Brown, B. (1990). Peer groups. In S. Feldman & G. Elliott (Eds.), *At the threshold: The developing adolescent* (pp. 171–196). Cambridge, MA: Harvard University Press.

Brown, B. (1996). Visibility, vulnerability, development, and context: Ingredients for a fuller understanding of peer rejection in adolescence. *Journal of Early Adolescence, 16,* 27–36.

Brown, B. (1999). "You're going out with who?": Peer group influences on adolescent romantic relationships. In W. Furman, B. Brown, & C. Feiring (Eds.). (1999). *Contemporary perspectives on adolescent romantic relationships* (pp. 291–329). New York: Cambridge University Press.

Brown, B., Clasen, D., & Eicher, S. (1986). Perceptions of peer pressure, peer conformity dispositions, and self-reported behavior among adolescents. *Developmental Psychology, 22,* 521–530.

Brown, B., Dolcini, M., & Leventhal, A. (1995, March). *The emergence of peer crowds: Friend or foe to adolescent health?* Paper presented at the biennial meetings of the Society for Research in Child Development, Indianapolis.

Brown, B., Freeman, H., Huang, B., & Mounts, N. (1992, March). *"Crowd hopping": Incidence, correlates and consequences of change in crowd affiliation during adolescence.* Paper presented at the biennial meetings of the Society for Research on Adolescence, Washington.

Brown, B., & Lohr, M. J. (1987). Peer group affiliation and adolescent self-esteem: An integration of ego-identity and symbolic interaction theories. *Journal of Personality and Social Psychology, 52,* 47–55.

Brown, B., Lamborn, S., & Newmann, F. (1992). "You live and you learn": The place of school engagement in the lives of teenagers. In F. Newmann (Ed.), *Student engagement and achievement in American high schools.* New York: Teachers College Press.

Brown, B., & Mounts, N. (1989, April). *Peer group structures in single versus multiethnic high schools.* Paper presented at the biennial meetings of the Society for Research in Child Development, Kansas City.

Brown, B., Mory, M., & Kinney, D. (1994). Casting crowds in a relational perspective: Caricature, channel, & context. In R. Montemayor, G. Adams, & T. Gullotta (Eds.), *Advances in adolescent development, Vol. 5: Personal relationships during adolescence.* Newbury Park, CA: Sage.

Brown, B., & Mounts, N., Lamborn, S., & Steinberg, L. (1993). Parenting practices and peer group affiliation in adolescence. *Child Development, 64,* 467–482.

Brown, B., Theobald, W., & Klute, C. (in press). Crowds, cliques, and friendship in adolescence. In G. Adams & M. Berzonsky (Eds.). *Handbook on adolescence.* New York: Blackwell.

Brown, J. (1994, February). *Adolescents' uses of mass media and bedroom culture.* Paper presented at the biennial meetings of the Society for Research on Adolescence, San Diego.

Brown, J., & Cantor, J. (2000a). An agenda for research on youth and the media. *Journal of Adolescent Health, 27,* 2–7.

Brown, J., & Cantor, J. (2000b). The mass media and adolescents' health. *Journal of Adolescent Health, 27,* supplement to August 2000 issue.

Brown, J., & Newcomer, S. (1991). Television viewing and adolescents' sexual behavior. *Journal of Homosexuality, 21,* 77–91.

Brown, J., & Witherspoon, E. (in press). The mass media and American adolescents' health. In Y. Kamalipour (Ed.), *Media, sex, violence and drugs in the global village.* Boulder, CO: Rowman & Littlefied.

Brown, J., White, A., & Nikopoulou, L. (1993). Disinterest, intrigue, resistance: Early adolescent girls' use of sexual media content. In B. Greenberg, J. Brown, & N. Buerkel-Rothfuss (Eds.), *Media, sex, and the adolescent* (pp. 177–195).

Brown, K., McMahon, R., Biro, F., Crawford, P., Schreiber, G., Similo, S. L., Waclawiw, M., & Striegel-Moore, R. (1998). Changes in self-esteem in black and white girls between the ages of 9 and 14 years: The NHLBI Growth and Health Study. *Journal of Adolescent Health, 23,* 7–19.

Brubacher, J., & Rudy, W. (1976). *Higher education in transition* (3rd ed.) New York: Harper & Row.

Bruch, H. (1973). *Eating disorders.* New York: Basic Books.

Brumberg, J. (1988). *Fasting girls: The emergence of anorexia as a modern disease.* Cambridge, MA: Harvard University Press.

Brumberg, J. (1997). *The body project: An intimate history of American girls.* New York: Random House.

Bruvold, W. (1993). A meta-analysis of adolescent smoking prevention programs. *American Journal of Public Health, 83,* 872–880.

Bryk, A., & Thum, Y. (1989). The effects of high school organization on dropping out: An exploratory investigation. *American Educational Research Journal, 26,* 353–383.

Buchanan, C., Eccles, J., & Becker, J. (1992). Are adolescents the victims of raging hormones? Evidence for activational effects of hormones on moods and behavior at adolescence. *Psychological Bulletin, 111,* 62–107.

Buchanan, C., Holmbeck, G., Allison, S., & Hughes, J. (1996, March). *Measuring beliefs about adolescence.* Paper presented at the biennial meetings of the Society for Research on Adolescence, Boston.

Buchanan, C., Maccoby, E., & Dornbusch, S. (1996). *Adolescents after divorce.* Cambridge, MA: Harvard University Press.

Buchanan, C., & Holmbeck, G. (1998). Measuring beliefs about adolescent personality and behavior. *Journal of Youth and Adolescence, 27,* 607–627.

Buchanan, C., & Maccoby, E., (1993, March). *Relationships between adolescents and their nonresidential parents: A comparison of nonresidential mothers and fathers.* Paper presented at the biennial meetings of the Society for Research in Child Development, New Orleans.

Buchanan, M., & Robbins, C. (1990). Early adult psychological consequences for males of adolescent pregnancy and its resolution. *Journal of Youth and Adolescence, 19,* 413–424.

Buechel, F., & Duncan, G. (1998). Do parents' social activities promote children's school attainments? Evidence from the German Socioeconomic Panel. *Journal of Marriage and the Family, 60,* 95–108.

Buehler, C. K., Krishnakumar, A., Anthony, C., Tittsworth, S., & Stone, G. (1994). Hostile interparental conflict and youth maladjustment. *Family Relations, 43,* 409–416.

Buehler, C., Krishnakumar, A., Stone, G., Anthony, C., Pemberton, S., Gerard, J., & Barber, B. (1998). Interparental conflict styles and youth problem behaviors: A two-sample replication study. *Journal of Marriage and the Family, 60,* 119–132.

Buhrmester, D. (1990). Intimacy of friendship, interpersonal competence, and adjustment during preadolescence and adolescence. *Child Development, 61,* 1101–1111.

Buhrmester, D. (1996). Need fulfillment, interpersonal competence, and the developmental contexts of early adolescent friendship. In W. Bukowski, A. Newcomb, & W. Hartup (Eds.), *The company they keep: Friendship in childhood and adolescence* (pp. 158–185). New York: Cambridge University Press.

Buhrmester, D., & Furman, W. (1987). The development of companionship and intimacy. *Child Development, 58,* 1101–1113.

Buhrmester, D., & Furman, W. (1990). Perceptions of sibling relationships during middle childhood and adolescence. *Child Development, 61,* 1387–1396.

Buhrmester, D., & Yin, J. (1997, April). *A longitudinal study of friends' influence on adolescents' adjustment.* Paper presented at the biennial meetings of the Society for Research in Child Development, Washington.

Bukowski, W. M., Sippola, L. K., & Hoza, B. (1999). Same and other: Interdependency between participation in same- and other-sex friendships. *Journal of Youth and Adolescence, 28*(4), 439–459.

Bukowski, W., Gauze, C., Hoza, B., & Newcomb, A. (1993). Differences and consistency between same-sex and other-sex peer relationships during early adolescence. *Developmental Psychology, 29,* 255–263.

Bukowski, W., Peters, P., Sippola, L., & Newcomb, A. (1993, March). *Patterns in the selection of same- and other-sex friends among aggressive and nonaggressive early adolescent boys and girls.* Paper presented at the biennial meetings of the Society for Research in Child Development, New Orleans.

Bukowski, W., Pizzamiglio, M., Newcomb, A., & Hoza, B. (1996). Popularity as an affordance for friendship: The link between group and dyadic experience. *Social Development, 5,* 189–202.

Bulcroft, R. (1991). The value of physical change in adolescence: Consequences for the parent-adolescent exchange relationship. *Journal of Youth and Adolescence, 20,* 89–106.

Bulcroft, R., Carmody, D., & Bulcroft, K. (1996). Patterns of parental independence giving to adolescents: Variations by race, age, and gender of child. *Journal of Marriage and the Family, 58,* 866–883.

Bumpass, L., & McLanahan, S. (1987, April). *Unmarried motherhood: A note on recent trends, composition and black-white differences.* Paper presented at the annual meetings of the Population Association of America, Chicago.

Burda, P., & Vaux, A. (1988). Social drinking in supportive contexts among college males. *Journal of Youth and Adolescence, 17,* 165–172.

Burleson, B. (1982). The development of comforting communication skills in childhood and adolescence. *Child Development, 53,* 1578–1588.

Burr, J., Hartman, J., & Matteson, D. (1999). Black suicide in U.S. metropolitan areas: An examination of the racial inequality and social integration-regulation hypotheses. *Social Forces, 77,* 1049–1080.

Butler, J., & Burton, L. (1990). Rethinking teenage childbearing: Is sexual abuse a missing link? *Family Relations, 39,* 73–80.

Butler, R., & Nissan, M. (1975). Who is afraid of success? And why? *Journal of Youth and Adolescence, 4,* 259–270.

Byrne, B., & Shavelson, R. (1996). On the structure of social self-concept for pre-, early-, and late-adolescents: A test of the Shavelson, Hubner, and Stanton (1976) model. *Journal of Personality and Social Psychology, 70,* 599–613.

Byrnes, J. (1997). *The nature and development of decision-making: A self-regulation model.* Hillsdale, NJ: Erlbaum.

Byrnes, J., & Takahira, S. (1993). Explaining gender differences on SAT-math items. *Developmental Psychology, 29,* 805–810.

Byrnes, J., Miller, D., & Schafer, W. (1999). Gender differences in risk taking: A metaanalysis. *Psychological Bulletin, 125,* 367–383.

Cairns, R., Cairns, B., & Neckerman, H. (1989). Early school dropout: Configurations and determinants. *Child Development, 60,* 1437–1452.

Cairns, R., Cairns, B., Neckerman, H., Gest, S., & Gariepy, J. (1988). Social networks and aggressive behavior: Peer support or peer rejection? *Developmental Psychology, 24,* 815–823.

Cairns, R., Leung, M., Buchanan, L., & Cairns, B. (1995). Friendships and social networks in childhood and adolescence: Fluidity, reliability, and interrelations. *Child Development, 66,* 1330–1345.

Caldwell, L., & Darling, N. (1999). Leisure context, parental control, and resistance to peer pressure as predictors of adolescent partying and substance use: An ecological perspective. *Journal of Leisure Research, 31,* 57–77.

Call, K., & McNall, M. (1992). Poverty, ethnicity, and youth adjustment: A comparison of poor Hmong and non-Hmong adolescents. In W. Meeus, M. de Goede, W. Knox, & K. Hurrelmann (Eds.), *Adolescence, careers, and cultures* (pp. 373–392). New York: de Gruyter.

Calverley, R., Fischer, K., & Ayoub, C. (1994). Complex splitting of self-representations in sexually abused adolescent girls. *Development and Psychopathology, 6,* 195–213.

Camarena, P., & Sarigiani, P. (1994, February). *Sexual victimization and psychological adjustment across adolescence.* Paper presented at the biennial meetings of the Society for Research on Adolescence, San Diego.

Cambell, C., & Schwartz, D. (1996). Prevalence and impact of exposure to interpersonal violence among suburban and urban middle school students. *Pediatrics, 98,* 396–402.

Campbell, A. (1968). The role of family planning in the reduction of poverty. *Journal of Marriage and the Family, 30,* 236–245.

Campbell, B. (1977). The impact of school desegregation: An investigation of three mediating factors. *Youth and Society, 9,* 79–111.

Campbell, E., Adams, G., & Dobson, W. (1984). Familial correlates of identity formation in late adolescence: A study of the predictive utility of connectedness and individuality in family relations. *Journal of Youth and Adolescence, 13,* 509–526.

Campbell, F., & Ramey, C. (1995). Cognitive and school outcomes for high-risk African-American students at middle adolescence: Positive effects of early intervention. *American Educational Research Journal, 32,* 743–772.

Campos, R., Raffaelli, M., Ude, W., Greco, M., Ruff, A., Rolf, J., Antunes, C., Halsey, N., Greco, D., & the Street Youth Study. (1994). Social networks and daily activities of street youth in Belo Horizonte, Brazil. *Child Development, 65,* 319–330.

Cantor, J. (2000). Media violence. *Journal of Adolescent Health, 27,* 30–34.

Cantwell, D., & Baker, L. (1991). Manifestations of depressive affect in adolescence: *Journal of Youth and Adolescence, 20,* 121–134.

Capaldi, D. (1991). Co-occurrence of conduct problems and depressive symptoms in early adolescent boys, I: Familial factors and general adjustment at grade 6. *Development and Psychopathology, 3,* 277–300.

Capaldi, D. (1992). Co-occurence of conduct problems and depressed mood in early adolescent boys, II: A two-year follow-up at grade 8. *Development and Psychopathology, 4,* 125–144.

Capaldi, D., & Clark, S. (1998). Prospective family predictors of aggression toward female partners for at-risk young men. *Developmental Psychology, 34,* 1175–1188.

Capaldi, D., Crosby, L., & Stoolmiller, M. (1996). Predicting the timing of first sexual intercourse for at-risk adolescent males. *Child Development, 67,* 344–359.

Capaldi, D., & Patterson, G. (1991). Relation of parental transitions to boys' adjustment problems, I: A linear hypothesis; II: Mothers at risk for transitions and unskilled parenting. *Developmental Psychology, 27,* 489–504.

Caplan, N., Choy, M., & Whitmore, J. (1992). Indochinese refugee families and academic achievement. *Scientific American,* February, 36–42.

Cappelleri, J., Eckenrode, J., & Powers, J. (1993). The epidemiology of child abuse: Findings from the Second National Incidence and Prevalence Study of Child Abuse and Neglect. *American Journal of Public Health, 83,* 1622–1624.

Carlo, G., Koller, S., Eisenberg, N., Da Silva, S., & Frohlich, C. (1996). A cross-national study of the relations among prosocial moral reasoning, gender role orientations, and prosocial behaviors. *Developmental Psychology, 32,* 231–240.

Carlson, E., Sroufe, L. A., Collins, W. A., Jimerson, S., Weinfield, N., Henninghausen, K., Egeland, B., Hyson, D., Anderson, F., & Meyer, S. (1999). Early environmental support and elementary school adjustment as predictors of school adjustment in middle adolescence. *Journal of Adolescent Research, 14,* 72–94.

Carnegie Council on Adolescent Development. (1989). *Turning points: Preparing youth for the 21st century.* New York: Carnegie Corporation of New York.

Carnegie Council on Adolescent Development. (1992). *A matter of time: Risk and opportunity in the after-school hours.* Washington, DC: Author.

Carns, D. (1973). Talking about sex: Notes on first coitis and the double sexual standard. *Journal of Marriage and the Family, 35,* 677–688.

Carr, M., Borkowski, J., & Maxwell, S. (1991). Motivational components of underachievement. *Developmental Psychology, 27,* 108–118.

Carr, R., Wright, J., & Brody, C. (1996). Effects of high school work experience a decade later: Evidence from the National Longitudinal Survey. *Sociology of Education, 69,* 66–81.

Carskadon, M., Acebo, C., Richardson, G., Tate, B., & Seifer, R. (1997). Long nights protocol: Access to circadian parameters in adolescents. *Journal of Biological Rhythms, 12,* 278–289.

Carson, D., Chowdhury, A., Perry, C., & Pati, C. (1999). Family characteristics and adolescent competence in India: Investigation of youth in southern Orissa. *Journal of Youth and Adolescence, 28,* 211–233.

Case, R. (1985). *Intellectual development: Birth to adulthood.* New York: Academic Press.

Casey, M., Nuttall, R., & Pezaris, E. (1999). Evidence in support of a model that predicts how biological and environmental factors interact to influence spatial skills. *Developmental Psychology, 35,* 1237–1247.

Casey, M., Nuttall, R., Pezaris, E., & Benbow, C. (1995). The influence of spatial ability on gender differences in mathematics college entrance test scores across diverse samples. *Developmental Psychology, 31,* 697–705.

Casper, L. (1990). Does family interaction prevent adolescent pregnancy? *Family Planning Perspectives, 22,* 109–114.

Casper, R., & Jabine, L. (1996). An eight-year follow-up: Outcome from adolescent compared to adult onset anorexia nervosa. *Journal of Youth and Adolescence, 25,* 599–617.

Caspi, A. (1997). Life-span personality development. In W. Damon (Series Editor) & N. Eisenberg (Volume Editor), *Handbook of child psychology, Vol. 3: Social, emotional, and personality development* (5th ed.) New York: Wiley.

Caspi, A., Elder, G., Jr., & Bem, D. (1987). Moving against the world: Life-course patterns of explosive children. *Developmental Psychology, 23,* 308–313.

Caspi, A., Henry, B., McGee, R., Moffitt, T., & Silva, P. (1995). Temperamental origins of child and adolescent behavior problems: From age three to age fifteen. *Child Development, 66,* 55–68.

Caspi, A., Lynam, D., Moffitt, T., & Silva, P. (1993). Unraveling girls' delinquency: Biological, dispositional, and contextual contributions to adolescent misbehavior. *Developmental Psychology, 29,* 19–30.

Caspi, A., & Moffitt, T. (1991). Individual differences and personal transitions: The sample case of girls at puberty. *Journal of Personality and Social Psychology, 61,* 157–168.

Caspi, A., & Silva, P. (1995). Temperamental qualities at age three predict personality traits in young adulthood: Longitudinal evidence from a birth cohort. *Child Development, 66,* 486–498.

Casteel, M. (1993). Effects of inference necessity and reading goal on children's inferential generation. *Developmental Psychology, 29,* 346–357.

Catsambis, S. (1992, March). *The many faces of tracking in middle school grades: Between-and within-school differentiation of students and resources.* Paper presented at the biennial meetings of the Society for Research on Adolescence, Washington.

Catsambis, S. (1994). The path to math: Gender and racial-ethnic differences in mathematics participation from middle school to high school. *Sociology of Education, 67,* 199–215.

Catterall, J. (1998). Risk and resilience in student transitions to high school. *American Journal of Education, 106,* 302–333.

Cauce, A. (1987). School and peer competence in early adolescence: A test of domain-specific self-perceived competence. *Developmental Psychology, 23,* 287–291.

Cauffman, E., & Steinberg, L. (1996). Effects of menarche, dating, and heterosocial involvement on dieting behavior in early adolescence. *Developmental Psychology, 32,* 631–635.

Cauffman, E., & Steinberg, L. (2000). (Im)maturity of judgment in adolescence: Why adolescents may be less culpable than adults. *Behavioral Sciences and the Law, 18,* 1–21.

Cauffman, E., Feldman, S., Waterman, J., & Steiner, H. (1998). Posttraumatic stress disorder among incarcerated females. *Journal of the American Academy of Child and Adolescent Psychiatry, 37,* 1209–1216.

Ceci, S., & Williams, W. (1999). Schooling, intelligence, and income. *American Psychologist, 52,* 1051–1058.

Centers for Disease Control. (2000a). Births: Preliminary data for 1999. *Vital Health Statistics Reports, 48,* 1–21.

Centers for Disease Control. (2000b). *Youth risk behavior surveillance, United States, 1999.* Washington, DC: U.S. Department of Health and Human Services.

Centers, N., & Weist, M. (1998). Inner city youth and drug dealing: A review of the problem. *Journal of Youth and Adolescence, 27,* 395–411.

Chalmers, D., & Lawrence, J. (1993). Investigating the effects of planning aids on adults' and adolescents' organisation of a complex task. *International Journal of Behavioural Development, 16,* 191–214.

Chamberlain, P., & Reid, J. (1998). Comparison of two community alternatives to incarceration for chronic juvenile offenders. *Journal of Consulting and Clinical Psychology, 66,* 624–633.

Chan, D. (1997). Depressive symptoms and perceived competence among Chinese secondary school students in Hong Kong. *Journal of Youth and Adolescence, 26,* 303–319.

Chandler, M. (1987). The Othello effect: Essay on the emergence and eclipse of skeptical doubt. *Human Development, 30,* 137–159.

Chao, R. (1994). Beyond parental control and authoritarian parenting style: Understanding Chinese parenting through the cultural notion of training. *Child Development, 65,* 1111–1119.

Chase-Landsdale, P., Brooks-Gunn, J., & Zamsky, E. (1994). Young African-American multigenerational families in poverty: Quality of mothering and grandmothering. *Child Development, 65,* 373–393.

Chassin, L., & Barrera, M., Jr. (1993). Substance use escalation and substance use restraint among adolescent children of alcoholics. *Psychology of Addictive Behaviors, 7,* 3–20.

Chassin, L., Curran, P., Hussong, A., & Colder, C. (1996). The relation of parent alcoholism to adolescent substance use: A longitudinal follow-up study. *Journal of Abnormal Psychology, 105,* 70–80.

Chassin, L., Pillow, D., Curran, P., Molina, B., & Barrera, M., Jr. (1993). Relation of parental alcoholism to early adolescent substance use: A test of three mediating mechanisms. *Journal of Abnormal Psychology, 102,* 3–19.

Chassin, L., Presson, C., Todd, M., Rose, J., & Sherman, S. (1998). Maternal socialization of adolescent smoking: The intergenerational transmission of parenting and smoking. *Developmental Psychology, 34,* 1189–1201.

Chassin, L., Rogosch, F., & Barrera, M., Jr. (1991). Substance use and symptomatology among adolescent children of alcoholics. *Journal of Abnormal Psychology, 100,* 449–463.

Chen, C., Greenberger, E., Lester, J., Dong, Q., & Guo, M. (1998). A cross-cultural study of family and peer correlates of adolescent misconduct. *Developmental Psychology, 34,* 770–781.

Chen, C., Lee, S., & Stevenson, H. (1996). Long-term prediction of academic achievement of American, Chinese, and Japanese adolescents. *Journal of Educational Psychology, 18,* 750–759.

Chen, C., & Stevenson, H. (1995). Motivation and mathematics achievement: A comparative study of Asian-American, Caucasian-American, and East Asian high school students. *Child Development, 66,* 1215–1234.

Chen, H., Mechanic, D., & Hansell, S. (1998). A longitudinal study of self-awareness and depressed mood in adolescence. *Journal of Youth and Adolescence, 27,* 719–734.

Chen, K., & Kandel, D. (1995). The natural history of drug use from adolescence to the mid-thirties in a general population sample. *American Journal of Public Health, 85,* 41–47.

Chen, X., Rubin, K., & Li, D. (1997). Relation between academic achievement and social adjustment: Evidence from Chinese children. *Developmental Psychology, 33,* 518–525.

Chen, X., Rubin, K., & Li, Z. (1995). Social functioning and adjustment in Chinese children: A longitudinal study. *Developmental Psychology, 31,* 531–539.

Chen, Z.-Y., & Dornbusch, S. M. (1998). Relating aspects of adolescent emotional autonomy to academic achievement and deviant behavior. *Journal of Adolescent Research, 13*(3), 293–319.

Cherlin, A., Chase-Landsdale, P., & McRae, C. (1998). Effects of parental divorce on mental health throughout the life course. *American Sociological Review, 63,* 239–249.

Cherlin, A., Furstenberg, F., Jr., Chase-Landsdale, L., Kiernan, K., Robins, P., Morrison, D., & Teitler, J. (1991). Longitudinal studies of effects of divorce on children in Great Britain and the United States. *Science, 252,* 1386–1389.

Cheung, Y. (1997). Family, school, peer, and media predictors of adolescent deviant behavior in Hong Kong, *Journal of Youth and Adolescence, 26,* 569–596.

Chilcoat, H., Dishion, T., & Anthony, J. (1995). Parent monitoring and the incidence of drug sampling in urban elementary school children. *American Journal of Epidemiology, 141,* 25–31.

Children's Defense Fund. (1989). Service opportunities for youths. Washington, DC: Author.

Chilman, C. (1986). Some psychosocial aspects of adolescent sexual and contraceptive behaviors in a changing American society. In J. Lancaster & B. Hamburg (Eds.), *School-age pregnancy and parenthood: Biosocial dimensions.* New York: Aldine de Gruyter.

Chilman, C. (1990). Promoting healthy adolescent sexuality. *Family Relations, 39,* 123–131.

Chisholm, L., & Hurrelmann, K. (1995). Adolescence in modern Europe: Pluralized transition patterns and their implications for personal and social risks. *Journal of Adolescence, 18,* 129–158.

Chou, C., Montgomery, S., Pentz, M., Rohrbach, L., Johnson, C., Flay, B., & MacKinnon, D. (1998). Effects of a community-based prevention program in decreasing drug use in high-risk adolescents. *American Journal of Public Health, 88,* 944–948.

Christopher, F. (1995). Adolescent pregnancy prevention. *Family Relations, 44,* 384–391.

Christopher, F. S., & Roosa, M. (1990). An evaluation of an adolescent pregnancy prevention program: Is "just say no" enough? *Family Relations, 39,* 68–72.

Chun, Y.-J., & MacDermid, S. M. (1997). Perceptions of family differentiation, individuation, and self-esteem among Korean adolescents. *Journal of Marriage and the Family, 59*(2), 451–462.

Chung, R., & Walkey, F. (1989). Educational and achievement aspirations of New Zealand Chinese and European secondary school students. *Youth and Society, 21,* 139–152.

Church, R. (1976). *Education in the United States.* New York: Free Press.

Cicchetti, D., & Toth, S. (1998). The development of depression in children and adolescents. *American Psychologist, 53,* 221–241.

Claes, M. (1998). Adolescents' closeness with parents, siblings, and friends in three countries: Canada, Belgium, and Italy. *Journal of Youth and Adolescence, 27,* 165–184.

Clancy, S., & Dollinger, S. (1993). Identity, self, and personality, I: Identity status and the five-factor model of personality. *Journal of Research on Adolescence, 3,* 227–246.

Clark, J., & Barber, B. (1994). Adolescents in postdivorce and always-married families: Self-esteem and perceptions of fathers' interest. *Journal of Marriage and the Family, 56,* 608–614.

Clark, R., & Delia, J. (1976). The development of functional persuasive skills in childhood and early adolescence. *Child Development, 47,* 1008–1014.

Clasen, D., & Brown, B. (1985). The multidimensionality of peer pressure in adolescence. *Journal of Youth and Adolescence, 14,* 451–468.

Clayton, R., & Bokemeier, J. (1980). Premarital sex in the seventies. *Journal of Marriage and the Family, 42,* 759–775.

Clingempeel, W., Colyar, J., Brand, E., & Hetherington, E. (1992). Children's relationships with maternal grandparents: A longitudinal study of family structure and pubertal status effects. *Child Development, 63,* 1404–1422.

Coe, C., Hayashi, K., & Levine, S. (1988). Hormones and behavior at puberty: Activation or concatenation. In M. Gunnar & W. A. Collins (Eds.), *The Minnesota Symposia on Child Psychology* (Vol. 21, pp. 17–41). Hillsdale, NJ: Erlbaum.

Cohen, Y. (1964). *The transition from childhood to adolescence.* Chicago: Aldine.

Coie, J., Lochman, J., Terry, R., & Hyman, C. (1992). Predicting early adolescent disorder from childhood aggression and peer rejection. *Journal of Consulting and Clinical Psychology, 60,* 783–792.

Coie, J., Terry, R., Lenox, K., Lochman, J., & Hyman, C. (1995). Childhood peer rejection and aggression as predictors of stable patterns of adolescent disorder. *Development and Psychopathology, 7,* 697–713.

Coiro, M., & Emery, R. (1996, March). *Adolescents' adjustment as a function of their involvement in post-divorce conflict.* Paper presented at the biennial meetings of the Society for Research on Adolescence, Boston.

Colby, A., & Kohlberg, L. (1987). *The measurement of moral judgment.* New York: Cambridge University Press.

Colby, A., Kohlberg, L., Gibbs, J., & Lieberman, M. (1983). *A longitudinal study of moral judgment.* Monographs of the Society for Research in Child Development, 48 (Serial No. 200).

Colder, C., Chassin, L., Stice, E., & Curran, P. (1997). Alcohol expectancies as potential mediators of parent alcoholism effects on the development of adolescent heavy drinking. *Journal of Research on Adolescence, 7,* 349–374.

Colder, C., & Stice, E. (1998). A longitudinal study of the interactive effects of impulsivity and anger on adolescent problem behavior. *Journal of Youth and Adolescence, 27,* 255–274.

Cole, D., & Jordan, A. (1995). Competence and memory: Integrating psychosocial and cognitive correlates of child depression. *Child Development, 66,* 459–473.

Cole, D., Martin, J., & Powers, B. (1997). A competency-based model of child depression: A longitudinal study of peer, parent, teacher, and self-evaluations. *Journal of Child Psychology and Psychiatry and Allied Disciplines, 38,* 505–514.

Cole, D., Martin, J., Peeke, L., Seroczynski, A., & Hoffman, K. (1998). Are cognitive errors of underestimation predictive or reflective of depressive symptoms in children: A longitudinal study. *Journal of Abnormal Psychology, 107,* 481–496.

Cole, D., Peeke, L., Dolezal, S., Murray, N., & Canzoniero, A. (1999). A longitudinal study of negative affect and self-perceived competence in young adolescents. *Journal of Personality and Social Psychology, 77,* 851–862.

Coleman, J. (1961). *The adolescent society.* Glencoe, IL: Free Press.

Coleman, J., Campbell, E., Hobson, C., McPartland, J., Mood, A., Weinfeld, F., & York, R. (1966). *Equality of educational opportunity.* Washington, DC: U.S. Government Printing Office.

Coleman, J., Hoffer, T., & Kilgore, S. (1982). *High school achievement: Public, Catholic and other private schools compared.* New York: Basic Books.

Coleman, J., & Hoffer, T. (1987). *Public and private high schools: The impact of communities.* New York: Basic Books.

Coleman, L. (1999). Comparing contraceptive use surveys of young people in the United Kingdom. *Archives of Sexual Behavior, 28,* 255–264.

Coley, R., & Chase-Lansdale, P. L. (1998). Adolescent pregnancy and parenthood: Recent evidence and future directions. *American Psychologist, 53,* 152–166.

Collaer, M., & Hines, M. (1995). Human behavioral sex differences: A role for gonadal hormones during early development? *Psychological Bulletin, 118,* 55–107.

Collins, W. A. (1988). Research on the transition to adolescence: Continuity in the study of developmental processes. In M. Gunnar & W. Collins (Eds.), *Minnesota Symposium on Child Psychology* (Vol. 21, pp. 1–15). Hillsdale, NJ: Erlbaum.

Collins, W. A. (1990). Parent-child relationships in the transition to adolescence: Continuity and change in interaction, affect, and cognition. In R. Montemayor, G. Adams, & T. Gullotta (Eds.), *Advances in adolescent development, Vol. 2: The transition from childhood to adolescence* (pp. 85–106). Beverly Hills, CA: Sage.

Collins, W. A., Maccoby, E., Steinberg, L., Hetherington, E. M., & Bornstein, M. (2000). Contemporary research on parenting: The case for nature and nurture. *American Psychologist, 55,* 218–232.

Collins, W. A., & Sroufe, L. A. (1999). Capacity for intimate relationships: A developmental construction. In W. Furman, B. Brown, & C. Feiring (Eds.), *Contemporary perspectives on adolescent romantic relationships* (pp. 125–147). New York: Cambridge University Press.

Collins, W., & Russell, G. (1991). Mother-child and father-child relationships in middle adolescence: A developmental analysis. *Developmental Review, 11,* 99–136.

Colten, M., Gore, S., & Aseltine, R., Jr. (1991). The patterning of distress and disorder in a community sample of high school aged youth. In M. Colten & S. Gore (Eds.), *Adolescent stress: Causes and consequences* (pp. 157–180). New York: Aldine de Gruyter.

Compas, B. (1987). Coping with stress during childhood and adolescence. *Psychological Bulletin, 101,* 393–403.

Compas, B., Connor, J., Saltzman, H., Thomsen, A., & Wadsworth, M. (in press). Coping with stress during childhood and adolescence: Problems, progress, and potential in theory and research. *Psychological Bulletin.*

Compas, B., Ey, S., & Grant, K. (1993). Taxonomy, assessment, and diagnosis of depression during adolescence. *Psychological Bulletin, 114,* 323–344.

Compas, B., Hinden, B., & Gerhardt, C. (1995). Adolescent development: Pathways and processes of risk and resilience. *Annual Review of Psychology, 46,* 265–293.

Compas, B., Malcarne, V., & Fondacaro, K., (1988). Coping with stress during childhood and adolescence. *Psychological Bulletin, 101,* 393–403.

Compas, B., Oppedisano, G., Connor, J., Gerhardt, C., Hinden, B., Achenbach, T., & Hammen, C. (1997). Gender differences in depressive symptoms in adolescence: Comparison of national samples of clinically referred and nonreferred youths. *Journal of Consulting and Clinical Psychology, 65,* 617–626.

Conant, J. (1959). *The American high school today.* New York: McGraw-Hill.

Condit, V. (1990). Anorexia nervosa: Levels of causation. *Human Nature, 1,* 391–413.

Conduct Problems Prevention Research Group. (1999). Initial impact of the Fast Track Prevention Trial for Conduct Problems: II. Classroom effects. *Journal of Consulting and Clinical Psychology, 67,* 648–657.

Conger, J. (1975). *Current issues in adolescent development. In Master lectures on developmental psychology.* Washington, DC: American Psychological Association.

Conger, K., & Conger, R. (1994). Differential parenting and change in sibling differences in delinquency. *Journal of Family Psychology, 8,* 287–302.

Conger, K., Conger, R., & Elder, G., Jr. (1994). Sibling relationships during hard times. In R. Conger & G. Elder, Jr. (Eds.), *Families in troubled times: Adapting to change in rural America* (pp. 235–252). New York: Aldine de Gruyter.

Conger, K., Conger, R., & Scaramella, L. (1997). Parents, siblings, psychological control, and adolescent adjustment. *Journal of Adolescent Research, 12,* 113–138.

Conger, R., Conger, K., Elder, G., Jr., Lorenz, F., Simons, R., & Whitbeck, L. (1992). A family process model of economic hardship and adjustment of early adolescent boys. *Child Development, 63,* 526–541.

Conger, R., Conger, K., Elder, G., Jr., Lorenz, F., Simons, R., & Whitbeck, L. (1993). Family economic stress and adjustment of early adolescent girls. *Developmental Psychology, 29,* 206–219.

Conger, R., Conger, K., Matthews, L., & Elder, G. H., Jr. (1999). Pathways of economic influence on adolescent adjustment. *American Journal of Community Psychology, 27,* 519–541.

Conger, R., Ge, X., Elder, G., Jr., Lorenz, F., & Simons, R. (1994). Economic stress, coercive family process, and developmental problems of adolescents. *Child Development, 65,* 541–561.

Conger, R., Patterson, G., & Ge, X. (1995). It takes two to replicate: A mediational model for the impact of parents' stress on adolescent adjustment. *Child Development, 66,* 80–97.

Connell, J., Halpern-Felsher, B., Clifford, E., Crichlow, W., & Usinger, P. (1995). Hanging in there: Behavioral, psychological, and contextual factors affecting whether African American adolescents stay in high school. *Journal of Adolescent Research, 10,* 41–63.

Connell, J., Spencer, M., & Aber, J. (1994). Educational risk and resilience in African-American youth: Context, self, action, and outcomes in school. *Child Development, 65,* 493–506.

Connolly, J., Craig, W., Goldberg, A., & Pepler, D. (1999). Conceptions of cross-sex friendships and romantic relationships in early adolescence. *Journal of Youth and Adolescence, 28*(4), 481–494.

Connolly, J., & Goldberg, A. (1999). Romantic relationships in adolescence: The role of friends and peers in their emergence and development. In W. Furman, B. Brown, & C. Feiring (Eds.), *Contemporary perspectives on adolescent romantic relationships* (pp. 266–290). New York: Cambridge University Press.

Connolly, J., & Johnson, A. (1993, March). *The psychosocial context of romantic relationships in adolescence.* Paper presented at the biennial meetings of the Society for Research in Child Development, New Orleans.

Connolly, J., & Konarski, R. (1994). Peer self-concept in adolescence: Analysis of factor structure and of associations with peer experience. *Journal of Research on Adolescence, 4,* 385–403.

Conseur, A., & Rivara, F. (1997). Maternal and perinatal risk factors for later delinquency. *Pediatrics, 99,* 785–790.

Consortium on Productivity in the Schools. (1995). Using what we have to get the schools we need: A productivity focus for American education. New York: Author, Institute on Education and the Economy, Teachers College, Columbia University.

Consortium on Renewing Education. (1998). *20/20 vision: A strategy for doubling America's academic achievement by the year 2020.* Nashville, TN: Peabody Center for Education Policy, Vanderbilt University.

Cook, T., Church, M., Ajanaku, S., Shadish, W., Jr., Kim, J., & Cohen, R. (1996). The development of occupational aspirations and expectations among inner-city boys. *Child Development, 67,* 3368–3385.

Cooley-Quille, M., & Lorion, R. (1999). Adolescents' exposure to community violence: Sleep and psychophysiological functioning. *Journal of Community Psychology, 27,* 367–375.

Coombs, R., Paulson, M., & Richardson, M. (1991). Peer vs. parental influence in substance use among Hispanic and Anglo children and adolescents. *Journal of Youth and Adolescence, 20,* 73–88.

Cooper, C. (1988). Commentary: The role of conflict in adolescent parent relationships. In M. Gunnar & W. A. Collin (Eds.), *Minnesota symposium on child psychology* (Vol. 21, pp. 181–187). Hillsdale, NJ: Erlbaum.

Cooper, C. (1994). Cultural perspectives on continuity and change in adolescents' relationships. In R. Montemayor, G. Adams, & T. Gullotta (Eds.), *Personal relationships during adolescence.* Thousand Oaks, CA: Sage.

Cooper, C., Baker, H., Polichar, D., & Welsh, M. (1994). Cultural perspectives on values and communication of adolescents with their fathers, mothers, siblings, and friends. In W. Collins & S. Shulman (Eds.), *New directions for child development: The role of fathers in adolescent development.* San Francisco: Jossey-Bass.

Cooper, C., Baker, H., Polichar, D., & Welsh, M. (1994). Values and communication of Chinese, European, Filipino, Mexican, and Vietnamese American adolescents with their families and friends. In S. Shulman & W. A. Collins (Eds.), *The role of fathers in adolescent development: New directions for child development* (pp. 73–89). San Francisco: Jossey-Bass.

Cooper, C., Carlson, C., Keller, J., Koch, P., & Spradling, V. (1993, March). *Conflict negotiation in early adolescence: Links between family and peer relational patterns.* Paper presented at the biennial meetings of the Society for Research in Child Development, New Orleans.

Cooper, C., Grotevant, H., & Condon, S. (1983). Individuality and connectedness in the family as a context for adolescent identity formation and role taking skill. In H. Grotevant & C. Cooper (Eds.), *Adolescent development in the family.* San Francisco: Jossey-Bass.

Cooper, C., & Grotevant, H. (1987). Gender issues in the interface of family experience and adolescents' friendship and dating identity. *Journal of Youth and Adolescence, 16,* 247–264.

Cooper, H., Charlton, K., Valentine, J., & Muhlenbruck, L. (2000). Making the most of summer school: A meta-analytic and narrative review. *Monographs of the Society for Research in Child Development, 65,* Serial No. 260.

Cooper, M. L., Shaver, P. R., & Collins, N. L. (1998). Attachment styles, emotion regulation, and adjustment in adolescence. *Journal of Personality and Social Psychology, 74*(5), 1380–1397.

Cornwell, G., Eggebeen, D., & Meschke, L. (1996). The changing family context of early adolescence. *Journal of Early Adolescence, 16,* 141–156.

Corville-Smith, J., Ryan, B., Adams, G., & Dalicandro, T. (1998). Distinguishing absentee students from regular attenders: The combined influence of personal, family, and school factors. *Journal of Youth and Adolescence, 27,* 629–640.

Costa, F., Jessor, R., Donovan, J., & Fortenberry, J. (1995). Early initiation of sexual intercourse: The influence of psychosocial unconventionality. *Journal of Research on Adolescence, 5,* 93–121.

Costa, F., Jessor, R., Fortenberry, J., & Donovan, J. (1996). Psychosocial conventionality, health orientation, and contraceptive use in adolescence. *Journal of Adolescent Health, 18,* 404–416.

Costello, E., Farmer, E. M., Angold, A., Burns, B., & Erkanli, A. (1997). Psychiatric disorders among American Indian and white youth in Appalachia: The great Smoky Mountains study. *American Journal of Public Health, 87,* 827–832.

Coughlin, C., & Vuchinich, S. (1996). Family experience in preadolescence and the development of male delinquency. *Journal of Marriage and the Family, 58,* 491–501.

Coulten, C., & Pandey, S. (1992). Geographic concentration of poverty and risk to children in urban environments. *American Behavioral Scientist, 35,* 238–257.

Courtney, M., & Cohen, R. (1996). Behavior segmentation by boys as a function of aggressiveness and prior information. *Child Development, 67,* 1034–1047.

Crandall, C. (1988). Social contagion of binge eating. *Journal of Personality and Social Psychology, 55,* 588–598.

Crane, J. (1991). The epidemic theory of ghettos and neighborhood effects on dropping out and teenage childbearing. *American Journal of Sociology, 96,* 1226–1259.

Creasey, G., & Kaliher, G. (1994). Age differences in grandchildren's perceptions of relations with grandparents. *Journal of Adolescence, 17,* 411–426.

Crick, N. (1996). The role of overt aggression, relational aggression, and prosocial behavior in the prediction of children's future social adjustment. *Child Development, 67,* 2317–2327.

Crick, N. (1997). Engagement in gender normative versus nonnormative forms of aggression: Links to social-psychological adjustment. *Developmental Psychology, 33,* 610–617.

Crick, N., Bigbee, M., & Howes, C. (1996). Gender differences in children's normative beliefs about aggression: How do I hurt thee? Let me count the ways. *Child Development, 67,* 1003–1014.

Crick, N., & Dodge, K. (1994). A review and reformulation of social information-processing mechanisms in children's social adjustment. *Psychological Bulletin, 115,* 74–101.

Crick, N., & Dodge, K. (1996). Social information-processing mechanisms in reactive and proactive aggression. *Child Development, 67,* 993–1002.

Crick, N., & Grotpeter, K. (1995). Relational aggression, gender, and social-psychological adjustment. *Child Development, 66,* 710–722.

Crisp, A. (1983). Some aspects of the psychopathology of anorexia nervosa. In P. Darby, P. Garfinkel, D. Garner, & D. Cosina (Eds.), *Anorexia nervosa: Recent developments in research* (pp. 15–28). New York: Alan R. Liss.

Crites, H. (1989). Career differentiation in adolescence. In D. Stern & D. Eichorn (Eds.), *Adolescence and work.* Hillsdale, NJ: Erlbaum.

Crittenden, P., Claussen, A., & Sugarman, D. (1994). Physical and psychological malteatment in middle childhood and adolescence. *Development and Psychopathology, 6,* 145–164.

Crockett, L., & Bingham, C. (1994, February). *Family influences on girls' sexual experience and pregnancy risk.* Paper presented at the biennial meetings of the Society for Research on Adolescence, San Diego.

Crockett, L., & Bingham, R. (2000). Anticipating adulthood: Expected timing of work and family transitions among rural youth. *Journal of Research on Adolescence, 10,* 151–172.

Crockett, L., & Dorn, L. (1987, April). *Young adolescents' pubertal status and reported heterosocial interaction.* Paper presented at the biennial meetings of the Society for Research in Child Development, Baltimore.

Crockett, L., Bingham, C., Chopak, J., & Vicary, J. (1996). Timing of first sexual intercourse: The role of social control, social learning and problem behavior. *Journal of Youth and Adolescence, 25,* 89–111.

Crockett, L., & Silbereisen, R. (Eds.). (2000). *Negotiating adolescence in times of social change.* New York: Cambridge University Press.

Crosbie-Burnett, M., & Giles-Sims, J. (1994). Adolescent adjustment and stepparenting styles. *Family Relations, 43,* 394–399.

Cross, W. (1978). The Thomas and Cook models of psychological nigrescence: A literature review. *Journal of Black Psychology, 4,* 13–31.

Crouter, A., Bumpus, M., Maguire, M., & McHale, S. (1999). Linking parents' work pressure and adolescents' well-being: Insights into dynamics in dual-earner families. *Developmental Psychology, 35,* 1453–1461.

Crouter, A., MacDermid, S., McHale, S., & Perry-Jenkins, M. (1990). Parental monitoring and perceptions of children's school performance and conduct in dual- and single-earner families. *Developmental Psychology, 26,* 649–657.

Crouter, A., Manke, B., & McHale, S. (1995). The family context of gender intensification in early adolescence. *Child Development, 66,* 317–329.

Crowe, P., Philbin, J., Richards, M., & Crawford, I. (1998). Adolescent alcohol involvement and the experience of social environments. *Journal of Research on Adolescence, 8,* 403–422.

Crystal, D., Chen, C., Fuligni, A., Stevenson, H., Hsu, C., Ko, H., Kitamura, S., & Kimura, S. (1994). Psychological maladjustment and academic achievement: A cross-cultural study of Japanese, Chinese, and American high school students. *Child Development, 65,* 738–753.

Crystal, D., Watanabe, H., Weinfurt, K., & Wu, C. (1998). Concepts of human differences: A comparison of American, Japanese, and Chinese children and adolescents. *Developmental Psychology, 34,* 714–722.

Csikszentmihalyi, M., & Larson, R. (1984). *Being adolescent.* New York: Basic Books.

Csikszentmihalyi, M., Larson, R., & Prescott, S. (1977). The ecology of adolescent activity and experience. *Journal of Youth and Adolescence, 6,* 281–294.

Cummings, E., Ballard, M., El-Sheikh, M., & Lake, M. (1991). Resolution and children's responses to interadult anger. *Developmental Psychology, 27,* 462–470.

Cummings, K., Pechacek, T., & Shopland, D. (1994). The illegal sale of cigarettes to U.S. minors: Estimates by state. *American Journal of Public Health, 84,* 300–302.

Cunningham, M. (1999). African-American adolescent males' perceptions of their community resources and constraints: A longitudinal analysis. *Journal of Community Psychology, 27,* 569–588.

Curran, P., Stice, E., & Chassin, L. (1997). The relation between adolescent alcohol use and peer alcohol use: A longitudinal random coefficients model. *Journal of Consulting and Clinical Psychology, 65,* 130–140.

Curtner-Smith, M., & MacKinnon-Lewis, C. (1994). Family process effects on adolescent males' susceptibility to antisocial peer pressure. *Family Relations, 43,* 462–468.

Cusick, P. A. (1973). *Inside high school.* New York: Holt, Rinehart & Winston.

Cutler, S., & Nolen-Hoeksema, S. (1991). Accounting for sex differences in depression through female victimization: Childhood sexual abuse. *Sex Roles, 24,* 425–438.

Cyranowski, J., & Frank, E. (2000). Adolescent onset of the gender difference in lifetime rates of major depression. *Archives of General Psychiatry, 57,* 21–27.

Dalton, S. (1992). Overuse injuries in adolescent athletes. *Sports Medicine, 13,* 58–70.

Daly, K. (1994). Adolescent perceptions of adoption. *Youth and Society, 25,* 330–350.

Damico, R. (1984). Does working in high school impair academic progress? *Sociology of Education, 57,* 157–164.

Damico, S., & Sparks, C. (1986). Cross-group contact opportunities: Impact on interpersonal relationships in desegregated middle schools. *Sociology of Education, 59,* 113–123.

D'Angelo, L., Getson, P., Luban, N., & Gayle, H. (1991). Human immunodeficiency virus infection in urban adolescents: Can we predict who is at risk? *Pediatrics, 88,* 982–986.

Daniels, D., Dunn, J., Furstenberg, F., Jr., & Plomin, R. (1985). Environmental differences within the family and adjustment differences within pairs of adolescent siblings. *Child Development, 56,* 764–774.

Danner, F., & Day, M. (1977). Eliciting formal operations. *Child Development, 48,* 1600–1606.

Darabi, K., & Ortiz, V. (1987). Childbearing among young Latino women in the United States. *American Journal of Public Health, 77,* 25–28.

Darling, N., Dowdy, B. B., Van Horn, M. L., & Caldwell, L. L. (1999). Mixed-sex settings and the perception of competence. *Journal of Youth and Adolescence, 28,* 461–480.

Darling, N., Hamilton, S., & Matsuda, S. (1990, March). *Functional roles and social roles: Adolescents' significant others in the United States and Japan.* Paper presented at the biennial meetings of the Society for Research on Adolescence, Atlanta.

Darling, N., & Steinberg, L. (1993). Parenting style as context: An integrative model. *Psychological Bulletin, 113,* 487–496.

Darling, N., & Steinberg, L. (1997). Community influences on adolescent achievement and deviance. In J. Brooks-Gunn, G. Duncan, & L. Aber (Eds.), *Neighborhood poverty: Context and consequences for children. Vol. 2: Conceptual,* *methodological, and policy approaches to studying neighborhoods* (pp. 120–131). New York: Russell Sage Foundation.

Dauber, S., Alexander, K., & Entwisle, D. (1996). Tracking and transitions through the middle grades: Channelling educational trajectories. *Sociology of Education, 69,* 290–307.

Davenport, E., Davison, M., Kuang, H., Ding, S., Kim, S., & Kwak, N. (1998). High school mathematics course-taking by gender and ethnicity. *American Educational Research Journal, 35,* 497–514.

Davies, P., & Cummings, M. (1994). Marital conflict and child adjustment: An emotional security hypothesis. *Psychological Bulletin, 116,* 387–411.

Davies, P., & Windle, M. (1997). Gender-specific pathways between maternal depressive symptoms, family discord, and adolescent adjustment. *Developmental Psychology, 33,* 657–668.

Davis, A., Rhodes, J., & Hamilton-Leaks, J. (1997). When both parents may be a source of support and problems: An analysis of pregnant and parenting female African American adolescents' relationships with their mothers and fathers. *Journal of Research on Adolescence, 7,* 331–348.

Davis, A., & Rhodes, J. (1994). African-American teenage mothers and their mothers: An analysis of supportive and problematic interactions. *Journal of Community Psychology, 22,* 12–19.

Davis, H., & Gergen, P. (1994). Self-described weight status of Mexican-American adolescents. *Journal of Adolescent Health, 15,* 407–409.

Davis, K., & Kirkpatrick, L. (1994). Attachment style, gender, and relationship stability: A longitudinal analysis. *Journal of Personality and Social Psychology, 66,* 502–512.

Dearden, K., Hale, C., & Woolley, T. (1995). The antecedents of teen fatherhood: A retrospective case-control study of Great Britain youth. *American Journal of Public Health, 85,* 551–554.

Deater-Deckard, K., & Plomin, R. (1999). An adoption study of etiology of teacher and parent reports of externalizing behavior problems in middle childhood. *Child Development, 70,* 144–154.

DeBaryshe, K., Patterson, G., & Capaldi, D. (1993). A performance model for academic achievement in early adolescent boys. *Developmental Psychology, 29,* 795–804.

DeBerry, K., Scarr, S., & Weinberg, R. (1996). Family racial socialization and ecological competence: Longitudinal assessments of African-American transracial adoptees. *Child Development, 67,* 2375–2399.

Deci, E., & Ryan, R. (1985). *Intrinsic motivation and self-determination in human behavior.* New York: Plenum.

Degirmencioglu, S., Tolson, J., & Urberg, K. (1993, March). *Stability of adolescent social networks over the school year.* Paper presented at the biennial meetings of the Society for Research in Child Development, New Orleans.

Degirmencioglu, S., Urberg, K., Tolson, J., & Richard, P. (1998). Adolescent friendship networks: Continuity and change over the school year. *Merrill-Palmer Quarterly, 44,* 313–337.

Degirmencioglu, S., & Urberg, K. (1994, February). *Cross-gender friendships in adolescence: Who chooses the "other"?* Paper presented at the biennial meetings of the Society for Research on Adolescence, San Diego.

Deihl, L., Vicary, J., & Deike, R. (1997). Longitudinal trajectories of self-esteem from early to middle adolescence and related psychosocial variables among rural adolescents. *Journal of Research on Adolescence, 7,* 393–411.

Dekovic, M. (1999). Risk and protective factors in the development of problem behavior during adolescence. *Journal of Youth and Adolescence, 28,* 667–685.

Demo, D., & Acock, A. (1996). Family structure, family process, and adolescent well-being. *Journal of Research on Adolescence, 6,* 457–488.

Demorest, A., Meyer, C., Phelps, E., Gardner, H., & Winner, E. (1984). Words speak louder than actions: Understanding deliberately false remarks. *Child Development, 55,* 1527–1534.

Denton, K., & Zarbatany, L. (1996). Age differences in support processes in conversations between friends. *Child Development, 67,* 1360–1373.

DeRosier, M., Kupersmidt, J., & Patterson, C. (1994). Children's academic and behavioral adjustment as a function of the chronicity and proximity of peer rejection. *Child Development, 65,* 1799–1813.

Deslandes, R., Potvin, P., & LeClerc, D. (1999). Family characteristics as predictors of school achievement: Parental involvement as a mediator. *McGill Journal of Education, 34,* 135–153.

Devereux, E. (1970). The role of peer group experience in moral development. In J. Hill (Ed.), *Minnesota symposium on child psychology* (Vol. 4). Minneapolis: University of Minnesota Press.

Deyhle, D. (1995). Navajo youth and Anglo racism: Cultural integrity and resistance. *Harvard Educational Review, 65,* 403–444.

Diamond, L. (1998). Development of sexual orientation among adolescent and young adult women. *Developmental Psychology, 34,* 1085–1095.

Diamond, L., Savin-Williams, R., & Dubé, E. (1999). Sex, dating, passionate friendships, and romance: Intimate peer relations among lesbian, gay, and bisexual adolescents. In W. Furman, B. Brown, & C. Feiring (Eds.), *Contemporary perspectives on adolescent romantic relationships* (pp. 175–210). New York: Cambridge University Press.

Diaz, R., & Berndt, T. (1982). Children's knowledge of a best friend: Fact or fancy? *Developmental Psychology, 18,* 787–794.

DiBlasio, F., & Benda, B. (1992). Gender differences in theories of adolescent sexual activity. *Sex Roles, 27,* 221–240.

DiClemente, R., Boyer, C., & Morales, E. (1988). Minorities and AIDS: Knowledge, attitudes, and misconceptions among black and Latino adolescents. *American Journal of Public Health, 78,* 55–57.

DiClemente, R., Lodico, M., Grinstead, O., Harper, G., Rickman, R., Evans, P., & Coates, T. (1996). African-American adolescents residing in high-risk urban environments do use condoms: Correlates and predictors of condom use among adolescents in public housing developments. *Pediatrics, 98,* 269–278.

Dielman, T. (1994). School-based research on the prevention of adolescent alcohol use and misuse: Methodological issues and advances. *Journal of Research on Adolescence, 4,* 271–293.

DiFranza, J., Savageau, J., & Aisquith, B. (1996). Youth access to tobacco: The effects of age, gender, vending machine locks, and "It's the Law" programs. *American Journal of Public Health, 86,* 221–224.

Dilorio, C., Kelley, M., & Hockenberry-Eaton, M. (1999). Communication about sexual issues: Mothers, fathers, and friends. *Journal of Adolescent Health, 24,* 181–189.

DiMaggio, P. (1982). Cultural capital and school success: The impact of status culture participation on the grades of U.S. high school students. *American Sociological Review, 47,* 189–201.

Dishion, T., & Andrews, D. (1995). Preventing escalation in problem behaviors with high-risk young adolescents: Immediate and 1-year outcomes. *Journal of Consulting and Clinical Psychology, 63,* 538–548.

Dishion, T., Andrews, D., & Crosby, L. (1995). Antisocial boys and their friends in early adolescence: Relationship characteristics, quality, and interactional process. *Child Development, 66,* 139–151.

Dishion, T., Capaldi, D., Spracklen, K., & Li, F. (1995). Peer ecology of male adolescent drug use. *Development and Psychopathology, 7,* 803–824.

Dishion, T., McCord, J., & Poulin, F. (1999). When interventions harm: Peer groups and problem behavior. *American Psychologist, 54,* 755–764.

Dishion, T. J., Capaldi, D. M., & Yoerger, K. (1999). Middle childhood antecedents to progressions in male adolescent substance use: An ecological analysis of risk and protection. *Journal of Adolescent Research, 14*(2), 175–205.

Dishion, T., Patterson, G., Stoolmiller, M., & Skinner, M. (1991). Family, school, and behavioral antecedents to early adolescent involvement with antisocial peers. *Developmental Psychology, 27,* 172–180.

Dittus, P., Jaccard, J., & Gordon, V. (1997). The impact of African American fathers on adolescent sexual behavior. *Journal of Youth and Adolescence, 26,* 445–465.

Dobkin, P., Tremblay, R., & Sacchitelle, C. (1997). Predicting boys' early-onset substance abuse from father's alcoholism, son's disruptiveness, and mother's parenting behavior. *Journal of Consulting and Clinical Psychology, 65,* 86–92.

Dobkin, P., Tremblay, R., Mässe, L., & Vitaro, F. (1995). Individual and peer characteristics in predicting boys' early onset of substance abuse: A seven-year longitudinal study. *Child Development, 66,* 1198–1214.

Dodge, K., & Coie, J. (1987). Social information-processing factors in reactive and proactive aggression in children's peer groups. *Journal of Personality and Social Psychology, 53,* 1146–1158.

Dodge, K., Price, J., Bachorowski, J., & Newman, J. (1990). Hostile attributional biases in severely aggressive adolescents. *Journal of Abnormal Psychology, 99,* 385–392.

Doherty, W., & Allen, W. (1994). Family functioning and parental smoking as predictors of adolescent cigarette use: A six-year prospective study. *Journal of Family Psychology, 8,* 347–353.

Donahue, M. (1994, February). *Positive youth development in religiously-based youth programs.* Paper presented at the biennial meetings of the Society for Research on Adolescence, San Diego.

Donnellan, M., Ge, X., & Wenk, E. (in press). Cognitive abilities in adolescence-limited and life-course-persistent criminal offenders. *Journal of Abnormal Psychology.*

Donnelly, B., & Voydanoff, P. (1996). Parenting versus placing for adoption: Consequences for adolescent mothers. *Family Relations, 42,* 427–434.

Donnelly, D., & Finkelhor, D. (1992). Does equality in custody arrangement improve the parent-child relationship? *Journal of Marriage and the Family, 54,* 837–845.

Donovan, J., & Jessor, R. (1985). Structure of problem behavior in adolescence and young adulthood. *Journal of Consulting and Clinical Psychology, 53,* 890–904.

Dorfman, L., Woodruff, K., Chavez, V., & Wallack, L. (1997). Youth and violence on local television news in California. *American Journal of Public Health, 87*(8), 1311–1316.

Dorius, G., Heaton, T., & Steffen, P. (1993). Adolescent life events and their association with the onset of sexual intercourse. *Youth and Society, 25,* 3–23.

Dorn, L. D., Nottelmann, E. D., Susman, E. J., Inoff-Germain, G., Cutler, G. B., Jr., & Chrousos, G. P. (1999). Variability in hormone concentrations and self-reported menstrual histories in young adolescents: Menarche as an integral part of a developmental process. *Journal of Youth and Adolescence, 28*(3), 283–304.

Dornbusch, S. (1994, February). *Off the track.* Presidential address to the Society for Research on Adolescence, San Diego.

Dornbusch, S., Carlsmith, J., Bushwall, S., Ritter, P., Leiderman, P., Hastorf, A., & Gross, R. (1985). Single parents, extended households, and the control of adolescents. *Child Development, 56,* 326–341.

Dornbusch, S., Carlsmith, J., Gross, R., Martin, J., Jennings, D., Rosenberg, A., & Duke, P. (1981). Sexual development, age, and dating: A comparison of biological and social influences upon one set of behaviors. *Child Development, 52,* 179–185.

Dornbusch, S., Mont-Reynaud, R., Ritter, P., Chen, Z., & Steinberg, L. (1991). Stressful events and their correlates among adolescents of diverse backgrounds. In M. Colten & S. Gore (Eds.), *Adolescent stress: Causes and consequences* (pp. 111–130). Hawthorne, NY: Aldine de Gruyter.

Dornbusch, S., Ritter, P., Liederman, P., Roberts, D., & Fraleigh, M. (1987). The relation of parenting style to adolescent school performance. *Child Development, 58,* 1244–1257.

Douvan, E., & Adelson, J. (1966). *The adolescent experience.* New York: Wiley.

Dowdy, B. B., & Kliewer, W. (1998). Dating, parent-adolescent conflict, and behavioral autonomy. *Journal of Youth and Adolescence, 27*(4), 473–492.

Downey, D. (1995). Understanding academic achievement among children in stephouseholds: The role of parental resources, sex of stepparent, and sex of child. *Social Forces, 73,* 875–894.

Downey, D., Ainsworth-Darnell, J., & Dufur, M. (1998). Sex of parent and children's well-being in single-parent households. *Journal of Marriage and the Family, 60,* 878–893.

Downey, G., Bonica, C., & Rincón, C. (1999). Rejection sensitivity and adolescent romantic relationships. In W. Furman, B. Brown, & C. Feiring (Eds.), *Contemporary perspectives on adolescent romantic relationships* (pp. 148–174). New York: Cambridge University Press.

Downey, G., Lebolt, A., Rincon, C., & Freitas, A. (1998). Rejection sensitivity and children's interpersonal difficulties. *Child Development, 69,* 1074–1091.

Dozier, M., & Kobak, R. (1992). Psychophysiology in attachment interviews: Converging evidence for deactivating strategies. *Child Development, 63,* 1473–2480.

Drumm, P., & Jackson, D. (1996). Developmental changes in questioning strategies during adolescence. *Journal of Adolescent Research,* 11, 285–305.

Dryfoos, J. (1990). *Adolescents at risk: Prevalence and prevention.* New York: Oxford University Press.

Dryfoos, J. (1993). Schools as places for health, mental health, and social services. *Teachers College Record, 94,* 540–567.

Dubas, J., Graber, J., & Petersen, A. (1991). A longitudinal investigation of adolescents' changing perceptions of pubertal timing. *Developmental Psychology, 27,* 580–586.

Dubé, E., & Savin-Williams, R. (1999). Sexual identity development among ethnic sexual-minority male youths. *Developmental Psychology, 35,* 1389–1398.

DuBois, D., Bull, C., Sherman, M., & Roberts, M. (1998). Self-esteem and adjustment in early adolescence: A social-contextual perspective. *Journal of Youth and Adolescence, 27,* 557–583.

DuBois, D., Eitel, S., & Felner, R. (1994). Effects of family environment and parent-child relationships on school adjustment during the transition to early adolescence. *Journal of Marriage and the Family, 56,* 405–414.

DuBois, D., Felner, R., Brand, S., & George, G. (1999). Profiles of self-esteem in early adolescence: Identification and investigation of adaptive correlates. *American Journal of Community Psychology, 27,* 899–932.

DuBois, D., Felner, R., Brand, S., Phillips, R., & Lease, A. (1996). Early adolescent self-esteem: A developmental-ecological framework and assessment strategy. *Journal of Research on Adolescence, 6,* 543–579.

DuBois, D., Felner, R., Meares, H., & Frier, M. (1994). Prospective investigation of the effects of socioeconomic disadvantage, life stress, and social support on early adolescent adjustment. *Journal of Abnormal Psychology, 103,* 511–522.

DuBois, D., Felner, R., Sherman, M., & Bull, C. (1994). Socioenvironmental experiences, self-esteem, and emotional/ behavioral problems in early adolescence. *American Journal of Community Psychology, 22,* 371–397.

DuBois, D., & Hirsch, B. (1990). School and neighborhood friendship patterns of blacks and whites in early adolescence. *Child Development, 61,* 524–536.

DuBois, D., Holloway, B., Valentine, J., & Cooper, H. (in press). Effectiveness of mentoring programs for youth: A meta-analytic review. *American Journal of Community Psychology.*

DuBois, D., & Tevendale, H. (1999). Self-esteem in childhood and adolescence: Vaccine or epiphenomenon? *Applied and Preventive Psychology, 8,* 103–117.

DuBois, D., Tevendale, H., Burk-Braxton, C., Swenson, L., & Hardesty, J. (2000). Self-system influences during early adolescence: Investigation of an integrative model. *Journal of Early Adolescence, 20,* 12–43.

Duckett, E., & Richards, M. (1995). Maternal employment and the quality of daily experience for young adolescents of single mothers. *Journal of Family Psychology, 9,* 418–432.

Dukes, R., Martinez, R., & Stein, J. (1997). Precursors and consequences of membership in youth gangs. *Youth and Society, 29,* 139–165.

Dumont, M., & Provost, M. (1999). Resilience in adolescents: Protective role of social support, coping strategies, self-esteem, and social activities on experience of stress and depression. *Journal of Youth and Adolescence, 28,* 343–363.

Duncan, G. (1994). Families and neighbors as sources of disadvantage in the schooling decisions of white and black adolescents. *American Journal of Education, 103,* 20–53.

Duncan, O., Featherman, D., & Duncan, B. (1972). *Socioeconomic background and achievement.* New York: Semmar Press.

Duncan, P., Ritter, P., Dornbusch, S., Gross, R., & Carlsmith, J. (1985). The effects of pubertal timing on body image, school behavior, and deviance. *Journal of Youth and Adolescence, 14,* 227–236.

Duncan, T., Duncan, S., & Hops, H. (1996). The role of parents and older siblings in predicting adolescent substance use: Modeling development via structural equation latent growth methodology. *Journal of Family Psychology, 10,* 158–172.

Dunn, J., Slomkowski, C., & Beardsall, L. (1994). Sibling relationships from the preschool period through middle childhood and early adolescence. *Developmental Psychology, 30,* 315–324.

Dunn, M., & Goldman, M. (1998). Age and drinking-related differences in the memory organization of alcohol expectancies in 3rd-, 6th-, 9th-, and 12th-grade children. *Journal of Consulting and Clinical Psychology, 66,* 579–585.

Dunn, S., Putallaz, M., Sheppard, B., & Lindstrom, R. (1987). Social support and adjustment in gifted adolescents. *Journal of Educational Psychology, 79,* 467–473.Dunphy, D. (1963). The social structure of urban adolescent peer groups. *Sociometry, 26,* 230–246.

Dunphy, D. (1969). *Cliques, crowds, and gangs.* Melbourne, Australia: Chesire.

DuRant, R., Cadenhead, C., Pendergrast, R., Slavens, G., & Linder, C. (1994). Factors associated with the use of violence among urban black adolescents. *American Journal of Public Health, 84,* 612–617.

DuRant, R., Getts, A., Cadenhead, C., & Woods, E. (1995). The association between weapon-carrying and the use of violence among adolescents living in or around public housing. *Journal of Adolescence, 18,* 579–592.

DuRant, R., Pendergrast, R., & Cadenhead, C. (1994). Exposure to violence and victimization and fighting behavior by urban black adolescents. *Journal of Adolescent Health, 15,* 311–318.

DuRant, R., Rome, E., Rich, M., Allred, E., Emans, S., & Woods, E. (1997). Tobacco and alcohol use behaviors portrayed in music videos: A content analysis. *American Journal of Public Health, 87,* 1131–1135.

DuRant, R., Treiber, F., Getts, A., McCloud, K., Linder, C., & Woods, E. (1996). Comparison of two violence prevention curricula for middle school adolescents. *Journal of Adolescent Health, 19,* 111–117.

Dusek, J., & Flaherty, J. (1981). The development of the self-concept during the adolescent years. *Monographs of the Society for Research in Child Development, 46*(191).

Dweck, C., & Light, B. (1980). Learned helplessness and intellectual achievement. In J. Garber & M. Seligman (Eds.), *Human helplessness.* New York: Academic Press.

Dweck, C., & Wortman, C. (1980). Achievement, test anxiety, and learned helplessness: Adaptive and maladaptive cognitions. In H. Krohne & L. Laux (Eds.), *Achievement, stress, and anxiety.* Washington, DC: Hemisphere.

Dyer, G., & Tiggemann, M. (1996). The effects of school environment on body concerns in adolescent women. *Sex Roles, 34,* 127–138.

Dyk, P., & Adams, G. (1990). Identity and intimacy: An initial investigation of three theoretical models using cross-lag panel correlations. *Journal of Youth and Adolescence, 19,* 91–110.

Earls, F., Cairns, R., & Mercy, J. (1993). The control of violence and the promotion of nonviolence in adolescents. In S. Millstein, A. Petersen, & E. Nightingale (Eds.), *Promoting the health of adolescents: New directions for the twenty-first century* (pp. 285–304). New York: Oxford University Press.

Early, D., & Eccles, J. (1994, February). *Predicting parenting behavior: The role of SES, neighborhood risk, and parental values.* Paper presented at the biennial meetings of the Society for Research on Adolescence, San Diego.

East, P. (1996a). Do adolescent pregnancy and childbearing affect younger siblings? *Family Planning Perspectives, 28,* 148–153.

East, P. (1996b). The younger sisters of childbearing adolescents: Their attitudes, expectations, and behaviors. *Child Development, 67,* 267–282.

East, P., & Blaustein, E. (1995, March). *Perceived timing of life-course transitions: Race differences in early adolescent girls' sexual, marriage, and childbearing expectations.* Paper presented at the biennial meetings of the Society for Research in Child Development, Indianapolis.

East, P., & Felice, M. (1992). Pregnancy risk among the younger sisters of pregnant and childbearing adolescents. *Developmental and Behavioral Pediatrics, 13,* 128–136.

East, P., & Felice, M. (1996). *Adolescent pregnancy and parenting: Findings from a racially diverse sample.* Mahwah, NJ: Erlbaum.

East, P., Felice, M., & Morgan, M. (1993). Sisters' and girlfriends' sexual and childbearing behavior: Effects on early adolescent girls' sexual outcomes. *Journal of Marriage and the Family, 55,* 953–963.

East, P., & Rook, K. (1992). Compensatory patterns of support among children's peer relationships: A test using school friends, nonschool friends, and siblings. *Developmental Psychology, 28,* 163–172.

Eaton, M. J., & Dembo, M. H. (1997). Differences in the motivational beliefs of Asian American and non-Asian students. *Journal of Educational Psychology, 89,* 433–440.

Ebata, A., & Moos, R. (1994). Personal, situational, and contextual correlates of coping in adolescence. *Journal of Research on Adolescence, 4,* 99–126.

Eccles, J. (1993, March). *Parents as gender-role socializers during middle childhood and adolescence.* Paper presented at the biennial meetings of the Society for Research in Child Development, New Orleans.

Eccles, J., & Barber, B. (1999). Student council, volunteering, basketball, or marching band: What kind of extracurricular involvement matters? *Journal of Adolescent Research, 14,* 10–43.

Eccles, J., Early, D., Frasier, K., Belansky, E., & McCarthy, K. (1997). The relation of connection, regulation, and support for autonomy to adolescents' functioning. *Journal of Adolescent Research, 12,* 263–286.

Eccles, J., Lord, S., & Midgley, C. (1991). What are we doing to early adolescents? The impact of educational contexts on early adolescents. *American Journal of Education, 99,* 521–542.

Eccles, J., Midgley, C., Wigfield, A., Buchanan, C., Reuman, D., Flanagan, C., & Mac Iver, D. (1993). Development during adolescence: The impact of stage-environment fit on young adolescents' experiences in schools and families. *American Psychologist, 48,* 90–101.

Eccles, J., Wigfield, A., & Schiefele, U. (1997). Motivation to succeed. In W. Damon (Series Editor) and N. Eisenberg (Volume Editor), *Handbook of child psychology: Vol. 3: Social, emotional, and personality development* (pp. 1017–1095). (5th ed.). New York: Wiley.

Economic Policy Institute. (1994). *The state of working in America, 1992–93.* Washington, DC: Author.

Edelman, P., & Ladner, J. (Eds.). (1991). *Adolescence and poverty: Challenge for the 90s.* Washington, DC: Center for National Policy Press.

Eder, D. (1985). The cycle of popularity: Interpersonal relations among female adolescents. *Sociology of Education, 58,* 154–165.

Eder, D., & Kinney, D. (1995). The effect of middle school extracurricular activities on adolescents' popularity and peer status. *Youth and Society, 26,* 298–324.

Eder, D., & Parker, S. (1987). The cultural production and reproduction of gender: The effect of extracurricular activities on peer-group culture. *Sociology of Education, 60,* 200–213.

Education Trust. (1996). *Education watch: The 1996 Education Trust state and national data book.* Washington, DC: Author.

Egan, S., & Perry, D. (1998). Does low self-regard invite victimization? *Developmental Psychology, 34,* 299–309.

Eggebeen, D., Snyder, A., & Manning, W. (1996). Children in single-father families in demographic perspective. *Journal of Family Issues, 17,* 441–465.

Eisenberg, N., Carlo, G., Murphy, B., & Van Court, P. (1995). Prosocial development in late adolescence: A longitudinal study. *Child Development, 66,* 1179–1197.

Eisenberg, N., Miller, P., Shell, R., McNalley, S., & Shea, C. (1991). Prosocial development in adolescence: A longitudinal study. *Developmental Psychology, 27,* 849–857.

Eisenstadt, S. (1956). *From generation to generation.* Glencoe, IL: Free Press.

Elder, G., Jr. (1974). *Children of the Great Depression.* Chicago: University of Chicago Press.

Elder, G., Jr. (1980). Adolescence in historical perspective. In J. Adelson (Ed.), *Handbook of adolescent psychology.* New York: Wiley.

Elder, G., Jr., & Ardelt, M. (1992, March). *Families adapting to economic pressure: Some consequences for parents and adolescents.* Paper presented at the biennial meetings of the Society for Research on Adolescence, Washington.

Elder, G., Jr., Caspi, A., & van Nguyen, T. (1986). Resourceful and vulnerable children: Family influences in stressful times. In R. Silbereisen, K. Eyferth, & G. Rudinger (Eds.), *Development as action in context.* Heidelberg, Germany: Springer.

Elder, G., Jr., Conger, R., Foster, E., & Ardelt, M. (1992). Families under economic pressure. *Journal of Family Issues, 13,* 5–37.

Elder, G., Jr., King, V., & Conger, R. (1996). Attachment to place and migration prospects: A developmental perspective. *Journal of Research on Adolescence, 6,* 397–425.

Elder, G., Jr., van Nguyen, T., & Caspi, A. (1985). Linking family hardship to children's lives. *Child Development, 56,* 361–375.

Elders, M., Perry, C., Eriksen, M., & Giovino, G. (1994). The report of the surgeon general: Preventing tobacco use among young people. *American Journal of Public Health, 84,* 543–547.

Eley, T., Lichenstein, P., & Stevenson, J. (1999). Sex differences in the etiology of aggressive and nonaggressive antisocial behavior: Results from two twin studies. *Child Development, 70,* 155–68.

Elkind, D. (1967). Egocentrism in adolescence. *Child Development, 38,* 1025–1034.

Elkind, D. (1978). Understanding the young adolescent. *Adolescence, 13,* 127–134.

Elkind, D. (1982). *The hurried child.* Reading, MA: Addison-Wesley.

Elkind, D. (1985). Egocentrism redux. *Developmental Review, 5,* 218–226.

Elkind, D., Barocas, R., & Rosenthal, R. (1968). Combinatorial thinking in adolescents from graded and ungraded classrooms. *Perceptual and Motor Skills, 27,* 1015–1018.

Elkins, I., McGue, M., & Iacono, W. (1997). Genetic and environmental influences on parent-son relationships: Evidence for increasing genetic influence during adolescence. *Developmental Psychology, 33,* 351–363.

Ellickson, P., Bell, R., & McGuigan, K. (1993). Preventing adolescent drug use: Long-term results of a junior high program. *American Journal of Public Health, 83,* 856–861.

Ellickson, P., Saner, H., & McGuigan, K. (1997). Profiles of violent youth: Substance use and other concurrent problems. *American Journal of Public Health, 87,* 985–991.

Elliott, B., & Richards, M. (1991, July). *Children and divorce: Educational performance and behaviour before and after parental separation.* Paper presented at the meetings of the International Society for the Study of Behavioural Development, Minneapolis.

Elliott, D., Huizinga, D., & Menard, S. (1989). *Multiple problem youth: Delinquency, substance abuse, and mental health problems.* New York: Springer-Verlag.

Elliott, D., & Morse, B. (1989). Delinquency and drug use as risk factors in teenage sexual activity. *Youth and Society, 21,* 32–57.

Elliott, D., & Wofford, S. (1991). *Adolescent employment.* Brief prepared for press release available from the authors. Boulder, CO: Institute of Behavioral Science, University of Colorado.

Ellis, B., & Garber, J. (2000). Psychosocial antecedents of variation in girls' pubertal timing: Maternal depression, stepfather presence, and marital and family stress. *Child Development, 71,* 485–501.

Ellis, B., McFadyen-Ketchum, S., Dodge, K., Pettit, G., & Bates, J. (1999). Quality of early family relationships and individual differences in the timing of pubertal maturation in girls: A longitudinal test of an evolutionary model. *Journal of Personality and Social Psychology, 77,* 387–401.

Elmen, J. (1991). Achievement orientation in early adolescence: Developmental patterns and social correlates. *Journal of Early Adolescence, 11,* 125–151.

Elo, I., King, R., & Furstenberg, F., Jr. (1999). Adolescent females: Their sexual partners and the fathers of their children. *Journal of Marriage and the Family, 61,* 74–84.

Ennett, S., & Bauman, K. (1994). The contribution of influence and selection to adolescent peer group homogeneity: The case of adolescent cigarette smoking. *Journal of Personality and Social Psychology, 67*, 653–663.

Ennett, S., & Bauman, K. (1996). Adolescent social networks: School, demographic, and longitudinal considerations. *Journal of Adolescent Research, 11*, 194–215.

Enright, R., Levy, V., Harris, D., & Lapsley, D. (1987). Do economic conditions influence how theorists view adolescents? *Journal of Youth and Adolescence, 16*, 541–560.

Ensminger, M. (1990). Sexual activity and problem behaviors among black, urban adolescents. *Child Development, 61*, 2032–2046.

Ensminger, M., Lamkin, R., & Jacobson, N. (1996). School leaving: A longitudinal perspective including neighborhood effects. *Child Development, 67*, 2400–2416.

Entwisle, D. (1990). Schools and the adolescent. In S. Feldman & G. Elliott (Eds.), *At the threshold: The developing adolescent* (pp. 197–224). Cambridge, MA: Harvard University Press.

Entwisle, D., & Hayduk, L. (1988). Lasting effects of elementary school. *Sociology of Education, 61*, 147–159.

Epstein, J. (1983a). The influence of friends on achievement and affective outcomes. In J. Epstein & N. Karweit (Eds.), *Friends in school* (pp. 177–200). New York: Academic Press.

Epstein, J. (1983b). Selecting friends in contrasting secondary school environments. In J. Epstein & N. Karweit (Eds.), *Friends in school*. New York: Academic Press.

Erel, O., & Burman, B. (1995). Interrelatedness of marital relations and parent-child relations: A meta-analytic review. *Psychological Bulletin, 118*, 108–132.

Erickson, M.F., Sroufe, L.A., & Egeland, B. (1985). The relationship between quality of attachment and behavior problems in preschool in a high-risk sample. Growing points of attachment theory and research. *Monographs of the Society for Research in Child Development, 50*, 147–193.

Erickson, P. (1994). Lessons from a repeat pregnancy prevention program for Hispanic teenage mothers in East Los Angeles. *Family Planning Perspectives, 26*, 174–178.

Erikson, E. (1959). Identity and the life cycle. *Psychological Issues, 1*, 1–171.

Erikson, E. (1963). *Childhood and society*. New York: Norton.

Erikson, E. (1968). *Identity: Youth and crisis*. New York: Norton.

Esbensen, F., Deschenes, E., & Winfree, L., Jr. (1999). Differences between gang girls and gang boys: Results from a multisite survey. *Youth and Society, 31*, 27–53.

Estrada, P. (1995). Adolescents' self-reports of prosocial responses to friends and acquaintances: The role of sympathy-related cognitive, affective, and motivational processes. *Journal of Research on Adolescence, 5*, 173–200.

Evans, D. (1993, March). *A model of structural self-complexity: Its relation to age, symptomatology and self-perception*. Paper presented at the biennial meetings of the Society for Research in Child Development, New Orleans.

Evans, E., Rutberg, J., Sather, C., & Turner, C. (1991). Content analysis of contemporary teen magazines for adolescent females. *Youth and Society, 23*, 99–120.

Evans, M. (1992, March). *Achievement and achievement-related beliefs in Asian and Western contexts: Cultural and gender differences*. Paper presented at the biennial meetings of the Society for Research on Adolescence, Washington.

Eveleth, P., & Tanner, J. (1990). *Worldwide variation in human growth* (2nd ed). New York: Cambridge University Press.

Everett, S., & Price, J. (1995). Students' perceptions of violence in the public schools: The MetLife survey. *Journal of Adolescent Health Care, 17*, 345–352.

Eyre, S., & Millstein, S. (1999). What leads to sex? Adolescent preferred partners and reasons for sex. *Journal of Research on Adolescence, 9*, 277–307.

Fagan, J. & Zimring, F. (Eds.). (2000). *The changing borders of juvenile justice: Transfer of adolescents to the criminal court*. Chicago: University of Chicago Press.

Fagot, B., Pears, K., Capaldi, D., Crosby, L., & Leve, C. (1998). Becoming an adolescent father: Precursors and parenting. *Developmental Psychology, 34*, 1209–1219.

Falk, R., & Wilkening, F. (1998). Children's construction of fair chances: Adjusting probabilities: *Developmental Psychology, 34*, 1340–1357.

Fallon, B. J., & Bowles, T. V. (1997). The effect of family structure and family functioning on adolescents' perceptions of intimate time spent with parents, siblings, and peers. *Journal of Youth and Adolescence, 26*, 25–43.

Fang, X., Stanton, B., Li, X., Feigelman, S., & Baldwin, R. (1998). Similarities in sexual activity and condom use among friends within groups before and after a risk-reduction intervention. *Youth and Society, 29*, 431–450.

Farel, A. (1982). *Early adolescence and religion: A status study*. Carrboro, NC: Center for Early Adolescence.

Farkas, G., Grobe, R., & Shuan, Y. (1990). Cultural resources and school success: Gender, ethnicity, and poverty groups within an urban school district. *American Sociological Review, 55*, 127–142.

Farrel, A. D., & White, K. S. (1998). Peer influences and drug use among urban adolescents: Family structure and parent-adolescent relationship as protective factors. *Journal of Consulting and Clinical Psychology, 66*, 248–258.

Farrell, A., & Danish, S. (1993). Peer drug associations and emotional restraint: Causes or consequences of adolescents' drug use? *Journal of Consulting and Clinical Psychology, 43*, 522–527.

Farrell, A., & Meyer, A. (1997). The effectiveness of a school-based curriculum for reducing violence among urban sixth-grade students. *American Journal of Public Health, 87*, 979–984.

Farrell, A., Danish, S., & Howard, C. (1992). Relationship between drug use and other problem behaviors in urban adolescents. *Journal of Consulting and Clinical Psychology, 60*, 705–712.

Farrell, M., & Rosenberg, S. (1981). *Men at midlife*. Boston: Auburn House.

Farrington, D. (1989). Early predictors of adolescent aggression and adult violence. *Violence and Victims, 4*, 79–100.

Farrington, D. (1991). Childhood aggression and adult violence: Early precursors and later-life outcomes. In D. Pepler & K. Rubin (Eds.). *The development and treatment of childhood aggression* (pp. 5–29). Hillsdale, NJ: Erlbaum.

Farrington, D., & West, D. (1991). The Cambridge Study in Delinquent Development: A long-term follow-up of 411 London males. In H. Kerner & G. Kaiser (Eds.), *Criminality: Personality, behavior, and life history* (pp. 115–138). New York: Springer Verlag.

Fasick, F. (1994). On the "invention" of adolescence. *Journal of Early Adolescence, 14*, 6–23.

Fauber, R., Forehand, R., McCombs, A., & Wierson, M. (1990). A mediational model of the impact of marital conflict on adolescent adjustment in intact and divorced families: The role of disrupted parenting. *Child Development, 61*, 1112–1123.

Faulkner, A., & Cranston, K. (1998). Correlates of same-sex sexual behavior in a random sample of Massachusetts high school students. *American Journal of Public Health, 88*, 262–266.

Featherman, D. (1980). Schooling and occupational careers: Constancy and change in worldly success. In O. Brim, Jr., & J. Kagan (Eds.), *Constancy and change in human development*. Cambridge, MA: Harvard University Press.

Federal Bureau of Investigation. (2000). *The school shooter: A threat assessment perspective*. Washington, DC: Author.

Federal Bureau of Investigation. (1999). *Uniform crime reports for the United States*. Washington, D.C.: U.S. Government Printing Office.

Federal Interagency Forum on Child and Family Statistics. (1997). *America's children: Key national indicators of well-being*. Washington, DC: Author.

Feingold, A. (1993). Cognitive gender differences: A developmental perspective. *Sex Roles, 29*, 91–112.

Feiring, C. (1993, March). *Developing concepts of romance from 15 to 18 years*. Paper presented at the biennial meetings of the Society for Research in Child Development, New Orleans.

Feiring, C. (1996). Concepts of romance in 15-year-old adolescents. *Journal of Research on Adolescence, 6*, 181–200.

Feiring, C. (1999a). Gender identity and the development of romantic relationships in adolescence. In W. Furman, B. Brown, & C. Feiring (Eds.), *Contemporary perspectives on adolescent romantic relationship* (pp. 211–232). New York: Cambridge University Press.

Feiring, C. (1999b). Other-sex friendship networks and the development of romantic relationships in adolescence, *Journal of Youth and Adolescence, 28*, 495–512.

Feiring, C., & Lewis, M. (1991). The transition from middle childhood to early adolescence: Sex differences in the social network and perceived self-competence. *Sex Roles, 24,* 489–510.

Feiring, C., & Lewis, M. (1993). Do mothers know their teenagers' friends? Implications for individuation in early adolescence. *Journal of Youth and Adolescence, 22,* 337–354.

Feld, B. (1997). Juvenile and criminal justice systems' responses to youth violence. In M. Tonry & M. Moore (Eds.), *Crime and justice* (Vol. 24). Chicago: University of Chicago Press.

Feldman, C., Stone, A., & Renderer, B. (1990). Stage, transfer, and academic achievement in dialect-speaking Hawaiian adolescents. *Child Development, 61,* 472–484.

Feldman, S., & Fisher, L. (1997). The effect of parents' marital satisfaction on young adults' adaptation: A longitudinal study. *Journal of Research on Adolescence, 7,* 55–80.

Feldman, S., & Gehring, T. (1988). Changing perceptions of family cohesion and power across adolescence. *Child Development, 59,* 1034–1045.

Feldman, S., & Quatman, T. (1988). Factors influencing age expectations for adolescent autonomy: A study of early adolescents and parents. *Journal of Early Adolescence, 8,* 325–343.

Feldman, S., & Rosenthal, D. (1994). Culture makes a difference . . . or does it? A comparison of adolescents in Hong Kong, Australia, and the United States. In R. Silbereisen & E. Todt (Eds.), *Adolescence in context: The interplay of family, school, peers, and work in adjustment* (pp. 25–45). New York: Springer-Verlag.

Feldman, S., & Rosenthal, D. (2000). The effect of communication characteristics on family members' perceptions of parents as sex educators. *Journal of Research on Adolescence, 10,* 119–150.

Feldman, S., & Wentzel, K. (1995). Relations of marital satisfaction to peer outcomes in adolescent boys: A longitudinal study. *Journal of Early Adolescence, 15,* 220–237.

Feldman, S., & Wood, D. (1994). Parents' expectations for preadolescent sons' behavioral autonomy: A longitudinal study of correlates and outcomes. *Journal of Research on Adolescence, 4,* 45–70.

Feldman, S., Rosenthal, D., Brown, N., & Canning, R. (1995). Predicting sexual experience in adolescent boys from peer rejection and acceptance during childhood. *Journal of Research on Adolescence, 5,* 387–411.

Felner, R., Brand, S., DuBois, D., Adan, A., Mulhall, P., & Evans, E. (1995). Socioeconomic disadvantage, proximal environmental experiences, and socio-emotional and academic adjustment in early adolescence: Investigation of a mediated effects model. *Child Development, 66,* 774–792.

Felson, R., Liska, A., South, S., & McNulty, T. (1994). The subculture of violence and delinquency: Individual vs. school context effects. *Social Forces, 73,* 155–173.

Felson, R., & Zielinski, M. (1989). Children's self-esteem and parental support. *Journal of Marriage and the Family, 51,* 727–735.

Fennema, E., & Sherman, J. (1977). Sex-related differences in mathematics achievement, spatial visualization, and affective factors. *American Educational Research Journal, 14,* 51–71.

Fergusson, D., & Horwood, L. (1995). Early disruptive behavior, IQ, and later school achievement and delinquent behavior. *Journal of Abnormal Child Psychology, 23,* 183–199.

Fergusson, D., & Lynskey, M. (1996). Alcohol misuse and adolescent sexual behaviors and risk taking. *Pediatrics, 98,* 91–96.

Fergusson, D., Lynskey, M., & Horwood, L. (1996a). Factors associated with continuity and changes in disruptive behavior patterns between childhood and adolescence. *Journal of Abnormal Child Psychology, 24,* 533–553.

Fergusson, D., Lynskey, M., & Horwood, L. (1996b). The short-term consequences of early-onset cannabis use. *Journal of Abnormal Child Psychology, 24,* 499–512.

Fergusson, D., Woodward, L., & Horwood, L. (1999). Childhood peer relationship problems and young people's involvement with deviant peers in adolescence. *Journal of Abnormal Child Psychology, 27,* 357–369.

Ferrell, J. (1995). Urban graffiti: Crime, control, and resistance. *Youth and Society, 27,* 73–92.

Ferrell, M., Tolone, W., & Walsh, R. (1977). Maturational and societal changes in the sexual double-standard: A panel analysis (1967–1971; 1970–1974). *Journal of Marriage and the Family, 39,* 255–271.

Field, T., Greenwald, P., Morrow, C., Healy, B., Foster, T., Guthertz, M., & Frost, P. (1992). Behavior state matching during interactions of preadolescent friends versus acquaintances. *Developmental Psychology, 28,* 242–250.

Filardo, E. (1996). Gender patterns in African American and white adolescents' social interactions in same-race, mixed-gender groups. *Journal of Personality and Social Psychology, 71,* 71–82.

Fincham, F. (1994). Understanding the association between marital conflict and child adjustment: Overview. *Journal of Family Psychology, 8,* 123–127.

Fine, G. (1981). Friends, impression management, and preadolescent behavior. In S. Asher & J. Gottman (Eds.), *The development of children's friendships.* Cambridge, England: Cambridge University Press.

Fine, G., Mortimer, J., & Roberts, D. (1990). Leisure, work, and the mass media. In S. Feldman & G. Elliott (Eds.), *At the threshold: The developing adolescent* (pp. 225–252). Cambridge, MA: Harvard University Press.

Fine, M., & Kurdek, L. (1995). Relation between marital quality and (step)parent-child relationship quality for parents and stepparents in stepfamilies. *Journal of Family Psychology, 9,* 216–223.

Finken, L., & Jacobs, J. (1996). Consultant choice across decision contexts: Are abortion decisions different? *Journal of Adolescent Research, 11,* 235–260.

Finn, C., Jr. (1991). *We must take charge: Our schools and our future.* New York: Free Press.

Finnegan, R., & Perry, D. (1993, March). *Preadolescents' self-reported attachments to their mothers and their social behavior with peers.* Paper presented at the biennial meetings of the Society for Research in Child Development, New Orleans.

Fischoff, B. (1988). Judgment and decision making. In R. Sternberg & E. Smith (Eds.), *The psychology of human thought* (pp. 153–187). New York: Cambridge University Press.

Fischoff, B., & Quadrel, M. (1995). Adolescent alcohol decisions. In G. Boyd, J. Howard, & R. Zucker (Eds.), *Alcohol problems among adolescents: Current directions in prevention research* (pp. 59–84). Hillsdale, NJ: Erlbaum.

Fisher, M., Golden, N., Katzman, D., Kriepe, R., Rees, J., Schebendach, J., Sigman, G., Ammerman, S., & Hoberman, H. (1995). Eating disorders in adolescents: A background paper. *Journal of Adolescent Health, 16,* 420–437.

Fisher, T. (1989). An extension of the findings of Moore, Peterson, and Furstenberg [1986] regarding family sexual communication and adolescent sexual behavior. *Journal of Marriage and the Family, 51,* 637–639.

Fitzpatrick, K. (1993). Exposure to violence and the presence of depression among low-income, African-American youth. *Journal of Consulting and Clinical Psychology, 61,* 528–531.

Fitzpatrick, K., & Yoels, W. (1992). Policy, school structure, and sociodemographic effects on statewide high school dropout rates. *Sociology of Education, 65,* 76–93.

Flammer, A., Alasker, F., & Noack, P. (1999). Time use by adolescents in an international perspective. I: The case of leisure activities. In F. Alasker & A. Flammer (Eds.) *The adolescent experience: European and American adolescents in the 1990s* (pp. 33–60). Hillsdale, NJ: Erlbaum.

Flanagan, C. (1990). Change in family work status: Effects on parent-adolescent decision making. *Child Development, 61,* 163–177.

Flanagan, C., & Galay, L. (1995). Reframing the meaning of "political" in research with adolescents. *Perspectives on Political Science, 24,* 34–41.

Flanagan, C., & Tucker, C. (1999). Adolescents' explanations for political issues: Concordance with their views of self and society. *Developmental Psychology, 35,* 1198–1209.

Flannery, D., Rowe, D., & Gulley, B. (1993). Impact of pubertal status, timing, and age on adolescent sexual experience and delinquency. *Journal of Adolescent Research, 8,* 21–40.

Flannery, D., Torquati, J., & Lindemeier, L. (1994). The method and meaning of emotional expression and experience during adolescence. *Journal of Adolescent Research, 9,* 8–27.

Flannery, D., Vazsonyi, A., & Rowe, D. (1996). Caucasian and Hispanic early adolescent substance use: Parenting, personality, and school adjustment. *Journal of Early Adolescence, 16,* 71–89.

Flannery, D., Vazsonyi, A., Torquati, J., & Fridrich, A. (1994). Ethnic and gender differences in risk for early adolescent substance use. *Journal of Youth and Adolescence, 23,* 195–213.

Flannery, D., Vazsonyi, A., Torquati, J., & Rowe, D. (1993, March). *Parenting, personality, and school influences on substance use in Caucasian and Hispanic early adolescents.* Paper presented at the biennial meetings of the Society for Research in Child Development, New Orleans.

Fletcher, A., Darling, N., Steinberg, L., & Dornbusch, S. (1995). The company they keep: Relation of adolescents' adjustment and behavior to their friends' perceptions of authoritative parenting in the social network. *Developmental Psychology, 31,* 300–310.

Fletcher, A., Elder, G., Jr., & Mekos, D. (2000). Parental influences on adolescent involvement in community activities. *Journal of Research on Adolescence, 10,* 29–48.

Flewelling, R., & Bauman, K. (1990). Family structure as a predictor of initial substance use and sexual intercourse in early adolescence. *Journal of Marriage and the Family, 52,* 171–181.

Flieller, A. (1999). Comparison of the development of formal thought in adolescent cohorts aged 10 to 15 years (1967–1996 and 1972–1993). *Developmental Psychology, 35,* 1048–1058.

Flynn, B., Worden, J., Secker-Walker, R., Pirie, P., Badger, G., Carpenter, J., & Geller, B. (1994). Mass media and school interventions for cigarette smoking prevention: Effects 2 years after completion. *American Journal of Public Health, 84,* 1148–1150.

Flynn, K., & Fitzgibbon, M. (1996). Body image ideals of low-income African American mothers and their preadolescent daughters. *Journal of Youth and Adolescence, 25,* 615–630.

Ford, C., & Beach, F. (1951). *Patterns of sexual behavior.* New York: Harper & Row.

Ford, D., & Harris, J. I. (1996). Perceptions and attitudes of black students toward school, achievement, and other educational variables. *Child Development, 67,* 1141–1152.

Ford, M. (1982). Social cognition and social competence in adolescence. *Developmental Psychology, 18,* 323–340.

Ford, M. (1987). Processes contributing to adolescent social competence. In M. Ford & D. Ford (Eds.), *Humans as self-constructing living systems.* Hillsdale, NJ: Erlbaum. pp. 199–233.

Fordham, C., & Ogbu, J. (1986). Black students' school success: Coping with the burden of "acting white." *Urban Review, 18,* 176–206.

Forehand, R., Armistead, L., & David, C. (1997). Is adolescent adjustment following parental divorce a function of predivorce adjustment? *Journal of Abnormal Child Psychology, 25,* 157–164.

Forehand, R., Biggar, H., & Kotchick, B. (1998). Cumulative risk across family stressors: Short- and long-term effects for adolescents. *Journal of Abnormal Child Psychology, 26,* 119–128.

Forehand, R., Miller, K., Dutra, R., & Chance, M. (1997). Role of parenting in adolescent deviant behavior: Replication across and within two ethnic groups. *Journal of Consulting and Clinical Psychology, 65,* 1036–1041.

Forehand, R., Neighbors, B., Devine, D., & Armistead, L. (1994). Interparental conflict and parental divorce: The additive, relative, and interactive effects on adolescents across four years. *Family Relations, 43,* 387–393.

Forehand, R., Thomas, A. M., Wierson, M., Brody, G., & Fauber, R. (1990). Role of maternal functioning and parenting skills in adolescent functioning following parental divorce. *Journal of Abnormal Psychology, 99,* 278–283.

Forehand, R., Wierson, M., Thomas, A., Fauber, R., Armistead, L., Kemptom, T., & Long, N. (1991). A short-term longitudinal examination of young adolescent functioning following divorce: The role of family factors. *Journal of Abnormal Child Psychology, 19,* 97–111.

Forgatch, M., DeGarmo, D., & Knutson, N. (1994, February). *Transitions within transitions: The impact of adolescence and family structure on boys' antisocial behavior.* Paper presented at the biennial meetings of the Society for Research on Adolescence, San Diego.

Forgatch, M., & Stoolmiller, M. (1994). Emotions as contexts for adolescent delinquency. *Journal of Research on Adolescence, 4,* 601–614.

Formoso, D., Ruiz, S., & Gonzales, N. (1997, March). *Parent-adolescent conflict: Resolution strategies reported with African-American, Mexican-American, and Anglo-American families.* Paper presented at the SRCD, Washington.

Forster, J., Murray, D., Wolfson, M., Blaine, T., Wagenaar, A., & Hennrikus, D. (1998). The effects of community policies to reduce youth access to tobacco. *American Journal of Public Health, 88,* 1193–1198.

Fortenberry, J., Costa, F., Jessor, R., & Donovan, J. (1997). Contraceptive behavior and adolescent lifestyles: A structural modeling approach. *Journal of Research on Adolescence, 7,* 307–329.

Foshee, V., Bauman, K., Arriaga, X., Helms, R., Koch, G., & Linder, G. (1998). An evaluation of "Safe Dates," an adolescent dating violence prevention program. *American Journal of Public Health, 88,* 45–50.

Foster, E. (1995). Why teens do not benefit from work experience programs: Evidence from brother comparisons. *Journal of Policy Analysis and Management, 14,* 393–414.

Foster, L., & Ritter, J. (1995, March). *Independence from parents as a predictor of happiness and life satisfaction.* Paper presented at the Society for Research in Child Development, Indianapolis.

Fowler, J. (1981). *Stages of faith.* New York: Harper & Row.

Frank, S., & Jackson, S. (1996). Family experiences as moderators of the relationship between eating symptoms and personality disturbance. *Journal of Youth and Adolescence, 25,* 55–72.

Frank, S., Pirsch, L., & Wright, V. (1990). Late adolescents' perceptions of their relationships with their parents: Relationships among deidealization, autonomy, relatedness, and insecurity and implications for adolescent adjustment and ego identity status. *Journal of Youth and Adolescence, 19,* 571–588.

Franklin, K., Janoff-Bulman, R., & Roberts, J. (1990). Long-term impact of parental divorce on optimism and trust: Changes in general assumptions or narrow beliefs? *Journal of Personality and Social Psychology, 59,* 743–755.

Franzoi, S., Davis, M., & Vasquez-Suson, K. (1994). Two social worlds: Social correlates and stability of adolescent status groups. *Journal of Personality and Social Psychology, 67,* 462–473.

Freeman, R., & Wise, D. (Eds.). (1982). *The youth labor market problem: Its nature, causes, and consequences.* Chicago: University of Chicago Press.

French, D., Conrad, J., & Turner, T. (1995). Adjustment of antisocial and nonantisocial rejected adolescents. *Development and Psychopathology, 7,* 857–874.

French, S., Story, M., Downes, B., Resnick, M., & Blum, R. (1995). Frequent dieting among adolescents: Psychosocial and health behavior correlates. *American Journal of Public Health, 85,* 695–701.

Freud, A. (1958). Adolescence. *Psychoanalytic Study of the Child, 13,* 255–278.

Freud, S. (1938). *An outline of psychoanalysis.* London: Hogarth Press.

Fried, M., & Fried, M. (1980). *Transitions: Four rituals in eight cultures.* New York: Norton.

Friedenberg, E. (1959). *The vanishing adolescent.* Boston: Beacon Press.

Friedenberg, E. (1967). *Coming of age in America.* New York: Vintage Books.

Friedman, M., & Brownell, K. (1995). Psychological correlates of obesity: Moving to the next research generation. *Psychological Bulletin, 117,* 3–29.

Frisch, R. (1983). Fatness, puberty, and fertility: The effects of nutrition and physical training on menarche and ovulation. In J. Brooks-Gunn & A. Petersen (Eds.), *Girls at puberty.* New York: Plenum.

Frome, P., & Eccles, J. (1996, March). *Gender-role identity and selfesteem.* Paper presented at the biennial meetings of the Society for Research on Adolescence, Boston.

Frost, J., & Forrest, J. (1995). Understanding the impact of effective teenage pregnancy prevention programs. *Family Planning Perspectives, 27,* 188–195.

Fuhrman, T., & Holmbeck, G. (1995). A contextual-moderator analysis of emotional autonomy and adjustment in adolescence. *Child Development, 66,* 793–811.

Fuligni, A. (1994, February). *Academic achievement and motivation among Asian-American and European-American early adolescents.* Paper presented at the biennial meetings of the Society for Research on Adolescence, San Diego.

Fuligni, A. (1997). The academic achievement of adolescents from immigrant families: The roles of family background, attitudes, and behavior. *Child Development, 68,* 351–363.

Fuligni, A. (1998). Authority, autonomy, and parent-adolescent conflict and cohesion: A study of adolescents from Mexican, Chinese, Filipino, and European backgrounds. *Developmental Psychology, 34,* 782–792.

Fuligni, A., & Eccles, J. (1992, March). *The effects of early adolescent peer orientation on academic achievement and deviant behavior in high school.* Paper presented at the biennial meetings of the Society for Research on Adolescence, Washington.

Fuligni, A., & Eccles, J. (1993). Perceived parent-child relationships and early adolescents' orientation toward peers. *Developmental Psychology, 29*, 622–632.

Fuligni, A., Eccles, J., & Barber, B. (1995). The long-term effects of seventh-grade ability grouping in mathematics. *Journal of Early Adolescence, 15*, 58–89.

Fuligni, A., & Stevenson, H. (1995). Time-use and mathematics achievement among American, Chinese, and Japanese high school students. *Child Development, 66*, 830–842.

Fuligni, A., Tseng, V., & Lam, M. (1999). Attitudes toward family obligations among American adolescents from Asian, Latin American, and European backgrounds. *Child Development, 70*, 1030–1044.

Fulton, A. (1997). Identity status, religious orientation, and prejudice. *Journal of Youth and Adolescence, 26*, 1–11.

Funk, J., Flores, G., Buchman, D., & Germann, J. (1999). Rating electronic games: Violence is in the eye of the beholder. *Youth and Society, 30*, 283–312.

Furbey, M., & Beyth-Marom, R. (1992). Risk-taking in adolescence: A decision-making perspective. *Developmental Review, 12*, 1–44.

Furman, B., Brown, B., & Feiring, C. (Eds.). (1999). *Contemporary perspectives on adolescent romantic relationships.* New York: Cambridge University Press.

Furman, W., & Buhrmester, D. (1985). Children's perceptions of the personal relationships in their social networks. *Developmental Psychology, 21*, 1016–1024.

Furman, W., & Simon, V. (1994). Cognitive representations of adolescent romantic relationships. In W. Furman, B. Brown, & C. Feiring (Ed.), *Contemporary perspectives on adolescent romantic relationships* (pp. 175–98). New York: Cambridge University Press.

Furman, W., & Wehner, E. (1994). Romantic views: Toward a theory of adolescent romantic relationships. In R. Montemayor (Ed.), *Advances in adolescent development*, Vol. 3 (pp. 168–195). Newbury Park, Calif.: Sage.

Furstenberg, F., Jr. (1990). Coming of age in a changing family system. In S. Feldman & G. Elliott (Eds.), *At the threshold: The developing adolescent* (pp. 147–170). Cambridge, MA: Harvard University Press.

Furstenberg, F., Jr. (1996, March). *Family management of adolescent success in inner-city Philadelphia.* Paper presented at the biennial meetings of the Society for Research on Adolescence, Boston.

Furstenberg, F., Jr., Brooks-Gunn, J., & Chase-Landsdale, L. (1989). Teenaged pregnancy and childbearing. *American Psychologist, 44*, 313–320.

Furstenberg, F., Jr., Brooks-Gunn, J., & Morgan, S. (1987). *Adolescent mothers in later life.* New York: Cambridge University Press.

Furstenberg, F., Jr., Cook, T., Eccles, J., Elder, G., Jr., & Sameroff, A. (1999). *Managing to make it: Urban families and adolescent success.* Chicago: University of Chicago Press.

Furstenberg, F., Jr., Geitz, L., Teitler, J., & Weiss, C. (1997). Does condom availability make a difference? An evaluation of Philadelphia's health resource centers. *Family Planning Perspectives, 29*, 123–127.

Furstenberg, F., Jr., Morgan, S. P., & Allison, P. (1987). Paternal participation and children's well-being after marital dissolution. *American Sociological Review, 52*, 695–701.

Fussell, M., & Greene, M. (in press). Demographic trends affecting youth around the world. *Journal of Research on Adolescence.*

Futterman, D., Hein, K., Reuben, N., Dell, R., & Shaffer, N. (1993). Human immunodeficiency virus–infected adolescents: The first 50 patients in a New York City program. *Pediatrics, 91*, 730–735.

Gaddis, A., & Brooks-Gunn, J. (1985). The male experience of pubertal change. *Journal of Youth and Adolescence, 14*, 61–70.

Gagne, E. (1985). *The cognitive psychology of school learning.* Boston: Little, Brown.

Gagnon, J. (1972). The creation of the sexual in early adolescence. In J. Kagan & R. Coles (Eds.), *Twelve to sixteen: Early adolescence.* New York: Norton.

Galambos, N., Almeida, D., & Petersen, A. (1990). Masculinity, femininity, and sex role attitudes in early adolescence: Exploring gender intensification. *Child Development, 61*, 1905–1914.

Galambos, N., & Garbarino, J. (1985). Adjustment of unsupervised children in a rural setting. *Journal of Genetic Psychology, 146*, 227–231.

Galambos, N., & Maggs, J. (1991). Out-of-school care of young adolescents and self-reported behavior. *Developmental Psychology, 27*, 644–655.

Galambos, N., & Silbereisen, R. (1987). Income change, parental life outlook, and adolescent expectations for job success. *Journal of Marriage and the Family, 49*, 141–149.

Galambos, N., Kolaric, G., & Maggs, J. (1994, February). *Adolescents' subjective age: An indicator of phenomenological maturity.* Paper presented at the biennial meetings of the Society for Research on Adolescence, San Diego.

Galambos, N., Kolaric, G., Sears, H., & Maggs, J. (1999). Adolescents' subjective age: An indicator of perceived maturity. *Journal of Research on Adolescence, 9*, 309–337.

Galambos, N., Sears, H., Almeida, D., & Kolaric, G. (1995). Parents' work overload and problem behavior in young adolescents. *Journal of Research on Adolescence, 5*, 201–223.

Galen, B., & Underwood, M. (1997). A developmental investigation of social aggression among children. *Developmental Psychology, 33*, 589–600.

Gallatin, J. (1975). *Adolescence and individuality.* New York: Harper & Row.

Gallup, G., & Bezilla, R. (1992). *The religious life of young Americans.* Princeton, NJ: Gallup Institute.

Galotti, K., Komatsu, L., & Voelz, S. (1997). Children's differential performance on deductive and inductive syllogisms. *Developmental Psychology, 33*, 70–78.

Gamoran, A. (1987). The stratification of high school learning opportunities. *Sociology of Education, 60*, 135–155.

Gamoran, A. (1992). The variable effects of high school tracking. *American Sociological Review, 57*, 812–828.

Gamoran, A. (1993). Alternative uses of ability grouping in secondary schools: Can we bring high-quality instruction to low-ability classes? *American Journal of Education, 102*, 1–22.

Gamoran, A. (1996). Curriculum standardization and equality of opportunity in Scottish secondary education: 1984–90. *Sociology of Education, 69*, 1–21.

Gamoran, A., & Mare, R. (1989). Secondary school tracking and educational inequality: Compensation, reinforcement, or neutrality? *American Journal of Sociology, 94*, 1146–1183.

Gans, J. (1990). *America's adolescents: How healthy are they?* Chicago: American Medical Association.

Garbarino, J., & Asp, C. (1981). *Successful schools and competent students.* Lexington, MA: Lexington Books.

Garbarino, J., Burston, N., Raber, S., Russell, R., & Crouter, A. (1978). The social maps of children approaching adolescence: Studying the ecology of youth development. *Journal of Youth and Adolescence, 7*, 417–428.

Garbarino, J., Wilson, J., & Garbarino, J. (1986). The adolescent runaway. In J. Garbarino & J. Sebes (Eds.), *Troubled youth, troubled families* (pp. 315–351). New York: Aldine de Gruyter.

Garber, J., Weiss, B., & Shanley, N. (1993). Cognitions, depressive symptoms, and development in adolescents. *Journal of Abnormal Psychology, 102*, 47–57.

Garcia Coll, C., Lamberty, G., Jenkins, R., McAdoo, H., Crnic, K., Wasik, B., & Vazquez Garcia, H. (1996). An integrative model for the study of developmental competencies in minority children. *Child Development, 67*, 1891–1914.

Gardner, H. (1983). *Frames of mind.* New York: Basic Books.

Gardner, R., Friedman, B., & Jackson, N. (1999). Body size estimations, body dissatisfaction, and ideal size preferences in children six through thirteen. *Journal of Youth and Adolescence, 28*(5), 603–618.

Gardner, W., & Herman, J. (1990). Adolescents' AIDS risk taking: A rational choice perspective. In W. Gardner, S. Millstein, & B. Wilcox (Eds.), *Adolescents in the AIDS epidemic* (pp. 17–34). San Francisco: Jossey-Bass.

Gardner, W., Scherer, D., & Tester, M. (1989). Asserting scientific authority: Cognitive development and adolescent legal rights. *American Psychologist, 44*, 895–902.

Gargiulo, J., Attie, I., Brooks-Gunn, J., & Warren, M. (1987). Girls' dating behavior as a function of social context and maturation. *Developmental Psychology, 23*, 730–737.

Garland, A., & Zigler, E. (1993). Adolescent suicide prevention: Current research and social policy implications. *American Psychologist, 48*, 169–182.

Garnefski, N., & Diekstra, R. (1997). "Comorbidity" of behavioral, emotional, and cognitive problems in adolescence. *Journal of Youth and Adolescence, 26,* 321–338.

Garnier, H., Stein, J., & Jacobs, J. (1997). The process of dropping out of high school: A 19-year perspective. *American Educational Research Journal, 34,* 395–419.

Gauze, C., Bukowski, W., Aquan-Assee, J., & Sippola, L. (1996). Interactions between family environment and friendship and associations with self-perceived well-being during early adolescence. *Child Development, 67,* 2201–2216.

Gavin, L., & Furman, W. (1989). Age differences in adolescents' perceptions of their peer groups. *Developmental Psychology, 25,* 827–834.

Gavin, L., & Furman, W. (1996). Adolescent girls' relationships with mothers and best friends. *Child Development, 67,* 375–386.

Gayle, H., Keeling, R., Garcia-Tunon, M., Kilbourne, B., Narkunas, J., Ingram, F., Rogers, M., & Curran, J. (1990). Prevalence of the human immunodeficiency virus among university students. *New England Journal of Medicine, 323,* 1538–1541.

Ge, X., & Conger, R. (1995, March). *Parents' depressive symptoms, hostile behaviors, and adolescent degressive symptoms.* Paper presented at the Society for Research in Child Development, Indianapolis.

Ge, X., Best, K., Conger, R., & Simons, R. (1994, February). *Parenting behaviors and the occurrence and co-occurrence of adolescent depressive symptoms and conduct problems.* Paper presented at the biennial meetings of the Society for Research on Adolescence, San Diego.

Ge, X., Best, K., Conger, R., & Simons, R. (1996). Parenting behaviors and the occurrence and co-occurrence of adolescent depressive symptoms and conduct problems. *Developmental Psychology, 32,* 717–731.

Ge, X., Conger, R., & Elder, G., Jr. (1996). Coming of age too early: Pubertal influences on girls' vulnerability to psychological distress. *Child Development, 67,* 3386–3400.

Ge, X., Conger, R., Cadoret, R., Neiderhiser, J., Yates, W., Throughton, E., & Stewart, M. (1996). The developmental interface between nature and nurture: A mutual influence model of child antisocial behavior and parent behaviors. *Developmental Psychology, 32,* 574–589.

Ge, X., Conger, R., Lorenz, F., Shanahan, M., & Elder, G., Jr. (1995). Mutual influences in parent and adolescent psychological distress. *Developmental Psychology, 31,* 406–419.

Ge, X., Lorenz, F., Conger, R., Elder, G., Jr., & Simons, R. (1994). Trajectories of stressful life events and depressive symptoms during adolescence. *Developmental Psychology, 30,* 467–483.

Gecas, V., & Seff, M. (1990). Families and adolescents: A review of the 1980s. *Journal of Marriage and the Family, 52,* 941–958.

Gerhardt, C., Compas, B., Connor, J., & Achenbach, T. (1999). Association of a mixed anxiety-depression syndrome and symptoms of major depressive disorder during adolescence. *Journal of Youth and Adolescence, 28,* 305–323.

Gerrard, M. (1987). Sex, sex guilt, and contraceptive use revisited: The 1980s. *Journal of Personality and Social Psychology, 52,* 975–980.

Gerrard, M., Gibbons, F., & Bushman, B. (1996). Relation between perceived vulnerability to HIV and precautionary sexual behavior. *Psychological Bulletin, 119,* 390–409.

Gest, S. (1997). Behavioral inhibition: Stability and associations with adaptation from childhood to early adulthood. *Journal of Personality and Social Psychology, 72,* 467–475.

Gfellner, B. (1994). A matched-group comparison of drug use and problem behavior among Canadian Indian and white adolescents. *Journal of Early Adolescence, 14,* 24–48.

Gibbons, F., Benbow, C., & Gerrard, M. (1994). From top dog to bottom half: Social comparison strategies in response to poor performance. *Journal of Personality and Social Psychology, 67,* 638–652.

Gil, A., Vega, W., & Dimas, J. (1994). Acculturative stress and personal adjustment among Hispanic adolescent boys. *Journal of Community Psychology, 22,* 43–54.

Gilligan, C. (1982). *In a different voice.* Cambridge, MA: Harvard University Press.

Gilligan, C. (1993). Joining the resistance: Psychology, politics, and girls. In L. Weis & M. Fine (Eds.), *Beyond silenced voices* (pp. 143–168). Albany: SUNY Press.

Gilligan, C., Lyons, N., & Hanmer, T. (Eds.). (1990). *Making connections: The relational worlds of adolescent girls at Emma Willard School.* Cambridge, MA: Harvard University Press.

Gillmore, M., Hawkins, J., Catalano, R., Jr., Day, L., Moore, M., & Abbott, R. (1991). Structure of problem behaviors in preadolescence. *Journal of Consulting and Clinical Psychology, 59,* 499–506.

Gillmore, M., Lewis, S., Lohr, M., Spencer, M., & White, T. (1997). Repeat pregnancies among adolescent mothers. *Journal of Marriage and the Family, 59,* 536–550.

Gillmore, M., Morrison, D., Lowery, C., & Baker, S. (1994). Beliefs about condoms and their association with intentions to use condoms among youths in detention. *Journal of Adolescent Health, 15,* 228–237.

Gillock, K., & Reyes, O. (1996). High school transition-related changes in urban minority students' academic performance and perceptions of self and school environment. *Journal of Community Psychology, 24,* 245–261.

Gilpin, E. A., Choi, W. S., Berry, C., & Pierce, J. P. (1999). How many adolescents start smoking each day in the United States? *Journal of Adolescent Health, 25,* 248–255.

Gilsanz, V., Roe, T., Mora, S., Costin, G., & Goodman, W. (1991). Changes in vertebral bone density in black girls and white girls during childhood and puberty. *New England Journal of Medicine, 325,* 1597–1600.

Ginsburg, G., & Bronstein, P. (1993). Family factors related to children's intrinsic/extrinsic motivational orientation and academic performance. *Child Development, 64,* 1461–1474.

Ginzberg, E. (1977). The job problem. *Scientific American, 237,* 43–51.

Giordano, P. (1995). The wider circle of friends in adolescence. *American Journal of Sociology, 101,* 661–697.

Gittler, J., Quigley-Rick, M., & Saks, M. (1990). *Adolescent health care decision making: The law and public policy.* Washington, DC: Carnegie Council on Adolescent Development.

Gjerde, P. (1995, March). *A typological analysis of girls' personality: A longitudinal study of developmental pathways.* Paper presented at the Society for Research in Child Development, Indianapolis.

Gjerde, P., Block, J., & Block, J. (1988). Depressive symptoms and personality during late adolescence: Gender differences in the externalization-internalization of symptom expression. *Journal of Abnormal Psychology, 97,* 475–486.

Gladstone, T., & Kaslow, N. (1995). Depression and attributions in children and adolescents: A meta-analytic review. *Journal of Abnormal Child Psychology, 23,* 597–606.

Glasgow, K., Dornbusch, S., Troyer, L., Steinberg, L., & Ritter, P. (1997). Parenting styles, adolescents' attributions, and educational outcomes in nine heterogeneous high schools. *Child Development, 68,* 507–529.

Glazer, R., & Bassok, M. (1989). *Learning theory and the study of instruction.* Annual Review of Psychology, 40. Palo Alto, CA: Annual Reviews.

Glei, D. (1999). Measuring contraceptive use patterns among teenage and adult women. *Family Planning Perspectives, 31,* 73–80.

Glenbard East Echo. (1984). *Teenagers themselves.* New York: Adama Books.

Glover, R., & Marshall, R. (1993). Improving the school-to-work transition of American adolescents. *Teachers College Record, 94,* 588–610.

Gold, M., & Yanof, D. (1985). Mothers, daughters, and girlfriends. *Journal of Personality and Social Psychology, 49,* 654–659.

Goleman, D. (1995). *Emotional intelligence.* New York: Bantam.

Golombok, S., & Tasker, F. (1996). Do parents influence the sexual orientation of their children? Findings from a longitudinal study of lesbian families. *Developmental Psychology, 32,* 3–11.

Gondoli, D., & Silverberg, S. (1997). Maternal emotional distress and diminished responsiveness: The mediating role of parenting efficacy and parental perspective taking. *Developmental Psychology, 33,* 861–868.

Gonzales, N., Cauce, A., Friedman, R., & Mason, C. (1996). Family, peer, and neighborhood influences on academic achievement among African-American adolescents: One-year prospective effects. *American Journal of Community Psychology, 24,* 365–387.

Gonzales, N., Cauce, A., & Mason, C. (1996). Interobserver agreement in the assessment of parental behavior and parent-adolescent conflict: African American mothers, daughters, and independent observers. *Child Development, 67,* 1483–1498.

Good, T., & Brophy, J. (1984). *Looking in classrooms.* New York: Harper & Row.

Goodchilds, J., & Zellman, G. (1984). Sexual signalling and sexual aggression in adolescent relationships. In N. M. Malamuth & E. D. Donnerstein (Eds.), *Pornography and sexual aggression.* New York: Academic Press.

Goodenow, C. (1992, April). *School motivation, engagement, and sense of belonging among urban adolescent students.* Paper presented at the annual meeting of the American Educational Research Association, San Francisco.

Goodlad, J. (1984). *A place called school.* New York: McGraw-Hill.

Goodman, E., & Cohall, A. (1989). Acquired immunodeficiency syndrome and adolescents: Knowledge, attitudes, beliefs, and behaviors in a New York City adolescent minority population. *Pediatrics, 84,* 36–42.

Goossens, L., Seiffge-Krenke, I., & Marcoen, A. (1992, March). *The many faces of adolescent egocentrism: Two European replications.* Paper presented at the biennial meetings of the Society for Research on Adolescence, Washington.

Goran, M., et al. (1998). Developmental changes in energy expenditure and physical activity in children: Evidence for a decline in physical activity in girls before puberty. *Pediatrics, 101*(5), 887–891.

Gordis, E., Margolin, G., & St. John, R. (1997). Marital aggression, observed parental hostility, and child behavior during triadic family interaction. *Journal of Family Psychology, 11,* 76–89.

Gordon, K. (1995). Self-concept and motivational patterns of resilient African American high school students. *Journal of Black Psychology, 21,* 239–255.

Gordon, M., & Miller, R. (1984). Going steady in the 1980s: Exclusive relationships in six Connecticut high schools. *Sociology and Social Research, 68,* 463–479.

Gordon, S., & Gilgun, J. (1987). Adolescent sexuality. In V. Van Hasselt & M. Hersen (Eds.), *Handbook of adolescent psychology.* New York: Pergamon.

Gore, S., & Aseltine, R., Jr. (1995). Protective processes in adolescence: Matching stressors with social resources. *American Journal of Community Psychology, 23,* 301–327.

Gore, T. (1987). *Raising PG kids in an X-rated society.* Nashville, TN: Abingdon Press.

Gorman-Smith, D., & Tolan, P. (1998). The role of exposure to community violence and developmental problems among inner-city youth. *Development and Psychopathology, 10,* 101–116.

Gorman-Smith, D., Tolan, P., Loeber, R., & Henry, D. (1998). Relation of family problems to patterns of delinquent involvement among urban youth. *Journal of Abnormal Child Psychology, 26,* 319–333.

Gottfredson, D. (1985). Youth employment, crime, and schooling: A longitudinal study of a national sample. *Developmental Psychology, 21,* 419–432.

Gottfredson, M., & Hirschi, T. (1990). *A general theory of crime.* Stanford, CA: Stanford University Press.

Gottfried, A., Fleming, J., & Gottfried, A. (1998). Role of cognitively stimulating home environment in children's academic intrinsic motivation: A longitudinal study. *Child Development, 69,* 1448–1460.

Gould, M., Wallenstein, S., & Kleinman, M. (1990). Time-space clustering of teenage suicide. *American Journal of Epidemiology, 131,* 71–78.

Gould, R. (1972). The phases of adult life. *American Journal of Psychiatry, 129,* 521–531.

Gowen, L., Hayward, C., Killen, J., Robinson, T., & Taylor, C. (1999). Acculturation and eating disorder symptoms in adolescent girls. *Journal of Research on Adolescence, 9,* 67–83.

Goyette, K., & Xie, Y. (1999). Educational expectations of Asian American youths: Determinants and ethnic differences. *Sociology of Education, 72,* 22–36.

Graber, J., Brooks-Gunn, J., & Warren, M. (1995). The antecedents of menarcheal age: Heredity, family environment, and stressful life events. *Child Development, 66,* 346–359.

Graber, J., & Brooks-Gunn, J. (1996). Transitions and turning points: Navigating the passage from childhood through adolescence. *Developmental Psychology, 32,* 768–776.

Graber, J., Brooks-Gunn, J., Paikoff, R., & Warren, M. (1994). Prediction of eating problems: An 8-year study of adolescent girls. *Developmental Psychology, 30,* 823–834.

Graber, J., Lewinsohn, P., Seeley, J., & Brooks-Gunn, J. (1997). Is psychopathology associated with the timing of pubertal development? *Journal of the American Academy of Child and Adolescent Psychiatry, 36,* 1768–1776.

Graber, J., Petersen, A., & Brooks-Gunn, J. (1996). Pubertal processes: Methods, measures, and models. In J. Graber, J. Brooks-Gunn, & A. Petersen (Eds.), *Transitions through adolescence: Interpersonal domains and context* (pp. 23–53). Mahwah, NJ: Erlbaum.

Graham, C. (1991). Menstrual synchrony: An update and review. *Human Nature, 2,* 293–311.

Graham, E. (1988, January 19). As kids gain power of purse, marketing takes aim at them. *Wall Street Journal,* pp. 1 and ff.

Graham, S. (1993, March). *Peer-directed aggression in African-American youth from an attributional perspective.* Paper presented at the biennial meetings of the Society for Research in Child Development, New Orleans.

Graham, S., & Hudley, C. (1994). Attributions of aggressive and nonaggressive African-American male early adolescents: A study of construct accessibility. *Developmental Psychology, 30,* 365–373.

Graham, S., & Juvonen, J. (1998). Self-blame and peer victimization in middle school: An attributional analysis. *Developmental Psychology, 34,* 587–599.

Graham, S., Hudley, C., & Williams, E. (1992). Attributional and emotional determinants of aggression among African-American and Latino young adolescents. *Developmental Psychology, 28,* 731–740.

Gray, M., & Steinberg, L. (1999). Adolescent romance and the parent-child relationship: A contextual perspective. In W. Furman, B. Brown, & C. Feiring (Eds.), *Contemporary perspectives on adolescent romantic relationships* (pp. 235–265). New York: Cambridge University Press.

Gray, P., & Feldman, J. (1997). Patterns of age mixing and gender mixing among children and adolescents at an ungraded democratic school. *Merrill-Palmer Quarterly, 43,* 67–86.

Gray, W., & Hudson, L. (1984). Formal operations and the imaginary audience. *Developmental Psychology, 20,* 619–627.

Gray-Little, B., & Carels, R. (1997). The effect of racial dissonance on academic achievement in elementary, junior high, and high school students. *Journal of Research on Adolescence, 7,* 109–131.

Gray-Little, B., & Hafdahl, A. (2000). Factors influencing racial comparisons of self-esteem: A quantitative review. *Psychological Bulletin, 126,* 26–54.

Graziano, W., Jensen-Campbell, L., & Finch, J. (1997). The self as a mediator between personality and adjustment. *Journal of Personality and Social Psychology, 73*(2), 392–404.

Green, R. (1980). Homosexuality. In H. Kaplan, A. Freedman, & B. Sadock (Eds.), *Comprehensive textbook of psychiatry* (Vol. 2, 3rd ed.). Baltimore: Williams & Wilkins.

Green, R. (1987). *The "sissy boy" syndrome and the development of homosexuality.* New Haven, CT: Yale University Press.

Greenberg, M., & Kusche, C. (1998). *Promoting alternative thinking strategies.* Boulder, CO: Institute of Behavioral Sciences, University of Colorado.

Greenberg, M., Siegel, J., & Leitch, C. (1983). The nature and importance of attachment relationships to parents and peers during adolescence. *Journal of Youth and Adolescence, 12,* 373–386.

Greenberger, E. (1982). Education and the acquisition of psychosocial maturity. In D. McClelland (Ed.), *The development of social maturity.* New York: Irvington.

Greenberger, E., & Chen, C. (1996). Perceived family relationships and depressed mood in early and late adolescence: A comparison of European and Asian Americans. *Developmental Psychology, 32,* 707–716.

Greenberger, E., & Sorenson, A. (1974). Toward a concept of psychosocial maturity. *Journal of Youth and Adolescence, 3,* 329–358.

Greenberger, E., & Steinberg, L. (1981). The workplace as a context for the socialization of youth. *Journal of Youth and Adolescence, 10,* 185–210.

Greenberger, E., & Steinberg, L. (1983). Sex differences in early work experience: Harbinger of things to come? *Social Forces, 62,* 467–486.

Greenberger, E., & Steinberg, L. (1986). *When teenagers work: The psychological and social costs of adolescent employment.* New York: Basic Books.

Greenberger, E., Chen, C., & Beam, M. R. (1998). The role of "very important" nonparental adults in adolescent development. *Journal of Youth and Adolescence, 27*(3), 321–343.

Greenberger, E., Chen, C., Tally, S., & Dong, Q. (2000). Family, peer, and individual correlates of depressive symptomatology among U.S. and Chinese adolescents. *Journal of Consulting and Clinical Psychology, 68,* 209–219.

Greenberger, E., Steinberg, L., & Ruggiero, M. (1982). A job is a job is a job . . . or is it? Behavioral observations in the adolescent workplace. *Work and Occupations, 9,* 79–96.

Greenberger, E., Steinberg, L., & Vaux, A. (1981). Adolescents who work: Health and behavioral consequences of job stress. *Developmental Psychology, 17,* 691–703.

Greenberger, E., Steinberg, L., Vaux, A., & McAuliffe, S. (1980). Adolescents who work: Effects of part-time employment on family and peer relations. *Journal of Youth and Adolescence, 9,* 189–202.

Gregory, L. (1995). The "turnaround" process: Factors influencing the school success of urban youth. *Journal of Adolescent Research, 10,* 136–154.

Grief, E., & Ulman, K. (1982). The psychological impact of menarche on early adolescent females: A review of the literature. *Child Development, 53,* 1413–1430.

Griesler, P., Kandel, D., & Davies, M. (1998). Maternal smoking in pregnancy, child behavior problems, and adolescent smoking. *Journal of Research on Adolescence, 8,* 159–185.

Grisso, T. (1999). Juvenile offenders and mental illness. *Psychiatry, Psychology, and Law, 6,* 143–151.

Grisso, T., & Schwartz, R. (2000). *Youth on trial.* Chicago: University of Chicago Press.

Grolnick, W., & Slowiaczek, M. (1994). Parents' involvement in children's schooling: A multidimensional conceptualization and motivational model. *Child Development, 65,* 237–252.

Grossman, D., Milligan, C., & Deyo, R. (1991). Risk factors for suicide attempts among Navajo adolescents. *American Journal of Public Health, 81,* 870–874.

Grossman, J. (Ed.). (1999). *Contemporary issues in mentoring.* Philadelphia: Public/Private Ventures.

Grossman, M., Chaloupka, F., Saffer, H., & Laixuthai, A. (1994). Effects of alcohol price policy on youth: A summary of economic research. *Journal of Research on Adolescence, 4,* 347–364.

Grotevant, H. (1997). Adolescent development in family contexts. In N. Eisenberg (Ed.), *Handbook of child psychology: Vol. 3: Social, emotional, and personality development* (5th ed, pp. 1097–1149). New York: Wiley.

Grotevant, H., & Cooper, C. (1986). Individuation in family relationships: A perspective on individual differences in the development of identity and role-taking skill in adolescence. *Human Development, 29,* 82–100.

Grotevant, H., & Cooper, C. (1988). The role of family experience in career exploration during adolescence. In P. Baltes, D. Featherman, & R. Lerner (Eds.), *Life-span development and behavior* (Vol. 8). pp 231–258, Hillsdale, NJ: Erlbaum.

Grotevant, H., & Durrett, M. (1980). Occupational knowledge and career development in adolescence. *Journal of Vocational Behavior, 17,* 171–182.

Grotevant, H., & Thorbecke, W. (1982). Sex differences in styles of occupational identity formation in late adolescence. *Developmental Psychology, 18,* 396–405.

Grotpeter, J., & Crick, N. (1996). Relational aggression, overt aggression, and friendship. *Child Development, 67,* 2328–2338.

Grumbach, M., Roth, J., Kaplan, S., & Kelch, R. (1974). Hypothalamic-pituitary regulation of puberty in man: Evidence and concepts derived from clinical research. In M. Grumbach, G. Grave, & F. Mayer (Eds.), *Control of the onset of puberty.* New York: Wiley.

Grych, J., & Fincham, F. (1992). Interventions for children of divorce: Toward greater integration of research and action. *Psychological Bulletin, 111,* 434–454.

Guberman, S. (1996). The development of everyday mathematics in Brazilian children with limited formal education. *Child Development, 67,* 1609–1623.

Guerra, N., & Slaby, R. (1990). Cognitive mediators of aggression in adolescent offenders, 2: Intervention. *Developmental Psychology, 26,* 269–277.

Guillen, E., & Barr, S. (1994). Nutrition, dieting, and fitness messages in a magazine for adolescent women, 1970–1990. *Journal of Adolescent Health, 15,* 464–472.

Guisinger, S., & Blatt, S. (1994). Individuality and relatedness: Evolution of a fundamental dialectic. *American Psychologist, 49,* 104–111.

Gunnoe, M. (1994, February). *Noncustodial mothers' and fathers' contributions to the adjustment of adolescents in stepfamilies.* Paper presented at the biennial meetings of the Society for Research on Adolescence, San Diego.

Gunnoe, M., Hetherington, E. M., & Reiss, D. (1999). Parental religiosity, parenting style, and adolescent social responsibility. *Journal of Early Adolescence, 19,* 199–225.

Guo, G. (1998). The timing of the influences of cumulative poverty on children's cognitive ability and achievement. *Social Forces, 77,* 257–287.

Guttmacher, S., Lieberman, L., Ward, D., Freudenberg, N., Radosh, A., & Des Jarlais, D. (1997). Condom availability in New York City public high schools: Relationships to condom use and sexual behavior. *American Journal of Public Health, 87,* 1427–1433.

Haan, N., Smith, M., & Block, J. (1968). Moral reasoning of young adults: Political-social behavior, family background, and personality correlates. *Journal of Personality and Social Psychology, 10,* 183–201.

Haapasalo, J., & Tremblay, R. (1994). Physically aggressive boys from ages 6 to 12: Family background, parenting behavior, and prediction of delinquency. *Journal of Consulting and Clinical Psychology, 62,* 1044–1052.

Hacker, D. (1994). An existential view of adolescence. *Journal of Early Adolescence, 14,* 300–327.

Hafetz, E. (1976). Parameters of sexual maturity in man. In E. Hafetz (Ed.), *Perspectives in human reproduction, Vol. 3: Sexual maturity: Physiological and clincial parameters.* Ann Arbor, MI: Ann Arbor Science Publishers.

Hagan, J., MacMillan, R., & Wheaton, B. (1996). New kid in town: Social capital and the life course effects of family migration on children. *American Sociological Review, 61,* 368–385.

Hale, S. (1990). A global developmental trend in cognitive processing speed. *Child Development, 61,* 653–663.

Hale, S., Bronik, M., & Fry, A. (1997). Verbal and spatial working memory in school-age children: Developmental differences in susceptibility to interference. *Developmental Psychology, 33,* 364–371.

Hall, G. S. (1904). *Adolescence.* New York: Appleton.

Hallinan, M. (1981). Recent advances in sociometry. In S. Asher & J. Gottman (Eds.), *The development of children's friendship.* New York: Cambridge University Press.

Hallinan, M. (1992). The organization of students for instruction in the middle school. *Sociology of Education, 65,* 114–127.

Hallinan, M. (1994). School differences in tracking effects on achievement. *Social Forces, 72,* 799–820.

Hallinan, M. (1996). Track mobility in secondary school. *Social Forces, 74,* 983–1002.

Hallinan, M., & Sorensen, A. (1987). Ability grouping and sex differences in mathematics achievement. *Sociology of Education, 60,* 63–72.

Hallinan, M., & Teixera, R. (1987). Opportunities and constraints: Black-white differences in the formation of interracial friendships. *Child Development, 58,* 1358–1371.

Hallinan, M., & Williams, R. (1989). Interracial friendship choices in secondary schools. *American Sociological Review, 54,* 67–78.

Halpern, C., & Udry, J. (1994, February). *Pubertal increases in body fat and implications for dieting, dating, and sexual behavior among black and white females.* Paper presented at the biennial meetings of the Society for Research on Adolescence, San Diego.

Halpern, C., Udry, J., & Suchindran, C. (1996, March). *Monthly measures of salivary testosterone predict sexual activity in adolescent males.* Paper presented at the biennial meetings of the Society for Research on Adolescence, Boston.

Halpern, C., Udry, J., Campbell, B., & Suchindran, C. (1999). Effects of body fat on weight concerns, dating, and sexual activity: A longitudinal analysis of black and white adolescent girls. *Developmental Psychology, 35,* 721–736.

Halpern-Felsher, B., & Cauffman, E. (in press). Costs and benefits of a decision: Decision-making competence in adolescents and adults. *Journal of Applied Developmental Psychology.*

Hamalainen, M., & Pulkkinen, L. (1996). Problem behavior as a precursor of male criminality. *Development and Psychopathology, 8,* 443–455.

Hamburg, D. (1986). *Preparing for life: The critical transition of adolescence.* New York: Carnegie Corporation of New York.

Hamill, S. (1994). Parent-adolescent communication in sandwich generation families. *Journal of Adolescent Research, 9,* 458–482.

Hamilton, C. (2000). Continuity and discontinuity of attachment from infancy through adolescence. *Child Development, 71,* 690–694.

Hamilton, S. (1990). *Apprenticeship for adulthood.* New York: Free Press.

Hamilton, S., & Hurrelmann, K. (1994). The school-to-career transition in Germany and the United States. *Teachers College Record, 96,* 329–344.

Hamilton, S., & Lempert, W. (1996). The impact of apprenticeship youth: A prospective analysis. *Journal of Research on Adolescence, 6,* 427–455.

Hanson, S. (1994). Lost talent: Unrealized educational aspirations and expectations among U. S. youths. *Sociology of Education, 67,* 159–183.

Hanson, S. (1996). Gender, family resources, and success in science. *Journal of Family Issues, 17,* 83–113.

Hanson, S., & Ginsburg, A. (1988). Gaining ground: Values and high school success. *American Educational Research Journal, 25,* 334–365.

Hanson, S., & Kraus, R. (1998). Women, sports, and science: Do female athletes have an advantage? *Sociology of Education, 71,* 93–110.

Hanson, T., McLanahan, S., & Thomson, E. (1996). Double jeopardy: Parental conflict and stepfamily outcomes for children. *Journal of Marriage and the Family, 58,* 141–154.

Hardesty, C., Wenk, D., & Morgan, C. (1995). Paternal involvement and the development of gender expectations in sons and daughters. *Youth and Society, 26,* 283–297.

Hardy, D., Astone, N., Brooks-Gunn, J., Shapiro, X., & Miller, X. (1998). Like mother, like child: Intergenerational patterns of age at first birth and associations with childhood and adolescent characteristics and adult outcomes in the second generation. *Developmental Psychology, 34,* 1220–1232.

Hardy, J., Duggan, A., Masnyk, K., & Pearson, C. (1989). Fathers of children born to young urban mothers. *Family Planning Perspectives, 21,* 159–163.

Harold, G., & Conger, R. (1997). Marital conflict and adolescent distress: The role of adolescent awareness. *Child Development, 68,* 333–350.

Harold, G., Fincham, F., Osborne, L., & Conger, R. (1997). Mom and dad are at it again: Adolescent perceptions of marital conflict and adolescent psychological distress. *Developmental Psychology, 33,* 333–350.

Harper, G., & Robinson, W. L. (1999). Pathways to risk among inner-city African-American adolescent females: The influence of gang membership. *American Journal of Community Psychology, 27,* 383–404.

Harris, J. (1995). Where is the child's environment? A group socialization theory of development. *Psychological Bulletin, 102,* 458–489.

Harris, J. R. (1998). *The nurture assumption: Why children turn out the way they do.* New York: Free Press.

Harris, K. (1999). The health status and risk behavior of adolescents in immigrant families. In D. Hernandez (Ed.), *Children of immigrants:* *Health, adjustment, and public assistance* (pp. 286–347). Washington, DC: National Academy Press.

Harris, M. (1994). Cholas, Mexican-American girls, and gangs. *Sex Roles, 30,* 289–301.

Hart, B., & Thompson, J. (1996). Gender role characteristics and depressive symptomatology among adolescents. *Journal of Early Adolescence, 16,* 407–426.

Hart, D., & Chmiel, S. (1992). Influence of defense mechanisms on moral judgment development: A longitudinal study. *Developmental Psychology, 28,* 722–730.

Hart, D., & Fegley, S. (1995). Prosocial behavior and caring in adolescence: Relations to self-understanding and social judgment. *Child Development, 66,* 1346–1359.

Hart, D., Fegley, S., & Brengelman, D. (1993). Perceptions of past, present, and future selves among children and adolescents. *British Journal of Developmental Psychology, 11,* 265–282.

Hart, D., Hofmann, V., Edelstein, W., & Keller, M. (1997). The relation of childhood personality types to adolescent behavior and development: A longitudinal study of Icelandic children. *Developmental Psychology, 33,* 195–205.

Hart, D., Keller, M., Edelstein, W., & Hofmann, V. (1998). Childhood personality influences on social-cognitive development: A longitudinal study. *Journal of Personality and Social Psychology, 74,* 1278–1289.

Harter, S. (1990). Identity and self development. In S. Feldman & G. Elliott (Eds.), *At the threshold: The developing adolescent* (pp. 352–387). Cambridge, MA: Harvard University Press.

Harter, S. (1998). The development of self-representations. In W. Damon (Series Editor) & N. Eisenberg (Volume Editor), *Handbook of child psychology: Vol. 3: Social, emotional, and personality development* (5th ed.) pp. 553–617. New York: Wiley.

Harter, S. (1999). *The construction of the self.* New York: Guilford.

Harter, S., Marold, D., Whitesell, N., & Cobbs, G. (1996). A model of the effects of parent and peer support on adolescent false self behavior. *Child Development, 67,* 360–374.

Harter, S., Waters, P., & Whitesell, N. (1998). Relational self-worth: Differences in perceived worth as a person across interpersonal contexts among adolescents. *Child Development, 69,* 756–766.

Harter, S., Waters, P., Whitesell, N., & Kastelic, D. (1998). Level of voice among female and male high school students: Relational context, support, and gender orientation. *Developmental Psychology, 34,* 892–901.

Harter, S., Whitesell, N., & Kowalski, P. (1991). *The effects of educational transitions on children's perceptions of competence and motivational orientation.* Manuscript submitted for publication. Department of Psychology, University of Denver.

Harter, S., & Monsour, A. (1992). Developmental analysis of conflict caused by opposing attributes in the adolescent self-portrait. *Developmental Psychology, 28,* 251–260.

Harter, S., Stocker, C., & Robinson, N. (1996). The perceived directionality of the link between approval and self-worth: The liabilities of a looking glass self orientation among young adolescents. *Journal of Research on Adolescence, 6,* 285–308.

Hartup, W. (1977). Adolescent peer relations: A look to the future. In J. Hill & F. Monks (Eds.), *Adolescence and youth in prospect.* Guildford, England: IPC Press.

Hartup, W. (1983). Peer relations. In E. M. Hetherington (Ed.), *Handbook of child psychology: Socialization, personality, and social development* (Vol. 4). New York: Wiley.

Hartup, W. (1992). Friendships and their developmental significance. In H. McGurk (Ed.), *Contemporary issues in childhood social development* (pp. 175–205). London: Routledge.

Hartup W. (1993). Adolescents and their friends. In B. Laursen (Ed.), *Close friendships during adolescence: New directions for child development* (pp. 3–22). San Francisco: Jossey-Bass.

Hartup, W. (1996). The company they keep: Friendships and their developmental significance. *Child Development, 67,* 1–13.

Hartup, W., & Stevens, N. (1997). Friendships and adaptation in the life course. *Psychological Bulletin, 121,* 335–370.

Hatzichristou, C., & Hopf, D. (1996). A multiperspective comparison of peer sociometric status groups in childhood and adolescence. *Child Development, 67,* 1085–1102.

Hauser, S. (1999). Understanding resilient outcomes: Adolescent lives across time and generations. *Journal of Research on Adolescence, 9,* 1–24.

Hauser, S., Book, B., Houlihan, J., Powers, S., Weiss-Perry, B., Follansbee, D., Jacobson, A., & Noam, G. (1987). Sex differences within the family: Studies of adolescent and parent family interactions. *Journal of Youth and Adolescence, 16,* 199–220.

Hauser, S., Powers, S., & Noam, G. (1991). *Adolescents and their families.* New York: Free Press.

Hauser, S., & Bowlds, M. (1990). Stress, coping, and adaptation. In S. Feldman & G. Elliott (Eds.), *At the threshold: The developing adolescent* (pp. 388–413). Cambridge, MA: Harvard University Press.

Hauser, S., & Kasendorf, E. (1983). *Black and white identity formation.* Malabar, FL: Robert E. Kreiger.

Hauser, S., & Safyer, A. (1994). Ego development and adolescent emotions. *Journal of Research on Adolescence, 4,* 487–502.

Hausman, A., Pierce, G., & Briggs, L. (1996). Evaluation of comprehensive violence prevention education: Effects on student behavior. *Journal of Adolescent Health, 19,* 104–110.

Hausser, D., & Michaud, P. (1994). Does a condom-promoting strategy (the Swiss STOP-AIDS Campaign) modify sexual behavior among adolescents? *Pediatrics, 93,* 580–585.

Havighurst, R. (1952). *Developmental tasks and education.* New York: McKay.

Hawdon, J. (1996). Deviant lifestyles: The social control of daily routines. *Youth and Society, 28,* 162–188.

Hawkins, J., Catalano, R., & Miller, J. (1992). Risk and protective factors for alcohol and other drug problems in adolescence and early adulthood: Implications for substance abuse prevention. *Psychological Bulletin, 112,* 64–105.

Hayes, C. (Ed.). (1987). *Risking the future: Adolescent sexuality, pregnancy, and childbearing* (Vol. 1). Washington, DC: National Academy Press.

Hayes, D., Wolfer, L., & Wolfe, M. (1996). Schoolbook simplification and its relation to the decline in SAT-verbal scores. *American Educational Research Journal, 33,* 489–508.

Hayward, C., Gotlib, I., Schraedley, P., & Litt, I. (1999). Ethnic differences in the association between pubertal status and symptoms of depression in adolescent girls. *Journal of Adolescent Health, 25,* 143–149.

Hayward, C., Killen, J., Wilson, D., Hammer, L., Litt, I., Kraemer, H., Haydel, F., Varady, A., & Taylor, B. (1997). Psychiatric risk associated with early puberty in adolescent girls. *Journal of the American Academy of Child and Adolescent Psychiatry, 36,* 255–261.

Hazan, C. (1994, February). *The role of sexuality in peer attachment formation.* Paper presented at the biennial meetings of the Society for Research on Adolescence, San Diego.

Hazard, B., & Lee, C. (1999). Understanding youth's health-compromising behaviors in Germany: An application of the risk-behavior framework. *Youth and Society, 30,* 348–366.

Hechinger, F. (1993). Schools for teenagers: An historic dilemma. *Teachers College Record, 94,* 522–539.

Hedges, L., & Nowell, A. (1995). Sex differences in mental test scores, variability, and numbers of high scoring individuals. *Science, 269,* 41–45.

Hedges, L., & Nowell, A. (1999). Changes in the black-white gap in achievement test scores. *Sociology of Education, 72,* 111–135.

Heimer, K., & Matsueda, R. (1994). Role-taking, role commitment, and delinquency: A theory of differential social control. *American Sociological Review, 59,* 365–390.

Hein, K. (1988a). *AIDS in adolescence: A rationale for concern.* Washington, DC: Carnegie Council on Adolescent Development.

Hein, K. (1988b). *Issues in adolescent health: An overview.* Washington, DC: Carnegie Council on Adolescent Development.

Hein, K., Dell, R., Futterman, D., Rotheram-Borus, M., & Shaffer, N. (1995). Comparison of HIV+ and HIV– adolescents: Risk factors and psychosocial determinants. *Pediatrics, 95,* 96–104.

Hektner, J. (1994, April). *When moving up implies moving out: How rural adolescents and their parents think about higher education and careers.* Paper presented at the annual meeting of the American Educational Research Association, New Orleans.

Helwig, C. (1995). Adolescents' and young adults' conceptions of civil liberties: Freedom of speech and religion. *Child Development, 66,* 152–166.

Helwig, C. (1997). The role of agent and social context in judgments of freedom of speech and religion. *Child Development, 68,* 484–495.

Hemmings, A. (1998). The self-transformations of African American achievers. *Youth and Society, 29,* 330–368.

Henderson, V., & Dweck, C. (1990). Motivation and achievement. In S. Feldman & G. Elliott (Eds.), *At the threshold: The developing adolescent* (pp. 308–329). Cambridge, MA: Harvard University Press.

Hendrick, S., & Hendrick, C. (1994, February). *Gender, sexuality, and close relationships.* Paper presented at the biennial meetings of the Society for Research on Adolescence, San Diego.

Henggeler, S. (1996). Treatment of violent juvenile offenders—We have the knowledge: Comment on Gorman-Smith et al. (1996). *Journal of Family Psychology, 10,* 137–141.

Henggeler, S., Melton, G., & Smith, L. (1992). Family prevention using multisystemic therapy: An effective alternative to incarcerating serious juvenile offenders. *Journal of Consulting and Clinical Psychology, 60,* 953–961.

Henry, B., Caspi, A., Moffitt, T., & Silva, P. (1996). Temperamental and familial predictors of violent and nonviolent criminal convictions: Age 3 to age 18. *Developmental Psychology, 32,* 614–623.

Henry, B., Caspi, A., Moffitt, T., Harrington, H., & Silva, P. (1999). Staying in school protects boys with poor self-regulation in childhood from later crime: A longitudinal study. *International Journal of Behavioral Development, 23,* 1049–1073.

Henry, B., Feehan, M., McGee, R., Stanton, W., Moffitt, T., & Silva, P. (1993). The importance of conduct problems and depressive symptoms in predicting adolescent substance use. *Journal of Abnormal Child Psychology, 21,* 469–480.

Henry, C., & Lovelace, S. (1995). Family resources and adolescent life satisfaction in remarried households. *Journal of Family Issues, 16,* 765–786.

Henshaw, S. (1995). The impact of requirements for parental consent on minors' abortions in Mississippi. *Family Planning Perspectives, 27,* 120–122.

Herman-Giddens, M., Sandler, A., & Friedman, N. (1988). Sexual precocity in girls: An association with sexual abuse? *American Journal of the Diseases of Childhood, 142,* 431–433.

Herman-Giddens, M., Slora, E., Wasserman, R., Bourdony, C., Bhapkar, M., Koch, G., & Hasemeier, C. (1997). Secondary sexual characteristics and menses in young girls seen in office practice: A study from the Pediatric Research in Office Settings Network. *Pediatrics, 88,* 505–512.

Herman-Stahl, M., Stemmler, M., & Petersen, A. (1995). Approach and avoidant coping: Implications for adolescent mental health. *Journal of Youth and Adolescence, 24,* 649–665.

Hernandez, D. (1997). Child development and the social demography of childhood. *Child Development, 68,* 149–169.

Hershberger, S., & D'Augelli, A. (1995). The impact of victimization on the mental health and suicidality of lesbian, gay, and bisexual youths. *Developmental Psychology, 31,* 65–74.

Hershberger, S., Pilkington, N., & D'Augelli, A. (1997). Predictors of suicide attempts among gay, lesbian, and bisexual youth. *Journal of Adolescent Research, 12,* 477–497.

Hess, R., Chih-Mei, C., & McDevitt, T. (1987). Cultural variations in family beliefs about children's performance in mathematics: Comparisons among People's Republic of China, Chinese-American, and Caucasian-American families. *Journal of Educational Psychology, 79,* 179–188.

Hetherington, E. M. (1981). Children and divorce. In R. Henderson (Ed.), *Parent-child interaction: Theory, research, and prospects.* New York: Academic Press.

Hetherington, E. M. (1991). The role of individual differences and family relationships in children's coping with divorce and remarriage. In P. Cowan & E. M. Hetherington (Eds.), *Advances in family research, Vol. 2: Family transitions.* Hillsdale, NJ: Erlbaum.

Hetherington, E. M. (1993). An overview of the Virginia longitudinal study of divorce and remarriage with a focus on early adolescence. *Journal of Family Psychology, 7,* 39–56.

Hetherington, E. M., Clingempeel, W., Anderson, E., Deal, J., Hagan, M., Hollier, E., & Lindner, M. (1992). Coping with marital transitions: A family systems perspective. *Monographs of the Society for Research in Child Development,* Serial No. 227.

Hetherington, E. M., & Stanley-Hagan, M. (1995). Parenting in divorced and remarried families. In M. Bornstein (Ed.), *Handbook of parenting, Volume 3: Status and social conditions of parenting* (pp. 233–254). Mahwah, NJ: Erlbaum.

Hetherington, E. M., Bridges, M., & Insabella, G. (1998). What matters? What does not? Five perspectives on the association between marital transitions and children's adjustment. *American Psychologist, 53,* 167–184.

Hetherington, E. M., Henderson, S., & Reiss, D. (1999). Adolescent siblings in stepfamilies: Family functioning and adolescent adjustment. *Monographs of the Society for Research in Child Development, 64,* Serial No. 259.

Hetherington, E. M., Reiss, D., & Plomin, R. (1994). *Separate social worlds of siblings: The impact of nonshared environment on development.* Hillsdale, NJ: Erlbaum.

Hibbard, R., Ingersoll, G., & Orr, D. (1990). Behavioral risk, emotional risk, and child abuse among adolescents in a nonclinical setting. *Pediatrics, 86,* 896–901.

Higgins, A., & Turnure, J. (1984). Distractibility and concentration of attention in children's development. *Child Development, 44,* 1799–1810.

Hightower, E. (1990). Adolescent interpersonal and familial predictors of positive mental health at midlife. *Journal of Youth and Adolescence, 19,* 257–276.

Hill, C. (1986). A developmental perspective on adolescent "rebellion" in the church. *Journal of Psychology and Theology, 14,* 306–318.

Hill, J. (1983). Early adolescence: A framework. *Journal of Early Adolescence, 3,* 1–21.

Hill, J., & Holmbeck, G. (1986). Attachment and autonomy during adolescence. In G. Whitehurst (Ed.), *Annals of child development.* Greenwich, CT: JAI Press.

Hill, J., & Holmbeck, G. (1987). Disagreements about rules in families with seventh-grade girls and boys. *Journal of Youth and Adolescence, 16,* 221–246.

Hill, J., & Lynch, M. (1983). The intensification of gender-related role expectations during early adolescence. In J. Brooks-Gunn & A. Petersen (Eds.), *Girls at puberty.* pp. 201–228. New York: Plenum.

Hill, J., & Palmquist, W. (1978). Social cognition and social relations in early adolescence. *International Journal of Behavioral Development, 1,* 1–36.

Hilsman, R., & Garber, J. (1995). A test of the cognitive diathesis-stress model of depression in children: Academic stressors, attributional style, perceived competence, and control. *Journal of Personality and Social Psychology, 69,* 370–380.

Hinden, B., Compas, B., Howell, D., & Achenbach, T. (1997). Covariation of the anxious-depressed syndrome during adolescence: Separating fact from artifact. *Journal of Consulting and Clinical Psychology, 65,* 6–14.

Hine, T. (1999). *The rise and fall of the American teenager.* New York: Bard Books.

Hines, A. (1997). Divorce-related transitions, adolescent development, and the role of the parent-child relationship: A review of the literature. *Journal of Marriage and the Family, 59,* 375–388.

Hingson, R., & Howland, J. (1993). Promoting safety in adolescents. In S. Millstein, A. Petersen, & E. Nightingale (Eds.), *Promoting the health of adolescents: New directions for the twenty-first century* (pp. 305–327). New York: Oxford University Press.

Hinshaw, S., Zupan, B., Simmel, C., Nigg, J., & Melnick, S. (1997). Peer status in boys with and without attention-deficit hyperactivity disorder: Predictions from overt and covert antisocial behavior, social isolation, and authoritative parenting beliefs. *Child Development, 68,* 886–896.

Hirsch, B., & DuBois, D. (1991). Self-esteem in early adolescence: The identification and prediction of contrasting longitudinal trajectories. *Journal of Youth and Adolescence, 20,* 53–72.

Hirsch, E. D. (1996). *The schools we need.* New York: Doubleday.

Hirschi, T. (1969). *Cause of delinquency.* Berkeley: University of California Press.

Hodges, E., Bouvin, M., Vitaro, F., & Bukowski, W. (1998). The power of friendship: Protection against an escalating cycle of peer victimization. *Developmental Psychology, 35,* 94–101.

Hodges, E., Finnegan, R., & Perry, D. (1999). Skewed autonomy-relatedness in preadolescents' conceptions of their relationships with mother, father, and best friend. *Developmental Psychology, 35,* 737–748.

Hodges, E., & Perry, D. (1999). Personal and interpersonal antecedents and consequences of victimization by peers. *Journal of Personality and Social Psychology, 76,* 677–685.

Hoffer, T. (1997). High school graduation requirements: Effects on dropping out and student achievement. *Teachers College Record, 98,* 584–607.

Hoffman, L. (1974). Effects of maternal employment on the child: A review of the research. *Developmental Psychology, 10,* 204–228.

Hoffman, L. (1977). Fear of success in 1965 and 1974: A follow-up study. *Journal of Consulting and Clinical Psychology, 45,* 310–321.

Hoffman, L. (1991). The influence of the family environment on personality: Accounting for sibling differences. *Psychological Bulletin, 110,* 187–203.

Hoffman, L. (1996). Progress and problems in the study of adolescence. *Developmental Psychology, 32,* 777–780.

Hoffman, S., Foster, E., & Furstenberg, F., Jr. (1993). Reevaluating the costs of teenage childbearing. *Demography, 30,* 1–13.

Hoge, D., Smit, E., & Hanson, S. (1990). School experiences and predicting changes in self-esteem of sixth- and seventh-grade students. *Journal of Educational Psychology, 82,* 117–127.

Hogue, A., & Steinberg, L. (1995). Homophily of internalized distress in adolescent peer groups. *Developmental Psychology, 31,* 897–906.

Holland, A., & Andre, T. (1994). Athletic participation and the social status of adolescent males and females. *Youth and Society, 25,* 388–407.

Holland, A., Sicotte, N., & Treasure, L. (1988). Anorexia nervosa: Evidence for a genetic basis. *Journal of Psychosomatic Research, 32,* 561–571.

Holland, J. (1985). *Making vocational choice: A theory of careers* (2nd ed.). Englewood Cliffs, NJ: Prentice-Hall.

Hollingshead, A. (1949/1975). *Elmtown's youth and Elmtown revisited.* New York: Wiley.

Holloway, S. (1988). Concepts of ability and effort in Japan and the United States. *Review of Educational Research, 58,* 327–345.

Holmbeck, G. (1996). A model of family relational transformations during the transition to adolescence: Parent-adolescent conflict and adaptation. In J. Graber, J. Brooks-Gunn, & A. Petersen (Eds.), *Transitions through adolescence: Interpersonal domains and context* (pp. 167–199). Mahwah, NJ: Erlbaum.

Holmbeck, G., & Hill, J. (1988). Storm and stress beliefs about adolescence: Prevalence, self-reported antecedents, and effects of an undergraduate course. *Journal of Youth and Adolescence, 17,* 285–306.

Holmbeck, G., & Hill, J. (1991). Conflictive engagement, positive affect, and menarche in families with seventh-grade girls. *Child Development, 62,* 1030–1048.

Holmbeck, G., & O'Donnell, K. (1991). Longitudinal study of discrepancies between maternal and adolescent perceptions of decision-making and desired behavioral autonomy. In R. Paikoff & W. A. Collins (Eds.), *New directions for child development: Shared views of the family during adolescence* (pp. 51–69). San Francisco: Jossey-Bass.

Holmbeck, G., Durbin, D., & Kung, E. (1995, March). *Attachment, astronomy, and adjustment before and after leaving home: Sullivan and Sullivan revisited.* Paper presented at the Society for Research in Child Development, Indianapolis.

Holmbeck, G., Shapera, W., Westhoven, V., Johnson, S., Millstein, R., & Hommeyer, J. (2000, March). *A longitudinal study of observed and perceived parenting behaviors and autonomy development in families of young adolescents with spina bifida.* Paper presented at the biennial meetings of the Society for Research on Adolescence, Chicago.

Holmen, T., Barrett-Connor, E., Holmen, J., & Bjerner, L. (2000). Health problems in teenage daily smokers versus nonsmokers, Norway, 1995–1997. *American Journal of Epidemiology, 151,* 148–155.

Holmes, S. (1994, July 20). Birthrate for unwed women up 70% since '83, study says. *New York Times,* pp. 1 and ff.

Holstein, C. (1972). The relation of children's moral judgment level to that of their parents and to communication patterns in the family. In R. Smart & M. Smart (Eds.), *Readings in child development and relationships.* New York: Macmillan.

Holtzman, D., & Rubinson, R. (1995). Parent and peer communication effects on AIDS-related behavior among U.S. high school students. *Family Planning Perspectives, 27,* 235–240, 268.

Hoover-Dempsey, K., & Sandler, H. (1995). Parental involvement in children's education: Why does it make a difference? *Teachers College Record, 97,* 310–331.

Horan, P., & Hargis, P. (1991). Children's work and schooling in the late nineteenth-century family economy. *American Sociological Review, 56,* 583–596.

Hoyt, S., & Scherer, D. (1998). Female juvenile delinquency: Misunderstood by the juvenile justice system, neglected by social science. *Law and Human Behavior, 22,* 81–107.

Hoza, B., Molina, B., Bukowski, W., & Sippola, L. (1995). Peer variables as predictors of later childhood adjustment. *Development and Psychopathology, 7,* 787–802.

Hudley, C. (1995). Assessing the impact of separate schooling for African American male adolescents. *Journal of Early Adolescence, 15,* 38–57.

Hudley, C. (1997). Supporting achievement beliefs among ethnic minority adolescents: Two case examples. *Journal of Research on Adolescence, 7,* 133–152.

Hughes, M., Furstenberg, F., Jr., & Teitler, J. (1995). The impact of an increase in family planning on the teenage population of Philadelphia. *Family Planning Perspectives, 27,* 60–65, 78.

Hughes, S., Power, T., & Francis, D. (1992). Defining patterns of drinking in adolescence: A cluster analytic approach. *Journal of Studies on Alcohol, 53,* 40–47.

Huizinga, D., & Elliot, D. (1985). *Juvenile offenders prevalence, offender incidence, and arrest rates by race.* Boulder, CO: Institute of Behavioral Science.

Humphries, L. (1988). Trends in levels of academic achievement of blacks and other minorities. *Intelligence, 12,* 231–260.

Hunt, M. (1974). *Sexual behavior in the 1970s.* Chicago: Playboy Press.

Hunter, F. (1984). Socializing procedures in parent-child and friendship relations during adolescence. *Developmental Psychology, 18,* 806–811.

Hunter, F., & Youniss, J. (1982). Changes in functions of three relations during adolescence. *Developmental Psychology, 18,* 806–811.

Hussong, A., Curran, P., & Chassin, L. (1998). Pathways of risk for accelerated heavy alcohol use among adolescent children of alcoholic parents. *Journal of Abnormal Child Psychology, 26,* 453–466.

Huston, A., & Alvarez, M. (1990). The socialization context of gender role development in early adolescence. In R. Montemayor, G. Adams, & T. Gullotta (Eds.), *Advances in adolescent development, Vol. 2: The transition from childhood to adolescence* (pp. 156–179). Beverly Hills, CA: Sage.

Huston, A., McLoyd, V., & Garcia Coll, C. (1994). Children and poverty: Issues in contemporary research. *Child Development, 65,* 275–282.

Huston, H., Anglin, D., & Pratts, M., Jr. (1994). Adolescents and children injured or killed in drive-by shootings in Los Angeles. *New England Journal of Medicine, 330,* 324–327.

Huttenlocher, P. (1994). Synaptogenesis, synapse elimination, and neural plasticity in human cerebral cortex. In C. Nelson (Ed.), Threats to optimal development: Integrating biological, psychological, and social risk factors. *Minnesota Symposium on Child Psychology, Volume 27,* (pp. 35–54). Hillsdale, NJ: Erlbaum.

Hyde, J., & Linn, M. (1988). Are there sex differences in verbal abilities? A meta-analysis. *Psychological Bulletin, 104,* 53–69.

Hymel, S., Bowker, A., & Woody, E. (1993). Aggressive versus withdrawn unpopular children: Variations in peer and self-perceptions in multiple domains. *Child Development, 64,* 879–896.

Hymel, S., Rubin, K., Rowden, L., & LeMare, L. (1990). Children's peer relationships: Longitudinal prediction of internalizing and externalizing problems from middle to late childhood. *Child Development, 61,* 2004–2021.

Inhelder, B., & Piaget, J. (1958). *The growth of logical thinking from childhood to adolescence.* New York: Basic Books.

Irwin, C., Jr. (1986). Biopsychosocial correlates of risk-taking behavior during adolescence: Can the physician intervene? *Journal of Adolescent Health Care, 7,* 82–96.

Irwin, C., Jr. (1993). Topical areas of interest for promoting health: From the perspective of the physician. In S. Millstein, A. Petersen, & E. Nightingale (Eds.), *Promoting the health of adolescents: New directions for the twenty-first century* (pp. 328–332). New York: Oxford University Press.

Isakson, K., & Jarvis, P. (1999). The adjustment of adolescents during the transition into high school: A short-term longitudinal study. *Journal of Youth and Adolescence, 28,* 1–26.

Ishiyama, I., & Chabassol, D. (1985). Adolescents' fear of social consequences of academic success as a function of age and sex. *Journal of Youth and Adolescence, 14,* 37–46.

Izard, M. (1990). Social influences on the reproductive success and reproductive endocrinology of prosimian primates. In F. Bercovitch & T. Zeigler (Eds.), *The socioendocrinology of primate reproduction* (pp. 159–186). New York: Alan R. Liss.

Jaccard, J., Dittus, P., & Gordon, V. (1996). Maternal correlates of adolescent sexual and contraceptive behavior. *Family Planning Perspectives, 28,* 159–165.

Jaccard, J., Dittus, P., & Gordon, V. (1998). Parent-adolescent congruency in reports of adolescent sexual behavior and in communications about sexual behavior. *Child Development, 69,* 247–261.

Jacklin, C. (1989). Female and male: Issues of gender. *American Psychologist, 44,* 127–133.

Jackson, A., & Hornbeck, D. (1989). Educating young adolescents. *American Psychologist, 44,* 831–836.

Jackson, L., Hodge, C., & Ingram, J. (1994). Gender and self-concept: A reexamination of stereotypic differences and the role of gender attitudes. *Sex Roles, 30,* 615–630.

Jacobs, J. (1991). Influence of gender stereotypes on parent and child mathematics attitudes. *Journal of Educational Psychology, 83,* 518–527.

Jacobs, J., & Eccles, J. (1992). The impact of mothers' gender-role stereotypic beliefs on mothers' and children's ability perceptions. *Journal of Personality and Social Psychology, 63,* 932–944.

Jacobs, J., & Portenza, M. (1991). The use of judgment heuristics to make social and object decisions: A developmental perspective. *Child Development, 62,* 166–178.

Jacobson, K., & Crockett, L. (2000). Parental monitoring and adolescent adjustment: An ecological perspective. *Journal of Research on Adolescence, 10,* 65–97.

Jacobsen, T., & Hofmann, W. (1997). Children's attachment representations: Longitudinal relations to school behavior and academic competency in middle childhood and adolescence. *Developmental Psychology, 35,* 703–710.

Jacobsen, T., Edelstein, W., & Hofmann, V. (1994). A longitudinal study of the relation between representations of attachment in childhood and cognitive functioning in childhood and adolescence. *Developmental Psychology, 30,* 112–124.

Jacobson, K., & Rowe, D. (1999). Genetic and environmental influences on the relationships between family connectedness, school connectedness, and adolescent depressed mood: Sex differences. *Developmental Psychology, 35,* 926–939.

Jahnke, H., & Blanchard-Fields, F. (1993). A test of two models of adolescent egocentrism. *Journal of Youth and Adolescence, 22,* 313–326.

Jakobsen, R., Rise, J., Aas, H., & Anderssen, N. (1997). Noncoital sexual interactions and problem behaviour among young adolescents: The Norwegian Longitudinal Health Behaviour Study. *Journal of Adolescence, 20,* 71–83.

Jang, S., & Thornberry, T. (1998). Self-esteem, delinquent peers, and delinquency: A test of the self-enhancement thesis. *American Sociological Review, 63,* 586–598.

Janosz, M., LeBlanc, M., Boulerice, B., & Tremblay, R. E. (1997). Disentangling the weight of school dropout predictors: A test on two longitudinal samples. *Journal of Youth and Adolescence, 26,* 733–762.

Jarrett, R. (1995). Growing up poor: The family experiences of socially mobile youth in low-income African American neighborhoods. *Journal of Adolescent Research, 10,* 111–135.

Jarvinen, D., & Nicholls, J. (1996). Adolescents' social goals, beliefs about the causes of social success, and satisfaction in peer relations. *Developmental Psychology, 32,* 435–441.

Jason, L., Berk, M., Schnopp-Wyatt, D., & Talbot, B. (1999). Effects of enforcement of youth access laws on smoking prevalence. *American Journal of Community Psychology, 27,* 143–160.

Jemmott, J., III, Jemmott, L., Fong, G., & McCaffree, K. (1999). Reducing HIV risk-associated sexual behavior among African American adolescents: Testing the generality of intervention effects. *American Journal of Community Psychology, 27,* 161–187.

Jenkins, P. (1995). School delinquency and school commitment. *Sociology of Education, 68,* 221–239.

Jessor, R. (1987). Risky driving and adolescent problem behavior: An extension of problem-behavior theory. *Alcohol, Drugs, and Driving, 3,* 1–11.

Jessor, R., Costa, F., Jessor, L., & Donovan, J. (1983). Time of first intercourse: A prospective study. *Journal of Personality and Social Psychology, 44,* 608–626.

Jessor, R., & Jessor, S. (1977). *Problem behavior and psychosocial development: A longitudinal study of youth.* New York: Academic Press.

Jessor, R., Turbin, M., & Costa, F. (1998). Protective factors in adolescent health behavior. *Journal of Personality and Social Psychology, 75,* 788–800.

Jessor, R., Van Den Bos, J., Vanderryn, J., Costa, F., & Turbin, M. (1995). Protective factors in adolescent problem behavior: Moderator effects and developmental change. *Developmental Psychology, 31,* 923–933.

Jeynes, W. (1999). Effects of remarriage following divorce on the academic achievement of children. *Journal of Youth and Adolescence, 28,* 385–393.

John, O., Caspi, A., Robins, R., Moffitt, T., & Stouthamer-Loeber, M. (1994). The "Little Five": Exploring the nomological network of the five-factor model of personality in adolescent boys. *Child Development, 65,* 160–178.

Johnson, E., & Meade, A. (1987). Developmental patterns of spatial ability: An early sex difference. *Child Development, 58,* 725–740.

Johnson, M., Beebe, T., Mortimer, J., & Snyder, M. (1998). Volunteerism in adolescence: A process perspective. *Journal of Research on Adolescence, 8,* 309–332.

Johnson, R., & Gerstein, D. (1998). Initiation of use of alcohol, cigarettes, marijuana, cocaine, and other substances in U.S. birth cohorts since 1919. *American Journal of Public Health, 88,* 27–33.

Johnson, R., Johnson, D., Wang, M., Smiciklas-Wright, H., & Guthrie, H. (1994). Characterizing nutrient intakes of adolescents by sociodemographic factors. *Journal of Adolescent Health, 15,* 149–154.

Johnson, S. (1975). *Update on education: A digest of the National Assessment of Education Progress.* Denver: Education Commission of the States.

Johnston, L., Bachman, G., & O'Malley, P. (1999). *Monitoring the future.* Ann Arbor, MI: Institute for Social Research.

Johnston, L., Bachman, J., & O'Malley, P. (1982). *Monitoring the Future: Questionnaire responses from the nation's high school seniors, 1981.* Ann Arbor, MI: Institute for Social Research.

Johnston, L., O'Malley, P., & Bachman, J. (1986). *Drug use among American high school students, college students, and other young adults: National trends through 1985.* Washington, DC: National Institute on Drug Abuse.

Jones, D., & Costin, S. (1993, March). *Helping orientations, sex role characteristics, and friendship satisfaction during preadolescence and adolescence.* Paper presented at the biennial meetings of the Society for Research in Child Development, New Orleans.

Jones, D., Costin, S., & Ricard, R. (1994, February). *Ethnic and sex differences in best friendship characteristics among African-American, Mexican-American, and European-American adolescents.* Paper presented at the biennial meetings of the Society for Research on Adolescence, San Diego.

Jones, E., et al. (1987). *Teenage pregnancy in industrialized countries.* New Haven, CT: Yale University Press.

Jones, G., & Dembo, M. (1989). Age and sex role differences in intimate friendships during childhood and adolescence. *Merrill-Palmer Quarterly, 35,* 445–462.

Jones, H. (1949). *Adolescence in our society.* In "The family in a democratic society" (anniversary papers of the Community Service Society of New York). New York: Columbia University Press.

Jones, J., Vanfossen, B., & Ensminger, M. (1995). Individual and organizational predictors of track placement. *Sociology of Education, 68,* 287–300.

Jones, M. (1957). The later careers of boys who were early- or late-maturing. *Child Development, 28,* 113–128.

Jones, M. (1965). Psychological correlates of somatic development. *Child Development, 36,* 899–911.

Jones, M., & Bayley, N. (1950). Physical maturing among boys as related to behavior. *Journal of Educational Psychology, 41,* 129–148.

Jones, M., & Mussen, P. (1958). Self-conceptions, motivations, and inter-personal attitudes of early- and late-maturing girls. *Child Development, 29,* 491–501.

Jones, N., Pieper, C., & Robertson, L. (1992). The effect of legal drinking age on fatal injuries of adolescents and young adults. *American Journal of Public Health, 82,* 112–115.

Jordan, A., & Cole, D. (1996). Relation of depressive symptoms to the structure of self-knowledge in childhood. *Journal of Abnormal Psychology, 105,* 530–540.

Jordan, W., Lara, J., & McPartland, J. (1996). Exploring the causes of early dropout among race-ethnic and gender groups. *Youth and Society, 28,* 62–94.

Jose, P., D'Anna, C., Cafasso, L., Bryant, F., Chiker, V., Gein, N., & Zhezmer, N. (1998). Stress and coping among Russian and American early adolescents. *Developmental Psychology, 34,* 757–769.

Josselson, R. (1980). Ego development in adolescence. In J. Adelson (Ed.), *Handbook of adolescent psychology* (pp. 188–210). New York: Wiley.

Josselson, R., Greenberger, E., & McConochie, D. (1977a). Phenomenological aspects of psychosocial maturity in adolescence, Part I: Boys. *Journal of Youth and Adolescence, 6,* 25–56.

Josselson, R., Greenberger, E., & McConochie, D. (1977b). Phenomenological aspects of psychosocial maturity in adolescence, Part II: Girls. *Journal of Youth and Adolescence, 6,* 145–167.

Jovanovic, J., & King, S. (1998). Boys and girls in the performance-based science classroom: Who's doing the performing? *American Educational Research Journal, 35,* 477–496.

Joyce, T., & Mocan, N. (1990). The impact of legalized abortion on adolescent childbearing in New York City. *American Journal of Public Health, 80,* 273–278.

Jozefowicz, D., Barber, B., Eccles, J., & Mollasis, C. (1994, February). *Relations between maternal and adolescent values and beliefs: Gender differences and implications for occupational choice.* Paper presented at the biennial meetings of the Society for Research on Adolescence, San Diego.

Juang, L., Lerner, J., McKinney, J., & von Eye, A. (1999). The goodness of fit in autonomy timetable expectations between Asian-American late adolescents and their parents. *International Journal of Behavioral Development, 23,* 1023–1048.

Juang, L., & Silbereisen, R. (1999). Supportive parenting and adolescent adjustment across time in former East and West Germany. *Journal of Adolescence, 22,* 719–736.

Jussim, L., & Eccles, J. (1992). Teacher expectations, II: Construction and reflection of student achievement. *Journal of Personality and Social Psychology, 63,* 947–961.

Juvonen, J., & Murdock, T. (1995). Grade-level differences in the social value of effort: Implications for self-presentation tactics of early adolescents. *Child Development, 66,* 1694–1705.

Kachur, S., Stennies, G., Powerll, K., Modzeleski, W., Stephens, R., Murphy, R., Kresnow, M., Sleet, D., & Lowry, R. (1996). School-associated violent deaths in the United States, 1992 to 1994. *Journal of the American Medical Association, 275,* 1729–1733.

Kagan, J., & Coles, R. (Eds.). (1972). *Twelve to sixteen: Early adolescence.* New York: Norton.

Kahn, J., Brindis, C., & Glei, D. (1999). Pregnancies averted among U.S. teenagers by the use of contraceptives. *Family Planning Perspectives, 31,* 29–34.

Kahn, S., Zimmerman, G., Csikszentmihalyi, M., & Getzels, J. (1985). Relations between identity in young adulthood and intimacy in midlife. *Journal of Personality and Social Psychology, 49,* 1316–1322.

Kahneman, D., Slovic, P., & Tversky, A. (Eds.). (1982). *Judgment under uncertainty: Heuristics and biases.* New York: Cambridge University Press.

Kail, R. (1991a). Developmental change in speed of processing during childhood and adolescence. *Psychological Bulletin, 109,* 490–501.

Kail, R. (1991b). Processing time declines exponentially during childhood and adolescence. *Developmental Psychology, 27,* 259–266.

Kail, R., & Hall, L. (1994). Processing speed, naming speed, and reading. *Developmental Psychology, 30,* 949–954.

Kalakoski, V., & Nurmi, J.-E. (1998). Identity and educational transitions: Age differences in adolescent exploration and commitment related to education, occupation, and family. *Journal of Research on Adolescence, 8,* 29–47.

Kalil, A., & Eccles, J. (1993, March). *The relationship of parenting style and conflict to maternal well-being in single and married mothers of school-aged children.* Paper presented at the biennial meetings of the Society for Research in Child Development, New Orleans.

Kalil, A., & Eccles, J. (1998). Does welfare affect family processes and adolescent adjustment? *Child Development, 69,* 1597–1613.

Kallen, D., & Stephenson, J. (1982). Talking about sex revisited. *Journal of Youth and Adolescence, 11,* 11–24.

Kalmuss, D., & Namerow, P. (1994). Subsequent childbearing among teenage mothers: The determinants of a closely spaced second birth. *Family Planning Perspectives, 26,* 149–153, 159.

Kalmuss, D., Namerow, P., & Bauer, U. (1992). Short-term consequences of parenting versus adoption among young unmarried women. *Journal of Marriage and the Family, 54,* 80–90.

Kandel, D. (1978). Homophily, selection, and socialization in adolescent friendships. *American Journal of Sociology, 84,* 427–436.

Kandel, D. (1980). Drug and drinking behavior among youth. *Annual Review of Sociology, 6,* 235–285.

Kandel, D., & Lesser, G. (1972). *Youth in two worlds.* San Francisco: Jossey-Bass.

Kandel, D., & Logan, J. (1984). Patterns of drug use from adolescence to young adulthood, I: Periods of risk for initiation, continued use, and discontinuation. *American Journal of Public Health, 74,* 660–666.

Kandel, D., & Wu, P. (1995). The contributions of mothers and fathers to the intergenerational transmission of cigarette smoking in adolescence. *Journal of Research on Adolescence, 5,* 225–252.

Kandel, D., Johnson, J., Bird, H., & Canino, G. (1997). Psychiatric disorders associated with substance use among children and adolescents: Findings from the Methods for the Epidemiology of Child and Adolescent Mental Disorders (MECA) Study. *Journal of Abnormal Child Psychology, 25,* 121–132.

Kandel, D., Raveis, V., & Davies, M. (1991). Suicidal ideation in adolescence: Depression, substance abuse, and other risk factors. *Journal of Youth and Adolescence, 20*, 289–310.

Kantor, H. (1994). Managing the transition from school to work: The false promise of youth apprenticeship. *Teachers College Record, 95*, 442–461.

Kantor, H., & Brenzel, B. (1992). Urban education and the "truly disadvantaged": The historical roots of the contemporary crisis, 1945–1990. *Teachers College Record, 94*, 278–314.

Kao, G. (1995). Asian Americans as model minorities? A look at their academic performance. *American Journal of Education, 103*, 121–159.

Kao, G. (1999). Psychological well-being and educational achievement among immigrant youth. In D. Hernandez (Ed.), *Children of immigrants: Health, adjustment, and public assistance* (pp. 410–477). Washington, DC: National Academy Press.

Kao, G., & Tienda, M. (1998). Educational aspirations of minority youth. *American Journal of Education, 106*, 349–384.

Kasen, S., Cohen, P., & Brook, J. (1998). Adolescent school experiences and dropout, adolescent pregnancy, and young adult deviant behavior. *Journal of Adolescent Research, 13*, 49–72.

Katainen, S., Raeikkoenen, K., & Keltikangas-Jaervinen, L. (1998). Development of temperament: Childhood temperament and the mother's childrearing attitudes as predictors of adolescent temperament in a 9-yr follow-up study. *Journal of Research on Adolescence, 8*, 485–509.

Katchadourian, H. (1990). Sexuality. In S. Feldman & G. Elliott (Eds.), *At the threshold: The developing adolescent* (pp. 330–351). Cambridge, MA: Harvard University Press.

Katz, M. (1975). *The people of Hamilton, Canada West: Family and class in a mid-nineteenth-century city.* Cambridge, MA: Harvard University Press.

Katz, P., & Ksansnak, K. (1994). Developmental aspects of gender role flexibility and traditionality in middle childhood and adolescence. *Developmental Psychology, 30*, 272–282.

Kaufman, K., Gregory, W., & Stephan, W. (1990). Maladjustment in statistical minorities within ethnically unbalanced classrooms. *American Journal of Community Psychology, 18*, 757–762.

Kavrell, A., & Petersen, A. (1984). Patterns of achievement in early adolescence. *Advances in Motivation and Achievement, 2*, 1–35.

Kazis, R. (1993). *Improving the transition from school to work in the United States.* Washington, DC: American Youth Policy Forum, Competitiveness Policy Council, and Jobs for the Future.

Keane, E., Dick, R., Bechtold, D., & Manson, S. (1996). Predictive and concurrent validity of the Suicidal Ideation Questionnaire among American Indian adolescents. *Journal of Abnormal Child Psychology, 24*, 735–747.

Keating, D. (1990). Adolescent thinking. In S. Feldman & G. Elliott (Eds.), *At the threshold: The Developing adolescent* (pp. 54–89). Cambridge, MA: Harvard University Press.

Keating, D. (1995). Habits of mind: Developmental diversity in competence and coping. In D. Detterman (Ed.), *Current topics in human intelligence: The role of the environment* (pp. 31–44). Norwood, NJ: Ablex.

Keating, D., & Hertzman, C. (Eds.) (2000). *Developmental health and the wealth of nations: Social, biological, and educational dynamics.* New York: Guilford.

Keenan, K., Loeber, R., Zhang, Q., Stouthamer-Loeber, M., & Van Kammen, W. (1995). The influence of deviant peers on the development of boys' disruptive and delinquent behavior: A temporal analysis. *Development and Psychopathology, 7*, 715–726.

Keener, D., & Boykin, K. (1996, March). *Parental control, autonomy, and adolescent ego development.* Paper presented at the biennial meetings of the Society for Research on Adolescence, Boston.

Keithly, D., & Deseran, F. (1995). Households, local labor markets, and youth labor force participation. *Youth and Society, 26*, 463–492.

Kelder, S., Perry, C., Klepp, K., & Lytle, L. (1994). Longitudinal tracking of adolescent smoking, physical activity, and food choice behaviors. *American Journal of Public Health, 84*, 1121–1126.

Kellam, S., & Anthony, J. (1998). Targeting early antecedents to prevent tobacco smoking: Findings from an epidemiologically based randomized field trial. *American Journal of Public Health, 88*, 1490–1495.

Kellam, S., Ling, X., Merisca, R., Brown, C., & Ialongo, N. (1998). The effect of the level of aggression in the first grade classroom on the course and malleability of aggressive behavior into middle school. *Development and Psychopathology, 10*, 165–185.

Keller, M., Edelstein, W., Schmid, C., Fang, F., & Fang, G. (1998). Reasoning about responsibilities and obligations in close relationships: A comparison across two cultures. *Developmental Psychology, 34*, 731–741.

Kelley, J., & de Armaa, A. (1989). Social relationships in adolescence: Skill development and training. In J. Worell & F. Danner (Eds.), *The adolescent as decision-maker.* San Diego: Academic Press.

Kelly, B., Huizinga, A., Thornberry, T., & Loeber, R. (1997, June). Epidemiology of serious violence. *OJJDP Juvenile Justice Bulletin.*

Keniston, K. (1970). Youth: A "new" stage of life. *American Scholar, 39*, 631–641.

Kenny, M. (1987). The extent and function of parental attachment among first-year college students. *Journal of Youth and Adolescence, 16*, 17–27.

Kerns, K. (1996). Individual differences in friendship quality: Links to child-mother attachment. In W. Bukowski, A. Newcomb, & W. Hartup (Eds.), *The company they keep: Friendship in childhood and adolescence* (pp. 137–157). New York: Cambridge University Press.

Kerr, M., & Stattin, H. (2000). What parents know, how they know it, and several forms of adolescent adjustment: Further support for a reinterpretation of monitoring. *Developmental Psychology, 36*, 366–380.

Kerr, M., Stattin, H., & Trost, K. (1999). To know you is to trust you: Parents' trust is rooted in child disclosure of information. *Journal of Adolescence, 22*, 737–752.

Kett, J. (1977). *Rites of passage: Adolescence in America, 1790 to the present.* New York: Basic Books.

Kilborn, P. (1996, November 27). Shifts in families reach a plateau, study says. *New York Times,* p. A16.

Kilgore, S. (1991). The organizational context of tracking in schools. *American Sociological Review, 56*, 189–203.

Killen, J., Robinson, T., Haydel, K., Hayward, C., Wilson, D., Hammer, L., Litt, I., & Taylor, C. (1997). Prospective study of risk factors for the initiation of cigarette smoking. *Journal of Consulting and Clinical Psychology, 65*, 1011–1016.

Killen, M., & Nucci, L. (1995). Morality, autonomy, and social conflict. In M. Killen & D. Hart (Eds.), *Morality in everyday life: A developmental perspective* (pp. 52–86). Cambridge, England: Cambridge University Press.

Killen, M., & Turiel, E. (1998). Adolescents' and young adults' evaluations of helping and sacrificing for others. *Journal of Research on Adolescence, 8*, 355–375.

Killian, K. (1994). Fearing fat: A literature review of family systems understandings and treatments of anorexia and bulimia. *Family Relations, 43*, 311–318.

Kilpatrick, D., Acierno, R., Saunders, B., Resnick, H., Best, C., & Schnurr, P. (2000). Risk factors for adolescent substance abuse and dependence: Data from a national sample. *Journal of Consulting and Clinical Psychology, 68*, 19–30.

Kim, J., Hetherington, E. M., & Reiss, D. (1999). Associations among family relationships, antisocial peers, and adolescents' externalizing behaviors: Gender and family type differences. *Child Development, 70*, 1209–1230.

Kimm, S. (1995). The role of dietary fiber in the development and treatment of childhood obesity. *Pediatrics, 96*, 1010–1014.

King, C., Akiyama, M., & Elling, K. (1996). Self-perceived competencies and depression among middle school students in Japan and the United States. *Journal of Early Adolescence, 16*, 192–210.

King, K., Balswick, J., & Robinson, I. (1977). The continuing premarital sexual revolution among college females. *Journal of Marriage and the Family, 39*, 455–459.

King, V., Elder, G. H., Jr., & Whitbeck, L. B. (1997). Religious involvement among rural youth: An ecological and life-course perspective. *Journal of Research on Adolescence, 7*, 431–456.

Kinney, D. (1993). From nerds to normals: The recovery of identity among adolescents from middle school to high school. *Sociology of Education, 66*, 21–40.

Kinsey, A., Pomeroy, W., & Martin, C. (1948). *Sexual behavior in the human male.* Philadelphia: Saunders.

Kirby, D., Korpi, M., Barth, R., & Cagampang, H. (1997). The impact of the Postponding Sexual Involvement curriculum among youths in California. *Family Planning Perspectives, 29,* 100–108.

Kirkendall, L. (1981). Sex education in the United States: A historical perspective. In L. Brown (Ed.), *Sex education in the eighties.* New York: Plenum.

Kisela, M., & Sturmer, P. (1993). Is society giving teenage fathers a mixed message? *Youth and Society, 24,* 487–501.

Kisker, E., & Brown, R. (1996). Do school-based health centers improve adolescents' access to health care, health status, and risk-taking behavior? *Journal of Adolescent Health, 18,* 335–343.

Kite, M. (1984). Sex differences in attitudes towards homosexuals: A meta-analytic review. *Journal of Homosexuality, 10,* 69–81.

Kitzmann, K., & Emery, R. (1994). Child and family coping one year after mediated and litigated child custody disputes. *Journal of Family Psychology, 8,* 150–159.

Klaczynski, P. (1997). Bias in adolescents' everyday reasoning and its relationship with intellectual ability, personal theories, and self-serving motivation. *Developmental Psychology, 33,* 273–283.

Klaczynski, P. (in press). Analytic and heuristic processing influences on adolescent reasoning and decision making. *Child Development.*

Klaczynski, P., & Gordon, D. (1996). Everyday statistical reasoning during adolescence and young adulthood: Motivational, general ability, and developmental influences. *Child Development, 67,* 2873–2891.

Klaczynzki, P., & Narasimham, G. (1998a). Development of scientific reasoning biases: Cognitive versus ego-protective explanations. *Developmental Psychology, 34,* 175–187.

Klaczynski, P., & Narasimham, G. (1998b). Representations as mediators of adolescent deductive reasoning. *Developmental Psychology, 34,* 865–881.

Klebanov, P., & Brooks-Gunn, J. (1992). Impact of maternal attitudes, girls' adjustment, and cognitive skills upon academic performance in middle and high school. *Journal of Research on Adolescence, 2,* 81–102.

Klepinger, D., Lundberg, S., & Plotnick, R. (1995). Adolescent fertility and the educational attainment of young women. *Family Planning Perspectives, 27,* 23–28.

Klerman, L. (1993). The influence of economic factors on health-related behaviors in adolescents. In S. Millstein, A. Petersen, & E. Nightingale (Eds.), *Promoting the health of adolescents: New directions for the twenty-first century* (pp. 38–57). New York: Oxford University Press.

Kliewer, W., & Sandler, I. (1992). Locus of control and self-esteem as moderators of stress-symptom relations in children and adolescents. *Journal of Abnormal Child Psychology, 20,* 393–413.

Kling, K., Hyde, J., Showers, C., & Buswell, B. (1999). Gender differences in self-esteem: A meta-analysis. *Psychological Bulletin, 125,* 470–500.

Kloep, M. (1995). Concurrent and predictive correlates of girls' depression and antisocial behaviour under conditions of economic crisis and value change: The case of Albania. *Journal of Adolescence, 18,* 445–458.

Kneisel, P. (1987, April). *Social support preferences of female adolescents in the context of interpersonal stress.* Paper presented at the biennial meetings of the Society for Research in Child Development, Baltimore.

Knight, G., Virdin, L., & Roosa, M. (1994). Socialization and family correlates of mental health outcomes among Hispanic and Anglo American children: Consideration of cross-ethnic scalar equivalence. *Child Development, 65,* 212–224.

Kobak, R., & Cole, H. (1994). Attachment and meta-monitoring: Implications for adolescent autonomy and psychopathology. In D. Cicchetti & S. Toth (Eds.), *Rochester symposium on developmental psychopathology, Vol. 5: Disorders and dysfunctions of the self* (pp. 267–297). Rochester, NY: University of Rochester Press.

Kobak, R., Cole, H., Ferenz-Gillies, R., Fleming, W., & Gamble, W. (1993). Attachment and emotion regulation during mother-teen problem-solving: A control theory analysis. *Child Development, 64,* 231–245.

Kobak, R., & Sceery, A. (1988). Attachment in late adolescence: Working models, affect regulation, and representations of self and others. *Child Development, 59,* 135–146.

Kobak, R., Sudler, N., & Gamble, W. (1992). Attachment and depressive symptoms during adolescence: A developmental pathways analysis. *Development and Psychopathology, 3,* 461–474.

Koch, P. (1993). Promoting healthy sexual development during early adolescence. In R. Lerner (Ed.), *Early adolescence: Perspectives on research, policy, and intervention* (pp. 293–307). Hillsdale, NJ: Erlbaum.

Koenig, L. (1995, March). *Change in self-esteem from 8th to 10th grade: Effects of gender and disruptive life events.* Paper presented at the biennial meetings of the Society for Research in Child Development, Indianapolis.

Koerner, S., Jacobs, S., & Raymond, M. (2000). When mothers turn to their adolescent daughters: Predicting daughters' vulnerability to negative adjustment outcomes. *Family Relations, 49,* 301–309.

Koff, E., & Rierdan, J. (1996). Premenarcheal expectations and postmenarcheal experiences of positive and negative menstrual related changes. *Journal of Adolescent Health, 18,* 286–291.

Kohlberg, L. (1976). Moral stages and moralization: The cognitive-development approach. In T. Lickona (Ed.), *Moral development and behavior.* New York: Holt, Rinehart & Winston.

Kohn, M. (1977). *Class and conformity* (2nd ed). Chicago: University of Chicago Press.

Koizumi, R. (1995). Feelings of optimism and pessimism in Japanese students' transition to junior high school. *Journal of Early Adolescence, 15,* 412–428.

Koo, H., Dunteman, G., George, C., Green, Y., & Vincent, M. (1994). Reducing adolescent pregnancy through a school- and community-based intervention: Denmark, South Carolina revisited. *Family Planning Perspectives, 26,* 206–211, 217.

Kosterman, R., Hawkins, J., Guo, J., Catalano, R., & Abbott, R. (2000). The dynamics of alcohol and marijuana initiation: Patterns and predictors of first use in adolescence. *American Journal of Public Health, 90,* 360–366.

Kowal, A., & Kramer, L. (1997). Children's understanding of parental differential treatment. *Child Development, 68,* 113–126.

Krevans, J., & Gibbs, J. (1996). Parents' use of inductive discipline: Relations to children's empathy and prosocial behavior. *Child Development, 67,* 3263–3277.

Krisberg, B., Schwartz, I., Fishman, G., Eisikovits, Z., & Guttman, E. (1986). *The incarceration of minority youth.* Minneapolis, MN: Hubert H. Humphrey Institute of Public Affairs, National Council on Crime and Delinquency.

Krishnakamur, A., & Buehler, C. (1996, March). *Interparental conflict styles and youth problem behaviors: The mediational role of parental behavioral control.* Paper presented at the biennial meetings of the Society for Research on Adolescence, Boston.

Kroger, J. (1993). The role of historical context in the identity formation process of late adolescence. *Youth and Society, 24,* 363–376.

Kroger, J. (1996). Identity, regression, and development. *Journal of Adolescence, 19,* 203–222.

Kroger, J., & Green, K. (1996). Events associated with identity status change. *Journal of Adolescence, 19,* 477–490.

Krosnick, J., & Judd, C. (1982). Transitions in social influence at adolescence: Who induces cigarette smoking? *Developmental Psychology, 18,* 359–368.

Kuhn, D., Garcia-Mila, M., Zohar, A., & Andersen, C. (1995). Strategies of knowledge acquistion. *Monographs of the Society for Research in Child Development, 60*(4) (Serial No. 245).

Kuhn, D., Langer, J., Kohlberg, L., & Haan, N. (1977). The development of formal operations in logical and moral judgment. *Genetic Psychology Monographs, 95,* 97–188.

Kupersmidt, J., Burchinal, M., Leff, S., & Patterson, C. (1992, March). *A longitudinal study of perceived support and conflict with parents from middle childhood through adolescence.* Paper presented at the biennial meetings of the Society for Research on Adolescence, Washington.

Kupersmidt, J., Burchinal, M., & Patterson, C. (1995). Developmental patterns of childhood peer relations as predictors of externalizing behavior problems. *Development and Psychopathology, 7,* 825–843.

Kupersmidt, J., & Coie, J. (1990). Preadolescent peer status, aggression, and school adjustment as predictors of externalizing problems in adolescents. *Child Development, 61,* 1350–1362.

Kurdek, L., & Fine, M. (1993). The relation between family structure and young adolescents' appraisals of family climate and parenting behavior. *Journal of Family Issues, 14,* 279–290.

Kurdek, L., & Fine, M. (1994). Family acceptance and family control as predictors of adjustment in young adolescents: Linear, curvilinear, or interactive effects. *Child Development, 65,* 1137–1146.

Kurdek, L., & Fine, M. (1995). Mothers, fathers, stepfathers, and siblings as providers of supervision, acceptance, and autonomy to young adolescents. *Journal of Family Psychology, 9,* 95–99.

Kurdek, L., Fine, M., & Sinclair, R. (1995). School adjustment in sixth graders: Parenting transitions, family climate, and peer norm effects. *Child Development, 66,* 430–445.

Kurdek, L., & Sinclair, R. (1988). Relation of eighth graders' family structure, gender, and family environment with academic performance and school behavior. *Journal of Educational Psychology, 80,* 90–94.

Kuttler, A. F., La Greca, A. M., & Prinstein, M. J. (1999). Friendship qualities and social-emotional functioning of adolescents with close, cross-sex friendships. *Journal of Research on Adolescence, 9*(3), 339–366.

Lahey, B., Goodman, S., Waldman, I., Bird, H., Canino, G., Jensen, P., Regier, D., Leaf, P., Gordon, R., & Applegate, B. (1999). Relation of age of onset to the type and severity of child and adolescent conduct problems. *Journal of Abnormal Child Psychology, 27,* 247–260.

Lahey, B., Loeber, R., Hart, E., Frick, P. Applegate, B., Zhang, Q., Green, S. & Russo, M. (1995). Four-uear longitudinal study of conduct disorder in boys: Patterns and predictors of persistence. *Journal of Abnormal Psychology, 104,* 83–93.

Laird, R., Pettit, G., Dodge, K., & Bates, J. (1999). Best friendships, group relationships, and antisocial behavior in early adolescence. *Journal of Early Adolescence, 19,* 413–437.

Lamborn, S., Dornbusch, S., & Steinberg, L. (1996). Ethnicity and community context as moderators of the relation between family decision-making and adolescent adjustment. *Child Development, 66,* 283–301.

Lamborn, S., Mounts, N., Brown, B., & Steinberg, L. (1992). Putting school in perspective: The influence of family, peers, extracurricular participation, and part-time work on academic engagement. In F. Newmann (Ed.), *Student engagement and achievement in American secondary schools* (pp. 153–181). New York: Teachers College Press.

Lamborn, S., Mounts, N., Steinberg, L., & Dornbusch, S. (1991). Patterns of competence and adjustment among adolescents from authoritative, authoritarian, indulgent, and neglectful families. *Child Development, 62,* 1049–1065.

Lamborn, S., & Steinberg, L. (1993). Emotional autonomy redux: Revisiting Ryan and Lynch. *Child Development, 64,* 483–499.

Landry, D., Kaeser, L., & Richards, C. (1999). Abstinence promotion and the provision of information about contraception in public school district sexuality education policies. *Family Planning Perspectives, 31,* 280–286.

Lang, S., Waller, P., & Shope, J. (1996). Adolescent driving: Characteristics associated with single-vehicle and injury crashes. *Journal of Safety Research, 27,* 241–257.

Langer, L., Tubman, J. G., & Duncan, S. (1998). Anticipated mortality, HIV vulnerability, and psychological distress among adolescents and young adults at higher and lower risk for HIV infection. *Journal of Youth and Adolescence, 27,* 513–538.

Langer, L., Zimmerman, R., & Katz, J. (1995). Virgins' expectations and nonvirgins' reports: How adolescents feel about themselves. *Journal of Adolescent Research, 10,* 291–306.

Lapsley, D. (1989). Continuity and discontinuity in adolescent social cognitive development. In R. Montemayor, G. Adams, & T. Gullota (Eds.), *Advances in adolescence research* (Vol. 2). Beverly Hills, CA: Sage.

Lapsley, D., Enright, R., & Serlin, R. (1985). Toward a theoretical perspective on the legislation of adolescence. *Journal of Early Adolescence, 5,* 441–466.

Lapsley, D., Flannery, D., Gottschlich, H., & Raney, M. (1996, March). *Sources of risk and resilience in adolescent mental health.* Paper presented at the biennial meetings of the Society for Research on Adolescence, Boston.

Lapsley, D., & Murphy, M. (1985). Another look at the theoretical assumption of adolescent egocentrism. *Developmental Review, 5,* 201–217.

Larkin, R. W. (1979). *Suburban youth in cultural crisis.* New York: Oxford.

Larson, M. (1996). Sex roles and soap operas: What adolescents learn about single motherhood. *Sex Roles, 35,* 97–110.

Larson, R. (1983). Adolescents' daily experience with family and friends: Contrasting opportunity systems. *Journal of Marriage and the Family, 45,* 739–750.

Larson, R. (1990). The solitary side of life: An examination of the time people spend alone from childhood to old age. *Developmental Review, 10,* 155–183.

Larson, R. (1995). Secrets in the bedroom: Adolescents' private use of media. *Journal of Youth and Adolescence, 24,* 535–550.

Larson, R. (1997). The emergence of solitude as a constructive domain of experience in early adolescence. *Child Development, 68,* 80–93.

Larson, R. (2000). Toward a psychology of positive youth development. *American Psychologist, 55,* 170–183.

Larson, R. (in press). Adolescence in the 21st century: A worldwide perspective. Introduction: Macro societal trends and the changing experiences of adolescence. In J. Mortimer & R. Larson (Eds.), *Reconstructing adolescence: Societal trends influencing the transition to adulthood.*

Larson, R., Clore, G., & Wood, G. (1999). The emotions of romantic relationships: Do they wreak havoc on adolescents? In W. Furman, B. Brown, & C. Feiring (Eds.), *Contemporary perspectives on adolescent romantic relationships* (pp. 19–49). New York: Cambridge University Press.

Larson, R., & Gillman, S. (1996, March). *Daily processes in single parent families.* Paper presented at the biennial meetings of the Society for Research on Adolescence, Boston.

Larson, R., & Ham, M. (1993). Stress and "storm and stress" in early adolescence: The relationship of negative events with dysphoric affect. *Developmental Psychology, 29,* 130–140.

Larson, R., & Lampman-Petraitis, C. (1989). Daily emotional states as reported by children and adolescents. *Child Development, 60,* 1250–1260.

Larson, R., & Richards, M. (Eds.). (1989). The changing life space of early adolescence. *Journal of Youth and Adolescence, 18*(6).

Larson, R., & Richards, M. (1991). Daily companionship in late childhood and early adolescence: Changing developmental contexts. *Child Development, 62,* 284–300.

Larson, R., & Richards, M. (1994a). *Divergent realities: The emotional lives of mothers, fathers, and adolescents.* New York: Basic Books.

Larson, R., & Richards, M. (1994b). Family emotions: Do young adolescents and their parents experience the same states? *Journal of Research on Adolescence, 4,* 567–583.

Larson, R., & Richards, M. (1998, Winter). Waiting for the weekend: Friday and Saturday night as the emotional climax of the week. *New Directions for Child and Adolescent Development,* 37–51.

Larson, R., Richards, M., Moneta, G., Holmbeck, G., & Duckett, E. (1996). Changes in adolescents' daily interactions with their families from ages 10 to 18: Disengagement and transformation. *Developmental Psychology, 32,* 744–754.

Larson, R., Richards, M., Sims, B., & Dworkin, J. (in press). How urban African-American young adolescents spend their time: Time budgets for locations, activities, and companionship. *American Journal of Community Psychology.*

Larson, R., & Verma, S. (1999). How children and adolescents spend time across the world: Work, play, and developmental opportunities. *Psychological Bulletin, 125,* 701–736.

Lau, S. (1989). Sex role orientation and domains of self-esteem. *Sex Roles, 21,* 415–422.

Lau, S. (1990). Crisis and vulnerability in adolescent development. *Journal of Youth and Adolescence, 19,* 111–132.

Laub, J., & Sampson, R. (1995). The long-term effect of punitive discipline. In J. McCord (Ed.), *Coercion and punishment in long-term perspectives* (pp. 247–258). New York: Cambridge University Press.

Lauritsen, J. (1994). Explaining race and gender differences in adolescent sexual behavior. *Social Forces, 72,* 859–884.

Laursen, B. (1993). The perceived impact of conflict on adolescent relationships. *Merrill-Palmer Quarterly, 39,* 535–550.

Laursen, B. (1995). Conflict and social interaction in adolescent relationships. *Journal of Research on Adolescence, 5,* 55–70.

Laursen, B. (1996). Closeness and conflict in adolescent peer relationships: Interdependence with friends and romantic partners. In W. Bukowski, A. Newcomb, & W. Hartup (Eds.), *The company they keep: Friendship in childhood and adolescence* (pp. 186–210). New York: Cambridge University Press.

Laursen, B., & Collins, W. (1994). Interpersonal conflict during adolescence. *Psychological Bulletin, 115*, 197–209.

Laursen, B., Coy, K., & Collins, W. A. (1998). Reconsidering changes in parent-child conflict across adolescence: A meta-analysis. *Child Development, 69*, 817–832.

Laursen, B., & Jensen-Campbell, L. (1999). The nature and functions of social exchange in adolescent romantic relationships. In W. Furman, B. Brown, & C. Feiring (Eds.), *Contemporary perspectives on adolescent romantic relationships* (pp. 50–74). New York: Cambridge University Press.

LaVoie, J. (1994). Identity in adolescence: Issues of theory, structure, and transition. *Journal of Adolescence, 17*, 17–28.

Lazarus, R., & Folkman, S. (Eds.). (1984). *Stress, appraisal, and coping.* New York: Springer-Verlag.

Leadbeater, B. (1996). School outcomes for minority-group adolescent mothers at 28 to 36 months postpartum: A longitudinal follow-up. *Journal of Research on Adolescence, 6*, 629–648.

Leadbeater, B., & Bishop, S. (1994). Predictors of behavior problems in preschool children of inner-city Afro-American and Puerto Rican adolescent mothers. *Child Development, 65*, 638–648.

Leadbeater, B., Blatt, S., & Quinlan, D. (1995). Gender-linked vulnerabilities to depressive symptoms, stress, and problem behaviors in adolescents. *Journal of Research on Adolescence, 5*, 1–29.

Leadbeater, B., Kuperminc, G., Blatt, S., & Hertzog, C. (1999). A multivariate model of gender differences in adolescents' internalizing and externalizing problems. *Developmental Psychology, 35*, 1268–1282.

Lee, M., & Larson, R. (1996). Effectiveness of coping in adolescence: The case of Korean examination stress. *International Journal of Behavioral Development, 19*, 851–869.

Lee, V., & Bryk, A. (1988). Curriculum tracking as mediating the social distribution of high school achievement. *Sociology of Education, 61*, 78–94.

Lee, V., & Bryk, A. (1989). A multilevel model of the social distribution of high school achievement. *Sociology of Education, 62*, 172–192.

Lee, V., Burkham, D., Zimiles, H., & Ladewski, B. (1994). Family structure and its effect on behavioral and emotional problems in young adolescents. *Journal of Research on Adolescence, 4*, 405–437.

Lee, V., & Burkham, D. (1992). Transferring high schools: An alternative to dropping out? *American Journal of Education, 100*, 420–453.

Lee, V., Croninger, R., Linn, E., & Chen, X. (1996). The culture of sexual harassment in secondary schools. *American Educational Research Journal, 33*, 383–417.

Lee, V., Marks, H., & Byrd, T. (1994). Sexism in single-sex and coeducational independent secondary school classrooms. *Sociology of Education, 67*, 92–120.

Lee, V., Smith, J., & Croninger, R. (1997). How high school organization influences the equitable distribution of learning in mathematics and science. *Sociology of Education, 70*, 128–150.

Lee, V., & Croninger, R. (1994). The relative importance of home and school in the development of literacy skills for middle-grade students. *American Journal of Education, 102*, 286–329.

Lee, V., & Smith, J. (1993). Effects of school restructuring on the achievement and engagement of middle-grade students. *Sociology of Education, 66*, 164–187.

Lee, V., & Smith, J. (1996). Collective responsibility for learning and its effects on gains in achievement for early secondary school students. *American Journal of Education, 104*, 103–147.

Lefkowitz, E., Romo, L., Corona, R., Au, T., & Sigman, M. (2000). How Latino American and European American adolescents discuss conflicts, sexuality, and AIDS with their mothers. *Developmental Psychology, 36*, 315–325.

Leibowitz, S. (1983). Hypothalamic catecholamine systems controlling eating behavior: A potential model for anorexia nervosa. In P. Darby, P. Garfinkel, D. Garner, & D. Cosina (Eds.), *Anorexia nervosa: Recent developments in research* (pp. 221–229). New York: Alan R. Liss.

Leming, J. (1987). Rock music and the socialization of moral values in early adolescence. *Youth and Society, 18*, 363–383.

Lempers, J., & Clark-Lempers, D. (1992). Young, middle, and late adolescents' comparisons of the functional importance of five significant relationships. *Journal of Youth and Adolescence, 21*, 53–96.

Lempers, J., Clark-Lempers, D., & Simmons, R. (1989). Economic hardship, parenting, and distress in adolescence. *Child Development, 60*, 25–49.

Lenhart, L., & Rabiner, D. (1995). An integrative approach to the study of social competence in adolescence. *Development and Psychopathology, 7*, 543–561.

Loeber, R., & Stouthamer-Loeber, M. (1986). Family factors as correlates and predictors of juvenile conduct problems and delinquency. In M. Tonry & N. Morris (Eds.), *Crime and justice* (Vol. 7, pp. 219–339). Chicago: University of Chicago Press.

Leon, G., Fulkerson, J., Perry, C., & Dube, A. (1994). Family influences, school behaviors, and risk for later development of an eating disorder. *Journal of Youth and Adolescence, 23*, 499–515.

Leon, G. R., Fulkerson, J. A., Perry, C. L., Keel, P. K., & Klump, K. L. (1999). Three to four year prospective evaluation of personality and behavioral risk factors for later disordered eating in adolescent girls and boys. *Journal of Youth and Adolescence, 28*, 181–196.

Lerner, J., Castellino, D., & Perkins, D. (1994, February). *The influence of adolescent behavioral and psychosocial characteristics on maternal behaviors*

and satisfaction. Paper presented at the biennial meetings of the Society for Research on Adolescence, San Diego.

Lerner, J., Hertzog, C., Hooker, K., Hassibi, M., & Thomas, A. (1988). A longitudinal study of negative emotional states and adjustment from early childhood through adolescence. *Child Development, 59*, 356–366.

Lesko, N. (1996). Denaturalizing adolescence: The politics of contemporary representations. *Youth and Society, 28*, 139–161.

Leslie, L. (1986). The impact of adolescent females' assessments of parenthood and employment on plans for the future. *Journal of Youth and Adolescence, 15*, 29–49.

Leventhal, H., & Keeshan, P. (1993). Promoting healthy alternatives to substance abuse. In S. Millstein, A. Petersen, & E. Nightingale (Eds.), *Promoting the health of adolescents: New directions for the twenty-first century* (pp. 260–284). New York: Oxford University Press.

Leventhal, T., & Brooks-Gunn, J. (2000). The neighborhoods they live in: The effects of neighborhood residence on child and adolescent outcomes. *Psychological Bulletin, 126*, 309–317.

Levesque, R. (1993). The romantic experience of adolescents in satisfying love relationships. *Journal of Youth and Adolescence, 22*, 219–251.

Levine, M., Smolak, L., & Hayden, H. (1994). The relation of sociocultural factors to eating attitudes and behaviors among middle school girls. *Journal of Early Adolescence, 14*, 471–490.

Levinson, D. (1978). *The seasons of a man's life.* New York: Knopf.

Levinson, R., Jaccard, J., & Beamer, L. (1995). Older adolescents' engagement in casual sex: Impact of risk perception and psychosocial motivations. *Journal of Youth and Adolescence, 24*, 349–364.

Levitt, M., Guacci-Franci, N., & Levitt, J. (1993). Convoys of social support in childhood and early adolescence: Structure and function. *Developmental Psychology, 29*, 811–818.

Levitz-Jones, E., & Orlofsky, J. (1985). Separation-individuation and intimacy capacity in college women. *Journal of Personality and Social Psychology, 49*, 156–169.

Lewin, K. (1948). *Resolving social conflict.* New York: Harper & Row.

Lewin, K. (1951). *Field theory and social science.* New York: Harper & Row.

Lewin, L., Davis, B., & Hops, H. (1999). Childhood social predictors of adolescent antisocial behavior: Gender differences in predictive accuracy and efficacy. *Journal of Abnormal Child Psychology, 27*, 277–292.

Lewin, T. (1997, October 1). Sexual abuse tied to 1 in 4 girls in teens. *New York Times*, p. A24.

Lewin-Epstein, N. (1981). *Youth employment during high school.* Washington, DC: National Center for Education Statistics.

Lewinsohn, P., Gotlib, I., & Seeley, J. (1997). Depression-related psychosocial variables: Are they specific to depression in adolescents? *Journal of Abnormal Psychology, 106*, 365–375.

Lewinsohn, P., Hops, H., Roberts, R., Seeley, J., & Andrews, J. (1993). Adolescent psychopathology, I: Prevalence and incidence of depression and other *DSM-III-R* disorders in high school students. *Journal of Abnormal Psychology, 102,* 133–144.

Lewinsohn, P., Roberts, R., Seeley, J., Rohde, P., Gotlib, I., & Hops, H. (1994). Adolescent psychopathology, II: Psychosocial risk factors for depression. *Journal of Abnormal Psychology, 103,* 302–325.

Lewinsohn, P., Rohde, P., Seeley, J., & Fischer, S. (1993). Age-cohort changes in the lifetime occurrence of depression and other mental disorders. *Journal of Abnormal Psychology, 102,* 110–120.

Lewis, C. (1981a). The effects of parental firm control. *Psychological Bulletin, 90,* 547–563.

Lewis, C. (1981b). How adolescents approach decisions: Changes over grades seven to twelve and policy implications. *Child Development, 52,* 538–544.

Lewis, C. (1987). Minors' competence to consent to abortion. *American Psychologist, 41,* 84–88.

Lewis, M., Feiring, C., & Rosenthal, S. (2000). Attachment over time. *Child Development, 71,* 707–720.

Lewis, M., Feiring, C., McGuffog, C., & Jaskir, J. (1984). Predicting psychopathology in six-year-olds from early social relations. *Child Development, 55,* 123–136.

Li, X., Stanton, B., Black, M., & Feigelman, S. (1996). Persistence of drug trafficking behaviors and intentions among urban African American early adolescents. *Journal of Early Adolescence, 16,* 469–487.

Lieberman, M., Doyle, A., & Markiewicz, D. (1999). Developmental patterns in security of attachment to mother and father in late childhood and early adolescence: Associations with peer relations. *Child Development, 70,* 202–213.

Lieu, T., Newacheck, P., & McManus, M. (1993). Race, ethnicity, and access to ambulatory care among U.S. adolescents. *American Journal of Public Health, 83,* 960–965.

Lightfoot, C. (1997). *The culture of adolescent risk-taking.* New York: Guilford.

Linn, M., & Songer, N. (1991). Cognitive and conceptual change in adolescence. *American Journal of Education, 99,* 379–417.

Linn, M., & Songer, N. (1993). How do students make sense of science? *Merrill-Palmer Quarterly, 39,* 47–73.

Linney, J., & Seidman, E. (1989). The future of schooling. *American Psychologist, 44,* 336–340.

Lipsey, M. (1997, May). *Can intervention rehabilitate serious delinquents? Research on a central premise of the juvenile justice system.* Paper presented at the Symposium on the Future of the Juvenile Court, University of Pennsylvania, Philadelphia.

Lipsitz, J. (1977). *Growing up forgotten.* Lexington, MA: Lexing-ton Books.

Litchfield, A., Thomas, D., & Li, B. (1997). Dimensions of religiosity as mediators of the relations between parenting and adolescent deviant behavior. *Journal of Adolescent Research, 12,* 199–226.

Little, T., Oettingen, G., Stetsenko, A., & Baltes, P. (1995). Children's action-control beliefs about school performance: How do American children compare with German and Russian children? *Journal of Personality and Social Psychology, 69,* 686–700.

Liu, X., Kaplan, H., & Risser, W. (1992). Decomposing the reciprocal relationships between academic achievement and general self-esteem. *Youth and Society, 24,* 123–148.

Livson, N., & Peskin, H. (1980). Perspectives on adolescence from longitudinal research. In J. Adelson (Ed.), *Handbook of adolescent psychology.* pp. 47–98. New York: Wiley.

Lochman, J. (1992). Cognitive-behavioral intervention with aggressive boys: Three-year follow-up and preventive effects. *Journal of Consulting and Clinical Psychology, 60,* 426–432.

Lochman, J., & Dodge, K. (1994). Social-cognitive processes of severely violent, moderately aggressive, and nonaggressive boys. *Journal of Consulting and Clinical Psychology, 62,* 366–374.

Lochman, J., & Dodge, K. (1998). Distorted perceptions in dyadic interactions of aggressive and nonaggressive boys: Effects of prior expectations, context, and boys' age. *Development and Psychopathology, 10,* 495–512.

Loeber, R., Russo, M., Stouthamer-Loeber, M., & Lahey, B. (1994). Internalizing problems and their relation to the development of disruptive behaviors in adolescence. *Journal of Research in Adolescence, 5,* 615–637.

Loeber, R., & Stouthamer-Loeber, M. (1986). Family factors as correlates and preictors of juvenile conduct problems and delinquency. In M. Tonry & N. Morris (Eds.), *Crime and justice* (Vol. 7). pp 219–339. Chicago: University of Chicago Press.

Loeber, R., & Stouthamer-Loeber, M. (1998). Development of juvenile aggression and violence: Some common misconceptions and controversies. *American Psychologist, 53,* 242–259.

Loeber, R., Wung, P., Keenan, K., Giroux, B., Stouthamer-Loeber, M., Van Kammen, W., & Maughan, B. (1993). Developmental pathways in disruptive child behavior. *Development and Psychopathology, 5,* 103–133.

Long, B. (1989). Heterosexual involvement of unmarried undergraduate females in relation to self-evaluations. *Journal of Youth and Adolescence, 18,* 489–500.

Lonigan, C., Carey, M., & Finch, A., Jr. (1994). Anxiety and depression in children and adolescents: Negative affectivity and the utility of self-reports. *Journal of Consulting and Clinical Psychology, 62,* 1000–1008.

Lord, S., Eccles, J., & McCarthy, K. (1994). Surviving the junior high transition: Family processes and self-perceptions as protective and risk factors. *Journal of Early Adolescence, 14,* 162–199.

Loredo, C., Reid, A., & Deaux, K. (1995). Judgments and definitions of sexual harassment by high school students. *Sex Roles, 32,* 29–45.

Louis, K., & Smith, B. (1992). Breaking the iron law of social class: The renewal of teachers' professional status and engagement. In F. Newmann (Ed.), *Student engagement and achievement in American high schools.* New York: Teachers College Press.

Lourenço, O., & Machado, A. (1996). In defense of Piaget's theory: A reply to 10 common criticisms. *Psychological Review, 103,* 143–164.

Lovitt, T. (1989). *Introduction to learning disabilities.* Boston: Allyn & Bacon.

Lowry, R., Holtzman, D., Truman, B., Kann, L., Collins, J., & Kolbe, L. (1994). Substance use and HIV-related sexual behaviors among U.S. high school students: Are they related? *American Journal of Public Health, 84,* 1116–1120.

Lucas, S. (1996). Selective attrition in a newly hostile regime: The case of 1980 sophomores. *Social Forces, 75,* 511–533.

Luo, Q., Urberg, K., Rao, P., & Fang, Z. (1995, March). *Selection of best friends among Chinese adolescents.* Paper presented at the biennial meetings of the Society for Research in Child Development, Indianapolis.

Luster, T., & McAdoo, H. (1995). Factors related to self-esteem among African American youths: A secondary analysis of the High/Scope Perry Preschool data. *Journal of Research on Adolescence, 5,* 451–467.

Luster, T., & Small, S. (1994). Factors associated with sexual risk-taking behaviors among adolescents. *Journal of Marriage and the Family, 56,* 622–632.

Luster, T., & Small, S. (1997). Sexual abuse history and problems in adolescence: Exploring the effects of moderating variables. *Journal of Marriage and the Family, 59,* 131–142.

Luthar, S. (1991). Vulnerability and resilience: A study of high-risk adolescents. *Child Development, 62,* 600–616.

Luthar, S. (1994, February). *Social competence of inner-city adolescents: A six-month prospective study.* Paper presented at the biennial meetings of the Society for Research on Adolescence, San Diego.

Luthar, S., & Cushing, G. (1997). Substance use and personal adjustment among disadvantaged teenagers: A six-month prospective study. *Journal of Youth and Adolescence, 26,* 353–372.

Luthar, S., & McMahon, T. (1996). Peer reputation among inner-city adolescents: Structure and correlates. *Journal of Research on Adolescence, 6,* 581–603.

Lynam, D. (1996). Early identification of chronic offenders: Who is the fledgling psychopath? *Psychological Bulletin, 120,* 209–234.

Lynn, D. (1966). The process of learning parental and sex-role identification. *Journal of Marriage and the Family, 28,* 446–470.

Lyon, J., Henggeler, S., & Hall, J. (1992). The family relations, peer relations, and criminal activities of Caucasian and Hispanic-American gang members. *Journal of Abnormal Child Psychology, 20,* 439–449.

Mac Iver, D., Stipek, D., & Daniels, D. (1991). Explaining within-semester changes in student effort in junior high school and senior high school courses. *Journal of Educational Psychology, 83,* 201–211.

Maccoby, E. (1990). Gender and relationships: A developmental account. *American Psychologist, 45,* 513–520.

Maccoby, E., & Jacklin, C. (1974). *The psychology of sex differences.* Stanford, CA: Stanford University Press.

Maccoby, E., & Martin, J. (1983). Socialization in the context of the family: Parent-child interaction. In E. M. Hetherington (Ed.), *Handbook of child psychology: Socialization, personality, and social development* (Vol. 4). pp. 1–101. New York: Wiley.

MacDonald, W., & DeMaris, A. (1995). Remarriage, stepchildren, and marital conflict: Challenges to the incomplete institutionalization hypothesis. *Journal of Marriage and the Family, 57,* 387–398.

MacKinnon-Lewis, C., Starnes, R., Volling, B., & Johnson, S. (1997). Perceptions of parenting as predictors of boys' sibling and peer relations. *Developmental Psychology, 33,* 1024–1031.

Macksoud, M., & Aber, J. (1996). The war experiences and psychosocial development of children in Lebanon. *Child Development, 67,* 70–88.

Madon, S., Jussim, L., & Eccles, J. (1997). In search of the powerful self-fulfilling prophecy. *Journal of Personality and Social Psychology, 72,* 791–809.

Maggs, J., Almeida, D., & Galambos, N. (1995). Risky business: The paradoxical meaning of problem behavior for young adolescents. *Journal of Early Adolescence, 15,* 344–362.

Maharaj, S., & Connolly, J. (1994). Peer network composition of acculturated and ethnoculturally-affiliated adolescents in a multicultural setting. *Journal of Adolescent Research, 9,* 218–240.

Mahoney, E. (1983). *Human sexuality.* New York: McGraw-Hill.

Mahoney, J. (2000). School extracurricular activity participation as a moderator in the development of antisocial patterns. *Child Development, 71,* 502–516.

Mahoney, J., & Cairns, R. (1997). Do extracurricular activities protect against early school dropout? *Developmental Psychology, 33,* 241–253.

Main, M., Kaplan, N., & Cassidy, J. (1985). Security in infancy, childhood and adulthood: A move to the level of representation. In I. Bretherton & E. Waters (Eds.), Growing points of attachment theory and research. *Monographs of the Society for Research on Child Development, 50,* 1–2, Serial No. 209, 66–106.

Malanchuk, O., & Eccles, J. (1999, April). *Determinants of self-esteem in African-American and white adolescent girls.* Paper presented at the biennial meetings of the Society for Research on Child Development, Albuquerque.

Males, M. (1996). *The scapegoat generation: America's war on adolescents.* Monroe, ME: Common Courage Press.

Males, M. (1998). *Framing youth: 10 myths about the next generation.* Monroe, ME: Common Courage Press.

Males, M., & Chew, K. (1996). The ages of fathers in California adolescent births. *American Journal of Public Health, 86,* 565–568.

Manegold, C. (1994, August 18). U.S. students are found gaining only in science. *New York Times,* p. A14.

Manlove, J. (1998). The influence of high school dropout and school disengagement on the risk of school-age pregnancy. *Journal of Research on Adolescence, 8,* 187–220.

Mannheim, K. (1952). The problem of generations. In K. Mannheim (Ed.), *Essays on the sociology of knowledge.* London: Routledge & Kegan Paul.

Manning, W., & Landale, N. (1996). Racial and ethnic differences in the role of cohabitation in premarital childbearing. *Journal of Marriage and the Family, 58,* 63–77.

Manning, W., & Lichter, D. (1996). Parental cohabitation and children's economic well-being. *Journal of Marriage and the Family, 58,* 998–1010.

Marcenko, M., Fishman, G., & Friedman, J. (1999). Reexamining adolescent suicidal ideation: A developmental perspective applied to a diverse population. *Journal of Youth and Adolescence, 28,* 121–138.

Marcia, J. (1966). Development and validation of ego identity status. *Journal of Personality and Social Psychology, 3,* 551–558.

Marcia, J. (1976). Identity six years after: A follow-up study. *Journal of Youth and Adolescence, 5,* 145–150.

Marcia, J. (1980). Identity in adolescence. In J. Adelson (Ed.), *Handbook of adolescent psychology.* pp. 159–187. New York: Wiley.

Marcotte, D. (1997). Treating depression in adolescence: A review of the effectiveness of cognitive-behavioral treatments. *Journal of Youth and Adolescence, 26,* 273–283.

Marini, M. (1984). The order of events in the transition to adulthood. *Sociology of Education, 57,* 63–84.

Marini, M., Fan, P., Finley, E., & Beutel, A. (1996). Gender and job values. *Sociology of Education, 69,* 49–65.

Marini, Z., & Case, R. (1994). The development of abstract reasoning about the physical and social world. *Child Development, 65,* 147–159.

Markovits, H., & Valchon, R. (1989). Reasoning with contrary-to-fact propositions. *Journal of Experimental Child Psychology, 47,* 398–412.

Markovits, H., & Valchon, R. (1990). Conditional reasoning, representation, and level of abstraction. *Developmental Psychology, 26,* 942–951.

Markovits, H., Venet, M., Janveau-Brennan, G., Malfait, N., Pion, N., & Vadeboncoeur, I. (1996). Reasoning in young children: Fantasy and information retrieval. *Child Development, 67,* 2857–2872.

Markstrom-Adams, C. (1989). Androgyny and its relation to adolescent psychological well-being: A review of the literature. *Sex Roles, 21,* 469–473.

Markstrom-Adams, C., & Adams, G. (1995). Gender, ethnic group, and grade differences in psychosocial functioning during middle adolescence. *Journal of Youth and Adolescence, 24,* 397–417.

Markus, H., & Nurius, P. (1986). Possible selves. *American Psychologist, 41,* 954–969.

Marsh, H. (1989). Age and sex effects in multiple dimensions of self-concept: Preadolescence to early adulthood. *Journal of Educational Psychology, 81,* 417–430.

Marsh, H. (1990). Casual ordering of academic self-concept and academic achievement: A multiwave, longitudinal panel analysis. *Journal of Educational Psychology, 82,* 646–656.

Marsh, H., Chessor, D., Craven, R., & Roche, L. (1995). The effects of gifted and talented programs on academic self-concept: The big fish strikes again. *American Educational Research Journal, 32,* 285–319.

Marsh, H., Kong, C., & Hau, K. (2000). Longitudinal multilevel models of the big-fish-little-pond effect on academic self-concept: Counterbalancing contrast and reflected-glory effects in Hong Kong schools. *Journal of Personality and Social Psychology, 78,* 337–349.

Marsh, H., & Yeung, A. S. (1998). Longitudinal structural equation models of academic self-concept and achievement: Gender differences in the development of math and English constructs. *American Educational Research Journal, 35,* 705–738.

Marshall, S. (1994, February). *Ethnic socialization of African American children: Implications for parenting, identity development and academic achievement.* Paper presented at the biennial meetings of the Society for Research on Adolescence, San Diego.

Marshall, S. (1995). Ethnic socialization of African American children: Implications for parenting, identity development, and academic achievement. *Journal of Youth and Adolescence, 24,* 377–396.

Marshall, W. (1978). Puberty. In F. Falkner & J. Tanner (Eds.), *Human growth* (Vol. 2). New York: Plenum.

Martin, B. (1990). The transmission of relationship difficulties from one generation to the next. *Journal of Youth and Adolescence, 19,* 181–200.

Martinez, R., & Dukes, R. (1997). The effects of ethnic identity, ethnicity, and gender on adolescent well-being. *Journal of Youth and Adolescence, 26,* 503–516.

Mason, C., Cauce, A., Gonzales, N., & Hiraga, N. (1996). Neither too sweet nor too sour: Problem peers, maternal control, and problem behavior in African American adolescents. *Child Development, 67,* 2115–2130.

Mason, C., Cauce, A., Gonzales, N., & Hiraga, Y. (1994). Adolescent problem behavior: The effect of peers and the moderating role of father absence and the mother-child relationship. *American Journal of Community Psychology, 22,* 723–743.

Mason, C., Cauce, A., Gonzales, N., Hiraga, Y., & Grove, K. (1994). An ecological model of externalizing behaviors in African-American adolescents: No family is an island. *Journal of Research on Adolescence, 4,* 639–655.

Massad, C. (1981). Sex role identity and adjustment during adolescence. *Child Development, 52,* 1290–1298.

Masten, A., Coatsworth, J., Neemann, J., Gest, S., Tellegen, A., & Garmezy, N. (1995). The structure and coherence of competence from childhood through adolescence. *Child Development, 66,* 1635–1659.

Masten, A., Hubbard, J., Gest, S., Tellegen, A., Garmezy, N., & Ramirez, M. (1999). Competence in the context of adversity: Pathways to resilience and maladaptation from childhood to late adolescence. *Development and Psychopathology, 11,* 143–169.

Masten, A., Miliotis, D., Graham-Bermann, S., Ramirez, M., & Neemann, J. (1993). Children in homeless families: Risks to mental health and development. *Journal of Consulting and Clinical Psychology, 61,* 335–343.

Matas, L., Arend, R., & Sroufe, L. (1978). Continuity in adaptation in the second year: The relationship between quality of attachment and later competence. *Child Development, 49,* 547–556.

Matthews, D., & Keating, D. (1995). Domain specificity and habits of mind: An investigation of patterns of high-level development. *Journal of Early Adolescence, 15,* 319–343.

Matza, M. (1990, November 24). More pre-teens drinking, more teens are alcoholics. *Philadelphia Inquirer,* p. 1–A1.

Mauldon, J., & Luker, K. (1996). The effects of contraceptive education on method use at first intercourse. *Family Planning Perspectives, 28,* 19–24, 41.

Mazor, A., & Enright, R. (1988). The development of the individuation process from a social cognitive perspective. *Journal of Adolescence, 11,* 29–47.

Mazor, A., Shamir, R., & Ben-Moshe, J. (1990). The individuation process from a social-cognitive perspective in kibbutz adolescents. *Journal of Youth and Adolescence, 19,* 73–90.

McCabe, K., Barnett, D., & Robbins, E. (1996, March). *Optimistic future orientation and adjustment among inner city African-American youth.* Paper presented at the biennial meetings of the Society for Research on Adolescence, Boston.

McCabe, M. (1984). Toward a theory of adolescent dating. *Adolescence, 19,* 159–169.

McCall, R., Applebaum, M., & Hogarty, P. (1973). Developmental changes in mental performance. *Monographs of the Society for Research in Child Development, 38* (Serial No. 150).

McCarthy, B., & Hagen, J. (1992). Mean streets: The theoretical significance of situational delinquency among homeless youth. *American Journal of Sociology, 98,* 597–627.

McCarthy, K., Lord, S., Eccles, J., Kalil, A., & Furstenberg, F., Jr. (1992, March). *The impact of family management strategies on adolescents in high risk environments.* Paper presented at the biennial meetings of the Society for Research on Adolescence, Washington.

McClelland, D. (1961). *The achieving society.* Princeton, NJ: Van Nostrand.

McClelland, D., Atkinson, J., Clark, R., & Lowell, E. (1953). *The achievement motive.* New York: Appleton-Century-Crofts.

McClintock, M. (1980). Major gaps in menstrual cycle research: Behavioral and physiological controls in a biological context. In P. Komenich, M. McSweeney, J. Noack, & N. Elder (Eds.), *The menstrual cycle* (Vol. 2, pp. 7–23). New York: Springer.

McClintock, M., & Herdt, G. (1996). Rethinking puberty: The development of sexual attraction. *Psychological Sciences, 5,* 178–183.

McCord, J. (1990). Problem behaviors. In S. Feldman & G. Elliott (Eds.), *At the threshold: The developing adolescent* (pp. 414–430). Cambridge, MA: Harvard University Press.

McCord, J. (1996a). Family as crucible for violence: Comment on Gorman-Smith et al. (1996). *Journal of Family Psychology, 10,* 147–152.

McCoy, J. (1996b, March). *Parents' involvement in youths' peer relationships as predictor of youths' later psychological well-being.* Paper presented at the biennial meetings of the Society for Research on Adolescence, Boston.

McCoy, J., Brody, G., & Stoneman, Z. (1994). A longitudinal analysis of sibling relationships as mediators of the link between family processes and youths' best friendships. *Family Relations, 43,* 400–408.

McCrae, R., & John, O. (1992). An introduction to the Five-Factor Model and its applications. *Journal of Personality, 60,* 175–215.

McCreary, M., Slavin, L., & Berry, E. (1996). Predicting problem behavior and self-esteem among African American adolescents. *Journal of Adolescent Research, 11,* 216–234.

McCullers, C. (1946). *The member of the wedding.* New York: Bantam.

McDermott, P., & Spencer, M. (1997). Racial and social class prevalence of psychopathology among school-age youth in the United States. *Youth and Society, 28,* 387–414.

McDonald, D., & McKinney, J. (1994). Steady dating and self-esteem in high school students. *Journal of Adolescence, 17,* 557–564.

McGee, L., & Newcomb, M. (1992). General deviance syndrome: Expanded hierarchical evaluations at four ages from early adolescence to adulthood. *Journal of Consulting and Clinical Psychology, 60,* 766–776.

McGee, R., Williams, S., & Feehan, M. (1992). Attention deficit disorder and age of onset of problem behaviors. *Journal of Abnormal Child Psychology, 20,* 487–502.

McGee, R., Wolfe, D., & Wilson, S. (1997). Multiple maltreatment experiences and adolescent behavior problems: Adolescents' perspectives. *Development and Psychopathology, 9,* 131–149.

McGue, M., Sharma, A., & Benson, P. (1996). The effects of common rearing on adolescent adjustment: Evidence from a U.S. adoption cohort. *Developmental Psychology, 32,* 604–613.

McGuire, S., Neiderhiser, J., Reiss, D., Hetherington, E. M., & Plomin, R. (1994). Genetic and environmental influences on perceptions of self-worth and competence in adolescence: A study of twins, full siblings, and step-siblings. *Child Development, 65,* 785–799.

McIntyre, J., & Dusek, J. (1995). Perceived parental rearing practices and styles of coping. *Journal of Youth and Adolescence, 24,* 499–510.

McKeown, R., Garrison, C., Jackson, K., Cuffe, S., Addy, C., & Waller, J. (1997). Family structure and cohesion, and depressive symptoms in adolescents. *Journal of Research on Adolescence, 7,* 267–281.

McLanahan, S., & Bumpass, L. (1988). Intergenerational consequences of family disruption. *American Journal of Sociology, 94,* 130–152.

McLoyd, V. (1990). The impact of economic hardship on black families and children: Psychological distress, parenting, and socioemotional development. *Child Development, 61,* 311–346.

McLoyd, V., Jayaratne, T., Ceballo, R., & Borquez, J. (1994). Unemployment and work interruption among African American single mothers: Effects on parenting and adolescent socioemotional functioning. *Child Development, 65,* 562–589.

McMaster, L., Connolly, J., & Craig, W. (1997, March). *Sexual harassment and dating violence among early adolescents.* Paper presented at the biennial meetings of the Society for Research in Child Development, Washington.

McNeal, J. (1995). Extracurricular activities and high school dropouts. *Sociology of Education, 68,* 62–81.

McNeal, R., Jr. (1997). Are students being pulled out of high school? The effect of adolescent employment on dropping out. *Sociology of Education, 70,* 206–220.

McNeil, L. (1984). *Lowering expectations: The impact of student employment on classroom knowledge.* Madison: Wisconsin Center for Education Research.

McNelles, L. R., & Connolly, J. A. (1999). Intimacy between adolescent friends: Age and gender differences in intimate affect and intimate behaviors. *Journal of Research on Adolescence, 9*(2), 143–159.

Mead, M. (1928). *Coming of age in Samoa.* New York: Morrow.

Mead, M. (1928/1978). *Culture and commitment.* Garden City, NY: Anchor.

Mechanic, D. (1983). Adolescent health and illness behavior: Review of the literature and a new hypothesis for the study of stress. *Journal of Human Stress, 9,* 4–13.

Mednick, S., Gabrielli, W., & Hitchings, B. (1987). Genetic factors in the etiology of criminal behavior. In S. Mednick, T. Moffitt, & S. Stack (Eds.), *The causes of crime: New biological approaches* (pp. 74–91). Cambridge, England: Cambridge University Press.

Medrich, E., Roizen, J., Rubin, V., & Buckley, S. (1982). *The serious business of growing up.* Berkeley: University of California Press.

Meeus, W., Iedema, J., & Vollebergh, W. (1999). Rejoinder: Identity formation rerevisited: A rejoinder to Waterman in developmental and cross-cultural issues. *Developmental Review, 19,* 480–496.

Mekos, D., Hetherington, E.M., & Reiss, D. (1996). Sibling differences in problem behavior and parental treatment in nondivorced and remarried families. *Child Development, 67,* 2148–2165.

Melby, J. (1995, March). *Early family and peer predictors of later adolescent tobacco use.* Paper presented at the biennial meetings of the Society for Research in Child Development, Indianapolis.

Melby, J., & Conger, R. (1996). Parental behaviors and adolescent academic performance: A longitudinal analysis. *Journal of Research on Adolescence, 6,* 113–137.

Melton, G. (1990). Knowing what we do know: APA and adolescent abortion. *American Psychologist, 45,* 1171–1173.

Menard, S., & Huizinga, D. (1994). Changes in conventional attitudes and delinquent behavior in adolescence. *Youth and Society, 26,* 23–53.

Merskin, D. (1999). Adolescence, advertising, and the ideology of menstruation. *Sex Roles, 40,* 941–957.

Merten, D. (1997). The meaning of meanness: Popularity, competition and conflict among junior high school girls. *Sociology of Education, 70,* 175–191.

Meuus, W., Iedema, J., Helsen, M., & Vollebergh, W. (1999). Patterns of adolescent identity development: Review of literature and longitudinal analysis. *Developmental Review, 19,* 419–461.

Meyer, L. (1994). *Teenspeak.* Princeton, NJ: Peterson's.

Meyer-Bahlburg, H., Ehrhardt, A., Rosen, L., Gruen, R., Veridiano, N., Vann, F., & Neuwalder, H. (1995). Prenatal estrogens and the development of homosexual orientation. *Developmental Psychology, 31,* 12–21.

Michael, R., Laumann, E., & Kolata, G. (1994). *Sex in America.* Boston: Little, Brown.

Mickelson, R. (1990). The attitude-achievement paradox among black adolescents. *Sociology of Education, 63,* 44–61.

Midgley, C., Arunkumar, R., & Urdan, T. (1996). "If I don't do well tomorrow, there's a reason: Predictors of adolescents' use of academic self-handicapping strategies," *Journal of Educational Psychology, 88,* 423–434.

Midgley, C., Feldlaufer, H., & Eccles, J. (1988). The transition to junior high school: Beliefs of pre- and post-transition teachers. *Journal of Youth and Adolescence, 17,* 543–562.

Midgley, C., & Urdan, T. (1995). Predictors of middle school students' use of self-handicapping strategies. *Journal of Early Adolescence, 15,* 389–411.

Mihalic, S., & Elliot, D. (1997). Short- and long-term consequences of adolescent work. *Youth and Society, 28,* 464–498.

Miller, B., & Moore, K. (1990). Adolescent sexual behavior, pregnancy, and parenting: Research through the 1980s. *Journal of Marriage and the Family, 52,* 1025–1044.

Miller, B., Norton, M., Curtis, T., Hill, E., Schvaneveldt, P., & Young, M. (1997). The timing of sexual intercourse among adolescents: Family, peer, and other antecedents. *Youth and Society, 29,* 54–83.

Miller, B., Norton, M., Fan, X., & Christopherson, C. (1998). Pubertal development, parental communication, and sexual values in relation to adolescent sexual behaviors. *Journal of Early Adolescence, 18,* 27–52.

Miller, D., & Byrnes, J. (1997). The role of contextual and personal factors in children's risk taking. *Developmental Psychology, 33,* 814–823.

Miller, J., & Yung, S. (1990). The role of allowances in adolescent socialization. *Youth and Society, 17,* 57–63.

Miller, J. B. (1986). *Toward a new psychology of women* (2nd ed.). Boston: Beacon Press.

Miller, K., Clark, L., & Moore, J. (1997). Sexual initiation with older male partners and subsequent HIV risk behavior among female adolescents. *Family Planning Perspectives, 29,* 212–214.

Miller, K., Forehand, R., & Kotchick, B. (1999). Adolescent sexual behavior in two ethnic minority samples: The role of family variables. *Journal of Marriage and the Family, 61,* 85–98.

Miller, K., Kotchick, B., Dorsey, S., Forehand, R., & Ham, A. (1998). Family communication about sex: What are parents saying and are their adolescents listening? *Family Planning Perspectives, 30,* 218–222, 235.

Miller, K., Levin, M., Whitaker, D., & Xu, X. (1998). Patterns of condom use among adolescents: The impact of mother-adolescent communication. *American Journal of Public Health, 88,* 1542–1544.

Miller, N. (1928). *The child in primitive society.* New York: Bretano.

Miller, N., Cowan, P., Cowan, C., Hetherington, E. M., & Clingempeel, W. (1993). Externalizing in preschoolers and early adolescents: A cross-study replication of a family model. *Developmental Psychology, 29,* 3–18.

Miller, P., & Simon, W. (1980). The development of sexuality in adolescence. In J. Adelson (Ed.), *Handbook of adolescent psychology* (pp. 383–407). New York: Wiley.

Miller, R., & Gordon, M. (1986). The decline in formal dating: A study in six Connecticut high schools. *Marriage and Family Review, 10,* 139–156.

Miller-Johnson, S., Winn, D., Coie, J., Hyman, C., Terry, R., Lochman, J., & Maumary-Gremaud, A. (1996, March). *Parenthood during the teen years: A developmental perspective on risk factors for childbearing.* Paper presented at the biennial meetings of the Society for Research on Adolescence, Boston.

Miller-Johnson, S., Winn, D., Coie, J., Maumary-Gremaud, A., Hyman, C., Retty, R., & Lochman, J. (1999). Motherhood during the teen years: A developmental perspective on risk factors for childbearing. *Development and Psychopathology, 11,* 85–100.

Miller-Jones, D. (1989). Culture and testing. *American Psychologist, 44,* 360–366.

Millstein, S., Petersen, A., & Nightingale, E. (Eds.). (1993). *Promoting the health of adolescents: New directions for the twenty-first century.* New York: Oxford University Press.

Minuchin, S., Rosman, B., & Baker, L. (1978). *Psychosomatic families: Anorexia nervosa in context.* Cambridge, MA: Harvard University Press.

Mitchell, B., Wister, A., & Burch, T. (1989). The family environment and leaving the parental home. *Journal of Marriage and the Family, 51,* 605–613.

Mitchell, C., & O'Nell, T. (1998). Problem and conventional behavior among American Indian adolescents: Structure and validity. *Journal of Research on Adolescence, 8,* 97–122.

Mitchell, C., O'Nell, T., Beals, J., Dick, R., Keane, E., & Manson, S. (1996). Dimensionality of alcohol use among American Indian adolescents: Latent structure, construct validity, and implications for developmental research. *Journal of Research on Adolescence, 6,* 151–180.

Mitchell, E. (Ed.). (1985). *Anorexia nervosa and bulimia: Diagnosis and treatment.* Minneapolis: University of Minnesota Press.

Modell, J., Furstenberg, F., Jr., & Hershberg, T. (1976). Social change and transitions to adulthood in historical perspective. *Journal of Family History, 1,* 7–32.

Modell, J., & Goodman, M. (1990). Historical perspectives. In S. Feldman & G. Elliott (Eds.), *At the threshold: The developing adolescent* (pp. 93–122). Cambridge, MA: Harvard University Press.

Moffitt, T. (1993). Adolescence-limited and life-course persistent antisocial behavior: A developmental taxonomy. *Psychological Review, 100,* 674–701.

Moffitt, T., Caspi, A., Belsky, J., & Silva, P. (1992). Childhood experience and the onset of menarche: A test of a sociobiological model. *Child Development, 63,* 47–58.

Moffitt, T., Caspi, A., Dickson, N., Silva, P., & Stanton, W. (1996). Childhood-onset versus adolescent-onset antisocial conduct problems in males: Natural history from ages 3 to 18 years. *Development and Psychopathology, 8,* 399–424.

Moffitt, T., Caspi, A., Harkness, A., & Silva, P. (1993). The natural history of change in intellectual performance: Who changes? How much? Is it meaningful? *Journal of Child Psychology and Psychiatry, 34,* 455–506.

Moffitt, T., & Silva, P. (1988). IQ and delinquency: A direct test of the differential detection hypothesis. *Journal of Abnormal Psychology, 97,* 330–333.

Molina, B., & Chassin, L. (1996). The parent-adolescent relationship at puberty: Hispanic ethnicity and parent alcoholism as moderators. *Developmental Psychology, 32,* 675–686.

Moll, R. (1986). *Playing the private college admissions game.* New York: Penguin.

Monck, E. (1991). Patterns of confiding relationships among adolescent girls. *Journal of Child Psychology and Psychiatry, 32,* 333–345.

Montemayor, R. (1982). The relationship between parent-adolescent conflict and the amount of time adolescents spend alone and with parents and peers. *Child Development, 53,* 1512–1519.

Montemayor, R. (1983). Parents and adolescents in conflict: All families some of the time and some families most of the time. *Journal of Early Adolescence, 3,* 83–103.

Montemayor, R. (1984). Maternal employment and adolescents' relations with parents, siblings, and peers. *Journal of Youth and Adolescence, 13,* 543–557.

Montemayor, R. (1986). Family variation in parent-adolescent storm and stress. *Journal of Adolescent Research, 1,* 15–31.

Montemayor, R., Brown, B., & Adams, G. (1985, April). *Changes in identity status and psychological adjustment after leaving home and entering college.* Paper presented at the biennial meetings of the Society for Research in Child Development, Toronto.

Montemayor, R., & Brownlee, J. (1987). Fathers, mothers, and adolescents: Gender-based differences in parental roles during adolescence. *Journal of Youth and Adolescence, 16,* 281–292.

Montemayor, R., & Eisen, M. (1977). The development of self-conceptions from childhood to adolescence. *Development Psychology, 13,* 314–319.

Montgomery, M. (1996). "The fruit that hangs highest": Courtship and chaperonage in New York high society, 1880–1920. *Journal of Family History, 21,* 172–191.

Montgomery, M. J., & Sorell, G. T. (1998). Love and dating experience in early and middle adolescence: Grade and gender comparisons. *Journal of Adolescence, 21*(6), 677–689.

Moore, K., Myers, D., Morrison, D., Nord, C., Brown, B., & Edmonston, B. (1993). Age at first childbirth and later poverty. *Journal of Research on Adolescence, 3,* 393–422.

Moore, K., Nord, C., & Peterson, J. (1989). Nonvoluntary sexual activity among adolescents. *Family Planning Perspectives, 21,* 110–114.

Moore, K, Peterson, J., & Furstenberg, F., Jr. (1986). Parental attitudes and the occurrence of early sexual activity. *Journal of Marriage and the Family, 48,* 777–782.

Moore, K., & Snyder, N. (1991). Cognitive attainment among firstborn children of adolescent mothers. *American Sociological Review, 56,* 612–624.

Moore, M. (1992). The family as portrayed on prime-time television, 1947–1990: Structure and characteristics. *Sex Roles, 26,* 41–62.

Moore, S. (1995). Girls' understanding and social construction of menarche. *Journal of Adolescence, 18,* 87–104.

Moore, S., & Gullone, E. (1996). Predicting adolescent risk behavior using a personalized cost-benefit analysis. *Journal of Youth and Adolescence, 25,* 343–359.

Moos, R. (1978). A typology of junior high and high school classrooms. *American Educational Research Journal, 15,* 53–66.

Morabia, A., Costanza, M., & World Health Organization Collaborative Study of Neoplasia and Steroid Contraceptives. (1998). International variability in ages at menarche, first livebirth, and menopause. *American Journal of Epidemiology, 148,* 1195–1205.

Morison, P., & Masten, A. (1991). Peer reputation in middle childhood as a predictor of adaptation in adolescence: A seven-year follow-up. *Child Development, 62,* 991–1007.

Morris, A., & Sloutsky, V. (1998). Understanding of logical necessity: Developmental antecedents and cognitive consequences. *Child Development, 69,* 721–741.

Morris, R., Harrison, E., Knox, G., Tromanhauser, E., Marquis, D., & Watts, L. (1995). Health risk behavioral survey from 39 juvenile correctional facilities in the United States. *Journal of Adolescent Health, 17,* 334–344.

Morrison, G. M., Laughlin, J., Miguel, S. S., Smith, D. C., & Widaman, K. (1997). Sources of support for school-related issues: Choices of Hispanic adolescents varying in migrant status. *Journal of Youth and Adolescence, 26*(2), 233–252.

Morrison, J., Payne, G., Barton, B., Khoury, P., & Crawford, P. (1994). Mother-daughter correlations of obesity and cardiovascular disease risk factors in black and white households: The NHLBI Growth and Health Study. *American Journal of Public Health, 84,* 1761–1767.

Mortimer, J., Finch, M., Shanahan, M., & Ryu, S. (1992). Adolescent work history and behavioral adjustment. *Journal of Research on Adolescence, 2,* 59–80.

Mortimer, J., & Lorence, J. (1979). Work experience and occupational value socialization: A longitudinal study. *American Journal of Sociology, 84,* 1361–1385.

Mortimer, J., Pimentel, E., Ryu, S., Nash, K., & Lee, C. (1996). Part-time work and occupational value formation in adolescence. *Social Forces, 74,* 1405–1418.

Mory, M. (1992, March). *"Love the ones you're with": Conflict and consensus in adolescent peer group stereotypes.* Paper presented at the biennial meetings of the Society for Research on Adolescence, Washington.

Mory, M. (1994, February). *When people form or perceive sets, they tend to be fuzzy: The case of adolescent crowds.* Paper presented at the biennial meetings of the Society for Research on Adolescence, San Diego.

Moses, A. (1999). Exposure to violence, depression, and hostility in a sample of inner city high school youth. *Journal of Adolescence, 22,* 21–32.

Mosher, W., & Bachrach, C. (1996). Understanding U.S. fertility: Continuity and change in the National Survey of Family Growth, 1988–1995. *Family Planning Perspectives, 28,* 4–12.

Moshman, D. (1993). Adolescent reasoning and adolescent rights. *Human Development, 36,* 27–40.

Mosteller, F., Light, R., & Sachs, J. (1996). Sustained inquiry in education: Lessons from skill grouping and class size. *Harvard Educational Review, 66,* 797–842.

Mott, F., Fondell, M., Hu, P., Kowaleski-Jones, P., & Menaghan, E. (1996). The determinants of first sex by age 14 in a high-risk adolescent population. *Family Planning Perspectives, 28,* 13–18.

Mounts, N., & Steinberg, L. (1995). An ecological analysis of peer influence on adolescent grade point average and drug use. *Developmental Psychology, 31,* 915–922.

Mukai, T. (1996). Mothers, peers, and perceived pressure to diet among Japanese adolescent girls. *Journal of Research on Adolescence, 6,* 309–324.

Muller, C. (1995). Maternal employment, parent involvement, and mathematics achievement among adolescents. *Journal of Marriage and the Family, 57,* 85–100.

Muller, C. (1998). Gender differences in parental involvement and adolescents' mathematics achievement. *Sociology of Education, 71,* 336–356.

Mullis, I., Dossey, J., Campbell, J., Gentile, C., O'Sullivan, C., & Latham, A. (1994). *NAEP 1992 trends in academic progress.* Washington, DC: U.S. Department of Education.

Munoz, R., & Amado, H. (1986). Anorexia nervosa: An affective disorder. In F. Larocca (Ed.), *Eating disorders* (pp. 13–19). San Francisco: Jossey-Bass.

Munsch, J., & Wampler, R. (1993). Ethnic differences in early adolescents' coping with school stress. *American Journal of Orthopsychiatry, 63,* 633–646.

Munsch, J., Liang, S., & DeSecottier, L. (1996, March). *Natural mentors: Who they are and the roles they fill: A gender and ethnic comparison.* Paper presented at the biennial meetings of the Society for Research on Adolescence, Boston.

Murdock, T. (1994, February). *Who are you and how do you treat me? Student withdrawal as motivated alienation.* Paper presented at the biennial meetings of the Society for Research on Adolescence, San Diego.

Murry, V. (1994). Black adolescent females: A comparison of early versus late coital initiators. *Family Relations, 43,* 342–348.

Murry, V. (1996). An ecological analysis of coital timing among middle-class African American adolescent females. *Journal of Adolescent Research, 43,* 400–408.

Musick, J. (1994). Grandmothers and grandmothers-to-be: Effects on adolescent mothers and adolescent mothering. *Infancy and Young Children, 6,* 1–9.

Mussen, P., & Jones, M. (1957). Self-conceptions, motivations, and interpersonal attitudes of late- and early-maturing boys. *Child Development, 28,* 243–256.

Mussen, P., & Jones, M. (1958). The behavior-inferred motivations of late- and early-maturing boys. *Child Development, 29,* 61–67.

Must, A., Jacques, P., Dallal, G., Bajema, C., & Dietz, W. (1992). Long-term morbidity and mortality of overweight adolescents. *New England Journal of Medicine, 327,* 1350–1355.

Myers, J., Lindentthal, J., & Pepper, M. (1975). Life events, social integration, and psychiatric symptomatology. *Journal of Health and Social Behavior, 16,* 421–429.

Mylod, D., Whitman, T., & Borkowski, J. (1997). Predicting adolescent mothers' transition to adulthood. *Journal of Research on Adolescence, 7,* 457–478.

Nagin, D., & Tremblay, R. (1999). Trajectories of boys' physical aggression, opposition, and hyperactivity on the path to physically violent and nonviolent juvenile delinquency. *Child Development, 70,* 1181–1196.

Nagin, D., Farrington, D., & Moffitt, T. (1995). Life-course trajectories of different types of offenders. *Criminology, 33,* 111–139.

Nagy, S., Adcock, A., & Nagy, C. (1994). A comparison of risky health behaviors of sexually active, sexually abused, and abstaining adolescents. *Pediatrics, 93*, 570–575.

Nagy, S., DiClimente, R., & Adcock, A. (1995). Adverse factors associated with forced sex among Southern adolescent girls. *Pediatrics, 96*, 944–946.

National Assessment of Educational Progress. (1999). *NAEP 1999 trends in academic progress.* Washington, DC: U.S. Department of Education.

National Center for Education Statistics. (1999a). *The condition of education.* Washington, DC: U.S. Department of Education.

National Center for Education Statistics. (1999b). *Digest of education statistics, 1999.* Washington, DC: U.S. Department of Education.

National Center for Vital Statistics. (2000). *Births, marriages, divorces, and deaths: Provisional data for September, 1999.* Washington, DC: Centers for Disease Control.

National Center on Education and the Economy. (1990). *America's choice: High skills or low wages!* Washington, DC: Author.

National Commission on Excellence in Education. (1983). *A nation at risk: The imperative for educational reform.* Washington, DC: U.S. Department of Education.

National Education Commission on Time and Learning. (1994). *Prisoners of time.* Washington, DC: U.S. Government Printing Office.

National Heart, Lung, and Blood Institute Growth and Health Study Research Group. (1992). Obesity and cardiovascular disease risk factors in black and white girls: The NHLBI Growth and Health Study. *American Journal of Public Health, 82*, 1613–1620.

National Research Council. (1993). *Losing generations.* Washington, DC: National Academy Press.

National Research Council. (1995). Immigrant children and their families: Issues for research and policy. *The Future of Children, 5*, 72–88.

National Research Council. (1998). *Protecting youth at work.* Washington, DC: National Academy Press.

Natriello, G., & McDill, E. (1986). Performance standards, student effort on homework, and academic achievement. *Sociology of Education, 59*, 18–31.

Natriello, G., Pallas, A., & Alexander, K. (1989). On the right track? Curriculum and academic achievement. *Sociology of Education, 62*, 109–118.

Neckerman, H., Cairns, B., & Cairns, R. (1993, March). *Peers and families: Developmental changes, constraints, and continuities.* Paper presented at the biennial meetings of the Society for Research in Child Development, New Orleans.

Needle, R., Su, S., & Doherty, W. (1990). Divorce, remarriage, and adolescent substance use: A prospective longitudinal study. *Journal of Marriage and the Family, 52*, 157–169.

Neemann, J., Hubbard, J., & Masten, A. (1995). The changing importance of romantic relationship involvement to competence from late childhood to late adolescence. *Development and Psychopathology, 7*, 727–750.

Neiderhiser, J., Pike, A., Hetherington, E. M., & Reiss, D. (1998). Adolescent perceptions as mediators of parenting: Genetic and environmental contributions. *Developmental Psychology, 34*, 1459–1469.

Neiderhiser, J., Reiss, D., Hetherington, E. M., Plomin, R. (1999). Relationships between parenting and adolescent adjustment over time: Genetic and environmental contributions. *Developmental Psychology, 35*, 680–692.

Neimark, E. (1975). Intellectual development during adolescence. In F. Horowitz (Ed.), *Review of child development research* (Vol. 4). Chicago: University of Chicago Press.

Neisser, U., Boodoo, B., Bouchard, T., Jr., Boykin, A., Brody, N., Ceci, S., Halpern, D., Loehlin, J., Perloff, R., Sternberg, R., & Urbina, S. (1966). Intelligence: Knowns and unknowns. *American Psychologist, 51*, 77–101.

Neugarten, B., & Datan, N. (1974). The middle years. In S. Arieti (Ed.), *American handbook of psychiatry* (Vol. 1, Part 3, 2nd ed.). New York: Basic Books.

Neumark-Sztainer, D., Story, M., Dixon, L., & Murray, D. (1998). Adolescents engaging in unhealthy weight control behaviors: Are they at risk for other health-compromising behaviors? *American Journal of Public Health, 88*(6), 952–955.

Neumark-Sztainer, D., Story, M., French, S., Cassuto, N., Jacobs, J.D., & Resnick, M. (1996). Patterns of health-compromising behaviors among Minnesota adolescents: Sociodemographic variations. *American Journal of Public Health, 86*, 1599–1606.

Newcomb, A., & Bagwell, C. (1995). Children's friendship relations: A meta-analytic review. *Psychological Review, 117*, 306–347.

Newcomb, M., & Bentler, P. (1988). Impact of adolescent drug use and social support on problems of young adults: A longitudinal study. *Journal of Abnormal Psychology, 97*, 64–75.

Newcomb, M., & Bentler, P. (1989). Substance use and abuse among children and teenagers. *American Psychologist, 44*, 242–248.

Newcomb, M., & Felix-Ortiz, M. (1992). Multiple protective and risk factors for drug use and abuse: Cross-sectional and prospective findings. *Journal of Personality and Social Psychology, 63*, 280–296.

Newcomb, M., Huba, G., & Bentler, P. (1983). Mothers' influence on the drug use of their children: Confirmatory tests of direct modeling and mediational theories. *Developmental Psychology, 19*, 714–726.

Newcombe, N., & Dubas, J. (1987). Individual differences in cognitive ability: Are they related to timing of puberty? In R. Lerner & T. Foch (Eds.), *Biological-psychosocial interactions in early adolescence,* (249–302). Hillsdale, NJ: Erlbaum.

Newcomer, S., & Udry, J. (1984). Mothers' influence on the sexual behavior of their teenage children. *Journal of Marriage and the Family, 42*, 477–485.

Newcomer, S., & Udry, J. (1985). Oral sex in an adolescent population. *Archives of Sexual Behavior, 14*, 41–56.

Newcomer, S., & Udry, J. (1988). Adolescents' honesty in a survey of sexual behavior. *Journal of Adolescent Research, 3*, 419–423.

Newman, B., & Newman, P. (1976). Early adolescence and its conflict: Group identity versus alienation. *Adolescence, 11*, 261–274.

Newman, R., & Schwager, M. (1995). Students' help seeking during problem solving: Effects of grade, goal, and prior achievement. *American Educational Research Journal, 32*, 352–376.

Newmann, F. (1992). Higher order thinking and prospects for classroom thoughtfulness. In F. Newmann (Ed.), *Student engagement and achievement in American high schools.* New York: Teachers College Press.

Newmann, F., Marks, H., & Gamoran, A. (1996). Authentic pedagogy and student performance. *American Journal of Education, 104*, 280–312.

Nichols, S., & Good, T. (1998). Students' perceptions of fairness in school settings: A gender analysis. *Teachers College Record, 100*, 369–401.

Nichter, M., Ritenbaugh, C., Nichter, M., Vukovic, N., & Aickin, M. (1995). Dieting and watching behaviors among adolescent females: Report of a multimethod study. *Journal of Adolescent Health, 17*, 153–162.

Nieto, M., Lambert, S., Briggs, E., McCoy, J., Brunson, L., & Aber, M. (1996, March). *Untangling the relationship between ethnic composition of neighborhood and school adjustment.* Paper presented at the biennial meetings of the Society for Research on Adolescence, Boston.

Nightingale, E., & Wolverton, L. (1993). Adolescent rolelessness in modern society. *Teachers College Record, 94*, 472–486.

Noack, P., Kracke, B., & Hofer, M. (1994, February). *The family context of rightist attitudes among adolescents in East and West Germany.* Paper presented at the biennial meetings of the Society for Research on Adolescence, San Diego.

Nock, S. (1998). The consequences of premarital fatherhood. *American Sociological Review, 63*, 250–263.

Noguera, P. (1995). Preventing and producing violence: A critical analysis of responses to school violence. *Harvard Educational Review, 65*, 189–212.

Nolen-Hoeksema, S., & Girgus, J. (1994). The emergence of gender differences in depression during adolescence. *Psychological Bulletin, 115*, 424–443.

Nolen-Hoeksema, S., Girgus, J., & Seligman, M. (1992). Predictors and consequences of childhood depressive symptoms: A 5-year longitudinal study. *Journal of Abnormal Psychology, 101*, 405–422.

Noller, P., & Callan, V. (1990). Adolescents' perceptions of the nature of their communication with parents. *Journal of Youth and Adolescence, 19*, 349–362.

Nottelmann, E. (1987). Competence and self-esteem during transition from childhood to adolescence. *Developmental psychology, 23,* 441–450.

Nottelmann, E., Inoff-Germain, G., Susman, E., & Chrousos, G. (1990). Hormones and behavior at puberty. In J. Bancroft & J. M. Reinisch (Eds.), *Adolescence and puberty* (pp. 88–123). New York: Oxford University Press.

Nurmi, J. (1993). Adolescent development in an age-graded context: The role of personal beliefs, goals, and strategies in the tackling of developmental tasks and standards. *International Journal of Behavioural Development, 16,* 169–189.

Nurmi, J., Onatsu, T., & Haavisto, T. (1995). Underachievers' cognitive and behavioral strategies: Self-handicapping at school. *Contemporary Educational Psychology, 20,* 188–200.

O'Beirne, H. (1994, February). *Differential correlates of male and female adolescents' sexual activity.* Paper presented at the biennial meetings of the Society for Research on Adolescence, San Diego.

O'Brien, D., & Overton, W. (1982). Conditional reasoning and the competence-performance issue: A developmental analysis of a training task. *Journal of Experimental Child Psychology, 34,* 274–290.

O'Brien, S., & Bierman, K. (1988). Conceptions and perceived influence of peer groups: Interviews with preadolescents and adolescents. *Child Development, 59,* 1360–1365.

O'Callaghan, M., Borkowski, J., Whitman, T., Maxwell, S., & Keogh, D. (1999). A model of adolescent parenting: The role of cognitive readiness to parent. *Journal of Research on Adolescence, 9,* 203–225.

O'Connor, T., Caspi, A., DeFries, J., & Plomin, R. (2000). Are associations between parental divorce and children's adjustment genetically mediated? An adoption study. *Developmental Psychology, 36,* 429–437.

O'Connor, T., Deater-Deckard, K., Fulker, D., Rutter, M., & Plomin, R. (1998). Genotype-environment correlations in late childhood and early adolescence: Antisocial behavioral problems and coercive parenting. *Developmental Psychology, 34,* 970–981.

O'Connor, T., Hetherington, E. M., Reiss, D., & Plomin, R. (1995). A twin-sibling study of observed parent-adolescent interactions. *Child Development, 66,* 812–829.

O'Donnell, J., Hawkins, J., & Abbott, R. (1995). Predicting serious delinquency and substance use among aggressive boys. *Journal of Consulting and Clinical Psychology, 63,* 529–537.

O'Malley, P., & Bachman, J. (1983). Self-esteem: Change and stability between ages 13 and 23. *Developmental Psychology, 19,* 257–268.

O'Malley, P., & Johnston, L. (1999). Drinking and driving among U.S. high school seniors, 1984–1997. *American Journal of Public Health, 89,* 678–684.

O'Neill, J. (1997, August 31). News is mixed on minorities' SATs. *Philadelphia Inquirer,* p. E2.

Oakes, J. (1990). Opportunities, achievement, and choice: Women and minority students in science and mathematics. *Review of Research in Education, 16,* 153–222.

Oakes, J. (1995). Two cities' tracking and within-school segregation. *Teachers College Record, 96,* 681–690.

Oakley, D., & Bogue, E. (1995). Quality of condom use as reported by female clients of a family planning clinic. *American Journal of Public Health, 85,* 1526–1530.

Obeidallah, D., McHale, S., & Silbereisen, R. (1996). Gender role socialization and adolescents' reports of depression: Why some girls and not others? *Journal of Youth and Adolescence, 25,* 775–786.

Oettinger, G. (1999). Does high school employment affect high school academic performance? *Industrial and Labor Relations Review, 53,* 136–151.

Ogbu, J. (1974). *The next generation: An ethnography of education in an urban neighborhood.* New York: Academic Press.

Ogbu, J. (1978). *Minority education and caste.* New York: Aca-demic Press.

Ohannessian, C., Lerner, R., Lerner, J., & von Eye, A. (1994). A longitudinal study of perceived family adjustment and emotional adjustment in early adolescence. *Journal of Early Adolescence, 14,* 371–390.

Orlofsky, J., Marcia, J., & Lesser, I. (1973). Ego identity status and the intimacy versus isolation crisis of young adulthood. *Journal of Personality and Social Psychology, 27,* 211–219.

Orr, D., Beiter, M., & Ingersoll, G. (1991). Premature sexual activity as an indicator of psychosocial risk. *Pediatrics, 87,* 141–147.

Orr, D., & Langefeld, C. (1993). Factors associated with condom use by sexually active male adolescents at risk for sexually transmitted disease. *Pediatrics, 91,* 873–879.

Orr, E., & Ben-Eliahu, E. (1993). Gender differences in idiosyncratic sex-typed self-images and self-esteem. *Sex Roles, 29,* 271–296.

Osgood, D., Johnston, L., O'Malley, P., & Bachman, J. (1988). The generality of deviance in late adolescence and early adulthood. *American Sociological Review, 53,* 81–93.

Osgood, D. W., Wilson, J., O'Malley, P., Bachman, J., & Johnston, L. (1996). Routine activities and individual deviant behavior. *American Sociological Review, 61,* 635–655.

Osipow, S. (1973). *Theories of career development* (2nd ed.). New York: Appleton-Century-Crofts.

Osofsky, J. (1995a). Children who witness domestic violence: The invisible victims. *Social Policy Report of SRCD, 9,* 1–16.

Osofsky, J. (1995b). The effects of exposure to violence on young children. *American Psychologist, 50,* 782–788.

Osofsky, J. (Ed.). (1997). *Children in a violent society.* New York: Guilford.

Oswald, H., Bahne, J., & Feder, M. (1994, February). *Love and sexuality in adolescence: Gender-specific differences in East and West Berlin.* Paper presented at the biennial meetings of the Society for Research on Adolescence, San Diego.

Overbaugh, K., & Allen, J. (1994). The adolescent athlete. Part II: Injury patterns and prevention. *Journal of Pediatric Health Care, 8,* 203–211.

Overton, W. (1990). Competence and procedures: Constraints on the development of logical reasoning. In W. Overton (Ed.), *Reasoning, necessity, and logic: Developmental perspectives* (pp. 1–32). Hillsdale, NJ: Erlbaum.

Overton, W., Ward, S., Noveck, I., Black, J., & O'Brien, D. (1987). Form and content in the development of deductive reasoning. *Developmental Psychology, 23,* 22–30.

Owen, J. (1995). *Why our kids don't study.* Baltimore: Johns Hopkins University Press.

Owens, T. (1994). Two dimensions of self-esteem: Reciprocal effects of positive self-worth and self-deprecation on adolescent problems. *American Sociological Review, 59,* 391–407.

Owens, T., Mortimer, J., & Finch, M. (1996). Self-determination as a source of self-esteem in adolescence. *Social Forces, 74,* 1377–1404.

Oyserman, D., & Markus, H. (1990). Possible selves and delinquency. *Journal of Personality and Social Psychology, 59,* 112–125.

Oyserman, D., Radin, N., & Benn, R. (1993). Dynamics in a three-generational family: Teens, grandparents, and babies. *Developmental Psychology, 29,* 564–572.

Ozer, E., MacDonald, T., & Irwin, C., Jr. (in press). Adolescent health care: Implications and projections for the new millennium. In J. Mortimer & R. Larson (Eds.), *Reconstructing adolescence: Societal trends influencing the transition to adulthood.*

Pabon, E., Rodriguez, O., & Gurin, G. (1992). Clarifying peer relations and delinquency. *Youth and Society, 24,* 149–165.

Paikoff, R., & Brooks-Gunn, J. (1991). Do parent-child relationships change during puberty? *Psychological Bulletin, 110,* 47–66.

Paikoff, R., Brooks-Gunn, J., & Warreen, M. (1991). Effects of girls' hormonal status on depressive and aggressive symptoms over the course of one year. *Journal of Youth and Adolescence, 20,* 191–216.

Paikoff, R., Carlton-Ford, S., & Brooks-Gunn, J. (1993). Mother-daughter dyads view the family: Associations between divergent perceptions and daughter well-being. *Journal of Youth and Adolescence, 22,* 473–492.

Paikoff, R., Parfenoff, S., Williams, S., McCormick, A., Greenwood, G., & Holmbeck, G. (1997). Parenting, parent-child relationships, and sexual possibility situations among urban African American preadolescents: Preliminary findings and implications for HIV prevention. *Journal of Family Psychology, 11,* 11–22.

Pallas, A., Natriello, G., & McDill, E. (1989). The changing nature of the disadvantaged population: Current dimensions and future trends. *Educational Researcher, 18,* 16–22.

Paquette, J., & Underwood, M. (1999). Gender differences in young adolescents' experiences of peer victimization: Social and physical aggression. *Merrill-Palmer Quarterly, 45,* 242–266.

Parke, R. (1988). Families in life-span perspective: A multilevel developmental approach. In E. M. Hetherington & M. Perlmutter (Eds.), *Child development in life-span perspective* (pp. 159–190). Hillsdale, NJ: Erlbaum.

Parke, R., & Buriel, R. (1977). Socialization in the family: Ethnic and ecological perspectives. In W. Damon (Series Ed.) & N. Eisenberg (Vol. Ed.), *Handbook of child psychology* (5th ed.). pp. 463–552. New York: Wiley.

Parke, R. D., & Buriel, R. (1998). Socialization in the family: Ethnic and ecological perspectives. In W. Damon (Series Ed.) & N. Eisenberg (Vol. Ed.), *Handbook of child psychology* (5th ed.). New York: Wiley.

Parker, J., & Asher, S. (1987). Peer acceptance and later personal adjustment. Are low accepted children at risk? *Psychological Bulletin, 102,* 357–389.

Parker, J., & Herrera, C. (1996). Interpersonal processes in friendship: A comparison of abused and nonabused children's experiences. *Developmental Psychology, 32,* 1025–1038.

Parker, J., & Seal, J. (1996). Forming, losing, renewing, and replacing friendships: Applying temporal parameters to the assessment of children's friendship experiences. *Child Development, 67,* 2248–2268.

Parker, J., Low, C., & Wargo, J. (1999, April). *Children's jealousy over their friends' friends: Personal and relational correlates in preadolescent and adolescent boys and girls.* Paper presented at the biennial meetings of the Society for Research in Child Development, Alburquerque.

Parker, S., Nichter, M., Nichter, M., Vuckovic, N., Sims, C., & Ritenbaugh, C. (1995). Body image and weight concerns among African American and white adolescent females: Differences which make a difference. *Human Organization, 54,* 103–114.

Parkhurst, J., & Asher, S. (1992). Peer rejection in middle school: Subgroup differences in behavior, loneliness, and interpersonal concerns. *Developmental Psychology, 28,* 231–241.

Parsons, J., Adler, T., & Kaczala, C. (1982). Socialization of achievement attitudes and beliefs: Parental influences. *Child Development, 53,* 310–321.

Parsons, T. (1949). The social structure of the family. In R. Anshen (Ed.), *The family: Its function and destiny.* New York: Harper & Row.

Paschall, M., Ennett, S., & Flewelling, R. (1996). Relationships among family characteristics and violent behavior by black and white male adolescents. *Journal of Youth and Adolescence, 25,* 177–197.

Paschall, M. J., & Hubbard, M. L. (1998). Effects of neighborhood and family stressors on African American male adolescents' self-worth and propensity for violent behavior. *Journal of Consulting and Clinical Psychology, 66*(5), 825–831.

Pasley, K., & Gecas, V. (1984). Stresses and satisfactions of the parental role. *Personnel and Guidance Journal, 2,* 400–404.

Pastore, D., Fisher, M., & Friedman, S. (1996a). Abnormalities in weight status, eating attitudes,

and eating behaviors among urban high school students: Correlations with self-esteem and anxiety. *Journal of Adolescent Health, 18,* 312–319.

Pastore, D., Fisher, M., & Friedman, S. (1996b). Violence and mental health problems among urban high school students. *Journal of Adolescent Health Care, 18,* 320–324.

Patrikakou, E. (1996). Investigating the academic achievement of adolescents with learning disabilities: A structural modeling approach. *Journal of Educational Psychology, 88,* 435–450.

Patterson, G. (1986). Performance models for antisocial boys. *American Psychologist, 41,* 432–444.

Patterson, G., DeBaryshe, B., & Ramsey, E. (1989). A developmental perspective on antisocial behavior. *American Psychologist, 44,* 329–335.

Patterson, G., DeGarmo, D., & Knutson, M. (2000). Hyperactive and antisocial behaviors: Comorbid or two points in the same process? *Development and Psychopathology, 12,* 91–106.

Patterson, G., Forgatch, M., Yoerger, K., & Stoolmiller, M. (1998). Variables that initiate and maintain an early-onset trajectory for juvenile offending. *Development and Psychopathology, 10,* 531–547.

Patterson, G., Reid, J., & Dishion, T. (1992). *Antisocial boys.* Eugene, OR: Castalia.

Patterson, G., & Stoolmiller, M. (1991). Replications of a dual failure model for boys' depressed mood. *Journal of Consulting and Clinical Psychology, 59,* 491–498.

Patterson, G., & Stouthamer-Loeber, M. (1984). The correlation of family management practices and delinquency. *Child Development, 55,* 1299–1307.

Patterson, G., & Yoerger, K. (1993, March). *Adolescent first arrest: One model or two?* Paper presented at the biennial meetings of the Society for Research in child Development, New Orleans.

Patton, W., & Mannison, M. (1995). Sexual coercion in high school dating. *Sex Roles, 33,* 447–457.

Paul, J. (1993). Childhood cross-gender behavior and adult homosexuality: The resurgence of biological models of sexuality. *Journal of Homosexuality, 24,* 41–54.

Paulsen, K., & Johnson, M. (1983). Sex role attitudes and mathematical ability in 4th-, 8th-, and 11th-grade students from a high socioeconomic area. *Developmental Psychology, 19,* 210–214.

Paulson, S. (1994). Relations of parenting style and parental involvement with ninth-grade students' achievement. *Journal of Early Adolescence, 14,* 250–267.

Pavlidis, K., & McCauley, E. (1995, March). *Autonomy and relatedness in family interactions with depressed adolescents.* Paper presented at the biennial meetings of the Society for Research in Child Development, Indianapolis.

Paxton, S., Wertheim, E., Gibbons, K., Szmukler, G., Hillier, L., & Petrovich, J. (1991). Body image satisfaction, dieting beliefs, and weight loss behaviors in adolescent girls and boys. *Journal of Youth and Adolescence, 20,* 361–380.

Penner, D., & Klahr, D. (1996). The interaction of domain-specific knowledge and domain-general discovery strategies: A study with sinking objects. *Child Development, 67,* 2709–2727.

Peplau, L., Garnets, L., Spalding, L., Conley, T., & Veniegas, R. (1998). A critique of Bem's "exotic becomes erotic" theory of sexual orientation. *Psychological Review, 105,* 387–394.

Peplau, L., Rubin, Z., & Hill, C. (1977). Sexual intimacy in dating relationships. *Journal of Social Issues, 33,* 86–109.

Perez-Febles, A., Allison, K., & Burton, L. (1999, April). *Sociocultural context and the construction of research questions: The case of adolescent childbearing.* Paper presented at the biennial meetings of the Society for Research on Child Development, Albuquerque.

Perkins, C. (1997). *Age patterns of victims of serious violent crime.* Washington, DC: U.S. Department of Justice.

Perkins, D., Luster, T., Villarruel, F., & Small, S. (1998). An ecological, risk-factor examination of adolescents' sexual activity in three ethnic groups. *Journal of Marriage and the Family, 60,* 660–673.

Perosa, L., Perosa, S., & Tam, H. (1996). The contribution of family structure and differentiation to identity development in females. *Journal of Youth and Adolescence, 25,* 817–837.

Perry, C., Williams, C., Veblen-Mortenson, S., Toomey, T., Komro, K., Anstine, P., McGivern, P., Finnegan, J., Forster, J., Wagenar, A., & Wolfson, M. (1996). Project Northland: Outcomes of a communitywide alcohol use prevention program during early adolescence. *American Journal of Public Health, 86,* 956–965.

Peskin, H. (1967). Pubertal onset and ego functioning: A psychoanalytic approach. *Journal of Abnormal Psychology, 72,* 1–15.

Peskin, H. (1973). Influence of the developmental schedule of puberty on learning and ego functioning. *Journal of Youth and Adolescence, 2,* 273–290.

Petersen, A. (1985). Pubertal development as a cause of disturbance: Myths, realities, and unanswered questions. *Genetic, Social, and General Psychology Monographs, 111,* 205–232.

Petersen, A. (1988). Adolescent development. *Annual Review of Psychology, 39,* 583–607.

Petersen, A., Compas, B., Brooks-Gunn, J., Stemmler, M., Ey, S., & Grant, K. (1993). Depression in adolescence. *American Psychologist, 48,* 155–168.

Petersen, A., & Taylor, B. (1980). The biological approach to adolescence: Biological change and psychological adaptation. In J. Adelson (Ed.), *Handbook of adolescent psychology* (pp. 117–115). New York: Wiley.

Peterson, P., Hawkins, J., Abbott, R., & Catalano, R. (1994). *Journal of Research on Adolescence, 4,* 203–227.

Petraitis, J., Flay, B., & Miller, T. (1995). Reviewing theories of adolescent substance use: Organizing pieces in the puzzle. *Psychological Bulletin, 117,* 67–103.

Pettit, G., Bates, J., Dodge, K, & Meece, D. (1999). The impact of after-school peer contact on early adolescent externalizing problems is moderated by parental monitoring, perceived neighborhood safety, and prior adjustment. *Child Development, 70,* 768–778.

Phelan, P., Yu, H., & Davidson, A. (1994). Navigating the psychosocial pressures of adolescence: The voices and experiences of high school youth. *American Educational Research Journal, 31,* 415–447.

Phillips, M. (1997). What makes schools effective? A comparison of the relationships of communitarian climate and academic climate to mathematics achievement and attendance during middle school. *American Educational Research Journal, 34,* 633–662.

Phillipsen, L. C. (1999). Associations between age, gender, and group acceptance and three components of friendship quality. *Journal of Early Adolescence, 19*(4), 438–464.

Phinney, J., & Alipuria, L. (1987, April). *Ethnic identity in older adolescents from four ethnic groups.* Paper presented at the biennial meetings of the Society for Research in Child Development, Baltimore.

Phinney, J., Cantu, C., & Kurtz, D. (1997). Ethnic and American identity as predictors of self-esteem among African American, Latino, and white adolescents. *Journal of Youth and Adolescence, 26,* 165–185.

Phinney, J., & Chavira, V. (1995). Parental ethnic socialization and adolescent coping with problems related to ethnicity. *Journal of Research on Adolescence, 5,* 31–53.

Phinney, J., & Devich-Navarro, M. (1997). Variations in bicultural identification among African American and Mexican American adolescents. *Journal of Research on Adolescence, 7,* 3–32.

Phinney, J., & Devich-Navarro, M., DuPont, S., Estrada, A., & Onwughala, M. (1994, February). *Bicultural identity orientations of African American and Mexican American adolescents.* Paper presented at the biennial meetings of the Society for Research on Adolescence, San Diego.

Phinney, J., Ferguson, D., & Tate, J. (1997). Intergroup attitudes among ethnic minority adolescents: A causal model. *Child Development, 68,* 955–969.

Pierce, J., & Gilpin, E. (1996). How long will today's new adolescent smoker be addicted to cigarettes? *American Journal of Public Health, 86,* 253–256.

Pierce, K. (1993). Socialization of teenage girls through teen-magazine fiction: The making of a new woman or an old lady? *Sex Roles, 29,* 59–68.

Pike, A., McGuire, S., Hetherington, E. M., Reiss, D., & Plomin, R. (1996). Family environment and adolescent depressive symptoms and antisocial behavior: A multivariate genetic analysis. *Developmental Psychology, 32,* 590–603.

Pilgrim, C., Luo, Q., Urberg, K. A., & Fang, X. (1999). Influence of peers, parents, and individual characteristics on adolescent drug use in two cultures. *Merrill-Palmer Quarterly, 45,* 85–107.

Pilkington, N., & D'Augelli, A. (1995). Victimization of lesbian, gay, and bisexual youth in community settings. *Journal of Community Psychology, 23,* 34–56.

Pine, D., Cohen, P., Gurley, D., Brook, J., & Ma, Y. (1998). The risk for early-adulthood anxiety and depressive disorders in adolescents with anxiety and depressive disorders. *Archives of General Psychiatry, 55,* 56–64.

Pine, D., Wasserman, G., Coplan, J., Fried, J., Huang, Y., Kassir, S., Greenhill, L., Shaffer, D., & Parsons, B. (1996). Platelet serotonin 2A (5HT$2A) receptor characteristics and parenting factors for boys at risk for delinquency: A preliminary report. *American Journal of Psychiatry, 153,* 538–544.

Pintrich, P., Roeser, R., & De Groot, E. (1994). Classroom and individual differences in early adolescents' motivation and self-regulated learning. *Journal of Early Adolescence, 14,* 139–161.

Pipher, M. (1994). *Reviving Ophelia.* New York: Putnam.

Piquero, A., & Chung, H. (in press). On the relationship between gender, early onset, and the seriousness of offending. *Journal of Criminal Justice.*

Pirog-Good, M. (1995). The family background and attitudes of teen fathers. *Youth and Society, 26,* 351–376.

Pleck, J., Sonenstein, F., & Ku, L. (1994). Problem behaviors and masculinity ideology in adolescent males. In R. Ketterlinus & M. Lamb (Eds.), *Adolescent problem behaviors: Issues and research* (pp. 165–186). Hillsdale, NJ: Erlbaum.

Plomin, R., & Daniels, D. (1987). Why are children in the same family so different from one another? *Behavioral and Brain Sciences, 10,* 1–60.

Plumert, J. (1994). Flexibility in children's use of spatial and categorical organizational strategies in recall. *Developmental Psychology, 30,* 738–747.

Plummer, D. (1995). Patterns of racial identity development of African American adolescent males and females. *Journal of Black Psychology, 21,* 168–180.

Poe-Yamagata, E., & Jones, M. (2000). *And justice for some: Differential treatment of minority youth in the justice system.* Washington, DC: Youth Law Center.

Polce-Lynch, M., Myers, B., Kilmartin, C., Forssmann-Falck, R., & Kliewer, W. (1998). Gender and age patterns in emotional expression, body image, and self-esteem: A qualitative analysis. *Sex Roles, 38,* 1025–1048.

Pong, S. (1997). Family structure, school context and eighth-grade math and reading achievement. *Journal of Marriage and the Family, 59,* 734–746.

Pong, S. (1998). The school compositional effect of single parenthood on 10th-grade achievement. *Sociology of Education, 71,* 23–42.

Pong, S., & Ju, D. (2000). The effects of change in family structure and income on dropping out in middle and high school. *Journal of Family Issues, 21,* 147–169.

Pope, A., & Bierman, K. (1999). Predicting adolescent peer problems and antisocial activities: The relative roles of aggression and dysregulation. *Developmental Psychology, 35,* 335–346.

Portes, A., & MacLeod, D. (1996). Educational progress of children of immigrants: The roles of class, ethnicity, and school context. *Sociology of Education, 69,* 255–275.

Poulin, F., Dishion, T. J., & Haas, E. (1999). The peer influence paradox: Friendship quality and deviancy training within male adolescent friendships. *Merrill-Palmer Quarterly, 45,* 42–61.

Powell, A., Farrar, E., & Cohen, D. (1985). *The shopping mall high school.* Boston: Houghton Mifflin.

Powers, S., & Wagner, M. (1984). Attributions for school achievement of middle school students. *Journal of Early Adolescence, 4,* 215–222.

Pratt, M., Filipovich, & Bountrogianni, M. (1995). Parenting style and parental beliefs and practices concerning school and home. *Alberta Journal of Educational Research, 41,* 175–187.

President's Science Advisory Committee. (1974). *Youth: Transition to adulthood.* Chicago: University of Chicago Press.

Prosser, E., & Carlson, C. (1999, April). *Ethnic differences in fluctuations in female self-esteem during early adolescence.* Paper presented at the biennial meetings of the Society for Research on Child Development, Albuquerque.

Public Agenda. (1997). *Getting by: What American teenagers really think about their schools.* New York: Author.

Public Agenda. (1999). *Kids these days '99: What Americans really think about the next generation.* New York: Author.

Pulkkinen, L. (1982). Self-control and continuity from childhood to adolescence. In P. Baltes & O. Brim (Eds.), *Life-span development and behavior* (Vol. 4). New York: Academic Press.

Purdie, N., Hattie, J., & Douglas, G. (1996). Student conceptions of learning and their use of self-regulated learning strategies: A cross-cultural comparison. *Journal of Educational Psychology, 88,* 87–100.

Quadrel, M., Fischoff, B., & Davis, W. (1993). Adolescent (in)vulnerability. *American Psychologist, 48,* 102–116.

Quintana, S., Castaneda-English, P., & Ybarra, V. C. (1999). Role of perspective-taking abilities and ethnic socialization in development of adolescent ethnic identity. *Journal of Research on Adolescence, 9,* 161–184.

Raeff, C. (1997). Individuals in relationships: Cultural values, children's social interactions, and the development of an American individualistic self. *Developmental Review, 17,* 205–238.

Raffaelli, M. (1997). Young adolescents' conflicts with siblings and friends. *Journal of Youth and Adolescence, 26*(5), 539–558.

Raffaelli, M., & Larson, R. (1987, April). *Sibling interactions in late childhood and early adolescence.* Paper presented at the biennial meetings of the Society for Research in Child Development, Baltimore.

Rastam, M., Gillberg, C., & Gillberg, I. (1996). A six-year follow-up study of anorexia nervosa subjects with teenage onset. *Journal of Youth and Adolescence, 25,* 439–453.

Rathunde, K. (1996). Family context and talented adolescents' optimal experience in school-related activities. *Journal of Research on Adolescence, 6,* 605–628.

Ravitch, D. (1995). *National standards in American education: A citizen's guide.* Washington, DC: Brookings.

Ravitch, D. (Ed.). (2001). *Brookings papers on education policy.* Washington, DC: Brookings Institution.

Reich, K., Oser, F., & Valentin, P. (1994). Knowing why I now know better: Children's and youth's explanations of their worldview changes. *Journal of Research on Adolescence, 4,* 151–173.

Reifman, A., & Windle, M. (1995). Adolescent suicidal behaviors as a function of depression, hopelessness, alcohol use, and social support: A longitudinal investigation. *American Journal of Community Psychology, 23,* 329–354.

Reimer, M. (1996a, March). *Shame-proneness and self-evaluation in adolescence.* Paper presented at the biennial meetings of the Society for Research on Adolescence, Boston.

Reimer, M. (1996b). "Sinking into the ground": The development and consequences of shame in adolescence. *Developmental Review, 16,* 321–363.

Reimer, M., Overton, W., Steidl, J., Rosenstein, D., & Horowitz, H. (1996). Familial responsiveness and behavioral control: Influences on adolescent psychopathology, attachment, and cognition. *Journal of Research on Adolescence, 6,* 87–112.

Reiss, D., Hetherington, E. M., Plomin, R., Howe, G., Simmens, S., Henderson, S., et al. (1995). Genetic questions for environmental studies. *Archives of General Psychiatry, 52,* 925–936.

Renken, B., Egeland, B., Marvinney, D., Mangelsdorf, S., & Sroufe, L. (1989). Early childhood antecedents of aggression and passive withdrawal in early elementary school. *Journal of Personality, 57,* 257–282.

Repetti, R. (1996). The effects of perceived daily social and academic failure experiences on school-age children's subsequent interactions with parents. *Child Development, 67,* 1467–1482.

Repinski, D., & Leffert, N. (1994, February). *Adolescents' relations with friends: The effects of a psychoeducational intervention.* Paper presented at the biennial meetings of the Society for Research on Adolescence, San Diego.

Reppucci, N. (1999). Adolescent development and juvenile justice. *American Journal of Community Psychology, 27,* 307–326.

Resnick, M., Bearman, P., Blum, R., Bauman, K., Harris, K., Jones, J., Tabor, J., Beuhring, T., Sieving, R., Shew, M., Ireland, M., Bearinger, L., & Udry, J. (1997). Protecting adolescents from harm: Findings from the National Longitudinal Study of Adolescent Health. *Journal of the American Medical Association, 278,* 823–832.

Resnick, M., & Blum, R. (1994). The association of consensual sexual intercourse during childhood with adolescent health risk and behaviors. *Pediatrics, 94,* 907–913.

Resnick, M., Blum, R., Bose, J., Smith, M., & Toogood, R. (1990). Characteristics of unmarried adolescent mothers: Determinants of child rearing versus adoption. *American Journal of Orthopsychiatry, 60,* 577–583.

Resnicow, K., Ross-Gaddy, D., & Vaughan, R. (1995). Structure of problem and positive behaviors in African American youths. *Journal of Consulting and Clinical Psychology, 63,* 594–603.

Rest, J. (1983). Morality. In J. Flavell & E. Markman (Eds.), *Handbook of child psychology, Vol. III: Cognitive development* (pp. 556–629). New York: Wiley.

Rest, J., Davison, M., & Robbins, S. (1978). Age trends in judging moral issues: A review of cross-sectional, longitudinal, and sequential studies of the Defining Issues Test. *Child Development, 49,* 263–279.

Reuman, D. (1989). How social comparison mediates the relation between ability-grouping practices and students' achievement expectancies in mathematics. *Journal of Educational Psychology, 81,* 178–189.

Reuter, M., & Conger, R. (1994, February). *Family dysfunction as a mediator in the relationship between parental substance use and adolescent substance use.* Paper presented at the biennial meetings of the Society for Research on Adolescence, San Diego.

Reviere, S., & Bakeman, R. (1992, March). *Measuring multicultural competence: American whites, American blacks, and immigrants.* Paper presented at the biennial meetings of the Society for Research on Adolescence, Washington.

Reyes, O., & Jason, L. (1993). Pilot study examining factors associated with academic success for Hispanic high school students. *Journal of Youth and Adolescence, 22,* 57–71.

Reynolds, A., & Temple, J. (1998). Extended early childhood intervention and school achievement: Age thirteen findings from the Chicago Longitudinal Study. *Child Development, 69,* 231–246.

Rhodes, J., Contreras, J., & Mangelsdorf, S. (1994). Natural mentor relationships among Latina adolescent mothers: Psychological adjustment, moderating processes, and the role of early parental acceptance. *American Journal of Community Psychology, 22,* 211–227.

Rhodes, J. E., Haight, W. L., & Briggs, E. C. (1999). The influence of mentoring on the peer relationships of foster youth in relative and nonrelative care. *Journal of Research on Adolescence, 9*(2), 185–201.

Rice, K. (1990). Attachment in adolescence: A narrative and meta-analytic review. *Journal of Youth and Adolescence, 19,* 511–538.

Rice, K., & Mulkeen, P. (1995). Relationships with parents and peers: A longitudinal study of adolescent intimacy. *Journal of Adolescent Research, 10,* 338–357.

Richards, M., Boxer, A., Petersen, A., & Albrecht, R. (1990). Relation of weight to body image in pubertal girls and boys from two communities. *Developmental Psychology, 26,* 313–321.

Richards, M., Crowe, P., Larson, R., & Swarr, A. (1998). Developmental patterns and gender differences in the experience of peer companionship during adolescence. *Child Development, 69,* 154–163.

Richards, M., & Duckett, E. (1994). The relationship of maternal employment to early adolescent daily experience with and without parents. *Child Development, 65,* 225–236.

Richards, M., & Larson, R. (1993). Pubertal development and the daily subjective states of young adolescents. *Journal of Research on Adolescence, 3,* 145–169.

Richards, M., Suleiman, L., Sims, B., & Sedeno, A. (1994, February). *Experiences of ethnically diverse young adolescents growing up in contexts of poverty, violence, and racism.* Paper presented at the biennial meetings of the Society for Research on Adolescence, San Diego.

Richardson, J., Dwyer, K., McGuigan, K., Hansen, W., Dent, C., Johnson, C., Sussman, S., Brannon, B., & Flay, B. (1989). Substance use among eighth-grade students who take care of themselves after school. *Pediatrics, 84,* 556–566.

Richardson, J., Radziszewska, B., Dent, C., & Flay, B. (1993). Relationship between after-school care of adolescents and substance use, risk taking, depressed mood, and academic achievement. *Pediatrics, 92,* 32–38.

Richardson, L. (1997, September 30). Condoms in school said not to affect teen-age sex rate. *New York Times,* p. A1 and ff.

Richardson, R. (1996, March). *Competence in the transition to adulthood: Exploring the influence of adolescent motherhood for low-income, urban, African-American women.* Paper presented at the biennial meetings of the Society for Research on Adolescence, Boston.

Rierdan, J., Koff, E., & Stubbs, M. (1989). Timing of menarche, preparation, and initial menstrual experience: Replication and further analyses in prospective study. *Journal of Youth and Adolescence, 18,* 413–426.

Rigsby, L., & McDill, E. (1975). Value orientations of high school students. In H. R. Stub (Ed.), *The sociology of education: A sourcebook* (3rd ed., pp. 53–74). Homewood, IL: Dorsey.

Riley, T., Adams, G., & Neilsen, E. (1984). Adolescent egocentrism: The association among imaginary audience behavior, cognitive development, and parental support and rejection. *Journal of Youth and Adolescence, 13,* 401–438.

Ringwalt, C., Greene, J., Robertson, M., & McPheeters, M. (1998). The prevalence of homelessness among adolescents in the United States. *American Journal of Public Health, 88,* 1325–1329.

Rivkin, S. (1994). Residential segregation and school integration. *Sociology of Education, 67,* 279–292.

Robbins, C., Kaplan, H., & Martin, S. (1985). Antecedents of pregnancy among unmarried adolescents. *Journal of Marriage and the Family, 47,* 567–583.

Roberts, D. (1993). Adolescents and the mass media: From "Leave It to Beaver" to "Beverly Hills 90210." *Teachers College Record, 94,* 629–644.

Roberts, D., Foehr, U., Rideout, V., & Brodie, M. (1999). *Kids and media @ the new millennium.* Menlo Park, CA: Kaiser Family Foundation.

Roberts, R., Roberts, C., & Chen, Y. (1997). Ethnocultural differences in prevalence of adolescent depression. *American Journal of Community Psychology, 25,* 95–110.

Robins, L. (1986). Changes in conduct disorder over time. In D. Farran & J. McKinney (Eds.), *Risk in intellectual and psychosocial development* (pp. 227–259). New York: Academic Press.

Robins, R., John, O., Caspi, A., Moffitt, T., & Stouthamer-Loeber, M. (1996). Resilient, overcontrolled, and undercontrolled boys: Three replicable personality types. *Journal of Personality and Social Psychology, 70,* 157–171.

Robinson, L., Klesges, R., Zbikowski, S., & Glaser, R. (1997). Predictors of risk for different stages of adolescent smoking in a biracial sample. *Journal of Consulting and Clinical Psychology, 65,* 653–662.

Robinson, N. (1995). Evaluating the nature of perceived support and its relation to perceived self-worth in adolescents. *Journal of Research on Adolescence, 5,* 253–280.

Robinson, N., Garber, J., & Hilsman, R. (1995). Cognitions and stress: Direct and moderating effects on depressive versus externalizing symptoms during the junior high school transition. *Journal of Abnormal Psychology, 104,* 453–463.

Robinson, T., Killen, J., Litt, I., Hammer, L., Wilson, D., Haydel, K., Hayward, C., & Taylor, B. (1996). Ethnicity and body dissatisfaction: Are Hispanic and Asian girls at increased risk for eating disorders? *Journal of Adolescent Health, 19,* 384–393.

Roderick, M. (1994). Grade retention and school dropout: Investigating the association. *American Educational Research Journal, 31,* 729–759.

Roderick, M., & Camburn, E. (1999). Risk and recovery from course failure in the early years of high school. *American Educational Research Journal, 36*(2), 303–343.

Rodgers, J. (1996). Sexual transitions in adolescence. In J. Graber, J. Brooks-Gunn, & A. Petersen (Eds.), *Transitions through adolescence: Interpersonal domains and context* (pp. 85–110). Mahwah, NJ: Erlbaum.

Rodgers, J., & Rowe, D. (1988). Influence of siblings on adolescent sexual behavior. *Developmental Psychology, 24,* 722–728.

Rodgers, J., & Rowe, D. (1993). Social contagion and adolescent sexual behavior: A developmental EMOSA model. *Psychological Review, 100,* 479–510.

Rodgers, K. (1999). Parenting processes related to sexual risk-taking behaviors of adolescent males and females. *Journal of Marriage and the Family, 61,* 99–109.

Rodkin, P., Farmer, T., Pearl, R., & Van Acker, R. (2000). Heterogeneity of popular boys: Antisocial and prosocial configurations. *Developmental Psychology, 36,* 14–24.

Rodman, H., Pratto, D., & Nelson, R. (1988). Toward a definition of self-care children: A commentary on Steinberg (1986). *Developmental Psychology, 24,* 292–294.

Roe, K. (1995). Adolescents' use of socially disvalued media: Towards a theory of media delinquency. *Journal of Youth and Adolescence, 24,* 617–631.

Roenkae, A., & Pulkkinen, L. (1998). Work involvement and timing of motherhood in the accumulation of problems in social functioning in young women. *Journal of Research on Adolescence, 8,* 221–239.

Roeser, R., & Eccles, J. (1998). Adolescents' perceptions of middle school: Relation to longitudinal changes in academic and psychological adjustment. *Journal of Research on Adolescence, 8,* 123–158.

Roeser, R., Eccles, J., & Freedman-Doan, C. (1999). Academic functioning and mental health in adolescence: Patterns, progressions, and routes from childhood. *Journal of Adolescent Research, 14,* 135–174.

Roeser, R., Eccles, J., & Sameroff, A. (1998). Academic and emotional functioning in early adolescence: Longitudinal relations, patterns, and prediction by experience in middle school. *Development and Psychopathology, 10,* 321–352.

Roeser, R., Lord, S., & Eccles, J. (1994, February). *A portrait of academic alienation in adolescence: Motivation, mental health, and family experience.* Paper presented at the biennial meetings of the Society for Research on Adolescence, San Diego.

Roeser, R., Midgley, C., & Urdan, T. (1996). Perceptions of the school psychological environment and early adolescents' psychological and behavioral functioning in school: The mediating role of goals and belonging. *Journal of Educational Psychology, 88,* 408–422.

Rogers, A. (1993). Voice, play, and a practice of ordinary courage in girls' and women's lives. *Harvard Educational Review, 63,* 265–295.

Rogers, J., Boruch, R., Stoms, G., & DeMoya, D. (1991). Impact of the Minnesota parental notification law on abortion and birth. *American Journal of Public Health, 81,* 294–298.

Rogers, M., & Holmbeck, G. (1997). Effects of brief interparental aggression on children's adjustment: The moderating role of cognitive appraisal and coping. *Journal of Family Psychology, 11,* 125–130.

Rogoff, B. (1997). Cognition as a collaborative process. In D. Kuhn & R. Siegler (Eds.), *Handbook of child psychology* (5th ed., Vol. 2). New York: Wiley.

Rohner, R., Bourque, S., & Elordi, C. (1996). Children's perceptions of corporal punishment, caretaker acceptance, and psychological adjustment in a poor, biracial Southern community. *Journal of Marriage and the Family, 58,* 842–852.

Rohner, R., & Pettengill, S. (1985). Perceived parental acceptance-rejection and parental control among Korean adolescents. *Child Development, 56,* 524–528.

Romer, D., Black, M., Ricardo, I., Feigelman, S., Kaljee, L., Galbraith, J., Nesbit, R., Hornik, R., & Stanton, B. (1994). Social influences on the sexual behavior of youth at risk for HIV exposure. *American Journal of Public Health, 84,* 977–985.

Ronka, A., & Pulkkinen, L. (1995). Accumulation of problems in social functioning in young adulthood: A developmental approach. *Journal of Personality and Social Psychology, 69,* 381–391.

Roosa, M., & Christopher, F. (1990). Evaluation of an abstinence-only adolescent pregnancy prevention program: A replication. *Family Relations, 39,* 363–367.

Rosario, M., Rotheram-Borus, M., & Reid, H. (1996). Gay-related stress and its correlates among gay and bisexual adolescents of predominantly black and Hispanic background. *Journal of Community Psychology, 24,* 136–159.

Roscigno, V., & Ainsworth-Darnell, J. (1999). Race, cultural capital and educational resources: Persistent inequalities and achievement returns. *Sociology of Education, 72,* 158–178.

Rose, J., Chassin, L., Presson, C., & Sherman, S. (1999). Peer influences on adolescent cigarette smoking: A prospective sibling analysis. *Merrill-Palmer Quarterly, 45,* 62–84.

Rose, R. (1988). Genetic and environmental variance in content dimensions of the MMPI. *Journal of Personality and Social Psychology, 55,* 302–311.

Rose, S., & Feldman, J. (1995). Prediction of IQ and specific cognitive abilities at 11 years from infancy measures. *Developmental Psychology, 31,* 685–696.

Rosen, B. (1956). The achievement syndrome: A psychocultural dimension of social stratification. *American Sociological Review, 21,* 203–211.

Rosen, B., & Aneshensel, C. (1975). The chameleon syndrome. *Journal of Marriage and the Family, 38,* 605–617.

Rosen, B., & D'Andrade, R. (1959). The psychosocial origins of achievement motivation. *Sociometry, 22,* 185–218.

Rosenbaum, E., & Kandel, D. (1990). Early onset of adolescent sexual behavior and drug involvement. *Journal of Marriage and the Family, 52,* 783–798.

Rosenbaum, J. (1976). *Making inequality: The hidden curriculum of high school tracking.* New York: Wiley.

Rosenbaum, J. (1996). Policy uses of research on the high school-to-work transition. *Sociology of Education, Extra Issue,* 102–122.

Rosenbaum, J., Stern, D., Hamilton, M., Hamilton, S., Berryman, S., & Kazis, R. (1992). *Youth apprenticeship in America: Guidelines for building an effective system.* Washington, DC: William T. Grant Foundation Commission on Youth and America's Future.

Rosenberg, M. (1975). The dissonant context and the adolescent self-concept. In S. Dragastin & G. Elder, Jr. (Eds.), *Adolescence in the life cycle.* Washington, DC: Hemisphere.

Rosenberg, M. (1986). Self concept from middle childhood through adolescence: In J. Suls & A. Greenwald (Eds.), *Psychological perspectives on the self* (Vol. 3). Hillsdale, NJ: Erlbaum.

Rosenberg, M., Schooler, C., & Schoenbach, C. (1989). Self-esteem and adolescent problems: Modeling reciprocal effects. *American Sociological Review, 54,* 1004–1018.

Rosenberg, M., Schooler, C., Schoenbach, C., & Rosenberg, F. (1995). Global self-esteem and specific self-esteem: Different concepts, different outcomes. *American Sociological Review, 60,* 141–156.

Rosenblum, G., & Lewis, M. (1999). The relations among body image, physical attractiveness, and body mass in adolescence. *Child Development, 70,* 50–64.

Rosenthal, D. (1994, February). *Gendered constructions of adolescent sexuality.* Paper presented at the biennial meetings of the Society for Research on Adolescence, San Diego.

Rosenthal, D., & Feldman, S. (1991). *The acculturation of Chinese immigrants: Effects on family functioning of length of residence in two cultural contexts.* Unpublished manuscript, Department of Psychology, University of Melbourne, Victoria, Australia.

Rosenthal, D., & Feldman, S. (1999). The importance of importance: Adolescents' perceptions of parental communication about sexuality. *Journal of Adolescence, 22,* 835–851.

Rosenthal, D., & Smith, A. (1997). Adolescent sexual timetable. *Journal of Youth and Adolescence, 26,* 619–636.

Rosenthal, D., Smith, A., & de Visser, R. (1999). Personal and social factors influencing age at first sexual intercourse. *Archives of Sexual Behavior, 28,* 319–333.

Rosenthal, R., & Jacobson, E. (1968). *Pygmalion in the classroom.* New York: Holt, Rinehart & Winston.

Roth, J., Brooks-Gunn, J., Murray, L., & Foster, W. (1998). Promoting healthy adolescents: Synthesis of youth development program evaluations. *Journal of Research on Adolescence, 8*(4), 423–459.

Rotheram-Borus, M., Hunter, J., & Rosario, M. (1994). Suicidal behavior and gay-related stress among gay and bisexual male adolescents. *Journal of Adolescent Research, 9,* 498–508.

Rotheram-Borus, M., & Koopman, C. (1991). Sexual risk behaviors, AIDS knowledge, and beliefs about AIDS among runaways. *American Journal of Public Health, 81,* 206–208.

Rotheram-Borus, M., Koopman, C., & Ehrhardt, A. (1991). Homeless youths and HIV infection. *American Psychologist, 46,* 1188–1197.

Rotheram-Borus, M., Marelich, W., & Srinivasan, S. (1999). HIV risk among homosexual, bisexual, and heterosexual male and female youths. *Archives of Sexual Behavior, 28,* 159–177.

Rotheram-Borus, M., & Phinney, J. (1990). Patterns of social expectations among black and Mexican-American children. *Child Development, 61,* 542–556.

Rotheram-Borus, M., Rosario, M., Van Rossem, R., Reid, H., & Gillis, R. (1995). Prevalence, course, and predictors of multiple problem behaviors among gay and bisexual male adolescents. *Developmental Psychology, 31,* 75–85.

Rousseau, J. (1762/1911). *Emile* (B. Foxley, trans.). London: Dent.

Rowan, B., Chiang, F., & Miller, R. (1997). Using research on employees' performance to study the effects of teachers on students' achievement. *Sociology of Education, 70,* 256–284.

Rowe, D., Rodgers, J., & Meseck-Bushey, S. (1992). Sibling delinquency and the family environment: Shared and unshared influences. *Child Development, 63,* 59–67.

Rowe, D., Rodgers, J., Meseck-Bushey, S., & St. John, C. (1989). Sexual behavior and nonsexual deviance: A sibling study of their relationship. *Developmental Psychology, 25,* 61–69.

Rowe, D., Vazsonyi, A., & Flannery, D. (1994). No more than skin deep: Ethnic and racial similarity in developmental processes. *Psychological Review, 101,* 396–413.

Roye, C., & Balk, S. (1996). The relationship of partner support to outcomes for teenage mothers and their children: A review. *Journal of Adolescent Health, 19,* 86–93.

Rubenstein, J., Heeren, T., Housman, D., Rubin, C., & Stechler, G. (1989). Suicidal behavior in "normal" adolescents: Risk and protective factors. *American Journal of Orthopsychiatry, 59,* 59–71.

Rubin, K., Chen, X., McDougall, P., Bowker, A., & McKinnon, J. (1995). The Waterloo Longitudinal Project: Predicting internalizing and externalizing problems in adolescence. *Development and Psychopathology, 7,* 751–764.

Rubin, K., LeMare, L., & Lollis, S. (1990). Social withdrawal in childhood: Developmental pathways to peer rejection. In S. Asher & J. Coie (Eds.), *Peer rejection in childhood* (pp. 217–249). New York: Cambridge University Press.

Rubin, Z. (1980). *Children's friendships.* Cambridge, MA: Harvard University Press.

Ruble, D., & Brooks-Gunn, J. (1982). The experience of menarche. *Child Development, 53,* 1557–1566.

Ruck, M., Abramovitch, R., & Keating, D. (1998). Children and adolescents' understanding of rights: Balancing nurturance and self-determination. *Child Development, 64,* 404–417.

Rudolph, K., & Hammen, C. (1999). Age and gender as determinants of stress exposure, generation, and reactions in youngsters: A transactional perspective. *Child Development, 70,* 660–677.

Rueter, M., & Conger, R. (1995a). Antecedents of parent-adolescent disagreements. *Journal of Marriage and the Family, 57,* 435–448.

Rueter, M., & Conger, R. (1995b). Interaction style, problem-solving behavior, and family problem-solving effectiveness. *Child Development, 66,* 98–115.

Rueter, M., & Conger, R. (1998). Reciprocal influences between parenting and adolescent problem-solving behavior. *Developmental Psychology, 34,* 1470–1482.

Ruggiero, M., Greenberger, E., & Steinberg, L. (1982). Occupational deviance among first-time workers. *Youth and Society, 13,* 423–448.

Ruggles, S. (1994). The origins of African-American family structure. *American Sociological Review, 59,* 136–151.

Rumbaut, R. (1996). The crucible within: Ethnic identity, self-esteem, and segmented assimilation among children of immigrants. *International Migration Review, 28,* 748–794.

Rumbaut, R. (1997). Assimilation and its discontents: Between rhetoric and reality. *International Migration Review, 31,* 923–960.

Rumbaut, R., & Cornelius, W. (Eds.). (1995). *California's immigrant children: Theory, research, and implications for educational policy.* San Diego: University of California, Center for U.S.-Mexican Studies.

Rumberger, R. (1995). Dropping out of middle school: A multilevel analysis of students of schools. *American Educational Research Journal, 32,* 583–625.

Rumberger, R., Ghatak, R., Poulos, G., Ritter, P., & Dornbusch, S. (1990). Family influences on dropout behavior in one California high school. *Sociology of Education, 63,* 283–299.

Rumberger, R., & Larson, K. (1998). Student mobility and the increased risk of high school dropout. *American Journal of Education, 107,* 1–35.

Rumberger, R., & Thomas, S. (2000). The distribution of dropout and turnover rates among urban and suburban high schools. *Sociology of Education, 73,* 39–67.

Russell, A., & Saebel, J. (1997). Mother-son, mother-daughter, father-son, and father-daughter: Are they distinct relationships? *Developmental Review, 17,* 111–147.

Russell, S. (1994). Life course antecedents of premarital conception in Great Britain. *Journal of Marriage and the Family, 56,* 480–492.

Russell, S., Elder, G., Jr., & Conger, R. (1997, April). *School transitions and academic achievement.* Paper presented at the biennial meetings of the Society for Research in Child Development, Washington.

Rutter, M. (1978). Protective factors in children's responses to stress and disadvantage. In M. Kent & J. Rolf (Eds.), *Primary prevention of psychopathology, Vol. 3: Promoting social competence and coping in children.* Hanover, NJ: University Press of New England.

Rutter, M. (1980). *Changing youth in a changing society: Patterns of adolescent development and disorder.* Cambridge, MA: Harvard University Press.

Rutter, M. (1983). School effects on pupil progress: Research findings and policy implications. *Child Development, 54,* 1–29.

Rutter, M. (1997). Nature-nurture integration: The example of antisocial behavior. *American Psychologist, 52,* 390–398.

Rutter, M., & Garmezy, N. (1983). Developmental psychopathology. In E. M. Hetherington (Ed.), *Handbook of child psychology, Vol. IV: Socialization, personality, and social development* (pp. 775–911). New York: Wiley.

Rutter, M., Graham, P., Chadwick, F., & Yule, W. (1976). Adolescent turmoil: Fact or fiction? *Journal of Child Psychiatry and Psychology, 17,* 35–56.

Ryan, R., & Lynch, J. (1989). Emotional autonomy versus detachment: Revisiting the vicissitudes of adolescence and young adulthood. *Child Development, 60,* 340–356.

Rys, G., & Bear, G. (1997). Relational aggression and peer relations: Gender and developmental issues. *Merrill-Palmer Quarterly, 43,* 87–106.

Sack, W., Clarke, G., & Seeley, R. (1996). Multiple forms of stress in Cambodian adolescent refugees. *Child Development, 67,* 107–116.

Safer, D. (1986). The stress of secondary school for vulnerable students. *Journal of Youth and Adolescence, 15,* 405–417.

Safren, S., & Heimberg, R. (1999). Depression, hopelessness, suicidality, and related factors in sexual minority and heterosexual adolescents. *Journal of Consulting and Clinical Psychology, 67,* 859–866.

Sagar, H., Schofield, J., & Snyder, H. (1983). Race and gender barriers: Preadolescent peer behavior in academic classrooms. *Child Development, 54,* 1032–1040.

Sagrestano, L., McCormick, S., Paikoff, R., & Holmbeck, G. (1999). Pubertal development and parent-child conflict in low-income, urban, African American adolescents. *Journal of Research on Adolescence, 9,* 85–107.

Salem, D., Zimmerman, M., & Notaro, P. (1998). Effects of family structure, family process, and father involvement on psychosocial outcomes among African American adolescents. *Family Relations, 47,* 331–341.

Salinger, J. (1951/1964). *The catcher in the rye.* New York: Bantam.

Salmivalli, C. (1998). Intelligent, attractive, well-behaving, unhappy: The structure of adolescents' self-concept and its relations to their social behavior. *Journal of Research on Adolescence, 8,* 333–354.

Samaniego, R., & Gonzales, N. (1999). Multiple mediators of the effects of acculturation status on delinquency for Mexican American adolescents. *American Journal of Community Psychology, 27,* 189–210.

Sampson, R. (1992). Family management and child development: Insights from social disorganization theory. In J. McCord (Ed.), *Advances in criminological theory* (Vol. 3). (pp. 63–93). New Brunswick, NJ: Transaction.

Sampson, R. (1997). Collective regulation of adolescent misbehavior: Validation results from eighty Chicago neighborhoods. *Journal of Adolescent Research, 12,* 227–244.

Sampson, R., & Groves, W. (1989). Community structure and crime: Testing social-disorganization theory. *American Journal of Sociology, 94,* 774–802.

Sampson, R., & Lamb, J. (1994). Urban poverty and the family context of delinquency: A new look at structure and process in a classic study. *Child Development, 65,* 523–540.

Sampson, R., Raudenbusch, S., & Earls, F. (1997, August 15). Neighborhoods and violent crime: A multilevel study of collective efficacy for children. *Science, 277,* 918–924.

Sandefur, G., McLanahan, S., & Wojtkiewicz, R. (1992). The effects of parental marital status during adolescence on high school graduation. *Social Forces, 71,* 103–121.

Sandfort, J., & Hill, M. (1996). Assisting young, unmarried mothers to become self-sufficient: The effects of different types of early economic support. *Journal of Marriage and the Family, 58,* 311–326.

Sandler, I., Tein, J., & West, S. (1994). Coping, stress, and the psychological symptoms of children of divorce: A cross-sectional and longitudinal study. *Child Development, 65,* 1744–1763.

Sandven, K., & Resnick, M. (1990). Informal adoption among black adolescent mothers. *American Journal of Orthopsychiatry, 60,* 210–224.

Santelli, J., Warren, C., Lowry, R., Sogolow, E., Collins, J., Kann, L., Kaufmann, R., & Celentano, D. (1997). The use of condoms with other contraceptive methods among young men and women. *Family Planning Perspectives, 29,* 261–267.

Savage, M., & Holcomb, D. (1999). Adolescent female athletes' sexual risk-taking behaviors. *Journal of Youth and Adolescence, 28,* 595–602.

Savage, M., & Scott, L. (1998). Physical activity and rural middle school adolescents. *Journal of Youth and Adolescence, 27*(2), 245–253.

Savin-Williams, R. (1988). Theoretical perspectives accounting for adolescent homosexuality. *Journal of Adolescent Health Care, 9,* 95–104.

Savin-Williams, R. (1994). Verbal and physical abuse as stressors in the lives of lesbian, gay male, and bisexual youths: Associations with school problems, running away, substance abuse, prostitution, and suicide. *Journal of Consulting and Clinical Psychology, 62,* 261–269.

Savin-Williams, R. (1998). The disclosure to families of same-sex attractions by lesbian, gay, and bisexual youths. *Journal of Research on Adolescence, 8,* 49–68.

Savin-Williams, R., & Berndt, T. (1990). Friendship and peer relations. In S. Feldman & G. Elliott (Eds.), *At the threshold: The developing adolescent* (pp. 277–307). Cambridge, MA: Harvard University Press.

Savin-Williams, R., & Demo, D. (1983). Situational and trastitutional determinants of adolescent self-feelings. *Journal of Personality and Social Psychology, 44,* 824–833.

Savin-Williams, R., & Demo, D. (1984). Developmental change and stability in adolescent self-concept. *Developmental Psychology, 20,* 1100–1110.

Scales, P. (1991). *A portrait of young adolescents in the 1990s: Implications for promoting healthy growth and development.* Chapel Hill, NC: Center for Early Adolescence.

Scales, P., & McEwin, C. (1994). *Growing pains: The making of America's middle school teachers.* Columbus, OH: National Middle School Association.

Scaramella, L., Conger, R., Simons, R., & Whitbeck, L. (1998). Predicting risk for pregnancy by late adolescence: A social contextual perspective. *Developmental Psychology, 34,* 1233–1245.

Scheer, S., & Unger, D. (1998). Russian adolescents in the era of emergent democracy: The role of family environment in substance use and depression. *Family Relations: Interdisciplinary Journal of Applied Family Studies, 47*(3), 297–303.

Scheier, L., & Botvin, G. (1998). Relations of social skills, personal competence, and adolescent alcohol use: A developmental exploratory study. *Journal of Early Adolescence, 18,* 77–114.

Schellenbach, C., Whitman, T., & Borkowski, J. (1992). Toward an integrative model of adolescent parenting. *Human Development, 35,* 81–99.

Scherer, D., & Gardner, W. (1990). Reasserting the authority of science. *American Psychologist, 45,* 1173–1174.

Schiff, A., & Knopf, I. (1985). The effects of task demands on attention allocation in children of different ages. *Child Development, 56,* 621–630.

Schiller, K. (1999). Effects of feeder patterns on students' transition to high school. *Sociology of Education, 72,* 216–233.

Schlegel, A., & Barry, H. (1991). *Adolescence: An anthropological inquiry.* New York: Free Press.

Schmitt-Rodermund, E., & Silbereisen, R. (1993, March). *Adolescents' age expectations during acculturation of German families from Eastern Europe.* Paper presented at the biennial meetings of the Society for Research in Child Development, New Orleans.

Schneider, B., & Shouse, R. (1991, April). *The work lives of eighth graders: Preliminary findings from the National Educational Longitudinal Study of 1988.* Paper presented at the biennial meetings of the Society for Research in Child Development, Seattle.

Schneider, B., Clegg, M., Byrne, B., Ledingham, J., & Crombie, G. (1989). Social relations of gifted children as a function of age and school program. *Journal of Educational Psychology, 81,* 48–56.

Schoenhals, M., Tienda, M., & Schneider, B. (1998). The educational and personal consequences of adolescent employment. *Social Forces, 77,* 723–762.

Schofield, J. (1981). Complementary and conflicting identities: Images and interaction in an interracial school. In S. Asher & J. Gottman (Eds.), *The development of children's friendships.* Cambridge, England: Cambridge University Press.

Schommer, M., Calvert, C., Gariglietti, G., & Baja, A. (1997). The development of epistemological beliefs among secondary school students: A longitudinal study. *Journal of Educational Psychology, 89,* 37–40.

Schonert-Reichl, K., & Elliott, J. (1994, February). *Rural pathways: Stability and change during the transition to young adulthood.* Paper presented at the biennial meetings of the Society for Research on Adolescence, San Diego.

Schreiber, G., Robins, M., Striegel-Moore, R., Obarzanek, E., Morrison, J., & Wright, D. (1996). Weight modification efforts reported by black and white preadolescent girls: National Heart, Lung, and Blood Institute Growth and Health Study. *Pediatrics, 98,* 63–70.

Schulenberg, J., & Bachman, J. (1993, March). *Long hours on the job? Not so bad for some adolescents in some types of jobs: The quality of work and substance use, affect, and stress.* Paper presented at the biennial meetings of the Society for Research in Child Development, New Orleans.

Schulenberg, J., Maggs, J., Dielman, T., Leech, S., Kloska, D., Shope, J., & Laetz, V. (1999). On peer influences to get drunk: A panel study of young adolescents. *Merrill-Palmer Quarterly, 45,* 108–142.

Schulenberg, J., Wadsworth, K., O'Malley, P., Bachman, J., & Jonston, L. (1996). Adolescent risk factors for binge drinking during the transition to young adulthood: Variable- and pattern-centered approaches to change. *Developmental Psychology, 32*, 659–674.

Schuster, M., Bell, R., Berry, S., & Kanouse, D. (1998). Impact of a high school condom availability program on sexual attitudes and behaviors. *Family Planning Perspectives, 30*, 67–72, 88.

Scott, C., & Owen, R. (1990, March). *Similarities and differences in sexuality socialization of males in three cultural/ethnic groups.* Paper presented at the biennial meetings of the Society for Research on Adolescence, Atlanta.

Scott, E., Reppucci, N., & Woolard, J. (1995). Evaluating adolescent decision making in legal contexts. *Law and Human Behavior, 19*, 221–244.

Sebald, H. (1986). Adolescents' shifting orientation toward parents and peers: A curvilinear trend over recent decades. *Journal of Marriage and the Family, 48*, 5–13.

Seginer, R. (1983). Parents' educational expectations and children's academic achievements: A literature review. *Merrill-Palmer Quarterly, 29*, 1–23.

Seginer, R. (1998). Adolescents' perceptions of relationships with older siblings in the context of other close relationships. *Journal of Research on Adolescence, 8*, 287–308.

Seguin, J., Pihl, J., Harden, P., Tremblay, R., & Boulerice, B. (1995). Cognitive and neuropsychological characteristics of physically aggressive boys. *Journal of Abnormal Psychology, 104*, 614–624.

Seidman, E., Aber, J., Allen, L., & French, S. (1996). The impact of the transition to high school on the self-system and perceived social context of poor urban youth. *American Journal of Community Psychology, 24*, 489–515.

Seidman, E., Allen, L., Aber, J., Mitchell, C., & Feinman, J. (1994). The impact of school transitions in early adolescence on the self-system and perceived social context of poor urban youth. *Child Development, 65*, 507–522.

Seidman, E., Yoshikawa, H., Roberts, A., Chesir-Teran, D., Allen, L., Friedman, J. L., & Aber, J. L. (1998). Structural and experiential neighborhood contexts, developmental stage, and antisocial behavior among urban adolescents in poverty. *Development and Psychopathology, 10*, 259–281.

Seitz, V., & Apfel, N. (1993). Adolescent mothers and repeated childbearing: Effects of a school-based intervention program. *American Journal of Orthopsychiatry, 63*, 572–581.

Seitz, V., & Apfel, N. (1994). Effects of a school for pregnant students on the incidence of low-birthweight deliveries. *Child Development, 65*, 666–676.

Sellers, D., McGraw, S., & McKinlay, J. (1994). Does the promotion and distribution of condoms increase teen sexual activity? Evidence from an HIV prevention program for Latino youth. *American Journal of Public Health, 84*, 1952–1959.

Sells, C., & Blum, R. (1996). Morbidity and mortality among U.S. adolescents: An overview of data and trends. *American Journal of Public Health, 86*, 513–519.

Selman, R. (1980). *The growth of interpersonal understanding: Developmental and clinical analyses.* New York: Academic Press.

Serovich, J., & Greene, K. (1997). Predictors of adolescent sexual risk taking behaviors which put them at risk for contracting HIV. *Journal of Youth and Adolescence, 26*, 429–444.

Sessa, F., & Steinberg, L. (1991). Family structure and the development of autonomy in adolescence. *Journal of Early Adolescence, 11*, 38–55.

Sethi, S., & Nolen-Hoeksema, S. (1997). Gender differences in internal and external focusing among adolescents. *Sex Roles, 37*, 687–700.

Sewell, W., & Hauser, R. (1972). Causes and consequences of higher education: Models of the status attainment process. *American Journal of Agricultural Economics, 54*, 851–861.

Sharabany, R., Gershoni, R., & Hofman, J. (1981). Girlfriend, boyfriend: Age and sex differences in intimate friendship. *Developmental Psychology, 17*, 800–808.

Sharma, A., McGue, M., & Benson, P. (1998). The psychological adjustment of United States adopted adolescents and their nonadopted siblings. *Child Development, 69*, 791–802.

Shaver, P., Furman, W., & Buhrmester, D. (1985). Transition to college: Network changes, social skills, and loneliness. In S. Duck & D. Perlman (Eds.), *Understanding personal relationships: An interdisciplinary approach* (pp. 193–219). London: Sage.

Shaw, M., & White, D. (1965). The relationship between child-parent identification and academic underachievement. *Journal of Clinical Psychology, 21*, 10–13.

Shayne, V., & Kaplan, B. (1988). AIDS education for adolescents. *Youth and Society, 20*, 180–208.

Shedler, J., & Block, J. (1990). Adolescent drug use and psychological health: A longitudinal inquiry. *American Psychologist, 45*, 612–630.

Sheeber, L., Hops, H., Alpert, A., Davis, B., & Andrews, J. (1997). Family support and conflict: Prospective relations to adolescent depression. *Journal of Abnormal Child Psychology, 25*, 333–344.

Sheeran, P., Abraham, C., & Orbell, S. (1999). Psychosocial correlates of heterosexual condom use: A meta-analysis. *Psychological Bulletin, 125*, 90–132.

Shih, T. (1998). Finding the niche: Friendship formation of immigrant adolescents. *Youth and Society, 30*, 209–240.

Shoop, D., & Davidson, P. (1994). AIDS and adolescents: The relation of parent and partner communication to adolescent condom use. *Journal of Adolescence, 17*, 137–148.

Shrum, W., Cheek, N., Jr., & Hunter, S. (1988). Friendship in school: Gender and racial homophily. *Sociology of Education, 61*, 227–239.

Shucksmith, J., Glendinning, A., & Hendry, L. (1997). Adolescent drinking behavior and the role of family life: A Scottish perspective. *Journal of Adolescence, 20*, 85–101.

Shulman, S., Laursen, B., Kalman, Z., & Karpovsky, S. (1997). Adolescent intimacy revisited. *Journal of Youth and Adolescence, 26*, 597–617.

Shulman, S., & Scharf, M. (2000). Adolescent romantic behaviors and perceptions: Age- and gender-related differences, and links with family and peer relationships. *Journal of Research on Adolescence, 10*, 99–118.

Siegel, J., Aneshensel, C., Taub, B., Cantwell, D., 7 Driscoll, A. (1998). Adolescent depressed mood in a multiethnic smaple. *Journal of Youth and Adolescence, 27*, 413–427.

Siegel, J., Yancey, A., Aneshensel, C., & Schuler, R. (1999). Body image, perceived pubertal timing, and adolescent mental health. *Journal of Adolescent Health, 25*, 155–165.

Siegel, L. (1994). Working memory and reading: A life-span perspective. *International Journal of Behavioural Development, 17*, 109–124.

Siegel, M., & Biener, L. (2000). The impact of an antismoking media campaign on progression to established smoking: Results of a longitudinal study. *American Journal of Public Health, 90*, 380–386.

Sieger, R. (1988). Individual differences in strategy choices: Good students, not-so-good students, and perfectionists. *Child Development, 59*, 833–851.

Siegler, R., Liebert, D., & Liebert, R. (1973). Inhelder and Piaget's pendulum problem: Teaching adolescents to act as scientists. *Developmental Psychology, 9*, 97–101.

Signorelli, N. (1993). Television and adolescents' perceptions about work. *Youth and Society, 24*, 314–341.

Silbereisen, R., Kracke, B., & Crockett, L. (1990, March). *Timing of maturation and adolescent substance use.* Paper presented at the biennial meetings of the Society for Research on Adolescence, Atlanta.

Silbereisen, R., Petersen, A., Albrecht, H., & Kracke, B. (1989). Maturational timing and the development of problem behavior: Longitudinal studies in adolescence. *Journal of Early Adolescence, 9*, 247–268, 1995.

Silbereisen, R., Schwarz, B., Nowak, M., Kracke, B., & von Eye, A. (1993, March). *Psychosocial adversities and timing of adolescent transitions: A comparison of the former East and West Germanies.* Paper presented at the biennial meetings of the Society for Research in Child Development, New Orleans.

Silberesien, R., Robins, L., & Rutter, M. (1995). Secular trends in substance use: Concepts and data on the impact of social change on alcohol and drug abuse. In M. Rutter & D. Smith (Eds.), *Psychosocial disorders in young people: Time trends and their origins.* New York: Wiley.

Silverberg, S. (1986). *Psychological well-being of parents with early adolescent children.* Unpublished doctoral dissertation, Department of Child and Family Studies, University of Wisconsin–Madison.

Silverberg, S., Marczak, M., & Gondoli, D. (1996). Maternal depressive symptoms and achievement-related outcomes among adolescent daughters: Variations by family structure. *Journal of Early Adolescence, 16,* 90–109.

Silverberg, S., & Steinberg, L. (1987). Adolescent autonomy, parent-adolescent conflict, and parental well-being. *Journal of Youth and Adolescence, 16,* 293–312.

Silverberg, S., Steinberg, L. (1990). Psychological well-being of parents at midlife: The impact of early adolescent children. *Developmental Psychology, 26,* 685–666.

Silverberg, S., Tennenbaum, D., & Jacob, T. (1992). Adolescence and family interaction. In V. Van Hasselt & M. Hersen (Eds.), *Handbook of social development: A lifespan perspective* (pp. 347–370). New York: Plenum.

Silverman, W., Kurtines, W., Ginsburg, G., Weems, C., Lumpkin, P., & Carmichael, D. (1999). Treating anxiety disorders in children with group cognitive-behavioral therapy: A randomized clinical trial. *Journal of Consulting and Clinical Psychology, 67,* 995–1003.

Silverstein, B., Perlick, D., Clauson, J., & McKoy, E. (1993). Depression combined with somatic symptomatology among adolescent females who report concerns regarding maternal achievement. *Sex Roles, 28,* 637–654.

Sim, H., & Vuchinich, S. (1996). The declining effects of family stressors on antisocial behavior from childhood to adolescence and early adulthood. *Journal of Family Issues, 17,* 408–427.

Sim, T. (2000). Adolescent psychosocial competence: The importance and role of regard for parents. *Journal of Research on Adolescence, 10,* 49–64.

Simmons, R., & Blyth, D. (1987). *Moving into adolescence.* New York: Aldine de Gruyter.

Simmons, R., & Rosenberg, F. (1975). Sex, sex roles, and self-image. *Journal of Youth and Adolescence, 4,* 229–258.

Simmons, R., Blyth, D., & McKinney, K. (1983). The social and psychological effects of puberty on white females. In J. Brooks-Gunn & A. Petersen (Eds.), *Girls at puberty* (pp. 229–272). New York: Plenum.

Simmons, R., Rosenberg, F., & Rosenberg, M. (1973). Disturbance in the self-image at adolescence. *American Sociological Review, 38,* 553–568.

Simon, W., & Gagnon, J. (1969). On psychosexual development. In D. Goslin (Ed.), *Handbook of socialization theory and research.* Chicago: Rand McNally.

Simons, R., Johnson, C., & Conger, R. (1994). Harsh corporal punishment versus quality of parental involvement as an explanation of adolescent maladjustment. *Journal of Marriage and the Family, 56,* 591–607.

Simons, R., Johnson, C., Beaman, J., Conger, R., & Whitebeck, L. (1996). Parents and peer group as mediators of the effect of community structure on adolescent problem behavior. *American Journal of Community Psychology, 24,* 145–171.

Simons, R., Lin, K., & Gordon, L. (1998). Socialization in the family of origin and male dating violence: A prospective study. *Journal of Marriage and the Family, 60,* 467–478.

Simons, R., Whitbeck, L., Beaman, J., & Conger, R. (1994). The impact of mothers' parenting, involvement by nonresidential fathers, and parental conflict on the adjustment of adolescent children. *Journal of Marriage and the Family, 56,* 356–374.

Simons, R., Whitbeck, L., Conger, R., & Chyi-In, W. (1991). Intergenerational transmission of harsh parenting. *Developmental Psychology, 27,* 159–171.

Simpson, H. (Ed.). (1996). *New to the road: Reducing the risks for young motorists.* Los Angeles: Youth Enhancement Service, UCLA School of Medicine.

Simpson, R. (1962). Parental influence, anticipatory socialization, and social mobility. *American Sociological Review, 27,* 517–522.

Singh, G., & Yu, S. (1996a). Trends and differentials in adolescent and young adult mortality in the United States, 1950 through 1993. *American Journal of Public Health, 86,* 560–564.

Singh, G., & Yu, S. (1996b). U.S. childhood mortality, 1950 through 1993: Trends and socioeconomic differentials. *American Journal of Public Health, 86,* 505–512.

Singh, K., & Hernandez-Gantes, V. (1996). The relation of English language proficiency to educational aspirations of Mexican-American eighth graders. *Journal of Early Adolescence, 16,* 253–273.

Singh, S., & Darroch, J. (1999). Trends in sexual activity among adolescent American women: 1982–1995. *Family Planning Perspectives, 31,* 212–219.

Sippola, L. K. (1999). Getting to know the "other": The characteristics and developmental significance of other-sex relationships in adolescence. *Journal of Youth and Adolescence, 28*(4), 407–418.

Skinner, B. F. (1953). *Science and human behavior.* New York: Free Press.

Slap, G., & Jablow, M. (1994). *Teenage health care.* New York: Pocket Books.

Slicker, E. (1998). Relationship of parenting style to behavioral adjustment in graduating high school seniors. *Journal of Youth and Adolescence, 27,* 345–372.

Small, S. (1988). Parental self-esteem and its relationship to childrearing practices, parent-adolescent interaction, and adolescent behavior. *Journal of Marriage and the Family, 50,* 1063–1072.

Small, S., & Silverberg, S., & Kerns, D. (1993). Adolescents' perceptions of the costs and benefits of engaging in health-compromising behaviors. *Journal of Youth and Adolescence, 22,* 73–87.

Small, S., Eastman, G., & Cornelius, S. (1988). Adolescent autonomy and parental stress. *Journal of Youth and Adolescence, 17,* 377–391.

Smetana, J. (1988a). Adolescents' and parents' conceptions of parental authority. *Child Development, 59,* 321–335.

Smetana, J. (1988b). Concepts of self and social convention: Adolescents' and parents' reasoning about hypothetical and actual family conflicts. In M. Gunnar & W. Collins (Eds.), *Minnesota symposium on child psychology* (Vol. 21, pp. 79–122). Hillsdale, NJ: Erlbaum.

Smetana, J. (1989). Adolescents' and parents' reasoning about actual family conflict. *Child Development, 59,* 1052–1067.

Smetana, J. (1994). Morality in context: Abstractions, applications, and ambiguities. In R. Vasta (Ed.), *Annals of child development* (Vol. 10, pp. 83–130). London: Jessica Kingsley.

Smetana, J. (1995). Parenting styles and conceptions of parental authority during adolescence. *Child Development, 66,* 299–316.

Smetana, J., & Asquith, P. (1994). Adolescents' and parents' conceptions of parental authority and personal autonomy. *Child Development, 65,* 1147–1162.

Smetana, J., & Bitz, B. (1996). Adolescents' conceptions of teachers' authority and their relations to rule violations in school. *Child Development, 67,* 1153–1172.

Smetana, J., & Gaines, C. (1999). Adolescent-parent conflict in middle-class African-American families. *Child Development, 70,* 1447–1463.

Smetana, J., Yau, J., Restrepo, A., & Braeges, J. (1991). Adolescent-parent conflict in married and divorced families. *Developmental Psychology, 27,* 1000–1010.

Smith, E. (1996, March). *Ethnic identity in African-American youth: Definition, components, and measurement.* Paper presented at the biennial meetings of the Society for Research on Adolescence, Boston.

Smith, E., & Udry, J. (1985). Coital and non-coital sexual behaviors of white and black adolescents. *American Journal of Public Health, 75,* 1200–1203.

Smith, E., & Zabin, L. (1993). Marital and birth expectations of urban adolescents. *Youth and Society, 25,* 62–74.

Smith, E., Udry, J., & Morris, N. (1985). Pubertal development and friends: A biosocial explanation of adolescent sexual behavior. *Journal of Health and Social Behavior, 26,* 183–192.

Smith, G., & Goldman, M. (1994). Alcohol expectancy theory and the identification of high-risk adolescents. *Journal of Research on Adolescence, 4,* 229–247.

Smith, G., Goldman, M., Greenbaum, P., & Christiansen, B. (1995). Expectancy for social facilitation from drinking: The divergent paths of high-expectancy and low-expectancy adolescents. *Journal of Abnormal Psychology, 104,* 32–40.

Smith, T. (1992). Gender differences in the scientific achievement of adolescents: Effects of age and parental separation. *Social Forces, 71,* 469–484.

Smith, T. (1993, March). *Federal employment training programs for youth: Failings and opportunities.* Paper presented at the biennial meetings of the Society for Research in Child Development, New Orleans.

Smolak, L., Levine, M., & Gralen, S. (1993). The impact of puberty and dating on eating problems among middle school girls. *Journal of Youth and Adolescence, 22,* 355–368.

Smoll, F., & Schutz, R. (1990). Quantifying gender differences in physical performance: A developmental perspective. *Developmental Psychology, 26,* 360–369.

Smollar, J., & Youniss, J. (1985, April). *Transformation in adolescents' perceptions of parents.* Paper presented at the biennial meetings of the Society for Research in Child Development, Baltimore.

Sobesky, W. (1983). The effects of situational factors on moral judgments. *Child Development, 54,* 575–584.

Solomon, R., & Liefeld, C. (1998). Effectiveness of a family support center approach to adolescent mothers: Repeat pregnancy and school drop-out rates. *Family Relations, 47,* 139–144.

Sommer, K., Whitman, T., Borkowski, J., Schellenbach, C., Maxwell, S., & Keogh, D. (1993). Cognitive readiness and adolescent parenting. *Developmental Psychology, 29,* 389–398.

Sommers, C. (2000). *The war against boys.* New York: Simon & Schuster.

Sonenstein, F., Ku, L., Lindberg, L., Turner, C., & Pleck, J. (1998). Changes in sexual behavior and condom use among teenaged males: 1988 to 1995. *American Journal of Public Health, 88,* 956–959.

Sorensen, R. (1973). *Adolescent sexuality in contemporary society.* New York: World Book.

Spear, P. (2000). The adolescent brain and age-related behavioral manifestations. *Neuroscience and Biobehavioral Reviews, 24,* 417–463.

Speicher, B. (1994). Family patterns of moral judgment during adolescence and early adulthood. *Developmental Psychology, 30,* 624–632.

Spence, J., & Helmreich, R. (1978). *Masculinity and femininity: Their psychological dimensions, correlates, and antecedents.* Austin: University of Texas Press.

Spencer, M., & Dornbusch, S. (1990). Challenges in studying minority youth. In S. Feldman & G. Elliott (Eds.), *At the threshold: The developing adolescent* (pp. 123–146). Cambridge, MA: Harvard University Press.

Spencer, M., & Markstrom-Adams, C. (1990). Identity processes among racial and ethnic minority children in America. Child Development, 61, 290–310.

Spieker, S., & Bensley, L. (1994). Roles of living arrangements and grandmother social support in adolescent mothering and infant attachment. *Developmental Psychology, 30,* 102–111.

Spielberger, C. (1966). The effects of anxiety on complex learning and academic achievement. In C. Spielberger (Ed.), *Anxiety and behavior.* New York: Academic Press.

Spingarn, R., & DuRant, R. (1996). Male adolescents involved in pregnancy: Associated health risk and problem behaviors. *Pediatrics, 98,* 262–268.

Sprecher, S., & Hatfield, E. (1996). Premarital sexual standards among U.S. college students: Comparison with Russian and Japanese students. *Archives of Sexual Behavior, 25,* 261–288.

Spreitzer, E. (1994). Does participation in interscholastic athletics affect adult development? *Youth and Society, 25,* 368–387.

Sroufe, L. A. (1979). The coherence of individual development. *American Psychologist, 34,* 834–841.

St. George, I., Williams, S., & Silva, P. (1994). Body size and menarche: The Dunedin study. *Journal of Adolescent Health, 15,* 573–576.

St. John, N. (1975). *School desegregation outcomes for children.* New York: Wiley.

St. Lawrence, J. (1993). African-American adolescents' knowledge, health-related attitudes, sexual behavior, and contraceptive decisions: Implications for the prevention of adolescent HIV infection. *Journal of Consulting and Clinical Psychology, 61,* 104–112.

St. Louis, M., Conway, M., Hayman, C., Miller, C., Petersen, L., & Dondero, T. (1991). Human immunodeficiency virus infection in disadvantaged adolescents. *Journal of the American Medical Association, 266,* 2387–2391.

St. Pierre, T., Mark, M., Kaltreider, D., & Aikin, K. (1997). Involving parents of high-risk youth in drug prevention. *Journal of Early Adolescence, 17,* 21–50.

Stack, S. (1994). The effect of geographic mobility on premarital sex. *Journal of Marriage and the Family, 56,* 204–208.

Stanger, C., Achenbach, T., & McConaughy, S. (1993). Three-year course of behavioral/emotional problems in a national sample of 4- to 16-year-olds, 3: Predictors of signs of disturbance. *Journal of Consulting and Clinical Psychology, 61,* 839–848.

Stanger, C., Achenbach, T., & Verhulst, F. (1997). Accelerated longitudinal comparisons of aggressive versus delinquent syndromes. *Development and Psychopathology, 9,* 43–58.

Stanton-Salazar, R., & Dornbusch, S. (1995). Social capital and the reproduction of inequality: Information networks among Mexican-origin high school students. *Sociology of Education, 68,* 116–135.

Stattin, H., & Magnusson, C. (1996). Leaving home at an early age among female adolescents: Antecedents, adolescent adjustment, and future life implications. *New Directions for Child Development, 71,* 53–69.

Stattin, H., & Magnusson, D. (1989). The role of early aggressive behavior in the frequency, seriousness, and types of later crime. *Journal of Consulting and Clinical Psychology, 57,* 710–718.

Stattin, H., & Magnusson, D. (1994, February). *Onset of official delinquency. Its co-occurrence in time with educational, behavioral, and interpersonal problems.* Paper presented at the biennial meetings of the Society for Research on Adolescence, San Diego.

Staub, E. (1996). Cultural-societal roots of violence. *American Psychologist, 51,* 117–132.

Stedman, L. (1998). An assessment of the contemporary debate over U.S. achievement. In D. Ravitch (Ed.), *The state of student performance in American schools: Brookings papers on education policy,* Vol. 1 (pp. 53–121). Washington, D.C.: Brookings Institution.

Steele, J., & Brown, J. (1995). Adolescent room culture: Studying media in the context of everyday life. *Journal of Youth and Adolescence, 24,* 551–576.

Stein, J., & Reiser, L. (1994). A study of white middle-class adolescent boys' responses to "semenarche" (the first ejaculation). *Journal of Youth and Adolescence, 23,* 373–384.

Stein, J., Newcomb, M., & Bentler, P. (1987). An 8-year study of multiple influences on drug use and drug use consequences. *Journal of Personality and Social Psychology, 53,* 1094–1105.

Stein, J., Newcomb, M., & Bentler, P. (1992). The effect of agency and communion on selfesteem: Gender differences in longitudinal data. *Sex Roles, 26,* 465–484.

Stein, N. (1995). Sexual harassment in shcool: The public performance of gendered violence. *Harvard Educational Review, 65,* 145–162.

Steinberg, L. (1981). Transformations in family relations at puberty. *Developmental Psychology 17,* 833–840.

Steinberg, L. (1986). Latchkey children and susceptibility to peer pressure: An ecological analysis. *Developmental Psychology, 22,* 433–439.

Steinberg, L. (1987a, September). Bound to bicker: Pubescent primates leave home for good reasons. Our teens stay with us and squabble. *Psychology Today,* pp. 36–39.

Steinberg, L. (1987b). Single parents, stepparents, and the susceptibility of adolescents to antisocial peer pressure. *Child Development, 58,* 269–275.

Steinberg, L. (1988). Reciprocal relation between parent-child distance and pubertal maturation. *Developmental Psychology, 24,* 122–128.

Steinberg, L. (1989). Pubertal maturation and parent-adolescent distance: An evolutionary perspective. In G. Adams, R. Montemayor, & T. Gullotta (Eds.), *Advances in adolescent development* (Vol. 1, pp. 71–79). Beverly Hills, CA: Sage.

Steinberg, L. (1990). Autonomy, conflict, and harmony in the family relationship. In S. Feldman & G. Elliott (Eds.), *At the threshold: The developing adolescent* (pp. 255–276). Cambridge, MA: Harvard University Press.

Steinberg, L. (1996). *Beyond the classroom: Why school reform has failed and what parents need to do.* New York: Simon & Schuster.

Steinberg, L. (1998). Standards outside the classroom. In D. Ravitch (Ed.), *The state of student performance in American schools: Brookings papers on education policy: Vol. 1* (pp. 319–357). Washington, DC: Brookings Institution.

Steinberg, L. (2000a, April 22) Software can't make school safe. *The New York Times,* p. A15.

Steinberg, L. (2000b). Youth violence: Do parents and families make a difference? *National Institute of Justice Journal, April,* 30–38.

Steinberg, L. (2001). We know some things: Adolescent-parent relationships in retrospect and prospect. *Journal of Research on Adolescence, 11,* 1–20.

Steinberg, L., & Avenevoli, S. (2000). The role of context in the development of psychopathology: A conceptual framework and some speculative propositions. *Child Development, 71,* 66–74.

Steinberg, L., & Cauffman, E. (1995). The impact of employment on adolescent development. In R. Vasta (Ed.), *Annals of child development* (Vol. 11, pp. 131–166). London: Jessica Kingsley.

Steinberg, L., & Cauffman, E. (1996). Maturity of judgment in adolescence: Psychosocial factors in adolescent decisionmaking. *Law and Human Behavior, 20,* 249–272.

Steinberg, L., & Dornbusch, S. (1991). Negative correlates of part-time work in adolescence: Replication and elaboration. *Developmental Psychology, 17,* 304–313.

Steinberg, L., & Silverberg, S. (1986). The vicissitudes of autonomy in early adolescence. *Child Development, 57,* 841–851.

Steinberg, L., & Silverberg, S. (1987). Influences on marital satisfaction during the middle stages of the family life cycle. *Journal of Marriage and the Family, 49,* 751–760.

Steinberg, L., & Steinberg, W. (1994). *Crossing paths: How your child's adolescence triggers your own crisis.* New York: Simon & Schuster.

Steinberg, L., Blinde, P., & Chan, K. (1984). Dropping out among language-minority youth. *Review of Educational Research, 54,* 113–132.

Steinberg, L., Dornbusch, S., & Brown, B. (1992). Ethnic differences in adolescent achievement: An ecological perspective. *American Psychologist, 47,* 723–729.

Steinberg, L., Elmen, J., & Mounts, N. (1989). Authoritative parenting, psychosocial maturity, and academic success among adolescents. *Child Development, 60,* 1424–1436.

Steinberg, L., Fegley, S., & Dornbusch, S. (1993). Negative impact of part-time work on adolescent adjustment: Evidence from a longitudinal study. *Developmental Psychology, 29,* 171–180.

Steinberg, L., Greenberger, E., Garduque, L., Ruggiero, M., & Vaux, A. (1982). Effects of working on adolescent development. *Developmental Psychology, 18,* 385–395.

Steinberg, L., Lamborn, S., Darling, N., Mounts, N., & Dornbusch, S. (1994). Over-time changes in adjustment and competence among adolescents from authoritative, authoritarian, indulgent, and neglectful families. *Child Development, 65,* 754–770.

Steinberg, L., Lamborn, S., Dornbusch, S., & Darling, N. (1992). Impact of parenting practices on adolescent achievement: Authoritative parenting, school involvement, and encouragement to succeed. *Child Development, 63,* 1266–1281.

Steinberg, L., Mounts, N., Lamborn, S., & Dornbusch, S. (1991). Authoritative parenting and adolescent adjustment across various ecological niches. *Journal of Research on Adolescence, 1,* 19–36.

Steiner, H., Cauffman, E., & Duxbury, E. (1999). Personality traits in juvenile delinquents: Relation to criminal behavior and recidivism. *Journal of the Academy of Child and Adolescent Psychiatry, 38,* 256–262.

Stephens, L. (1996). Will Johnny see Daddy this week? An empirical test of three theoretical perspectives of postdivorce contact. *Journal of Family Issues, 17,* 466–494.

Stern, D., Finkelstein, N., Stone, J., Latting, J., & Dornsife, C. (1994). *Research on school-to-work transition programs in the United States.* Berkeley, CA: National Center for Research in Vocational Education.

Sternberg, R. (1977). *Intelligence, information processing, and analogical reasoning: The componential analysis of human abilities.* Hillsdale, NJ: Erlbaum.

Sternberg, R. (1988). *The triarchic mind.* New York: Viking Penguin.

Sternberg, R. (1994). Commentary: Reforming school reform: Comments on multiple intelligences. *Teachers College Record, 95,* 561–569.

Sternberg, R., & Nigro, G. (1980). Developmental patterns in the solution of verbal analogies. *Child Development, 51,* 27–38.

Sternberg, R., & Rifkin, B. (1979). The development of analogical reasoning processes. *Journal of Experimental Child Psychology, 27,* 195–232.

Stetsenko, A. (in press). Adolescence in Russia: Current status and recent trends. In B. Brown, R. Larson, & T. Saraswathi (Eds.), *Worlds of adolescence: Global similarities and differences in the experience of adolescence.*

Stevens, J. (1988). Social support, locus of control, and parenting in three low-income groups of mothers: Black teenagers, black adults, and white adults. *Child Development, 59,* 635–642.

Stevenson, D., & Baker, D. (1987). The family-school relation and the child's school performance. *Child Development, 58,* 1348–1357.

Stevenson, D., Schiller, K., & Schneider, B. (1994). Sequences of opportunities for learning. *Sociology of Education, 67,* 184–198.

Stevenson, H. (1994). Extracurricular programs in East Asian schools. *Teachers College Record, 95,* 389–407.

Stevenson, H., & Stigler, J. (1992). *The learning gap: Why our schools are failing and what we can learn from Japanese and Chinese education.* New York: Simon & Schuster.

Stevenson, H. C., Davis, G., Weber, E., Weiman, D., & Abdul-Kabir, S. (1995). HIV prevention beliefs among urban African-American youth. *Journal of Adolescent Health, 16,* 316–323.

Stevenson, H. C., Reed, J., Bodison, P., & Bishop, A. (1997). Racism stress management: Racial social beliefs and the experience of depression and anger in African American youth. *Youth and Society, 29,* 197–222.

Stevenson, H.C. (1998). Raising safe villages: Cultural-ecological factors that influence the emotional adjustment of adolescents. *Journal of Black Psychology, 24,* 44–59.

Stice, E., & Barrera, M., Jr. (1995). A longitudinal examination of the reciprocal relations between perceived parenting and adolescents' substance use and externalizing behaviors. *Developmental Psychology, 31,* 322–334.

Stice, E., & Gonzales, N. (1998). Adolescent temperament moderates the relation of parenting to antisocial behavior and substance use. *Journal of Adolescent Research, 13,* 5–31.

Stice, E., Cameron, R., Killen, J., Hayward, C., & Taylor, C. (1999). Naturalistic weight-reduction efforts prospectively predict growth in relative weight and onset of obesity among female adolescents. *Journal of Consulting and Clinical Psychology, 67*(6), 967–974.

Stier, D., Leventhal, J., Berg, A., Johnson, L., & Mezger, J. (1993). Are children born to young mothers at increased risk of maltreatment? *Pediatrics, 91,* 642–648.

Stipek, D., & Gralinski, J. (1996). Children's beliefs about intelligence and school performance. *Journal of Educational Psychology, 88,* 397–407.

Stock, J., Bell, M., Boyer, D., & Connel, F. (1997). Adolescent pregnancy and sexual risk-taking among sexually abused girls. *Family Planning Perspectives, 29,* 200–203, 227.

Stoller, C., Offer, D., Howard, K., & Koenig, L. (1996). Psychiatrists' concept of adolescent self-image. *Journal of Youth and Adolescence, 25,* 273–284.

Strasburger, V., & Donnerstein, E. (1999). Children, adolescents, and the media: Issues and solutions. *Pediatrics, 103,* 129–139.

Strauss, M., & Yodanis, C. (1996). Corporal punishment in adolescence and physical assaults on spouses in later life: What accounts for the link? *Journal of Marriage and the Family, 58,* 825–841.

Strober, M., Freeman, R., Bower, S., & Rigali, J. (1996). Binge eating in anorexia nervosa predicts later onset of substance use disorder: A ten-year prospective, longitudinal follow-up of 95 adolescents. *Journal of Youth and Adolescence, 25,* 519–532.

Strouse, J., Goodwin, M., & Roscoe, B. (1994). Correlates of attitudes toward sexual harassment among early adolescents. *Sex Roles, 31,* 559–577.

Studer, M., & Thornton, A. (1987). Adolescent religiosity and contraceptive usage. *Journal of Marriage and the Family, 49,* 117–128.

Stukas, A., Jr., Clary, E., & Synder, M. (1999). Service learning: Who benefits are why. *Social Policy Report of the Society for Research in Child Development, 13.*

Stumpf, H., & Stanley, J. (1996). Gender-related differences on the College Board's Advanced Placement and Achievement tests, 1982–1992. *Journal of Educational Psychology, 88,* 353–364.

Sucoff, C., & Upchurch, D. (1998). Neighborhood context and the risk of childbearing among metropolitan-area black adolescents. *American Sociological Review, 63,* 571–585.

Sue, S., & Okazaki, S. (1990). Asian-American educational achievements: A phenomenon in search of an explanation. *American Psychologist, 45,* 913–920.

Sui-Chu, E., & Willms, J. (1996). Effects of parental involvement on eighth-grade achievement. *Sociology of Education, 69,* 126–141.

Sullivan, H. S. (1953a). *Conceptions of modern psychiatry.* New York: Norton.

Sullivan, H. S. (1953b). *The interpersonal theory of psychiatry.* New York: Norton.

Sullivan, K., & Sullivan, A. (1980). Adolescent-parent separation. *Developmental Psychology, 16,* 93–99.

Sum, A., & Fogg, W. (1991). The adolescent poor and the transition to early adulthood. In P. Edelman & J. Ladner (Eds.), *Adolescence and poverty: Challenge for the 90s* (pp. 37–110). Washington, DC: Center for National Policy Press.

Summers, P., Forehand, R., Armistead, L., & Tannenbaum, L. (1998). Parental divorce during early adolescence in Caucasian families: The role of family process variables in predicting the long-term consequences for early adult psychosocial adjustment. *Journal of Consulting and Clinical Psychology, 66,* 327–336.

Summerville, M., & Kaslow, N. (1993, March). *Racial differences in psychological symptoms, cognitive style, and family functioning in suicidal adolescents.* Paper presented at the biennial meetings of the Society for Research in Child Development, New Orleans.

Super, D. (1967). *The psychology of careers.* New York: Harper & Row.

Surbey, M. (1987). Anorexia nervosa, amenorrhea, and adaptation. *Ethology and Sociobiology, 8,* 475–515.

Surbey, M. (1990). Family composition, stress, and human menarche. In F. Bercovitch & T. Zeigler (Eds.), *The socioendocrinology of primate reproduction* (pp. 1–25). New York: Alan R. Liss.

Suris, J., Resnick, M., Cassuto, N., & Blum, R. (1996). Sexual behavior of adolescents with chronic disease and disability. *Journal of Adolescent Health, 19,* 124–131.

Susman, E. (1997). Modeling developmental complexity in adolescence: Hormones and behavior in context. *Journal of Research on Adolescence, 7,* 283–306.

Susman, E., Dorn, L., Inoff-Germain, G., Nottelmann, E., & Chrousos, G. (1997). Cortisol reactivity, distress behavior, and behavioral and psychological problems in young adolescents: A longitudinal perspective. *Journal of Research on Adolescence, 7,* 81–105.

Susman, E., Inhoff-Germain, G., Nottelmann, E., Loriaux, D., Cutler, G., Jr. & Chrousos, G. (1987). Hormones, emotional dispositions, and aggressive attributes in young adolescents. *Child Development, 58,* 1114–1134.

Susman, E., Koch, P., Maney, D., & Finkelstein, J. (1993). Health promotion in adolescence: Developmental and theoretical considerations. In R. Lerner (Ed.), *Early adolescence: Perspectives on research, policy, and intervention* (pp. 247–260). Hillsdale, NJ: Erlbaum.

Sussman, S., Dent, C., McAdams, L., Stacy, A., Burton, D., & Flay, B. (1994). Group self-identification and adolescent cigarette smoking: A 1-year prospective study. *Journal of Abnormal Psychology, 103,* 576–580.

Swarr, A., & Richards, M. (1996). Longitudinal effects of adolescent girls' pubertal development, perceptions of pubertal timing, and parental relations on eating problems. *Developmental Psychology, 32,* 636–646.

Szeszulski, P., Martinez, A., & Reyes, B. (1994, February). *Patterns and predictors of self-satisfaction among culturally diverse high school students.* Paper presented at the biennial meetings of the Society for Research on Adolescence, San Diego.

Tanner, D. (1972). *Secondary education.* New York: Macmillan.

Tanner, J. (1972). Sequence, tempo, and individual variation in growth and development of boys and girls aged twelve to sixteen. In J. Kagan & R. Coles (Eds.), *Twelve to sixteen: Early adolescence.* New York: Norton.

Taris, T., & Semin, G. (1997). Parent-child interaction during adolescence, and the adolescent's sexual experience: Control, closeness, and conflict. *Journal of Youth and Adolescence, 26,* 373–398.

Tasker, F., & Richards, M. (1994). Adolescents' attitudes toward marriage and marital prospects after parental divorce: A review. *Journal of Adolescent Research, 9,* 340–362.

Taylor, R. (1996). Adolescents' perceptions of kinship support and family management practices: Association with adolescent adjustment in African American families. *Developmental Psychology, 32,* 687–695.

Taylor, R., & Roberts, D. (1995). Kinship support and maternal and adolescent well-being in economically disadvantaged African-American families. *Child Development, 66,* 1585–1597.

Taylor, R., Casten, R., & Flickinger, S. (1993). The influence of kinship social support on the parenting experiences and psychosocial adjustment of African-American adolescents. *Developmental Psychology, 29,* 382–388.

Taylor, R., Casten, R., Flickinger, S., Roberts, D., & Fulmore, C. (1994). Explaining the school performance of African-American adolescents. *Journal of Research on Adolescence, 4,* 21–44.

Taylor, R., Roberts, D., & Jacobson, L. (1997). *Stressful life events, parenting, and adolescent adjustment among low income African-American families.* Unpublished manuscript, Department of Psychology, Temple University.

Teachman, J. (1996). Intellectual skill and academic performance: Do families bias the relationship? *Sociology of Education, 69,* 35–48.

Teachman, J. (1997). Gender of siblings, cognitive achievement, and academic performance: Familial and nonfamilial influences on children. *Journal of Marriage and the Family, 59,* 363–374.

Teachman, J., Paasch, K., & Carver, K. (1996). Social capital and dropping out of school early. *Journal of Marriage and the Family, 58,* 773–783.

Telljohann, S., & Price, J. (1993). A qualitative examination of adolescent homosexuals' life experiences: Ramifications for secondary school personnel. *Journal of Homosexuality, 26,* 41–56.

Terrell, N. (1997). Street life: Aggravated and sexual assaults among homeless and runaway adolescents. *Youth and Society, 28,* 267–290.

Teti, D., & Lamb, M. (1989). Socioeconomic and marital outcomes of adolescent marriage, adolescent childbirth, and their co-occurrence. *Journal of Marriage and the Family, 51,* 203–212.

Tevendale, H., DuBois, D., Lopez, C., & Prindiville, S. (1997). Self-esteem stability and early adolescent adjustment: An exploratory study. *Journal of Early Adolescence, 17,* 216–237.

Thomas, G., Farrell, M., & Barnes, G. (1996). The effects of single-mother families and nonresident fathers on delinquency and substance abuse in black and white adolescents. *Journal of Marriage and the Family, 58,* 884–894.

Thomson, E., Hanson, T., & McLanahan, S. (1994). Family structure and child well-being: Economic resources vs. parental behaviors. *Social Forces, 73,* 221–242.

Thompson, L., Riggs, P., Mikulich, S., & Crowley, T. (1996). Contribution of ADHD symptoms to substance problems and delinquency in conduct-disordered adolescents. *Journal of Abnormal Child Psychology, 24,* 325–347.

Thompson, R., & Larson, R. (1995). Social context and the subjective experience of different types of rock music. *Journal of Youth and Adolescence, 24,* 731–744.

Thompson, R., & Zuroff, D. C. (1999). Dependency, self-criticism, and mothers' responses to adolescent sons' autonomy and competence. *Journal of Youth and Adolescence, 28,* 365–384.

Thompson, S., Sargent, R., & Kemper, K. (1996). Black and white adolescent males' perceptions of ideal body size. *Sex Roles, 34,* 391–406.

Thornberry, T., Smith, C., & Howard, G. (1997). Risk factors for teenage fatherhood. *Journal of Marriage and the Family, 59,* 505–522.

Thornton, A., & Camburn, D. (1989). Religious participation and adolescent sexual behavior and attitudes. *Journal of Marriage and the Family, 51,* 641–653.

Thornton, A., Orbuch, T. L., and Axinn, W. G. (1995). Parent-child relationships during the transition to adulthood. *Journal of Family Issues, 16,* 538–564.

Thornton, M., Chatters, L., Taylor, R., & Allen, W. (1990). Sociodemographic and environmental correlates of racial socialization by black parents. *Child Development, 61,* 401–409.

Thurber, C. (1995). The experience and expression of homesickness in preadolescent and adolescent boys. *Child Development, 66,* 1162–1178.

Tiezzi, L., Lipshutz, J., Wrobleski, N., Vaughan, R., & McCarthy, J. (1997). Pregnancy prevention among urban adolescents younger than 15: Results of the "In Your Face" program. *Family Planning Perspectives, 29,* 173–176, 197.

TIMSS. (1997). *TIMSS highlights of international results.* Chestnut Hill, MA: TIMSS International Study Center, Boston College.

Tisak, M., Tisak, J., & Rogers, M. (1994). Adolescents' reasoning about authority and friendship relations in the context of drug usage. *Journal of Adolescence, 17,* 265–282.

Tobin-Richards, M. (1985, April). *Sex differences and similarities in heterosexual activity in early adolescence.* Paper presented at the biennial meetings of the Society for Research in Child Development, Toronto.

Toch, T. (1993). Violence in schools. *U.S. News and World Report, 115,* 31–37.

Tolan, P., & Thomas, P. (1995). The implications of age of onset for delinquency risk, II: Longitudinal data. *Journal of Abnormal Child Psychology, 23,* 157–181.

Tolman, D. (1993, March). *"When my body says yes": Adolescent girls' experiences of sexual desire.* Paper presented at the biennial meetings of the society for Research in Child Development, New Orleans.

Tolson, J., Halliday-Scher, K. & Mack, V. (1994, February). *Similarity and friendship quality in African-American adolescents.* Paper presented at the biennial meetings of the Society for Research on Adolescence, San Diego.

Torney-Purta, J. (1990). Youth in relation to social institutions. In S. Feldman & G. Elliott (Eds.), *At the threshold: The developing adolescent* (pp. 457–478). Cambridge, MA: Harvard University Press.

Torney-Purta, J. (1992). Cognitive representations of the political system in adolescents: The continuum from pre-novice to expert. In H. Haste & J. Torney-Purta (Eds.), *The development of political understanding* (pp. 11–25). San Francisco: Jossey-Bass.

Treaster, J. (1994, February 1). Survey finds marijuana use is up in high schools. *New York Times,* pp. A1 and ff.

Treboux, D., & Busch-Rossnagel, N. (1990). Social network influences on adolescent sexual attitudes and behaviors. *Journal of Adolescent Research, 5,* 175–189.

Tremblay, R., Masse, L., Vitaro, F., & Dobkin, P. (1995). The impact of friends' deviant behavior on early onset of delinquency: Longitudinal data from 6 to 13 years of age. *Development and Psychopathology, 7,* 649–667.

Tremblay, R., Pagani-Kurtz, L., Masse, L., Vitaro, F., & Pihl, R. (1995). A bimodal preventive intervention for disruptive kindergarten boys: Its impact through mid-adolescence. *Journal of Consulting and Clinical Psychology, 63,* 560–568.

Trent, K., & Crowder, K. (1997). Adolescent birth intentions, social disadvantage and behavioral outcomes. *Journal of Marriage and the Family, 59,* 523–535.

Trent, K., & Harlan, S. (1994). Teenage mothers in nuclear and extended households: Differences by marital status and race/ethnicity. *Journal of Family Issues, 15,* 309–337.

Trickett, P., McBride-Chang, C., & Putnam, F. (1994). The classroom performance and behavior of sexually abused females. *Development and Psychopathology, 6,* 183–194.

Trussell, J. (1989). Teenage pregnancy in the United States. *Family Planning Perspectives, 21,* 262–269.

Tschann, J., & Adler, N. (1997). Sexual self-acceptance, communication with partner, can contraceptive use among adolescent females: A longitudinal study. *Journal of Research on Adolescence, 7,* 413–430.

Tubman, J., Windle, M., & Windle, R. (1996). The onset and cross-temporal patterning of sexual intercourse in middle adolescence: Prospective relations with behavioral and emotional problems. *Child Development, 67,* 327–343.

Tucker, C., Barber, B., & Eccles, J. (1997). Advice about life plans and personal problems in late adolescent sibling relationships. *Journal of Youth and Adolescence, 26,* 63–76.

Turiel, E. (1978). The development of concepts of social structure: Social convention. In J. Glick & K. A. Clarke-Stewart (Eds.), *The development of social understanding.* New York: Gardner.

Turkheimer, E., & Waldron, M. (2000). Nonshared environment: A theoretical, methodological, and quantitative review. *Psychological Bulletin, 126,* 78–108.

UCLA Higher Education Research Institute. (1999). *American freshman 1998.* Los Angeles: Author.

UCLA Higher Education Research Institute. (2000). *American freshman 1999.* Los Angeles: Author.

Udry, J. (1987). Hormonal and social determinants of adolescent sexual initiation. In J. Bancroft (Ed.), *Adolescence and puberty.* New York: Oxford University Press.

Udry, J., & Billy, J. (1987). Initiation of coitus in early adolescence. *American Sociological Review, 52,* 841–855.

Udry, J., & Billy, J., Morris, N., Gruff, T., & Raj, M. (1985). Serum androgenic hormones motivate sexual behavior in boys. *Fertility and Sterility, 43,* 90–94.

Udry, J., Halpern, C., & Campbell, B. (1991, April). *Hormones, pubertal development, and sexual behavior in adolescent females.* Paper presented at the biennial meetings of the Society for Research in Child Development, Seattle.

Udry, J., Talbert, L., & Morris, N. (1986). Biosocial foundations for adolescent female sexuality. *Demography, 23,* 217–230.

Uhlenberg, P., & Eggebeen, D. (1986). The declining well-being of American adolescents. *Public Interest, 82,* 25–38.

Underwood, M., Kupersmidt, J., & Coie, J. (1996). Childhood peer sociometric status and aggression as predictors of adolescent childbearing. *Journal of Research on Adolescence, 6,* 201–223.

Unger, J., Kipke, M., Simon, T., Montgomery, S., & Johnson, C. (1997). Homeless youths and young adults in Los Angeles: Prevalence of mental health problems and the relationship between mental health and substance abuse disorders. *American Journal of Community Psychology, 25,* 371–394.

United Nations Population Division. (1976). *Population by sex and age for regions and countries, 1950–2000, as assessed in 1973: Median variant.* New York: United Nations Department of Social and Economic Affairs.

Upchurch, D., Aneshensel, C., Sucoff, C., & Levy-Storms, L. (1999). Neighborhood and family contexts of adolescent sexual activity. *Journal of Marriage and the Family, 61,* 920–933.

Upchurch, D., Levy-Storms, L., Sucoff, C., & Aneshensel, C. (1998). Gender and ethnic differences in the timing of first sexual intercourse. *Family Planning Perspectives, 30,* 121–127.

Urberg, K., Degirmencioglu, S., & Pilgrim, C. (1997). Close friend and group influence on adolescent cigarette smoking and alcohol use. *Developmental Psychology, 33,* 834–844.

Urberg, K., Degirmencioglu, S., Tolson, J., & Halliday-Scher, K. (1995). The structure of adolescent peer networks. *Developmental Psychology, 31,* 540–547.

U.S. Bureau of the Census. (1994). *Who's minding the kids?* Washington, DC: Author.

U.S. Bureau of the Census. (1996). *Statistical abstract of the United States.* Washington, DC: Author.

U.S. Bureau of the Census. (1999a). *Current population survey, March 1999.* Washington, DC: U.S. Department of Commerce.

U.S. Bureau of the Census. (1999b). *Statistical abstract of the United States.* Washington, DC: U.S. Department of Commerce.

U.S. Bureau of the Census. (1999c). *Young adults living at home: 1960 to present.* Washington, DC: U.S. Bureau of the Census (Internet release date: January 7, 1999).

U.S. Bureau of the Census. (2000). *Projections of the total resident population by 5-year age groups, and sex with special age categories: Middle series, 1999 to 2100.* Washington, DC: U.S. Department of Commerce.

U.S. Department of Commerce, Bureau of the Census. (1940). *Characteristics of the population.* Washington, DC: U.S. Government Printing Office.

Usmiani, S., & Daniluk, J. (1997). Mothers and their adolescent daughters: Relationship between self-esteem, gender role identity, and body image. *Journal of Youth and Adolescence, 26,* 45–62.

Valois, R., Oeltmann, J., Waller, J., & Hussey, J. (1999). Relationship between number of sexual intercourse partners and selected health risk behaviors among public high school adolescents. *Journal of Adolescent Health, 25,* 328–335.

Van Hoof, A. (1999). The identity status field re-reviewed: An update of unresolved and neglected issues with a view on some alternative approaches. *Developmental Review, 19,* 497–556.

van Wel, F. (1994). "I count my parents among my best friends": Youths' bonds with parents and friends in The Netherlands. *Journal of Marriage and the Family, 56,* 835–843.

Vandell, D., & Corasaniti, M. (1988). The relation between third graders' after-school care and social, academic, and emotional functioning. *Child Development, 59,* 868–875.

Vandell, D., & Ramanan, J. (1991). Children of the National Longitudinal Survey of Youth: Choices in after-school care and child development. *Developmental Psychology, 27,* 637–643.

Vandewater, E., & Lansford, J. (1998). Influences of family structure and parental conflict on children's well-being. *Family Relations, 47,* 323–330.

Vanfossen, B., Jones, J., & Spade, J. (1987). Curriculum tracking and status maintenance. *Sociology of Education, 60,* 104–122.

Varenne, H. (1982). Jocks and freaks: The symbolic structure of the expression of social interaction among American senior high school students. In G. Spindler (Ed.), *Doing the ethnography of schooling* (pp. 213–235). New York: Holt, Rinehart & Winston.

Vaughan, R., McCarthy, J., Armstrong, B., Walter, H., Waterman, P., & Tiezzi, L. (1996). Carrying and using weapons: A survey of minority junior high school students in New York City. *American Journal of Public Health, 86,* 568–572.

Vega, W., Gil, A., & Zimmerman, R. (1993). Patterns of drug use among Cuban-American, African-American, and white non-Hispanic boys. *American Journal of Public Health, 83,* 257–259.

Vega, W., Khoury, E., Zimmerman, R., Gil, A., & Warheit, G. (1995). Cultural conflicts and problem behaviors of Latino adolescents in home and school environments. *Journal of Community Psychology, 23,* 167–179.

Velez, W. (1989). High school attrition among Hispanic and non-Hispanic white youths. *Sociology of Education, 62,* 119–133.

Vera Institute of Justice. (1990). *The male role in teenage pregnancy and parenting.* New York: Author.

Verkuyten, M. (1995). Self-esteem, self-concept stability, and aspects of ethnic identity among minority and majority youth in The Netherlands. *Journal of Youth and Adolescence, 24,* 155–185.

Vicary, J., Klingaman, L., & Harkness, W. (1995). Risk factors associated with date rape and sexual assault of adolescent girls. *Journal of Adolescence, 18,* 289–306.

Vigersky, R. (Ed.). (1977). *Anorexia nervosa.* New York: Raven Press.

Vispoel, W., & Austin, J. (1995). Success and failure in junior high school: A critical incident approach to understanding students' attributional beliefs. *American Educational Research Journal, 32,* 377–412.

Vitaro, F., Tremblay, R., Kerr, M., Pagani, L., & Bukowski, W. (1997). Disruptiveness, friends' characteristics, and delinquency in early adolescence: A test of two competing models. *Child Development, 68,* 676–689.

Voelkl, K. (1997). Identification with school. *American Journal of Education, 105,* 294–318.

Voyer, D., Voyer, S., & Bryden, M. (195). Magnitude of sex differences in spatial abilities: A meta-analysis and consideration of critical variables. *Psychological Bulletin, 117,* 250–270.

Vuchinich, S., Angeletti, J., & Gatherum, A. (1996). Context and development in family problem solving with preadolescent children. *Child Development, 67,* 1276–1288.

Vuchinich, S., Bank, L., & Patterson, G. (1992). Parenting, peers, and the stability of antisocial behavior in preadolescent boys. *Developmental Psychology, 28,* 510–521.

Vuchinich, S., Hetherington, E.M., Vuchinich, R., & Clingempeel, W. (1991). Parent-child interaction and gender differences in early adolescents' adaptation to stepfamilies. *Developmental Psychology, 27,* 618–626.

Vygotsky, L. (1930/1978). *Mind in society.* Cambridge, MA: Harvard University Press.

Waber, D. (1977). Sex differences in mental abilities, hemispheric lateralization, and rate of physical growth at adolescence. *Developmental Psychology, 13,* 29–38.

Wagner, B. (1997). Family risk factors for child and adolescent suicidal behavior. *Psychological Bulletin, 121,* 246–298.

Wagner, B., Cohen, P., & Brook, J. (1996). Parent/adolescent relationships: Moderators of the effects of stressful life events. *Journal of Adolescent Research, 11,* 347–374.

Wainer, H., & Steinberg, L. (1992). Sex differences in performance on the mathematics section of the Scholastic Aptitude Test: A bidirectional validity study. *Harvard Educational Review, 62,* 323–336.

Waite, L., Goldscheider, F., & Witsberger, C. (1986). Nonfamily living and the erosion of traditional family orientations among young adults. *American Sociological Review, 51,* 541–554.

Walberg, H. (1998). *Spending more while learning less.* New York: Thomas B. Fordham Foundation.

Waldman, I. (1996). Aggressive boys' hostile perceptual and response biases: The role of attention and impulsivity. *Child Development, 67,* 1015–1033.

Walker, L., & Taylor, J. (1991a). Family interaction and the development of moral reasoning. *Child Development, 62,* 264–283.

Walker, L., & Taylor, J. (1991b). Stage transitions in moral reasoning: A longitudinal study of developmental processes. *Developmental Psychology, 27,* 330–337.

Walker, L., de Vries, B., & Trevethan, S. (1987). Moral stages and moral orientations in real-life and hypothetical dilemmas. *Child Development, 58,* 842–858.

Wall, J., Power, T., & Arbona, C. (1993). Susceptibility to antisocial peer pressure and its relation to acculturation in Mexican-American adolescents. *Journal of Adolescent Research, 8,* 403–418.

Wallace-Broscious, A. Serafica, F., & Osipow, S. (1994). Adolescent career development: Relationships to self-concept and identity status. *Journal of Research on Adolescence, 4,* 127–149.

Wallerstein, J., & Blakeslee, S. (1989). *Second chances.* New York: Ticknor & Fields.

Wallerstein, J., & Kelly, J. (1974). The effects of parental divorce: The adolescent experience. In E. Anthony & A. Koupernik (Eds.), *The child in his family: Children as a psychiatric risk* (Vol. 3). New York: Wiley.

Wang, M., Fitzhugh, E., Westerfield, R., & Eddy, J. (1995). Family and peer influences on smoking behavior among American adolescents: An age trend. *Journal of Adolescent Health, 16,* 200–203.

Wångby, M., Bergman, L., & Magnusson, D. (1999). Development of adjustment problems in girls: What syndromes emerge? *Child Development, 70,* 678–699.

Ward, M. (1995). Talking about sex: Common themes about sexuality in the prime-time television programs children and adolescents view most. *Journal of youth and Adolescence, 24,* 595–615.

Ward, S., & Overton, W. (1990). Semantic familiarity, relevance, and the development of deductive reasoning. *Developmental psychology, 26,* 488–493.

Warneke, C., & Cooper, S. (1994). Child and adolescent drownings in Harris Country, Texas, 1983 through 1990. *American Journal of Public Health, 84,* 593–598.

Warner, B., & Weist, M. (1996). Urban youth as witnesses to violence: Beginning assessment and treatment effects. *Journal of Youth and Adolescence, 25,* 361–377.

Warren, C., Santelli, J., Everett, S., Kann, L., Collins, J., Cassell, C., Morris, L., & Kolbe, L. (1998). Sexual behavior among U.S. high school students, 1990–1995. *Family Planning Perspectives, 30,* 170–172, 200.

Warren, J. (1996). Educational inequality among white and Mexican-orign adolescents in the American Southwest: 1990. *Sociology of Education, 69,* 142–158.

Washington Post. (1994, April 24). Specialists, youngsters paint disturbing portrait of teen sex in the '90s, pp. A1 and ff.

Wasserman, G., Rauh, V., Brunelli, S., Garcia-Castro, M., & Necos, B. (1990). Psychosocial attributes and life experiences of disadvantaged minority mothers: Age and ethnic variations. *Child Development, 61,* 566–580.

Waterman, A. (1982). Identity development from adolescence to adulthood: An extension of theory and a review of research. *Developmental Psychology, 18,* 341–358.

Waterman, A. (1999a). Commentary: Identity, the identity statuses, and identity status development: A contemporary statement. *Developmental Review, 19,* 591–621.

Waterman, A. (1999b). Issues of identity formation revisited: United States and the Netherlands. *Developmental Review, 19,* 462–479.

Waterman, A., & Goldman, J. (1976). A longitudinal study of ego identity development at a liberal arts college. *Journal of Youth and Adolescence, 5,* 361–369.

Waterman, A., Geary, P., & Waterman, A. (1974). A longitudinal study of changes in ego identity status from the freshman to the senior year at college. *Developmental Psychology, 10,* 387–392.

Waters, E., Merrick, S., Treboux, D., Crowell, J., & Albersheim, L. (2000). Attachment security in infancy and early adulthood: A twenty-year longitudinal study. *Child Development, 71,* 684–689.

Watson, D., & Kendall, P. (1989). Understanding anxiety and depression: Their relation to negative and positive affective states. In P. Kendall (Ed.), *Anxiety and depression* (pp. 3–26). New York: Academic Press.

Weiner, I. (1980). Psychopathology in adolescence. In J. Adelson (Ed.), *Handbook of adolescent psychology* (pp. 447–471). New York:Wiley.

Weinfeld, N., Sroufe, A., & Egeland, B. (2000). Attachment from infancy to early adulthood in a high-risk sample: Continuity, discontinuity, and their correlates. *Child Development, 71,* 695–702.

Weinfield, N. S., Ogawa, J. R., & Sroufe, L. A. (1997). Early attachment as a pathway to adolescent peer competence. *Journal of Research on Adolescence, 7,* 241–265.

Weinraub, M., & Gringlas, M. (1995). Single parenthood. In M. Bornstein (Ed.), *Handbook of parenting, Volume 3: Status and social conditions of parenting* (pp. 65–88). Mahwah, NJ: Erlbaum.

Weisner, T., & Garnier, H. (1995, March). *Family values and nonconventional family lifestyles: An 18-year longitudinal study at adolescence.* Paper presented at the biennial meetings of the Society for Research in Child Development, Indianapolis.

Weiss, L., & Schwartz, J. (1996). The relationship between parenting types and older adolescents' personality, academic achievement, adjusment, and substance use. *Child Development, 67,* 2101–2114.

Weiss, R. (1974). The provisions of social relationships. In Z. Rubin (Ed.), *Doing unto others.* Englewood Cliffs, NJ: Prentice-Hall.

Weiss, R. (1979). Growing up a little faster: The experience of growing up in a single parent household. *Journal of Social Issues, 35,* 97–111.

Weissberg, R., Caplan, M., & Harwood, R. (1991). Promoting competent young people in competence-enhancing environments: A systems-based perspective on primary prevention. *Journal of Consulting and Clinical Psychology, 59,* 830–841.

Weist, M., Freedman, A., Paskewitz, D., Proescher, E., & Flaherty, L. (1995). Urban youth under stress: Empirical identification of protective factors. *Journal of Youth and Adolescence, 24,* 705–729.

Weisz, J., McCabe, M., & Dennig, M. (1994). Primary and secondary control among children undergoing medical procedures: Adjustment as a function of coping style. *Journal of Consulting and Clinical Psychology, 62,* 324–332.

Weisz, J., Weiss, B., Han, S., Granger, D., & Morton, T. (1995). Effects of psychotherapy with children and adolescents revisited: A meta-analysis of treatment outcome studies. *Psychological Bulletin, 117,* 450–468.

Wells, A. (1995). Reexamining social science research on desegregation: Long-versus short-term effects. *Teachers College Record, 96,* 691–706.

Wells, A., & Serna, I. (1996). The politics of culture: Understanding local political resistance to detracking in racially mixed schools. *Harvard Educational Review, 66,* 93–118.

Wentzel, K. (1989). Adolescent classroom goals, standards for performance, and academic achievement: An interactionist perspective. *Journal of Educational Psychology, 81,* 131–142.

Wentzel, K. (1994a). Family functioning and academic achievement in middle school: A social-emotional perspective. *Journal of Early Adolescence, 14,* 268–291.

Wentzel, K. (1994b). Relations of social goal pursuit to social acceptance, classroom behavior, and perceived social support. *Journal of Educational Psychology, 86,* 173–182.

Wentzel, K. (1998). Social relationships and motivation in middle school: The role of parents, teachers, and peers. *Journal of Educational Psychology, 90,* 202–209.

Wentzel, K., & Asher, S. (1995). The academic lives of neglected, rejected, popular, and controversial children. *Child Development, 66,* 754–763.

Wentzel, K., & Caldwell, K. (1997). Friendships, peer acceptance, and group membership: Relations to academic achievement in middle school. *Child Development, 68,* 1198–1209.

Wentzel, K., & Erdley, C. (1993). Strategies for making friends: Relations to social behavior and peer acceptance in early adolescence. *Developmental Psychology, 29,* 819–826.

Wentzel, K. R. (1997). Student motivation in middle school: The role of perceived pedagogical caring. *Journal of Educational Psychology, 89,* 411–419.

Werner, E., & Smith, R. (1982). *Vulnerable but invincible: A longitudinal study of resilient children.* New York: McGraw-Hill.

Westoff, C. (1988). Unintended pregnancy in America and abroad. *Family Planning Perspectives, 20,* 254–261.

Wetzel, J. (1987). *American youth: A statistical snapshot.* New York: William T. Grant Foundation Commission on Work, Family, and Citizenship.

Whillits, F. (1988). Adolescent behavior and adult success and well-being. *Youth and Society, 20,* 68–69.

Whitaker, D., Miller, K., May, D., & Levin, M. (1999). Teenage partners' communication about sexual risk and condom use: The importance of parent-teenager discussions. *Family Planning Perspectives, 31,* 117–121.

Whitbeck, L., Conger, R., Simons, R., & Kao, M. (1993). Minor deviant behaviors and adolescent sexuality. *Youth and Society, 25,* 24–37.

Whitbeck, L., Hoyt, D., & Ackley, K. (1996, March). *Abusive family backgrounds and later victimization among runaway and homeless adolescents.* Paper presented at the biennial meetings of the Society for Research on Adolescence, Boston.

Whitbeck, L., Hoyt, D., & Ackley, K. (1997). Abusive family backgrounds and later victimization among runaway and homeless adolescents. *Journal of Research on Adolescence, 7,* 375–392.

Whitbeck, L., Hoyt, D., & Yoder, K. (1999). A risk-amplification model of victimization and depressive symptoms among runaway and homeless adolescents. *American Journal of Community Psychology, 27,* 273–296.

Whitbeck, L., Hoyt, D., Miller, M., & Kao, M. (1992). Parental support, depressed affect, and sexual experience among adolescents. *Youth and Society, 24,* 166–177.

Whitbeck, L., Yoder, K., Hoyt, D., & Conger, R. (1999). Early adolescent sexual activity: A developmental study. *Journal of Marriage and the Family, 61,* 934–946.

White, J., Moffitt, T., & Silva, P. (1989). A prospective replication of the protective effects of IQ in subjects at high risk for juvenile delinquency. *Journal of Consulting and Clinical Psychology, 57,* 719–724.

White, J., Moffitt, T., Caspi, A., Bartusch, D., Needles, D., & Stouthamer-Loeber, M. (1994). Measuring impulsivity and examining its relationship to delinquency. *Journal of Abnormal Psychology, 103,* 192–205.

White, K., Speisman, J., & Costos, D. (1983). Young adults and their parents. In H. Grotevant & C. Cooper (Eds.), *Adolescent development in the family.* San Francisco: Jossey-Bass.

White, L., & Brinkerhoff, D. (1981). The sexual division of labor: Evidence from childhood. *Social Forces, 60,* 170–181.

Whitebeck, L., Simons, R., & Kao, M. (1994). The effects of divorced mothers' dating behaviors and sexual attitudes on the sexual attitudes and behaviors of their adolescent children. *Journal of Marriage and the Family, 56,* 615–621.

Whitesell, N., & Harter, S. (1996). The interpersonal context of emotion: Anger with close friends and classmates. *Child Development, 67,* 1345–1359.

Whiting, B., & Whiting, J. (1975). *Children of six cultures.* Cambridge, MA: Harvard University Press.

Wichstrom, L. (1999). The emergence of gender difference in depressed mood during adolescence: The role of intensified gender socialization. *Developmental Psychology, 35,* 232–245.

Widmer, E. (1997). Influence of older siblings on initiation of sexual intercourse. *Journal of Marriage and the Family, 59,* 928–938.

Widom, C., & Kuhns, J. (1996). Childhood victimization and subsequent risk for promiscuity, prostitution, and teenage pregnancy: A prospective study. *American Journal of Public Health, 86,* 1607–1612.

Wigfield, A., & Eccles, J. (1994). Children's competence beliefs, achievement values, and general self-esteem: Change across elementary and middle school. *Journal of Early Adolescence, 14,* 107–138.

Wigfield, A., Eccles, J., Mac Iver, D., Reuman, D., & Midgley, C. (1991). Transitions during early adolescence: Changes in children's domain-specific self-perceptions and general self-esteem across the transition to junior high school. *Developmental Psychology, 27,* 552–565.

Wilcox, W. (1998). Conservative Protestant childrearing: Authoritarian or authoritative? *American Sociological Review, 63,* 796–809.

Wilkinson, D., & Fagan, J. (1996). The role of firearms in violence "scripts": The dynamics of gun events among adolescent males. *Law and Contemporary Problems, 59,* 55–89.

William T. Grant Foundation Commission on Work, Family, and Citizenship. (1988). *The forgotten half: Non-college youth in America.* Washington, DC: Author.

Williams, J., & Dunlop, L. (1999). Pubertal timing and self-reported delinquency among male adolescents. *Journal of Adolescence, 22,* 157–171.

Williamson, J., Borduin, C., & Howe, B. (1991). The ecology of adolescent maltreatment: A multilevel examination of adolescent physical abuse, sexual abuse, and neglect. *Journal of Consulting and Clinical Psychology, 59,* 449–457.

Wills, T., & Cleary, S. (1996). How are social support effects mediated? A test with parental support and adolescent substance use. *Journal of Personality and Social Psychology, 71,* 937–952.

Wills, T., McNamara, G., Vaccaro, D., & Hirky, A. (1996). Escalated substance use: A longitudinal grouping analysis from early to middle adolescence. *Journal of Abnormal Psychology, 105,* 166–180.

Wills, T., Windle, M., & Cleary, S. (1998). Temperament and novelty seeking in adolescent substance use: Convergence of dimensions of temperament with constructs from Cloninger's theory. *Journal of Personality and Social Psychology, 74,* 387–406.

Wilson, F. (1985). The impact of school desegregation programs on white public-school enrollment, 1968–1976. *Sociology of Education, 58,* 137–153.

Wilson, M., & Daly, M. (1985). Competitiveness, risk taking, and violence: The young male syndrome. *Ethology and Sociobiology, 6,* 59–73.

Wilson, P., & Wilson, J. (1992). Environmental influences on adolescent educational aspirations: A logistic transform model. *Youth and Society, 24,* 52–70.

Wilson, T., & Linville, P. (1985). Improving the performance of college freshmen with attributional techniques. *Journal of Personality and Social Psychology, 49,* 287–293.

Wilson, W. (1987). *The truly disadvantaged: The inner city, the underclass, and public policy.* Chicago: University of Chicago Press.

Windle, M. (1989). Substance use and abuse among adolescent runaways: A four-year follow-up study. *Journal of Youth and Adolescence, 18,* 331–344.

Windle, M. (1994). A study of friendship characteristics and problem behaviors among middle adolescents. *Child Development, 65,* 1764–1777.

Windle, M., & Windle, R. (1996). Coping strategies, drinking motives, and stressful life events among middle adolescents: Associations with emotional and behavioral problems and with academic functioning. *Journal of Abnormal Psychology, 105,* 551–560.

Windle, M., Miller-Tutzauer, C., & Barnes, G. (1991). Adolescent perceptions of help-seeking resources for substance abuse. *Child Development, 62,* 179–189.

Winfree, J., Backstrom, T., & Mays, G. (1994). Social learning theory, self-reported delinquency, and youth gangs: A new twist on a general theory of crime and delinquency. *Youth and Society, 26,* 147–177.

Wintemute, G., Kraus, J., Teret, S., & Wright, M. (1987). Drowning in childhood and adolescence: A population-based study. *American Journal of Public Health, 77,* 830–832.

Winterbottom, M. (1958). The relation of need for achievement to learning experiences in independence and mastery. In J. Atkinson (Ed.), *Motives in fantasy, action, and society.* Princeton, NJ: Van Nostrand.

Wintre, M., Hicks, R., McVey, G., & Fox, J. (1988). Age and sex differences in choice of consultant for various types of problems. *Child Development, 59,* 1046–1055.

Wojtkiewicz, R., & Donato, K. (1995). Hispanic educational attainment: The effects of family background and nativity. *Social Forces, 74,* 559–574.

Wolf, A., Gortmaker, S., Cheung, L., Gray, H., Herzog, D., & Colditz, G. (1993). Activity, inactivity, and obesity: Racial, ethnic, and age differences among schoolgirls. *American Journal of Public Health, 83,* 1625–1627.

Wolfe, D., Wekerle, C., Reitzel-Jaffe, D., & Lefebvre, L. (1998). Factors associated with abusive relationships among maltreated and nonmaltreated youth. *Development and Psychopathology, 10,* 61–85.

Wolfe, S., & Truxillo, C. (1996, March). *The relationship between decisional control, responsibility and positive and negative outcomes during early adolescence.* Paper presented at the biennial meetings of the Society for Research on Adolescence, Boston.

Wolfer, L., & Moen, P. (1996). Staying in school: Maternal employment and the timing of black and white daughters' school exit. *Journal of Family Issues, 17,* 540–560.

Wolfson, A., & Carskadon, M. (1998). Sleep schedules and daytime functioning in adolescents. *Child Development, 69,* 875–887.

Wolk, L., & Rosenbaum, R. (1995). The benefits of school-based condom availability: Cross-sectional analysis of a comprehensive high school-based program. *Journal of Adolescent Health, 17,* 184–188.

Wong, C., Crosnoe, R., Laird, J., & Dornbusch, S. (in press). Relations with parents and teachers, susceptibility to friends' negative influences, and adolescent deviance. *Journal of Adolescent Research.*

Wong, M., & Csikszentmihalyi, M. (1991). Affiliation motivation and daily experience: Some issues on gender differences. *Journal of Personality and Social Psychology, 60,* 154–164.

Wood, P., & Clay, W. (1996). Perceived structural barriers and academic performance among American Indian high school students. *Youth and Society, 28,* 40–61.

Wood, P., & Clay, W. (1996). Perceived structural barriers and academic performance among American Indian high school students. *Youth and Society, 28,* 40–61.

Woodward, L., & Fergusson, D. (1999). Childhood peer relationship problems and psychosocial adjustment in late adolescence. *Journal of Abnormal Child Psychology, 27,* 87–104.

Wright, J., Cullen, F., & Williams, N. (1997). Working while in school and delinquent involvement: Implications for social policy. *Crime and Delinquency, 43,* 203–221.

Wright, L., Frost, C., & Wisecarver, S. (1993). Church attendance, meaningfulness of religion, and depressive symptomatology among adolescents. *Journal of Youth and Adolescence, 22,* 559–568.

Wu, L., & Anthony, J. (1999). Tobacco smoking and depressed mood in late childhood and early adolescence. *American Journal of Public Health, 89,* 1837–1840.

Yamaguchi, K., & Kandel, D. (1987). Drug use and other determinants of premarital pregnancy and its outcome: A dynamic analysis of competing life events. *Journal of Marriage and the Family, 49,* 257–270.

Yankelovich, D. (1974). *The new morality: A profile of American youth in the 1970s.* New York: McGraw-Hill.

Yates, M., & Youniss, J. (1996). Community service and political-moral identity in adolescents. *Journal of Research on Adolescence, 6,* 271–284.

Yau, J., & Smetana, J. (1996). Adolescent-parent conflict among Chinese adolescents in Hong Kong. *Child Development, 67,* 1262–1275.

YMCA. (2000). *Telephone survey conducted for the White House Conference on Teenagers.* Chicago: Author.

Yoder, K., Hoyt, D., & Whitbeck, L. (1998). Suicidal behavior among homeless and runaway adolescents. *Journal of Youth and Adolescence, 27,* 753–771.

Yoon, K., Eccles, J., Wigfield, A., & Barber, B. (1996, March). *Developmental trajectories of early to middle adolescents' academic achievement and motivation.* Paper presented at the biennial meetings of the Society for Research on Adolescence, Boston.

Yoshikawa, H. (1994). Prevention as cumulative protection: Effects of early family support and education on chronic deliquency and its risks. *Psychological Bulletin, 115,* 28–54.

Young, H., & Ferguson, L. (1979). Developmental changes through adolescence in the spontaneous nomination of reference groups as a function of decision context. *Journal of Youth and Adolescence, 8,* 239–252.

Youniss, J., & Ketterlinus, R. (1987). Communication and connectedness in mother- and father-adolescent relationships. *Journal of Youth and Adolescence, 16,* 265–292.

Youniss, J., & Smollar, J. (1985). *Adolescent relations with mothers, fathers, and friends.* Chicago: University of Chicago Press.

Zabin, L., Astone, N., & Emerson, M. (1993). Do adolescents want babies? The relationship between attitudes and behavior. *Journal of Research on Adolescence, 3,* 67–86.

Zabin, L., Hirsch, M., & Emerson, M. (1989). When urban adolescents choose abortion: Effects on education, psychological status and subsequent pregnancy. *Family Planning Perspectives, 21,* 248–255.

Zabin, L. S., Sedivy, V., & Emerson, M. (1994). Subsequent risk of childbearing among adolescents with a negative pregnancy test. *Family Planning Perspectives, 26,* 212–217.

Zahn-Waxler, C., Klimes-Dougan, B., & Slattery, M. (in press). Internalizing problems of childhood and adolescence: Prospects, pitfalls, and progress in understanding the development of anxiety and depression. *Development and Psychopathology.*

Zavela, K., Battistich, V., Dean, B., Flores, R., Barton, R., & Delaney, R. (1997). Say Yes First: A longitudinal, school-based alcohol and drug prevention project for rural youth and families. *Journal of Early Adolescence, 17,* 67–96.

Zeldin, R., Small, S., & Savin-Williams, R. (1982). Prosocial interactions in two mixed-sex adolescent groups. *Child Development, 53,* 1492–1498.

Zelnick, M., & Kantner, L. (1973). Sex and contraception among unmarried teenagers. In C. Westoff et al. (Eds.), *Toward the end of growth: Population in America.* Englewood Cliffs, NJ: Prentice-Hall.

Zeman, J., & Shipman, K. (1997). Social-contextual influences on expectancies for managing anger and sadness: The transition from middle childhood to adolescence. *Developmental Psychology, 33,* 917–924.

Zillman, D. (2000). Influence of unrestrained access to erotica on adolescents' and young adults' dispositions toward sexuality. *Journal of Adolescent Health, 27,* 41–44.

Zima, B., Wells, K., & Freeman, H. (1994). Emotional and behavioral problems and severe academic delays among sheltered homeless children in Los Angeles County. *American Journal of Public Health, 84,* 260–264.

Zimiles, H., & Lee, V. (1991). Adolescent family structure and educational progress. *Developmental Psychology, 27,* 314–320.

Zimmer-Gembeck, M. J. (1999). Stability, change and individual differences in involvement with friends and romantic partners among adolescent females. *Journal of Youth and Adolescence, 28,* 419–438.

Zimmerman, M., Copeland, L., Shope, J., & Dielman, T. (1997). A longitudinal study of self-esteem: Implications for adolescent development. *Journal of Youth and Adolescence, 26,* 117–141.

Zimmerman, M., Ramirez-Valles, J., Washienko, K., Walter, B., & Dyer, S. (1996). The development of a measure of enculturation for Native American youth. *American Journal of Community Psychology, 24,* 295–301.

Zimmerman, R., Sprecher, S., Langer, L., & Holloway, C. (1995). Adolescents' perceived ability to say "no" to unwanted sex. *Journal of Adolescent Research, 10,* 383–399.

Zimring, F. (1982). *The changing legal world of adolescence.* New York: Free Press.

Zimring, F. (1998). *American youth violence.* New York: Oxford University Press.

Zollo, P. (1999). *Wise up to teens: Insights into marketing and advertising to teenagers* (2nd ed.). Ithaca, NY: New Strategist.

Zuckerman, M. (Ed.). (1983). *Biological basis of sensation seeking, impulsivity, and anxiety.* Hillsdale, NJ: Erlbaum.

Credits

Introduction

Table 1.1 From: C. Buchanan and G. Holmbeck, "Measuring Beliefs about Adolescent Personality and Behavior." JOURNAL OF YOUTH AND ADOLESCENCE 27, 607-627, 1997. Reprinted by permission of Plenum Publishers and the author.

Chapter 1

Figure 1.1 From: M. Grumbach, J. Roth, S. Kaplan, and R. Kelch. Hypothalamic-pituitary regulation of puberty in man: Evidence and concepts derived from clinical research. In M. Grumbach, G. Grave and F. Mayer (Eds.) CONTROL OF THE ONSET OF PUBERTY. Copyright © 1974. Reprinted by permission of Lippincott Williams & Wilkins.   **Figure 1.2** From: W. Marshall, Puberty. In F. Faulkner and J. Tanner (eds.) HUMAN GROWTH, Vol 2. Copyright 1978. Reprinted by permission of Plenum Publishers.   **Figure 1.3** From: M. Grumbach, J. Roth, S. Kaplan, and R. Kelch. Hypothalamic-pituitary regulation in man: Evidence and concepts derived from clinical research. In M. Grumbach, G. Grave & F. Mayer (eds.) CONTROL OF THE ONSET OF PUBERTY. Copyright © 1974. Reprinted by permission of Lippincott Williams & Wilkins.   **Figure 1.4** From: N. Morris & J. Udry. Validation of a self-administered instrument to assess stage of adolescent development. JOURNAL OF YOUTH AND ADOLESCENCE 9, 271-280, 1980. Reprinted by permission of Plenum Publishers.   **Figure 1.5** From: W. Marshall & J. Tanner, Variations in the pattern of pubertal change in girls. ARCHIVE OF DISEASE OF CHILDHOOD, 44, 130. Copyright 1969. Reprinted by permission of BMJ Publishing Group.   **Figure 1.6** From: M. Herman-Giddens, E. Slora, R. Wasserman, C. Bourdony, M. Bhapkar, G. Koch, and C. Hasemeir, "Secondary sexual characteristics and menses in young girls seen in office practice: A study from the Pediatric Research in Office Settings Network." Reprinted by permission of PEDIATRICS, Vol. 88, pp 505-512, figure 4, 1997.   **Figure 1.7** From: P. Eveleth and J. Tanner, WORLD-WIDE VARIATION IN HUMAN GROWTH. Copyright 1976. Reprinted by permission of Cambridge University Press.   **Figure 1.8** From: P. Eveleth and J. Tanner, WORLDWIDE VARIATION IN HUMAN GROWTH. Copyright 1976. Reprinted by permission of Cambridge University Press.   **Figure 1.10(a-b)** Fluctuations in two adolescents' moods over the course of a week. From BEING ADOLESCENT: CONFLICT AND GROWTH IN THE TEENAGE YEARS by Mihaly Csikszentmihali and Reed Larson. Copyright © 1984 by Basic Books, Inc. Reprinted by permission of Basic Books, a subsidiary of Perseus Books Group, LLC.   **Figure 1.11** From: C. Halpern, J. Udry, B. Campbell, and C. Suchindran. Effects of Body Fat on weight concerns, dating, and sexual activity: A longitudinal analysis of black and white adolescent girls. *Development Psychology,* 35, 721-736. © 1999 by The American Psychological Association. Reprinted by permission.   **Table 1.1** From: B. Goldstein, INTRODUCTION TO HUMAN SEXUALITY. Copyright © 1976. Reprinted by permission of Star Publishing Company, Belmont, CA. **Table 1.2** From: Patricia Bence. Patterns of the experience of mood. Paper presented at the biennial meetings of the Society for Research on Adolescence. Washington, March, 1992.

Chapter 2

Figure 2.2 From: N. Bayley, "Consistency and variability in the growth of intelligence from birth to eighteen years." JOURNAL OF GENETIC PSYCHOLOGY, 75, 165-196. Reprinted with permission of the Helen Dwight Reid Educational Foundation. Published by Heldref Publications, 1319 Eighteenth Street NW, Washington, DC 20036-1802. Copyright © 1949.   **Figure 2.3** From: R. McCall, M. Applebaum and P. Hogarty. Developmental changes in mental performance. Monographs of the Society for the Research in Child Development, 38, Serial No. 150. Copyright © 1973. Reprinted by permission of the Society for Research in Child Development. **Figure 2.4** From: N. Bayley, "Consistency and variability in the growth of intelligence from birth to eighteen years." JOURNAL OF GENETIC PSYCHOLOGY, 75, 165-196. Reprinted with permission of the Helen Dwight Reid Educational Foundation. Published by Heldref Publications, 1319 Eighteenth Street NW, Washington, DC 20036-1802. Copyright © 1949.   **Figure 2.5** From: Baruch Fiscoff, et al. J. Howard, and R. Zucker, ALCOHOL PROBLEMS AMONG ADOLESCENTS: CURRENT DIRECTIONS IN PREVENTION RESEARCH, pp 59-84. Copyright © 1995. Reprinted by permission of Lawrence Erlbaum Associates, Inc.

Chapter 3

Figure 3.1 From: L. Chisholm & K. Hurrelman. Adolescence in modern Europe: Pluralized transition patterns and their implications for personal and social risks. JOURNAL OF ADOLESCENCE, 18. Copyright 1995. Reprinted by permission.   **Figure 3.2** From: J. Arnett. "Learning to Stand Alone." HUMAN DEVELOPMENT, 41, pp 295-315. Copyright © 1998. Reprinted by permission of S. Karger AG Basel.   **Figure 3.3** From: L. Chisholm & K. Hurrelman. Adolescence in modern Europe: Pluralized transition patterns and their implications for personal and social risks. JOURNAL OF ADOLESCENCE, 18. Copyright 1995. Reprinted by permission.   **Figure 3.4** From: L. Chisholm & K. Hurrelman. Adolescence in modern Europe: Pluralized transition patterns and their implications for personal and social risks. JOURNAL OF ADOLESCENCE, 18. Copyright 1995. Reprinted by permission.   **Box figure 3.2** From: H. Stattin & C. Magnusson. Leaving home at an early age among females: Antecedents, adolescent adjustment & future life implications. In J.A. Graber & J.S. Dubas (eds.), Leaving home: Understanding the transitions to adulthood. NEW DIRECTIONS Copyright © 1996. Reprinted by permission.   **Figure 3.5** From: J. Wetzel. American Youth: A statistical snapshot. William T. Grant Foundation Commission on Work, Family, and Citizenship. Copyright 1988. Reprinted by permission.   **Figure 3.6** From: A. Sum & W. Fogg. The adolescent poor and the transition to early adulthood, pp 37-110 in P. Edelman & J. Ladner (eds.) ADOLESCENCE AND POVERTY: CHALLENGES FOR THE 90S. Copyright 1991. Reprinted by permission of the Center for National Policy Press, Washington, DC.

Chapter 4

Figure 4.1 From: R. Larson, M. Richards, G. Moneta, G. Holmbeck & E. Duckett. Changes in their families from ages 10 to 18:

Disengagement and transformation. DEVELOPMENTAL PSY-CHOLOGY, 32, 744- 754. Copyright 1996 by the American Psychological Association. Reprinted by permission. **Figure 4.2** Adapted from: Stice and Gonzales. JOURNAL OF ADOLESCENT RESEARCH. Copyright January 1998. **Figure 4.3** From: E. Maccoby and J. Martin. Socialization in the context of the family: Parent-child interaction. In E.M. Heatherington (ed.) HANDBOOK OF CHILD PSYCHOLOGY: SOCIALIZATION, PERSONALITY, AND SOCIAL DEVELOPMENT, Vol. 4, Copyright 1983. Reprinted by permission of John Wiley & Sons, Inc. **Figure 4.4** From: W. Furman & D. Buhmester. Children's perceptions of the personal relationships in their social networks. DEVELOPMENTAL PSYCHOLOGY, 21, 1016-1024. Copyright 1985 American Psychological Association. Reprinted by permission. **Figure 4.6** From: D. Hernandez. Child development and the social demography of childhood. CHILD DEVELOPMENT, 67. Copyright 1997. Reprinted by permission of the Society for Research in Child Development. **Figure 4.7** From: D. Hernandez. Child development and the social demography of childhood. CHILD DEVELOPMENT, 67. Copyright 1997. Reprinted by permission of the Society for Research in Child Development. **Figure 4.8** From: Andrew J. Cherlin, P. Lindsay Chase-Lansdale, & Christine McRae. Effects of Parental Divorce on Mental Health Throughout the Life Course. AMERICAN SOCIOLOGICAL REVIEW, 63, 239-249. Copyright 1998. Reprinted by permission of the American Sociological Association. **Figure 4.9** From: R. Conger, K. Conger, G. Elder, Jr., F. Lornez, R. Simons, & L. Whitebeck. Family economic stress and adjustment of early adolescent girls. DEVELOPMENTAL PSYCHOLOGY, 29, 206-219. Copyright 1993 by the American Psychological Association. Reprinted by permission. **Box 4.2** From: P. Amato & B. Keith. Parental divorce and the well-being of children: A meta-analysis. PSYCHOLOGICAL BULLETIN, 110, 26-46. Copyright 1991 by the American Psychological Association. Reprinted by permission.

Chapter 5

Figure 5.1 From: R. Larson & M. Richards. Waiting for the weekend. NEW DIRECTIONS FOR CHILD AND ADOLESCENT DEVELOPMENT, Winter, 37-51. Copyright 1998. Reprinted by permission of Jossey-Bass, Inc., a subsidiary of John Wiley & Sons, Inc. **Figure 5.3** From: R. Larson & M. Richards. Daily companionship in late childhood and early adolescence: Changing developmental contexts. CHILD DEVELOPMENT, 62, 284-300. Copyright 1991. Reprinted by permission of the Society for Research in Child Development. **Figure 5.4** From: S. Ennett & K. Bauman. "Adolescent social networks: School, demographic, and longitudinal considerations." JOURNAL OF ADOLESCENT RESEARCH, 11, 194-215. Copyright 1996. Reprinted by permission of Sage Publications, Inc. **Figure 5.5** From: B. Brown, M. Mory, & D. Kinney, "Casting crowds in relational perspective: Caricature, channel, and context." In R. Montemayor, G. Adams, and T. Gullotta (eds.). ADVANCES IN ADOLESCENT DEVELOPMENT, Vol 5: Personal relationships during adolescence. Reprinted by permission of Sage Publications, Inc. **Figure 5.6** From: B. Brown. Peer Groups, pp171-196 in S. Feldman & G. Elliot (eds.), AT THE THRESHOLD: THE DEVELOPING ADOLESCENT, Harvard University Press. Copyright 1990. Reprinted by permission of the author. **Box 5.1** From: D. Kinney. From nerds to normals: The recovery of identity among adolescents from middle school to high school. SOCIOLOGY OF EDUCATION (1993), 66, 21-40.

Chapter 6

Figure 6.1 Reprinted by permission of the William T. Grant Foundation. **Figure 6.2** From: R. Roeser, J. Eccles, & C. Freedman-Doan. Academic functioning and mental health. JOURNAL OF ADOLESCENT RESEARCH, 14, 135-174. Copyright 1999. Reprinted by permission of Sage Publications, Inc. **Figure 6.3** From: R. Roesser, C. Midgley, & T. Urdan Perceptions of the school psychological environment & early adolescents' psychological and behavioral functioning in school: The mediating role of goals and belonging. JOURNAL OF EDUCATIONAL PSYCHOLOGY 88,408-422. Copyright 1996 by the American Psychology Association. Reprinted by permission. **Figure 6.4** From: R. Larson & M. Richards. "Waiting for the Weekend." NEW DIRECTIONS FOR CHILD & ADOLESCENT DEVELOPMENT, Winter, 37-51. Copyright 1998. Reprinted by permission of Jossey-Bass, Inc., a subsidiary of John Wiley & Sons, Inc. **Figure 6.6** From: H. Cooper, K. Charlton, J. Valentine & L. Muhlenbruck. Making the most of summer school: A meta-analytic and narrative review. MONOGRAPHS OF THE SOCIETY FOR RESEARCH IN CHILD DEVELOPMENT, 65. serial no. 260. Copyright 2000. Reprinted by permission of SOCIETY FOR RESEARCH IN CHILD DEVELOPMENT. **Box 6.2** From: L. Jussim and J. Eccles. Teacher expectations II: Construction and reflection of student achievement. JOURNAL OF PERSONALITY AND SOCIAL PSYCHOLOGY, 63, 947-961. Copyright 1992 by the American Psychological Association. Reprinted by permission.

Chapter 7

Figure 7.2 From: R. Larson, M. Richards, B. Sims, J. Dworkin. How Urban African-American young adolescents spend their time: Time budgets for locations, activities, and companionship. AMERICAN JOURNAL OF COMMUNITY PSYCHOLOGY. **Box 7.2 and box figure 7.2** From: R. Larson & M. Richards. Daily companionship in late childhood and early adolescence: Changing developmental contexts. CHILD DEVELOPMENT, 62, Copyright 1991. Reprinted by permission of the Society for Research in Child Development. **Figure 7.3** From: R. Larson. Toward a psychology of positive youth development. AMERICAN PSYCHOLOGIST, 55, 170-183. Copyright 2000 by the American Psychological Association. Reprinted by permission. **Figure 7.5** From: G. Pettit, J. Bates, K. Dodge, and D. Meece. The impact of after-school peer contact on early adolescent externalizing problems is moderated by parental monitoring, perceived neighborhood safety, and prior adjustment. CHILD DEVELOPMENT, 70, 768-778. Copyright 1999. Reprinted by permission of Society for Research in Child Development. **Figure 7.6** From: D. Roberts, U. Foehr, V. Rideout, & M. Brodie. Media availability in children's bedrooms by age. Kids and the Media @ the New Millennium. Copyright 1999. Reprinted by permission of The Henry J. Kaiser Family Foundation.

Chapter 8

Figure 8.1 From: Susan Harter. THE CONSTRUCTION OF THE SELF. Copyright 1999. Reprinted by permission of the Guilford Press. **Figure 8.2** Adapted from: B. Hirsch & D. Dubois. "Self-esteem in early adolescence: The identification and prediction of contrasting longitudinal trajectories," JOURNAL OF YOUTH & ADOLESCENCE, 20, 53-72. Copyright 1991. Reprinted by permission of Plenum Publishers. **Figure 8.2** From: Susan Harter. THE CONSTRUCTION OF THE SELF. Copyright 1999. Reprinted by permission of the Guilford Press. **Figure 8.4** From: K. Brown, R. McMahon, F. Biro,

Chapter 9

Chapter 10

Chapter 11

Chapter 12

motivation: A longitudinal study. CHILD DEVELOPMENT, 69, 1448-1460. Copyright 1998. Reprinted by permission of the Society for Research in Child Development.

Chapter 13

Box figure 13.1 From: L. Wichstrøm. The emergence of gender difference in depressed mood during adolescence: The role of intensified gender socialization. DEVELOPMENTAL PSYCHOLOGY, 35, 232-245. Copyright 1999 by the American Psychological Association. Reprinted by permission.   **Table 13.2** from: The Diagnostic and Statistical Manual of Mental Disorders, Fourth Edition, Text Revision, 380-381. Copyright 2000 by the American Psychiatric Association. Reprinted by permission.

Photos

PO1 Will McIntyre/Photo Researchers.   **CO1** Tony Freeman/PhotoEdit. **CO2** Will McIntyre/Photo Researchers.   **CO3** David Young Wolff/PhotoEdit.   **PO2** Mark Richards/PhotoEdit.   **CO4** Lawrence Migdale/Stock Boston.   **CO5** Richard Hutchings/Photo Researchers.   **CO6** Mark Richards/PhotoEdit.   **CO7** Tony Freeman/PhotoEdit.   **PO3** Steve Skjold/PhotoEdit.   **CO8** Paul Conklin/PhotoEdit.   **CO9** Bob Daemmrich/Stock Boston.   **CO10** Steve Skjold/PhotoEdit.   **CO11** Perlstein/Jerrican/Photo Researchers. **CO12** Alan Oddie/PhotoEdit.   **CO13** Paul Conklin/PhotoEdit.

Subject Index

Page numbers followed by *i* indicate illustrations; page numbers followed by *t* indicate tables; page numbers followed by *f* indicate figures.